LABOR LAW

EDITORIAL ADVISORY BOARD

LABOR LAW

Cases, Materials, and Problems

Third Edition

Bernard D. Meltzer

Distinguished Service Professor of Law
University of Chicago

Stanley D. Henderson

F.D.G. Ribble Professor of Law
University of Virginia

LITTLE, BROWN AND COMPANY   Boston and Toronto

Library of Congress Catalog Card No. 84-81751

ISBN 0-316-56647-0

Second Printing

HAM

Published simultaneously in Canada
by Little, Brown & Company (Canada) Limited

Printed in the United States of America

SUMMARY OF CONTENTS

TABLE OF CONTENTS

vii

CHAPTER 3

THE BASIC STATUTORY MACHINERY FOR PROTECTING AND REGULATING ORGANIZATION AND COLLECTIVE ACTION

CHAPTER 4

PROTECTION OF THE ORGANIZING PROCESS AGAINST INTERFERENCE

CHAPTER 5

PROTECTION OF THE ORGANIZING AND BARGAINING PROCESS AGAINST "DISCRIMINATION"   199

CHAPTER 6

DETERMINATION OF REPRESENTATIVE
STATUS   349

CHAPTER 7

THE REGULATION OF COLLECTIVE ACTION BY LABOR ORGANIZATIONS

CHAPTER 9

REGULATION OF THE BARGAINING PROCESS

CHAPTER 10

THE ENFORCEMENT OF COLLECTIVE AGREEMENTS

CHAPTER 11

THE INDIVIDUAL AND COLLECTIVE ACTION   1125

CHAPTER 12

REGULATION OF UNION GOVERNMENT AND ADMINISTRATION

PREFACE

These materials are primarily concerned with current regulation of the conflicting interests involved in the organization and exercise of power in labor-management relations in the private sector. Understanding of that regulation is obviously promoted by placing it in its historical and social context. Accordingly, despite the risks involved, we include a nutshell treatment of the history of the American labor movement. We also introduce difficult questions concerning the accomplishments, costs, and limitations of contemporary collective bargaining. Such questions are often central to the adjudicative, legislative, and bargaining process and will retain their importance long after some details of current regulation disappear. In short, this volume, like prior editions, is designed as a lawyer's book, but one that reaches to the basic issues embedded in the regulation of labor relations and the work of those who administer, and who are subject to, that regulation.

It is clear to us that a study of the basic issues of labor law must take account of the functioning of legal institutions generally and the role and limits of the law in enforcing legislated standards. Consequently, this book invites consideration of the proper coordination among tribunals for adjudication — courts, administrative agencies, and arbitrators. It also draws attention to the nature and consequences of the National Labor Relations Board's approaches to precedent, "politics," and proliferation of regulatory detail. And it introduces the grievance-arbitration process, not only because of its importance in labor-management relations, but also because it raises procedural and substantive questions central to all modes of adjudication.

We have in general followed the organization of the previous editions. It has worked for us and, apparently, for our students and those teaching colleagues who have shared their experiences with us. Several organizational changes have, however, resulted from our decision, first, to omit any systematic treatment of public-sector labor relations and, second, to delete treatment of the standards for determining "discrimination" under Title VII of the Civil Rights Act of 1964 and related regulation. These changes reflect both the explosive growth in those areas and the development of separate courses for them.

Nonetheless, we have expanded, as well as relocated, the materials on the interplay and tensions between Title VII and basic elements of our collective bargaining system, such as exclusive representation, seniority, and arbitration. Thus,

Emporium Capwell Co. v. Western Addition Community Organization now appears, inter alia, under "Protected Activities." Other old and new landmarks, such as Alexander v. Gardner-Denver Co. and W.R. Grace & Co. v. Local 759, Rubber Workers, appear in a new section ("Arbitration and External Law"), along with the NLRB's recent decisions on deference to arbitration (United Technologies Corp. and Olin Corp).

Throughout, we have also given more attention to the following matters: (1) the influence of NLRA developments on application of the Railway Labor Act and vice versa; (2) remedial problems; (3) general questions of administrative law raised in labor cases; and (4) basic employment developments, such as restrictions on the employment-at-will doctrine in the nonunionized sector.

In order to deal with the large volume of new developments, we have made greater use of summaries of cases and of titled Notes designed to supply essential information or to summarize developments. Teachers familiar with the book will see that space for new and significant developments was made available by deleting expendable parts of materials retained from earlier editions.

We have sought to make the principal cases the main source of problems for discussion, with the other material designed to support and deepen discussion of those problems. Even though we have shortened some of the Notes, we have continued to use the Notes to put the hard questions lurking in the principal cases. We have found that such questions encourage reflection on the determinants, voiced and unvoiced, of decisions, on their soundness and implications, and on how labor law responds to economic, social, and political changes. Nevertheless, we recognize that, because of differences in course time and approach, teachers' and students' use of questions in the Notes will vary. Consequently, we have sought to present the principal cases and the expository comments so that they would raise, independently of the related Notes, the central issues involved.

It is a pleasure to record our indebtedness to colleagues who have directly and indirectly helped us to shape these materials. Aaron Director, while trying to teach the elder editor some economics, unsettled many of his assumptions and helped develop his distrust of sentimental pieties. Dennis Carlton, now a colleague at the University of Chicago Graduate School of Business, has continued that education and has left his traces on these materials. John F. Burton, Jr., Professor, New York State School of Industrial and Labor Relations, updated materials on union membership (now in Chapter 1) and the section in Chapter 2 on the "Economic Impact of Unions." Martin Schneid of the NLRB's Chicago office has been a font of information concerning NLRB procedures. The late Bernard Dunau and former NLRB Chairman Frank McCulloch, once Virginia colleagues of the junior editor, are owed special thanks for insights and guidance that reach far beyond labor law and the covers of this book.

We are especially indebted to many labor law teachers for their helpful suggestions and their encouragement. Naturally, our own students have also helped to refine these materials. We are especially grateful to Carrie Huff, Maris Rogdon, Roy Underhill (recent graduates of the University of Chicago Law School), and Darilyn Bock (a member of its Class of 1986), and to Patricia K. Epps, David Carter, David

Leitch (recent graduates of the University of Virginia Law School), and Jill Powell (a member of its Class of 1986), who assisted in our research and in the preparation of this volume for publication.

Our secretaries, Sharon Mikulich, in Chicago, and Gloria Kelarakis, in Charlottesville, earned our thanks for unfailing skill in typing and preparing the final manuscript, and for support and good cheer along the way.

Several miscellaneous signposts are in order: Collateral citations have been deleted from opinions, without showing ellipses. Occasionally, edited materials have been reparagraphed. The Statutory Supplement, which is separately bound, contains a supplementary bibliography as well as statutory and other reference materials. Finally, although cases reported after May 31, 1984 have not been systematically covered, important Supreme Court decisions and some NLRB decisions reported through mid-July 1984 are reflected in this volume.

Bernard D. Meltzer
February 1985   *Stanley D. Henderson*

ACKNOWLEDGMENTS

We appreciate the permission of the following publishers, authors, and periodicals (in addition to those specifically noted in the text) to reprint excerpts from their publications:

Feller, The Coming End of Arbitration's Golden Age, Proc., Natl. Acad. of Arbitrators, 29th Ann. Meeting, pp. 97-112 (1976). Reprinted with permission of The Bureau of National Affairs, Inc.

Freeman and Medoff, The Two Faces of Unionism, The Public Interest, No. 57, pp. 69-92 (1979). Reprinted with permission.

Meltzer, Labor Unions, Collective Bargaining and the Antitrust Law, Journal of Law and Economics, vol. 6, pp. 154-160 (R.H. Coase ed. 1963). Reprinted with permission of The University of Chicago Press.

A. Rees, The Economics of Trade Unions, pp. 99, 194-195 (1962). Reprinted with permission of The University of Chicago Press.

Ross, Comments on Kadish, The Criminal Law and Industrial Discipline as Sanctioning Systems: Some Comparative Observations, Proc., Natl. Acad. of Arbitrators, 17th Ann. Meeting, p. 144 (1964). Reprinted with permission of The Bureau of National Affairs, Inc.

Simons, Some Reflections on Syndicalism, Journal of Political Economy, vol. 52, pp. 1-25 (1944). Reprinted with permission of The University of Chicago Press.

Wallen, How Issues of Subcontracting and Plant Removal Are Handled by Arbitrators, Industrial and Labor Relations Review, vol. 19, no. 2, p. 266 (January 1966). Copyright © 1966 by Cornell University. All rights reserved. Reprinted with permission.

LABOR LAW

CHAPTER 1

HISTORICAL AND INSTITUTIONAL FRAMEWORK

A. THE DEVELOPMENT OF AMERICAN LABOR UNIONS

At the beginning of the nineteenth century, the existence and development of American labor unions were threatened by an ill-defined doctrine of criminal conspiracy. Today unions are, in general, secure and important centers of private power,[a] enjoying affirmative legal protection and widespread social approval.[b] Even a necessarily compressed review of that transformation is likely to deepen understanding of current and future problems in labor relations.

More specifically, the history in this chapter, which draws on familiar sources, is designed to promote an appreciation of the following considerations, among others: (1) the persistence of the problems raised for public policy and private adjustment in labor relations; (2) sources of current attitudes, symbols, and slogans, such as "government by injunction," which frequently are more closely related to historical grievances than to contemporary conditions; (3) the roots of current rivalries and conflicts within the labor movement; (4) the diversity of institutions and relationships with which labor law and policy must grapple; (5) the ebb and flow of market unionism and of social reform; (6) the tension between marketwide unionization and the

---

[a] "Power," as used in labor relations and elsewhere, is an excessively vague term that calls for specification: "power to do what?" As used here, "union power" refers to the capacity of organization to improve the terms and conditions of employment for members of a bargaining unit, to cut off the supply of goods and services, and (occasionally) to challenge the state's monopoly of force.

[b] It should, however, be noted that there is a growing literature reflecting increasing concern about the social costs of major strikes, the tensions between strong unions and a price system, and the limitations of collective bargaining in dealing with the problems of poverty, economic recession, and racial justice.

1

commitment to competition in product markets; (7) the risk that widespread and disruptive economic warfare will trigger legislative restrictions; and (8) the limits of law in dealing with substantial aggregations of private power that are organized to achieve their ends by economic warfare, and that at the same time are enjoined by their own ideology and by law to practice internal democracy.

Although guilds of craftsmen can be traced back to a much earlier period, trade unions in the United States did not begin to develop until the end of the eighteenth century. Unions first emerged in the larger cities because relatively large numbers of employees were engaged in the same occupations, and there distinct classes of employees and employers first evolved. Organization initially embraced skilled workers. Such workers had the education necessary for organizing and running a union, and they desired to safeguard their investment in their apprenticeship. The relative scarcity of skilled workers impeded their replacement and increased the power of their organization.[c]

The early unions were highly unstable. They were often formed to press a particular demand, such as increased wages during a period of rising prices. Organization frequently disappeared along with the occasion that generated it, because of a lack of continuing interest on the part of the members or because of employer or judicial hostility. In addition, during depressions members drifted away because workers, pressed by job scarcity, sought to protect individual interests rather than those of the group. Thus, until the 1930s, "The overshadowing problem of the American labor movement [was] the problem of staying organized."[d]

Until the 1820s, unions were essentially local organizations limited to workers in a particular craft or skill. In 1827 the first central labor union, The Mechanics Union of Trade Associations, was formed in Philadelphia. That federation consisted of representatives of a number of trades. Such organizations of unions, embracing a variety of occupations and industries within a city, still exist (e.g., the Chicago Federation of Labor). Although such federations contain groups that lack a common economic interest and do not serve as agents for collective bargaining, they may furnish support to striking locals and speak for unions on community and political issues. The Philadelphia federation, despite a constitutional inhibition against political activity, called

[c] In the colonial period, masters or businessmen workers in various trades had combined to secure and maintain a jurisdictional monopoly and better prices. See R. Morris, Government and Labor in Early America 136 (1965). Such activities may later have served as a model for similar activities by journeymen. Prior to the American Revolution, combination by the latter to secure better working conditions was "excessively rare."

[d] See S. Perlman, A Theory of the Labor Movement 162 (1928).

for the election of a local ticket selected by the Working Men's Party, the first labor party in the world.

In the next few years, workingmen's parties emerged in other cities and supported, among other measures, free public schools, shorter hours, and mechanics' lien laws. Those parties soon disappeared because of factionalism and the blandishments of the established parties. Nevertheless, labor's early political efforts highlighted social evils that were eventually ameliorated.

In the 1830s, city centrals or "trades' unions" were formed in a number of eastern cities and became the basis for a geographically broader organization. In 1834 a conference of delegates from these trades' unions led to the formation of the first national labor organization in the United States, the National Trades' Union, the only union that to date has consisted of a federation of city centrals. After an appeal by that union, in 1840 President Van Buren, by executive order, established the ten-hour day for government employees without any reduction in their daily pay. That order, issued after the Congress had rejected a plea for a reduced workweek, was invoked as support for similar demands by nongovernmental employees. The National Trades' Union disappeared, however, before that demand was granted. Like many local unions, it was a casualty of the serious depression that began in 1837.

In the 1840s, unions were isolated and relatively weak. Labor embarked on a broader reform movement, which contrasted with the job-centered "business unionism" that was later to become dominant. Much of the leadership of the labor movement consisted of intellectuals rather than manual workers. The leadership sought to remedy the evils of a competitive economy by supporting consumers' and producers' cooperatives, land reform, and a fundamental reorganization of the money and credit system. Producers' cooperatives had, at best, ephemeral successes; most of them failed because of bad management or inadequate capital, and the few survivors refused to admit new employees and eventually became ordinary profit-seeking enterprises.

The first permanent national unions were formed in the 1850s, beginning with the National Typographical Union in 1852. A national union was originally a federation of local unions representing one craft or occupation in various localities.[e] An important stimulus to the development of national unions arose from the improvement in transportation and communication through the growth of railroads. Formation of such unions was, in part, an effort to deal with problems caused by the flow of goods produced at low wages into markets offering goods produced in high-wage areas. Such unions

---

[e] The term "international" was used to indicate affiliation with Canadian unions. Today the terms "national" and "international" are interchangeable.

were also formed in response to problems raised by the movement of workers to new locations where they sought admission to the local of their trade. Rules for the admission of migratory workers were an important concern of many early national unions. Today the national union in the mass-production industries is generally the most important unit of organization; in such industries it is usually more realistic to view the local as a subordinate division of the national union rather than to consider the national as a federation of locals. By contrast, in the construction trades, locals play a critically important role in bargaining and in other activities.

The strong demand for labor and the inflation accompanying the Civil War promoted the growth of established unions and the formation of new ones, both nationally and locally. In 1866 another central federation of American labor unions, the National Labor Union, was formed. It was a loose association of national unions, central federations, local unions, and various social reform groups. During the six turbulent years of its existence, it was primarily committed to social reforms. That commitment, which ran counter to the more immediate interests of some of the union's constituents, contributed to its early collapse.

The Civil War also accelerated developments that were to influence significantly the workplace and union development. War profits laid the basis for increased capital formation and industrialization. New technology further stimulated two great capital-goods industries—iron-steel and machinery. Industrial establishments increased in size, and larger enterprises were employing a larger proportion of the workers. As cities became more important, a growing number of urban workers became completely dependent upon wages. Those forces, and particularly the increased scale of enterprises, ended the personal relationship between employer and employed that was typical of smaller enterprises. Although the real wages of industrial workers had increased appreciably in the period immediately following the Civil War, the growth of large-scale enterprises appeared to reinforce the claim that the individual worker suffered from an inherent bargaining disadvantage—a claim that, incidentally, Adam Smith had voiced.

In the 1870s, financial panic and depression again took its toll of unions. During that period, labor-management relations were turbulent. Substantial paralysis of traffic and extensive disruption resulted from large-scale railroad strikes in protest against wage cuts. After riots in several cities, federal troops and state militia were called out "to restore order." Few railroad workers had been organized, and the strikes appeared to be largely spontaneous. They were unsuccessful, partly because violence alienated public opinion.

The 1870s also saw the prosecution of the Molly Maguires, a secret organization formed in the Pennsylvania coal fields. The Mollies were neither a labor organization nor the forerunner of one, but they became a labor legend. They sought to punish harsh or arbitrary supervisors and generally to protect their members against oppression. A Pinkerton agent infiltrated the organization and secured evidence for the prosecution of certain Mollies, whose members had been considered responsible for violence and terrorism in the coal fields. A series of trials beginning in 1876 resulted in the death sentence for nineteen Mollies and in conviction of others for perjury and other offenses.

Between the formation and collapse of the National Labor Union, another effort to unite workers for economic and political action led to the formation of the Noble Order of the Knights of Labor, founded in 1869 as a secret society. The depression of 1870 contributed to its growth. The Knights began to abandon their secrecy in 1879, and the organization grew rapidly in the next few years. The preamble to its constitution embodied themes familiar in the literature of protest:

> The alarming development and aggressiveness of great capitalists and corporations, unless checked, will inevitably lead to the pauperization and hopeless degradation of the toiling masses. It is imperative, if we desire to enjoy the full blessings of life, that a check be placed upon unjust accumulation and the power for evil of aggregated wealth. This much-desired object can be accomplished only by the united efforts of those who obey the divine injunction: "In the sweat of thy face thou shalt eat bread."[f]

The Knights differed from most early organizations in several respects. They admitted not only skilled craftsmen but also the unskilled, women, farmers, and some persons such as self-employed businessmen. Lawyers, doctors, liquor dealers, and other "non-workingmen" were ineligible. The Knights also emphasized political action and producer cooperation rather than collective bargaining and, in principle, opposed strikes and depended instead on legislation and education to achieve their aims. In practice, the Knights achieved their greatest successes when some of their district assemblies, representing railroad workers of a particular craft or occupation, won major strikes against wage cuts and discriminatory discharges.

The Noble Order of the Knights of Labor achieved its most dramatic success in 1885 when various railroads controlled by Jay Gould, a symbol of unrestrained economic power, agreed to end discrimination against striking members of the Knights. Thereafter, the organization's prestige and membership soared and, in 1886, reached a peak of 700,000 — almost seven times the 1885 membership.

[f]See L. Hacker, The Triumph of American Capitalism 408 (1940).

The decline of the Knights was even swifter than their rise. The Noble Order embraced a variety of groups and interests difficult to reconcile. It suffered from weak and inexperienced leadership. It also was hurt by the Haymarket riot,[g] which turned public opinion against all protest movements and stiffened employer resistance — even though Powderly, the Knights' leader, declined to support a request for a pardon of the convicted defendants. In the second half of 1886, the Knights were also involved in important strikes that ended disastrously for labor and resulted in the loss of many members. The virtual disappearance of the Knights by the 1890s marked a major turning point in the history of American unions. Never again was a major union to advocate primary reliance on social reform and producer cooperation rather than on collective bargaining backed by economic weapons.

The Knights had become involved in jurisdictional controversies with craft unions and had recruited their members. As a defensive measure, those unions called a convention in 1881 and formed the Federation of Organized Trades and Labor Unions, which was reorganized in 1886 as the American Federation of Labor. That federation, at first, largely appealed to craft unions. Its leaders, including Samuel Gompers, its first president, rejected the more utopian and radical features of earlier movements. The new federation adopted what Selig Perlman described as "a philosophy of pure wage consciousness," which accepted capitalism and sought to enlarge "the bargaining power of the wage earner in the sale of his labor."[h] The principles announced by Gompers included: (1) autonomy in the internal affairs of each affiliated international union; (2) exclusive jurisdiction for each affiliate; (3) avoidance of a permanent commitment to any political party and the use of labor's political influence to support its friends and punish its enemies regardless of their party affiliations; (4) the principle of voluntarism, i.e., the improvement of wages and hours through trade unions, as distinguished from legislative action.[i] Those principles were so attractive that all national unions

[g] The riot occurred in Chicago on May 4, 1886, after a strike for the eight-hour day that had been settled and then resumed after the employer insisted on retaining strikebreakers. Local anarchist leaders were addressing a mass meeting called to protest the death of strikers killed after violence on a picket line. While the police were advancing to break up the meeting, a bomb killed one policeman and wounded others. There were additional deaths on both sides in the fighting that followed. Eight anarchists were convicted of the bombing; seven were condemned to death; of these, two were reprieved, one committed suicide in prison, and four were hanged. Governor John Peter Altgeld of Illinois later pardoned the three surviving prisoners on the ground that the evidence had not connected the defendants with the bomb-throwing and that the jury had been improperly drawn and had been prejudiced. See generally H. David, The History of the Haymarket Riot (1936).

[h] S. Perlman, supra note d, at 197-207 (1928).

[i] See I. Bernstein, The Lean Years 91 (1960), quoted in Peters, Recent Literature in American Labor History, Proc., 18th Ann. Meeting, Indus. Rel. Research Assn. 333, 334

of any importance, except those representing railroad-operating employees, soon joined the new federation.

The Federation failed to secure the affiliation of at least one of the railroad brotherhoods because of Gompers' insistence on the elimination, from national union constitutions, of provisions discriminating against blacks[j] — discrimination which was to persist on the railroads and lead to landmark litigation in the 1940s. The AFL at first denied admission to unions whose constitutions explicitly provided for discrimination. But opposition to Gompers' policy caused him to modify it in order to increase the strength of the Federation.

Despite the victory for craft unionism reflected in the success of the Federation, the United Mine Workers in 1890 finally succeeded in organizing the first permanent industrial union, embracing coal miners in the bituminous and anthracite fields. Later, the AFL was to recognize the UMW's right to organize certain skilled workers in and around the mining industry, despite rival jurisdictional claims of craft unions.

In the depression of 1893, the AFL and other major unions lost less ground than they had lost in any previous major downturn. The union movement in the 1890s suffered, however, some famous defeats. Carnegie Steel broke a strike precipitated by wage cuts at Homestead, Pa., after importing Pinkerton guards, who fought gun battles with the strikers, and after widespread violence led to intervention by the state militia.[k] Another celebrated defeat resulted from a strike in 1894, also precipitated by wage cuts and involving the workers in the Pullman car shops. That strike spread to the

---

(1965): "Gompers accepted capitalism not because he considered it an ideal system for the worker but because it was here and here to stay. The job for labor was to make the best of it pragmatically. The house of Utopia would take care of itself; philosophers might debate its furnishings but busy unionists had no time for idle speculation. Conflict between the classes was endemic under capitalism but was not class struggle in the Marxist sense. Rather it was a contest over how the economic pie would be cut. Here labor's aim was both clear and simple: 'More, more, more, now.'

"The foundation of power was economic organization. Workers, therefore, must engage in voluntary self-organization to make sure that they got 'more.' For the worker the supreme loyalty must be to the union; for the union, supreme loyalty must be to the economic advancement of the worker. For the organization this loyalty must be exclusive, uncontaminated — 'pure and simple.' Nonworkers who intervened in union affairs were meddlers; Gompers viewed with suspicion intellectuals, well-intentioned reformers, and Socialists. 'Voluntarism' was the key word in his philosophy, and self-organization of the working class lay at its base. 'Gompers,' John R. Commons observed, 'became even more class conscious than Marx himself.'"

Beginning in 1906, the Federation's political action broadened and began to embrace middle class progressive policies. The New Deal period marked a substantial increase in labor's commitment to both legislative action and partisan politics. See J. Greenstone, Labor in American Politics 25-36, 39-41 (1977).

[j] See H. Pelling, American Labor 84, 90 (1960).
[k] See L. Wolff, Lockout (1965).

railways when the American Railway Union, an industrial union led by Eugene V. Debs, instituted a boycott against trains carrying Pullman cars. That boycott led to a substantial paralysis of the railways and to the hiring of replacements for the strikers. Violence and destruction of property increased, and the Attorney General of the United States took an extraordinary step that became a decisive factor in the failure of the boycott; he directed the United States Attorney in Chicago to seek an injunction in the federal court for northern Illinois. That court issued a sweeping injunction against Debs, other union officials, and against "all other persons combining and conspiring with them, and to all other persons, whosoever, to desist and refrain from, in any way or manner, interfering with, hindering, obstructing, or stopping any of the business of any of the following named railroads."[1] The next day, the United States marshal reported that the injunction could not be enforced without the use of federal troops. President Cleveland ordered federal troops into Chicago, over the objection of Governor Altgeld, who previously had called out the National Guard.

Judicial and executive intervention contributed to the defeat of the Pullman strike, but labor achieved gains important for the long run. Debs' subsequent imprisonment for contempt of court, which was upheld by the Supreme Court,[m] drew attention to the increasing use and abuse of injunctions in labor disputes — a use that had become more frequent in the 1880s as court-appointed railroad receivers had resorted to courts to restrain striking employees from destroying railroad property and interfering with railroad operations. In addition, the report on the Chicago strike by the commission appointed by President Cleveland criticized the company's opposition to collective bargaining as "behind the age," supported the full recognition of labor unions by law, and made other recommendations favorable to unions that ultimately were to be enacted into law.

Union membership grew rapidly during the prosperity that followed the depression of the mid-1890s; from 1897 to 1904, the reported membership of national and international unions increased from 447,000 to about 2,000,000. In 1904, unions suffered membership losses, and thereafter the rapid growth rate in union membership declined. That decline has been attributed in part to the bitter opposition of employer groups, their aggressive support of the open shop (the nonunion shop), blacklists of unionists, and the use of yellow-dog contracts.

The AFL and its philosophy of business unionism was also challenged by radical movements, including the Industrial Workers of the World (IWW), formed in 1905. The IWW developed a militant syndicalism, encompassing strikes and other forms of direct action designed to eliminate

[1]See United States v. Debs, 64 F.724, 726 (N.D. Ill. 1894).
[m]See In re Debs, 158 U.S. 564 (1895).

the wage system and to replace existing governmental organs by organization of workers along industrial lines. Early in its history, most of its strength was in the West, especially among lumberjacks and migratory workers. It did, however, support several large, spontaneous, and successful strikes in the East. Nevertheless, its radical program appeared to divert it from building a permanent organization. It opposed American participation in World War I and military conscription. Those positions, along with mob violence against the IWW, federal prosecution of its leaders for hampering the government's war efforts, and state "criminal syndicalism" statutes, contributed to its virtual disappearance in the postwar period. Socialists, although a minority group, from 1890 to 1918 also occasionally challenged the AFL's established leadership and played a significant role in keeping the issue of industrial unionism alive.

Immediately prior to World War I, unionization and efforts to achieve collective bargaining had been accompanied by widespread turbulence and violence on both sides, suppression of unionists' civil liberties, frequent use of troops, and fears of violent social upheaval. In an effort to determine the underlying causes of industrial strife, Congress in 1912 established a United States Commission on Industrial Relations, a tripartite body with broad investigatory authority. 37 Stat. 415 (1912). Although the commission issued three separate statements, a staff report signed by its chairman and three labor representatives and issued in 1915 was considered by the public to be the "official" viewpoint. That report identified four major causes of unrest and proposed specific remedies later to be embodied into law. (1) Workers had not received a fair share of the nation's wealth; between one-fourth and one-third of families employed in manufacturing earned "less than enough to support them in anything like a comfortable, decent condition." Tenant farmers were "badly housed, ill-nourished, badly educated, and hopeless." (2) The growth of large corporations and the separation of corporate ownership and control had widened the gulf between owners, on one side, and workers and management, on the other, and had made bargaining by individual employees impossible. (3) Inequality of income had reduced mass purchasing power and had led to periodic layoffs. (4) Labor's right to organize had been denied. The report advocated constitutional amendments and new laws to protect the right of organization and collective bargaining, and it recommended that the Federal Trade Commission be empowered to investigate and prosecute all unfair labor practices. It also advocated a sharply graduated inheritance tax and a ceiling on individual inheritances.[n] The commission was, however, silent about the problems of black workers.

[n] Professor Magruder has summarized the findings contained in the reports of a variety of federal commissions established to inquire into strikes and labor conditions: "[E]mployees will not submit to a reign of industrial absolutism; . . . efforts by employers to suppress bona fide

In the prewar period the President, Congress, and state legislatures took action favorable to the interests of workers and organized labor. Near the end of his term President Taft signed the law creating the present Department of Labor. 37 Stat. 736 (1913). In 1914 Congress enacted the Clayton Act,° which declared generally that unions were not to be regarded as illegal combinations in restraint of trade and which also appeared to impose substantial restrictions on the issuance of labor injunctions. Gompers hailed the Clayton Act as labor's Magna Carta, but restrictive interpretation by the Supreme Court was to disappoint labor's hopes. The states enacted a body of protective legislation dealing with child labor, compulsory school attendance, women's hours, workmen's compensation, and minimum wage laws, which, incidentally, were opposed by the AFL as well as by employers.

World War I and its immediate aftermath brought additional successes for the union movement. Membership increased rapidly, from about two and a half million in 1914 to about five million in 1920. That growth was aided by a strong demand for workers and by rising prices, which produced both discontent and opportunities for unions to secure increases in money wages. Furthermore, the National War Labor Board legitimated organization by recognizing the "right of workers to organize in trade unions and to bargain collectively through chosen representatives." Although that board had lacked enforcement power, the President exercised his war powers to secure obedience to its decisions, threatening recalcitrant workers with conscription and in several cases seizing the plants of defiant employers. The policy of affirmative protection of organizational interests was abandoned soon after the war, but it survived in the railroad industry, and during the Great Depression it was to become the cornerstone of national labor policy.

The wartime increase in union membership had been concentrated in relatively few trades, and the trade union movement had not organized the unskilled workers in heavy industries. The AFL's effort in 1917-1918 to organize the basic steel industry failed. Elbert Gary of the United States Steel Company, which dominated that industry, first stated that the corporation "does not confer . . . with or combat labor unions as such"ᵖ and later insisted that the unions lacked authority to speak for their men. Some em-

---

organization of employees are bound ultimately to fail and, meanwhile to provoke the bitterest industrial unrest. . . . [T]he sooner employers abandon the stupid battle over 'recognition,' and negotiate collective agreements with labor unions as a matter of course, the better will be the outlook for stabilizing labor relations on a healthy basis; . . . the policy of the law, therefore, should be to encourage the development of strong labor organizations." Magruder, A Half Century of Legal Influence upon the Development of Collective Bargaining, 50 Harv. L. Rev. 1071, 1078 (1937).

°See infra pp. 27-28.
ᵖP. Taft, The AFL in the Time of Gompers 387 (1957).

ployers resisted unionization with familiar weapons: espionage, discharge of union sympathizers, and other acts of intimidation and suppression. A strike called in 1919, despite Gompers' urging of caution and President Wilson's request for postponement, was honored by a majority of the steel workers in every region, and in seven weeks there were 367,000 strikers, according to union estimates. Violence erupted in many areas; twenty people, including eighteen strikers, were killed, and martial law was imposed in some areas. Replacements made the strike increasingly ineffective, and early in 1920 it was called off.

The failure of that strike has been attributed in part to the public hysteria about radicalism, which in the case of the steel campaign had been stimulated by the leadership role of William Z. Foster, who had advocated syndicalism and who later was to be nominated for the Presidency by the Communist Party of the United States. In addition, the craft orientation of the AFL leadership appeared to have been a factor in the failure of the organizing efforts in steel. The major cause of failure was, however, the determined and effective opposition of the employers.

While the steel strike was in progress, the first Industrial Conference was convened by President Wilson, who was seeking to maintain the wartime truce between labor and management. The labor and public representatives approved a resolution that would have recognized employee rights to bargain through representatives of their own choosing. The employer representatives rejected that resolution; they were unwilling to encourage "outside" unions and would have supported employee free choice only if it were confined to representatives on the company payroll. Since the conference rules required unanimity, that resolution, and ultimately the conference, failed.

The failure of the steel strike and the conference was followed by a general decline for unions. In contrast to their gains in prior periods of prosperity, unions did not benefit from the vigorous economic activity and the stable prices that prevailed from 1923 to 1929. Union membership decreased from about five million in 1920 to about three and a half million in 1929. Employers used the carrot as well as the stick; they began to establish special personnel staffs and to adopt policies of "welfare capitalism," including profit-sharing, plant councils or shop committees, insurance plans, company housing, and recreation. All those measures were not necessarily designed to abort independent unionism, but, together with the general increase in wages and reduction in the standard workweek accompanying increased productivity, they encouraged many unorganized workers to stay that way.

Setbacks to organization were also attributed to the characteristics of some unions. Their increasing size and age had led to increased centralization of power among full-time officials, who were often less interested in working-class solidarity and democratic control than were the volunteers whom they had replaced. Furthermore, various forms of graft, corruption, and extortion developed, particularly in the construction trades. Those circumstances, along with a decline of missionary zeal on the part of the unions, diluted their appeal to some workers.

The Great Depression, which began in 1929, initially had a seriously adverse effect on unions. In 1933 the unemployed — union and nonunion —numbered thirteen million. Reported union membership fell by almost 20 percent in four years and probably understated the actual decline. Unions, anxious to hide their weakness, kept unemployed members on their rolls even though they did not pay dues. Moreover, many unions were forced to accept wage cuts, which in practice were greater than those announced.

The early losses during the first phase of the depression were, however, soon replaced by dramatic gains. The upheaval of the thirties, which rocked and then reshaped the foundations of our society, led to significant changes in opinion and law, including the Wagner Act, which gave moral approval and legal protection to unionization and collective bargaining. Although that legislation touched off vigorous employer resistance, it was a factor in the doubling of union membership from 1933 to 1937. Nevertheless, it should be noted that organizational successes in rubber, autos, and steel (referred to below) were achieved prior to the decision in NLRB v. Jones & Laughlin Steel Corp., 301 U.S. 1 (1937), which upheld the constitutionality of the Wagner Act. It has, accordingly, been forcefully suggested that "one of the most prevalent myths shared by labor historians is that labor could not have achieved its historic breakthrough of 1936-1937 without the decisive help of the Wagner Act and other New Deal legislation such as the NRA."[q]

That breakthrough was linked to another important development of the 1930s, the formation of the CIO and the rise of the great industrial unions. The bitter conflict within the union movement, touched off by those developments, was foreshadowed by the formation of local industrial unions in various industries, including autos and rubber. The AFL granted so-called federal charters to such unions, directly affiliating them with the AFL, as distinguished from existing national unions. The aim of those new locals, to represent all the workers in the plants involved, conflicted with the traditional jurisdictional claims of the established craft unions — claims that were unacceptable both to the new unions and to older industrial unions, including the United Mine Workers led by John L. Lewis.

[q]Peters, supra note i, at 341.

During the 1935 convention of the AFL, the issues involved could no longer be compromised or evaded, and the position of the craft unions was upheld by the convention. The industrial unionists, led by John L. Lewis, thereupon formed the Committee for Industrial Organization. Although that committee was formed within the framework of the AFL, the executive council of the AFL stigmatized it as a "dual organization" and ordered it to disband. Upon the Committee's refusal, its constituent unions were expelled from the AFL. In 1938 the insurgent group changed its name to the Congress of Industrial Organizations (CIO) and operated as a rival federation until the AFL-CIO merger in 1955.

The new industrial unions, upon being denied recognition in autos and rubber, resorted to a dramatic form of the strike, which, in 1936, had been used in the rubber industry and which had previously been used in the United States and Europe. Strikers occupied struck plants and were supplied by sympathizers outside the plants. Although the sit-down strike was uniformly held to be illegal,[r] it contributed to the recognition of unions in the auto and rubber industries, including the celebrated recognition by General Motors after a sit-down strike at the Flint Works in Michigan.

The CIO had also launched an organizing campaign in the basic steel industry through a new organization, the Steel Workers Organizing Committee (SWOC), to which John L. Lewis and the United Mine Workers (UMW) supplied staff and funds. In 1937, the United States Steel Corporation voluntarily recognized SWOC and signed an agreement providing wage increases and other concessions. Other steel producers were, however, more stubborn. Their resistance led to strikes marked by violent incidents, including the "Memorial Day Massacre" on May 30, 1937, at the South Chicago plant of the Republic Steel Company, where ten strikers were killed by police gunfire. SWOC lost the Little Steel strike. However, organizational activity in the little steel companies continued, and in 1941 they recognized SWOC.[s]

The CIO emerged as a political as well as an economic rival of the AFL and generally was bolder and more vigorous in its political action. Its leaders were prominent in the formation in 1936 of Labor's Non-Partisan League. The UMW, led by John L. Lewis, contributed close to half a million dollars to the League's efforts in connection with the national elections in 1936. Labor's vigorous support of the Democratic ticket was, presumably, a factor in Roosevelt's sweeping victory.

In 1940, Lewis switched his support to the Republican candidate after

---

[r] See McClintock, Injunctions Against Sit-down Strikes, 23 Iowa L. Rev. 149, 150 (1938); NLRB v. Fansteel Metallurgical Co., 306 U.S. 240 (1939).
[s] See W. Galenson, The CIO Challenge to the AFL 115-116 (1960).

Roosevelt had rejected Lewis as his running mate and the Democrats had rejected Lewis' suggestion that Roosevelt should not be nominated for a third term. After Roosevelt's victory, Lewis, redeeming his preelection pledge, refused to continue as head of the CIO.

The expansion of political activities and expenditures by labor led to divisions between the AFL and the CIO, in part because Lewis permitted key positions to be filled by Communists, who exploited their influence to serve the Communist movement. The political developments sketched above were to be a factor in the passage of legislation, in 1947 and 1959, directed against certain political expenditures by unions and control of unions by Communists.

On the economic front, the challenge of the CIO and the protection to organization afforded by the Wagner Act stimulated new vigorous organizational campaigns by the AFL. The older federation soon made up for its loss of members to the CIO. Some AFL successes resulted from voluntary recognition by employers who wished to forestall bargaining with CIO unions, reputedly more militant than their AFL rivals. The rivalry between the two federations also blurred the distinction between craft and industrial unions, since the AFL, as a competitive measure, allowed craft unions to charter industrial locals.

That rivalry also complicated the administration of the Wagner Act by the National Labor Relations Board. The Board in determining appropriate units for elections and bargaining was faced with a continuing controversy between constituents of the two federations. The AFL's charge of the Board's pro-CIO bias accompanied employer allegations of the Board's pro-labor bias. Those complaints were ultimately to contribute to amendments of the Wagner Act, made by the Taft-Hartley Act (1947), which changed both the statutory machinery for resolving representation questions and the Board's internal structure.

World War II, like World War I, was a period of growth for the union movement. President Roosevelt promised to maintain the protections provided by the Wagner Act and the Fair Labor Standards Act, including premium pay for overtime. Unions, in turn, gave no-strike pledges designed to avoid interference with war production. The prestige of the union movement was enhanced by the appointment of union leaders to important posts in mobilization agencies. The National War Labor Board, a tripartite agency, was established "for adjusting and settling labor disputes which might interrupt work which contributes to the effective prosecution of the war." Later, the board's responsibility was extended to include wage stabilization as well as dispute settlement. It sought to "stabilize" wages without freezing them. Its basic guidelines were embodied in "the Little Steel formula," which in general sought to limit wage increases to those warranted by the 15 percent increase in the cost of living between January 1941 and May 1942.

Although labor's no-strike pledge was substantially honored in the early part of the war, a substantial number of stoppages, many of them wildcat, occurred later. John L. Lewis and the UMW attacked the entire principle of wage stabilization and called a strike in the bituminous coal fields. That strike prompted the President to threaten to deny draft exemptions to strikers under forty-five and led to the seizure of the mines and a face-saving concession in the form of a substantial, if somewhat disguised, wage increase. Lewis' behavior contributed to the enactment of the War Labor Disputes Act (Smith-Connally Act), 57 Stat. 163 (1943), over a presidential veto. This act authorized the President to seize any war plant threatened by stoppages, provided for the maintenance of preexisting conditions of employment unless otherwise directed by the National War Labor Board, and made strikes against government-operated plants punishable by fine and imprisonment. The act, which was effective only during the war period, required a strike vote before a strike could take place and by implication permitted strikes approved by a majority vote in enterprises not being operated by the government. It also placed restrictions on union political expenditures.

The war precipitated serious ideological conflict within the CIO. Communists had achieved strategic positions in the CIO and some of its constituent unions, partly because of John L. Lewis' mistaken notion that he could use the organizing skills of Communists and also control them. Beginning in 1935, Communists espoused a "People's Front" policy, designed to organize diverse groups in the "drive against fascism." The Russian-German Pact of 1939 produced a sharp shift in the party line. Communists in the labor movement strongly opposed American preparedness and aid to the Allies and were charged with fomenting strikes in defense plants for the purpose of sabotaging such aid. After the German attack on the Soviet Union, Communists in unions again sharply changed direction. They became "superpatriots" and attacked unions pressing for wage increases and other union objectives. There were bitter contests between Communists and non-Communists for control, which in some unions were won by Communists and their sympathizers.[t]

In 1949 the CIO expelled several unions on charges of Communist domination. Some of the expelled unions are still in existence, including the United Electrical Workers (which claimed 160,000 members in 1958) and

---

[t]"Communist" efforts to secure influence within the NLRB and the effect of the employment of party members by the NLRB are treated by E. Latham, The Communist Controversy in Washington, ch. 5 (1966).

the Mine, Mill and Smelter Workers (which claimed 100,000), which is now merged with the Steelworkers Union. These unions deny that they are under Communist control, and their day-to-day operations do not now differ substantially from those of other unions.

Postwar reconversion was accompanied by a wave of long and stubborn strikes, which involved over three million workers in 1945 and which affected many important industries, including coal, electrical manufacturing, oil refining, longshoremen, railroads, and steel. In 1946 the Government took vigorous action to end the most significant strikes — those in coal and railroads. The coal strike led to government seizure and to the imposition of fines on John L. Lewis and on the union for violating an injunction against the strike.[u] Those strikes stimulated widespread support for curbing the power of, and "abuses" by, organized labor and contributed to the passage of the Taft-Hartley Act in 1947.

The war period had also stimulated efforts to reunify the AFL and CIO. Those efforts gained additional momentum as a result of the enactment of Taft-Hartley and the subsequent reelection of Senator Taft despite labor's efforts to defeat him. In 1955, after the death of their respective presidents (Green and Murray), the two federations merged and became the American Federation of Labor and the Congress of Industrial Organizations (AFL-CIO). Merger did not, however, end jurisdictional conflicts between craft and industrial unions or, indeed, among craft unions.

Soon after the merger, congressional investigations highlighted corruption and malpractices in some unions. Although those problems had long plagued American unions, the disclosures of the 1950s provoked particularly strong public and official concern. In response, the AFL-CIO adopted Codes of Ethical Practices dealing with a variety of malpractices and conflicts of interests by union officials and providing for suspension or expulsion of offending internationals.

In 1957 the AFL-CIO expelled three unions, including the Teamsters, its largest affiliate, for noncompliance with those codes. The expulsion of the Teamsters resulted from its refusal to oust its president, James Hoffa, who had been the subject of unfavorable publicity.[v] That expulsion reflected both the traditional autonomy of national unions and the crudeness of the expulsion weapon. James Hoffa continued in power. The AFL-CIO lost 1.5 million members and $750,000 in annual revenue. The Teamsters, moreover, continued to grow at a faster rate than the AFL-CIO.

Congress was unwilling to rely on self-policing by unions, and in 1959

---

[u] See United States v. UMW and United States v. Lewis, 330 U.S. 258 (1947).

[v] National Labor Relations Board, Legislative History of the Labor-Management Reporting and Disclosure Act of 1959, at 419-420 (1959).

enacted the Landrum-Griffin Act, the first comprehensive regulation of internal union affairs by the federal government.

During the early 1960s unions did much better in bargaining than in organizing. Their impressive bargaining gains, together with rising prices, led the Council of Economic Advisors to promulgate guidelines for the purpose of moderating price and wage increases. But between 1960 and 1965, the total number of union members did not increase even though the work force increased by five million.[w] This organizational failure has been explained on a variety of grounds, including the following: (1) an increase in the number and proportion of white-collar workers, who are harder to organize; (2) increased affluence; (3) disclosures of union corruption and maladministration; (4) a growing conviction that union power had been exercised without regard to the public interest and a growing concern about the social costs of strikes; (5) increased centralization of union government and a wider gulf between the rank and file and their leaders; (6) the age and complacency of leaders in the union movement; (7) the weakening of traditional sources of union support because of the responsibility of some unions for racial discrimination.

Although labor organization lagged in the 1960s, other organizations concerned with anti-poverty campaigns and civil rights grew in number and in influence. Furthermore, widespread discussion of the extent of, and the remedies for, poverty reflected a broad concern about the problems of the disadvantaged. That concern was reinforced by new political forces, including the removal of voting disqualifications of blacks and the increasing interest of students and other groups in the expansion and reform of programs of welfare and social insurance.

This new mood was reflected in a broad range of social legislation and executive action, which in general was part of President Johnson's program for a Great Society and his war on poverty.[x] That legislation dealt with the following, among other matters: manpower development and training, area redevelopment, economic opportunity for the disadvantaged, increases in minimum wages, expanded coverage of the Fair Labor Standards Act, improvement of Social Security benefits, and Medicare for the aged. In addition, the President and Congress took action directed at barring discrimination based on race and other invidious grounds, on the part of employers or unions. Executive Order No. 10,925 (1961), 3 C.F.R. §448

---

[w] Exec. Order No. 10,988 (1962), 3 C.F.R. §521 (1959-1963 comp.), issued by President Kennedy, reflected a policy favorable to unionization and limited collective bargaining by federal employees. It contributed to a substantial increase of unionization and collective action throughout the whole public sector.

[x] S. Levitan, The Great Society's Poor Law, A New Approach to Poverty (1969).

(1959-1963 comp.), issued by President Kennedy, included an obligation to take "affirmative action" as well as the obligation imposed by previous executive orders requiring government contractors to refrain from racial and related forms of discrimination in employment. Furthermore, Title VII of the Civil Rights Act of 1964, 42 U.S.C. §§2000c to 2000c-15, proscribed such discrimination by employers and unions regardless of whether government contractors were involved.

Beginning in 1966, the UAW and particularly its president, Walter Reuther, launched a campaign of public criticism against the AFL-CIO, which exposed not only divisions within the labor movement but also Reuther's disappointment in the failure of private and public policies to be more effective in helping the disadvantaged. That campaign culminated in the UAW's formal disaffiliation[y] from the AFL-CIO in 1968 and the creation of the Alliance for Labor Action by the UAW and the Teamsters. In 1972, after Reuther's death, the Alliance was dissolved, because of strains caused by the UAW's support of the United Farm Workers in their dispute with the Teamsters and also because of the UAW's financial problems.

The year 1971 marked the first peacetime use of comprehensive and direct wage and price controls, which were not dismantled until 1974. The 1972 presidential campaign was unusual because organized labor, in the main, did not support the Democratic nominee.

The 1960s marked the beginning of a period of unusual growth for public employee unions — in numbers, legal recognition and protection, in strikes (generally illegal), in employee benefits, and in public concern about the appropriate policies for public employee labor relations. This concern was intensified by New York City's economic problems and financial collapse in 1975, to which the city's labor relations policies had contributed, along with other important causes. The financial problems of the cities, along with increasing strikes, contributed to both harder bargaining by public employers and reduced public sympathy and support for governmental employees.

There was also scant support from the public — or the labor movement — when the Professional Air Traffic Controllers Organization, on August 3, 1981, launched the first completely nationwide and undisguised strike against the federal government. This strike, a felony under federal law, was a disaster for the strikers as well as the union. The strikers were fired and replaced, and proposals for their reinstatement rejected.

Observers have disagreed over whether the government's unusually tough response was a significant factor in the hard bargaining by private firms

[y]For an AFL-CIO "white paper" concerning that disaffiliation, see To Clear the Record, AFL-CIO Executive Council Report on the Disaffiliation of the UAW (1969).

in the 1980s. A recession, along with stiff foreign competition, led to plant closings and mass layoffs in some industries, such as autos and steel, where unions had been strong. Consequently, some unions accepted wage freezes or cutbacks as well as changes in inefficient work rules. In exchange, management sometimes accepted new restrictions on layoffs and plant closures, and new forms of participation by union officials and by employees within and outside the union structure. Thus UAW President C. Douglas Fraser became a member of Chrysler's board of directors, and employee groups explored measures for improving their work product and environment. There was debate over whether these developments signalled the beginning of longer term labor-management cooperativeness or were only a temporary phenomenon. There were also suggestions that management had unwisely compromised "managerial prerogatives" and entrepreneurial freedom. See generally Proc., 35th Ann. Meeting, Indus. Rel. Research Assn. (Dec. 1982).

We conclude this historical sketch with a closer look at data on union membership.[z]

As already suggested, the enactment of the National Labor Relations Act in 1935 was followed by sharp increases in union membership (see Table 1). Union membership as a percentage of nonagricultural employment continued to grow until 1945, when it reached 35.5 percent. After fluctuating between 31 to 35 percent for a decade, the percentage of unionized nonagricultural workers began to decline in 1955, and by 1978 had dropped to 23.6 percent, the level of the late 1930s. The union organizing record is not quite so bleak in light of the growth of the membership of the National Education Association and other organizations that sometimes function as unions. In 1980, members of labor organizations (unions and bargaining associations) totalled 22,366,000 or 20.9 percent of the labor force and 24.7 percent of nonagricultural employment. Nevertheless, even with the more comprehensive concept of labor organization, membership has declined from 30.0 percent of employees in 1970 to 24.7 percent in 1980.

Table 2 suggests factors in the percentage decline of employees organized. (Unfortunately, the data have to be presented in two noncompatible panels because the Department of Labor has discontinued certain data series.) In manufacturing, the traditional union stronghold, total employment has grown slowly, and the number of members and the percentage organized have shrunk. In nonmanufacturing, which includes construction,

[z] This material on union membership has been prepared by John F. Burton, Jr., Professor, New York State School of Industrial and Labor Relations, Cornell University. Professor Burton's contributions to this book also include the materials on the Economic Impact of Unions. See Chapter 2, p. 59.

TABLE 1
Membership as a Proportion of the Labor Force, 1930-1980

Year	Total Membership[1] (thousands)	Total Labor Force		Employees in Non-agricultural Establishments	
		Number (thousands)	Percent Members	Number (thousands)	Percent Members
Panel A: Membership in Unions					
1930	3401	50080	6.8	29424	11.6
1935	3584	53140	6.7	27053	13.2
1936	3989	53740	7.4	29082	13.7
1937	7001	54320	12.9	31026	22.6
1938	8034	54950	14.6	29209	27.5
1939	8763	55600	15.8	30618	28.6
1940	8717	56180	15.5	32376	26.9
1945	14322	65300	21.9	40394	35.5
1950	14267	63858	22.3	45222	31.5
1953	16948	66560	25.5	50232	33.7
1954	17022	66993	25.4	49022	34.7
1955	16802	68077	24.7	50675	33.2
1960	17049	72142	23.6	54234	31.4
1965	17299	77178	22.4	60815	28.4
1970	19381	85903	22.6	70920	27.3
1975	19611	94793	20.7	76945	25.5
1976	19634	96917	20.3	79382	24.7
1977	19695	99534	19.8	79382	24.8
1978	20246	102537	19.7	85763	23.6
Panel B: Membership in Labor Organizations					
1970	21248	85903	24.7	70880	30.0
1975	22361	94793	23.6	77364	28.9
1976	22662	96917	23.4	80048	28.3
1977	22456	99534	22.6	82423	27.2
1978	22757	102537	22.2	86697	26.2
1979	22579	104996	21.5	89886	25.1
1980	22366	106821	20.9	90657	24.7

Source: Union data from Handbook of Labor Statistics, 1979, Table 165. Labor organization data from Directory of U.S. Labor Organizations (1982-83 ed.), Table 2.

[1] Membership includes total reported membership excluding Canada. Also included are members of directly affiliated local unions. Members of single-firm unions are excluded.

TABLE 2
Membership by Industry Division, 1956-1980

Panel A: Membership in Unions

Year	Manufacturing			Nonmanufacturing			Government		
	Employees (1,000's)	Members (1,000's)	Percentage Organized	Employees (1,000's)	Members (1,000's)	Percentage Organized	Employees (1,000's)	Members (1,000's)	Percentage Organized
1956	17,243	8,839	51.3%	27,848	8,350	30.0%	7,278	915	12.6%
1958	15,945	8,359	52.4	27,540	8,574	31.1	7,839	1,035	13.2
1960	16,796	8,591	51.1	29,040	8,375	28.8	8,353	1,070	12.8
1962	16,853	8,050	47.8	29,806	8,289	27.8	8,890	1,225	13.8
1964	17,274	8,342	48.3	31,413	8,125	25.9	9,596	1,453	15.1
1966	19,214	8,769	45.6	33,903	8,640	25.5	10,784	1,717	15.9
1968	19,781	9,218	46.6	36,277	8,837	24.4	11,839	2,155	18.2
1970	19,367	9,173	47.4	38,959	9,198	23.6	12,554	2,318	18.5
1972	19,151	8,920	46.6	41,190	9,458	23.0	13,334	2,460	18.4
1974	20,077	9,144	45.5	44,018	9,520	21.6	14,170	2,920	20.6
1976	18,997	8,568	45.1	45,514	9,549	21.0	14,871	3,012	20.3
1978	20,505	8,119	39.6	50,520	9,997	19.8	15,672	3,625	23.1

Panel B: Organized Employed Wage and Salary Workers, May 1980

	Manufacturing			Nonmanufacturing			Public Administration		
1980	20,976	6,771	32.3%	61,246	11,512	18.8%	5,364	1,812	33.8%

Sources: Union membership: U.S. Dept. of Labor, Bureau of Labor Statistics, Directory of National Unions and Employee Associations 1979, Table 15. Employment, Panel A: Employment and Earnings, Nov. 1982, Table B-1. The nonmanufacturing division employment figures do not include agricultural employees.

Organized Employed Wage and Salary Workers and Employment, Panel B: BNA, Directory of U.S. Labor Organizations (1982-83 ed.), Tables 8 and 9.

trade, and services, the proportion of unionized workers has also fallen sharply. Between 1956 and 1978, there were 22.7 million jobs created, but unions gained only about 1.6 million members, in effect organizing less than 8 percent of all new jobs. This adverse record reflects factors such as the increase of nonproduction employees and the dispersion of manufacturing firms to the south and rural areas. Some argue that unions' recent lack of success is also due to more aggressive antiunion activities by employers.

Recently unions have achieved their principal successes in the government sector, where total employment more than doubled between 1956 and 1978. Even more dramatic has been the quadrupling of union membership in this sector between 1956 and 1978. The importance of government unions and bargaining organizations for recent membership gains is evident in Table 3. Although three of the four largest bargaining organizations have their membership predominantly in the private sector, the three fastest growing organizations are in the public sector (the Service Employees, the fourth most rapidly growing organization, also has a substantial number of members in the public sector). In contrast, all four of the organizations that experienced the most rapid declines between 1970 and 1980 have their membership predominantly in the private sector. As Table 2 indicates, almost three-quarters of all new union members in the 1956 to 1978 period were in the public sector.

In connection with the data on the extent of union membership, one oversimplified assumption should be avoided, i.e., that the number or percentage of organized workers is an adequate index of the influence of organized labor. Such an assumption ignores the following factors: (1) Unorganized workers within a bargaining unit are directly affected by collective bargaining. (2) The terms of employment for a bargaining unit are likely to have important consequences for other employees of the same employer who are not represented by a union. For example, clerical employees in a manufacturing industry, such as automobiles, may be affected by the bargain worked out for the bargaining unit covering production workers. Similarly, the bargain for an organized plant may directly affect the terms of employment in unorganized plants of the same employer. (3) Unorganized enterprises may be influenced by patterns set by organized employers, sometimes because of the fear of organization if nonunion firms do not match union settlements. (4) All enterprises, organized and unorganized, are affected by the impact of wages, employment, and output in the bargaining unit, which in turn affects the supply of labor elsewhere. (5) Finally, the economic power of particular unions is determined not by the extent of organization in general, but by factors such as the extent of organization of enterprises

TABLE 3

Membership of Four Largest Unions in 1980 and of Four Unions with
Largest Increase and Decrease in Membership, 1970-1980

	Membership (in thousands)		Change	
Union	1970	1980	Number	Percent
Largest				
1. Teamsters	1,829	1,891	62	3.4
2. National Education Association	1,100	1,684	584	53.1
3. Automobile Workers	1,486	1,357	−129	−8.7
4. Food and Commercial[1]	1,099	1,300	201	18.3
Fastest Growing				
1. State, County	444	1,098	654	147.3
2. National Education Association	1,100	1,684	584	53.1
3. Teachers (AFT)	205	551	346	168.8
4. Service Employees	435	650	215	49.4
Fastest Declining				
1. Steelworkers[2]	1,410	1,238	−172	−12.2
2. Automobile Workers	1,486	1,357	−129	−8.7
3. Ladies' Garment	442	323	−119	−26.9
4. Machinists	865	754	−111	−12.8

[1] Membership figure for 1970 derived by combining pre-merger membership of Retail Clerks International Union and Amalgamated Meat Cutters and Butcher Workmen of North America.

[2] Membership figure for 1970 derived by combining pre-merger membership of United Steelworkers of America and International Union of District 50, Allied and Technical Workers of the U.S. and Canada.

serving a given product market and the elasticity of the demand for their products.

B.   THE DEVELOPMENT OF A NATIONAL LABOR POLICY

In the early American cases, union activities were subjected to a doctrine of criminal conspiracy, which in England had been embodied in the Combination Acts of 1799 and 1800 and possibly in its common law before. See R. Morris, Government and Labor in Early America 207 (Octagon ed.

1965). In the first reported American labor case, Philadelphia Cordwainers (Commonwealth v. Pullis, Phila. Mayor's Court, 1806), 3 J. Commons & E. Gilmore, A Documentary History of American Industrial Society 59-248 (1910), Recorder Levy charged the jury that "A combination of workmen to raise their wages may be considered in a two fold point of view: one is to benefit themselves . . . the other is to injure those who do not join their society. The rule of law condemns both." Despite this sweeping charge, the defendants, as the Recorder also noted, had struck to enforce a closed shop. See Nelles, The First American Labor Case, 41 Yale L.J. 165 (1931).

The early *Cordwainers* cases discussed issues that are vital today: the employer's role and prerogatives in responding to market forces, the community's interest in lower costs, the rights of employees objecting to forced union membership.

Commonwealth v. Hunt, 45 Mass. (4 Met.) 111 (1842), was an important factor in the decline of the criminal conspiracy doctrine. Chief Justice Shaw's opinion, relying on a technical construction of the indictment, reversed a verdict of guilty based on the enforcement of a closed shop against a dissident worker, by a strike threat. Shaw also pointed to justifications for familiar union objectives, and his opinion has been hailed as arresting the use of the criminal conspiracy doctrine and inviting, instead, consideration of the justification for particular union purposes and the propriety of the means used. See L. Levy, The Law of the Commonwealth and Chief Justice Shaw, ch. II (1965); but cf. J. Landis & M. Manoff, Cases on Labor Law 35 (2d ed. 1942).

In states other than Massachusetts, application of the criminal conspiracy doctrine continued as, e.g., in State v. Donaldson, 32 N.J.L. 151 (Sup. Ct. 1867), until the labor injunction emerged as an effective weapon against harms attributed to labor unions.

The use of collective action to achieve union objectives typically inflicts harm — in the short run at least — on employers, nonunion employees, rival unions, or the general public. After the early doctrine of criminal conspiracy lapsed, courts employed a variety of approaches in determining whether the infliction of such harm was tortious. The prevailing judicial test focused on the issue of whether the means employed or the purpose sought was "improper" or illegal; in either event, liability would attach. That test plainly called for a clean distinction between the ends and means involved, but, in practice, courts frequently scrambled those matters by treating collective activities, such as strikes, as "coercive" or "oppressive" when they were directed at questionable purposes.

Even when means and ends were sharply differentiated, the application of the illegal-purpose test bristled with difficulties. The underlying issue was, of course, whether the harm inflicted on others by the attainment of a given union objective was justified by the union's competing interest. The resolution of such issues, Holmes observed,[a] involved fundamental questions of policy that were not answerable by simple jural tools. But such realism was only the beginning of analysis, for it answered neither the question of whether courts should adopt a hands-off attitude with respect to union purposes nor what the criteria for judicial intervention should be. Courts in general undertook to regulate union objectives but failed to furnish intelligible criteria for distinguishing between purposes related to strengthening organization and those related to achieving more immediate gains for employees. The result was a chaotic jurisprudence bristling with attenuated distinctions in a single jurisdiction and conflicting results in different jurisdictions.

The foundations of contemporary regulation of labor relations were established by the enactment of the Norris-LaGuardia Act in 1932 and the Wagner Act in 1935. Although the Great Depression provided the immediate impetus for those statutes, their underlying policy had been in the making for many years. Long before the depression, an impressive number of national commissions had called for a reconstruction of national policy. There had been, moreover, a variety of state and federal measures designed to protect unions against employer opposition and judicial restraints. Such measures had been directed at outlawing employer weapons, such as yellow-dog contracts and blacklisting; restricting the use of labor injunctions; and establishing mediation and arbitration machinery. Courts nullified some of those reforms on constitutional grounds or limited their reach by restrictive construction. Nevertheless, such measures reflected the growing acceptance of the legitimacy of unions, their increased political power, the costs of repressive policies, the validity of labor's historic grievances, and legislative responsibility for the basic policy issues. In the 1930s, Congress sought to consolidate and extend the bits and pieces of antecedent reforms and to avoid nullification or restrictive construction by the judiciary. A brief treatment of the earlier efforts of reform, by congressional and presidential action, is appropriate background for consideration of the current regulatory framework.

[a] Dissenting in Vegelahn v. Guntner, 167 Mass. 92, 102, 105-106, 44 N.E. 1077, 1079, 1080 (1896).

1. Railway Labor Legislation

Legislative and executive action designed to protect labor organization was first directed at the railroads. Such measures reflected the importance of railroad transportation to the national welfare, the authority of Congress over interstate transportation, and the strength of the railway unions. The Erdman Act, 30 Stat. 424 (1898), based on an earlier statute, strengthened provisions for arbitration of railway labor disputes and established the policy of government mediation and conciliation. That statute also made it a misdemeanor for an employer to condition employment on the execution of a yellow-dog contract or to engage in discrimination, actual or threatened, against employees because of their union membership. That antidiscrimination provision was, however, invalidated in Adair v. United States, 208 U.S. 161 (1908), as an arbitrary interference with liberty of contract violative of the Fifth Amendment and as beyond the commerce power.

During World War I, the government, while operating the railroads, announced a policy of protecting the employees' right to unionize; it also established boards of adjustment to deal with problems arising in the interpretation and administration of collective-bargaining agreements. Those wartime practices continued into the postwar period and, in general, received statutory support in the Transportation Act of 1920, 41 Stat. 456. The provisions of that statute were, however, not backed by sanctions, and the determinations of the boards it created were appeals only to moral obligation and public opinion. See Pennsylvania R.R. v. United States R.R. Lab. Bd., 261 U.S. 72 (1923).

The labor provisions of that act were replaced by the Railway Labor Act of 1926, 45 U.S.C. §§151-163, which had been agreed upon by the railroads and the interested unions. The 1926 act imposed a duty on the parties "to make and maintain agreements concerning rates of pay, rules and working conditions." It prohibited "interference, influence, or coercion by either party over the self-organization or designation of representatives by the other," without, however, specifying any enforcement machinery. The Supreme Court provided such machinery in Texas & N.O.R.R. v. Railway Clerks, 281 U.S. 548 (1930), by affirming an injunction against inducement and coercion, including discriminatory discharge of employees, designed to supplant an established national union with a company union. The Court (at 571) dismissed the Adair case as inapplicable, stating that the statute "does not interfere with the normal exercise of the right of the carrier to select its employees or to discharge them" but is aimed only "at the interference with the right of employees to have representatives of their own choosing." The

Court also dismissed §20 of the Clayton Act on the ground that injunctive relief was necessary to avoid irreparable injury to a property right, and it expressed doubt whether that section "can be regarded as limiting the authority of the court to restrain the violation of an explicit provision of an act of Congress."

In 1934 the Railway Labor Act was amended in order to meet certain objections voiced by railway labor unions, among others. Prohibitions were enacted against the use of a carrier's funds to maintain or assist labor organizations (including company unions) or to induce employees to join, or abstain from joining, such organizations. The National Mediation Board was authorized to conduct elections or to use other appropriate means of ascertaining the kind of labor organization desired by a majority of the employees in a craft or class. Local adjustment boards were replaced by a National Railroad Adjustment Board (NRAB) to be composed of eighteen representatives, nine chosen by the carriers and nine by the unions. The NRAB had different divisions with jurisdiction over different occupations. In the event of a deadlock among NRAB members, they were to select a neutral referee or have one assigned by the National Mediation Board. The 1934 act has remained substantially intact until the present. In 1936 most of its provisions were made applicable to interstate air carriers (45 U.S.C. §§181-188); and in 1951 it was amended to authorize union shop and check-off provisions (45 U.S.C. §152). In 1966 it was again amended to provide for the establishment of special adjustment boards, at the request of either unions or carriers, to limit sharply the scope of judicial review of awards and to permit judicial review at the instance of employees and unions as well as carriers (45 U.S.C. §153).

2.   The Norris-LaGuardia Act

National labor legislation of general application was initially designed to limit "government by injunction" and to restrict the application of the Sherman Act to union activities. The provisions of the Clayton Act (1914) directed at those ends were, however, largely nullified by legislative ambiguity and restrictive judicial interpretation. In 1932 Congress responded to the continuing criticism of labor injunctions by enacting the Norris-LaGuardia Act. That statute was narrowly drawn as a limitation on the jurisdiction of the federal courts to issue injunctions in labor disputes. Its limitations on their face were neutral, applying to nonviolent pressures by both management and labor. But the injunction had been a one-sided device, restricting labor's weapons, often on the basis of ex parte proceedings and boilerplate affidavits, while leaving management's substantially untouched; and the statute, despite its formal mutuality, was designed to promote unionization and more effective collective bargaining by freeing unions from hostile judicial intervention. Norris-LaGuardia has been characterized as a revolutionary statute even though its direct impact was limited. It applied only to diversity cases and to a narrow range of cases involving federal statutes impinging on labor relations, but its indirect impact was substantial. It was an eloquent legislative indictment of judicial treatment of union activity. Its preamble proclaimed a moral justification for unionization, collective bargaining, and concerted activity —and foreshadowed the affirmative protection soon to be granted by the Wagner Act. Like the Clayton Act, Norris-LaGuardia became the model for state legislation. Finally, it was in time to be invoked as support for a substantial immunity of unions from the Sherman Act.

3.   The Wagner Act and Its Immediate Precursors

The initial New Deal effort to supplement the benevolent neutrality of the Norris-LaGuardia Act with governmental protection for unionization and collective bargaining consisted of §7(a) of the National Industrial Recovery Act of 1933 (48 Stat. 213). Whether that section imposed a duty on employers to bargain with the representatives of their employees was uncertain. Such a duty was recognized by the National Labor Board, created by the President to enforce §7(a). That board was superseded in 1934 by the (first) National Labor Relations Board, appointed by the President on the basis of a joint resolution of Congress (48 Stat. 1183) and the NIRA. The new Board developed a body of case law concerning the duty to bargain that was invoked in the legislative debate preceding the enactment of the Wagner Act and in the interpretation of that statute. The 1934 Board ceased operations after the NIRA was invalidated in Schechter Poultry Corp. v. United States, 295 U.S. 495 (1935).

Soon after the demise of the NIRA, the policy of §7(a) was clarified and extended by the Wagner Act. Incidentally, although that act has been acclaimed as one of the enduring accomplishments of the New Deal, President Roosevelt's attitude toward the Wagner bill has been described as, at best, ambivalent, and his eleventh-hour endorsement as a grudging acceptance of the inevitable. See Keyserling, The Wagner Act: Its Origin and Current Significance, 29 Geo. Wash. L. Rev. 199, 202-203 (1960).

The Wagner Act provided affirmative legal protection against the exercise of employer power to frustrate the organization of employees for collective bargaining. In relatively simple, if elastic, provisions, the Act in general barred employer discrimination on account of, or interference with, organizational activities and other concerted activities by employees. It also imposed on employers an enforceable duty to bargain with unions chosen by a majority of employees in an appropriate unit, and it provided for machinery to determine such units and to ascertain employee preferences. The preference of the majority in general bound not only the employer but also other employees. A validly selected representative had a right to bargain, and a duty to bargain fairly, on behalf of all members of the unit; the employer in general had a correlative duty to bargain with the majority representative and with no one else. Enforcement of the statute devolved on a three-member Board that discharged the functions of both prosecutor and judge. Final orders of the Board were subject to judicial review and did not constitute the basis for any sanctions until they were judicially enforced.

There were manifest tensions in the means employed in the Norris-La-Guardia and Wagner acts to achieve their common purpose. Under Norris-LaGuardia, government was to keep the peace but otherwise to permit a "free struggle" in which economic power, rather than employee preferences, was to be decisive. Under the Wagner Act, government was to restrain employer power in order to protect employee preferences for unionization and collective bargaining and was, indeed, to rely on the injunction as the enforcement mechanism. That act, moreover, left untouched union pressures that could also pose a threat to employee self-determination. Such peaceful pressures, although wholly compatible with the philosophy of Norris-LaGuardia, could enforce demands on employers incompatible with their duties under the Wagner Act.

The legislative debates preceding the passage of the Wagner Act had identified the tensions between laissez faire as to union pressures and regulation of employer power. Critics of the proposed legislation had objected to its one-sidedness; they had also urged the need for disclosure of union financing and for anti-racketeering measures. But such problems had been tabled for reassessment when unions were no longer engaged in a bitter fight for recognition and survival. See Magruder, A Half Century of Legal Influence on the Development of Collective Bargaining, 50 Harv. L. Rev. 1071 (1937).

4.   The Taft-Hartley Act

Twelve years later such reassessment was reflected in the Taft-Hartley Act, enacted in 1947 over President Truman's veto. That act had been preceded by a bitter and extravagant debate, in the course of which the proposed legislation had been condemned as "the slave labor act." An important factor in its enactment had been, as already indicated, a rash of postwar strikes, which had deepened concern about union "power" and which had caused unions to be blamed for price increases and dislocations that were inevitable incidents of the reconversion period.

The Taft-Hartley Act was a comprehensive and complex statute, the provisions of which will be treated in detail in the materials below. At this point our principal concern will be with the changes reflected by the statute in the premises and objectives of the national labor policy.

The Taft-Hartley Act left virtually intact the employer unfair labor practices proscribed by the Wagner Act. It also reaffirmed the prior endorsement of collective bargaining, subject only to a condition that could have been fairly read into the Wagner Act — that such bargaining should rest on the uncoerced preferences of the majority of the employees concerned. That reaffirmation, at a time when unions were under severe attack, was an eloquent recognition that collective bargaining through the freely chosen representatives of employees had become a central value of our society and that its legal protection had, so far as one could see, become a permanent feature of national policy. Thus the Taft-Hartley Act, despite the bitter controversy that it precipitated, reflected a national consensus about the general desirability of collective bargaining through freely chosen representatives — a consensus that was later to be respected by even the most vocal critics of some aspects of labor-management relations. In the light of those considerations, it is difficult to accept the suggestion that the statute represented "a fundamental change in philosophy which rejects outright the policy of encouraging collective bargaining." See Cox, Some Aspects of the National Labor Relations Act (Pt. I), 61 Harv. L. Rev. 1, 24 (1947). The fundamental change in policy reflected by Taft-Hartley was of a different order. The national government acknowledged responsibility for regulating the means used and the objectives pursued by the beneficiaries of the Wagner Act. Congress sought to discharge this responsibility through provisions that defined and proscribed unfair labor practices by labor organizations. These provisions, which were part of Title I of Taft-Hartley, constituted the most important changes made by the new legislation. They prohibited so-called "bad practices" by unions, including coercion of employees, secondary boycotts, and work-assignment disputes.

Other amendments to the Wagner Act, also embodied in Title I of Taft-Hartley, may be briefly mentioned at this point. Section 9 was amended by imposing restrictions on the NLRB's conduct of representation proceedings and by conditioning the utilization of the Board's representation and unfair labor practices machinery by unions on their furnishing certain financial reports and on their principal officers' filing affidavits disclaiming their membership in the Communist party. The NLRB was also increased from three to five members. The prosecutive and judicial functions regarding unfair labor practices were separated by conferring upon the Board's General Counsel final authority to investigate charges and to issue complaints.

In addition to those and other amendments to the Wagner Act, Taft-Hartley dealt with a variety of matters: Title II established the Federal Mediation and Conciliation Service (FMCS) as an independent agency and also established procedures for dealing with national emergency disputes. Title III provided for suits in federal courts to enforce collective bargaining agreements and for damage actions in both state and federal courts for certain unfair labor practices. It also restricted employer payments to employee representatives and health and welfare funds, and prohibited certain union political contributions and strikes by government employees.

5. The Labor-Management Reporting and Disclosure Act of 1959

This statute (LMRDA) broke new ground by subjecting union internal affairs to direct and comprehensive federal regulation. The immediate momentum for such regulation had been provided by the Senate Select Committee on Improper Activities in the Labor-Management Field (the McClellan Committee). That committee had disclosed the existence of various abuses within some unions, including misuse and embezzlement of union funds, a lack of internal democracy and procedural decency, and collusion with (and payoffs by) management. The LMRDA contains a broad variety of provisions designed to curb such abuses.

The statute also contained various amendments to the NLRA. It tightened the secondary boycott provisions, restricted organizational and recognition picketing, and conferred upon states jurisdiction over cases declined by the NLRB. As a sweetener to unions, the statute granted workers replaced during an economic strike voting rights in elections conducted by the NLRB.

Although the revelations of the McClellan Committee provided the impetus for the 1959 act, that statute, like the Wagner Act, was the culmination of developments with a considerable history. The democratic ideal had been an important source of support for the union movement. The plant had been analogized to the larger society; and participation by employees, through their representatives, in shaping the industrial code that so pervasively affected their lives had been justified as "industrial democracy" and had been linked to the larger values of a democratic order.

The ideal of democracy was closely connected with the ideal of fiduciary responsibility. Union government, like political government, was supposed to protect the welfare of the group and not to line the pockets of the leadership. Furthermore, pervasive common law doctrines imposed special responsibilities on those who acted for others in ordinary commercial activities. Such doctrines had a special force in relation to a movement that had elements of a genuine crusade on behalf of the disinherited and that had flourished in part because of the legal protection afforded by national legislation. It was natural that the law should be invoked to purify the institutions that it had sponsored.

Finally, the spread of union security arrangements, as well as the use of questionable organizational techniques such as organizational picketing, had increased the number of captive union members. Such compulsion gave added force to demands for protecting all members against internal tyranny and dishonesty.

6.   Title VII of the Civil Rights Act of 1964

This act provided comprehensive remedies against racial and other forms of invidious discrimination. The Equal Opportunity Act of 1972 expanded Title VII's coverage and modified its enforcement procedures. The values reflected in those statutes also stimulated the development of overlapping remedies based on other statutes and the Constitution.

7.   Direct Federal Regulation of the Employment Relation

The foregoing legislation proscribes the use of certain invidious criteria (such as race) in connection with employment, or protects certain processes (such as collective bargaining) but does not directly regulate the terms and conditions of employment. An important body of federal law provides for such regulation.

Among the most important is the Fair Labor Standards Act (wage and hour law) of 1938, as amended, 29 U.S.C. §§201-219. It prescribes minimum wages, requires premium pay for overtime work, provides for exemptions from the minimum rate for learners, the handicapped, etc., prohibits child labor under some circumstances and regulates it in others; its coverage has been extended by successive amendments. In National League of Cities v. Usery, 426 U.S. 833 (1976), the Supreme Court (5 to 4) invalidated the extension of coverage to state and local government employees, at least if they were performing "integral governmental functions," as distinguished, presumably, from "proprietary functions."[b]

The Davis-Bacon Act of 1931, as amended, 40 U.S.C. §276(a), applies to all contracts in excess of $2000 to which the United States or the District of Columbia is a party and which involve the construction or alteration of public buildings or public works. The Secretary of Labor is authorized by the act to determine the prevailing area wage rate for each group of workers and impose such wage rates as minimal. The standards of the Davis-Bacon Act and related statutes — the Anti-Kickback Act of 1934, 18 U.S.C. §874, and the Contract Work Hours Standards Act of 1962, 40 U.S.C. §§327-332 — have been extended to cover work performed pursuant to various federal loan, guarantee, and grant-in-aid programs for the states.

The Walsh-Healey Public Contracts Act of 1936, as amended, 41 U.S.C. §§35-45, applies to work done on United States Government contracts of $10,000 or more for materials and supplies, etc., and authorizes the Secretary of Labor to determine prevailing minimum wages on the basis of prevailing wage rates.

The depression of the 1930s marked a new phase in the acceptance of national responsibility for dealing with economic insecurity. The permanent measures initiated in that period include the Railroad Retirement Act of 1935, 49 Stat. 967; this replaced the 1934 act invalidated by the Supreme Court decision in R.R. Retirement Bd. v. Alton R.R., 295 U.S. 330 (1935), and established a special retirement system for railroad workers. A special system of unemployment insurance for railroad workers was adopted in 1938. In 1946 the railroad programs were expanded to provide survivor and disability benefits.

Of more general importance was the enactment of the Social Security Act of 1935, 42 U.S.C.A. §§301 et seq. That statute, as amended, constitutes the basis for a comprehensive system of old-age and survivor benefits financed by payroll taxes on employers and employees; that statute was also the basis for a nationwide system of unemployment insurance financed by employer payroll taxes.

Although detailed consideration of the statutes mentioned above is beyond the scope of this book, it is appropriate to suggest certain relationships between such direct regulation of labor standards and labor relations statutes:

[b] But cf. EEOC v. Wyoming, 460 U.S. 226 (1983).

(1) Direct regulation supplements the efforts of relatively weak unions in low-wage industries to improve the employment conditions of their constituents. (2) Some of those statutes, e.g., the Fair Labor Standards Act, raise issues similar to those raised by the exertion of union power, e.g., the impact of regulation on employment opportunities of marginal workers. (3) Such statutes in other countries have provided protections secured in the United States by collective bargaining and constitute a theoretical alternative to collective bargaining as a means of securing some benefits for employees. (4) The current desirability of some of those statutes (e.g., Davis-Bacon and Walsh-Healey) has been questioned on the ground that subsequent developments, including the increased power of organized labor and particularly of construction workers, have undermined the original reasons for enactment. See, e.g., C. Christenson & R. Myren, Wage Policy under the Walsh-Healey Public Contracts Act: A Critical Review (1966); A. Thieblot, Jr., The Davis-Bacon Act (1975).

Two other far-reaching federal statutes will be dealt with only incidentally. The Occupational Safety and Health Act of 1970 (OSHA), 29 U.S.C. §§651-678, authorizes the Secretary of Labor to adopt and to enforce safety and health standards for the workers' protection. The Employee Retirement Income Security Act of 1974 (ERISA), 29 U.S.C. §§1001-1381, vastly expands federal regulation of pension and welfare plans.

CHAPTER 2

WORKERS, UNIONS, AND THE ECONOMY: AN OVERVIEW

In a classic article Professor Hoxie wrote:

> [T]he union problem is neither simple nor unitary. It is not a mere question of wages and hours, of shop conditions and the narrow economic rights of employer and employee, and it cannot be resolved by a mere resort to economic theory. . . . It is a complex of economic, legal, ethical and social problems which can be understood and met only by knowing the facts and the genesis of the viewpoint of organized labor in all its reach, diversity, contradictoriness and shifting character, and by considering this viewpoint in relation to developing social conditions and social standards.[a]

See generally, T. Kochan, Collective Bargaining and Industrial Relations (1980). This chapter introduces some of the questions suggested by Hoxie —those concerning the rationale for unionization and collective bargaining, and the impact of unions on other workers and the general public. These questions are presented at this point because of the pervasive impact of varying answers on the development of both the broad policies and specific elements of labor-management regulation.

Senate Committee on Education & Labor
S. Rep. No. 573 on S. 1958,[b] 74th Cong., 1st Sess. 1-4 (1935)

Industrial peace. The first objective of the bill is to promote industrial peace. The challenge of economic unrest is not new. During the period from 1915 through 1921 there were on the average 3,043 strikes per year, involv-

[a] Hoxie, Trade Unionism in the United States: General Character and Types, 22 J. Pol. Econ. 207 (1914), reprinted in Landmarks in Political Economy 67, 71 (E. Hamilton, A. Rees, & H. Johnson eds. 1962).
[b] This was the bill introduced by Senator Wagner on February 21, 1935, which after minor amendments became the original NLRA.

35

ing the vacating of 1,745,000 jobs and the loss of 50,242,000 working days every 12 months. From 1922 through 1926 the annual average totaled 1,050 strikes, 775,000 strikers, and 17,050,000 working days lost. From 1927 through 1931 the yearly average for disputes was 763, for the employees leaving their work 275,000, and for days lost 5,665,000. In 1933 over 813,137 workers were drawn into strikes, and in 1934 the number rose to 1,277,344. In this two-year period over 32,000,000 working days were lost because of labor controversies. While exactitude is impossible, reliable authority has it that, over a long range of time, the losses due to strikes in this country have amounted to at least $1,000,000,000 per year. And no one can count the cost in bitterness of feeling, in inefficiency, and in permanent industrial dislocation.

Prudence forbids any attempt by the Government to remove all the causes of labor disputes. Disputes about wages, hours of work, and other working conditions should continue to be resolved by the play of competitive forces, so far as the provisions of codes of fair competition are not controlling. This bill in no respect regulates or even provides for supervision on wages or hours, nor does it establish any form of compulsory arbitration.

But many of the most fertile sources of industrial discontent can be segregated into a single category susceptible to legislative treatment. Competent students of industrial relations have estimated that at least 25 percent of all strikes have sprung from failure to recognize and utilize the theory and practices of collective bargaining, under which are subsumed the rights of employees to organize freely and to deal with employers through representatives of their choosing. . . . [O]f the 6,355 new cases received by the regional agencies of the present National Labor Relations Board during the second half of 1934, the issue of collective bargaining was paramount in 2,330, or about 74 [sic] percent.

It is thus believed feasible to remove the provocation to a large proportion of the bitterest industrial outbreaks by giving definite legal status to the procedure of collective bargaining and by setting up machinery to facilitate it. Furthermore, by establishing the only process through which friendly negotiations or conferences can operate in modern large-scale industry, there should be a tremendous lessening of the strife that has resulted from failure to adjust wage and hour disputes. . . . [T]he committee believes that the present bill, by promoting peace in industry, will confer mutual benefits upon employers, workers, and the general public.

Economic adjustment. The second major objective of the bill is to encourage, by developing the procedure of collective bargaining, equality of bargaining power which is a prerequisite to equality of opportunity and freedom of contract. The relative weakness of the isolated wage earner caught in the complex of modern industrialism has become such a common-place of our economic literature and political vocabulary that it needs no exposition. This relative weakness of position has been intensified by the technological forces driving us toward greater concentration of business, by the tendency of the courts to narrow the application of the antitrust laws, and more recently by the policy of the Government in encouraging cooperative activity among trade and industrial groups.

Congress long ago recognized that it must play some part in redressing this inequality of bargaining power. A ready example has been the extensive role played by the Federal Government in the railroad industry. . . . Another instance is the Norris-LaGuardia Act. And a marked enlargement of Federal activity in the field of labor relations was one of the consequences of the nation-wide depression beginning in 1929.

Between 1929 and February 1933, the index of industrial production dropped from 119 to 63, while construction activities fell from 117 to 19, and commodity prices from 95.3 to 59.8. Payrolls receded from 107 to 40. In the 3 years following 1929, the income received by individuals in the United States shrank from 81 billion dollars to 49, a reduction of 40 percent. At the height of the crisis, from 12 to 16 million people were unemployed.

While neither economists nor statesmen agreed entirely as to the causes or remedies for the depression, the overwhelming preponderance acknowledged that the disregard of economic forces for state lines, the interpenetration of various industries throughout the country, and the nation-wide character of the prolonged calamity made national action essential. To speed business revival Congress, therefore, abetted nation-wide cooperation among businessmen to outlaw unfair trade practices, to rationalize production, and to coordinate the distribution of goods. Supplementary to this, Congress accepted and acted upon the tested hypothesis that the depression had been provoked and accentuated by a long-continued and increasing disparity between production and consumption; that this disparity had resulted from a level of wages that did not permit the masses of consumers to relieve the market of an ever-increasing flow of goods; and that even businessmen who recognized these evils — and very many of them did — were powerless to act because of the uncontrolled competition in regard to wages and other working conditions. Having in mind both the temporary expediency of priming the pump of business and the permanent objective of crystallizing anti-depressive forces for the future, Congress commenced the regulation of minimum wages and maximum hours to stabilize competitive conditions and to spread adequate consumer purchasing power throughout the nation at large.

Congress recognized at the outset, however, that governmental regulation of wages and working conditions was not a complete solution, and that far from being a substitute for self-help by industry and labor, it was merely a bedrock upon which both might build. In order that industry might help itself, there was some relaxation of the antitrust laws; in order that labor might help itself, the prospectus of collective bargaining was set forth in Section 7(a) of the National Industrial Recovery Act (48 Stat. 198), supplemented in June 1934 by Public Resolution 44 (48 Stat. 1183), providing for governmentally supervised elections of representatives of employees.

Whatever divergence of opinion there may be as to the validity of some of the steps in the program above discussed, the committee believes that the desirability of collective bargaining, as it bears upon industrial peace and equality of bargaining power, is sufficiently well established and sufficiently divorced from the temporary aspects of the present economic situation to justify its affirmance in adequate and permanent Federal law. . . .

NOTES

1. The "purchasing power" theory referred to in the foregoing report, and the related idea that general increases in wages are an effective antidepression measure, have for some time been rejected by many economists. See Dunlop, American Wage Determination and the Economics of Liberalism, in Wage Determination and the Economics of Liberalism 34,44 (U.S. Chamber of Commerce 1947) and the excerpt from the Simons article, immediately below.

2. The idea that unorganized employees suffer from an inherent bargaining disadvantage has a long history going back at least to Adam Smith's The Wealth of Nations, Book I, ch. VIII (Modern Library ed. 1937), and has been an important element of the justification for labor organization. See, e.g., American Steel Foundries Co. v. Tri-City Cent. Trades Council, 257 U.S. 184, 204 (1921). That idea has been supported by a variety of contentions, including the following: Employers expressly or tacitly combine to keep wages low; employers can wait, while employees cannot withhold services because of lack of reserves and because labor is "perishable"; labor is consistently and almost uniquely overstocked; the worker is relatively uninformed about alternative opportunities; because of attachment to a particular workplace, the individual employee is reluctant to move. Attempts have been made to refine the discussion of bargaining power by considering whether the pertinent product market is essentially competitive or monopolistic, whether a given labor market is characterized by monopsony, whether general economic activity is high or low, and whether the skill of particular workers is substantially independent of a particular enterprise.

3. The general idea of labor's inherent bargaining disadvantage and the propositions invoked to support that idea have, however, been questioned on both empirical and conceptual grounds by economists with varying views concerning the costs and benefits of labor organization. See, e.g., W. Hutt, The Theory of Collective Bargaining (Am. ed. 1954); F. Machlup, The Political Economy of Monopoly, chs. 9-10 (1952); J. Dunlop, Wage Determination Under Trade Unions, ch. 5 (1944); Mason, The Monopolistic Power of Labor Unions, 79 Monthly Lab. Rev. 161, 162 (1956).

Students should consider the content and validity of the bargaining power doctrine in examining not only the materials in this section but also the issues raised throughout this book as to whether particular accretions to union or employer power are desirable.

Simons, Some Reflections on Syndicalism
52 J. Pol. Econ. 1 (1944)[c]

Questioning the virtues of the organized labor movement is like attacking religion, monogamy, motherhood, or the home. . . . One simply cannot argue that organization is injurious to labor; one is either for labor or against it, and the test is one's attitude toward unionism. But . . . my central interest, and the criterion in terms of which I wish to argue, is a maximizing of aggregate labor income and a minimizing of inequality. If unionism were good for labor as a whole, that would be the end of the issue for me, since the community whose welfare concerns us is composed overwhelmingly of laborers.

Our problem here, at bottom, is one of broad political philosophy. Advocates of trade unionism are, I think, obligated morally and intellectually to present a clear picture of the total political-economic system toward which they would have us move. For my part, I simply cannot conceive of any tolerable or enduring order in which there exists widespread organization of workers along occupational, industrial, functional lines. Sentimentalists view such developments merely as a contest between workers who earn too little and enterprises which earn too much; and, unfortunately, there has been enough monopsony in labor markets to make this view superficially plausible, through not enough to make it descriptively important. What we generally fail to see is the identity of interest between the whole community and enterprises seeking to keep down costs. Where enterprise is competitive — and substantial, enduring restraint of competition in product markets is rare — enterprisers represent the community interest effectively; indeed,

[c]Reprinted in H. Simons, Economic Policy for a Free Society 121 (Director ed. 1947).

they are merely intermediaries between consumers of goods and sellers of services. Thus we commonly overlook the conflict of interest between every large organized group of laborers and the community as a whole. What I want to ask is how this conflict can be reconciled, how the power of strongly organized sellers can be limited out of regard for the general welfare. No insuperable problem arises so long as organization is partial and precarious, so long as most unions face substantial nonunion competition, or so long as they must exercise monopoly powers sparingly because of organizational insecurity. Weak unions have no large monopoly powers. But how does a democratic community limit the demands and exactions of strong, secure organizations? Looking at the typographers, the railway brotherhoods, and metropolitan building trades, among others, one answers simply: "It doesn't!" . . .

All the grosser mistakes in economic policy, if not most manifestations of democratic corruption, arise from focusing upon the interests of people as producers rather than upon their interests as consumers, that is, from acting on behalf of producer minorities rather than on behalf of the whole community as sellers of services and buyers of products. One gets the right answers usually by regarding simply the interests of consumers, since we are all consumers; and the answers reached by this approach are presumably the correct ones for laborers as a whole. . . .

. . . [L]abor monopolies and labor "states" may readily become a problem which democracy simply cannot solve at all. There must be effective limitations upon their powers; but I do not see how they can be disciplined democratically save by internal competition or how that discipline can be effected without breaking down organization itself. Here, possibly, is an awful dilemma: democracy cannot live with tight occupational monopolies; and it cannot destroy them, once they attain great power, without destroying itself in the process. If democratic governments cannot suppress organized extortion and preserve their monopoly of violence, they will be superseded by other kinds of government. . . .

Every organized group of sellers is typically in a position to gain by raising prices and restricting sales. . . . When organization becomes widespread, however, the common interest in increased production may greatly outweigh particular interests in restriction, even for those practicing restriction. . . .

Monopoly power must be abused. It has no use save abuse. Some people evidently have believed that labor organizations should have monopoly powers and be trusted not to use them. Collective bargaining, for the Webbs, was evidently a scheme whereby labor monopolies were to raise wages to competitive levels, merely counteracting monopsony among buyers, but eschewing further exercise of organizational powers. A trade-unionism affecting wages and working rules only within such limits, and doing all the many other good things that unions can do, would be a blessing all around.[5] . . . But monopsony in the labor market is, I think, very unsubstantial or transitory; and it is romantic and unreasonable to expect organizations to exercise powers only within limits consistent with the common interest. All bargaining power is monopoly power. Such power, once attained, will be used as fully as its conservation permits and also used continuously for its own accretion and consolidation. . . .

Patently restrictive practices are now commonly deplored and, perhaps because unnecessary, seem somewhat on the wane. But there have been many cases of severe limitations upon entry — high initiation fees, excessive periods of apprenticeship and restrictions upon numbers of apprentices, barriers to movement between related trades, and, of course, make-work restrictions, cost-increasing working rules, and prohibition of cost-reducing innovations, notably in the building trades — not to mention racial and sex discriminations against which effective competition in labor markets is probably a necessary, if not a sufficient, protection.

It is not commonly recognized, however, that control of wage rates *is* control of entry, especially where seniority rules are in force and, even failing such rules, where qualitative selection is important and turnover itself very costly to firms. If able to enforce standard rates, experienced, established workers can insulate themselves from the competition of new workers merely by making their cost excessive, that is, by establishing labor costs and wage

---

[5] It has seemed best in this essay simply to recognize that unions perform many useful functions and render many valuable services besides those having to do with wage rates, labor costs, restrictive practices, and monopoly or bargaining power — without attempting to detail or to appraise the salutary activities or aspects of activities. This deliberate omission implies no inclination to question or to minimize the good things of unionism, but merely a disposition to emphasize considerations and aspects which are the proper and special business of economists as such. To stress those things which are especially amenable to quantitative or abstract analysis is not to imply that others are unimportant. . . .

I wish I could honestly and tactfully propose that large unions be protected and fostered in their good functions and deprived of their socially bad ones (monopoly power). Like others, I can *wish* for this solution, but, also like others, I cannot honestly propose it, for I have no notion *how* it could be done. Politicians may go on advocating schemes defined merely in terms of everyone's ends, without any reference to means or implementation — and fearlessly opposing sin in general. Professors, after a prodigious spree, should now eschew such rhetorical intoxicants and go back to work. However, it is perhaps not merely wishful to suggest that many of the good features of unionism *could* be preserved, and monopoly powers perhaps kept within reason, by limiting the size of unions and proscribing collusion among them. Having said this, one must pause for riotous heckling about "company unions" and then try calmly to assert that the case against company unions is strongest when asserted only against bad ones and, like the case against means tests, is not impressive when stated categorically or when supported only by bad (i.e., historical) evidence.

expectations which preclude expansion of production or employment in their field. . . . Wage control, determining a major element in operating cost, also determines the rate at which a whole industry will expand or, more likely, with strong organization, the rate of contraction. . . .

The situation is more complicated . . . where unions do permit and facilitate entry, that is, where work is shared equally between newcomers and others. Here the advantages of high wages are dissipated by the sharing of unemployment; and annual wages may even drop below a competitive level, if workers value leisure highly or are usually able to find other remunerative work during their periods of layoff. The outcome resembles that of the pure cartel among enterprises where price is fixed by voluntary agreement, output divided by quotas, and newcomers admitted freely and granted quotas on the same basis as old firms. No one gains, and everybody as consumer loses. There is great social wastage of resources, of labor in one case, of investment in the other; and the two wastes are likely to occur together, as in coal-mining.

. . . Personnel experts tell us that qualitative dispersion in labor markets is enormous; that among workers regarded as belonging to the same class (i.e., apart from the upgrading that accompanies large increases of employment) the best workers are worth several times as much to a firm as are the poorer ones. In any case, it is instructive to consider an analogy in agricultural policy to the device of the standard rate in unionized industry.

It is a familiar axiom that the existence of poorer grades of land serves to keep down rents on the better grades. The poorer grades, adding to output, keep down product prices and thus diminish productivity and rents of other land. Suppose now that wheat producers, protected by prohibitive tariffs, should organize and prohibit, by nightriding or by securing appropriate legislation, the use for wheat-raising of any land whose net annual rental value is less than $10 per acre. (Thus renters could not use land for wheat unless they paid at least $10 per acre; and owners could so use their own land only if annual net returns averaged above $10 per acre.) The effects of such a measure would be fairly complex, since some land excluded at the start would become eligible for use after output fell and price rose; but its virtues for owners of the best land, and its grave diseconomies for the community, are obvious enough. No one (outside the Department of Agriculture) would purport to defend such a policy or suggest that it would be less objectionable if extended to cover all forms of agriculture. In principle, however, there is little to distinguish it from the standard wage in industry. . . .

The case for differentiation according to differences in living costs is commonly conceded in principle and need not detain us here. Trade unionists will deplore any such concession as a confession of weakness or as impractical and, since it is clearly contrary to the interests of established workers and established centers in most cases, may be expected to prevent it if they have the power to do so. Moreover, the principle is much less simple and definite than it seems to most people, for even rough estimate of the relative value of money as between distant places is nearly impossible.

Even with such differentiation, however, the argument for standardization of wage rates between communities comes near to denying all advantages of interregional trade and is fundamentally on a level with the preposterous Republican (and Democratic!) principles of tariff policy. If standard wage rates are desirable, then tariffs should everywhere be adjusted to offset all differences in labor cost between domestic and foreign producers. . . . If fully applied in tariff policy, it would practically prohibit all trade and all territorial specialization. One difference here may, however, be noted. If a domestic industry and its workers are protected by duties which compensate for wage differences, say, in Argentina, Argentinean workers are excluded from an American product market. If American workers can enforce their wage rates on Argentinean and other producers, they get both the American and the Argentinean markets — if they are superior workers and/or if they have access here to better and more abundant capital and management. If northern enterprises and workers can enforce northern wages in particular southern industries, they can largely exclude southern enterprises and workers from both northern and southern markets. . . .

The public interest demands free exchange and free movement of workers among occupations. Above all, it demands the easiest possible access by workers in low-wage occupations to highly productive and unusually remunerative employment. Unionism implies ability of established workers in high-wage areas and occupations to insulate themselves from competition, excluding inexperienced new workers and qualitatively inferior labor from their markets. It enables an aristocracy of labor to build fences around its occupations, restricting entry, raising arbitrarily the costs and prices of its products, and lowering the wages and incomes of those outside, and of the poor especially.

. . . [L]et me propose, as something better than half-truth, the generalization that, by and large, employers get the kind of labor they pay for. Highest enterprise earnings usually go with highest wage rates; and so-called marginal firms commonly pay both their workers and their owners rather poorly. Some people deduce from these facts . . . that wage increases, whether enforced by legislation or by unions, will be relatively costless, forcing economies in management and improvement in methods. This argument, unfortunately, can also be employed to demonstrate that excises are the best device of taxation, since, as some classical writers argued incautiously, they tend to be absorbed by inducing more economical methods of production! But the phenomenon in the labor market is not hard to explain on other grounds.

As between firms and even between industries, large differences in wage rates may persist without corresponding differences in costs. A single firm, offering higher wages than its competitors, may get better morale and cooperation which are well worth the cost; and surely it will be able to enlist and maintain a qualitatively superior labor force. A whole industry may accomplish the same thing, competing for labor with other industries. . . . Thus, wage concessions to organized groups may at the outset cost nothing at all, to a firm as against other firms or to an industry as against other industries. All that happens is that quality standards are raised and inferior workers more rigidly excluded. But downgrading cannot go on forever; the trick works only if it is confined to a few cases; we should guard here against fallacies of composition. . . . When all industry or many industries try the trick, poorer labor is simply frozen out and driven into unemployment or into much less remunerative and less socially productive employment where standards are less severe. In the old days the steel industry, the garment industry, and coal-mining, with all their abuses, did absorb and train a great mass of low-grade immigrant labor. What industries will do this job for us in the future? . . .

Consider also the untoward effect of standard rates on new and venturesome enterprise. The most vital competition commonly arises from firms content to experiment with new locations and relatively untrained labor. Such enterprises must offer workers better terms than they have received in alternative previous employment but cannot offer the wages paid to highly specialized, selected workers in established centers. If compelled to offer such terms, they will not arise. Yet it is obviously one of the finest services of new and venturesome enterprise to find better uses for existing labor and to employ more productively than theretofore labor resources which need not be confined to activities of low value. Indeed, every new firm must do this in large measure. Old established firms have skimmed off the cream of the labor supply and have trained their workers to a substantial superiority over the inexperienced. If potential competitors must pay the same wages as old firms, the established enterprises will be nearly immune to new competition, just as high-grade workers are immune to the competition of poorer grades. . . .

Let me now propose some generalizations about wages and ideal wage policy, whether for a democratic capitalism or for a democratic socialism. To avoid the confusion and sophistry of "purchasing-power" arguments, we may simply abstract from monetary disturbances and deflation, supposing that the government successfully maintains a sound and highly stable currency. . . .

The proper wage in any area or occupational category is the lowest wage which will bring forth an adequate supply of labor in competition with other employment opportunities. "Adequate supply" is ambiguous as it stands but will usually be interpreted correctly if not defined. It may, of course, be defined as the supply necessary to equate the productivity of transferable labor as between the industry or occupation in question and other alternative employments. In other words, it is the wage which will permit the maximum transfer of workers from less attractive, less remunerative, less productive employments. . . . We imply that any wage is excessive if more qualified workers are obtainable at that wage than are employed — provided only that the industry is reasonably competitive as among firms. Reduction of rates would permit workers to enter who otherwise would be compelled to accept employment less attractive to them and less productive for the community or to accept involuntary unemployment. This amounts to saying that any relative wage may be presumed to be too high if it requires the support of force (organization) or law.

The basic principle here is freedom of entry — freedom of migration, between localities, between industries, between occupational categories. If such freedom is to exist — and it is limited inevitably by costs and by defects of training and experience — wages must fall to accommodate new workers in any area to which many qualified persons wish to move. Freedom of migration implies freedom of qualified workers, not merely to seek jobs but to get them; free entry implies full employment for all qualified persons who wish to enter. Whether the wage permits an adequate family scale of living, according to social service workers, is simply irrelevant — as, indeed, are the net earnings of employers. What really matters is the judgment of workers who would be excluded by an excessive wage as to the *relative* merits of the employment in question and of employment in the less attractive alternatives actually open to them. Other things equal, the wage is too high if higher than the wage in actually alternative employments. Ethically, one cannot go beyond the opinion of qualified workers seeking to transfer. If in large numbers they prefer employment here to the alternatives and cannot get it, the wage is excessive. A case may be made for supplementing, by governmental expenditure, the family incomes of workers of low productivity, but not for keeping them idle or for confining them to less productive as against more productive employment.[11] . . .

---

[11] Perhaps the best investment by government in better labor standards is improvement of labor exchanges and public employment agencies, facilitation of labor mobility and migration, and systematic informing of enterprisers about areas of labor redundancy, actual and prospective. Labor markets can and should be made more competitive among firms, industries, and localities and more flexible, as well as less monopolistic, on the supply line. All this is proper and urgent public business.

Unionism is only incidentally a means of raising labor incomes at the expense of profits or property income. Profits are usually a small moiety, sometimes positive and often negative; and all property income is a margin whose reduction by particular wage increases reacts promptly and markedly upon employment, production, and product price. Increased labor cost in particular areas has its impact upon earnings; but, as with excise taxes, the burden or incidence quickly transfers to the buyer of products, if not to sellers of services, via output changes.

. . . The semblance of struggle between labor and capital conceals the substantial conflict between a labor monopoly and the community; between organized workers and consumers; and especially between established workers in more remunerative occupations and workers elsewhere. The masses of the unorganized and unorganizable lose as consumers; they lose by being denied access to higher-wage areas; and they lose by an artificial abundance of labor in the markets where they must sell. . . . And let no one infer that their problem would be solved if they too were organized. The monopoly racket, like that of tariffs and subsidies, works only so long as it is exceptional — works only to advantage minorities relatively, with over-all diseconomy and loss.[12] . . .

Gradual secular increase is to be expected in a progressive economy. But note the awful effects of adjusting *relative* wages continuously to relative earnings. Even in a vigorous and healthy system, some industries and employments will always be contracting, relatively and absolutely. Given free markets, the slack will readily be taken up by industries where demand conditions are improving. . . .

With strong organization, established workers in expansible employments are in a position to prevent expansion and must do so to capture for themselves the full advantage of favorable changes affecting their industry or product market. Ethically, they should share their gains with the community as consumers and with outside workers for whom expansion of output would permit transfer from less remunerative employment. But no group will practice such sharing if it has power to prevent it. . . .

[12] One may recognize the possibility that, with wide or universal organization of workers, federations of unions might enforce some moderation of wage demands and of exclusive, restrictive practices among the labor aristocracies. Such internal discipline among and between unions is a real contingency in small, homogeneous nations like Sweden (especially if complemented by a strong free-trade tradition). In a vast nation or a culturally heterogeneous population, the possibility may be dismissed as utterly unsubstantial. Moreover, the development of such effective "regulation" would involve radical constitutional change in the political system, i.e., reduction of the Congress or national legislature to a status not unlike that of the British crown.

It is interesting to note that Swedish co-operatives have at times discharged functions of our Antitrust Division — which is not a decisive reason for abolishing that agency here!

The situation here is especially alarming when one considers it from the viewpoint of enterprises or investors. In a free-market world, every commitment of capital is made in the face of enormous uncertainties. One may lose heavily or gain vastly, depending on unpredictable (uninsurable) contingencies. For reasonably intelligent investors, however, the gamble, with free markets, is a fairly even one, with chances of gain balancing roughly the risks of loss — relative to a conservative commitment, say, in government bonds. The willingness to take chances, to venture with one's property, especially in new and novel enterprises, of course, is the very basis of our whole economic and political system. It is now gravely jeopardized by developments which tend ominously to diminish the chances of gain relative to the chances of loss. . . .

[T]here are no absolute rights; and the right of voluntary association must always be qualified, inter alia, by prohibitions against monopolizing — against collusive action among sellers. Failing ability to use violence or to threaten it effectively, particular organizations could not practice heavy extortion or sustain it indefinitely; but they could often tax the community substantially for a time and subject it to substantial, if minor, disturbances. The grave diseconomies of the theorist's pure cartel situation, in labor and other markets, are relevant to real situations, actual and possible; and protection of the public interest demands limitation of the right of association where the association is of people as suppliers of particular commodities or services.[13]

. . . [L]abor organization without large powers of coercion and intimidation is an unreal abstraction. Unions now have such powers; they always have had and always will have, so long as they persist in their present form. Where the power is small or insecurely possessed, it must be exercised overtly and extensively; large and unchallenged, it becomes like the power of strong government, confidently held, respectfully regarded, and rarely displayed conspicuously. . . . However, they necessarily restrict drastically the normal flows of trade, destroying general prosperity in their struggle for relative advantage, and reducing enterprisers and investors to a defensive, defeatist task of withdrawing their property, on the least unfavorable terms obtainable politically, into the dubious security of government bonds. . . .

The obvious struggle within particular industries over division of earnings tends largely to obscure the more substantial identity of interest and functional complementarity of labor and employer organizations. Popularly regarded and defended as counterpoises to industrial concentration of enter-

---

[13] Dr. Gerhard Meyer reminds me that all this is admirably stated in Dicey, Law and Opinion in England (2d ed.), esp. pp. 150 ff., 190 ff., and 467 ff. Dicey in turn reminds me that perhaps everything I have tried to say was better said by Bentham and the Benthamites.

prise monopoly, unions in fact serve mainly to buttress effective monopoly in product markets where it already obtains and to call it into existence when it does not. Labor leaders have, indeed, a quite normal appetite for monopoly prices and for monopoly profits which bargaining power permits them to appropriate and to distribute among their members. . . .

Freeman & Medoff, The Two Faces of Unionism*
57 The Public Interest 69, 70-83, 85-88, 91-92 (1979)[d]

Trade unions are the principal institution of workers in modern capitalist societies, as endemic as large firms, oligopolistic organization of industries, and governmental regulation of free enterprise. But for over 200 years, since the days of Adam Smith, there has been widespread disagreement about the effects of unions on the economy. On the one side, such economists as John Stuart Mill, Alfred Marshall, and Richard Ely (one of the founders of the American Economic Association) viewed unions as having major positive effects on the economy. On the other side, such economists as Henry Simons and Fritz Machlup have stressed the adverse effects of unions on productivity. . . . Economists today generally treat unions as monopolies whose sole function is to raise wages. Since monopolistic wage increases are socially deleterious — in that they can be expected to induce both inefficiency and inequality — most economic studies implicitly or explicitly judge unions as having a negative impact on the economy.

Our research demonstrates that this view of unions as organizations whose chief function is to raise wages is seriously misleading. For in addition to raising wages, unions have significant non-wage effects which influence diverse aspects of modern industrial life. By providing workers with a voice both at the workplace and in the political arena, unions can and do affect positively the functioning of the economic and social systems. . . .

One key dimension of the new work on trade unionism can best be understood by recognizing that societies have two basic mechanisms for dealing with divergences between desired social conditions and actual conditions. The first is the classic market mechanism of exit and entry, individual mobility: The dissatisfied consumer switches products; the diner whose soup is too salty seeks another restaurant; the unhappy couple divorces. In the labor market, exit is synonymous with quitting, while entry consists of new

* Reprinted with permission of the authors from: The Public Interest, No. 57 (Fall 1979), pp. 69-93. © 1979 by National Affairs, Inc.

[d][For a fuller treatment of this topic, see R. Freeman & J. Medoff, What Do Unions Do? (1984) — Eds.]

hires by the firm. By leaving less-desirable jobs for more-desirable jobs, or by refusing bad jobs, individuals penalize the bad employer and reward the good — leading to an overall improvement in the efficiency of the social system. . . .

There is, however, a second mode of adjustment. This is the political mechanism, which Albert Hirschman termed "voice" in his important book, Exit, Voice, and Loyalty [1970]. "Voice" refers to the use of direct communication to bring actual and desired conditions closer together. . . .

In the job market, voice consists of discussing with an employer conditions that ought to be changed, rather than quitting the job. In modern industrial economies, and particularly in large enterprises, a trade union is the vehicle for collective voice — that is, for providing workers as a group with a means of communicating with management.

Collective rather than individual bargaining with an employer is necessary for effective voice at the workplace for two reasons. First, many important aspects of an industrial setting are "public goods," which affect the well-being (negatively or positively) of every employee. As a result, the incentive for any single person to express his preferences, and invest time and money to change conditions (for the good of all), is reduced. Safety conditions, lighting, heating, the speed of a production line, the firm's policies on layoffs, work-sharing, cyclical-wage adjustment, and promotion, its formal grievance procedure and pension plan — all obviously affect the entire workforce in the same way that defense, sanitation, and fire protection affect the entire citizenry. "Externalities" (things done by one individual or firm that also affect the well-being of another, but for which the individual or firm is not compensated or penalized) and "public goods" at the workplace require collective decision-making. Without a collective organization, the incentive for the individual to take into account the effects of his or her actions on others, or express his or her preferences, or invest time and money in changing conditions, is likely to be too small to spur action. . . .

A second reason collective action is necessary is that workers who are not prepared to exit will be unlikely to reveal their true preferences to their bosses, for fear of some sort of punishment. . . .

The collective nature of trade unionism fundamentally alters the operation of a labor market and, hence, the nature of the labor contract. In a nonunion setting, where exit and entry are the predominant forms of adjustment, the signals and incentives to firms depend on the preferences of the "marginal" worker, the one who will leave (or be attracted) by particular conditions or changes in conditions. The firm responds primarily to the needs of this marginal, generally younger and more mobile worker and can within some bounds ignore the preferences of "infra-marginal," typically older workers, who — for reasons of skill, knowledge, rights that cannot be readily transferred to other enterprises, as well as because of other costs associated with changing firms — are effectively immobile. In a unionized setting, by contrast, the union takes account of the preferences of *all* workers to form an average preference that typically determines its position at the bargaining table. Because unions are political institutions with elected leaders, they are likely to be responsive to a different set of preferences from those that dominate in a competitive labor market.

. . . When issues involve sizeable fixed costs or "public goods," a calculus based on the average preference can lead to a contract which, ignoring distributional effects, is socially more desirable than one based on the marginal preference — that is, it may even be economically more "efficient."

As a voice institution, unions also fundamentally alter the social relations of the workplace. Perhaps most importantly, a union constitutes a source of worker power in a firm, diluting managerial authority and offering members a measure of due process, in particular through the union innovation of a grievance and arbitration system. . . . [T]he entire industrial jurisprudence system — by which many workplace decisions are based on negotiated rules (such as seniority) instead of supervisory judgment (or whim), and are subject to challenge through the grievance/arbitration procedure — represents a major change in the power relations within firms. As a result, in unionized firms workers are more willing and able to express discontent and to object to managerial decisions. . . .

Another crucial point about unions is that their effects will depend upon the response of management. . . . If management uses the collective-bargaining process to learn about and improve the operation of the workplace and the production process, unionism can be a significant plus that improves managerial efficiency. On the other hand, if management reacts negatively to collective bargaining or is prevented by unions from reorganizing the work process, unionism can have a negative effect on the performance of the firm. . . . The economic impact of bargaining and the nature of industrial relations depend on the policies and actions of both. It is for this reason that we use the two terms "collective voice" and "institutional response" to refer to the second view of unionism under consideration. . . .

In the monopoly view, unions reduce society's output in three ways. First, union-won wage increases cause a misallocation of resources by inducing organized firms to hire fewer workers, to use more capital per worker, and to hire higher quality workers than is socially efficient. Second, union contract provisions — such as limits on the loads that can be handled by workers, restrictions on tasks performed, featherbedding, and so forth — reduce the output that should be forthcoming from a given amount of capital and labor. Third, strikes called to force management to accept union demands cause a substantial reduction in gross national product.

By contrast, the collective-voice/institutional-response model directs attention to the important ways in which unionism can raise productivity. First of all, unionism should reduce "quits." As workers' voice increases in an establishment, less reliance need be placed on the exit and entry mechanism to obtain desired working conditions. Since hiring and training costs are lowered and the functioning of work groups is less disrupted when "quit" rates are low, unionism can actually raise efficiency.

The fact that senior workers are likely to be relatively more powerful in enterprises where decisions are based on voice instead of exit and entry points to another way in which unions can raise productivity. Under unionism, promotions and other rewards tend to be less dependent in any precise way on individual performance and more dependent on seniority. As a result, in union plants feelings of rivalry among individuals are likely to be less pronounced than in nonunion plants and the amount of informal training and assistance that workers are willing to provide one another is greater. (The importance of seniority in firms in Japan, together with the permanent employment guaranteed many workers there, have often been cited as factors increasing the productivity of Japanese enterprises.) It is, of course, also important to recognize that seniority can reduce productivity by placing individuals in jobs for which they are not qualified.

Unionism can also raise efficiency by pressuring management into tightening job-production standards and accountability, in an effort to respond to union demands while maintaining profits. . . . This appears to occur largely because modern personnel practices are forced on the firm and traditional paternalism is discarded. Management's ability to make such improvements is a function of the union's cooperation, since the union can perform a helpful role in explaining changes in the day-to-day routine. One recent study supportive of this view reports that while union workers spend more time on formal breaks, they spend *less* time on informal ones and report working harder than nonunion workers.[1]

Finally, under the voice view, the collective bargaining apparatus opens

---

[1] It is important to recognize that productivity gains, from improved methods of management in the face of unionism, run counter to the standard assumption of neoclassical economics that all enterprises operate at peak efficiency. It is, however, consistent with the "satisfieing" models of firms developed by the recent Nobel Prize winner Herbert Simon and other analysts and with the model of X-inefficiency put forth by Harvey Leibenstein. In these models, firms strive for maximum efficiency only when they are under severe pressure from competitors, unions, or other external forces.

an important communication channel between workers and management, one likely to increase the flow of information between the two, and possibly improve the productivity of the enterprise.

What does the evidence reveal on these points? Most of the econometric analysis of unions has focused on the question of central concern to the monopoly view: How large is the union wage effect? In his important book, Unionism and Relative Wages [1963], H. Gregg Lewis summarized results of this analysis through the early 1960's, concluding that, while differing over time and across settings, the union wage effect averages on the order of 10 to 15 percent. That is, as a result of collective bargaining, a union member makes about 10 to 15 percent more than an otherwise comparable worker who is not a member. Later work, using larger data files which have information permitting more extensive controls and employing more complex statistical techniques, tends to confirm Lewis's generalization. While unions in some environments raise wages by an enormous amount, the average estimated union wage effect is by no means overwhelming.

As predicted by the monopoly wage model, the capital-labor ratio and average "quality" of labor both appear to be somewhat greater than "optimal" in union settings. However, the total loss in output due to this misallocation of resources appears to be miniscule; an analysis done by Albert Rees suggests that the loss is less than 0.3 percent of the gross national product. [Rees, The Effects of Unions on Resource Allocation, in Readings in Labor Market Analysis 489, 494 (J. Burton et al. eds. 1971).] For 1975, that would have amounted to $21.00 per person in the U.S. Even this estimate may be too high if one considers the other important and relevant distortions in the economy.

One of the central tenets of the collective-voice/institutional-response model is that among workers receiving the same pay, unions reduce employee turnover and its associated costs by offering "voice" as an alternative to exit. Our own research, using newly available information on the job changes and employment status of thousands of individuals and industry-level turnover rates, shows that, with diverse factors (including wages) held constant, unionized workers do have significantly lower quit rates than non-union workers who are comparable in other respects. . . . [R. Freeman, The Exit-Voice Tradeoff in the Labor Market: Unionism, Job Tenure, Quits, and Separations, 94 Q. J. of Econ. 643 (1980).] Moreover, consistent with the claim that unions provide better representation for workers with greater seniority, the evidence suggests a larger reduction in exit and a larger increase in job tenure for older male workers than for younger male workers. . . .

Our analyses of newly available data on unionism and output per worker

TABLE III
Estimates of the Impact of Unionism on Productivity*

Setting	Estimated Increase or Decrease in Output per Worker Due to Unionism
All 2-digit Standard Industrial Classification (SIC) manufacturing industries[1]	20 to 25%
Wooden household furniture[2]	15
Cement[3]	6 to 8
Underground bituminous coal, 1965[4]	25 to 30
Underground bituminous coal, 1975[4]	−20 to −25

* Sources: All calculations are based on the analyses cited below, which control for capital-labor ratios and diverse other factors that may influence productivity.

[1] From C. Brown and J. Medoff, "Trade Unions in the Production Process," Journal of Political Economy, June 1978, pp. 355-378.

[2] From J. Frantz, "The Impact of Trade Unions on Productivity in the Wood Household Furniture Industry," Senior Honors Thesis, Harvard University, March 1976.

[3] From K. Clark, "Unions and Productivity in the Cement Industry," Doctoral Thesis, Harvard University, September 1978.

[4] From R. B. Freeman, J. L. Medoff, and M. Connerton, "Industrial Relations and Productivity; A Study of the U.S. Bituminous Coal Industry," in progress.

in many establishments or sectors suggests that the monopoly view of unions as a major deterrent to productivity is erroneous. In some settings, unionism leads to *higher* productivity, not only because of the greater capital intensity and higher labor quality, but also because of what can best be termed institutional-response factors.

Table III summarizes the available estimates of the union productivity effect. The calculations in the table are based on statistical analyses that relate output per worker to unionization, controlling for capital per worker, the skill of workers (in some of the analyses), and other relevant factors. While all of the studies are subject to some statistical problems and thus must be treated cautiously, a general pattern emerges. In manufacturing, productivity in the organized sector appears to be substantially higher than in the unorganized sector, by an amount that could roughly offset the increase in total costs attributable to higher union wages.

. . . Kim Clark, in his study of the cement industry [in The Impact of Unionization on Productivity: A Case Study, 33 Indus. & Lab. Rel. Rev. 451 (1980)], noted that from his discussions with individuals at recently organized plants, it appeared that the entrance of a union was usually followed by major alterations in operations. Interestingly, the enterprise typically changed plant management, suggesting that the union drive was an important signal to top management of ineffective lower-level managerial personnel: The drive thus provided valuable information or shock of a distinctive kind. Perhaps most importantly, the discussions with union and management officials in the cement industry indicated that firms often adopted more efficiency-oriented and less paternalistic personnel policies in response to unionism in order to raise productivity and meet higher wage demands.

On the other side of the picture, our analysis (with Marguerite Connerton) of productivity in organized and unorganized underground bituminuous coal mines indicates that as industrial relations in the union sector deteriorated in the late 1960's and 1970's, unionism became associated with negative productivity effects. . . .

. . . If the increase in productivity is greater than the increase in average unit costs due to the union wage effect, then the profit rate will increase; if not, the rate of profit will fall. There is limited tentative evidence that, on average, net profits are reduced somewhat by unionism, particularly in oligopolistic industries, though there are notable exceptions. At present, there is no definitive accounting of what proportion of the union wage effect comes at the expense of capital, other labor, or consumers, and what portion is offset by previously unexploited possibilities for productivity improvements.

Finally, it is important to note that despite what some critics of unions might claim, strikes do not seem to cost society a substantial amount of goods and services. For the economy as a whole, the percentage of total working time lost directly to strikes during the past two decades has never been greater than 0.5 percent and has averaged about 0.2 percent. . . .

Data on the remuneration of individual workers and on the expenditures for employees by firms show that the proportion of compensation allotted to fringe benefits is markedly higher for organized blue-collar workers than for similar nonunion workers. . . . While some of the difference is attributable to the higher wages paid to union workers (since higher-wage workers generally "buy" more fringes), . . . much of the difference is in fact due to the effect of unionism. . . . [T]he greatest increases in fringes induced by unionism are for deferred compensation, which is generally favored by older, more stable employees. This is consistent with the view that unions are more responsive to senior, less-mobile workers.

Studies concerning workers' preferences for fringes, and managers' awareness of these preferences, provide support for the claim that a union can provide management with information that affects the composition of the pay package. . . . Equally important is the apparent role of unions in evaluating the complex costs and prospective advantages of modern fringe benefits and transmitting these facts to their members. It is unlikely that an individual worker will invest the time required to evaluate alternative compensation packages. Unions, however, can hire the lawyers, actuaries, and other experts necessary to perform these analyses. . . . One of the striking implications of the monopoly view, which runs counter to popular thought, is that union wage gains increase inequality in the labor market. According to the monopoly model, the workers displaced from unionized firms as a result of union wage gains raise the supply of labor to nonunion firms, which can therefore be expected to reduce wages. Thus in the monopoly view unionized workers are likely to be made better off at the expense of nonunion workers. The fact that organized blue-collar workers would tend to be more skilled and higher paid than other blue-collar workers even in the absence of unionism implies further that unionism benefits "labor's elite" at the expense of those with less skill and earning power. Since many people have supported unions in the belief they reduce economic inequality, evidence that unions have the opposite effect would be a strong argument against the union movement.

In fact, the collective-voice/institutional-response model suggests very different effects on equality than does the monopoly view. Given that union decisions are based on a political process, and given that the majority of union members are likely to have earnings below the mean (including white-collar workers) in any workplace, unions can be expected to seek to reduce wage inequality. Union members are also likely to favor a less-dispersed distribution of earnings for reasons of ideology and organizational solidarity. Finally, by its nature, collective bargaining reduces managerial discretion in the wage-setting process, and this should also reduce differences among similarly situated workers.

Two common union wage policies exemplify unions' efforts to reduce economic inequality. The first is the long-standing policy of pushing for "standard rates" — uniform rates for comparable workers across establishments, and for given occupational classes within establishments. While many large nonunion enterprises today also employ formal wage-setting practices, personal differentials based on service, performance, favoritism, or other factors are more common in the nonunion than in the union sector. For example, so-called "merit" plans for wage adjustment appear to be less prevalent in the union sector. In the 1970's, while about 43 percent of all companies offered plant employees "wage adjustment based on a merit plan," only 13 percent of major union contracts mentioned these plans. Overall, according to Slichter, Healy, and Livernash [in The Impact of Collective Bargaining on Management 602, 606 (1960)], "the influence of unions has clearly been one of minimizing and eliminating judgment-based differences in pay for individuals employed on the same job" and of "removing ability and performance judgments as a factor in individual pay for job performance." One important potential result of these policies is a reduction of inequality, possibly at the expense of efficiency, which may be lessened because the reward for individual effort is reduced. Another important potential result of this policy is that wage discrimination against minorities is likely to be less in unionized than in nonunionized settings.

Union policies favoring seniority in promotion, and job-posting and bidding systems in which workers are informed about new openings and can bid for promotions, can also be expected to have egalitarian consequences. The possibility that arbitrary supervisory judgments will determine the career of a worker is greatly reduced by the development of formal rules which treat each worker identically. . . .

Our empirical estimates, based on new data, show that standardization policies have substantially reduced wage inequality, and that this effect dominates the monopoly wage effect. [R. Freeman, Unionism and the Dispersion of Wages, 34 Indus. & Lab. Rel. Rev. 3 (1980).] When, for instance, the distribution of earnings for male blue-collar workers is graphed, the results for unionized workers in both the manufacturing and nonmanufacturing sectors show a much narrower distribution, compressed at the extremes and radically peaked in the middle. For nonunion workers, by contrast, the graphs show a much more dispersed pattern of earnings.

In addition to reducing earnings inequality among blue-collar workers, union wage policies contribute to the equalization of wages by decreasing the differential between covered blue-collar workers and uncovered white-collar workers. In manufacturing, though white-collar workers earn an average of 49 percent more than blue-collar workers, our estimates indicate that in unionized enterprises this premium is only 32 percent; in the nonmanufacturing sector, where white-collar workers average 31 percent more in earnings than blue-collar workers, the estimated differential is only 19 percent where there are unions.

But to obtain the net effect of unionism on earnings inequality it is necessary to add the *decrease* in inequality due to wage standardization and the *decrease* due to the reduction in the white-collar/blue-collar differential to the *increase* due to the greater wages of blue-collar union workers. Our calculations show clearly that the *dominant* influence affecting earnings inequality is the standardization of rates within the union sector. As a result of the large reduction in inequality attributable to standard-rate policies, the variance in the natural logarithm of earnings (a common measure of inequality) is reduced by 21 percent in manufacturing and by 27 percent in the nonmanufacturing sector. . . .

There is a history of conflict between trade-union seniority rules and affirmative-action programs and of discrimination by craft unions. But empirical evidence, as Orley Ashenfelter [in Racial Discrimination and Trade

Unionism, 80 J. Pol. Econ. 435 (1972)] was first to note, shows clearly that on average, unions aid black workers and reduce differences based on race. Unions affect the distribution of earnings between blacks and whites in at least three ways.

First, because blacks are actually more likely than whites to be union members, they are more likely to benefit from union wage gains. In the 1973-to-1975 period, 30 percent of black workers were organized compared to 24 percent of white workers. The greater degree of organization among blacks reflects the fact that they are overrepresented among blue-collar factory workers and underrepresented among the less organized white-collar workers. . . .

Second, unionization reduces discriminatory differences within organized firms through the standard-rate and promotion-by-seniority policies described earlier. While organized black workers make less than organized white workers, the differential is smaller than among unorganized workers. Estimates using data from the 1973 to 1975 May Current Population Surveys show that among all unionized blue-collar workers in the private sector, the hourly wage for blacks was about 9 percent lower than for whites. Among comparable nonunion workers, the figure was about 15 percent. Seniority rules, which are often regarded as inimical to the interests of black workers because they conflict with affirmative-action programs, should in the long run be beneficial to blacks. . . .

Third, an analysis by Duane Leigh [in Unions and Nonwage Racial Discrimination, 32 Indus. & Lab. Rel. Rev. 439 (1979)] of the effect of unionism on the quit rates of black and white workers shows that, with wages held constant, the turnover of blacks is as much reduced by unions as is the turnover of whites. This implies that the non-wage benefits associated with unionism improve conditions as much for blacks as for whites. . . .

If, in addition to its negative monopoly effects, trade unionism is associated with substantial positive effects on the operation of the economy and on the performance of firms, why do so many U.S. firms oppose unions so vehemently? . . .

First, the bulk of the economic gains that spring from unionism accrue to workers and not to owners or managers. Managers are unlikely to see any personal benefits in their subordinates' unionization, but are likely to be quite aware of the costs: a diminution of their power, the need to work harder, the loss of operating flexibility, and the like.

Second, though productivity might typically be higher in union than in otherwise comparable nonunion work settings, so too are wages. It would seem, given the objectives and actions of most unions, that the rate of return on capital would be lower under collective bargaining, although there are important exceptions. Thus, there is risk in unionization; the firm may be able to rationalize operations, have good relations with the union, and maintain its profit rate — or it may not. In addition, while the total cost of strikes to society as a whole has been shown to be quite small, the potential cost to a particular firm can be substantial. Since managers — like most other people — dislike taking risks, we would expect opposition to unions even if on average the benefits to firms equal the costs. Moreover, given the wide-ranging differences in the effects of unions on economic performance, at least some managerial opposition surely arises from enterprises in which the expected benefits of collective bargaining are small but the expected costs high. . . .

Third, management may find unionism expensive, difficult, and very threatening in its initial stages, when modes of operation must be altered if efficiency is to be improved. New and different types of management policies are needed under unionism, and these require either changes in the behavior of current management, or . . . a new set of managers.

Finally, U.S. management has generally adopted an ideology of top-down enlightened control, under which unions are seen as both a cause and an effect of managerial failure. In this view, unions interfere with management's efforts to carry out its social function of ensuring that goods and services are produced efficiently. In addition, because unions typically come into existence as a result of management's mistakes in dealing with its workforce, managers frequently resent what unionization implies about their own past performances.

NOTES

1. Freeman and Medoff (F & M) have raised questions that bear on important policy issues. Addison & Barnett, in The Impact of Unions on Productivity, 20 Brit. J. Indus. Rel. 145 (1982), have, however, questioned both the underlying analytical model and the conclusions reached in this and similar studies. They make the following observations, among others: (a) The suggestion that unionization causes a reduction in quit rates ignores that workers with a low propensity to quit may be more susceptible to unionization. Id. at 152. (b) There is little hard evidence that organized firms outcompete unorganized ones and strong evidence the other way. Id. at 151, 155, 158-159. (c) F & M provide no data to support their theory that the higher productivity reported for unionized firms is attributable to better management, morale, and communication, rather than to other equally plausible factors. Id. at 152. Thus they do not examine, e.g., the impact of

grievance adjustments on absenteeism, effort, and other aspects of productivity. Addison and Barnett state, however (p. 159): "While considerable doubt must attach to the specific estimates, [F & M] have demonstrated the important point that unions need not necessarily have a deleterious effect on productivity."

2. Freeman and Medoff found that in general the rate of return on capital is lower under collective bargaining. Does that finding suggest that the lower quit rate results from premium wage rates and that the improved morale imputed to unionization does not in turn bring about increased productivity commensurate with the increased wages?

3. Assume that the pertinent data showed that labor unions, like monopoly firms, produced results that were generally "economically inefficient." Would it follow that the general policy of protecting employee self-determination and majority rule (embodied in the Wagner Act, as amended) should be abandoned or redirected towards achieving greater efficiency? See infra pp. 66-67.

4. As you examine the materials below on existing regulation, consider the potential significance of Freeman and Medoff's thesis for legislative or adjudicative developments. Consider, for example, its potential impact on (a) limitations on union organizational pressures — limitations that have been opposed on the ground that the spread of organization is necessary to protect union gains against the cost advantages enjoyed by nonunion competitors (see Chapter 7(C), (E), and (F)); (b) the scope of bargaining units (see Chapter 6(A) (2)); (c) the desirability of upholding the legality of less adversarial relationships between unions and management (see Chapter 4 (C)).

Burton, Economic Impact of Unions[e]

1. *Introduction.* Doctrinal arguments about the economic impacts of unions have been supplemented by a large, complex, and conflicting body of empirical studies. These notes attempt to summarize briefly the most generally accepted findings of these studies. For an extensive introduction to this literature, see R. Ehrenberg & R. Smith, Modern Labor Economics, especially ch. 12 (1982). See also D. Mitchell, Collective Bargaining and the Economy, and R. Freeman and J. Medoff, The Impact of Collective Bar-

[e] [This material was prepared for this book by John F. Burton, Jr., Professor, New York State School of Industrial and Labor Relations, Cornell University. Professor Burton also provided the data on union membership that appears in Chapter 1, pp. 19-23. Naturally, we are grateful for Professor Burton's valuable and generous collaboration. — EDS.]

gaining: Illusion or Reality?, both in J. Stieber et al., U.S. Industrial Relations 1950-1980: A Critical Assessment (1981).

2. *Relative wages.* Wages may vary among workers along several dimensions. Interindustry wage differentials are the relative wage levels of different industries for workers in the same occupational category and geographic area. Interfirm wage differentials measure the relative wage levels for workers in the same occupation, geographic area, and industry, but in different firms. Occupational differentials measure the relative wage levels of different occupational groups in the same plant. Geographical wage differentials measure the relative wage levels of workers in the same industry and occupation, but in different geographical areas. Personal differentials are the relative wage levels of workers who are in the same plant and occupation, but who differ in age, sex, race, or other personal characteristics. These wage differentials are discussed in L. Reynolds & C. Taft, The Evolution of Wage Structure 9-10 (1956).

Unions can affect each of the foregoing wage differentials. A simple example involving interindustry wage differentials, adapted from A. Rees, The Economics of Trade Unions 72 (1977), illustrates a relative wage effect of unions of approximately 17 percent.

	Wages when neither industry unionized	Wages after Industry A is unionized
Industry A	$4.80	$5.60
Industry B	$4.00	$4.00
Interindustry Wage Differential	$\frac{\$4.80}{\$4.00} = 1.20$	$\frac{\$5.60}{\$4.00} = 1.40$

$$\text{Relative wage effect of unions} = \frac{1.40}{1.20} = 1.17 \text{ or } 17\%$$

As the example indicates, determination of the net impact of unions on relative wages must first isolate any interindustry wage differentials associated with factors other than unionization. The list of candidates, all with supporters and detractors, is long: industry profitability, the degree to which industry output is concentrated in a few sellers, the growth of industry employment and productivity, and working conditions. Similar factors would have to be accounted for before the unions' impact on interfirm, occupational, or the other types of wage differentials could be measured.

Some scholars argue that factors such as unattractive working conditions cause higher wages, which in turn attract unions, and that once this direction of causation is recognized, much or all of the apparent influence of unions on wages is eliminated. Empirical studies relying on this approach are examined in C. Parsley, Labor Unions and Wages: A Survey, 18 Journal of Economic Literature 1 (1980). The statistical technique used in these studies is criticized as unreliable by Freeman and Medoff, supra, at 86; the balance of this note relies primarily on empirical studies in which unions are assumed to cause higher wages rather than vice-versa.

The most generally accepted estimate of the relative wage impact of unions on interindustry wage differentials, once the other factors affecting industry wages have been accounted for, is about 10-20 percent. This estimate applies to periods of relatively stable prices and high employment. There are exceptions even during such periods: The United Mine Workers, e.g., had an impact of 30 percent or more in the mid-1950s, at least partly because they were willing to ignore the impact of their wage policies on employment opportunities. Other unions have had a relative wage impact considerably less than 10 percent, often because they have organized economically declining industries. See Rees, supra, at 73-74.

The union impact on interindustry wage differentials varies, depending on general economic conditions. The key appears to be that collective bargaining, which often results in multi-year contracts, slows down wage adjustments by unionized firms. The result is that the relative wage advantage of unions declines in periods of very low unemployment and rapid inflation because nonunion wages surge. By contrast, in recessions the union relative wage impact is enhanced; for nonunion wages respond to unfavorable labor market conditions much more rapidly than do union wages, apparently because of both the strong opposition of unions to wage decreases and the influence of multi-year contracts.

Another important dimension of the union impact on relative wages concerns interfirm wage differentials. Such a differential may be most significant when the union organizes only part of an industry. When the products of such an industry compete in a national market, the union impact on wages in the organized firms is limited because the high prices that would result from substantial wage gains would have a severe impact on sales and ultimately on employment in the unionized sector of the industry, at least, if there is no compensating productivity gain. The inability of the textile unions to obtain wages much above the wages received in the nonunion sector of the industry illustrates this constraint on union influence. In contrast, the construction industry's product generally does not compete in a national market. Even though construction unions have not organized all sections of the country, they have used their bargaining power in well organized areas. Consequently, wages have differed between the unionized and nonunionized sectors of the construction industry by 30 percent or more. Rees, supra, at 73.

Over time, estimates of the relative wage impact of unions have tended to attribute increasing impacts to unions. In his first edition of The Economics of Trade Unions 79 (1962), Rees estimated that the average effect of all American unions on the wages of their members relative to nonunion members was between 10 and 15 percent. This range was close to H. G. Lewis' estimate for years immediately preceding Rees' 1962 edition. H. G. Lewis, Unionism and Relative Wages in the United States, 5 (1963). In his 1977 edition, Rees (at 74) increased his estimate of the average effect to 15 to 20 percent. He attributed this difference more to the availability of new data than to a belief that union power has been increasing.

Ehrenberg and Smith, supra, at 356, estimate the average effect of unions on wages in recent years as 10 to 20 percent; Mitchell, supra, at 10, estimates 20 to 30 percent for production and nonsupervisory workers in the late 1970s. Both studies discuss an apparent widening of the differential during the 1970s that is not attributable only to better data. A persuasive explanation is the relatively high unemployment rates during the decade, an environment that normally enhances the union relative wage advantage. There may, however, be limits to the relationship between higher unemployment rates and a larger union relative wage effect. Concessionary union contracts in the early 1980s in such depressed industries as auto, steel, and trucking may portend a collapse of the union wage advantage in severe recessions.

Most studies of the union effect on relative wages have ignored fringe benefits, but recent studies suggest that unions have an even greater impact on fringe benefits than on wages. For example, Freeman and Medoff, supra, at 54, report that for one group of blue-collar workers the union wage advantage was 8 to 15 percent while union fringe benefits were 28 to 36 percent higher. As Ehrenberg and Smith, supra, at 359 indicate, studies ignoring fringes may understate the total union/nonunion differential in compensation.

3. *Resource allocation.* Differences in wages and fringes among industries and firms affect the relative costs of production, the relative prices of goods, and ultimately, affect patterns of consumption. One concern of economists is that unions may distort the appropriate set of wage differentials and therefore impede the most desirable or efficient allocation of resources in the economy.

Most economists believe that the most desirable set of wage differentials is embedded in the model of "pure and perfect competition." This model has an equilibrium where interindustry and interfirm wage differentials would be eliminated, although occupational and personal wage differentials within a nonhomogeneous work force would persist. Critics have attacked the assumptions of this model and its exclusive concern with consumer welfare and its disregard of producer interests. See, e.g., N. Chamberlain & J. Kuhn, Collective Bargaining, ch. 13 (1965).

Even if the competitive model with its focus on consumer welfare is accepted as an appropriate norm, it is arguable that the union impact on wage differentials is desirable. Largely because interfirm wage differentials appeared to be much greater among nonunion firms than the competitive model suggested they should be, and because unions appeared substantially to reduce such differentials, Reynolds and Taft, supra, at 194, concluded that " . . . one can make a strong case that unionism has at any rate not worsened the wage structure. We are inclined to be more venturesome than this, and to say that its net effect has been beneficial."

Other scholars, such as Rees, have disagreed, probably because they believe that the union impact on interindustry wage differentials is greater than do Reynolds and Taft, who found this impact to have been "minor." But even Rees indicated that the combined cost of union effects on interindustry and interfirm wage differentials and the resultant impact on resource allocation were less than 0.3 percent of the gross national product. Rees concluded that another avenue by which unions affect resource allocation — direct restrictions of output through control of manning requirements, the work pace, and work practices — probably resulted in losses exceeding the social losses from relative wage effects. Rees, The Effects of Unions on Resource Allocation, 6 J. of Law and Economics 69 (1963).

In recent years, several labor economists have presented evidence that some unions have increased productivity. This view has been given its widest dissemination by R. Freeman and J. Medoff (excerpts from their "Two Faces of Unionism" appear earlier in this chapter). As Freeman and Medoff note, however, in some industries, such as bituminous coal, unionized workers have been less productive in recent years. Moreover, even if unionized workers on average are more productive than other workers, Ehrenberg and Smith, supra, at 362, indicate that there is no consensus about whether the higher productivity more than offsets losses of output caused both by union effects on wage structure and union strike activity. It is instructive that Freeman and Medoff in their 1981 study (at 61) report that the rate of return on capital is lower in unionized settings, apparently because productivity in unionized firms is not sufficiently higher than elsewhere to offset the higher compensation and greater capital intensiveness in unionized firms.

4. *Average wage level.* There is no necessary connection between the union impact on relative wages and the union impact on average wages. For example, a union might organize industry C and push up wages, thereby displacing workers who move to industry D and depress wages. The average

wage in the economy would remain constant even though the union had had a relative wage impact. Similarly, after a union organizes industry E and pushes wages up, employers in industry F respond with a proportional wage increase in order to forestall unionization: The average wage in the economy increases because of the union, even though it has not had any relative wage impact.

The most reliable way to determine the impact of unions on the general wage level is to investigate that question directly, and not to infer the impact from unions' relative wage effect. But direct investigation is difficult. Part of this difficulty involves theoretical questions, such as the relationship between union wage gains and increases in the money supply needed to finance those gains. See Rees (1977), ch. V. Even at the empirical level, however, it is difficult to isolate the union impact on the general wage level, largely because so many other variables have been proposed as determinants of wage changes. Candidates in recent years include profits; labor turnover; unemployment levels; changes in the levels of unemployment, employment, prices, and productivity; and qualitative improvements in the labor force.

That unions are not the dominant influence on wages is suggested by the data in Section A of this chapter, which show in the last two decades a continuing decline in the proportion of the labor force organized even though, during the same period, the rate of increase in wages has gone through several cycles. There is, however, some evidence, that unions play a secondary role in determining the rate of changes in the general wage level. Isolating the influence of unions on the general level of wages is complicated by the widespread use of multiple year contracts, which tend to postpone and limit the effect of labor market conditions on wages for workers represented by unions. On the other hand, cost-of-living provisions in many contracts make the wages responsive to price changes during the life of these contracts. In some circumstances, such as an unanticipated decrease in unemployment, these features of collective bargaining may actually restrain wage increases for union workers, while in other circumstances, such as periods when unemployment is rapidly increasing because of governmental anti-inflation policies, these features may prolong inflation. The various relationships among wages, prices, and collective bargaining are explored at length by D. Mitchell, who finds little support among economists for the proposition that collective bargaining can initiate inflation (supra, at 25) and no general answer to the question of whether unions make it more or less difficult to halt ongoing inflation (supra, at 33). A somewhat different conclusion was reached by Ehrenberg and Smith, supra at 485, who suggested that the increasing prevalence of cost-of-living clauses during the 1970s contributed to the economy's inflationary tendency. The difference in these viewpoints should not obscure the central point: The major determinants of wage increases and inflation are factors such as monetary and fiscal policy and the state of the labor market, while the independent role of unions and collective bargaining is at best secondary.

5. *Income distribution.* One way that unions might affect income distribution would be to increase the share of national income going to wages and salaries, as distinguished from rent, interest, and profits. There is, however, no necessary connection between the union impact on wages and the size of labor's share of national income. For example, if unions increase wages by 10 percent and employers respond by increasing prices by 10 percent, all the relative shares of national income could remain constant. Even if employers do not meet a wage increase with a proportionate price increase, labor's share need not increase. If employers respond to a wage increase by a shift to capital goods and a reduction in the number of workers hired, the ratio of the total wage bill to the national income could remain the same.

These and other possible employer reactions to union wage gains probably explain the empirical evidence that fails to demonstrate any significant union effect on labor's share of national income. There has been a long run tendency for labor's share to rise, largely explained, however, by changes in the relative importance of various sectors of the economy. Thus, over the last 50 years there has been a substantial decline in the importance of the agricultural sector (where wages represent only about 15 to 20 percent of income) and a substantial increase in the importance of the manufacturing sector (where about 75 percent of income is paid out as wages). Within the unionized sectors (construction, mining, manufacturing, and communication), there was during 1919-1969, no significant trend in labor's relative share of income. See F. Marshall, V. Briggs, & A. King, Labor Economics: Wages, Employment & Trade Unionism, ch. 14 (4th ed. 1980).

The relative wage gains of union workers thus appear to be largely at the expense of nonunion workers rather than capital. Whether unions narrowed or widened income distribution within the wage earners class depends on whether unions organized low wage workers and closed the gap between them and the average worker or whether unions organized high wage workers and widened the gap between them and the average worker.

On this issue, many scholars have changed their views in recent years. The prior view is represented by Rees (1977), supra at 93:

Perhaps the best summary statement that can be made from the available evidence about the effect of unions on the size distribution of income is that unions have probably raised many higher income workers from an initial position somewhat above the middle of the income distribution to a present position closer to the top. They have narrowed the gap between the best paid manual workers and the very rich, and widened the gap between these workers and the very poor. This effect cannot be completely described by calling it either an increase or a decrease in the equality of income distribution, though it seems closer to the latter than to the former.

The current view, represented by Ehrenberg and Smith, supra, at 358, is that "on balance unions appear to reduce wage dispersion in the United States." That view has been vigorously advanced by Freeman and Medoff, who report:

[U]nion wage policies appear to contribute to the equalization of wages by decreasing the differential between covered blue-collar workers and noncovered white-collar workers. If we add the apparent decrease in inequality due to wage standardization and the apparent decrease due to reduction in the white-collar/blue-collar differential to the apparent increase due to the greater wages of blue-collar union workers, we find that the apparent net effect of unionism is to reduce total wage inequality. [Freeman and Medoff, supra, at 55.]

6. *Evaluation of the economic impact of unions.* Since these notes have paid considerable attention to Rees' views, his opinion of the union's role in American society may be of interest:

If the union is viewed solely in terms of its effect on the economy, it must in my opinion be considered an obstacle to the optimum performance of our economic system. It alters the wage structure in a way that impedes the growth of employment in sectors of the economy where productivity and income are naturally high and that leaves too much labor in low income sectors of the economy like southern agriculture and the least skilled service trades. It benefits most those workers who would in any case be relatively well off, and while some of this gain may be at the expense of the owners of capital, most of it must be at the expense of consumers and the lower-paid workers. Unions interfere blatantly with the use of the most productive techniques in some industries, and this effect is probably not offset by the stimulus to higher productivity furnished by some other unions.

Many of my fellow economists would stop at this point and conclude that unions are harmful and that their power should be curbed. I do not agree that one can judge the value of a complex institution from so narrow a point of view. Other aspects of unions must also be considered. The protection against the abuse of managerial authority given by seniority systems and grievance procedures seems to me to be a union accomplishment of the greatest importance. So too is the organized representation in public affairs given the worker by the political activities of unions. If, as most of us believe, America should continue to have political democracy and a free enterprise economy, it is essential that the great mass of manual workers be committed to the preservation of this system and that they should not, as in many other democracies, constantly be attempting to replace it with something radically different. Yet such a commitment cannot exist if workers feel that their rights are not respected and they do not get their fair share of the rewards of the system. By giving workers protection against arbitrary treatment by employers, by acting as their representative in politics, and by reinforcing their hope of continuous future gain, unions have helped to assure that the basic values of our society are widely diffused and that our disagreements on political and economic issues take place within a broad framework of agreement. If the job rights won for workers by unions are not conceded by the rest of society simply because they are just, they should be conceded because they help to protect the minimum consensus that keeps our society stable. In my judgment, the economic losses imposed by unions are not too high a price to pay for their successful performance of this role. [Rees (1977), supra, at 186-187.]

NOTES

1. Minimum wage legislation raises issues similar to those raised by the preceding materials. Economists disagree concerning the desirability and effect of such legislation. Its opponents argue that in competitive labor markets the number of jobs declines with an effective increase in minimum wages that is not nullified by inflation. They concede that in monopsonistic labor markets such increases do not necessarily cause unemployment but may, under certain conditions, increase the number of jobs. See Stigler, The Economics of Minimum Wage Legislation, 36(1) Am. Econ. Rev. 358 (1946).[f] But such conditions, they insist, are rarely satisfied; accordingly, opponents have concluded that minimum wage legislation is likely to disemploy marginal workers, such as unskilled teenagers — who are supposed to be beneficiaries of such laws. Id. at 360-361.

The foregoing position has been challenged on the following grounds: It ignores imperfections in the labor market and the "real world," particularly the increases in productivity and employment following increases in the statutory minima. See, e.g., Blum, Minimum-Wage Legislation: Another View, in Labor and the National Economy 49, 50 (W. Bowen ed. 1965). But even such criticism appears to recognize that increased minima do increase

---

[f] That article contains, at 365, what may have been the first proposal for a negative income tax.

industry's incentive for displacing workers by resorting to improved technology, and that the displaced workers may not be reabsorbed. Id. at 51 n.3.

2. Empirical studies seeking to isolate the impact of increased minima have produced conflicting and uncertain conclusions. Goldfarb, The Policy Content of Quantitative Minimum Wage Research, 27 Indus. Rel. Research Assn. Proc. 261, 263 (1974). But cf. id. at 266. Studies of teenage employment do, however, suggest a disemployment effect. Id. at 266; Brozen, The Effect of Statutory Minimum Wage Increases on Teen-Age Employment, 12 J. Law & Econ. 108 (1968); Kosters & Welch, The Effects of Minimum Wages on the Distribution of Changes in Aggregate Employment, 62 Am. Econ. Rev. 323 (1972). Although these studies have been questioned on technical grounds (Goldfarb at 266), concern about disemployment effects, especially on teenagers and marginal workers, persists and has been reflected in continuing efforts to legislate teenage wage differentials.

For a recent effort, see H.R. 485, 98th Cong., 1st Sess. (1983) (proposed amendments to the Fair Labor Standards Act (FLSA) permitting employers to hire individuals under age 19 at 85 percent of the otherwise applicable minimum wage for up to 365 days and to employ full-time students of any age for a maximum of 20 hours per week at that rate). See also Guzzardi, How to Deal with The New Unemployment, 94 Fortune, Oct. 1976, at 132. For an exploration of various aspects of teenage unemployment, see The Youth Labor Market Problem: Its Nature, Causes, and Consequences (R. Freeman & D. Wise eds. 1982), especially the introductory essay by the editors at 1-16; Hall, The Minimum Wage and Job Turnover in Markets for Young Workers at 475-492, and Comments on Hall's thesis at 492-497.

What impact might teenage differentials have on the employment of unskilled adults? Would the high incidence of crime among teenagers support such a differential even if it merely redistributed unemployment?

3. In order to promote employment of some marginal workers, §14 of the FLSA authorizes the Secretary of Labor to issue certificates permitting students and the handicapped, among others, to work at subminimum wages. As of 1975, more than 700,000 workers, of whom 515,000 were full-time students, were certified under §14. Dept. of Labor, Employment Statistics Admin., Workers Certification Under §14 F.L.S.A. 8 (1976).

CHAPTER 3

THE BASIC STATUTORY MACHINERY FOR PROTECTING AND REGULATING ORGANIZATION AND COLLECTIVE ACTION

A. NLRB MACHINERY AND PROCEDURE

The National Labor Relations Act (NLRA), as amended, is administered in the first instance by the National Labor Relations Board (NLRB). The Board's principal functions are to conduct secret-ballot elections on the question of whether employees wish to be represented by a union in dealing with their employers, and to prevent and remedy violations of the NLRA ("unfair labor practices") by both employers and unions.[a] Although, strictly speaking, the NLRB consists of five members, "Board," as used in the preceding sentence and colloquially, generally refers to the total agency process, including the office of the General Counsel, the approximately 33 regional offices, and the Division of Judges; in 1972, the designation "Trial Examiner" was changed to "Administrative Law Judge" (ALJ).

Members of the NLRB are appointed to five-year terms by the President, subject to Senate confirmation. The Board operates through three-member panels, which dispose of routine cases. Each Board member has approximately twenty legal assistants (directed by a chief counsel), who assist in the preparation of opinions, among other matters. The NLRB's Solicitor, who is selected by and is responsible to the entire Board, is its legal advisor and consultant.

In response to charges of Board bias under the Wagner Act, the Taft-

---

[a] The other principal statute protecting organizational interests, the Railway Labor Act (RLA), as amended, relies on quite different machinery and is considerably less detailed in its regulation than is the NLRA. The RLA establishes administrative machinery only for representation issues and bargaining impasses; its prohibitions (see §2) are enforced by criminal penalties. Courts, without explicit statutory authorization, have supplemented those penalties by issuing injunctions against both employers and unions at the instance of private parties. The RLA, as well as the NLRA, is reproduced in the separately bound Statutory Supplement to this casebook.

Hartley amendments (now embodied in NLRA §§3, 4) provided for strict and unique separation of adjudicative and prosecuting functions.[b] The latter are now the responsibility of the General Counsel. He is not appointed by the Board, as is the practice in other agencies, but by the President, with the Senate's consent, for a four-year term. Section 3(d) of the NLRA provides that the General Counsel "shall exercise general supervision over all attorneys employed by the Board (other than [ALJs] and legal assistants to Board members) and over employees in the regional offices." Section 3(d) also gives him final authority over the investigation of charges filed by aggrieved persons, the issuance of complaints, and their prosecution before the Board. Authority over issuance of complaints, except in cases "involving novel and complex issues," is exercised in the first instance by the directors of the Board's regional offices;[c] their refusals to issue complaints are, however, subject to review by the General Counsel.

The General Counsel's refusal to issue a complaint, or to withdraw a complaint previously issued, is not reviewable either by the Board or, in general, by the courts. See NLRB v. Sears Roebuck & Co., 421 U.S. 132, 138 (1975); but cf. Rosenbloom, A New Look at the General Counsel's Unreviewable Discretion Not to Issue a Complaint Under the NLRA, 89 Yale L.J. 1349 (1977). The General Counsel has, however, developed procedures for informing a charging party of the reasons for the refusal of regional offices to issue a complaint, as well as procedures for appeals to his office from such refusals. These procedures have been praised as uniquely effective for "structuring prosecutorial discretion." See K. Davis, Discretionary Justice 205-207 (1969). In *Sears Roebuck*, supra, the Court held that advice and appeals memoranda explaining General Counsel decisions to withhold a complaint, as distinguished from such memoranda explaining decisions to file a complaint, are "final opinions" and not protected against disclosure under the Freedom of Information Act by the statutory exemption for "intra-agency memoranda."

The General Counsel does not initiate unfair labor practice cases on his own motion.[d] Such cases begin with the filing of a charge. "Any person" may, under the Board's Rules and Regulations (§102.9), file a charge in the

---

[b]Prior to those amendments, the NLRB had, in practice, separated its prosecuting and adjudicating functions by internal staff divisions that satisfied the requirements of the Administrative Procedure Act. For a discussion of the factors behind, and the controversy surrounding, the 1947 changes in Board structure and alternatives thereto, see Subcomm. on Admin. Prac. & Proc. of Senate Comm. on the Judiciary, 86th Cong., 2d Sess., Report on the Regulatory Agencies to the President-Elect (Landis Report), 59 (Comm. Print 1960).

[c]See NLRB, Statement of Procedures, Series 8, as amended, §101.8.

[d]Representation cases are handled differently from unfair labor practice cases. See Chapter 6.

Regional Office for the area where the unfair labor practice allegedly occurred. Employees in the regional offices investigate charges and discuss
them informally with the parties involved. Resultant settlements, both before
and after the issuance of a complaint, together with withdrawals and dismissal
of charges, dispose of the bulk of charges, as much as 94.3 percent in the fiscal
year ending September 1981. See 46 N.L.R.B. Ann. Rep. 5 (1981).

Formal proceedings are begun by the issuance of a complaint, specifying the charged violations of the Act and the time and place of hearing.
Section 10(b) of the Act provides that "no complaint shall issue based upon
any unfair labor practice occurring more than six months prior to the filing of
the charge with the Board." This section is subject to the general rule that a
federal limitation statute begins to run only when the claimant discovers, or in
the exercise of reasonable diligence, should have discovered, the misconduct;
and that fraudulent concealment preventing timely discovery tolls the statute. See NLRB v. Don Burgess Constr. Co., 596 F.2d 378 (9th Cir. 1979).
After a complaint is issued, the Board may, and in some cases must (see
§§10(j), 10(1)), apply to a federal district court for temporary relief against
continuation of the unfair labor practice. Discretionary applications for such
injunctive relief, though infrequent, have increased in recent years. (There
were 58 §10(j) proceedings in fiscal 1981. 46 N.L.R.B. Ann. Rep. 225
(1981).)

A hearing on a complaint is held before an ALJ, usually in or close to the
city where the unfair labor practice is alleged to have occurred. (ALJs are
appointed by the Board from a roster compiled by the Civil Service Commission, but they are independent of the Board and can be removed only for
"good cause" by that commission.) A complaint is prosecuted for the Board
by an attorney from a Regional Office. The charging party may intervene,
and its lawyers may participate in the proceedings.

Section 10(b), as amended in 1947, requires the Board "insofar as
practicable" to apply the rules of evidence governing the trial of civil cases in
the federal district courts. After evidence has been taken, both parties have a
right to present oral argument to the ALJ and to file a written brief.

Section 10(b) has been invoked, largely by employers, in attempts at
prehearing discovery of employees' statements to Board agents.[e] The Board
has, however, generally been able to block such discovery, urging that it
would inhibit employees' cooperation with NLRB representatives. See generally Garvey, Prehearing Discovery in NLRB Proceedings, 26 Lab. L.J.
710 (1975). In NLRB v. Robbins Tire & Rubber Co., 437 U.S. 214 (1978),
the Court interpreted Exemption 7A of the Freedom of Information Act,

---

[e] For the status of requests by employers charged with unfair labor practices (or by their
counsel) to employees for copies of their statements to Board agents, see infra p. 137.

which covers investigatory records whose disclosure would "interfere with enforcement proceedings," and held that under that exemption the NLRB, "at least until the completion of the Board's hearing," could properly deny prehearing disclosure of statements made by any prospective witnesses in pending unfair labor practice proceedings, without a particularized showing of probable interference.

After the hearing is concluded, the ALJ files a "Decision" setting forth his findings of fact and proposed disposition of the case. If exceptions to the "Decision" are not filed, it will normally be adopted by the Board. If exceptions are filed, the Board will review the case, usually on the basis of briefs and without oral argument; the opportunity to present oral arguments must be specifically requested in writing but is rarely granted and frequently waived by the parties. Section 10(c) of the statute describes the burden of persuasion applicable to the Board's findings and confers broad remedial authority on the Board.

Cases ready for NLRB review are assigned to individual members in rotation. Each member, with his legal assistants, determines whether an assigned case is routine, to be decided by a three-member panel, or important enough to warrant full Board consideration. Draft opinions, prepared by each member's legal assistants, circulate to all five Board members, any one of whom may ask for consideration by the full Board.

For a more detailed description of the Board's operations, see 1976 Interim Report and Recommendations of the Chairman's Task Force on the NLRB, 93 L.R.R. 22, 264-268 (Nov. 15, 1976); E. Miller, An Administrative Appraisal of the NLRB (3d ed. 1981).

B.   NLRB CASE LOAD AND DELAY

The NLRB has adopted a policy of declining to exercise jurisdiction over some classes of cases falling within its statutory jurisdiction. See Chapter 8(A). Despite that policy, the Board faced an increasing intake of representation and unfair labor practice cases even before its jurisdiction was significantly expanded in the 1970s by legislation extending NLRA coverage to postal and health care employees. In fiscal 1980 the Board's total intake at all levels was 57,381 cases, a 71 percent increase over 1970. Furthermore, that intake involved over 44,000 unfair labor practice cases, which require more staff time than representation cases. 45 N.L.R.B. Ann. Rep. 1 (1980). In

1980 the Board issued 1,857 decisions in contested cases, including 1,181 unfair labor practice decisions. Id. at 18. Most of the remaining contested cases involved representation issues. The number of decisions issued by the Board appears far to exceed that of any other regulatory agency or federal court.

During 1980, the median number of days from the filing of a charge to the issuance of a complaint was approximately 46 (id. at 12); the median number of days from the filing of a charge to the filing of a Board order was approximately 484 for unfair labor practice cases (id. at 294). Additional delays may, of course, result from judicial proceedings to review or enforce Board orders. For the twelve-month period ending June 30, 1980, the median time interval from the filing of the complete record to final disposition in the United States courts of appeals was 11.8 months for all federal administrative agency cases. 1980 Ann. Rep. of the Dir., Admin. Office of the United States 10-11 (1980).

It is clear that delay surrounding the disposition of contested NLRB cases is an important obstacle to the effectiveness of the statutory machinery. Delays prior to submission of unfair practice cases to the Board may be reduced by larger appropriations and staff. But delays at the Board level appear to be inherent in the NLRB's work load and structure. President Kennedy sent to Congress "Reorganization Plan No. 5 of 1961 (NLRB)," which would have authorized the Board to delegate to trial examiners the authority to make initial decisions in unfair labor practice cases, subject to a discretionary review on the basis of standards to be formulated by the Board. That plan was, however, defeated in the House of Representatives.[f]

The substantial delays between a meritorious charge and a remedy may well increase with the Board's steadily increasing case load. The delay factor should be carefully weighed in appraising: (1) the Board's expansion of its regulation to matters that arguably, at least, are remote from the central concerns of the statute (e.g., the details of the bargaining process); (2) the multiplication of standards of adjudication that involve slippery and burdensome evidentiary issues; (3) the Board's tendency to change, again and again, its rules or doctrines, through adjudication rather than rule-making and the encouragement to litigation resulting from that tendency; (4) the desirability of greater use of temporary injunctive relief against alleged unfair practices on the basis of §10(j) of the Act; and (5) an increase in temporary relief by courts of appeals on the basis of §10(e).

[f]For a statement of the competing considerations and of alternatives for dealing with the delay problem, see ABA Lab. Rel. Sec., Rep. of the Comm. on Prac. and Proc. under the Natl. Lab. Rel. Act 224 (Comm. Rep. 1966); 1976 Interim Report and Recommendations of the Chairman's Task Force on the NLRB, 93 L.R.R. 221 (Nov. 15, 1976).

C.   ENFORCEMENT AND JUDICIAL REVIEW

An unfair labor practice order by the NLRB is not self-executing; if compliance is not forthcoming, the Board must seek enforcement of its order by petitioning the appropriate United States court of appeals (see NLRA §10(e)). The NLRB conducts more litigation in the courts of appeals than any other federal agency (449 NLRB-related decisions in fiscal 1980, most of which were §10(e) enforcement actions). An enforcement order entered by the court of appeals operates like an injunction, and its violation is punishable by an action for contempt.

"Any person aggrieved" by a Board order, including respondents and charging parties, may also seek judicial review in the federal appeals courts. Under NLRA §10(f), an aggrieved or losing party is provided a wider choice of forums for review than is the Board when it seeks enforcement. Rival appellants from Board orders have occasionally engaged in elaborately planned races in order to obtain a desired forum. See, e.g., International Union of Electrical Workers v. NLRB, 343 F.2d 327 (D.C. Cir. 1965). Furthermore, a party, even though granted virtually the whole remedy it requested, has been held to be "aggrieved" by what the Board did not grant and, accordingly, eligible to enter the forum-shopping race. See Oil, Chemical & Atomic Workers Local 6-418 v. NLRB, 694 F.2d 1289 (D.C. Cir. 1982). One proposed reform would eliminate an aggrieved party's unqualified right to review in the D.C. Circuit. That proposal appears to have been inspired in part by the conviction of management lawyers that that court in the 1960s had a pro-union bias. Union lawyers appear to have shared that conviction. See, e.g., ABA Lab. Rel. Sec., Rep. of the Comm. on Prac. and Proc. under the Natl. Lab. Rel. Act 235-239 (Comm. Rep. 1966).

The right to intervene in review or enforcement proceedings exists for both the respondent acquitted of unfair labor practice charges before the Board and the charging party whose charges have been upheld by the Board. See UAW v. Scofield, 382 U.S. 205 (1965). The charging party may not, however, maintain a contempt action for violation of a judicially-enforced Board order; only the NLRB has standing to initiate contempt proceedings. See Amalgamated Utility Workers v. Consolidated Edison Co., 309 U.S. 261 (1940). Also, the charging party's recognized right to intervene in enforcement or review proceedings has generally not been extended to Board-initiated contempt actions. This view is criticized in Bartosic & Lanoff, Escalating the Struggle Against Taft-Hartley Contemnors, 39 U. Chi. L. Rev. 255, 266-275 (1972).

Several studies of the delay problem have recommended that NLRB orders should be subject to automatic judicial enforcement unless a person aggrieved by a final order petitions for review within a specified period. See, e.g., Advisory Panel on Labor-Management Relations Law, Organization and Procedure of the NLRB Report to Senate Comm. on Labor and Public Welfare, S. Doc. No. 81, 86th Cong., 2d Sess. 16, 25 (1960). See also Recommendations and Reports of the Administrative Conference of the United States 23, 238 (1970).

D.   THE SCOPE OF REVIEW: THE BOARD AND ADMINISTRATIVE LAW JUDGES, COURTS AND THE BOARD

Final disposition of a complaint may involve the disposition of several kinds of issues, including (1) issues of "historic fact," i.e., what happened, with what motivation; (2) the specific impact or general significance of the historic facts; and (3) the applicability of elastic or ambiguous statutory language. Naturally, there may be disagreement with respect to such determinations among an ALJ, the Board, and the reviewing court. Universal Camera Corp. v. NLRB, 340 U.S. 474 (1951), is a leading case concerning the impact of amendments to the Wagner Act on the interrelationships and responsibilities of those tribunals. Students of administrative law need no reminder of the importance of that case; it deserves the careful attention of students of labor law because it increases the importance of ALJs' resolutions of certain kinds of issues and sets forth a general framework for judicial review of NLRB determinations.

   Section 10(e) of the Wagner Act had provided that "the findings of the Board as to the facts, if supported by evidence, shall be conclusive." The Administrative Procedure Act (1946) provided that the reviewing court should set aside agency action "unsupported by substantial evidence" and that in making the foregoing determinations, "the court shall review the whole record or such portions thereof as may be cited by any party. . . ." Section 10(e), as amended by the Taft-Hartley Act, provided that the "findings of the Board with respect to questions of fact if supported by substantial evidence *on the record considered as a whole* shall be conclusive." (Emphasis added.)

   In *Universal Camera* the Supreme Court considered the impact of the Taft-Hartley amendments on the scope of judicial review. The issue was whether a supervisory employee had been discharged as a reprisal for his testimony supporting the union's position in an NLRB representation proceeding, or solely because he subsequently had accused the personnel manager of drunkenness. The Trial Examiner (now ALJ) had credited the employer's testimony, had found that antiunion animus had not entered into the discharge, and had recommended the dismissal of the complaint. The Board, in a divided opinion, made the opposite finding and held the discharge to be a violation of the Act. The Second Circuit, with Judge Learned Hand speaking for the majority, affirmed the Board but also expressed misgivings about the Board's assessment of the evidence.[g]

Judge Hand observed that the addition of the words "on the record considered as a whole" to §10(e) had apparently been designed to change what might have been the understanding of some courts, i.e: "if any passage could be found in the testimony to support a finding, the review was to stop, no matter how much other parts of the testimony contradicted, or outweighed, it." He concluded, however, that the additional language had not broadened judicial review but had only made explicit what had previously been implied.

Judge Hand found the uncertainties as to the reviewing function particularly acute when, as in *Universal Camera*, the NLRB had reversed a finding of a Trial Examiner on an issue that had turned essentially on credibility of witnesses. The judge concluded, however, that he could not attach any weight to the difference between the examiner and the Board with respect to such an issue. His argument went like this: The power of decision was lodged in the Board. If its finding, absent a contrary finding by the examiner, was supported by substantial evidence, the examiner's contrary finding did not reduce the substantiality of the supporting evidence. In Judge Hand's view, there was no intermediate ground between according no weight to the examiner's contrary finding or treating it as unassailable as a master's finding, i.e., reversible only if "clearly erroneous." Judge Hand rejected the latter approach on the ground that it required a plainer basis than the statute contained. Nevertheless, he recognized that the printed record before the Board would not preserve all the evidence on which an examiner bases his findings and suggested that it would be erroneous for the Board totally to disregard the examiner's finding.

The Supreme Court, in an opinion by Mr. Justice Frankfurter, agreed with Judge Hand's conclusion that §10(e), as amended, requires reviewing courts to consider not only evidence in support of a finding, viewed in isolation, but also anything in the record that fairly detracts from the weight of such evidence. But the Justice indicated that the amendment had enlarged the judicial function and required courts to "assume more responsibility for

[g]NLRB v. Universal Camera Corp., 179 F.2d 749 (2d Cir. 1950).

the reasonableness and fairness of Labor Board decisions than some courts have shown in the past." Nevertheless, he recognized that the statute did not authorize courts to weigh competing inferences or to "displace the Board's choice between two fairly conflicting views, even though the court would justifiably have made a different choice had the matter been before it de novo." The Board's findings, he concluded, "are entitled to respect; but they must nonetheless be set aside when the record before a court of appeals clearly precludes the Board's decision from being justified by a fair estimate of the worth of the testimony of witnesses or its informed judgment on matters within its special competence or both."

The Court disagreed with Judge Hand's views that the scope of review had not been changed and that the Board's reversal of a Trial Examiner should be disregarded by a reviewing court. (Two justices dissented on the latter point.) Although the Court conceded that its requirement that reviewing courts take account of such reversals would introduce an "unruly factor" into judicial review, it supported its position on two principal and interrelated grounds: (1) The examiner's report was part of the "record," which §10(e) required a reviewing court to consider; (2) the pertinent legislative history indicated that the enhancement of the examiner's status had been an important legislative purpose. The Court declared that the examiner's findings, when rejected by the Board, need not be given "more weight than in reason and in the light of judicial experience they deserve." And it emphasized that "the significance of his report, of course, depends largely on the importance of credibility in the particular case."

Upon remand, the Second Circuit, "upon giving weight to the examiner's findings," concluded that its first decision had been wrong and that the complaint should have been dismissed.[h] Judge Hand, moreover, appeared to define the function of the reviewing courts even more broadly than Mr. Justice Frankfurter's language warranted. Thus Judge Hand, after referring to the greater autonomy that reviewing courts had been directed to exercise, stated:

> Presumably, that does not extend to those issues on which the Board's specialized experience equips it with major premises inaccessible to judges, but as to matters of common knowledge we are to use a somewhat stiffer standard. Just where the Board's specialized experience ends it may no doubt be hard to say; but we are to find the boundary and beyond it to deem ourselves as competent as the Board to pass upon issues of fact. We hold that all the issues at bar are beyond the boundary and for that reason we cannot accept the Board's argument that we are not in as good a position as itself to decide what witnesses were more likely to be telling the truth. [190 F.2d at 430.]

[h] NLRB v. Universal Camera Corp., 190 F.2d 429, 431 (2d Cir. 1951).

And with respect to the point that had precipitated the remand, the reviewing court's disregard of the examiner's finding, Judge Hand seemed to read the Supreme Court as having altered the "substantial evidence" formula, for he declared: "Perhaps as good a way as any to state the change effected by the amendment is to say that we are not to be reluctant to insist that an examiner's findings on veracity must not be overruled without a very substantial preponderance in the testimony as recorded." That alteration of the "substantial evidence" formula was, however, rejected by the Supreme Court in FCC v. Allentown Broadcasting Co., 349 U.S. 358, 364 (1955). See also NLRB v. Interboro Contractors, Inc., 388 F.2d 495, 499 (2d Cir. 1967). Courts, however, have less discretion to overturn an ALJ than the Board, whose policy is not to overrule ALJ "credibility" determinations unless incorrectness is shown by "a clear preponderance of evidence." See IUE Local 745 (McGraw Edison), 263 N.L.R.B. No. 193, 111 L.R.R.M. 1046 (1982); Kopack v. NLRB, 668 F.2d 946, 953 (7th Cir. 1982).

The distinction between issues turning on credibility and those involving expertise has been justifiably emphasized by both Judge Hand and Justice Frankfurter. Nevertheless, these types of issues are not nicely discrete but coalesce in the process of judgment. Assume, for example, that an employer is charged with firing one Smith as reprisal for his adherence to the union. The employer establishes that Smith had spoiled a substantial amount of raw material and testifies that the spoilage was the only reason for the discharge. The ALJ credits that testimony and recommends dismissal of the complaint. The Board is skeptical of that recommendation and the assessment of credibility on which it rests, on the ground that insights about industrial relations convince it that the spoilage was not so excessive as to have been the sole reason for discharge. Is the pivotal question before the Board one of "credibility," "common knowledge," or "expertise"? See generally Kopack v. NLRB, supra, at 953-954, for an exploration of the difficulties resulting from efforts to separate demeanor-based findings of "credibility" from inferences from the entire record.

Universal Camera dealt with the reviewing function only with respect to "questions of fact," as distinguished from "questions of law," "mixed questions of law and fact," "policy," "discretionary" judgments, and so on. The classification of issues before reviewing courts into one or another of those categories appears to be related to the scope of judicial review. Thus review will be most expansive when the disputed issue is labeled as one of "law." But those categories, in the context of NLRB decisions, as elsewhere, do not have a clear analytic content, and they often appear to be used as convenient rationalizations for judicial practices that seem to rest on other grounds, such as the importance of the issues involved and the judicial response to the merits of the Board's decision, characterization of the issue aside.[i] Thus, where courts reverse the Board, they tend to characterize issues in such a way as to warrant broad judicial review, e.g., by denominating the issue as one of "law." See NLRB v. Babcock & Wilcox Co., infra p. 161. Where, however, Board decisions are affirmed, the issue may be characterized as one involving "expertise" or the balancing of conflicting interests within the Board's special competence, and, accordingly, calling for limited judicial review. See NLRB v. Erie Resistor Corp., infra p. 305.

Even though a court of appeals rejects the Board's interpretation of the Act, the Board often refuses to acquiesce, thereby provoking harsh judicial criticism (e.g., Yellow Taxi Co. of Minneapolis v. NLRB, noted infra p. 711), as well as acute discomfort for the lawyers defending NLRB refusals to honor "circuit law" before the circuit involved. Judicial umbrage, although understandable, ignores the Board's responsibility for unified administration, the role of intercircuit conflict in obtaining a grant of certiorari, and the possibility that the Supreme Court may reject positions approved by all circuits passing on an issue. See NLRB v. Southland Mfg. Co., 201 F.2d 244, 246 (4th Cir. 1952); Zimmerman & Dunn, Relations Between the NLRB and the Court of Appeal: A Tale of Acrimony and Accommodation, 8 Employee Rel. L.J. 4, 20 (1982).

Even though the NLRB was established almost 50 years ago, disagreement persists regarding the functions to be discharged by the NLRB and the relationship of those functions to the legislative and judicial process. See Winter, Judicial Review of Agency Decisions: The Labor Board and the Court, 1968 Sup. Ct. Rev. 53. The principal issue as to the Board's functions, stated somewhat generally, is whether the Board should behave essentially as a court and should make policy only within the interstices of the statute, or whether the statute has granted the Board more expansive policy-making functions. In this connection, periodic amendments to the NLRA, as well as the fleshing-out of the bare bones of the statute by administration, are relevant to the issue of whether the Board's freedom to alter its rules should be narrowed by the passage of time. A related issue is the extent to which the Board, reconstituted after shifts in national administrations, should be free to reverse prior decisions, not only because experience has revealed their inadequacy or because of underlying changes in conditions, but also because a new Board (Republican or Democrat) strikes a different balance between conflicting interests or attempts to respond to a new national "mood."

---

[i] The analytic content of the categories involved and the tensions between analysis and practice have been discussed in an extensive and subtle literature. See, e.g., L. Jaffe, Judicial Control of Administrative Action, chs. 14-15 (1965). Cf. K. Davis, Administrative Law Treatise, chs. 29-30 (1958).

The Supreme Court has not provided answers to the foregoing questions, even though they are of critical importance for the scope of judicial review, the function of which is to insure that the NLRB operates within the framework prescribed by Congress. Thus, if the NLRB is to have a larger policy-making function than a court (as is usually conceded) or if it is to be a politically responsive agency (a considerably more controversial point), the scope of judicial review would be limited. Furthermore, if the Board, as a properly politically responsive or policy-making agency, is to be free to reverse any of its own decisions that have not been affirmed by the Supreme Court, judicial affirmance of a particular decision as a correct exercise of agency discretion, rather than as a result compelled by the statute, should not necessarily preclude future modification by the Board. Although the Court has implicitly sanctioned such modifications (see NLRB v. Weingarten, infra p. 1181), it has not squarely confronted the other, even larger, issues as to the Board's functions, and a coherent approach to them is yet to emerge.

CHAPTER 4

PROTECTION OF THE ORGANIZING PROCESS AGAINST INTERFERENCE

The Wagner Act was designed to eliminate the guerrilla warfare that, as Chapter 1 indicated, had accompanied struggles over organization in the United States. Section 7 of that act broadly affirmed the rights of self-determination and concerted activity, and §8 implemented those rights by proscribing a broad range of employer activities that had operated to impede unionization.[a] Furthermore, §8, and subsection 8(1) particularly, was deliberately elastic so that it could be used to strike down new forms of interference that were likely to develop and that might not fit neatly under the more specific provisions of subsections (2)-(5). H.R. Rep. No. 969, 74th Cong., 1st Sess. 15 (1935).

These sweeping and pliable restrictions were to require the Board and the courts to strike a balance between legitimate employer interests and conflicting interests in employee self-determination and organization. Campaigns typically waged by employers and unions prior to a Board-conducted election spawned many problems of accommodation and led to an elaborate system of rules regulating pre-election conduct. That body of regulation does not rest solely on the unfair labor practice provisions of §8. Section 9 of the Act, which authorizes the NLRB to conduct union representation elections, quickly became an important supplementary basis for the policing of elections.

This chapter will examine the regulation, under the NLRA, of (1) pre-election campaign statements and tactics, (2) employer restrictions on

---

[a] Old antiunion tactics have not, of course, disappeared. In 1952, a Senate subcommittee reported: "In stopping a union-organizing campaign, employers will use some or all of the following methods: surveillance of organizers and union adherents; propaganda through rumors, letters, news stories, advertisements, speeches to the employees; denial of free speech and assembly to the union; organization of the whole community for antiunion activity; labor espionage; discharges of union sympathizers; violence and gunplay; injunctions; the closing or moving of the mill; endless litigation." Senate Subcomm. of the Comm. on Labor & Public Welfare, Report on Labor-Management Relations in the Southern Textile Industry, 82d Cong., 2d Sess., 54-55 (1952).

81

the use of company premises for organizational purposes, and (3) employer assistance to unions that threatens the integrity of collective bargaining. These topics embrace only some of the activities that are central to the organizational process. Deferred for treatment later are, for example, discriminatory discharges and other employer reprisals against collective action, as well as organizational picketing and boycotts by unions. Students should return to the questions raised by this chapter after considering the total body of regulation bearing on the organizational process.

Students should also seek to identify and to scrutinize both the purposes ascribed to the body of regulation presented here and the behavioral assumptions on which that regulation appears to rest. These assumptions have been questioned by J. Getman, S. Goldberg, & J. Herman, Union Representation Elections: Law and Reality (1976), whose findings are described infra pp. 115-117. (But cf. Lachman, Freedom of Speech in Union Representation Elections: Employer Campaigning and Employee Response, 1982 Am. B. Research J. 755.) Other useful discussions of the Board's regulation of campaigning include R. Williams, P. Janus, & K. Huhn, NLRB Regulation of Election Conduct (1974); Bok, The Regulation of Campaign Tactics in Representation Elections Under the National Labor Relations Act, 78 Harv. L. Rev. 38 (1964).

A.   REGULATION OF CAMPAIGN TECHNIQUES

NLRB v. Golub Corp.
388 F.2d 921 (2d Cir. 1967)

[The Board had held that the employer had violated §§8(a)(5) and 8(a)(1) of the Act. The court, denying validity to certain union authorization cards that the Board had counted toward a majority, denied enforcement of the §8(a)(5) order on the ground that the union had not acquired a valid card-based majority at the time of its demand for recognition. The court then turned to the Board's finding that the employer's letters and speeches to employees constituted violations of §8(a)(1).]

FRIENDLY, J. . . . In contrast to many §8(a)(1) proceedings, the violations here found consisted solely of writings and a speech addressed to the employees as a group — there was no finding of interrogation or surveillance, of discriminatory discharge, or of the grant of benefits. The case thus sharply raises the issue how far the Board may go in curbing speech consistently with §8(c) and the First Amendment.

The Board had no criticism of the company's letters of February 11 and 12, and only faulted portions of the letters of February 2 and 8 and a rather small part of Golub's speech of February 16. To quote simply the contested passages would create a false impression; it is necessary to place them in their setting by summarizing the entire communications.

The February 2 letter began by telling the employees of the forthcoming election. It accused the union of making false promises which "you can easily find out about . . . from others" and of picking on a single store to avoid a vote for all the chain's employees. It assured employees that the ballot would be absolutely secret, that they were "protected by law from anyone who attempts to interfere with your making a free choice," and that they were not bound by having signed a union card. It then went on to say "To get you to vote for them, the Union has been making many promises — promises to make demands which could be excessive. Companies that have been forced to meet excessive Union demands have been known to be forced out of business. The employees at the other local chain (Saveway) were not fooled by Union promises and flatly rejected them just a short time ago."[7] After arguing that union membership would mean dues, assessments, other financial burdens, and possibly sympathy strikes, the letter continued:

> The retail food business is the most competitive business in the world. Customers, not Unions, help pay your wages. We bring customers into our stores if we attract them with competitive prices. Even the large chains cannot meet these Union demands without making drastic adjustments because they also have to remain competitive. Large chains which have been forced to sign up with the Unions have been known to increase the workload of all their individual employees by reducing the number of employees in order to offset the higher costs. They find that they have to get the same amount of work done by fewer people to remain competitive.[8]

In conclusion the company promised to write again and asked the employees to keep an open mind.

The February 8 letter began by asking the employees to "look at the true facts of what outside interference would mean to you." The first set of facts consisted of the payment of dues and other union obligations, much as the earlier letter had depicted. Then came a paragraph found to have violated §8(a)(1) which we quote in the margin.[9] The letter went on to challenge "two

---

[7] The last two sentences were found to have violated §8(a)(1).

[8] The last two sentences were found to have violated §8(a)(1).

[9] "2. What does the choice of a union do to personal relationships? It means the end of a close relationship between you and your manager — or other management personnel. You certainly must recall that from time to time you may have asked the manager for some special personal arrangement or privilege which he probably gladly granted, such as time off when

false arguments" — that employees who did not sign up or vote for the union would be fired if the union won and that Central's owners really wanted a union. It urged employees not to put their future in the hands of union representatives with little interest in their needs or problems, and warned that a union might cook up a dispute "just to 'keep the pot boiling' or perhaps to help one of their favorites in your store," and that choice of a union "possibly could mean long drawn out strikes." It told the employees who planned to make their careers with the company that they did not need a union "to get the greatest benefits which this company can give and which it gives without unions" and appealed to those employees who were working their way through school or college not to foist a burden on their fellows. The letter concluded by asking how a union can "truthfully promise job security," arguing that "their exorbitant, excessive and outlandish demands often result in layoffs and even force companies out of business," and that job security really rested in sales and service to customers. Golub promised to write again, and requested the employees to "keep an open mind until the election."

Only two excerpts [in Golub's long February 16 speech] were found to have violated §8(a)(1). The first we quote in the margin.[10] In the second Golub dealt with the small 1% profit margin characteristic of grocery chains and the correspondingly narrow leeway for "many additional unrealistic demands which add to your overhead and expenses." He then told of a large chain which had raised prices after negotiating a union contract and as a result had been required to discharge around 25% of its help and make the remaining staff "do a tougher job because they have got to do the work those who were let out have to do," and of another market, and also a discount store, that were being forced out of business due to a union contract.

. . . [T]he basic issue is whether an employer coerces his employees in

---

your children were sick, weddings, for haircuts, a school prom, emergencies at home, and to catch up on studies. If there were a union contract, such personal privileges most likely could not be granted. Special privileges could be forbidden under a contract and be in violation of the contract. In such cases, we could not deal directly with you, but only through your union representative. You will not be able to solve problems directly as we have been doing. Do not be fooled by those who tell you otherwise — especially those fellow employees who might try to *frighten* you into thinking that they can control your job."

[10] "We have never had tensions or misunderstanding. We have always been able to talk them out, and they are here. They bring in these tensions and these difficulties which you would be subject to under their regime. Now, don't forget also that if they were to come in that many of the human things that we are now doing as a matter of course would no longer be possible if they were here under contract. Many of the little human things like we do, like giving you privileges where you want to go out to dances or if you have to play in a basketball game, or a child is sick, or of a dozen reasons. We will always give you reasonable consideration. Under a contract we would be subject to the rules of that contract. If we did these things, we could be charged with favoritism, we would be violating our contract. These things could well go by the board as a result. . . . "

the exercise of §7 rights, as forbidden by §8(a)(1), when he prophesies that unionization will decrease or wholly eliminate work opportunities, increase workloads, or create greater rigidity in personnel relationships, or whether such predictions come within the protection [of] §8(c). . . . While the answer would seem easy enough, the trend of Board decisions toward ever increasing restrictions on employer speech makes it desirable to attain perspective by a brief historical survey.

Under the Wagner Act, which contained §8(a)(1) but nothing like §8(c), the Board condemned almost any antiunion expression by an employer. It was sustained against First Amendment attack by some courts including this one, on the basis that employer arguments have "an ambivalent character." Since "what to an outsider will be no more than the vigorous presentation of a conviction, to an employee may be the manifestation of a determination which it is not safe to thwart," we held that "the Board must decide how far the second aspect obliterates the first," with the substantial evidence rule available to support its decision. NLRB v. Federbush Co., 121 F.2d 954, 957 (2d Cir. 1941). The Supreme Court evidently thought otherwise. NLRB v. Virginia Electric & Power Co., 314 U.S. 469 (1941), dealt with the employer notices pointing out that in the fifteen years since an organization had failed, confidence and understanding had reigned without the existence of a labor organization in any department. It went on to state that the company would freely entertain employee grievances and that it believed the mutual interest of all could "best be promoted through confidence and cooperation." The Board found the communications a violation of §8(1). The Court interpreted the words of the Wagner Act to avoid constitutional doubts arising from the First Amendment. It held that speech, which by its own terms was not coercive, did not violate the Act unless part of a course of conduct that was coercive.[12] As the Board appeared to have found the employer's words had violated the Act in and of themselves, the Court remanded to the Board so that it could determine whether the totality of the employer's conduct, of which his communications were a part, coerced its employees in violation of the statute. The Board later held that it did. See Virginia Electric & Power Co. v. NLRB, 319 U.S. 533 (1943).

This decision and the Board's rather halting response to it . . . constituted the background for §8(c) of the Taft-Hartley Act. The Hartley bill as passed by the House provided that "Expressing any views, argument, or opinion, or the dissemination thereof, whether in written, printed, graphic or

---

[12] The Court, in a dictum in Thomas v. Collins, 323 U.S. 516, 537 (1945), interpreted *Virginia Electric* as deciding that an employer's attempts to persuade employees to join or not to join a union are "within the First Amendment's guaranty" and can be restricted only when "other things are added which bring about coercion, or give it that character."

visual form, if it does not by its own terms threaten force or economic reprisal," shall not constitute or be evidence of an unfair labor practice. H.R. Rep. No. 3020, 80th Cong., 1st Sess., §8(d)(1) (1947).[b] The reference in the bill as passed by the Senate was less clear, reading:

> The Board shall not base any finding of unfair labor practice upon any statement of views or arguments, either written or oral, if such statement contains under all the circumstances no threat, express or implied, of reprisal or force, or offer, express or implied, of benefit; Provided, That no language or provision of this section is intended to nor shall it be construed or administered so as to abridge or interfere with the right of either employers or employees to freedom of speech as guaranteed by the first amendment to the Constitution of the United States. H.R. 3020, as passed Senate, §8(c).[c]

The Conference Committee eliminated both the "by its own terms" of the House bill and the "under all the circumstances" and the unnecessary proviso of the Senate bill. While the Act thus went less far than the House bill, the detailed analysis of the compromise which Senator Taft submitted makes clear that, at the very least, the final form limits the extent to which context can be used to impart sinister meanings to innocuous words:

[b][Concerning that provision, H.R. Rep. No. 245, 80th Cong., 1st Sess. 33, stated: " . . . Although the Labor Board says it does not limit free speech, its decisions show that it uses against people what the Constitution says they can say freely. Thus, if an employer criticizes a union, and later a foreman discharges a union official for gross misconduct, the Board may say that the official's misconduct warranted his being discharged, but 'infer,' from what the employer said, perhaps long before, that the discharge was for union activity, and reinstate the official with back pay. . . . The bill corrects this, providing that nothing that anyone says shall constitute or be evidence of an unfair labor practice unless it, by its own express terms, threatens force or economic reprisal. This means that a statement may not be used against the person making it unless it, standing alone, is unfair within the express terms of Sections 7 and 8 of the amended act." — EDS.]

[c][S. Rep. No. 105, 80th Cong., 1st Sess. 23, gave the following explanation of the purpose of the foregoing provision: "Another amendment to this section would insure both to employers and labor organizations full freedom to express their views to employees on labor matters, refrain from threats of violence, intimation of economic reprisal, or offers of benefit [sic]. The Supreme Court in Thomas v. Collins (323 U.S. 516) held, contrary to some earlier decisions of the Labor Board, that the Constitution guarantees freedom of speech on either side in labor controversies. . . .

"The Board has placed a limited construction upon these decisions by holding such speeches by employers to be coercive if the employer was found guilty of some other unfair labor practice even though severable or unrelated (Monumental Life Insurance, 69 N.L.R.B. 247) or if the speech was made in the plant on working time (Clark Brothers, 70 N.L.R.B. 60). The committee believes these decisions to be too restrictive and, in this section, provides that if, under all the circumstances, there is neither an expressed or implied threat of reprisal, force, or offer of benefit, the Board shall not predicate any finding of unfair labor practice upon the statement. The Board, of course, will not be precluded from considering such statements as evidence." — EDS.]

The House conferees were of the opinion that the phrase "under all the circumstances" in the Senate amendment was ambiguous and might be susceptible of being construed as approving certain Board decisions which have attempted to circumscribe the right of free speech where there were also findings of unfair labor practices. Since this was certainly contrary to the intent of the Senate, . . . the Senate conferees acceded to the wish of the House group that the intent of this section be clarified. 93 Cong. Rec. 6601 (1947).

In its Annual Report for 1948 the Board announced that §8(c)

appears to enlarge somewhat the protection accorded by the original statute and to grant immunity beyond that contemplated by the free speech guarantees of the Constitution. For example, the *Clark Bros.* "compulsory audience" doctrine has been held to be invalidated by this section of the act. Nor can a noncoercive speech any longer be held to violate the act because at other times, and on other occasions, the employer has committed other unfair labor practices. *However, words and conduct may be so intertwined as to be considered a single coercive act.* Thus where an employer delivered a speech to his employees impressing them with the fact that a union was an unnecessary outside influence which he preferred not to have in his plant, and immediately thereafter polled the employees on whether he should "step out completely and let the business go on its own power," the board found that the speech and the poll together constituted a threat that, if the employees voted for the union, the employer might discontinue operations. The speech and poll jointly were therefore found to violate §8(a)(1) of the act.

13 N.L.R.B. Ann. Rep. 49-50 (1948). (Emphasis supplied.) The Board can draw no comfort here from the sentence we have italicized since the company is not claimed to have indulged in any conduct violative of §8(a)(1) other than its communications to employees.

In the light of this history and the Supreme Court's more recent warning of the dangers of ever finding an unfair labor practice in employer argument alone, see NLRB v. Exchange Parts Co., 375 U.S. 405 (1964), we find the approach here taken unacceptable. In holding the passages we have cited to be violations, the Trial Examiner stated simply that "the letters and speech . . . were calculated to create and instill in the minds of employees a fear of loss of privileges and economic suffering as a result of their adherence to the Union, and constituted interferences, restraint, and coercion within the meaning of §8(a)(1) of the Act." This is reading the Act as if §8(c) did not exist; while there is a risk that an employer's prediction of adverse consequences from unionization may be taken as a threat to produce them, to hold that this danger alone suffices to convert a prediction into a threat of reprisal would go back to the very position of the early 1940s which §8(c) was adopted to change. . . . Only if respondent's words contained a "threat of reprisal" did they go beyond the bounds of §8(c). But, as the dictionaries tell us, a "threat of reprisal" means a "threat of retaliation" and this in turn means not a prediction that adverse consequences will develop but a threat that they will be deliberately inflicted in return for an injury—"to return evil for evil." Whatever vitality decisions . . . giving weight to an agency's construction of statutory language may have generally, . . . such considerations have little weight when the statute being enforced approaches the limits of constitutional power. In such a case we encounter the overriding principle of construction requiring that statutes be read so as to avoid serious constitutional doubt. . . .

The error of the Board in finding violations of the Act in the two passages from the letter of February 2 and the second set of remarks in the speech of February 16 predicting loss of work, harder work, or even a close-down as a result of unionization is apparent. Nothing in these communications could reasonably be interpreted as a threat to make the employees' lot harder in retaliation for their voting for the union [citing cases]. The only fair reading is that the employer would take these steps solely from economic necessity and with regret. NLRB v. S & H Grossinger's, Inc., 372 F.2d 26 (2d Cir. 1967), is very much in point. There the Board had found a violation of §8(a)(1) in employer statements that unionization would result in "less steady work" and that, although the employees always had had the security of their jobs, "under union conditions, we never know." 156 N.L.R.B. 233, 241 (1965). This court, speaking through Judge Hays, refused enforcement saying, in language equally applicable here, that "the statements did not suggest that the Grossinger management would seek to bring about any of the unfortunate conditions which they feared might occur." Still more recently, in NLRB v. River Togs, Inc., 382 F.2d 198, 202 (2d Cir. 1967), we noted that "Although the Board apparently thinks workers should be shielded from such disconcerting information, an employer is free to tell his employees what he reasonably believes will be the likely economic consequences of unionization that are outside his control, as distinguished from threats of economic reprisal to be taken solely on his own volition." While, as the last quoted extract suggests, what is in form a prediction could so far outrun any possible basis for it that the Board might be justified in concluding a threat was intended, . . . this is a principle that must be kept within narrow limits not here approached. Congress did not intend the Board to act as a censor of the reasonableness of statements by either party to a labor controversy even if it constitutionally could. See Linn v. United Plant Guard Workers, 383 U.S. 53 (1964). We need not here consider whether the Board may set aside an election, under the principle of General Shoe Corp., 77 N.L.R.B. 124

(1948), because of an unfounded prophecy not containing a threat of reprisal. . . .

Although the case as to the prediction of the effect of unionization on
the grant of special privileges is a shade closer, we reach the same conclusion.
Golub's speech made it clear enough that he would not aim to withdraw
special privileges if a union contract were signed, and certainly not to withdraw them in retaliation for the union contract, but that he feared that the
rules of the contract or the union's administration of it might forbid giving
such benefits to one employee unless they were uniformly given to all. The
same is true of the letter of February 8 when this is read as a whole. While
these fears may have been unwarranted, they were not shown to have so far
transcended the bounds of reason as to justify the Board in finding them to be
disguised threats of reprisal. . . .

Enforcement denied.

HAYS, J., dissenting. The majority opinion demonstrates once more the
inescapable truth that United States Circuit Judges safely ensconced in their
chambers do not feel threatened by what employers tell their employees. An
employer can dress up his threats in the language of prediction ("You will
lose your job" rather than "I will fire you") and fool judges. He doesn't fool
his employees; they know perfectly clearly what he means. . . .

The error into which the majority falls is to believe that one can identify
threatening language regardless of the circumstances in which the language
is used and regardless of the ears to which it is directed. A dictionary definition will suffice because it makes no difference whether the words are addressed to a judge or to a machine hand, they must mean the same thing.

It is astonishing to find that the ears of employees are so exquisitely
attuned to every nuance of meaning in the employer's letters and speeches,
but that when it comes to the union's representations these same employees
are "ordinary working people unversed in the 'witty diversities' of labor law,"
NLRB v. S. E. Nichols Co., 380 F.2d 438, 442 (2d Cir. 1967), so dull and
stupid that the union can easily pull the wool over their eyes. Employees who
have not the slightest difficulty in distinguishing between a "prediction" and
a "threat," are unable to read union authorization cards with even that degree
of understanding which human beings ordinarily exercise. Surely enforcement of the Board's orders has not become a game of "Heads I win, tails you
lose."

The extent to which the majority will go in defending the employer's
rights is indicated by their treatment of the employer's threats to discontinue
making "special personal arrangement[s]" and granting privileges "such as
time off when your children [are] sick, weddings, for haircuts, a school prom,
emergencies at home, and to catch up on studies." These "fears" (of the

employer!) may have been "unwarranted" says the majority, but "they were not shown" to be unreasonable. If it is not obvious on its face that no employee would believe that the *union* would interfere with his taking time off for a haircut, and that the employees undoubtedly (and correctly) understood that it was the *employer* who was going to withdraw these privileges, then certainly such a matter ought to be left to the Board's expertise, without requiring a "showing" that the Board was right. . . .

NOTES

1. Section 8(c) provides not only that communications privileged under that section shall not constitute an unfair labor practice but also that such communications shall not be evidence thereof. During the legislative debate, that evidentiary role was assailed as contrary to the rules of evidence generally applicable to criminal and civil trials. See, e.g., remarks of Senator Morse, NLRB, 2 Legislative History of the LMRA 1555 (1948). Senator Taft responded to that criticism as follows:

. . . The conferees had in mind a number of Board decisions in which, because of the fact that an employer has at some time committed an unfair labor practice, a speech by him, innocuous in itself, has been held not to be privileged. The conferees did not believe that past misconduct should deprive either employees or labor organizations of the privilege of exercising constitutional rights. There have also been a number of decisions by the Board in which discharges of employees, even though there was no evidence, in the surrounding circumstances, of discrimination, have been deemed unfair labor practices simply because at one time or another the employer has expressed himself as not in favor of unionization of his employees. The object of this section, therefore, is to make it clear that decisions of this sort cannot be made under the conference bill.

It has been argued, however, that the prohibition against using expressions of opinion as evidence goes much further than the rules with respect to admissibility in a criminal or civil trial. Senators making this argument overlook the fact that the privilege of this subsection is limited to expression of "view, arguments, or opinion." It has no application to statements which are acts in themselves or contain directions or instructions. These, of course, could be deemed admissions and hence competent under the well-recognized exception to the hearsay rule.

Numerous comparisons with criminal and civil trials have been made. Consider a more exact comparison. A man is on trial for selling liquor illegally. The fact that he argued against adoption of the Volstead Act would scarcely be permitted to be used in evidence against him. In a murder trial in which defendant is accused of killing a Republican Senator, his political views or opinions would not be competent testimony. Yet the Board has permitted employers' expressions of opinion on unionism to be used to sustain the theory that he was guilty of violations of the National Labor Relations Act. [NLRB, 2 Legislative History of the LMRA 1624 (1948).]

What criticisms, if any, would be warranted by the foregoing comments or the rule of exclusion embodied in §8(c)?

2. After an organizing campaign began, the employer fired one Eager, ostensibly for violating a plant rule that had not been enforced for some time. The next day the employer posted the following notice on the employee bulletin board: "I've treated you fairly and will continue to do so, no matter what. But a union in this plant would not be good for you or for the company. Don't sign up with dues-hungry union bosses." Did the posting of the notice violate the NLRA? Would the notice be evidence that the discharge had been prompted by Eager's support of the union and had, accordingly, violated §8(a)(3)?

3. Ordinarily, the Board does not concern itself with the actual effects of speech or other conduct. See 33 NLRB Ann. Rep. 60 (1968). In determining whether disputed communications are coercive, should the Board attempt to assess the actual impact of specific conduct on the employees involved? What weight, if any, should be given to the general social context of an election campaign, e.g., a southern mill town dominated by the employer, or a northern industrial complex with a strong, accepted tradition of unionization? If the general social context is to be considered, how are the relevant data to be presented to the NLRB and the reviewing courts?

4. Under §8(c), the Board, noting that "words and conduct may be so intertwined as to be considered a single coercive act," continued to apply the totality-of-conduct approach. See 13 NLRB Ann. Rep. 49-50 (1948). The courts in general approved this approach as required by the statutory protection of free choice. See, e.g., NLRB v. Kropp Forge Co., 178 F.2d 822 (7th Cir. 1949), cert. denied, 340 U.S. 810 (1950); Irving Air Chute Co. v. NLRB, 350 F.2d 176 (2d Cir. 1965); but cf. NLRB v. Rockwell Mfg. Co., 271 F.2d 109 (3d Cir. 1959).

5. The problem raised by Golub, whether statements on their face involve "coercion" or promises of "benefit," has bristled with difficulties characteristic of all efforts to regulate speech and compounded in this context by the brinkmanship of antiunion employers seeking to exploit §8(c) to the hilt. The cases below reflect the fluctuating responses to such difficulties by Board members who have attached different weights to unionization and free

communication, respectively — and who were appointed by administrations with different political obligations and attitudes with respect to unionization.

General Shoe Corp., 77 N.L.R.B. 124 (1948). The employer's pre-election campaign had consisted mainly of "vigorously disparaging statements" about the union. In a proceeding consolidating the union's charges of unfair labor practices and its objections to the election which it had lost, the Board found only two isolated instances of §8(1) coercion of individual employees. It also held the employer's many antiunion statements to be protected by §8(c) and thus "excluded from . . . consideration in an unfair labor practice case." Turning to the union's objections to the election, the Board found it unnecessary,

> in *this* part of the case, to pass upon or adopt the Trial Examiner's finding that the respondent violated the Act by the actions of its supervisors in visiting the individual employees at their homes after working hours for the purpose of dissuading them from selecting the Union . . . , or by the action of its president in summoning the employees, in groups of 20 to 25, to his office on the eve of the election for the purpose of reading to them an antiunion speech.

Nevertheless, the Board ordered the election set aside, explaining:
     ". . . Conduct that creates an atmosphere which renders improbable a free choice will sometimes warrant invalidating an election, even though that conduct may not constitute an unfair labor practice. An election can serve its true purpose only if the surrounding conditions enable employees to register a free and untrammeled choice for or against a bargaining representative. For this reason the Board has sometimes set elections aside . . . in the absence of any charges or proof of unfair labor practice. When a record reveals conduct so glaring that it is almost certain to have impaired employees' freedom of choice, we have set an election aside and directed a new one.[d] . . .
     "On this record, therefore, although the respondent's activities immediately before the election . . . are not held to constitute unfair labor practices . . . , certain of them created an atmosphere calculated to prevent a free and untrammeled choice by the employees. . . . The significant element is the method selected by this Company's president to express his antiunion views to the employees on the day before the election. He had them brought to his own office in some 25 groups of 20 to 25 individuals, and there, in the very room which each employee must have regarded as the locus

---

[d] [See note e below. — EDS.]

of final authority in the plant, read every small group the same intemperate antiunion address. In our opinion, this *conduct*, and the Employer's instructions to its foremen to propagandize employees in their homes, went so far beyond the presently accepted custom of campaigns directed at employees' reasoning faculties that we are not justified in assuming that the election results represented the employees' own true wishes.

"We do not subscribe to the view . . . that the criteria applied by the Board in a representation proceeding to determine whether certain alleged misconduct interfered with an election need necessarily be identical to those employed in testing whether an unfair labor practice was committed, although the result will ordinarily be the same.[10] In election proceedings, it is the Board's function to provide a laboratory in which an experiment may be conducted, under conditions as nearly ideal as possible, to determine the uninhibited desires of the employees. It is our duty to establish those conditions; it is also our duty to determine whether they have been fulfilled. When, in the rare extreme case, the standard drops too low, because of our fault or that of others, the requisite laboratory conditions are not present and the experiment must be conducted over again. That is the situation here.

"We find that the circumstances surrounding the election . . . raise substantial doubt[e] as to whether [its results reflect] the employees' free choice. . . . Accordingly, we shall order it set aside. . . . "

Members Reynolds and Gray, dissenting in part: " . . . Clearly if the calling of small groups of employees into the respondent's office and visiting of individual employee's homes by supervisors is to be deemed conduct precluding the free expression of choice by employees in an election, it would be only logical to conclude that the employment of such 'method' by an

---

[10] The dissenting opinion seems to be predicated on the general proposition that only conduct declared unlawful by the Act is a valid ground for setting aside an election held under the Board's auspices. Yet, in apparent inconsistency, our colleagues concede that certain circumstances . . . may afford "unquestionable justification" for setting aside an election "as not reflecting the free choice of representatives contemplated by the Act," notwithstanding the fact that they do not constitute unfair labor practices.

It should be noted that Congress only applied the new §8(c) to unfair labor practice cases. Matters which are not available to prove a violation of law, and therefore to impose a penalty upon a respondent, may still be pertinent, if extreme enough, in determining whether an election satisfies the Board's own administrative standards. This is borne out . . . by the very fact that the Board occasionally . . . set aside an election under the original Wagner Act because of union misconduct at a time when that misconduct could not have constituted a violation of law.

[e] [Observe the different burdens of persuasion expressed by the Board in the text accompanying notes d and e, respectively. The latter formulation imposes a burden much lighter than that recognized by courts generally. See, e.g., NLRB v. Advanced Systems, Inc., 681 F.2d 570 (9th Cir. 1982); Daylight Grocery Co. v. NLRB, 678 F.2d 905 (11th Cir. 1982). — Eds.]

employer to express its views is sufficiently coercive to be violative of the Act. But no such conclusion is reached by our colleagues. Indeed, in our opinion, it is difficult to see how such a finding could be made in the face of a contrary intent by Congress in [enacting §8(c)]. . . .

". . . The instant case . . . presents no conduct such as the Act prohibits on the part of an employer, but rather the kind to which it specifically lends protection. It is paradoxical, to say the least, that now, after Congress has so strongly rejected the Board's prior construction of the Act in its relation to the Constitutional guarantee of free speech, that this Board should construe privileged expressions of opinion as creating an atmosphere which prevents employees from freely expressing their choice of representatives in a Board-conducted election. If the expression or dissemination of views, arguments, or opinion by an employer is to be afforded the full freedom which the amended Act envisages, it follows that the Board cannot justify setting aside elections merely because the employer avails himself of the protection which the statute specifically provides."

NOTES

1. Reviewing courts have, in general, upheld the NLRB's laboratory conditions approach as compatible with §8(c) and the First Amendment. See Bausch & Lomb, Inc. v. NLRB, 451 F.2d 873, 878 (2d Cir. 1971). Do you agree? The Board has declared: "Conduct violative of §8(a)(1) is, *a fortiori*, conduct which interferes with the exercise of a free and untrammeled [election] choice. . . . This is so because the test of conduct which may interfere with 'laboratory conditions' . . . is considerably more restrictive than the test of conduct which amounts to interference, restraint, or coercion [under] §8(a)(1)." Dal-Tex Optical Co., 137 N.L.R.B. 1782, 1786-1787 (1962). Should a pre-election unfair labor practice automatically constitute grounds for setting aside an election? Suppose, for example, that the evidence is clear that the violation had no effect on the outcome of the election? The Board's policy is described in Custom Trim Products, 255 N.L.R.B. 787 (1981). The materials in Chapter 6 will return to the point that representation proceedings under the Act involve only the question of whether "laboratory conditions" have been disturbed and do not involve determinations of whether unfair labor practices have been committed.

2. *General Shoe* involved specific findings of objectionable pre-election conduct. Could an employer's overall campaign against the union warrant invalidating an election even though no specific employer conduct is sufficient in and of itself to have that effect? See Rosewood Mfg. Co., 263

N.L.R.B. 420 (1982) (employer repeatedly linked selection of the union with unprofitability, low productivity, plant closure, and loss of jobs); Turner Shoe Co., Inc. and Carmen Athletic Industries, Inc., 249 N.L.R.B. 144 (1980).

3. Before, during, and after an election scheduled for 5:00-7:00 p.m., employees on their way to or from the polls came into a bar close to the polling place. A union official, who had not previously announced free drinks at the bar for employees, told arrivals "drinks are on my tab." He paid for drinks for 12 to 15 of the 18 voters, telling them "not to forget how to vote"; no voter got drunk. Did the union, a 13-5 election victor, destroy "laboratory conditions"? Any difference in your answer if the union had announced in advance and served free Pepsi and tuna sandwiches at the same location? Should a court of appeals defer to, or second guess, the Board's certification of the union when it is challenged in an appeal from the Board's unfair labor practice order? Cf. NLRB v. Labor Services, Inc., 721 F.2d 13 (1st Cir. 1983).

4. After an election is erroneously upset under *General Shoe*, the union wins a second election conducted within a year of the first one. The employer refuses to bargain with the union despite its certification, and in the resulting §8(a)(5) unfair labor practice proceeding urges that the first election was valid and that the second election was, accordingly, barred by §9(c)(3). Would the acceptance of the employer's contention warrant his refusal to bargain with the union despite its demonstration of majority support in the second election? What would be the justification for permitting such refusals?

NLRB v. Gissel Packing Co.
395 U.S. 575 (1969)

[Each of four cases before the Court raised the question of the validity of a bargaining order entered (under §8(a)(5)) against an employer who had both rejected a recognition demand by a union with an authorization card-based majority and engaged in an antiunion campaign involving unfair labor practices. The portion of the Court's opinion considering the bargaining order appears at p. 442, infra. Here the Court deals with the reach of §8(c) and the First Amendment — a question raised by the Sinclair Company, a petitioner challenging the finding that its communications to employees violated §8(a)(1).]

WARREN, C. J. . . . In July 1965, the Int. Brotherhood of Teamsters, Local Union No. 404, began an organizing campaign among petitioner's Holyoke employees and by the end of the summer had obtained authorization cards from 11 of the Company's 14 journeymen wire weavers choosing the Union as their bargaining agent. On September 20, the Union notified petitioner that it represented a majority of its wire weavers, requested that the Company bargain with it, and offered to submit the signed cards to a neutral third party for authentication. After petitioner's president declined the Union's request a week later, claiming, *inter alia*, that he had a good faith doubt of majority status because of the cards' inherent unreliability, the Union petitioned, on November 8, for an election. . . .

When petitioner's president first learned of the Union's drive in July, he talked with all of his employees in an effort to dissuade them from joining a union. He particularly emphasized the results of the long 1952 strike, which he claimed "almost put our company out of business," and expressed worry that the employees were forgetting the "lessons of the past." He emphasized, secondly, that the Company was still on "thin ice" financially, that the Union's "only weapon is to strike," and that a strike "could lead to the closing of the plant," since the parent company had ample manufacturing facilities elsewhere. He noted, thirdly, that because of their age and the limited usefulness of their skills outside their craft, the employees might not be able to find reemployment if they lost their jobs as a result of a strike. Finally, he warned those who did not believe that the plant could go out of business to "look around Holyoke and see a lot of them out of business." The president sent letters to the same effect to the employees in early November, emphasizing that the parent company had no reason to stay in Massachusetts if profits went down.

During the two or three weeks immediately prior to the election on December 9, the president sent the employees a pamphlet captioned: "Do you want another 13-week strike?" stating, *inter alia*, that: "We have no doubt that the Teamsters Union can again close the Wire Weaving Department and the entire plant by a strike. We have no hopes that the Teamsters Union Bosses will not call a strike. . . . The Teamsters Union is a strike-happy outfit." Similar communications followed in late November, including one stressing the Teamsters' "hoodlum control." Two days before the election, the Company sent out another pamphlet that was entitled: "Let's Look at the Record," and that purported to be an obituary of companies in the Holyoke-Springfield, Massachusetts, area that had allegedly gone out of business because of union demands, eliminating some 3,500 jobs; the first page carried a large cartoon showing the preparation of a grave for the Sinclair Company and other headstones containing the names of other plants allegedly victimized by the unions. Finally, on the day before the election, the president made another personal appeal to his employees to reject the Union. He repeated that the Company's financial condition was precarious;

that a possible strike would jeopardize the continued operation of the plant; and that age and lack of education would make reemployment difficult. The Union lost the election 7 to 6, and then filed both objections to the election and unfair labor practice charges which were consolidated for hearing before the trial examiner.

The Board agreed with the trial examiner that the president's communications with his employees, when considered as a whole, "reasonably tended to convey to the employees the belief or impression that selection of the Union in the forthcoming election could lead [the Company] to close its plant, or to the transfer of the weaving production, with the resultant loss of jobs to the wire weavers." Thus, the Board found that under the "totality of the circumstances" petitioner's activities constituted a violation of §8(a)(1) of the Act. The Board further agreed with the trial examiner that petitioner's activities, because they "also interfered with the exercise of a free and untrammeled choice in the election," and "tended to foreclose the possibility" of holding a fair election, required that the election be set aside. . . . [T]he First Circuit sustained the Board's findings and conclusions and enforced its order in full. 397 F.2d 157. . . .

. . . [A]n employer's free speech right to communicate his views to his employees is firmly established and cannot be infringed by a union or the Board. Thus, §8(c) merely implements the First Amendment.

Any assessment of the precise scope of employer expression, of course, must be made in the context of its labor relations setting. Thus, an employer's rights cannot outweigh the equal rights of the employees to associate freely, as those rights are embodied in §7 and protected by §8(a)(1) and the proviso to §8(c). And any balancing of those rights must take into account the economic dependence of the employees on their employers, and the necessary tendency of the former, because of that relationship, to pick up intended implications of the latter that might be more readily dismissed by a more disinterested ear. Stating these obvious principles is but another way of recognizing that what is basically at stake is the establishment of a nonpermanent, limited relationship between the employer, his economically dependent employee and his union agent, not the election of legislators or the enactment of legislation whereby that relationship is ultimately defined and where the independent voter may be freer to listen more objectively and employers as a class freer to talk. Cf. New York Times Co. v. Sullivan, 376 U.S. 254 (1964).[f]

[f][In Virginia State Bd. of Pharmacy v. Virginia Citizens Consumers Council, Inc., 425 U.S. 748 (1976), the Court, in invalidating a state prohibition of price-advertising of prescription drugs by pharmacists, extended some First Amendment protection to "commercial speech." Although disclaiming any intention to deal with labor cases, the Court referred to

Within this framework, we must reject the Company's challenge to the decision below and the findings of the Board on which it was based. The standards used below for evaluating the impact of an employer's statements are not seriously questioned by petitioner and we see no need to tamper with them here. Thus, an employer is free to communicate to his employees any of his general views about unionism or any of his specific views about a particular union, so long as the communications do not contain a "threat of reprisal or force or promise of benefit." He may even make a prediction as to the precise effects he believes unionization will have on his company. In such a case, however, the prediction must be carefully phrased on the basis of objective fact to convey an employer's belief as to demonstrably probable consequences beyond his control or to convey a management decision already arrived at to close the plant in case of unionization. See Textile Workers v. Darlington Mfg. Co., 380 U.S. 263, 274, n.20 (1965). If there is any implication that an employer may or may not take action solely on his own initiative for reasons unrelated to economic necessities and known only to him, the statement is no longer a reasonable prediction based on available facts but a threat of retaliation based on misrepresentation and coercion, and as such without the protection of the First Amendment. We therefore agree with the court below that "[c]onveyance of the employer's belief, even though sincere, that unionization will or may result in the closing of the plant is not a statement of fact unless, which is most improbable, the eventuality of closing is capable of proof." 397 F.2d 157, 160. As stated elsewhere, an employer is free only to tell "what he reasonably believes will be the likely economic consequences of unionization that are outside his control," and not "threats of economic reprisal to be taken solely on his own volition." NLRB v. River Togs, Inc., 382 F.2d 198, 202 (2d Cir. 1967).

Equally valid was the finding by the court and the Board that petitioner's statements and communications were not cast as a prediction of "demonstrable 'economic consequences,'" 397 F.2d, at 160, but rather as a threat of retaliatory action. The Board found that petitioner's speeches, pamphlets, leaflets, and letters conveyed the following message: that the company was in a precarious financial condition; that the "strike-happy" union would in all likelihood have to obtain its potentially unreasonable demands by striking, the probable result of which would be a plant shutdown, as the past history of labor relations in the area indicated; and that the employees in such a case

---

them as illustrating the extension of First Amendment protections to essentially private and economic speech. Rehnquist, J., dissenting, stated that the Court's decision presumably would require the reevaluation of prior labor decisions invalidating NLRB elections because of truthful but implicitly coercive statements, e.g., that unionization leads to plant closings. — Eds.]

would have great difficulty finding employment elsewhere. In carrying out its duty to focus on the question: "[W]hat did the speaker intend and the listener understand?" (A. Cox, Law and the National Labor Policy 44 (1960)), the Board could reasonably conclude that the intended and understood import of that message was not to predict that unionization would inevitably cause the plant to close but to threaten to throw employees out of work regardless of the economic realities. In this connection, we need go no further than to point out (1) that petitioner had no support for its basic assumption that the union, which had not yet even presented any demands, would have to strike to be heard, and that it admitted at the hearing that it had no basis for attributing other plant closings in the area to unionism; and (2) that the Board has often found that employees, who are particularly sensitive to rumors of plant closings take such hints as coercive threats rather than honest forecasts.

Petitioner argues that the line between so-called permitted predictions and proscribed threats is too vague to stand up under traditional First Amendment analysis and that the Board's discretion to curtail free speech rights is correspondingly too uncontrolled. It is true that a reviewing court must recognize the Board's competence in the first instance to judge the impact of utterances made in the context of the employer-employee relationship, see NLRB v. Virginia Electric & Power Co., 314 U.S. 469, 479 (1941). But an employer, who has control over that relationship and therefore knows it best, cannot be heard to complain that he is without an adequate guide for his behavior. He can easily make his views known without engaging in " 'brinkmanship' " when it becomes all too easy to "overstep and tumble [over] the brink," Wausau Steel Corp. v. NLRB, 377 F.2d 369, 372 (7th Cir. 1967). At the least he can avoid coercive speech simply by avoiding conscious overstatements he has reason to believe will mislead his employees. . . .

NOTES

1. A company vice-president in his pre-election speech to assembled employees said:

> . . . [T]here is no magic in unions. If a company is competitive, if it manu-
> factures a good product [efficiently] . . . , there is going to be job security
> whether [or not] you have a union. . . . I have dealt with a number of
> unions in which I have had to shut down plants, or move them elsewhere. I've
> sat at the bargaining table and told [a] union that you'll either have to agree to
> the company's position or we'll shut the plant down. They didn't believe me
> and we shut the plant down. These are not threats, these are simply facts

showing what I think all of you really understand. Whether [or not] you have a union, a company must remain competitive and it must grow if it is going to succeed.

The Board found in this passage an unlawful threat of plant closure. A reviewing court, although upholding NLRB findings of other company unfair labor practices and purporting to apply the customary "totality" test, saw only protected speech in this passage. The court, citing *Gissel*, emphasized that the remarks "did not contain any implication that the company would shut down its plants 'on its own initiative for reasons unrelated to economic necessities'" and that "in fact, [the vice-president] was careful to state that his remarks were not threats but simply his view of the possible economic consequences of a union victory." NLRB v. Intertherm, Inc., 596 F.2d 267 (8th Cir. 1979).

Do you agree with the court's application of *Gissel*? In order to avert serious risk of an unfair labor practice, would it be a good idea for the company to revise the quoted statement before using it again? If so, what revisions would you propose? (In NLRB v. Village IX, Inc., 723 F.2d 1360, 1368 (7th Cir. 1983), the court, protecting a speech like that in *Intertherm*, declared:

[The employer] provided objective support for his prediction of the consequences of unionizing [his restaurant] by pointing to the competitive nature of the restaurant business and to the fact that only one restaurant in [the city] was unionized and it was doing badly. More was not required in the circumstances; we do not read *Gissel* to require the employer to develop detailed advance substantiation in the manner of the Federal Trade Commission, . . . at least for predictions founded on common sense and general experience. A small [restaurant] should not have to hire a high-powered consultant to make an econometric forecast of the probable consequences of unionization on the restaurant business in [a particular locality].

Do you agree that one unionized restaurant doing badly constitutes "objective support"?)

2. In American Greetings Corp., 146 N.L.R.B. 1440 (1964), the question was whether an employer, not charged with §8(a)(1) violations, had nevertheless destroyed "laboratory conditions" by a campaign stressing the inevitability of strikes, violence, and loss of employment. The Board declared:

In cases in which the Board [has] set aside an election [because of an employer's having indicated the futility of unionization], the employer had stated, either expressly or by clear implication, that it would not bargain in good faith with a union even if it were selected by the employees. . . . [Unlike the situation where the strike issue is raised as a "straw man" to frighten employees, here] the Employer related the strike and violence issues to the Petitioner's own strike record. That record was relevant to the election issues before the employees. Moreover, the Petitioner could have, and in fact, did, answer this Employer contention with its own version of its record. In these circumstances, neither the fact that the Employer also discussed a strike in a nearby plant in which Petitioner was not involved, nor the fact that the Employer's development of the strike theme pointed up to employees that in light of Petitioner's own strike record, their selection of Petitioner might lead to their involvement in strikes, violence, and loss of jobs to replacements, is a sufficient basis for finding that the Employer's conduct exceeded the bounds of permissible electioneering.

Should it matter that the employer's statements were half-truths or conveyed a distorted picture of collective bargaining? Would the impact on the employees be likely to be different had an employer described the harms from organization as "possible" rather than as "probable" or "inevitable"?

3. Under what circumstances should an employer's statement that bargaining with a union would begin "from scratch," "from ground zero," or "with a blank sheet of paper" be held to violate the Act or to destroy laboratory conditions? In evaluating such statements, the NLRB purports to distinguish situations in which such remarks in context could be read as a threat to discontinue existing benefits from situations in which the remarks merely describe bargaining strategy or merely tell employees that unionization alone is no guarantee of increased benefits. See Host International, Inc., 195 N.L.R.B. 348 (1972). A "reprisal" rationale appears to explain why bargaining-from-scratch statements are viewed with suspicion and often found objectionable. See Plastronics, Inc., 233 N.L.R.B. 155, 156 (1977) (threats to take away existing benefits and to bargain from scratch leave employees "with the impression that what they may ultimately receive [through collective bargaining] depends in large measure upon what the [u]nion can induce the employer to restore"); see also TRW-United Greenfield Division v. NLRB, 637 F.2d 410 (5th Cir. 1981).

4. For a time, the Board was of the view that a union agent's pre-election threats of bodily harm or property damage must be aimed at the election itself in order to interfere with "laboratory conditions"; thus, a threat of reprisals against employees for failing to cooperate with the union during a strike at some unspecified time in the future was not deemed grounds for upsetting an election. Hickory Springs Mfg. Co., 239 N.L.R.B. 641 (1978). Discarding this view as "unrealistic," the NLRB presently finds that such

threats tend to interfere with both free campaigning and uncoerced voting. See Indus. Disposal Serv., 266 N.L.R.B. No. 22, 112 L.R.R.M. 1257 (1983). Does this approach unduly limit a union's campaign on the theme of its ability to stand up to an employer in collective bargaining?

Luxuray of N.Y. v. NLRB, 447 F.2d 112 (2d Cir. 1971). The issue was whether the Board erred in finding that the company had violated §8(a)(1) by showing to its employees a popular antiunion film entitled "And Women Must Weep." Prior to showing the film, a company official had read a prepared statement that the film, even though a dramatization by professional actors, told a true story. Concluding, he had observed that similar events "could happen to us people, our community, our friends." The court, quoting Southwire Co. v. NLRB, 383 F.2d 235, 239-240 (5th Cir. 1967), described the film as follows:

> It is in color. It tells the story of a strike in Princeton, Indiana. . . . The film is narrated by one of the actresses who plays the part of the wife of a minister whose parishioners are involuntarily involved in the strike as members of the union. They are among the union members who are dictatorily mistreated by the majority of the union members. . . .
>
> Among other baneful events, the film shows picket line violence, the minister being jeered, smashed windshields, slashed tires, and upturned automobiles, all caused by the majority members of the union. The minister's wife is threatened by an anonymous caller who announces that her home will be the next to be bombed. The minister is shown with a rifle, sitting through the night, in an effort to protect his family. The climax of the fray is reached when the strikers fire into the trailer home of a dissenting union member and a bullet strikes his baby in the head. The film closes with the end of the strike and with the announcement that the baby will live. The closing words of the narrator are: "All you have to do is ask yourself, could my town be next? And if you think that the answer of what happened to us couldn't happen to you, remember that is what we thought in the beginning. Must you wait to come face to face with tyranny as we did."

Joining at least two other circuits in rejecting the Board's condemnation of the showing of the film as an unfair labor practice, the court reasoned:
". . . Relying primarily on NLRB v. Gissel Packing Co., 395 U.S. 575 (1969), the Board appears to advance two theories under which showing the film might be found unlawful under the Act: (1) That, especially in light of [the company's] introductory remarks, the film impliedly made 'representations as to the dire results of unionization which are both factually unsupportable and coercively misleading.' (2) That the violence and misconduct

depicted in the movie is unlikely to occur absent either knowing acquiescence or active encouragement by the employer — thus, by this latter theory, the employer in effect threatened to encourage union violence, for example by refusing to bargain collectively, should the instant union win the election. We believe that both theories fail. . . .

". . . [A] mere expression of antiunion sentiment by an employer is an exercise of free speech protected by at least §8(c) and most likely by the First Amendment. The film, in the context of its showing, cannot even be said to have implied a 'prediction.' A fairer characterization would be that by showing the film, the employer expressed an opinion that in the past local union officials have abused their power and called wild-cat strikes to the detriment of the union membership, and that similar abuses might accompany unionization in the future. . . . Thus, the film is a one-sided brief against unionism, devoid of significant rational content perhaps, but nonetheless not reasonable to be construed as threatening retaliation or force. Nowhere in the film does the employer or his representative appear or make any representation. . . .

"Moreover, the union does not contend that it lacked the opportunity to make its own case. In fact, it made use of the film, entitled "Anatomy of a Lie," designed to refute "And Women Must Weep." "Anatomy" apparently has been shown by other unions in the past to neutralize the effect of its antiunion counterpart. It is primarily the responsibility of employees, and not of the Board, to evaluate the merit of competing propaganda. . . . The import of a threat of force by an employer with power to inflict severe economic injury on a disfavored employee lies largely in the manifest fact that such threats are unanswerable by the union. That is not the case here. . . ."

Hays, J., concurring in part, dissenting in part: ". . . We are not called upon to decide whether the showing of this film would interfere with, restrain or coerce United States circuit judges. . . . The question is what effect the film would be likely to have on the employees of Luxuray. . . . "And Women Must Weep" does not deal with 'objective fact' or 'demonstrably probable consequences.' It contains grossly melodramatic distortions which the employer not only did not attempt to verify, but which he magnified by telling the employees that the incidents pictured in the film were 'actually true' and that what 'happened in that movie could happen to us people, our community, our friends.'

"The Board seems to me to have been acting well within its powers when it found that by showing this film to a captive audience of people who were economically dependent on the employer and who had a 'necessary tendency . . . to pick up intended implications of the [employer] that might be more readily dismissed by a more disinterested ear,' NLRB v. Gissel

Packing Co., supra, 395 U.S. at 617, the employer was in fact communicating a threat of retaliatory action. The Board's view that the film, in the employer-employee context, implies that the company will by *its* behavior, act in a way that will bring about the type of confrontation depicted there, is by no means so unsupportable as to justify setting aside the Board's order. . . ."

NOTES

1. Experiments have raised questions as to the accuracy of the Board's assumptions about the persuasive impact of "And Women Must Weep," whether it is shown alone or along with the standard rebuttal film, "The Anatomy of a Lie" (which, incidentally, was prepared by the International Association of Machinists, the union involved in the strike that was the purported basis for "Weep"). See Field & Field, " . . . And Women Must Weep" v: "Anatomy of a Lie": An Empirical Assessment of Two Labor Relations Propaganda Films, 1 Pepperdine L. Rev. 21 (1973).

2. For a time, Board panels divided on whether showing "And Women Must Weep" or similar films constitutes either a violation of §8(a)(1) or a ground for setting aside an election. The divisions concerned the extent to which the Board should use a totality-of-circumstances approach and take account of such matters as other unfair labor practices. See Sylacauga Garment Co., 210 N.L.R.B. 501 (1974). In Litho Press of San Antonio, 211 N.L.R.B. 1014 (1974), *enforced*, 512 F.2d 72 (5th Cir. 1975), a Board majority overruled inconsistent cases and held that "the showing of 'And Women Must Weep' is neither violative of the Act nor a sufficient basis for setting aside an election." The Board has extended this view to a more recent and equally popular antiunion film, "The Springfield Gun." See Sab Harmon Industries, 252 N.L.R.B. 953 (1980).

NLRB v. Bancroft Mfg. Co.
516 F.2d 436 (5th Cir. 1975), *cert. denied*, 424 U.S. 914 (1976)

[The Board had overruled the company's objections to an election won by the union, 361 to 286, and held the company's refusal to bargain a violation of §8(a)(5) of the Act. The court here reviews the Board's finding that the union's conduct did not constitute an inflammatory or impermissible appeal to racial prejudice.]

GOLDBERG, J. . . . Forty-three percent of the Company's workforce . . . were black people, so that much of the Union's organizing effort was devoted to convincing the blacks that their interests would best be served by choosing the Union. . . . The Company contends that the Union's actions in this regard amounted to an inflammatory appeal to racial passion which caused the very large number of black employees to vote for the Union on the basis of racial considerations alone. The major support for this theory is provided by the Board's finding that Union organizer Sylvester Hicks, a black man, warned black employees on several occasions that "if the blacks did not stay together as a group and the Union lost the election, all the blacks would be fired" . . . [and] that "seemingly the trend was . . . that the blacks were going to be laid off if they didn't stick together and try to get the plant organized to where they would have some protection. . . . " Finally, a rumor had it that the Company would give an automobile to a friendly black employee, J. C. Butler, if Butler helped to swing the black vote. At a meeting attended by a large number of white and black employees, Rev. Harry Buie, a black minister employed by the Delta Ministry (an anti-poverty organization) and invited by the Union to assist in the campaign, commented . . . that "it had been called to his attention that an employee was to be given a car to swing the black vote. He understood that he was a soul brother and the part that hurt him so bad was that it would be a sold out soul brother."

The Company complains that the remarks of Hicks and Buie were grossly inaccurate and were calculated to instill in the black employees the conviction that their employer held blacks in low esteem and intended to discriminate against them in an invidious manner. The racially-oriented propaganda, the Company contends, was so likely to impair the blacks' capacity for a reasoned decision that the election must be set aside. The [ALJ] found, however — and the Board agreed — that these remarks were unimportant and not unreasonable in the particular situation, and that even if the statements were untrue, they had not exercised a significant influence on the results of the voting.

The NLRB first enunciated a policy for dealing with racially inflammatory remarks in representation campaigns in Sewell Mfg. Co., 1962, 138 N.L.R.B. 66, . . . [where] a Mississippi employer conducted a strident anti-union campaign on the theme that since the union seeking to represent its employees supported the struggle for equal civil rights for black citizens, a vote for the union was tantamount to a vote for an integrated society, a goal the employer assumed its all-white workforce rejected. . . . The Board . . . voided the election, finding that the employer had deliberately sought to overstress and exacerbate racial feelings by irrelevant, inflammatory appeals. . . . The NLRB reasoned:

We take it as datum that prejudice based on color is a powerful emotional force. We think it also indisputable that a deliberate appeal to such prejudice is not intended or calculated to encourage the reasoning faculty.

What we have said indicates our belief that appeals to racial prejudice on matters unrelated to the election issues or to the union's activities are not mere "prattle" or puffing. They have no place in Board electoral campaigns. They inject an element which is destructive of the very purpose of an election. They create conditions which make impossible a sober, informed exercise of the franchise. The Board does not intend to tolerate as "electoral propaganda" appeals or arguments which can have no purpose except to inflame the racial feelings of voters in the election.

This is not to say that a relevant campaign statement is to be condemned because it may have racial overtones. . . .

We would be less than realistic if we did not recognize that such statements, even when moderate and truthful, do in fact cater to racial prejudice. Yet we believe that they must be tolerated because they are true and because they pertain to a subject concerning which employees are entitled to have knowledge — the union's position on racial matters.

So long, therefore, as a party limits itself to *truthfully* setting forth another party's position on matters of racial interest and does not deliberately seek to overstress and exacerbate racial feelings by irrelevant, inflammatory appeals, we shall not set aside an election on this ground. However, the burden will be on the party making use of a racial message to establish that it was truthful and germane, and where there is doubt as to whether the total conduct of such party is within the described bounds, the doubt will be resolved against him.

138 N.L.R.B. at 71-72.

On the same day that *Sewell* was decided, the Board concluded that employer literature not dissimilar to that used in *Sewell* fell within permissible bounds because the statements were made in a generally temperate fashion. Allen-Morrison Sign Co., Inc., 1962, 138 N.L.R.B. 73. In this spirit, the Board has consistently approved union campaigns which stress black racial pride, the past history of discrimination against blacks in American society or the present disadvantaged status of blacks as a class, where the statements do not claim special privileges for blacks, on the theory that such statements are true and that economic issues, even racially-oriented ones, properly form the core content of representation contests. Baltimore Luggage Co., 1967, 162 N.L.R.B. 1230, *enforced*, 4 Cir. 1967, 387 F.2d 744; Aristrocrat Linen Supply Co., Inc., 1965, 150 N.L.R.B. 1448; Archer Laundry Co., 1965, 150 N.L.R.B. 1427. . . . [g]

[g][In *Archer Laundry*, a union seeking to organize Baltimore laundry workers who were predominantly black invoked the theme of racism as well as civil rights. One union leaflet captioned "What Does Martin Luther King Have to Say About Labor Unions?" concluded:

Sewell requires the party making a racially-oriented statement to demonstrate the truth of the statement, and we believe that the Union has failed to discharge that burden here. Union Organizer Hicks based his comments on the possibility of discriminatory discharges or layoffs of blacks on the fact that several recent layoffs had affected many more blacks than whites, and on his belief that the percentage of blacks in the workforce had recently declined from 38% to 34%. In fact, the layoffs were apparently made on the basis of seniority and the proportion of black employees remained near 43% at all times relevant to our inquiry. In other words, there is no evidence that the Company intended to or did in fact treat its black employees unfairly. With respect to Buie's comment about the "sold out soul brother," the most that can be said for it is that the accusation was based on second- or third-hand hearsay, that Buie did not attempt to verify the accuracy of the rumor before making his accusations, and that employee Butler eventually *purchased* an automobile from the Company, apparently at near-market value, as he had done once several years before this representation campaign.

The Board decided that Hicks' statements about mass black firings were not really false but were instead reasonable predictions of future events based on the Company's recent history of layoffs. The problem with this reasoning is that however plausible or commonplace the statements may have been, the fact remains that Hicks and Buie were wrong, and that their comments could have led black employees to infer that the Company would discriminate against them although there was no evidence to support such a conclusion. This is not a case . . . in which union organizers tell black employees that (white) employers in general have tended to discriminate against blacks; this is a case where the employees were told that *their* employer discriminated against *them* in a particular fashion.

Where racial remarks are injected into an election contest, but do not form the core or theme of the campaign as they did in *Sewell*, the court's analysis of their effect should follow a two-step process. First, were the statements racially inflammatory? If they were, then the test for truth and relevancy must be made as *Sewell* describes. Second, if the remarks were not racially inflammatory, then the statements should be reviewed under the familiar standards applied to any other type of alleged material misrepresentation.

"The labor hater is always a twin-headed creature spewing anti-Negro talk from one mouth and anti-union propaganda from the other." Another exhorted: "Be a free person, not a 'handkerchiefhead Uncle Tom.'" Other leaflets featured illustrations of police dogs and police brutality. The Board, in rejecting the employer's objection to the election, reasoned that the union campaign appealed to "racial self-consciousness" rather than to racial hatred. — Eds.]

. . . [W]e find substantial evidence to support the determination of the [ALJ] and the Board that the disputed statements did not so taint the campaign with racial passion as to make a fair election impossible. . . . This campaign was waged in a bargaining unit which was 57% white and 43% black. As a matter of common sense, any attempt by the Union to set black against white would have been suicidal. . . . There is no evidence that the Union sought to incite blacks against whites; at no time were there either acts or threats of inter-racial violence. . . . [T]here was no racially-oriented campaign; the vast bulk of the literature on both sides was devoted to the economic issues ordinarily found in representation contests. . . . The NLRB found Buie's remarks to be nothing more than the sort of inter-employee squabbling that so often occurs in campaigns.

The next step is to review the record to determine if racial inflammation resulted from the interjection of these remarks. Both the [ALJ] and the Board concluded that none of the disputed statements could be characterized as racially inflammatory. We agree. The statements of Hicks and Buie were neither variations on a Union theme nor attempts to incite racial passions. Rather, they were more in the nature of asides addressed to a particular group of employees in the context of a campaign aimed at securing the adherence of all employees to the Union. Although we cannot condone the Union's somewhat cavalier attitude toward truth in the sensitive area of race relations, this record does not disclose that the disputed statements had an inflammatory effect on the black employees.

This then leads us to the second step of the process required here. The Union made material misrepresentations of fact during the campaign, hence we must decide whether the election must be set aside on that account. In Hollywood Ceramics, 1962, 140 N.L.R.B. 221, the NLRB adopted a four-pronged test for evaluating questionable campaign communications which we have applied in numerous cases . . . : (1) whether there has been a misrepresentation of a material fact; (2) whether the misrepresentation came from a party who was in a position to know the truth or who had special knowledge of the facts; (3) whether the other party had adequate opportunity to reply and to correct the misrepresentation; and (4) whether the employees had independent knowledge of the misrepresented facts, so that they could effectively evaluate the propaganda. . . .

We have already determined that the statements of Hicks and Buie were material misrepresentations, . . . and we will assume *arguendo* that the employees had no independent knowledge either of the discharge-layoff situation or of the circumstances surrounding employee Butler's purchase of an automobile from the Company, so that the fourth criterion is also weighted against the Union. On the other hand, neither the Union in general nor Hicks in particular were in a position to know the Company's future plans regarding layoffs or discharges. . . . [W]e cannot say that the Board was unreasonable in its determination that the employees most likely regarded the statements only as slightly credible Union propaganda and valued them accordingly. With respect to Buie's remarks, Hicks immediately asked several employees to check the accuracy of the rumors, thus considerably diminishing the impact of Buie's comments, and nothing more was said by any Union agent regarding employee Butler and his automobile-to-be. In sum, the second factor in our calculus weighs against the Union, but not decisively.

Of controlling importance to our decision, however, is the fact that although the Company never replied directly either to Hicks or to Buie, the Company was well aware that the Union was appealing to the racial pride of its black employees, and the Company attempted to rebut those appeals in its own communications. Company literature stressed over and over again that an employee's job depended solely on his or her own efficiency and the Company's ability to compete in the industry. Company fliers were replete with magazine and newspaper articles chronicling union discrimination against blacks in all parts of the nation. The Company's president personally made a strong plea for employee loyalty, condemning racial bigotry, reminding the employees of the Company's fair labor policies, and expressing both his displeasure at the Union's mention of racial issues ("I don't know of anything that a man can do that is dirtier than this.") and his satisfaction that "our black employees are not being fooled by this talk." These vigorous Company rejoinders offered the employees an opportunity to view the Hicks and Buie remarks in the context of avowal and denial in which representation elections are customarily conducted. These rebuttals and the Union's adequate margin of victory (56% of the vote) convince us that the Board did not abuse its broad discretion in representation matters by finding that the Company had failed to show that the Union's statements so lowered the tone of the campaign that the free choice of a majority of the employees cannot be determined from the election results. . . .

Enforced.

NOTES

1. The Board's decision in *Bancroft* seems clearly to have rested on an application of the rule of the *Sewell* case. Is that the rule used by the court of appeals in affirming the Board? If not, how should the court have proceeded? Students should recall their courses in Administrative Law, specifically the problem of SEC v. Chenery Corp., 318 U.S. 80 (1943), 332 U.S. 194

(1947), and the fundamental proposition of *Chenery I* (318 U.S. at 95):
" . . . [A]n administrative order cannot be upheld unless the grounds upon
which the agency acted in exercising its powers were those upon which its
action can be sustained." Assume that *Chenery* is neglected occasionally in
labor cases. What is your hunch about why this happens? Do "efficiency"
considerations explain it?

2. With respect to issues such as race, is a requirement of "temperate"
rather than "inflammatory" electioneering likely to affect voting? If not,
what is your surmise about the Board's reasons for drawing that distinction?
See Note, 72 Yale L.J. 1243, 1250-1253 (1963).

3. In Vanasco v. Schwartz, 401 F. Supp. 87 (E.D.N.Y. 1975), affirmed on appeal without opinion, 423 U.S. 1041 (1976), a three-judge
district court held provisions of a New York fair campaign statute (and of the
Code adopted thereunder by the State Board of Elections) to be violative of
the First Amendment. Those provisions barred candidates campaigning for
public office from making "attacks on a candidate based on race, sex, religion,
or ethnic background" through literature, the media, or "otherwise." Also
barred were "misrepresentations" of a candidate's position, voting record,
party affiliation, or qualifications. Violators were, inter alia, subject to judicially enforceable fines. The district court, stressing the broad protection
normally given to campaign speech, held that the speech forbidden by the
challenged provisions did not lose First Amendment protection under the
"actual malice" standard of New York Times v. Sullivan, 376 U.S. 254
(1964). Regarding the prohibition of attacks based on race, etc., the court
stated:

> . . . It is a blanket prohibition against any attacks on a candidate's race,
> sex, religion or ethnic background. Justification for such a sweeping prohibi-
> tion rests on the assumption that this Code section focuses only on attributes
> which are completely unrelated to any candidate's "fitness for office." Such an
> assumption is an exercise in self-delusion. The Supreme Court has recognized
> that "[g]iven the realities of our political life, it is by no means easy to see what
> statements about a candidate might be altogether without relevance to his
> fitness for the office he seeks." Monitor Patriot Co. v. Roy, 401 U.S. 265, 275
> (1970). Attempts to create a "public sector"-"private sector" dichotomy were
> characterized as "syllogistic manipulation[s]" by the Court. 401 U.S. at 273. It
> would be a retreat from reality to hold that voters do not consider race, religion,
> sex or ethnic background when choosing political candidates. Speech is often
> provocative and indeed offensive, Cantwell v. Connecticut, 310 U.S. 296
> (1940); Terminiello v. Chicago, 337 U.S. 1 (1949), . . . but unless it falls
> into one of those "well defined and narrowly limited classes" of unprotected
> speech (e.g., 'fighting words') it enjoys constitutional protection. New York's

attempt to eliminate an entire segment of protected speech from the arena of public debate is clearly unconstitutional.

Note: The Vicarious Responsibility of Employers and Unions

The involvement of an "outsider" in the election campaign in *Bancroft* raises the general question of the responsibility of employers and unions for the conduct of non-parties that affects the labor-management relationship. This question, which, of course, arises in many labor law contexts, will be introduced here and raised at various points later in this book — e.g., the materials on union violence (see Chapter 7(D)) and on discrimination in the operation of hiring halls (see Chapter 11(B)).

The Wagner Act provided the basis for expansive vicarious responsibility by defining "employer," in §2(2), to include "any person acting in the interest of an employer, either directly or indirectly." It should be observed that imputation of responsibility to an "employer" thus involves a double effect: Any person for whose conduct an employer is responsible also becomes an "employer" subject to the proscriptions and remedies of the Act.

The Taft-Hartley amendments in 1947 substituted the more restrictive language now in §2(2), which incorporates the common law "rules" of agency as the test of employer responsibility. This change reflected dissatisfaction with what was deemed to have been the Board's excesses in imputing responsibility to employers. See H.R. Rep. No. 244, 80th Cong., 1st Sess. 18 (1947).

The 1947 amendments also added §2(13), which provides that "the question of whether the specific acts performed were actually authorized or subsequently ratified shall not be controlling" in determining "agency." That section was designed to supersede, under the LMRA, the limitations on union responsibility embodied in §6 of the Norris-LaGuardia Act and to subject unions, as well as employers, to the "ordinary common-law rules of agency." See H.R. Conf. Rep. No. 510, 80th Cong., 1st Sess. 36 (1947); 93 Cong. Rec. 700 (1947). An important effect of §2(13) was to make clear that "apparent authority" is available to charge a union with the unauthorized acts of its authorized representatives, even actions taken in violation of a union's express instructions. See, e.g., NLRB v. Georgetown Dress Corp., 537 F.2d 1239 (4th Cir. 1976).

It is difficult to determine what specific impact the 1947 amendments have had, or, indeed, were "intended" to have, on employer responsibility. In J.S. Abercrombie Co., 83 N.L.R.B. 524, 529 (1949), *review denied*, 180

F.2d 578 (5th Cir. 1950), the Board, citing cases antedating the 1947 amendments, stated: "the test applied by the Board, with the approval of the courts, in determining whether an employer is responsible for coercive statements by a supervisor is not whether the statements were, in fact, within the scope of the supervisor's employment, but whether the employees have just cause to believe that the supervisor is acting on behalf of management. . . . " Accordingly, the Board stated that, absent special circumstances, an employer is responsible for coercive statements and other conduct of a supervisor. A test of "just cause to believe" means, of course, that formal supervisory status is not required in order to have employer responsibility; any individual reasonably understood by the workforce to act for management in the circumstances would be an agent of the employer.

Such a test also permits employers to limit their responsibilities even for supervisors' actions. Thus, where top management has directed supervision not to interfere with organizational activity and has promptly advised employees of such directions, an employer may avoid responsibility for coercive statements by such "subordinate" supervisors. See NLRB v. Cleveland Trust Co., 214 F.2d 95, 101-102 (6th Cir. 1954) (reversing the NLRB). Moreover, a disavowal of a supervisor's unlawful conduct, if communicated promptly and unequivocally may preclude remedial action against the employer. See Broyhill Co., 260 N.L.R.B. 1366 (1982); NLRB v. Miami Coca Cola Bottling Co., 222 F.2d 341 (5th Cir. 1955) (Board finding of employer responsibility for supervisor's assault on union organizer set aside; strong, prompt repudiation and disciplining of supervisor removes basis for employees' believing they are subject to employer coercion); Graves Trucking, Inc. v. NLRB, 692 F.2d 470 (7th Cir. 1982) (employer's isolated disapproval of supervisor's prior assault, not disclosed to all affected employees and coupled with reiteration of supervisor's authority, insufficient for repudiation). Despite communication to employees of advance notices and prompt disavowals, an employer would presumably be responsible for extensive or systematic coercion by supervisors since employees are likely to discount employer protestations that are regularly disregarded.

Where non-supervisory employees are involved, responsibility for their coercive statements or conduct is usually not imputed to the employer unless the employee has some special relationship with management or unless management has instigated, or by inaction condoned, the conduct. See General Tire & Rubber Co., 149 N.L.R.B. 474, 476-477 (1964); J.D. Newell, Inc., 99 N.L.R.B. 61 (1952) (employer responsible when an employee, upon inquiring what would happen if a union representative was whipped, was told by the manager "[a]s long as you stick to personal affairs — don't involve me or the company — it is plumb all right with me.")

Efforts to impose responsibility on unions for activities of employees who have no position in the union frequently fail — absent proof of union authorization or ratification. For example, solicitation of authorization cards by employees, standing alone, does not make those employees union agents; thus, their coercive statements are not imputable to the union. See Davlan Engineering, Inc., 262 N.L.R.B. 850 (1982).

Where "outsiders" such as citizens' committees or news media have threatened a plant closing and other reprisals for unionization, responsibility has not been imputed to an employer absent a showing that the employer instigated or aided the outside activity, or failed to disavow it under circumstances that made such failure a tacit adoption. See Livingston Shirt Corp., 107 N.L.R.B. 400 (1953); NLRB v. Lake Butler Apparel Co., 392 F.2d 76 (5th Cir. 1968). In Amalgamated Clothing Workers v. NLRB, 371 F.2d 740 (D.C. Cir. 1966), an employer was held responsible for the threats of an outside businessman made at a company open house and not disavowed by the company. Local businessmen had brought the company to the small town, endorsed its notes, and, in general, had reflected an identity of interest with the company. The court, noting that the company itself had delicately implied "benefits" and "portents of reprisal," stated that, in such a setting, "responsibility" for an outsider's conduct is not controlled by "refinements of the law of agency" or by "rigid application of principles of respondeat superior." 371 F.2d at 744.

Outsiders' conduct, even though it is not imputed to a union or employer, may nevertheless destroy laboratory conditions and warrant setting aside an election. See, e.g., Daylight Grocery Co., Inc. v. NLRB, 678 F.2d 905 (11th Cir. 1982) (anonymous threats may be basis for overturning election when atmosphere of confusion and fear of reprisals results). Even with the agency issue removed, the status of an outsider is relevant in assessing the coercive impact or potential of the objectionable speech or conduct. See NLRB v. Katz, 701 F.2d 703 (7th Cir. 1983) (Catholic priest addressing largely Catholic audience at union meeting in Catholic church); NLRB v. Payless Cashway Lumber Store, 508 F.2d 24 (8th Cir. 1974) (city's acting mayor addressing election-eve union meeting). But the principal significance of a failure to attribute conduct to a party is that, in proceedings to upset an election, less weight normally is given to conduct of third persons than to employer or union conduct. This approach, which is extended to the pro-union activities of employees, is supported on the ground that conduct not attributable to a party to an election is less likely to affect its outcome. See NLRB v. Eskimo Radiator Mfg. Co., 688 F.2d 1315 (9th Cir. 1982); Zieglers Refuse Collectors v. NLRB, 639 F.2d 1000 (3d Cir. 1981). Even though outsiders' misconduct generally must be more aggravated to taint an election, a union's failure to disavow an employee's threats against other employees, particularly threats of violence, may provide a basis for upsetting an election without regard to whether the employee was a union agent. See NLRB v. Urban Telephone Corp., 449 F.2d 239 (7th Cir. 1964). See also NLRB v. Katz, 701 F.2d 703, 708 (7th Cir. 1983) ("we query whether the Union should be permitted to profit from [union adherents' threats of violence and retaliation] and yet disavow responsibility for it"; election won by union may, however, be upset without finding of union responsibility, particularly where the election unit is "small" (here, 30 voters) and the victory margin one vote).

Note: Campaign Misrepresentations — Empirical Research and Its Impact

As *Bancroft* indicates, the Board in Hollywood Ceramics Co., 140 N.L.R.B. 220 (1962), announced that it would be more vigorous in policing pre-election factual misrepresentations. The union had won an election after last-minute handbilling that grossly understated the employer's wage scale, then compared that deflated figure with wages in unionized plants. The Board set the election aside, finding it "obvious" that votes cast on the basis of seriously inaccurate or misleading campaign statements could not represent "the kind of choice envisaged by the Act." The Board announced this general formula:

> [A]n election should be set aside only where there has been a misrepresenta-
> tion or other similar campaign trickery, which involves a substantial departure
> from the truth, at a time which prevents the other party or parties from making
> an effective reply, so that the misrepresentation, whether deliberate or not,
> may reasonably be expected to have a significant impact on the election.

Hollywood Ceramics drew continuing criticism within and outside the Board.[h] In Shopping Kart Food Market, Inc., 228 N.L.R.B. 1311 (1977), the Board (3 to 2) overruled *Hollywood Ceramics* and announced that it would no longer set aside elections on the basis of misleading campaign statements. Less than two years later, in General Knit of California, Inc., 239 N.L.R.B. 619 (1978), the Board (again 3 to 2, after a change in membership) abandoned *Shopping Kart* and reinstated the rule of *Hollywood Ceramics*.

Criticism of the *Hollywood Ceramics* rule emphasized that the required analysis of the truth or falsity of campaign assertions created serious adminis-

---

[h] The pertinent history is traced in Grunewald, Empiricism in NLRB Election Regulation: *Shopping Kart* and *General Knit* in Retrospect, 4 Indus. Rel. L.J. 161 (1981).

trative problems. In addition, critics challenged the behavioral assumptions implicit in the policy itself, particularly the basic assumption that free choice is easily impaired by what is said during election campaigns. An important challenge to the latter assumption appeared in a major empirical study published in the mid-1970s, J. Getman, S. Goldberg, & J. Herman, Union Representation Elections: Law and Reality (1976) [hereinafter cited as Study]. That study called for the elimination of the *Hollywood Ceramics* doctrine as a part of a broader recommendation for deregulation, namely, that campaign communications should not serve as a basis for the NLRB's vacating of elections or its finding of unfair labor practices. Study at 150.

The Getman study challenged the empirical basis for the Board's regulation of speech, including not only untrue assertions but actual or implied threats of economic retaliation. The study also challenged other Board approaches, including its issuance of bargaining orders against employers whose statutory violations were followed by loss of elections by unions. See Chapter 6(B). Accordingly, we present a summary of key aspects of the study's design, its findings, and its reception by the Board.

The study sought to determine the effects of pre-election campaigns, particularly conduct unlawful under §8, on voting behavior. The authors' principal data sources consisted of two waves of deep interviews with voters in 31 NLRB elections held in midwestern states during 1972 and 1973. (These elections were selected primarily because they were likely to prompt vigorous and possibly unlawful campaigns — and they did so. Study at 34.) A total of 1,239 employees were interviewed soon after the election date was set and again immediately after the election. The first interview was designed to determine how the employees felt about their working conditions ("job satisfaction") and about unions in general, and how they intended to vote. At a second interview, the employees were asked to recall the content of the campaign and to disclose how they had voted and why.[i]

The authors concluded that, contrary to the NLRB's behavioral assumptions, an election campaign plays only a limited role in the employees' ultimate vote. The study's findings included the following:

1. Employees' attitudes toward current working conditions and unions in general produce durable predispositions to vote for or against representation. Of those employees who declared a firm intention to vote when initially

---

[i]The authors' summary of their purposes behind these interviews states: "As a result of these interviews, we knew what had taken place in the campaign. We knew what parts of the campaign had made an impression on employees, and what parts had not — what they remembered of the campaign, and what they did not. Finally, we knew which employees voted as they had intended prior to the campaign, and which did not. Thus, we were in a position to study the relationship between voter intent, different types of campaigning, and actual vote." Goldberg, Getman, & Brett, Union Representation Elections: Law and Reality — The Authors Respond to the Critics, 79 Mich. L. Rev. 564, 569 (1981).

interviewed, 87 percent carried out that intention. Furthermore, the votes of 81 percent of the interviewees were correctly predicted on the basis of their pre-campaign declarations (13 percent voted contrary to their original declarations and 6 percent said they were initially undecided). Study at 60-66, 103.

2. Forty-three percent of the interviewees had been union members on other jobs; parents or spouses of 75 percent had been union members; and 30 percent had voted in previous NLRB elections. Hence, the authors found little basis for assuming that employees are generally unsophisticated about union-management relations. Study at 66-68.

3. Employees "cannot meaningfully be described as having been attentive to the campaign"; immediately after the election they could recall comparatively few of the issues raised by the parties' respective campaigns. Study at 76. Indeed, only half the interviewees knew that the union had claimed that the wages it had secured elsewhere were higher than the employer's — an apparently important claim, which had been made in 22 of the 31 elections; and less than a quarter could recall the claim with any accuracy. Study at 82.

4. Although there was no significant difference in pro-company and pro-union voters' familiarity with the company's campaign, pro-union voters were significantly more familiar than pro-company voters with the union campaign. Study at 85. This difference was attributed to the company's advantage in reaching employees:

> A far larger proportion of employees attend company meetings (83 percent) than attend union meetings (36 percent). Furthermore, those who attend union meetings tend to be union supporters. This is not true of company meetings. Regardless of intent, attendance at meetings is significantly related to familiarity. . . . [W]hen the employer can hold campaign meetings on working time and premises and the union cannot, the union is at a substantial disadvantage in achieving meaningful communication with employees. . . . [Study at 96.]

5. The company ultimately secured the vote of a substantial majority of both those employees who voted contrary to their originally stated intent (13 percent) and those initially undecided (6 percent). Yet there was no evidence that those employees were more familiar with, or influenced by, the content of the company campaign than were those who did not switch to the company. In contrast, the switchers and the undecided who moved to a union vote were significantly more familiar with the union campaign than those who voted company — apparently because of more frequent attendance at union meetings. Nevertheless, the authors concluded that the influence of

the union's campaign on employees who are initially undecided or intend to vote company "is not strong," and that there were too few of these voters switching to the union — approximately 5 percent of the total sample — to make a difference in many elections. It should be noted, however, that the votes of these 19 percent of the employees (13 percent switchers and 6 percent undecided) determined the outcome in 9 of the 31 elections (29 percent). Study at 103.[j] Furthermore, the study does not indicate whether the fact of the campaign — apart from its content — influenced these voters. Study at 103-108.[k]

6. At election time the union's average loss of card-signers was 4 percent for all elections, but 35 percent for the five most successful company campaigns. Similarly, across all elections, an average of 72 percent of the card-signers voted union; in those five most successful company campaigns, only 37 percent of the card-signers and 4 percent of the non-signers did so. Study at 100-103.

7. There was no evidence that unlawful campaign practices — e.g., threats or acts of reprisal or promises or grants of benefit — affected employee voting behavior more than did lawful campaigning. Study at 129-30.

The study concentrated on campaigning that constitutes an unfair labor practice under §8; there was no attempt to measure directly the impact of campaign practices that, although falling short of illegality, are held to destroy "laboratory conditions" and to warrant the Board's setting an election aside. Thus the study does not directly answer the question of whether employers, through less coercive strategies, might avoid the backlash effect that may arise from employer violations of §8. See Lachman, Freedom of Speech in Union Representation Elections, 1982 Am. B. Research J. 755, 779-781; but see Goldberg, et al., 79 Mich. L. Rev. at 570-576.

The 1977 *Shopping Kart* decision marked the Board's first response to the Getman group's research. The Board's lead opinion in *Shopping Kart*, endorsed by Members Penello and Walther, highlighted the "many difficulties" in administering the *Hollywood Ceramics* policy; the opinion also

[j] The study has been criticized for failing to focus on the possibility that a shift of votes by small numbers of critically-located voters could have had a significant effect on the number of union victories (unions won only 8 of the 31 elections studied). See, e.g., Weiler, Promises to Keep: Securing Workers' Rights to Self-Organization Under the NLRA, 96 Harv. L. Rev. 1769, 1784-1785 (1983) ("A shift of only 2% of the total votes cast in the thirty-one elections, if those 2% had been carefully allocated, would have been sufficient to provide . . . eight additional [union] victories.").

[k] Another study, in its early stages, has found "tentative evidence" of correlations between certain employer campaign practices or tactics — e.g., use of an outside consultant — and election success. See Murrmann & Porter, Employer Campaign Tactics and NLRB Election Outcomes: Some Preliminary Evidence, Proc., 35th Ann. Meeting, Ind. Rel. Research Assn. 67 (1982).

accepted the study's basic finding regarding the modest influence of campaigns, as well as its plea that employees be treated as adults. But the commitment to the Getman study's essential thesis was in fact quite circumscribed. For Penello and Walther, while rejecting *Hollywood Ceramics*, left undisturbed other Board rules and assumptions, such as those involving alleged employer threats, declaring that "[w]e shall, of course, continue our policy of overseeing other campaign conduct which interferes with employee free choice outside the area of misrepresentations."

Then-Chairman Murphy, concurring in *Shopping Kart*, agreed that the Board must recognize the employees' ability to evaluate campaign propaganda but did not refer to the Getman study. Member Fanning, dissenting in part, criticized the study's sample and, rejecting the authors' interpretations of their data, urged that the study supported the view that significant numbers of voters are influenced by the election campaign (noting, e.g., "the 5 percent of voters who appear to have admitted changing their minds due to the campaign" and the "22 percent 'precise' recall . . . of the wages-elsewhere issue"). Member Jenkins, in a separate dissent, mounted a sharp but general attack on the study.

For a forceful criticism of the Board's treatment of the study in *Shopping Kart*, coupled with proposals of less adversarial alternatives, see Shapiro, Why Do Voters Vote?, 86 Yale L.J. 1532 (1977).[1]

---

[1] Professor Shapiro says in part (86 Yale at 1543-1545): " . . . [W]hatever position one may take on the merits, it is hard to view the Board's approach in the *Shopping Kart* case as anything but misguided . . . [T]he majority simply referred to the study without any consideration of its strengths and weaknesses; the dissenters . . . tried only to score debaters' points against it without any pretense at objectivity. And the crucial swing voter did not explicitly address herself to the study at all. . . . Since it dealt with one of the less important rules governing campaign practices, *Shopping Kart* was not in any event the best vehicle for considering the study's significance, and simply led to an unexplained affirmation of other existing rules. . . . And the dissenters, while defending their own assumptions about what may influence a voter's decision, made only a halting attempt to support the *Hollywood Ceramics* rule on grounds quite unrelated to those assumptions.

"There could hardly be a better illustration of the inappropriateness of squeezing considerations of legislative policy into the unaccommodating mold of an adjudication. Instead of a full and open discussion . . . of the study's methodology and conclusions, of its relevance to all of the Board's rules in the area of campaign practices, and of the question whether some or all of these rules may find their justification on other grounds, we have little more than an endorsement of the study by two members of a three-member majority in a case in which it may not even have been addressed by the litigants. . . .

"What would be the advantages of a rule-making proceeding [rather than adjudication] in considering whether any changes in the Board's election policies should be made? . . . [T]here would be considerable value in subjecting a specific proposal to comment by all interested persons, in allowing free discussion of the [Getman study's] data and conclusions and their application to *all* relevant Board rules unimpeded by the confines of a particular case, and in being able to consider submissions without the restrictions of the rules of evidence applicable in a trial-type adjudicatory hearing. [And] if the Board itself had its own

In *General Knit*, the Board (3 to 2) discarded *Shopping Kart* (before its second birthday). The majority opinion made these objections to the Getman study:[m]

> . . . [It] was not designed to investigate the actual reasons for the reaction of voters to the campaigns, and theirs is by no means the only possible conclusion to be drawn from the data. The results of 43 years of conducting elections . . . convince us that employees are influenced by certain . . . campaign statements. Even the authors acknowledged that, of the 19 percent, those who ultimately voted against the union may have been influenced by the employer's campaign, even though they did not recall specific issues.
>
> The authors' final recommendations, including the suggested deregulation of misrepresentations, were based on their findings *vis-a-vis* the 81 percent of voters rather than the 19 percent. Such a narrow focus might have been warranted if the authors had concluded either that the votes of the 19 percent had not affected the results of a significant number of elections or that the 19 percent, in deciding how to vote, had not based that decision on information provided during the campaign. . . .
>
> Even if this particular study were clearly supportive of all of the authors' conclusions, however, we would still not find it an adequate ground for rejecting a rule which had been well established for 15 years. While we welcome research from the behavioral sciences, 1 study of only 31 elections in 1 area of the country — although it may provide food for thought — is simply not sufficient to disprove the assumptions upon which the Board has regulated election conduct, especially since, in our experience, statements made by either side can significantly affect voter preference.

---

unit capable of assessing empirical data and of conducting research, . . . such a unit could make a valuable contribution to the rulemaking proceedings."

[For a proposal that the Board's empirical capabilities be enhanced by its creating an empirical research unit, see Roomkin & Abrams, Using Behavioral Evidence in NLRB Regulation: A Proposal, 90 Harv. L. Rev. 1441 (1977). Because of its history, §4(a) of the Act, which prohibits the Board's appointment of individuals for "economic analysis," might presently be a legal impediment to research-unit proposals. See F. McCulloch & T. Bornstein, The National Labor Relations Board 29-47 (1974). — EDS.]

[m] Critics had raised a number of questions about the study, including the authors' sample, methodology, conclusions and recommendations for changes in Board doctrine. See Eames, An Analysis of the Union Voting Study from a Trade-Unionist's Point of View, 28 Stan. L. Rev. 1181 (1976); Flanagan, The Behavioral Foundations of Union Election Regulation, 28 Stan. L. Rev. 1195 (1976); Goetz & Wike, Book Review, 25 Kan. L. Rev. 375 (1977); Kochan, Legal Nonsense, Empirical Examination and Policy Evaluation, 29 Stan. L. Rev. 1115 (1977); Miller, The Getman, Goldberg and Herman Questions, 28 Stan. L. Rev. 1163 (1976); Peck, Book Review, 53 U. Wash. L. Rev. 197 (1977); Phalen, The Demise of Hollywood Ceramics, 46 U. Cin. L. Rev. 450 (1977); Roomkin, Book Review, 27 Case W. Res. L. Rev. 1056 (1977). A defense of the study can be found in Goldberg, Getman, & Brett, Union Representation Elections: Law and Reality — The Authors Respond to the Critics, 79 Mich. L. Rev. 564 (1981).

In 1981, the Board returned to the issue of campaign misrepresentations in the case below.

Midland National Life Insurance Co.
263 N.L.R.B. 127 (1982)

[The Board, finding unfair labor practices and objectionable campaigning by the employer, upset an election held on April 28, 1978, and won by the employer, 127 to 75. Following court enforcement of the Board's order against the employer, a second election was held on October 16, 1980. There were 107 votes for and 107 votes against the union, which again filed objections to the election. The Board, rejecting the Hearing Officer's recommendations, overruled the union's objections and certified the results of the second election. Chairman Van de Water and Members Zimmerman and Hunter joined in the Board's opinion.]

I

. . . On the afternoon of October 15, 1980, the day before the election, the Employer distributed campaign literature to its employees with their paychecks. One of the distributions was a six-page document which included photographs and text depicting three local employers and their involvements with the Petitioner. The document also contained a reproduction of a portion of the Petitioner's 1979 financial report (hereinafter LMRDA report) submitted to the Department of Labor pursuant to the provisions of the Labor Management Reporting and Disclosure Act of 1959. The Petitioner learned of the document the next morning, 3 1/2 hours before the polls were to open.

The first subject of the document, Meilman Food, Inc., was portrayed in "recent" pictures as a deserted facility, and was described in accompanying text as follows: "They too employed between 200 and 300 employees. This Local 304A struck this plant — violence ensued. *Now all of the workers are gone!* What did the Local 304A do for them? Where is the 304A union job security?" (Emphasis in original.) Jack Smith, the Petitioner's business representative, testified that Local 304A, the Petitioner, had been the representative of Meilman's employees, but that neither the Petitioner nor Meilman's employees had been on strike when the plant closed. He added that the employees had been working for at least 1 1/2 years following the strike and prior to the closure of the facility.

. . . [The] document [also referred to] Luther Manor Nursing Home and Blue Cross/Blue Shield. The text accompanying the pictures of Luther Manor explained that:

[a]lmost a year ago this same union that tells you they will "make job security" (we believe you are the only ones who can do that) and will get you more pay, told the employees of LUTHER MANOR (again, here in Sioux Falls) . . . the union would get them a contract with job security and more money. Unfortunately Local 304A did not tell the Luther Manor employees what year or century they were talking about. Today the employees have no contract. Most of the union leaders left to work elsewhere. Their job security is the same (depends upon the individual as it always has). There has been no change or increase in wages or hours. The union has sent in three different sets of negotiators. Again, promises and performance are two different things. All wages, fringes, working conditions are remaining the same while negotiations continue.

The text accompanying the pictures of Blue Cross stated that "this same Local union won an election at Blue Cross/Blue Shield after promising less restrictive policies, better pay and more job security. Since the election a good percentage of its former employees are no longer working there. Ask them! The employees have been offered a wage increase — *next year* of 5%. . . ." (Emphasis in original.)

Smith testified that the Petitioner took over negotiations at Luther Manor and at Blue Cross on or about July 1, 1980, after the Petitioner had merged with Retail Clerks, Local 1665, and that Retail Clerks, Local 1665, not the Petitioner, had conducted the prior negotiations and won the election at Blue Cross.

. . . [T]he Hearing Officer concluded that, in its description of Meilman Food, the Employer intended to instill in the minds of its employees the false impression that the Petitioner had conducted a strike at Meilman, that violence had ensued, and that, as a direct result of the strike, all of the employees at Meilman were terminated. . . . [T]he Hearing Officer [also] found that the Employer had misrepresented the labor organization involved [at Luther Manor and Blue Cross]. . . .

The Employer's distribution also [reproduced] a portion of the Petitioner's 1979 LMRDA report. . . . Three entries on the reproduced page were underlined: total receipts, reported at $508,946; disbursements "On Behalf of Individual Members," reported at zero; and total disbursements, reported at $492,701. Other entries on the reproduced page showed disbursements of $93,185 to officers, and $22,662 to employees. The accompanying text stated that $141,000 of the Petitioner's funds went to "union officers and officials and those who worked for them," and that "NOTHING — according to the report they filed with the U.S. Government — was spent 'on behalf of the individual members' [sic]."

The Hearing Officer found that the report actually showed that the

Petitioner disbursed only $115,847 to its officers and employees, a difference of $25,000, and that the Employer's statement attributed 19 percent more in income to the officials and employees than was actually received. He further found that, while the report showed that no sums had been spent "on behalf of the individual members," the instructions for the LMRDA report require that entry to reflect disbursements for "other than normal operating purposes," and that the Employer failed to include this fact in its distribution.

. . . [T]he Hearing Officer concluded that the document distributed by the Employer contained numerous misrepresentations of fact of a substantial nature designed to portray the Petitioner as . . . staffed by highly paid officials and employees who were ineffectual as bargaining representatives, and that as a consequence employees would suffer with respect to job security and compensation. The Hearing Officer also determined . . . that the Petitioner did not become aware of [the document] until approximately 10 a.m. election day, 2 1/2 hours before the preelection conference and 3 1/2 hours before the polls were to open, and that . . . the Petitioner did not have sufficient time to respond effectively. Applying the standard found in General Knit of California, Inc.,[8] and Hollywood Ceramics Co., Inc.,[9] the Hearing Officer . . . recommended that the objection be sustained and that a third election be directed.

We have decided to reject the Hearing Officer's recommendations and to certify the results of the election. We do so because, after painstaking evaluation . . . we have resolved to return to the sound rule announced in Shopping Kart Food Market, Inc.,[10] and to overrule *General Knit* and *Hollywood Ceramics*. . . .

II

During the years under the Wagner Act, the Board made no attempt to regulate campaign propaganda, and concerned itself solely with conduct which might tend to coerce employees in their election choice. . . . Following the enactment of the Taft-Hartley amendments, the Board continued to disregard issues concerning the truth or falsity of campaign propaganda.[11] . . . In an apparent effort to remove itself further from controversies of this nature, the Board also imposed a duty upon the parties to correct "inaccurate or untruthful statements by any of them." Id.

[8] 239 N.L.R.B. 619 (1978).
[9] 140 N.L.R.B. 221 (1962).
[10] 228 N.L.R.B. 1311 (1977).
[11] In considering the Taft-Hartley amendments to the Act, Congress expressed no disapproval of the Board's refusal to regulate such campaign propaganda, and in fact sought to reduce even further the Board's ability to restrict speech by enacting Sec. 8(c). See NLRB v. The Golub Corporation, 388 F.2d 921 (2d Cir. 1967).

Even as it was refusing to consider the truth or falsity of campaign propaganda, the Board announced its "laboratory conditions" standard. General Shoe Corp., 77 N.L.R.B. 124 (1948). . . . However, as was subsequently explained in The Liberal Market, Inc., 108 N.L.R.B. 1481, 1482 (1954), the Board had a realistic recognition that elections did "not occur in a laboratory where controlled or artificial conditions may be established," and that, accordingly, the Board's goal was "to establish ideal conditions insofar as possible," and to assess "the actual facts in the light of realistic standards of human conduct." Id.

. . . [T]he Board recognized a limited exception to its general rule barring an examination of the effect of the truth or falsity of campaign propaganda upon the election results. Thus, where it appeared that employees were deceived as to the source of campaign propaganda by trickery or fraud, and that they could therefore neither recognize nor evaluate propaganda for what it was, the Board set aside the election. United Aircraft Corp., 103 N.L.R.B. 102 (1953). . . . In those situations, the Board found that election standards had been "lowered . . . to a level which impaired the free and informed atmosphere requisite to an untrammeled expression of choice by the employees." 103 N.L.R.B. at 105.

It was not until 20 years after the Board began establishing standards for elections that it deviated from its practice of refusing to consider the truth or falsity of campaign propaganda. In The Gummed Products Co., 112 N.L.R.B. 1092 (1955), the Board set aside an election where the union deliberately misrepresented wage rates it had negotiated with another employer. Recognizing that it "normally [would] not censor or police preelection propaganda by parties to elections, absent threats or acts of violence," the Board noted that "some limits" had been imposed. "Exaggerations, inaccuracies, partial truths, name-calling, and falsehoods, while not condoned, may be excused as legitimate propaganda, provided they are not so misleading as to prevent the exercise of free choice by employees in the election of their bargaining representative. The ultimate consideration is whether the challenged propaganda has lowered the standards of campaigning to the point where it may be said that the uninhibited desires of the employees cannot be determined in an election." Id. at 1093-1094.

[The opinion here traces developments from Hollywood Ceramics through Shopping Kart and General Knit.]

Many lessons and conclusions can be drawn from this summary of the Board's past practice regarding the role of misrepresentations in Board elections. . . . [R]easonable, informed individuals . . . have differed in their assessment of the effect of misrepresentations on voters and in their views of the Board's proper role in policing such misrepresentations. No one can or does dispute the ultimate purpose of this controversy, that is the necessity of Board procedures which insure the fair and free choice of a bargaining representative. The sole question facing us is how that "fair and free choice" is best assured.

III

. . . Congress has entrusted a wide degree of discretion to the Board to establish the procedures necessary to insure the fair and free choice of bargaining representatives by employees. NLRB v. A. J. Tower Co., 329 U.S. 324, 330 (1946). . . . [We] find that the rule we announce today constitutes . . . a [justifiable and reasonable adjustment] of our democratic electoral processes. By returning to the sound principles espoused in *Shopping Kart*, not only do we alleviate the many difficulties attending the *Hollywood Ceramics* rule, but we also insure the certainty and finality of election results, and minimize unwarranted and dilatory claims attacking those results.

. . . As an initial matter, it is apparent that reasonable, informed individuals can differ on the multitude of subjective issues encompassed in [the *Hollywood Ceramics*] rule. When does a particular statement involve a "substantial" departure from the "truth"? Under what conditions has there been time for an "effective reply"? May the misrepresentation "reasonably be expected" to have a "significant impact" upon the election? As Professor Derek C. Bok concluded [see supra p. 82, at 85] . . . , restrictions on the content of campaign propaganda requiring truthful and accurate statements "resist every effort at a clear formulation and tend inexorably to give rise to vague and inconsistent rulings which baffle the parties and provoke litigation."

The Board's experience under the *Hollywood Ceramics* rule bears this out. As was found in *Shopping Kart*, although the adoption of the *Hollywood Ceramics* rule "was premised on assuring employee free choice its administration has in fact tended to impede the attainment of that goal. The ill effects of the rule include extensive analysis of campaign propaganda, restriction of free speech, variance in application as between the Board and the courts, increasing litigation, and a resulting decrease in the finality of election results."[15]

In sharp contrast to the *Hollywood Ceramics* standard, *Shopping Kart*

---

[15] 228 N.L.R.B. at 1312. Our dissenting colleagues choose to ignore all of the bases for our determination to overrule *General Knit* except that of administrative convenience. We reject the characterization that our only purpose is to cut down the level of litigation of election objections, though we agree that is one worthy goal served by our decision today.

"draws a clear line between what is and what is not objectionable."[16] Thus, "elections will be set aside 'not on the basis of the *substance* of the representation, but the deceptive *manner* in which it was made.' . . . As long as the campaign material is what it purports to be, i.e., mere propaganda of a particular party, the Board would leave the task of evaluating its contents solely to the employees."[17] Where, due to forgery, no voter could recognize the propaganda "for what it is," Board intervention is warranted. Further, unlike *Hollywood Ceramics*, the rule in *Shopping Kart* lends itself to definite results which are both predictable and speedy. The incentive for protracted litigation is greatly reduced, as is the possibility of disagreement between the Board and the courts. Because objections alleging false or inaccurate statements can be summarily rejected at the first stage of Board proceedings, the opportunity for delay is almost nonexistent.[18] Finally, the rule in *Shopping Kart* "furthers the goal of consistent and equitable adjudications" by applying uniformly to the objections of both unions and employers.

. . . [W]e also consider [the *Hollywood Ceramics* rule] to [reflect] an unrealistic view of the ability of voters to assess misleading campaign propaganda. . . . The "protectionism" propounded by the . . . rule is simply not warranted. On the contrary, as we found in *Shopping Kart*, "we believe that Board rules in this area must be based on a view of employees as mature individuals who are capable of recognizing campaign propaganda for what it is and discounting it."

This fact is apparently recognized to a certain extent even under *Hollywood Ceramics*. Thus, although the Board determined that a substantial misrepresentation had been made, the election would not be set aside if it also appeared that there had been ample time to respond. This result would obtain no matter how egregious the error or falsity, and regardless of whether in fact a response had been made.

We appreciate that today's decision is likely to cause concern, just as did *General Knit's* quick retreat from *Shopping Kart* in 1978. Accordingly, we

---

[16] General Knit of California, Inc., 239 N.L.R.B. 619, 629 (1978) (Member Penello dissenting).

[17] Id.

[18] The figures cited by our dissenting colleagues purporting to compare the "number of elections in which allegations of misleading statements were ruled upon" before and after *Shopping Kart* hardly establish that the policy change we enunciate today will not have the desired effects. That parties continued to file misrepresentation objections in 1978 simply demonstrated their acknowledgment of the reality that *Shopping Kart* could be overturned by a shift of one Board Member. In fact, that is what occurred when former Member Truesdale replaced former Member Walther on the Board. In any event, had our dissenting colleagues been more amenable to giving *Shopping Kart* a reasonable chance to take life, perhaps their point might have some merit.

do not take this step lightly. We take it because of our emphatic belief that the rule in *Shopping Kart* is the most appropriate accommodation of all the interests here involved. . . . Weighing the benefits flowing from reinstatement of the *Shopping Kart* rule against the possibility that some voters may be misled by erroneous campaign propaganda, a result that even *Hollywood Ceramics* permits, we find that the balance unquestionably falls in favor of implementing the standard [of] *Shopping Kart*.

. . . As is obvious from today's decision, the policy views of the Board have changed. We cannot permit earlier decisions to endure forever if, in our view, their effects are deleterious and hinder the goals of the Act. The nature of administrative decisionmaking relies heavily upon the benefits of the cumulative experience of the decisionmakers. . . .

In sum, we rule today that we will no longer probe into the truth or falsity of the parties' campaign statements, and that we will not set elections aside on the basis of misleading campaign statements.[24] We will, however, intervene in cases where a party has used forged documents which render the voters unable to recognize propaganda for what it is. Thus, we will set an election aside not because of the substance of the representation, but because of the deceptive manner in which it was made, a manner which renders employees unable to evaluate the forgery for what it is. As [under] *Shopping Kart*, we will continue to protect against other campaign conduct, such as threats, promises, or the like, which interferes with employee free choice.

Accordingly, inasmuch as the Petitioner's objection alleges nothing more than misrepresentations, it is hereby overruled.[26] . . .

---

[24] In accordance with our usual practice, we shall apply our new policy not only "to the case in which the issue arises," but also "to all pending cases in whatever stage." Deluxe Metal Furniture Co., 121 N.L.R.B. 995, 1006-1007 (1958). See, generally, former Member Penello's dissenting opinion in Blackman-Uhler Chemical Division — Synalloy Corp., 239 N.L.R.B. 637, 638 (1978), applying the balancing test set forth by the Supreme Court in Securities & Exchange Commission v. Chenery Corp., 332 U.S. 194, 203 (1947). As former Member Penello pointed out, applying the *Shopping Kart* standard retroactively imposes no substantial hardship on the objecting party. On the other hand, failure to do so would be contrary to the "statutory design." *Chenery*, supra. For, as discussed above, we believe that, on balance, the *Hollywood Ceramics* rule operates more to frustrate than to further the fundamental statutory purpose of assuring employee free choice.

[For an illustration of the effects on pending cases of the Board's movement from *Shopping Kart* to *Hollywood Ceramics* and back again, see Mosey Mfg. Co. v. NLRB, 701 F.2d 610 (7th Cir. 1983) (en banc), where, because of delay attributed to the Board's gyrations, a divided court refused to remand for a third round of review proceedings. — Eds.]

[26] With respect to the LMRDA report, our dissenting colleagues' attempted analogy to the rule set forth in Formco, Inc., 233 N.L.R.B. 61 (1977), misses the mark. . . . *Formco* clearly is inapposite, since here there is no Board document involved. In any event, there is no basis for describing — as the dissenters do — the Employer's presentation of the Form LM-2 excerpt as "an elaborately conceived fraud." The portion of the form distributed by the Employer appeared exactly as submitted by the Petitioner. We categorically reject the dis-

Members Fanning and Jenkins, dissenting. . . . In reestablishing the *Shopping Kart* rule, the present majority adds nothing to the debate that has accompanied the seesawing of Board doctrine in this area. Instead, the majority reiterates the familiar theme of the "unrealistic view of the ability of voters to assess misleading campaign propaganda" . . . and the promise of elimination of delays caused by the processing of misrepresentation objections.

. . . [*Hollywood Ceramics*] represented the accumulated wisdom and experience of several generations of Board Members.[28] . . . And the stated policies behind *Hollywood Ceramics* belie the majority's claim that it is based on an over-protectionist, condescending view of employees:

> . . . The Board has limited its intervention . . . because an election by secret ballot, conducted under Government auspices, should not be lightly set aside, and because we realize that additional elections upset the plant routine and prevent stable labor-management relations. We are also aware that absolute precision of statement and complete honesty are not always attainable in an election campaign, nor are they expected by the employees. Election campaigns are often hotly contested and feelings frequently run high. At such times a party may, in its zeal, overstate its own virtues and the vices of the other without essentially impairing "laboratory conditions." Accordingly, in reaching its decision in cases where objections to elections have been filed alleging that one party misrepresented certain facts, the Board must balance the right of the employees to an untrammeled choice, and the right of the parties to wage a free and vigorous campaign with all the normal legitimate tools of electioneering. [140 N.L.R.B. at 223-224.]

What the majority does now is to give up, in the interest of possibly reducing litigation, a speculative thing at best, any attempt to balance the rights of the employees and the campaigners.[30] However, their goal, which,

---

senters' suggestion that any misrepresentation of any document constitutes a fraud. Their novel position in this regard finds no support in the law, and they make no attempt to muster such support.

[28] . . . [W]e decidedly reject the majority's contention that, prior to *Gummed Products*, the Board had a rigid rule similar to the majority's present position. To the contrary, in United Aircraft Corp., 103 N.L.R.B. 102, 104 (1953), the Board, summarizing earlier decisions, recognized a limit to the condonation of propaganda where it is " 'so misleading' as to prevent the exercise of a free choice by employees in the selection of their bargaining representative"; that policing would be withheld only if the propaganda remains within "bounds"; and that "the question to be decided is 'one of degree.' " . . .

[30] We find incomprehensible the majority's additional suggestion that the *Shopping Kart* rule (presumably as compared with the *Hollywood Ceramics* rule) " 'furthers the goal of consistent and equitable adjudications' by applying uniformly to the objections of both unions and employers." To our knowledge, no rule ever contemplated by the Board has treated misrepresentations by unions and employers differently.

as the Board noted in *General Knit*, must never take precedence over preservation of the integrity of the electoral process, seems to have eluded the Board's prior attempt under *Shopping Kart*. For, according to an internal audit conducted for the General Counsel, the number of elections in which allegations of misleading statements were ruled on increased from 327 in 1976, the year before *Shopping Kart* was decided, to 357 in 1978, the first full year after *Shopping Kart* was in effect, this despite a decrease (from 8,899 to 8,464) in the total number of elections conducted in those respective years.

. . . It is apparent that the system contemplated by . . . the Act for representation elections has survived reasonably well during the decades in which the Board has taken a role in insuring the integrity of its elections. Indeed, the majority does not suggest deregulating the election process other than with respect to misrepresentations. . . . [W]e are especially puzzled by the distinction the majority draws between forgery, which it will regulate, and other kinds of fraud, which it will not. The majority states that forgeries "render the voters unable to recognize the propaganda for what it is." Yet it is precisely the Board's traditional perception that there are some misrepresentations which employees can recognize "for what they are" and others which, in the Board's considered judgment, they cannot, that has made the *Hollywood Ceramics* doctrine so effective. . . . Employees' free choice in elections, the only reason we run elections, must necessarily be inhibited, distorted, and frustrated by [the majority's] new rule. To the majority, this is less important than the freedom to engage in lies, trickery, and fraud. Under the new rule, important election issues will be ignored in favor of irresponsible charges and deceit. Under *Hollywood Ceramics*, the Board did not attempt to sanitize elections completely but only to keep the campaign propaganda within reasonable bounds. Those bounds have now disappeared. Why?

Albeit today's American employees may be better educated, in the formal sense, than those of previous generations, and may be in certain respects more sophisticated, we do not honor them by abandoning them utterly to the mercies of unscrupulous campaigners, including the expert cadre of professional opinion molders who devise campaigns for many of our representation elections. In political campaigns, which are conducted over a much longer period of time and are subject to extensive media scrutiny, the voters have ready access to independent sources of information concerning the issues. In representation campaigns, they do not. Thus, it has been observed that: "Promises are often written on the wind, but statements of fact are the stuff upon which men and women make serious value judgements . . . [and] rank and file employees must largely depend upon the company and union to provide the data. . . ."[32] As we said in our dissent in *Shopping Kart*, the very high level of participation in Board elections as compared with political elections speaks well for the Board's role in insuring a measure of responsibility in campaigning.[33] . . . [A]bsent some external restraint, the campaigners will have little incentive to refrain from any last-minute deceptions that might work to their short-term advantage. . . .

[In] the instant case, . . . [there] were substantial misrepresentations concerning the central issue in the choice of a bargaining representative — its effectiveness. But the Employer did not limit itself to simple misrepresentations. It . . . engaged in an elaborately conceived fraud [regarding] an excerpt from the [required] Form LM-2 financial report. . . . Line 71 of the form, showing union disbursements "on behalf of individual members," appears to show that the Union made no such disbursements during the reporting year. The Employer both underlined that item and emphasized it in a separate notation. The Employer contrasted this negative disbursement figure with a figure which overstated by 19 percent the moneys paid to union officers and "those that worked for them." . . . What the excerpt and the Employer's notations concealed, however, was that the Labor Department's instructions for completing line 71 specifically exclude from disbursements "on behalf of individual members" all normal operating expenses. Thus, while a reader in possession of the instructions might realize that the Union's operating expenses, including salaries for the Union's staff, are incurred with the objective of benefiting all the members, the Employer carefully disguised this fact, egregiously distorted what the Union does with its members' money, and ingeniously made the Union itself appear to be the source of this misinformation. In addition, how many employees are going to read and understand this complicated form?

The Employer's fraudulent misstatement of the contents of this Government document is analogous to the mischaracterization of this Board's documents, and is at least equally objectionable. See Formco, Inc., 233 N.L.R.B. 61 (1977). Here, in sum, we have a fraudulent misrepresentation of a most serious and extreme nature, forming part of a series of material misrepresentations. Such conduct can hardly have failed to affect the elec-

[32] J. I. Case Co. v. NLRB, 555 F.2d 202, 205 (8th Cir. 1977).
[33] Perhaps it is not practicable to regulate political campaign propaganda as the Board traditionally has policed representation campaigns, because elected Government positions must be filled within a very brief period after the election. As noted above, however, our system of majority collective-bargaining representation has not been endangered by *Hollywood Ceramics*.

tion, especially since, with a tally of 107 to 107, the change of a single vote may have changed the outcome.

The majority through this decision is giving our election processes . . . over to the possible excesses of the participants and eliminating the Board from its statutory oversight responsibilities. Why? Accordingly, we must dissent.

NOTES

1. Is there an explanation for the *Midland* Board's failure to rely on the Getman voting study (indeed, even to mention it)?

2. Is an intelligent guess possible as to which party's interest will, in general, suffer or benefit from the overruling of *Hollywood Ceramics?* Presumably, Professors Getman, Goldberg, and Herman would say that neither side would suffer much. Do you agree? (Judge Aldrich, concurring in NLRB v. New Columbus Nursing Home, 720 F.2d 726, 730 (5th Cir. 1983), included among his criticisms of *Midland* a prediction that it would operate as "basically a pro-union rule," because "unions are the ones more likely to take advantage" of the decision. Why doesn't *Midland* tempt employers at least as much, if not more, than it tempts unions?)

3. Assume the correctness of the Getman study's conclusions downplaying the influence of campaign statements on voter behavior.[n] Would it necessarily follow that the study's deregulation proposals should be accepted? Would such deregulation invite greater excesses in campaigning, which in turn might impair future relationships between labor and management? Does NLRB regulation of campaigns have important effects that are independent of actual impact on voting behavior? If so, does the effort to preserve any such independent effects, by regulating speech, involve excessive costs?

A principal argument of supporters of *Hollywood Ceramics* within the Board — Member Fanning, for example — has been that certain misrepresentations must be prohibited in order to "preserve the integrity of the Board's electoral process." This claim seems to place great value on appearances (e.g., the appearance of election "fairness"); it also seems to be

---

[n] One critic has argued against the assumption as follows: "It may be legitimate for Getman and his coauthors to conclude that their own data do not demonstrate with certainty that employer coercion affects employee voting, but it is entirely unjustified to infer from that fact alone that the contrary is true. The failure to find a statistically significant connection between employer intimidation and employee votes in this limited sample neither proves that there is no such relationship nor provides a basis on which to argue that we may safely abandon efforts to protect employee choice." Weiler, Promises to Keep: Securing Workers' Rights to Self-Organization Under the NLRA, 96 Harv. L. Rev. 1769, 1783 (1983).

grounded in considerations not likely to show up in empirical data on employee voting behavior. Do you have any surmises about those considerations? Who are the people in need of reassurance from the NLRB? Does justification of Board regulation on an "integrity" rationale involve more than symbolic values? See generally Miller, The Getman, Goldberg and Herman Questions, 28 Stan. L. Rev. 1173 (1976).

4. After *Midland*, the Board, expanding its deregulation, concluded (3 to 2) that its *Formco* doctrine should be discarded and that campaigners' misstatements as to actions by the Board should be treated like other misrepresentations. The case, Affiliated Midwest Hospital, Inc., 264 N.L.R.B. No. 146, 111 L.R.R.M. 1425 (1982), involved a union leaflet that obviously misrepresented the Board's disposition of unfair labor practice charges brought against the employer. In finding the misrepresentation unobjectionable under *Midland*, the majority branded as "erroneous" the Board's earlier extension of the exception for altered Board documents to cases of mischaracterization of action reflected in Board documents, distinguishing the two situations on grounds that a mischaracterization neither injects the Board itself into the campaign (there is "only one party's representation of the Board's action") nor conveys the impression of Board bias in favor of one party (a finding for or against a party in a document "does not indicate that the Board has taken any view with respect to the course the employees should take in an election"). In addition, the majority rejected outright the *Formco* premise that misstatements concerning NLRB processes are not easily neutralized by the affected party's reply. Members Fanning and Jenkins, dissenting, asked why the majority "would condemn any misrepresentation of Board proceedings accomplished by the use of an altered Board document but condone the same misrepresentation when made on a separate sheet of paper." If this is the distinction made by the decision, is it justified?

5. Reviewing courts generally recognize a right to an evidentiary hearing for a party whose election objections raise "substantial and material issues of fact" that would, if resolved in the objector's favor, warrant setting aside the election. In Anchor Inns, Inc. v. NLRB, 644 F.2d 292 (3d Cir. 1981), the Board had refused to decide whether evidence presented in the objector's affidavits was itself sufficient to require a hearing on the factual issues raised. Instead, the Board awaited the results of the Regional Director's ex parte investigation before resolving the hearing issue. This procedure was found to be inadequate. The court ruled that the objector's allegations must be taken as true in determining the substantiality and materiality of factual issues raised by an objection. Accord, NLRB v. Claxton Mfg. Co., 613 F.2d 1364 (5th Cir. 1980) (once the right to a hearing is established by prima facie evidence of substantiality, "the investigation is not a substitute for it"). On the standard

of review of Board denials of a hearing on claims of election misconduct, see NLRB v. ARA Services, Inc., 717 F.2d 57 (3d Cir. 1983) (en banc).

Teamsters, Local 633 v. NLRB
509 F.2d 490 (D.C. Cir. 1974)

[In late 1970, Bulk Haulers, a non-unionized company, employed Hall, a member of Local 633, and then McKay, as drivers. Both men were supervised by Therriault. In November 1971, following a dispute between Hall and Therriault over late deliveries, Hall contacted Local 633 and arranged a meeting at his home, which McKay attended. Hall also discussed the union with other company drivers. During this period Therriault called McKay into his office and questioned him about the union. Hall was discharged a few days later. The NLRB, adopting the Trial Examiner's findings and order, held that neither the questioning of McKay nor the discharge of Hall violated the Act. The opinion below reviews the Board's determination that the interrogation of McKay did not violate §8(a)(1); the court's treatment of Hall's discharge is omitted.]

BAZELON, J. . . . Therriault initiated the questioning by calling McKay into the company's conference room. Therriault then asked McKay whether McKay had been approached by the union, adding that McKay did not have to answer this question if he did not wish to. McKay stated in response that he had indeed been approached by the union. Therriault then remarked that he expected that sooner or later Bulk Haulers would go union but that McKay would be wise to ensure that the benefits obtained through unionization were sufficient to offset any union dues. Therriault also stated that if the union came in, the senior driver would get the better work, if that driver wanted it, and that McKay who was relatively less senior "could come up short." The trial examiner found that the questioning was limited and that Therriault, by assuring McKay that he did not have to answer his question, "blunted what otherwise might have been the coercive nature of the inquiry." The trial examiner further found that statements relating to the adverse effects of a union seniority system were permissible predictions with a reasonable basis in fact and thus were legally protected speech under §8(c) of [the Act].

We begin . . . [with] the nature of the §8(a)(1) offense of "coercive interrogation." The policy of §8(a)(1) is to protect employee free choice in the decision whether to accept union representation, a free choice explicitly preserved in §7 . . . and implicit in a number of related areas of national labor policy. The specific focus of §8(a)(1) is the prohibition of the use of employer economic power to interfere with this free choice. But neither

§8(a)(1) or its union counterpart, §8(b)(1), could reasonably be read to eliminate employer and union attempts to persuade workers of the benefits or costs of accepting the union. First, such a result would lead to the absurd conclusion that free choice means a relatively uninformed choice and, second, the result would be inconsistent with §8(c) of the Act which implements traditional First Amendment policies.[9] The burden of §8(a)(1) is thus to distinguish between employer attempts to persuade workers of the disadvantages of unionization and employer attempts to use their economic power to "coerce" workers into voting against the union. But, as should be immediately obvious, there is no clear cut distinction between these two kinds of activity. There is always an iron "fist inside the velvet glove"[10] of persuasion. Established First Amendment doctrine would seem to indicate that this inability to easily distinguish protected from non-protected speech is cause for restricting the government's ability to remedy the non-protected speech, but the Supreme Court has expressly rejected that analogy [in *Gissel*]. . . .

The Board has since the inception of the [NLRA] recognized that interrogation by an employer of a worker's attitude toward the union and that statements by the employer about what might happen if the union is selected as the representative of the employees have a tendency to coerce workers in the exercise of their §7 rights.[14] The Labor Board and the courts have over the years crystallized a number of "factors" to be considered in determining whether employer questioning and predictions as to the consequences of unionization pass beyond permissible persuasion into impermissible use of employer economic power. A number of these factors were enunciated in the leading case of Bourne v. NLRB, 332 F.2d 47, 48 (2d Cir. 1964).[15] . . . [W]e think that [the *Bourne*] factors supply the proper starting place[17]

[9] *See* NLRB v. Gissel Packing Co., 395 U.S. 575, 617 (1969).

[10] NLRB v. Exchange Parts Co., 375 U.S. 405, 409 (1964).

[14] *See* NLRB v. Virginia Elec. & Power Co., 314 U.S. 469 (1941); Blue Flash Express, Inc., 109 N.L.R.B. 591 (1954). . . .

[15] . . . The original *Bourne* factors are as follows:

(1) The background, i. e. is there a history of employer hostility and discrimination?

(2) The nature of the information sought, e. g. did the interrogator appear to be seeking information on which to base taking action against individual employees?

(3) The identity of the questioner, i. e. how high was he in the company hierarchy?

(4) Place and method of interrogation, e.g. was employee called from work to the boss's office? Was there an atmosphere of "unnatural formality"?

(5) Truthfulness of the reply.

[17] There is nothing in Local 49, Operating Engrs. v. NLRB, 122 U.S. App. D.C. 314, 353 F.2d 852, 856 (1965), *on remand* Struksnes Construction Co., 165 N.L.R.B. No. 102 (1967), *approved* NLRB v. Gissel Packing Co., 395 U.S. 575, 609, . . . which is inconsistent with *Bourne*. The *Struksnes* case concerned an employer poll of his employees to determine majority sentiment. This Court refused to accept the Board's position based on its loss in NLRB v. Lorben Corp., 345 F.2d 346 (2d Cir. 1965) that an employer poll was not [*sic*] a violation of §8(a)(1) simply because the employer did not inform the employees of the

for . . . analysis of whether particular employer questioning was in the totality of circumstances "coercive" or merely persuasive. Passing from the coercive nature *vel non* of questioning about an employee's attitude toward a union to employer statements as to the effect of unionization, the recent decision in . . . [*Gissel*] establishes that such statements must be either non-coercive or a prediction "carefully phrased on the basis of objective fact to convey an employer's belief as to demonstrably probable consequences beyond his control. . . . "[18] Whether statements as to the effect of unionization are coercive involves an inquiry essentially similar to that suggested in *Bourne*.

It is apparent . . . that the type of inquiry mandated by *Bourne* and related cases was not conducted here. The trial examiner properly considered the extent of the questioning by Therriault. Surely, an isolated and limited set of questions would not rise to the level of employer "coercion." However, the trial examiner did not stop there but also stated that Therriault "by assuring McKay that he need not answer unless he wanted to . . . blunted what otherwise might have been the coercive nature of the inquiry." We find this conclusion highly problematic. Without a supporting discussion of the totality of circumstances surrounding the questioning, we are not prepared to hold that the bare "assurance" that the employee need not answer is sufficient to eliminate what would otherwise be employer economic coercion. We think the Board should conduct a more searching inquiry into the nature of the questioning and the circumstances in which it was conducted before concluding the questioning was not coercive. As to Therriault's prediction that McKay might "come up short" because of union seniority provisions, we are not prepared to evaluate this statement under the *Gissel* test until the Board has more fully considered whether the circumstances of the questioning were coercive. We also note that there was no evidence in the record to support the trial examiner's conclusion that Therriault had a reasonable basis

---

purpose of the poll and assure them that there would be no retaliation. This Court remanded the case to the Board to develop specific standards to govern employer polls. The Supreme Court approved the Board's remand effort apparently as a "safe harbor" for the employer who, under prior Board authorization card practice, might be between the devil and the deep blue sea when deciding whether to recognize an authorization card proffer. NLRB v. Gissel Packing Co., supra at 609. . . . The need for this safe harbor is considerably lessened by the Board's new practice on authorization cards announced at oral argument in *Gissel*, 395 U.S. at 594. . . . In any event, we do not think that the specific holding in *Struksnes* can overcome the weight of §8(a)(1) precedent recognized in the reasoning of *Gissel*. . . .

[18] The relation between this "test" under §8(a)(1) and the general *Bourne* analysis of coercive circumstances is not clear from the decided cases which variously merge the two and treat each as an independent ground for refusing to find a §8(a)(1) violation. One possible view is that this specific *Gissel* test quoted in the text is a per se rule for determining whether one particular statement (as opposed to a set of coercive circumstances) is coercive. . . .

in fact for his suggestion that the union might bring in a seniority system which would disadvantage McKay. [Thus the better course of action] is to remand . . . to the Board for a more complete evaluation of Therriault's questioning of McKay in light of . . . this opinion. This remand is consistent with the holding in *Gissel* that the Labor Board must in the first instance perform the extremely delicate task [of] distinguishing employer coercion from employer persuasion.

A consideration of the vagaries of this task compels us to suggest to the Board the beginnings of a principled approach to distinguishing coercion from persuasion. This approach, it would seem, is also instructive on the similarly delicate issue of whether a statement is a "prediction" or a "threat of retaliation." A §8(a)(1) violation based on speech alone is made out solely by reference to imminent coercive actions. Speech which carries a message of actual coercion is more than pure speech and thus is subject to balance with other important social interests. The Congress has concluded that the right of workers to freely associate for their economic betterment is of more social importance than the employer's free speech rights when that speech is backed by a threat of action. The Supreme Court has let that judgment stand [in *Gissel*]. But coercion must surely be interpreted to mean more than a persuasive argument that certain events will occur which are distasteful *to the listener*. Rather coercion is defined by reference to the will of the speaker — does the speaker intend to perform an act for no other reason than that the listener is in favor of the union?[25] Of course, the speaker's intent must be inferred from the circumstances as they appear to the reasonable person. Thus, to take examples from a recurrent §8(a)(1) problem, employer assertions that "serious harm" will result from unionization are generally not an

---

[25] "When the employer declares that he will have to move or close down if the union comes in and obtains higher wages, union organizers can reply that their negotiators will take account of the company's position and endeavor not to induce its departure from the area. Under these circumstances, the arguments on both sides are legitimate and the voters are free to choose between them. But if the employees are led to believe that the company will simply close down automatically if the union is selected, they are left with a devastating and improper assertion which the organizer is unable to rebut save by pointing out that the employer cannot carry out his plan without violating the law. Rightly or wrongly, this is an argument that will often make little or no impression on the voters." Bok, 78 Harv. L. Rev. [at] 77. This view of the §8(a)(1) principle, when applied to employer speech, was adopted in Luxuray of New York v. NLRB, 447 F.2d 112, 117 (2d Cir. 1971) and is implied in [*Gissel*] ("If there is any implication that an employer may or may not take action solely on his own initiative for reasons unrelated to economic necessities and known only to him, the statement is no longer a reasonable prediction. . . . ").

Viewed in this context, §8(a)(1) pure speech violations are really an inchoate form of actions which if completed would violate §8(a)(1) or (3) under established doctrine.

unfair labor practice while assertions that the employer will "bargain from scratch" are unfair labor practices.[26]

. . . [W]e reverse the Board's determination that Therriault did not violate §8(a)(1) by questioning Stephen McKay and remand for further consideration. . . .

NOTES

1. In Struksnes Construction Co., 165 N.L.R.B. 1062 (1967), mentioned by Judge Bazelon in *Local 633* (note 17), the Board adopted the following standards for determining the legality of polls of employees regarding their support of a union: "Absent unusual circumstances, the polling of employees by an employer will be violative of Section 8(a)(1) . . . unless the following safeguards are observed: (1) the purpose of the poll is to determine the truth of a union's claim of majority, (2) this purpose is communicated to the employees, (3) assurances against reprisals are given, (4) the employees are polled by secret ballot, and (5) the employer has not engaged in unfair labor practices or otherwise created a coercive atmosphere." Is there any significant difference between the *Struksnes* test and the approach taken in *Local 633*, based on the *Bourne* factors? As *Local 633* illustrates, courts of appeal have generally begun with the *Bourne* factors — despite the Supreme Court's seeming approval of *Struksnes*, in *Gissel*. See Utrad Corp. v. NLRB, 454 F.2d 520 (7th Cir. 1971).

2. Once a NLRB election is pending, an employer who polls employees on the representation question will probably be held to have engaged in election interference whether or not there is a specific finding of coercion. See generally Offner Electronics, Inc., 127 N.L.R.B. 991 (1960). Similar polling by a union has, however, been held not to warrant upsetting an election. What basis, if any, is there for this difference in treatment? See Springfield Discount, Inc., 195 N.L.R.B. 921 n.4 (1972), *enforced*, 82 L.R.R.M. 2173 (7th Cir. 1973). Polling will be examined again (see Chapter 6(A)), in the context of an employer's questioning an incumbent union's continuing support among the employees.

3. Does an employer's questioning of his employees as to their union sympathies necessarily "interfere with, restrain, or coerce" under §8(a)(1)? What if, in a specific instance, the employee questioned is a known, self-

---

[26] . . . *See also* the "propaganda movie" cases: Luxuray of New York v. NLRB, 447 F.2d 112, 117 (2d Cir. 1971). . . .

avowed union supporter and the employer simply inquires as to his reasons for supporting the union? In PPG Industries, Inc., 251 N.L.R.B. 1146 (1980), the NLRB decided that initiating such questioning of even known adherents in and of itself violates the Act. PPG was overruled (3 to 1) in 1984, in favor of a test of whether, "under all the circumstances," an interrogation reasonably tends to be coercive. Rossmore House, 269 N.L.R.B. No. 198, 115 L.R.R.M. 1025 (1984) (citing Bourne for "relevant areas of inquiry"). In Rossmore, both the majority and the dissenter (who adhered to PPG) contended that the other had "ignored the reality of the workplace." What is your assessment of "reality" when the interrogated employee openly supports the union? Is uncommitted?

4. The question of unlawful interrogation arises frequently in the context of an attorney's interview of employees for the purpose of preparing a defense to unfair labor practice charges before the Board. In general, the Board has been strict — too strict, in the view of some courts — in applying its standard "Miranda"-type safeguards against coercion in such cases, particularly requirements of assurances against reprisals and of disclosure of the purpose and voluntary nature of the interview. See Standard-Coosa-Thatcher, Inc., 257 N.L.R.B. 304 (1981); W.W. Grainger, Inc., 255 N.L.R.B. 1106 (1981), enforcement denied, 677 F.2d 557 (7th Cir. 1982). When attorneys' investigatory or prehearing interviews include questioning of employees about their statements given to Board agents, the Board, with disagreement from some courts, has tended to condemn the questioning even though it was accompanied by the required explanations and assurances. See Braswell Motor Freight Lines, Inc., 156 N.L.R.B. 671 (1966), enforced 386 F.2d 190 (6th Cir. 1967); NLRB v. Tamper, Inc., 522 F.2d 711 (4th Cir. 1976). There is some uncertainty on the question whether employers' requests for copies of employees' written statements to Board agents are per se §8(a)(1) violations. See NLRB v. Maxwell, 637 F.2d 698 (9th Cir. 1981) (finding support for a stringent rule in the Supreme Court's Robbins Tire holding (437 U.S. 214) that employees' prehearing statements to the Board are exempt from disclosure under the Freedom of Information Act); NLRB v. Martin A. Gleason, Inc., 534 F.2d 466 (2d Cir. 1976) (rejecting Board's per se rule and permitting nonthreatening requests by employer preparing for trial).

5. A strike appears to be imminent, and the employer, in order to plan production, wishes to ask existing employees, and applicants for employment who would replace strikers, whether they would cross a picket line and work during the strike. The employer also wishes to avoid violating the NLRA. What advice would you give him? See NLRB v. Transportation Manage-

ment Corp., 686 F.2d 63 (1st Cir. 1982) (legitimate reasons for wishing to obtain information as to employees' strike intentions will not save a poll that fails to satisfy established safeguards); W.A. Sheaffer Pen Co., 199 N.L.R.B. 242 (1972), *enforced*, 486 F.2d 180 (8th Cir. 1973).

6. It is generally recognized that photographing employees engaged in peaceful picketing has, like interrogation as to union sympathies, a tendency to interfere with the exercise of protected employee rights. Thus, an employer is usually required to provide a substantial justification for its photographing of employee picketing. Presumably, violence or other picketline misconduct would warrant the taking of pictures. In what other circumstances should photography of protected activities be permitted? See, e.g., United States Steel Corp. v. NLRB, 682 F.2d 98 (3d Cir. 1982); NLRB v. Colonial Haven Nursing Home, Inc., 542 F.2d 691 (7th Cir. 1976). Should a union's taking of photographs as employees leave the plant during an organizational campaign be a violation of §8(B)(1)(A) or a basis for overturning an election? See Spring City Knitting Co. v. NLRB, 647 F.2d 1011 (9th Cir. 1981).

NLRB v. Exchange Parts Co.
375 U.S. 405 (1964)

HARLAN, J. This case presents a question concerning the limitations which §8(a)(1) . . . places on the right of an employer to confer economic benefits on his employees shortly before a representation election. The precise issue is whether that section prohibits the conferral of such benefits, without more, where the employer's purpose is to affect the outcome of the election. . . .

The respondent, Exchange Parts Company, is engaged in the business of rebuilding automobile parts in Fort Worth, Texas. Prior to November 1959 its employees were not represented by a union. On November 9, 1959, the International Brotherhood of Boilermakers, Iron Shipbuilders, Blacksmiths, Forgers and Helpers, AFL-CIO, advised Exchange Parts that the union was conducting an organizational campaign at the plant and that a majority of the employees had designated the union as their bargaining representative. On November 16 the union petitioned . . . for a representation election. The Board conducted a hearing on December 29, and on February 19, 1960, issued an order directing . . . an election. . . . The election was held on March 18, 1960.

At two meetings on November 4 and 5, 1959, C. V. McDonald, the Vice-President and General Manager of Exchange Parts, announced to the employees that their "floating holiday" in 1959 would fall on December 26 and that there would be an additional "floating holiday" in 1960. On February 25, six days after the Board issued its election order, Exchange Parts held a dinner for employees at which Vice-President McDonald told the employees that they could decide whether the extra day of vacation in 1960 would be a "floating holiday" or would be taken on their birthdays. The employees voted for the latter. McDonald also referred to the forthcoming representation election as one in which, in the words of the trial examiner, the employees would "determine whether . . . [they] wished to hand over their right to speak and act for themselves." He stated that the union had distorted some of the facts and pointed out the benefits obtained by the employees without a union. He urged all the employees to vote in the election.

On March 4, Exchange Parts sent its employees a letter which spoke of "the *Empty Promises* of the Union" and "the *fact* that *it is the Company that puts things in your envelope*. . . ." After mentioning a number of benefits, the letter said: "The Union can't put any of those things in your envelope — *only the Company can do that*."[2] Further on, the letter stated: " . . . [I]t didn't take a Union to get any of those things and . . . it won't take a Union to get additional improvements in the future." Accompanying the letter was a detailed statement of the benefits granted by the company since 1949 and an estimate of the monetary value of such benefits to the employees. Included in the statement of benefits for 1960 were the birthday holiday, a new system for computing overtime during holiday weeks which had the effect of increasing wages for those weeks, and a new vacation schedule which enabled employees to extend their vacations by sandwiching them between two weekends. Although Exchange Parts asserts that the policy behind the latter two benefits was established earlier, it is clear that the letter of March 4 was the first general announcement of the changes to the employees. In the ensuing election the union lost.

The Board, affirming the findings of the trial examiner, found that the announcement of the birthday holiday and the grant and announcement of overtime and vacation benefits were arranged by Exchange Parts with the intention of inducing the employees to vote against the union. It found that this conduct violated §8(a)(1) . . . and issued an appropriate order. On the Board's petition for enforcement of the order, the Court of Appeals rejected the finding that the announcement of the birthday holiday was timed to influence the outcome of the election. It accepted the Board's findings with respect to the overtime and vacation benefits, and the propriety of those findings is not in controversy here. However, noting that "the benefits were put into effect unconditionally on a permanent basis, and no one has sug-

---

[2] The italics appear in the original letter.

gested that there was any implication the benefits would be withdrawn if the workers voted for the union," 304 F.2d 368, 375, the court denied enforcement of the Board's order. It believed that it was not an unfair labor practice under §8(a)(1) for an employer to grant benefits to its employees in these circumstances. We think the Court of Appeals was mistaken in concluding that the conferral of employee benefits while a representation election is pending, for the purpose of inducing employees to vote against the union, does not "interfere with" the protected right to organize.

. . . We have no doubt that [§8(a)(1)] prohibits not only intrusive threats and promises but also conduct immediately favorable to employees which is undertaken with the express purpose of impinging upon their freedom of choice for or against unionization and is reasonably calculated to have that effect. In Medo Photo Supply Corp. v. Labor Board, 321 U.S. 678, 686, this Court said: "The action of employees with respect to the choice of their bargaining agents may be induced by favors bestowed by the employer as well as by his threats or domination." Although in that case there was already a designated bargaining agent and the offer of "favors" was in response to a suggestion of the employees that they would leave the union if favors were bestowed, the principles which dictated the result there are fully applicable here. The danger inherent in well-timed increases in benefits is the suggestion of a fist inside the velvet glove. Employees are not likely to miss the inference that the source of benefits now conferred is also the source from which future benefits must flow and which may dry up if it is not obliged.[3] The danger may be diminished if, as in this case, the benefits are conferred permanently and unconditionally. But the absence of conditions or threats pertaining to the particular benefits conferred would be of controlling significance only if it could be presumed that no question of additional benefits or renegotiation of existing benefits would arise in the future; and, of course, no such presumption is tenable.

Other Courts of Appeals have found a violation of §8(a)(1) in the kind of conduct involved here. . . . It is true, as the court below pointed out, that in most cases of this kind the increase in benefits could be regarded as "one part of an overall program of interference and restraint by the employer," 304 F.2d, at 372, and that in this case the questioned conduct stood in isolation. Other unlawful conduct may often be an indication of the motive behind a grant of benefits while an election is pending, and to that extent it is relevant to the legality of the grant; but when as here the motive is otherwise estab-

---

[3] The inference was made almost explicit in Exchange Parts' letter to its employees of March 4, already quoted, which said: "The Union can't put any of those . . . [benefits] in your envelope—*only the Company can do that.*" (Original italics.) We place no reliance, however, on these or other words of the respondent dissociated from its conduct. . . .

lished, an employer is not free to violate §8(a)(1) by conferring benefits simply because it refrains from other, more obvious violations. We cannot agree with the Court of Appeals that enforcement of the Board's order will have the "ironic" result of "discouraging benefits for labor." 304 F.2d, at 376. The beneficence of an employer is likely to be ephemeral if prompted by a threat of unionization which is subsequently removed. Insulating the right of collective organization from calculated good will of this sort deprives employees of little that has lasting value.

Reversed.

NOTES

1. Compare the Court's assumptions in the principal case with the following statement in a speech by N. C. Weston, Director of the United States Steelworkers District 35, set forth in 75 L.R.R. (BNA) 280-282 (Nov. 20, 1970):

> In an effort to defeat the union in organizational campaigns, the companies have given wage increases prior to the representation elections. Instead of buying the vote of the youth, it has served only to whet his appetite. He votes for the union more readily, for he is convinced that with the power of the union he can do at least twice as well no later than the first week following the election.

2. Getman, Goldberg, and Herman recommend that grants and promises of benefits not be grounds for setting aside an election or for finding a violation of §8(a)(1). The authors conceded, but were not concerned by, the possibility of a resulting increase in explicit promises and grants of benefit. They stated (Study at 160):

> An employee is free to choose union representation despite [such] promises or grants. . . . He may not lawfully be penalized for doing so. If . . . an employee wishes to rely on the employer's promises or grants of benefit as a reason for rejecting union representation, his decision would appear wholly free. A contrary conclusion [maintained by the Board] could rest only on an assumption that promises or grants of benefit will be understood by employees to contain an implied threat of reprisal (the "fist inside the velvet glove theory") or that employees are incapable of maintaining a previously formulated intention to vote union, however strongly held, in the face of a grant or promise of benefits designed to persuade them to vote company. Neither of these assumptions is supported by the data.

Is this argument supported by the 1947 amendments to §7, providing that the rights of employees to abstain from, and to participate in, concerted activities are in general to be coequal? What of the preference for collective action in §1 of the Act?

3. During 1976-1983, the employer, on the basis of an annual wage survey, granted wage increases to all employees during the first week of April. An election petition covering employees in the shipping department was filed on December 8, 1983, and an election conducted on May 26, 1984. During the first week in April 1984, on the basis of the customary wage survey, the employer instituted annual wage increases for only those departments not involved in the pending election proceedings, including departments already represented by the petitioning union. At the same time, the employer distributed a notice that wage adjustments for employees involved in the election proceedings were being postponed, on advice of counsel, in order to avoid the appearance of vote-buying and possible unfair labor practices. The union lost the election and objected thereto on the basis of the foregoing notice. The Regional Director sustained that objection but was overruled by the NLRB, which found that the notice was not intended to, and did not operate to, influence the election or disparage the union. The Board also disclaimed any suggestion that it would necessarily have been "objectionable" for the employer to have made its annual wage adjustments at the usual time. See Uarco, Inc., 169 N.L.R.B. 1153 (1968); Sugardale Foods, Inc., 221 N.L.R.B. 1228 (1976) (emphasizing, in following *Uarco*, possible differences in amounts of the raises). In Russell Stover Candies, Inc., 221 N.L.R.B. 441, 444 (1975), the Board reaffirmed as a settled proposition: "[A]n employer, when confronted by a union organizing campaign, must proceed as it would have done had the union not been conducting its campaign." In practice, will it be easy to follow this advice when past wage increases have involved substantial discretion? For judicial recognition of an employer's risk of a potential " 'damned if you do, damned if you don't' situation," see J. J. Newberry v. NLRB, 645 F.2d 148, 151 (2d Cir. 1981).

4. Does §8(c) of the Act call for the result in *Exchange Parts*, at least as to a "promise of benefit"? What significance flows from the applicability of §8(c) to §8(b), as well as to §8(a), and from the difference in wording of §§8(a)(1) and 8(b)(1)?

5. In Marine World USA, 251 N.L.R.B. 1211 (1980), which involved inter-union rivalry, the Board, on remand from the court of appeals, reversed its prior finding that §8(a)(1) had been violated by two announcements to employees concerning withholding of a wage increase. The employer, seeking to grant an unscheduled wage increase during an election campaign involving an incumbent and a rival union, had sought both unions' consent to

the increase. The rival union consented but the incumbent refused, requesting instead discussions. Apparently believing that bargaining with the incumbent would be unlawful, the employer then distributed to the employees two written announcements that the incumbent union's failure to consent had precluded the unscheduled wage increase. The Board, accepting as the law of the case the remanding court's analysis (that speech that might otherwise be unlawful under §8(a)(1) cannot, in view of §8(c), be the basis of a violation unless the speech amounts to a "threat" or "promise"), reasoned as follows:

> Respondent's announcements clearly were calculated to disparage the incumbent Union . . . and to discourage membership therein. However, even considering the announcements in the context of Respondent's overall campaign in which it openly favored the rival Union, the announcements do not suggest, either expressly or impliedly, that Respondent would retaliate against the employees and deny them a wage increase if the incumbent Union won the election. Nor can the announcements be read to suggest that Respondent would reward the employees with increased benefits if they voted to defeat the incumbent Union. Thus . . . although the announcements were critical of the incumbent Union, a threat of reprisal or force or promise of benefit by Respondent cannot be inferred from the surrounding circumstances. Given this, the announcements cannot be found unlawful under the analysis applied by the court.

Assume that the employer grants a regularly scheduled benefit, or a wage increase designed only to maintain real purchasing power in the face of inflation — despite the refusal of a union seeking recognition to consent. Under §8(c), should the legality of the employer's action depend on whether he makes "propaganda" out of the union's refusal when he grants the benefit (or when he announces that it would not be forthcoming)? See Simpson Electric Co. v. NLRB, 654 F.2d 15 (7th Cir. 1981); American Telecommunications Corp., 249 N.L.R.B. 1135 (1980).

6. An employer frequently campaigns by linking the future to the past — i.e., by stressing to employees its record of benefits compared with the industry's unionized plants, or the performance elsewhere of the union in question. Such statements are permissible unless found to promise, expressly or impliedly, a continuance of past benefits only in the absence of a union. Furthermore, the Board has sometimes condemned the promise of the same level of benefits, whether a union is present, as a statement of the "futility" of union representation (see Note 3, supra p. 101). Such condemnation has extended, for example, to a statement that the company's unrepresented employees have received benefits equal to those of its represented em-

ployees. Compare Galbreath & Co., 266 N.L.R.B. No. 18, 112 L.R.R.M. 1279 (1983), with Pacific Telephone Co., 256 N.L.R.B. 449 (1981), and American Telecommunications Corp., 249 N.L.R.B. 1135 (1980). An employer's general promises of an even better future are also permitted, even though such promises are prompted by an organizational campaign. See, e.g., Coverall Rental Serv., Inc., 205 N.L.R.B. 880 (1973) (employer referred to employee interviews with employment relations consultant, hired before election, and agreed to "share" consultant's forthcoming recommendations with employees and asked for opportunity to "work together" for "job security" and for "good helpful supervisors and direct communication").

Additional complications arise because employer statements about employment conditions often appear to be at least implied promises of specific improvements. A finding of such a promise raises other problems: Was it made for the purpose of encouraging employees to reject the union? Should the finding of such a purpose always be necessary for a violation, or should a violation turn on the impact on employee free choice rather than the employer's motive? Pertinent problems are illustrated by situations involving preelection discussions in which employees may advise employers of complaints about specific conditions (for example, wages) or about a general lack of effective communication procedures. If the company elects to discuss such complaints fully, what is it permitted to say about meritorious ones that invite remedial action? Must the company state that the law requires "no promises" regarding employee complaints? Indeed, would such a statement be lawful? And even though the company merely listens more attentively to such complaints, would such a preelection improvement of communications be a proscribed "benefit"? See generally Uarco, Inc., 216 N.L.R.B. 1 (1974); Jackson & Heller, Promises and Grants of Benefits Under the NLRA, 131 U. Pa. L. Rev. 1 (1982).

7. A union begins an organizing campaign but does not file a petition for an election. Is the employer who knows about the campaign barred from promising or granting benefits exceeding past practices? If so, for how long? See Alumbaugh Coal Corp., 247 N.L.R.B. 895 (1980), enforced as modified, 635 F.2d 1380 (8th Cir. 1980); California Pellet Mill Co., 219 N.L.R.B. 435 (1975).

NLRB v. Savair Mfg. Co.
414 U.S. 270 (1973)

DOUGLAS, J. . . . Respondent filed objections to the election [won by the union, 22 to 20] but . . . a hearing officer found against respondent and the Board certified the Union as the representative of the employees in that unit. Respondent, however, refused to bargain. . . . The Court of Appeals denied enforcement of the [Board's bargaining order]. 470 F.2d 305. . . . We affirm.

It appeared that prior to the election, "recognition slips" were circulated among employees. An employee who signed the slip before the election[4] became a member of the Union and would not have to pay what at times was called an "initiation fee" and at times a "fine." If the Union was voted in, those who had not signed a recognition slip would have to pay.

The actual solicitation of signatures on the "recognition slips" was not done by Union officials. Union officials, however, explained to employees at meetings that those who signed the slips would not be required to pay an initiation fee, while those who did not would have to pay. Those officials also picked out some five employees to do the soliciting and authorized them to explain the Union's initiation-fee policy. Those solicited were told that there would be no initiation fee charged those who signed the slip before the election. Under the bylaws of the Union, an initiation fee apparently was not to be higher than $10; but the employees who testified at the hearing (1) did not know how large the fee would be and (2) said that their understanding was that the fee was a "fine" or an "assessment."

One employee, Donald Bridgeman, testified that he signed the slip to avoid paying the "fine" if the Union won. He got the message directly from an employee picked by the Union to solicit signatures on the "slips." So did Thomas Rice, another employee.

The Board originally took the position that preelection solicitation of memberships by a union with a promise to waive the initiation fee of the union was not consistent with a fair and free choice of bargaining representatives. Lobue Bros., 109 N.L.R.B. 1182. Later in DIT-MCO, Inc., 163 N.L.R.B. 1019, the Board explained its changed position as follows:

> We shall assume, *arguendo*, that employees who sign cards when offered a waiver of initiation fees do so solely because no cost is thus involved; that they in fact do not at that point really want the union to be their bargaining representative. The error of the *Lobue* premise can be readily seen upon a review of the consequences of such employees casting votes for or against union representation. Initially, it is obvious that employees who have received or been promised free memberships will not be required to pay an initiation fee, *whatever the outcome of the vote*. If the union wins the election, there is by

[4]The question for review presented by the Board is whether the "Board properly concluded that a union's offer to waive initiation fees for all employees who sign union authorization cards *before a Board representation election*, if the union wins the election, does not tend to interfere with employee free choice in the election." (Emphasis added.) . . .

postulate no obligation; and if the union loses, *there is still no obligation*, because compulsion to pay an initiation fee arises under the Act only when a union becomes the employees' representative and negotiates a valid union-security agreement. Thus, whatever kindly feeling toward the union may be generated by the cost-reduction offer, when consideration is given only to the question of initiation fees, it is completely illogical to characterize as improper inducement or coercion to vote "Yes" a waiver of something that can be avoided simply by voting "No."

The illogic of *Lobue* does not become any more logical when other consequences of a vote for representation are considered. Thus, employees know that if a majority vote for the union, it will be their exclusive representative, and, provided a valid union-security provision is negotiated, they will be obliged to pay dues as a condition of employment. Thus, viewed solely as a financial matter, a "no" vote will help to avoid any subsequent obligations, a "yes" may well help to incur such obligations. In these circumstances, an employee who did not want the union to represent him would hardly be likely to vote for the union just because there would be no initial cost involved in obtaining membership. Since an election resulting in the union's defeat would entail not only no initial cost, but also insure that no dues would have to be paid as a condition of employment, the financial inducement, if a factor at all, would be in the direction of a vote against the union, rather than for it.

Id., at 1021-1022.

. . . [T]he Board's analysis ignores the realities of the situation. Whatever his true intentions, an employee who signs a recognition slip prior to an election is indicating to other workers that he supports the union. His outward manifestation of support must often serve as a useful campaign tool in the union's hands to convince other employees to vote for the union, if only because many employees respect their coworkers' views on the unionization issue. By permitting the union to offer to waive an initiation fee for those employees signing a recognition slip prior to the election, the Board allows the union to buy endorsements and paint a false portrait of employee support during its election campaign.

That influence may well have been felt here for, as noted, there were 28 who signed up with the Union before the election petition was filed with the Board and either seven or eight more who signed up before the election. We do not believe that the statutory policy of fair elections . . . permits endorsements, whether for or against the union, to be bought and sold in this fashion.

In addition, while it is correct that the employee who signs a recognition slip is not legally bound to vote for the union and has not promised to do so in any formal sense, certainly there may be some employees who would feel obliged to carry through on their stated intention to support the union. And on the facts of this case, the change of just one vote would have resulted in a 21 to 21 election rather than a 22 to 20 election.

Any procedure requiring a "fair" election must honor the right of those who oppose a union as well as those who favor it. The Act is wholly neutral when it comes to that basic choice. By §7 of the Act employees have the right not only to "form, join, or assist" unions but also the right "to refrain from any or all of such activities." . . . There is no explicit provision which makes "interference" by a union with the right of an employee to "refrain" from union activities an unfair labor practice.

Section 8(c), however, provides: "The expressing of any views, argument, or opinion, or the dissemination thereof, whether in written, printed, graphic, or visual form, shall not constitute or be evidence of an unfair labor practice under any of the provisions of this subchapter, *if such expression contains no threat of reprisal or force or promise of benefit.*" . . . (emphasis added).

Whether it would be an "unfair" labor practice for a union to promise a special benefit to those who sign up for a union seems not to have been squarely resolved.[6] The right of free choice is, however, inherent in the principles reflected in §9(c)(1)(A). . . .

The latent potential of [the] alternative use of authorization cards [as a basis for a bargaining order] cautions us to treat the solicitation of authorization cards in exchange for consideration of fringe benefits granted by the union as a separate step protected by the same kind of moral standard that governs elections themselves.

The Board in its supervision of union elections may not sanction procedures that cast their weight for the choice of a union and against a nonunion shop or for a nonunion shop and against a union.

In the *Exchange Parts* case we said that, although the benefits granted by the employer were permanent and unconditional, employees were "not likely to miss the inference that the source of benefits now conferred is also the source from which future benefits must flow and which may dry up if it is not obliged." 375 U.S., at 409. If we respect, as we must, the statutory right of employees to resist efforts to unionize a plant, we cannot assume that unions exercising powers are wholly benign towards their antagonists whether they

_____

[6] . . . The NLRB itself has recognized in other contexts that promising or conferring benefits may unduly influence representation elections. See e.g., Wagner Electric Corp., 167 N.L.R.B. 532, 533 (grant of life insurance policy to those who signed with union before representation election "subjects the donees to a constraint to vote for the donor union"); General Cable Corp., 170 N.L.R.B. 1682 ($5 gift to employees by union before election, even when not conditioned on outcome of election, was inducement to cast ballots favorable to union); Teletype Corp., 122 N.L.R.B. 1594 (payment of money by rival unions to those attending preelection meetings).

be nonunion protagonists or the employer. The failure to sign a recognition slip may well seem ominous to nonunionists who fear that if they do not sign they will face a wrathful union regime, should the union win. That influence may well have had a decisive impact in this case where a change of one vote would have changed the result.

Affirmed.

WHITE, J., with whom BRENNAN and BLACKMUN, JJ., join, dissenting. . . .

I

It is well established that an "unconditional" offer to waive initiation fees, where the waiver offer is left open for some period of time after the election, is not coercive and does not constitute an unfair labor practice. . . . [The] initiation fee is created by the union and represents a self-imposed barrier to entry. There is no evidence that the fee was normally imposed for the sole purpose of removing it during a labor campaign. A different case might be put if the union purported to remove a nonexistent fee or artificially inflated the fee so as to misrepresent the benefit tendered by its removal. . . . Similarly, it is established that the union can promise employees to obtain wage increases or other benefits if it is elected as a bargaining representative. . . .

It must be obvious that these waivers of fees are a form of economic inducement, as the opinion for the Court employs that term. Undoubtedly an offer to reduce the cost of joining the union makes the union a more attractive possibility and may influence an employee to vote for the union, though one would assume, in view of the other costs and benefits at stake, that this consideration will be marginal. Similarly, if the union represents to the employees that it will attempt to secure higher wages, an employee's calculations of costs and benefits will be altered, but in that instance the union is merely stating the obvious; indeed, the promise of higher wages is the primary rationale of the existence of the union. In any event, these forms of inducement are valid.

In the instant case, an offer which by its terms expires with the conclusion of the election is also a form of economic inducement. But insofar as the offer might affect the calculation of costs and benefits of joining the union, its effect is the same as an offer which does not expire until some time after the election. The inability to distinguish between these two situations, at least where small fees are involved and where the sole source of concern is pure financial inducement, led the Board to conclude in *DIT-MCO* that "an employee who did not want the union to represent him would hardly be likely to vote for the union just because there would be no initial cost involved in obtaining membership." 163 N.L.R.B., at 1022.

The majority places heavy reliance on the supposed analogy between the waiver of fees in this case and an actual increase in benefits made by an employer during the course of an election campaign. NLRB v. Exchange Parts Co., 375 U.S. 405 (1964). . . . A number of important differences exist between that case and the instant one. First, the employer actually gave his employees substantial increased benefits, whereas here the benefit is only contingent and small; the union glove is not very velvet. Secondly, in the union context, the fist is missing. When the employer increased benefits, the threat was made "that the source of benefits now conferred is also the source from which future benefits must flow and which may dry up if it is not obliged." Ibid. The Union, on the other hand, since it was not the representative of the employees, and would not be if it were unsuccessful in the election, could not make the same threat by offering a benefit which it would take away if it *lost* the election. A union can only make its own victory more desirable in the minds of the employees.[4]

II

If pure economic inducement in the form of lowering anticipated costs of joining the union is not to be considered coercive, one must focus on the special dangers, if any, presented by the conditional offer, an analysis not undertaken by the majority. It has been proposed that the conditional offer is specially to be proscribed because of the interjection of a new consideration into the voting choice of an employee: how probable it is that the union will win or lose the election. NLRB v. Gafner Automotive & Machine, Inc., 400 F.2d, at 13 (Phillips, J., concurring); Amalgamated Clothing Workers v. NLRB, 345 F.2d, at 268 (Friendly, J., concurring). The argument might be that an employee who estimates that the costs of joining the union exceed the benefits, even taking into account the reduced initiation fees available by signing a card, will still sign the card, as a hedge, because of his prediction that the union will win the election.[5] A statement of the theory carries with it its

---

[4] The Court cannot ignore the fact, as well, that §1 of the [NLRA] declared the congressional policy of "encouraging the practice and procedure of collective bargaining." . . . This preference is only one of opportunity and the free choice of the employee must be protected, but restrictions on the communications of the union as to potential benefits may unduly prevent the intelligent exercise of such choice. The employer may garner loyalty through his actions and record of past performance for his own employees; the union can only sell employees the future.

[5] This possibility of hedging is to some extent borne out by the record. Although the Court cannot know what the correlation was between signed cards and votes for the Union,

own disproof. The special inducement is to sign the card, not to vote for the union. The majority decision collapses these two choices into one, and is thus untenable. The majority assumes, contrary to fact, that the employee has joined the Union by signing the authorization card. This is only true, however, if the Union wins the election and signs a collective contract, and the employee can still seek to prevent that outcome by casting his vote against the Union in a secret ballot. The testimony was clear that if the Union loses the election, the employee who signs the card incurs no obligation to the Union. The expressed preference in the . . . Act for secret ballot elections assumes that voters may act differently in private than in public, and ordinarily guarantees to employees the ability to make a secret choice. It is, therefore, important to highlight the fact that the Board in *DIT-MCO* assumed, *arguendo,* "that employees who sign cards when offered a waiver of initiation fees do so solely because no cost is thus involved; that they in fact do not at that point really want the union to be their bargaining representative." 163 N.L.R.B., at 1021.

There is no need to consider here, as does the majority, whether the Union could achieve recognition on the basis of authorization cards secured, in part, by an offer of fee waiver. Of course, a card majority cannot serve as a basis for §8(a)(5) bargaining order under NLRB v. Gissel Packing Co., 395 U.S. 575, 614-616 (1969), unless the employer has committed serious unfair labor practices. It may be that even given a serious unfair labor practice on the part of the employer, these cards could not serve as a basis for recognition. In this case, however, the Board's bargaining order was based on the vote of a secret ballot election, and the Court must supply the connective between the decision to sign a card and the decision to vote for the Union. This connective can only be supplied by some rather speculative counter-rational psychological assumptions, i.e., that a person who signs the card *will* vote for the union.[7] The Board assumes that such is not the case, and I am not prepared to

---

we do know that not everyone who signed cards voted for the Union. Twenty-eight persons plus signed cards . . . and only 22 voted for the Union. Moreover, there is testimony that some employees discussed the hedge. "Of course some of us fellows did say to other fellows that were really against it [the Union] and *have always been against it* you better sign your ticket and turn it in because if you didn't if it does get voted in, if the majority of the men vote the union in, at least you have to pay your dues which is very natural but you wouldn't have to pay no initiation fee." . . . (Emphasis added.)

[7] It is certainly arguable that such a connection can be made when the union pays a person cash to vote for or assist the union. The benefit of the union has been tendered and the employee may well feel he has incurred a moral obligation to vote for the union. See, e.g., Wagner Electric Corp., 167 N.L.R.B. 532, 533 (1967) (grant of life insurance policy to those who signed with union before representation election "subjects the donees to a constraint to vote for the donor union"). See also Collins & Aikman Corp. v. NLRB, 383 F.2d 722

upset the Board's judgment on this matter.[8] The majority opinion stresses the fact that the margin of Union victory was only two votes, and thus suggests that the "psychological connective" may explain the outcome indicating that it *"may well have* had a decisive impact" (emphasis added). But there is no evidence to this effect, and definitions of unfair practices which become a function of the outcome of an election are subject to severe problems of administration. The Board, in my judgment, is entitled to regulate elections on standard theories of coercion.

III

Since the case for coercion arising out of the conditional offer is speculative, and since the alteration of the calculus of costs and benefits is marginal where a small fee is involved, the issue here resolves into the proper allocation of institutional responsibility between an administrative agency and a reviewing court. The Board, upon reflection and study, has concluded that the conditional offer is not coercive within the meaning of §7. This represented a basic change in policy. . . . Such revisions are especially likely in the regulation of labor elections, due to the substantial problems in deciding what is likely to interfere with employee free choice. . . .

[O]ne cannot ask the agency to do the impossible. When choosing between alternative contentions of coercion, the agency must make judgments based on available knowledge. . . . Recognition of this discretion has been a recurrent theme in this Court's review of Board decisions. . . . There is certainly a conflicting interest between the union's right to make itself attractive to employees without misrepresentation and the employee's unfettered choice to vote for or against the union. I think it is rational for the Board to conclude on the basis of the facts presented that the decision of the Union to waive small fees was not coercive within the meaning of §7. . . .

(CA4th 1967) (payment of $7 to employee to be observer at election); NLRB v. Commercial Letter, Inc., 455 F.2d 109 (CA8th 1972) (excessive payments to union members to attend meetings). In *Wagner*, supra, the Board distinguished the initiation fee decision in DIT-MCO, Inc., 163 N.L.R.B. 1019 (1967), on the ground that there was no immediate improvement in an employee's economic situation when fees are waived.

[8] The majority in its conclusion seems to articulate still another theory of coercion: "The failure to sign a recognition slip may well seem ominous to nonunionists who fear that if they do not sign they will face a wrathful union regime, should the union win." This theory, of course, assumes a card signer will vote for the union. Moreover, this problem is fundamental in labor elections, at the outset, when cards are collected for the purpose of holding an election pursuant to the necessary showing of support, and, at the conclusion, if the union wins, when those who oppose the union must still decide to join the union or face the union's wrath. One could easily argue that at least an equal deterrent to signing the card is the wrathful employer if the union *loses* the election.

B. ACCOMMODATION OF ORGANIZATIONAL INTERESTS AND PROPERTY RIGHTS

The preceding section dealt with employer measures designed or operating to make the case against unionization. This section is concerned with employer restrictions on the use of company premises or "property" by proponents of unionization. Plainly, such restrictions and, indeed, a broad range of employer policies, "interfere" with the "rights" affirmed by §7. But a literal application of §8(1), leading to the outlawing of all employer policies that do in fact constitute "interference," would completely subordinate the employer's (and the community's and the employees') interest in efficiency and security to organizational interests. The Board, rejecting such literalism, has sought to reconcile competing interests.

That process involves at least three inquiries of ascending difficulty: first, pinpointing as precisely as possible the conflicting interests; second, determining their legitimacy under the statute; and third, determining which legitimate interest should be paramount or what balance should be struck. This section will illustrate the familiar difficulties in balancing interests by adjudication under a statute that necessarily embodied only the most general and elastic guideposts.

For discussions of the problems involved, see (in addition to the references supra p. 82) Fanning, Union Solicitation and Distribution of Literature on the Job — Balancing the Rights of Employers and Employees, 9 Ga. L. Rev. 367 (1975); Gould, The Question of Union Activity on Company Property, 18 Vand. L. Rev. 73 (1964).

Republic Aviation Corp. v. NLRB
324 U.S. 793 (1945)

REED, J. In the *Republic Aviation Corporation* case, the employer, a large and rapidly growing military aircraft manufacturer, adopted, well before any union activity at the plant, a general rule against soliciting which read as follows: "Soliciting of any type cannot be permitted in the factory or offices." . . . The Republic plant was located in a built-up section of Suffolk County, New York. An employee persisted after being warned of the rule in soliciting union membership in the plant by passing out application cards to employees on his own time during lunch periods. The employee was discharged for infraction of the rule and, as the [NLRB] found, without discrimination on the part of the employer toward union activity.

Three other employees were discharged for wearing UAW-CIO union steward buttons in the plant after being requested to remove the insignia. The union was at that time active in seeking to organize the plant. The reason which the employer gave for the request was that, as the union was not then the duly designated representative of the employees, the wearing of the steward buttons in the plant indicated an acknowledgment by the management of the authority of the stewards to represent the employees in dealing with the management and might impinge upon the employer's policy of strict neutrality in union matters and might interfere with the existing grievance system of the corporation.

The Board was of the view that wearing union steward buttons by employees did not carry any implication of recognition of that union by the employer where, as here, there was no competing labor organization in the plant. The discharges of the stewards, however, were found not to be motivated by opposition to the particular union or, we deduce, to unionism.

The Board determined that the promulgation and enforcement of the "no solicitation" rule violated §8(1) of the [NLRA] as it interfered with, restrained and coerced employees in their rights under §7 and discriminated against the discharged employee under §8(3). It determined also that the discharge of the stewards violated §§8(1) and 8(3). As a consequence of its conclusions as to the solicitation and the wearing of the insignia, the Board entered the usual cease and desist order and directed the reinstatement of the discharged employees with back pay and also the rescission of "the rule against solicitation in so far as it prohibits union activity and solicitation on company property during the employees' own time." 51 N.L.R.B. 1186, 1189. The Circuit Court of Appeals for the Second Circuit affirmed, 142 F.2d 193. . . .

In the case of *Le Tourneau Company of Georgia,* two employees were suspended two days each for distributing union literature or circulars on the employees' own time on company owned and policed parking lots, adjacent to the company's fenced-in plant, in violation of a long standing and strictly enforced rule, adopted prior to union organization activity about the premises, which read as follows: "In the future no Merchants, Concern, Company, or Individual or Individuals will be permitted to distribute, post, or otherwise circulate handbills or posters, or any literature of any description, on Company property without first securing permission from the Personnel Department." . . . The rule was adopted to control littering and petty pilfering from parked autos by distributors. The Board determined that there was no union bias or discrimination by the company in enforcing the rule.

The company's plant for the manufacture of earth-moving machinery and other products for the war is in the country on a six thousand acre tract. The plant is bisected by one public road and built along another. There is one hundred feet of company-owned land for parking or other use between the highways, and the employee entrances to the fenced enclosures where the work is done, so that contact on public ways or on noncompany property with employees at or about the establishment is limited to those employees, less than 800 out of 2100, who are likely to walk across the public highway near the plant on their way to work, or to those employees who will stop their private automobiles, buses or other conveyances on the public roads for communications. The employees' dwellings are widely scattered.

The Board found that the application of the rule to the distribution of union literature by the employees on company property which resulted in the layoffs was an unfair labor practice under §§8(1) and 8(3). Cease and desist, and rule rescission orders, with directions to pay the employees for their lost time, followed. 54 N.L.R.B. 1253. The Circuit Court of Appeals for the Fifth Circuit reversed the Board, 143 F.2d 67, and we granted certiorari because of conflict with the *Republic* case. 323 U.S. 698.

These cases bring here for review the action of the . . . Board in working out an adjustment between the undisputed right of self-organization assured to employees under the Wagner Act and the equally undisputed right of employers to maintain discipline in their establishments. Like so many others, these rights are not unlimited in the sense that they can be exercised without regard to any duty which the existence of rights in others may place upon employer or employee. Opportunity to organize and proper discipline are both essential elements in a balanced society.

The Wagner Act did not undertake the impossible task of specifying in precise and unmistakable language each incident which would constitute an unfair labor practice. On the contrary, that Act left to the Board the work of applying the Act's general prohibitory language in the light of the infinite combinations of events which might be charged as violative of its terms. Thus a "rigid scheme of remedies" is avoided and administrative flexibility within appropriate statutory limitations obtained to accomplish the dominant purpose of the legislation. Phelps Dodge Corp. v. Labor Board, 313 U.S. 177, 194. So far as we are here concerned, that purpose is the right of employees to organize for mutual aid without employer interference. This is the principle of labor relations which the Board is to foster.

The gravamen of the objection of both Republic and Le Tourneau to the Board's orders is that they rest on a policy formulated without due administrative procedure. To be more specific it is that the Board cannot substitute its knowledge of industrial relations for substantive evidence. The contention is that there must be evidence before the Board to show that the rules and orders of the employers interfered with and discouraged union organization in the circumstances and situation of each company. Neither in the *Republic* nor the *Le Tourneau* cases can it properly be said that there was evidence or a finding that the plant's physical location made solicitation away from company property ineffective to reach prospective union members. Neither of these is like a mining or lumber camp where the employees pass their rest as well as their work time on the employer's premises, so that union organization must proceed upon the employer's premises or be seriously handicapped.

. . . [The] statutory plan for an adversary proceeding requires that the Board's orders on complaints of unfair labor practices be based upon evidence which is placed before the Board by witnesses who are subject to cross-examination by opposing parties. Such procedure strengthens assurance of fairness by requiring findings on known evidence. [Cases cited.] Such a requirement does not go beyond the necessity for the production of evidential facts, however, and compel evidence as to the result which may flow from such facts. An administrative agency with power after hearings to determine on the evidence in adversary proceedings whether violations of statutory commands have occurred may infer within the limits of the inquiry from the proven facts such conclusions as reasonably may be based upon the facts proven. One of the purposes which lead to the creation of such boards is to have decisions based upon evidential facts under the particular statute made by experienced officials with an adequate appreciation of the complexities of the subject which is entrusted to their administration. . . .

In the *Republic* . . . case the evidence showed that the petitioner was in early 1943 a nonurban manufacturing establishment for military production which employed thousands. It was growing rapidly. Trains and automobiles gathered daily many employees for the plant from an area on Long Island, certainly larger than walking distance. The rule against solicitation was introduced in evidence and the circumstances of its violation by the dismissed employee after warning was [sic] detailed.

As to the employees who were discharged for wearing the buttons of a union steward, the evidence showed in addition the discussion in regard to their right to wear the insignia when the union had not been recognized by the petitioner as the representative of the employees. Petitioner looked upon a steward as a union representative for the adjustment of grievances with the management after employer recognition of the stewards' union. Until such recognition petitioner felt it would violate its neutrality in labor organization if it permitted the display of a steward button by an employee. From its point of view, such display represented to other employees that the union already was recognized.

No evidence was offered that any unusual conditions existed in labor relations, the plant location or otherwise to support any contention that conditions at this plant differed from those occurring normally at any other large establishment.

The *Le Tourneau . . .* case also is barren of special circumstances. The evidence which was introduced tends to prove the simple facts heretofore set out as to the circumstances surrounding the discharge of the two employees for distributing union circulars.

These were the facts upon which the Board reached its conclusions as to unfair labor practices. The Intermediate Report in the *Republic Aviation* case, 51 N.L.R.B. at 1195, sets out the reason why the rule against solicitation was considered inimical to the right of organization.[6] This was approved by the Board. The Board's reasons for concluding that the petitioner's insistence that its employees refrain from wearing steward buttons appear at page 1187 of the report.[7] In the *Le Tourneau Company* case the discussion of the reasons underlying the findings was much more extended. 54 N.L.R.B. 1253, 1258, et seq. We insert in the note below a quotation which shows the character of the Board's opinion.[8] Furthermore, in both opinions of the

---

[6] 51 N.L.R.B. 1195: "Thus, under the conditions obtaining in January 1943, the respondent's employees, working long hours in a plant engaged entirely in war production and expanding with extreme rapidity, were entirely deprived of their normal right to 'full freedom of association' in the plant on their own time, the very time and place uniquely appropriate and almost solely available to them therefor. The respondent's rule is therefore in clear derogation of the rights of its employees guaranteed by the Act."

[7] We quote an illustrative portion. 51 N.L.R.B. 1187-1188: "We do not believe that the wearing of a steward button is a representation that the employer either approves or recognizes the union in question as the representative of the employees, especially when, as here, there is no competing labor organization in the plant. Furthermore, there is no evidence in the record herein that the respondent's employees so understood the steward buttons or that the appearance of union stewards in the plant affected the normal operation of the respondent's grievance procedure. On the other hand, the right of employees to wear union insignia at work has long been recognized as a reasonable and legitimate form of union activity, and the respondent's curtailment of that right is clearly violative of the Act."

[8] 54 N.L.R.B. at 1259-1260: "As the Circuit Court of Appeals for the Second Circuit has held, 'It is not every interference with property rights that is within the Fifth Amendment . . . Inconvenience, or even some dislocation of property rights, may be necessary in order to safeguard the right to collective bargaining.' The Board has frequently applied this principle in decisions involving varying sets of circumstances, where it has held that the employer's right to control his property does not permit him to deny access to his property to persons whose presence is necessary there to enable the employees effectively to exercise their right to self-organization and collective bargaining, and in those decisions which have reached the courts, the Board's position has been sustained. Similarly, the Board has held that, while it was 'within the province of an employer to promulgate and enforce a rule prohibiting union

Board full citation of authorities was given, including the Matter of Peyton Packing Co., 49 N.L.R.B. 828, 50 N.L.R.B. 355, hereinafter referred to.

The Board has fairly, we think, explicated . . . the theory which moved it to its conclusions in these cases. The excerpts from its opinions just quoted show this. The reasons why it has decided as it has are sufficiently set forth. We cannot agree, as Republic urges, that in these present cases reviewing courts are left to "sheer acceptance" of the Board's conclusions or that its formulation of policy is "cryptic." . . .

Not only has the Board in these cases sufficiently expressed the theory upon which it concludes that rules against solicitation or prohibitions against the wearing of insignia must fall as interferences with union organization, but, in so far as rules against solicitation are concerned, it had theretofore succinctly expressed the requirements of proof which it considered appropriate to outweigh or overcome the presumption as to rules against solicitation. In the Peyton Packing Company case, 49 N.L.R.B. 828, at 843, hereinbefore referred to, the presumption adopted by the Board is set forth.[10] . . .

In the *Republic Aviation* case, petitioner urges that irrespective of the validity of the rule against solicitation, its application in this instance did not violate §8(3) . . . because the rule was not discriminatorily applied against union solicitation but was impartially enforced against all solicitors. It seems clear, however, that if a rule against solicitation is invalid as to union solicitation on the employer's premises during the employee's own time, a discharge because of violation of that rule discriminates within the meaning of §8(3) in that it discourages membership in a labor organization.

Republic Aviation Corporation v. National Labor Relations Board is affirmed.

---

solicitation during working hours,' it was 'not within the province of an employer to promulgate and enforce a rule prohibiting union solicitation by an employee outside of working hours, although on company property,' the latter restriction being deemed an unreasonable impediment to the exercise of the right to self-organization."

[10] 49 N.L.R.B. at 843-844: "The Act, of course, does not prevent an employer from making and enforcing reasonable rules covering the conduct of employees on company time. Working time is for work. It is therefore within the province of an employer to promulgate and enforce a rule prohibiting union solicitation during working hours. Such a rule must be presumed to be valid in the absence of evidence that it was adopted for a discriminatory purpose. It is no less true that time outside working hours, whether before or after work, or during luncheon or rest periods, is an employee's time to use as he wishes without unreasonable restraint, although the employee is on company property. It is therefore not within the province of an employer to promulgate and enforce a rule prohibiting union solicitation by an employee outside of working hours, although on company property. Such a rule must be presumed to be an unreasonable impediment to self-organization and therefore discriminatory in the absence of evidence that special circumstances make the rule necessary in order to maintain production or discipline."

National Labor Relations Board v. Le Tourneau Company of Georgia is reversed.

Roberts, J., dissents in each case.

NOTES

1. In a decision reversing the NLRB, an employer was held entitled to prohibit employees, during an organizational campaign, from wearing buttons during working time reading: "Don't Be a Scab. Join the Union." Caterpillar Tractor Co. v. NLRB, 230 F.2d 357 (7th Cir. 1956). (For a well-known definition of "scab," see Branch 496, Letter Carriers v. Austin, infra p. 743.) Is *Caterpillar Tractor* compatible with the principle, recognized in *Republic Aviation*, that the wearing of a union button at work is presumptively protected by the Act?

The Board's view is that customer contact is not, in and of itself, a "special circumstance" justifying a total ban on wearing union buttons. Assume that two waitresses are engaged in organizing the employees of a posh and expensive restaurant; the manager prohibits their wearing of four-inch buttons which state: "Help us organize this sweat shop." Has the Act been violated? See NLRB v. Rooney, 677 F.2d 44 (9th Cir. 1982). What if the same button had been worn by employees required to wear identical uniforms and assigned to the drive-through window at McDonald's? See Burger King Corp., 265 N.L.R.B. 1507 (1982), *enforcement denied*, 725 F.2d 1053 (6th Cir. 1984). Should it make a difference in either of these cases if the four-inch button had simply stated: "Win with the Union"? See Virginia Elec. & Power Co., 703 F.2d 79 (4th Cir. 1983).

2. To be presumptively valid, a rule restricting organizational activity must state with reasonable clarity that it does not apply during periods when employees are not scheduled for work — e.g., lunch and break periods. Overruling T.R.W., Inc., 257 N.L.R.B. 442 (1981), which had rejected an earlier NLRB distinction between "working time" and "working hours," the Board has returned to the view that restrictions on "working time" are presumptively valid because this phrase is commonly understood to cover only periods of actual work, whereas rules applying to "working hours" are presumptively invalid for failing to exclude from coverage employees' own time on company premises. The presumption activated by a "working hours" rule may, of course, be rebutted by evidence of practices or oral communications allowing solicitation during employees' free time. See Our Way, Inc., 268 N.L.R.B. No. 61, 115 L.R.R.M. 1009 (1983). In determining whether a no-solicitation rule is overly broad (and thus an unfair labor

practice), the Board takes the view that ambiguous language is to be resolved against the employer. J.C. Penney Co., 266 N.L.R.B. No. 210, 113 L.R.R.M. 1117 (1983). Should employees subject to a work rule have any obligation to seek clarification of ambiguities? See NLRB v. Village IX, Inc., 723 F.2d 1360 (7th Cir. 1983).

3. The Board has distinguished between oral solicitation and distribution of literature by employees and has recognized the presumptive validity of plant rules restricting such "distribution" to *nonworking areas* of the plant regardless of whether such distribution occurs during nonworking time. For the purpose of this distinction, the handing out of union solicitation cards, as distinguished from handbilling, is deemed a form of solicitation. See Stoddard-Quirk Mfg. Co., 138 N.L.R.B. 615 (1962) (two members dissenting). If, as the *Stoddard-Quirk* majority emphasized, distributing is different because it involves a littering problem, should that problem be met, as the dissent urged, by prohibiting littering rather than distribution?

4. Broader restrictions on solicitation and distribution are presumptively valid in special circumstances. Thus, the unusual risks to goodwill posed by organizational campaigns in department stores have led to the validating of rules banning employee-solicitation, even during nonworking time, on selling floors and other areas frequented by the public. See G.C. Murphy Co., 171 N.L.R.B. 370 (1968), *enforced*, 422 F.2d 685 (D.C. Cir. 1969); May Dept. Stores Co., 59 N.L.R.B. 976 (1944), *enforced*, 154 F.2d 533 (8th Cir.), *cert. denied*, 329 U.S. 725 (1946). (This presumption apparently is applicable to all retailers.) Similarly, distribution of union literature may be completely banned in all retail customer areas even when customers are absent. See Bankers Club, Inc., 218 N.L.R.B. 11 (1975).

5. In the hospital context, the Board has departed somewhat from the department store precedents. While permitting a total ban of solicitation (even during nonworking time) in strictly patient-care areas, such as patients' rooms and diagnostic areas, the Board has characterized as presumptively invalid a similar ban in "visitor-access" or "patient-access" areas — e.g., cafeterias or lounges. St. John's Hospital, 222 N.L.R.B. 1150 (1976), *enforcement granted in part and denied in part*, 557 F.2d 1368 (10th Cir. 1977). The Board's position was approved by the Supreme Court in Beth Israel Hospital v. NLRB, 437 U.S. 483 (1978), where the hospital had enforced a rule prohibiting union solicitation and distribution by employees in its cafeteria, restricting such activities to locations next to employees' lockers and rest rooms. Only about 600 of the 2,200 regular employees were accessible to solicitation in the scattered locker areas. A union survey had shown that of the cafeteria's patrons, 77 percent were employees while 9 percent were visitors and 1.5 percent patients.

For discussion of presumptions appropriate for various public areas of hospitals, see NLRB v. Baptist Hospital, Inc., 442 U.S. 773 (1979); Comment, Union Solicitation in the Health Care Industry: Guidelines for the Labor Law Practitioner, 15 St. Mary's L.J. 123 (1983).

6. Disparate treatment of pro-union activity in the content or application of rules against solicitation or distribution normally constitutes an unfair labor practice. Some employer favoritism toward charitable solicitation has, however, been tolerated on the ground that a few beneficent acts do not constitute "discriminatory" enforcement. See, e.g., Emerson Elec. Co., 187 N.L.R.B. 294 (1970). See also Hammary Mfg. Corp., Div. of U.S. Industries, 265 N.L.R.B. 57 (1982) (rule containing single exception for United Way campaign held not per se unlawful, Member Jenkins objecting, in dissent, that statutorily protected solicitation had been banned under the disputed rule while charitable solicitation on a comparable scale had been permitted). Where, however, incidents of charitable or beneficent solicitation cannot be dismissed as "isolated," enforcement of a rule against union-solicitation may constitute unlawful discrimination. See Serv-Air, Inc., 175 N.L.R.B. 801 (1969) (on remand from Serv-Air, Inc. v. NLRB, 395 F.2d 557 (10th Cir. 1968), cert. denied, 395 U.S. 840 (1968)). Does this position lend force to Jenkins' Hammary dissent? Should an employer be faulted for "discriminatory" application where a facially-valid rule is prompted by an organizational campaign and is enforced initially against union solicitation? See State Chemical Co., 166 N.L.R.B. 455 (1967), enforced (silentio), 404 F.2d 1382 (6th Cir. 1968); NLRB v. Roney Plaza Apts., 597 F.2d 1046 (5th Cir. 1979).

NLRB v. Magnavox Co., 415 U.S. 322 (1974). An incumbent union had for many years acquiesced in a company rule banning employee distribution of literature on all company property, including nonworking areas. The collective bargaining agreements between the parties had, however, entitled the union to post notices on company bulletin boards. The NLRB, concluding that a bargaining representative may not waive employees' rights to distribute organizational literature on company property, whether the literature supports or opposes the incumbent union, held that the company's rejection of the union's request for a change in the no-distribution rule violated §8(a)(1). The Board emphasized that its concern was "solely with the exercise by *employees* of their §7 rights," and that its decision did not license the distribution of "institutional" — as distinguished from purely "organizational" — literature of the acquiescent union. 195 N.L.R.B. 265, 266 n.9 (1972). Reversing the Sixth Circuit, which had recognized a union's broad authority contractually to waive employees' on-premises distribution rights, the Supreme Court held that the no-distribution rule was invalid whether applied to supporters or opponents of the incumbent union and that an employer is not protected against an unfair labor practice by a union's acquiescence in an excessively broad rule. The Court did not mention the NLRB's distinction between different types of literature.

NOTES

1. Is there a satisfactory basis for distinguishing between the validity of an incumbent union's waiver of the right (a) to distribute literature and (b) to strike to enforce the terms of a collective agreement? See Note, 56 Iowa L. Rev. 152 (1970). Should the approach in *Magnavox* operate presumptively to invalidate contractual prohibitions against any distribution on company property of communications regarding internal union affairs, such as elections of union officers or dues increases? See, e.g., General Motors Corp. v. NLRB, 512 F.2d 447 (6th Cir. 1975).

2. A two-year collective bargaining agreement between an employer and an NLRB-certified union contains the following clause: "During the term of this Agreement, no union other than the employees' certified representative shall be granted access to the Employer's premises or bulletin boards; provided, however, that the certified representative's exclusive right of access shall not affect the statutory rights of employees to make distributions or solicitations on the Employer's premises." Does *Magnavox* answer the question whether this provision violates the NLRA? Cf. Perry Educ. Assn. v. Perry Local Educators' Assn., 103 S.Ct. 948 (1983), where the Court, holding that the First Amendment was not violated by a bargaining agreement's grant to a recognized public-sector union of an exclusive right of access to teachers' mailboxes and interschool mail systems, noted (at 958 n.11) that exclusive access provisions for private-sector bargaining representatives "have yet to be expressly approved."

NLRB v. Babcock & Wilcox Co.
351 U.S. 105 (1956)

REED, J. In each of these cases the employer refused to permit distribution of union literature by nonemployee union organizers on company-owned parking lots. The [NLRB] . . . found in each case that it was unreasonably difficult for the union organizer to reach the employees off company property and held that, in refusing the unions access to parking lots, the employers had unreasonably impeded their employees' right to self-organization in violation of §8(a)(1). . . .

The plant involved in No. 250, Labor Board v. Babcock & Wilcox Co., is a [manufacturing] company . . . located on a 100-acre tract about one mile from a community of 21,000 people. Approximately 40% of the 500 employees live in that town and the remainder live within a 30-mile radius. More than 90% of them drive to work in private automobiles and park on a company lot that adjoins the fenced-in plant area. The parking lot is reached only by a driveway 100 yards long which is entirely on company property excepting for a public right-of-way that extends 31 feet from the metal of the highway to the plant's property. Thus, the only public place in the immediate vicinity of the plant area at which leaflets can be effectively distributed to employees is that place where this driveway crosses the public right-of-way. Because of the traffic conditions at that place the Board found it practically impossible for union organizers to distribute leaflets safely to employees . . . as they enter or leave the lot. The Board noted that the company's policy on such distribution had not discriminated against labor organizations and that other means of communication, such as the mail and telephones, as well as the homes of the workers, were open to the union.[1] The employer justified its refusal to allow distribution of literature on company property on the ground that it had maintained a consistent policy of refusing access to all kinds of pamphleteering and that such distribution of leaflets would litter its property.

The Board found that the parking lot and the walkway from it to the gatehouse, where employees punched in for work, were the only "safe and practicable" places for distribution of union literature. The Board viewed the place of work as so much more effective a place for communication of information that it held the employer guilty of an unfair labor practice for refusing limited access to company property to union organizers. It therefore ordered the employer to rescind its no-distribution order for the parking lot and walkway, subject to reasonable and nondiscriminating [sic] regulations "in the interest of plant efficiency and discipline, but not as to deny access to union representatives for the purpose of effecting such distribution." 109 N.L.R.B., at 486.

---

[1] "*Other union contacts with employees:* In addition to distributing literature to some of the employees, as shown above, during the period of concern herein the Union has had other contacts with some of the employees. It has communicated with over 100 employees . . . on three different occasions by sending literature to them through the mails. Union representatives have communicated with many . . . employees by talking with them on the streets of Paris, by driving to their homes and talking with them there, and by talking with them over the telephone. All of these contacts have been for the purpose of soliciting the adherence and membership of the employees in the Union." 109 N.L.R.B., at 492-493.

. . . [T]he Court of Appeals for the Fifth Circuit . . . refused enforcement on the ground that the statute did not authorize the Board to impose a servitude on the employer's property where no employee was involved. Labor Board v. Babcock & Wilcox Co., 222 F.2d 316.

The conditions and circumstances involved in No. 251, Labor Board v. Seamprufe, Inc., and No. 422, Ranco, Inc. v. Labor Board, are not materially different, except that *Seamprufe* involves a plant employing approximately 200 persons and in the *Ranco* case it appears that union organizers had a better opportunity to pass out literature off company property. The Board likewise ordered these employers to allow union organizers limited access to company lots. The orders were in substantially similar form as that in the *Babcock & Wilcox* case. . . . [T]he Tenth Circuit in No. 251, Labor Board v. Seamprufe, Inc., 222 F.2d 858, refused enforcement on the ground that a nonemployee can justify his presence on company property only "as it bears a cogent relationship to the exercise of the employees' guaranteed right of self-organization." These "solicitors were therefore strangers to the right of self-organization, absent a showing of nonaccessibility amounting to a handicap to self-organization." Id., at 861. The . . . Sixth Circuit in No. 422 granted enforcement. Labor Board v. Ranco, Inc., 222 F.2d 543. The per curiam opinion depended upon its decision in Labor Board v. Monarch Tool Co., 210 F.2d 183, a case in which only employees were involved; Labor Board v. Lake Superior Lumber Corporation, 167 F.2d 147, an isolated lumber camp case; and our Republic Aviation Corp. v. Labor Board, 324 U.S. 793. It apparently considered, as held in the *Monarch Tool* case, supra, at 186, that the attitude of the employer in the *Ranco* case was an "unreasonable impediment to the freedom of communication essential to the exercise of its employees' rights to self organization." Because of the conflicting decisions on a recurring phase of enforcement of the National Labor Relations Act, we granted certiorari. 350 U.S. 818, 894.

In each of these cases the Board found that the employer violated §8(a)(1). . . . These holdings were placed on the Labor Board's determination in LeTourneau Company of Georgia, 54 N.L.R.B. 1253. In the *Le-Tourneau* case the Board balanced the conflicting interests of employees to receive information on self-organization on the company's property from fellow employees during nonworking time, with the employer's right to control the use of his property and found the former more essential in the circumstances of that case. . . . [T]he Board said: "Upon all the above considerations, we are convinced, and find, that the respondent, in applying its 'no-distributing' rule to the distribution of union literature by its employees on its parking lots has placed an unreasonable impediment on the freedom of communication essential to the exercise of its employees' right to self-organization," 54 N.L.R.B., at 1262. This Court affirmed the Board. Republic Aviation Corp. v. Labor Board, 324 U.S. 793, 801 et seq. . . . .

The Board has applied its reasoning in the *LeTourneau* case without distinction to situations where the distribution was made, as here, by nonemployees. . . .

In these present cases the Board has set out the facts that support its conclusions as to the necessity for allowing nonemployee union organizers to distribute union literature on the company's property. In essence they are that nonemployee union representatives, if barred, would have to use personal contacts on streets or at home, telephones, letters or advertised meetings to get in touch with the employees. The force of this position in respect to employees isolated from normal contacts has been recognized by this Court and by others. See Republic Aviation Corporation v. Labor Board, supra, at 799, note 3. . . . We recognize, too, that the Board has the responsibility of "applying the Act's general prohibitory language in the light of the infinite combinations of events which might be charged as violative of its terms." Labor Board v. Stowe Spinning Co., 336 U.S. 226, 231. We are slow to overturn an administrative decision.

It is our judgment, however, that an employer may validly post his property against nonemployee distribution of union literature if reasonable efforts by the union through other available channels of communication will enable it to reach the employees with its message and if the employer's notice or order does not discriminate against the union by allowing other distribution. In these circumstances the employer may not be compelled to allow distribution even under such reasonable regulations as the orders in these cases permit.

This is not a problem of always open or always closed doors for union organization on company property. Organization rights are granted to workers by the same authority, the National Government, that preserves property rights. Accommodation between the two must be obtained with as little destruction of one as is consistent with the maintenance of the other. The employer may not affirmatively interfere with organization; the union may not always insist that the employer aid organization. But when the inaccessibility of employees makes ineffective the reasonable attempts by nonemployees to communicate with them through the usual channels, the right to exclude from property has been required to yield to the extent needed to permit communication of information on the right to organize.

The determination of the proper adjustments rests with the Board. Its rulings, when reached on findings of fact supported by substantial evidence on the record as a whole, should be sustained by the courts unless its conclusions rest on erroneous legal foundations. Here the Board failed to make a distinction between rules of law applicable to employees and those applicable to nonemployees.

The distinction is one of substance. No restriction may be placed on the employees' right to discuss self-organization among themselves, unless the employer can demonstrate that a restriction is necessary to maintain production or discipline. Republic Aviation Corp. v. Labor Board, 324 U.S. 793, 803. But no such obligation is owed nonemployee organizers. Their access to company property is governed by a different consideration. The right of self-organization depends in some measure on the ability of employees to learn the advantages of self-organization from others. Consequently, if the location of a plant and the living quarters of the employees place the employees beyond the reach of reasonable union efforts to communicate with them, the employer must allow the union to approach his employees on his property. No such conditions are shown in these records.

The plants are close to small well-settled communities where a large percentage of the employees live. The usual methods of imparting information are available. . . . The various instruments of publicity are at hand. Though the quarters of the employees are scattered they are in reasonable reach. The Act requires only that the employer refrain from interference, discrimination, restraint or coercion in the employees' exercise of their own rights. It does not require that the employer permit the use of its facilities for organization when other means are readily available.

Labor Board v. Babcock & Wilcox Co., No. 250, is Affirmed.

Labor Board v. Seamprufe, Inc., No. 251, is Affirmed.

Ranco, Inc. v. Labor Board, No. 422, is Reversed.

Harlan, J., took no part in the consideration or decision of these cases.

NOTES

1. Given employees' rights to engage in oral solicitation and to distribute literature on employer premises, is the exclusion of nonemployee organizers, as in *Babcock & Wilcox*, likely to make any practical difference in the success of organizational campaigns?

2. Issues of access to employer premises by nonemployee organizers arise in a broad spectrum of situations ranging from isolated lumber camps (where the employer must grant access) to plants in urban centers that do not involve any special obstacles to communications with employees (where access usually is not required). For a useful discussion of the variables involved in a case falling between these extremes, see the ALJ's report in S & H Grossinger's, Inc., 156 N.L.R.B. 233 (1965), *enforced as modified,*

372 F.2d 26 (2d Cir. 1967). In general, union organizers seeking access to an employer's property have not been able to meet the *Babcock & Wilcox* test. See, e.g., Monogram Models, Inc., 192 N.L.R.B. 705, 706 (1971) (rejecting a proposed "big city rule" based on the claim that employees in a metropolitan area are generally inaccessible, and declaring that the test is "not one of relative convenience, but rather whether 'the location of a plant and the living quarters of the employees place [them] beyond the reach of reasonable union efforts. . . . ' "). But see Scholle Chem. Corp., 192 N.L.R.B. 724 (1971), *enforced*, 82 L.R.R.M. 2410 (7th Cir. 1972), *cert. denied*, 414 U.S. 909 (1973). One question that seems to have divided courts is whether a union can satisfy its burden of showing the ineffectiveness of the "usual channels" of communication without having made a significant organizational effort through those channels. Should the answer to that question depend on whether the delay and expense of a trial run appears to be warranted by the probable success of alternative means of communication in reaching the employees? See Husky Oil, Inc., v. NLRB, 669 F.2d 643 (10th Cir. 1982); Hutzler Bros. Co. v. NLRB, 630 F.2d 1012 (4th Cir. 1980).

3. In NLRB v. Stowe Spinning Co., 336 U.S. 226 (1949), a union organizer sought to use the only available meeting hall in a company town. That hall had been built by the company for, and leased to, the Patriotic Order of Sons of America. The president of the Order had given the organizer permission to use the hall, but the company had rescinded that permission. Previously, the company had not interfered with the Order's decisions permitting other groups to use the hall. The Court sustained the Board's finding of an unfair labor practice in the company's discriminatory treatment of the union. (a) Would the company have violated the Act had it previously denied use of the hall to all persons and groups? (b) Whether or not a company town is involved, does the principle underlying *Stowe Spinning* extend to an unrecognized union's right to post organizational notices and materials on an employer's plant bulletin boards? See, e.g., Union Carbide Corp. v. NLRB, 714 F.2d 657 (6th Cir. 1983). What if the bulletin boards were being posted by rival employee factions?

4. As will appear from Chapter 7(B), public access to an area of an employer's property, at the employer's invitation, has been considered relevant by both the NLRB and the courts in applying the balancing test of *Babcock & Wilcox*. The Board, however, has gone further than some courts and has concluded that a nonemployee no-solicitation rule applicable to the public restaurant of a retail store is unlawfully broad without regard to the *Babcock & Wilcox* criteria. In Montgomery Ward & Co., 256 N.L.R.B. 800 (1981), where an employer applied its blanket rule to prohibit union organizers from meeting (by appointment) with off-duty employees in the store's

public cafeteria, the Board reasoned that the *Babcock & Wilcox* rationale typically controls in situations where organizers use "private" property, to which the public is not invited, in a manner inconsistent with the property's intended purpose. Here, organizers had complied with established Board law in such locations (they had not table-hopped, attempted to distribute litera-ture, spoken to on-duty employees, or created any disturbance); hence, they were attempting to use the cafeteria, "public" property, in a manner consis-tent with its purpose — "personal discussion while dining." Accordingly, the organizers were entitled to access to the cafeteria as members of the general public; they did not need to demonstrate the ineffectiveness of other means of communication. The Seventh Circuit upheld the Board's finding of a viola-tion of §8(a)(1), but rejected the contention that *Babcock & Wilcox* is not applicable in these circumstances. In its view, *Babcock & Wilcox* is the starting point for analysis of any solicitation activity by nonemployees, and public access to employer premises is relevant in balancing organizational and property interests. Montgomery Ward & Co. v. NLRB, 692 F.2d 1115 (7th Cir. 1982). See also Ameron Automotive Centers, 265 N.L.R.B. 511 (1982).

5. For consideration of whether the First Amendment protects access to private property for purposes of union activity, see Hudgens v. NLRB, infra p. 496.

NLRB v. United Steelworkers of America
357 U.S. 357 (1958)

FRANKFURTER, J. . . . No. 81. — In April of 1953 the respondent Steelworkers instituted a campaign to organize the employees of respondent NuTone, Inc., a manufacturer of electrical devices. In the early stages of the campaign, supervisory personnel of the company interrogated employees and solicited reports concerning the organizational activities of other em-ployees. Several employees were discharged; the Board later found that the discharges had been the result of their organizational activities. In June the company began to distribute, through its supervisory personnel, literature that, although not coercive, was clearly antiunion in tenor. In August, while continuing to distribute such material, the company announced its intention of enforcing its rule against employees' posting signs or distributing literature on company property or soliciting or campaigning on company time. The rule, according to these posted announcements, applied to "all employees — whether they are for or against the union." Later the same month a represen-tation election was held, which the Steelworkers lost.

In a proceeding before the Board commenced at the instance of the Steelworkers, the company was charged with a number of violations of the Act alleged to have taken place both before and after the election, including the discriminatory application of the no-solicitation rule. The Board found that the preelection interrogation and solicitation by supervisory personnel and the discharge of employees were unfair labor practices; it also found that the company had, in violation of the Act, assisted and supported an employee organization formed after the election. However, the Board dismissed the allegation that the company had discriminatorily enforced its no-solicitation rule. 112 N.L.R.B. 1153. . . . The Court of Appeals concluded that it was an unfair labor practice for the company to prohibit the distribution of organizational literature on company property during nonworking hours while the company was itself distributing antiunion literature; and it directed that the Board's order be modified accordingly and enforced as modified. 243 F.2d 593 [D.C. Cir.].

No. 289. — In the fall of 1954 the Textile Workers conducted an organizational campaign at several of the plants of respondent Avondale Mills. A number of individual employees were called before supervisory personnel of the company, on the ground that they had been soliciting union membership, and informed that such solicitation was in violation of plant rules and would not be tolerated in the future. The rule had not been promulgated in written form, but there was evidence that it had been previously invoked in a nonorganizational context. During this same period, both in these interviews concerning the rule and at the employees' places of work, supervisory personnel interrogated employees concerning their organizational views and activities and solicited employees to withdraw their membership cards from the union. This conduct was in many cases accompanied by threats that the mill would close down or that various employee benefits would be lost if the mill should become organized. Subsequently three employees, each of whom had been informed of the no-solicitation rule, were laid off and eventually discharged for violating the rule.

. . . The Board found that the interrogation, solicitation and threatening of employees by the company's supervisory personnel were unfair labor practices. Moreover, it found that resort to the no-solicitation rule and discharge of the three employees for its violation were discriminatory and therefore in violation of the Act; it further held that, even if the rule had not been invoked discriminatorily, the discharge of one of the employees had resulted solely from his organizational activities apart from any violation of the rule and was therefore an unfair labor practice. The Board ordered the cessation of these practices and the reinstatement of the discharged employees. 115 N.L.R.B. 840. Upon the Board's petitioning for enforcement in the Court of Appeals for the Fifth Circuit, the company contested only the portions of the Board's findings and order relating to the rule and the discharges. The Court enforced the uncontested portions of the order but, finding insufficient evidence of discrimination in the application of the no-solicitation rule, denied enforcement to the portion of the order relating to the rule and to two of the discharges. As to the third discharge, the court agreed with the Board that it was the result of discrimination unrelated to a violation of the rule, and the court enforced the portion of the Board's order directing the employee's reinstatement. 242 F.2d 669. . . .

. . . In neither of the cases before us did the party attacking the enforcement of the no-solicitation rule contest its validity. Nor is the claim made that an employer may not, under proper circumstances, engage in noncoercive antiunion solicitation; indeed, his right to do so is protected by the so-called "employer free speech" provision of §8(c) of the Act. Contrariwise, as both cases before us show, coercive antiunion solicitation and other similar conduct run afoul of the Act and constitute unfair labor practices irrespective of the bearing of such practices on enforcement of a no-solicitation rule. The very narrow and almost abstract question here derives from the claim that, when the employer himself engages in antiunion solicitation that if engaged in by employees would constitute a violation of the rule — particularly when his solicitation is coercive or accompanied by other unfair labor practices — his enforcement of an otherwise valid no-solicitation rule against the employees is itself an unfair labor practice. We are asked to rule that the coincidence of these circumstances necessarily violates the Act, regardless of the way in which the particular controversy arose or whether the employer's conduct to any considerable degree created an imbalance in the opportunities for organizational communication. For us to lay down such a rule of law would show indifference to the responsibilities imposed by the Act primarily on the Board to appraise carefully the interests of both sides of any labor-management controversy in the diverse circumstances of particular cases and in light of the Board's special understanding of these industrial situations.

There is no indication in the record in either of these cases that the employees, or the union on their behalf, requested the employer, himself engaging in antiunion solicitation, to make an exception to the rule for prounion solicitation. There is evidence in both cases that employers had in the past made exceptions to their rules for charitable solicitation. Notwithstanding the clear antiunion bias of both employers, it is not for us to conclude as a matter of law — although it might well have been open to the Board to conclude as a matter of industrial experience — that a request for a similar qualification upon the rule for organizational solicitation would have been rejected. Certainly the employer is not obliged voluntarily and without any request to offer the use of his facilities and the time of his employees for prounion solicitation. He may very well be wary of a charge that he is interfering with, or contributing support to, a labor organization in violation of §8(a)(2) of the Act.

No attempt was made in either of these cases to make a showing that the no-solicitation rules truly diminished the ability of the labor organizations involved to carry their messages to the employees. Just as that is a vital consideration in determining the validity of a non-solicitation rule, see Republic Aviation Corp. v. Labor Board, supra, at 797-798; Labor Board v. Babcock & Wilcox Co., supra, at 112, it is highly relevant in determining whether a valid rule has been fairly applied. Of course the rules had the effect of closing off one channel of communication; but the Taft-Hartley Act does not command that labor organizations as a matter of abstract law, under all circumstances, be protected in the use of every possible means of reaching the minds of individual workers, nor that they are entitled to use a medium of communication simply because the employer is using it. Cf. Bonwit Teller, Inc., v. Labor Board, 197 F.2d 640, 646; Labor Board v. F. W. Woolworth Co., 214 F.2d 78, 84 (concurring opinion). No such mechanical answers will avail for the solution of this nonmechanical, complex problem in labor-management relations. If, by virtue of the location of the plant and of the facilities and resources available to the union, the opportunities for effectively reaching the employees with a prounion message, in spite of a no-solicitation rule, are at least as great as the employer's ability to promote the legally authorized expression of his antiunion views, there is no basis for invalidating these "otherwise valid" rules. The Board, in determining whether or not the enforcement of such a rule in the circumstances of an individual case is an unfair labor practice, may find relevant alternative channels available for communications on the right to organize. When this important issue is not even raised before the Board and no evidence bearing on it adduced, the concrete basis for appraising the significance of the employer's conduct is wanting.

We do not at all imply that the enforcement of a valid no-solicitation rule by an employer who is at the same time engaging in antiunion solicitation may not constitute an unfair labor practice. All we hold is that there must be some basis, in the actualities of industrial relations, for such a finding. The records in both cases — the issues raised in the proceedings — are barren of the ingredients for such a finding. Accordingly the judgment in No. 81 is reversed, insofar as it sets aside and requires the Board to modify its order, and the cause is remanded to the Court of Appeals for proceedings not inconsistent with this opinion; in all other respects, it is affirmed. The judgment in No. 289 is affirmed.

Black and Douglas, JJ., would affirm the judgment in No. 81 for the reasons set forth in the opinion of the Court of Appeals, 243 F.2d 593.

Black and Douglas, JJ., join in the dissent in No. 289, Labor Board v. Avondale Mills.

WARREN, C. J., dissenting in part and concurring in part. . . . There is no issue in this case [*Avondale Mills*] of balancing the employee's rights under §7 with the employer's right to promote "the legally authorized expression of his antiunion views." The only expression of views carried on by Avondale Mills was a series of threats against the union. Far from being "legally authorized," this expression of views constituted an unfair labor practice by itself. Thus we are not concerned in this case with the possibility of curtailing legitimate employer expression in violation of either the First Amendment or §8(c) of the [NLRA]. . . .

In *United Steelworkers*, I concur in the result. The . . . Board declined to hold that the enforcement of an employer's no-distribution rule against a union was an unfair labor practice even though it was coupled with an antiunion campaign. The Court of Appeals reversed the Board on this point, modifying the Board's order accordingly. This Court sustains the Board. It is conceded that the enforcement of this no-distribution rule against the union is not by itself an unfair labor practice. The Board determined that the employer's expressions of his antiunion views were noncoercive in nature. This fact creates a vital distinction between this case and *Avondale Mills*. Being noncoercive in nature, the employer's expressions were protected by §8(c) . . . and so cannot be used to show that the contemporaneous enforcement of the no-distribution rule was an unfair labor practice.

I dissent from the judgment in No. 289, *Avondale Mills*, and concur in the result in No. 81, *United States Steelworkers*.

NOTES

1. Is the Court's emphasis on the union's failure (a) to request an exception to the employer's rules and (b) to show that those rules "truly diminished" the union's organizational ability consistent with the provisions of §8(c)?

2. Getman, Goldberg, and Herman, supra p. 115, found that familiarity with a party's campaign was strongly correlated with attendance at that party's meetings, that attendance at union meetings was significantly related to switching to the union, and that 83 percent of their employee sample had attended company meetings while only 36 percent (typically employees already committed to the union) had attended union meetings. (Study at 95-96; 104-105.) These data led them to conclude that an organizational

imbalance resulted from an employer's addressing a captive audience on working time and premises while denying the union an equal opportunity and that, accordingly, the *Nutone* decision was wrong. (Id. at 96, 156-159.) The authors conceded, however, that their recommendation of equal on-premises opportunities rested in part on their general commitment to equal access to electorates rather than on empirical data regarding employer impact on captive audiences. (Id. at 157.)

3. Under the "equal opportunity" rule of Bonwit-Teller, Inc., 96 N.L.R.B. 608 (1951), an employer, although permitted to assemble and address a captive audience, violated the Act by denying the union's request to reply under similar circumstances. In Livingston Shirt Corp., 107 N.L.R.B. 400, 409 (1953), a reconstituted Board, finding "nothing improper in an employer's refusing to grant to the union a right equal to his own in his plant," abandoned the *Bonwit-Teller* rule and required an employer to grant such requests to reply only in "special circumstances," namely, when an employer maintains "either an unlawful broad no-solicitation rule (prohibiting union access to company premises on other than working time) or a privileged no-solicitation rule (broad, but not unlawful because of the character of the business)." In later cases, the Board found that the *Nutone* emphasis on "an imbalance in organizational communication" reinforced the *Bonwit-Teller* exception resting on an employer's enforcement of a broad but privileged (or an unlawful) rule. See, e.g., Montgomery Ward & Co. v. NLRB, 339 F.2d 889 (6th Cir. 1965). What is the rationale for concluding that the maintenance of a broad but privileged no-solicitation rule constitutes "special circumstances" calling for union access to company premises in order to respond to a captive audience speech? Is that conclusion compatible with §8(c)? Cf. Miami Herald Publishing Co. v. Tornillo, 418 U.S. 241 (1974).

4. Apart from the question whether an employer's ban of union representatives is itself an unfair labor practice, the problem of union access to company property arises in the context of the NLRB's authority to take affirmative action to remedy other §§8(a)(1) and 8(a)(3) violations of the Act. Where an employer's response to an organizing effort is a series of unlawful acts, typically serious in nature, the Board has ordered certain forms of union access to the employer's premises as a remedial measure—e.g., access to plant bulletin boards, to nonworking areas during nonworking periods, or to a worktime forum to reply to any captive audience speeches. Such access is usually limited to the site at which the unfair labor practices were committed. Is it understandable why the Board maintains that such orders do not require a showing that the union has no other reasonable means of reaching the employees? For a thorough discussion of access remedies, see United Steel-

workers v. NLRB (Florida Steel Corp.), 646 F.2d 616 (D.C. Cir. 1981). See also Note, NLRB Orders Granting Unions Access to Company Property, 68 Cornell L. Rev. 895 (1983).

5. In Peerless Plywood Co., 107 N.L.R.B. 427, 429 (1953), the Board adopted the rule that "employers and unions alike will be prohibited from making election speeches on company time to massed assemblies of employees within 24 hours before the scheduled . . . election." A last-minute speech on company time, the Board reasoned, tends to create "a mass psychology" incompatible with "sober and thoughtful choice" and to give an "unfair advantage" to the party who enjoys the last opportunity to talk to the voters. (What of last-minute speeches in union halls?) Thus, violation of this rule was made a basis for upsetting an election but not for a finding of an unfair labor practice. Are the premises for *Peerless Plywood* intact after the Board's *Midland* decision on last-minute misrepresentations? (*Peerless Plywood* leaves untouched many forms of campaigning during the twenty-four hours preceding an election. For example, an employer's brief expressions of hope and appreciation for a "no" vote, made to individual employees at their work stations within twenty-four hours of the election, have been held not to amount to "speeches to a massed assembly" within the meaning of *Peerless Plywood*. See Land O'Frost of Arkansas, Inc., 252 N.L.R.B. 1 (1980).)

Excelsior Underwear Inc.
156 N.L.R.B. 1236 (1966)

[After a consent election in which 246 of 247 eligible employees voted and 206 votes were against the union, the union filed objections based, inter alia, on the employer's failure to supply the union with the employees' names and addresses so as to facilitate the union's reply to the employer's antiunion letter. The Regional Director recommended that the objections be overruled. The Chamber of Commerce, the National Assn. of Manufacturers, the AFL-CIO, and various international unions, pursuant to the Board's invitation, filed amicus curiae briefs and participated in oral argument.]

. . . [E]ach of these cases poses the question whether an employer's refusal to provide a union with the names and addresses of employees eligible to vote in a representation election should be grounds on which to set that election aside. The Board has not in the past set elections aside on this ground. . . .

We are persuaded . . . that higher standards of disclosure than we have heretofore imposed are necessary, and that prompt disclosure of the information here sought by the Petitioners should be required in all representation elections. Accordingly, we now establish a requirement that will be applied in all election cases. That is, within seven days after the Regional Director has approved a consent-election agreement entered into by the parties . . . , or after the Regional Director or the Board has directed an election . . . , the employer must file with the Regional Director an election eligibility list, containing the names and addresses of all the eligible voters. The Regional Director, in turn, shall make this information available to all parties in the case. Failure to comply with this requirement shall be grounds for setting aside the election whenever proper objections are filed.[5]

The considerations that impel us to adopt the foregoing rule are these: . . . [W]e regard it as the Board's function to conduct elections in which employees have the opportunity to cast their ballots for or against representation under circumstances that are free not only from interference, restraint, or coercion violative of the Act, but also from other elements that prevent or impede a free and reasoned choice.[7] Among the factors that undoubtedly tend to impede such a choice is a lack of information with respect to one of the choices available. In other words, an employee who has had an effective opportunity to hear the arguments concerning representation is in a better position to make a more fully informed and reasonable choice. Accordingly, we think that it is appropriate for us to remove the impediment to communication to which our new rule is directed.

. . . [A]n employer, through his possession of employee names and home addresses as well as his ability to communicate with employees on plant premises, is assured of the continuing opportunity to inform the entire electorate of his views. . . . [A] labor organization, whose organizers normally have no right of access to plant premises,[9] has no method by which it can be certain of reaching all the employees with its arguments in favor of representation. . . . This is not, of course, to deny the existence of various means by which a party *might* be able to communicate with a substantial portion of the electorate even without possessing their names and addresses. It is rather to say what seems to us obvious — that the access of *all* employees to such communications can be insured only if all parties have the names and addresses of all the voters.[10] In other words, by providing all parties with

[5] However, the rule we have here announced is to be applied prospectively only. It will not apply in the instant cases but only in those elections that are directed, or consented to, subsequent to 30 days from the date of this Decision. We impose this brief period of delay to insure that all parties to forthcoming representation elections are fully aware of their rights and obligations as here stated.

[7] See General Shoe Corporation, 77 N.L.R.B. 124, 126-127.

[9] NLRB v. The Babcock & Wilcox Company, 351 U.S. 105.

[10] A union that does not know the names or addresses of some of the voters may seek to communicate with them by distributing literature on sidewalks or street corners adjoining the employer's premises or by utilizing the mass media of communication. The likelihood that *all*

employees' names and addresses,[14] we maximize the likelihood that all the voters will be exposed to the arguments for, as well as against, union representation. . . .

A requirement that all participants in an election contest have the opportunity to ascertain the names and addresses of the voters is not uncommon. Lists of registered voters in public elections are open to inspection and copying by the public. . . . Any candidate for union office is entitled to have the union distribute his campaign literature to all members.[17] . . . As one thoughtful commentator has stated: "Since the opportunity for both sides to reach all the employees is basic to a fair and informed election, the reasons for requiring disclosure seem just as strong as those leading to similar requirements under other provisions of the law."[18]

. . . As noted (supra) an employer is presently under no obligation to supply an election eligibility list until shortly before the election. The list, when made available, not infrequently contains the names of employees unknown to the union and even to its employee supporters. The reasons for

---

employees will be reached by these methods is, however, problematical at best. See NLRB v. United Aircraft Corp., et al., 324 F.2d 128, 130 (C.A. 2d), *cert. denied* 376 U.S. 951. Personal solicitation on plant premises by employee supporters of the union, while vastly more satisfactory than the above methods, suffers from the limited periods of nonworking time available for solicitation (generally and legally forbidden during working time, Peyton Packing Company, Inc., 49 N.L.R.B. 828, 843) and, in a large plant, the sheer physical problems involved in communicating with fellow employees.

[14] . . . [I]t should be noted that the requirement here imposed applies equally to the case in which an election has been directed upon a petition by an employee or group of employees who seek to decertify an existing bargaining representative or to rescind that representative's authority to enter into a union-security agreement of the sort otherwise authorized by §8(a)(3) of the Act. In these latter cases, the petitioning employees would be entitled to the names and addresses of their fellow employees as an aid in their efforts to communicate their arguments against continued union representation or continuance of an existing union-security agreement. Similarly, the union, as a party to the election, would be entitled to employees' names and addresses so as to communicate its position. In short, the disclosure requirement here adopted applies whenever a Board election has been scheduled and insures all parties to the election, whatever their viewpoint, of an opportunity to communicate with the electorate. The only exception is in the expedited election conducted pursuant to §8(b)(7)(C). In this situation, we believe that the time span between the direction of election and the conduct thereof is too brief, taking into account the time required for the employer to compile and file a list of names and addresses, for the union to be able to make any meaningful use of this information. [This footnote number has been relocated in the text. — Eds.]

[17] 29 U.S.C. §481(c).

[18] Bok, The Regulation of Campaign Tactics in Representation Elections under the National Labor Relations Act, 78 Harv. L. Rev. 38, 99-100 (1964); Cf. Summers, Judicial Regulation of Union Elections, 70 Yale L. J. 1221, 1227-1228 (1961). Another manifestation of the concept that all participants in an election should have access to the electorate is embodied in 47 U.S.C. §315(a), which provides for equal time for political candidates on radio and television.

this are, in large part, the same as those that make it difficult for a union to obtain, other than from the employer, the names of all employees; i.e., large plants with many employees unknown to their fellows, employees on layoff status, sick leave, military leave, etc. With little time (and no home addresses) with which to satisfy itself as to the eligibility of the "unknowns," the union is forced either to challenge all those who appear at the polls whom it does not know or risk having ineligible employees vote. The effect of putting the union to this choice, we have found, is to increase the number of challenges, as well as the likelihood that the challenges will be determinative of the election, thus requiring investigation and resolution by the Regional Director or the Board. Prompt disclosure of employee names as well as addresses will, we are convinced, eliminate the necessity for challenges based solely on lack of knowledge as to the voter's identity. Furthermore, bona fide disputes between employer and union over voting eligibility will be more susceptible of settlement without recourse to the formal and time-consuming challenge procedures of the Board if such disputes come to light early in the election campaign. . . .

The arguments against imposing a requirement of disclosure are of little force especially when weighed against the benefits resulting therefrom. Initially, we are able to perceive no substantial infringement of employer interests that would flow from such a requirement. A list of employee names and addresses is not like a customer[s] list, and an employer would appear to have no significant interest in keeping the names and addresses of his employees secret (other than a desire to prevent the union from communicating with his employees — an interest we see no reason to protect). Such legitimate interest in secrecy as an employer may have is, in any event, plainly outweighed by the substantial public interest in favor of disclosure. . . .

The main arguments that have been presented to us by the Employers and the amici curiae supporting the Employers relate not to any infringement of *employer* rights flowing from a disclosure requirement but rather to an asserted infringement of *employee* rights. . . . We regard this argument as without merit. An employee's failure to provide a union with his name and address, whether due to inertia, fear of employer reprisal, or an initial predisposition to vote against union representation, is not, as we view it, an exercise of the §7 rights to refrain from union activity. Rather, in the context with which we are here concerned — a Board-conducted representation election — an employee exercises this right by voting for or against union representation.

Similarly, we reject the argument that to provide the union with employee names and addresses subjects employees to the dangers of harassment and coercion in their homes. We cannot assume that a union, seeking to obtain employees' votes in a secret ballot election, will engage in conduct of this nature; if it does, we shall provide an appropriate remedy. We do not, in any event, regard the mere possibility that a union will abuse the opportunity to communicate with employees in their homes as sufficient basis for denying this opportunity altogether. . . .

The argument is also made (by the Employer in the *Excelsior* case) that under the decisions of the Supreme Court in NLRB v. The Babcock & Wilcox Company, and NLRB v. United Steelworkers of America (Nutone Inc.), the Board may not require employer disclosure of employee names and addresses unless, in the particular case involved the union would otherwise be unable to reach the employees with its message. . . .

Initially, as we read *Babcock* and *Nutone*, the existence of alternative channels of communication is relevant only when the opportunity to communicate made available by the Board would interfere with a significant employer interest — such as the employer's interest in controlling the use of property owned by him. Here, as we have shown, the employer has no significant interest in the secrecy of employee names and addresses. Hence, there is no necessity for the Board to consider the existence of alternative channels of communication before requiring disclosure of that information. Moreover, even assuming that there is some legitimate employer interest in nondisclosure, we think it relevant that the subordination of that interest which we here require is limited to a situation in which employee interests in self-organization are shown to be substantial. For, whenever an election is directed (the precondition to disclosure) the Regional Director has found that a real question concerning representation exists; when the employer consents to an election, he has impliedly admitted this fact. The opportunity to communicate on company premises sought in *Babcock* and *Nutone* was not limited to the situation in which employee organizational interests were substantial; i.e., in which an election had been directed; we think that on this ground also the cases are distinguishable. Finally, both *Babcock* and *Nutone* dealt with the circumstances under which the Board might find an employer to have committed an unfair labor practice in violation of §8 of the Act, whereas the instant cases pose the substantially distinguishable issue of the circumstances under which the Board may set aside an election. "[T]he test of conduct which may interfere with the 'laboratory conditions' for an election is considerably more restrictive than the test of conduct which amounts to interference, restraint, or coercion which violates §8(a)(1)."[24] Whether or not an employer's refusal to disclose employee names and addresses after an

[24] Dal-Tex Optical Company, Inc., 137 N.L.R.B. 1782, 1786-1787; see also General Shoe Corporation, 77 N.L.R.B. 124, 126-127.

election is directed would constitute "interference, restraint, or coercion" within the meaning of §8(a)(1) . . . , despite the existence of alternative channels of communication open to the union, is a question on which we express no view because it is not before us. . . .

Finally, we . . . do not limit the disclosure requirement to the situation in which the employer has mailed antiunion literature to employees' homes . . . because we believe that access to employee names and addresses is fundamental to a fair and free election regardless of whether the employer has sent campaign propaganda to employees' homes. We do not limit the requirement of disclosure to furnishing employee names and addresses to a mailing service . . . because this would create difficult practical problems and because we do not believe that the union should be limited to the use of the mails in its effort to communicate with the entire electorate.[27]

[The Board certified that a majority of valid ballots had not been cast for the unions participating in each of the elections involved.]

NOTES

1. In NLRB v. Wyman-Gordon Co., 394 U.S. 759 (1969), the Supreme Court, despite substantial disagreement as to whether the Board in *Excelsior* had met the rulemaking requirements of the Administrative Procedure Act (and, if not, the significance of any such failure), ruled that the names-and-addresses requirement was valid and enforceable by subpoena under §11(1) of the NLRA.

2. In General Electric Co., 156 N.L.R.B. 1247 (1966), decided the same day as *Excelsior*, petitioning unions urged the NLRB to overrule *Livingston Shirt* and to reinstate the "equal opportunity" doctrine of *Bonwit Teller*. The Board rejected this suggestion, stating (at 1251): "In light of the increased opportunities for employees' access to communications which should flow from *Excelsior*, but with which we have, as yet, no experience, . . . we prefer to defer any reconsideration of current Board doctrine in the area of plant access until after the effects of *Excelsior* become known."

---

[27] . . . In the briefs and arguments of the Employers and *amici curiae* supporting the Employers, much has been made of Board decisions setting aside representation elections because an employer or his agents called on all or a majority of employees in their homes in the period preceding the election. . . . The argument is made that it would be inequitable for the Board to preclude employers from visiting employees in their homes and at the same time insist that unions be furnished with employee names and addresses so that they may engage in home visits. The short answer to this argument is that employers are free to communicate with their employees in the plant; a union, as a practical matter, is severely limited in its efforts at inplant communications. . . .

Given the complex of variables affecting the effectiveness of communications, is it difficult to understand why the NLRB has yet to announce whether "the effects" of the *Excelsior* rule, in general or in any particular situation, have "become known"? Getman, Goldberg, & Herman found that employees who received letters or other written material had a significantly greater familiarity with the campaign, both company and union claims, than those who did not, and that, apparently because of the *Excelsior* rule, unions were able to reach nearly as many employees with written material as did employers. (Study at 89-90.)

3. Should adoption of the *Excelsior* rule result in applications of §8(a)(1) and the "laboratory conditions" formula that would give an employer greater latitude in making "dire predictions" of the possible consequences of a union victory and union policies, at least where the union has time to reply?

C. EMPLOYER DOMINATION AND ASSISTANCE OF UNIONS

Section 8(a)(2) of the Act was directed at the so-called company union problem. A "company union" typically has been a union confined to the employees of a single employer and unaffiliated with another union. Such unions, although sometimes independent of the employer, were frequently established by employers in order to obtain subservient organizations and to convert collective bargaining into a "colloquy between one side of [the employer's] mouth and the other." See R. Brooks, Unions of Their Own Choosing 68-69 (1939). In the period immediately before the Wagner Act, many single-firm unions are said to have participated in such abuses, and the term "company union" had acquired a negative connotation. See H. Millis & R. Montgomery, Organized Labor 879-886 (1945). The enactment of the Wagner Act led employers to sponsor or assist company unions as a shield against outside unions. See Crager, Company Unions Under the NLRA, 40 Mich. L. Rev. 831-833 (1942).

Section 8(a)(2), like §2, Fourth of the Railway Labor Act, attacked such spurious forms of organization and collective bargaining by supplementing the general prohibition of employer interference (§8(a)(1)) with a proscription against employer support or domination. In disposing of the large volume of resultant litigation, the NLRB applied three general propositions, supported by the pertinent legislative history. First, unaffiliated unions were to be legal if freely chosen by the employees without employer pressure or interference. Second, an employee representative supported or dominated by the employer "cannot command, even if deserving it, the full confidence" of the workers it represents. See S. Report No. 573, 74th Cong., 1st Sess. 9-11 (1935). Third, the question of domination or improper interference was to be "one of fact in each case." See also 3 NLRB Ann. Rep. 28-29, 108, 112-126 (1938).

There has been a sharp decline in blatant employer abuses and in §8(a)(2) charges.° Nevertheless, investigations by the "McClellan Committee" in the late 1950s indicated the persistence, or at least the revival, of old abuses. That committee reported that some of the most respected names in American business had resorted to notorious "middlemen" in order to create employee organizations subservient to employers. See Select Senate Comm. on Improper Activities in the Labor or Management Field, Interim Report, Rep. No. 1417, 85th Cong., 2d Sess. 255, 256, 298-299, 300 (1958). For recent examples of employers' efforts to direct employees into a "preferred" union, see Hirsch v. Trim Lean Meat Products, 479 F. Supp. 1351 (D. Del. 1979); Hartz Mountain Corp., 228 N.L.R.B. 492 (1977), *enforced sub nom.* District 65, Distributive Workers v. NLRB, 593 F.2d 1155 (D.C. Cir. 1978).

Recent economic difficulties have spurred discussion of the need to reexamine the adversarial model of labor-management relations that exists in this country.ᴾ There have been appeals for more cooperation in collective bargaining in order to deal with problems in unionized industries that have suffered from lower-cost competition. Similarly, there has been a renewed interest in other forms of worker participation and representation in both organized and unorganized settings. See generally I. Siegel & E. Weinberg, Labor-Management Cooperation: The American Experience 99-200

°In 1980, for example, only 3.1 percent of the more than 30,000 unfair labor practice cases against employers included allegations of a §8(a)(2) violation. 45 NLRB Ann. Rep. 243 (1980). Such charges accounted for approximately 20 percent of the complaint proceedings against employers during the years immediately following passage of the Wagner Act. See 3 NLRB Ann. Rep. 28 (1938). See also Kesselring & Brinker, Employer Domination Under Section 8(a)(2), 30 Lab. L.J. 340, 341-342 (1979) (during period 1950-1974, employer formation or initiation of a union was an issue in only 129 of the 832 NLRB decisions under §8(a)(2)).

ᴾThe scope of current discussions of collective bargaining is indicated by Forst, Labor Union Representation on Boards of Corporate Competitors: An Antitrust Analysis, 7 J. Corp. L. 421 (1982); McCormick, Union Representatives as Corporate Directors: The Challenge to the Adversarial Model of Labor Relations, 15 U. Mich. J.L. Ref. 219 (1982); Note, Worker Ownership and Section 8(a)(2) of the National Labor Relations Act, 91 Yale L.J. 615 (1982). Doubts regarding the effectiveness of more collaborative approaches are developed in Levitan & Johnson, Labor and Management: The Illusion of Cooperation, Harv. Bus. Rev., Sept.-Oct. 1983, at 8.

(1982); K. Bradley & A. Gelb, Worker Capitalism — The New Industrial Relations (1983) (dealing with various forms of employee ownership of companies). As the case immediately following illustrates, §8(a)(2) may impede unilateral management efforts to establish cooperative and participatory employee arrangements.

NLRB v. Streamway Div., Scott & Fetzer Co.
691 F.2d 288 (6th Cir. 1982)

ENGEL, J. . . . [T]he United Auto Workers, in October 1976 and again in November 1977, failed to obtain majority support for its efforts to be certified as the collective bargaining agent for the Company's production and maintenance employees.[1] The Union filed no objections to the conduct of either election, and no unfair labor charges emerged [from] those elections.

In March, 1977, the Company established and outlined the structure of the [In-Plant Representation Committee (hereinafter "the Committee")]. . . . [A] notice to all hourly employees [stated that] a working committee was intended to be established as a part of the Company's program to develop "more readily accessible channels of communications within Manufacturing Operations" and "to provide coordination between plant personnel and management."

The expressed goal of the Committee was "to provide an informal yet orderly process for communicating Company plans and programs; defining and identifying problem areas and eliciting suggestions and ideas for improving operations." . . . Initially, one general meeting and one departmental meeting in each of the four departments in the Company was to be held each month. The committee was to include eight employee representatives [elected from departments], and management personnel would be present at both general and departmental meetings.

The Company avowedly planned that the Committee would "provide to as many employees as possible the opportunity of direct input." It therefore set forth a rotating schedule of initial terms to be served which varied from three to six months, with all terms thereafter to be three months in duration. To maximize employee participation . . . , no employee was to serve, other than the initial term, for more than three months in a calendar year. At the time of the second UAW certification election in February 1978, the Committee had been operating for several months. . . .

. . . [U]nfair labor practice charges were filed against the Company in

[1] The Union filed election petitions on these dates. The record does not disclose when the first election was held; the second was held in January 1978.

October and November, 1978 and in January, 1979. The [ALJ] found that the Company dominated and interfered with the Committee, which he determined was a labor organization as defined in §2(5) of the Act. . . .[q] The Board adopted the ALJ's order [and now petitions for enforcement].

Section 8(a)(2) . . . prohibits domination or support of a "labor organization." The Board upheld the ALJ's determination that the Committee formed by the Company was a "labor organization" as defined in §2(5) of the Act, which provides:

> The term "labor organization" means any organization of any kind, or any agency or employee representation committee or plan, in which employees participate *and which exists for the purpose*, in whole or in part, *of dealing with employers* concerning grievances, labor disputes, wages, rates of pay, hours of employment, or conditions of work. (emphasis added.)

We think there is little question that if it is a "labor organization" under §2(5), . . . the Committee was dominated by the Company. It was expressly mandated by the Company, and the Company controlled its composition and its meetings. Therefore, we think it follows that if the Committee was in fact a labor organization, the Company was guilty of a violation of §8(a)(2). . . . We are, however, convinced that the Committee was not, under any enlightened view of the Act, a labor organization as above defined.

Because a labor organization is defined as an "organization of any kind" for purposes of the Act, the recurrent question is whether an organization exists to "deal" with employers regarding conditions of work. The term "dealing" in the Act was interpreted in NLRB v. Cabot Carbon Co., 360 U.S. 203 (1958). . . . [A]n employee committee had been established and endowed with the responsibility to handle grievances. It also made and discussed proposals respecting a wide variety of the aspects of the company's employee relationships, including seniority, job classifications, job bidding, make-up time, overtime records, time cards, merit systems, vacations, sick leave, and the like. The committee was instrumental in altering several conditions of work. Members of the local committee formulated a list of

[q] [The ALJ's decision reveals that elections of representatives to the in-plant committee were conducted on company time, with ballots prepared, distributed, and counted by management. Furthermore, the ALJ had relied heavily on the testimony of the company's president, which the ALJ summarized as follows: "[He] specifically acknowledged that a purpose of the committee was . . . that the employees would have a vehicle to complain about conditions of employment. . . . [He] clearly indicate[d] that working conditions were something the representatives were supposed to talk about in meetings. Indeed, he testified that he elicited comments from each representative individually because some people were reluctant to speak out. It is further clear that [he] intended the [committee] members to act in a 'representative' capacity . . . ," 249 N.L.R.B. 396, 400-401 (1980). — Eds.]

proposals which they presented directly to the Director of Industrial Relations. . . . Because its powers did not expressly include "bargaining," the Fifth Circuit held that the committee was not a labor organization. 256 F.2d 281 (5th Cir. 1958). . . . [I]t found that "dealing with" was synonymous with "bargaining with" and was therefore limited to committees which actually engaged in collective bargaining.

In reversing, Justice Whittaker . . . emphasized that the final text of the Act expressly rejected more restrictive language which would have defined labor organizations as groups engaging in collective bargaining;[8] he concluded that the term "dealing" should be more broadly construed. Finding that the "Committee undertook the 'responsibility to,' and did 'handle grievances,'" 360 U.S. at 213, Justice Whittaker concluded that "it is plain as words can say that these committees existed, at least in part, for the purposes 'of dealing with employers concerning grievances. . . .' This alone brings these committees squarely within the statutory definition of 'labor organizations.'" Id.

Justice Whittaker went on to observe that the meetings consisted of a series of "proposals and requests with respect to matters covering nearly the whole scope of the employment relationship." Id. at 214. Although Justice Whittaker stressed the continuous course of contacts between the committee and both local and central management, and stated that "dealing" often involves making recommendations, he did not indicate the limitations, if any, upon the meaning of "dealing" under the statute. Because the Supreme Court has not spoken further on this issue, the question of how much interaction is necessary before dealing is found is unresolved.

Our circuit has been quick to find that "advisory committees" were company dominated labor organizations where in fact a pattern of dealing existed. For example, in NLRB v. General Shoe, 192 F.2d 504 (6th Cir. 1954), a series of committees, including an Advisory Committee and a Grievance Committee, were set up to consider a myriad of employment conditions. . . . We found that the Advisory Committee was itself a labor organization when viewed against the background evidence presented, because it "handled suggestions and questions," and it served as both an

---

[8] The Court also rejected an argument that labelling employee committees as labor organizations "would prevent employers and employees from discussing matters of mutual interest concerning the employment relationship, and would thus abridge freedom of speech. . . . " 360 U.S. at 218. It stated that the Board's order did not bar such speech; instead, it "merely preclude[d] the employers from dominating, interfering with or supporting such employee committees which Congress has defined to be labor organizations." We think the same analysis would apply to the Company's contention that the proviso to §8(a)(2), allowing employees to confer with employers, precludes a finding that an employee committee is a labor organization.

"advisor" on company policy and as a means of communication for employees. . . .

At the same time, logic and experience under the Act . . . dictate that not all management efforts to communicate with employees concerning company personnel policy are forbidden on pain of violating the Act. An overly broad construction of the statute would be as destructive of the objects as the Act as ignoring the provision entirely. Thus there is particular force in the logic of Judge John Minor Wisdom, dissenting in N.L.R.B. v. Walton Mfg. Co., 289 F.2d 177, 182 (5th Cir. 1961):

> To my mind an inflexible attitude of hostility toward employee committees defeats the Act. It erects an iron curtain between employer and employees, penetrable only by the bargaining agent of a certified union, if there is one, preventing the development of a decent, honest, constructive relationship between management and labor. The Act encourages collective bargaining, as it should, in accordance with national policy. The Act does not encourage compulsory membership in a labor organization. The effect of the Board's policy here is to force employees to form a labor organization, regardless of the wishes of the employees in the particular plant, if there is so much as an intention by an employer to allow employees to confer with management on any matter that can be said to touch, however slightly, their "general welfare". There is nothing in *Cabot Carbon*, or in the Labor Management Act, or in any other law that makes it wrong for an employer "to work together" with employees for the welfare of all. There is nothing wrong — provided that the committee through which employer and employees work is not in fact a labor organization within the meaning of Sections 2(5) . . . and 8(a)(2) and is not used by the employer to infringe on labor's right of self-government and other rights in violation of Section 8(a)(1).

Somewhat similar considerations have influenced decisions of both our circuit and the Board itself. Two Sixth Circuit cases considering whether labor organizations were dominated illustrate our more recent attitude toward the meaning of §8(a)(2). . . . In Modern Plastics v. NLRB, 379 F.2d 201 (6th Cir. 1967), our court joined a minority of circuits indicating that the adversarial model of labor relations is an anachronism. There the court rejected a Board finding that an organization was dominated by the company merely because of the weakness of the organization. The committee received no dues and did not operate under a constitution or bylaws. The company paid for food and drink and compensated committee members for time spent attending meetings. These facts, the Board held, indicated company domination of the committee. Our circuit disagreed, observing that the strength or weakness of the committee, if it were truly representative of the employee, was a matter of little concern to the Board or to the Act itself;

the real question was whether the company dominated the decisions of the committee. . . . In Federal-Mogul Corp., Coldwater Distribution Center Division v. NLRB, 394 F.2d 915 (6th Cir. 1968), where it was shown that committee members were compensated by the company for time spent at meetings and that the committee had no formal constitution or bylaws and did not collect dues, our court held that it was not the potential for control that the Act declared unlawful. "It is only when management's activities actually undermine the integrity of the employees' freedom of choice and independence in dealing with their employer that such activities fall within the proscriptions of the Act." 394 F.2d at 921.

Modern Plastics and *Federal-Mogul* presuppose the existence of a labor organization and consider domination, which is not the focus of our inquiry here.[9] They indicate, however, that our circuit is willing to reject a rigid interpretation of the statute and instead consider whether the employer's behavior fosters employee free expression and choice as the Act requires.

Although the Board has generally interpreted the term "labor organizations" broadly, it too recognizes that employee committees may communicate with the employer without violating the Act. In General Foods Corporation and American Federation of Grain Millers, AFL-CIO and Its Local 70, 231 N.L.R.B. No. 122 (1977), the Board found that committees established by the employer were not labor organizations. The company had established teams, divided according to job assignments. Each team, acting by consensus, made job assignments, assigned job rotations and scheduled overtime. Each team had meetings to discuss such topics as a compensation system and the objectives of each team or group of employees. A psychologist was hired to improve internal communications among team members and to build "trust levels" among the teams, and members discussed conditions of work such as compensation at their meetings. Notwithstanding the facial similarity between this activity and the language of the Act, the Board adopted the trial examiner's finding that the teams were not labor organizations. Although the examiner stressed that the committees were merely administrative subdivisions of employees and did not serve in a representative capacity, he also found significant that:

. . . [T]he teams herein were not established to head off incipient organizing drives by outside unions nor did they come into existence as a result of any unrest in the bargaining unit which was sensed by Respondent.

[9] At least one commentator has construed *Modern Plastics* and other "cooperation" cases to suggest a new standard for illegal domination, based upon the intent to coerce. See Note, New Standards for Domination and Support Under Section 8(a)(2), 82 Yale L.J. 510, 519-525 (1973).

231 N.L.R.B. No. 122 at 1234.

A case presenting facts similar to those here is Mercy-Memorial Hospital Corporation and Local 79, Service Employees International Union, AFL-CIO, 231 N.L.R.B. No. 182 (1977). There a group was designated to investigate grievances and to render decisions, but the Board nonetheless determined that it was not a labor organization. Again the Board . . . accepted the employer's argument that the committee existed not to deal with management but to give employees a voice in resolving the grievances of fellow employees. More important for our purposes here, the examiner determined that the committee was not a labor organization even though a policy statement provided that "the committee does have the right and the obligation to recommend to the director of personnel and all other administrative heads . . . any changes in rules, regulations, and standards" and the committee actually made recommendations regarding conditions of employment. Clearly, then, communication between a committee and management does not itself bestow labor organization status upon a group.

Our facts here do not fit precisely within either *Cabot Carbon* or within those of *General Foods* and *Mercy-Memorial*. Nevertheless, an examination of the record as a whole satisfies us that the limited functions of the Committee here more closely resemble those in the latter decisions. As in *General Foods*, the Committee was a part of a company plan to determine employee attitudes regarding working conditions and other problems in an accurate and effective way, for the Company's self-enlightenment, rather than a method by which to pursue a course of dealings. Although we acknowledge that the difference between communication of ideas and a course of dealings at times is seemingly indistinct, we believe, nevertheless, that it is vital here.

Although *Cabot Carbon* cautions against a restrictive reading of the term "dealing," it involved a more active, ongoing association between management and employees, which the term dealing connotes, than is present here. The Board offered no evidence of a continuous interaction between employer and committee other than recital of the committee's purpose to "allow employees to question, complain about, or raise matters concerning conditions of employment," and that the committee actually complained. Whatever the reach of *Cabot Carbon* beyond the facts of that case, we do not think it applies here. We cannot accept the Board's suggestion that *Cabot Carbon* should be read so broadly as to call any group discussing issues related to employment a labor organization.

Several factors convince us that the committee is not a labor organization. The continuous rotation of Committee members to ensure that many employees participate makes the Committee resemble more closely the employee groups speaking directly to management on an individual, rather than a representative, basis as in *General Foods*. Moreover, the ALJ determined he could find no employer hostility or anti-union animus in the present case. . . . The Board offers no evidence connecting the creation of the committee to the organizational drive that occurred months afterward. The Board in *General Foods* considered whether anti-union sentiment existed at the time the committees were formed. Similarly, in both *Modern Plastics* and *Federal-Mogul* our court considered lack of anti-union animus to be a factor in the determination that the employer's activities comported with the purposes of the Act.

Finally, neither the employees, nor the Committee, nor, so far as we can ascertain, the union involved in two certification elections, seems to have considered that the Committee even remotely resembled a labor organization in the ordinary sense of the term. . . . If the Committee were in fact a labor organization within the meaning of the Act, its members or the company on its behalf might have been expected to have interposed this as a bar to the efforts to seek certification of the UAW as collective bargaining agent. No such action occurred here, and the election was held without incident and objection, resulting in the defeat of the union. *Federal-Mogul* indicates that unless employees are encouraged "in the mistaken belief that [a committee is] truly representative and afford[s] an agency for collective bargaining," no interference with employee choice, essential to a finding that the Act has been violated, occurs. 394 F.2d at 918.[11] The Board offers no evidence that anyone viewed the committee as anything more than a communicative device. . . .

We recognize that the facts here have not precisely arisen before. We also recognize, however, as does the Board, that at some point a literal translation of §2(5) will frustrate the very purposes of the Act itself. This, we think, has occurred here.

Two certification elections have occurred in the span of time covered by this litigation. No unfair labor charges were filed. Those elections provided the employees with an uncoerced opportunity to make an intelligent choice between the status quo and the alternative benefits of a formal contract, reached after collective bargaining through a local organization of their choice. Clearly those employees have exercised their option to dispense with the benefit of the formal collective bargaining agreement through a labor organization. Just as the Act provides democratic machinery to protect the

---

[11] Our analysis therefore is not altered by the fact that the Company changed the vacation policy following discussions with the committee. An isolated incident does not convert the Committee into a labor organization. *See Mercy-Hospital Corp.*, supra, 231 N.L.R.B. at 1121; *General Foods*, supra, 231 N.L.R.B. at 1235.

employees' choice to bargain collectively, so equally it protects the employees' right to forego those benefits, if in their judgment their interests are best served by this course. There has been no evidence of Company hostility toward the union and no evidence that the Company itself interfered with any exercise of employee rights to bargain collectively, unless it might be said that an enlightened personnel policy led them to be content with the status quo. This was their choice. We see no reason under the Act to disturb that choice or to tip the scales against it and in favor of that which the employees themselves have twice rejected. . . .

Enforcement is denied.

COHN, J., dissenting in part. . . . I believe my colleagues give too little weight to the . . . Board's determination that the In-Plant Representation Committee was a "labor organization." . . . My reading of the record supports the Board's conclusion that the committee was a labor organization as defined in §2(5) as interpreted by the Supreme Court in [*Cabot Carbon*]. . . .

However much there may be a need for "bona fide, socially desirable employee committee[s] or joint employer-employee committee[s] that [are] something less than a labor organization and something more than a Great Books Study Group," NLRB v. Walton Manufacturing Co., 289 F.2d 177, 182 (5th Cir. 1961) (Wisdom, J., dissenting in part), that objective should not be achieved by overly restricting the definition of a labor organization. Rather, I believe, the test to be emphasized is employer domination, Section 8(a)(1), (2) of the National Labor Relations Act. . . .

NOTES

1. Should a plant committee's presentation to management of employees' "views" on working conditions, without specific recommendations for accommodating those views, constitute "dealing" under §2(5)? The Board has answered "yes," relying on the *Cabot Carbon* proposition that the term "dealing" is broader than the term "collective bargaining." Thompson Ramo Wooldridge, Inc. (Dage Television Division), 132 N.L.R.B. 993 (1961), *enforced*, 305 F.2d 807 (7th Cir. 1962). Are you satisfied with the *Streamway* court's efforts to distinguish "communication of ideas" from "dealing"?

2. Was the court in *Streamway* on solid ground in using decisions on "domination" — e.g., *Modern Plastics* and *Federal-Mogul* — to support its resolution of the "labor organization" issue? Did the court effectuate its own "enlightened" social purposes or Congress'? Was the court sufficiently def-

erential to the Board? See generally, Hogler, Employee Involvement Programs and NLRB v. Scott & Fetzer Co.: The Developing Interpretation of Section 8(a)(2), 35 Lab. L.J. 21 (1984).

3. *Streamway* appears to give great weight to "employee free choice" under §8(a)(2) and, specifically, in relation to the threshold question of what constitutes a "labor organization." Can the justification for this interpretation be found in the section itself? If consideration of employee preferences is proper (even on the definitional question), is it clear that the In-Plant Representation Committee was the "choice" of the Streamway employees? See Note, Collective Bargaining as an Industrial System: An Argument Against Judicial Revision of Section 8(a)(2) of the National Labor Relations Act, 96 Harv. L. Rev. 1662 (1983) (criticizing judicial preoccupation with employee preferences rather than arms-length collective bargaining); but see Note, New Standards for Domination and Support Under Section 8(a)(2), 82 Yale L.J. 510 (1973) (criticizing the Board's approach as reflecting only an adversarial model of labor relations while disregarding employee satisfaction with other forms of representation).

4. In Sparks Nugget, Inc., 230 N.L.R.B. 275 (1977), *enforced sub nom.* NLRB v. Silver Spur Casino, 623 F.2d 571 (9th Cir. 1980), *cert. denied*, 451 U.S. 906 (1981), the employer established an "impartial Employees Council" for resolving grievances that supervisors could not settle. Employees in each department elected their own council representative. When hearing specific grievances, the council consisted of the grievant's elected representative, the employer's industrial relations director (who served as chairman), and a third member, selected by these two, from the management of a department other than the grievant's. The Board held that the council, since it adjudicated rather than advocated, did not "deal with" management but performed a management function. Hence, the employer's creation and domination of the council (even in the context of other unfair labor practices) did not violate §8(a)(2). Is it likely that the rationale of this decision will apply to many employee committees outside the grievance context? Cf. Note, Does Employer Implementation of Employee Production Teams Violate Section 8(a)(2) of the National Labor Relations Act? 49 Ind. L.J. 516, 531-536 (1974).

5. At the outset of a union's organizing campaign, the employer, in casual conversation with some of his employees, stated: "I hope there won't ever be a union in this plant. But if there has to be one, I would prefer that you employees form your own union rather than bring one in from the outside." Should §8(c) protect this statement from challenge under §8(a)(1) or §8(a)(2)? Cf. Texaco, Inc. v. NLRB, 722 F.2d 1226 (5th Cir. 1984).

6. The Labor Management Cooperation Act of 1978, Pub. L. No.

95-524, §6(c)(2), 92 Stat. 2020, was enacted to add §205A to the LMRA. This legislation authorizes the Federal Mediation and Conciliation Service (FMCS) to provide financial and other assistance in the creation of joint labor-management committees organized for the purposes of "improving labor management relationships, job security, organizational effectiveness, enhancing economic development or involving workers in decisions affecting their jobs including improving communication with respect to subjects of mutual interest and concern." A committee limited to a single plant is not eligible for assistance if the plant's employees are unorganized and not covered by a collective bargaining agreement. While an unorganized employer may participate in an area or industry wide committee, such committees qualify for assistance only if all unions representing the employees of other employer-members participate. Committees found to have been created for the purpose of "interfer[ing] with collective bargaining" or "discourag[ing] the exercise of [§7] rights" are expressly denied assistance.

Does the federal assistance made available by this statute encroach on §8(a)(2)'s policy of "employee free choice"? For a report on the activities of some of the 21 committees awarded §205A grants during the first two years of the FMCS Cooperation Program, see 113 L.R.R. 134 (1983). Cf. Jackson, An Alternative to Unionization and the Wholly Unorganized Shop: A Legal Basis for Sanctioning Joint Employer-Employee Committees and Increasing Employee Free Choice, 28 Syracuse L. Rev. 809 (1977).

7. Employer payments to union officials while on union business raise questions under NLRA, §8(a)(2); LMRA, §302; and LMRDA, §§202 and 203. But payments for time spent on grievance adjustment and, indeed, for full time company-paid union grievance representatives, are not uncommon. See Dwyer, Employer-Paid "Union Time" Under the Federal Labor Laws, 12 Lab. L.J. 236 (1961). Would it be material that payments by a firm covered, in part, time spent on bargaining units outside that firm? See N.L.R.B. Gen. Coun. Advice Mem. No. 30-CA-3614, in Bemis Mfg. Co., 93 L.R.R.M. 1332 (1976).

8. In some industries supervisors commonly maintain union membership, for job security and other reasons. Hence there is a risk that participation by supervisors in the internal affairs of unions — e.g., holding union office or voting in internal union elections — will be found to violate §8(a)(2), particularly if such supervisors occupy "high level" positions with the employer. See, e.g., Schwenk Inc., 229 N.L.R.B. 640 (1977); Note, 75 Harv. L. Rev. 1443 (1962).

In addition, participation by supervisors in efforts to organize employees may constitute a violation of §8(a)(2) and, as noted earlier in the representation context (see supra p. 112), may also constitute a basis for dismissing an election petition or for invalidating an election. Such results usually are based on a finding either that employees were led to believe that supervisors were acting for the employer (and, thus, that their employer favored the union) or that employees' support of the union was prompted by fear of reprisals by union-oriented supervisors. Here, too, the Board will consider the level of a supervisor's managerial authority. See, e.g., Gary Aircraft Corp., 220 N.L.R.B. 187 (1975) (declining to upset union-won election where pro-union supervisors would not have been viewed as employer's alter ego given employer's own extensive antiunion campaign; employee fear of reprisal unlikely since "low-level" supervisor's authority extended to only small fraction of employees). The Board's "major-minor" distinction, in this context, has been rejected by some courts as substituting labels for actual inquiries into the coercive potential of supervisory conduct. See ITT Lighting Fixtures v. NLRB, 712 F.2d 40, 44 (2d Cir. 1983) (faulting Board for basing distinction between supervisors on "power to retaliate" without considering "power to reward"), cert. denied, 104 S. Ct. 2361 (1984). But see Fall River Sav. Bank v. NLRB, 649 F.2d 50, 57 (1st Cir. 1981) (NLRB entitled to infer lack of coercion from low-level supervisors' limited retaliatory power).

Note: Remedies Under Section 8(a)(2)

Prior to the Taft-Hartley Act, the NLRB would typically order the "disestablishment" of an unaffiliated union found to have been "dominated" by an employer. That remedy operated to bar the union, in perpetuum, from being recognized by the offending employer. When, however, the "dominated union" was affiliated with a national union, the Board would order that recognition be withheld pending certification. The Board's rationale was that a union affiliated with an international beyond the employer's control could not be "permanently subjugated." Reading the 1947 amendment to §10(c) of the NLRA as excluding such disparate treatment, the Board in Carpenter Steel Co., 76 N.L.R.B. 670, 673 (1948), announced the following approach:

> In all cases in which we find that an employer has dominated, or interfered with, or contributed support to a labor organization, or has committed any of these proscribed acts, we will find such conduct a violation of §8(a)(2) of the Act, as amended in 1947, regardless of whether the organization involved is affiliated. Where we find that an employer's unfair labor practices have been so extensive as to constitute *domination* of the organization, we shall order its disestablishment, whether or not it be affiliated. The Board believes that disestablishment is still necessary as a remedy, in order effectively to remove the consequences of an employer's unfair labor practices . . . in those cases,

perhaps few in number, in which an employer's control of *any* labor organization has extended to the point of actual domination. But when the Board finds that an employer's unfair labor practices were limited to interference and support and never reached the point of domination, we shall only order that recognition be withheld until certification, again without regard to whether or not the organization happens to be affiliated. Subsequent representation proceedings in such situations will be governed, of course, by the provisions of §9(c)(2).

Disestablishment orders have run against not only the tainted union but also any "successor thereto." But the Board has indicated that an organization may escape its predecessor's taint if the employer, "prior to the formation of the successor, has established a clear line of fracture between the two organizations by publicly and unequivocally disestablishing the old organization and by assuring the employees of their freedom from further interference with their choice of bargaining representative." 16 N.L.R.B. Ann. Rep. 102 (1951). See also NLRB v. O.E. Szekely & Assoc., Inc., 259 F.2d 652 (6th Cir. 1958) (disestablishment order against "successor" does not preclude employees, acting independently of the employer, from immediately forming another labor organization).

Where the only illegal acts have occurred outside §10(b)'s six-month limitation period, such acts cannot serve as a valid basis for a §8(a)(2) complaint. See, e.g., Mt. Clements Metal Products Co., 126 N.L.R.B. 1297 (1960). Nevertheless, in determining whether conduct within the limitation period justifies a finding of unlawful domination, the Board, relying on the Supreme Court's interpretation of §10(b) in Local Lodge 1424, IAM v. NLRB (Bryan Mfg. Co.), 362 U.S. 411 (1960), will consider evidence of antecedent events insofar as it sheds light on the employer's later conduct. See NLRB v. Erie Marine, Inc., 465 F.2d 104 (3d Cir. 1972); 25 N.L.R.B. Ann. Rep. 61, 125 (1961).

International Ladies' Garment Workers Union v. NLRB
366 U.S. 731 (1961)

CLARK, J. We are asked to decide . . . whether it was an unfair labor practice for both an employer and a union to enter into an agreement under which the employer recognized the union as exclusive bargaining representative of certain of his employees, although in fact only a minority of those employees had authorized the union to represent their interests. The Board found that by extending such recognition, even though done in the good-faith belief that the union had the consent of a majority of employees in the appropriate bargaining unit, the employer interfered with the organizational rights of his employees in violation of §8(a)(1) . . . and that such recognition also constituted unlawful support to a labor organization in violation of §8(a)(2). In addition, the Board found that the union violated §8(b)(1)(A) by its acceptance of exclusive bargaining authority at a time when in fact it did not have the support of a majority of the employees, and this in spite of its bona fide belief that it did. Accordingly, the Board ordered the unfair labor practices discontinued and directed the holding of a representation election.[r] The Court of Appeals, by a divided vote, granted enforcement, 280 F.2d 616 [D.C. Cir.]. . . . We agree with the Board and the Court of Appeals that such extension and acceptance of recognition constitute unfair labor practices, and that the remedy provided was appropriate.

In October 1956 the petitioner union initiated an organizational campaign at Bernhard-Altmann Texas Corporation's knitwear manufacturing plant in San Antonio, Texas. No other labor organization was similarly engaged at that time. During the course of that campaign, on July 29, 1957, certain of the company's Topping Department employees went on strike in protest against a wage reduction. That dispute was in no way related to the union campaign, however, and the organizational efforts were continued during the strike. Some of the striking employees had signed authorization cards solicited by the union during its drive, and, while the strike was in progress, the union entered upon a course of negotiations with the employer. As a result of those negotiations, held in New York City where the home offices of both were located, on August 30, 1957, the employer and union signed a "memorandum of understanding." In that memorandum the company recognized the union as exclusive bargaining representative of "all production and shipping employees." The union representative asserted that the union's comparison of the employee authorization cards in its possession with the number of eligible employees [that] representatives of the company furnished it indicated that the union had in fact secured such cards from a majority of employees in the unit. Neither employer nor union made any effort at that time to check the cards in the union's possession against the employee roll, or otherwise, to ascertain with any degree of certainty that the union's assertion, later found by the Board to be erroneous, was founded on fact rather than upon good-faith assumption. The agreement, containing no union security provision, called for the ending of the strike and for certain improved wages and conditions of employment. It also provided that a "formal agreement containing these terms" would "be promptly drafted . . . and signed by both parties within the next two weeks."

[r] [As the next page of this case indicates, the Board did not order an election but made recognition of the union contingent on its certification by the NLRB. See Bernhard-Altmann Texas Corp., 122 N.L.R.B. 1289, 1294-1297 (1959). — EDS.]

Thereafter, on October 10, 1957, a formal collective bargaining agreement, embodying the terms of the August 30 memorandum, was signed by the parties. . . . It is not disputed that as of execution of the formal contract the union in fact represented a clear majority of employees in the appropriate unit. In upholding the complaints filed against the employer and union by the General Counsel, the Board decided[6] that the employer's good-faith belief that the union in fact represented a majority of employees in the unit on the critical date of the memorandum of understanding was not a defense, "particularly where, as here, the Company made no effort to check the authorization cards against its payroll records." 122 N.L.R.B. 1289, 1292. Noting that the union was "actively seeking recognition at the time such recognition was granted," and that "the Union was [not] the passive recipient of an unsolicited gift bestowed by the Company," the Board found that the union's execution of the August 30 agreement was a "direct deprivation" of the nonconsenting majority employees' organizational and bargaining rights. . . . Accordingly, the Board ordered the employer to withhold all recognition from the union and to cease giving effect to agreements entered into with the union; the union was ordered to cease acting as bargaining representative of any of the employees until such time as a Board-conducted election demonstrated its majority status, and to refrain from seeking to enforce the agreements previously entered. . . .

At the outset, we reject as without relevance to our decision the fact that, as of the execution date of the formal agreement on October 10, petitioner represented a majority of the employees. As the Court of Appeals indicated, the recognition of the minority union on August 30, 1957, was "a fait accompli depriving the majority of the employees of their guaranteed right to choose their own representative." 280 F.2d, at 621. It is, therefore, of no consequence that petitioner may have acquired by October 10 the necessary majority if, during the interim, it was acting unlawfully. Indeed, such acquisition of majority status itself might indicate that the recognition secured by the August 30 agreement afforded petitioner a deceptive cloak of authority with which to persuasively elicit additional employee support.

. . . Likewise, no question of picketing is presented. Lastly, the violation which the Board found was the grant by the employer of exclusive representation status to a minority union, as distinguished from an employer's bargaining with a minority union for its members only. Therefore, the exclusive representation provision is the vice in the agreement, and discussion of "collective bargaining," as distinguished from "exclusive rec-

---

[6]Member Fanning agreed with a majority of the Board that the employer violated §8(a)(1) and (2), but dissented as to the finding of union violation of §8(b)(1)(A). 122 N.L.R.B. 1289, 1297.

ognition," is pointless.[8] Moreover, the insistence that we hold the agreement valid and enforceable as to those employees who consented to it must be rejected. On the facts shown, the agreement must fail in its entirety. It was obtained under the erroneous claim of majority representation. Perhaps the employer would not have entered into it if he had known the facts. Quite apart from other conceivable situations, the unlawful genesis of this agreement precludes its partial validity.

In their selection of a bargaining representative, §9(a) of the Wagner Act guarantees employees freedom of choice and majority rule. J. I. Case Co. v. Labor Board, 321 U.S. 332, 339. In short, as we said in Brooks v. Labor Board, 348 U.S. 96, 103, the Act placed "a nonconsenting minority under the bargaining responsibility of an agency selected by a majority of the workers." Here, however, the reverse has been shown to be the case. Bernhard-Altmann granted exclusive bargaining status to an agency selected by a minority of its employees, thereby impressing that agent upon the nonconsenting majority. There could be no clearer abridgment of §7 of the Act, assuring employees the right "to bargain collectively through representatives of their own choosing" or "to refrain from" such activity. It follows, without need of further demonstration, that the employer activity found present here violated §8(a)(1). . . . Section 8(a)(2) of the Act makes it an unfair labor practice for an employer to "contribute . . . support" to a labor organization. The law has long been settled that a grant of exclusive recognition to a minority union constitutes unlawful support in violation of that section, because the union so favored is given "a marked advantage over any other in securing the adherence of employees." Labor Board v. Pennsylvania Greyhound Lines, 303 U.S. 261, 267. In the Taft-Hartley Law, Congress added §8(b)(1)(A) to the Wagner Act, prohibiting, as the Court of Appeals held, "unions from invading the rights of employees under §7 in a fashion comparable to the activities of employers prohibited under §8(a)(1)." 280 F.2d, at 620. It was the intent of Congress to impose upon unions the same restrictions which the Wagner Act imposed on employers with respect to violations of employee rights.

The petitioner, while taking no issue with the fact of its minority status on the critical date, maintains that both Bernhard-Altmann's and its own good-faith beliefs in petitioner's majority status are a complete defense. To countenance such an excuse would place in permissibly careless employer

[8] Relying upon reference to §9 decertification proceedings, petitioner contends that such a contract with a minority union does not prevent employees from exercising complete freedom. The availability of such a remedy is doubtful in view of the Board's position that the "contract bar" defense prevents a showing of lack of majority status at the time a contract was made. See In re Columbia River Salmon & Tuna Packers Assn., 91 N.L.R.B. 1424, and cases cited therein.

and union hands the power to completely frustrate employee realization of the premise of the Act — that its prohibitions will go far to assure freedom of choice and majority rule in employee selection of representatives. We find nothing in the statutory language prescribing scienter as an element of the unfair labor practices here involved. The act made unlawful by §8(a)(2) is employer support of a minority union. Here that support is an accomplished fact. More need not be shown. . . .

This conclusion . . . places no particular hardship on the employer or the union. It merely requires that recognition be withheld until the Board-conducted election results in majority selection of a representative. The Board's order here, as we might infer from the employer's failure to resist its enforcement, would apparently result in similarly slight hardship upon it. We do not share petitioner's apprehension that holding such conduct unlawful will somehow induce a breakdown, or seriously impede the progress of collective bargaining. If an employer takes reasonable steps to verify union claims, themselves advanced only after careful estimate — precisely what Bernhard-Altmann and petitioner failed to do here — he can readily ascertain their validity and obviate a Board election. We fail to see any onerous burden involved in requiring responsible negotiators to be careful, by cross-checking, for example well-analyzed employer records with union listings on authorization cards. Individual and collective employee rights may not be trampled upon merely because it is inconvenient to avoid doing so. Moreover, no penalty is attached to the violation. Assuming that an employer in good faith accepts or rejects a union claim of majority status, the validity of his decision may be tested in an unfair labor practice proceeding. If he is found to have erred in extending or withholding recognition, he is subject only to a remedial order requiring him to conform his conduct to the norms set out in the Act, as was the case here. No further penalty results. We believe the Board's remedial order is the proper one in such cases. . . .

Affirmed.

DOUGLAS, J., with whom BLACK, J., concurred, dissenting in part. I think the Court is correct insofar as it sets aside the exclusive recognition clause in the contract. I think it is incorrect in setting aside the entire contract. *First*, that agreement secured valuable benefits for the union's members regarding wages and hours, work standards and distribution, discharge and discipline, holidays, vacations, health and welfare fund, and other matters. Since there was no duly selected representative for all the employees authorized in accordance with the Act, it certainly was the right of the employee union members to designate the union or any other appropriate person to make this contract they desired. To hold the contract void as to the union's voluntary members seems to me to go beyond the competency of the Board under the Act and to be unsupported by any principle of contract law. Certainly there is no principle of justice or fairness with which I am familiar that requires these employees to be stripped of the benefits they acquired by the good-faith bargaining of their designated agent. Such a deprivation gives no protection to the majority who were not members of the union and arbitrarily takes from the union members their contract rights. . . .

The present case is unique. The findings are that both the employer and the union were in "good faith" in believing that the union represented a majority of the workers. Good-faith violations of the Act are nonetheless violations; and the present violation warrants disestablishment of the union as a majority representative. But this good-faith mistake hardly warrants full and complete disestablishment, heretofore reserved for flagrant violations of the Act. Its application here smacks more of a penalty than of a remedial measure.

I think this union is entitled to speak for its members until another union is certified as occupying the bargaining field. That is its common-law right in no way diluted or impaired by the Act.

NOTES

1. A collective agreement between parties to an established bargaining relationship may contain a promise by the employer to remain "neutral" in any organizing campaign conducted by the union in the future at other plants operated, or subsequently opened, by the employer. Although such clauses vary in nature and scope, the typical neutrality pledge contemplates that the employer will not answer or oppose the union's organizational campaign. (a) Should an employer's agreement to refrain from taking a stand against a union constitute illegal "assistance" or "support" of that union under §8(a)(2)? (b) Is "employee free choice" impaired when an employer's views on a particular union and the representation issue in general are withheld from his employees? (c) If a contractual pledge of neutrality is enforceable against the employer, in what forum should enforcement occur and what is an appropriate remedy for the employer's breach of contract? See UAW v. Dana Corp., 679 F.2d 634 (6th Cir. 1982), *vacated as moot*, 697 F.2d 718 (1983) (en banc); Dana Corp., 76 Lab. Arb. 125 (1981) (Mittenthal, Arb.). For a critical assessment of neutrality agreements, see Kramer, Miller & Bierman, Neutrality Agreements: The New Frontier in Labor Relations — Fair Play or Foul? 23 B.C.L. Rev. 39 (1981). Cf. NLRB v. Magnavox Co., supra p. 160.

2. An employer's obligation to remain neutral in the face of competing union claims for recognition is examined in Chapter 6(A).

3. For consideration of a "prehire" agreement with a minority union in the construction industry, authorized by §8(f) of the Act, see Chapter 11(B), p. 1197.

CHAPTER 5

PROTECTION OF THE ORGANIZING AND BARGAINING PROCESS AGAINST "DISCRIMINATION"

As indicated in Chapter 4, the proscription against "discrimination" in §8(3) of the Wagner Act was designed to curb an employer's control over jobs as a weapon against organization and other "concerted activities" protected by §7. Such "discrimination" had taken many different forms, but its proto-type had been the discharge of (or refusal to hire) individuals for belonging to, or actively supporting, a union. After the Wagner Act, only in the rarest case would an employer, with primitive candor, tell an employee that his discharge was "because of the union." Such reprisals were almost always ostensibly based on other and lawful grounds, such as inefficiency or breach of plant rules. When an employer was accused of discharges or other discipline in violation of §8(3) [now §8(a)(3)], the question for adjudication was typically one of fact, i.e., whether the stated reason for discipline had been the true reason or only a pretext for reprisals prompted by employee activities protected by the statute. Such questions generally turned on the employer's motivations, and their resolution, although of critical importance to the interests at stake and to the achievement of the statutory purposes, rarely raised important or difficult issues of construction.

Significant interpretive issues, however, arose more frequently when employer action was avowedly a response to "concerted activities," but was defended as necessary for the protection of a firm's legitimate interests. The cases raised three principal difficulties: First, "concerted activities," read literally, encompassed a broad range of means — from peaceful persuasion to violence — directed at a variety of ends. Consequently, if the interest in joint action was to be reconciled with competing interests, such as industrial order and efficiency, it was necessary to determine which of the range of activities concerted in fact would be given legal protection by insulating them against the employer's economic sanctions. The second difficulty was that §8(a)(3) proscribed "discrimination" without defining either "discrimination" or the additional circumstances necessary to complete a violation of that section. Third, even when legally protected activities were involved, an employer, although barred from engaging in reprisals or "discrimination," could, in response to such activities, take certain countermeasures to protect his legitimate interests. For example, an employer could not lawfully discharge employees for engaging in an economic strike not barred by an agreement or by §8(d) of the Act; yet, he could lawfully hire permanent replacements even though such replacements might substantially "interfere" with the protected activity of striking and have the same practical consequences on strikers as discharge. In determining what measures an employer might lawfully adopt to counter legally protected economic pressure by employees, the Board and the courts had to confront difficulties arising from permitting some countermeasures while prohibiting "discrimination." Finally, although acts of discipline violative of §8(a)(3) also violated derivatively §8(a)(1), the converse, as we shall see, was not necessarily true. Hence, the question arose as to the independent significance of §8(a)(1) in appraising employer conduct that deprived unionized employees of jobs or of particular job benefits.

This chapter will deal with the foregoing issues as they arise in a variety of functional contexts, ranging from preorganizational situations to situations involving an established union whose role is apparently accepted by the employer but whose demands are being resisted. For useful general discussions, see Getman, §8(a)(3) of the NLRA and the Effort to Insulate Free Employee Choice, 32 U. Chi. L. Rev. 735 (1965); Getman, The Protection of Economic Pressure by Section 7 of the National Labor Relations Act, 115 U. Pa. L. Rev. 1195 (1967); Christensen & Svanoe, Motive and Intent in the Commission of Unfair Labor Practices: The Supreme Court and Fictive Formality, 77 Yale L.J. 1269 (1968).

A.   "PROTECTED" ACTIVITIES: AN OVERVIEW

NLRB v. City Disposal Systems, Inc.
104 S. Ct. 1505 (1984)

BRENNAN, J. James Brown . . . was discharged when he refused to drive a truck that he . . . believed to be unsafe because of faulty brakes. Article XXI of the collective-bargaining agreement between respondent and [Teamsters] Local 247, which covered Brown, provides:

[t]he Employer shall not require employees to take out on the streets or highways any vehicle that is not in safe operating condition or equipped with

safety appliances prescribed by law. It shall not be a violation of the Agreement where employees refuse to operate such equipment unless such refusal is unjustified.[1]

The question . . . is whether Brown's honest and reasonable assertion of his right to be free of the obligation to drive unsafe trucks constituted "concerted activit[y]" within the meaning of §7 of the [NLRA]. . . .

I

. . . Respondent, City Disposal System, Inc., hauls garbage for the City of Detroit . . . , to a land fill about 37 miles away. . . . James Brown was assigned to truck No. 245. On Saturday, May 12, 1979, Brown observed that a fellow driver had difficulty with the brakes of . . . truck No. 244. As a result of the brake problem, truck No. 244 nearly collided with Brown's truck. After unloading their garbage at the land fill, Brown and the driver of truck No. 244 brought No. 244 to respondent's truck-repair facility, where they were told that the brakes would be repaired either over the weekend or in the morning of Monday, May 14.

Early in the morning of Monday, May 14, while transporting a load of garbage to the land fill, Brown experienced difficulty with one of the wheels of his own truck — No. 245 — and brought that truck in for repair. . . . Brown was told that, because of a backlog at the facility, No. 245 could not be repaired that day. Brown reported the situation to his supervisor, Otto Jasmund, who ordered Brown to punch out and go home. Before Brown could leave, however, Jasmund changed his mind and asked Brown to drive truck No. 244 instead. Brown refused, explaining that "there's something wrong with that truck . . . with the brakes . . . there was a grease seal or something leaking causing it to be affecting the brakes." Brown did not, however, explicitly refer to Article XXI of the collective-bargaining agreement or to the agreement in general. In response to Brown's refusal to drive truck No. 244, Jasmund angrily told Brown to go home. At that point, an argument ensued and Robert Madary, another supervisor, intervened, repeating Jasmund's request that Brown drive truck No. 244. Again, Brown refused, explaining that No. 244 "has got problems and I don't want to drive it." Madary replied that half the trucks had problems and that if respondent tried to fix all of them it would be unable to do business. He went on to tell Brown that "[w]e've got all this garbage out here to haul and you tell me about you

[1] Article XXI also provides that "[t]he Employer shall not ask or require any employee to take out equipment that has been reported by any other employee as being in an unsafe operating condition until same has been approved as being safe by the mechanical department."

don't want to drive." Brown responded, "Bob, what you going to do, put the garbage ahead of the safety of the men?" Finally, Madary went to his office and Brown went home. Later that day, Brown received word that he had been discharged. . . .

. . . [The next day] Brown filed a written grievance, pursuant to the collective-bargaining agreement, asserting that truck No. 244 was defective, that it had been improper for him to have been ordered to drive the truck, and that his discharge was therefore also improper. The union, however, found no objective merit in the grievance and declined to process it.

On September 7, 1979, Brown filed [a] charge with the NLRB. . . . The [ALJ] found that Brown had been discharged for refusing to operate truck No. 244, that Brown's refusal was covered by §7 . . . , and that respondent had therefore [violated] §8(a)(1). The ALJ held that an employee who acts alone in asserting a contractual right can nevertheless be engaged in concerted activity within the meaning of §7. . . . The NLRB adopted the findings and conclusions of the ALJ and ordered that Brown be reinstated with backpay.

. . . [T]he Court of Appeals disagreed with the ALJ and the Board.[a] Finding that Brown's refusal to drive truck No. 244 was an action taken solely on his own behalf, the [court] concluded that the refusal was not a concerted activity within the meaning of §7. This holding followed the court's prior decision in ARO, Inc. v. NLRB, 596 F.2d 713 (CA6 1979), in which the Court of Appeals had held:

> For an individual claim or complaint to amount to concerted action under the Act it must not have been made solely on behalf of an individual employee, but it must be made on behalf of other employees or at least be made with the object of inducing or preparing for group action and have some arguable basis in the collective bargaining agreement.

Id., at 718.

II

. . . The NLRB's decision in this case applied the Board's longstanding "*Interboro* doctrine," under which an individual's assertion of a right grounded in a collective-bargaining agreement is recognized as "concerted

---

[a] [The Court here noted that at least four other circuits had agreed with the Court of Appeals, while three circuits had accepted the Board's contrary view that "concerted activities" includes an individual's assertion of a right grounded in the bargaining agreement. — Eds.]

activit[y]" and therefore accorded the protection of §7.[6] See Interboro Contractors, Inc., 157 N.L.R.B. 1295, 1298 (1966), *enforced*, 388 F.2d 495 (CA2 1967). . . . The Board has relied on two justifications for the doctrine: First, the assertion of a right contained in a collective-bargaining agreement is an extension of the concerted action that produced the agreement . . . ; and second, the assertion of such a right affects the rights of all employees covered by the collective-bargaining agreement.

We have often reaffirmed that the task of defining the scope of §7 "is for the Board to perform in the first instance . . . ," Eastex, Inc. v. NLRB, 437 U.S. 556, 568 (1978), and, on an issue that implicates its expertise in labor relations, a reasonable construction by the Board is entitled to considerable deference. . . . The question . . . is thus narrowed to whether the Board's application of §7 to Brown's refusal to drive truck No. 244 is reasonable. . . .

A

. . . The term "concerted activit[y]" is not defined in the Act but it clearly enough embraces the activities of employees who have joined together in order to achieve common goals. See, e.g., Meyers Industries, 268 N.L.R.B. No. 73, at 3 (1984). What is not self-evident from the language of the Act, however, . . . is the precise manner in which particular actions of an individual employee must be linked to the actions of fellow employees in order to permit it to be said that the individual is engaged in concerted activity. . . .

Although one could interpret the phrase, "to engage in concerted activities," to refer to a situation in which two or more employees are working together at the same time and the same place toward a common goal, the language of §7 does not confine itself to such a narrow meaning. In fact, §7 itself defines both joining and assisting labor organizations — activities in which a single employee can engage — as concerted activities.[8] Indeed, even the courts that have rejected the *Interboro* doctrine recognize the possibility that an individual employee may be engaged in concerted activity when he acts alone. They have limited their recognition of this type of concerted

---

[6]The NLRB has recently held that, where a group of employees are not unionized and there is no collective-bargaining agreement, an employee's assertion of a right that can only be presumed to be of interest to other employees is not concerted activity. Meyers Industries, 268 N.L.R.B. No. 73 (1984). The Board, however, distinguished that case from the cases involving the *Interboro* doctrine, which is based on the existence of a collective-bargaining agreement. The *Meyers* case is thus of no relevance here.

[8]Section 7 lists these and other activities initially and concludes the list with the phrase "*other* concerted activities," thereby indicating that the enumerated activities are deemed to be "concerted."

activity, however, to two situations: (1) that in which the lone employee intends to induce group activity, and (2) that in which the employee acts as a representative of at least one other employee. See, e.g., Aro, Inc. v. NLRB, 596 F.2d, at 713, 717 (CA6 1979); NLRB v. Northern Metal Co., 440 F.2d 881, 884 (CA3 1971). The disagreement over the *Interboro* doctrine, therefore, merely reflects differing views regarding the nature of the relationship that must exist between the action of the individual employee and the actions of the group in order for §7 to apply. We cannot say that the Board's view of that relationship, as applied in the *Interboro* doctrine, is unreasonable.

The invocation of a right rooted in a collective-bargaining agreement is unquestionably an integral part of the process that gave rise to the agreement. That process — beginning with the organization of a union, continuing into the negotiation of a collective-bargaining agreement, and extending through the enforcement of the agreement — is a single, collective activity. Obviously, an employee could not invoke a right grounded in a collective-bargaining agreement were it not for the prior negotiating activities of his fellow employees. Nor would it make sense for a union to negotiate a collective-bargaining agreement if individual employees could not invoke the rights thereby created against their employer. Moreover, when an employee invokes a right grounded in the collective-bargaining agreement, he does not stand alone. Instead, he brings to bear on his employer the power and resolve of all his fellow employees. When, for instance, James Brown refused to drive a truck he believed to be unsafe, he was in effect reminding his employer that he and his fellow employees, at the time their collective-bargaining agreement was signed, had extracted a promise from City Disposal that they would not be asked to drive unsafe trucks. He was also reminding his employer that if it persisted in ordering him to drive an unsafe truck, he could reharness the power of that group to ensure the enforcement of that promise. It was just as though James Brown was reassembling his fellow union members to reenact their decision not to drive unsafe trucks. A lone employee's invocation of a right grounded in his collective-bargaining agreement is, therefore, a concerted activity in a very real sense.

Furthermore, the acts of joining and assisting a labor organization, which §7 explicitly recognizes as concerted, are related to collective action in essentially the same way that the invocation of a collectively bargained right is related to collective action. When an employee joins or assists a labor organization, his actions may be divorced in time, and in location as well, from the actions of fellow employees. Because of the integral relationship among the employees' actions, however, Congress viewed each employee as engaged in concerted activity. The lone employee could not join or assist a labor organization were it not for the related organizing activities of his fellow employees. Conversely, there would be limited utility in forming a labor organization if other employees could not join or assist the organization once it is formed. Thus, the formation of a labor organization is integrally related to the activity of joining or assisting such an organization in the same sense that the negotiation of a collective-bargaining agreement is integrally related to the invocation of a right provided for in the agreement. In each case, neither the individual activity nor the group activity would be complete without the other.[10]

The *Interboro* doctrine is also entirely consistent with the purposes of the Act. . . . Although . . . there is nothing in the legislative history of §7 that specifically expresses the understanding of Congress in enacting the "concerted activities" language, the general history of §7 reveals no inconsistency between the *Interboro* doctrine and congressional intent. That history begins in the early days of the labor movement, when employers invoked the common law doctrines of criminal conspiracy and restraint of trade to thwart workers' attempts to unionize. See Automobile Workers, Local 232 v. Wisconsin Employment Relations Board (Briggs & Stratton), 336 U.S. 245, 257-258 (1949). As this Court recognized in NLRB v. Jones & Laughlin Steel Corp., 301 U.S. 1, 33 (1937), a single employee at that time "was helpless in dealing with an employer, . . . he was dependent ordinarily on his daily wage for the maintenance of himself and his family; . . . if the employer refused to pay him the wages that he thought fair, he was nevertheless unable to leave the employ and resist arbitrary and unfair treatment; . . . union was essential to give laborers opportunity to deal on an equality with their employer."

[10]Of course, at some point an individual employee's actions may become so remotely related to the activities of fellow employees that it cannot reasonably be said that the employee is engaged in concerted activity. For instance, the Board has held that if an employer were to discharge an employee for purely personal "griping," the employee could not claim the protection of §7. See, e.g., Capital Ornamental Concrete Specialties, Inc., 248 N.L.R.B. 851 (1980).

In addition, although the Board relies entirely on its interpretation of §7 as support for the *Interboro* doctrine, it bears noting that under §8(a)(1), an employer commits an unfair labor practice if he or she "interfere[s] with, [or] restrain[s]" concerted activity. It is possible, therefore, for an employer to commit an unfair labor practice by discharging an employee who is not himself involved in concerted activity, but whose actions are related to other employees' concerted activities in such a manner as to render his discharge an interference or restraint on those activities. In the context of the *Interboro* doctrine, for instance, even if an individual's invocation of rights provided for in a collective-bargaining agreement, for some reason, were not concerted activity, the discharge of that individual would still be an unfair labor practice if the result were to restrain or interfere with the concerted activity of negotiating or enforcing a collective-bargaining agreement.

Congress's first attempt to equalize the bargaining power of management and labor, and its first use of the term "concert" in this context, came in 1914 with the enactment of §§6 and 20 of the Clayton Act, which exempted from the antitrust laws certain types of peaceful union activities. . . . There followed, in 1932, the Norris-LaGuardia Act, which declared [§2] that "the individual . . . worker shall be free from the interference, restraint, or coercion, of employers . . . in self-organization or in *other concerted activities for the purpose of collective bargaining or other mutual aid or protection*." (emphasis added). This was the source of the language enacted in §7. It was adopted first in §7(a) of the National Industrial Recovery Act and then, in 1935, in §7 of the NLRA. . . .

. . . [I]t is evident that, in enacting §7 of the NLRA, Congress sought generally to equalize the bargaining power of the employee with that of his employer by allowing employees to band together in confronting an employer regarding the terms and conditions of their employment. There is no indication that Congress intended to limit this protection to situations in which an employee's activity and that of his fellow employees combine with one another in any particular way. Nor, more specifically, does it appear that Congress intended to have this general protection withdrawn in situations in which a single employee, acting alone, participates in an integral aspect of a collective process. Instead, what emerges from the general background of §7 — and what is consistent with the Act's statement of purpose — is a congressional intent to create an equality in bargaining power between the employee and the employer throughout the entire process of labor organizing, collective bargaining, and enforcement of collective-bargaining agreements.

The Board's *Interboro* doctrine, based on a recognition that the potential inequality in the relationship between the employee and the employer continues beyond the point at which a collective-bargaining agreement is signed, mitigates that inequality throughout the duration of the employment relationship, and is, therefore, fully consistent with congressional intent. Moreover, by applying §7 to the actions of individual employees invoking their rights under a collective-bargaining agreement, the *Interboro* doctrine preserves the integrity of the entire collective-bargaining process; for by invoking a right grounded in a collective-bargaining agreement, the employee makes that right a reality, and breathes life, not only into the promises contained in the collective-bargaining agreement, but also into the entire process envisioned by Congress as the means by which to achieve industrial peace.

To be sure, the principal tool by which an employee invokes the rights granted him in a collective-bargaining agreement is the processing of a grievance according to whatever procedures his collective-bargaining agreement establishes. No one doubts that the processing of a grievance in such a manner is concerted activity within the meaning of §7. . . . Indeed, it would make little sense for §7 to cover an employee's conduct while negotiating a collective-bargaining agreement, including a grievance mechanism by which to protect the rights created by the agreement, but not to cover an employee's attempt to utilize that mechanism to enforce the agreement.

In practice, however, there is unlikely to be a bright-line distinction between an incipient grievance, a complaint to an employer, and perhaps even an employee's initial refusal to perform a certain job that he believes he has no duty to perform. It is reasonable to expect that an employee's first response to a situation that he believes violates his collective-bargaining agreement will be a protest to his employer. Whether he files a grievance will depend in part on his employer's reaction and in part upon the nature of the right at issue. In addition, certain rights might not be susceptible of enforcement by the filing of a grievance. In such a case, the collective-bargaining agreement might provide for an alternative method of enforcement, as did the agreement involved in this case, or the agreement might be silent on the matter. Thus, for a variety of reasons, an employee's initial statement to a employer to the effect that he believes a collectively bargained right is being violated, or the employee's initial refusal to do that which he believes he is not obligated to do, might serve as both a natural prelude to, and an efficient substitute for, the filing of a formal grievance. As long as the employee's statement or action is based on a reasonable and honest belief that he is being, or has been, asked to perform a task that he is not required to perform under his collective-bargaining agreement, and the statement or action is reasonably directed toward the enforcement of a collectively bargained right, there is no justification for overturning the Board's judgment that the employee is engaged in concerted activity, just as he would have been had he filed a formal grievance.

The fact that an activity is concerted, however, does not necessarily mean that an employee can engage in the activity with impunity. An employee may engage in concerted activity in such an abusive manner that he loses the protection of §7. See, e.g., Crown Central Petroleum Corp. v. NLRB, 430 F.2d 724, 729 (CA5 1970). . . . Cf. Eastex, Inc. v. NLRB, 437 U.S. 556 (1978) (finding concerted activity nonetheless unprotected); NLRB v. Babcock & Wilcox Co., 351 U.S. 105 (1956) (same). Furthermore, if an employer does not wish to tolerate certain methods by which employees invoke their collectively bargained rights, he is free to negotiate a provision in his collective-bargaining agreement that limits the availability of such methods. . . . Whether Brown's action in this case was unprotected, however, is not before us.

B

Respondent argues that the *Interboro* doctrine undermines the arbitration process by providing employees with the possibility of provoking a discharge and then filing an unfair labor practice claim. This argument, however, misses the mark for several reasons. First, an employee who purposefully follows this route would run the risk that the Board would find his actions concerted but nonetheless unprotected, as discussed above.

Second, the *Interboro* doctrine does not shift dispute resolution from the grievance and arbitration process to NLRB adjudication in any way that is different from the alternative position adopted by the Court of Appeals, and pressed upon us by respondent. . . . [T]he Court of Appeals would allow a finding of concerted activity if two employees together invoke a collectively bargained right, if a lone employee represents another employee in addition to himself when he invokes the right, or if the lone employee invokes the right in a manner that is intended to induce at least one other employee to join him. In each of these situations, however, the underlying substance of the dispute between the employees and the employer is the same as when a single employee invokes a collectively bargained right by himself. In each case the employees are claiming that their employer violated their collective-bargaining agreement, and if the complaining employee or employees in those situations are discharged, their unfair labor practice action would be identical to an action brought by an employee who has been discharged for invoking a collectively bargained right by himself. Because the employees in each of these situations are equally well positioned to go through the grievance and arbitration process, there is no basis for singling out the *Interboro* doctrine as undermining that process any more than would the approach of respondent and the Courts of Appeals that have rejected the doctrine.

Finally, and most importantly, to the extent that the factual issues raised in an unfair labor practice action have been, or can be, addressed through the grievance process, the Board may defer to that process. See Collyer Insulated Wire, 192 N.L.R.B. 837 (1971); Spielberg Manufacturing Co., 112 N.L.R.B. 1080 (1955). There is no reason, therefore, for the Board's interpretation of "concerted activit[y]" in §7 to be constrained by a concern for maintaining the integrity of the grievance and arbitration process.

III

. . . Respondent argues that Brown's action was not concerted because he did not explicitly refer to the collective-bargaining agreement as a basis for his refusal to drive the truck. The Board, however, has never held that an employee must make such an explicit reference for his actions to be covered by the *Interboro* doctrine, and we find that position reasonable. . . . As long as the nature of the employee's complaint is reasonably clear to the person to whom it is communicated, and the complaint does, in fact, refer to a reasonably perceived violation of the collective-bargaining agreement, the complaining employee is engaged in the process of enforcing that agreement. In the context of a workplace dispute, where the participants are likely to be unsophisticated in collective-bargaining matters, a requirement that the employee explicitly refer to the collective-bargaining agreement is likely to serve as nothing more than a trap for the unwary.

Respondent further argues that the Board erred in finding Brown's action concerted based only on Brown's reasonable and honest belief that truck No. 244 was unsafe. Respondent bases its argument on the language of the collective-bargaining agreement, which provides that an employee may refuse to drive an unsafe truck "unless such refusal is unjustified." In the view of respondent, this language allows a driver to refuse to drive a truck only if the truck is objectively unsafe. Regardless of whether respondent's interpretation of the agreement is correct, a question as to which we express no view, this argument confuses the threshold question whether Brown's conduct was concerted with the ultimate question whether that conduct was protected. The rationale of the *Interboro* doctrine compels the conclusion that an honest and reasonable invocation of a collectively bargained right constitutes concerted activity, regardless of whether the employee turns out to have been correct in his belief that his right was violated. See supra, Part II. No one would suggest, for instance, that the filing of a grievance is concerted only if the grievance turns out to be meritorious. As long as the grievance is based on an honest and reasonable belief that a right had been violated, its filing is a concerted activity because it is an integral part of the process by which the collective-bargaining agreement is enforced. The same is true of other methods by which an employee enforces the agreement. On the other hand, if the collective-bargaining agreement imposes a limitation on the means by which a right may be invoked, the concerted activity would be unprotected if it went beyond that limitation.

. . . [B]ecause Brown reasonably and honestly invoked his right to avoid driving unsafe trucks, his action was concerted. It may be that the collective-bargaining agreement prohibits an employee from refusing to drive a truck that he reasonably believes to be unsafe, but that is, in fact, perfectly safe. If so, Brown's action was concerted but unprotected. . . . [H]owever, the only issue before this Court and the only issue passed upon by the Board or the Court of Appeals is whether Brown's action was concerted, not whether it was protected.

IV

. . . [W]e accept the Board's conclusion that James Brown was engaged in concerted activity when he refused to drive truck No. 244. We therefore reverse the judgment of the Court of Appeals and remand the case for further proceedings consistent with this opinion, including an inquiry into whether respondent may continue to defend this action on the theory that Brown's refusal to drive truck No. 244 was unprotected, even if concerted.

O'CONNOR, J., with whom BURGER, C. J., and POWELL and REHNQUIST, JJ., join, dissenting. . . . Although the concepts of individual action for personal gain and "concerted activity" are intuitively incompatible, the Court today defers to the Board's judgment that the *Interboro* doctrine is necessary to safeguard the exercise of rights previously won in the collective bargaining process. Since I consider the *Interboro* doctrine to be an exercise in undelegated legislative power by the Board, I respectfully dissent.

In my view, the fact that the right the employee asserts ultimately can be grounded in the collective bargaining agreement is not enough to make the individual's self-interested action concerted. If it could, then *every* contract claim could be the basis for an unfair labor practice complaint. But the law is clear that an employer's alleged violation of a collective agreement cannot, by itself, provide the basis for an unfair labor practice complaint. See NLRB v. C & C Plywood, 385 U.S. 421, 427-428 (1967). . . . Congress expressly decided that, "[o]nce [the] parties have made a collective bargaining contract[,] the enforcement of that contract should be left to the usual processes of the law and not to the . . . Board." H. R. Conf. Rep. No. 510, 80th Cong., 1st Sess., 42 (1946). . . .

Of course, the Board has considerable discretion to act on contractual matters which are incident to unfair labor practice proceedings. See NRLB v. C & C Plywood, supra. But the fact that the Board can resolve contractual matters incident to unfair labor practice disputes does not give it authority to make unfair labor practice claims out of the contractual disputes themselves. The statutory authority to interpret *some* contract provisions is not authority to resolve *all* labor contract disputes. Congress' decision not to give the Board this broad power indicates that it considered the difference between individual and concerted activity to be a meaningful one. . . .

This Court has previously recognized that the labor laws were designed to encourage employees to act together. See, e.g., NLRB v. Weingarten, Inc., 420 U.S. 251, 260-264 (1975). Even a single employee acting in good faith and asserting a right contained in the collective bargaining agreement may be too fearful, inarticulate, or lacking in skill to relate accurately either the event being investigated or the relevant extenuating factors. Other disinterested employees, especially knowledgeable union stewards, can assist the employee and the employer in eliciting the relevant facts and in preventing misunderstandings and hard feelings. The participation of other employees may save production time, reduce administrative expenses, and avoid unnecessary discharges and disciplinary action. By providing an increased degree of statutory coverage to employees participating in that process, the labor laws encourage and preserve the "practice and procedure of collective bargaining." Emporium Capwell Co. v. Western Addition Community Organization, 420 U.S. 50, 62 (1975). The fact that two employees receive coverage where one acting alone does not is therefore entirely consistent with the labor laws' emphasis on collective action. . . .

The Court and the Board insist that, because the group has previously expressed interest in the right now being asserted, the individual's self-interested expression must be treated as "concerted" to ensure that meaning is given to the contract rights. This argument is mistaken. It confuses the employees' substantive contract entitlements with the process by which those entitlements are to be vindicated. When employees act together in expressing a mutual concern, contractual or otherwise, their action is "concerted" and the statute authorizes them to seek vindication through the Board's administrative processes. In contrast, when an employee acts alone in expressing a personal concern, contractual or otherwise, his action is not "concerted;" in such cases, the statute instructs him to seek vindication through his union, and where necessary, through the courts. See Republic Steel Corp. v. Maddox, 379 U.S. 650 (1965); Hines v. Anchor Motor Freight, Inc., 424 U.S. 554 (1976). Under either scenario, the integrity of the rights won in the collective bargaining process and the rights of all other employees are preserved. The question is whether these rights will be vindicated by administrative or by private and judicial processes. . . .

. . . [T]he Interboro doctrine makes little sense when applied to the facts of this case. There is no evidence that employee James Brown discussed the truck's alleged safety problem with other employees, sought their support in remedying the problem, or requested their or his union's assistance in protesting to his employer. He did not seek to warn others of the problem or even initially to file a grievance through his union. He simply asserted that the truck was not safe enough for *him* to drive. James Brown was not engaging in "concerted activity" in any reasonable sense of the term. . . . The fact that the right asserted can be found in the collective bargaining agreement may be relevant to whether activity of that type should be "protected," but not to whether it is "concerted." . . .

I do not mean to imply . . . that conduct should not be considered "concerted" because it is engaged in by only a single employee. The crucial issue is . . . the precise nature of the relationship that must exist between the action of an individual employee and the actions of the group. An employee certainly engages in "concerted activity" when he acts with or expressly on behalf of one or more of the other employees. And, as several of the courts of appeals have concluded, the statutory language can even be stretched to cover an individual who takes action with the proven object of inducing, initiating, or preparing for group action. See, e.g., Aro, Inc. v. NLRB, 596 F.2d 713, 717 (CA6 1979); NLRB v. Northern Metal Co., 440 F.2d 881, 884 (CA3 1971); see also Kohls v. NLRB, 629 F.2d 173, 176-177 (CADC 1980). But it stretches the language past its snapping point to cover an employee's action that is taken solely for personal benefit. . . .

NOTES

1. In Alleluia Cushion Co., 221 N.L.R.B. 999 (1975), an employee in an unorganized plant, acting solely from his own concerns about plant safety and without seeking or obtaining support from any other employee, sought to enforce state safety regulations applicable to the plant by writing to the appropriate regulatory agency. The NLRB, stressing the common interest of all workers in job safety and state and federal legislation on the subject, found "constructive concerted" activity. It reasoned that, absent evidence of overt disavowal, the consent of coworkers (and thus concert of action) emanated from an individual's efforts to enforce statutes designed to benefit all employees.

City Disposal emphasized that the NLRA was designed to redress the individual employee's power imbalance. Does that emphasis undercut the Board's approach in Alleluia, where government regulation aimed at the imbalance was already in place?

2. While City Disposal was pending in the Court, a newly-constituted NLRB, dividing 3 to 1, repudiated the theory of "constructive concerted" activity and overruled Alleluia "and its progeny." Meyers Industries, Inc., 268 N.L.R.B. No. 73, 115 L.R.R.M. 1025 (1984). The case involved a truck driver discharged for his complaints about the safety of the truck he was required to drive, including a complaint filed with a state safety commissioner following an accident, and for refusing to drive the truck after the accident. The majority, although "outraged" by the employer's conduct, held that the discharge did not violate the Act because the driver's actions were not in concert with other employees. The Board, distinguishing situations where there is a bargaining agreement (and disclaiming any intention to deal with

the *Interboro* doctrine), adopted what it termed an "objective" standard of concerted activity:

> In general, to find an employee's activity to be "concerted," we shall require that it be engaged in with or on the authority of other employees, and not solely by and on behalf of the employee himself. . . . It will no longer be sufficient for the General Counsel to set out the subject matter that is of alleged concern to a theoretical group and expect to establish concert of action thereby.

Does the relevant language of §7 support the respective tests of *City Disposal* and *Meyers?* Should it be material to "concertedness" whether two employees, independently and without knowledge of each other's conduct, individually make the same complaint to management about a working condition?

3. When complaints of an individual concern working conditions in a plant that has no union or collective agreement, should the analysis differ from that applied when a plant is covered by a bargaining agreement or the subject matter of the complaint is subject to external regulation? After *Alleluia*, the NLRB extended §7 protection to a variety of individual actions involving neither resort to a regulatory agency nor a matter the subject of legislation. See, e.g., Steere Dairy, Inc., 237 N.L.R.B. 1350 (1978) (single employee's walkout to protest changes in plant job duties). See also Air Surrey Corp., 229 N.L.R.B. 1014 (1977), *enforcement denied*, 601 F.2d 256 (6th Cir. 1979) (employee's inquiry at employer's bank to determine existence of funds to cover upcoming payroll checks, which had been dishonored in the past, presumed supported by fellow employees as effort to secure employer's compliance with state banking statutes).

4. Some courts, confronting a single-employee complaint or protest in unorganized shops, have read "concertedness" to require that individual activity "look toward group action." See, e.g., Mushroom Transp. Co. v. NLRB, 330 F.2d 683, 685 (3d Cir. 1964) (if there is no "object of initiating or inducing or preparing for group action," an individual's activity is "more than likely to be mere 'griping' "). This view is usually attributed to the express language of §7 — "the right to . . . engage in . . . concerted activities." A well-known example is Ontario Knife Co. v. NLRB, 637 F.2d 840 (2d Cir. 1980), where the court limited §7 "to its terms" in all cases not involving the assertion of rights under a bargaining agreement. Judge Friendly, for the court, emphasized that §7 was based on §2 of the Norris-LaGuardia Act and that close adherence to the statutory text of §7 was supported by the history of Norris-LaGuardia, designed, as it was, to protect against injunction of collective activity promoting either unionization or bargaining demands.

As a policy matter, what justification is there for reading into §7 the limitation reflected in *Ontario Knife?* After *City Disposal*, is the "adhere-to-statutory-text" argument still convincing in unorganized settings?

For a useful discussion calling for an expansive reading of §7, see Gorman & Finkin, The Individual and the Requirement of "Concert" Under the National Labor Relations Act, 130 U. Pa. L. Rev. 286 (1981).

5. Section 502 of the NLRA provides that "the quitting of labor by an employee or employees in good faith because of abnormally dangerous conditions for work . . . [shall not] be deemed a strike under this Act." As we shall see (Gateway Coal Co. v. UMW, infra p. 1037), the principal purpose of the section is to provide a shelter against claims that work stoppages violate either a contractual no-strike pledge or a provision of §8(b) of the Act. In *Meyers*, the Board noted but did not address §502 (nor was §502 raised in *City Disposal*); nevertheless, the language of the section ("an employee or employees") appears to reach an individual acting alone.

Does §502 modify §7? Assuming these two provisions create separate NLRA protections, do they take precedence over OSHA regulation of the work place? For a "no" answer to the first question and a "yes" to the second, see NLRB v. Tamara Foods, Inc., 692 F.2d 1171 (8th Cir. 1982), *cert. denied*, 103 S. Ct. 2089 (1983). See generally Note, Refusals of Hazardous Work Assignments: A Proposal for a Uniform Standard, 81 Colum. L. Rev. 544 (1981).

Eastex, Inc. v. NLRB
437 U.S. 556 (1978)

POWELL, J. . . . [Petitioner] manufactures paper products in Silsbee, Tex. Since 1954, petitioner's production employees have been represented by Local 801 of the United Paperworkers International Union. . . . Since Texas is a "right-to-work" State by statute, Local 801 is barred from obtaining an agreement with petitioner requiring all production employees to become union members.

In March 1974, officers of Local 801, seeking to strengthen employee support for the union and perhaps recruit new members in anticipation of upcoming contract negotiations with petitioner, decided to distribute a union newsletter to petitioner's production employees. . . . The first and fourth sections urged employees to support and participate in the union and, more generally, extolled the benefits of union solidarity. The second section encouraged employees to write their legislators to oppose incorporation of the state "right-to-work" statute into a revised state constitution then under consideration, warning that incorporation would "weaken[] Unions and improv[e] the edge business has at the bargaining table." The third section noted that the President recently had vetoed a bill to increase the federal minimum wage from $1.60 to $2.00 per hour, compared this action to the increase of prices and profits in the oil industry under administration policies, and admonished, "As working men and women we must defeat our enemies and elect our friends. If you haven't registered to vote, please do so today." . . .

[In March and April 1974 certain employees as well as union officers were denied permission by the company to distribute the newsletter in the plant's nonworking areas. The union filed unfair labor practice charges.]

At a hearing on the charge, [the company's personnel director] testified that he had no objection to the first and fourth sections of the newsletter. He had denied permission to distribute the newsletter because he "didn't see any way in which [the second and third sections were] related to our association with the Union." The [ALJ] held that although not all of the newsletter had immediate bearing on the relationship between petitioner and Local 801, distribution of all its contents was protected under §7 as concerted activity for the "mutual aid or protection" of employees. Because petitioner had presented no evidence of "special circumstances" to justify a ban on the distribution of protected matter by employees in nonworking areas during nonworking time, the [ALJ] held that petitioner had violated §8(a)(1). . . . The Board affirmed . . . and adopted [the ALJ's] recommended order. Eastex, Inc., 215 N.L.R.B. 271 (1974).

The Court of Appeals enforced the order. Eastex, Inc. v. NLRB, 550 F.2d 198 (5th Cir. 1977). It rejected petitioner's argument that the "mutual aid or protection" clause of §7 protects only concerted activity by employees that is directed at conditions that their employer has the authority or power to change or control. Without expressing an opinion as to the full range of §7 rights "when exercised off the employer's property," id., at 202, the court purported to balance those rights against the employer's property rights and concluded that "whatever is reasonably related to the employees' *jobs* or to their status as employees in the plant may be the subject of such handouts as we treat of here, distributed on the plant premises in such a manner as not to interfere with the work. . . ." Id., at 203 (emphasis in original). The court further held that all of the material in the newsletter here met this test. Id., at 204-205.[9] . . . We affirm.

Two distinct questions are presented. The first is whether, apart from

[9]The court went on to disapprove the alternative ground for the Board's decision, . . . stating that "the presence of some §7 protected material will not rescue that which is significantly not protected." 550 F.2d, at 205. We do not find it necessary to express an opinion as to the correctness of this statement. In an opinion denying rehearing and rehearing en banc, the court reaffirmed that it had balanced the employer's and employees' rights, and it deleted two references in its first opinion to the First Amendment. Eastex, Inc. v. NLRB, 556 F.2d 1280 (5th Cir. 1977).

the location of the activity, distribution of the newsletter is the kind of concerted activity that is protected from employer interference by §§7 and 8(a)(1) of the National Labor Relations Act. If it is, then the second question is whether the fact that the activity takes place on petitioner's property gives rise to a countervailing interest that outweighs the exercise of §7 rights in that location. . . . We address these questions in turn.

A

. . . Petitioner contends that the activity here is not within the "mutual aid or protection" language [of §7] because it does not relate to a "specific dispute" between employees and their own employer "over an issue which the employer has the right or power to affect." In support of its position, petitioner asserts that the term "employees" in §7 refers only to employees of a particular employer, so that only activity by employees on behalf of themselves or other employees of the same employer is protected. Petitioner also argues that the term "collective bargaining" in §7 "indicates a direct bargaining relationship whereas 'other mutual aid or protection' must refer to activities of a similar nature. . . . " Thus, in petitioner's view, under §7 "the employee is only protected for activity within the scope of the employment relationship." Petitioner rejects the idea that §7 might protect any activity that could be characterized as "political," and suggests that the discharge of an employee who engages in any such activity would not violate the Act.[11]

We believe that petitioner misconceives the reach of the "mutual aid or protection" clause. The "employees" who may engage in concerted activities for "mutual aid or protection" are defined by §2(3) of the Act, to "include any employee, and shall not be limited to the employees of a particular employer, unless the Act explicitly states otherwise. . . . " This definition was intended to protect employees when they engage in otherwise proper concerted activities in support of employees of employers other than their own. In recognition of this intent, the Board and the courts long have held that the "mutual aid or protection" clause encompasses such activity. Petitioner's argument on this point ignores the language of the Act and its settled construction.

We also find no warrant for petitioner's view that employees lose their

[11] See Tr. of Oral Arg. 17:

"*Question:* [Suppose the] Union is banding together and they all want to oppose right-to-work laws, and they pass out literature out on the public street; and the employer says, 'I just don't like you fellows getting into this kind of business, I'm going to fire you.' Now, is that an unfair labor practice?

Mr. Abercrombie: Your honor, we would submit that it was not, that political activity is not protected under Section 7."

protection under the "mutual aid or protection" clause when they seek to improve terms and conditions of employment or otherwise improve their lot as employees through channels outside the immediate employee-employer relationship. The 74th Congress knew well enough that labor's cause often is advanced on fronts other than collective bargaining and grievance settlement within the immediate employment context. It recognized this fact by choosing, as the language of §7 makes clear, to protect concerted activities for the somewhat broader purpose of "mutual aid or protection" as well as for the narrower purposes of "self-organization" and "collective bargaining." Thus, it has been held that the "mutual aid or protection" clause protects employees from retaliation by their employers when they seek to improve working conditions through resort to administrative and judicial forums,[15] and that employees' appeals to legislators to protect their interests as employees are within the scope of this clause. To hold that activity of this nature is entirely unprotected — irrespective of location or the means employed — would leave employees open to retaliation for much legitimate activity that could improve their lot as employees. As this could "frustrate the policy of the Act to protect the right of workers to act together to better their working conditions," NLRB v. Washington Aluminum Co., 370 U.S. 9, 14 (1962), we do not think that Congress could have intended the protection of §7 to be as narrow as petitioner insists.[17]

It is true . . . that some concerted activity bears a less immediate

---

[15] . . . We do not address here the question of what may constitute "concerted" activities in this context. Cf. NLRB v. Weingarten, Inc., 420 U.S. 251, 260-261 (1975).

[17] Petitioner relies upon [two] cases said to construe §7 more narrowly than do we. . . . [B]oth quote the same treatise for the proposition that to be protected under §7, concerted activity must seek "a specific remedy" for a "work-related complaint or grievance." 509 F.2d, at 813, and 497 F.2d, at 1202-1203, quoting 18B Business Organizations, T. Kheel, Labor Law §10.02[3], at 10-21 (1973). It was unnecessary in those cases to decide whether the protection of §7 went beyond the treatise's formulation, for the activity in both cases was held to be protected. Moreover, in stating its "rule," the treatise relied upon takes no note of the cases cited in [this opinion]. Compare R. Gorman, Labor Law 296-302 (1976). The . . . Sixth and Ninth Circuits themselves have taken a broader view of the "mutual aid or protection" clause than the reference to the treatise in the above-cited cases would seem to suggest. See, e.g., Kellogg Co. v. NLRB, 457 F.2d 519, 522-523 (6th Cir. 1972), and cases there cited; Kaiser Engineers v. NLRB, 538 F.2d 1379, 1384-1385 (9th Cir. 1976). . . .

This leaves only G & W Electric Specialty Co. v. NLRB, 360 F.2d 873 (7th Cir. 1966), which refused to enforce a Board order because the concerted activity there — circulation of a petition concerning management of an employee-run credit union — "involved no request for any action upon the part of the Company and did not concern a matter over which the Company had any control." Id., at 876. G & W Electric cites no authority for its narrowing of §7 and it ignores a substantial weight of authority to the contrary, including the Seventh Circuit's own prior holding in Fort Wayne Corrugated Paper Co. v. NLRB, 111 F.2d 869, 874 (1940). . . . We therefore do not view any of these cases as persuasive authority for petitioner's position.

relationship to employees' interests as employees than other such activity. We may assume that at some point the relationship becomes so attenuated that an activity cannot fairly be deemed to come within the "mutual aid or protection" clause. It is neither necessary nor appropriate, however, for us to attempt to delineate precisely the boundaries of the "mutual aid or protection" clause. That task is for the Board to perform in the first instance as it considers the wide variety of cases that come before it.[18] . . . To decide this case, it is enough to determine whether the Board erred in holding that distribution of the second and third sections of the newsletter is for the purpose of "mutual aid or protection."

The Board determined that distribution of the second section, urging employees to write their legislators to oppose incorporation of the state "right-to-work" statute into a revised state constitution, was protected because union security is "central to the union concept of strength through solidarity" and "a mandatory subject of bargaining in other than right-to-work states." 215 N.L.R.B., at 274. The newsletter warned that incorporation could affect employees adversely "by weakening Unions and improving the edge business has at the bargaining table." The fact that Texas already has a "right-to-work" statute does not render employees' interest in this matter any less strong, for, as the Court of Appeals noted, it is "one thing to face a legislative scheme which is open to legislative modification or repeal" and "quite another thing to face the prospect that such a scheme will be frozen in a concrete constitutional mandate." 550 F.2d, at 205. We cannot say that the Board erred in holding that this section of the newsletter bears such a relation to employees' interests as to come within the guarantee of the "mutual aid or protection" clause. . . .

The Board held that distribution of the third section, criticizing a presidential veto of an increase in the federal minimum wage and urging employees to register to vote to "defeat our enemies and elect our friends,"

---

[18] See Ford Motor Co., 221 N.L.R.B. 663, 666 (1975), *enforced*, 546 F.2d 418 (3rd Cir. 1976) (holding distribution on employer's premises of a "purely political tract" unprotected even though "the election of any political candidate may have an ultimate effect on employment conditions"); cf. Ford Motor Co. (Rouge Complex), 233 N.L.R.B. No. 102 (1977), decision of [ALJ], at 8 (concession of General Counsel that distributions on employer's premises of literature urging participation in Revolutionary Communist Party celebration, and of Party's newspaper, were unprotected). The Board has not yet made clear whether it considers distributions like those in the above-cited cases to be unprotected altogether, or only on the employer's premises.

In addition, even when concerted activity comes within the scope of the "mutual aid or protection" clause, the forms such activity permissibly may take may well depend on the object of the activity. "The argument that the employer's lack of interest or control affords a legitimate basis for holding that a subject does not come within 'mutual aid or protection' is unconvincing. The argument that economic pressure should be unprotected in such cases is more convincing." Getman, The Protection of Economic Pressure by Section 7 of the National Labor Relations Act, 115 U. Pa. L. Rev. 1195, 1221 (1967).

was protected despite the fact that petitioner's employees were paid more than the vetoed minimum wage. It reasoned that the "minimum wage inevitably influences wage levels derived from collective bargaining, even those far above the minimum," and that "concern by [petitioner's] employees for the plight of other employees might gain support for them at some future time when they might have a dispute with their employer." 215 N.L.R.B., at 274. We think that the Board acted within the range of its discretion in so holding. Few topics are of such immediate concern to employees as the level of their wages. The Board was entitled to note the widely recognized impact that a rise in the minimum wage may have on the level of negotiated wages generally, a phenomenon that would not have been lost on petitioner's employees. The union's call, in the circumstances of this case, for these employees to back persons who support an increase in the minimum wage, and to oppose those who oppose it, fairly is characterized as concerted activity for the "mutual aid or protection" of petitioner's employees and of employees generally.

In sum, we hold that distribution of both the second and the third sections of the newsletter is protected under the "mutual aid or protection" clause of §7.[20]

B

The question that remains is whether the Board erred in holding that petitioner's employees may distribute the newsletter in nonworking areas of petitioner's property during nonworking time. Consideration of this issue must begin with the Court's decisions in Republic Aviation Corp. v. NLRB, 324 U.S. 793 (1945), and NLRB v. Babcock & Wilcox Co., 351 U.S. 105 (1956). . . . The Court recently has emphasized the distinction between the two cases: "A wholly different balance was struck when the organizational activity was carried on by employees already rightfully on the employer's property, since the employer's management interests rather than his property interests were there involved." Hudgens v. NLRB, 424 U.S. 507, 521-522, n.10 (1976); see also Central Hardware Co. v. NLRB, 407 U.S. 539, 543-545 (1972). It is apparent that the instant case resembles *Republic Aviation* rather closely. . . .

---

[20] Petitioner argues that the "right to work" and minimum wage issues are "political," and that advancing a union's political views is not protected by §7. As almost every issue can be viewed by some as political, the clear purpose of the "mutual aid or protection" clause would be frustrated if the mere characterization of conduct or speech removed it from the protection of the Act. . . . Moreover, what may be viewed as political in one context can be viewed quite differently in another. There may well be types of conduct or speech that are so purely political or so remotely connected to the concerns of employees as employees as to be beyond the protection of the clause. But this is a determination that should be left for case-by-case consideration. . . .

The only possible ground of distinction is that part of the newsletter in this case does not address purely organizational matters, but rather concerns other activity protected by §7. The question, then, is whether this difference required the Board to apply a different rule here than it applied in *Republic Aviation*.

Petitioner contends that the Board must distinguish among distributions of protected matter by employees on an employer's property on the basis of the content of each distribution. Echoing its earlier argument, petitioner urges that the *Republic Aviation* rule should not be applied if a distribution "does not involve a request for any action on the part of the employer, or does not concern a matter over which the employer has any degree of control." . . . In petitioner's view, distribution of any other matter protected by §7 would be an "unnecessary intrusion on the employer's property rights," . . . in the absence of a showing by employees that no alternative channels of communication with fellow employees are available.

We hold that the Board was not required to adopt this view in the case at hand. In the first place, petitioner's reliance on its property right is largely misplaced. Here, as in *Republic Aviation*, petitioner's employees are "already rightfully on the employer's property," so that in the context of this case it is the "employer's management interests rather than [its] property interests" that primarily are implicated. *Hudgens*, supra, 424 U.S. at 521-522, n.10. As already noted, petitioner made no attempt to show that its management interests would be prejudiced in any way by the exercise of §7 rights proposed by its employees here. Even if the mere distribution by employees of material protected by §7 can be said to intrude on petitioner's property rights in any meaningful sense, the degree of intrusion does not vary with the content of the material. Petitioner's only cognizable property right in this respect is in preventing employees from bringing literature onto its property and distributing it there — not in choosing which distributions protected by §7 it wishes to suppress.

On the other side of the balance, it may be argued that the employees' interest in distributing literature that deals with matters affecting them as employees, but not with self-organization or collective bargaining, is so removed from the central concerns of the Act as to justify application of a different rule than in *Republic Aviation*. Although such an argument may have force in some circumstances, see *Hudgens*, supra, 424 U.S., at 522, the Board to date generally has chosen not to engage in such refinement of its rules regarding the distribution of literature by employees during nonworking time in nonworking areas of their employer's property. We are not prepared to say in this case that the Board erred in the view it took.

It is apparent that the complexity of the Board's rules and the difficulty of the Board's task might be compounded greatly if it were required to distinguish not only between literature that is within and without the protection of §7, but also among subcategories of literature within that protection. In addition, whatever the strength of the employees' §7 interest in distributing particular literature, the Board is entitled to view the intrusion by employees on the property rights of their employer as quite limited in this context as long as the employer's management interests are adequately protected. . . .

We need not go so far in this case, however, as to hold that the *Republic Aviation* rule properly is applied to every in-plant distribution of literature that falls within the protective ambit of §7. This is a new area for the Board and the courts which has not yet received mature consideration. . . . For this reason, we confine our holding to the facts of this case.

Petitioner concedes that its employees were entitled to distribute a substantial portion of this newsletter on its property. In addition, as we have held above, the sections to which petitioner objected concern activity which petitioner, in the absence of a countervailing interest of its own, is not entitled to suppress. Yet petitioner made no attempt to show that its management interests would be prejudiced in any manner by distribution of these sections, and in our view any incremental intrusion on petitioner's property rights from their distribution together with the other sections would be minimal. Moreover, it is undisputed that the Union undertook the distribution in order to boost its support and improve its bargaining position in upcoming contract negotiations with petitioner. Thus, viewed in context, the distribution was closely tied to vital concerns of the Act. In these circumstances, we hold that the Board did not err in applying the *Republic Aviation* rule to the facts of this case. The judgment of the Court of Appeals therefore is affirmed.

[White, J., concurring, acknowledged the difficulty of explaining why an employer was required to permit distributions on his property about subjects unrelated to his relationship with his employees simply because of the union's convenience and the absence of interference with management interests. But he was content to affirm in the absence of evidence as to whether the employer's work force as a whole and the general public were deeply divided regarding the union's goals and whether the employer wished to avoid the appearance of taking sides.]

REHNQUIST, J., with whom the CHIEF JUSTICE joins, dissenting. . . .

The Court today cites no case in which it has ever held that anyone, whether an employee or a nonemployee, has a protected right to engage in anything other than organizational activity on an employer's property. The simple question before us is whether Congress has authorized the Board to displace an employer's right to prevent the distribution on his property of political material concerning matters over which he has no control.[3] In eschewing any analysis of this question, in deference to the supposed expertise of the Board, the Court permits a " 'yielding' of property rights" which is certainly not "temporary"; and I cannot conclude that the deprivation of such a right of property can be dismissed as "minimal." It may be that Congress has power under the Commerce Clause to require an employer to open his property to such political advocacy, but, if Congress intended to do so, "such a legislative intention should be found in some definite and unmistakable expression." *Fansteel*, supra, 306 U.S., at 255. Finding no such expression in the Act, I would not permit the Board to balance away petitioner's right to exclude political literature from its property.

I would reverse the judgment of the Court of Appeals.

NOTES

1. In performing the case-by-case delineation authorized by *Eastex*, the Board has said that it is attempting to place union "political" communications along a continuum, with one end (the unprotected end) encompassing literature designed principally to induce votes for specific candidates and the other end (the protected end) covering literature designed principally to educate employees on issues that might affect their employment conditions. At least one union has argued (unsuccessfully) that this is a "we-know-it-when-we-see-it" approach that leaves both employees and employers without standards to guide their conduct. See Local 174, UAW v. NLRB, 645 F.2d 1151 (D.C. Cir. 1981). Do you agree that a union lacks guidance in drafting leaflets for in-plant distribution?

2. Was the company's cause helped by its answer to the question asked from the bench, in footnote 11 of the *Eastex* opinion?

3. If leaflets are sufficiently work-related to qualify for in-plant distribution under *Eastex*, under what circumstances should protection be forfeited because the leaflets also contain offensive or provocative language? Presum-

---

[3] The Court's complaint that "almost every issue can be viewed by some as political," contrasts markedly with its earlier assurance, in another context, that "commonsense" distinctions may be drawn between political speech and commercial speech. Ohralik v. Ohio State Bar Assn., 98 S. Ct. 1912 at 1918. In any case, there is little difficulty in determining whether the employer has the power to affect those matters of which his employees complain. Where he does not, there is no reason to require him to permit such advocacy on his property, even though such activity might arguably be protected under §7 if committed elsewhere.

ably distributions exhorting the employees to violence or other misconduct need not be tolerated. But what of obscenities, abusive epithets, incendiary rhetoric, or calls for employees to unite with communist groups for a "violent struggle against capitalistic bosses"? Cf. NLRB v. New York Univ. Medical Center, 702 F.2d 284 (2d Cir. 1981). Some employers have attempted to set limits through no-distribution rules, such as the following: "No employee is permitted to bring in or distribute, at any time on Company property, literature which is libelous, defamatory, scurrilous, abusive or insulting, or any literature which would tend to disrupt order, discipline or production within the plant." What facts might determine this rule's validity? See Great Lakes Steel v. NLRB, 625 F.2d 131 (6th Cir. 1980).

4. In Plastilite Corp., 153 N.L.R.B. 180 (1965), *enforced in relevant part*, 375 F.2d 343 (8th Cir. 1967), employees struck in protest after a minor supervisor had been discharged for reasons unrelated to his supervisory functions. The Board, applying its *Dobbs House* doctrine (135 N.L.R.B. 885 (1962), *enforcement denied*, 325 F.2d 531 (5th Cir. 1963)), held that strike to be protected, noting that the supervisor's ability directly affected the performance of the employees' functions, thereby legitimizing their concern about the supervisor's identity. The Board also indicated that a strike against the appointment or termination of a high-level supervisor would raise a different question. Should §7 protection in this context depend on the moderation of the concerted action (e.g., was a walkout "reasonable" in the circumstances?) or on the rank of the supervisor involved, as distinguished from the impact of the supervisor's performance on employees' job interests? There has been continuing disagreement between the Board and the courts on this question, as well as on the application of the Board's *Dobbs House* test in specific cases — i.e., whether employees who protest management changes in supervisory personnel are in fact protesting conditions of "their own employment." See, e.g., NLRB v. Sheraton Puerto Rico Corp., 651 F.2d 49 (1st Cir. 1981); Henning & Cheadle, Inc. v. NLRB, 522 F.2d 1050 (7th Cir. 1975). For the relevance of §8(b)(1)(B) of the Act to these issues, see Chapter 12, p. 1282.

5. Two employees who have no complaints about their own working conditions or the effects of the employer's policies on them personally engage in on-the-job criticism of the employer in an effort to affect "managerial philosophy and policies." Does *Eastex* protect such activity? See Good Samaritan Hosp. and Health Center, 265 N.L.R.B. 618 (1982). For consideration of the First Amendment rights of public employees to comment on internal office matters and to criticize superiors, see Connick v. Myers, 103 S. Ct. 1684 (1983).

Elk Lumber Co.
91 N.L.R.B. 333 (1950)

[The complaint charged that the employer had violated §§8(a)(1) and 8(a)(3) by discharging employees for protesting a unilateral change in their rate of pay.]

On January 3, 1949, as a result of certain physical improvements in the plant, the Respondent changed the method of loading. . . . As a result, the work of the carloaders was both easier and more steady.

At the same time, the Respondent unilaterally changed the rate of pay of the carloaders to $1.52 1/2 an hour. [Previously, on an incentive basis, they had averaged $2.71 an hour.] Some of the carloaders thereupon decided among themselves that it was sufficient to load one car a day, and proceeded to work at approximately that rate until February 7. The rate was adopted, according to their testimony, because it was the quota at other plants in the same area, and because they "thought one carload was a good day's work at a dollar and a half." Admittedly, they could have loaded more cars in a day, would have done so for more pay, and knew that the Respondent was not satisfied with their production.

The Respondent did not at any time set a quota for the carloading operation or warn the carloaders that they would be discharged if they failed to increase their production. However, on February 1, 1949, George C. Flanagan, the Respondent's vice-president and manager, invited them to dinner at his house to discuss the situation. During the course of the discussion, he asked them for suggestions for improving production. One of them, apparently speaking for and with the approval of the entire group that had engaged in the slowdown, suggested that the Respondent either return to the piecework rate of pay or increase the hourly rate, and made it clear that the men did not intend to increase their production unless they were given a corresponding increase in pay. Flanagan said that he would investigate the practice at another mill in the vicinity, which he was about to visit, and would report back to them. Thereafter, he visited the mill in question, but he made no report.

On February 7, 1949, the five carloaders named in the complaint, who had not struck but continued to work at their own chosen pace in the interim, were given their final checks. Kennedy, the planing mill superintendent, merely told one of them that "we can't make it go that way, so we have got to find some new faces." . . .

The Respondent contends, and the Trial Examiner apparently found, that the five carloaders were discharged, not for having engaged in concerted activities, as alleged in the complaint, but because their production was not satisfactory. It is clear, however, that their failure to produce was the result of an agreement to slow down. In our opinion, therefore, the only question presented is whether this conduct was a form of concerted activity protected by the Act. We believe, contrary to the contention of the General Counsel, that it was not.

Section 7 of the Act guarantees to employees the right to engage in concerted activities for the purpose of collective bargaining or other mutual aid or protection. However, both the Board and the courts have recognized that not every form of activity that falls within the letter of this provision is protected.[6] The test, as laid down by the Board in the *Harnischfeger Corporation* case [9 N.L.R.B. 676], and referred to with apparent approval by the Supreme Court in the recent *Wisconsin* case,[8] is whether the particular activity involved is so indefensible as to warrant the employer in discharging the participating employees. Either an unlawful objective or the adoption of improper means of achieving it may deprive employees engaged in concerted activities of the protection of the Act.

Here, the objective of the carloaders' concerted activity — to induce the Respondent to increase their hourly rate of pay or to return to the piecework rate — was a lawful one. To achieve this objective, however, they adopted the plan of decreasing their production to the amount they considered adequate for the pay they were then receiving. In effect, this constituted a refusal on their part to accept the terms of employment set by their employer without engaging in a stoppage, but to continue rather to work on their own terms. The courts, in somewhat similar situations, have held that such conduct is justifiable cause for discharge. Thus, in the *Conn* case,[9] . . . the Seventh Circuit found that the employer was justified in discharging employees who refused to work overtime, saying:

> We are aware of no law or logic that gives the employee the right to work upon terms prescribed solely by him. That is plainly what was sought to be done in this instance. It is not a situation in which employees ceased work in protest against conditions imposed by the employer, but one in which the employees sought and intended to work upon their own notion of the terms which should prevail. If they had a right to fix the hours of their employment, it would follow that a similar right existed by which they could prescribe all conditions and regulations affecting their employment.

[6] International Union, UAWA, AF of L, Local 232, et al. v. Wisconsin Employment Relations Board, et al., 336 U.S. 245, and cases therein cited.
[8] See footnote 6, supra.
[9] C. G. Conn, Ltd. v. NLRB, 108 F.2d 390 (7th Cir.), cited with approval by the Supreme Court in the *Wisconsin* case, supra.

And in the *Montgomery Ward* case,[10] in which employees at one of the employer's plants refused to process orders from another plant where a strike was in progress, the Court of Appeals . . . said:

> It was implied in the contract of hiring that these employees would do the work assigned to them in a careful and workmanlike manner; that they would comply with all reasonable orders and conduct themselves so as not to work injury to the employer's business; that they could serve faithfully and be regardful of the interests of the employer during the term of their service, and carefully discharge their duties to the extent reasonably required . . . Any employee may, of course, be lawfully discharged for disobedience of the employer's directions in breach of his contract . . . While these employees had the undoubted right to go on a strike and quit their employment, they could not continue to work and remain at their positions, accept the wages paid them, and at the same time select what part of their allotted tasks they cared to perform of their own volition, or refuse openly or secretly, to the employer's damage, to do other work.

We believe that the principle of these decisions is applicable to the situation before us, and that, under the circumstances, the carloaders' conduct justified their discharge.

The General Counsel contends, however, that "if such activity [a slowdown] is to be condemned by the Board, it should only be done after there has been a deliberate refusal to do the Employer's bidding," and that here, "at the time of discharge there still had been no failure to comply with any command of management." In support of this contention, he asserts that "after the outset of this slowdown, the Employer obviously acquiesced in it and made no protest"; and that it "did not set a definite rate [of production], nor did it make any statement as to what rate of production was considered accurate"; and that it discharged the men "without any warning or reason being given."

On the record before us, however, we find no convincing evidence that the Respondent at any time acquiesced in the slowdown. On the contrary, it appears from the testimony regarding the dinner meeting on February 1, that the Respondent was concerned about the reduced production and was attempting to find some way of increasing it.

Furthermore, although the Respondent admittedly did not tell the carloaders how many cars a day they were expected to load, and, so far as the present record shows, did not warn them that they would be discharged if they did not increase their production, it is clear that the men knew that the

---

[10] NLRB v. Montgomery Ward & Co., 157 F.2d 486 (8th Cir.).

rate they had adopted was not satisfactory. Despite this knowledge, they continued to load fewer cars a day than they could have loaded, or than they would have loaded, for more money. Under these particular circumstances, we regard it as immaterial that the Respondent had given them no express order as to the amount of work required, or any warning that they would be discharged if they failed to meet the requirement.

We therefore find that the Respondent did not violate the Act by discharging the five carloaders named in the complaint. . . .

NOTES

1. In Polytech, Inc., 195 N.L.R.B. 695 (1972), the Board found a violation of §8(a)(1) in a two-day suspension of all employees in a department for refusing to work overtime in protest against recent assignments of substantial overtime under fatiguing and difficult working conditions. Noting that the overtime refusal had been an isolated protest by unrepresented employees without structured grievance procedures, the Board sought to synthesize previous decisions regarding partial stoppages by announcing "a presumption that a single concerted refusal to work overtime is [protected] . . . and that [that] presumption should be deemed rebutted . . . only when the evidence demonstrates that the stoppage is part of a plan or pattern of intermittent action . . . inconsistent with a genuine strike or genuine performance by employees of the work normally expected of them by the employer." In fashioning this rule, the Board stated (at 696) that "we are guided, in the main," by NLRB v. Washington Aluminum Co., 370 U.S. 9 (1962), which, it said, "held that when a group of unrepresented employees spontaneously ceased work [and went home] after reporting to their jobs because of an unsatisfactory condition in the plant [the absence of heat on a bitterly cold morning], their concerted action was entitled to the Act's protection — and this even though the stoppage occurred without any advance notice to the employer and there had been no prior demand for a change in the prevailing working conditions."

Is Polytech distinguishable from Washington Aluminum? From Elk Lumber?

2. Even if "slowdowns" are normally unprotected, did special circumstances in Elk Lumber support a different result? Despite an employee's unprotected activity, the NLRB may order his reinstatement on the basis of the doctrine of "condonation" whereby an employer is held to waive his rights to discipline if he expressly or impliedly forgave employee misconduct. Claims of condonation have usually arisen in strike situations, typically when

an employer invites strikers to return to work without reserving his right to discipline them for strike misconduct. See, e.g., NLRB v. Marshall Car Wheel and Foundry Co., 218 F.2d 409 (5th Cir. 1955). In NLRB v. Colonial Press, Inc., 509 F.2d 850 (8th Cir. 1975), employees lawfully discharged for engaging in "long meetings on company time" alleged that the employer had invited them to return to work during a subsequent unfair labor practice strike by other employees. The court rejected the Board's finding that general statements ("my door is always open") had constituted a reemployment offer and held, alternatively, that such an offer would not justify reinstatement since those lawfully discharged were no longer "employees" under the NLRA. Consequently, proof of the employees' acceptance of the employer's offer, by returning to work during the strike, would have been necessary before reinstatement could have been based on "condonation." Does the court's characterization of the discharged workers as nonemployees reflect adequate concern for the statutory purposes? Does §10(c) cast any light on the question involved in Colonial Press?

For general discussions of "condonation," see 88 Harv. L. Rev. 1903 (1975) [noting Colonial Press]; Note, The Condonation Doctrine: The Search for a Rationale, 110 U. Pa. L. Rev. 879 (1962).

3. For criticism of Elk Lumber and of the law's traditional approach to similar job actions by employees, see J. Atleson, Values and Assumptions in American Labor Law 44-66 (1983).

4. The protected status of an employee's refusal to cross picket lines is dealt with in Chapter 7(E), p. 617.

NLRB v. Local 1229, IBEW
346 U.S. 464 (1953)

[After an impasse in negotiations for a renewal agreement with the Jefferson Standard Broadcasting Co., members of Local 1229, which represented 22 television technicians, engaged in the activities described below.]

BURTON, J. July 9, 1949, the union began daily peaceful picketing of the company's station. Placards and handbills on the picket line charged the company with unfairness to its technicians and emphasized the company's refusal to renew the provision for arbitration of discharges. The placards and handbills named the union as the representative of the WBT technicians. The employees did not strike. They confined their respective tours of picketing to their off-duty hours and continued to draw full pay. There was no violence or threat of violence and no one has taken exception to any of the above conduct.

But on August 24, 1949, a new procedure made its appearance. Without warning, several of its technicians launched a vitriolic attack on the quality of the company's television broadcasts. Five thousand handbills were printed over the designation "WBT TECHNICIANS." These were distributed on the picket line, on the public square two or three blocks from the company's premises, in barber shops, restaurants and busses. Some were mailed to local businessmen. The handbills made no reference to the union, to a labor controversy or to collective bargaining. They read:

IS CHARLOTTE A SECOND-CLASS CITY?
You might think so from the kind of Television programs being presented by the Jefferson Standard Broadcasting Co. over WBTV. Have you seen one of their television programs lately? Did you know that all the programs presented over WBTV are on film and may be from one day to five years old. There are no local programs presented by WBTV. You cannot receive the local baseball games, football games or other local events because WBTV does not have the proper equipment to make these pickups. Cities like New York, Boston, Philadelphia, Washington receive such programs nightly. Why doesn't the Jefferson Standard Broadcasting Company purchase the needed equipment to bring you the same type of programs enjoyed by other leading American cities? Could it be that they consider Charlotte a second-class community and only entitled to the pictures now being presented to them?

WBT TECHNICIANS

This attack continued until September 3, 1949, when the company discharged ten of its technicians, whom it charged with sponsoring or distributing these handbills. The company's letter discharging them tells its side of the story.[4]

[4] Dear Mr. . . . ,

When you and some of our other technicians commenced early in July to picket against this Company, we felt that your action was very ill-considered. We were paying you a salary of . . . per week, to say nothing of other benefits which you receive as an employee of our Company. . . . Yet when we were unable to agree upon the terms of a contract with your Union, you began to denounce us publicly as "unfair."

And ever since early July while you have been walking up and down the street with placards and literature attacking us, you have continued to hold your job and receive your pay and all the other benefits. . . .

Even when you began to put out propaganda which contained many untruths about our Company and great deal of personal abuse and slander, we still continued to treat you exactly as before. For it has been our understanding that under our labor laws, you have a very great latitude in trying to make the public believe that your employer is unfair to you.

Now, however, you have turned from trying to persuade the public that we are unfair *to you* and are trying to persuade the public that we give inferior service *to them*.

. . . [A]fter hearing, a trial examiner . . . [recommended] that all of those discharged be reinstated with back pay. . . . The Board found that one of the discharged men had neither sponsored nor distributed the "Second-Class City" handbill and ordered his reinstatement with back pay. It then found that the other nine had sponsored or distributed the handbill and held that the company, by discharging them for such conduct, had not engaged in an unfair labor practice. The Board, accordingly, did not order their reinstatement. One member dissented. . . . Under §10(f) of the Taft-Hartley Act, the union petitioned the Court of Appeals . . . for a review of the Board's order and for such a modification of it as would reinstate all ten of the discharged technicians with back pay. That court remanded the cause to the Board for further consideration and for a finding as to the "unlawfulness" of the conduct of the employees which had led to their discharge. . . . 202 F.2d 180 [D.C. Cir.][7] We granted certiorari because of the importance of the case in the administration of the Taft-Hartley Act.

In its essence, the issue is simple. It is whether these employees, whose contracts of employment had expired, were discharged "for cause." They were discharged solely because at a critical time in the initiation of the company's television service, they sponsored or distributed 5,000 handbills making a sharp, public, disparaging attack upon the quality of the company's product and its business policies, in a manner reasonably calculated to harm the company's reputation and reduce its income. The attack was made by

---

While we are struggling to expand into and develop a new field, and incidentally losing large sums of money in the process, you are busy trying to turn customers and the public against us in every possible way, even handing out leaflets on the public streets advertising that our operations are "second-class," and endeavoring in various ways to hamper and totally destroy our business. Certainly we are not required by law or common sense to keep you in our employment and pay you a substantial salary while you thus do your best to tear down and bankrupt our business.

You are hereby discharged from our employment. Although there is nothing requiring us to do so, and the circumstances certainly do not call for our doing so, we are enclosing a check payable to your order for two weeks' advance or severance pay.

Very truly yours,
Jefferson Standard Broadcasting Company
By: Charles H. Crutchfield.

[7] The Court of Appeals said:

"Protection under §7 . . . is withdrawn only from those concerted activities which contravene either (a) specific provisions or basic policies of the Act or related federal statutes, or (b) specific rules of other federal or local law that is not incompatible with the Board's governing statute. . . .

"We think the Board failed to make the finding essential to its conclusion that the concerted activity was unprotected. Sound practice in judicial review of administrative orders precludes this court from determining 'unlawfulness' without a prior consideration and finding by the Board." 202 F.2d, at 188, 189.

them expressly as "WBT TECHNICIANS." It continued ten days without indication of abatement. The Board found that —

> It [the handbill] occasioned widespread comment in the community and caused Respondent to apprehend a loss of advertising revenue due to dissatisfaction with its television broadcasting service.
> In short, the employees in this case deliberately undertook to alienate their employer's customers by impugning the technical quality of his product. As the Trial Examiner found, they did not misrepresent, at least wilfully, the facts they cited to support their disparaging report. And their ultimate purpose — to extract a concession from the employer with respect to the terms of their employment — was lawful. That purpose, however, was undisclosed; the employees purported to speak as experts, in the interest of consumers and the public at large. They did not indicate that they sought to secure any benefit for themselves, *as employees*, by casting discredit upon their employer.

94 N.L.R.B., at 1511.

The company's letter shows that it interpreted the handbill as a demonstration of such detrimental disloyalty as to provide "cause" for its refusal to continue in its employ the perpetrators of the attack. We agree.

Section 10(c) of the Taft-Hartley Act expressly provides that: "No order of the Board shall require the reinstatement of any individual as an employee who has been suspended or discharged, or the payment to him of any back pay, if such individual was suspended or discharged for cause." There is no more elemental cause for discharge of an employee than disloyalty to his employer. It is equally elemental that the Taft-Hartley Act seeks to strengthen, rather than to weaken, that cooperation, continuity of service and cordial contractual relation between employer and employee that is born of loyalty to their common enterprise.

Congress, while safeguarding, in §7, the right of employees to engage in "concerted activities for the purpose of collective bargaining or other mutual aid or protection," did not weaken the underlying contractual bonds and loyalties of employer and employee. The conference report that led to the enactment of the law said:

> [T]he courts have firmly established the rule that under the existing provisions of section 7 . . . employees are not given any right to engage in unlawful or other improper conduct. . . .
> . . . Furthermore, in §10(c) of the amended act, as proposed in the conference agreement, it is specifically provided that no order of the Board shall require the reinstatement of any individual or the payment to him of any back pay if such individual was suspended or discharged for cause, and this, of course, applies with equal force whether or not the acts constituting the cause for discharge were committed in connection with a concerted activity.

H.R. Rep. No. 510, 80th Cong., 1st Sess. 38-39.

This has been clear since the early days of the Wagner Act. In 1937, Chief Justice Hughes, writing for the Court, said:

> The Act does not interfere with the normal exercise of the right of the employer to select its employees or to discharge them. The employer may not, under cover of that right, intimidate or coerce its employees with respect to their self-organization and representation, and, on the other hand, the Board is not entitled to make its authority a pretext for interference with the right of discharge when that right is exercised for other reasons than such intimidation and coercion.

Labor Board v. Jones & Laughlin, 301 U.S. 1, 45-46. . . .

Many cases reaching their final disposition in the Courts of Appeals furnish examples emphasizing the importance of enforcing industrial plant discipline and of maintaining loyalty as well as the rights of concerted activities. The courts have refused to reinstate employees discharged for "cause" consisting of insubordination, disobedience or disloyalty. In such cases, it often has been necessary to identify individual employees, somewhat comparable to the nine discharged in this case, and to recognize that their discharges were for causes which were separable from the concerted activities of others whose acts might come within the protection of §7. It has been equally important to identify employees, comparable to the tenth man in the instant case, who participated in simultaneous concerted activities for the purpose of collective bargaining or other mutual aid or protection but who refrained from joining the others in separable acts of insubordination, disobedience or disloyalty. In the latter instances, this sometimes led to a further inquiry to determine whether their concerted activities were carried on in such a manner as to come within the protection of §7. [Cases cited.]

. . . The legal principle that insubordination, disobedience or disloyalty is adequate cause for discharge is plain enough. The difficulty arises in determining whether, in fact, the discharges are made because of such a separable cause or because of some other concerted activities engaged in for the purpose of collective bargaining or other mutual aid or protection which may not be adequate cause for discharge. . . .

In the instant case the Board found that the company's discharge of nine offenders resulted from their sponsoring and distributing the "Second-Class City" handbills . . . , issued in their name as the "WBT TECHNICIANS." Assuming that there had been no pending labor controversy, the conduct of the "WBT TECHNICIANS" from August 24 through September 3 unquestionably would have provided adequate cause for their disciplinary discharge within the meaning of §10(c). Their attack related itself to no labor practice of the company. It made no reference to wages, hours or working conditions. The policies attacked were those of finance and public relations for which management, not technicians, must be responsible. The attack asked for no public sympathy or support. It was a continuing attack, initiated while off duty, upon the very interests which the attackers were being paid to conserve and develop. Nothing could be further from the purpose of the Act than to require an employer to finance such activities. Nothing would contribute less to the Act's declared purpose of promoting industrial peace and stability.[12]

The fortuity of the coexistence of a labor dispute affords these technicians no substantial defense. While they were also union men and leaders in the labor controversy, they took pains to separate those categories. In contrast to their claims on the picket line as to the labor controversy, their handbill of August 24 omitted all reference to it. The handbill diverted attention from the labor controversy. It attacked public policies of the company which had no discernible relation to that controversy. The only connection between the handbill and the labor controversy was an ultimate and undisclosed purpose or motive on the part of some of the sponsors that, by the hoped-for financial pressure, the attack might extract from the company some future concession. A disclosure of that motive might have lost more public support for the employees than it would have gained, for it would have given the handbill more the character of coercion than of collective bargaining. Referring to the attack, the Board said "In our judgment, these tactics, in the circumstances of this case, were hardly less 'indefensible' than acts of physical sabotage." 94 N.L.R.B., at 1511. In any event, the findings of the Board effectively separate the attack from the labor controversy and treat it solely as one made by the company's technical experts upon the quality of the company's product. As such, it was as adequate a cause for the discharge of its sponsors as if the labor controversy had not been pending. The technicians, themselves, so handled their attack as thus to bring their discharge under §10(c).

The Board stated "We . . . do not decide whether the disparagement of product involved here would have justified the employer in discharging the employees responsible for it, had it been uttered in the context of a conventional appeal for support of the union in the labor dispute." Id., at 1512, n.18. This underscored the Board's factual conclusion that the attack of August 24 was not part of an appeal for support in the pending dispute. . . .

We find no occasion to remand this cause to the Board for further specificity of findings. Even if the attack were to be treated, as the Board has

---

[12] " . . . An employee can not work and strike at the same time. He can not continue in his employment and openly or secretly refuse to do his work. He can not collect wages for his employment, and, at the same time, engage in activities to injure or destroy his employer's business." Hoover Co. v. Labor Board, 191 F.2d 380, 389. . . .

not treated it, as a concerted activity wholly or partly within the scope of those mentioned in §7, the means used by the technicians in conducting the attack have deprived the attackers of the protection of that section, when read in the light and context of the purpose of the Act.

Accordingly, the order of the Court of Appeals remanding the cause to the [NLRB] is set aside, and the cause is remanded to the Court of Appeals with instructions to dismiss respondent's petition to modify the order of the Board. . . .

FRANKFURTER, J., whom BLACK and DOUGLAS, JJ., join, dissenting. . . . On this central issue — whether the Court of Appeals rightly or wrongly found that the Board applied an improper criterion — this Court is silent. It does not support the Board in using "indefensible" as the legal litmus nor does it reject the Court of Appeals' rejection of that test. This Court presumably does not disagree with the assumption of the Court of Appeals that conduct may be "indefensible" in the colloquial meaning of that loose adjective, and yet be within the protection of §7.

Instead, the Court, relying on §10(c) which permits discharges "for cause," points to the "disloyalty" of the employees and finds sufficient "cause" regardless of whether the handbill was a "concerted activity" within §7. Section 10(c) does not speak of discharge "for disloyalty." If Congress had so written that section, it would have overturned much of the law that had been developed by the Board and the courts in the twelve years preceding the Taft-Hartley Act. The legislative history makes clear that Congress had no such purpose but was rather expressing approval of the construction of "concerted activities" adopted by the Board and the courts. Many of the legally recognized tactics and weapons of labor would readily be condemned for "disloyalty" were they employed between man and man in friendly personal relations. In this connection it is significant that the ground now taken by the Court, insofar as it is derived from the provision of §10(c) relating to discharge "for cause," was not invoked by the Board in justification of its order.

To suggest that all actions which in the absence of a labor controversy might be "cause" — or, to use the words commonly found in labor agreements, "just cause" — for discharge should be unprotected, even when such actions were undertaken as "concerted activities, for the purpose of collective bargaining," is to misconstrue legislation designed to put labor on a fair footing with management. Furthermore, it would disregard the rough and tumble of strikes, in the course of which loose and even reckless language is properly discounted.

"Concerted activities" by employees and dismissal "for cause" by employers are not dissociated legal criteria under the Act. They are like the two halves of a pair of shears. Of course, as the Conference Report on the

Taft-Hartley Act said, men on strike may be guilty of conduct "in connection with a concerted activity" which properly constitutes "cause" for dismissal and bars reinstatement. But §10(c) does not obviate the necessity for a determination whether the distribution of the handbill here was a legitimate tool in a labor dispute or was so "improper," as the Conference Report put it, as to be denied the protection of §7 and to constitute a discharge "for cause." It is for the Board, in the first instance, to make these valuations, and a court of appeals does not travel beyond its proper bounds in asking the Board for greater explicitness in light of the correct legal standards for judgment.

The Board and the courts of appeals will hardly find guidance for future cases from this Court's reversal of the Court of Appeals, beyond that which the specific facts of this case may afford. More than that, to float such imprecise notions as "discipline" and "loyalty" in the context of labor controversies, as the basis of the right to discharge, is to open the door wide to individual judgment by Board members and judges. One may anticipate that the Court's opinion will needlessly stimulate litigation.

NOTES

1. During a strike prompted by a bargaining impasse, the company, a paint manufacturer, continued to operate with supervisors. Thereupon, various strikers distributed circulars entitled "Beware Paint Substitute." Those circulars, after referring to the strike, advised customers that the company was not manufacturing paint with "the well-trained, experienced employees who have made the paint you have always bought" and warned that other paint might peel and crack. The circular concluded with the statement that customers would be told when they could again buy paint made by the company's regular employees. A majority of the Board, finding no decisive differences from the situation in *Local 1229*, upheld the employer's discharge of the strikers who had distributed the circulars. Patterson Sargent Co., 115 N.L.R.B. 1627 (1956). Do you agree?

2. Unionized employees of a parent company were engaged in an economic strike against their employer. Supporting that effort, unorganized employees of a wholly-owned subsidiary came to work displaying signs on their autos calling for a boycott of the parent's product. The subsidiary, whose principal customer was the parent, enforced against its employees a total ban of such signs on its property, contending that the display of the boycott signs was "indefensible" under the rule of *Local 1229*. Has the subsidiary unlawfully interfered with protected activity? See Coors Container Co. v. NLRB, 628 F.2d 1283 (10th Cir. 1980).

3. In determining whether public disparagement of the employer con-

stitutes "disloyalty," should it be decisive that employees' statements were truthful or, at the least, not made in reckless disregard of the truth? See Linn v. United Plant Guard Workers, Local 114, reproduced infra p. 742.

4. Apart from the requirements of §8(d) of the Act or contractual restrictions, a union generally can lawfully strike without notice to the employer and at a time when a strike will inflict the maximum damage on the business. Indeed, the lockout cases (see pp. 316-332 infra) make clear that the issue of whether the employer or the union can determine the timing of a stoppage designed to break a bargaining impasse may have a critical bearing on their respective power positions. But where a precipitate strike may damage physical equipment, limits have been imposed. In NLRB v. Marshall Car Wheel and Foundry Co., 218 F.2d 409 (5th Cir. 1955), a strike, without advance notice, by 45 percent of the employees was deliberately timed for peak operations, when a failure to pour molten iron out of a furnace would have caused serious damage to the plant's equipment. Although other employees and supervisors averted any damage, the strike was held unprotected. The court stated that the Board had acknowledged that employees who deliberately time a strike so as to create a risk of substantial property damage engage in unprotected activity and are subject to discharge. To avoid damage to plant equipment from sudden or unregulated stoppage, some agreements, e.g., in basic steel, specify the plant-protection arrangements to be made prior to a strike.

Is there any basis for distinguishing the *Marshall Foundry* case from the following: active sabotage by striking employees, a strike against a department store during the Christmas shopping season, a sudden strike by restaurant workers responsible for placing perishable products under refrigeration, or a sudden strike by employees assembling the sections of a Sunday newspaper. See NLRB v. A. Lasaponara & Sons, Inc., 541 F.2d 992, 998 (2d Cir. 1976); NLRB v. Cowles Publishing Co., 214 F.2d 708 (9th Cir. 1954), *cert. denied*, 348 U.S. 876 (1954). In connection with these questions, consider NLRB v. Insurance Agents Intl., 361 U.S. 477 (1960), reproduced infra p. 830.

Emporium Capwell Co. v. Western Addition Community Organization
420 U.S. 50 (1975)

MARSHALL, J. This litigation presents the question whether, in light of the national policy against racial discrimination in employment, the National Labor Relations Act protects concerted activity by a group of minority

employees to bargain with their employer over issues of employment discrimination. The [NLRB] held that the employees could not circumvent
their elected representative to engage in such bargaining. The Court of
Appeals . . . reversed and remanded, holding that in certain circumstances
the activity would be protected. . . . We now reverse.

I

The Emporium Capwell Co. (Company) operates a department store in San
Francisco. . . . [I]t was a party to the collective bargaining agreement negotiated by the San Francisco Retailer's Council, of which it was a member, and
the Department Store Employees Union (Union) which represented all
stock and marking area employees of the Company. The agreement, in
which the Union was recognized as the sole collective bargaining agency for
all covered employees, prohibited employment discrimination by reason of
race, color, creed, national origin, age, or sex, as well as union activity. It had a
no-strike or lockout clause, and it established grievance and arbitration machinery for processing any claimed violation of the contract, including a
violation of the antidiscrimination clause.

On April 3, 1968, a group of Company employees covered by the
agreement met with the secretary-treasurer of the Union, Walter Johnson, to
present a list of grievances including a claim that the Company was discriminating on the basis of race in making assignments and promotions. The
Union official agreed to take certain of the grievances and to investigate the
charge of racial discrimination. He appointed an investigating committee and
prepared a report on the employees' grievances, which he submitted to the
Retailer's Council and which the Council in turn referred to the Company.
The report described "the possibility of racial discrimination" as perhaps the
most important issue raised by the employees and termed the situation at the
Company as potentially explosive if corrective action were not taken. It
offered as an example of the problem the Company's failure to promote a
Negro stock employee regarded by other employees as an outstanding candi-
date but a victim of racial discrimination.

Shortly after receiving the report, the Company's labor relations director met with Union representatives and agreed to "look into the matter" of
discrimination and see what needed to be done. Apparently unsatisfied with
these representations, the Union held a meeting in September attended by
Union officials, Company employees, and representatives of the California
Fair Employment Practices Committee (FEPC) and the local antipoverty
agency. The secretary-treasurer of the Union announced that the Union had
concluded that the Company was discriminating, and that it would process
every such grievance through to arbitration if necessary. Testimony about

the Company's practices was taken and transcribed by a court reporter, and the next day the Union notified the Company of its formal charge and demanded that the joint union-management Adjustment Board be convened "to hear the entire case."

At the September meeting some of the Company's employees had expressed their view that the contract procedures were inadequate to handle a systemic grievance of this sort; they suggested that the Union instead begin picketing the store in protest. Johnson explained that the collective agreement bound the Union to its processes and expressed his view that successful grievants would be helping not only themselves but all others who might be the victims of invidious discrimination as well. The FEPC and antipoverty agency representatives offered the same advice. Nonetheless, when the Adjustment Board meeting convened on October 16, James Joseph Hollins, Tom Hawkins, and two other employees whose testimony the Union had intended to elicit refused to participate in the grievance procedure. Instead, Hollins read a statement objecting to reliance on correction of individual inequities as an approach to the problem of discrimination at the store and demanding that the president of the Company meet with the four protestants to work out a broader agreement for dealing with the issue as they saw it. The four employees then walked out of the hearing.

Hollins attempted to discuss the question of racial discrimination with the Company president shortly after the incidents of October 16. The president refused to be drawn into such a discussion but suggested to Hollins that he see the personnel director about the matter. Hollins, who had spoken to the personnel director before, made no effort to do so again. Rather, he and Hawkins and several other dissident employees held a press conference on October 22 at which they denounced the store's employment policy as racist, reiterated their desire to deal directly with "the top management" of the Company over minority employment conditions, and announced their intention to picket and institute a boycott of the store. On Saturday, November 2, Hollins, Hawkins, and at least two other employees picketed the store throughout the day and distributed at the entrance handbills urging consumers not to patronize the store.[2] Johnson encountered the picketing em-

---

[2] The full text of the handbill read:
"**BEWARE****BEWARE****BEWARE**
"EMPORIUM SHOPPERS
" 'Boycott Is On'   'Boycott Is On'   'Boycott Is On'
    "For years at The Emporium black, brown, yellow and red people have worked at the lowest jobs, at the lowest levels. Time and time again we have seen intelligent, hard working brothers and sisters denied promotions and respect.
    "The Emporium is a 20th Century colonial plantation. The brothers and sisters are being treated the same way as our brothers are being treated in the slave mines of Africa.

ployees, again urged them to rely on the grievance process, and warned that they might be fired for their activities. The pickets, however, were not dissuaded, and they continued to press their demand to deal directly with the Company president.

On November 7, Hollins and Hawkins were given written warnings that a repetition of the picketing or public statements about the Company could lead to their discharge. When the conduct was repeated the following Saturday, the two employees were fired.

Western Addition Community Organization (hereinafter respondent), a local civil rights association of which Hollins and Hawkins were members, filed a charge against the Company with the National Labor Relations Board. . . . After a hearing, the NLRB Trial Examiner found that the discharged employees had believed in good faith that the Company was discriminating against minority employees, and that they had resorted to concerted activity on the basis of that belief. He concluded, however, that their activity was not protected by §7 of the Act and that their discharges did not, therefore, violate §8(a)(1).

The Board, after oral argument, adopted the findings and conclusions of its Trial Examiner and dismissed the complaint. Among the findings adopted by the Board was that the discharged employees' course of conduct "was no mere presentation of a grievance but nothing short of a demand that the [Company] bargain with the picketing employees for the entire group of minority employees."[5] The Board concluded that protection of such an attempt to bargain would undermine the statutory system of bargaining through an exclusive, elected representative, impede elected unions' efforts at bettering the working conditions of minority employees, "and place on the Employer an unreasonable burden of attempting to placate self-designated representatives of minority groups while abiding by the terms of a valid

---

"Whenever the racist pig at The Emporium injures or harms a black sister or brother, they injure and insult all black people. THE EMPORIUM MUST PAY FOR THESE INSULTS. Therefore, we encourage all of our people to take their money out of this racist store, until black people have full employment and are promoted justly through out The Emporium.

"We welcome the support of our brothers and sisters from the churches, unions, sororities, fraternities, social clubs, Afro-American Institute, Black Panther Party, W.A.C.O. and the Poor Peoples Institute."

[5] 192 N.L.R.B., at 185. The evidence marshaled in support of this finding consisted of Hollins' meeting with the Company president in which he said that he wanted to discuss the problem perceived by minority employees; his statement that the pickets would not desist until the president treated with them; Hawkins' testimony that their purpose in picketing was to "talk to the top management to get better conditions"; and his statement that they wanted to achieve their purpose through "group talk and through the president if we could talk to him," as opposed to use of the grievance-arbitration machinery.

bargaining agreement and attempting in good faith to meet whatever demands the bargaining representative put forth under that agreement."[6]

On respondent's petition for review the Court of Appeals reversed and remanded. The court was of the view that concerted activity directed against racial discrimination enjoys a "unique status" by virtue of the national labor policy against discrimination, as expressed in both the NLRA, see United Packinghouse Workers v. NLRB, 416 F.2d 1126, *cert. denied*, 396 U.S. 903 (1969), and in Title VII of the Civil Rights Act of 1964, and that the Board had not adequately taken account of the necessity to accommodate the exclusive bargaining principle of the NLRA to the national policy of protecting action taken in opposition to discrimination from employer retaliation. The court recognized that protection of the minority-group concerted activity involved in this case would interfere to some extent with the orderly collective bargaining process, but it considered the disruptive effect on that process to be outweighed where protection of minority activity is necessary to full and immediate realization of the policy against discrimination. In formulating a standard for distinguishing between protected and unprotected activity, the majority held that the "Board should inquire, in cases such as this, whether the union was actually remedying the discrimination to the *fullest extent possible, by the most expedient and efficacious means*. Where the union's efforts fall short of this high standard, the minority group's concerted activities cannot lose [their] §7 protection."[8] Accordingly, the court remanded the case for the Board to make this determination and, if it found in favor of the employees, to consider whether their particular tactics were so disloyal to their employer as to deprive them of §7 protection under our decision in NLRB v. Electrical Workers, 346 U.S. 464 (1953).[9]

---

[6] The Board considered but stopped short of resolving the question of whether the employees' invective and call for a boycott of the Company bespoke so malicious an attempt to harm their employer as to deprive them of the protection of the Act. The Board decision is therefore grounded squarely on the view that a minority group member may not bypass the Union and bargain directly over matters affecting minority employees, and not at all on the tactics used in this particular attempt to obtain such bargaining.

Member Jenkins dissented on the ground that the employees' activity was protected by §7 because it concerned the terms and conditions of their employment. Member Brown agreed but expressly relied upon his view that the facts revealed no attempt to bargain "but simply to urge [the Company] to take action to correct conditions of racial discrimination which the employees reasonably believed existed at the Emporium." 192 N.L.R.B., at 179.

[8] 485 F.2d, at 931 (emphasis in original). We hasten to point out that it had never been determined in any forum, at least as of the time that Hollins and Hawkins engaged in the activity for which they were discharged, that the Company had engaged in any discriminatory conduct. The Board found that the employees believed that the Company had done so, but that no evidence introduced in defense of their resort to self-help supported this belief.

[9] Judge Wyzanski dissented insofar as the Board was directed on remand to evaluate the adequacy of the Union's efforts in opposing discrimination. He was of the view that minority concerted activity against discrimination would be protected regardless of the Union's efforts.

II

. . . [T]he Board found that the employees were discharged for attempting to bargain with the Company over the terms and conditions of employment as they affected racial minorities. Although the Court of Appeals expressly declined to set aside this finding, respondent has devoted considerable effort to attacking it in this Court, on the theory that the employees were attempting only to present a grievance to their employer within the meaning of the first proviso to §9(a).[12] We see no occasion to disturb the finding of the Board. The issue, then, is whether such attempts to engage in separate bargaining are protected by §7 of the Act or proscribed by §9(a).

A

. . . [The rights guaranteed by §7] are, for the most part, collective rights, rights to act in concert with one's fellow employees; they are protected not for their own sake but as an instrument of the national labor policy of minimizing industrial strife "by encouraging the practice and procedure of collective bargaining."

Central to the policy of fostering collective bargaining, where the employees elect that course, is the principle of majority rule. . . . [In] establishing a regime of majority rule, Congress sought to secure to all members of the unit the benefits of their collective strength and bargaining power, in full awareness that the superior strength of some individuals or groups might be subordinated to the interest of the majority. As a result, "[t]he complete satisfaction of all who are represented is hardly to be expected." Ford Motor Co. v. Huffman, 345 U.S. 330, 338 (1953).

The Court most recently had occasion to reexamine the underpinnings of the majoritarian principle in NLRB v. Allis-Chalmers Mfg. Co., 388 U.S. 175 (1967). In that case employees in two local unions had struck their common employer to enforce their bargaining demands for a new contract. In each local at least the two-thirds majority required by the constitution of the international union had voted for the strike, but some members nonethe-

---

[12] . . . Respondent clearly misapprehends the nature of the "right" conferred by this section. The intendment of the proviso is to permit employees to present grievances and to authorize the employer to entertain them without opening itself to liability for dealing directly with employees in derogation of the duty to bargain only with the exclusive bargaining representative, a violation of §8(a)(5). The Act nowhere protects this "right" by making it an unfair labor practice for an employer to refuse to entertain such a presentation, nor can it be read to authorize resort to economic coercion. This matter is fully explicated in Black-Clawson Co. v. Machinists, 313 F.2d 179 (CA 2d Cir. 1962). If the employees' activity in the present litigation is to be deemed protected, therefore, it must be so by reason of the reading given to the main part of §9(a), in light of Title VII and the national policy against employment discrimination, and not by burdening the proviso to that section with a load it was not meant to carry.

less crossed the picket lines and continued to work. When the union later tried and fined these members, the employer charged that it had violated §8(b)(1)(A) by restraining or coercing the employees in the exercise of their §7 right to refrain from concerted activities. In holding that the unions had not committed an unfair labor practice by disciplining the dissident members, we approached the literal language of §8(b)(1)(A) with an eye to the policy within which it must be read:

> National labor policy has been built on the premise that by pooling their economic strength and acting through a labor organization freely chosen by the majority, the employees of an appropriate unit have the most effective means of bargaining for improvements in wages, hours, and working conditions. The policy therefore extinguishes the individual employee's power to order his own relations with his employer and creates a power vested in the chosen representative to act in the interests of all employees. . . .

In vesting the representatives of the majority with this broad power Congress did not, of course, authorize a tyranny of the majority over minority interests. First, it confined the exercise of these powers to the context of a "unit appropriate for the purposes of collective bargaining," i.e., a group of employees with a sufficient commonality of circumstances to ensure against the submergence of a minority with distinctively different interests in the terms and conditions of their employment. Second, it undertook in the 1959 Landrum-Griffin amendments . . . to assure that minority voices are heard as they are in the functioning of a democratic institution. Third, we have held, by the very nature of the exclusive bargaining representative's status as representative of *all* unit employees, Congress implicitly imposed upon it a duty fairly and in good faith to represent the interests of minorities within the unit. And the Board has taken the position that a union's refusal to process grievances against racial discrimination, in violation of that duty, is an unfair labor practice. Hughes Tool Co., 147 N.L.R.B. 1573 (1964); see Miranda Fuel Co., 140 N.L.R.B. 181 (1962), *enforcement denied*, 326 F.2d 172 (CA 2d Cir. 1963). Indeed, the Board has ordered a union implicated by a collective bargaining agreement in discrimination with an employer to propose specific contractual provisions to prohibit racial discrimination. See Local Union No. 12, United Rubber Workers of America v. NLRB, 368 F.2d 12 (CA 5th Cir. 1966) (*enforcement granted*).

B

Against this background of long and consistent adherence to the principle of exclusive representation tempered by safeguards for the protection of minority interests, respondent urges this Court to fashion a limited exception to that principle: employees who seek to bargain separately with their employer as to the elimination of racially discriminatory employment practices peculiarly affecting them,[15] should be free from the constraints of the exclusivity principle of §9(a). Essentially because established procedures under Title VII or, as in this case, a grievance machinery, are too time consuming, the national labor policy against discrimination requires this exception, respondent argues, and its adoption would not unduly compromise the legitimate interests of either unions or employers.[16]

Plainly, national labor policy embodies the principles of nondiscrimination as a matter of highest priority, Alexander v. Gardner-Denver Co., 415 U.S. 36, 47 (1974), and it is a commonplace that we must construe the NLRA in light of the broad national labor policy of which it is a part. These general principles do not aid respondent, however, as it is far from clear that separate bargaining is necessary to help eliminate discrimination. Indeed, as the facts of this litigation demonstrate, the proposed remedy might have just the opposite effect. The collective bargaining agreement involved here prohibited without qualification all manner of invidious discrimination and made any claimed violation a grievable issue. The grievance procedure is directed precisely at determining whether discrimination has occurred. That orderly determination, if affirmative, could lead to an arbitral award enforceable in court. Nor is there any reason to believe that the processing of grievances is inherently limited to the correction of individual cases of discrimination. Quite apart from the essentially contractual question of whether the Union could grieve against a "pattern or practice" it deems inconsistent with the nondiscrimination clause of the contract, one would hardly expect

[15] As respondent conceded at oral argument, the rule it espouses here would necessarily have equal application to any identifiable group of employees — racial or religious groups, women, etc. — that reasonably believed themselves to be the object of invidious discrimination by their employer. As seemingly limited by the Court of Appeals, however, such a group would have to give their elected representative an opportunity to adjust the matter in some way before resorting to self-help.

[16] Our analysis of respondent's argument in favor of the exception makes it unnecessary either to accept or reject its factual predicate, viz., that the procedures now established for the elimination of discrimination in employment are too cumbersome to be effective. We note, however, that the present record provides no support for the proposition. Thus, while respondent stresses the fact that Hollins and Hawkins had brought their evidence of discrimination to the Union in April 1968 but did not resort to self-help until the following October, it overlooks the fact that although they had been in contact with the state Fair Employment Practices Commission they did not file a charge with that agency or the Equal Employment Opportunity Commission (EEOC). Further, when they abandoned the procedures to which the Union was bound because they thought "the union was sort of putting us off and on and was going into a lot of delay that we felt was unnecessary," . . . it was at the very moment that the Adjustment Board had been convened to hear their testimony.

an employer to continue in effect an employment practice that routinely results in adverse arbitral decisions.

The decision by a handful of employees to bypass the grievance procedure in favor of attempting to bargain with their employer, by contrast, may or may not be predicated upon the actual existence of discrimination. An employer confronted with bargaining demands from each of several minority groups would not necessarily, or even probably, be able to agree to remedial steps satisfactory to all at once. Competing claims on the employer's ability to accommodate each group's demands, e.g., for reassignments and promotions to a limited number of positions, could only set one group against the other even if it is not the employer's intention to divide and overcome them. Having divided themselves, the minority employees will not be in position to advance their cause unless it be by recourse seriatim to economic coercion, which can only have the effect of further dividing them along racial or other lines. Nor is the situation materially different where, as apparently happened here, self-designated representatives purport to speak for all groups that might consider themselves to be victims of discrimination. Even if in actual bargaining the various groups did not perceive their interests as divergent and further subdivide themselves, the employer would be bound to bargain with them in a field largely preempted by the current collective bargaining agreement with the elected bargaining representative. In this instance we do not know precisely what form the demands advanced by Hollins, Hawkins, et al. would take, but the nature of the grievance that motivated them indicates that the demands would have included the transfer of some minority employees to sales areas in which higher commissions were paid. Yet the collective bargaining agreement provided that no employee would be transferred from a higher-paying to a lower-paying classification except by consent or in the course of a layoff or reduction in force. The potential for conflict between the minority and other employees in this situation is manifest. With each group able to enforce its conflicting demands—the incumbent employees by resort to contractual processes and the minority employees by economic coercion—the probability of strife and deadlock is high; the likelihood of making headway against discriminatory practices would be minimal.

. . . The court below minimized the impact on the Union in this case by noting that it was not working at cross-purposes with the dissidents, and that indeed it could not do so consistent with its duty of fair representation and perhaps its obligations under Title VII. As to the Company, its obligations under Title VII are cited for the proposition that it could have no legitimate objection to bargaining with the dissidents in order to achieve full compliance with that law.

This argument confuses the employees' substantive right to be free of racial discrimination with the procedures available under the NLRA for securing these rights. Whether they are thought to depend upon Title VII or have an independent source in the NLRA,[23] they cannot be pursued at the expense of the orderly collective bargaining process contemplated by the NLRA. The elimination of discrimination and its vestiges is an appropriate subject of bargaining, and an employer may have no objection to incorporating into a collective agreement the substance of his obligation not to discriminate in personnel decisions; the Company here has done as much, making any claimed dereliction a matter subject to the grievance-arbitration machinery as well as to the processes of Title VII. But that does not mean that an employer may not have strong and legitimate objections to bargaining on several fronts over the implementation of the right to be free of discrimination for some of the reasons set forth above. Similarly, while a union cannot lawfully bargain for the establishment or continuation of discriminatory practices, . . . it has a legitimate interest in presenting a united front on this as on other issues and in not seeing its strength dissipated and its stature denigrated by subgroups within the unit separately pursuing what they see as separate interests. When union and employer are not responsive to their legal obligations, the bargain they have struck must yield pro tanto to the law, whether by means of conciliation through the offices of the EEOC, or by means of federal court enforcement at the instance of either that agency or the party claiming to be aggrieved. . . .

III

Even if the NLRA, when read in the context of the general policy against discrimination, does not sanction these employees' attempt to bargain with the Company, it is contended that it must do so if a specific element of that policy is to be preserved. The element in question is the congressional policy of protecting from employer reprisal employee efforts to oppose unlawful discrimination, as expressed in §704(a) of Title VII. Since the discharged employees here had, by their own lights, "opposed" discrimination, it is argued that their activities "fell plainly within the scope of," and their discharges therefore violated, §704(a). The notion here is that if the discharges did not also violate §8(a)(1) of the NLRA, then the integrity of §704(a) will be seriously undermined. We cannot agree.

[23] See United Packinghouse Workers v. NLRB, 416 F.2d 1126, *cert. denied*, 396 U.S. 903 (1969); Local Union No. 12, United Rubber Workers of America v. NLRB, 368 F.2d 12 (CA 5th Cir. 1966).

Even assuming that §704(a) protects employees' picketing and instituting a consumer boycott of their employer,[25] the same conduct is not necessarily entitled to affirmative protection from the NLRA. Under the scheme of that Act, conduct which is not protected concerted activity may lawfully form the basis for the participants' discharge. That does not mean that the discharge is immune from attack on other statutory grounds in an appropriate case. If the discharges in these cases are violative of §704(a) of Title VII, the remedial provisions of that title provide the means by which Hollins and Hawkins may recover their jobs with backpay.

Respondent objects that reliance on the remedies provided by Title VII is inadequate effectively to secure the rights conferred by Title VII. There are indeed significant differences between proceedings initiated under Title VII and an unfair labor practice proceeding. Congress chose to encourage voluntary compliance with Title VII by emphasizing conciliatory procedures before federal coercive powers could be invoked. Even then it did not provide the EEOC with the power of direct enforcement, but made the federal courts available to the agency or individual to secure compliance with Title VII. By contrast, once the General Counsel of the NLRB decides to issue a complaint, vindication of the charging party's statutory rights becomes a public function discharged at public expense, and a favorable decision by the Board brings forth an administrative order. As a result of these and other differences, we are told that relief is typically available to the party filing a charge with the NLRB in a significantly shorter time, and with less risk, than obtains for one filing a charge with the EEOC.

Whatever its factual merit, this argument is properly addressed to the Congress and not to this Court or the NLRB. In order to hold that employer conduct violates §8(a)(1) of the NLRA *because* it violates §704(a) of Title VII, we would have to override a host of consciously made decisions well within the exclusive competence of the legislature.[26] This obviously, we cannot do.

[25] The NLRB argues that §704(a) is directed at protecting access to the EEOC and federal courts. Pettway v. American Cast Iron Pipe Co., 411 F.2d 998 (CA 5th Cir. 1969). We have previously had occasion to note that "[n]othing in Title VII compels an employer to absolve and rehire one who has engaged in . . . deliberate, unlawful activity against it." McDonnell Douglas Corp. v. Green, 411 U.S. 792, 803 (1973). Whether the protection afforded by §704(a) extends only to the right of access or well beyond it, however, is not a question properly presented by these cases. Nor is it an appropriate question to be answered in the first instance by the NLRB. Questions arising under Title VII must be resolved by the means that Congress provided for that purpose. . . .

[26] In Alexander v. Gardner-Denver Co., 415 U.S., at 48 n.9, we had occasion to refer to Senator Clark's interpretive memorandum stating that "[n]othing in Title VII or anywhere else in this bill affects rights and obligations under the NLRA. . . ." Since the Senator's remarks were directed to the suggestion that enactment of Title VII would somehow constrict

Reversed.

[The dissenting opinion of Douglas, J., is omitted.]

NOTES

1. In Frank Briscoe, Inc. v. NLRB, 637 F.2d 946 (3d Cir. 1981), the Board had found (a) that the almost simultaneous filing of similar complaints with the EEOC by five black workers had constituted "concerted activity" protected under the NLRA, and (b) that the employer had retaliated against the five complainants by not recalling them from layoff, thereby violating §8(a)(1). The court, affirming these findings, relied on the legislative history of Title VII and the *Emporium* decision to support its further conclusion that the NLRB's jurisdiction over interference with activity protected under §7 of the NLRA is not foreclosed by the existence of a Title VII remedy under §704(a). The court stated (at 952-953):

> . . . [C]ertain conduct may be protected by both statutes, and thus an employee may resort to the remedies of either statute. . . . [W]e emphasize that we are not holding that all conduct protected by §704(a) is necessarily protected by §8(a)(1). . . . [H]ere the mere fact that the concerted activity was manifested in the form of filing EEOC complaints does not convert the employees' complaint under the NLRA into one exclusively under Title VII.

Should the NLRB, in deciding protection vel non under the NLRA, be entitled to, required to, or permitted to give effect to the policies embodied in Title VII, §704(a)?

2. Suppose the employer in *Emporium* had been found guilty of "discrimination" in violation of Title VII. Any difference in result? Would your answer be affected by the nature and seriousness of the violation? See generally Meltzer, The National Labor Relations Act and Racial Discrimination: The More Remedies, the Better? 42 U. Chi. L. Rev. 1 (1974); Lopatka, Protection Under the National Labor Relations Act and Title VII of the Civil Rights Act for Employees who Protest Discrimination in Private Employment, 50 N.Y.U.L. Rev. 1179 (1975).

3. On the Title VII question not addressed in footnote 25 of *Emporium* (i.e., permissible forms of employee "opposition" under §704(a)), see

---

an employee's access to redress under other statutory regimes, we do not take them as foreclosing the possibility that in some circumstances rights created by the NLRA and related laws affecting the employment relationship must be broadened to accommodate the policies of Title VII.

EEOC v. Crown Zellerbach Corp., 720 F.2d 1008 (9th Cir. 1983) (black employees' letter to their employer's customer, protesting affirmative action award from the customer (the local school board) to the employer, was neither "disloyal" nor "unreasonable" under §704(a) and thus constituted protected "opposition" to the employer's practices).

NLRB v. Shop Rite Foods, Inc., 430 F.2d 786 (5th Cir. 1970). During negotiations with a newly certified union, Shop Rite concluded that merchandise was being deliberately damaged in order to exert bargaining pressure and discharged an apparently guilty employee. A minority of the employees walked out in protest against that discharge and, perhaps, against the employer's refusal to discuss it with union officials and ten other employees in the manager's office. A union official advised the employees to picket while he sought strike authorization. The union denied such authorization and ordered the men back to work, but the employer denied the employees' request for reinstatement. In reversing the Board's finding that the strike had been protected, the court retreated from its approach in NLRB v. R.C. Can Co., 328 F.2d 974 (5th Cir. 1964), which, in keeping with the NLRB's customary distinction between unauthorized strikes that undermine the union's position and those that do not, had accorded protection to minority strikes supporting union objectives. The court stated (at 790):

> If union objectives are characterized in general terms—such as wages, job security . . . —one can assume that in a great majority of instances minority action will be consistent with one or more of those objectives. If R.C. Can is not applied with great care it would allow minority action in a broad range of situations and permit unrestrained undercutting of collective bargaining.

In the instant case, the court (passing over a statement by the local's chief steward that the discharged employee "hadn't done this" and that the company "was asking for trouble") stated that the union had not made a challenge of the discharge an "established objective" and had not approved the strike. In denying controlling effect to the absence of a collective agreement, the court emphasized the sensitivity of bargaining negotiations and the timing of the walkout just after the submission of the company's final offer.

NOTES

1. Suppose the minority group walkout in *Shop Rite Foods* had been triggered by the employer's unilateral change in lunch-period rules at a time

when the employer and the union were bargaining on that subject, among others. Should the presence of a bargaining representative remove such wildcat activity from §7's protection of "other concerted activities for the purpose of . . . mutual aid or protection"? See Chicago Rehabilitation Center v. NLRB, 710 F.2d 397 (7th Cir. 1983), *cert. denied,* 104 S. Ct. 1414 (1984), where the court, indicating that the employer's changing of the lunch rules was "a circumvention of the policies of the Act," declared (at 402):

> Although §9(a) qualifies §7, it qualifies the part of §7 that gives workers the right to bargain collectively. It does not — not explicitly anyway — qualify their §7 right to engage in other concerted activities for mutual aid or protection. Unless, therefore, a wildcat strike is called for the purpose of asserting a right to bargain collectively in the union's place or is likely, regardless of its purpose, to impair the union's performance as exclusive bargaining representative, §9(a) does not put the strikers beyond the pale of §7.

2. For discussion of group activities not sanctioned by the bargaining representative, see Cantor, Dissident Worker Action, After *The Emporium,* 29 Rutgers L. Rev. 35 (1975); Atleson, Work Group Behavior and Wildcat Strikes: The Causes and Functions of Industrial Civil Disobedience, 34 Ohio St. L.J. 751 (1973).

Mastro Plastics Corp. v. NLRB
350 U.S. 270 (1956)

[The employer and a Carpenters' local were parties to a collective bargaining agreement, terminating on November 30 and containing a no-strike pledge. In August of 1950, a rival union, believed by the employer to be Communist-dominated, began an organizational campaign designed to displace the incumbent union. The employer gave a third union (Pulp Workers, Local 318) active and unlawful assistance in its attempt to secure majority status. On October 10, the Carpenters served a sixty-day notice requesting modification of the contract. On November 10, the employer discharged one Ciccone because of his support of the Carpenters. This discharge precipitated a strike that began prior to both the contract termination date and the expiration of the sixty-day period. According to the Board's findings, confirmed on appeal, that strike was not called in support of contract demands but was a protest against, and an attempt to remedy, the employer's unfair labor practices. Four months after the strike began, the strikers made an unconditional offer to return to work, but they were denied reinstatement and were discharged. The employer was charged with a violation of §§8(a)(1),(2), and (3). The Board's reinstatement of the strikers was affirmed by the court of appeals.]

BURTON, J. . . . [Petitioners'] first affirmative defense was that the waiver of the right to strike, expressed by their employees in their collective bargaining contract, applied to strikes not only for economic benefits but to any and all strikes by such employees, including strikes directed solely against unfair labor practices of the employer.

Petitioners' other principal defense was that the existing strike began during the statutory waiting period initiated by the employees' request for modification of the contract and that, by virtue of §8(d) of the Act, the strikers had lost their status as employees. That defense turned upon petitioners' interpretation of §8(d), applying it not only to strikes for economic benefits but to any and all strikes occurring during the waiting period, including strikes solely against unfair labor practices of the employer. . . .

Apart from the issues raised by petitioners' affirmative defenses, the proceedings reflect a flagrant example of interference by the employers with the expressly protected right of their employees to select their own bargaining representative. The findings disclose vigorous efforts by the employers to influence and even to coerce their employees to abandon the Carpenters as their bargaining representatives and to substitute Local 318. Accordingly, unless petitioners sustain at least one of their affirmative defenses, they must suffer the consequences of their unfair labor practices violating §8(a)(1), or (2) or (3) of the Act. . . .

In the absence of some contractual or statutory provision to the contrary, petitioners' unfair labor practices provide adequate ground for the orderly strike that occurred here. Under those circumstances, the striking employees do not lose their status and are entitled to reinstatement with back pay, even if replacements for them have been made. Failure of the Board to enjoin petitioners' illegal conduct or failure of the Board to sustain the right to strike against that conduct would seriously undermine the primary objectives of the Labor Act. . . . While we assume that the employees, by explicit contractual provision, could have waived their right to strike against such unfair labor practices and that Congress, by explicit statutory provision, could have deprived strikers, under the circumstances of this case, of their status as employees, the questions before us are whether or not such a waiver was made by the Carpenters in their 1949-1950 contract and whether or not such a deprivation of status was enacted by Congress in §8(d) of the Act, as amended in 1947.

I. *Does the collective-bargaining contract waive the employees' right to strike against the unfair labor practices committed by their employers?* The answer turns upon the proper interpretation of the particular contract before us. Like other contracts, it must be read as a whole and in the light of the law relating to it when made. . . .

On the premise of fair representation, collective bargaining contracts frequently have included certain waivers of the employees' right to strike and of the employers' right to lockout to enforce their respective economic demands during the term of those contracts. *Provided the selection of the bargaining representative remains free,* such waivers contribute to the normal flow of commerce and to the maintenance of regular production schedules. Individuals violating such clauses appropriately lose their status as employees.

The waiver in the contract before us, upon which petitioners rely, is as follows:

> 5. The Union agrees that during the term of this agreement, there shall be no interference of any kind with the operations of the Employers, or any interruptions or slackening of production of work by any of its members. The Union further agrees to refrain from engaging in any strike or work stoppage during the term of this agreement. . . .

Petitioners argue that the words "any strike" leave no room for interpretation and necessarily include all strikes, even those against unlawful practices destructive of the foundation on which collective bargaining must rest. We disagree. We believe that the contract, taken as a whole, deals solely with the economic relationship between the employers and their employees. It is a typical collective bargaining contract dealing with terms of employment and the normal operations of the plant. It is for one year and assumes the existence of a lawfully designated bargaining representative. Its strike and lockout clauses are natural adjuncts of an operating policy aimed at avoiding interruptions of production prompted by efforts to change existing economic relationships. The main function of arbitration under the contract is to provide a mechanism for avoiding similar stoppages due to disputes over the meaning and application of the various contractual provisions.

To adopt petitioners' all-inclusive interpretation of the clause is quite a different matter. That interpretation would eliminate, for the whole year, the employees' right to strike, even if petitioners, by coercion, ousted the employees' lawful bargaining representative and, by threats of discharge, cause the employees to sign membership cards in a new union. Whatever may be said of the legality of such a waiver when explicitly stated, there is no adequate basis for implying its existence without a more compelling expression of it than appears in §5 of this contract. . . .

It is suggested that §13 of the Act . . . precludes reliance by the Board upon the Act for support of its interpretation of the strike-waiver clause. That section provides that "Nothing in this Act, except as specifically provided for herein, shall be construed so as either to interfere with or impede or diminish in any way the right to strike, or to affect the limitations or qualifications on that right." . . . On the basis of the above language, petitioners claim that because the contract-waiver clause prohibits all strikes of every nature, nothing in the Act may be construed to affect the "limitations or qualifications" which the contract thus places on that right. Such a claim assumes the point at issue. The Board relies upon the context of the contract and upon the language of the clause itself, rather than upon the statute, to define the kind of strike that is waived.

As a matter of fact, the initial provision in §13 that nothing in the Act "shall be construed so as either to interfere with or impede or diminish in any way the right to strike" adds emphasis to the Board's insistence upon preserving the employees' right to strike to protect their freedom of concerted action. Inasmuch as strikes against unfair labor practices are not anywhere specifically excepted from lawful strikes, §13 adds emphasis to the congressional recognition of their propriety.

For the reasons stated above and those given by the Board and the court below, we conclude that the contract did not waive the employees' right to strike solely against the unfair labor practices of their employers.

II. *Does §8(d) of the National Labor Relations Act, as amended, deprive individuals of their status as employees if, within the waiting period prescribed by §8(d)(4), they engage in a strike solely against unfair labor practices of their employers?* Here again the background is the dual purpose of the Act (1) to protect the right of employees to be free to take concerted action as provided in §§7 and 8(a), and (2) to substitute collective bargaining for economic warfare in securing satisfactory wages, hours of work and employment conditions. Section 8(d) seeks to bring about the termination and modification of collective bargaining agreements without interrupting the flow of commerce or the production of goods, while §§7 and 8(a) seek to insure freedom of concerted action by employees at all times.

The language in §8(d) especially relied upon by petitioners is as follows: "Any employee who engages in a strike within the sixty-day period specified in this subsection shall lose his status as an employee of the employer engaged in the particular labor dispute, for the purposes of §§8, 9, and 10 of this Act, as amended. . . ."

Reading the clause in conjunction with the rest of §8, the Board points out that "the sixty-day period" referred to is the period mentioned in paragraph (4) of §8(d). That paragraph requires the party giving notice of a desire to *"terminate or modify"* such a contract, as part of its obligation to bargain under §8(a)(5) or §8(b)(3), to continue "in full force and effect, without resorting to strike or lockout, all the terms and conditions of the existing contract for a period of sixty days after such notice is given or until the expiration date of such contract, whichever occurs later." Section 8(d) thus seeks, during this natural renegotiation period, to relieve the parties from the economic pressure of a strike or lockout in relation to the subjects of negotiation. The final clause of §8(d) also warns employees that, if they join a proscribed strike, they shall thereby lose their status as employees and, consequently, their right to reinstatement.

The Board reasons that the words which provide the key to a proper interpretation of §8(d) with respect to this problem are "termination or modification." Since the Board expressly found that the instant strike was *not to terminate or modify* the contract, but was designed instead to protest the unfair labor practices of petitioners, the loss-of-status provision of §8(d) is not applicable. We sustain that interpretation. Petitioners' construction would produce incongruous results. It concedes that prior to the 60-day negotiating period, employees have a right to strike against unfair labor practices designed to oust the employees' bargaining representative, yet petitioners' interpretation of §8(d) means that if the employees give the 60-day notice of their desire to modify the contract, they are penalized for exercising that right to strike. This would deprive them of their most effective weapon at a time when their need for it is obvious. Although the employees' request to modify the contract would demonstrate their need for the services of their freely chosen representative, petitioners' interpretation would have the incongruous effect of cutting off the employees' freedom to strike against unfair labor practices aimed at that representative. This would relegate the employees to filing charges under a procedure too slow to be effective. The result would unduly favor the employers and handicap the employees during negotiation periods contrary to the purpose of the Act. There also is inherent inequity in any interpretation that penalizes one party to a contract for conduct induced solely by the unlawful conduct of the other, thus giving advantage to the wrongdoer.

Petitioners contend that, unless the loss-of-status clause is applicable to unfair labor practice strikes, as well as to economic strikes, it adds nothing to the existing law relating to loss of status. Assuming that to be so, the clause is justifiable as a clarification of the law and as a warning to employees against engaging in economic strikes during the statutory waiting period. Moreover, in the face of the affirmative emphasis that is placed by the Act upon freedom of concerted action and freedom of choice of representatives, any limitation on the employees' right to strike against violations of §§7 and 8(a), protecting those freedoms, must be more explicit and clear than it is here in order to restrict them at the very time they may be most needed.

There is sufficient ambiguity here to permit consideration of relevant legislative history. While such history provides no conclusive answer, it is consistent with the view taken by the Board and by the Courts of Appeals for the Second and Seventh Circuits.

Senator Ball, who was a manager for the 1947 amendments in the Senate and one of the conferees on the bill, stated that §8(d) made mandatory what was already good practice and was aimed at preventing such interruptions of production as the "quickie strikes" occasionally used to gain economic advantages. . . .

One minority report suggested a fear that §8(d) would be applicable to unfair practice strikes. The suggestion, however, was not even made the subject of comment by the majority reports or in the debates. An unsuccessful minority cannot put words into the mouths of the majority and thus, indirectly, amend a bill.

The record shows that the supporters of the bill were aware of the established practice which distinguished between the effect on employees of engaging in economic strikes and that of engaging in unfair practice strikes. If Congress had wanted to modify that practice, it could readily have done so by specific provision. Congress cannot fairly be held to have made such an intrusion on employees' rights, as petitioners claim, without some more explicit expression of its purpose to do so than appears here. . . .

As neither the collective bargaining contract nor §8(d) . . . stands in the way, the judgment of the Court of Appeals is

Affirmed.

FRANKFURTER, J., whom MINTON and HARLAN, JJ., join, dissenting. . . . Since §8 [under the Wagner Act] did not place any duties upon employees or unions, most peaceful collective action was protected under §7, because most peaceful activity did not infringe some implicit federal labor policy or some other federal policy, such as that represented by the statute against mutiny.

The Taft-Hartley Act changed the situation. Section 8 of the Wagner Act was amended and duties were placed upon unions. Collective action which violates any of these duties is of course activity unprotected by §7. See Cox, The Right to Engage in Concerted Activities, 26 Ind. L.J. 319, 325-333 (1951). One of these new union duties, and an important one, is contained in §8(d): unions may not strike to enforce their demands during the 60-day "cooling-off" period.

By reason of this new enactment, participating workers would not be engaged in a protected activity under §7 by striking for the most legitimate economic reasons during the 60-day period. The strike would be in violation of the provision of that section which says that during the period there shall be no resort to a strike. The employer could discharge such strikers without violating §8. This would be so if §8 were without the loss-of-status provision. The Board would be powerless to order reinstatement under §10. The loss-of-status provision in §8(d) does not curtail the Board's power, since it did not have power to order reinstatement where a strike is resorted to for economic reasons before the 60-day period has expired. In such a situation the striker has no rights under §§8 and 10. Yet the Board would have us construe the loss-of-status provision as applicable only to the economic striker and qualifying a power which the Board does not have.

It is with respect to the unfair-labor-practice striker that the provision serves a purpose. This becomes clear if we assume that there were no such provision and examine the consequences of its absence. On such an assumption, a strike based on an unfair labor practice by the employer during the 60-day period may or may not be a protected activity under §7. If it is, obviously discharged strikers would be entitled to reinstatement. The strike would not be a §7 activity, however, if, for example, it were in breach of a no-strike clause in the contract which extends to a work stoppage provoked by an employer unfair labor practice, cf. Labor Board v. Sands Mfg. Co., 306 U.S. 332, 344, or if the no-strike clause in §8(d)(4) (not to be confused with the loss-of-status provision) extends to such a work stoppage. However, even if the strike is not a §7 activity, the Board in the unfair-labor-practice strike situation as distinguished from the economic strike situation, may in its discretion order the discharged participants reinstated. This is so because of the antecedent employer unfair practice which caused the strike, and which gave employees rights under §8. If the Board finds that reinstatement of such strikers is a remedy that would effectuate the policies of the Act, it has the power under §10(c) to issue the necessary order.

This would not be the case, however, if the loss-of-status provision were held applicable to unfair-labor-practice strikes, because participating workers would lose their rights as "employees" for the purposes of §§8 and 10. Under the Act only "employees" are eligible for reinstatement. The unfair-labor-practice strike, then, is the one situation where loss of status for the purposes of §§8 and 10 is of significance. At any rate, we have not been advised of any other situation to which the provision would apply.

We are therefore confronted with the demonstrable fact that if the provision stripping strikers of their status as employees during the 60-day period is to have any usefulness at all and not be an idle collection of words, the fact that a strike during that period is induced by the employer's unfair labor practice is immaterial. Even though this might on first impression seem an undesirable result, it is so only by rejecting the important considerations in promoting peaceful industrial relations which might well have determined the action of Congress. In the first place, the Congress may have set a very high value on peaceful adjustments, i.e., the absence of strikes. One may take judicial notice of the fact that this consideration was at the very forefront of the thinking and feeling of the Eightieth Congress. And there is another consideration not unrelated to this. While in a particular case the cause of a strike may be clear, and in a particular case there may be no controversy regarding the circumstances which prove that an employer committed an unfair labor practice, as a matter of experience that is not always true; indeed often it is not true. One of the sharpest controversies, one of the issues most difficult of determination, is the very question of what precipitated a work stoppage. This is especially true where a new contract is being negotiated. It is not at all unreasonable, therefore, to find a congressional desire to preclude litigation over what all too often is a contentious subject and to deter all strikes during the crucial period of negotiation. . . .

NOTES

1. In a series of cases beginning with Arlan's Department Store of Michigan, Inc., 133 N.L.R.B. 802, 807 (1961), the NLRB has derived from *Mastro Plastics* the proposition that under a general no-strike agreement only strikes protesting "non-serious" employer unfair labor practices lose the protection of the NLRA. See, e.g., the *Dow Chemical* litigation noted in Chapter 10, p. 1067. Is the NLRB's *Arlan's* doctrine a fair reading of *Mastro Plastics?* Does that opinion indicate how one is to distinguish between "serious" and "non-serious" employer unfair labor practices? Would the general law of contracts support that distinction?

2. An employer fired several employees for striking in protest over the employer's unlawful discharge of a union supporter. The collective bargaining agreement barred strikes over discharges prior to exhaustion of the contractually prescribed grievance procedure. The NLRB noted that recourse to the grievance procedure would have taken only five days and that the antecedent unfair labor practice had not threatened the union's existence. Despite the absence of an explicit contractual waiver of the right to strike against an unfair labor practice, the Board upheld the discharge of the strikers, on the ground that their failure to resort to the grievance procedure made their strike unprotected. See Mid-West Metallic Prod., Inc., 121 N.L.R.B. 1317 (1958). See also Caterpillar Tractor Co. v. NLRB, 658 F.2d 1242, 1247 (7th Cir. 1981), where the no-strike clause provided: "The

company agrees that there will be no 'lockout' of its employees, and the Union agrees that there will be no strike or stoppage of work until all peaceable means, as enumerated in the grievance procedure of this agreement, of reaching a mutually satisfactory decision on any and all problems have been tried." The court, finding the clause "more specific" than the one at issue in *Mastro Plastics*, interpreted it to involve a waiver of the employees' right to strike in response to a "non-serious" §8(a)(5) violation (company's ending the practice of permitting voluntary employee transfers to a lower job classification), while the union and the employer were attempting to resolve the dispute through the grievance procedure.

Local 833, UAW v. NLRB (The Kohler Case)
300 F.2d 699 (D.C. Cir. 1962), *cert. denied*, 370 U.S. 911 (1962)

BAZELON, J. These are petitions for review and enforcement of an order of the National Labor Relations Board concerning a strike by Local 833, UAW-AFL-CIO, against the Kohler Company. The strike began on April 5, 1954, and was still unsettled when the Board issued its order on August 26, 1960. The dispute has a long and bitter history — more typical of "a bygone era" — which is set forth in detail in the Board's decision. Kohler Co., 128 N.L.R.B. 1062 (1960). In this opinion we relate only those facts required to understand the issues we consider.

I. THE BOARD'S DECISION AND ORDER

The Board found that a disagreement over contract terms and not Kohler's alleged refusal to bargain caused the strike, but that it was prolonged by such refusals on and after June 1, 1954. On that date Kohler granted a three-cent wage increase to nonstriking employees working under the conditions specified in an expired contract, but failed to make a similar offer to the Union. The Board also found that Kohler subsequently refused to bargain in good faith in the following respects, among others: by unilaterally putting into effect a second wage increase; by discharging striking employees and transferring nonstriking employees without notification to or consultation with the Union; and by refusing to furnish wage information pertinent to the negotiations. The Board also determined that Kohler violated §8(a)(3) and (1) of the Act . . . by discriminatorily treating some employees and unlawfully discharging others because of their participation in strike activities. In addition, the Board found that after June 1, 1954, Kohler interfered with, restrained, and coerced its employees in the exercise of their right to join labor unions and bargain collectively by engaging in surveillance and antiunion espionage, evicting certain strikers from Company-owned dwellings, and other conduct violating §8(a)(1) of the Act.

Having concluded that Kohler's unfair labor practices on and after June 1, 1954, converted what the Board thought had been an economic strike into an unfair labor practice strike, the Board issued a remedial order directing the Company, inter alia, to reinstate strikers replaced after the June 1 unilateral wage increase, excepting, however, employees discharged on March 1, 1955, for misconduct in connection with the strike.

II.   KOHLER'S PETITION FOR REVIEW IN NO. 16182

In No. 16182 Kohler seeks review of the Board's adverse determinations. We think they are amply supported by the record considered as a whole and that Kohler's attack must fail. . . .

III.   THE UNION'S PETITION FOR REVIEW IN NO. 15961

In No. 15961 the Union challenges the Board's refusal to reinstate seventy-seven employees discharged for misconduct. It alleges that the Board failed to balance that misconduct against the Company's unfair labor practices. This balancing, it contends, is required by the statutory command that the Board's remedy "effectuate the policies of the [Act]. . . ." NLRB v. Thayer Co., 213 F.2d 748 (1st Cir.), cert. denied, 348 U.S. 883 (1954). The Union also contends that the Board should have found that Kohler failed, both in form and substance, to bargain in good faith in the unsuccessful negotiations which culminated in the 1954 strike and that the walkout was therefore an unfair labor practice strike from its inception on April 5, 1954. In the absence of such a finding, the Board ordered reinstatement only of employees whose jobs were filled after June 1, 1954. Had it found that Kohler's unfair labor practices caused the walkout on April 5, it might have ordered reinstatement of all strikers replaced by nonstrikers at any time during the dispute.[5] More-over, if the *Thayer* doctrine is valid, the Board should have balanced Kohler's unfair labor practices against the discharged strikers' misconduct whether it occurred either before or after June 1, 1954.[6]

A.   THE DISCHARGES FOR MISCONDUCT

We first set forth the facts relevant to the union's request that the Board be directed to reconsider its decision not to reinstate seventy-seven strikers

---

[5] See Mastro Plastics Corp. v. NLRB, 350 U.S. 270, 278 (1956). . . .

[6] We assume without deciding that *Thayer* principles would not govern reinstatement of employees discharged during the time, if any, before the stoppage became an unfair labor practice strike.

discharged for misconduct. Their misconduct occurred in connection with three series of incidents.

First, forty-four discharges were based on participation in "belly-to-back" mass picketing ranging from presence on the picket line to a physical assault upon a nonstriker. The Board found that from April 5 through May 28 this picketing prevented any person who did not have a Union pass from entering Kohler's plants. The second series of incidents involved demonstrations by large, jeering crowds outside the homes of nonstrikers during the month of August, 1954. Some strikers who actively participated in the demonstrations and others who were merely present in the crowds were discharged. The third series of incidents took place near Kohler's employment office in December 1954 and January 1955 when a group of Union pickets hindered applicants from entering by blocking, pushing, and shoving some of them and by forcing others to walk around the pickets. Kohler discharged the participants. The last two series of incidents accounted for twenty-one discharges. The remaining twelve dischargees were members of the Union's strike committee which the Board found instigated some of the misconduct.

The trial examiner found that some of these employees had been discharged for activity which did not constitute misconduct or which Kohler had condoned. Accordingly, he recommended their reinstatement. But the Board reversed the examiner's findings. We put aside the Union's attack upon the Board's reasons for reversal, and turn to the Union's contention that, in any event, we should direct the Board to reconsider the reinstatement issue in light of the *Thayer* doctrine.

B.   THE APPLICATION OF THE THAYER DOCTRINE

Thayer holds that where an employer who has committed unfair labor practices discharges employees for unprotected acts of misconduct, the Board must consider both the seriousness of the employer's unlawful acts and the seriousness of the employees' misconduct in determining whether reinstatement would effectuate the policies of the Act. Those policies inevitably come into conflict when both labor and management are at fault. To hold that employee "misconduct" automatically precludes compulsory reinstatement ignores two considerations which we think important. First, the employer's antecedent unfair labor practices may have been so blatant that they provoked employees to resort to unprotected action. Second, reinstatement is the only sanction which prevents an employer from benefiting from his unfair labor practices through discharges which may weaken or destroy a union. In the Matter of H. N. Thayer Co., 115 N.L.R.B. 1591, 1605-1606

(1956) (dissenting opinion). But sanctions other than discharge — criminal prosecutions, civil suits, union unfair labor practice proceedings and the *possibility* of discharge — are available to prevent or remedy certain employee misconduct. Hart & Pritchard, The Fansteel Case: Employee Misconduct and the Remedial Powers of the National Labor Relations Board, 52 Harv. L. Rev. 1275, 1319 (1939).[b] . . . Hence automatic denial of reinstatement prevents the Board from protecting the rights of employees, but may not be essential to the protection of legitimate interests of employers and the public. We conclude that the teaching of the *Thayer* case is sound and must be followed in order to assure the Board's compliance with the statutory command that its remedial orders effectuate the policies of the Act.

The record indicates that the Board disregarded the *Thayer* doctrine. Despite exceptions taken by both the Union and the general counsel to the trial examiner's express refusal to follow *Thayer*, the Board's decision refers neither to the doctrine nor to the considerations it requires. On the contrary, the Board held that strikers who did not themselves obstruct applicants but were present at the employment office picketing could not be reinstated because they were engaged in unprotected activity.[16] That approach to formulating the remedy for an employer's antecedent unfair labor practice was specifically disapproved by *Thayer*. In ordering the Board to reconsider its determination not to reinstate certain employees who had engaged in unprotected acts of misconduct, the *Thayer* court reasoned that where the issue is simply whether a discharge was an attempt to coerce employees in the exercise of their rights under §7, a finding that an employee was fired for participation in unprotected activity ends the inquiry; but where there has been an antecedent employer unfair labor practice, a finding that employees have engaged in unprotected activity is only the first step in determining whether reinstatement is appropriate.[18] We think that view of the Board's remedial powers is correct. . . .

[b] [In *Fansteel*, a celebrated case, the Court, disagreeing with the Board, denied relief to strikers discharged for engaging in a nine-day, violent, physically destructive "sit in," even though it had been provoked by the employer's serious unfair labor practices. See NLRB v. Fansteel Metallurgical Corp., 306 U.S. 240 (1939). The Board has been divided and unclear on the protected status of brief, nondestructive sit-ins or "work ins." See Advance Indus. Div.-Overhead Door Corp., 220 N.L.R.B. 431 (1975), *enforcement denied*, 540 F.2d 878 (7th Cir. 1976); cf. Peck Inc., 226 N.L.R.B. 1174, 1176 (1976). — Eds.]

[16] The Union attacks this finding, citing, inter alia, International Ladies' Garment Workers Union v. National Labor Relations Board, 237 F.2d 545 (1956). In that case, we held that the Board erred in imputing the misconduct of some employees on the picket line to other employees who were present but who did not participate in acts of misconduct. We express no opinion concerning the applicability of that case to the facts of the present case. We assume that on the remand in this case the Board will consider it in assessing the seriousness of the misconduct.

[18] The *Thayer* court referred to "well-behaved" picket lines in which 103 employees had

C. APPLICATION OF THE DISCHARGE "FOR CAUSE" PROVISION OF §10(c)

In its brief and argument before this court, the Board urges that balancing union and employer misconduct is unnecessary here since §10(c) precludes reinstatement of employees "discharged for cause." It now contends that the acts of misconduct which it found were committed by the discharged employees constituted "cause." But in its decision the Board did not mention the "for cause" provision of §10(c). Nor did it allude to factors which may be relevant considerations under that provision, such as the employer's unfair labor practices, each employee's job history, and the relationship between the acts of misconduct and fitness for continued service. Thus it clearly appears that the Board did not rely on §10(c) in refusing reinstatement.

Ordinarily "the grounds upon which an administrative order must be judged are those upon which the record discloses that its action was based," Securities & Exchange Commn. v. Chenery Corp., 318 U.S. 80, 87 (1943). We could sustain the Board's order upon a ground which it did not consider only if that ground were one "within the power of . . . appellate court to formulate." Clearly, whether these employees' misconduct constituted "cause" for discharge under §10(c) — like the question whether death arose out of and in the course of employment under the Longshoremen's and Harbor Workers' Act, 33 U.S.C.A. §901 et seq. — is governed by "standards [which] are not so severable from the experience of industry nor of such a nature as to be peculiarly appropriate for independent judicial ascertainment as [a] 'questions of law.'" That determination lies within the special competence of the Board. The Board failed to make it and we cannot supply it. Therefore, we cannot say that §10(c) would prevent the Board from ordering reinstatement if it were to find that to do so would effectuate the policies of the Act.

D. THE BOARD'S DETERMINATION THAT KOHLER BARGAINED IN GOOD FAITH DURING THE 1954 NEGOTIATIONS

The Union's second contention, mentioned earlier, is that the Board's finding that Kohler bargained in good faith during the 1954 negotiations cannot be sustained because in making that determination the Board viewed the negotiations in isolation, ignoring the Company's pre-1953 history of antiunion activities and three unfair labor practices committed during the negotiations. We think that contention is sound. . . .

---

participated and for which they had been discharged. Since peaceful picketing is protected activity, the court upheld the Board's reinstatement of these employees. But the court also directed the Board to reconsider its refusal to reinstate certain other employees who had engaged in admittedly unprotected acts of misconduct. It is this portion of the *Thayer* opinion, to which the character of the picket lines is not relevant, which we follow here.

IV. CONCLUSION AND THE BOARD'S PETITION FOR ENFORCEMENT IN NO. 16031

Since we find the Board's order directing Kohler to take affirmative action and to refrain from engaging in enumerated unfair labor practices is supported by substantial evidence, the Board's petition for enforcement will be granted. So much of its order as denies reinstatement to seventy-seven discharged employees will be set aside and the case remanded for further proceedings in light of this opinion and for modification of the Board's order if necessary. Any order of the Board entered pursuant to our remand will be reviewable or enforceable, as the case may be, on petition to this court. . . .

[The opinion of Miller, J., dissenting from both the enforcement of the Board's order and the setting aside of the Board's denial of reinstatement to the seventy-seven discharged employees, is omitted.]

NOTES

1. Was it proper for the court of appeals to conclude both that the Board must follow *Thayer* and that the "for cause" provision of §10(c) had not been relied on by the Board and therefore could not be considered by the court? The Supreme Court has frequently affirmed the NLRB's broad discretion with respect to remedial action. See, e.g., Phelps Dodge Corp. v. NLRB, 313 U.S. 177 (1941), noted infra p. 275. Is that approach relevant to the propriety of the *Kohler* court's embracing the *Thayer* doctrine without the benefit of the Board's views? What hypothesis do you have about the reasons for the court's treatment of these questions in *Kohler*?

2. In Blades Mfg. Corp., 144 N.L.R.B. 561 (1963), *enforcement denied*, 344 F.2d 998 (8th Cir. 1965), the Board announced its acquiescence in the *Thayer* doctrine.

3. In *Kohler*, on remand, 148 N.L.R.B. 1434 (1964), *aff'd by an equally divided court*, 345 F.2d 748 (D.C. Cir.), *cert. denied*, 382 U.S. 836 (1965), the Board, rejecting its earlier finding, characterized the 1954 strike as an unfair labor practice strike, ab initio. It denied reinstatement only to those strikers discharged for engaging in violent physical assaults on nonstrikers or in threats of violence against members of their families. For those strikers reinstated, the Board tolled back pay from September 1, 1960, the date of the strikers' unconditional request for reinstatement, to January 26, 1962, the date of the decision in the principal case, which fully apprised the

company of the controlling legal principles. Member Leedom, dissenting on several grounds, urged independently that back pay should run only from the date of the Board's supplemental decision (September 29, 1964), in accordance with the Board's precedents (see Walls Mfg. Co., 137 N.L.R.B. 1317 (1962), *enforced*, 321 F.2d 753 (D.C. Cir.), *cert. denied*, 375 U.S. 923 (1963)). The final *Kohler* back pay settlement was for $4.5 million. 31 N.L.R.B. Ann. Rep. 13 (1966).

4. Only serious misconduct during a strike has excluded a striker from the Act's protections. The exclusionary test is typically stated in general terms: whether a striker's misconduct "render[s] [him] unfit for further service." NLRB v. Illinois Tool Works, 153 F.2d 811, 815-816 (7th Cir. 1946). See also Coronet Casuals, Inc., 207 N.L.R.B. 304, 305 (1973) (expressing concern that the "right to strike . . . would be unduly jeopardized if any misconduct, without regard for [its] seriousness . . . , would deprive the employee of [statutory protections]").

In Associated Grocers of New England v. NLRB, 526 F.2d 1333 (1st Cir. 1977), the court denied enforcement to a Board order rescinding the discharge of an economic striker who, in the presence of 30 to 40 pickets, had told three job applicants not to go through the gate if they valued their lives, dissuading one of them from doing so. The court rejected as too rigid the Board's established doctrine that verbal threats lose the protection of §7 only when "accompanied . . . by physical acts or gestures that would provide added emphasis or meaning to [the] words." Noting that context could provide credibility, the court approved "an objective standard denying protection to misconduct that in the circumstances reasonably tends to coerce or intimidate . . . "; hence, verbal threats, even if ineffective, would not necessarily be protected by §7. In 1984, the Board, relying in part on *Associated Grocers*, rejected its own "acts or gestures" doctrine and adopted a similar "objective" test for determining the coerciveness of strike-related threats. Clear Pine Mouldings, Inc., 268 N.L.R.B. No. 173, 115 L.R.R.M. 1113 (1984) (two of the four members concurred in result, adopting only *Associated Grocers'* reasoning and test, rather than the plurality's controversial dicta, which included a vigorous rejection of the *Thayer* doctrine). Is NLRB v. Gissel Packing Co., supra p. 95, relevant to the *Associated Grocers'* approach?

Following the NLRB's reversal of position in *Clear Pine Mouldings*, the Supreme Court vacated the grant of certiorari in a case involving verbal threats by strikers, ordering a remand to the Board for further consideration in light of *Clear Pine Mouldings*. See Woodkraft Div., Georgia Kraft Co. v. NLRB, 104 S. Ct. 1673 (1984).

B.   THE ELEMENTS OF PROSCRIBED "DISCRIMINATION"

1.   Reprisals Against Protected Activities

Transportation Management Corp.
256 N.L.R.B. 101 (1981)

. . . The [ALJ] found, and we agree, that Respondent discharged employee Santillo in violation of §§8(a)(3) and (1). . . . We arrive at that conclusion by applying to the facts of this case the test we have recently enunciated . . . in *Wright Line, Inc.*[4] In the application of this test, the first element to be determined is whether the General Counsel has established a *prima facie* case for the finding of a violation.

In this regard the General Counsel established by credible evidence that Santillo was a leading union activist and . . . was the one responsible for first contacting the Union. Respondent soon became aware of Santillo's role as union activist by its unlawful interrogation of employees. Thus, in a conversation between Respondent's manager, Patterson, and employee Baer, Patterson stated that he had heard that Santillo had started the Union and that he (Patterson) considered Santillo to be "two faced" and threatened to get even with him. In another conversation between Patterson and employee West, Patterson asked West, "What's with Sam and the Union" and Patterson promised to remember Santillo's union activity when Santillo wanted privileges.

The foregoing evidence establishes beyond doubt that Respondent had knowledge of Santillo's union activity and that it intended to retaliate against Santillo because of these actions. It also demonstrates that Respondent evidenced a strong union animus. Finally, Santillo was discharged the day after Patterson made his threat to "get even" with Santillo. In such circumstances, we find that the General Counsel has established by strong and credible evidence a *prima facie* case for finding that Santillo was discharged in violation of §8(a)(3). . . .

The only remaining question, therefore, is whether Respondent has shown, by other evidence, that Santillo's discharge would have occurred without regard to these considerations. Respondent offers three reasons to justify Santillo's discharge. The first is that he left the keys in his bus on the day of his discharge, which is a violation of company policy. The evidence

---

[4]Wright Line, a Division of Wright Line, Inc., 251 N.L.R.B. 1083 (1980).

shows, however, that it is a common practice among the drivers to leave the keys in their buses and, in Santillo's case, we have Patterson's admission that he had decided to discharge Santillo before he had any knowledge that the keys had been left in the bus. Accordingly, we conclude, as did the [ALJ], that this is nothing more than a purely pretextual reason which does more to detract from the lawfulness of the discharge than support it.

The second reason offered by Respondent was that Santillo was "stealing time" by taking unauthorized coffeebreaks. . . . [T]he [pertinent] evidence shows that Santillo did in fact take coffeebreaks, but this was a normal practice among the drivers. The evidence further shows that such practices were tolerated unless these breaks affected the driver's ability properly to perform his job functions. In situations where the taking of such breaks adversely affected the driver's job performance, Respondent's practice was to change the driver's route, increase the number of children to be delivered, or refuse to pay the driver who was taking unauthorized time. In no such instance is there any evidence of disciplinary action being taken, much less any suspension or discharge.

The third and last reason relied on by Respondent was Santillo's practice of stopping off at his home before reporting at the garage which Respondent also characterized as "stealing time." The evidence establishes that Santillo, in fact, did engage in such a practice and there is no showing that Respondent either directly or indirectly condoned . . . [it]. On the other hand, when Respondent finally became convinced that Santillo was taking unauthorized time, Respondent did not confront him with the evidence or warn him of possible disciplinary action. Nor did Respondent follow its regular procedure of three written warnings before discharge.

On the basis of this evidence, we conclude that Respondent has failed to meet its burden of overcoming the General Counsel's *prima facie* case by establishing by competent evidence that Santillo would have been discharged, even absent his union activities. Accordingly, we find . . . that Respondent discharged Santillo in violation of §§8(a)(3) and (1) of the Act.

NOTES

1. In formulating the *Wright Line* test, the NLRB drew on the Supreme Court's analysis in Mount Healthy City Board of Education v. Doyle, 429 U.S. 274 (1977). Doyle, an untenured public school teacher, was not retained for reasons presented to him in writing, including: (a) his use of obscene language and gestures in the school cafeteria, and (b) his disclosure to a local radio station of a change in the school's dress code for teachers.

Doyle's suit for reinstatement alleged that the nonrenewal of his contract contravened the First and Fourteenth Amendments. The Supreme Court upheld this contention with respect to the second reason cited by the school board but rejected the view that Doyle could prevail by establishing that constitutionally protected conduct had played a role (even a "substantial" role) in the nonrenewal. Rather, the Court, reversing and remanding the decision in favor of Doyle, ruled that the school board should have been permitted to avoid liability by showing that it would have reached the same decision solely on the basis of the unprotected conduct. The Court reasoned as follows (pp. 285-286):

> A rule of causation which focuses solely on whether protected conduct played a part, "substantial" or otherwise, in a decision not to rehire, could place an employee in a better position as a result of the exercise of constitutionally protected conduct than he would have occupied had he done nothing. . . . The constitutional principle at stake is sufficiently vindicated if . . . an employee is placed in no worse a position than if he had not engaged in the [protected] conduct. A borderline or marginal candidate should not have the employment question resolved against him because of constitutionally protected conduct. But that same candidate ought not to be able, by engaging in such conduct, to prevent his employer from assessing his performance record and reaching a decision not to rehire on the basis of that record, simply because the protected conduct makes the employer more certain of the correctness of its decisions.

Thus, *Mount Healthy* responded to the problems of "dual motivation" cases with a procedure for shifting the "burden of proof": "Initially, . . . the burden was properly placed upon respondent [Doyle] to show that his conduct was constitutionally protected, and that this conduct was a 'substantial factor' in the [school's] decision not to rehire him. Respondent having carried that burden, however, the District Court should have gone on to determine whether the [school board] had shown by a preponderance of the evidence that it would have reached the same decision . . . even in the absence of the protected conduct." 429 U.S. at 287.

In *Wright Line*, the NLRB concluded that the *Mount Healthy* procedure "accommodates the legitimate competing interests inherent in dual motivation cases, while . . . [effectuating] the policies and objectives of §8(a)(3)."ᶜ 251 N.L.R.B. at 1088-1089. The Board also declared that appli-

---

ᶜ[In adopting a burden-shifting analysis in §8(a)(3) cases, the Board relied on NLRB v. Great Dane Trailers, infra p. 334, which, the Board said (at 1088), contains the principle that "the employer has to make the proof." There will be an opportunity to pursue this point when *Great Dane* is reached. — EDS.]

cation of the *Mount Healthy* test under §8(a)(3) would eliminate the need to distinguish between "pretext" and "dual motive" cases and thus reduce preexisting confusion. The Board stated (pp. 1084; 1089 n.14):

> . . . [T]he evidence may reveal . . . that the [employer's] asserted justification [for its action] is a sham in that the purported rule or circumstance advanced . . . did not exist, or was not, in fact, relied upon. When this occurs, the reason advanced by the employer may be termed pretextual. Since no legitimate business justification for the discipline exists, there is, by strict definition, no dual motive. The pure dual motive case presents a different situation. . . . [T]he discipline decision involves two factors. The first is a legitimate business reason. The second . . . [is] the employer's reaction to its employees' engaging in union or other protected activities. . . .
> Unfortunately, the distinction between a pretext case and a dual motive case is sometimes difficult to discern. This is especially true since the . . . designation seldom can be made until after the presentation of all relevant evidence. The conceptual problems . . . can be eliminated if one views the employer's asserted justification as an affirmative defense. Thus, in a pretext situation, the employer's affirmative defense of business justification is wholly without merit. If, however, the affirmative defense has at least some merit a "dual motive" may exist and the issue becomes one of the sufficiency of proof necessary for the employer's affirmative defense to be sustained. . . .
> . . . [I]n those instances where, after all the evidence has been submitted, the employer has been unable to carry its burden, we will not seek to quantitatively analyze the effect of the unlawful cause once it has been found. It is enough that the employees' protected activities are causally related to the employer action which is the basis of the complaint. Whether that "cause" was the straw that broke the camel's back or a bullet between the eyes, if it was enough to determine events, it is enough to come within the proscription of the Act.

In NLRB v. Wright Line, 662 F.2d 899 (1st Cir. 1981), the Board's order was enforced on the ground that the record justified a finding, by a preponderance of the evidence, that the discharge had resulted from union activity. Nevertheless, the First Circuit rejected the Board's formulation of the *Wright Line* test, holding that, after the General Counsel's presentation of a prima facie case of unlawful motive, the Board could shift to the employer only the burden of production, not the burden of persuasion, regarding the claim that the discharge would have occurred irrespective of the unlawful motive.

2. The First Circuit, in *Transportation Management*, also denied enforcement, per curiam, reiterating its position in *Wright Line* — i.e., the NLRB lacked statutory authority to require the company to overcome the

General Counsel's prima facie case by establishing that Santillo would have been discharged even absent his union activities. NLRB v. Transportation Management Corp., 674 F.2d 130 (1st Cir. 1982). Breyer, J., wrote a thoughtful concurrence. Id. at 132.

NLRB v. Transportation Management Corp.
103 S. Ct. 2469 (1983)

WHITE, J. . . . . [In response to] a complaint alleging that an employee was discharged because of his union activities, the employer may assert legitimate motives for his decision. In *Wright Line*, 251 N.L.R.B. 1083 (1980), *enforced*, 662 F.2d 899 (CA1 1981), *cert. denied*, 455 U.S. 989 (1982), the [NLRB] reformulated the allocation of the burden of proof in such cases. It determined that the General Counsel carried the burden of persuading the Board that an anti-union animus contributed to the employer's decision to discharge an employee, a burden that does not shift, but that the employer, even if it failed to meet or neutralize the General Counsel's showing, could avoid the finding that it violated the statute by demonstrating by a preponderance of the evidence that the worker would have been fired even if he had not been involved with the Union. The question presented . . . is whether the burden placed on the employer in *Wright Line* is consistent with §§8(a)(1) and 8(a)(3), as well as with §10(c) of the NLRA, which provides that the Board must prove an unlawful labor practice by a "preponderance of the evidence."

. . . [The ALJ] determined by a preponderance of the evidence that Patterson [who supervised Santillo and other drivers] clearly had an anti-union animus and that Santillo's discharge was motivated by a desire to discourage union activities. [The Court here summarized the ALJ's findings.] While acknowledging that Santillo had engaged in some unsatisfactory conduct, the ALJ was not persuaded that Santillo would have been fired had it not been for his union activities.

The Board affirmed, adopting with some clarification the ALJ's findings and conclusions and expressly applying its *Wright Line* decision. It stated that respondent had failed to carry its burden of persuading the Board that the discharge would have taken place had Santillo not engaged in activity protected by the Act. The First Circuit . . . , relying on its previous decision rejecting the Board's *Wright Line* test, . . . refused to enforce the Board's order and remanded for consideration of whether the General Counsel had proved by a preponderance of the evidence that Santillo would not have been fired had it not been for his union activities. 674 F.2d 130. . . . We now reverse. . . .

Under [§§7, 8(a)(1), and 8(a)(3)] it is undisputed that if the employer fires an employee for having engaged in union activities and has no other basis for the discharge, or if the reasons that he proffers are pretextual, the employer commits an unfair labor practice. He does not violate the NLRA, however, if any anti-union animus that he might have entertained did not contribute at all to an otherwise lawful discharge for good cause. Soon after the passage of the Act, the Board held that it was an unfair labor practice for an employer to discharge a worker where anti-union animus actually contributed to the discharge decision. Consumers Research, Inc., 2 N.L.R.B. 57, 73 (1936); Louisville Refining Co., 4 N.L.R.B. 844, 861 (1938), *enforced*, 102 F.2d 678 (CA6), *cert. denied*, 308 U.S. 568 (1939). . . . In *Consumers Research*, the Board rejected the position that "antecedent to a finding of violation of the Act, it must be found that the sole motive for discharge was the employee's union activity." It explained that "[s]uch an interpretation is repugnant to the purpose and meaning of the Act, and . . . may not be made." Ibid. In [NLRB] Third Annual Report 70 (1938), the Board stated, "Where the employer has discharged an employee for two or more reasons, and one of them is union affiliation or activity, the Board has found a violation [of §8(a)(3)]." . . . This construction of the Act — that to establish an unfair labor practice the General Counsel need show by a preponderance of the evidence only that a discharge is in any way motivated by a desire to frustrate union activity — was plainly rational and acceptable. The Board has adhered to that construction of the Act since that time.

At the same time, there were decisions indicating that the presence of an anti-union motivation in a discharge case was not the end of the matter. An employer could escape the consequences of a violation by proving that without regard to the impermissible motivation, the employer would have taken the same action for wholly permissible reasons. . . . [4]

The Courts of Appeals were not entirely satisfied with the Board's approach to dual-motive cases. The Board's *Wright Line* decision in 1980 was an attempt to restate its analysis in a way more acceptable to the Courts of Appeals. The Board held that the General Counsel of course had the burden of proving that the employee's conduct protected by §7 was a substantial or a

---

[4] The Board argues that its approach to mixed-motive cases was known to Congress and ratified by the passage of the [LMRA] (1947), which was reenacted in §§8(a)(1) and 8(a)(3) almost without material change. We need not pass on this submission, since we find nothing in the legislative history of the LMRA that calls into question the decisions of the Board relevant to the issue before us now. The issue after, as well as before, the passage of the LMRA is whether the Board's construction of §8(a) is sufficiently rational to be acceptable in the courts. We do note that nowhere in the legislative history is reference made to any of the mixed-motive cases decided by the Board or by the Courts. . . .

motivating factor in the discharge.[5] Even if this was the case, and the employer failed to rebut it, the employer could avoid being held in violation of §§8(a)(1) and 8(a)(3) by proving by a preponderance of the evidence that the discharge rested on the employee's unprotected conduct as well and that the employee would have lost his job in any event. It thus became clear, if it was not clear before, that proof that the discharge would have occurred in any event and for valid reasons amounted to an affirmative defense on which the employer carried the burden of proof by a preponderance of the evidence. "The shifting burden merely requires the employer to make out what is actually an affirmative defense. . . . " *Wright Line*, supra, at 1088, n. 11; see also id., at 1084, n. 5.

The . . . First Circuit refused enforcement of the *Wright Line* decision because in its view it was error to place the burden on the employer to prove that the discharge would have occurred had the forbidden motive not been present. The General Counsel, the Court of Appeals held, had the burden of showing not only that a forbidden motivation contributed to the discharge but also that the discharge would not have taken place independently of the protected conduct of the employee. The Court of Appeals was quite correct, and the Board does not disagree, that throughout the proceedings, the General Counsel carries the burden of proving the elements of an unfair labor practice. Section 10(c) expressly directs that violations may be adjudicated only "upon the preponderance of the testimony" taken by the Board. The Board's rules also state "the Board's attorney has the burden of pro[ving] violations of Section 8." 29 CFR §101.10(b). We are quite sure, however, that the Court of Appeals erred in holding that §10(c) forbids placing the burden on the employer to prove that absent the improper motivation he would have acted in the same manner for wholly legitimate reasons.

As we understand the Board's decisions, they have consistently held that the unfair labor practice consists of a discharge or other adverse action that is based in whole or in part on anti-union animus — or as the Board now puts it, that the employee's protected conduct was a substantial or motivating factor

---

[5] The Board has not purported to shift the burden of persuasion on the question of whether the employer fired Santillo at least in part because he engaged in protected activities. The General Counsel satisfied his burden in this respect and no one disputes it. Thus, Texas Department of Community Affairs v. Burdine, 450 U.S. 248 (1981), is inapposite. In that case, which involved a claim of racial discrimination in violation of Title VII of the Civil Rights Acts of 1964, the question was who had "[t]he ultimate burden of persuading the trier of fact that the defendant intentionally discriminated against the plaintiff. . . . " 450 U.S. 253. The Court discussed only the situation in which the issue is whether either illegal or legal motives, but not both, were the "true" motives behind the decision. It thus addressed the pretext case.

in the adverse action. The General Counsel has the burden of proving these elements under §10(c). But the Board's construction of the statute permits an employer to avoid being adjudicated a violator by showing what his actions would have been regardless of his forbidden motivation. It extends to the employer what the Board considers to be an affirmative defense but does not change or add to the elements of the unfair labor practice that the General Counsel has the burden of proving under §10(c).[6] We assume that the Board could reasonably have construed the Act in the manner insisted on by the Court of Appeals. We also assume that the Board might have considered a showing by the employer that the adverse action would have occurred in any event as not obviating a violation adjudication but as going only to the permissible remedy, in which event the burden of proof could surely have been put on the employer. The Board has instead chosen to recognize, as it insists it has done for many years, what it designates as an affirmative defense that the employer has the burden of sustaining. We are unprepared to hold that this is an impermissible construction of the Act. "[T]he Board's construction here, while it may not be required by the Act, is at least permissible under it . . . ", and in these circumstances its position is entitled to deference. NLRB v. Weingarten, Inc., 420 U.S. 251, 266-267 (1975); NLRB v. Erie Resistor Corp., 373 U.S. 221, 236 (1963).

[6] The language of the [NLRA] requiring that the Board act on a preponderance of the testimony taken was added by the [LMRA] in 1947. A closely related provision directed that no order of the Board reinstate or compensate any employee who was fired for cause. Section 10(c) places the burden on the General Counsel only to prove the unfair labor practice, not to disprove an affirmative defense. Furthermore, it is clear from the legislative history of the [LMRA] that the drafters of §10(c) were not thinking of the mixed motive case. Their discussions reflected the assumption that discharges were either "for cause" or punishment for protected activity. Read fairly, the legislative history does not indicate whether, in mixed motive cases, the employer or the General Counsel has the burden of proof on the issue of what would have happened if the employer had not been influenced by his unlawful motives; on that point the legislative history is silent.

The "for cause" proviso was not meant to apply to cases in which both legitimate and illegitimate causes contributed to the discharge, see infra. The amendment was sparked by a concern over the Board's perceived practice of inferring from the fact that someone was active in a union that he was fired because of anti-union animus even though the worker had been guilty of gross misconduct. The House Report explained the change in the following terms:

> A third change forbids the Board to reinstate an individual unless the weight of the evidence shows that the individual was not suspended or discharged for cause. In the past, the Board, admitting that an employee was guilty of gross misconduct, nevertheless frequently reinstated him, "inferring" that, because he was a member or an official of a union, this, not his misconduct, was *the* reason for his discharge.

H.R. Rep. No. 245, 80th Cong., 1st Sess., at 42 (April 11, 1947) (emphasis added). The proviso was thus a reaction to the Board's readiness to infer anti-union animus from the fact that the discharged person was active in the union, and thus has little to do with the situation in which the Board has soundly concluded that the employer had an anti-union animus and that such feelings played a role in a worker's discharge.

The Board's allocation of the burden of proof is clearly reasonable in this context, for the reason stated in NLRB v. Remington Rand, 94 F.2d 862, 872 (CA2), *cert. denied*, 304 U.S. 576 (1938), a case on which the Board relied when it began taking the position that the burden of persuasion could be shifted. E.g., Eagle-Picher Mining & Smelting [16 N.L.R.B. 727, 801 (1939), *enforced in relevant part*, 119 F.2d 903 (8th Cir. 1941)]. The employer is a wrongdoer; he has acted out of a motive that is declared illegitimate by the statute. It is fair that he bear the risk that the influence of legal and illegal motives cannot be separated, because he knowingly created the risk and because the risk was created not by innocent activity but by his own wrongdoing.

In Mount Healthy City Board of Education v. Doyle, 429 U.S. 274 (1977), we found it prudent, albeit in a case implicating the Constitution, to set up an allocation of the burden of proof which the Board heavily relied on and borrowed from in its *Wright Line* decision. . . . The analogy to *Mount Healthy* drawn by the Board was a fair one.[7]

For these reasons, we conclude that the Court of Appeals erred in refusing to enforce the Board's orders, which rested on the Board's *Wright Line* decision.

. . . At least two of the transgressions that purportedly would have in any event prompted Santillo's discharge were commonplace, and yet no

---

[7] Respondents also argue that placement of the burden of persuasion on the employer contravenes §10(b) of the Act and §7(d) of the Administrative Procedure Act. Section 10(b) provides that the Federal Rules of Evidence apply to board proceedings insofar as practicable. Respondent contends that Federal Rule of Evidence 301 requires that the burden of persuasion rest on the General Counsel. Rule 301 provides:

> In all civil actions and proceedings not otherwise provided for by Act of Congress or by these rules, a presumption imposes on the party against whom it is directed the burden of going forward with evidence to rebut or meet the presumption, but does not shift to such party the burden of proof in the sense of the risk of nonpersuasion, which remains throughout the trial upon the party on whom it was originally cast.

The Rule merely defines the term "presumption." It in no way restricts the authority of a court or an agency to change the customary burdens of persuasion in a manner that otherwise would be permissible. Indeed, were respondent correct, we could not have assigned to the defendant the burden of persuasion on one issue in Mount Healthy Board of Education v. Doyle, 429 U.S. 274 (1977).

Section 7(d) of the Administrative Procedure Act provides that the proponent of an order has the burden of proof. Since the General Counsel is the proponent of the order, asserts respondent, the General Counsel must bear the burden of proof. Section 7(d), however, determines only the burden of going forward, not the burden of persuasion. Environmental Defense Fund, Inc. v. Environmental Protection Agency, 548 F.2d 998, 1004, 1013-1015 (CADC 1976), *cert denied sub nom.*, Velsicol Chemical Corp. v. Environmental Protection Agency, 431 U.S. 925 (1977).

transgressor had ever before received any kind of discipline. Moreover, the employer departed from its usual practice in dealing with rules infractions; indeed, not only did the employer not warn Santillo that his actions would result in being subjected to discipline, it never even expressed its disapproval of his conduct. In addition, Patterson, the person who made the initial decision to discharge Santillo, was obviously upset with Santillo for engaging in such protected activity. It is thus clear that the Board's finding that Santillo would not have been fired even if the employer had not had an anti-union animus was "supported by substantial evidence on the record considered as a whole."

Accordingly, the judgment is Reversed.

NOTES

1. Under §10(c) should the General Counsel win if, after both sides have rested, the evidence on whether the discharge would have occurred, absent the protected activity, is in "equipoise"?

2. Will "equipoise" cases occur often? Is *Transportation Management* such a case? Assume that it is unlikely that the evidence in "dual motivation" cases will often be deemed in "equipoise" by the NLRB. Does that assumption support or undercut the Board's *Wright Line* test?

3. During an organizational campaign, an employer informs you of the following: Eager, a leading supporter of the union, has gotten quite sloppy in his work, and, despite warnings, his rate of materials spoilage has stayed excessively high. The employer asks whether he could fire Eager without serious risk of an unfair labor practice order that would be judicially enforceable. What additional information would you ask for and why?

The above situation suggests the following questions:

What is the probable effect of *Transportation Management* on settlement of charges against an employer? On appellate review of Board determinations that an employer had failed to carry his *Wright Line* burden of persuasion? Suppose, for example, a reviewing court concludes that the employer had carried that burden but that the Board erroneously applied *Wright Line*. Would the court necessarily reverse the Board's determination? See Humes Elec., Inc. v. NLRB, 715 F.2d 468, 472-473 (9th Cir. 1983) (Sneed, J., concurring); Behring International, Inc. v. NLRB, 714 F.2d 291, 292 (3d Cir. 1983) (reconsideration, in light of *Transportation Management*, led to upholding of Board's decision that certain layoffs violated §8(a)(3); court declared that allocation of ultimate burden could be determinative "in a case as close as this one"), *cert. denied*, 104 S. Ct. 979 (1984).

4. In Texas Dept. of Community Affairs v. Burdine, 450 U.S. 248 (1981), which is characterized as "inapposite" in *Transportation Management* (footnote 5), the Court defined the probative burdens in cases alleging disparate treatment violative of Title VII of the Civil Rights Act of 1964, stating (pp. 252-253):

> First, the plaintiff has the burden of proving by the preponderance of the evidence a prima facie case of discrimination. Second, if the plaintiff succeeds in proving the prima facie case, the burden shifts to the defendant "to articulate some legitimate, nondiscriminatory reason for the employee's rejection." [McDonnell Douglas Corp. v. Green, 411 U.S. 792, 802 (1973).] Third, should the defendant carry this burden, the plaintiff must then have an opportunity to prove by a preponderance of the evidence that the legitimate reasons offered by the defendant were not its true reasons, but were a pretext for discrimination. . . . The ultimate burden of persuading the trier of fact that the defendant intentionally discriminated against the plaintiff remains at all time with the plaintiff. . . . See generally 9 Wigmore, Evidence §2489 (3d ed. 1940) (the burden of persuasion "never shifts").

Is the formulation in *Burdine* consistent with that in *Mount Healthy* and *Transportation Management?* If not, is there any justification in policy for different approaches under Title VII and the NLRA?

5. The Board in *Wright Line* plainly sought to diminish the importance, under §8(a)(3), of any distinction between "pretext" and "dual motive" cases. Do the *Wright Line* test and *Transportation Management* eliminate that distinction altogether? For an example of the complications resulting from efforts by a court of appeals to apply that distinction, see NLRB v. Charles Batchelder Co., 646 F.2d 33 (2d Cir. 1981).

6. After security guards reported that two strikers had thrown rocks in the direction of the guards and company offices, the employer fired the strikers. The NLRB ordered reinstatement and backpay, finding that the evidence showed only that the employees had thrown unidentified objects, and not what, how hard, or at whom. The court held that "substantial evidence does not support the conclusion that the two employees did not engage in misconduct serious enough to justify their discharge." The court also ruled more generally that once an employer shows his good faith belief that employees engaged in misconduct justifying their discharge, the General Counsel has the burden of showing that no misconduct had occurred or that it did not justify the discharge. See Schreiber Mfg., Inc. v. NLRB, 725 F.2d 413 (6th Cir. 1984). Is the court's approach consistent with *Transportation Management?*

Note: Remedial Problems

1.   THE SCOPE OF NLRB AUTHORITY

In Phelps Dodge Corp. v. NLRB, 313 U.S. 177 (1941), the Court, recognizing the NLRB's broad remedial authority under §10(c), upheld a §8(a)(3) order calling for the hiring of applicants for employment who had been rejected because of their union affiliations, even though the applicants in the interim had obtained substantially equivalent employment elsewhere. For the interpretive questions involved, see §2(3), which refers to an "employee" as a person "who has not obtained . . . other regular and substantially equivalent employment," and §10(c), which speaks of "reinstatement of employees." The Court reasoned that the hiring order, although not necessary to protect the rejected applicants against monetary loss, was warranted because the Act was designed to effectuate the public policy in favor of self-organization and was not confined to remedying private losses. The Court also held that the computation of lost pay should reflect a deduction not only of the actual earnings of the discriminatee, but also of the amounts he had failed to earn without excuse. Despite the Court's affirmation of the Board's remedial discretion, it rejected the Board's contention that such a requirement for mitigating damages would be administratively burdensome.

2.   THE BACK PAY REMEDY

The *Phelps Dodge* decision (313 U.S. at 194) defined the remedial goal in §8(a)(3) cases as "a restoration of the situation, as nearly as possible, to that which would have obtained but for the illegal discrimination." Thus, an employee discriminatorily denied benefits given to others will receive those benefits at the NLRB's direction. If an employee is discriminatorily discharged, the usual remedy is an order of reinstatement and an award of back pay from the date of the discharge to the date of an offer of reinstatement, the event which ordinarily tolls an employer's financial liability. When an employer appeals from a Board reinstatement order, the back pay period is extended to the time of court of appeals' enforcement of the Board's unfair labor practice order.

The amount of back pay, which is customarily determined at the "compliance stage" (a separate NLRB proceeding following issuance of the order on the unfair labor practice charge, or, if the Board's order is appealed, following court enforcement), has been governed by changing rules. Prior to 1950, the Board would calculate the difference between what a victim of discrimination would have earned and his actual earnings from other employment during the entire period from the discharge to an offer of reinstatement. In F.W. Woolworth Co., 90 N.L.R.B. 289 (1950), the Board ruled that computation of loss of earnings should be on a quarterly basis so that excess earnings in one quarter would not reduce back pay liability accrued in a previous quarter; the new formula was designed to destroy any incentive for delaying reinstatement in order to reduce previously accrued back pay liability. In NLRB v. Seven-Up Bottling Co., 344 U.S. 344 (1953), the Supreme Court approved the *Woolworth* formula but indicated that it might properly be modified when a seasonal industry is involved. The quarterly method of computation is deemed appropriate even though its application results in an award of back pay to an employee whose total interim earnings exceed what he would have earned in the job from which he was discharged. See Nelson Metal Fabricating, 259 N.L.R.B. 1023 (1982), *enforced*, 111 L.R.R.M. 2280 (3d Cir. 1982).

In 1962, the NLRB began to add interest to back pay awards; this practice has been upheld as "remedial," rather than "punitive." See Philip Carey Mfg. Co. v. NLRB, 331 F.2d 720, 729-731 (6th Cir. 1964), *cert. denied*, 379 U.S. 888 (1964). In Florida Steel Corp., 231 N.L.R.B. 651 (1977), the Board announced its adoption of the interest rate formula used by the Internal Revenue Service, which involves annual adjustments that reflect changes in money market rates; during 1982, the rate was 20 percent.

Despite its "remedial" rather than "punitive" approach, the Supreme Court has upheld the Board's practice of not reducing back pay awards by unemployment compensation payments received by discriminatees. NLRB v. Gullet Gin Co., 340 U.S. 361 (1951). What justification is there for such a result, which appears to give the employee a financial windfall? By contrast, is the Board's *Wright Line* test designed to avoid a windfall for employees who violate plant rules?

Once the General Counsel has established the gross amount of back pay lost by a claimant, the employer bears the burden of persuasion with respect to the claimant's failure to mitigate his losses. See Southern Household Prod. Co., 203 N.L.R.B. 881 (1973). In accordance with the usual mitigation principle, an employee who has made reasonable efforts to find substantially equivalent employment will not be found to have willfully incurred a loss of earnings. Nevertheless, while discriminatees generally may hold out for jobs that are "substantially equivalent," where reasonable efforts have not produced such jobs for long periods, courts have occasionally ruled that an employee's sights should have been lowered and have modified back pay orders accordingly. See, e.g., NLRB v. Madison Courier, Inc., 505 F.2d 391 (D.C. Cir. 1974). For a discussion of these problems, as well as a comprehensive treatment of the back pay remedy in general, see Fuchs, Kelleher & Pye, Back Pay Revisited, 15 B.C. L. Rev. 227 (1973).

3.   Judicial Review of the Back Pay Remedy

Sure-Tan, Inc. v. NLRB, 104 S. Ct. 2803 (1984), involved the Board's remedial authority, the reviewing authority of the courts, and the interplay of immigration policy and the NLRA. The Court sustained, as compatible with both immigration policy and the NLRA, the NLRB's position that illegal aliens could be "employees" entitled to NLRA protection. Consequently, the employer's instigating the deportation of such aliens, in reprisal for their support of a union (which had won a Board election), constituted an unlawful "constructive discharge." The Court reasoned this way: Hiring an illegal alien is not a crime. The Board's position, if known by employers, would reduce their incentives for such hiring and, presumably, aliens' incentives for illegal entry, and would also help avoid creating an underclass of alien workers whose substandard benefits undercut unions and collective bargaining.

Nonetheless, the Court (by Justice O'Connor) vacated modifications which the Board had made in its original order at the suggestion of the Seventh Circuit, but had supported before the Supreme Court. These modifications called for keeping open for four years the employer's reinstatement offers, writing them in Spanish, and having their deliveries verified by a receipt; the Seventh Circuit had also called for an award of six months' back pay. (The Board had rejected, as "unnecessarily speculative," the ALJ's recommendation of four weeks' back pay as a minimum.) The Court's reasoning included these considerations: The Seventh Circuit, in expanding the Board's remedy, had exceeded its own reviewing authority and had compelled the Board to exceed its remedial authority. A "proposed remedy must be tailored to the unfair labor practice it is intended to redress." But the instant back pay remedy was incompatible with "the [NLRA's] general reparative policies." It was "pure speculation," unsupported by any record evidence of the circumstances, including the job prospects of the deported employees before their apprehension. The Board's compliance proceeding, and not courts of appeals, should determine the amount of back pay. Similarly, the other modifications of the Board's order by the Seventh Circuit, although unobjectionable in themselves, exceeded the limits of judicial review.

Brennan, J., joined by Marshall, Blackmun, and Stevens, JJ., agreed that the illegal aliens were protected "employees" but dissented from the Court's position on the remedy. He urged the following grounds: The Court's new standard — "sufficiently tailored" — abandoned its former requirement that an opponent of a back pay order show that the order seeks "ends other than those which can fairly be said to effectuate the policies of the Act." The

Court created a "disturbing anomaly" by first holding that the NLRA protects illegal aliens and then denying them any effective remedy for a violation of their rights.

Powell, J., joined by Rehnquist, J., dissented from the holding that the NLRA protected illegal aliens, urging that it was unlikely that Congress intended so to protect persons wanted for violation of our criminal laws. He agreed, however, with the Court's vacating of the modifications in the Board's original remedy, observing that the Court thereby reduced incentives for illegal entry.

Cf. Pyler v. Doe, 457 U.S. 202 (1982), invalidating (5-4), as a denial of equal protection, a Texas statute that withheld from local school districts state funds for the education of children who were illegal aliens and authorized local districts not to enroll such children.

In *Sure-Tan*, what factors would you expect to have shaped the views of the plurality? the dissenters? Does Pyler v. Doe suggest considerations that might have been influential? With *Sure-Tan*, cf. NLRB v. Bridge & Iron Wkrs. Local 480, 104 S. Ct. 2081 (1984) (error for a court of appeals to restrict back pay to charging parties injured by union's discrimination against nonmembers and to eliminate back pay for "others similarly situated" because of the Board's delays in specifying amounts due them; employees "may not be punished for the Board's nonfeasance").

4.   SUGGESTIONS FOR MORE EFFECTIVE REMEDIES

Back pay orders, despite their potentially substantial amounts,[d] have sometimes failed to deter continuing discrimination by the same employer. Furthermore, Board remedies for violations of §8(a)(1) may be even less effective restraints on recidivism, for they frequently do not include monetary payments. These considerations have led to suggestions for more effective Board remedies (see, e.g., Note, The Need for Creative Orders Under Section 10(c) of the National Labor Relations Act, 112 U. Pa. L. Rev. 69 (1963)), including greater use of the Board's discretionary power to petition a federal district court for interim injunctive relief under §10(j) of the Act. See Samoff, NLRB Priority and Injunctions for Discriminatory Discharges, 31 Lab. L.J. 54 (1980); Siegel, Section 10(j) of the National Labor Relations Act: Suggested Reforms for an Expanded Use, 13 B.C. Ind. & Com. L. Rev. 457 (1972). The Getman voting study, supra p. 115, suggested these alterna-

---

[d]In fiscal 1980, the NLRB awarded an all-time high of $32,135,914 in back pay to 15,566 discriminatees; the back pay remedy was used in nearly 4,000 cases closed during the year. In addition, 10,033 employees were offered reinstatement in connection with unfair labor practice cases closed in 1980; 89 percent of the offers were accepted. See 45 N.L.R.B. Ann. Report 13-14; 248-249 (1980). Cf. Stephens & Chaney, A Study of the Reinstatement Remedy Under the National Labor Relations Act, 25 Lab. L.J. 31 (1974).

tives to the issuance of *Gissel* bargaining orders (pp. 155-156): (1) The Board could be required to institute immediate injunctive proceedings in order to obtain reinstatement of any employee discharged during an organizational campaign, with the employer assigned the burden of proving the absence of a discriminatory motive for the discharge; and (2) back pay awards for employees found to have been discriminatorily discharged during such campaigns might be three times the amount of actual lost earnings. Similar proposals were included in the Labor Reform Act of 1978, which the 95th Congress failed to adopt. See S. Rep. No. 95-628, 95th Cong., 2d Sess. (1978); H. Rep. No. 8410, 95th Cong., 1st Sess. (1977). What impact, if any, are such remedies likely to have on plant operations or an employer's treatment of a campaigning union?

The Board's efforts to devise so-called extraordinary remedies for discriminatory discharges coupled with other "massive violations" are illustrated by United Dairy Farmers Coop. Assn., 242 N.L.R.B. 1025 (1979), *remanded*, 633 F.2d 1054 (3d Cir. 1980); NLRB v. J.P. Stevens & Co., 464 F.2d 1326 (2d Cir. 1972), *cert. denied*, 410 U.S. 926 (1973); J.P. Stevens & Co. v. NLRB, 406 F.2d 1017 (4th Cir. 1968). See generally, D. McDowell & K. Huhn, NLRB Remedies for Unfair Labor Practices (1976); Note, J.P. Stevens: Searching for a Remedy to Fit the Wrong, 55 N.C. L. Rev. 696 (1977). For a useful discussion of the standards for interim injunctive relief under §§10(1) and 10(j), respectively, see Maram v. Universidad Interamericana De Puerto Rico, Inc., 722 F.2d 953 (1st Cir. 1983).

Radio Officers' Union v. NLRB
347 U.S. 17 (1954)

REED, J. The necessity for resolution of conflicting interpretations by Courts of Appeals of §8(a)(3) of the [NLRA] . . . impelled us to grant certiorari in these three cases. . . .

Teamsters. Upon the basis of a charge filed by Frank Boston, a truck driver employed by Byers Transportation Company and a member of [Teamsters] Local Union No. 41, the General Counsel of the [NLRB] issued a complaint against the union alleging violation of §§8(b)(1)(A) and 8(b)(2) . . . by causing the company to discriminate against Boston by reducing his seniority standing because of Boston's delinquency in paying his union dues. . . .

The Board found that the union, as exclusive bargaining representative of the teamsters in the company's employ, had in 1949 negotiated a collective-bargaining agreement with the company which governed working conditions on all over-the-road operations of the company. This agreement established a seniority system under which the union was to furnish periodically to the company a seniority list and provided that "any controversy over the seniority standing of any employee on this list shall be referred to the Union for settlement." Union security provisions of the agreement were not effective due to lack of authorization then required by §8(a)(3) of the Act. The seniority list therefore included both union members and nonmembers. Each new employee of the company, after a thirty-day trial period, was placed at the bottom of this list, and such employee would gradually advance in position as senior members were either removed from the list or reduced in their position on it. Position upon the seniority list governed the order of truck-driving assignments, the quality of such assignments, and the order of layoff.

The bylaws of [Local 41] provided that "any member, under contract, one month in arrears for dues shall forfeit all seniority rights. . . . " A member's dues were payable on the first day of each month, and he was deemed "in arrears" for any month's dues on the second day of the following month. Boston did not pay his dues for June 1950 until July 5, 1950. When the union transmitted a new seniority list to the company on the following July 15, Boston, who had previously been eighteenth on the list, was reduced to fifty-fourth, the bottom position on the list. As a result of such reduction Boston was denied driving assignments he would otherwise have obtained and for which he would have received compensation.

Upon these facts . . . the Board found that the union had violated §§8(b)(1)(A) and 8(b)(2). . . . As to the former, the Board held that the union's reduction of Boston's seniority restrained and coerced him in the exercise of his right to refrain from assisting a labor organization guaranteed by §7. The Board held that, "absent a valid contractual union-security provision, Boston had the absolute protected right under the Act to determine how he would handle his union affairs without risking any impairment of his employment rights and that the Union had no right at any time whether Boston was a member or not a member to make his employment status to any degree conditional upon the payment of dues. . . . " As to the latter, the Board concluded that the union had caused the company to discriminate against Boston and adopted the Trial Examiner's finding that "the normal effect of the discrimination against Boston was to encourage nonmembers to join the Union, as well as members to retain their good standing in the Union, a potent organization whose assistance is to be sought and whose opposition is to be avoided. The Employer's conduct tended to encourage membership in the Union. Its discrimination against Boston had the further effect of enforcing rules prescribed by the Union, thereby strengthening the Union in its control over its members and its dealings with their employers and was thus calculated to encourage all members to retain their membership and good standing either through fear of the consequences of losing membership or seniority privileges or through hope of advantage in staying in. . . ."

The Board entered an order requiring the union to cease and desist from the unfair labor practices found and from related conduct; to notify Boston and the company that the union withdraws its request for the reduction of Boston's seniority and that it requests the company to offer to restore Boston to his former status; to make Boston whole for any losses of pay resulting from the discrimination; and to post appropriate notices of compliance.

The [Eighth Circuit] denied the Board's petition to enforce its order. The court held that "the evidence here abundantly supports the finding of the Board that the respondent caused or attempted to cause the employer to discriminate against Boston in regard to 'tenure . . . or condition of employment,' " but "discrimination alone is not sufficient" and "we can find no substantial evidence to support the conclusion that the discrimination . . . did or would encourage or discourage membership in any labor organization." This conclusion was reached because "the testimony of Boston . . . shows clearly that this act neither encouraged nor discouraged his adhesion to membership in the respondent union" and because, assuming the effect of the discrimination on other employees was relevant, the court found no evidence to support a conclusion that such employees were so encouraged or discouraged. We granted the Board's petition for certiorari.

Radio Officers. Upon the basis of a charge filed by William Christian Fowler, a member of The Radio Officers' Union of the Commercial Telegraphers Union, AFL, the General Counsel . . . issued a complaint against the union alleging violation of §§8(b)(1)(A) and 8(b)(2) . . . by causing the A. H. Bull Steamship Company to discriminatorily refuse on two occasions to employ Fowler. No complaint was issued against the company because Fowler filed no charge against it. . . .

The Board found that at the time the transactions giving rise to this case occurred the union had a collective bargaining contract with a number of steamship concerns including the Bull Steamship Company covering the employment of radio officers on ships of the contracting companies. Pertinent provisions in this contract are:

> Section 1. The Company agrees when vacancies occur necessitating the employment of Radio Officers, to select such Radio Officers who are members of the Union in good standing, when available, on vessels covered by this Agreement, provided such members are in the opinion of the Company qualified to fill such vacancies.
> Section 6. The Company shall have the right of free selection of all its

Radio Officers and when members of the Union are transferred, promoted, or hired the Company agrees to take appropriate measures to assure that such members are in good standing, and the Union agrees to grant all members of the Union in good standing the necessary "clearance" for the position to which the Radio Officer has been assigned. If a member is not in good standing, the Union will so notify the Company in writing.

The union's contention that this contract provided for a hiring hall under which complete control over selection of radio officers to be hired by any company was given to the union was rejected by the Trial Examiner and by a majority of the Board. Such an agreement would have legalized the actions of the union in this case.[e] But the Board concluded, primarily from the last sentence of §6 of the contract, that the contract "was clear on its face and did not provide for any hiring hall arrangement" and that it therefore was not improper for the Trial Examiner to exclude evidence that general, although not universal, practice had been for radio officers to be assigned to employers by the union.

The Board also found that: On February 24, 1948, the company telegraphed an offer of a job as radio officer on the company's ship *S. S. Frances* to Fowler, who had often previously been employed by the company; Fowler had notified the company that he would accept the job; the company then informed Kozel, the radio officer on the previous voyage of the ship, that he was being replaced by "a man with senior service in the company"; Fowler reported to the *Frances* without seeking clearance from the union and Kozel reported such action to the union; the union secretary wired Fowler that he had been suspended from membership for "bumping" another member and taking a job without clearance and notified the company that Fowler was not in good standing in the union; the union secretary had no authority to effect such a suspension, the suspension was void and Fowler was in good standing in the union at all times material in this case; express requests to the union for clearance of Fowler for employment on the *Frances* by the company and by Fowler were subsequently refused, the union secretary stating that he would never again clear Fowler for a position with that company although Fowler would be cleared for jobs with other employers; unable to obtain clearance for Fowler, the company gave the job to another man supplied by the union, and Fowler returned to his home in Florida; on April 22, 1948, Fowler returned to New York and again advised the company that he was available for work before reporting to the union; the union secretary told Fowler he was being

---

[e] [The Court indicated that if the agreement had provided for complete union control over hiring of radio officers, the legality of that provision would have been saved by the grandfather clause in §102 of the LMRA. — EDS.]

made "a company stiff" and adhered to his position that he would not clear Fowler for work with that company; clearance sought by the company for Fowler for a job on the S. S. *Evelyn* was subsequently refused, and another man was dispatched to the job by the union. . . .

Gaynor. Upon the basis of charges filed by Sheldon Loner, a nonunion employee of Gaynor News Company, the General Counsel . . . issued a complaint against the company alleging inter alia violation of §§8(a)(1), (2) and (3) of the Act by granting retroactive wage increases and vacation payments to employees who were members of the Newspaper and Mail Deliverers' Union . . . and refusing such benefits to other employees because they were not union members. . . .

The Board found that in 1946 the company . . . entered into a collective-bargaining agreement respecting delivery-department employees with the union. This agreement provided for specified wages and paid vacations, and also provided for a closed shop, i.e., restricting employment by the company to members of the union. The agreement, however, permitted the employment by the company of nonunion employees pending such time as the union could supply union employees. This provision was necessary because the union was closed, ordinarily admitting to membership only first-born legitimate sons of members. The company at all pertinent times had nonunion as well as union employees in its delivery department. This original agreement was subsequently extended to 1948 and a supplementary agreement was executed by the parties in 1947 providing that in the event the parties negotiated a new contract, the wage rates set therein would be retroactive for three months. In October 1948 the company and the union entered into such a new contract which included an invalid union-security clause[32] and provided for increased wage and vacation benefits. In this agreement the company expressly recognized the union as exclusive bargaining agent of all employees in the delivery department. In compliance with the 1947 supplementary agreement, the company in November 1948 made lump-sum payments to its union employees of the differential between the old and new wage rates for the three months' retroactive period. Further payments were subsequently made to union members to compensate for differences in vacation benefits under the two contracts even though the supplementary agreement made no reference to such benefits. The company refused to make similar payments to any of its nonunion employees on the grounds that it was not contractually bound to do so, and, in its business judgment, did not choose to do so.

---

[32] This clause requiring all new employees to become union members within thirty days was not authorized as then required by §8(a)(3).

The Board concluded that, since nothing in the supplementary agreement prohibited equal payment to nonunion employees, "the contract affords no defense to the allegation that the Respondent unlawfully engaged in disparate treatment of employees on the basis of union membership or lack of it . . . ," and held that the company had violated the Act as alleged. The company's arguments that its actions had not violated §8(a)(3) because "the record is barren of any evidence that the discriminatory treatment of nonunion employees encouraged them to join the union" or had such purpose, and that there could be no such evidence because all the nonunion employees had previously sought membership in the union and been denied because of the union's closed policy, were rejected. The Board adopted the Trial Examiner's finding that "it is obvious that the discrimination with respect to retroactive wages and vacation benefits had the natural and probable effect not only of encouraging nonunion employees to join the Union, but also of encouraging union employees to retain their union membership." We assume this concedes that the employer acted from self-interest and not to encourage unionism. An order was entered requiring the company to cease and desist from the unfair labor practices found and from related conduct; to make whole Loner and all other nonunion employees similarly situated for any loss of pay they have suffered by reason of the company's discrimination against them; and to post appropriate notices of compliance.

The Court of Appeals [Second Circuit] . . . [enforced] all parts of the order pertinent here. On the issue of the legality of the discrimination, the court distinguished Labor Board v. Reliable Newspaper Delivery, Inc., 187 F.2d 547, involving actions closely paralleling the company's here by another company dealing with the same union, stating, "there discrimination resulted from what the court considered the entirely legal action of the minority union in asking special benefits for its members only. The union made no pretense of representing the majority of employees or of being the exclusive bargaining agent in the plant. The other nonunion employees, reasoned the Court, were quite able to elect their own representative and ask for similar benefits. Not so here. The union here represented the majority of employees and was the exclusive bargaining agent for the plant. Accordingly, it could not betray the trust of nonunion members, by bargaining for special benefits to union-members only, thus leaving the nonunion members with no means of equalizing the situation." 197 F.2d, at 722. The court continued, in answer to the company's contention that its action "had neither the purpose nor the effect required by §8(a)(3)": "discriminatory conduct, such as that practiced here, is inherently conducive to increased union membership. In this respect, there can be little doubt that it 'encourages' union membership, by increasing the number of workers who would like to join and/or their quantum of desire. It may well be that the union, for reasons of its own, does not want new members at the time of the employer's violations and will reject all applicants. But the fact remains that these rejected applicants have been, and will continue to be, 'encouraged,' by the discriminatory benefits, in their desire for membership. This backlog of desire may well, as the Board argues, result in action by nonmembers to 'seek to break down membership barriers by any one of a number of steps, ranging from bribery to legal action.' A union's internal politics are by no means static; changes in union entrance rules may come at any time. If and when the barriers are let down, among the new and now successful applicants will almost surely be large groups of workers previously 'encouraged' by the employer's illegal discrimination. We do not believe that, if the union-encouraging effect of discriminatory treatment is not felt immediately, the employer must be allowed to escape altogether. If there is a reasonable likelihood that the effects may be felt years later, then a reasonable interpretation of the Act demands that the employer be deemed a violator." 197 F.2d, at 722-723. We granted the company's petition for certiorari.

I.   Meaning of "Membership"

. . . These are the first cases to reach us involving application of this section or its predecessor to the problem of encouragement of union membership by employers. We have on many occasions considered aspects of the application of these sections to actions by employers aimed at discouragement of union membership. . . .

In past cases we have been called upon to clarify the terms "discrimination" and "membership in any labor organization." Discrimination is not contested in these cases: involuntary reduction of seniority, refusal to hire for an available job, and disparate wage treatment are clearly discriminatory. But the scope of the phrase "membership in any labor organization" is in issue here. Subject to limitations, we have held that phrase to include discrimination to discourage participation in union activities as well as to discourage adhesion to union membership.

Similar principles govern the interpretation of union membership where encouragement is alleged. The policy of the Act is to insulate employees' jobs from their organizational rights. Thus §§8(a)(3) and 8(b)(2) were designed to allow employees to freely exercise their right to join unions, be good, bad, or indifferent members, or abstain from joining any union without imperiling their livelihood. The only limitation Congress has chosen to impose on this right is specified in the proviso to §8(a)(3). . . .

From the foregoing it is clear that the Eighth Circuit too restrictively interpreted the term "membership" in *Teamsters*. Boston was discriminated against by his employer because he was delinquent in a union obligation. Thus he was denied employment to which he was otherwise entitled, for no reason other than his tardy payment of union dues. The union caused this discrimination by applying a rule apparently aimed at encouraging prompt payment of dues. The union's action was not sanctioned by a valid union security contract, and, in any event, the union did not choose to terminate Boston's membership for his delinquency. Thus the union by requesting such discrimination, and the employer by submitting to such an illegal request, deprived Boston of the right guaranteed by the Act to join in or abstain from union activities without thereby affecting his job. A fortiori the Second Circuit correctly concluded in *Radio Officers* that such encouragement to remain in good standing in a union is proscribed. . . .

II

A.   NECESSITY FOR PROVING EMPLOYER'S MOTIVE

The language of §8(a)(3) is not ambiguous. The unfair labor practice is for an employer to encourage or discourage membership by means of discrimination. Thus this section does not outlaw all encouragement or discouragement of membership in labor organizations; only such as is accomplished by discrimination is prohibited. Nor does this section outlaw discrimination in employment as such; only such discrimination as encourages or discourages membership in a labor organization is proscribed.

The relevance of the motivation of the employer in such discrimination has been consistently recognized under both §8(a)(3) and its predecessor. In the first [NLRA] case to reach the Court . . . , Labor Board v. Jones & Laughlin Steel Corp., 301 U.S. 1, in which we upheld the constitutionality of §8(3), we said with respect to limitations placed upon employers' right to discharge by that section that "the [employer's] true purpose is the subject of investigation with full opportunity to show the facts." Id., at 46. In another case the same day [Associated Press v. Labor Board, 301 U.S. 103, 132] we found the employer's "real motive" to be decisive and stated that "the act permits a discharge for any reason other than union activity or agitation for collective bargaining with employees." . . .

That Congress intended the employer's purpose in discriminating to be controlling is clear. The Senate Report on the Wagner Act said: "Of course nothing in the bill prevents an employer from discharging a man for incompetence; from advancing him for special aptitude; or from demoting him for failure to perform." . . . With this consistent interpretation of that section before it, Congress, as noted above, chose to retain the identical language in its 1947 amendments. No suggestion is found in either the reports or hearings on those amendments that the section had been too narrowly construed. . . .

B. PROOF OF MOTIVE

But it is also clear that specific evidence of intent to encourage or discourage is not an indispensable element of proof of violation of §8(a)(3). This fact was recognized in the House Report on the Wagner Act when it was stated that under §8(3) "agreements more favorable to the majority than to the minority are impossible. . . . " Both the Board and the courts have recognized that proof of certain types of discrimination satisfies the intent requirement. This recognition that specific proof of intent is unnecessary where employer conduct inherently encourages or discourages union membership is but an application of the common-law rule that a man is held to intend the foreseeable consequences of his conduct. . . . Thus an employer's protestation that he did not intend to encourage or discourage must be unavailing where a natural consequence of his action was such encouragement or discouragement. Concluding that encouragement or discouragement will result, it is presumed that he intended such consequence. In such circumstances intent to encourage is sufficiently established. Our decision in Republic Aviation Corp. v. Labor Board, 324 U.S. 793, relied upon by the Board to support its contention that employers' motives are irrelevant under §8(a)(3), applied this principle. That decision dealt primarily with the right of the Board to infer discouragement from facts proven for purposes of proof of violation of §8(3). In holding that discharges and suspensions of employees under company "no solicitation" rules for soliciting union membership, in the circumstances disclosed, violated §8(3), we noted that such employer action was not "motivated by opposition to the particular union or, we deduce, to unionism" and that "there was no union bias or discrimination by the company in enforcing the rule." But we affirmed the Board's holding that the rules involved were invalid when applied to union solicitation since they interfered with the employees' right to organize. Since the rules were no defense and the employers intended to discriminate solely on the ground of such protected union activity, it did not matter that they did not intend to discourage membership since such was a foreseeable result.

In *Gaynor*, the Second Circuit also properly applied this principle. The court there held that disparate wage treatment . . . based solely on union membership status is "inherently conducive to increased union membership." In holding that a natural consequence of discrimination, based solely on union membership or lack thereof, is discouragement or encouragement of membership in such union, the court merely recognized a fact of common experience — that the desire of employees to unionize is directly proportional to the advantages thought to be obtained from such action. No more striking example of discrimination so foreseeably causing employee response as to obviate the need for any other proof of intent is apparent than the payment of different wages to union employees doing a job than to nonunion employees doing the same job. . . .

. . . According to the reasoning of the Second Circuit, however, disparate payments based on contract are illegal only when the union, as bargaining agent for both union and nonunion employees, betrays its trust and obtains special benefits for the union members. That court considered such action unfair because such employees are not in a position to protect their own interests. Thus, it reasoned, if a union bargains only for its own members, it is legal for such union to cause an employer to give, and for such employer to give, special benefits to the members of the union for if nonmembers are aggrieved they are free to bargain for similar benefits for themselves.

We express no opinion as to the legality of disparate payments where the union is not exclusive bargaining agent, since that case is not before us. We do hold that in the circumstances of this case, the union being exclusive bargaining agent for both member and nonmember employees, the employer could not, without violating §8(a)(3), discriminate in wages solely on the basis of such membership even though it had executed a contract with the union prescribing such action. . . . Such discriminatory contracts are illegal and provide no defense to an action under §8(a)(3). See Steele v. Louisville & Nashville R. Co., 323 U.S. 192. . . .

III.   POWER OF BOARD TO DRAW INFERENCES

Petitioners in *Gaynor* and *Radio Officers* contend that the Board's orders in these cases should not have been enforced by the Second Circuit because the records do not include "independent proof that encouragement of Union membership actually occurred." . . .

We considered this problem in the *Republic Aviation* case. . . . [We stated:]

An administrative agency with power after hearings to determine on the evidence in adversary proceedings whether violations of statutory commands have occurred may infer within the limits of the inquiry from the proven facts such conclusions as reasonably may be based upon the facts proven. One of the purposes which lead to the creation of such boards is to have decisions based upon evidential facts under the particular statute made by experienced officials with an adequate appreciation of the complexities of the subject which is entrusted to their administration. . . .

324 U.S., at 798, 800. . . . [W]e but restated a rule familiar to the law and followed by all fact-finding tribunals — that it is permissible to draw on experience in factual inquiries. . . .

In Universal Camera Corp. v. Labor Board, 340 U.S. 474, we carefully considered this legislative history and interpreted it to express dissatisfaction with too restricted application of the "substantial evidence" test of the Wagner Act. We noted, however, that sufficiency of evidence to support findings of fact was not involved in the *Republic Aviation* case, and stated that the amendment was not "intended to negative the function of the Labor Board as one of those agencies presumably equipped or informed by experience to deal with a specialized field of knowledge, whose findings within that field carry the authority of an expertness which courts do not possess and therefore must respect." There is nothing in the language of the amendment itself that suggests denial to the Board of power to draw reasonable inferences. It is inconceivable that the authors of the reports intended such a result, for a fact-finding body must have some power to decide which inferences to draw and which to reject. We therefore conclude that insofar as the power to draw reasonable inferences is concerned, Taft-Hartley did not alter prior law.

The Board relies heavily upon the House Report on §8(3), which stated that the section outlawed discrimination "which tends to 'encourage or discourage membership in any labor organization'" for its conclusion that only a tendency to encourage or discourage membership is required by §8(a)(3). We read this language to mean that subjective evidence of employee response was not contemplated by the drafters, and to accord with our holding that such proof is not required where encouragement or discouragement can be reasonably inferred from the nature of the discrimination.

Encouragement and discouragement are "subtle things" requiring "a high degree of introspective perception." Cf. Labor Board v. Donnelly Garment Co., 330 U.S. 219, 231. But . . . it is common experience that the desire of employees to unionize is raised or lowered by the advantages thought to be attained by such action. Moreover, the Act does not require that the employees discriminated against be the ones encouraged for purposes of violations of §8(a)(3). Nor does the Act require that this change in employees' "quantum of desire" to join a union have immediate manifestations.

Obviously, it would be gross inconsistency to hold that an inherent effect of certain discrimination is encouragement of union membership, but that the Board may not reasonably infer such encouragement. We have held that a natural result of the disparate wage treatment in *Gaynor* was encouragement of union membership; thus it would be unreasonable to draw any inference other than that encouragement would result from such action. The company complains that it could have disproved this natural result if allowed to prove that Loner, the employee who filed the charges against it, had previously applied for and been denied membership in the union. But it is clear that such evidence would not have rebutted the inference: not only would it have failed to disprove an increase in desire on the part of other employees, union members or nonmembers, to join or retain good standing in the union, but it would not have shown lack of encouragement of Loner. In rejecting this argument the Second Circuit noted that union admission policies are not necessarily static and that employees may be encouraged to join when conditions change. This proved to be an accurate prophecy regarding the Newspaper and Mail Deliverers' Union, involved in this case, for in 1952 it altered its admission policy to allow membership of "all steady situation holders," thus admitting many employees not previously eligible.

The circumstances in *Radio Officers* and *Teamsters* are nearly identical. In each case the employer discriminated upon the instigation of the union. The purposes of the unions in causing such discrimination clearly were to encourage members to perform obligations or supposed obligations of membership. Obviously, the unions would not have invoked such a sanction had they not considered it an effective method of coercing compliance with union obligations or practices. Both Boston and Fowler were denied jobs by employers solely because of the union's actions. Since encouragement of union membership is obviously a natural and foreseeable consequence of any employer discrimination at the request of a union, those employers must be presumed to have intended such encouragement. It follows that it was eminently reasonable for the Board to infer encouragement of union membership, and the Eighth Circuit erred in holding encouragement not proved.

[In Part IV of its opinion, the Court rejected the following contentions of the union in *Radio Officers*: that (1) it was error for the Board to proceed against a union charged with a violation of §8(b)(2) without joining the employer and (2) absent a finding of a violation of §8(a)(3) by, and a reinstatement order against, the offending employer, the Board lacked authority to require back pay from the union, under §8(b)(2).]

FRANKFURTER, J., concurring. . . . The lower courts have given conflicting interpretations to the phrase, "by discrimination . . . to encourage or discourage membership in any labor organization," contained in §8(a)(3). We should settle this conflict without giving rise to avoidable new controversies.

The phrase in its relevant setting is susceptible of alternative constructions of decisively different scope:

(a) On the basis of the employer's disparate treatment of his employees standing alone, or as supplemented by evidence of the particular circumstances under which the employer acted, it is open for the Board to conclude that the conduct of the employer tends to encourage or discourage union membership, thereby establishing a violation of the statute.

(b) Even though the evidence of disparate treatment is sufficient to warrant the Board's conclusion set forth in (a), there must be a specific finding by the Board in all cases that the actual aim of the employer was to encourage or discourage union membership.

I think (a) is the correct interpretation. In many cases a conclusion by the Board that the employer's acts are likely to help or hurt a union will be so compelling that a further and separate finding characterizing the employer's state of mind would be an unnecessary and fictive formality. In such a case the employer may fairly be judged by his acts and the inferences to be drawn from them.

Of course, there will be cases in which the circumstances under which the employer acted serve to rebut any inference that might be drawn from his acts of alleged discrimination standing alone. For example, concededly a raise given only to union members is prima facie suspect; but the employer, by introducing other facts, may be able to show that the raise was so patently referable to other considerations, unrelated to his views on unions and within his allowable freedom of action, that the Board could not reasonably have concluded that his conduct would encourage or discourage union membership.

In sum, any inference that may be drawn from the employer's alleged discriminatory acts is just one element of evidence which may or may not be sufficient, without more, to show a violation. But that should not obscure the fact that this inference may be bolstered or rebuted by other evidence which may be adduced, and which the Board must take into consideration. The Board's task is to weigh everything before it, including those inferences which, with its specialized experience, it believes can fairly be drawn. On the basis of this process, it must determine whether the alleged discriminatory acts of the employer were such that he should have reasonably anticipated that they would encourage or discourage union membership.

What I have written and the Court's opinion, as I read it, are not in disagreement. In any event, I concur in its judgment.

Burton and Minton, JJ., having joined in the opinion of the Court, also join this opinion.

[Black, J., with whom Douglas, J., joined, dissented, urging that §8(a)(3) "forbids an employer to discriminate" only when he does so *in order to* "encourage or discourage" union membership and that the evidence did not establish, and, indeed, may have controverted, the existence of the proscribed purpose.]

NOTES

1. Where a discharge for noncompliance with union security provisions results solely from a union's violations of §§8(b)(1)(A) and 8(b)(2) and the employer is innocent of wrongdoing, the Board's remedy is a back pay order against the union for all lost wages and benefits to the date the wrongfully discharged employee is reinstated or obtains substantially equivalent employment elsewhere. See Sheet Metal Workers (Zinsco Elec. Products), 254 N.L.R.B. 773 (1981) (discarding rule that union's back pay liability is tolled five days after notice to employer of withdrawal of objections to employee's reinstatement), *enforced in relevant part*, 716 F.2d 1249 (9th Cir. 1983).

2. Collective bargaining agreements sometimes grant "superseniority" (that is, seniority preferences or credits) to employees who serve as the union's representatives in the plant. Superseniority, by its terms, operates with respect to contractual benefits affected by seniority — e.g., shift, overtime, or holiday work assignments. Such clauses quite obviously "discriminate" on grounds forbidden by §8(a)(3), as well as "encourage membership." Nevertheless, in Dairylea Cooperative, Inc., 219 N.L.R.B. 656 (1975), *enforced*, 531 F.2d 1162 (2d Cir. 1976), the Board found that some job protection for union shop stewards "benefit[s] all unit employees" by furthering "the effective administration of bargaining agreements on the plant level." Accordingly, the Board ruled, contractual superseniority for union stewards is "presumptively valid" when limited to layoff and recall situations, but such provisions become presumptively invalid when extended to other job benefits. After some indecision, the Board has taken the position that layoff and recall superseniority accorded to union officials generally is an unjustifiable §8(a)(3) discrimination — unless such officials in fact do what stewards do, handle plant grievances and "on-the-job" contract administration. Gulton Electro-Voice, Inc., 266 N.L.R.B. No. 84, 112 L.R.R.M. 1361 (1983), *enforced sub nom.* Local 900, Electrical Workers v. NLRB, 727 F.2d 1184 (D.C. Cir. 1984).

We shall see later that §8(a)(3) restricts an employer's use of superseniority as a weapon against the union and its members. What is it that distinguishes the disparate treatment sanctioned in *Dairylea*? See NLRB v. Erie Resistor Corp., reproduced infra p. 305; NLRB v. Great Dane Trailers, reproduced infra p. 334.

NLRB v. Burnup & Sims, 379 U.S. 21 (1964). The employer discharged two employees after he had been told that, while recruiting during an organizing campaign, they had threatened to use dynamite, if necessary, to achieve recognition. The Board found that the reported threat had not been made, ruled that the employer's honest belief to the contrary was not a defense, concluded that the discharges had violated both §8(a)(1) and §8(a)(3), and ordered reinstatement and back pay. The Court affirmed the Board's order solely on the basis of §8(a)(1), stating (pp. 22-24):

> We find it unnecessary to reach . . . §8(a)(3) for . . . §8(a)(1) was plainly violated, whatever the employer's motive. . . . A protected activity acquires a precarious status if innocent employees can be discharged while engaging in it, even though the employer acts in good faith. It is the tendency of [such] discharges to weaken or destroy the §8(a)(1) right that is controlling. We are not in the realm of managerial prerogatives. . . . Had the alleged dynamiting threats been wholly disassociated from §7 activities quite different considerations might apply.

Harlan, J., concurring in part and dissenting in part, stressed the business justification for the employer's action (to avoid dynamiting of the plant) and concluded: "I do not believe this case presents the rare situation in which the Board can ignore motive."

NOTES

1. Why do you suppose the Court avoided the §8(a)(3) questions in *Burnup & Sims?* Is there an interpretation of "discrimination" and "to encourage or discourage" that would have warranted a finding of a violation of that section? As you study the remainder of this chapter, consider what are to be the respective roles of §§8(a)(1) and 8(a)(3) when an employer is charged with reprisals or unlawful countermeasures against employees who have engaged in protected activities.

2. Questions concerning the respective roles of §§8(a)(1) and 8(a)(3) and the content to be poured into "discrimination" are also involved in cases dealing with hiring halls and with disparate treatment of employees based on race and other invidious or arbitrary criteria. See Teamsters, Local 357 v. NLRB, 365 U.S. 667 (1961), reproduced infra p. 1221, and Packinghouse Workers v. NLRB, 416 F.2d 1126, 1135 (D.C. Cir. 1969), *cert. denied,* 396 U.S. 903 (1969), referred to infra p. 1134. In *Local 357,* the dissent urged that under §8(a)(3) "the word 'discrimination,' . . . as the Board points

out, . . . includes not only distinctions contingent upon 'the presence or absence of union membership,' . . . but all differences in treatment regardless of their basis." In *Packinghouse Workers* the court declared that discrimination against employees on the basis of race violates §8(a)(1) because (1) it creates an unjustified clash of interests among groups of employees and thereby hampers concerted action, and (2) it engenders apathy or docility among its victims, inhibiting them from asserting their rights against the discriminator and from exercising their §7 rights.

If these approaches were followed, would the NLRA operate as a Fair Employment Practices act? As a substitute for Title VII of the Civil Rights Act of 1964? For example, would the *Packinghouse Workers* formula apply to a "sweatshop employer" who egregiously overworked and underpaid some of his employees but not others? If these approaches would convert the NLRA into an FEP act, would that be a desirable development?

3. The Supreme Court's elusive and shifting treatment of "motive," "intent," and "purpose" has been the subject of extensive and subtle discussion. See the references cited at p. 200, supra, and Oberer, The Scienter Factor in §§8(a)(1) and (3) of the Labor Act: Of Balancing, Hostile Motive, Dogs and Tails, 52 Cornell L.Q. 491 (1967).

Textile Workers Union v. Darlington Mfg. Co.
380 U.S. 263 (1965)

HARLAN, J. . . . Darlington Manufacturing Company was a South Carolina corporation operating one textile mill. A majority of Darlington's stock was held by Deering Milliken, a New York "selling house" marketing textiles produced by others. Deering Milliken in turn was controlled by Roger Milliken, president of Darlington, and by other members of the Milliken family. The National Labor Relations Board found that the Milliken family, through Deering Milliken, operated 17 textile manufacturers, including Darlington, whose products, manufactured in 27 different mills, were marketed through Deering Milliken.

In March 1956 petitioner, Textile Workers Union, initiated an organizational campaign at Darlington which the company resisted vigorously in various ways, including threats to close the mill if the union won a representation election. On September 6, 1956, the union won an election by a narrow margin. When Roger Milliken was advised of the union victory, he decided to call a meeting of the Darlington board of directors to consider closing the mill. Mr. Milliken testified before the Labor Board:

I felt that as a result of the campaign that had been conducted and the promises and statements made in these letters that had been distributed [favoring unionization], that if before we had had some hope, possible hope of achieving competitive [costs] . . . by taking advantage of new machinery that was being put in, that this hope had diminished as a result of the election because a majority of the employees had voted in favor of the union. . . .

The board of directors met on September 12 and voted to liquidate the corporation, an action which was approved by the stockholders on October 17. The plant ceased operations entirely in November, and all plant machinery and equipment were sold piecemeal at auction in December.

The union filed charges with the Labor Board claiming that Darlington had violated §§8(a)(1) and (3) . . . by closing its plant; and §8(a)(5) by refusing to bargain with the union after the election.[5] The Board, by a divided vote, found that Darlington had been closed because of the antiunion animus of Roger Milliken, and held that to be a violation of §8(a)(3). The Board also found Darlington to be part of a single integrated employer group controlled by the Milliken family through Deering Milliken; therefore Deering Milliken could be held liable for the unfair labor practices of Darlington. Alternatively, since Darlington was a part of the Deering Milliken enterprise, Deering Milliken had violated the Act by closing part of its business for a discriminatory purpose. The Board ordered back pay for all Darlington employees until they obtained substantially equivalent work or were put on preferential hiring lists at the other Deering Milliken mills. Respondent Deering Milliken was ordered to bargain with the union in regard to details of compliance with the Board order. 139 N.L.R.B. 241.

On review, the Court of Appeals, sitting en banc, set aside the order and denied enforcement by a divided vote. 325 F.2d 682. The Court of Appeals held that even accepting arguendo the Board's determination that Deering Milliken had the status of a single employer, a company has the absolute right to close out a part or all of its business regardless of antiunion motives. The court therefore did not review the Board's finding that Deering Milliken was a single integrated employer. We granted certiorari to consider the important

---

[5] The union asked for a bargaining conference on September 12, 1956 (the day that the board of directors voted to liquidate), but was told to await certification by the Board. The union was certified on October 24, and did meet with Darlington officials in November, but no actual bargaining took place. The Board found this to be a violation of §8(a)(5). Such a finding was in part based on the determination that the plant closing was an unfair labor practice, and no argument is made that §8(a)(5) requires an employer to bargain concerning a purely business decision to terminate his enterprise. Cf. Fibreboard Paper Products Corp. v. Labor Board, 379 U.S. 203.

questions involved. We hold that so far as the Labor Relations Act is concerned, an employer has the absolute right to terminate his entire business for any reason he pleases, but disagree with the Court of Appeals that such right includes the ability to close part of a business no matter what the reason. We conclude that the cause must be remanded to the Board for further proceedings.

Preliminarily it should be observed that both petitioners argue that the Darlington closing violated §8(a)(1) as well as §8(a)(3). . . . We think, however, that the Board was correct in treating the closing only under §8(a)(3).[8] Section 8(a)(1) provides that it is an unfair labor practice for an employer "to interfere with, restrain, or coerce employees in the exercise of" §7 rights. Naturally, certain business decisions will, to some degree, interfere with concerted activities by employees. But it is only when the interference with §7 rights outweighs the business justification for the employer's action that §8(a)(1) is violated. See, e.g., Labor Board v. Steelworkers, 357 U.S. 357; Republic Aviation Corp. v. Labor Board, 324 U.S. 793. A violation of §8(a)(1) alone therefore presupposes an act which is unlawful even absent a discriminatory motive. Whatever may be the limits of §8(a)(1), some employer decisions are so peculiarly matters of management prerogative that they would never constitute violations of §8(a)(1), whether or not they involved sound business judgment, unless they also violated §8(a)(3). Thus it is not questioned in this case that an employer has the right to terminate his business, whatever the impact of such action on concerted activities, if the decision to close is motivated by other than discriminatory reasons.[10] But such action, if discriminatorily motivated, is encompassed within the literal language of §8(a)(3). We therefore deal with the Darlington closing under that section.

I

We consider first the argument, advanced by the petitioner union but not by the Board, and rejected by the Court of Appeals, that an employer may not go completely out of business without running afoul of the Labor Relations Act if such action is prompted by a desire to avoid unionization. Given the

---

[8] The Board did find that Darlington's discharges of employees following the decision to close violated §8(a)(1). . . .

[10] It is also clear that the ambiguous act of closing a plant following the election of a union is not, absent an inquiry into the employer's motive, inherently discriminatory. We are thus not confronted with a situation where the employer "must be held to intend the very consequences which foreseeably and inescapably flow from his actions . . . ." (Labor Board v. Erie Resistor Corp., 373 U.S. 221, 228), in which the Board could find a violation of §8(a)(3) without an examination into motive. See Radio Officers v. Labor Board, 347 U.S. 17, 42-43; Teamsters Local v. Labor Board, 365 U.S. 667, 674-676.

Board's findings on the issue of motive, acceptance of this contention would carry the day for the Board's conclusion that the closing of this plant was an unfair labor practice, even on the assumption that Darlington is to be regarded as an independent unrelated employer. A proposition that a single businessman cannot choose to go out of business if he wants to would represent such a startling innovation that it should not be entertained without the clearest manifestation of legislative intent or unequivocal judicial precedent so construing the Labor Relations Act. We find neither.

. . . [T]here is not the slightest indication in the history of the Wagner Act or of the Taft-Hartley Act that Congress envisaged any such result under either statute.

As for judicial precedent, the Board recognized that "[t]here is no decided case directly dispositive of Darlington's claim that it had an absolute right to close its mill, irrespective of motive." 139 N.L.R.B., at 250. . . .

The AFL-CIO suggests in its amicus brief that Darlington's action was similar to a discriminatory lockout, which is prohibited " 'because designed to frustrate organizational efforts, to destroy or undermine bargaining representation, or to evade the duty to bargain.' " One of the purposes of the Labor Relations Act is to prohibit the discriminatory use of economic weapons in an effort to obtain future benefits. The discriminatory lockout designed to destroy a union, like a "runaway shop," is a lever which has been used to discourage collective employee activities in the future. But a complete liquidation of a business yields no such future benefit for the employer, if the termination is bona fide.[14] It may be motivated more by spite against the union than by business reasons, but it is not the type of discrimination which is prohibited by the Act. The personal satisfaction that such an employer may derive from standing on his beliefs and the mere possibility that other employers will follow his example are surely too remote to be considered dangers at which the labor statutes were aimed.[15] Although employees may be prohibited from engaging in a strike under certain conditions, no one would consider it a violation of the Act for the same employees to quit their employment en masse, even if motivated by a desire to ruin the employer. The very permanence of such action would negate any future economic benefit to the employees. The employer's right to go out of business is no different.

---

[14] The Darlington property and equipment could not be sold as a unit, and were eventually auctioned off piecemeal. We therefore are not confronted with a sale of a going concern, which might present different considerations under §§8(a)(3) and (5). Cf. John Wiley & Sons, Inc. v. Livingston, 376 U.S. 543; Labor Board v. Deena Artware, Inc., 361 U.S. 398.

[15] Cf. NLRA §8(c). Different considerations would arise were it made to appear that the closing employer was acting pursuant to some arrangement or understanding with other employers to discourage employee organizational activities in their businesses.

We are not presented here with the case of a "runaway shop," whereby Darlington would transfer its work to another plant or open a new plant in another locality to replace its closed plant.[f] Nor are we concerned with a shutdown where the employees, by renouncing the union, could cause the plant to reopen. Such cases would involve discriminatory employer action for the purpose of obtaining some benefit from the employees in the future. We hold here only that when an employer closes his entire business, even if the liquidation is motivated by vindictiveness toward the union, such action is not an unfair labor practice.[20]

II

While we thus agree with the Court of Appeals that viewing Darlington as an independent employer the liquidation of its business was not an unfair labor practice, we cannot accept the lower court's view that the same conclusion necessarily follows if Darlington is regarded as an integral part of the Deering Milliken enterprise.

The closing of an entire business, even though discriminatory, ends the employer-employee relationship; the force of such a closing is entirely spent as to that business when termination of the enterprise takes place. On the other hand, a discriminatory partial closing may have repercussions on what remains of the business, affording employer leverage for discouraging the free exercise of §7 rights among remaining employees of much the same kind as that found to exist in the "runaway shop" and "temporary closing" cases. . . . Moreover, a possible remedy open to the Board in such a case, like remedies available in the "runaway shop" and "temporary closing" cases, is to order reinstatement of the discharged employees in the other parts

---

[f][For an example of a "runaway shop" found to have been motivated by a desire to escape the union and not by economic factors, see Local 57, International Ladies Garment Union v. NLRB (Garwin Corp.), reproduced infra p. 462. — Eds.]

[20]Nothing we have said in this opinion would justify an employer's interfering with employee organizational activities by threatening to close his plant, as distinguished from announcing a decision to close already reached by the board of directors or other management authority empowered to make such a decision. We recognize that this safeguard does not wholly remove the possibility that our holding may result in some deterrent effect on organizational activities independent of that arising from the closing itself. An employer may be encouraged to make a definitive decision to close on the theory that its mere announcement before a representation election will discourage the employees from voting for the union, and thus his decision may not have to be implemented. Such a possibility is not likely to occur, however, except in a marginal business; a solidly successful employer is not apt to hazard the possibility that the employees will call his bluff by voting to organize. We see no practical way of eliminating this possible consequence of our holding short of allowing the Board to order an employer who chooses so to gamble with his employees not to carry out his announced intention to close. We do not consider the matter of sufficient significance in the overall labor-management relations picture to require or justify a decision different from the one we have made.

of the business. No such remedy is available when an entire business has been terminated. By analogy to those cases involving a continuing enterprise we are constrained to hold, in disagreement with the Court of Appeals, that a partial closing is an unfair labor practice under §8(a)(3) if motivated by a purpose to chill unionism in any of the remaining plants of the single employer and if the employer may reasonably have foreseen that such closing would likely have that effect.

While we have spoken in terms of a "partial closing" in the context of the Board's finding that Darlington was part of a larger single enterprise controlled by the Milliken family, we do not mean to suggest that an organizational integration of plants or corporations is a necessary prerequisite to the establishment of such a violation of §8(a)(3). If the persons exercising control over a plant that is being closed for antiunion reasons (1) have an interest in another business, whether or not affiliated with or engaged in the same line of commercial activity as the closed plant, of sufficient substantiality to give promise of their reaping a benefit from the discouragement of unionization in that business; (2) act to close their plant with the purpose of producing such a result; and (3) occupy a relationship to the other business which makes it realistically foreseeable that its employees will fear that such business will also be closed down if they persist in organizational activities, we think that an unfair labor practice has been made out.

Although the Board's single employer finding necessarily embraced findings as to Roger Milliken and the Milliken family which, if sustained by the Court of Appeals, would satisfy the elements of "interest" and "relationship" with respect to other parts of the Deering Milliken enterprise, that and the other Board findings fall short of establishing the factors of "purpose" and "effect" which are vital requisites of the general principles that govern a case of this kind.

Thus, the Board's findings as to the purpose and foreseeable effect of the Darlington closing pertained *only* to its impact on the Darlington employees. No findings were made as to the purpose and effect of the closing with respect to the employees in the other plants comprising the Deering Milliken group. It does not suffice to establish the unfair labor practice charged here to argue that the Darlington closing necessarily had an adverse impact upon unionization in such other plants. We have heretofore observed that employer action which has a foreseeable consequence of discouraging concerted activities generally does not amount to a violation of §8(a)(3) in the absence of a showing of motivation which is aimed at achieving the prohibited effect. See Teamsters Local v. Labor Board, 365 U.S. 667, and the concurring opinion therein, at 677. In an area which trenches so closely upon otherwise legitimate employer prerogatives, we consider the absence of Board findings on this score a fatal defect in its decision. The Court of

Appeals for its part did not deal with the question of purpose and effect at all, since it concluded that an employer's right to close down his entire business because of distaste for unionism, also embraced a partial closing so motivated.

Apart from this, the Board's holding should not be accepted or rejected without court review of its single employer finding, judged, however, in accordance with the general principles set forth above. Review of that finding, which the lower court found unnecessary on its view of the cause, now becomes necessary in light of our holding in this part of our opinion, and is a task that devolves upon the Court of Appeals in the first instance. Universal Camera Corp. v. Labor Board, 340 U.S. 474.

In these circumstances, we think the proper disposition of this cause is to require that it be remanded to the Board so as to afford the Board the opportunity to make further findings on the issue of purpose and effect. See, e.g., Labor Board v. Virginia Elec. & Power Co., 314 U.S. 469, 479-480. This is particularly appropriate here since the cases involve issues of first impression. If such findings are made, the cases will then be in a posture for further review by the Court of Appeals on all issues. Accordingly, without intimating any view as to how any of these matters should eventuate, we vacate the judgments of the Court of Appeals and remand the cases to that court with instructions to remand them to the Board for further proceedings consistent with this opinion. . . .

Stewart and Goldberg, JJ., took no part in the consideration or decision of these cases.

[On remand, the Trial Examiner concluded that the evidence did not establish a violation under the Court's tests. In rejecting that conclusion, the Board relied on Roger Milliken's antiunion speeches to Kiwanis clubs and other nonemployee groups and stated that the legislative background of §8(c) indicated that it "left unrestricted the Board's right to consider employer statements for purposes for which they ordinarily would be admissible in courts of law." The Board's order was enforced (5 to 2) by the Court of Appeals for the Fourth Circuit sitting en banc; in January of 1969 the Supreme Court denied the company's request to review the decision. Darlington Mfg. Co. v. NLRB, 397 F.2d 760 (4th Cir. 1968), cert. denied, 393 U.S. 1023 (1969). The back pay phase of Darlington began in the early 1970s, involved 400 hearing days spread over a period of years, and produced a record that reached 37,000 pages. On December 3, 1980, the NLRB's General Counsel announced the company's agreement to his proposed back pay settlement of $5,000,000, which the affected employees also approved. See generally NLRB Office of the General Counsel, Release No. 1625, Dec. 3, 1980; Eames, The History of the Litigation of Darlington as an Exercise in Administrative Procedure, 5 U. Tol. L. Rev. 595 (1974); Dallas & Schaffer, Whatever Happened to the Darlington Case? 24 Lab. L.J. 3 (1973).]

NOTES

1. Suppose that during the preelection period an employer who owns only one plant includes in a speech to his employees the following statement from the Court's *Darlington* opinion: "When an employer closes his entire business, even if the liquidation is motivated by vindictiveness toward the union, such action is not an unfair labor practice." Would the Board upset an election lost by the union? Would knowledge of an employer's right to close down if the union won be relevant to the employees' voting decision(s)? If such information is relevant, what is the basis for the Board's barring, under §8 or §9, an employer from telling his employees of his right to close down? Cf. Paoli Chair Co., 231 N.L.R.B. 539 (1977).

2. All drivers employed by R, a small trucker, were members of the Teamsters. R hired two mechanics for his newly established truck servicing department. A month later, these mechanics joined the Teamsters, and the latter's business agent asked for bargaining rights and showed R contracts reflecting wage rates for mechanics approximately 30 percent higher than R's scale. R's service operation was already costing him as much as he had previously paid for outside servicing. Shortly after the union's request, R shut down his service department, dismissed the mechanics, and returned to outside servicing. (1) Under *Darlington*, has R committed any unfair labor practices? (2) Should the closing of the unionized part of a business because higher costs are expected after its unionization be unlawful? Does such a closing reflect "antiunion animus"? (3) Is the Board's *Wright Line* approach relevant in cases governed by *Darlington?* For guidance on the §8(a)(3) issues presented by closings, relocations, or consolidations, see Weather Tamer, Inc. v. NLRB, 676 F.2d 483 (11th Cir. 1982); George Lithograph Co., 204 N.L.R.B. 431 (1973); NLRB v. Rapid Binding, Inc., 293 F.2d 170 (2d Cir. 1961); NLRB v. Adkins Transfer Co., 226 F.2d 324 (6th Cir. 1955).

2. Collective Bargaining, Strikes, and Countervailing Employer Action

NLRB v. Mackay Radio & Telegraph Co.
304 U.S. 333 (1938)

[The Mackay Company, a communications enterprise, employed in its San Francisco office about sixty supervisors, operators, and clerks, many of whom were members of Local No. 3 of the American Radio Telegraphists Association, a national union. After unsuccessful negotiations in New York, between the national union and Mackay's parent company for an agreement covering marine and point-to-point operators, the national union called a "general strike," in which Local 3 participated. Mackay, in order to maintain operations, brought in employees from other offices to fill the strikers' places in San Francisco. The strike was unsuccessful. In response to the strikers' inquiries, Mackay stated that they could return in a body, except for eleven strikers who would have to file applications for reinstatement. Thereafter, only five of the replacements wished to remain in San Francisco, and six of the special group of eleven strikers were allowed to return to work, together with the others. The remaining five, who had been prominent in union activities, were denied reinstatement. The Board held that this denial constituted a violation of §§8(1) and 8(3) and ordered reinstatement, with back pay, of the five strikers. The court of appeals denied enforcement of the Board's order and was, in turn, reversed by the Supreme Court. The Court concluded that the strikers remained "employees" under §2(3) of the Act and that the evidence supported the Board's finding of discrimination in the denial of reinstatement to the five strikers.]

ROBERTS, J. . . . But it is said the record fails to disclose what caused these negotiations to fail or to show that the respondent was in any wise in fault in failing to comply with the union's demands; and, therefore, for all that appears, the strike was not called by reason of fault of the respondent. The argument confuses a current labor dispute with an unfair labor practice defined in §8 of the Act. True there is no evidence that respondent had been guilty of any unfair labor practice prior to the strike, but within the intent of the Act there was an existing labor dispute in connection with which the strike was called. The finding is that the strike was deemed "advisable in view of the unsatisfactory state of the negotiations" in New York. It was unnecessary for the Board to find what was in fact the state of the negotiations in New York when the strike was called, or in so many words that a labor dispute as defined by the Act existed. The wisdom or unwisdom of the men, their justification or lack of it, in attributing to respondent an unreasonable or arbitrary attitude in connection with the negotiations, cannot determine whether, when they struck, they did so as a consequence of or in connection with a current labor dispute.

. . . Nor was it an unfair labor practice to replace the striking employees with others in an effort to carry on the business. Although §13 provides, "Nothing in this Act shall be construed so as to interfere with or impede or diminish in any way the right to strike," it does not follow that an employer, guilty of no act denounced by the statute, has lost the right to protect and continue his business by supplying places left vacant by strikers. And he is not bound to discharge those hired to fill the places of strikers, upon the election of the latter to resume their employment, in order to create places for them. The assurance by respondent to those who accepted employment during the strike that if they so desired their places might be permanent was not an unfair labor practice nor was it such to reinstate only so many of the strikers as there were vacant places to be filled. But the claim put forward is that the unfair labor practice indulged by the respondent was discrimination in reinstating striking employees by keeping out certain of them for the sole reason that they had been active in the union. As we have said, the strikers retained, under the Act, the status of employees. Any such discrimination in putting them back to work is, therefore, prohibited by §8. . . .

As we have said, the respondent was not bound to displace men hired to take the strikers' places in order to provide positions for them. It might have refused reinstatement on the ground of skill or ability, but the Board found that it did not do so. It might have resorted to any one of a number of methods of determining which of its striking employees would have to wait because five men had taken permanent positions during the strike, but it is found that the preparation and use of the list, and the action taken by respondent, were with the purpose to discriminate against those most active in the union. There is evidence to support these findings.

NOTES

1. In *Mackay Radio*, the Board had reserved the question of the legality of permanently replacing economic strikers; disposition of that question had not been necessary to the Board's decision condemning the denial of reinstatement to some strikers on the basis of their union activities. See Mackay Radio & Telegraph Co., 1 N.L.R.B. 201, 216-222 (1936). Should the Court have ruled on that far-reaching issue without the benefit of the Board's "expertise"? For a vigorous criticism of the Court's dictum, see J. Atleson, Values and Assumptions in American Labor Law 21-24 (1983) (noting that the General Counsel's brief to the Court, apparently relying on a position taken by the NLRB's predecessor, the NLB, had conceded an employer's right to hire permanent replacements, though the Board had not passed on the issue). Cf. C. Perry, A. Kramer, & T. Schneider, Operating During Strikes 35-37 (1982).

2. In assessing the Court's resolution of the replacement issue, consider §§7, 8, and 13 of the NLRA. Do they provide a clear basis for that resolution? Consider also the following statement by Andrew Carnegie, quoted in L. Wolff, Lockout 28 (1965):

I would have the public give due consideration to the terrible temptation to which the workingman on a strike is sometimes subjected. To expect that one dependent on his daily wage for the necessaries of life will stand by peaceably, and see a new man employed in his stead is to expect much. The poor man may have a wife and children dependent on his labor. Whether medicine for a sick child, or even nourishing food for a delicate wife, is procurable, depends upon his steady employment. . . . No wise employer will lightly lose his old employees. Length of service counts for much in many ways. Calling upon strange men should be the last resort.

3. Assume that the strike in *Mackay Radio* was successful and that the company, in order to end the strike and the bargaining dispute, had entered into a settlement agreement incorporating Local 3's demand that the permanent replacements be displaced by strikers. Would such an agreement be a violation of the Act by the company or the union? What are the relevant sections? See Bio-Science Laboratories, 209 N.L.R.B. 796, 797 (1974); Portland Stereotypers' Union (Journal Publishing Co.), 137 N.L.R.B. 782 (1962); Belknap, Inc. v. Hale, 103 S. Ct. 3172 (1983), reproduced infra p. 790, on the question of the rights of displaced replacements under state law.

4. With respect to the employer's right to replace, a distinction must be drawn between economic strikes and unfair labor practice strikes, i.e., a strike called or prolonged because of the employer's unfair labor practice. A strike may be caused both by a bargaining impasse and by an unfair labor practice. Such a strike is deemed an unfair labor practice strike unless the employer shows that the strike would have occurred even in the absence of his unfair labor practice. See NLRB v. Wooster Div. of Borg-Warner Corp., 236 F.2d 898 (6th Cir. 1956), *aff'd and modified on other grounds*, 356 U.S. 342 (1958), applied by the Board, after remand, 121 N.L.R.B. 1492 (1958). Similarly, if an employer commits unfair labor practices during an economic strike, a finding of a causal connection between the employer's conduct and a continuation of the strike will convert the stoppage into an unfair labor practice strike and strikers who are replaced thereafter are treated as unfair labor practice strikers. See National Car Rental System v. NLRB, 594 F.2d 1203, 1206 (8th Cir. 1979); Local 833, UAW v. NLRB (Kohler Co.), supra p. 257. An employer is required to displace even permanent replacements in order to make room for unfair labor practice strikers (as distinguished from economic strikers) who have made an unconditional application for reinstatement. Is this distinction between the two classes of strikers sound? Should back pay for unfair labor practice strikers begin as of the time that such strikes began or, as is the case with economic strikers, at the time of an unconditional application for reinstatement for jobs to which they are entitled? See Stewart,

Conversion of Strikes: Economic to Unfair Labor Practice: I & II, 45 Va. L. Rev. 1322 (1959), 49 Va. L. Rev. 1297 (1963).

5. In Abilities & Goodwill, Inc., 241 N.L.R.B. 27 (1979), *enforcement denied on other grounds,* 612 F.2d 6 (1st Cir. 1979), the NLRB overruled a 30-year-old rule and held that strikers unlawfully discharged during a lawful strike should be treated like any other unlawfully discharged employee and should, in general, be entitled to back pay from the time of the discharge rather than (as had been the case) only from the time of a striker's application for reinstatement. The Board's majority reasoned that it is uncertain whether discharged strikers are not working voluntarily, i.e., because of the strike, rather than because the discharge showed the futility of applying for reinstatement. Since that uncertainty results from the employer's misconduct, it seems equitable, the Board urged, to require the employer to rescind the discharge in order to cut off back pay. Courts have generally approved the *Abilities & Goodwill* remedy. See NLRB v. Trident Seafoods Corp., 642 F.2d 1148 (9th Cir. 1981); NLRB v. Lyon & Ryan Ford, Inc., 647 F.2d 745 (7th Cir. 1981), *cert. denied,* 454 U.S. 894 (1981) (adding that even under *Abilities & Goodwill* an employer can present evidence that the employee would have refused a reinstatement offer even if made; thus, back pay liability is avoided if the employer "can affirmatively establish that the unlawful discharge did not prevent the employee from returning to work").

NLRB v. Erie Resistor Corp.
373 U.S. 221 (1963)

WHITE, J. The question before us is whether an employer commits an unfair labor practice under §8(a) of the [NLRA] . . . when he extends a 20-year seniority credit to strike replacements and strikers who leave the strike and return to work. The . . . Third Circuit in this case joined the Ninth Circuit, Labor Board v. Potlatch Forests, Inc., 189 F.2d 82 (and see Labor Board v. Lewin-Mathes, 285 F.2d 329, from the Seventh Circuit), to hold that such super-seniority awards are not unlawful absent a showing of an illegal motive on the part of the employer. 303 F.2d 359. The Sixth Circuit, Swarco, Inc., v. Labor Board, 303 F.2d 668, and the National Labor Relations Board are of the opinion that such conduct can be unlawful even when the employer asserts that these additional benefits are necessary to continue his operations during a strike. To resolve these conflicting views upon an important question in the administration of the [NLRA], we brought the case here. . . .

Erie Resistor Corporation and Local 613 of the [IUEW] were bound by a collective bargaining agreement which was due to expire on March 31, 1959. In January 1959, both parties met to negotiate new terms but, after extensive bargaining, they were unable to reach agreement. Upon expiration of the contract, the union, in support of its contract demands, called a strike which was joined by all of the 478 employees in the unit.

The company, under intense competition and subject to insistent demands from its customers to maintain deliveries, decided to continue production operations. Transferring clerks, engineers and other nonunit employees to production jobs, the company managed to keep production at about 15% to 30% of normal during the month of April. On May 3, however, the company notified the union members that it intended to begin hiring replacements and that strikers would retain their jobs until replaced. The plant was located in an area classified by the United States Department of Labor as one of severe unemployment and the company had in fact received applications for employment as early as a week or two after the strike began.

Replacements were told that they would not be laid off or discharged at the end of the strike. To implement that assurance, particularly in view of the 450 employees already laid off on March 31, the company notified the union that it intended to accord the replacements some form of superseniority. At regular bargaining sessions between the company and the union, the union made it clear that, in its view, no matter what form the superseniority plan might take, it would necessarily work an illegal discrimination against the strikers. As negotiations advanced on other issues, it became evident that superseniority was fast becoming the focal point of disagreement. On May 28, the company informed the union that it had decided to award 20 years'[3] additional seniority both to replacements and to strikers who returned to work, which would be available only for credit against future layoffs and which could not be used for other employee benefits based on years of service. The strikers, at a union meeting the next day, unanimously resolved to continue striking now in protest against the proposed plan as well.

The company made its first official announcement of the superseniority plan on June 10, and by June 14, 34 new employees, 47 employees recalled from layoff status and 23 returning strikers had accepted production jobs. The union, now under great pressure, offered to give up some of its contract demands if the company would abandon superseniority or go to arbitration on the question, but the company refused. In the following week, 64 strikers returned to work and 21 replacements took jobs, bringing the total to 102

---

[3] The figure of 20 years was developed from a projection, on the basis of expected orders, of what the company's work force would be following the strike. As of March 31, the beginning of the strike, a male employee needed seven years' seniority to avoid layoff and a female, nine years.

replacements and recalled workers and 87 returned strikers. When the number of returning strikers went up to 125 during the following week, the union capitulated. A new labor agreement on the remaining economic issues was executed on July 17, and an accompanying settlement agreement was signed providing that the company's replacement and job assurance policy should be resolved by the [NLRB] and the federal courts but was to remain in effect pending final disposition.

Following the strike's termination, the company reinstated those strikers whose jobs had not been filled (all but 129 were returned to their jobs). At about the same time, the union received some 173 resignations from membership. By September of 1959, the production unit work force had reached a high of 442 employees, but by May of 1960, the work force had gradually slipped back to 240. Many employees laid off during this cutback period were reinstated strikers whose seniority was insufficient to retain their jobs as a consequence of the company's superseniority policy.

The union filed a charge . . . alleging that awarding superseniority during the course of the strike constituted an unfair labor practice and that the subsequent layoff of the recalled strikers pursuant to such a plan was unlawful. The Trial Examiner found that the policy was promulgated for legitimate economic reasons,[4] not for illegal or discriminatory purposes, and recommended that the union's complaint be dismissed. The Board could not agree with the Trial Examiner's conclusion that specific evidence of subjective intent to discriminate against the union was necessary to finding that superseniority granted during a strike is an unfair labor practice. Its consistent view, the Board said, had always been that superseniority, in circumstances such as these, was an unfair labor practice. The Board rejected the argument that superseniority granted during a strike is a legitimate corollary of the employer's right of replacement under Labor Board v. Mackay Radio & Tel. Co., 304 U.S. 333, and detailed at some length the factors which to it indicated that "superseniority is a form of discrimination extending far beyond the employer's right of replacement sanctioned by Mackay, and is, moreover, in direct conflict with the express provisions of the Act prohibiting discrimination." Having put aside *Mackay*, the Board went on to deny "that specific evidence of Respondent's discriminatory motivation is required to establish the alleged violations of the Act," relying upon Radio Officers v.

---

[4] The Examiner had relied upon the company's employment records for his conclusion that the replacement program was ineffective until the announcement of the superseniority awards. The General Counsel, to show that such a plan was not necessary for that purpose, pointed to the facts that the company had 300 unprocessed job applications when the strike ended, that the company declared to the union it could have replaced all the strikers and that the company did not communicate its otherwise well-publicized policy to replacements before they were hired but only after they accepted jobs.

Labor Board, 347 U.S. 17, Republic Aviation Corp. v. Labor Board, 324 U.S. 793, and Teamsters Local v. Labor Board, 365 U.S. 667. Moreover, in the Board's judgment, the employer's insistence that its overriding purpose in granting superseniority was to keep its plant open and that business necessity justified its conduct was unacceptable since "to excuse such conduct would greatly diminish, if not destroy, the right to strike guaranteed by the Act, and would run directly counter to the guarantees of §§8(a)(1) and (3) that employees shall not be discriminated against for engaging in protected concerted activities." Accordingly, the Board declined to make findings as to the specific motivation of the plan or its business necessity in the circumstances here.

The Court of Appeals rejected as unsupportable the rationale of the Board that a preferential seniority policy is illegal however motivated.

> We are of the opinion that inherent in the right of an employer to replace strikers during a strike is the concomitant right to adopt a preferential seniority policy which will assure the replacements some form of tenure, provided the policy is adopted *solely* to protect and continue the business of the employer. . . . Whether the policy adopted by the Company in the instant case was illegally motivated we do not decide. The question is one of fact for decision by the Board.

303 F.2d at 364. It consequently denied the Board's petition for enforcement and remanded the case for further findings.

We think the Court of Appeals erred in holding that, in the absence of a finding of specific illegal intent, a legitimate business purpose is always a defense to an unfair labor practice charge. Cases in this Court dealing with unfair labor practices have recognized the relevance and importance of showing the employer's intent or motive to discriminate or to interfere with union rights. But specific evidence of such subjective intent is "not an indispensable element of proof of violation." Radio Officers v. Labor Board, 347 U.S. 17, 44. "Some conduct may by its very nature contain the implications of the required intent; the natural foreseeable consequences of certain action may warrant the inference. . . . The existence of discrimination may at times be inferred by the Board, for 'it is permissible to draw on experience in factual inquiries.'" Teamsters Local v. Labor Board, 365 U.S. 667, 675.

Though the intent necessary for an unfair labor practice may be shown in different ways, proving it in one manner may have far different weight and far different consequences than proving it in another. When specific evidence of a subjective intent to discriminate or to encourage or discourage union membership is shown, and found, many otherwise innocent or ambiguous actions may, without more, be converted into unfair labor practices [citing cases involving the discharge of employees, the subcontracting of union work, and the movement of a plant to another town]. Such proof itself is normally sufficient to destroy the employer's claim of a legitimate business purpose, if one is made, and provides strong support to a finding that there is interference with union rights or that union membership will be discouraged. Conduct which on its face appears to serve legitimate business ends in these cases is wholly impeached by the showing of an intent to encroach upon protected rights. The employer's claim of legitimacy is totally dispelled.

The outcome may well be the same when intent is founded upon the inherently discriminatory or destructive nature of the conduct itself. The employer in such cases must be held to intend the very consequences which foreseeably and inescapably flow from his actions and if he fails to explain away, to justify or to characterize his actions as something different than they appear on their face, an unfair labor practice charge is made out. Radio Officers v. Labor Board, supra. But, as often happens, the employer may counter by claiming that his actions were taken in the pursuit of legitimate business ends and that his dominant purpose was not to discriminate or to invade union rights but to accomplish business objectives acceptable under the Act. Nevertheless, his conduct *does* speak for itself — it *is* discriminatory and it *does* discourage union membership and whatever the claimed overriding justification may be, it carries with it unavoidable consequences which the employer not only foresaw but which he must have intended. As is not uncommon in human experience, such situations present a complex of motives and preferring one motive to another is in reality the far more delicate task, reflected in part in decisions of this Court, of weighing the interests of employees in concerted activity against the interest of the employer in operating his business in a particular manner and of balancing in the light of the Act and its policy the intended consequences upon employee rights against the business ends to be served by the employer's conduct.[8] This

---

[8] In a variety of situations, the lower courts have dealt with and rejected the approach urged here that conduct otherwise unlawful is automatically excused upon a showing that it was motivated by business exigencies. Thus, it has been held that an employer cannot justify the discriminatory discharge of union members upon the ground that such conduct is the only way to induce a rival union to remove a picket line and permit the resumption of business, Labor Board v. Star Publishing Co., 97 F.2d 465, or rearrange the bargaining unit because of an expected adverse effect on production, Allis-Chalmers Mfg. Co. v. Labor Board, 162 F.2d 435, or defend a refusal to bargain in good faith on the ground that unless the employer's view prevails dire consequences to the business will follow, Labor Board v. Harris, 200 F.2d 656, or refuse exclusive recognition to a union for fear that such recognition will bring reprisals from rival unions, McQuay-Norris Mfg. Co. v. Labor Board, 116 F.2d 748, *cert. denied*, 313 U.S. 565; . . . or discriminate in his business operations against employees of rival unions or without union affiliation solely in order to keep peace in the plant and avoid disruption of business, Wilson & Co., Inc., v. Labor Board, 123 F.2d 411. . . . Indeed, many employers

essentially is the teaching of the Court's prior cases dealing with this problem and, in our view, the Board did not depart from it.

The Board made a detailed assessment of superseniority and, to its experienced eye, such a plan had the following characteristics:

(1) Superseniority affects the tenure of all strikers whereas permanent replacement, proper under *Mackay*, affects only those who are, in actuality, replaced. It is one thing to say that a striker is subject to loss of his job at the strike's end but quite another to hold that in addition to the threat of replacement, all strikers will at best return to their jobs with seniority inferior to that of the replacements and of those who left the strike.

(2) A superseniority award necessarily operates to the detriment of those who participated in the strike as compared to nonstrikers.

(3) Superseniority made available to striking bargaining unit employees as well as to new employees is in effect offering individual benefits to the strikers to induce them to abandon the strike.

(4) Extending the benefits of superseniority to striking bargaining unit employees as well as to new replacements deals a crippling blow to the strike effort. At one stroke, those with low seniority have the opportunity to obtain the job security which ordinarily only long years of service can bring, while conversely, the accumulated seniority of older employees is seriously diluted. This combination of threat and promise could be expected to undermine the strikers' mutual interest and place the entire strike effort in jeopardy. The history of this strike and its virtual collapse following the announcement of the plan emphasize the grave repercussions of superseniority.

(5) Superseniority renders future bargaining difficult, if not impossible, for the collective bargaining representative. Unlike the replacement granted in *Mackay* which ceases to be an issue once the strike is over, the plan here creates a cleavage in the plant continuing long after the strike is ended. Employees are henceforth divided into two camps: those who stayed with the union and those who returned before the end of the strike and thereby gained extra seniority. This breach is reemphasized with each subsequent layoff and stands as an ever-present reminder of the dangers connected with striking and with union activities in general.

In the light of this analysis, superseniority by its very terms operates to discriminate between strikers and nonstrikers, both during and after a strike, and its destructive impact upon the strike and union activity cannot be

---

doubtless could conscientiously assert that their unfair labor practices were not malicious but were prompted by their best judgment as to the interests of their business. Such good-faith motive itself, however, has not been deemed an absolute defense to an unfair labor practice charge.

doubted. The origin of the plan, as respondent insists, may have been to keep production going and it may have been necessary to offer superseniority to attract replacements and induce union members to leave the strike. But if this is true, accomplishment of respondent's business purpose inexorably was contingent upon attracting sufficient replacements and strikers by offering preferential inducements to those who worked as opposed to those who struck. We think the Board was entitled to treat this case as involving conduct which carried its own indicia of intent and which is barred by the Act unless saved from illegality by an overriding business purpose justifying the invasion of union rights. The Board concluded that the business purpose asserted was insufficient to insulate the superseniority plan from the reach of §8(a)(1) and §8(a)(3), and we turn now to a review of that conclusion.

The Court of Appeals and respondent rely upon *Mackay* as precluding the result reached by the Board but we are not persuaded. Under the decision in that case an employer may operate his plant during a strike and at its conclusion need not discharge those who worked during the strike in order to make way for returning strikers. It may be, as the Court of Appeals said, that "such a replacement policy is obviously discriminatory and may tend to discourage union membership." But *Mackay* did not deal with superseniority, with its effects upon all strikers, whether replaced or not, or with its powerful impact upon a strike itself. Because the employer's interest must be deemed to outweigh the damage to concerted activities caused by permanently replacing strikers does not mean it also outweighs the far greater encroachment resulting from superseniority in addition to permanent replacement.

We have no intention of questioning the continuing vitality of the *Mackay* rule, but we are not prepared to extend it to the situation we have here. To do so would require us to set aside the Board's considered judgment that the Act and its underlying policy require, in the present context, giving more weight to the harm wrought by superseniority than to the interest of the employer in operating its plant during the strike by utilizing this particular means of attracting replacements. We find nothing in the Act or its legislative history to indicate that superseniority is necessarily an acceptable method of resisting the economic impact of a strike, nor do we find anything inconsistent with the result which the Board reached. On the contrary, these sources are wholly consistent with, and lend full support to, the conclusion of the Board.

. . . Section 13 makes clear that although the strike weapon is not an unqualified right, nothing in the Act except as specifically provided is to be construed to interfere with this means of redress, H.R. Conf. Rep. No. 510, 80th Cong., 1st Sess. 59, and §2(3) preserves to strikers their unfilled positions and status as employees during the pendency of a strike. S. Rep. No. 573, 74th Cong., 1st Sess. 6. This repeated solicitude for the right to strike is predicated upon the conclusion that a strike when legitimately employed is an economic weapon which in great measure implements and supports the principles of the collective bargaining system.

While Congress has from time to time revamped and redirected national labor policy, its concern for the integrity of the strike weapon has remained constant. Thus when Congress chose to qualify the use of the strike, it did so by prescribing the limits and conditions of the abridgement in exacting detail, e.g., §§8(b)(4), 8(d), by indicating the precise procedures to be followed in effecting the interference, e.g., §10(j), (k), (1), . . . and by preserving the positive command of §13 that the right to strike is to be given a generous interpretation within the scope of the Labor Act. The courts have likewise repeatedly recognized and effectuated the strong interest of federal labor policy in the legitimate use of the strike. . . .

Accordingly, in view of the deference paid the strike weapon by the federal labor laws and the devastating consequences upon it which the Board found was and would be precipitated by respondent's inherently discriminatory superseniority plan, we cannot say the Board erred in the balance which it struck here. Although the Board's decisions are by no means immune from attack in the courts as cases in this Court amply illustrate, e.g., Labor Board v. Babcock & Wilcox Co., 351 U.S. 105; Labor Board v. United Steelworkers, 357 U.S. 357; Labor Board v. Insurance Agents, 361 U.S. 477, its findings here are supported by substantial evidence, Universal Camera Corp. v. Labor Board, 340 U.S. 474, its explication is not inadequate, irrational or arbitrary, . . . and it did not exceed its powers or venture into an area barred by the statute. . . . The matter before the Board lay well within the mainstream of its duties. It was attempting to deal with an issue which Congress had placed in its hands and "where Congress has in the statute given the Board a question to answer, the courts will give respect to that answer." Labor Board v. Insurance Agents, supra, at 499. Here, as in other cases, we must recognize the Board's special function of applying the general provisions of the Act to the complexities of industrial life, . . . and of "[appraising] carefully the interests of both sides of any labor-management controversy in the diverse circumstances of particular cases" from its special understanding of "the actualities of industrial relations." Labor Board v. United Steelworkers, supra, at 362-363. "The ultimate problem is the balancing of the conflicting legitimate interests. The function of striking that balance to effectuate national labor policy is often a difficult and delicate responsibility, which the Congress committed primarily to the National Labor Relations Board, subject to limited judicial review." Labor Board v. Truck Drivers Union, 353 U.S. 87, 96.

Consequently, because the Board's judgment was that the claimed business purpose would not outweigh the necessary harm to employee rights — a judgment which we sustain — it could properly put aside evidence of respondent's motive and decline to find whether the conduct was or was not prompted by the claimed business purpose. We reverse the judgment of the Court of Appeals and remand the case to that court since its review was a limited one and it must now reach the remaining questions before it, including the propriety of the remedy which at least in part turns upon the Board's construction of the settlement agreement as being no barrier to an award not only of reinstatement but of backpay as well.

Reversed and remanded.

HARLAN, J., concurring. I agree with the Court that the Board's conclusions respecting this 20-year "superseniority" plan were justified without inquiry into the respondents' motives. However, I do not think that the same thing would necessarily be true in all circumstances, as for example with a plan providing for a much shorter period of extra seniority. Being unsure whether the Court intends to hold that the Board has power to outlaw *all* such plans, irrespective of the employer's motives and other circumstances, or only to sustain its action in the particular circumstances of *this* case, I concur in the judgment.

NOTES

1. Is the Board's distinguishing of *Mackay* convincing? If the Board's goal is to maintain a balance of power in an economic contest, is the Court's acquiescence consistent with its treatment of the Board's approach in the lockout cases below, *American Ship* and *Brown?* See also NLRB v. Insurance Agents Intl. Union, reproduced infra p. 830.

2. When an employer cannot secure replacements without offering them some form of superseniority, what is the basis for characterizing superseniority as "discriminatory" and as carrying its own indicia of intent (presumably malignant)?

3. At the conclusion of an economic strike, the company and the union entered into a collective agreement granting superseniority to replacements and to strikers who had abandoned the strike and returned to work; the grant was applicable to layoffs, preferred shifts, job transfers, and vacation times. Does *Erie Resistor* govern even though the superseniority plan was agreed to by the bargaining representative and did not come into existence until the strike had ended? The answer was "yes" in Great Lakes Carbon Corp. v. NLRB, 360 F.2d 19 (4th Cir. 1966). Do you agree?

NLRB v. Fleetwood Trailer Co., 389 U.S. 375 (1967). The employer, after a strike by about 50 percent of his work force, maintained operations at a temporarily reduced rate with the help of replacements. When the strike ended, the employer stated that reinstatement of the strikers was not then possible because of a production cutback. Two months later, the employer, in accordance with his continuing intention, increased production to the prestrike level. Although the strikers had made known their continuing desire for reinstatement, new employees were hired for jobs for which the strikers were qualified. Invoking *Erie Resistor* and NLRB v. Great Dane Trailers, infra p. 334, the Court upheld the Board's finding of violations of §§8(a)(1) and 8(a)(3), reasoning as follows: A striker remains an "employee" under §2(3) of the Act until he has secured regular and substantially equivalent employment. The failure to reinstate had discouraged employees from engaging in protected activity. Accordingly, a violation of §§8(a)(1) and 8(a)(3) was established unless the employer discharged his burden of showing legitimate and substantial business justification, such as the replacement of all strikers or the elimination of jobs by changes in production. Absent such a showing, the employer, without regard to his intent or antiunion motivation, had violated the Act. Harlan, J., concurring, also emphasized the statutory preservation of a striker's employee status. He reasoned that it was wholly inconsistent with that status to treat the temporary production cutback as the equivalent of job abolition or permanent replacement. Accordingly, he concluded that the employer had erred in treating the strikers as applicants for employment entitled only to nondiscriminatory consideration. Given the employer's disregard for his obligations to strikers, the problems of "employer motivation" or "legitimate business justification" were not, in the justice's view, involved in the case.

NOTES

1. In Laidlaw Corp., 171 N.L.R.B. 1366 (1968), *enforced*, 414 F.2d 99 (7th Cir. 1969), *cert. denied*, 397 U.S. 920 (1970), the Board, relying on *Fleetwood Trailer*, ruled that "economic strikers who unconditionally apply for reinstatement at a time when their positions are filled by permanent replacements: (1) remain employees; and (2) are entitled to full reinstatement upon the departure of replacements unless they have in the meantime acquired regular and substantially equivalent employment, or . . . the failure to offer full reinstatement was for legitimate and substantial business reasons." The *Laidlaw* doctrine has generated the following questions, among others: (a) For how long must an employer seek out replaced strikers

as vacancies arise? (b) May an employer require periodic notice of strikers' desires to maintain their recall rights? (c) May a strike settlement agreement validly limit those recall rights?

On these questions, see United Aircraft Corp., 192 N.L.R.B. 382 (1971), *enforced in part sub nom.*, IAM v. United Aircraft Corp., 534 F.2d 422 (2d Cir. 1975), *cert. denied*, 429 U.S. 825 (1976); Brooks Research & Mfg., Inc., 202 N.L.R.B. 634 (1973). For an argument against the waiving of *Laidlaw* rights, see Finkin, The Truncation of *Laidlaw* Rights by Collective Agreements, 3 Ind. Rel. L.J. 591 (1979).

2. An economic striker (J) returns to work during a strike. J has less seniority than S, another striker. Later S asks for reinstatement when the employer has no vacancies. Does the NLRA require reinstatement of S even though J would be displaced? Should it matter whether J returned to work as a permanent replacement for S or merely returned to his prestrike position? See Machinists, Dist. 8 v. J.L. Clark Co., 471 F.2d 694, 698 (7th Cir. 1972) (declaring that *Mackay* "was not intended to give an employer discretion as to which strikers he would reinstate"). In II & F Binch Co. v. NLRB, 456 F.2d 357 (2d Cir. 1972), the court ruled that strikers' reinstatement requests did not require an employer who had transferred his own employees into strikers' jobs to retransfer them to their former jobs, which were open, since the transferees would have quit or have been disaffected if retransferred. The court reserved the "different question" that would have been raised if an employee had transferred simply to accommodate the employer and would have cheerfully returned to his former position. See also George Banta Co. v. NLRB, 686 F.2d 10 (D.C. Cir. 1982), *cert. denied*, 103 S. Ct. 1770 (1983) (assigning each early-returning striker his prestrike job classification and wage rate regardless of company's production requirements or the work the employee performed during strike, while assigning full-term strikers reinstated at strike's end the remaining work at appropriate classification and wage rate, unlawfully burdens the right to strike within meaning of *Erie Resistor*).

3. In the event of a layoff following an economic strike in which permanent replacements were hired, does *Erie Resistor* mean that the replacements will be the first to be laid off? When recalls from layoff begin, do unreinstated strikers have a right of recall (i.e., reinstatement) ahead of laid-off replacements with less seniority? Ahead of laid-off reinstated strikers with less seniority?

In determining whether a striker's right to reinstatement is activated by layoff and recall, (a) Is the governing precedent *Mackay* or *Erie Resistor?* (b) Is the question as to what constitutes a *Laidlaw* "vacancy" or "job opening" important? See Giddings & Lewis, Inc. v. NLRB, 675 F.2d 926 (7th

Cir. 1982); Randall, Div. of Textron v. NLRB, 687 F.2d 1240 (8th Cir. 1982), *cert. denied*, 103 S. Ct. 1892 (1983); MCC Pacific Valves, 244 N.L.R.B. 931 (1979), *enforced in part*, 665 F.2d 1053 (9th Cir. 1981).

American Ship Building Co. v. NLRB
380 U.S. 300 (1965)

STEWART, J. . . . The question presented is that expressly reserved in Labor Board v. Truck Drivers Local Union, 353 U.S. 87, 93; namely, whether an employer commits an unfair labor practice under [§§8(a)(1) and 8(a)(3)] of the Act when he temporarily lays off or "locks out" his employees during a labor dispute to bring economic pressure in support of his bargaining position. . . .

The American Ship Building Company operates four shipyards on the Great Lakes — at Chicago, at Buffalo, and at Toledo and Lorain, Ohio. The company is primarily engaged in the repairing of ships, a highly seasonal business concentrated in the winter months when the freezing of the Great Lakes renders shipping impossible. What limited business is obtained during the shipping season is frequently such that speed of execution is of the utmost importance to minimize immobilization of the ships.

Since 1952 the employer has engaged in collective bargaining with a group of eight unions. . . . [T]he employer had contracted with the unions on five occasions, each agreement having been preceded by a strike. The particular chapter of the collective bargaining history with which we are concerned opened shortly before May 1, 1961, when the unions notified the company of their intention to seek modification of the current contract, due to expire on August 1.

. . . [O]n August 9, after extended negotiations, the parties separated without having resolved substantial differences on the central issues dividing them and without having specific plans for further attempts to resolve them — a situation which the trial examiner found was an impasse. Throughout the negotiations, the employer displayed anxiety as to the unions' strike plans, fearing that the unions would call a strike as soon as a ship entered the Chicago yard or delay negotiations into the winter to increase strike leverage. The union negotiator consistently insisted that it was his intention to reach an agreement without calling a strike; however, he did concede incomplete control over the workers — a fact borne out by the occurrence of a wildcat strike in February 1961. Because of the danger of an unauthorized strike and the consistent and deliberate use of strikes in prior negotiations, the employer remained apprehensive of the possibility of a work stoppage.

In light of the failure to reach an agreement and the lack of available work, the employer decided to lay off certain of its workers. On August 11 the employees received a notice which read: "Because of the labor dispute which has been unresolved since August 1, 1961, you are laid off until further notice." The Chicago yard was completely shut down and all but two employees laid off at the Toledo yard. A large force was retained at Lorain to complete a major piece of work there and the employees in the Buffalo yard were gradually laid off as miscellaneous tasks were completed. Negotiations were resumed shortly after these layoffs and continued for the following two months until a two-year contract was agreed upon on October 27. The employees were recalled the following day.

Upon claims filed by the unions, the General Counsel of the Board issued a complaint charging the employer with violations of §§8(a)(1), (3), and (5). The trial examiner found that although there had been no work in the Chicago yard since July 19, its closing was not due to lack of work. Despite similarly slack seasons in the past, the employer had for 17 years retained a nucleus crew to do maintenance work and remain ready to take such work as might come in. The examiner went on to find that the employer was reasonably apprehensive of a strike at some point. Although the unions had given assurances that there would be no strike, past bargaining history was thought to justify continuing apprehension that the unions would fail to make good their assurances. It was further found that the employer's primary purpose in locking out its employees was to avert peculiarly harmful economic consequences which would be imposed on it and its customers if a strike were called either while a ship was in the yard during the shipping season or later when the yard was fully occupied. The examiner concluded that the employer: "was economically justified and motivated in laying off its employees when it did, and that the fact that its judgment was partially colored by its intention to break the impasse which existed is immaterial in the peculiar and special circumstances of this case. Respondent, by its actions, therefore, did not violate §§8(a)(1), (3), and (5) of the Act."

A three-to-two majority of the Board rejected the trial examiner's conclusion that the employer could reasonably anticipate a strike. Finding the unions' assurances sufficient to dispel any such apprehension, the Board was able to find only one purpose underlying the layoff: a desire to bring economic pressure to secure prompt settlement of the dispute on favorable terms. The Board did not question the examiner's finding that the layoffs had not occurred until after a bargaining impasse had been reached. Nor did the Board remotely suggest that the company's decision to lay off its employees was based either on union hostility or on a desire to avoid its bargaining obligations under the Act. The Board concluded that the employer "by curtailing its operations at the South Chicago yard with the consequent layoff of the employees, coerced employees in the exercise of their bargaining rights in violation of §8(a)(1) of the Act, and discriminated against its employees within the meaning of §8(a)(3) of the Act." 142 N.L.R.B., at 1364-1365.

The difference between the Board and the trial examiner is thus a narrow one turning on their differing assessments of the circumstances which the employer claims gave it reason to anticipate a strike. Both the Board and the examiner assumed, within the established pattern of Board analysis, that if the employer had shut down its yard and laid off its workers solely for the purpose of bringing to bear economic pressure to break an impasse and secure more favorable contract terms, an unfair labor practice would be made out.

> The Board has held that, absent special circumstances, an employer may not during bargaining negotiations either threaten to lock out or lock out his employees in aid of his bargaining position. Such conduct the Board has held presumptively infringes upon the collective bargaining rights of employees in violation of §8(a)(1) and the lockout, with its consequent layoff, amounts to discrimination within the meaning of §8(a)(3). In addition, the Board has held that such conduct subjects the Union and the employees it represents to unwarranted and illegal pressure and creates an atmosphere in which the free opportunity for negotiation contemplated by §8(a)(5) does not exist.

Quaker State Oil Refining Corp., 121 N.L.R.B. 334, 337.

The Board has, however, exempted certain classes of lockouts from proscription. "Accordingly, it has held that lockouts are permissible to safeguard against . . . loss where there is reasonable ground for believing that a strike was threatened or imminent." Ibid. Developing this distinction in its rulings, the Board has approved lockouts designed to prevent seizure of a plant by a sitdown strike, Link-Belt Co., 26 N.L.R.B. 227; to forestall repetitive disruptions of an integrated operation by "quickie" strikes, International Shoe Co., 93 N.L.R.B. 907; to avoid spoilage of materials which would result from a sudden work stoppage, Duluth Bottling Assn., 48 N.L.R.B. 1335; and to avert the immobilization of automobiles brought in for repair, Betts Cadillac Olds, Inc., 96 N.L.R.B. 268. In another distinct class of cases the Board has sanctioned the use of the lockout by a multiemployer bargaining unit as a response to a whipsaw strike against one of its members. Buffalo Linen Supply Co., 109 N.L.R.B. 447, rev'd sub nom. Truck Drivers Union v. Labor Board, 231 F.2d 110, rev'd, 353 U.S. 87.[7]

---

[7] The Board's initial view was that such lockouts are unlawful. Morand Bros. Beverage Co., 91 N.L.R.B. 409; Davis Furniture Co., 100 N.L.R.B. 1016. The Board later embraced the contrary view, *Buffalo Linen Supply Co.*, supra, a position earlier taken by the Ninth Circuit in reversing the *Davis Furniture* case sub nom. Leonard v. Labor Board, 205 F.2d 355 (1953).

In analyzing the status of the bargaining lockout under §§8(a)(1) and (3) . . . , it is important that the practice with which we are here concerned be distinguished from other forms of temporary separation from employment. No one would deny that an employer is free to shut down his enterprise temporarily for reasons of renovation or lack of profitable work unrelated to his collective bargaining situation. Similarly, we put to one side cases where the Board has concluded on the basis of substantial evidence that the employer has used a lockout as a means to injure a labor organization or to evade his duty to bargain collectively. Hopwood Retinning Co., 4 N.L.R.B. 922; Scott Paper Box Co., 81 N.L.R.B. 535. What we are here concerned with is the use of a temporary layoff of employees solely as a means to bring economic pressure to bear in support of the employer's bargaining position, after an impasse has been reached. This is the only issue before us, and all that we decide.[8]

To establish that this practice is a violation of §8(a)(1), it must be shown that the employer has interfered with, restrained, or coerced employees in the exercise of some right protected by §7 of the Act. The Board's position is premised on the view that the lockout interferes with two of the rights guaranteed by §7: the right to bargain collectively and the right to strike. In the Board's view, the use of the lockout "punishes" employees for the presentation of and adherence to demands made by their bargaining representatives and so coerces them in the exercise of their right to bargain collectively. It is important to note that there is here no allegation that the employer used the lockout in the service of designs inimical to the process of collective bargaining. There was no evidence and no finding that the employer was hostile to its employees' banding together for collective bargaining or that the lockout was designed to discipline them for doing so. It is therefore inaccurate to say that the employer's intention was to destroy or frustrate the process of collective bargaining. What can be said is that it intended to resist the demands made of it in the negotiations and to secure modification of these demands. We cannot see that this intention is in any way inconsistent with the employees' rights to bargain collectively.

Moreover, there is no indication, either as a general matter or in this specific case, that the lockout will necessarily destroy the unions' capacity for effective and responsible representation. The unions here involved have vigorously represented the employees since 1952, and there is nothing to show that their ability to do so has been impaired by the lockout. Nor is the lockout one of those acts which are demonstrably so destructive of collective

---

[8]Contrary to the views expressed in a concurring opinion filed in this case, we intimate no view whatever as to the consequences which would follow had the employer replaced its employees with permanent replacements or even temporary help. Cf. Labor Board v. Mackay Radio & Telegraph Co., 304 U.S. 333.

bargaining that the Board need not inquire into employer motivation, as might be the case, for example, if an employer permanently discharged his unionized staff and replaced them with employees known to be possessed of a violent antiunion animus. Cf. Labor Board v. Erie Resistor Corp., 373 U.S. 221. The lockout may well dissuade employees from adhering to the position which they initially adopted in the bargaining, but the right to bargain collectively does not entail any "right" to insist on one's position free from economic disadvantage. Proper analysis of the problem demands that the simple intention to support the employer's bargaining position as to compensation and the like be distinguished from a hostility to the process of collective bargaining which could suffice to render a lockout unlawful. See Labor Board v. Brown, 380 U.S. 278.

The Board has taken the complementary view that the lockout interferes with the right to strike protected under §§7 and 13 of the Act in that it allows the employer to preempt the possibility of a strike and thus leave the union with "nothing to strike against." Insofar as this means that once employees are locked out, they are deprived of their right to call a strike against the employer because he is already shut down, the argument is wholly specious, for the work stoppage which would have been the object of the strike has in fact occurred. It is true that recognition of the lockout deprives the union of exclusive control of the timing and duration of work stoppages calculated to influence the result of collective bargaining negotiations, but there is nothing in the statute which would imply that the right to strike "carries with it" the right exclusively to determine the timing and duration of all work stoppages. The right to strike as commonly understood is the right to cease work — nothing more. No doubt a union's bargaining power would be enhanced if it possessed not only the simple right to strike but also the power exclusively to determine when work stoppages should occur, but the Act's provisions are not indefinitely elastic, content-free forms to be shaped in whatever manner the Board might think best conforms to the proper balance of bargaining power.

Thus, we cannot see that the employer's use of a lockout solely in support of a legitimate bargaining position is in any way inconsistent with the right to bargain collectively or with the right to strike. Accordingly, we conclude that on the basis of the findings made by the Board in this case, there has been no violation of §8(a)(1).

Section 8(a)(3) prohibits discrimination in regard to tenure or other conditions of employment to discourage union membership. Under the words of the statute there must be both discrimination and a resulting discouragement of union membership. It has long been established that a finding of violation under this section will normally turn on the employer's motivation. See Labor Board v. Brown, 380 U.S. 278; Radio Officers' Union v. Labor Board, 347 U.S. 17, 43. . . . Thus when the employer discharges a union leader who has broken shop rules, the problem posed is to determine whether the employer has acted purely in disinterested defense of shop discipline or has sought to damage employee organization. It is likely that the discharge will naturally tend to discourage union membership in both cases, because of the loss of union leadership and the employees' suspicion of the employer's true intention. But we have consistently construed the section to leave unscathed a wide range of employer actions taken to serve legitimate business interests in some significant fashion, even though the act committed may tend to discourage union membership. See, e.g., Labor Board v. Mackay Radio & Telegraph Co., 304 U.S. 333, 347. Such a construction of §8(a)(3) is essential if due protection is to be accorded the employer's right to manage his enterprise. See Textile Workers v. Darlington Mfg. Co., 380 U.S. 263.

This is not to deny that there are some practices which are inherently so prejudicial to union interests and so devoid of significant economic justification that no specific evidence of intent to discourage union membership or other antiunion animus is required. In some cases, it may be that the employer's conduct carries with it an inference of unlawful intention so compelling that it is justifiable to disbelieve the employer's protestations of innocent purpose. Radio Officers' Union v. Labor Board, supra, at 44-45; Labor Board v. Erie Resistor Corp., supra. Thus where many have broken a shop rule, but only union leaders have been discharged, the Board need not listen too long to the plea that shop discipline was simply being enforced. In other situations, we have described the process as the "far more delicate task . . . of weighing the interests of employees in concerted activity against the interest of the employer in operating his business in a particular manner. . . ." Labor Board v. Erie Resistor Corp., supra, at 229.

But this lockout does not fall into that category of cases arising under §8(a)(3) in which the Board may truncate its inquiry into employer motivation. As this case well shows, use of the lockout does not carry with it any necessary implication that the employer acted to discourage union membership or otherwise discriminate against union members as such. The purpose and effect of the lockout were only to bring pressure upon the union to modify its demands. Similarly, it does not appear that the natural tendency of the lockout is severely to discourage union membership while serving no significant employer interest. In fact, it is difficult to understand what tendency to discourage union membership or otherwise discriminate against union members was perceived by the Board. There is no claim that the employer locked out only union members, or locked out any employee simply because he was a union member; nor is it alleged that the employer conditioned rehiring upon resignation from the union. It is true that the employees suffered economic disadvantage because of their union's insistence on demands unacceptable to the employer, but this is also true of many steps which an employer may take during a bargaining conflict, and the existence of an arguable possibility that someone may feel himself discouraged in his union membership or discriminated against by reason of that membership cannot suffice to label them violations of §8(a)(3) absent some unlawful intention. The employer's permanent replacement of strikers ([*Mackay Radio*], supra), his unilateral imposition of terms (Labor Board v. Tex-Tan, Inc., 318 F.2d 472, 479-482), or his simple refusal to make a concession which would terminate a strike — all impose economic disadvantage during a bargaining conflict, but none is necessarily a violation of §8(a)(3).

To find a violation of §8(a)(3), then, the Board must find that the employer acted for a proscribed purpose. Indeed, the Board itself has always recognized that certain "operative" or "economic" purposes would justify a lockout. But the Board has erred in ruling that only these purposes will remove a lockout from the ambit of §8(a)(3), for that section requires an intention to discourage union membership or otherwise discriminate against the union. There was not the slightest evidence and there was no finding that the employer was actuated by a desire to discourage membership in the union as distinguished from a desire to affect the outcome of the particular negotiations in which it was involved. We recognize that the "union membership" which is not to be discouraged refers to more than the payment of dues and that measures taken to discourage participation in protected union activities may be found to come within the proscription. Radio Officers' Union v. Labor Board, supra, at 39-40. However, there is nothing in the Act which gives employees the right to insist on their contract demands, free from the sort of economic disadvantage which frequently attends bargaining disputes. Therefore, we conclude that where the intention proven is merely to bring about a settlement of a labor dispute on favorable terms, no violation of §8(a)(3) is shown.

The conclusions which we draw from analysis of §§8(a)(1) and (3) are consonant with what little of relevance can be drawn from the balance of the statute and its legislative history. In the original version of the Act, the predecessor of §8(a)(1) declared it an unfair labor practice "[t]o attempt, by interference, influence, restraint, favor, coercion, or lockout, or by any other means, to impair the right of employees guaranteed in section 4."[11] Promi-

---

[11] 1 Legislative History of the National Labor Relations Act, 1935, 3 (hereafter Leg. Hist.). Section 4 of the bill provided: "Employees shall have the right to organize and join labor organizations, and to engage in concerted activities, either in labor organizations or

nent in the criticism leveled at the bill in the Senate Committee hearings was the charge that it did not accord even-handed treatment to employers and employees because it prohibited the lockout while protecting the strike. In the face of such criticism, the Committee added a provision prohibiting employee interference with employer bargaining activities[13] and deleted the reference to the lockout.[14] A plausible inference to be drawn from this history is that the language was deleted to mollify those who saw in the bill an inequitable denial of resort to the lockout, and to remove any language which might give rise to fears that the lockout was being proscribed per se. It is in any event clear that the Committee was concerned with the status of the lockout and that the bill, as reported and as finally enacted, contained no prohibition on the use of the lockout as such.

Although neither §8(a)(1) nor §8(a)(3) refers specifically to the lockout, various other provisions of the [Act] do refer to the lockout, and these references can be interpreted as a recognition of the legitimacy of the device as a means of applying economic pressure in support of bargaining positions. Thus [§8(d)(4)] prohibits the use of a strike or lockout unless requisite notice procedures have been complied with; [§203(c) of Title II of Taft-Hartley] directs the Federal Mediation and Conciliation Service to seek voluntary resolution of labor disputes without resort to strikes or lockouts; and [§§206, 207 of that Title] authorize procedures whereby the President can institute a board of inquiry to forestall certain strikes or lockouts. The correlative use of the terms "strike" and "lockout" in these sections contemplates that lockouts will be used in the bargaining process in some fashion. This is not to say that these provisions serve to define the permissible scope of a lockout by an employer. That, in the context of the present case, is a question ultimately to be resolved by analysis of §§8(a)(1) and (3).

The Board has justified its ruling in this case and its general approach to the legality of lockouts on the basis of its special competence to weigh the competing interests of employers and employees and to accommodate these interests according to its expert judgment. "The Board has reasonably concluded that the availability of such a weapon would so substantially tip the scales in the employer's favor as to defeat the Congressional purpose of placing employees on a par with their adversary at the bargaining table." To buttress its decision as to the balance struck in this particular case, the Board

otherwise, for the purposes of organizing and bargaining collectively through representatives of their own choosing or for other purposes of mutual aid or protection." Ibid.

[13] S. 2926, §3(2): "It shall be an unfair labor practice [f]or employees to attempt, by interference or coercion, to impair the exercise by employers of the right to join or form employer organizations and to designate representatives of their own choosing for the purpose of collective bargaining." 1 Leg. Hist. 1087.

[14] S. 2926, §3(1). . . .

points out that the employer has been given other weapons to counterbalance the employees' power of strike. The employer may permanently replace workers who have gone out on strike, or, by stockpiling and subcontracting, maintain his commercial operations while the strikers bear the economic brunt of the work stoppage. Similarly, the employer can institute unilaterally the working conditions which he desires once his contract with the union has expired. Given these economic weapons, it is argued, the employer has been adequately equipped with tools of economic self-help.

There is of course no question that the Board is entitled to the greatest deference in recognition of its special competence in dealing with labor problems. In many areas its evaluation of the competing interests of employer and employee should unquestionably be given conclusive effect in determining the application of §§8(a)(1), (3), and (5). However, we think that the Board construes its functions too expansively when it claims general authority to define national labor policy by balancing the competing interests of labor and management.

While a primary purpose of the [NLRA] was to redress the perceived imbalance of economic power between labor and management, it sought to accomplish that result by conferring certain affirmative rights on employees and by placing certain enumerated restrictions on the activities of employers. . . . The central purpose of these provisions was to protect employee self-organization and the process of collective bargaining from disruptive interferences by employers. Having protected employee organization in countervailance to the employers' bargaining power, and having established a system of collective bargaining whereby the newly coequal adversaries might resolve their disputes, the Act also contemplated resort to economic weapons should more peaceful measures not avail. Sections 8(a)(1) and (3) do not give the Board a general authority to assess the relative economic power of the adversaries in the bargaining process and to deny weapons to one party or the other because of its assessment of that party's bargaining power. Labor Board v. Brown, 380 U.S. 278. In this case the Board has, in essence, denied the use of the bargaining lockout to the employer because of its conviction that use of this device would give the employer "too much power." In so doing, the Board has stretched §§8(a)(1) and (3) far beyond their functions of protecting the rights of employee organization and collective bargaining. What we have recently said in a closely related context is equally applicable here:

> [W]hen the Board moves in this area . . . it is functioning as an arbiter of the sort of economic weapons the parties can use in seeking to gain acceptance of their bargaining demands. It has sought to introduce some standard of properly "balanced" bargaining power, or some new distinction of justifiable

and unjustifiable, proper and "abusive" economic weapons into . . . the Act. . . . We have expressed our belief that this amounts to the Board's entrance into the substantive aspects of the bargaining process to an extent Congress has not countenanced.

Labor Board v. Insurance Agents' International Union, 361 U.S. 477, 497-498.

We are unable to find that any fair construction of the provisions relied on by the Board in this case can support its finding of an unfair labor practice. Indeed, the role assumed by the Board in this area is fundamentally inconsistent with the structure of the Act and the function of the sections relied upon. The deference owed to an expert tribunal cannot be allowed to slip into a judicial inertia which results in the unauthorized assumption by an agency of major policy decisions properly made by Congress. Accordingly, we hold that an employer violates neither §8(a)(1) nor §8(a)(3) when, after a bargaining impasse has been reached, he temporarily shuts down his plant and lays off his employees for the sole purpose of bringing economic pressure to bear in support of his legitimate bargaining position.

Reversed.

[WHITE, J., joined in reversing the Board on the ground that the closing of the shipyard had resulted from the lack of repair work caused by the bargaining deadlock and the fear of a strike rather than from an effort to exert economic pressure against the union. After urging that the Court had unnecessarily reached the issue of the validity of bargaining lockouts, he expressed his dissent from the Court's general position.]

. . . [T]he legal status of the bargaining lockout, as the Court indicated in Labor Board v. Truck Drivers Union, 353 U.S. 87, 96, is to be determined by "the balancing of the conflicting legitimate interests."

The Board has balanced these interests here — the value of the lockout as an economic weapon against its impact on protected concerted activities, including the right to strike, for which the Act has special solicitude, Labor Board v. Erie Resistor Corp., 373 U.S. 221, 234 — and has determined that the employer's interest in obtaining a bargaining victory does not outweigh the damaging consequences of the lockout. It determined that for an employer to deprive employees of their livelihood because of demands made by their representatives and in order to compel submission to the employer's demands, coerces employees in their exercise of the right to bargain collectively and discourages resort to that right. And this interferes with the right to strike, sharply reducing the effectiveness of that weapon and denying the union control over the timing of the economic contest. The Court rejects this reasoning on the ground that the lockout is not conduct "demonstrably so destructive of collective bargaining that the Board need not inquire into employer motivation." . . . Since the employer's true motive is to bring about settlement of the dispute on favorable terms, there can be no substantial discouragement of union membership or interference with concerted activities. And the right to strike is only the right to cease work, which the lockout only encourages rather than displaces.

This tour de force denies the Board's assessment of the impact on employee rights and this truncated definition of the right to strike, nowhere supported in the Act, is unprecedented. Until today the employer's true motive or sole purpose has not always been determinative of the impact on employee rights. Republic Aviation Corp. v. Labor Board, 324 U.S. 793; Radio Officers' Union v. Labor Board, 347 U.S. 17; Labor Board v. Truck Drivers Union, 353 U.S. 87; Labor Board v. Erie Resistor Corp., 373 U.S. 221; Labor Board v. Burnup & Sims, Inc., 379 U.S. 21. The importance of the employer's right to hire replacements to continue operations, or of his right to fire employees he has good reason to believe are guilty of gross misconduct was not doubted in *Erie Resistor* and *Burnup & Sims*. Nonetheless the Board was upheld in its determination that the award of superseniority to strike replacements and discharge of the suspected employee were unfair labor practices. Of course, such conduct is taken in the pursuit of legitimate business ends, but nonetheless the "conduct *does* speak for itself . . . it carries with it unavoidable consequences which the employer not only foresaw but which he must have intended." *Erie Resistor*, 373 U.S., at 228. I would have thought it apparent that loss of jobs for an indefinite period, and the threatened loss of jobs, which the Court's decision assuredly sanctions, cf. Textile Workers Union v. Darlington Mfg. Co., decided today, ante, at 274, n.20, because of the union's negotiating activity, itself protected conduct under §7, hardly encourage affiliation with a union.

If the Court means what it says today, an employer may not only lock out after impasse consistent with §§8(a)(1) and (3), but replace his locked-out employees with temporary help, cf. Labor Board v. Brown [p. 273, infra] or perhaps permanent replacements, and also lock out long before an impasse is reached. Maintaining operations during a labor dispute is at least equally as important an interest as achieving a bargaining victory, see [Labor Board v. Mackay Radio], and a shutdown during or before negotiations advances an employer's bargaining position as much as a lockout after impasse. And the hiring of replacements is wholly consistent with the employer's intent "to resist the demands made of it in the negotiations and to secure modification of these demands." I would also assume that under §§8(a)(1) and (3) he may lock out for the sole purpose of resisting the union's assertion of grievances under a collective bargaining contract, absent a no-lockout clause. Given these legitimate business purposes, there is no antiunion motivation, and absent such motivation, a lockout cannot be deemed destructive of employee rights. "[I]nquiry into employer motivation" may not be truncated. "Proper analysis of the problem demands that the simple intention to support the employer's bargaining position as to compensation and the like be distinguished from a hostility to the process of collective bargaining which could suffice to render a lockout unlawful." Ante, at 309. . . . The balance and accommodation of "conflicting legitimate interests" in labor relations does not admit of a simple solution and a myopic focus on the true intent or motive of the employer has not been the determinative standard of the Board or this Court. As the Court points out, there are things an employer may do for business reasons which are inconsistent with a rigid or literal interpretation of employee rights under the Act, such as the right to hire strike replacements. [Labor Board v. Mackay Radio]. But there are just as clearly others which he may not. *Republic Aviation*, 324 U.S. 793; *Erie Resistor*, 373 U.S. 221; *Burnup & Sims*, 379 U.S. 21. A literal interpretation will not suffice to reconcile these cases, nor to justify the result in the present case. For in saying an employer may lock out all his employees, the Court fully ignores the most explicit statutory right of employees "to refrain from any or all [concerted] activities." Nor can these cases be explained by the Court's test that employer conduct is not proscribed unless it is "inherently so prejudicial to union interests and so devoid of significant economic justification," ante, at 311, that true motivation need not be independently shown. The test is clearly one of choosing among several motivations or purposes and weighing the respective interests of employers and employees. And I think that is the standard the Court applies to the bargaining lockout in this case, but without heeding the fact the balance is for the Board to strike in the first instance.

. . . [I]nsistence on a reasoned decision is a foremost function of judicial review, especially where conflicting significant interests are sought to be accommodated. Compare Securities & Exchange Commn. v. Chenery Corp., 318 U.S. 80, with Securities & Exchange Commn. v. Chenery Corp., 332 U.S. 194. But this function is not to reject the Board's reasoned assessment of the impact of a particular economic weapon on employee rights. It is certainly not to restrike the balance which the Board has reached.

[Goldberg, J., with whom Warren, C. J., joined, concurred in result on the ground that the lockout had been permissible on the basis of the Board's settled doctrine permitting lockouts designed to avoid unusual operational problems or economic loss where there is reasonable ground for believing that a strike is threatened or imminent. The opinion then criticized the Court's treatment of the significance of antiunion motivation or its absence as contrary to past decisions and emphasized the desirability of weighing legitimate conflicting interests in variant lockout situations, rather than announcing a simple, general formula.]

NOTES

1. Is there any basis in the language of the statute, particularly §8(d), for holding an "impasse" to be a prerequisite for the legality of a bargaining lockout while exempting strikes from that requirement? If not, what considerations bear on that question? In Darling & Co., 171 N.L.R.B. 801 (1968), the Board (4 to 1) ruled that the absence of an impasse, although a factor in determining whether a lockout was unlawfully motivated, does not per se illegalize a lockout and upheld the disputed lockout on the ground that the strike history of the bargaining unit justified employer concern about a strike timed to occur during his busy season. This decision was affirmed in Lane v. NLRB, 418 F.2d 1208 (D.C. Cir. 1969), which emphasized that lockouts must be examined under the principles of *Great Dane Trailers*; it noted that the union was "strong" and had been recognized for a substantial period, and referred to the admonition of Goldberg, J., in *American Ship*, against definitive formulas. In the light of the remedies for unlawful lockouts, consider the difficulties raised by the approach of the circuit court.

2. See generally Bernhardt, Lockouts: An Analysis of Board and Court Decisions Since *Brown* and *American Ship*, 57 Cornell L. Rev. 211 (1972); Baird, Lockout Law: The Supreme Court and the NLRB, 38 Geo. Wash. L. Rev. 396 (1970); Oberer, Lockouts and the Law: The Impact of *American Ship Building* and *Brown Food*, 51 Cornell L.Q. 193 (1966); Meltzer, The Lockout Cases, 1965 Sup. Ct. Rev. 87.

NLRB v. Brown[g]
380 U.S. 278 (1965)

[The union, after a deadlock in contract negotiations, struck Food Jet, Inc., a member of a multiemployer bargaining unit that for many years had bargained with the union. During the strike, the unstruck members of the unit imposed a lockout. Despite the strike, Food Jet continued to operate using supervisors and other temporary replacements. By similar expedients,

---

[g] [It would be useful at this point to read the materials, pp. 410-412 infra, dealing with the prerequisites for the creation of multiemployer units. — Eds.]

the other employers, after their lockout, also continued to operate but advised the union and their regular employees that the latter would be recalled when the strike ended. When the parties reached an agreement, which retained the union-shop clause of the prior agreement, all regular employees were reinstated. The Board, although upholding the struck employer's use of replacements, condemned their use by the unstruck employers as a violation of §§8(a)(1) and 8(a)(3). Brown Food Stores, 137 N.L.R.B. 73, 76 (1962) (two members dissenting). The Tenth Circuit denied enforcement (319 F.2d 7 (1963)) and was affirmed by the Supreme Court.]

BRENNAN, J. . . . The Board's decision does not rest upon independent evidence that the respondents acted either out of hostility toward the Local or in reprisal for the whipsaw strike. It rests upon the Board's appraisal that the respondents' conduct carried its own indicia of unlawful intent, thereby establishing, without more, that the conduct constituted an unfair labor practice. It was disagreement with this appraisal, which we share, that led the Court of Appeals to refuse to enforce the Board's order. . . .

In the circumstances of this case, we do not see how the continued operations of respondents and their use of temporary replacements imply hostile motivation any more than the lockout itself; nor do we see how they are inherently more destructive of employee rights. Rather, the compelling inference is that this was all part and parcel of respondents' defensive measure to preserve the multiemployer group in the face of the whipsaw strike. Since Food Jet legitimately continued business operations, it is only reasonable to regard respondents' action as evincing concern that the integrity of the employer group was threatened unless they also managed to stay open for business during the lockout. For with Food Jet open for business and respondents' stores closed, the prospect that the whipsaw strike would succeed in breaking up the employer association was not at all fanciful. The retail food industry is very competitive and repetitive patronage is highly important. Faced with the prospect of a loss of patronage to Food Jet, it is logical that respondents should have been concerned that one or more of their number might bolt the group and come to terms with the Local, thus destroying the common front essential to multiemployer bargaining. The Court of Appeals correctly pictured the respondents' dilemma in saying, "If . . . the struck employer does choose to operate with replacements and the other employers cannot replace after lockout, the economic advantage passes to the struck member, the non-struck members are deterred in exercising the defensive lockout, and the whipsaw strike . . . enjoys an almost inescapable prospect of success." 319 F.2d, at 11. Clearly respondents' continued operations with the use of temporary replacements following the lockout were wholly consistent with a legitimate business purpose.

Nor are we persuaded by the Board's argument that justification for the inference of hostile motivation appears in the respondents' use of temporary employees rather than some of the regular employees. It is not common-sense, we think, to say that the regular employees were "willing to work at the employers' terms." 137 N.L.R.B., at 76. It seems probable that this "willing-ness" was motivated as much by their understandable desire to further the objective of the whipsaw strike — to break through the employers' united front by forcing Food Jet to accept the Local's terms — as it was by a desire to work for the employers under the existing unacceptable terms. As the Board's dissenting members put it, "These employees are willing only to receive wages while their brethren in the rest of the association-wide unit are exerting whipsaw pressure on one employer to gain benefits that will ultimately accrue to all employees in the association-wide unit, including those here locked out." 137 N.L.R.B., at 78. Moreover, the course of action to which the Board would limit the respondents would force them into the position of aiding and abetting the success of the whipsaw strike and consequently would render "largely illusory," 137 N.L.R.B., at 78-79, the right of lockout recognized by *Buffalo Linen*; the right would be meaningless if barred to non-struck stores that find it necessary to operate because the struck store does so.

. . . Continued operations with the use of temporary replacements may result in the failure of the whipsaw strike, but this does not mean that the employers' conduct is demonstrably so destructive of employee rights and so devoid of significant service to any legitimate business end that it cannot be tolerated consistently with the Act. Certainly then, in the absence of eviden-tiary findings of hostile motive, there is no support for the conclusion that respondents violated §8(a)(1).

Nor does the record show any basis for concluding that respondents violated §8(a)(3). Under that section both discrimination and a resulting discouragement of union membership are necessary, but the added element of unlawful intent is also required. In *Buffalo Linen* itself the employers treated the locked-out employees less favorably because of their union mem-bership, and this may have tended to discourage continued membership, but we rejected the notion that the use of the lockout violated the statute. The discriminatory act is not by itself unlawful unless intended to prejudice the employees' position because of their membership in the union; some ele-ment of antiunion animus is necessary. See Radio Officers' Union v. Labor Board, 347 U.S. 17, 42-44. . . . We have determined that the "real mo-tive" of the employer in an alleged §8(a)(3) violation is decisive; if any doubt still persisted, we laid it to rest in Radio Officers' Union v. Labor Board, supra, where we concluded that Congress clearly intended the employer's purpose in discriminating to be controlling. Id., at 44. See also Textile Workers v. Darlington Mfg. Co., ante, at 275, 276; American Ship Building Co. v. Labor Board, post, at 311-313; Local 357, International Brotherhood of Teamsters v. Labor Board, 365 U.S. 667, 674-676.

We recognize that, analogous to the determination of unfair practices under §8(a)(1), when an employer practice is inherently destructive of employee rights and is not justified by the service of important business ends, no specific evidence of intent to discourage union membership is necessary to establish a violation of §8(a)(3). This principle, we have said, is "but an application of the common-law rule that a man is held to intend the foreseeable consequences of his conduct." Radio Officers' Union v. Labor Board, supra, at 45. For example, in Labor Board v. Erie Resistor Corp., supra, we held that an employer's action in awarding superseniority to employees who worked during a strike was discriminatory conduct that carried with it its own indicia of improper intent. The only reasonable inference that could be drawn by the Board from the award of superseniority — balancing the prejudicial effect upon the employees against any asserted business purpose — was that it was directed against the striking employees because of their union membership; conduct so inherently destructive of employee interests could not be saved from illegality by an asserted overriding business purpose pursued in good faith. But where, as here, the tendency to discourage union membership is comparatively slight, and the employers' conduct is reasonably adapted to achieve legitimate business ends or to deal with business exigencies, we enter into an area where the improper motivation of the employers must be established by independent evidence. When so established, antiunion motivation will convert an otherwise ordinary business act into an unfair labor practice. Labor Board v. Erie Resistor Corp., supra, at 227, and cases there cited.

. . . While the use of temporary nonunion personnel in preference to the locked-out union members is discriminatory, we think that any resulting tendency to discourage union membership is comparatively remote, and that this use of temporary personnel constitutes a measure reasonably adapted to the effectuation of a legitimate business end. Here discontent on the part of the Local's membership in all likelihood is attributable largely to the fact that the membership was locked out as the result of the Local's whipsaw stratagem. But the lockout itself is concededly within the rule of *Buffalo Linen.* We think that the added dissatisfaction, with its resultant pressure on membership, attributable to the fact that the nonstruck employers remain in business with temporary replacements is comparatively insubstantial. . . .

When the resulting harm to employee rights is thus comparatively slight, and a substantial and legitimate business end is served, the employers' conduct is prima facie lawful. Under these circumstances the finding of an unfair labor practice under §8(a)(3) requires a showing of improper subjective intent. Here, there is no assertion by either the union or the Board that the respondents were motivated by antiunion animus, nor is there any evidence that this was the case.

[Goldberg, J., joined by Warren, C. J., filed a concurring opinion; White, J., dissented.]

NOTES

1. Lockouts, although arising from the common interests of employers, may go beyond the scope of an established multiemployer unit and may occur before an impasse confronts the employer(s) taking lockout action. For example, the Detroit Evening News and the Detroit Free Press have bargained jointly with most unions, but separately, though concurrently, with the Teamsters, whose agreements with both papers have had a common expiration date. In October 1967 the Teamsters presented both employers with demands for new agreements. Subsequently, both employers learned that ten of the eighteen issues under discussion with the Teamsters were common to both negotiations, and that three of the common issues were "vital." The employers agreed that they would not yield on any of those three issues, that a strike against one on those issues would be followed by a lockout, and that this agreement for unified action should not be disclosed to the union. The Teamsters struck the Free Press and immediately thereafter indicated to the News that it would be struck if it failed to agree to the three vital demands which had been rejected by the Free Press. The Teamsters representative had discussed a further meeting with the News representative, who, after a delay of several days, stated that he could not see any benefit in setting up another meeting. The next day, the News ceased publication. After the lockout had continued for three days, both papers settled with the Teamsters. Was the News' lockout an unfair labor practice? What factors should be considered in determining the legality of such "supportive lockouts"? See The Evening News Assn., 166 N.L.R.B. 219 (1967), *aff'd sub nom.* Newspaper Drivers v. NLRB, 404 F.2d 1159 (6th Cir. 1968), *cert. denied*, 395 U.S. 923 (1969).

2. Employers in various industries have agreed to "mutual aid pacts," which call for nonstruck employers to pay to struck employers a share of the increased revenues accruing to the former because of a strike or which provide for payments to the struck firm out of "insurance funds" contributed

by the participating employers. In Operating Engineers Local 12, 187 N.L.R.B. 430 (1970), the NLRB held that employer strike insurance programs are not subjects of mandatory bargaining and that a union's insistence on the elimination of such insurance violated §8(b)(3). Cf. Air Line Pilots Assn. v. CAB, 502 F.2d 453 (D.C. Cir. 1974), cert. denied, 420 U.S. 972 (1976), where the court upheld CAB approval of the airlines' mutual aid pact, as consistent with the national policy permitting parties to marshall economic resources to resolve labor disputes. Issues raised by such arrangements are discussed in Unterberger & Koziara, The Demise of Airline Strike Insurance, 34 Indus. & Lab. Rel. Rev. 82 (1980); Levine & Helly, The Airlines' Mutual Aid Pact: A Deterrent to Collective Bargaining, 28 Lab. L.J. 44 (1977); Comment, 60 Colum. L. Rev. 205 (1960).

3. In American Cyanamid Co. v. NLRB, 592 F.2d 356 (7th Cir. 1979), the court upheld the Board's finding that the company had violated the Act by rejecting strikers' unconditional back-to-work offers, made after the union had rejected the company's request for both a one-year ban on strikes and the union's waiver of other statutory rights. The court concluded that the company had failed to substantiate its claim that the back-to-work offer had not been in good faith but was a "Trojan Horse" — a claim based on the strike's length and violence, the importance of the struck plant's operation to the rest of the company, and the danger and costliness of even a partial shutdown. The court also rejected the company's contention that its right to lockout implied the right to impose reasonable conditions on ending any lockout. Although finding "some appeal" in this "novel" claim, the court referred to the difficulties it posed under the court's own holding in Inland Trucking Co. v. NLRB (see infra p. 342), which had condemned the use of temporary replacements following an offensive lockout. The court noted that because the strikers here had been engaged in an unfair labor strike their unconditional back-to-work offer had entitled them to reinstatement. Hence, there was no need to decide "under what circumstances an employer might be able to convert an economic strike to a permissible lockout or what conditions, if any, short of reaching agreement on the economic issues, it might attach to ending such a lockout."

What considerations bear on the resolution of those questions? Cf. Blue Grass Provisions Co. v. NLRB, 636 F.2d 1127 (6th Cir. 1980) (company's pre-impasse subcontracting of unit work in violation of §8(a)(5) is not made lawful by characterizing conduct as "lockout"; company failed to demonstrate business interests sufficient to justify impact on employee rights of even a lockout). In American Cyanamid, the back pay award settlement was approximately $10,500,000, plus $1,400,000 in interest. Daily Lab. Rep. No. 247, Dec. 22, 1979, p. A-8. See also Inter-Collegiate Press, infra p. 341.

NLRB v. Great Dane Trailers
388 U.S. 26 (1967)

WARREN, C. J. . . . The issue here is whether, in the absence of proof of an antiunion motivation, an employer may be held to have violated §§8(a)(3) and (1) . . . when it refused to pay striking employees vacation benefits accrued under a terminated collective bargaining agreement while it announced an intention to pay such benefits to striker replacements, returning strikers, and nonstrikers who had been at work on a certain date during the strike.

The respondent company and the union entered into a collective bargaining agreement which was effective by its terms until March 31, 1963. The agreement contained a commitment by the company to pay vacation benefits to employees who met certain enumerated qualifications. In essence, the company agreed to pay specified vacation benefits to employees who, during the preceding year, had worked at least 1,525 hours. It was also provided that, in the case of a "lay-off, termination or quitting," employees who had served more than 60 days during the year would be entitled to prorata shares of their vacation benefits. Benefits were to be paid on the Friday nearest July 1 of each year.

The agreement was temporarily extended beyond its termination date, but on April 30, 1963, the union gave the required 15 days' notice of intention to strike over issues which remained unsettled at the bargaining table. Accordingly, on May 16, 1963, approximately 350 of the company's 400 employees commenced a strike which lasted until December 26, 1963. The company continued to operate during the strike, using nonstrikers, persons hired as replacements for strikers, and some original strikers who had later abandoned the strike and returned to work.[4] On July 12, 1963, a number of the strikers demanded their accrued vacation pay from the company. The company rejected this demand, basing its response on the assertion that all contractual obligations had been terminated by the strike and, therefore, none of the company's employees had a right to vacation pay. Shortly thereafter, however, the company announced that it would grant vacation pay — in the amounts and subject to the conditions set out in the expired agreement — to all employees who had reported for work on July 1, 1963. The company denied that these payments were founded on the agreement and stated that they merely reflected a new "policy" which had been unilaterally adopted.

---

[4] All strikers had been replaced by October 8, 1963. After their replacement, some strikers were rehired by the company, apparently as new employees.

. . . [T]he Court of Appeals held that, although discrimination between striking and nonstriking employees had been proved, the Board's
conclusion that the company had committed an unfair labor practice was not
well-founded inasmuch as there had been no affirmative showing of an
unlawful motivation to discourage union membership or to interfere with the
exercise of protected rights. Despite the fact that the company itself had not
introduced evidence of a legitimate business purpose underlying its discriminatory action, the Court of Appeals speculated that it might have been
motivated by a desire "(1) to reduce expenses; (2) to encourage longer tenure
among present employees; or (3) to discourage early leaves immediately
before vacation periods." Believing that the possibility of the existence of
such motives was sufficient to overcome the inference of an improper motive
which flowed from the conduct itself, the court denied enforcement of the
order. 363 F.2d 130 (1966). We granted certiorari to determine whether the
treatment of the motivation issue by the Court of Appeals was consistent with
recent decisions of this Court.

The unfair labor practice charged here is grounded primarily in
§8(a)(3)[h] which requires specifically that the Board find a discrimination and
a resulting discouragement of union membership. . . . There is little question but that the result of the company's refusal to pay vacation benefits to
strikers was discrimination in its simplest form. . . . Some employees who
met the conditions specified in the expired collective bargaining agreement
were paid accrued vacation benefits in the amounts set forth in that agreement, while other employees who also met the conditions but who had
engaged in protected concerted activity were denied such benefits. Similarly,
there can be no doubt but that the discrimination was capable of discouraging
membership in a labor organization within the meaning of the statute.
Discouraging membership in a labor organization "includes discouraging
participation in concerted activities . . . such as a legitimate strike." Labor
Board v. Erie Resistor Corp., 373 U.S. 221, 233 (1963). The act of paying
accrued benefits to one group of employees while announcing the extinction
of the same benefits for another group of employees who are distinguishable

---

[h] [In Knuth Bros., 229 N.L.R.B. 1204 (1977), *enforced*, 584 F.2d 813 (7th Cir. 1978),
the employer denied vacation benefits to economic strikers who had been replaced before the
date when benefits for the previous year accrued under the established vacation policy. The
Board concluded that there was no basis for finding a §8(a)(3) violation since nonstrikers
terminated before the accrual date were also denied pro rata payments. Nevertheless, the
Board (2 to 1) found a violation of §8(a)(1), suggesting that although replaced strikers were
not denied vacation benefits "because" of their protected activities, denial was "a consequence of" such activities. The dissenter invoked *Great Dane*. Does the Board's distinction
involve a genuine difference? — EDS.]

only by their participation in protected concerted activity surely may have a discouraging effect on either present or future concerted activity.

But inquiry under §8(a)(3) does not usually stop at this point. The statutory language "discrimination . . . to . . . discourage" means that the finding of a violation normally turns on whether the discriminatory conduct was motivated by an antiunion purpose. American Ship Building Co. v. Labor Board, 380 U.S. 300 (1965). It was upon the motivation element that the Court of Appeals based its decision not to grant enforcement, and it is to that element which we now turn. In three recent opinions we considered employer motivation in the context of asserted §8(a)(3) violations. American Ship Building Co. v. Labor Board, supra; Labor Board v. Brown, 380 U.S. 278 (1965); and Labor Board v. Erie Resistor Corp., supra. We noted in *Erie Resistor*, at 227, that proof of an antiunion motivation may make unlawful certain employer conduct which would in other circumstances be lawful. Some conduct, however, is so "inherently destructive of employee interests" that it may be deemed proscribed without need for proof of an underlying improper motive. Labor Board v. Brown, at 287; American Ship Building Co. v. Labor Board, at 311. That is, some conduct carries with it "unavoidable consequences which the employer not only foresaw but which he must have intended" and thus bears "its own indicia of intent." Labor Board v. Erie Resistor Corp., at 228, 231. If the conduct in question falls within this "inherently destructive" category, the employer has the burden of explaining away, justifying or characterizing "his actions as something different than they appear on their face," and if he fails, "an unfair labor practice charge is made out." Id., at 228. And even if the employer does come forward with counter explanations for his conduct in this situation, the Board may nevertheless draw an inference of improper motive from the conduct itself and exercise its duty to strike the proper balance between the asserted business justifications and the invasion of employee rights in light of the Act and its policy. Id., at 229. On the other hand, when "the resulting harm to employee rights is . . . comparatively slight, and a substantial and legitimate business end is served, the employers' conduct is prima facie lawful," and an affirmative showing of improper motivation must be made. Labor Board v. Brown, at 289; American Ship Building Co. v. Labor Board, at 311-313.

From this review of our recent decisions, several principles of controlling importance here can be distilled. First, if it can reasonably be concluded that the employer's discriminatory conduct was "inherently destructive" of important employee rights, no proof of an antiunion motivation is needed and the Board can find an unfair labor practice even if the employer introduces evidence that the conduct was motivated by business considerations.

Second, if the adverse effect of the discriminatory conduct on employee rights is "comparatively slight," an antiunion motivation must be proved to sustain the charge *if* the employer has come forward with evidence of legitimate and substantial business justifications for the conduct. Thus, in either situation, once it has been proved that the employer engaged in discriminatory conduct which could have adversely affected employee rights to *some* extent, the burden is upon the employer to establish that he was motivated by legitimate objectives since proof of motivation is most accessible to him.

Applying the principles to this case then, it is not necessary for us to decide the degree to which the challenged conduct might have affected employee rights. As the Court of Appeals correctly noted, the company came forward with no evidence of legitimate motives for its discriminatory conduct. 363 F.2d, at 134. The company simply did not meet the burden of proof, and the Court of Appeals misconstrued the function of judicial review when it proceeded nonetheless to speculate upon what *might have* motivated the company. Since discriminatory conduct carrying a potential for adverse effect upon employee rights was proved and no evidence of a proper motivation appeared in the record, the Board's conclusions were supported by substantial evidence, Universal Camera Corp. v. Labor Board, 340 U.S. 474 (1951), and should have been sustained.

The judgment of the Court of Appeals is reversed and the case is remanded with directions to enforce the Board's order.

HARLAN, J., with whom STEWART, J., joins, dissenting. [The dissent criticized the Court's premise that vacation benefits had accrued under the agreement, urged that the Board and the court of appeals had properly disregarded the contract issue and that the only issue properly before the Court was whether the employer's unilaterally declared vacation policy violated §8(a)(3), absent a showing of improper motivation. Excerpts from the dissent follow.]

. . . In the Court's view an employer must "come forward with evidence of legitimate and substantial business justifications" whenever any of his actions are challenged in a §8(a)(3) proceeding. Prior to today's decision, §8(a)(3) violations could be grouped into two general categories: those based on actions serving no legitimate business purposes or actions inherently severely destructive of employee rights where improper motive could be inferred from the actions themselves, and, in the latter instance, even a legitimate business purpose could be held by the Board not to justify the employer's conduct, Labor Board v. Erie Resistor Corp., 373 U.S. 221; and those not based on actions "demonstrably so destructive of employee rights and so devoid of significant service to any legitimate business end," where independent evidence evincing the employer's antiunion animus would be required to find a violation. Labor Board v. Brown, 380 U.S. 278, 286. The Court is unable to conclude that the employer's conduct in this case falls into the first category, and has proposed its rule as an added gloss on the second whose contours were fixed only two years ago in *Brown*.

Under today's formulation, the Board is required to find independent evidence of the employer's antiunion motive only when the employer has overcome the presumption of unlawful motive which the Court raises. This alteration of the burden in §8(a)(3) cases may either be a rule of convenience important to the resolution of this case alone or may, more unfortunately, portend an important shift in the manner of deciding employer unfair labor practice cases under §8(a)(3). In either event, I believe it is unwise.

The "legitimate and substantial business justifications" test may be interpreted as requiring only that the employer come forward with a non-frivolous business purpose in order to make operative the usual requirement of proof of antiunion motive. If this is the result of today's decision, then the Court has merely penalized Great Dane for not anticipating this requirement when arguing before the Board. Such a penalty seems particularly unfair in view of the clarity of our recent pronouncements that "the Board must find from evidence independent of the mere conduct involved that the conduct was primarily motivated by an antiunion animus," Labor Board v. Brown, 380 U.S., at 288, and that "the Board must find that the employer acted for a proscribed purpose." American Ship Building Co. v. Labor Board, 380 U.S. 300, 313.

On the other hand, the use of the word "substantial" in the burden of proof formulation may give the Board a power which it formerly had only in §8(a)(3) cases like *Erie Resistor*, supra. The Board may seize upon that term to evaluate the merits of the employer's business purposes and weigh them against the harm that befalls the union's interests as a result of the employer's action. If this is the Court's meaning, it may well impinge upon the accepted principle that "the right to bargain collectively does not entail any 'right' to insist on one's position free from economic disadvantage." American Ship Building Co. v. Labor Board, supra, at 309. Employers have always been free to take reasonable measures which discourage a strike by pressuring the economic interests of employees, including the extreme measure of hiring permanent replacements, without having the Board inquire into the "substantiality" of their business justifications. Labor Board v. Mackay Radio & Telegraph Co., 304 U.S. 333. If the Court means to change this rule, though I assume it does not, it surely should not do so without argument of the point by the parties and without careful discussion.

In my opinion, the Court of Appeals correctly held that this case fell into the category in which independent evidence of antiunion motive is required to sustain a violation. As was pointed out in the Court of Appeals opinion, a number of legitimate motives for the terms of the vacation policy could be inferred, 363 F.2d, at 134, and an unlawful motive is not the sole inference to be drawn from the conduct. Nor is the employer's conduct here, like the superseniority plan in *Erie Resistor*, supra, such that an unlawful motive can be found by "an application of the common-law rule that a man is held to intend the foreseeable consequences of his conduct." Radio Officers v. Labor Board, 347 U.S. 17, 45. The differences between the facts of this case and those of *Erie Resistor*, are, as the parties recognize, so significant as to preclude analogy. Unlike the granting of superseniority, the vacation pay policy here had no potential long-term impact on the bargaining situation. The vacation policy was not employed as a weapon against the strike as was the superseniority plan. Notice of the date of required presence for vacation pay eligibility was not given until after the date had passed. The record shows clearly that Great Dane had no need to employ any such policy to combat the strike, since it had successfully replaced almost all of the striking employees.[4] The Trial Examiner rejected all union claims that particular actions by Great Dane demonstrated antiunion animus. In these circumstances, the Court of Appeals correctly found no substantial evidence of a violation of §8(a)(3).

Plainly the Court is concerned lest the strikers in this case be denied their "rights" under the collective bargaining agreement that expired at the commencement of the strike. Equally plainly, a suit under §301 is the proper manner by which to secure these "rights," if they indeed exist. I think it inappropriate to becloud sound prior interpretations of §8(a)(3) simply to reach what seems a sympathetic result.

NOTES

1. Both the majority and dissenters agreed on the existence of two categories of conduct differentiated by the severity of injury to employee interests. Is the application of that distinction administratively feasible? Are the differential consequences of inclusion in one category or the other warranted by the language of §§8(a)(3) or 8(a)(1)? Consistent with the Court's prior emphasis on motive? With the imposition of the burden of persuasion on the General Counsel by §10(c) of the Act? Would it be preferable for the Court to abandon the motive test and to recognize explic-

---

[4] By July 1, 1963, almost 75% of the striking employees had been replaced. By August 1, 1963, when the dispute over vacation pay was coming to a head almost 90% had been replaced. All strikers had been replaced by October 8, 1963.

itly that legality turns on a judgment of whether injury to union or employee interests is warranted by countervailing employer interests; and that "motive" is a "fictive formality" rationalizing results reached by such a balancing approach? Should the NLRB have the same latitude in balancing interests in the bargaining context as it has been accorded in the organizational context? See generally Janofsky, New Concepts in Interference and Discrimination Under the NLRA: The Legacy of *American Ship Building* and *Great Dane Trailers*, 70 Colum. L. Rev. 81 (1970); Christensen & Svanoe, Motive and Intent in the Commission of Unfair Labor Practices, 77 Yale L.J. 1269, 1314-1332 (1968).

2. If the company in *Great Dane* had come forward with evidence demonstrating that (a) the refusal to pay vacation benefits was based solely on a "good faith" interpretation of the expired contract and (b) its reading of the contract was "reasonable and at least arguably correct," would the company have discharged the burden of proof assigned by the Court? If these proofs had been sufficient to show proper motivation, does it follow that no unfair labor practice was committed? Compare Vesuvius Crucible Co. v. NLRB, 668 F.2d 162 (3d Cir. 1981), with Midstate Tel. Corp. v. NLRB, 706 F.2d 401 (2d Cir. 1983). In NLRB v. Sherwin Williams Co., 714 F.2d 1095 (11th Cir. 1983), the Board had found that the company's termination of disability payments during an economic strike was unlawfully intended to coerce strikers by imposing a sanction against disabled (and thus nonstriking) employees. The court, finding that the company's action was based both on the terms of the disability plan and on its consistent past practice of suspending disability benefits during strikes, rejected the Board's conclusion that the company had failed to prove a legitimate business motive for its conduct. Applying the *Great Dane* analysis, the court stressed the lack of evidence that the company's past practice had "hindered future bargaining or created continuing obstacles to the future exercise of . . . employees' rights"; hence the termination could not be characterized as "inherently destructive."

3. During a seven-week strike, there was damage to automobiles of nonstrikers as well as strikers and to the homes of some nonstrikers. Upon the settlement of the strike, the employer, pursuant to a decision made but not disclosed during the strike, gave a $100 bonus to each nonstriker for risking "their health, property and peace of mind." The Board held that (1) the bonus payment violated §8(a)(1) in that it created a divisive wedge in the work force and demonstrated the special rewards for refraining from protected strike activity in the future, and (2) the employer's unilateral action and its refusal to comply with union requests for information regarding payment of the bonus independently violated §8(a)(5). The Board's remedial

order required, inter alia, payment of $100 plus interest to each striker. Aero-Motive Mfg. Co., 195 N.L.R.B. 790 (1972), *enforced,* 475 F.2d 27 (6th Cir. 1973). *Accord,* NLRB v. Rubatex Corp., 601 F.2d 147, 151 (4th Cir. 1979) ("payment of an equivalent bonus to the striking employees would seem to be the most effective and least disruptive of the alternatives," even though it requires the company to pay over $82,000 plus interest).

4. In light of *Erie Resistor* and *Great Dane,* what types of benefits may an employer lawfully withhold from striking employees? May an employer withhold not only wages but also "service credits" that affect strikers' seniority standing, the length of paid vacations, or the size of retirement benefits? See General Electric Co., 80 N.L.R.B. 510 (1948); Illinois Bell Tel. Co., 179 N.L.R.B. 681 (1969), *petition to review denied,* 446 F.2d 815 (7th Cir. 1971), *cert. denied,* 404 U.S. 1059 (1972); Texaco, Inc. v. NLRB, 700 F.2d 1039 (5th Cir. 1983). What criteria should determine whether a struck employer's withholding of employment or of benefits is a "penalty" for legally protected activity or a privileged response to business considerations?

The problem of workable criteria is illustrated by the litigation over the application of otherwise lawful probationary rules to economic strikers — for example, requiring probationary employees to begin the company's standard probationary period anew upon return from a strike. See Freezer Queen Foods, Inc., 249 N.L.R.B. 330 (1980). An employer who treats striking probationary employees as "new hires" is likely to have difficulty under the *Great Dane* formula, unless such treatment is permitted by a collective agreement or established plant practice. Does the difficulty arise because such conduct is "inherently destructive" of employee rights? See Kansas City Power & Light Co. v. NLRB, 641 F.2d 553 (8th Cir. 1981). Are cases involving probationary employees distinguishable from situations where an employer reduces or denies noncontractual bonus payments to economic strikers because their productivity has declined as a result of a prolonged strike? What if the prolonged strike is caused by the employer's unfair labor practice? Cf. Pittsburgh-Des Moines Steel Co. v. NLRB, 284 F.2d 74 (9th Cir. 1960).

Inter-Collegiate Press, Graphic Arts Div. v. NLRB
486 F.2d 837 (8th Cir. 1973), *cert. denied,* 416 U.S. 938 (1974)

GIBSON, J. . . . [The ALJ] concluded that he was bound by the Board's decision in Inland Trucking Co., 179 N.L.R.B. 350 (1969), and found that the Company had violated [§§8(a)(1) and (3)] by its use of temporary replacements [after a lawful lockout]. A majority of the Board disagreed and ordered the complaint dismissed. Inter-Collegiate Press, 199 N.L.R.B. No. 35 (1972).[i]

. . . In Inland Trucking Co. v. NLRB, 440 F.2d 562, 565 (7th Cir.), *cert. denied*, 404 U.S. 858 (1971), the Seventh Circuit concluded: "[T]hat a lockout in the circumstances at bar, accompanied by continued operation with replacement labor, is, per se, an interference with protected employee rights, and accordingly, per se, an unfair labor practice under §158(a)(1)."

. . . Inland supports the Union's position, but we do not think it conforms with the Supreme Court's opinions touching this issue and decide it would be improper for us at this time to adopt a per se rule. To do so would remove the development of the law in this area from the special competence of the Board, which has been proceeding on a case-by-case basis to adjudicate the impact of hiring temporary replacements during a lawful lockout by balancing the interests of employees and employers and thereby fashioning a national body of labor law. . . .

. . . Admittedly, the conduct in question has some effect upon protected employee rights, but we are not prepared to say absolutely that a lockout plus the hiring of temporary replacements is conduct so "inherently destructive" of employee rights to warrant a reviewing court in promulgating a per se rule when the Board itself has chosen not to do so. To the extent that *Inland Trucking* is interpreted as setting forth a per se rule, it has been criticized by commentators,[4] and to follow that path would seem to ignore the caution raised in American Ship Bldg. v. NLRB, 380 U.S. 300, 337-338 (1965) (Goldberg, J., concurring), that "the problem of lockouts requires 'an evolutionary process,' not 'a quick, definitive formula,' for its answer." It was also unnecessary to the decision reached in *Inland* to announce a per se rule, since the court went on to find a lack of any legitimate and substantial business justification for the employer's conduct, which would warrant a finding of a violation of the Act under the test of NLRB v. Great Dane Trailers, Inc., 388 U.S. 26, 34 (1967).

Since we deem a per se approach inappropriate, we think it important to relate in some detail the facts of this case. The Company prints scholastic year books and graduation announcements at its plant in Mission, Kansas. The

---

[i][Two Board members maintained that employment of temporary replacements following a lawful lockout always constituted a violation; and two members, that it never did so. Chairman Miller, rejecting both those approaches, urged that *Brown Food* and *Great Dane* required a case-by-case balancing of interests. In upholding Inter-Collegiate's use of temporary replacements, the Chairman relied on reasons similar to those invoked by the reviewing court. See 199 N.L.R.B. 177 (1972). — EDS.]

[4]Note, Lockouts — Employers' Lockout with Temporary Replacements is an Unfair Labor Practice, 85 Harv. L. Rev. 680, 683-685 (1972); Note, 50 Tex. L. Rev. 552, 556-558 (1972).

Union represents all the full-time and permanent seasonal employees in the cover and bindery departments, and those in the announcement department, who perform paper cutting, finishing, and packaging work. In February, 1967, the Union was recognized as the bargaining representative of the above employees. After seven months of negotiations in 1967 during which a two week strike occurred, agreement was reached between the Union and the Company on a collective bargaining contract that expired August 31, 1970.

Negotiations on a new contract began July 7, 1970.[7] Fourteen bargaining sessions were held after this date until the Company lockout October 16th. It is uncontroverted that the Company and the Union were at impasse in their negotiations by October 15th, for on that date a federal mediator stated that further bargaining would be "an exercise in futility." The Company locked out all employees represented by the Union on October 16th, after being informed that morning that the Company's last contract proposal was unacceptable and the Union had no proposals to make. . . .

The Union had been made aware as early as September 16th that the Company was considering a lockout, but no progress was made on any of the unresolved issues from that date until the date of the lockout. The parties and the Board are in agreement that the lockout was entirely legal at its inception. . . .

. . . The lockout failed to bring about any fruitful negotiations or agreements and effected no change in the Union's bargaining position. A substantial backlog of work had accumulated in the areas manned by locked out employees, and a failure to resolve the impasse before the Company's busy season would have prevented the Company from meeting its delivery schedules. Competitors were contacting Inter-Collegiate's customers and informing them that there would be late deliveries because of the labor dispute, and these customers were threatening to take their business elsewhere unless the Company could guarantee timely delivery. During the time when the Company's busy season was approaching, the Company's salesmen were warning of a substantial loss of customers and good will unless the labor dispute was resolved.

Inter-Collegiate is engaged in a highly seasonal business. It prepares yearbooks and announcements that must be delivered around the time of school graduations in May and June. . . . [T]he Company has a peak period between February and June of each year, when it operates at over 100% of its plant's capacity (by use of overtime) and adds approximately 300 seasonal employees to its permanent work force of 200. . . . Any disruption has serious consequences for the Company's ability to meet its guaranteed deliv-

[7] Dates hereafter are in 1970 unless otherwise indicated.

ery schedules. During the previous busy season the Company had been struck by a different union, and this strike disrupted deliveries and caused the cancellation of some contracts. . . .

The Company believed, we feel with justification, that the Union's strategy was to continue negotiations, while working without a contract, into the busy season when a strike or threat of a strike would have left the Company with little choice but to meet the Union's demands. This had been the scenario for the other union's strike during the last busy season. . . .

The Company, therefore, on November 9th, offered to end the lockout if the Union would agree to a no-strike commitment for the coming busy season. The Union made a counter-proposal whereby it would agree to the no-strike commitment if the Company agreed to sign a contract acceptable to the Union by July 1, 1971. No agreement was reached by the parties. Thereafter, on November 23rd, the Company informed the Union that it would begin hiring temporary replacements unless a contract was signed or a no-strike commitment given by November 30. The Union and the employees were informed that the replacements were to be used only for the duration of the labor dispute, and in any event, their employment would not continue past June 21, 1971. The Company did hire replacements beginning November 30, resumed full production December 1, and continued the lockout until June 1, 1971, at which time the Company offered to reinstate all the locked out employees.

The evidence clearly indicates that the employer's use of the temporary replacements was motivated only by legitimate and substantial business reasons. . . .

We now turn to an analysis of the lockout with the delayed temporary replacement of employees. . . . We note first the argument of the Union that while a "defensive" lockout plus the hiring of temporary replacements may be upheld, citing NLRB v. Brown, 380 U.S. 278 (1965), an "offensive" lockout plus the hiring of temporary replacements is violative of §§8(a)(1) and (3). . . . We do not think a pro forma application of the labels "offensive" and "defensive" to a lockout assists in the analysis required to determine the legality of the conduct involved.[9] . . . Eschewing the use of labels

---

[9] As was stated in Laclede Gas Co. v. NLRB, 421 F.2d 610, 615 n.11 (8th Cir. 1970):
"Characterizing a lockout as 'defensive' or 'offensive' is a difficult task at best. . . .

" 'Moreover, and more important, whatever the determination in a particular case might be, the fact remains that the defensive lockout has its primary significance as an attempt to improve the employer's bargain. If that proposition be conceded . . . it undermines the basic distinction which the Board has sought to maintain in the lockout context — that is, the distinction between . . . [offensive and defensive lockouts]. . . . ' Meltzer, Lockouts Under the LRMA: New Shadows on an Old Terrain, 28 U. Chi. L. Rev. 614, 621 (1961)." . . .

"offensive" or "defensive," we think the legality of an employer's conduct in a lockout should be determined by principles set out by the Supreme Court in NLRB v. Great Dane Trailers, Inc., 388 U.S. at 34.

Great Dane involved a claimed §8(a)(3) violation. However, NLRB v. Fleetwood Trailer Co., 389 U.S. 375, 380 (1967), indicates that the above principles are applicable in determining whether a §8(a)(1) violation exists as well. The complaint in this case charges violations of both §8(a)(1) and §8(a)(3).

If the employer's conduct is deemed "inherently destructive," it will be a violation of the Act under the first test in *Great Dane*. The phrase "inherently destructive" is not easily susceptible of precise definition. . . . We should not attempt to complete a catalog of actions that might be regarded as "inherently destructive," but rather must determine whether the conduct in this case should be so viewed. One commentator suggests that "inherently destructive" conduct is that which creates visible and continuing obstacles to the future exercise of employee rights.[11] The impact of a lockout, as recognized by another commentator, is more likely to be on the union's bargaining position than on the employees' allegiance to the union, at least where there is a history of bargaining relations between the parties.[12]

There has been no showing that the Union's position as bargaining agent was jeopardized or that it has suffered any diminution in its capacity to effectively represent the employees. . . . Although 15 employees did not return to work after the lockout ended, this was apparently because they had found other jobs. There is no indication that any of the union employees who did return has disavowed his union membership. The Board did not find the conduct here to be "inherently destructive," and we are not inclined to disturb this finding under the circumstances of this case.

The considerations which motivated the Court in NLRB v. Brown, 380 U.S. at 288-289, to conclude that the use of temporary replacements had a "comparatively slight" effect on employee rights are present here. First, the replacements were expressly hired only for the duration of the labor dispute, and a definite date was given for their termination even if the dispute was not resolved. This was communicated to both the union and the employees. Second, at all times the option was available to the employees to return to work by simply agreeing to the employer's terms, which were better than those in the old contract. Third, the employer had already agreed to continue in effect the union-security clause from the old contract. Thus, we conclude that the employer's conduct did not have "unavoidable consequences

[11] Note, 85 Harv. L. Rev. supra at 686.
[12] Getman, Section 8(a)(3) of the NLRA and the Effort to Insulate Free Employee Choice, 32 U. Chi. L. Rev. 735, 751 (1951).

. . . which he must have intended," *Erie Resistor*, 373 U.S. at 228, and therefore was not "inherently destructive."

Conduct having even a "comparatively slight" impact on employee rights may be a violation of §8(a)(3), unless the employer has established a legitimate and substantial business justification. *Great Dane*, 388 U.S. at 34. Here the employer has established a legitimate and substantial business justification for his conduct, and there is no evidence of any unlawful motivation. . . .

The Union argues that the conduct here is violative of §8(a)(1) because of the coercion inherent when the employees are deprived of their income while the company continues to operate. . . . We recognize that there is coercion present when the employer locks out his employees, and it may be magnified when the employer continues operations with temporary employees.[14] The coercion, however, is to force acceptance of the employer's bargaining proposals, not to deter employees from the exercise of their rights. . . .

It must be conceded that the use of a lockout in support of a legitimate bargaining position is not inconsistent with the right to bargain collectively or the right to strike. *American Ship Bldg.*, at 310. The hiring of temporary replacements does no more than increase the pressure upon the employees to settle the dispute, while perhaps easing the pressure on the employer. Such pressure is surely no greater than that caused by stockpiling and subcontracting, *American Ship Bldg.*, at 316, or the shifting of production to other plants during the lockout, Ruberoid Corp., 167 N.L.R.B. 987 (1967), which have been found lawful during a bargaining lockout. . . .

Neither the Board nor the courts should sit as arbiters of the permissible economic weapons available to the parties in a labor dispute. . . . Here, since no antiunion animus or hostile motivation has been shown and the employer has established a legitimate and substantial business justification, we agree with the Board that there is no §8(a)(1) violation merely because the Company may have increased the economic pressure on the Union by continued operation with temporary replacements. To find otherwise would be taking upon ourselves a general authority to assess the bargaining power of the parties to a dispute and to attempt to redress what we might perceive to be

---

[14] We note in passing that the returns of continued operation with temporary employees may not be such as to lead most employers to take such a step. There was evidence in this case that Inter-Collegiate lost approximately $120,000 as a direct result of using temporary employees. In addition, replacements for highly skilled jobs may be hard to locate, or the cost of training replacements merely for the duration of a labor dispute may be prohibitively high. In view of the above and the fact that the employer will have to prove legitimate and substantial business justification for his conduct, it is unlikely an employer would hire temporary replacements during an otherwise lawful lockout unless motivated by business exigencies. . . .

a relative imbalance in bargaining power by finding a violation of §8(a)(1). Such a method of decision has been denied even to the Board. *American Ship Bldg.*, 380 U.S. at 317. The balancing of bargaining power denied to the Board must be contrasted with the Board's authority to balance "conflicting legitimate interests." *Erie Resistor*, 373 U.S. at 236. This is what the Board has done in this case.

Finding no violation of §§8(a)(1) or (3) in the facts of this case, we affirm the Board's dismissal of the complaint.

NOTES

1. Following unproductive negotiations and the expiration of a collective bargaining agreement, the employer unilaterally terminated non-negotiated insurance plans. The employer urged that under the lockout cases such a reduction of economic benefits was a permissible method of resolving a bargaining impasse. In rejecting that contention and finding a violation of §8(a)(5), the Board distinguished a lockout from such withdrawal of employment benefits, urging that the latter generated more hostility and gave a windfall to the employer until the dispute was settled. Borden, Inc., 196 N.L.R.B. 1170 (1972); see also United States Pipe and Foundry Co., 180 N.L.R.B. 325 (1969), *enforced sub nom.* Local 155, Molders v. NLRB, 442 F.2d 742 (D.C. Cir. 1971). But cf. NLRB v. Insurance Agents Intl. Union, reproduced infra p. 830.

2. In Johns-Manville Products v. NLRB, 557 F.2d 1126 (5th Cir.), *cert. denied*, 436 U.S. 956 (1978), the court, reversing the Board, upheld an employer who, after his lockout, hired permanent replacements without prior notification to the union. The court found that the employees' in-plant sabotage during negotiations had amounted to "an in-plant strike" and that the severity of their conduct justified the employer's countermeasures. The court also noted that substantial losses had accompanied operations with temporary replacements and that the union had denied the company's allegations about damage and ignored its request for help in identifying those responsible. Judge Wisdom, dissenting, criticized the majority's treatment of the sabotage as a strike; would have limited employer reprisals to identified offenders; and, using *Great Dane's* balancing approach, would have sustained the Board's condemnation of the resort to permanent replacements following the offensive lockout, given that the company had not previously threatened replacement in order to break the bargaining impasse.

In determining the legality of hiring replacements, should substantial violence by employees, designed to exert bargaining pressure on their employer, be treated differently from a conventional strike? Should it be material in such a case that (as in *Johns-Manville*) the employer shut down completely before hiring replacements? Is the approach in that case consistent with the general rule restricting discipline for unprotected activities to identified participants? Cf. Methodist Hospital of Kentucky, Inc. v. NLRB, 619 F. 2d 563 (6th Cir.), *cert. denied*, 449 U.S. 889 (1980).

CHAPTER 6

DETERMINATION OF REPRESENTATIVE STATUS

An employer may recognize a union as the bargaining representative for a group of employees who fill a specified pool of jobs, such as production and maintenance. (Such a pool of jobs, rather than the employees filling them, constitutes a "bargaining unit.") As we have seen, lawful recognition does not require a Board election and formal certification of the union as the majority representative in a bargaining unit. Recognition may instead be based on an informal showing of support, such as authorization cards. Such informal recognition is, however, open to challenge on the ground that the union lacked majority support when it was recognized or was otherwise tainted by unlawful employer domination or assistance. Recourse to the NLRB's election machinery (provided by §9) and Board certification of a winning union provides a defense against such challenges. Furthermore, under §§9(c)(3), 8(b)(4)(C), and 8(b)(7)(B) of the Act, as amended, an election provides special protections to an employer and to a winning union that are not available in the event of informal recognition.

When an employer declines to extend informal recognition, a union may activate the Board's election machinery by filing a petition under §9(c)(1). Under the Wagner Act, the Board initially would entertain an election petition from an employer only if it alleged that two or more unions had made conflicting representation claims on the petitioner. The 1947 amendments authorized employer petitions even though only one union had requested recognition.

Another significant 1947 amendment (§9(c)(1)(A)(ii)) authorized employees to file petitions for decertification, alleging that a substantial number of unit employees assert that an incumbent union no longer has majority support. Decertification petitions are in general governed by the rules applicable to other election petitions filed under §9. See generally Krupman & Rasin, Decertification Removing the Shroud, 30 Lab. L.J. 231 (1979). During the last decade, the number of decertification elections has increased substantially, and the percentage of such elections lost by unions has in-

349

creased slightly. See 35 N.L.R.B. Ann. Rep. 181 (1970); 45 N.L.R.B. Ann. Rep. 273 (1980). Presumably, recent union losses are related to the malaise generated by a sluggish economy and by employer pressures for "give-backs" in collective bargaining negotiations.

See generally J. Feerick, H. Baer, & J. Arfa, NLRB Representation Elections — Law, Practice & Procedure (1980); E. Miller, An Administrative Appraisal of the NLRB, ch. II (rev. ed. 1980).

Administration of the election machinery constitutes an important part of the Board's business. In 1980 alone, the Board closed approximately 13,540 representation cases, almost 8,200 of them by election, 45.7 percent of which unions won — the first year in the last nine that unions won more elections than in the previous year. See 44 N.L.R.B. Ann. Rep. 19 (1979). Nonetheless, the unions' 1980 success rate was much lower than the 55 percent rate of ten years ago. See 35 N.L.R.B. Ann. Rep. 178-179 (1970); 45 N.L.R.B. Ann. Rep. 2-3, 14-16 (1980). Representation decisions manifestly have important effects on free and informed choice, and on the structure, stability, and power dimensions of collective bargaining if a union is certified.

Pursuant to authority granted by the 1959 amendment to §3(b), the NLRB in 1961 delegated most of its powers over representation matters to its 33 Regional Directors, who, subject to the Board's discretionary and limited review, play a leading role in processing such cases. See NLRB, Rules and Regulations, Series 8, as amended, §102.67. That delegation, which the Board described as one of its most far-reaching steps in election cases, has been followed by a considerable reduction in the time required for disposing of representation cases. In 1961, the median interval between the filing of a representation petition and a Board decision was 89 days; in 1980, the median interval between the filing of a petition and a decision by the Regional Director was 38 days. See 45 N.L.R.B. Ann. Rep. 15, 226 (1980). Regional offices issued 1,971 representation decisions in contested cases in fiscal 1980; Board review was sought in 798 of those cases and granted in 101 of them. In fiscal 1980, an additional 155 decisions were issued by the Board. Id. at 245.

A.   NLRB ELECTIONS

1.   Bars to Elections

Satisfaction of the requirements of §9(c)(1) does not necessarily lead to a Board-conducted election. Section 9(c)(3) (as we have seen) and, more importantly, the Board through its discretionary authority, have established certain "bars to proceeding." These bars reflect an effort to strike a proper balance among a cluster of competing interests: stable labor relations, conservation of public as well as private resources, fair representation, and employee self-determination. The Board's decisions in this area have changed quickly. A perennial question has been whether changes should be made through the Board's exercise of its rulemaking authority under §6 of the Act rather than by case-by-case adjudication. Cf. NLRB v. Wyman Gordon, noted supra p. 178. See generally Bernstein, The NLRB's Adjudication-Rule Making Dilemma Under the Administrative Procedure Act, 79 Yale L.J. 571 (1970); Williams, The NLRB and Administrative Rulemaking, Southwestern Legal Foundation, 16 Inst. on Labor Law 209 (1970); Kahn, The NLRB and Higher Education: The Failure of Policymaking Through Adjudication, 21 UCLA L. Rev. 63 (1973).

a. Lack of Substantial Support

The Board will not proceed to an election on a petition filed by a union (or on a decertification petition) unless the petition has "substantial support," which usually means support by at least 30 percent of the employees in the unit involved.[a] Such a showing is usually made by the submission of authorization cards or union membership cards, which the Board's field representative checks against the employer's payroll records. This requirement is designed to conserve the Board's resources, as well as those of the parties, by screening out petitions with little prospect of success. The Board's longstanding practice has been to consider the determination of substantial support exclusively an administrative matter that is not litigable by the parties, at least in a representation proceeding.[b] Courts, in upholding the Board's practice, have rejected the contention that the reference to substantial support in §9(c)(1) (added in 1947) makes record evidence of such support a jurisdictional prerequisite for a certification. See NLRB v. J.I. Case Co., 201 F.2d 597 (9th Cir. 1953).

b. Pending Unfair Labor Practice Charges

The NLRB generally will abate a representation case while unfair labor practice charges affecting the unit are pending and when the charging party is

---

[a] Employer petitions are not subject to that requirement. See NLRA §9(c)(1) and NLRB Statements of Procedure, Series 8, as amended, §101.18.

[b] When an employer's unfair labor practice appears to turn on the existence of substantial support for one of several rival unions, should the employer be bound by the Board's administrative determination?

a party to the representation case. Furthermore, even though the charging party is not a party to the representation case, the election machinery will generally be suspended following charges of violations of §§8(a)(2), 8(a)(5), 8(b)(3) or 8(b)(7). See NLRB Field Manual §11730 (rev. ed. 1971).

This abatement policy, although not prescribed by the Act, appears to promote employee free choice, which presupposes that the effects of unlawful conduct have been neutralized. Nevertheless, in some cases the "blocking charge" rule may impede free choice by inviting charges as a dilatory tactic. Mechanical application of the rule can lead to judicial correction, on the ground that such application is inconsistent with §9(c)(1) (see Hamil v. Youngblood, 96 L.R.R.M. 3016 (N.D. Okla. 1977)), or that unexplained delays in Board processing of a blocking charge constitutes a denial of due process (see Sparks Nugget, Inc. v. Scott, 116 L.R.R.M. 2405 (D.C. Nev. 1984). Courts are, however, generally reluctant to intervene. See, e.g., Bishop v. NLRB, 502 F.2d 1024 (5th Cir. 1974). Cf. Leedom v. Kyne, infra p. 434.

The dismissal of a charge found groundless permits the election machinery to operate. The Board may also proceed to an election when the charging party executes a "Request to Proceed," or when, as to some charges, the Regional Director finds that an election would be fair despite the unremedied conduct. Such requests do not constitute a waiver of the right to challenge the subsequent election or to proceed with the unfair labor practice charge thereafter. Charges under §§8(a)(2), 8(a)(5), or 8(b)(3) are, however, treated differently, and a charging party's request to go forward with an election despite the pendency of such charges will normally be rejected. The charging party may, however, unblock the election machinery by agreeing to withdraw such charges as a basis for either challenging the election or unfair labor practice proceedings. See NLRB Field Manual, §11730 (rev. ed. 1971); Carlson Furn. Indus., Inc., 157 N.L.R.B. 851 (1966).

c.   An Existing Agreement

The Board's "contract-bar" doctrine, which is designed to promote stable labor relations, generally bars an election among employees covered by a valid and operative collective agreement of reasonable duration.

To operate as a bar, an agreement must cover an appropriate unit, be in writing, properly executed and binding; it must contain "substantial terms and conditions of employment" sufficient "to stabilize the bargaining relationship"; it will not be a bar if it deals only with wages, if it is confined to "members only," or if it lacks a termination date. See Cind-R-Lite Co., 239

N.L.R.B. 1255 (1979). Unless an agreement by its terms makes ratification by members a condition precedent to its validity, nonratification will not preclude bar effect. See Appalachian Shale Prod. Co., 121 N.L.R.B. 1160 (1958); Stur-Dee Health Products, 248 N.L.R.B. 1100 (1980) (bar effect given to agreement arising from established relationship and providing for grievance arbitration along with no-strike pledge, union security, and various fringe items but leaving wages for arbitral determination).

The Board's approach to problems raised by agreements or relationships involving illegal clauses or practices has been fluid. Thus, in Paragon Prod. Corp., 134 N.L.R.B. 662 (1961), the Board, in an overruling decision, held that a contract would be given bar effect despite an allegedly invalid union security provision, unless that provision was clearly invalid on its face or had been held unlawful in an unfair labor practice proceeding; consequently, evidence as to practice under the disputed provision would not be received.

In Food Haulers, Inc., 136 N.L.R.B. 394 (1962), the Board abandoned an earlier decision and held that an agreement would serve as a bar even though it contained a "hot cargo clause" unlawful under §8(e). The Board reasoned that such an agreement, unlike an illegal union security clause, does not restrain freedom of choice; to deny bar effect would, in substance, invalidate the entire contract and would involve a more drastic remedy than that imposed in unfair labor practice proceedings, namely, the invalidation of only the offending clause. Is the Board's reasoning persuasive? Does such tinkering with the details of these rules invite litigation over relatively minor issues?

In Pioneer Bus Co., 140 N.L.R.B. 54 (1962), bar effect was denied to separate agreements for black and white workers, worked out in separate employer meetings with black and white representatives, even though the agreements contained virtually identical terms. See the materials on the duty of fair representation in Chapter 11.

Currently, a contract for a fixed term will bar a petition filed by a rival union for only three years even though the contract term is longer and even though contracts for a longer term are customary in the industry or area involved. General Cable Corp., 139 N.L.R.B. 1123 (1962), modifying Pacific Coast Assn. of Pulp & Paper Mfg., 121 N.L.R.B. 990, 992-993 (1958). Both the employer and the certified representative who are parties to a longer term agreement are, however, barred from filing a petition during its term. Montgomery Ward & Co., 137 N.L.R.B. 346 (1962).

A petition by a rival union, by the employer, or by employees seeking decertification, generally must be filed no more than 90, and no less than 60, days prior to the expiration date of the contract (or so much of its term as does not exceed three years). This 60-day period constitutes an "insulated period," during which petitions will not be considered timely filed. After an agreement expires, petitions filed prior to the execution of a new contract are timely. When an agreement provides for automatic renewal unless a timely forestalling notice is given, the insulated period begins 60 days prior to the expiration of the agreement's initial term regardless of the time specified for that notice. See Deluxe Metal Furn. Co., 121 N.L.R.B. 995, 1000 (1958).

The Board has, however, established a special rule for health care institutions, in response to the 1974 amendments to NLRA, §8(d). Under those amendments, a party desiring termination or modification of a collective agreement applicable to employees of such institutions must give 90 (rather than 60) days' notice to that effect to the other party. The Board, accordingly, increased the insulated period for health care institutions from 60 to 90 days and provided that the open period in which petitions could be filed would include an additional 30 days, but not more than 120 days, prior to the termination of the agreement. See 40 N.L.R.B. Ann. Rep. 22 (1976).

"Premature extension" of a prior agreement consists of its extension, with or without modifications, prior to the beginning of the insulated period as measured by the original agreement. Despite a "premature extension," a petition is timely if filed prior to the beginning of the insulated period measured by the unextended contract. If, however, a petition is filed later, the extended agreement will constitute a new bar. See Republic Aviation, 122 N.L.R.B. 998 (1959).

These rules are designed to reduce the disruption caused by organizational activities conducted long before the contract expiration date; to provide a period shortly before that date during which renewal agreements may be negotiated free from the pressures generated by rival petitions; to furnish outside unions with a precise time chart; and to conserve the time of the regional offices.

(1) Lifting the Contract Bar

In Hershey Chocolate Corp., 121 N.L.R.B. 901 (1958), the AFL-CIO expelled the Bakery and Confectionery Workers (BCW) for corruption and chartered the American Bakery and Confectionery Workers (ABC) as an AFL-CIO affiliate, with substantially the same jurisdiction previously granted the BCW. Shortly thereafter, on December 28, 1957, at a membership meeting (on 10 days' written notice), the members of BCW Local 464 voted 829 to 1 to disaffiliate from BCW and to affiliate with ABC, to transfer all property and contract rights from the BCW to ABC Local 464, and to retain all officers of the BCW local as officers of the ABC local. On December 30, the latter, after learning that its request for a charter had been granted by the AFL-CIO, advised the employer of the change in affiliation and indicated that it intended to observe the collective agreement, which did not expire until December 31, 1958, and expected the employer to do the same.

On December 30, 1957, the BCW appointed a trustee for BCW Local 464, and about 50 of the 2,000 members of that local expressed their continued loyalty. After the employer had filed an election petition on January 9, 1958, the trustee advised the employer of his willingness to administer the collective agreement and requested a meeting.

The Board, invoking the schism doctrine, held that the unexpired agreement did not bar an election. The Board stated that a prerequisite for a schism is "a basic intraunion conflict . . . over policy at the highest level of an international union . . . or within a federation, which results in a disruption of existing intraunion relationships." In addition, in order to lift the contract bar, the employees in the unit must have had an opportunity to express their judgment on the conflict, preferably at an open meeting after due notice that its purpose is to take disaffiliation action for reasons relating to the basic intraunion conflict, and such membership action must be taken "within a reasonable period of time" after the conflict occurs and must cause "confusion unstabilizing the bargaining relationship." See generally Summers, Union Schism in Perspective: Flexible Doctrines, Double Standards and Projected Answers, 45 Va. L. Rev. 261, 273 (1959).

In *Hershey*, the Board also reaffirmed that bar effect will be denied to a contract with a defunct union, i.e., one unable or unwilling to represent the employees. The Board emphasized that "temporary inability to function" or loss of all members in the unit does not constitute defunctness.

In American Sunroof Corp.-West Coast, Inc., 243 N.L.R.B. 1128 (1979), the employees, seeking to abrogate the union shop provision of the collective bargaining agreement, filed a petition under §9(e)(1). In apparent retaliation, the incumbent union filed a disclaimer of any interest in representing the employees. Another union filed a petition for an election, and the Board held that the disclaimer lifted the contract bar, noting the absence of any collusion between the two unions. See also NLRB v. Circle A&W Products Co., 647 F.2d 924 (9th Cir.), *cert. denied*, 454 U.S. 1054 (1981), upholding the Board's approach in a similar situation.

In General Extrusion Co., 121 N.L.R.B. 1165 (1958), the Board declared:

A contract does not bar an election if executed (1) before any employees had been hired or (2) prior to a substantial increase in personnel. When the question of a substantial increase in personnel is in issue, a contract will bar an election only if at least 30 percent of the complement employed at the time of the hearing had been employed at the time the contract was executed, *and* 50 percent of the job classifications in existence at the time of the hearing were in existence at the time the contract was executed.

In the absence of a collective agreement, impending expansion of the work force will constitute a separate ground for barring an election and for dismissing a petition as untimely if the existing employees are not "representative" of job skills of the projected work force and are not a "substantial" part thereof. See A. O. Smith, 100 N.L.R.B. 1329 (1952), 102 N.L.R.B. 1116 (1953); Endicott Johnson de Puerto Rico, Inc., 172 N.L.R.B. 1676, 1677, n.3 (1968), declaring that the criteria announced in *General Extrusion* govern only contract-bar questions and not whether an election should be held in all expanding units. See also Clement-Blythe Companies, 182 N.L.R.B. 502 (1970) (disclaiming "hard and fast" rules and suggesting that §§8(e) and (f), particularly, favor early elections in the construction industry).

Is there any basis for applying different standards to the situations illustrated by *General Extrusion* and *Endicott Johnson?*

(2)   The Effect of an Intervening Certification

In American Seating Co., 106 N.L.R.B. 250 (1953), the UAW, the certified representative of all the employer's production and maintenance workers, had entered into a three-year collective agreement. At a time when such agreements were not a bar for their full term, the Board conducted an election and certified the Pattern Makers union as the representative of the employer's pattern makers. The Board declined to decide the effect of the intervening certification on the unexpired agreement but declared:

> The purpose of . . . holding a contract of unreasonable duration not a bar . . . is the democratic one of insuring to employees the right at reasonable intervals of reappraising and changing, if they so desire, their union representation. . . . Strikes for a change of representatives are thereby reduced and the effects of employee dissatisfaction with their representatives are mitigated. But, if a newly chosen representative is to be hobbled in the way proposed by the Respondent, a great part of the benefit to be derived from the no-bar rule will be dissipated. There is little point in selecting a new bargaining representative which is unable to negotiate new terms and conditions of employment for an extended period of time.
>
> We hold that, for the reasons which led the Board to adopt the rule that a

contract of unreasonable duration is not a bar to a new determination of representatives, such a contract may not bar full statutory collective bargaining, including the reduction to writing of any agreement reached, as to any group of employees in an appropriate unit covered by such contract, upon the certification of a new collective-bargaining representative for them. Accordingly, we find that by refusing . . . to bargain with the Pattern Makers . . . , the Respondent violated §8(a)(5) and (1) of the Act.

NOTES

1. Assume that an outside union wins an election after the NLRB holds the contract bar inapplicable because of disclaimer by, or defunctness of, or a schism involving, the incumbent union. Should the winning union be required to assume the unexpired agreement? Are the foregoing situations — involving deficiencies in the incumbent union — distinguishable from those where the contract bar is held inapplicable because of deficiencies in the characteristics of the contract? See Comment, Enforcing the Existing Agreement after the NLRB Waives the Contract-Bar Rule, 131 U. Pa. L.Rev. 457 (1982).

2. In both situations below assume that the disputed conduct occurs before the expiration of the agreement between American Seating and the UAW, but after the Pattern Makers have been certified:

(a) The agreement between the UAW and the company banned all strikes during the term of the agreement. The company and the Pattern Makers bargained in good faith but deadlocked over changes in the agreement proposed by the Pattern Makers. Would a strike by the Pattern Makers to secure those changes violate the no-strike clause, or §8(b)(3) and §8(d) of the Act? See Jacobs Mfg. Co. and NLRB v. Lion Oil Co. in Chapter 9(E), infra.

(b) When the Pattern Makers were certified, the company suddenly began to experience serious losses, and the inflation rate was much less than the UAW's and the company's estimate when they had reached their agreement. The company and the Pattern Makers bargained in good faith but deadlocked over the company's request for deferring a wage increase fixed by the agreement. The company thereupon unilaterally suspended that increase, advising the employees and the Pattern Makers union that the company's losses left it no alternative. Has the company violated the agreement or §§8(a)(5) and 8(d)? Would it be material that the UAW had agreed to suspend the contractual wage increase for the employees in the unit that it continued to represent?

d. Legitimacy and Disqualification of the Union Representative

In general the Board will not deny a union either a place on the ballot or certification, on the ground of the union's prior misfeasance or unfitness. Cf. LMRDA, §504(a). The Board may, however, revoke a certification because of a union's postcertification misconduct.

(1) Union Corruption

The NLRB will not entertain claims that a union should be disqualified because it has been an ineffectual or corrupt representative, or its officials have criminal records, or they have misappropriated union funds. Without considering evidence regarding such claims, the Board will place a union on the ballot if (apart from such claims) such action is appropriate and will certify the union if certification is otherwise appropriate. The Board has, however, reserved authority (which it has rarely exercised) to revoke a previously issued certification if a labor organization "fails to fulfill its statutory obligations" as an exclusive bargaining representative. See Alto Plastics Manufacturing Corp., 136 N.L.R.B. 850, 854 (1962).

The NLRB's precertification hands-off approach contrasts with that of the New York State Board of Labor Relations, which excludes from the ballot so-called labor organizations that have engaged in a variety of corrupt practices at the expense of the employees involved. The formal rationale for such exclusion is that such organizations, which are often "paper locals," are not "labor organizations" within the meaning of the New York statute. See Helsid Realty Corp., 22 S.L.R.B. 326 (N.Y. 1959); K. Hanslowe, Procedures and Policies of the New York State Labor Relations Board 15-19 (1964). Cf. §7103(A)(4) of the Federal Civil Service Reform Act of 1978, which excludes from the scope of "labor organization" an organization that denies membership on the basis of race, sex, creed, or other similarly unacceptable criteria; and §7120 of that Act, which provides that an agency shall accord recognition only "to a labor organization that is free from corrupt influences and influences opposed to basic democratic principles."

If the New York rationale were adopted under the NLRA, would a corrupt "paper" local be subject to the proscriptions of §8(b)?

(2) Racial and Other Invidious Discrimination

In Handy Andy, Inc., 228 N.L.R.B. 447 (1977), the Board, abandoning its prior approach, declared that it would not consider evidence of racial or other invidious discrimination by a union outside the unit in question before certifying the union as a bargaining representative. Instead, the Board would consider only "proof of . . . dereliction as to unit employees in a *revocation* proceeding." Id. at 453 (emphasis added). See also Bell & Howell Co. v. NLRB, 598 F.2d 136 (D.C. Cir. 1979), *cert. denied*, 442 U.S. 942 (1979) (involving alleged union discrimination against women; generally approving the Board's approach); but see NLRB v. Mansion House Center Management Corp., 473 F.2d 471 (8th Cir. 1973). The Board's role in combatting discrimination obviously became much less important after the enactment of the Civil Rights Act of 1964, Title VII of which bars discrimination on account of race, sex, and other unacceptable criteria. For an analysis of the Board's antidiscrimination role, see Meltzer, The National Labor Relations Act and Racial Discrimination: The More Remedies, the Better? 42 U. Chi. L. Rev. 1 (1974). But see Note, The Inevitable Interplay of Title VII and the National Labor Relations Act: A New Role for the NLRB, 123 U. Pa. L. Rev. 158 (1974).

(3) Conflict of Interest

In St. John's Hospital & Health Center, 264 N.L.R.B. 990 (1982), the Board, extensively reviewing its decisions, dismissed an election petition by the California Nurses Association (CNA), because it controlled a nurse registry service that made revenue-producing referrals to the instant hospital, among other employers. The Board's lengthy and divided opinions suggest that the dismissal rested on stricter conflict-of-interest standards than those previously applied.

CNA represented hospital "employees" and also operated nurse registry services through CNA-controlled separate corporations. The registries referred nurses for duty at both hospitals and private homes. Private duty referrals depended largely on hospital recommendations and represented a significant percentage of agency referrals. CNA members paid the registry 4 percent, and nonmembers, 8 percent, of their total fee.

Prior to CNA's organizational campaign at St. John's, 80 percent of CNA's referrals from the regional registry was to St. John's. Thereafter, that registry lost substantial revenue because the hospital stopped referring patients to, or seeking temporary staff from, CNA's registry.

In dismissing CNA's election petition, the Board stressed that CNA, because of its desire for revenue from the registry services, might not engage in arm's-length bargaining but might instead subordinate the employees' job interests to CNA's business interests.

The majority, rejecting the dissenter's contention that the registry was merely a hiring hall, stressed that CNA did not refer exclusively to employers signatory to collective agreements with CNA. The majority observed that if there had been such exclusivity, "the registry might well be a hiring hall, which would not pose the [instant] conflict."

Member Fanning, the dissenter, noted the lack of evidence as to the amount of referral revenues and urged that the employer had not met its "considerable burden" of establishing a "clear and present" danger of disqualifying conflict. Fanning emphasized that "the majority's new standard" would require disqualification of unions charging a fee for all referrals from "a nonexclusive hiring hall," which he described as one in which an employer, pursuant to a collective bargaining agreement, seeks and gets referrals from the union but may reject the individuals referred and hire from other sources.

(a) Has the majority in *St. John's* adequately answered Fanning's argument that stressed the Board's failure to condemn conventional hiring halls on conflict-of-interest grounds? For material on the impact of the Act on hiring halls, see Chapter 11(B).

(b) What grounds, if any, are there for distinguishing between hiring halls in the construction trade and the CNA registry? Would the acceptability of such a distinction be affected by the number and percentages of firms and employees using each of the union registries? By the supply of qualified labor available from other sources?

(c) What considerations might explain the Board's different treatment of disqualification claims based on alleged conflicts-of-interest and claims based on union corruption or racial discrimination in admitting members?

Compare *St. John's* with the approach in Sierra Vista Hospital, 241 N.L.R.B. 631 (1979). The Board, prompted by judicial disapproval, abandoned its practice of granting conditional certification to labor organizations composed in part of supervisors. In *Sierra Vista*, because of certification, that practice had been conditioned on delegation by the union, a statewide nurses association, of its bargaining authority to a local autonomous chapter controlled by nonsupervisory employees. The Board gave this explanation for its change of position: The issue of whether an association is a "labor organization," under §2(5) of the Act, is separate from whether participation of supervisors disqualifies a "labor organization" from serving as a bargaining representative. Such participation might infringe on the employees' right to a representative concerned solely with their interests or on the employer's interest in loyalty from its own supervisors. Furthermore, although participation by supervisors of a third-party employer (one not involved in the bargaining sought by a labor organization) does not involve the danger that the employer may be "bargaining with itself," such participation might deny employees a representative with undivided concern for their interests. Since there is no "inherent" conflict between supervisors and employees in bargaining, an employer invoking conflict of interest in justification for a particular refusal to bargain will have to show that the "danger of a conflict of interest is clear and present" — a heavy burden likely to forestall measurably dilatory litigation. Such eligibility issues will be considered in representation proceedings despite the general rule excluding from such proceedings unfair labor practice issues of a kind sometimes embedded in issues of qualification. The Board rescinded its prior certification and its refusal-to-bargain order against the hospital, and directed a hearing to determine whether conflict of interest called for denial of certification. Member Truesdale, dissenting in part, urged immediate certification, and litigation in an unfair labor practice proceeding of any issue raised by the supervisors' participation.

e. Prior Certification or Recognition

Brooks v. NLRB
348 U.S. 96 (1954)

FRANKFURTER, J. The [NLRB] conducted a representation election in petitioner's Chrysler-Plymouth agency on April 12, 1951. [Machinist's] District Lodge No. 727 won by a vote of eight to five, and the Labor Board certified it as the exclusive bargaining representative on April 20. A week after the election and the day before the certification, petitioner received a handwritten letter signed by nine of the 13 employees in the bargaining unit stating: "We, the undersigned majority of the employees . . . are not in favor of being represented by Union Local No. 727 as a bargaining agent."

Relying on this letter and the decision of the . . . Sixth Circuit in Labor Board v. Vulcan Forging Co., 188 F.2d 927, petitioner refused to bargain with the union. The Labor Board found that petitioner had thereby committed an unfair labor practice in violation of §§8(a)(1) and 8(a)(5) . . . and the Court of Appeals for the Ninth Circuit enforced the Board's order to bargain, 204 F.2d 899. . . .

The issue before us is the duty of an employer toward a duly certified bargaining agent if, shortly after the election which resulted in the certification, the union has lost, without the employer's fault, a majority of the employees from its membership.

Under the original Wagner Act, the Labor Board was given the power to certify a union as the exclusive representative of the employees in a bargaining unit when it had determined, by election or "any other suitable method," that the union commanded majority support. §9(c). . . . In exercising this authority the Board evolved a number of working rules, of which the following are relevant to our purpose:

(a) A certification, if based on a Board-conducted election, must be honored for a "reasonable" period, ordinarily "one year," in the absence of "unusual circumstances."

(b) "Unusual circumstances" were found in at least three situations: (1) the certified union dissolved or became defunct; (2) as a result of a schism, substantially all the members and officers of the certified union transferred their affiliation to a new local or international; (3) the size of the bargaining unit fluctuated radically within a short time.

(c) Loss of majority support after the "reasonable" period could be questioned in two ways: (1) employer's refusal to bargain, or (2) petition by a rival union for a new election.

(d) If the initial election resulted in a majority for "no union," the election — unlike a certification — did not bar a second election within a year.

The Board uniformly found an unfair labor practice where, during the so-called "certification year," an employer refused to bargain on the ground that the certified union no longer possessed a majority. While the courts in the main enforced the Board's decision, they did not commit themselves to one year as the determinate content of reasonableness. The Board and the courts proceeded along this line of reasoning:

(a) In the political and business spheres, the choice of the voters in an election binds them for a fixed time. This promotes a sense of responsibility in the electorate and needed coherence in administration. These considerations are equally relevant to healthy labor relations.

(b) Since an election is a solemn and costly occasion, conducted under safeguards to voluntary choice, revocation of authority should occur by a procedure no less solemn than that of the initial designation. A petition or a public meeting — in which those voting for and against unionism are disclosed to management, and in which the influences of mass psychology are present — is not comparable to the privacy and independence of the voting booth.

(c) A union should be given ample time for carrying out its mandate on behalf of its members, and should not be under exigent pressure to produce hothouse results or be turned out.

(d) It is scarcely conducive to bargaining in good faith for an employer to know that, if he dillydallies or subtly undermines, union strength may erode and thereby relieve him of his statutory duties at any time, while if he works conscientiously toward agreement, the rank and file may, at the last moment, repudiate their agent.

(e) In situations, not wholly rare, where unions are competing, raiding and strife will be minimized if elections are not at the hazard of informal and short-term recall.

Certain aspects of the Labor Board's representation procedures came under scrutiny in the Congress that enacted the Taft-Hartley Act in 1947. . . . Congress was mindful that, once employees had chosen a union, they could not vote to revoke its authority and refrain from union activities, while if they voted against having a union in the first place, the union could begin at once to agitate for a new election. The [NLRA] was amended to provide that (a) employees could petition the Board for a decertification election, at which they would have an opportunity to choose no longer to be represented by a union, [§9(c)(1)(A)(ii)]; (b) an employer, if in doubt as to the majority claimed by a union without formal election or beset by the conflicting claims of rival unions, could likewise petition the Board for an election, [§9(c)(1)(B)]; (c) after a valid certification or decertification election had been conducted, the Board could not hold a second election in the same bargaining unit until a year had elapsed, [§9(c)(3)]; (d) Board certification could only be granted as the result of an election, [§9(c)(1)], though an employer would presumably still be under a duty to bargain with an uncertified union that had a clear majority. . . .

The Board continued to apply its "one-year certification" rule after the Taft-Hartley Act came into force, except that even "unusual circumstances" no longer left the Board free to order an election where one had taken place within the preceding 12 months. . . .

The issue is open here. No case touching the problem has directly presented it. In Franks Bros. v. Labor Board, 321 U.S. 702, we held that where a union's majority was dissipated after an employer's unfair labor practice in refusing to bargain, the Board could appropriately find that such conduct had undermined the prestige of the union and require the employer to bargain with it for a reasonable period despite the loss of majority. And in Labor Board v. Mexia Textile Mills, Inc., 339 U.S. 563, we held that a claim of an intervening loss of majority was no defense to a proceeding for enforcement of an order to cease and desist from certain unfair labor practices.

Petitioner contends that whenever an employer is presented with evidence that his employees have deserted their certified union, he may forthwith refuse to bargain. In effect, he seeks to vindicate the rights of his employees to select their bargaining representative. If the employees are dissatisfied with their chosen union, they may submit their own grievance to the Board. If an employer has doubts about his duty to continue bargaining, it is his responsibility to petition the Board for relief, while continuing to bargain in good faith at least until the Board has given some indication that his claim has merit. Although the Board may, if the facts warrant, revoke a certification or agree not to pursue a charge of an unfair labor practice, these are matters for the Board; they do not justify employer self-help or judicial intervention. The underlying purpose of this statute is industrial peace. To allow employers to rely on employees' rights in refusing to bargain with the formally designated union is not conducive to that end, it is inimical to it. Congress has devised a formal mode for selection and rejection of bargaining agents and has fixed the spacing of elections, with a view of furthering industrial stability and with due regard to administrative prudence.

We find wanting the arguments against these controlling considerations. In placing a nonconsenting minority under the bargaining responsibility of an agency selected by a majority of the workers, Congress has discarded common-law doctrines of agency. It is contended that since a bargaining agency may be ascertained by methods less formal than a supervised election, informal repudiation should also be sanctioned where decertification by another election is precluded. This is to make situations that are different appear the same. Finally, it is not within the power of this Court to require the Board, as is suggested, to relieve a small employer, like the one involved in this case, of the duty that may be exacted from an enterprise with many employees.

To be sure, what we have said has special pertinence only to the period during which a second election is impossible. But the Board's view that the one-year period should run from the date of certification rather than the date of election seems within the allowable area of the Board's discretion in carrying out congressional policy. See Phelps Dodge Corp. v. Labor Board, 313 U.S. 177, 192-197. . . . Otherwise, encouragement would be given to management or a rival union to delay certification by spurious objections to the conduct of an election and thereby diminish the duration of the duty to bargain. Furthermore, the Board has ruled that one year after certification the employer can ask for an election or, if he has fair doubts about the union's continuing majority, he may refuse to bargain further with it. This, too, is a matter appropriately determined by the Board's administrative authority. . . .

Affirmed.

NOTES

1. Would an employer with "doubts about his duty to continue bargaining" early in the certification year be helped if he followed Justice Frankfurter's advice?

2. During the period in which §9(c)(3) or the Board's policy bars an

election, should a union be able to compel recognition by demonstrating majority status by other means? Consider the results of the following cases in the light of *Brooks*.

(a) Following an independent union's certification and seven months of bargaining, the parties were at an impasse. Thereupon, at a formal meeting a majority of the independent's members voted by secret ballot for its dissolution, for the designation of a local of an international as their bargaining representative, and for a transfer of the independent's treasury to that local. The employer, advised of that vote, stopped checking off dues for the independent but refused to recognize the local. The Board held (3 to 2) that that refusal, although occurring during the independent's certification year, violated §8(a)(5). The majority reasoned that under the "unusual circumstances" doctrine the independent's defunctness relieved the employer of his duty to bargain with it and that the employer lacked a good faith doubt with respect to majority support of the newly designated local. See Rocky Mountain Phosphates, Inc., 138 N.L.R.B. 292 (1962). What risks does such a result impose on employers? Would it be preferable to uphold the employer's refusal until the newly designated union secured from the NLRB an amendment of the certification?

(b) In an election in Conren Inc. v. NLRB, 368 F.2d 173 (7th Cir. 1966), *cert. denied*, 386 U.S. 974 (1967), the employees chose "no union" rather than the Retail Clerks or the Teamsters. Nine months later the Retail Clerks obtained a clear authorization-card majority. The employer urged that under §9(c)(3) he had no duty to bargain with a union that, during the year after an election, evidenced its majority support by other means. The court (2 to 1) affirmed the Board's finding of a §8(a)(5) violation and declared that §9(c)(3) barred only a second election, as distinguished from other means of establishing majority support.

Is *Conren* fairly distinguishable from *Mountain Phosphates?* Suppose the employer in *Conren*, instead of invoking §9(c)(3), had urged that the union's election defeat had reinforced his doubts about the reliability of authorization cards; any difference in result? Cf. NLRB v. Gissel Packing Co., reproduced infra p. 442, and Linden Lumber v. NLRB, noted infra p. 458.

3. Section 8(b)(4)(C) of the Act bars recognition strikes and picketing by an outside union when another union has been certified, and §303 provides for recovery of damages caused by such strikes or picketing. Parks v. Atlanta Printing Pressman, 243 F.2d 284 (5th Cir.), *cert. denied*, 354 U.S. 937 (1957), held that the loss of the certified union's majority was not a defense against an action for damages for a recognition strike called by another union after the expiration of the certification year. If, under such

circumstances, employers are not required to respect certification for bargaining purposes, should a rival union be required to do so? Could an employer lawfully recognize the uncertified union under the circumstances described above? See RCA Del Caribe, Inc., reproduced infra p. 372.

Mar-Jac Poultry, 136 N.L.R.B. 785 (1962). On March 1, 1960, a union certified on November 17, 1959, requested the employer to bargain. On June 8, 1960, the union filed a refusal-to-bargain charge and, on August 9, the employer entered into a settlement agreement calling for good-faith bargaining with the union. On November 7, 1960, the Regional Director issued a letter of compliance. Such bargaining went forward during the six months after the settlement, but in March 1961, the employer petitioned for an election to determine whether the union still retained its majority status. The Board ruled that the petition should be dismissed for the following reason:

> To permit the Employer now to obtain an election would be to allow it to take advantage of its own failure to carry out its statutory obligation contrary to the very reasons for the establishment of the rule that a certification requires bargaining for at least one year. We shall, therefore, in this and similar cases revealing similar inequities, grant the union a period of at least one year of actual bargaining from the date of the settlement agreement.

NOTE

See also Lamar Hotel & Restaurant Employees, 137 N.L.R.B. 226 (1962), *enforced*, 328 F.2d 600 (5th Cir. 1964), *cert. denied*, 379 U.S. 817 (1965), applying the *Mar-Jac* principle so as to extend the certification year for a period equal to that during which the employer refused to bargain. Does tacking on two discrete bargaining periods, totaling one year, achieve the purpose of the rule granting a certified union the right to bargain without interruption during the year following certification? See Pepe, Certification-Year Rule and the *Mar-Jac Poultry* Extension, 19 Lab. L.J. 335, 347-351 (1968).

Pennco, Inc.
250 N.L.R.B. 716 (1980), *enforced*, 684 F.2d 340 (6th Cir. 1982), *cert. denied*, 459 U.S. 994 (1982)

. . . [T]he Union began an economic strike on May 18, 1977, at Respondent's Ashland, Kentucky, plant and established a picket line. As a result of incidents on the picket line the . . . Circuit Court of Boyd County, Kentucky, issued a restraining order in July 1977.

During the last pay period prior to the strike, Respondent employed 173 bargaining unit members. By November 3, 1977, the pay period after the expiration of the 1-year certification period, there were 257 employees in the bargaining unit on the payroll, of whom 47 had been on the payroll prior to the strike. All the employees working in Respondent's plant during the strike had to cross the union picket line.

Respondent withdrew recognition from the Union in November 1977. The strike continued until September 15, 1978, when the Union removed its pickets and 42 employees unconditionally offered to return to work. At no time between November 1, 1976, and the time of the hearing in this case did the Union abandon the bargaining unit or relinquish its interest in negotiating a collective-bargaining agreement on behalf of unit employees.

In addition to the facts set forth in our earlier Decision,[c] the parties have stipulated that 109 employees failed to report to work upon commencement of the strike and 109 employees remained on strike when Respondent withdrew recognition. Further, all of the striking employees — and 25 employees who left their employment with Respondent between May 18 and November 5, 1977, for reasons other than the strike — were replaced by Respondent prior to the withdrawal of recognition. The parties state that they have no affirmative evidence that any strikers abandoned their status as strikers as of the time recognition was withdrawn.

In our original Decision, we found that since the evidence presented by Respondent was insufficient to support its asserted good-faith doubt of the Union's majority status, Respondent had not rebutted the Union's continuing presumption of majority status. Upon reconsideration of our original Decision and consideration of the further stipulation of the parties, we reaffirm our previous Decision. . . .

. . . Upon expiration of the certification year, the presumption of majority status continues but becomes rebuttable. An employer who wishes to withdraw recognition from a certified union after a year may rebut the presumption in one of two ways: (1) by showing that on the date recognition was withdrawn the union did not in fact enjoy majority support, or (2) by presenting evidence of a sufficient objective basis for a reasonable doubt of the union's majority status at the time the employer refused to bargain.

The presumption of continuing majority status essentially serves two important functions of Federal labor policy. First, it promotes continuity in bargaining relationships. . . . The resulting industrial stability remains a

---

[c][The Board, sua sponte, had decided to reconsider its original decision (242 N.L.R.B. 467 (1979)), so advised the parties, and received a supplemental stipulation. — EDS.]

primary objective of the Wagner Act, and to an even greater extent, the Taft-Hartley Act. Second, [that] presumption . . . protects the express statutory right of employees to designate a collective-bargaining representative of their own choosing, and to prevent an employer from impairing that right without some objective evidence that the representative the employees have designated no longer enjoys majority support.

 . . . [I]n light of the dual policies underlying the presumption, the employer's burden [of rebuttal] is a heavy one. Thus, "it is insufficient . . . that the employer merely intuits nonsupport," and good-faith doubt "may not depend solely on unfounded speculation or a subjective state of mind."

A corollary of the overall presumption of continuing majority status is that, again absent evidence to the contrary, new employees are presumed to support the incumbent union in the same ratio as those they replace. Respondent contends, however, that it had sufficient objective evidence to establish its good-faith doubt of majority status since its new employees should be presumed *not* to support the Union because they crossed the union picket line. The thrust of this argument is either that the presumption of majority status does not extend to employees in the event of a strike, or that that presumption may be rebutted by the countervailing presumption that Respondent would have us adopt.

We reject Respondent's contentions. Clearly, Respondent is in error if it is contending that the presumption of majority status does not apply in the event of a strike where strike replacements and other new employees cross a picket line. The Board has long held that this presumption applies as a matter of law, and it is incumbent upon Respondent to rebut it even, and perhaps especially, in the event of a strike. Similarly, Respondent is in error if it is urging the Board to permit it to rebut the presumption of majority status with its own presumption for it "misconceives the nature of the employer's burden of proof . . . this burden can be sustained only by objective evidence and presumptions do not provide such evidence." Certainly in nonstrike circumstances Respondent would be required to rebut the presumption of majority status based on objective evidence, and we see no persuasive reason to make an exception here.

Indeed, the policies which underline the heavy burden of proof imposed on an employer in order to rebut the presumption of continuing majority status are particularly compelling when a strike is involved. In this regard, the right of employees to engage in concerted activities such as economic strikes is protected, *inter alia*, by §§7 and 13 of the Act. . . . Although employees have the right to engage in economic strikes they exercise this right at the risk of permanent replacement. Respondent, in effect, is asking us to add to this risk the potential additional loss of the employees' collective-bargaining representative based solely on a presumption Respondent would have us draw. Thus, adoption of Respondent's presumption would allow an employer to withdraw recognition and eliminate a union as its employee's representative as soon as an economic strike commences and a number of employees equivalent to the number on strike are willing to cross a picket line. Such an additional burden on the employees' right to strike would effectively impair that right, and disturb the delicate balance of competing weapons which the Board and the courts have recognized in the labor relations arena.

Further, the presumption that Respondent urges us to adopt is not a persuasive one. In this regard, the Board has held, with court approval, that an employee's return to work during a strike does not provide a reasonable basis for presuming that he has repudiated the union as his bargaining representative. Absent supporting evidence it may mean no more than that he was forced to return to work for financial reasons or that he did not support that particular strike. Similarly, the Board, with court approval, has held that a replacement hired for a striking employee cannot, without more, be presumed to reject the union as his bargaining representative. Such a worker also may be compelled to seek employment, or may disapprove of the strike in question, but would support other union initiatives. Thus, in light of this uncertainty as to the reasons employees cross a picket line, Respondent's presumption alone is clearly not sufficient to rebut the presumption of majority status nor its corollary that new employees, including strike replacements, are presumed to support the Union in the same ratio as those they replace.

Finally, we note that Respondent has offered no other evidence supporting a "presumption" that the union lost its majority status. Thus, it has not shown that any of its employees who crossed the picket line, in fact, did not support the Union.[16] This lack of corroborative evidence further undermines the utility of the inference Respondent would have us draw and its assertion of good-faith doubt of majority status.[17]

---

[16] Although Respondent emphasizes . . . that only 42 striking employees sought reinstatement at the conclusion of the strike, Respondent withdrew recognition from the Union approximately 10 months prior to the end of the strike and so cannot rely on the number of strikers offering to return to work as an objective consideration underlying its asserted good-faith doubt at the time it withdrew recognition.

Respondent additionally contends that . . . violence . . . on the picket line crossed by its employees rendered the support of these employees for the Union even more unlikely. However, in view of the speculative nature of the employees' reasons for crossing the picket line, the occurrence of [such] violence is, at best, one factor weakening the presumption of majority status but not alone rebutting it.

[17] We note . . . that this case is distinguishable from Beacon Upholstery Company, Inc., 226 N.L.R.B. 1360 (1976). In that case striking employees had been lawfully discharged

In view of the foregoing, we conclude that Respondent has failed to meet its burden of establishing a good-faith doubt based on objective considerations of the Union's majority status as of the time it withdrew recognition from the Union. Accordingly, we affirm our previous Decision and Order in which we found that Respondent's withdrawal of recognition from the Union and refusal to supply the Union with a copy of one of its two health insurance plans were violative of §8(a)(5) and (1) of the Act. . . .

[In NLRB v. Pennco, Inc., 684 F.2d 340 (6th Cir. 1982), the court enforced the Board's order, emphasizing these considerations: The picket line violence had ended approximately 3 1/2 months before the withdrawal of recognition, and there was no evidence as to how many of the employees working on the day recognition was withdrawn had also been working when violence had occurred. At most, 109 of the 257 replacements would have lost their jobs to strikers following a strike settlement. Furthermore, there was no evidence that any particular replacement knew of that prospect.[d]

The court declined to accept either of the two conflicting presumptions, stating that "neither is justified under the stipulated facts." The court added (at 343):

> . . . the evidence demonstrated by Pennco is sufficient only to put the parties in equipoise. Yet, equipoise is not enough for Pennco to demonstrate by objective evidence a good faith doubt as to the Union's majority status. Pennco would need some further evidence of union non-support in order to shift the burden to the Board to prove the Union in fact had majority status on the critical day. See Automated Business Systems v. NLRB, 497 F.2d 262 (6th Cir. 1974).

White, J., joined by Blackmun and Rehnquist, JJ., dissented from the Supreme Court's denial of certiorari in *Pennco* (see 459 U.S. 994-996 (1982)). Justice White noted that several circuits, in part because of the specific facts of the cases before them, had rejected the Board's presumption

---

and were no longer in the bargaining unit. Here, the bargaining unit is composed of striking employees and their replacements. . . . Thus, their interests are not as divergent as those of the two groups in *Beacon Upholstery*. Accordingly, we are unwilling to presuppose, as Respondent would have us do, that the Union would be unable to accommodate the apparently conflicting interests of the striking and nonstriking employees, particularly in light of the Union's statutory duty of fair representation requiring it to serve the interests of all bargaining unit employees fairly and in good faith.

[d][In I.T. Services, 263 N.L.R.B. 1183 (1982), the Board, in upholding the employer's withdrawal of recognition, relied in part on the presence of factors missing in *Pennco*: first, the replacements (who outnumbered the returned strikers) knew that the union wanted them dismissed; second, picket line violence, for which the union was responsible, had been directed at the replacements throughout the 11-month strike. The Board, however, carefully noted that it had also relied on all other factors mentioned by the ALJ. — EDS.]

regarding strike replacements' support of an incumbent union and had accepted the antithetical presumption. He urged that review was justified by the conflict among the circuits and between the circuits and the NLRB, and by the need for a uniform resolution of the important issues presented.]

NOTES

1. A court of appeals' dictum in *Pennco* indicated that even if a respondent's evidence of good faith doubt was sufficient to rebut the presumption of continuing support, such evidence would not be an absolute defense if the General Counsel produced evidence that the union had in fact represented a majority of employees on the refusal-to-bargain date. 684 F.2d at 343. The Board itself has wavered as to whether an employer's proof of a good faith doubt should, as the Board said in *Pennco*, constitute an absolute defense. See, e.g., Automated Business Systems, 205 N.L.R.B. 532 (1973), which discusses prior Board cases and adopts the absolute defense rule; the court of appeals denied enforcement on other grounds, but apparently rejected the absolute defense position. See 497 F.2d 262, 270, 271 n.7 (6th Cir. 1974).

Seemingly, the acceptance of evidence of a good faith doubt as an absolute defense lightens the employer's burden. But the difference, if any, between the two approaches depends largely on the strictness of the requirements for employer proof of an objectively based "good faith doubt." Indeed, it is fairly arguable that those requirements have become so strict that the Board finds the presumption rebutted only by proof of the incumbent's lack of majority support and not merely by a good faith doubt of the continuation of such support. See Thomas Industries, Inc. v. NLRB, 687 F.2d 863, 867 (6th Cir. 1982); Comment, Application of the Good-Faith-Doubt Test to the Presumption of Continued Majority Status of Incumbent Unions, 1981 Duke L.J. 718, 724, 727.

2. In assessing the Board's standards for proving good faith doubt and its fluctuations as to whether such proof constitutes an absolute defense, what factors do you consider significant? What argument(s), if any, might be drawn from the controversy over the respective voting rights of economic strikers and their replacements? On the question of voting rights, see infra p. 429.

3. As will appear later in this chapter, an employer is not required to recognize a union for the first time merely because the employer has independent knowledge of the union's majority support in an appropriate unit. What is the reason for focusing on the employer's knowledge in determining whether the presumption of continuing majority support has been rebutted

and the employer's obligation to recognize an incumbent union extinguished?

4. In order to harmonize its approach in representation and §8(a)(5) cases, respectively, the Board ruled that an employer's election petition questioning an incumbent union's majority status would be dismissed unless the petitioner, by objective evidence, demonstrated reasonable grounds for doubting the incumbent's majority status. See United States Gypsum, 157 N.L.R.B. 652 (1962). See also Dresser Industries, Inc., 264 N.L.R.B. 1088 (1982), referred to infra p. 378. Furthermore, the Board has held that an employer's noncoercive and otherwise valid poll of employees, if conducted without a reasonable basis for doubting the union's continuing majority, violates the Act and does not validate a refusal to bargain even if the poll discloses the incumbent's lack of majority support. See Montgomery Ward & Co., 210 N.L.R.B. 717 (1974); Forbidden City Restaurant, 265 N.L.R.B. 409 (1982). Some courts have, however, upheld otherwise valid polls on "substantial objective evidence of a loss of union support" (such as decline in membership), even though the evidence is insufficient to justify withdrawal. See Thomas Industries, Inc. v. NLRB, 687 F.2d 863, 868 (6th Cir. 1982). In *Thomas Industries*, "immediately before" the poll the employer had delivered an antiunion but noncoercive speech on company property and time. Should it be material to the legality of the poll or the subsequent withdrawal of recognition that the union's president also spoke to the employees before the poll? Cf. NLRB v. A.W. Thompson, Inc., 651 F.2d 1141, 1145 (5th Cir. 1981) (legality conditioned, in part, on employer's giving notice of poll to the union). Why a notice requirement? More generally, why permit — or bar — otherwise valid polls of an incumbent union's support when a Board election would be precluded?

Students should reexamine the issues raised by *Pennco* in light of *RCA del Caribe* and *Bruckner Nursing Home*, which follow immediately.

RCA Del Caribe, Inc.
262 N.L.R.B. 963 (1982)

[After Respondent recognized the IBEW in 1971, those parties entered into successive collective bargaining agreements covering Respondent's production and maintenance (P&M) employees. Negotiations to replace the agreement expiring on January 2, 1975, began in November 1974 and continued through January 8, 1975. On January 9, 1975, the employees, with the IBEW's authorization, began an economic strike against Respondent. On January 27, a rival union, the Union Independiente, filed an election petition with the NLRB, covering the P&M unit. Respondent refused to negotiate with the IBEW while the petition was pending; consequently, on February 24, the IBEW submitted to the Respondent valid authorization sheets from 157 of the 227 P&M employees. After determining that the 157 signatures were genuine, on February 25 Respondent resumed negotiations with the IBEW at the latter's request; on February 26, the parties executed a renewal agreement which, inter alia, retained the prior union security clause and raised wages. After the parties stipulated the facts and waived a hearing before an ALJ, an order was issued transferring the proceeding to the Board.]

. . . In this and a companion case, Abraham Grossman d/b/a Bruckner Nursing Home, 262 N.L.R.B. 955 (1982), we endeavor . . . to redefine the Board's longstanding *Midwest Piping* doctrine.[e] . . . In *Bruckner*, we set forth a new policy with respect to the requirements of employer neutrality in rival union initial organizing situations. In this case, we shall reexamine the law applicable to situations wherein an incumbent union is challenged by an "outside" union.

. . . The Board reversed itself in Shea Chemical Corporation [121 N.L.R.B. 1027 (1958)] and held that an employer faced with a pending petition from an outside union must cease bargaining with the incumbent and maintain . . . strict neutrality with respect to both the incumbent and the challenging labor organization, until such time as one or the other has been certified following a Board-conducted election. As in the *Midwest Piping* initial organizing cases, the reasons for requiring strict employer neutrality and a Board-conducted election in the incumbent setting have been the Board's concern that employees should have the greatest possible freedom in the selection and . . . retention of their collective-bargaining representatives. To this end, the Board has held that the continued negotiation of a contract with an incumbent union in the face of a validly supported petition was not the conduct of a neutral employer. The Board did, however, provide that the incumbent could still process grievances and otherwise act as the exclusive representative of employees in the unit involved. . . .

. . . [I]t has become increasingly evident that the Board's efforts to promote employee free choice have been at a price to the stability of collective-bargaining relationships. In particular, the *Shea Chemical* adaptation of *Midwest Piping* has failed to accord incumbency the advantages which in nonrival situations the Board has encouraged in the interest of industrial stability. The recognition of the special status of an incumbent union indi-

---

[e] [See 63 N.L.R.B. 1060 (1945). The instant opinion noted several circuits' rejection of that doctrine. — EDS.]

cates a judgment that, having once achieved the mantle of exclusive bargaining representative, a union ought not to be deterred from its representative functions even though its majority status is under challenge. . . .

Because *Midwest Piping* focused on a legitimate concern for preserving the right of employees to change their bargaining representative, the Act's concern for stability in collective-bargaining relationships embodied in the doctrine of the presumption of continuing majority status was not given its due. While the filing of a valid petition may raise a doubt as to majority status, the filing, in and of itself, should not overcome the strong presumption in favor of the continuing majority status of the incumbent and should not serve to strip it of the advantages and authority it could otherwise legitimately claim.

We have concluded that requiring an employer to withdraw from bargaining after a petition has been filed is not the best means of assuring employer neutrality. . . . Unlike initial organizing situations, an employer in an existing collective-bargaining relationship cannot observe strict neutrality. In many situations, as here, the incumbent challenged by an outside union is in the process of — perhaps close to completing — negotiation of a contract when the petition is filed. If an employer continues to bargain, employees may perceive a preference for the incumbent union, whether or not the employer holds that preference. On the other hand, if an employer withdraws from bargaining, particularly when agreement is imminent, this withdrawal may more emphatically signal repudiation of the incumbent and preference for the rival. Again, it may be of little practical consequence to the employees whether the employer actually intended this signal or was compelled by law to withdraw from bargaining. We further recognize that an employer may be faced with changing economic circumstances which could require immediate response and commensurate changes in working conditions. . . . Thus, to prohibit negotiations until the Board has ruled on the results of a new election might work an undue hardship on employers, unions, and employees. Under the circumstances, we believe preservation of the status quo through an employer's continued bargaining with an incumbent is the better way to approximate employer neutrality.

For the foregoing reasons, we have determined that the mere filing of a representation petition by an outside, challenging union will no longer require or permit an employer to withdraw from bargaining or executing a contract with an incumbent union.[12] Under this rule, an employer will not violate Section 8(a)(2) by postpetition negotiations or execution of a contract

---

[12] We hereby overrule *Shea Chemical,* supra, to the extent it is inconsistent with this Decision and Order.

with an incumbent, but an employer will violate Section 8(a)(5) by withdrawing from bargaining based solely on the [filing of a] petition . . . by an outside union. . . .[13]

. . . It should be clear that our new rule does not have the effect of insulating incumbent unions from a legitimate outside challenge . . . [A] timely filed petition will put an incumbent to the test of demonstrating that it still is the majority choice. . . . Unlike before, however, . . . an incumbent will retain its earned right to demonstrate its effectiveness . . . at the bargaining table. An outside union and its employee supporters will now be required to take their incumbent opponent as they find it — as the previously elected majority representative.[14]

Although some courts of appeals have suggested that an employer could extinguish the question concerning representation raised by the filing of a petition merely by satisfying itself that it was still negotiating with a majority representative, as Respondent here did, we emphasize that the Board will continue to process valid petitions timely filed by outside unions and to conduct the election as expeditiously as possible. To do otherwise would make the difficult task of unseating an incumbent almost impossible, and would too often have the further effect of making the filing of a petition during the "open period" a nullity. If the incumbent prevails in the election held, any contract executed with the incumbent will be valid and binding. If the challenging union prevails, however, any contract executed with the incumbent will be null and void.

. . . [W]hile Union Independiente filed a valid petition during the open period, Respondent's continued negotiations and execution of a contract with the incumbent IBEW were not violations of the Act within the meaning of Section 8(a)(2).[16] Accordingly, we shall dismiss the complaint in its entirety.

Chairman VAN DE WATER, dissenting: . . . The [requirement of neutrality pending an election embodied in *Midwest Piping*] does not prejudice any party. The only effect of this requirement is a minimal delay in selecting the bargaining representative — a delay which the Supreme Court [in Lin-

---

[13] Of course, this rule will not preclude an employer from withdrawing recognition in good faith based on other objective considerations. See, e.g., United States Gypsum Company, 157 N.L.R.B. 652 (1966). . . .

[14] Chairman Van de Water, in his dissent, treats an incumbent union as nothing more than "one of the claimants to majority status." He ignores the plain fact that the incumbent is the claimant whose majority status has been demonstrated, and that the Board presumes that majority status to continue in the absence of objective factors indicating its loss.

[16] In reaching this conclusion, we did not rely on the [IBEW's submission of] valid authorization sheets . . . since we do not believe an incumbent union is required to reaffirm its status after a petition has been filed.

den Lumber Div., Summer & Co. v. NLRB, 419 U.S. 301 (1974)] has found to be compatible with the goal of stable industrial relations. Furthermore, the conclusiveness of election results reinforces stability in labor relations[20] at the same time it furthers employee rights . . . at the heart of the Act. . . .

. . . [T]hat an incumbent union is one of the claimants to majority status is all the more reason to impose the requirement of neutrality.[22] For an incumbent bargaining representative enjoys certain inherent advantages over an outside challenger. An incumbent, through its stewards and other . . . representatives, is present in the plant, involved in the day-to-day workplace and worklives of the employees. It is also reasonable to presume that an incumbent has a legitimacy in the eyes of the employees by the very fact that the employer . . . deals with it as the employees' bargaining representative. . . .

. . . [A]n employer may prefer to displace the incumbent union. . . . [B]y engaging in either lawful hard bargaining or unlawful surface bargaining, the employer might cause the employees to become disenchanted with the incumbent. . . . Equally, an employer may wish to retain the current union relationship in the face of a challenge by a rival union which the employer may consider a more powerful or effective employee representative — resulting in the employer's giving up a past hard bargaining stance to gain employee favoritism for the incumbent as a means toward foreseeable longer term employer gain. Hence, the majority's allowance of continuing incumbent bargaining after a rival petition has been filed, whether or not the incumbent is able to secure a majority of signatures requesting continuance of bargaining, places the employer in a position to maneuver employee sentiments.

There are other practical considerations as well for imposing a requirement of neutrality. . . . Obviously, an incumbent union's bargaining leverage is limited when a substantial number of employees have indicated a desire to be represented by a rival union. And, an employer who doubts the incumbent's majority status and who does not have a preference between the

[20] The majority herein and some courts have . . . suggested that stability . . . is undermined and that bargaining relationships are disrupted by application of the *Midwest Piping* doctrine. See, e.g., NLRB v. Peter Paul, Inc., 467 F.2d 700 (9th Cir. 1972). . . . In my judgment, their assessments are incorrect. Further, I believe their approach fails to consider . . . that Congress provided that a Board election be the sole forum for deciding the question concerning representation raised by a petition, and ignores *Linden Lumber*'s admonition that elections are the favored means for resolving such questions.

[22] As a clarification to employees the Board can modify . . . the "Notice of Election" to explain that Board law requires the temporary suspension of bargaining pending the employees' decision regarding which labor organization will represent them. [This footnote number has been relocated. — EDS.]

competing unions may well hesitate to conclude an agreement with the incumbent for fear of later learning that it must bargain with another union. Thus, there may be a negligible chance of progress in bargaining. In these circumstances, such bargaining would be an exercise in futility for both parties, the results of which would be frustration, waste of time, and division of energy between bargaining and campaigning. Predictably, the denouement would be lengthy and costly 8(a)(5) litigation — which could be of no conceivable benefit to the employer, the union, or the employees. . . .

Member JENKINS, dissenting. . . . While I share the majority's concerns for the Board's unsuccessful enforcement efforts . . . , I believe we can resolve that through fine tuning of *Midwest Piping* rather than . . . resorting to a major overhaul. . . . [W]e have applied the doctrine too [mechanically]. . . . [W]e have failed to define just what constitutes a substantial claim [of a real question concerning representation]. It is our error of regarding even *de minimis* support for a competing union as sufficient to halt the bargaining relationship which has caused the courts to reject our views. That problem can be solved simply by requiring substantial employee support for the rival union before we would proceed to conduct a Board election. I propose a 15-percent showing of employee support for a rival union as the requirement for holding such an election. For, I view a 15-percent showing in a two-union contest as approximately equivalent to the Board's current 30-percent administrative requirement (for elections involving a single union), based on my observation of the frequency of dual cards and the presence of some hardcore opponents of any union in the usual employee complement. . . .

NOTES

1. The Board states that a contract executed with an incumbent "will be null and void" if the outside union wins the election. Is that view reconcilable with the Board's approach in *American Seating*, supra p. 356?

2. Is an employer who thinks about the *Del Caribe* approach likely to be concerned that a victorious outside union will seek to improve the package secured by the incumbent? Could that prospect encourage an employer to hold something back, something to give to the rival if it should win the election? Is that consideration relevant to the choice between the majority and dissenting views in *Del Caribe?*

3. After the union's certification on July 1, 1976, the parties during four bargaining sessions over a ten-month period agreed on a broad range of issues but not a complete package. On July 2, 1977, a decertification petition

was filed, with notice to the employer. Referring to that petition, the employer thereupon advised the union that bargaining was suspended pending resolution of the representation question. The employer's lawyer also advised union counsel that the employer was relying on Telautograph, Inc., 199 N.L.R.B. 892 (1972), which, the lawyer stated, precludes bargaining with an incumbent or other union pending resolution of a decertification petition. The union filed a §8(a)(5) charge against the employer.

Assume that the decertification petition had been supported by (a) 51 percent of the unit, (b) 30 percent of the unit, or (c) 15 percent of the unit, and the matter comes to the Board shortly after its decision in *Del Caribe*. In each of those situations, how should the complaint be disposed of and what Board order, if any, should issue? See generally Dresser Industries, Inc., 264 N.L.R.B. 1088 (1982) (overruling *Telautograph* for reasons stated in *Del Caribe*); and N.T. Enloe Memorial Hospital, 250 N.L.R.B. 583 (1980), *enforced* 682 F.2d 790 (9th Cir. 1982), holding that an employer's petition, coupled with advice from the Regional Director's office that a real question of representation had been raised, did not constitute reasonable grounds for doubting the incumbent's continuing majority support. The court of appeals observed (at 794) that the case did not involve rival unions, or a decertification petition. Is there any basis for the distinction implicit in the court's observation?

4. See generally, Getman, The Midwest Piping Doctrine: An Example of the Need for Appraisal of Labor Board Dogma, 31 U. Chi. L. Rev. 292 (1964).

Bruckner Nursing Home, 262 N.L.R.B. 955 (1982). In early September 1974, Local 144 of the Hotel, Hospital, Nursing Home & Allied Health Services Union ("Local 144") advised the employer of its card-based majority and scheduled an impartial card count. Thereupon, Local 1115, Joint Board, Nursing Home & Hospital Employees Division ("Local 1115"), told the employer of its competing organizing campaign and objected to his recognizing another union. On September 23, Local 1115 filed with the NLRB charges of unlawful interference by the employer and Local 144. The impartial count, on September 27, showed that Local 144 had cards from over 80 percent of the 125 employees, while Local 1115 had only two cards. Nevertheless, the employer rejected Local 144's recognition request, pending disposition of Local 1115's charges. Several weeks after these charges were dismissed, the employer recognized Local 144, and on December 18, 1974 executed a collective bargaining agreement with that local. Local 1115 then filed additional unfair labor practice charges. Neither local had filed a representation petition. The ALJ found that Local 1115's representation claim had been "colorable," concluded that the employer, by executing an agreement in the face of a real question of representation, had violated §8(a)(2), and recommended that the employer be ordered to cease giving effect to the agreement and to withhold recognition from Local 144, pending its certification by the Board.

In a decision issued the same day as *Del Caribe*, the Board ordered dismissal of the complaint, reasoning as follows: In *Midwest Piping*, the employer had been found guilty of unlawful assistance because, prior to a Board-conducted election, he had recognized one of two unions, both of which had filed representation petitions and had campaigned extensively. In subsequent cases the Board had applied *Midwest Piping* even though an election petition had not been filed, finding a violation when an employer, relying on an informal showing of support, had recognized one union despite another union's representation claim that was not "clearly unsupportable" or "naked." These uncertain standards had enabled unions with only meager support to frustrate the statutory purposes by blocking bargaining by a union enjoying majority support. Furthermore, many courts had rejected this extension of *Midwest Piping* as well as the Board's premise that authorization cards were too unreliable to be controlling when rival unions were involved.

Accordingly, the Board revised its prior approach, stating:

> [W]e will no longer find 8(a)(2) violations in rival union, initial organizing situations when an employer recognizes a labor organization which represents an uncoerced, unassisted majority, before a valid petition for an election has been filed with the Board. However, once notified of a valid petition, an employer must refrain from recognizing any of the rival unions. . . .

The Board also acknowledged, but rejected, the view expressed by some courts that a pending election petition does not itself render unlawful an employer's recognition of one of several competing unions.

NOTES

1. Is the Board's approach in *Bruckner* sound? What considerations might lie behind an employer's voluntary recognition of one union despite awareness of a rival union's organizing effort? Are those considerations inconsistent with the Act's policy of furthering employee free choice?

2. An employer has 100 production employees. On December 1, Union A asks the employer for a bargaining session and tenders undeniable evidence that 60 production employees have signed valid authorization cards. On December 3, Union B tells the employer that it has just begun to

organize the production employees, but is making good progress. Neither union files an election petition. On December 4, the employer recognizes Union A and enters into a three-year contract covering the production employees. Has the Act been violated?

2.   "Appropriate Units" for Election and Bargaining

Before an election can be held, an electoral unit must be determined. The NLRA, as amended (§9(c)(4)), provides for unit determination by agreement of the parties, subject to the Board's rules and regulations, or by the Board (§9(b)). Pursuant to the 1961 delegation, the Board acts initially through the Regional Directors. In most cases, the parties reach agreement,[f] and the agreed-upon unit is accepted by the Regional Director unless the unit is manifestly inappropriate.

In contested cases, the unit is determined on the basis of a hearing held before a hearing officer, usually the field examiner to whom the petition was assigned for investigation. The hearing, which purports to be nonadversary in character, is part of the investigation in which the primary interest of the Board agents is said to be to insure that the record contains a full statement of facts.[g] Transcripts of hearings are submitted to the Regional Director without recommendations.

Unit determinations have always involved important and thorny issues for the Board. Frequently, such determinations, like the drawing of election districts in other contexts, have been decisive in determining whether there would be any collective bargaining at all in a plant or enterprise. Unions and employers have sought to gerrymander accordingly. Furthermore, when an election leads to the certification of one or more unions, the unit (or units) shapes the scope of the unions' bargaining authority, the concomitant duty of fair representation, and the structure for bargaining, as well as the extent and legality of strikes and lockouts. Unit determination has important consequences on the character of bargaining structures, the accommodation of the interests of skilled and unskilled workers, work-assignment disputes between unions, the impact of antitrust laws on labor relations, and the relative power

---

[f] In 1980 there were 6,672 election agreements, comprising 80 percent of the cases closed by elections of all kinds. See 45 N.L.R.B. Ann. Rep. 263 (1980). There are two kinds of consent procedures: (1) consent election followed by the Regional Director's determination of disputes concerning the validity of the election, the more frequently used procedure; and (2) the consent-election agreement (or stipulation) followed by Board determination of such disputes. See NLRB, Statements of Procedure, Series No. 8, as amended, §101.19.

[g] NLRB, Statements of Procedure, Series No. 8, as amended, §101.20. Should the primary interest of Board agents, including the General Counsel, be different in unfair labor practice proceedings?

of labor and management. See Livernash, The Relation of Power to the Structure and Process of Collective Bargaining, 6 J. Law & Econ. 10 (1963); Leslie, Labor Bargaining Units, 70 Va. L. Rev. 353 (1984) (an exploration of the relationship of NLRB unit criteria to models of union activity and labor markets). Such determinations may also affect the degree of competition within the economy although that consideration has not been the Board's concern. As already indicated, bargaining for a particular unit may have an impact on labor-management relations that extends far beyond that unit.

Section 9(b) of the Wagner Act gave the Board extremely broad discretion in the choice of units, from "an employer unit, craft unit, plant unit, or subdivision thereof."[h] The Taft-Hartley amendments to §9(b) imposed specific limitations of varying clarity upon that discretion. Nevertheless, as the following excerpt indicates, the Board retains broad latitude in this area.

NLRB Annual Report
Vol. 14, pp. 32-33 (1949)

. . . [T]he 1947 amendments to the act have, in the main, left unchanged the familiar basic tests of appropriateness [previously] formulated by the Board. Thus, in resolving unit issues, the Board is still guided by the fundamental concept that only employees having a substantial mutuality of interest in wages, hours, and working conditions, as revealed by the type of work they perform, should be appropriately grouped in a single unit. . . . Chief among these criteria of appropriateness are: (1) the extent and type of union organization[25] and the history of collective bargaining in behalf of the employees involved or other employees of the same employer or of other employers in the same industry; (2) the duties, skill, wages, and working conditions of the employees; (3) the relationship between the proposed unit or units and the employer's organization, management, and operation of his business, including the geographical location of the various plants involved; and (4) the desires of the employees themselves.

---

[h] Cf. §§2, 4, and 9 of the Railway Labor Act, providing for designation by a majority of any "craft or class" and conferring authority over representation disputes on the National Mediation Board. It should also be observed that the National Mediation Board is not required to, but may in its discretion, make the employer a party to unit determinations. See Brotherhood of Ry. & S.S. Clerks v. Association for the Benefit of Non-Contract Employees, 380 U.S. 650, 666-667 (1965); SMB Stage Line v. Natl Mediation Bd., 574 F.2d 394, 399 (1978), cert. denied, 439 U.S. 881 (1978).

[25] Subsec. 9(c)(5) provides: "In determining whether a unit is appropriate for the purposes specified in subsec. (b) [of sec. 9] the extent to which the employees have organized shall not be controlling." However, the extent of employee organization is still *one* of several factors to be weighed in determining the appropriateness of a unit. . . .

[See generally J. Abodeely, R. Hammer, & A. Sandler, The NLRB and the Appropriate Bargaining Unit (rev. ed. 1981).]

a.   Craft, Departmental, or Industrial Unit

Early in its history, the Board, faced with the rival claims of craft unions and the industrial unions sponsored by the CIO, tended to select large units when one union appeared to have a majority in such units. See Jones, Self-Determination vs. Stability of Labor Relations, 58 Mich. L. Rev. 313, 315 (1960). After protests by the AFL, the Board reconsidered that policy and held "Globe elections" on the basis of its landmark decision in Matter of Globe Mach. & Stamping Co., 3 N.L.R.B. 294 (1937). In that case, almost all the employees belonged to one of four unions seeking initial certification and disputing the appropriate unit. The Auto Workers (CIO) requested a unit for all production and maintenance ("P & M") workers; two AFL craft unions urged a unit for metal polishers and punch press operators, respectively; and an AFL federal union requested a unit for all the P & M workers remaining after the craft units had been carved out. The membership rolls of the four unions were in such confusion that an accurate determination of the employees' preferences was not possible. The polishing and punch press work had been done in separate and defined areas, required some, but not a high degree of skill, and involved the transfer of men from that work to other departments of the plant. Production was so highly integrated that a stoppage in one department would have shut down the whole plant. Finally, the history of organization and bargaining was inconclusive since both craft and plantwide negotiations had been successful.

The Board concluded that the considerations supporting each of the four proposed units were evenly balanced and that under such circumstances the "determining factor" should be the wishes of the employees themselves. Accordingly, the Board ordered three separate elections: (1) among the polishers, (2) among the punch press operators, and (3) among the rest of the P & M workers, declaring (at p. 300): "On the results of these elections will depend the determination of the appropriate unit for purposes of collective bargaining. Such of the groups as do not choose the UAWA will constitute separate and distinct appropriate units, and such as do choose the UAWA will together constitute a single appropriate unit."

Vote tallying and ballot forms for Globe-type elections raise complex questions. One underlying question is (a) whether employees in the putatively separate (or S) unit(s) should be included in the larger unit if a majority of those voting in the S unit does not support separate representation or, instead, (b) whether a requirement for such inclusion should be an affirmative vote in its favor. Although language in *Globe* could be read as adopting alternative (b), the Board's practice in *Globe* elections is to pool the S-votes with the votes in the rest of the more inclusive unit if a majority of S-voters does not support separate representation.

The form of the ballot in a *Globe* election also involves a potential ambiguity: The S group may choose among (a) the S union, (b) the I union (seeking the more inclusive unit), and (c) "neither." Such a ballot denies members of the S group an opportunity to show preferences beyond their first; thus it does not permit them to show that if the S union does not get a majority, their second choice would be the I union. A related difficulty arises when a majority of the S unit votes for the I union but that union does not get a majority in the larger unit. The S vote is, of course, ambiguous. It is not clear whether its vote for I was a vote for separate representation by I, or rather a vote for representation by I provided that I secured a majority in the overall unit. See J.I. Case Co., 87 N.L.R.B. 692 (1949), certifying an industrial union solely as the representative of a craft group, following a *Globe* election. Furthermore, where a *Globe* election involves several unions seeking to represent only a craft or departmental unit, the vote may show a majority in favor of separate representation even though none of the unions gets a majority and one of them gets fewer votes than "No Union." In such a situation, the *Globe* election resolves only the unit question and not the question concerning representation. In the subsequent election directed at the latter question, all the unions who sought to represent the separate unit, including the union that received fewer votes than "No Union," would be on the ballot. The §9(c)(3) period would, moreover, start running from the time of the subsequent election, rather than the time of the *Globe* election. See BP Alaska, 234 N.L.R.B. 125 (1978).

Although the *Globe* doctrine invoked the workers' desires and purported to reflect the Board's neutrality, that doctrine also met the desires of the AFL. Furthermore, "desires of the men themselves" was an elusive and question-begging phrase until the question "what men" was anwered. Many unskilled and semiskilled workers might desire to enlist the economic power of the skilled craftsmen. On the other hand, the latter might desire to avoid what they feared would be a dilution of their power if they became minorities in a larger unit that might, for example, narrow differentials by bargaining for cents-per-hour increases rather than percentage increases.

Board Member Edwin Smith, who had concurred in the *Globe* decision, soon dissented from its application, on several grounds: It constituted an abdication of the Board's judicial function; it disregarded the interests of the mass of employees; and it increased the risks of strikes by small but powerful craft unions that could close down an entire plant.[i] Smith urged that the statute required that "pseudo-democratic method" should be subordinated to "united economic strength" and to industrial peace.[j]

Such criticisms led the Board to modify its position by developing "the *American Can* doctrine," under which it would refuse, in general, to sever a craft from an industrial unit with a successful bargaining history.[k] The *American Can* doctrine operated to exclude the AFL from the mass production industries, which had been organized by the CIO, and naturally generated strong objections by the AFL. These objections were followed first by the Board's relaxation of its nonseverance rule, and then by a 1947 amendment of the Act: §9(b)(2). That amendment was far weaker than the AFL's proposal, which would have required the creation of a craft unit whenever a majority of a craft desired separate representation; nevertheless, it appeared designed to facilitate craft severance. The merger of the AFL-CIO in 1955 and interunion no-raiding agreements have softened some craft-industrial rivalries. But such rivalries persist and continue to generate problems about the impact of §9(b). The materials below deal with the Board's fluctuating responses to the issues involved.

Mallinckrodt Chemical Works
162 N.L.R.B. 387 (1966)

[The Regional Director had directed an election on the basis of the IBEW's petition, described below. After the employer requested review of that decision, the Board remanded for further hearings and subsequently determined that "no question . . . concerning the representation of certain of the [employer's] employees exists" and dismissed the petition.]

---

[i] Allis-Chalmers Mfg. Co., 4 N.L.R.B. 159, 175-177 (1937). The Board's use of *Globe* "elections" was upheld in NLRB v. Underwood Mach. Co., 179 F.2d 118 (1st Cir. 1949), enforcing 79 N.L.R.B. 1287 (1948), which involved only one union but more than one "appropriate unit," and which rejected an employer's contention that a *Globe* election involved an improper delegation to employees of the Board's authority to determine the appropriate unit.

[j] *Globe* elections, although used most frequently in disputes pitting craft against industrial units, are in some circumstances used when either a group of plants or a division thereof would be appropriate. See *Underwood Mach. Co.*, supra; Martin-Marietta Corp., 139 N.L.R.B. 925 (1962).

[k] See Milton Bradley Co., 15 N.L.R.B. 938 (1939); American Can Co., 13 N.L.R.B. 1252 (1939).

Petitioner seeks a unit composed of: All instrument mechanics, their apprentices and helpers in the Employer's instrument department at the Weldon Spring, Missouri, location. Although the Petitioner has asserted at the hearing and in its brief that it seeks severance of the instrument mechanics as a "functionally distinct and homogeneous traditional departmental group" and not as a craft — a contention upon which it based its motion for reconsideration of the Board's order granting review — it has also . . . asserted its willingness to "go along with any other unit that the Board may determine to be appropriate."

[Here the opinion described the employer's operations and the duties, the location, and supervision of the instrument mechanics, concluding that the instrument makers "constitute an identifiable group of skilled employees similar to groups we have previously found to be journeymen or craft instrument mechanics."]

WHETHER PETITIONER QUALIFIES AS A TRADITIONAL REPRESENTATIVE OF INSTRUMENT MECHANICS

. . . [A]lthough Petitioner did not as of the time of the hearing represent any instrument mechanics in separate craft units, it did number, among its members, employees performing duties similar to those regularly assigned to the instrument mechanics in this case. Petitioner is also a party to collective bargaining agreements which assign the exclusive performance of instrumentation work to employees classified as electricians. Petitioner is a party to one collective bargaining agreement which provides for the maintenance of an apprenticeship program for training electricians in certain functions which, in this case, are performed by the Employer's instrument mechanics. Twelve members of Petitioner have taken courses in instrumentation work presented at a St. Louis high school; the course, however, was not confined solely to instruction in all the various types of instrument work, but appears to have placed primary emphasis on work of the electrician craft. In addition to the foregoing, Petitioner relies upon the fact that its parent organization, International Brotherhood of Electrical Workers, AFL-CIO, has often participated in proceedings and been granted representation rights for separate units of instrument mechanics.

The foregoing, in our view, falls short of establishing that Petitioner qualifies as a traditional representative of instrument mechanics of the kind involved in this case. However, for reasons stated below, we do not now view the Petitioner's failure to satisfy the traditional representative test as it has developed since the *American Potash* decision as in itself a decisive ground for dismissal.

RECONSIDERATION OF THE *AMERICAN POTASH* DOCTRINE [107 N.L.R.B. 1418 (1954)]

. . . [I]t is appropriate to set forth the nature of the issue confronting the Board in making unit determinations in severance cases. Underlying such determinations is the need to balance the interest of the employer and the total employee complement in maintaining the industrial stability and resulting benefits of an historical plant-wide bargaining unit as against the interest of a portion of such complement in having an opportunity to break away from the historical unit by a vote for separate representation. The Board does not exercise its judgment lightly in these difficult areas. Each such case involves a resolution of "what would best serve the working man in his effort to bargain collectively with his employer, and what would best serve the interest of the country as a whole."[6] It is within the context of this declared legislative purpose that Congress has delegated to the Board the obligation to determine appropriate bargaining units. . . .

The cohesiveness and special interest of a craft or departmental group seeking severance may indicate the appropriateness of a bargaining unit limited to that group. However, the interests of all employees in continuing to bargain together in order to maintain their collective strength, as well as the public interest and the interests of the employer and the plant union in maintaining overall plant stability in labor relations and uninterrupted operation of integrated industrial or commercial facilities, may favor adherence to the established patterns of bargaining.

The problem of striking a balance has been the subject of Board and Congressional concern since the early days in the administration of the Wagner Act. In the *American Can* decision, the Board refused to allow craft severance in the face of a bargaining history on a broader basis. This so-called *American Can* doctrine was not, however, rigidly applied to rule out all opportunities for craft severance. Nevertheless, when Congress amended the Wagner Act in 1947 by enactment of the Taft-Hartley Act, it added a proviso to §9(b), stating in pertinent part: "The Board shall . . . not decide that any craft unit is inappropriate on the ground that a different unit has been established by a prior Board determination, unless a majority of the employees in the proposed craft unit vote against separate representation."

Though the legislative history indicates that this proviso grew out of Congressional concern that the *American Can* doctrine unduly restricted the rights of craft employees to seek separate representation, it is equally clear that Congress did not intend to take away the Board's discretionary authority

---

[6]NLRB v. Pittsburgh Plate Glass Company, 270 F.2d 167, 173 (4th Cir.), *cert. denied*, 361 U.S. 943.

to find craft units to be inappropriate for collective bargaining purposes if a review of *all* the facts, both pro and con severance, led to such result. [Quoting from Senate Report No. 105 on S.1126, submitted by Senator Taft.] . . .

This conclusion is further buttressed by the fact that the House Bill provisions[10] making the granting of severance mandatory were rejected by Congress in favor of the present provision which, as Senator Taft described it . . . requires the Board to exercise its "discretion to review all the facts."

Shortly after the enactment of §9(b)(2), the Board, in the *National Tube* case [76 N.L.R.B. 1199 (1948)], dismissed a craft severance petition filed on behalf of a group of bricklayer craftsmen who were employed in the basic steel industry. . . . [T]he Board concluded that:

> (1) the only restriction imposed by §9(b)(2) is that a prior Board determination cannot be the basis for denying separate representation to a craft group; (2) under the language of the statute there is nothing to bar the Board from considering either a prior determination or the bargaining history of a particular employer as a factor, even if not controlling, in determining the appropriateness of a proposed craft unit; (3) there is nothing in either statute or legislative history to preclude the Board from considering or giving such weight as it deems necessary to the factors of bargaining history in an industry, the basic nature of the duties performed by the craft employees in relation to those of the production employees, the integration of craft functions with the overall production process of the employer, and many other circumstances upon which the Board has customarily based its determination as to the appropriateness or inappropriateness of a proposed unit.

The bricklayer unit was there found to be inappropriate because of the existence of such a pattern and history of bargaining in the basic steel industry and because the functions of the craft bricklayers were intimately connected with the basic steel production process which was highly integrated in nature. In subsequent cases, the same grounds were relied upon for denying the formation of craft units in the wet milling, basic aluminum, and lumbering industries.

In the *American Potash* decision, the Board, in effect, reversed the *National Tube* decision as to both the proper construction of §9(b)(2) and the propriety of denying craft severance on the basis of integrated production processes in an industry where the prevailing pattern of bargaining is industrial in character. . . .

---

[10] See H.R. 3020, §9(f)(2), 1 Leg. Hist. 188-189. See, also, Hearings before the Senate Committee on S. 55, etc., 80th Cong., 1st Sess., pp. 1007 et seq. (1947), for a proposal by the President of the American Federation of Labor which would have made the establishment of craft units mandatory unless the craft employees rejected separate representation.

It is apparent that the decision in *American Potash* was predicated in substantial part on the view that §9(b)(2) virtually forecloses discretion and compels the Board to grant craft severance. This view represented an almost diametrically opposite construction of the statute from that adopted by the Board in *National Tube*. . . . [W]e believe the revised construction of the statute adopted in *American Potash* was erroneous, a belief apparently shared by the Court of Appeals for the Fourth Circuit. "The Board was right . . . [in the *National Tube* decision] in reaching the conclusion that the addition of subsection 2 of §9(b) created no ambiguity. As amended, §9(b) does not strip the Board of its original power and duty to decide in each case what bargaining unit is most appropriate. . . . The amended section expressly requires the Board to decide *in each case* what unit would be most appropriate to effectuate the overall purpose of the Act to preserve industrial peace."

Rejecting, as we do, the statutory interpretation on which the *American Potash* decision is premised, . . . we now consider whether the tests laid down in the *American Potash* case nevertheless permit a satisfactory resolution of the issues posed in severance cases. We find that they do not. *American Potash* established two basic tests: (1) the employees involved must constitute a true craft or departmental group, and (2) the union seeking to carve out a craft or departmental unit must be one which has traditionally devoted itself to the special problems of the group involved. These tests do serve to identify and define those employee groups which normally have the necessary cohesiveness and special interests to distinguish them from the generality of production and maintenance employees. . . . However, they do not consider the interests of the other employees and thus do not permit a weighing of the craft group against the competing interests favoring continuance of the established relationship. . . .

Furthermore, the *American Potash* decision makes arbitrary distinctions between industries by forbidding the application of the *National Tube* doctrine to other industries whose operations are as highly integrated, and whose plant-wide bargaining patterns are as well established, as is the case in the so-called "National Tube" industries.[1] In fact, the *American Potash* decision is inherently inconsistent in asserting that ". . . it is not the province of this Board to dictate the course and pattern of labor organization in

---

[1] [The industries immunized against craft severance were steel, aluminum, lumber, and wet milling. The criticism in the text of the arbitrariness of the distinction between those and substantially similar industries echoes the court's objection in Pittsburgh Plate Glass Co., 270 F.2d 167, 174, 175 (4th Cir. 1959), *cert. denied*, 361 U.S. 943 (1960). The court also suggested that the immunity had been based on prior Board determinations rejecting craft representation and was, accordingly, a violation of the second proviso to §9(b)(2). — EDS.]

our vast industrial complex," while, at the same time, establishing rules which have that very effect. . . .

It is patent, from the foregoing, that the *American Potash* tests do not effectuate the policies of the Act. We shall, therefore, no longer allow our inquiry to be limited by them. Rather, we shall, as the Board did prior to *American Potash*, broaden our inquiry to permit evaluation of all considerations relevant to an informed decision in this area. The following areas of inquiry are illustrative of those we deem relevant:

1. Whether or not the proposed unit consists of a distinct and homogeneous group of skilled journeymen craftsmen performing the functions of their craft on a nonrepetitive basis, or of employees constituting a functionally distinct department, working in trades or occupations for which a tradition of separate representation exists.

2. The history of collective bargaining of the employees sought and at the plant involved, and at other plants of the employer, with emphasis on whether the existing patterns of bargaining are productive of stability in labor relations, and whether such stability will be unduly disrupted by the destruction of the existing patterns of representation.

3. The extent to which the employees in the proposed unit have established and maintained their separate identity during the period of inclusion in a broader unit, and the extent of their participation or lack of participation in the establishment and maintenance of the existing pattern of representation and the prior opportunities, if any, afforded them to obtain separate representation.

4. The history and pattern of collective bargaining in the industry involved.

5. The degree of integration of the employer's production processes, including the extent to which the continued normal operation of the production processes is dependent upon the performance of the assigned functions of the employees in the proposed unit.

6. The qualifications of the union seeking to "carve out" a separate unit, including that union's experience in representing employees like those involved in the severance action.[15]

In view of the nature of the issue posed by a petition for severance, the foregoing should not be taken as a hard and fast definition or an inclusive or exclusive listing of the various considerations involved in making unit deter-

---

[15] With respect to this factor, we shall no longer require, as a sine qua non for severance, that the petitioning union qualify as a "traditional representative" in the *American Potash* sense. The fact that a union may or may not have devoted itself to representing the special interests of a particular craft or traditional departmental group of employees is a factor which will be considered in making our unit determinations in this area.

minations in this area. No doubt other factors worthy of consideration will appear in the course of litigation. We emphasize the foregoing to demonstrate our intention to free ourselves from the restrictive effect of rigid and inflexible rules in making our unit determinations. Our determinations will be made only after a weighing of all relevant factors on a case-by-case basis, and we will apply the same principles and standards to all industries.[17]

. . . [W]e conclude that it will not effectuate the policies of the Act to permit the disruption of the production and maintenance unit by permitting Petitioner to "carve out" a unit of instrument mechanics. Our conclusion is predicated on the following considerations.

The Employer is engaged in the production of uranium metal. It is the only enterprise in the country which is engaged in all phases of such production. All of its finished product is sold to the Atomic Energy Commission. Continued stability in labor relations at such facilities is vital to our national defense.

The Employer produces uranium metal by means of a highly integrated continuous flow production system which the record herein shows is beyond doubt as highly integrated as are the production processes of the basic steel, basic aluminum, wet milling, and lumbering industries. The process itself is largely dependent upon the proper functioning of a wide variety of instrument controls which channel the raw materials through the closed pipe system and regulate the speed of flow of the materials as well as the temperatures within different parts of the system. These controls are an integral part of the production system. The instrument mechanics' work on such controls is therefore intimately related to the production process itself. Indeed, in performing such work, they must do so in tandem with the operators of the controls to insure that the system continues to function while new controls are installed, and existing controls are calibrated, maintained, and repaired.

The instrument mechanics have been represented as part of a production and maintenance unit for the last 25 years. The record does not demonstrate that their interests have been neglected by their bargaining representative. In fact, the record shows that their pay rates are comparable to those received by the skilled electricians who are currently represented by the Petitioner, and that such rates are among the highest in the plant. The instrument mechanics have their own seniority for purposes of transfer, layoff, and recall. Viewing this long lack of concern for maintaining and preserving a separate group identity for bargaining purposes, together with

---

[17]To the extent that *American Potash* forecloses inquiry into all relevant factors, and to the extent that it limits consideration of the factors of industry bargaining history and integration of operations to cases arising in the so-called *National Tube* industries, it is overruled. . . .

the fact that Petitioner has not traditionally represented the instrument mechanic craft, we find that the interests served by maintenance of stability in the existing bargaining unit of approximately 280 production and maintenance employees outweigh the interests served by affording the 12 instrument mechanics an opportunity to change their mode of representation.

We conclude that the foregoing circumstances present a compelling argument in support of the continued appropriateness of the existing production and maintenance unit for purposes of collective bargaining, and against the appropriateness of a separate unit of instrument mechanics. . . . [W]e have not overlooked . . . that the instrument mechanics do constitute an identifiable group of skilled journeymen mechanics, similar to groups the Board heretofore has found entitled to severance from an overall unit. However, it appears that the separate community of interests which these employees enjoy by reason of their skills and training has been largely submerged in the broader community of interests which they share with other employees by reason of long and uninterrupted association in the existing bargaining unit, the high degree of integration of the employer's production processes, and the intimate connection of the work of these employees with the actual uranium metal-making process itself.[18] We find, accordingly, that the unit sought by the Petitioner is inappropriate for the purposes of collective bargaining. We shall, therefore, dismiss the petition.

Member FANNING, dissenting: Although I join my colleagues in reviewing and revising the Board's craft severance policies, I find myself in disagreement with them as to the circumstances in which it will effectuate the policies of the Act to deny skilled craft employees the opportunity to break away from industrial units in order to protect their special interests through separate representation. I deem it desirable to set forth with some particularity the considerations which will henceforth guide me in making unit determinations in severance cases.

First, however, I wish to stress my rejection of the plain implication in the majority opinion that the *American Potash* doctrine necessarily precludes

---

[18]Nor have we overlooked the fact that the Employer's powerhouse employees and electricians have been permitted to sever themselves from the existing unit. However, in directing a severance election for the powerhouse employees, the Board noted that these employees worked in locations segregated from work locations of other employees, and that the powerhouse employees had virtually no daily contact with other employees. See 76 N.L.R.B. 1055. We do not regard our decision in the instant case as being necessarily inconsistent with this previous action of the Board. In directing a severance election for electricians, a majority of the participating Board Members expressly refused to consider the effect or weight to be given to the integrated nature of the Employer's operations or to the existence of an industrial pattern of bargaining in the "chemical" industry. See 129 N.L.R.B. 312. For reasons already noted, we can give no precedential weight to this decision.

the Board from exercising its statutory responsibility to make informed determinations as to whether employees in a proposed craft unit may constitute an appropriate bargaining unit in a particular case. . . .

. . . I think it manifest from the language of 9(b) and the proviso under consideration that Congress did not enact into law the requirement that craft employees always be given an opportunity to vote for separate representation. It is also apparent, however, that the wording of the proviso did not in any way dilute the strength of the presumption running in favor of the appropriateness of craft units, whether that issue is presented in a severance case or in one involving the initial organization of the employees involved. . . .

. . . [T]he effectuation of Congressional intention in this area can best be achieved by placing upon the parties who would deny separate representation to craft employees, the burden of demonstrating that the separate community of interests normally possessed by craftsmen has become submerged in the larger community of interests of the employees in the broader unit. . . . I do not believe that such burden is met merely by a showing of a bargaining history on a broader basis, no matter how long it has endured. I believe there must be a showing that the bargaining history has, because of the nature and quality of the representation afforded craft employees, contributed to a strengthening of their ties and interests with those of the other employees, or that the history and pattern of representation in the industry involved is one of plant-wide, rather than craft or departmental representation. . . .

Similarly, I am not persuaded that the fact that craft employees work in close association with other employees in operating and maintaining a highly integrated production system necessarily destroys their right to seek representation in a separate unit. I recognize, however, that the separate identity of craft employees may be destroyed, or their separate community of interests submerged in the broader community of interests shared by all employees in the plant, in particular circumstances. For example, where the exigencies of a particular integrated production system are such as to require of craft employees: direct participation in the production process itself; the repetitive performance of routine tasks at more or less fixed work stations along the assembly line or channel of flow; or the acquisition of special skills in addition to those acquired in the course of normal training and experience in their craft, in order to enable them to work on their employer's specialized equipment; I believe it fair to conclude that the equities weigh in favor of maintaining the existing pattern of representation. . . .

I find that the Employer and the Intervenor have not met the burden of proving that instrument mechanics should be denied the opportunity to obtain separate representation by Petitioner. Thus, the record demonstrates, in the words of the majority opinion, that: ". . . the instrument mechanics are skilled workmen who work under separate supervision and we find that the instrument mechanics constitute an identifiable group of skilled employees similar to groups we have previously found to be journeymen or craft instrument mechanics." . . . Thus, like the electricians whose unit is found appropriate in the companion *DuPont* case, 162 N.L.R.B. No. 49, issued this date, the instrument mechanics are separately supervised and work from a shop separate from other departments at the Employer's premises. They report to this shop at the start of their work day and return there at the end of the day. The instrument mechanics have their own, highly specialized equipment, and their work tasks require the exercise of the traditional skills of the instrument mechanics craft. Although almost 75 percent of the repairs performed by the instrument mechanics occur on the production line, and though their work is intimately related to the successful operation of the Employer's uranium production process, the job requirements of the instrument mechanics and production operators "are clearly defined and do not overlap." Nor can it be found that the nature and extent of the instrument mechanics' duties in the production areas negate their craft status, for in DuPont, over 90 percent of the electricians' working time is spent in production areas in coordination with the tasks of production operators.

The record thus reveals that the Employer's instrument mechanics constitute a functionally distinct group of skilled craftsmen who have never been afforded an opportunity to decide for themselves whether they wish to be represented for collective bargaining purposes in a separate unit by a union which, in their opinion, will better represent their separate interests as craft employees.

[The dissent next considered the three grounds invoked by the majority.]

The record will not support the claim that maintenance of stability in the Employer's labor relations depends on the continued inclusion of the instrument mechanics in the production and maintenance unit. The pattern of representation at this plant is *not* one based solely on production and maintenance unit bargaining. Separate units for licensed stationary engineers, powerhouse employees, and electricians have been severed from the overall unit. . . . There is no evidence in the record that such multiunit bargaining has been productive of instability in the Employer's labor relations, or that, generally, craft representation is an unstabilizing and disruptive force in labor relations.

Nor do I believe that the appropriateness of a separate unit of instrument mechanics is negated by the degree of integration of the Employer's production processes and the intimate connection of the work of these employees with actual uranium metalmaking process, particularly when this decision is viewed together with the companion *DuPont* decision. . . . [T]he degree of operational and functional integration in *DuPont* is at least as great as in the instant case. Yet, in *DuPont*, the majority rejects the Employer's contention that the operational and functional integration at its plant has so blended the interests of the electricians with those of the other maintenance and production employees that only an overall unit is appropriate. . . .

If the majority's conclusion in the *DuPont* case is sound, and I believe it is, it cannot in logic rely on the integration of operations at the instant plant as a basis for finding that the instrument mechanics have lost their separate community of interest. In any event, this record fails to demonstrate that the integrated nature of the Employer's production processes has resulted either in the direct utilization of the instrument mechanics in the production process, or in the utilization of these employees' skills in routine and repetitive work at fixed stations on the channel of flow; nor has it been shown that the instrument mechanics required additional training beyond that normally required of craft instrument mechanics in order to enable them to work on the various instruments and controls which regulate the flow of raw materials through the production process. In view of these circumstances, and in view of the absence of evidence demonstrating that the integrated nature of the Employer's operations has made collective bargaining on the present multiunit basis unworkable, I can not agree with my colleagues that integration of the Employer's operations is a factor weighing against the appropriateness of the instrument mechanics' unit in this case.

Finally, I do not view the 25-year bargaining history for the production and maintenance unit as supporting the finding that a separate unit of instrument mechanics is inappropriate. Examination of that history reveals . . . that other units have been severed therefrom without noticeable loss in the collective strength of the production and maintenance employees, and I venture the opinion that the severance of these 12 instruments mechanics would not weaken the capability of the 280 production and maintenance employees to bargain effectively in the future. Moreover, there is no indication in this record that the inclusion of the instrument mechanics in the larger unit has resulted in a loss of separate identity; indeed, the very factors cited by the majority for their conclusion that the needs of the instrument mechanics have not been neglected by the Intervenor also indicate that the Employer and the Intervenor continue to recognize their separate identity and special interests. Accordingly, in the absence of evidence compelling the conclusion that the instrument mechanics do not, as craftsmen, share a community of interests separate and distinct from the community of interests they share with other employees in the existing production and maintenance unit, I believe this is a situation in which §9(b)(2) contemplates that a craft unit can not be found to be inappropriate unless the employees in the proposed unit vote against separate representation. . . .

NOTES

1. In evaluating the Board's specific criteria and their relevance, consider the following questions:

(a) What is meant by "stability" in the second criterion? On what basis will the Board predict whether such "stability will be unduly disrupted"? When there are strong craft grievances, is it equally possible that failure to sever will be disruptive?

(b) What is the relevance of "participation or lack thereof" in the third criterion? Would participation in the union be evidence that the craft group that now supports severance found plant-wide representation unsatisfactory? Would nonparticipation reflect the craft's conviction that it would have been hopeless to attempt to protect its interests while submerged in a larger group? Does the relatively sparse participation by rank and file members in all unions raise a question about the realism of the third criterion?

(c) Why should the history of other employers in the same industry be a factor in curtailing self-determination by smaller groups of a particular employer?

(d) Is the emphasis on integration of processes designed primarily to protect the employer's interests, the employees', or the public's? Under §9 of the Act, is each of these considerations relevant? Is each equally weighty?

(e) Why should the Board, rather than the employees directly affected, determine the qualifications of the would-be representative?

2. *Mallinckrodt* and its progeny are discussed in J. Abodeely, R. Hammer, & A. Sandler, The NLRB and the Appropriate Bargaining Unit 94-111 (rev. ed. 1981); Sharp, Craft Certification: New Expansion of an Old Concept, 33 Ohio St. L.J. 102 (1972).

3. On the basis of the *American Potash* doctrine, the Board in 1955 directed an election that resulted in severance of both a unit of powerhouse employees and a unit of electricians and that led to the certification of separate unions as representatives of each of those units. After *Mallinckrodt*, the employer involved and the union representing the remaining production and maintenance employees want to include those separate units in an overall production and maintenance unit. Assume that the Board on the basis

of *Mallinckrodt* would now deny severance to those units if the issue of severance were now being raised for the first time. What steps are open to the employer and the plant union to reverse the prior severance, and what is the likelihood of success? Cf. NLRB v. Industrial Rayon Corp., 291 F.2d 809 (4th Cir. 1961).

4. Assume that the Mallinckrodt plant was not previously organized. The IBEW petitions for a separate unit of electricians and instrument mechanics, and the operating engineers for a separate unit of powerhouse employees; the chemical workers petition for a unit of all production and maintenance employees, including the employees to be included in the separate units sought by the other unions. Is the disposition of those petitions controlled by the approach adopted in the principal case? Do the majority and the dissent agree on the relevance of that approach to such petitions? What considerations should control the issues raised by those petitions? Cf. E.I. DuPont de Nemours & Co., 162 N.L.R.B. 413 (1966).

NLRB v. Mercy Hospital Assn.
606 F.2d 22 (2d Cir. 1979), *cert. denied*, 445 U.S. 971 (1980)

[An Operating Engineers' local petitioned for an election in a unit of the hospital's 23 maintenance employees, who had 17 job titles. The hospital, a nonprofit facility with 1,287 full- and part-time employees, objected that that unit contravened the congressional "directive" against undue unit proliferation in health care facilities. The Regional Director, however, upheld the unit, and the Board denied review of his direction of an election. The local won the election and was certified, but the hospital refused to bargain. The court declined to enforce the Board's bargaining order and remanded to the Board "for consideration of the propriety of the certified unit under a standard affording appropriate deference to the mandate of Congress."]

MULLIGAN, J. . . . [A]n assessment of the propriety of the Board's unit determination must take place in the context of the 1974 amendment extending coverage of the Act to non-profit hospitals which had been previously exempted by the Taft-Hartley Act. The amendment was prompted by the conclusion of Congress that there was "no acceptable reason why 1,427,012 employees of . . . non-profit, non-public hospitals . . . should continue to be excluded from the coverage and protections of the Act." S. Rep. No. 93-766, 93d Cong., 2d Sess. (1974), reprinted in 2 [1974] U.S. Code Cong. & Admin. News, pp. 3946, at 3948. At the same time, however, Congress was concerned that work stoppages arising out of inter-union jurisdictional disputes and the reluctance of many union members to cross the picket lines of other unions posed serious threats to uninterrupted patient care. See id. at 3948-3952. Sensitivity to such dangers resulted in the incorporation into the amendment of a number of mandatory procedures, including strike notice requirements for unions representing employees of health care institutions. Id. at 3951.

In addition, Senator Taft offered a provision which would have prevented Board approval of more than the following four bargaining units in any health care institution: (1) professional employees, (2) technical employees, (3) clerical employees, (4) maintenance and service employees. S. 2292, 93d Cong., 1st Sess. (1973). While this specific limitation on the Board's discretion was not adopted, congressional concern for the underlying problem was embodied in a directive inserted in both the House and Senate Reports accompanying the final version of the bill:

> Due consideration should be given by the Board to preventing proliferation of bargaining units in the health care industry. In this connection, the Committee notes with approval the recent Board decisions in Four Seasons Nursing Center, 208 N.L.R.B. 403 (1974), and Woodland Park Hospital, 205 N.L.R.B. 888 (1973), as well as the trend toward broader units enunciated in Extendicare of West Virginia, 203 N.L.R.B. 1232 (1973).[1]
>
> [1] By our reference to *Extendicare*, we do not necessarily approve all of the holdings of that decision.

S. Rep. No. 93-766, 93d Cong., 2d Sess. (1974), reprinted in [1974] U.S. Code Cong. & Admin. News, pp. 3946, at 3950; H.R.Rep. No. 93-1051, 93d Cong., 2d Sess. 7 (1974).

Senators Taft and Williams, co-sponsors of the 1974 amendment to the Act, explained this directive during floor discussion on the bill. Senator Taft stated:

> . . . this is a sound approach and a constructive compromise, as the Board should be permitted some flexibility in unit determination cases. I cannot stress enough, however, the importance of great caution being exercised by the Board in reviewing unit cases in this area. Unwarranted unit fragmentation leading to jurisdictional disputes and work stoppages must be prevented.
>
> The administrative problems from a practical operational viewpoint and labor relation [sic] viewpoint must be considered by the Board on this issue. Health-care institutions must not be permitted to go the route of other industries, particularly the construction trades, in this regard.

120 Cong. Rec. 12944-12945 (1974). He further observed that

> every effort should be made to prevent a proliferation of bargaining units in the health care field and this was one of the central issues leading to agreement on

this legislation. In this area there is a definite need for the Board to examine the public interest in determining appropriate bargaining units.

S. Rep. No. 93-766, 93d Cong., 2d Sess. at 255 (1974); accord, 120 Cong. Rec. 22949 (1974) (remarks of Congressman Ashbrook).

The legislative history of the 1974 amendment clearly reveals that Congress expected the Board, when determining in its discretion an appropriate bargaining unit in a health care institution, to give substantial weight to the public interest in preventing unit fragmentation. Indeed, in Shriner's Hospital, 217 N.L.R.B. 806 (1975), decided soon after enactment of the 1974 amendment, the Board seemed to perceive the congressional mandate in precisely that way. . . .

In later decisions, however, the Board has been less solicitous of the directive of Congress.[2] As a consequence two circuit courts of appeals have denied enforcement of bargaining orders requiring hospitals to bargain with Board-certified units. In St. Vincent's Hospital v. NLRB [567 F.2d 588 (3d Cir. 1977)], the Board had certified a bargaining unit consisting of boiler operators and three other maintenance workers in a hospital employing some 280 employees. The Third Circuit found that in approving the unit the Board had relied only on traditional industrial standards under which the employees in the unit could have been found to possess a sufficiently separate community of interest to justify certification. The Court refused to approve the Board's bargaining order and stated that

> . . . the factors of amount of contact between workers, separate immediate supervision, and the special skills of certain crafts must be put in balance against the public interest in preventing fragmentation in the health care field. A mechanical reliance on traditional patterns based on licensing, supervision, skills and employee joint activity simply does not comply with congressional intent to treat this unique field in a special manner.

Id. at 592.

[The court here found even more pertinent the denial of enforcement in NLRB v. West Suburban Hospital, 570 F.2d 213 (7th Cir. 1978), because of the Board's "mere lip-service" to the relevance of the Congressional

---

[2] In Long Island College Hospital v. NLRB, supra, 566 F.2d at 843, we observed that the Board's decisions in this area had fallen into disarray. Of the rulings there collected, the Board had rejected bargaining units limited to maintenance employees 11 times and approved them only four times, including the later reversed decision in West Suburban Hospital, 224 N.L.R.B. 1349 (1976), enforcement denied, 570 F.2d 213 (7th Cir. 1978). Subsequently the Board has approved separate maintenance units with increasing frequency. . . .

admonition without any specification as to how its determination implemented that admonition.]

In response to such judicial criticism . . . , the Board in Alleghany General Hospital, 239 N.L.R.B. No. 104 (1978) . . . re-examined at length the legislative history of the 1974 amendment. Over a vigorous dissent by member Penello, the Board concluded that it gave sufficient deference to the congressional admonition against undue proliferation of bargaining units in health care institutions by applying to proposed hospital bargaining units the same community of interest approach ordinarily utilized for unit determinations in an industrial context. The Board reasoned that the congressional directive was really meant to forestall the grouping of health care institution employees by virtually *every* professional interest or job classification as has occurred, for example, in the construction industry. Id. at 9-11. Since application of a community of interest test, however, has not generally resulted in such fragmentation of bargaining units in the industrial setting, the Board concluded that the sole use of that standard for determining hospital bargaining units satisfied the mandate of the 1974 amendment. Id. at 19.

We disagree. Our reading of the legislative history leads us to conclude that in the 1974 amendment Congress was expressing concern not only that health care institutions be spared the egregious unit proliferation of the construction trades but that less extreme unit fragmentation arising from application of usual industrial unit criteria could also impede effective delivery of health care services. . . .

Thus, we hold along with our sister circuits that when the Board makes a unit determination for health care institution employees, traditional community of interest factors "must be put in balance against the public interest in preventing fragmentation in the health care field." The Board in its decision must specify "the manner in which its unit determination . . . implement[s] or reflect[s] that admonition. . . ." NLRB v. West Suburban Hospital, supra, 570 F.2d at 216.

Such a course was not followed in the case before us. The Board's conclusion that maintenance department employees should be represented by a separate bargaining unit was premised solely on analysis of traditional criteria: (1) lack of operational and functional integration with other employees, (2) prevalent functional integration within the maintenance department itself, (3) skill and experience of the maintenance employees, (4) supervision by a separate supervisory hierarchy, and (5) generally higher wage rates of maintenance employees in comparison to service employees. The regional director, whose opinion was adopted without further elaboration by the Board, ruled that the presence of the above factors demonstrated a "community of interest sufficiently separate and distinct from the service and other Hospital employees to justify a separate maintenance unit." The decision's single reference to the congressional admonition against proliferation of bargaining units was the conclusory observation that the congressional directive did "not preclude the appropriateness of a maintenance unit." This does not comply with the congressional concern . . . which requires an independent evaluation of the factors in this particular hospital. . . .

NOTES

1. For a comprehensive review of the pertinent legislative history, including not altogether consistent statements made before and after both the issuance of the Conference Report and the enactment of the health care amendment, see Bumpass, Appropriate Bargaining Units in Health Care Institutions: An Analysis of Congressional Intent and its Implementation by the NLRB, 20 B.C. L. Rev. 867 (1979). For a review of the cases dealing with the health care amendment, see Comment, Labor Relations in the Health Care Industry, 54 Tul. L. Rev. 416, 423-438 (1980).

2. In St. Francis Hospital, 265 N.L.R.B. 1025 (1982), the Board, although again upholding a hospital maintenance unit, accepted judicial criticism that its rhetoric had not honored the Congressional antiproliferation admonition. Defending its results, however, the Board attempted to satisfy its critics by announcing that its prior decisions were explicable by a two-step test, which it would explicitly apply in the future: Absent "extraordinary and compelling circumstances," a unit would not be upheld unless (1) it was one of seven that the Board's experience had shown "may" be appropriate; and unless (2) the unit also satisfied the traditional community-of-interest test. The provisionally appropriate seven consisted of employees falling in the following categories: physicians, registered nurses, other professionals, technical staff, business office clericals, service and maintenance staff, and maintenance workers.

Chairman Van de Water and Member Hunter, dissenting, charged that the majority's purported reformulation, as well as their seven categories of employees, reflected the same community-of-interest test that the majority were purporting to modify. The Chairman suggested that only two units — all professional and all nonprofessional employees — should be presumptively valid, and that in considering a smaller proposed unit, the appropriate question is not whether the employees in the proposed unit share a community of interest but whether they reflect a "disparity of interest" sufficient to warrant separating them from a potentially larger unit. Member Hunter agreed with the "disparity-of-interest" test but rejected any particular number of presumptively appropriate units.

(a) Can you give any precise content to the distinction between a "disparity-of-interest" and a "community-of-interest" approach? Cf. The Trustees of the Masonic Hall and Asylum Fund v. NLRB, 699 F.2d 626 (2d Cir. 1982) (upholding a unit of service and maintenance employees comprised of 400 of a nursing home's total of 475 nonsupervisory employees, even though the Board had not explicitly addressed the size and inclusiveness of the unit — factors that the court stressed; also approving the Board's rejection of the "disparity-of-interest" test on the ground that it is already encompassed by the traditional community-of-interest approach).

(b) Is any bargaining unit likely to be free from some disparity of interests among employees? In health care facilities, what is the probable impact of the directive against undue "unit proliferation" on the success of organizational campaigns? On the number and scope of stoppages? On employee claims of a breach of the duty of fair representation by incumbent unions?

3. Does "undue proliferation" refer merely to the absolute number of units in the institution involved or rather to the number of such units relative to either the size of the institution or the heterogeneity of its work force? Cf. NLRB v. Res-Care, Inc., 705 F.2d 1461 (7th Cir. 1983). In view of changing technology, is a presumption of appropriateness stated in numerical terms desirable? Without an indication of the evidence requisite for rebuttal, does a numerical approach substantially reduce uncertainty surrounding the anti-proliferation admonition? Would a numerical approach unfairly "discriminate" against units proposed when an institution's "quota" is close to being, or actually is, full?

b. Single or Multilocation Units

Where organizing campaigns involve a multiestablishment company, the NLRB must determine whether an employer-wide unit, all of the subdivisions within a given geographical area, a single plant or store, or even a subdivision thereof, constitutes an appropriate unit. (The Railway Labor Act, by contrast, has been interpreted as precluding the National Mediation Board (NMB) from forming a unit out of less than an entire system. See Switchmen's Union v. NMB, 320 U.S. 297 (1943).) Such determinations involve sharp conflicts of interest. A union may prefer a smaller unit in order to avoid the expense or difficulty of mounting a successful campaign on a broader front. Employers may, of course, prefer the larger unit for those reasons and because it conforms to an administrative structure centralizing labor relations and providing for interchange of employees. Incumbent unions in all or a group of plants may also wish to preserve the larger unit, not only to complicate a rival's organizing job, but also to avoid the dilution of bargaining power that may result when an employer with a group of autonomous or unintegrated plants offsets a stoppage or higher costs in one plant by shifting orders to other locations. On the other hand, where one of a group of plants has been organized by one union, and the rest of the plants by another, the first union might of course lose its representative rights if the multiplant unit were recognized. Similarly, the original designation or maintenance of a multiplant unit might subject an unorganized plant to the union's bargaining authority.

The Board's approach to multiestablishment units has fluctuated. Where a union had organized one of several establishments, the Board tended to uphold a union's request for a smaller unit, even when that request seemed to be dictated by the extent of that union's organization. See 4 N.L.R.B. Ann. Rep. 90 (1940). Where the petitioning union had achieved a company-wide majority but had failed to organize one or more plants, the Board tended at first to designate the larger unit but, beginning in 1940, was inclined toward granting self-determination on a plant basis. See Brooks & Thompson, Multiplant Units: The NLRB's Withdrawal of Free Choice, 20 Indus. & Lab. Rel. Rev. 363, 364, 366-368 (1967). The Board generally blocked efforts to sever a plant from a preexisting multiplant unit. Since such units had typically been established by the incumbent union and the employer, without determining the sentiments of the employees, the Board's antiseverance policy has been criticized as destructive of free choice. Id. at 373.

The Taft-Hartley amendments did not deal specifically with multiplant units. Section 9(c)(5), a response to alleged gerrymandering by the Board, was, however, designed to limit the Board's discretion regarding unit determinations in general, and, more particularly, those involving multilocation firms. The materials below introduce the unit problems raised by proceedings involving such firms and by §9(c)(5), generally.

NLRB v. Purity Food Stores, Inc.
376 F.2d 497 (1st Cir. 1967), *cert. denied*, 389 U.S. 959 (1967)

WOODBURY, J. This court on a previous petition for enforcement affirmed the Board's findings that the respondent had improperly interfered with its employees' efforts to organize by surveillance and overly hostile anti-union talk in violation of §8(a)(1) of the [Act]. But the court was dissatisfied with the Board's determination that only the Peabody store in the respondent's supermarket chain constituted an appropriate collective bargaining unit. Wherefore the court declined to enforce the Board's order to bargain collectively [150 N.L.R.B. 1523 (1965)] and remanded to the Board for further proceedings. NLRB v. Purity Food Stores, Inc., 354 F.2d 926 (C.A. 1, 1965). The Board, in spite of this court's statement that "in our opinion it would be difficult to find a more integrated operation, or less difference among employees," . . . in a supplemental decision and order [160 N.L.R.B. 651 (1966)] reaffirmed its previous determination that the respondent's Peabody store constituted an appropriate collective bargaining unit and has again petitioned for enforcement.

The respondent operates a chain of seven supermarkets in Massachusetts. All stores are located north of Boston and all are within a 30-mile radius of the respondent's central office in Chelmsford. All stores are located in relatively small communities, the largest being Peabody with a population as of the 1960 federal census of 32,202.

On May 13 and 14, 1964, a majority of the full and regular part-time employees at the respondent's Peabody market signed cards requesting representation by Local 1435, Retail Clerks International Association, AFL-CIO. No effort was made at that time to organize the clerks at any of the other 6 markets in the chain. The sole question here is whether the employees at that market constitute an appropriate collective bargaining unit.

In its supplemental decision the Board made more specific and detailed findings of fact than it vouchsafed in its original decision. It found, as the evidence clearly requires, that the respondent's merchandising practices are highly centralized. Specifically, the Board found substantially as follows: The respondent's central office determines the merchandise to be sold in the stores, how the stock shall be displayed and fixes uniform sales prices throughout the chain. Promotional sales, when held, take place uniformly in all seven stores. All merchandise is purchased and paid for by the respondent's central office. All vendors are selected by central office executives who negotiate prices which are not disclosed to local store managers. Except for purely local news media . . . all radio advertising and advertising in Boston metropolitan newspapers identify the locations of all seven stores. Local store managers have the responsibility of keeping the shelves in their stores stocked. To accomplish this they have authority to order goods from the vendors selected by the central office and to transfer stock from store to store as required which, the Board found, "is frequent and continuing." From October, 1962, to May, 1964, 162,311 units of groceries were transferred between stores.

Administratively the respondent's operation is also centralized. Certain central office executives are assigned responsibility for purchasing specific categories of merchandise, such as meats, groceries, produce, etc. for all seven stores, and each such executive has responsibility for supervising his category of merchandise in all seven stores.

In addition to his chain-wide duties each executive also is assigned over-all responsibility for the operation of a specific store or stores. Thus one Goggins, the executive responsible for buying groceries for all stores and for the grocery departments in all stores, has over-all responsibility for the respondent's stores in Peabody and Billerica. He therefore spends part of his time in the central office and part of his time in the various stores with the major part of his out-of-office time in the two stores in his particular charge.[2] The Board found that respondent's telephone expense of about $1,500 per month showed a "close and continuing liaison" between the stores and between the stores and the central office.

Daily receipts from all seven stores are transferred to the respondent's general bank account. Employee security is handled by a single officer at the central office. Insurance of every kind is contracted for centrally and is applicable to the chain as a whole. All refrigeration maintenance work, electrical work and laundering of uniforms is done for all stores under contracts with outside contractors.

Finally, and of primary significance, the respondent's personnel practices and procedures are also both centralized and integrated. The Board found that employees in certain departments (i.e., meat, produce and delicatessen), are hired by the central office executives responsible for purchasing and merchandising those products for the chain. Some full-time grocery clerks are hired at the store by the central office executive having over-all charge of the store, and others are hired at the central office in Chelmsford and assigned to whatever store may be shorthanded. Some part-time employees are hired by the local store managers but most of them are hired by the central office executive responsible for the store. In a footnote appended to those findings the Board noted that although there was testimony showing a general policy of central hiring of meat, delicatessen and produce employees for the chain, specific testimony showed that of about 107 employees at the Peabody store "all part-timers are hired at the store, and only 3 or 4 full-time employees were hired centrally and referred to that store." The significance of the place of hiring escapes us. What is significant is that

---

[2] The Board in another footnote conceded that Goggins "is actively engaged in day-to-day supervision" of the Peabody store. However, it rejected the respondent's assertion that he and the other central office executives actively supervised the day-to-day activities in their respective departments in all seven stores. It said that although there was testimony to that effect, "it strains credulity to conclude that the executives, rather than the store manager and department heads, are, in addition to their other duties, actively engaged in hour-by-hour or day-by-day supervision of the various departments throughout the chain."

employees are not hired by local store managers, except apparently for a few casual part-timers, but are hired by central office executives.

All cashiers are hired and trained by a central office executive who determines after a trial period whether a cashier is to be retained in employment. All employment is effectuated on the basis of uniform application forms prepared by the central office, and all new employees are given the company's employee manual. Almost all firing is handled by the central office executive in charge of the particular store involved, or at least after consultation with him. The testimony is that local store managers may discharge on their own responsibility only for "some outrageous activity."

At the end of each week time cards are sent from all stores to the central office where all personnel records are kept and from which all pay checks are issued. Job classifications and wage rates in each classification apply uniformly in all stores. General wage increases, when granted, apply to the employees in all stores. Fringe benefits such as paid vacations and holidays, sickness and accident insurance benefits, Blue Cross and Blue Shield and a profit-sharing retirement plan apply uniformly in all stores. Paid vacations are based on the individual employee's continuous employment in the chain and when two employees in the same category in the same store apply for the same vacation period, the central office gives first choice to the employee with the greater chain-wide seniority.

There are approximately 400 employees in the respondent's chain and there have been "numerous transfers," both temporary and permanent, from one to another of the seven stores, usually for the respondent's business convenience. During the two-year period from June 1962 to May 30, 1964, there were 557 transfers, 118 being in to and out of the Peabody store. Moreover, some employees regularly divide their normal work week between two stores, and frequently an employee, in addition to working his normal work week in one store, works overtime in another. In all such cases the employee is paid by a single check issued from respondent's central office.

The Board said that it agreed with the respondent "that the record fairly construed reveals that operation of its various stores is accomplished through a substantial degree of centralized control." And it said that it was "mindful" that unit findings ought not to ignore the desirability of accommodating the opportunity of employees to organize with management's ability to run its business and that it was in "complete agreement" with this court's statement in its earlier opinion that "there should be some . . . consideration given to the employer's side of the picture, the feasibility, and the disruptive effects of piecemeal unionization." Nevertheless the Board reaffirmed its previous determination that the Peabody store alone constituted an appropriate unit for bargaining.

The Board rested its conclusion basically on lack of store-wide bargaining history[3] and on its view that the Peabody store was so economically independent of the other retail stores and possessed such "significant autonomy" within the respondent's over-all operation that separation of that store from the others for purposes of collective bargaining would not obstruct centralized control and effective operation of the chain. We cannot agree.

It seems to us obvious that in view of the frequent interchange of employees from store to store, either permanently or for part-time work, only friction between employees and chaos in labor relations could possibly result if some employees were under union rules as to wages, hours, seniority, grievance procedures, etc. when the employees working beside them in the same category were not. The Board's conclusion to the contrary flies in the face of reality.

The evidence and the Board's specific findings based thereon disclose a small, compact, homogeneous, centralized and integrated operation. . . . Under some circumstances a single store in a retail chain may constitute an appropriate bargaining unit. But on the evidence and findings in this case we can see no rational basis for fractionating the respondent's organization for purposes of collective bargaining.

We do not lightly disagree with the Board in matters of unit determination. We are not unaware of the difficulties involved in making unit determinations which will "assure to employees the fullest freedom" in exercising their right to organize as required by §9(b) of the Act without running afoul of §9(c)(5) . . . forbidding the Board to treat the extent to which employees have organized as "controlling." And we recognize the particular difficulties involved in making unit determinations in the retail chain store industry which will protect employees' statutory rights while at the same time giving the employer reasonably adequate protection from the "disruptive effects of piecemeal unionization" to quote this court's previous opinion. See 79 Harv. L. Rev. 811. Nor are we unaware that §9(b) . . . confers broad discretion on the Board in unit determination and that its determinations invoke "of necessity a large measure of informed discretion and the decision of the Board, if not final, is rarely to be disturbed." Packard Motor Car Co. v. NLRB, 330 U.S. 485, 491 (1947).

Nevertheless the Board must articulate substantial reasons for its unit determinations. NLRB v. Metropolitan Life Insurance Co., 380 U.S. 438 (1965). No such reasons have been offered. The "independence" of the stores in the Purity chain amounts to no more than a few miles of physical

---

[3] This is true so far as it goes but it does not mention the failure of the Union to organize the stores in a consent chainwide election in 1961.

separation and the consequent division of a few ministerial responsibilities. This is far from enough. NLRB v. Frisch's Big Boy Ill-Mar, Inc., 356 F.2d 895 (C.A. 7, 1966). The Board's simple declaration that single store units are considered "presumptively appropriate" adds nothing, especially since the Board declared as recently as 1963 that "*the* appropriate bargaining unit in retail chain operations should embrace the employees of all stores within an employer's administrative or geographical area." Weis Markets, Inc., 142 N.L.R.B. 708, 710 (emphasis added). To be sure the selection of an appropriate bargaining unit gives the majority of employees within that unit the bargaining representative they desire. But this selection may also affect the employer, employees excluded from the unit but affected by the selection, and minority employees within the selected unit.

Section 10(e) of the Act clothes the courts of appeals with authority to enter decrees "enforcing, modifying, and enforcing as so modified, or setting aside in whole or in part the order of the Board." We have a statutory duty to perform in the premises and when, as here, we are unable to avoid the conclusion that the Board's unit determination simply does not square with its specific findings, we would not perform our statutory function should we enforce. [Board order set aside.]

NOTES

1. What connection, if any, is there between the provisions of §9(b) and the aspects of the employer's operations relied on by the court? Was there a conflict between the employees' "fullest freedom" to exercise their statutory rights and the employer's internal organization? If so, under the statute, which of those competing interests should get preponderant weight?

2. Compare Friendly Ice Cream Corp. v. NLRB, 705 F.2d 570 (1st Cir. 1983). The Board, finding appropriate a unit consisting of the employees of a single restaurant within a multistate chain of 605 restaurants, had certified the union after a 11-10 vote in its favor. Although upholding that unit, the court acknowledged that the "administration of the Friendly chain is a casebook study in centralized control." The court, however, "distinguished" *Purity II* on the following grounds: The Board's failure to take note of the evidence of employee interchange among a group made up of 99 of Friendly's restaurants was justified since neither party had proposed that group as an alternative unit. The court's reliance in *Purity II* on evidence of employee interchange among all seven grocery stores had been warranted by the Board's underlying "presumption that an appropriate unit should encompass an employer's administrative or geographical area. . . ." Contrari-

wise, in *Friendly Ice Cream*, because of the Board's current presumption that a single store is an appropriate bargaining unit, "evidence pertaining to an area larger than the proposed single store has decidedly less relevance." The court added:

> In making a unit determination, the Board's primary duty is to effect the Act's overriding policy of assuring employees the fullest freedom in exercising *their right to bargain collectively*. (Italics supplied.) . . . [T]he Board must also respect the interest of an integrated multi-unit employer in maintaining enterprise-wide labor relations. NLRB v. Solis Theatre Corp., 403 F.2d 381, 382 (2d Cir. 1968). Accordingly the Board must grant some minimum consideration to the employer's interest in avoiding the disruptive effects of piecemeal unionization.

3. Is there justification for the court's statement that the Act reflects "the overriding policy of assuring employees the fullest freedom in exercising their right to bargain collectively"? See §9(b), §7, as amended, §9(c)(5), §1 of the Act, and *Savair Manufacturing*, supra p. 144; see also NLRB v. Res-Care Inc., 705 F.2d 1461 (7th Cir. 1983), seemingly in accord with the First Circuit's dictum.

(a) Would the single-minded enforcement of the "overriding policy" expressed in *Friendly Ice Cream* multiply small units, including one-member units (which the Board declines to recognize), without sufficient regard for the interests of other potential employee units or of employers seeking both to align bargaining and operational groupings and to avoid undue unit proliferation?

(b) Given the conflicting pull of the pertinent statutory provisions and the breadth of the Board's authority, the standard for judicial review of Board unit determinations is justifiably quite deferential, requiring an "abuse of discretion" for reversal. Did the court of appeals appear to be applying an equally deferential standard in both *Purity II* and *Friendly Ice Cream*?

Note: Accretion and Unit Clarification

A unionized employer, by adding employees with new skills in an existing plant or by establishing or acquiring a new plant or facility, may generate a question of "accretion," i.e., whether a new and identifiable group of employees should be incorporated into an existing bargaining unit or whether, instead, an election should be held to determine their preferences. The NLRB's accretion guidelines resemble, but do not coincide with, unit determination criteria. Thus, even though it would be appropriate to have either (1) a preexisting unit, expanded by accretion to include a new plant, or (2) a separate unit for that plant, the Board tends to deny accretion. The reason for such restrictions is that "accreted" employees, unlike those involved in an initial representation election, are absorbed into a larger unit without participating in an election proceeding. See Melbet Jewelry, 180 N.L.R.B. 107, 110 (1969).

The accretion issue arising from the formation of a wholly owned subsidiary or from the acquisition of another commonly owned subsidiary (or operation) may be coupled with the question of which entities or operations should be deemed a "single employer."[m] Those two questions must, of course, be kept separate: The determination that several subsidiaries constitute a "single employer" does not necessarily mean that they also constitute a single bargaining unit, or that a collective agreement or a bargaining duty applicable to one part of a "single employer" encompasses other parts. Cases arising from "double-breasted" operations in the construction business (commonly owned unionized and nonunion operations) have emphasized that point. See Carpenters Local 1846 v. Pratt-Farnsworth, 690 F.2d 489, 494-509 (5th Cir. 1982). See also Chapter 11(B).

An accretion question may be raised by various initiatives: a charge under §8(a)(2) or §8(a)(5); a petition to the Board for an election covering potentially accretable employees; or a petition for unit clarification, which may be filed whether the union has been certified or is currently recognized but uncertified. See NLRB, Statements of Procedure, Series 8, as amended, §101.17. Similarly, accretion questions may arise in arbitration or in actions under §301 of the Act, in connection with a claim that an employer's failure to apply a collective agreement to "accreted" employees violated the agreement. See Associated General Contractors of California v. California State Council, infra p. 675. Such litigation in turn may raise troublesome issues concerning the NLRB's primary jurisdiction, explored in Chapter 10.

NLRB Annual Report
Vol. 17, pp. 68-69 (1952)

. . . [I]n certain industries, company-wide or multiplant units are generally favored. Foremost among such industries are public utilities, such as power, telephone, and gas companies, where it has long been the Board's policy to establish system-wide or multiplant units whenever feasible. This

---

[m] That characterization is also important in determining whether the Act's proscriptions against "secondary boycotts" shield one part of a company from labor disputes arising in a geographically separate part. See Chapter 7, infra.

policy is based upon the highly integrated and interdependent character of public utility operations and the high degree of coordination among the employees required by the type of service rendered. The Board, therefore, has held that where a labor organization is prepared to represent utility employees on a system-wide basis, a system-wide utility unit is ordinarily appropriate notwithstanding a bargaining history on a narrower basis. But when no union sought a system-wide representation, a unit limited to a single station of an electric utility with an 8-year bargaining history was held appropriate.

The Board similarly favors system-wide and division-wide units of employees in the transportation industry. . . .

c.   Multiemployer Units

There are estimates that approximately 40 percent of employees covered by collective agreements are in multiemployer units,[n] in which a single master agreement is worked out for the employer group (perhaps supplemented by individual agreements dealing with the problems of particular employers). Such units are predominantly local; they exist in building construction, retail stores, and many service and other industries with large numbers of relatively small firms operating in local labor and "product" markets. There are also multiemployer units organized on a regional basis, e.g., in longshore, maritime, coal mining, and men's and women's clothing. In only a few situations is there multiemployer bargaining on a national basis, e.g., glass containers, elevator construction, and pottery. In industries dominated by relatively few firms, such bargaining has rarely developed. Far more significant and widespread in such industries is "pattern-following," i.e., the spread throughout the industry of a bargain worked out with one employer.

The formation of multiemployer units has been explained largely as an effort by employers to blunt the power of unions by preventing them from singling out one employer, extracting concessions from him by actual or threatened strikes, and thereafter relying on the coercive impact of the initial bargains to secure the same concessions from competitors. See Kerr &

---

[n] See Committee on Econ. Dev., The Public Interest in National Labor Policy 131 (1961); U.S. Bureau of Labor Statistics Dept. of Labor, Bull. No. 2065, Characteristics of Major Collective Bargaining Agreements — January 1, 1978, at 12, table 1.8 (1980) (recent survey of major collective bargaining agreements (those covering 1,000 or more employees) finding that of 1,536 major agreements, 648 (42 percent) were multiemployer agreements, covering 3,238,400 employees). The advantages to management and labor offered by multiemployer units are noted in Charles D. Bonanno Linen Service, Inc. v. NLRB, reproduced immediately below.

Fisher, Multi-Employer Bargaining: The San Francisco Experience, in Insights Into Labor Issues 25-61 (R. Lester & J. Shister eds. 1948). The multiemployer unit is designed to avoid such whipsawing and to expand the scope of an actual or threatened stoppage and thereby to increase its costs to the union and the employees involved. Such expansion may also reduce the pressure that otherwise would operate on a single struck employer to settle in order to avoid giving his competitors an opportunity to divert his customers.

This conventional explanation has been supplemented by another point that is not wholly consistent, i.e., such bargaining permits employer concessions that would otherwise be withheld only out of fear that competitors might make a better bargain. Insofar as that point is valid, it would appear to strengthen rather than weaken the union's hand. Some economists have, indeed, turned the conventional explanation on its head by suggesting that multiemployer bargaining increases the union's relative power. See Haberler, Wage Policy, Employment and Economic Stability, in The Impact of the Union 41 (D. Wright ed. 1951). In that connection it is relevant that unions, as well as employers, must under the NLRA consent to the initial formation of multiemployer units and that in some cases unions play the leading role in their formation. This necessity for mutual consent sharpens the issue as to whose power is increased by multiemployer units in differing economic and organizational contexts as well as the issue of why consent to such arrangements is given if it increases the bargaining power of an adversary. See Charles D. Bonanno Linen Service, Inc. v. NLRB, infra p. 415, at n.3; Meltzer, Single-Employer and Multi-Employer Lockouts Under the Taft-Hartley Act, 24 U. Chi. L. Rev. 70, 85-86 (1956).

Multiemployer bargaining has long been a controversial matter. Its defenders have emphasized, among other considerations, its contribution to wage uniformity among competitors in product markets, to "responsible bargaining," and to "industrial peace." Its opponents have decried such uniformity and have urged that it bars entry of new firms and promotes monopoly in both labor and product markets. This debate is summarized in H. Davey, Contemporary Collective Bargaining 50-54 (1951). See also Note, 43 Ill. L. Rev. 877 (1949). Several empirical studies of selected instances of multiemployer bargaining concluded that the fears surrounding it are exaggerated and have predicted that such bargaining is likely to spread in the United States, as it has in Sweden, Great Britain, and other European countries. See Kerr & Fisher, Multi-Employer Bargaining: The San Francisco Experience, in Insights into Labor Issues 25-61 (R. Lester & J. Shister eds. 1948); R. Lester & E. Robie, Wages under National and Regional Collective Bargaining (1946). But more recent studies, although emphasizing the dearth of data, have questioned the existence of any trend toward such bargaining. See, e.g., Henle, Union Policy and Size of Bargaining Unit, in The Structure of Collective Bargaining 107, 119 (A. Weber ed. 1961).

The NLRB has not dealt recently with these broad questions raised by multiemployer bargaining. The pertinent Board guidelines are suggested by the following excerpt from its 23rd Annual Report 36-37 (1958):

> In dealing with requests for multiemployer units, the Board is primarily guided by the rule that a single-employer unit is presumptively appropriate and that to establish a contested claim for a broader unit a controlling history of collective bargaining on such a basis by the employers and the union involved must be shown.[59] But no controlling weight was given to multiemployer bargaining which was preceded by a long history of single-employer bargaining, was of brief duration, did not result in a written contract of substantial duration, and was not based on any Board unit finding.
>
> The existence of a controlling multiemployer bargaining history may also depend on whether the employer group has in fact bargained jointly or on an individual basis. Generally, the Board will find that joint bargaining is established where the employers involved have for a substantial period directly participated in joint bargaining or delegated the power to bind them in collective bargaining to a joint agent, have executed the resulting contract, and have not negotiated on an individual basis. Execution of the contract by each employer separately does not preclude a finding of a multiemployer bargaining history where the employers are clearly shown to have participated in a pattern of joint bargaining.[o]
>
> A multiemployer unit may include only employers who have participated in and are bound by joint negotiations. The mere adoption of a group contract by an employer who has not participated in joint bargaining directly or through an agent, or has indicated his intention not to be bound by future group negotiations, is insufficient to permit his inclusion in a proposed multiemployer unit.

Charles D. Bonanno Linen Service, Inc. v. NLRB
454 U.S. 404 (1982)

WHITE, J. The issue here is whether a bargaining impasse justifies an employer's unilateral withdrawal from a multiemployer bargaining unit. The

---

[59] . . . Where the petitioner and employer seek a multiemployer unit and no union seeks to represent a smaller unit, collective bargaining history is not a prerequisite to the appropriateness of the requested multiemployer unit. Calumet Contractors Assn., 121 N.L.R.B. No. 16.

[o][For an illustration of the difficulties involved in determining whether the evidence justifies a finding of "an unequivocal intention to be bound by group action," see Crane Sheet Metal, Inc. v. NLRB, 675 F.2d 256 (10th Cir. 1982). — EDS.]

National Labor Relations Board (Board) concluded that an employer attempting such a withdrawal commits an unfair labor practice in violation of §§8(a)(5) and 8(a)(1) of the [Act], by refusing to execute the collective bargaining agreement later executed by the union and the multiemployer association. The Court of Appeals for the First Circuit enforced the Board's order. 630 F.2d 25 (1980). . . . We granted certiorari to resolve the conflict among the circuits on this important question of federal labor law. We affirm the judgment of the Court of Appeals.

I

. . . Petitioner, Charles D. Bonanno Linen Service, Inc. (Bonanno), is a Massachusetts corporation engaged in laundering, renting, and distributing linens and uniforms. Teamsters Local No. 25 (Union) represents its drivers and helpers as well as those of other linen supply companies in the area. For several years, Bonanno has been a member of the New England Linen Supply Association (Association), a group of 10 employers formed to negotiate with the Union as a multiemployer unit and a signatory of the contracts negotiated between the Union and the Association. On February 19, 1975, Bonanno authorized the Association's negotiating committee to represent it in the anticipated negotiations for a new contract. Bonanno's president became a member of the committee.

The Union and the Association held 10 bargaining sessions during March and April. On April 30, the negotiators agreed upon a proposed contract, but four days later the Union members rejected it. By May 15, according to the stipulations of the parties, the Union and the Association had reached an impasse over the method of compensation: the Union demanded that the drivers be paid on commission, while the Association insisted on continuing payment at an hourly rate.

Several subsequent meetings failed to break the impasse. On June 23, the Union initiated a selective strike against Bonanno. In response, most of [the] Association members locked out their drivers. Despite sporadic meetings, the stalemate continued throughout the summer. During this period two of the employers met secretly with the Union, presumably in an effort to reach a separate settlement. These meetings, however, never reached the level of negotiations.

Bonanno hired permanent replacements for all of its striking drivers. On November 21, it notified the Association by letter that it was "withdrawing from the association with respect to negotiations at this time because of an ongoing impasse with Teamsters Local 25." Bonanno mailed a copy of its revocation letter to the Union and read the letter over the phone to a Union representative.

Soon after Bonanno's putative withdrawal, the Association ended the lockout. It told the Union that it wished to continue multiemployer negotiations. Several negotiating sessions took place between December and April, without Bonanno participating. In the middle of April, the Union abandoned its demand for payment on commission and accepted the Association's offer of a revised hourly wage rate. With this development, the parties quickly agreed on a new contract, dated April 23, 1976, and given retroactive effect to April 18, 1975.

Meanwhile, on April 9, 1976, the Union had filed the present action, alleging that Bonanno's purported withdrawal from the bargaining unit constituted an unfair labor practice. In a letter dated April 29, the Union informed Bonanno that because the Union had never consented to the withdrawal, it considered Bonanno to be bound by the settlement just reached. In a reply letter, Bonanno denied that it was bound by the contract.

An [ALJ] concluded, after a hearing, that no unusual circumstances excused Bonanno's withdrawal from the multiemployer bargaining unit. The Board affirmed, ordering Bonanno to sign and implement the contract retroactively. In a supplemental decision, the Board explained the basis of its decision that Bonanno's attempt to withdraw from the multiemployer was untimely and ineffective. 243 N.L.R.B. 1093 (1979). The Court of Appeals enforced the Board's order. 630 F.2d 25 (1980).

II

The standard for judicial review of the Board's decision in this case was established by Labor Board v. Truck Drivers Union, 353 U.S. 87 (1957) (Buffalo Linen). There, the Union struck a single employer during negotiations with a multiemployer bargaining association. The other employers responded with a lockout. Negotiations continued, and an agreement was reached. The Union, claiming that the lockout violated its rights under §§7 and 8 of the Act, then filed charges with the Board. The Board rejected the claim, but the Court of Appeals held that the lockout was an unfair practice.

This Court in turn reversed. That the Act did not expressly authorize or deal with multiemployer units or with lockouts in that context was recognized. Nonetheless, multiemployer bargaining had "long antedated the Wagner Act" and had become more common as employers, in the course of complying with their duty to bargain under the Act, "sought through group bargaining to match increased union strength." 353 U.S., at 94-95. . . . Furthermore, at the time of the debates on the Taft-Hartley amendments, Congress had rejected a proposal to limit or outlaw multiemployer bargaining. The debates and their results offered "cogent evidence that in many industries multiemployer bargaining was a vital factor in the effectuation of the national policy of promoting labor peace through strengthened collective bargaining." 353 U.S., at 95.[3] Congress' refusal to intervene indicated that it intended to leave to the Board's specialized judgment the resolution of conflicts between union and employer rights that were bound to arise in multiemployer bargaining. In such situations, the Court said,

> The ultimate problem is the balancing of the conflicting legitimate interests. The function of striking that balance to effectuate national labor policy is often a difficult and delicate responsibility, which the Congress committed primarily to the National Labor Relations Board, subject to limited judicial review.

353 U.S., at 96. Thus, the Court of Appeals' rejection of the Board's justification of the lockout as an acceptable effort to maintain the integrity of the multiemployer unit and its refusal to accept the lockout as a legitimate response to the whipsaw strike had too narrowly confined the exercise of the Board's discretion. 353 U.S., at 97.

Multiemployer bargaining has continued to be the preferred bargaining mechanism in many industries, and as *Buffalo Linen* predicted, it has raised a variety of problems requiring resolution. One critical question concerns the rights of the union and the employers to terminate the multiemployer bargaining arrangement. Until 1958, the Board permitted both employers and the Union to abandon the unit even in the midst of bargaining. Bearing & Rim Supply Co., 107 N.L.R.B. 101, 102-103 (1953). . . . But in Retail Associates, Inc., 120 N.L.R.B. 388 (1958), the Board announced guidelines for withdrawal from multiemployer units. These rules, which reflect an increasing emphasis on the stability of multiemployer units, permit any party to withdraw prior to the date set for negotiation of a new contract or the date on which negotiations actually begin, provided that adequate notice is given. Once negotiations for a new contract have commenced, however, with-

---

[3] As the Court of Appeals explained in this case,

"Multiemployer bargaining offers advantages to both management and labor. It enables smaller employers to bargain 'on an equal basis with a large union' and avoid 'the competitive disadvantages resulting from nonuniform contractual terms.' NLRB v. Truck Drivers Local 449, 353 U.S., 87, 96, . . . (1957). At the same time, it facilitates the development of industry-wide, worker benefit programs that employers otherwise might be unable to provide. More generally, multiemployer bargaining encourages both sides to adopt a flexible attitude during negotiations; as the Board explains, employers can make concessions 'without fear that other employers will refuse to make similar concessions to achieve a competitive advantage,' and a union can act similarly 'without fear that the employees will be dissatisfied at not receiving the same benefits which the union might win from other employers.' Brief, at 10. Finally, by permitting the union and employers to concentrate their bargaining resources on the negotiation of a single contract, multiemployer bargaining enhances the efficiency and effectiveness of the collective bargaining process and thereby reduces industrial strife." 630 F.2d, at 28.

drawal is permitted only if there is "mutual consent" or "unusual circumstances" exist. Id., at 395.

The Board's approach in *Retail Associates* has been accepted in the
courts, as have its decisions that unusual circumstances will be found where
an employer is subject to extreme financial pressures or where a bargaining
unit has become substantially fragmented. But as yet there is no consensus as
to whether an impasse in bargaining in a multiemployer unit is an unusual
circumstance justifying unilateral withdrawal by the Union or by an employer. After equivocating for a time, the Board squarely held that an impasse
is not such an unusual circumstance. Hi-Way Billboards, Inc., 206 N.L.R.B.
22 (1973). The [Fifth Circuit] refused enforcement of that decision, 500
F.2d 181 (CA5 1974), although it has since modified its views and now
supports the Board. Similar decisions by the Board were also overturned by
the Courts of Appeals in three other circuits. . . . [I]n this case, the Board
[reaffirmed] its position that an impasse is not an unusual circumstance
justifying withdrawal. Its decision was sustained and enforced by the [First
Circuit].

III

We agree with the Board and with the Court of Appeals. The Board has
recognized the voluntary nature of multiemployer bargaining. It neither
forces employers into multiemployer units nor erects barriers to withdrawal
prior to bargaining. At the same time, it has sought to further the utility of
multiemployer bargaining as an instrument of labor peace by limiting the
circumstances under which any party may unilaterally withdraw during
negotiations. Thus, it has reiterated the view expressed in *Hi-Way Billboards*
that an impasse is not sufficiently destructive of group bargaining to justify
unilateral withdrawal. As a recurring feature in the bargaining process, impasse is only a temporary deadlock or hiatus in negotiations "which in almost
all cases is eventually broken either through a change of mind or the application of economic force." Charles D. Bonanno Linen Service, 243 N.L.R.B.
1093, 1093-1094 (1979). Furthermore, an impasse may be "brought about
intentionally by one or both parties as a device to further, rather than destroy,
the bargaining process." Id., at 1094. Hence, "there is little warrant for
regarding an impasse as a rupture of the bargaining relation which leaves the
parties free to go their own ways." Ibid. As the Board sees it, permitting
withdrawal at impasse would as a practical matter undermine the utility of
multiemployer bargaining.[8]

---

[8] The Board explains that if withdrawal were permitted at impasse, the parties would
bargain under the threat of withdrawal by any party who was not completely satisfied with the
results of the negotiations. That is, parties could precipitate an impasse in order to escape any

Of course, the ground rules for multiemployer bargaining have not come into being overnight. They have evolved and are still evolving, as the Board, employing its expertise in the light of experience, has sought to balance the "conflicting legitimate interests" in pursuit of the "national policy of promoting labor peace through strengthened collective bargaining." *Buffalo Linen*, supra, 353 U.S., at 96, 97. The Board might have struck a different balance from the one it has, and it may be that some or all of us would prefer that it had done so. But assessing the significance of impasse and the dynamics of collective bargaining is precisely the kind of judgment that *Buffalo Linen* ruled should be left to the Board. We cannot say that the Board's current resolution of the issue is arbitrary or contrary to law.

If the Board's refusal to accept an impasse, standing alone, as an unusual circumstance warranting withdrawal were the only issue in this case, we would affirm without more. But several Courts of Appeals have rejected *Hi-Way Billboards* on the grounds that impasse may precipitate a strike against one or all members of the unit and that upon impasse the Board permits the union to execute interim agreements with individual employers. These Courts of Appeals consider the possibility of such events as sufficient grounds for any employer in the unit to withdraw.

In *Beck Engraving Company* [522 F.2d 475 (3d Cir. 1975)], for example, the Court of Appeals for the Third Circuit held that an impasse followed by a selective strike justified unilateral withdrawal from the bargaining unit. Because at that juncture labor relations law, as interpreted by the Board, would permit the union to execute an interim agreement with the struck employer, the Court of Appeals concluded that the union and the employer entering into such an agreement would be given unfair advantage against other employers if the latter were not permitted to withdraw from the unit. The Court of Appeals thought the employer's right to withdraw and the union's privilege of executing interim contracts should mature simultaneously. It concluded that the Board's approach too drastically upset the bargaining equilibrium to be justified in the name of maintaining the stability of the bargaining unit.

The Board's reasons for adhering to its *Hi-Way Billboards* position are telling. They are surely adequate to survive judicial review. First, it is said that strikes and interim agreements often occur in the course of negotiations prior to impasse and that neither tactic is necessarily associated with impasse. Second, it is "vital" to understand that the Board distinguishes "between

---

agreement less favorable than the one expected. In addition, it is precisely at and during impasse, when bargaining is temporarily replaced by economic warfare, that the need for a stable, predictable bargaining unit becomes acute in order that the parties can weigh the costs and possible benefits of their conduct.

interim agreements which contemplate adherence to a final unitwide contract and are thus not antithetical to group bargaining and individual agreements which are clearly inconsistent with, and destructive of, group bargaining." 243 N.L.R.B. at 1096. . . .

On the other hand, where the union, not content with interim agreements that expire with the execution of a unitwide contract, executes separate agreements that will survive unit negotiations, the union has so "effectively fragmented and destroyed the integrity of the bargaining unit," id., as to create an "unusual circumstance" under *Retail Associates* rules. Cf. Typographic Service Co., 238 N.L.R.B. 1565 (1978). Furthermore, the Board has held that the execution of separate agreements that would permit either the union or the employer to escape the binding effect of an agreement resulting from group bargaining is a refusal to bargain and an unfair labor practice on the part of both the union and any employer executing such an agreement. Teamsters Union Local No. 378 (Olympia Automobile Dealers Assn.), 243 N.L.R.B. 1086 (1979). The remaining members of the unit thus can insist that parties remain subject to unit negotiations in accordance with their original understanding.

The Board therefore emphatically rejects the proposition that the negotiation of truly interim, temporary agreements, as distinguished from separate, final contracts, are "inconsistent with the concept of multiemployer bargaining units." Charles D. Bonanno Linen Service, 243 N.L.R.B. 1093, 1096 (1979). Although interim agreements establish terms and conditions of employment for one or more employer members of the unit pending the outcome of renewed group bargaining, all employers, including those executing interim agreements, have an "equivalent stake" in the final outcome because "the resulting group agreement would then apply to all employers, including each signer of an interim agreement." Ibid. Such interim arrangements "preclude a finding that the early signers had withdrawn from the unit." Ibid. Although the Board concedes that interim agreements exert economic pressure on struck employers, this fact should no more warrant withdrawal than the refusal of one employer to join with others in a lockout.[9]

---

[9] The Board adopts the language of the First Circuit below: "the uneven application of economic pressure *per se* is not inconsistent with multiemployer bargaining." 630 F.2d, at 33. In addition, it points out that the employer also has additional weapons at its disposal for exerting economic pressure. It can engage in a lockout, make unilateral changes in working conditions if they are consistent with the offers the union has rejected, hire replacements to counter the loss of striking employees, and try to blunt the effectiveness of an anticipated strike by stockpiling inventories, readjusting contract schedules, or transferring work from one plant to another. The Board further notes that interim agreements do not always have the effect the Union desires. The signing of an interim agreement may not weaken the association's determination to resist the union's demands, see Plumbers & Steamfitters Union No. 323

In any event, the Board's view is that interim agreements, on balance, tend to deter rather than promote unit fragmentation since they preserve a continuing mutual interest by all employer members in a final association-wide contract.

The Board also rests on this Court's admonition that the Board should balance "conflicting legitimate interests" rather than economic weapons and bargaining strength. Its conclusion is that the interest in unit stability, recognized as a major consideration by both *Buffalo Linen* and NLRB v. Brown, 380 U.S. 278 (1965), adequately justifies enforcement of the obligation to bargain despite the execution of a temporary agreement.

Of course, no interim or separate agreements were executed in this case. But neither did the impasse initiate any right to execute an agreement inconsistent with the duty to abide by the results of group bargaining. Some Courts of Appeals, taking a different view of the interests involved, question the legitimacy of enforcing the duty to bargain where impasse has occurred and interim agreements have been or may be executed. . . . The balance [the Board] has struck is not inconsistent with the terms or purposes of the Act, and its decision should therefore be enforced.

IV

The Chief Justice, in dissent, is quite right that this case turns in major part on the extent to which the courts should defer to the Board's judgment with respect to the critical factors involved. . . . But The Chief Justice does not suggest that the Board seeks here to promote illegitimate ends. Both he and the Board strive to further labor peace through effective collective bargaining. Hence, if the Board's assessment of the impact of impasse and interim agreements on those goals is accepted, it is plain that its decision in this case is consistent with its mandate and promotes the underlying Congressional purpose.

The Chief Justice, candidly accepting that the issue is one of balancing the legitimate interests involved, nonetheless disputes the Board's judgment regarding the underlying factors with respect to what would best serve the statutory goals. He rejects the Board's assessment of the significance of impact and interim agreements in the multiemployer bargaining context and substitutes his own views. For example, he finds that the impasse in this case "was no 'temporary deadlock or hiatus in negotiations' as the Board claims;

(P.H.C. Mechanical Contractors), 191 N.L.R.B. 592 (1971), and the eventual contract settlement may have terms more favorable to the employers than the interim agreements, requiring the union to give up its temporary gains, see Associated Shower Door Co., 205 N.L.R.B. 677 (1973), *enforced on other grounds*, 512 F.2d 230 (CA9), *cert. denied*, 423 U.S. 893 (1975). . . .

this was instead a complete breakdown in negotiations coupled with a prolonged strike and lock-out." Post, at 730.[10] He also states, contrary to the Board's judgment, that when the parties have remained at impasse for a long period, "withdrawal of one or a few employers may facilitate rather than frustrate bargaining." . . . Thus, The Chief Justice avers, it would be "more consistent with [the goals of industrial peace] to permit withdrawal and allow negotiation of separate agreements than to force the parties into escalated economic warfare." . . .

The Chief Justice may be quite right. There is obviously room for differing judgments. . . . But the dissenting Justices would have us substitute our judgment for those of the Board with respect to the issues that Congress intended the Board should resolve. This we are unwilling to do. If the courts are to monitor so closely the agency's assessment of the kind of factors involved in this case, the role of the judiciary in administering regulatory statutes will be enormously expanded and its work will become more complex and time-consuming. We doubt that this is what Congress intended in subjecting the Board to judicial review. Indeed, we so held in *Buffalo Linen*.

We agree that the [NLRA] does not constitute the Board as an "arbiter of the sort of economic weapons the parties can use in seeking to gain acceptance of their bargaining demands," NLRB v. Insurance Agents' International Union, AFL-CIO (Prudential Ins. Co.), 361 U.S. 477, 497 (1960), or give "the Board a general authority to assess the relative economic power of the adversaries in the bargaining process and to deny weapons to one party or the other because of its assessment of the party's bargaining power," American Ship Building v. NLRB, 380 U.S. 300, 317 (1965). But the Board has refused to enter that proscribed area, despite the urging of several Courts of Appeal. Instead, it looked at its statutory mandate and duty — to promote labor peace through strengthened collective bargaining — in developing its rule.

In *Brown* itself the Court disagreed with the Board and held that no unfair labor practice occurred when members of a multiemployer unit hired temporary replacements following a lockout. Maintaining the stability of the multiemployer unit was the key to that decision: the Court reasoned that without temporary replacements "the prospect that the whipsaw strike would succeed in breaking up the employer association was not at all fanciful." *Brown*, supra, 380 U.S., at 284. In contrast to its action in *Brown*, the Board in this case has developed a rule which, although it may deny an employer a

---

[10] The dissent here ignores *Buffalo Linen*'s recognition of whipsawing as a legitimate weapon of economic persuasion in the course of collective bargaining. See *Buffalo Linen*, supra, 353 U.S., at 90, n.7.

particular economic weapon, does so in the interest of the proper and pre-
eminent goal, maintaining the stability of the multiemployer unit. Because
the Board has carefully considered the effect of its rule on that goal, we should
defer to its judgment.

Affirmed.

STEVENS, J., concurring. . . . The Court's holding does not preclude
an employer from explicitly conditioning its participation in group bargaining on any special terms of its own design. Presumably, an employer could
refuse to participate in multiemployer bargaining unless the union accepted
the employer's right to withdraw from the bargaining unit should an impasse
develop. The union or the other members of the bargaining unit of course
may reject such a condition; in such a case, however, the employer simply
would be forced to choose between agreeing to be bound by the terms of
group negotiation without a right of withdrawal at impasse, or forgoing the
advantages of multiemployer bargaining and bargaining on its own.

BURGER, C. J. with whom REHNQUIST, J., joins, dissenting. . . . The
Court holds that the occurrence of an impasse, without more, does not
automatically trigger a right of an employer to withdraw from a multiemployer bargaining unit. If the Court went no further, my objections would be
minimal. In this case, however, there was much more than a mere impasse.
At the time of the petitioner's withdrawal from the bargaining unit, the
negotiations had been stalemated for more than six months, a selective strike
and unit-wide lockout had kept employees away from their jobs for five
months, and there were no signs that the parties would return to the bargaining table. This was no "temporary deadlock or hiatus in negotiations" as the
Board claims; this was instead a complete breakdown in negotiations coupled
with a prolonged strike and lockout.[3] Nevertheless, the Court holds employers in the multiemployer group could not withdraw.

The Court then goes on, stating that even when the union negotiates
separate "interim" agreements with individual employers the remaining
employers cannot withdraw from the bargaining group. Thus, with all of the
members of a multiemployer group closed down or crippled by a strike or a
lockout, the union is permitted to "divide and conquer" by coming to terms
with some of the employers, allowing them to resume operations with a full
staff. With one or more competitors fully back in business, the ability of the
remaining employers to resist the union demands becomes greatly — and
unfairly — diminished. Unable to withdraw, the remaining employers have
no defense; they are forced either to submit to the union's demands or to
allow fellow members of the group to profit from the strike or lockout. The

---

[3] As the Board conceded during oral argument, its rule, now endorsed by this Court,
prohibits withdrawal even if an impasse and a strike or lockout lasts as long as two years.

effect of today's decision is "to deny self-help by employers when legitimate interests of employees and employers collide." NLRB v. Truck Drivers, Union, 353 U.S. 87, 96 (1957) *(Buffalo Linen)*. . . .

II

. . . The Court's deferral to the Board's conclusion that its rules advance the national labor policy by enhancing stability and promoting collective bargaining represents just the kind of uncritical judicial rubber-stamping we have often condemned. NLRB v. Brown [380 U.S. 278], at 291.

Contrary to the Board's conclusory statements, accepted by the Court, employers who execute interim agreements do not have an equivalent stake in promptly securing a reasonable final agreement. Such employers are able to operate fully while their competitors are hampered by a strike or defensive lockout; employers covered by interim agreements have a natural economic interest in prolonging the deadlock, thereby increasing their competitive advantage over the employers who remain in the multiemployer group.

The Court also accepts the Board's naked assertion that "interim agreements . . . deter rather than promote unit fragmentation." It is difficult to imagine an event more likely to fragment a multiemployer group than a union's successful whipsawing. Certainly employers will be reluctant to continue their association with other employers who are now encouraged by the Board — and by this Court — selfishly to permit themselves to be used to force the group to yield to the union demands.[4]

Even without the negotiation of interim agreements, when the parties have remained at impasse for a lengthy period, withdrawal of one or a few employers may facilitate rather than frustrate bargaining. The present case is illustrative. Bargaining between the Teamsters and the association was at a stalemate when Bonanno Linen decided to withdraw. That withdrawal did not cause the immediate "disintegration" of the bargaining unit, but instead provided the impetus for the union and the remaining employers ultimately to return to the bargaining table and reach agreement. Thus, Bonanno Linen's withdrawal can be seen as fostering the group collective bargaining

---

[4]The Court places great reliance on the notion that the union is only allowed to negotiate interim agreements with individual employers and that negotiation of permanent separate agreements not tied to the final association agreement would permit the remaining employers to withdraw from the unit. This reliance may be misplaced. In Tobey Fine Papers of Kansas City, 245 N.L.R.B. 1393 (1979), *enforced*, 659 F.2d 841 (CA8 1981), the Board did not permit an employer to withdraw from a multiemployer group even though two of the 14 members (representing 42% of the group's employees) had withdrawn with union consent and negotiated separate, permanent agreements. The Board held that "it does not follow *ipso facto* that execution of individual separate final contracts with [withdrawn] Association members either proves an intent to destroy, or necessarily causes the fragmentation of, a multiemployer unit." 245 N.L.R.B., at 1395.

process rather than hindering it. In any event, an employer's withdrawal from the multiemployer group is no more disruptive of the bargaining process than union's decision to use "divide and conquer" tactics.

Industrial peace, it must be remembered, is the primary objective of the federal labor laws. . . . When a union and a group of employers have reached an impasse and further negotiations would appear to be an exercise in futility, it is more consistent with that goal to permit withdrawal and allow negotiation of separate agreements than to force the parties into escalated economic warfare. Because of differing concerns, it is likely that employers will be able to negotiate agreements individually even though efforts to reach a group agreement failed. By instead forcing the parties to use their economic weapons, the Board's rule runs counter to the Congressional goal of industrial peace.

III

In addition to arguing that its rule barring withdrawal upon impasse enhances the stability of multiemployer groups and promotes collective bargaining, the Board contends that an impasse is neither sufficiently unusual nor adequately determinable to support withdrawal. "Impasse" is a term of art in labor law; the presence of an impasse triggers other important consequences. At impasse, for example, either party may decline to negotiate further. . . . In addition, at impasse an employer may unilaterally make changes in terms and conditions of employment provided that the changes are consistent with the proposals it made at the bargaining table. . . .

Because unions and employers have important rights which arise upon impasse, the Board and the courts have acquired considerable experience in determining whether an impasse exists. . . . It makes little sense to say, as the Board does here, that on the one hand an impasse is too common and indeterminable to permit withdrawal from a multiemployer bargaining unit while on the other hand maintaining that an impasse is sufficiently momentous and ascertainable to allow employers to stop bargaining and make unilateral changes. Moreover, if the Board, after nearly 40 years of dealing with the concept, finds impasse too ill-defined to permit withdrawal, it is high time that the Board exercise its presumed expertise and establish more definite guidelines to identify impasse. Unions and employers are entitled to that guidance.

The Court also accepts the Board's contention that "impasse may be 'brought about intentionally by one of the parties,'" and asserts that "permitting withdrawal at impasse would as a practical matter undermine the utility of multiemployer bargaining." The Court explains that permitting withdrawal upon impasse would allow employers to "precipitate an impasse in order to escape any agreement less favorable than the one expected." This argument ignores a basic element of impasse: impasse is reached only when a stalemate — a breakdown in bargaining — occurs after good-faith negotiations. . . . Intentionally refusing to agree in order to create an impasse and thus facilitate withdrawal — or trigger any of the other rights available upon impasse — is hardly good-faith bargaining. . . . The Board has ample means to deal with feigned bargaining.

IV

I would have little difficulty with a rule that a brief cessation of bargaining, without more, does not trigger a right to withdraw from a multiemployer bargaining unit. But the Board has gone much further. No impasse, we are told, no matter how long it lasts or how far apart the parties remain, permits withdrawal. Employers may not withdraw even after the union has negotiated separate agreements with some of the employers in order to force the others in the group into compliance. Absent a more reasonable alternative than that offered by the Board, I would adopt the rule of the Second, Third, and Ninth Circuits and permit withdrawal upon impasse.

[O'Connor, J., in a dissenting opinion joined by Powell, J., joined in the introduction and Part I of the Chief Justice's dissent. She objected, however, to the Chief Justice's and the majority's "absolute positions." She called on the Board to examine all circumstances surrounding an impasse in order to determine whether it was "temporary" or whether, as the Board might have found in *Bonanno*, it constituted a "complete breakdown" and an "unusual circumstance" warranting withdrawal.]

NOTES

1. Early in 1982, counsel for the Bonanno firm advised the authors as follows: (a) The status of the company's permanent replacements had not been considered by the Board or the courts. The Board's order did, however, require the company to make whole the employees in the association-wide bargaining unit for "any loss of pay" resulting from the company's "refusal to sign and implement the [Association] agreement." 229 N.L.R.B. 629, 633 (1977); *aff'd* 243 N.L.R.B. 1093, 1097 (1979); (b) It remained to be determined, presumably by the Board, whether the union still represents Bonanno employees; (c) The Association, whose 1976 agreement the Board imposed on Bonanno, expired in 1979, when the contract expired.

Was the ultimate question in *Bonanno* whether the respondent was going to bargain as part of, and to be bound by the contract of, the multiemployer group, or rather whether the respondent was to be completely free from any bargaining duty to the union involved? See the *Pennco* litigation, supra p. 366. See also NLRB v. John J. Corbett Press, Inc., 401 F.2d 673 (2d Cir. 1968).

2. Bonanno was awarded approximately $124,000 as compensatory damages in an action against Local 125, among others, resulting from serious violence, actual and threatened, during the selective strike authorized or ratified by the union; the violence included physical damage to Bonanno's trucks and plant, and threats of physical injury to employees that culminated in brutal attacks against substitute drivers and a security guard. Bonanno himself and his supervisory and professional employees were also the targets of threats. See Charles D. Bonanno Linen Service, Inc. v. McCarthy, 550 F.Supp. 231 (D.C. Mass. 1982), *aff'd in part and reversed in part*, 708 F.2d 1 (1st Cir. 1983), *cert. denied*, 114 L.R.R.M. 2976 (1983).

Should the "unusual circumstances" justification for withdrawal include serious and antecedent union violence? Should serious union violence, whether before or after withdrawal, constitute a defense against a bargaining order? Cf. NLRB v. Triumph Curing Center, 571 F.2d 462 (9th Cir. 1978).

3. In NLRB v. Siebler Heating & Air Conditioning, 563 F.2d 366 (8th Cir. 1977), the court, reversing the Board, upheld withdrawal by residential contractors from a multiemployer unit after negotiations for a renewal agreement began. The court recognized that dissatisfaction with the results of group bargaining does not justify withdrawal but found "unusual circumstances" in the association's failure fairly to represent the defectors, specifically in sacrificing their interests to the majority by feebly supporting the defectors' efforts to get a lower wage rate for certain residential construction in order to meet nonunion competition.

Should the failure of an employer's bargaining representative to give adequate weight to the employer's distinctive problems affect the employer's obligations to the union with respect to the scope of the bargaining unit? After you have examined the union's duty of fair representation (Chapter 11) and the preemption materials (Chapter 8), consider whether there should be a similar duty in the context of multiemployer bargaining and whether its breach should be actionable, as well as a justification for withdrawal, by the aggrieved employer.

4. Under the Multiemployer Pension Plan Amendments Act of 1980, Pub. L. No. 96-364, 94 Stat. 1208 (1980), withdrawal from a multiemployer unit, even though proper under the NLRA, will, in general, require a withdrawing employer to fund a share of the unfunded vested benefits of the multiemployer plan. "Withdrawal" for this purpose may also arise from decertification of a union previously representing employees covered by the

multiemployer plan, plant closure, or sale of assets. Plainly, the 1980 Act, which can only be mentioned here, impinges substantially on rights conferred by the NLRA. See, particularly, 26 U.S.C. §§412(b)(7), 414, 418-418E, 4971, 4975, 6511 (Supp. V, 1981).

5. All members of a multiemployer unit have, for many years, bargained with a union through their association. Recently, these members agreed to bylaws barring any individual firm from abandoning a lawful lockout or from entering into "interim" or "separate" agreements without the permission of the multiemployer association's executive committee, which, under the applicable bylaws, is to be the exclusive bargaining agent for all the member firms. Prior to the time set for negotiations for a renewal agreement, the union was formally advised of those bylaws. Following protracted negotiations and compliance with the notice and waiting periods of §8(d) of the Act, the union called a strike against Target, Inc., a member of the unit. The association's executive committee, pursuant to the bylaws, then activated a lockout by all members of the unit.

(a) Would those bylaws affect the legality, under the NLRA, of another unit member's lifting the lockout and executing either an "interim agreement" or a "separate agreement" with the union, without prior permission from the association's executive committee? See NLRB v. Teamsters Local No. 378, 672 F.2d 741 (9th Cir. 1982) (remanding the Board's order in Olympia Automobile Dealers Assn., 243 N.L.R.B. 1086 (1979), which was cited with approval in *Bonanno*). Would your answer be affected by the union's ignorance of these bylaws? By the employers' having conditioned their acceptance of the multiemployer unit on its operating under those bylaws and the union's acceptance of that condition?

(b) If a defecting employer abandoned the group lockout or made a separate deal with the union, what forum, if any, would grant specific enforcement of the obligations embodied in the bylaws, including, e.g., an order requiring the defector to resume the defensive lockout and to disregard any agreement with the union not permitted by the executive committee? Students should return to this question after examining the preemption materials in Chapter 8.

(c) Assume that all members of the association have also agreed to a bylaw barring resignations from the association after negotiations for a collective bargaining agreement have begun and providing for specified fines against members who violate bylaw provisions barring individual deals with the union. Would the existence of such bylaws or the attempt to enforce them in state courts violate the NLRA? Students should return to this question after examining in Chapter 13 the materials on union fines against members defecting from a strike.

Note: Coalition or Coordinated Bargaining

We have seen that employers, in connection with multiemployer bargaining, have drawn on considerations typically invoked by unions — the need for redressing power imbalances and for protection against divide-and-conquer tactics. Unions have stressed similar considerations in connection with "coordinated or coalition bargaining." These terms are sometimes used interchangeably to describe various forms of cooperative communication or parallel action by unions that are bargaining for different bargaining units of the same employer. "Coordinated bargaining," however, would better describe communication among different bargaining representatives who nevertheless retain the power of independent decision-making. "Coalition bargaining," by contrast, would fairly describe an effort by unions to force the consolidation of separate bargaining units. Such efforts are more likely to run afoul of the rule that makes it unlawful for a union to insist on, or strike for, the expansion of the bargaining unit certified by the NLRB or agreed to by the union and the employer. See Douds v. International Longshoremen's Assn, 241 F.2d 278 (2d Cir. 1957).

General Electric Co. v. NLRB, 412 F.2d 512 (2d Cir. 1969), involved the interplay of that rule and interunion cooperative arrangements. The IUE, which represented about 90,000 GE employees in 150 bargaining units, had formed a Committee for Collective Bargaining (CCB) with seven other international unions, whose locals had agreements with GE covering seven separate bargaining units. CCB's avowed purposes included the coordination of bargaining with GE and Westinghouse (GE's chief competitor), the formulation of national goals, and the creation of reciprocal support among the participating unions, which represented GE employees in 50 states. The court of appeals upheld the NLRB's position that it was proper for the IUE to include on its bargaining committee representatives of the seven other unions. Consequently, GE's refusal to bargain with the "mixed committee" violated §8(a)(5).

Although, as the GE case indicates, unions have been given considerable leeway in choosing their bargaining representatives, the Board and courts have rebuffed direct efforts by unions to consolidate separate bargaining units of a single employer. See Oil, Chemical and Atomic Wkrs. v. NLRB, 486 F.2d 1266 (D.C. Cir. 1973) (affirming the Board's decision that upheld a company's refusal to bargain at a single time and place with international union and its locals, regarding pension benefits for 19 separate bargaining units represented by locals of the international union).

Similarly, in Operating Engrs. Local 428 (Phelps Dodge Corp.), 184 N.L.R.B. 976 (1970), enforcement denied, 470 F.2d 722 (3d Cir.), cert.

denied, 409 U.S. 1059 (1972), the Board held that a group of unions representing different bargaining units had violated §8(b)(3) by insisting, in effect, on company-wide bargaining. That holding rested on these findings: The unions had pursued their previously disclosed purpose of merging separate units into a company-wide one (1) by demanding, and striking for, most favored nation clauses and a limited no-strike clause permitting employees in one unit to remain on strike pending settlement in other units, and (2) by subsequently withdrawing those demands and substituting a demand for simultaneous settlement in all units. The court, however, denied enforcement, noting the Board's failure to characterize the unions' demands as nonmandatory or to find that the unions had "bargained in bad faith." Rather, the court added, the Board in effect had held that the union had used mandatory items to achieve a nonmandatory purpose, the enlargement of the bargaining unit. The court, concluding that the record did not support the Board's finding, declared that parallel bargaining to an impasse on mandatory subjects, despite its extra-unit effects, is not evidence of an attempt to merge separate bargaining units. On the Board's petition, the court deleted a portion of its original opinion (459 F.2d 374) characterizing the demands withdrawn by the unions as mandatory subjects of bargaining, thereby leaving open the possibility of holding nonmandatory insistence on simultaneous settlements or contemporaneous expiration dates. See 80 L.R.R.M. 2620 (3d Cir. 1972).

Is there any functional difference between the unions' bargaining position (or positions) in *Phelps Dodge* and a demand for a company-wide unit?

For a review of coordinated and coalition bargaining, see Note, Coordinated-Coalition Bargaining: Theory, Legality, Practice and Economic Effects, 55 Minn. L. Rev. 599 (1971). See also Comment, De Facto Coalition Bargaining, 62 Geo. L.J. 325 (1973).

3. Conduct of Representation Elections

Objections to elections based on departures from "laboratory conditions" were dealt with in Chapter 4. This section deals with other grounds for such objections and with recurring problems of some significance.

NLRB Annual Report
Vol. 31, p. 59 (1967)

Section 9(c)(1) of the Act provides that if, upon a petition filed, a question of representation exists, the Board must resolve it through an election by secret ballot. The election details are left to the Board. Such matters as voting eligibility, timing of elections, and standards of election conduct are subject to rules laid down in the Board's Rules and Regulations and in its decisions. Board elections are conducted in accordance with strict standards designed to assure that the participating employees have an opportunity to determine, and to register a free and untrammeled choice in the selection of, a bargaining representative. Any party to an election who believes that the standards have not been met may file timely objections to the election with the regional director under whose supervision it was held. In that event, the regional director may, as the situation warrants, either make an administrative investigation of the objections or hold a formal hearing to develop a record as the basis for decision. If the election was held pursuant to a consent-election agreement authorizing a determination by the regional director, the regional director will then issue a decision on the objections which is final. If the election was held pursuant to a consent agreement authorizing a determination by the Board, the regional director will then issue a report on objections which is then subject to exceptions by the parties and decision by the Board. However, if the election was one directed by the Board, the regional director may (1) either make a report on the objections, subject to exceptions with the decision to be made by the Board, or (2) dispose of the issues by issuing a decision, which is then subject to limited review by the Board.[p]

a. Voting Eligibility of Replacements and Economic Strikers

In A. Sartorius & Co., 10 N.L.R.B. 493, 495 (1938), the Board held that strikers and not their replacements were entitled to vote, urging that voting by replacements would obstruct strike settlements. In 1941, the Board overruled *Sartorius* and held that permanent replacements, as well as strikers, were entitled to vote. Rudolph Wurlitzer Co., 32 N.L.R.B. 163 (1941). The Taft-Hartley Act, by adding §9(c)(3), denied voting rights to permanently replaced strikers, primarily on the ground that they lacked any expectancy of employment. See generally Note, 16 U. Chi. L. Rev. 537 (1949).

After President Eisenhower condemned §9(c)(3) as "union busting," it was amended in 1959 so as to give replaced economic strikers a qualified right to vote. In the light of §9(c)(3), as amended, consider the following questions:

1. An employer and a union had bargained during December 1982 without reaching agreement. On January 1, 1983, 10 percent of the unit

[p][The Board's election forms and procedures are described in J. Feerick, H. Baer, & J. Arfa, NLRB Representation Elections, Law, Practice & Procedure, ch. 7 (1980). —Eds.]

walked out; on January 15, the union called a strike, and an additional 50 percent of the employees walked out. The employer continued to operate with the rest of the unit supplemented by replacements. By December 15, 1983, virtually all the strikers had obtained other substantially equivalent jobs. The union picketed the employer sporadically, but no negotiations have taken place since June 1983. On December 15, 1983, the Board directed an election to be held on January 2, 1984. Which of the employees who walked out, if any, would be entitled to vote?

2. Assume that an economic strike began more than a year before an election. In determining the voting eligibility of replaced strikers or strikers unreplaced because of reduced operations, what weight would you attach to the following considerations: (a) *Fleetwood Trailer*, supra p. 314, and *Laidlaw*, supra p. 314, were decided after the 1959 amendment to §(9)(c)(3), and Congress in 1959 seemed to believe that the replacement of economic strikers ended their job rights; (b) Can particular strikers, because of attrition rates, have "a reasonable expectancy of re-employment in the near future"? Cf. Clipper Corp., 195 N.L.R.B. 634 (1972); Globe Molded Plastics Co., 200 N.L.R.B. 377 (1972); Gulf States Paper Corp., 219 N.L.R.B. 206 (1975).

3. During an economic strike, strikers engaged in misconduct that would have constituted "cause" for discharge under §10(c), but they have not been replaced or discharged prior to an election held six months after the beginning of the strike. Are they entitled to vote? See Union Mfg. Co. v. NLRB, 221 F.2d 532 (D.C. Cir.), *cert. denied*, 349 U.S. 921 (1955).

b.   The Majority Sufficient for Certification

A majority of the votes cast, rather than a majority of eligible voters, is sufficient for certification under both the NLRA and the Railway Labor Act. See NLRB v. Deutsch Co., 265 F.2d 473 (9th Cir. 1959), *cert. denied*, 361 U.S. 963, *rehg. denied*, 362 U.S. 945 (1960); Virginian Ry. v. System Federation, 300 U.S. 515 (1937). The National Mediation Board will, however, not certify unless a majority of the employees in the unit participate in the election. Pan Am. Airways, Inc., NMB, Case No. R-1818 (1947). See Brotherhood of Ry. & S.S. Clerks v. Assn. for Benefit of Non-Contract Emp., 380 U.S. 650, 657, 669-670 (1965). The NLRB requires only participation by a "representative group." See Northwest Packing Co., 65 N.L.R.B. 890 (1946) (participation of 40 out of 218 employees, 21 voting for CIO union, 19 for AFL union, and none voting for "no union," in a mail election while plant is shut down, does not constitute "representative vote" and is not sufficient predicate for certification); Stiefel Constr. Corp., 65 N.L.R.B. 925 (1946) (14 votes out of 45 eligible voters — 13 for CIO union, 1 for AFL, 0 for "no union" — in a mail election constitutes a "representative" vote). Cf. NLRB v. W.S. Hatch Co., 474 F.2d 558 (9th Cir. 1973) (upholding vacating of first election and bargaining order based on a second election, on the basis of Board finding that significant number of employees was deprived of voting opportunity by virtue of employer's refusal to hold first election by mail and absence of 5 of 13 bargaining unit employees on temporary assignment).

If an NLRB election involves two or more labor organizations, the ballot contains a slot for "neither" or "none" as well as slots for each of the rival organizations. Under the Railway Labor Act, the NMB does not provide a ballot with a "no union" box, and "if the employee refuses to vote, he is treated as having voted for no representation." See Brotherhood of Ry. & S.S. Clerks v. Assn. for Benefit of Non-Contract Emp., 380 U.S. 650, 672 n.1 (1965).[q] In an action (consolidated with the foregoing case) to enjoin the use of the NMB ballot, United Air Lines in its brief to the Supreme Court urged (at 51-54):

> Assume a craft or class of 13 employees, 6 of whom desire no representation, 4 desire Union A and *no other*, and 3 desire Union B and *no other*. The fact that an employee may prefer no representation rather than representation by a union to which he has been opposed in a hotly contested campaign is neither unrealistic nor unusual.
>
> Under the new Mediation Board form of ballot, as well as the old, the 6 who desire no representation can manifest this desire only by not participating in the election. The remaining 7 employees will then cast 4 valid ballots for Union A and 3 valid ballots for Union B. Since 7 employees — or a majority of the 13 — have participated in the election, the election is valid under the Board's procedures. A majority of those participating, or 4, will then determine the representative. Hence Union A will be the representative for all 13 employees, although it was the choice of only 4.
>
> If under the same circumstances the National Labor Relations Board were to conduct the election the results would be different. The 6 employees

[q] Before reaching the merits, the Court declared that a carrier's participation in representation proceedings was a matter within the NMB's discretion and not a matter of right. The Court considered the ballot question because it had been raised by an association of employees, albeit one that had disclaimed interest in recognition. Nevertheless, the Court's decision has been read as an implicit holding that a carrier, even though generally lacking standing to participate in NMB representation proceedings, has standing to challenge NMB decisions concerning the certification of representatives of the carrier's employees. See British Airways Board v. Natl. Mediation Bd., 685 F.2d 52, 55 (2d Cir. 1982); International In-Flight Catering v. Natl. Mediation Bd., 555 F.2d 712, 719 (9th Cir. 1977).

who wanted no representation could cast valid ballots for "no union;" 4 would vote for Union A and 3 for Union B. Since no choice would have a majority of the total votes cast, under run-off procedures, Union B, having the lowest number of votes, would be dropped and a run-off election would be held between the choices of Union A and 'no union.' Now the 6 employees would be joined by the 3 who voted for Union B and preferred no representation rather than Union A, and the vote would be the same 4 for Union A and 9 for 'no union.'[21]

The government's answer to this example — which was set out in United's complaint . . . — and a similar one used by Judge Youngdahl in his opinion . . . is that the example argues conclusions from facts. An equally valid assumption might be made, suggests the government, that the supporters of Union B might prefer Union A to no union (NMB Brief, 30 n.8).

But this answer pinpoints the vice in the Board's failure to allow a chance for a 'no' vote to be cast. There is no possible way of knowing whether the nonvoters were motivated by indifference or by a desire to have no representation; and neither is it possible to know how those who voted for Union B would vote in a run-off between Union A and no union.

The fact is that unless a representative receives an absolute majority of the total eligible to vote there is no valid conclusion that can be drawn from the Board's election. We do not argue that a representative must get such a vote for the election to meet the statutory requirement that the representative be determined by a majority of the employees. We would not even contend that an election is invalid simply because a majority of those eligible to vote did not participate. We do say that unless the choice of casting a valid ballot against representation is available then no valid conclusions can be drawn about the desires or presumed desires of a majority of the employees.[22]

The result of the Board's position is a perfect paradox: the certification of a union receiving less than a majority of the number eligible to vote is justified

[21] The run-off procedures of the [NLRB] have varied, as the government states (NMB Brief, 30 n.8). However, at all times since the "no" has appeared on the NLRB ballot, the "no" choice would appear on the run-off ballot if it received a plurality of the votes cast. The Mediation Board run-off rules provide that the two highest choices will appear on the run-off ballot (29th NMB Annual Report (1963), p. 36). The Mediation Board does not tell us here whether it would allow a "no" choice to appear on a run-off ballot if a majority participated in the election, but the number not participating exceeded the number voting for any one choice — as in the example cited above. Such a run-off should be allowed if not voting is "treated as the equivalent of a vote against representation." (NMB Brief, 30.)

[22] Significantly, in the only judicial examination of the Mediation Board's form of ballot prior to this litigation, the district court for the Northern District of New York held, in McNulty v. National Mediation Board, 18 F. Supp. 494 (N.D.N.Y., 1936), that the Mediation Board's failure to provide space in its ballot for a "no" union note precluded a clear expression of majority will and that, therefore, a certification resulting from an election based upon that form of ballot was not entitled to judicial enforcement. The Board does not consider the McNulty case as binding on it since it was not a party to the suit. . . .

on the ground that the non-voter is presumed to assent to the will of the majority of the voters (Virginian Railway case, 300 U.S. 515, 560); yet the employee who wants no representation is told the only way he can manifest that desire is by not voting; but under the initial presumption, by not voting he binds himself to the choice of the majority of those who do vote for representation.

If the Mediation Board really means that not voting is the equivalent of voting 'no', then the question put by Judge Youngdahl to government counsel should be answered: 'If you say that it is the same, why aren't you willing to agree to it?'

Without confronting *United*'s arguments, the Court upheld the disputed ballot as within the NMB's statutory authority. See 380 U.S. 650, 668-671 (1965). Stewart, J., dissented, urging that the ballot form resulted from the NMB's mistaken view that it had a duty to encourage collective bargaining; he would have remanded the ballot question for the NMB's reconsideration.

With respect to the foregoing controversy, what disposition by the NMB and the Court, respectively, would you favor? Cf. Leedom v. Kyne, reprinted below.

4. Judicial Review of Representation Proceedings

The Supreme Court has held that NLRB representation determinations, such as directions of elections in an "appropriate unit," are not "final orders," judicially reviewable under §§10(e) and (f) of the Act. See AFL v. NLRB, 308 U.S. 401, 409-411 (1940); Boire v. Greyhound Corp., 376 U.S. 473, 476-477 (1964) (Douglas, J., dissenting). Furthermore, §9 of the Act is silent about judicial review of Board representation orders or determinations.

To secure review of such decisions under §10(e) or §10(f), an aggrieved party must become the target of an NLRB unfair labor practice order whose validity depends on the propriety of the prior representation determination. When a court is to review an unfair labor practice order under §10, §9(d) requires that the record in the representation case be included in the record of the unfair labor practice case, filed with the court. A common instance of such indirect review involves an employer who, aggrieved by the Board's unit determination, declines to bargain with the union certified by the Board as the bargaining representative for the unit in question. If an unfair labor practice proceeding then occurs, the Board (which, at least as to §8(a)(5) charges, generally declines to relitigate issues resolved in the representation proceeding)[r] will issue a bargaining order against the employer. Judicial review of that order will then encompass scrutiny of the underlying representation decision (or decisions) on which the unfair labor practice order rests.

The materials below present the reasons for permitting only this indirect review of §9 determinations under §10 of the Act, and also introduce extraordinary situations in which a federal district court directly reviews representation determinations, independently of the review provisions of the NLRA. See generally Goldberg, District Court Review of NLRB Representation Proceedings, 42 Ind. L.J. 455 (1967); Note, Leedom v. Kyne and the Implementation of a National Labor Policy, 1981 Duke L.J. 853.

Leedom v. Kyne
358 U.S. 184 (1958)

WHITTAKER, J. . . . Buffalo Section, Westinghouse Engineers Association, Engineers and Scientists of America, a voluntary unincorporated labor organization, hereafter called the Association, was created for the purpose of promoting the economic and professional status of the nonsupervisory professional employees of Westinghouse Electric Corporation at its plant in Cheektowaga, New York, through collective bargaining with their employer. In October 1955, the Association petitioned the [NLRB] for certification as the exclusive collective bargaining agent of all nonsupervisory professional employees, being then 233 in number, . . . [at the Cheektowaga plant]. . . . A hearing was held by the Board upon that petition. A competing labor organization was permitted by the Board to intervene. It asked the Board to expand the unit to include employees in five other categories who performed technical work and were thought by it to be "professional employees" within the meaning of §2(12) of the Act. . . . The Board found that they were not professional employees within the meaning of the Act. However, it found that nine employees in three of those categories should nevertheless be included in the unit because they "share a close community of employment interests with [the professional employees, and their inclusion would not] destroy the predominantly professional character of such a unit." The Board, after denying the Association's request to take a vote

---

[r] A Board regulation bars relitigating, in any "related subsequent unfair labor practice proceeding," any issue that was, or could have been, raised in the representation proceeding. See NLRB Rules & Regulations, Series 8, as amended, §102.67(f). This restriction has been lifted when, for example, the validity of a charge of employer discrimination under §8(a)(3) turns on the propriety of the Board's classification of the alleged discriminatee in a prior representation proceeding. See Rock Hill Telephone Co., 234 N.L.R.B. 690 (1978), enforced, 605 F.2d 139 (4th Cir. 1979).

among the professional employees to determine whether a majority of them favored "inclusion in such unit," included the 233 professional employees and the nine nonprofessional employees in the unit and directed an election to determine whether they desired to be represented by the Association, by the other labor organization, or by neither. The Association moved the Board to stay the election and to amend its decision by excluding the nonprofessional employees from the unit. The Board denied that motion and went ahead with the election at which the Association received a majority of the valid votes cast and was thereafter certified. . . .

Thereafter respondent, individually, and as president of the Association, brought this suit in the District Court against the members of the Board, alleging the foregoing facts and asserting that the Board had exceeded its statutory power in including the professional employees, without their consent, in a unit with nonprofessional employees in violation of §9(b)(1) which commands that the Board "shall not" do so, and praying, among other things, that the Board's action be set aside. . . .

On the Board's appeal it did not contest the trial court's conclusion that the Board, in commingling professional with nonprofessional employees in the unit, had acted in excess of its powers and had thereby worked injury to the statutory rights of the professional employees. Instead, it contended only that the District Court lacked jurisdiction to entertain the suit. The Court of Appeals held that the District Court did have jurisdiction and affirmed its judgment. 249 F.2d 490. . . .

Petitioners, members of the Board, concede here that the District Court had jurisdiction of the suit under §24(8) of the Judicial Code, 28 U.S.C. §1337, unless the review provisions of the [NLRA] destroyed it. In American Federation of Labor v. Labor Board, 308 U.S. 401, this Court held that a Board order in certification proceedings under §9 is not "a final order" and therefore is not subject to judicial review except as it may be drawn in question by a petition for enforcement or review of an order, made under §10(c) of the Act, restraining an unfair labor practice. But the Court was at pains to point out in that case that "[t]he question [there presented was] distinct from . . . whether petitioners are precluded by the provisions of the Wagner Act from maintaining an independent suit in a district court to set aside the Board's action because contrary to the statute. . . ." Id., at 404. . . .

The record in this case squarely presents the question found not to have been presented by the record in American Federation of Labor v. Labor Board, supra. This case, in its posture before us, involves "unlawful action of the Board [which] has inflicted an injury on the [respondent]." Does the law, "apart from the review provisions of the . . . Act," afford a remedy? We think the answer surely must be yes. This suit is not one to "review," in the sense of that term as used in the Act, a decision of the Board made within its jurisdiction. Rather it is one to strike down an order of the Board made in excess of its delegated powers and contrary to a specific prohibition in the Act. Section 9(b)(1) is clear and mandatory. It says that, in determining the unit appropriate for the purposes of collective bargaining, "the Board *shall not* (1) decide that any unit is appropriate for such purposes if such unit includes both professional employees and employees who are not professional employees unless a majority of such professional employees vote for inclusion in such unit." (Emphasis added.) Yet the Board included in the unit employees whom it found were not professional employees, after refusing to determine whether a majority of the professional employees would "vote for inclusion in such unit." Plainly, this was an attempted exercise of power that had been specifically withheld. It deprived the professional employees of a "right" assured to them by Congress. Surely, in these circumstances, a Federal District Court has jurisdiction of an original suit to prevent deprivation of a right so given. . . .

In Switchmen's Union v. National Mediation Board, 320 U.S. 297, this Court held that the District Court did not have jurisdiction of an original suit to review an order of the National Mediation Board determining that all yardmen of the rail lines operated by the New York Central system constituted an appropriate bargaining unit, because the Railway Labor Board had acted within its delegated powers. But in the course of that opinion the Court announced principles that are controlling here.

> If the absence of jurisdiction of the federal courts meant a sacrifice or obliteration of a right which Congress had created, the inference would be strong that Congress intended the statutory provisions governing the general jurisdiction of those courts to control. That was the purport of the decisions of this Court in Texas & New Orleans R. Co. v. Brotherhood of Clerks, 281 U.S. 548, and Virginian R. Co. v. System Federation, 300 U.S. 515. In those cases it was apparent that but for the general jurisdiction of the federal courts there would be no remedy to enforce the statutory commands which Congress had written into the Railway Labor Act. The result would have been that the "right" of collective bargaining was unsupported by any legal sanction. That would have robbed the Act of its vitality and thwarted its purpose.

Id., at 300.

Here, differently from the *Switchmen's* case, "absence of jurisdiction of the federal courts" would mean "a sacrifice or obliteration of a right which Congress" has given professional employees, for there is no other means, within their control (American Federation of Labor v. Labor Board, supra), to protect and enforce that right. And "the inference [is] strong that Congress intended the statutory provisions governing the general jurisdiction of those courts to control." 320 U.S., at 300. This Court cannot lightly infer that Congress does not intend judicial protection of rights it confers against agency action taken in excess of delegated powers. . . .

Where, as here, Congress has given a "right" to the professional employees it must be held that it intended that right to be enforced, and "the courts . . . encounter no difficulty in fulfilling its purpose." Texas & New Orleans R. Co. v. Railway Clerks, supra, at 568.

The Court of Appeals was right in holding, in the circumstances of this case, that the District Court had jurisdiction of this suit, and its judgment is
Affirmed.

BRENNAN and FRANKFURTER, JJ., dissenting. The legislative history of the Wagner Act, and of the Taft-Hartley amendments, shows a considered congressional purpose to restrict judicial review of [NLRB] representation certifications to review in the Courts of Appeals in the circumstances specified in §9(d). The question was extensively debated when both Acts were being considered, and on both occasions Congress concluded that, unless drastically limited, time-consuming court procedures would seriously threaten to frustrate the basic national policy of preventing industrial strife and achieving industrial peace by promoting collective bargaining. . . .

The Court today opens a gaping hole in this congressional wall against direct resort to the courts. . . .

There is nothing in the legislative history to indicate that the Congress intended any exception from the requirement that collective bargaining begin without awaiting judicial review of a Board certification or the investigation preceding it. Certainly nothing appears that an exception was intended where the attack upon the Board's action is based upon an alleged misinterpretation of the statute. The policy behind the limitation of judicial review applies just as clearly when the challenge is made on this ground. Plainly direct judicial review of a Board's interpretation of the statute is as likely to be as drawn out, and thus as frustrative of the national policy, as is review of any other type of Board decision. . . .

I daresay that the ingenuity of counsel will, after today's decision, be entirely adequate to the task of finding some alleged "unlawful action," whether in statutory interpretation or otherwise, sufficient to get a foot in a District Court door under 28 U.S.C. §1337. Even when the Board wins such a case on the merits, as in Inland Empire Council, while the case is dragging through the courts the threat will be ever present of the industrial strife sought to be averted by Congress in providing only drastically limited judicial review under §9(d). Both union and management will be able to use the tactic of litigation to delay the initiation of collective bargaining when it suits their purposes. A striking example of this was recently disclosed to the Select Committee of the Senate on Improper Activities in the Labor or Management Field. A union, by challenging Board certification proceedings in the District Courts, was able to extend a representation proceeding to over six months, even though only seven employees were involved and they did not support the union. By the time that the Board was able to certify a representative of the employees, the industrial strife of those six months had forced the employer out of business. Thus collective bargaining was prevented, the basic purpose of the LMRA was frustrated, and the result was serious hardship to both the employer and employees. . . .

It is no support for the Court's decision that the respondent union may suffer hardship if review under 28 U.S.C. §1337 is not open to it. The Congress was fully aware of the disadvantages and possible unfairness which could result from the limitation on judicial review enacted in §9(d). The House proposal for direct review of Board certifications in the Taft-Hartley amendments was based in part upon the fact that, under the Wagner Act, the operation of §9(d) was "unfair to . . . the union that loses, which has no appeal at all no matter how wrong the certification may be; [and to] the employees, who also have no appeal. . . ." Congress nevertheless continued the limited judicial review provided by §9(d) because Congress believed the disadvantages of broader review to be more serious than the difficulties which limited review posed for the parties. Furthermore, Congress felt that the Board procedures and the limited review provided in §9(d) were adequate to protect the parties.

The Court supports its decision by stating that Switchmen's Union v. National Mediation Board, supra, "announced principles that are controlling here." This is true, but I believe that those principles lead to, indeed compel, a result contrary to that reached by the Court. In that case, the Switchmen's Union sought to challenge in a District Court the certification of an employee representative by the National Mediation Board under the Railway Labor Act. The Board certified the Brotherhood of Railroad Trainmen as representative for all the yardmen of the rail lines operated by the New York Central system. The Switchmen's Union contended that yardmen of certain designated parts of the system should be permitted to vote for separate representatives instead of being compelled to take part in a system-wide election. The Board rejected this contention of the Switchmen's Union upon the ground that the Railway Labor Act did not authorize the Board to determine a unit of less than the entire system. The Board's interpretation was that the "Railway Labor Act vests the Board with no discretion to split a single carrier. . . ." Switchmen's case, 320 U.S., at 309. This Court held that the action of the Switchmen's Union was not cognizable in a District Court. The Court held that the Railway Labor Act, read in the light of its history, disclosed a congressional intention to bar direct review in the District Courts of certifications by the Mediation Board. This was held notwithstanding the fact that the certification was based on an alleged misinterpretation of the Act.

This same reasoning has striking application in this case. The [NLRA] provides that the Labor Board "shall decide in each case . . . the unit appropriate for the purposes of collective bargaining," §9(b), but also provides that the Board "shall not . . . decide that any unit is appropriate . . . if such unit includes both professional employees and employees who are not professional employees unless a majority of such professional employees vote for inclusion in such unit. . . ." §9(b)(1). The Board, in making the certification in dispute, has interpreted these provisions as requiring the approval of the professional employees of a mixed bargaining unit of professionals and nonprofessionals only when the professionals are a minority in the unit, since only in such a case would they need this protection against the ignoring of their particular interests. This interpretation is the basis of respondent union's complaint in its action under 28 U.S.C. §1337 in the District Court. But an alleged error in statutory construction was also the basis of the District Court action in the *Switchmen's* case. Thus the two cases are perfectly parallel. And just as surely as in the case of the Mediation Board under the Railway Labor Act, the Congress has barred District Court review of [NLRB] certifications under the Labor Management Relations Act. The history of the controversy over direct judicial review which I have canvassed shows with a clarity perhaps not even as true of the Mediation Board that the [NLRB] was the "precise machinery," 320 U.S., at 301, selected by Congress for the purpose of determining a certification and that "there was to be no dragging out of the controversy into other tribunals of law." Id., at 305. Congress evidenced its will definitely and emphatically "by the highly selective manner in which Congress . . . provided for judicial review of administrative orders of determinations under the Act." Id., at 305. Review is confined to review in a Court of Appeals in the circumstances specified in §9(d).

The Court seizes upon the language in *Switchmen's*. "If the absence of jurisdiction of the federal courts meant a sacrifice or obliteration of a right which Congress had created, the inference would be strong that Congress intended the statutory provisions governing the general jurisdiction of those courts to control." 320 U.S., at 300. . . . The Court used the "sacrifice or obliteration" language solely to distinguish the situation where Congress created a "right" but no tribunal for its enforcement. This was the case in

Texas & New Orleans R. Co. v. Brotherhood of Railway Clerks, 281 U.S. 548, and Virginian R. Co. v. System Federation, 300 U.S. 515. In the *Texas* case, the employer was attempting to prevent the organization of its employees in violation of §2 of the Railway Labor Act, which provided that the employees could select representatives "without interference, influence, or coercion" by the employer. There was no agency designated to enforce this policy of the Act, and unless the courts provided sanctions against the outlawed activity, there would be no official sanctions to prevent it. . . .

But here, as the Congress provided the Mediation Board under the Railway Labor Act, the Congress has provided an agency, the NLRB, to protect the "right" it created under the National Labor Relations Act. Congress has in addition enacted "an appropriate safeguard and opportunity to be heard" in procedures to be followed by the Board. It has indeed gone further than in the Railway Labor Act. Whereas no judicial review of any kind was there provided, some, although limited, judicial review is provided under §9(d). This was considered by Congress as "a complete guarantee against arbitrary action by the Board." Plainly we have here a situation where it may be said precisely as in *Switchmen's* that "Congress for reasons of its own decided upon the method for protection of the 'right' it created. It selected the precise machinery and fashioned the tool which it deemed suited to that end." . . .

I would reverse and remand the case to the District Court with instructions to dismiss the complaint for lack of jurisdiction of the subject matter.

NOTES

1. If the dissenters' views had prevailed, could the Association have secured judicial review by means other than an action for an injunction?

2. A union complains that a rival was certified on the basis of a unit determination that plainly violated a specific provision of the Act, e.g., the provision as to *Globe* elections for professional employees. Consider, in the light of §§8(b)(7)(B) and 8(b)(4)(C) and LMRA §303, whether the aggrieved union could secure judicial review on the basis of Leedom v. Kyne. Compare Cannery Warehousemen, etc. v. Haigh Berberian, Inc., 623 F.2d 77, 80-81 (9th Cir. 1980), and United Federation of College Teachers, Local 1460 v. Miller, 479 F.2d 1074, 1079 (2d Cir. 1973), with NLRB v. Interstate Dress Carriers, Inc., 610 F.2d 99, 108-109 (3d Cir. 1979).

3. A representation election was held on a union's petition. The union lost (119 to109) and filed objections, alleging, inter alia, that an NLRB agent in charge of the election had given a worker a ballot premarked "No," had

lunched with management on election day, had protested union challenges of ballots, and, after the election, had what appeared to be crumpled ballots in his brief case. After investigation, the Regional Director found no misconduct and recommended that the union's objections be overruled. The Board, although upholding that finding, set aside the first election and ordered a new one, observing that "the mere appearance of irregularity in a Board agent's conduct of an election departs from the standards the Board seeks to maintain in assuring the integrity and secrecy of its elections and constitutes a basis for setting aside the election." The company, relying primarily on §§9(e)(1) and (2), sued in a federal district court to compel the Board to certify the election results and to enjoin the second election directed by the Board. The court, rejecting the suggestion that an employer could not invoke Leedom v. Kyne, granted the relief requested. See Bullard Co. v. NLRB, 253 F. Supp. 391 (D.D.C. 1966). Is that decision consistent with Leedom v. Kyne?

B.   UNFAIR LABOR PRACTICE PROCEEDINGS

Although a Board election is generally the most reliable way to determine whether a union has majority support in a given unit, it is not the only road to representative status. We have seen that an employer is entitled to grant voluntary recognition to a union with majority support in an appropriate unit, provided that recognition does not "interfere" with the organizational interests of a rival union. See Bruckner Nursing Home, supra p. 378. Indeed, under the *Joy Silk* rule (discussed in the case below), now largely discarded, an employer committed an unfair labor practice by refusing "in bad faith" to recognize a union; bad faith was found either because the employer had no reason to doubt the union's majority or because the employer's subsequent unfair labor practices were deemed to have been directed at eroding such a majority.

The Board formerly had limited bargaining orders based on such findings by holding, in Louis Aiello, 110 N.L.R.B. 1365, 1370 (1954), that a union's participation in an election after an employer's denial of recognition barred postelection §8(a)(5) charges based on the employer's preelection conduct known to the union. But in Bernel Foam Products Co., 146 N.L.R.B. 1277 (1964), the Board overturned *Aiello*, finding nothing inconsistent in a union's filing of an election petition (thereby asserting the existence of a question concerning representation) and, after losing an election, filing a refusal to bargain charge together with other unfair labor practice charges. The Board, however, soon made it clear that a §8(a)(5) order, based on preelection conduct, could issue only if the Board had set aside the election. See Irving Air Chute Co., 149 N.L.R.B. 627, 630 (1964), *enforced*, 350 F.2d 176 (2d Cir. 1965).[5]

These developments appeared to stimulate preelection solicitation of authorization cards by unions. For a union could gain bargaining status by winning the election, or, having lost the election and having it vacated, the union might secure a bargaining order on the basis of the employer's unfair practices. Not surprisingly, after *Bernel Foam* there was an increase in bargaining orders conferring initial representative status. The materials below explore the rationale for, and the restrictions on, such orders.

NLRB v. Gissel Packing Co.
395 U.S. 575 (1969)

WARREN, C. J. . . . The specific questions facing us here are whether the duty to bargain can arise without a Board election under the Act; whether union authorization cards, if obtained from a majority of employees without misrepresentation or coercion, are reliable enough generally to provide a valid, alternate route to majority status; whether a bargaining order is an appropriate and authorized remedy where an employer rejects a card majority while at the same time committing unfair labor practices that tend to undermine the union's majority and make a fair election an unlikely possibility; and whether certain specific statements made by an employer to his employees constituted such an election-voiding unfair labor practice and thus fell outside the protection of the First Amendment and §8(c) of the Act. . . . For reasons given below, we answer each of these questions in the affirmative. . . .

[The Court's discussion of the First Amendment and §8(c) appears at p. 95, supra.]

Nos. 573 AND 691

In each of the cases from the Fourth Circuit, the course of action followed by the Union and the employer and the Board's response were similar. In each

---

[5]But cf. Peoples Gas System, 238 N.L.R.B. 1008, 1010-1011 (1978), *enforcement denied*, 629 F.2d 35 (D.C. Cir. 1980), dispensing with the requirement recognized in *Air Chute*, when an incumbent union alleging the illegality of an employer's withdrawal of prior recognition had failed to object to an election that it had lost.

When an employer commits an unfair labor practice during the "critical period," i.e., after the filing of the election petition and before the holding of the election, the Board ordinarily vacates the election and orders a new one. When, however, it appears virtually impossible that the violation affected the results of the election, the Board will not upset the election. See Custom Trim Products, 255 N.L.R.B. 787 (1981).

case, the Union waged an organizational campaign, obtained authorization cards from a majority of employees in the appropriate bargaining unit, and then, on the basis of the cards, demanded recognition by the employer. All three employers refused to bargain on the ground that authorization cards were inherently unreliable indicators of employee desires; and they either embarked on, or continued, vigorous antiunion campaigns that gave rise to numerous unfair labor practice charges. In *Gissel*, where the employer's campaign began almost at the outset of the Union's organizational drive, the Union (petitioner in No. 691), did not seek an election, but instead filed three unfair labor practice charges against the employer, for refusing to bargain in violation of §8(a)(5), for coercion and intimidation of employees in violation of §8(a)(1), and for discharge of Union adherents in violation of §8(a)(3). In *Heck's* an election sought by the Union was never held because of nearly identical unfair labor practice charges later filed by the Union as a result of the employer's antiunion campaign, initiated after the Union's recognition demand. And in *General Steel*, an election petitioned for by the Union and won by the employer was set aside by the Board because of the unfair labor practices committed by the employer in the pre-election period.

In each case, the Board's primary response was an order to bargain directed at the employers, despite the absence of an election in *Gissel* and *Heck's* and the employer's victory in *General Steel*. More specifically, the Board found in each case (1) that the Union had obtained valid authorization cards[4] from a majority of the employees in the bargaining unit and was thus entitled to represent the employees for collective bargaining purposes; and (2) that the employer's refusal to bargain with the Union in violation of §8(a)(5) was motivated, not by a "good faith" doubt of the Union's majority status, but by a desire to gain time to dissipate that status. The Board based its conclusion as to the lack of good faith doubt on the fact that the employers had committed substantial unfair labor practices during their antiunion campaign efforts to resist recognition. Thus, the Board found that all three employers had engaged in restraint and coercion of employees in violation of §8(a)(1) — in *Gissel*, for coercively interrogating employees about Union activities, threatening them with discharge, and promising them benefits; in *Heck's*, for coercively interrogating employees, threatening reprisals, creating the appearance of surveillance, and offering benefits for opposing the

---

[4]The cards used . . . unambiguously authorized the Union to represent the signing employee for collective bargaining purposes; there was no reference to elections. Typical of the cards was the one used in the Charleston campaign in *Heck's*, and it stated in relevant part:

"Desiring to become a member of the above Union of the International Brotherhood of Teamsters, Chauffeurs, Warehousemen and Helpers of America, I hereby make application for admission to membership. I hereby authorize you, your agents or representatives to act for me as collective bargaining agent on all matters pertaining to rates of pay, hours, or any other conditions of employment."

Union; and in *General Steel*, for coercive interrogation and threats of reprisals, including discharge. In addition, the Board found that the employers in *Gissel* and *Heck's* had wrongfully discharged employees for engaging in Union activities in violation of §8(a)(3). And, because the employers had rejected the card-based bargaining demand in bad faith, the Board found that all three had refused to recognize the Unions in violation of §8(a)(5).

Only in *General Steel* was there any objection by an employer to the validity of the cards and the manner in which they had been solicited, and the doubt raised by the evidence was resolved in the following manner. The customary approach of the Board in dealing with allegations of misrepresentation by the Union and misunderstanding by the employees of the purpose for which the cards were being solicited has been set out in Cumberland Shoe Corp., 144 N.L.R.B. 1268 (1963) and reaffirmed in Levi Strauss & Co., 172 N.L.R.B. No. 57, 68 L.R.R.M. 1338 (1968). Under the *Cumberland Shoe* doctrine, if the card itself is unambiguous (i.e., states on its face that the signer authorizes the Union to represent the employee for collective bargaining purposes and not to seek an election), it will be counted unless it is proved that the employee was told that the card was to be used *solely* for the purpose of obtaining an election. In *General Steel*, the trial examiner considered the allegations of misrepresentation at length and, applying the Board's customary analysis, rejected the claims with findings that were adopted by the Board and are reprinted in the margin.[5]

Consequently, the Board ordered the companies to cease and desist from their unfair labor practices, to offer reinstatement and back pay to the employees who had been discriminatorily discharged, to bargain with the Unions on request, and to post the appropriate notices.

On appeal, [the Fourth Circuit], in curiam opinions in each of the three cases (398 F.2d 336, 337, 339), sustained the Board's findings as to the §§8(a)(1) and (3) violations, but rejected the Board's findings that the employers' refusal to bargain violated §8(a)(5) and declined to enforce those portions of the Board's orders directing the respondent companies to bargain in good faith. . . . [The court's position was] that the 1947 Taft-Hartley

---

[5] "Accordingly, I reject Respondent's contention 'that if a man is told that his card will be secret, or will be shown only to the Labor Board for the purpose of obtaining election, that this is the absolute equivalent of telling him that it will be used "only" for purposes of obtaining an election.'

"With respect to 97 employees . . . Respondent in its brief contends, in substance, that their cards should be rejected because each of these employees was told *one or more* of the following: (1) that the card would be used to get an election (2) that he had the right to vote either way, even though he signed the card (3) that the card would be kept secret and not shown to anybody except to the Board in order to get an election. For reasons heretofore explicated, I conclude that these statements, singly or jointly, do not foreclose use of the cards for the purpose designated on their face."

amendments to the Act, which permitted the Board to resolve representation disputes by certification under §9(c) only by secret ballot election, withdrew from the Board the authority to order an employer to bargain under §8(a)(5) on the basis of cards, in the absence of NLRB certification, unless the employer knows independently of the cards that there is in fact no representation dispute. The court held that the cards themselves were so inherently unreliable that their use gave an employer virtually an automatic, good faith claim that such a dispute existed, for which a secret election was necessary. Thus, these rulings established that a company could not be ordered to bargain unless (1) there was no question about a Union's majority status (either because the employer agreed the cards were valid or had conducted his own poll so indicating), or (2) the employer's §§8(a)(1) and (3) unfair labor practices committed during the representation campaign were so extensive and pervasive that a bargaining order was the only available Board remedy irrespective of a card majority. . . .

No. 585

. . . In July 1965, [Teamsters, Local Union No. 404] began an organizing campaign among petitioner's Holyoke employees and by the end of the summer had obtained authorization cards from 11 of the Company's 14 journeymen wire weavers choosing the Union as their bargaining agent. On September 20, the Union notified petitioner that it represented a majority of its wire weavers, requested that the Company bargain with it, and offered to submit the signed cards to a neutral third party for authentication. After petitioner's president declined the Union's request a week later, claiming, *inter alia*, that he had a good faith doubt of majority status because of the cards' inherent unreliability, the Union petitioned, on November 8, for an election that was ultimately set for December 9.

. . . The Union lost the election 7 to 6, and then filed both objections to the election and unfair labor practice charges which were consolidated for hearing before the trial examiner.

The Board agreed with the trial examiner that the president's communications with his employees, when considered as a whole, "reasonably tended to convey to the employees the belief or impression that selection of the Union in the forthcoming election could lead [the Company] to close its plant, or to the transfer of the weaving production, with the resultant loss of jobs to the wire weavers." Thus, the Board found that under the "totality of the circumstances" petitioner's activities constituted a violation of §8(a)(1) of the Act. The Board further agreed with the trial examiner that petitioner's activities, because they "also interfered with the exercise of a free and untrammeled choice in the election," and "tended to foreclose the possibility" of holding a fair election, required that the election be set aside. The Board also found that the Union had a valid card majority . . . when it demanded recognition initially and that the Company declined recognition, not because of a good faith doubt as to the majority status, but, as the §8(a)(1) violations indicated, in order to gain time to dissipate that status — in violation of §8(a)(5). Consequently, the Board set the election aside, entered a cease-and-desist order, and ordered the Company to bargain on request.

On appeal, the [First Circuit] sustained the Board's findings and conclusions and enforced its order in full. 397 F.2d 157. . . .

II

In urging us to reverse the Fourth Circuit and to affirm the First Circuit, the [NLRB] contends that we should approve its interpretation and administration of the duties and obligations imposed by the Act in authorization card cases. The Board argues (1) that unions have never been limited under §9(c) of either the Wagner Act or the 1947 amendments to certified elections as the sole route to attaining representative status. Unions may, the Board contends, impose a duty to bargain on the employer under §8(a)(5) by reliance on other evidence of majority employee support, such as authorization cards. Contrary to the Fourth Circuit's holding, the Board asserts, the 1947 amendments did not eliminate the alternative routes to majority status. The Board contends (2) that the cards themselves, when solicited in accordance with Board standards which adequately insure against union misrepresentation, are sufficiently reliable indicators of employee desires to support a bargaining order against an employer who refuses to recognize a card majority in violation of §8(a)(5). The Board argues (3) that a bargaining order is the appropriate remedy for the §8(a)(5) violation, where the employer commits other unfair labor practices that tend to undermine union support and render a fair election improbable.

Relying on these three assertions the Board asks us to approve its current practice, which is briefly as follows. When confronted by a recognition demand based on possession of cards allegedly signed by a majority of his employees, an employer need not grant recognition immediately, but may, unless he has knowledge independently of the cards that the union has a majority, decline the union's request and insist on an election, either by requesting the union to file an election petition or by filing such a petition himself under §9(c)(1)(B). If, however, the employer commits independent and substantial unfair labor practices disruptive of election conditions, the Board may withhold the election or set it aside, and issue instead a bargaining order as a remedy for the various violations. A bargaining order will not issue, of course, if the union obtained the cards through misrepresentation or coercion or if the employer's unfair labor practices are unrelated generally to the representation campaign. Conversely, the employers in these cases urge us to adopt the views of the Fourth Circuit.

. . . [T]he Union, petitioner in No. 691, argues that we should accord a far greater role to cards in the bargaining area than the Board itself seeks in this litigation. In order to understand the differences between the Union and the Board, it is necessary to trace the evolution of the Board's approach to authorization cards from its early practice to the position it takes on oral argument before this Court. Such an analysis requires viewing the Board's treatment of authorization cards in three separate phases: (1) under the *Joy Silk* doctrine, (2) under the rules of the *Aaron Brothers* case, and (3) under the approach announced at oral argument before this Court.

The traditional approach utilized by the Board for many years has been known as the *Joy Silk* doctrine. Joy Silk Mills, Inc., 85 N.L.R.B. 1263 (1949), *enforced*, 185 F.2d 732 (1950). Under that rule, an employer could lawfully refuse to bargain with a union claiming representative status through possession of authorization cards if he had a "good faith doubt" as to the union's majority status; instead of bargaining, he could insist that the union seek an election in order to test out his doubts. The Board, then, could find a lack of good faith doubt and enter a bargaining order in one of two ways. It could find (1) that the employer's independent unfair labor practices were evidence of bad faith, showing that the employer was seeking time to dissipate the union's majority. Or the Board could find (2) that the employer had come forward with no reasons for entertaining any doubt and therefore that he must have rejected the bargaining demand in bad faith. An example of the second category was Snow & Sons, 134 N.L.R.B. 709 (1961), *enforced*, 308 F.2d 687 (C.A. 9th Cir. 1962), where the employer reneged on his agreement to bargain after a third party checked the validity of the card signatures and insisted on an election because he doubted that the employees truly desired representation. The Board entered a bargaining order with very broad language to the effect that an employer could not refuse a bargaining demand and seek an election instead "without a valid ground therefor," 134 N.L.R.B., at 710-711.

The leading case codifying modifications to the *Joy Silk* doctrine was *Aaron Brothers*, 158 N.L.R.B. 1077 (1966). There the Board made it clear that it had shifted the burden to the General Counsel to show bad faith and that an employer "will not be held to have violated his bargaining obligation . . . simply because he refuses to rely upon cards, rather than an election, as the method for determining the union's majority." 158 N.L.R.B., at 1078. Two significant consequences were emphasized. The Board noted (1) that not every unfair labor practice would automatically result in a finding of bad faith and therefore a bargaining order; the Board implied that it would find bad faith only if the unfair labor practice was serious enough to have the tendency to dissipate the union's majority. The Board noted (2) that an employer no longer needed to come forward with reasons for rejecting a bargaining demand. The Board pointed out, however, that a bargaining order would issue if it could prove that an employer's "course of conduct" gave indications as to the employer's bad faith. As examples of such a "course of conduct," the Board cited *Snow & Sons*, supra. . . .

Although the Board's brief before this Court generally followed the approach as set out in *Aaron Brothers*, supra, the Board announced at oral argument that it had virtually abandoned the *Joy Silk* doctrine altogether. Under the Board's current practice, an employer's good faith doubt is largely irrelevant, and the key to the issuance of a bargaining order is the commission of serious unfair labor practices that interfere with the election processes and tend to preclude the holding of a fair election. Thus, an employer can insist that a union go to an election, regardless of his subjective motivation, so long as he is not guilty of misconduct; he need give no affirmative reasons for rejecting a recognition request, and he can demand an election with a simple "no comment" to the union. The Board pointed out, however, (1) that an employer could not refuse to bargain if he *knew*, through a personal poll for instance, that a majority of his employees supported the union, and (2) that an employer could not refuse recognition initially because of questions as to the appropriateness of the unit and then later claim, as an afterthought, that he doubted the union's strength. . . .

[The Court here reserved the question decided later in *Linden Lumber*, infra p. 458, i.e., whether an employer confronted with a bargaining demand supported by a card-based majority must either recognize the union or file a petition for an NLRB election.]

III

A

The first issue facing us is whether a union can establish a bargaining obligation by means other than a Board election and whether the validity of alternate routes to majority status, such as cards, was affected by the 1947 Taft-Hartley amendments. The most commonly traveled[7] route for a union

---

[7] In 1967, for instance, the Board conducted 8,116 elections but issued only 157 bargaining orders based on a card majority. Levi Strauss & Co., 172 N.L.R.B. No. 57, 68 L.R.R.M. 1338, 1342, n.9 (1968). . . . The number of card cases that year, however, represents a rather dramatic increase over previous years, from 12 such cases in 1964, 24 in 1965, and about 117 in 1966. Browne, Obligation to Bargain on Basis of Card Majority, 3 Ga. L. Rev. 334, 347 (1969).

to obtain recognition as the exclusive bargaining representative of an unorganized group of employees is through the Board's election and certification procedures under §9(c) . . . ; it is also, from the Board's point of view, the preferred route. A union is not limited to a Board election, however, for, in addition to §9, the present Act provides in §8(a)(5), as did the Wagner Act in §8(5), that "[i]t shall be an unfair labor practice for an employer . . . to refuse to bargain collectively with the representatives of his employees, subject to the provisions of §9(a)." Since §9(a), in both the Wagner Act and the present Act, refers to the representative as the one "designated or selected" by a majority of the employees without specifying precisely how that representative is to be chosen, it was clearly recognized that an employer had a duty to bargain whenever the union representative presented "convincing evidence of majority support." Almost from the inception of the Act, then, it was recognized that a union did not have to be certified as the winner of a Board election to invoke a bargaining obligation; it could establish majority status by other means under the unfair labor practice provision of §8(a)(5) — by showing convincing support, for instance, by a union-called strike or strike vote, or, as here, by possession of cards signed by a majority of the employees authorizing the union to represent them for collective bargaining purposes.

. . . We have consistently accepted this interpretation of the Wagner Act and the present act, particularly as to the use of authorization cards. . . . [T]he 1947 amendments weaken rather than strengthen the position taken by the employers here and the Fourth Circuit below. An early version of the bill in the House would have amended §8(5) of the Wagner Act to permit the Board to find a refusal-to-bargain violation only where an employer had failed to bargain with a union "currently recognized by the employer or certified as such [through an election] under section 9." Section 8(a)(5) of H.R. 3020, 80th Cong., 1st Sess. (1947). The proposed change, which would have eliminated the use of cards, was rejected in Conference (H.R. Conf. Rep. No. 510, 80th Cong., 1st Sess., 41 (1947)), however, and we cannot make a similar change in the Act simply because, as the employers assert, Congress did not expressly approve the use of cards in rejecting the House amendment. Nor can we accept the Fourth Circuit's conclusion that the change was wrought when Congress amended §9(c) to make election the sole basis for *certification* by eliminating the phrase "any other suitable method to ascertain such representatives," under which the Board had occasionally used cards as a certification basis. A certified union has the benefit of numerous special privileges which are not accorded unions recognized voluntarily or under a bargaining order and which, Congress could determine, should not be dispensed unless a union has survived the crucible of a secret ballot election.

The employers rely finally on the addition to §9(c) of subparagraph (B), which allows an employer to petition for an election whenever "one or more individuals or labor organizations have presented to him a claim to be recognized as the representative defined in section 9(a)." That provision was not added, as the employers assert, to give them an absolute right to an election at any time; rather, it was intended, as the legislative history indicates, to allow them, after being asked to bargain, to test out their doubts as to a union's majority in a secret election which they would then presumably not cause to be set aside by illegal antiunion activity. We agree with the Board's assertion here that there is no suggestion that Congress intended §9(c)(1)(B) to relieve any employer of his §8(a)(5) bargaining obligation where, without good faith, he engaged in unfair labor practices disruptive of the Board's election machinery. And we agree that the policies reflected in §9(c)(1)(B) fully support the Board's present administration of the Act . . . ; for an employer can insist on a secret ballot election, unless, in the words of the Board, he engages "in contemporaneous unfair labor practices likely to destroy the union's majority and seriously impede the election." . . .

B

We next consider the question whether authorization cards are such inherently unreliable indicators of employee desires that, whatever the validity of other alternate routes to representative status, the cards themselves may never be used to determine a union's majority and to support an order to bargain. In this context, the employers urge us to take the step the 1947 amendments and their legislative history indicate Congress did not take, namely, to rule out completely the use of cards in the bargaining arena. Even if we do not unhesitatingly accept the Fourth Circuit's view in the matter, the employers argue, at the very least we should overrule the *Cumberland Shoe* doctrine . . . and establish stricter controls over the solicitation of the cards by union representatives.

The objections to the use of cards voiced by the employers and the Fourth Circuit boil down to two contentions: (1) that, as contrasted with the election procedure, the cards cannot accurately reflect an employee's wishes, either because an employer has not had a chance to present his views and thus a chance to insure that the employee choice was an informed one, or because the choice was the result of group pressures and not individual decision made in the privacy of a voting booth; and (2) that quite apart from the election comparison, the cards are too often obtained through misrepresentation and coercion which compound the cards' inherent inferiority to the election process. Neither contention is persuasive, and each proves too much. The Board itself has recognized, and continues to do so here, that secret elections are generally the most satisfactory — indeed the preferred — method of ascertaining whether a union has majority support. The acknowledged superiority of the election process, however, does not mean that cards are thereby rendered totally invalid, for where an employer engages in conduct disruptive of the election process, cards may be the most effective — perhaps the only — way of assuring employee choice. As for misrepresentation, in any specific case of alleged irregularity in the solicitation of the cards, the proper course is to apply the Board's customary standards (to be discussed more fully below) and rule there was no majority if the standards were not satisfied. It does not follow that because there are some instances of irregularity, the cards can never be used; otherwise, an employer could put off his bargaining obligation indefinitely through continuing interference with elections.

That the cards, though admittedly inferior to the election process, can adequately reflect employee sentiment when that process has been impeded, needs no extended discussion, for the employers' contentions cannot withstand close examination. The employers argue that their employees cannot make an informed choice because the card drive will be over before the employer has had a chance to present his side of the unionization issues. Normally, however, the union will inform the employer of its organization drive early in order to subject the employer to the unfair labor practice provisions of the Act; the union must be able to show the employer's awareness of the drive in order to prove that his contemporaneous conduct constituted unfair labor practices on which a bargaining order can be based if the drive is ultimately successful. . . . Further, the employers argue that without a secret ballot an employee may, in a card drive, succumb to group pressures or sign simply to get the union "off his back" and then be unable to change his mind as he would be free to do once inside a voting booth. But the same pressures are likely to be equally present in an election, for election cases arise most often with small bargaining units where virtually every voter's sentiments can be carefully and individually canvassed. And no voter, of course, can change his mind after casting a ballot in an election even though he may think better of his choice shortly thereafter.

The employers' second complaint, that the cards are too often obtained through misrepresentation and coercion, must be rejected also in view of the Board's present rules for controlling card solicitation, which we view as adequate to the task where the cards involved state their purpose clearly and unambiguously on their face. We would be closing our eyes to obvious difficulties, of course, if we did not recognize that there have been abuses, primarily arising out of misrepresentation by union organizers as to whether the effect of signing a card was to designate the union to represent the employee for collective bargaining purposes or merely to authorize it to seek an election to determine that issue. And we would be equally blind if we did not recognize that various courts of appeals and commentators have differed significantly as to the effectiveness of the Board's *Cumberland Shoe* doctrine to cure such abuses. . . .

We need make no decision as to the conflicting approaches used with regard to dual-purpose cards, for in each of the five organization campaigns in the four cases before us the cards used were single-purpose cards, stating clearly and unambiguously on their face that the signer designated the union as his representative. And even the view forcefully voiced by the Fourth Circuit below that unambiguous cards as well present too many opportunities for misrepresentation comes before us somewhat weakened in view of the fact that there were no allegations of irregularities in four of those five campaigns (*Gissel*, the two *Heck's* campaigns, and *Sinclair*). Only in *General Steel* did the employer challenge the cards on the basis of misrepresentations. There, the trial examiner, after hearing testimony from over 100 employees and applying the traditional Board approach concluded that "all of these employees not only intended, but were fully aware, that they were thereby designating the Union as their representative." Thus, the sole question before us, raised in only one of the four cases here, is whether the *Cumberland Shoe* doctrine is an adequate rule under the Act for assuring employee free choice.

In resolving the conflict among the circuits in favor of approving the Board's *Cumberland* rule, we think it sufficient to point out that employees should be bound by the clear language of what they sign unless that language is deliberately and clearly canceled by a union adherent with words calculated to direct the signer to disregard and forget the language above his signature. There is nothing inconsistent in handing an employee a card that says the signer authorizes the union to represent him and then telling him that the card will probably be used first to get an election. . . . We cannot agree with the employers here that employees as a rule are too unsophisticated to be bound by what they sign unless expressly told that their act of signing represents something else. . . .

We agree, however, with the Board's own warnings in Levi Strauss & Co., 172 N.L.R.B. 732 and n.7 (1968), that in hearing testimony concerning a card challenge, trial examiners should not neglect their obligation to ensure employee free choice by a too easy mechanical application of the *Cumberland* rule. We also accept the observation that employees are more likely than not, many months after a card drive and in response to questions by company counsel, to give testimony damaging to the union, particularly where company officials have previously threatened reprisals for union activity in violation of §8(a)(1). We therefore reject any rule that requires a probe of an employee's subjective motivations as involving an endless and unreliable inquiry. . . . We emphasize that the Board should be careful to guard against an approach any more rigid than that in *General Steel*. And we reiterate that nothing we say here indicates our approval of the *Cumberland Shoe* rule when applied to ambiguous, dual-purpose cards.

The employers argue as a final reason for rejecting the use of the cards that they are faced with a Hobson's choice under current Board rules and will almost inevitably come out the loser. They contend that if they do not make an immediate, personal investigation into possible solicitation irregularities to determine whether in fact the union represents an uncoerced majority, they will have unlawfully refused to bargain for failure to have a good faith doubt of the union's majority; and if they do make such an investigation, their efforts at polling and interrogation will constitute an unfair labor practice in violation of §8(a)(1) and they will again be ordered to bargain. As we have pointed out, however, an employer is not obligated to accept a card check as proof of majority status, under the Board's current practice, and he is not required to justify his insistence on an election by making his own investigation of employee sentiment and showing affirmative reasons for doubting the majority status. See Aaron Brothers, 158 N.L.R.B. 1077, 1078. If he does make an investigation, the Board's recent cases indicate that reasonable polling in this regard will not always be termed violative of §8(a)(1) if conducted in accordance with the requirements set out in Struksnes Construction Co., 165 N.L.R.B. 1062 (1967). And even if an employer's limited interrogation is found violative of the Act, it might not be serious enough to call for a bargaining order. . . . As noted above, the Board has emphasized that not "any employer conduct found violative of §8(a)(1) of the Act, regardless of its nature or gravity, will necessarily support a refusal-to-bargain finding," *Aaron Brothers*, supra, at 1079.

C

Remaining before us is the propriety of a bargaining order as a remedy for a §8(a)(5) refusal to bargain where an employer has committed independent unfair labor practices which have made the holding of a fair election unlikely or which have in fact undermined a union's majority and caused an election to be set aside. We have long held that the Board is not limited to a cease-and-desist order in such cases, but has the authority to issue a bargaining order without first requiring the union to show that it has been able to maintain its majority status. And we have held that the Board has the same authority even where it is clear that the union, which once had possession of cards from a majority of the employees, represents only a minority when the bargaining order is entered. Franks Bros. Co. v. NLRB, 321 U.S. 702 (1944). We see no reason now to withdraw this authority from the Board. If the Board could enter only a cease-and-desist order and direct an election or a rerun, it would in effect be rewarding the employer and allowing him "to profit from [his] own wrongful refusal to bargain," *Franks Bros.*, supra, at 704, while at the same time severely curtailing the employees' right freely to determine whether they desire a representative. The employer could continue to delay or disrupt the election process and put off indefinitely his obligation to bargain,[30] and any election held under these circumstances would not be likely to demonstrate the employees' true, undistorted desires.[31]

The employers argue that the Board has ample remedies, over and above the cease-and-desist order, to control employer misconduct. The Board can, they assert, direct the companies to mail notices to employees, to read notices to employees during plant time and to give the union access to employees during working time at the plant, or it can seek a court injunctive order under §10(j), as a last resort. In view of the Board's power, they conclude, the bargaining order is an unnecessarily harsh remedy that need-lessly prejudices employees' §7 rights solely for the purpose of punishing or restraining an employer. Such an argument ignores that a bargaining order is designed as much to remedy past election damage as it is to deter future misconduct. If an employer has succeeded in undermining a union's strength and destroying the laboratory conditions necessary for a fair election, he may see no need to violate a cease-and-desist order by further unlawful activity.

---

[30] The Board indicates here that its records show that in the period between January and June 1968, the median time between the filing of an unfair labor practice charge and a Board decision in a contested case was 388 days. But the employer can do more than just put off his bargaining obligation by seeking to slow down the Board's administrative processes. He can also affect the outcome of a rerun election by delaying tactics, for figures show that the longer the time between a tainted election and a rerun, the less are the union's chances of reversing the outcome of the first election. See n.31, infra.

[31] A study of 20,153 elections held between 1960 and 1962 shows that in the 267 cases where rerun elections were held over 30% were won by the party who caused the election to be set aside. See Pollitt, NLRB Re-Run Elections: A Study, 41 N.C.L. Rev. 209, 212 (1963). The study shows further that certain unfair labor practices are more effective to destroy election conditions for a longer period of time than others. For instance, in cases involving threats to close or transfer plant operations, the union won the rerun only 29% of the time, while threats to eliminate benefits or refuse to deal with the union if elected seemed less irremediable with the union winning the rerun 75% of the time. Id., at 215-216. Finally, time appears to be a factor. The figures suggest that if a rerun is held too soon after the election before the effects of the unfair labor practices have worn off, or too long after the election when interest in the union may have waned, the chances for a changed result occurring are not as good as they are if the rerun is held sometime in between those periods. Thus, the study showed that if the rerun is held within 30 days of the election or over nine months after, the chances that a different result will occur are only one in five; when the rerun is held within 30-60 days after the election, the chances for a changed result are two in five. Id., at 221. [Pollitt's methodology is criticized in Getman & Goldberg, The Myth of Labor Board Expertise, 39 U. Chi. L. Rev. 681, 691-694 (1972). —EDS.]

The damage will have been done, and perhaps the only fair way to effectuate employee rights is to reestablish the conditions as they existed before the employer's unlawful campaign. There is, after all, nothing permanent in a bargaining order, and if, after the effects of the employer's acts have worn off, the employees clearly desire to disavow the union, they can do so by filing a representation petition.

. . . Despite our reversal of the Fourth Circuit below in Nos. 573 and 691 on all major issues, the actual area of disagreement between our position here and that of the Fourth Circuit is not large as a practical matter. While refusing to validate the general use of a bargaining order in reliance on cards, the Fourth Circuit nevertheless left open the possibility of imposing a bargaining order, without need of inquiry into majority status on the basis of cards or otherwise, in "exceptional" cases marked by "outrageous" and "pervasive" unfair labor practices. Such an order would be an appropriate remedy for those practices, the court noted, if they are of "such a nature that their coercive effects cannot be eliminated by the application of traditional remedies, with the result that a fair and reliable election cannot be had." NLRB v. Logan Packing Co., 386 F.2d 562, 570 (C.A. 4th Cir. 1967). . . . The Board itself, we should add, has long had a similar policy of issuing a bargaining order, in the absence of a §8(a)(5) violation or even a bargaining demand, when that was the only available, effective remedy for substantial unfair labor practices. . . .

The only effect of our holding here is to approve the Board's use of the bargaining order in less extraordinary cases marked by less pervasive practices which nonetheless still have the tendency to undermine majority strength and impede the election processes. The Board's authority to issue such an order on a lesser showing of employer misconduct is appropriate, we should reemphasize, where there is also a showing that at one point the union had a majority; in such a case, of course, effectuating ascertainable employee free choice becomes as important a goal as deterring employer misbehavior. In fashioning a remedy in the exercise of its discretion, then, the Board can properly take into consideration the extensiveness of an employer's unfair practices in terms of their past effect on election conditions and the likelihood of their recurrence in the future. If the Board finds that the possibility of erasing the effects of past practices and of ensuring a fair election (or a fair rerun) by the use of traditional remedies, though present, is slight and that employee sentiment once expressed through cards would, on balance, be better protected by a bargaining order, then such an order should issue.

We emphasize that under the Board's remedial power there is still a third category of minor or less extensive unfair labor practices, which, because of their minimal impact on the election machinery, will not sustain a bargaining order. There is, the Board says, no *per se* rule that the commission of any unfair practice will automatically result in a §8(a)(5) violation and the issuance of an order to bargain. See *Aaron Brothers*, supra.

With these considerations in mind, we turn to an examination of the orders in these cases. In *Sinclair*, No. 585, the Board made a finding, left undisturbed by the First Circuit, that the employer's threats of reprisal were so coercive that, even in the absence of a §8(a)(5) violation, a bargaining order would have been necessary to repair the unlawful effect of those threats. The Board therefore did not have to make the determination called for in the intermediate situation above that the risks that a fair rerun election might not be possible were too great to disregard the desires of the employees already expressed through the cards. . . .

In the three cases in Nos. 573 and 691 from the Fourth Circuit, on the other hand, the Board did not make a similar finding that a bargaining order would have been necessary in the absence of an unlawful refusal to bargain. Nor did it make a finding that, even though traditional remedies might be able to ensure a fair election, there was insufficient indication that an election (or a rerun in *General Steel*) would definitely be a more reliable test of the employees' desires than the card count taken before the unfair labor practices occurred. The employees argue that such findings would not be warranted, and the court below ruled in *General Steel* that available remedies short of a bargaining order could guarantee a fair election. 398 F.2d 339, 340, n.3. We think it possible that the requisite findings were implicit in the Board's decisions below to issue bargaining orders (and to set aside the election in *General Steel*); and we think it clearly inappropriate for the court below to make any contrary finding on its own. Because the Board's current practice at the time required it to phrase its findings in terms of an employer's good or bad faith doubts (see Part II, supra), however, the precise analysis the Board now puts forth was not employed below, and we therefore remand these cases for proper findings. . . .

NOTES

1. Underlying the materials below (especially Note 2) is the question whether a bargaining order is essentially an additional remedy for violations of §§8(a)(1)-(4) of the Act rather than a remedy for refusals to bargain in violation of §8(a)(5). Consider the compatibility of such an additional remedy with both the strictures against "punitive remedies" and the Act's emphasis on employee self-determination.

2. On February 1, 1984, a union requested recognition in an appropriate unit and (truthfully) advised the employer of its valid card majority. The

employer promptly said "No." On February 2, 1984, a supervisor asked several employees their opinion of "the union business" and received non-committal replies. On February 6, 1984, a management consultant, following a three-month study of the employer's wage costs and those of his competitors, (truthfully) advised the employer that his wages would have to be cut by 19 percent if he were to remain competitive. On February 8, the employer instituted such a cut. On February 10, the employer asked employees suspected of having attended a union meeting whether the union bosses were promising "pie-in-the-sky." Later he threatened many employees with plant closure if the union came in; he also discharged well-known union supporters. The question is whether, in addition to issuing a bargaining order based on serious violations of §§8(a)(1) and 8(a)(3), the Board should also find a violation of §8(a)(5) and make that finding the basis for a back pay order remedying the employer's unilateral wage cutting. How should that issue be resolved? See Trading Port, Inc., 219 N.L.R.B. 298 (1975); Local 669 v. NLRB (John Cuneo, Inc.), 681 F.2d 11 (D.C. Cir. 1982), cert. denied, 103 S. Ct. 831 (1983), enforcing a Board order, retroactive to the date the union requested recognition, for reinstatement of employees engaging in a subsequent recognition strike, on the ground that that strike was an unfair labor practice strike from its inception. [Rehnquist, J., joined by Powell, J., dissenting from denial of certiorari, expressed concern that "the bargaining order has been sanctioned without a finding that the special circumstances required by Gissel exist" and stating that the Court should review the propriety of that approach.]

   To what date should a bargaining order be retroactive: (a) when the employer declined to recognize; (b) when its unlawful conduct began; (c) when it succeeded in undermining the union's preexisting majority; or (d) when its conduct became "outrageous" in cases in which the union never had majority support—assuming that bargaining orders will be granted under such circumstances?

   3. In Gourmet Foods, 270 N.L.R.B. No. 113, 116 L.R.R.M. 1105 (1984), Chairman Dotson and Members Hunter and Dennis agreed to the overruling of prior Board decisions, including Conair Corp., 261 N.L.R.B. 1189 (1982), enforcement denied (2-1), 721 F.2d 1355 (D.C. Cir. 1983), and held that the Act did not authorize the issuance of a bargaining order in favor of a union that never had majority support in an appropriate unit, regardless of the outrageousness of the employer's unfair labor practices. Two members maintained that even if statutory authority existed, the Board, in its discretion, should not exercise it. Member Zimmerman dissented with respect to both positions adopted by the plurality, noting that courts of appeal had upheld the Board's authority. The division in the Board turned on the

weight to be given to the principle of majority rule, in light of H.K. *Porter*, infra p. 844. Is that principle decisive, as the majority urged, or is the crucial issue the appropriate way to protect that principle when an employer's "outrageous" misconduct is found to preclude a fair election?

On §10(j) injunctions against employers vulnerable to *Gissel*-type bargaining orders, see Seeler v. Trading Post, Inc., 517 F.2d 33 (2d Cir. 1975); Boire v. Pilot Freight Carriers, Inc., 515 F.2d 1185 (5th Cir. 1975), *rehg. denied*, 521 F.2d 795, *cert. denied*, 426 U.S. 934 (1976). See generally Note, The Propriety of Section 10(j) Bargaining Orders in *Gissel* Situations, 82 Mich. L. Rev. 112 (1983).

4. In Linden Lumber Div., Summer & Co. v. NLRB, 419 U.S. 301 (1974), the Court (5-4), reversing 487 F.2d 1099 (D.C. Cir. 1973), upheld two Board rulings. First, an employer, otherwise guiltless of unfair labor practices, does not violate §8(a)(5) merely by refusing to recognize a union even though the employer at the time had "independent knowledge" of the union's valid card majority. Second, notwithstanding such independent knowledge, the union seeking recognition (rather than the employer) has the burden of filing an election petition. The Court reserved (419 U.S. at 310, n.10) "the question whether the same result obtains if the employer breaches his agreement to permit majority status to be determined by means other than a Board election. See Snow & Sons, 134 N.L.R.B. 709 (1961), *enf'd*, 308 F.2d 687 (CA9 1962)."

5. In Kroger Co., 219 N.L.R.B. 331 (1975), a collective agreement provided for recognition of the union in stores added by the employer to the division covered by the agreement. The employer declined to honor the additional-store clause even though the union tendered proof of (and had) valid card majorities among the stores' employees. The Board (3-2), reversing its original decision after remand by the D.C. Circuit, found a violation of §8(a)(5). The majority conceded that the stores could not be "accreted" since they might have constituted separate appropriate units, but read the additional-stores clause as effectively waiving the employer's right to insist on an election subject to the condition implied by the Board, "as a matter of law," that the union would supply proof of majority status.

(a) In the light of the question reserved in *Linden Lumber*, consider whether the majority position in *Kroger* is inconsistent (as a dissenter urged) with that decision.

(b) Does the Board's honoring of the modified additional-stores clause give adequate weight to the employees' interest in self-determination? Cf. *Magnavox*, supra p. 160; Penn Traffic Co., 219 N.L.R.B. 189 (1975); and the material on accretion, supra p. 408.

6. Suppose an employer's unfair labor practices appear to have been a factor in the loss of an incumbent union's majority and the employer declines

to bargain. Should a bargaining order be issued without regard to the serious-ness of the employer's antecedent misconduct or should the *Gissel* "guide-lines" be applied? See Daisy's Originals, Inc. v. NLRB, 468 F.2d 493, 501-502 (5th Cir. 1972) (*Gissel* guidelines for unions seeking initial recogni-tion should be equally applicable to loss of majorities by incumbents). This ruling is criticized in Note, 122 U. Pa. L. Rev. 207 (1973). Reconsider the Notes following *Bonanno*, supra p. 424.

Larid Printing, Inc.
264 N.L.R.B. 369 (1982)

. . . [T]he ALJ properly found that Respondent engaged in numerous violations of the Act in its effort to defeat the Union. These include interro-gations; threats of plant closure, loss of benefits, and harsher working condi-tions; prohibition against talking about the Union on Respondent's premises; requirement that loans be immediately repaid; and discharges of two em-ployees. In addition, we have found herein further violations of the Act including more instances of interrogation, statements blaming the loss of benefits and promotions on the Union, additional threats of plant closure, unspecified reprisals, discharge, and reduction of employee complement, and creation of the impression of surveillance.

The [ALJ] further found that, prior to September 3, a majority of the employees in the appropriate unit had designated, by . . . valid authoriza-tion cards, the Union as their bargaining representative, that Respondent received a demand for recognition on September 23, and that Respondent refused the Union's demand on that date. He concluded that the unfair labor practices that he found "eroded the Union's established majority and ren-dered it unlikely that even with the aid of conventional remedies a fair election could be held in the future." Therefore, based on the authorization cards, he recommended issuance of a bargaining order. We agree that a bargaining order is necessary to remedy fully Respondent's unlawful conduct and to effectuate the policies and purposes of the Act.

The Board has long recognized that certain conduct, such as threats of plant closing and loss of employment, is among the most serious and flagrant forms of interference with §7 rights. E.g., Irving N. Rothkin d/b/a Irv's Market, 179 N.L.R.B. 832 (1969), *enfd.* 434 F.2d 1051 (6th Cir. 1970). The Supreme Court has agreed that such threats are among the less remedi-able unfair labor practices. N.L.R.B. v. Gissel Packing Co., Inc., 395 U.S. 575, 611, fn. 31 (1969). The unlawful discharge of union adherents is misconduct which the Board and courts have long classified as going "to the very heart of the Act." See, e.g., N.L.R.B. v. Entwistle Manufacturing Co.,

120 F.2d 532, 536 (4th Cir. 1941). As the Second Circuit has noted, these "hallmark" violations are likely "to have a coercive effect on employees and to remain in their memories for a long period." N.L.R.B. v. Jamaica Towing, Inc., 632 F.2d 208, 213 (1980). Here, Respondent engaged in extensive unfair labor practices, several of which clearly constitute "hallmark" violations: two threats of plant closure, one of which was made to all the employees assembled; a threat of reduction in the employee complement, again made to all employees; a threat of discharge; and actual discharge of two principal union advocates. The court stated in *Jamaica Towing* that such "hallmark" violations will support the issuance of a bargaining order unless some significant mitigating circumstances are present.

No such circumstances exist in this case. To the contrary, we note that the unit here was comprised of only 19 employees and that many of the violations were committed by Respondent's president, Sarner. Clearly, an employer's unlawful conduct is heightened when it is directed at such a relatively small employee complement and when it is committed by a high-level management official.

In concluding that a bargaining order is warranted here, we have followed the Supreme Court's admonition to consider "the extensiveness of [Respondent's] unfair labor practices in terms of their past effect on election conditions and the likelihood of their recurrence in the future." N.L.R.B. v. Gissel, supra at 614. . . . [I]mmediately after receiving notice of the union campaign Respondent embarked upon . . . "a course of conduct designed to thwart the Union's efforts." This unlawful conduct . . . continued during the pendency of the Union's [election] objections when Respondent unlawfully discharged employees Beaudrot and Edwards. Given the swiftness with which Respondent reacted to the organizational effort and the fact that additional violations were committed during the postelection period, the likelihood of Respondent again engaging in illegal conduct is clearly present.

Thus, we are convinced, given the nature and extent of Respondent's unfair labor practices, that traditional remedies would be unlikely to dissipate the effects of Respondent's unlawful conduct. We therefore conclude . . . that majority employee sentiment (reflected by valid authorization cards) will be better protected by a bargaining order than by direction of an election.

NOTES

1. In *Gissel* "Class II" cases ("pervasive" but not "outrageous" unfair labor practices), the existence of majority support, usually established by authorization cards, appears to be a prerequisite for a bargaining order. The

Board's approach postulates that "hallmark offenses" are more likely both to destroy a preexisting majority and to preclude a fair election in the future, i.e., one free from the continuing effects of past employer misconduct. Do these premises seem intuitively correct? Do they have any empirical basis? Consider the conclusion of the Getman Study, supra p. 115, that serious employer violations are no more likely to have an adverse impact on union electioneering than less serious ones. The study recommended that bargaining orders be eliminated as a remedy for unlawful campaigning, or, if retained, that they be used solely to deter specific predetermined unlawful conduct, such as discriminatory discharges, and be imposed only if objective and publicized criteria were met (Study at 150, n.21).

2. In General Stencils, Inc., 195 N.L.R.B. 1109 (1972), *enforcement denied* (2-1), 472 F.2d 170 (2d Cir. 1972), the Board, on remand, reaffirmed a bargaining order; the court had previously denied enforcement (438 F.2d 894 (1971)) on the ground that the Board had not adequately explained its inconsistent decisions regarding bargaining orders. NLRB Chairman Edward B. Miller, dissenting from the issuance of the bargaining order, made these points: Only two categories of conduct should per se justify a *Gissel* Class II bargaining order, (1) the improper "grant of significant benefits," and (2) "repeated violations of §8(a)(3)." 195 N.L.R.B. at 112. In the latter context, actions must be sharply distinguished from alleged threats, because threats require the Board to consider whether they were uttered, the extent of their dissemination, and their impact on employees. Here, a bargaining remedy should be denied because there was no evidence that a single threat made to only one employee, shortly before he resigned, had been communicated to other employees.

3. The Third Circuit has been divided over when *Gissel* orders are appropriate and over the propriety of a requirement that the Board (or the ALJ) "articulate" the justification for preferring a bargaining order to a new election. See NLRB v. Eastern Steel, 671 F.2d 104 (3d Cir. 1982). The requirement of articulation is designed, among other things, to elicit a showing that a bargaining order is needed to remedy past misconduct rather than merely to serve as a deterrent in the future. See, e.g., NLRB v. World Carpets, Inc., 463 F.2d 57, 62 n.6 (2d Cir. 1972); New Alaska Development Corp. v. NLRB, 441 F.2d 491 (7th Cir. 1971). If the purpose in a given case is remedial, i.e., to displace an election process deemed still tainted by the employer's misconduct, what consideration should the Board (or a reviewing court) give to events subsequent to the employer's misconduct, including employee turnover unrelated to such misconduct, lapse of time, and removal of supervisors and managers directly responsible for the prior misconduct? Some courts, in denying enforcement of bargaining orders, have admonished the Board for failing to address such factors. See, e.g., NLRB v.

Windsor Industries, 730 F.2d 860 (2d Cir. 1984); NLRB v. Armcor Industries, Inc., 227 N.L.R.B. 1543 (1977), *enforcement denied*, 535 F.2d 239 (3d Cir. 1978) (en banc). See generally Comment, "After All, Tomorrow is Another Day": Should Subsequent Events Affect the Validity of Bargaining Orders? 31 Stan. L. Rev. 505 (1979).

Local 57, International Ladies Garment Union v. NLRB (Garwin Corp.)
374 F.2d 295 (D.C. Cir. 1967), *cert. denied*, 387 U.S. 942 (1967)

[The Board found that the employer, in order to escape the union and his obligations under the collective agreement, had closed its New York plant, discharged its employees, and had resumed substantially the same operations in Florida. The Board, accordingly, found violations of §§8(a)(1), (3), and (5) of the Act.]

BURGER, J. To redress the injuries occasioned by this "runaway," the Board ordered the Employer to offer full reinstatement to its workers and to compensate them for any loss of earnings resulting from the discrimination against them. It further ordered the employer to bargain with the Union either at the New York plant, if it returned there, or at the new Florida location, irrespective of whether the Union had majority status. . . .

The Board reasoned that this remedy was necessary to deprive the company of the "fruits" of its illegal acts — i.e., escape from the New York union. Although the examiner acknowledged that this remedy impinged on "the rights of new employees innocent of wrongdoing," the Board concluded that "on balance" the Florida employees' §7 right to choose their own bargaining representative (or to have none at all) "must yield to the statutory objective of fashioning a meaningful remedy for the unfair labor practices found." We disagree. . . .

. . . The Board argues that the remedy in this case is proper since it restores the status quo by removing from the company the benefit of its misdeeds. However, an examination of the purpose of this doctrine and an analysis of the record of this case demonstrate that, as applied here, the remedy does not effectuate a policy of the Act and indeed violates one of the Act's most basic policies, i.e., employee freedom to select a bargaining agent. . . .

The Board has traditionally required an employer to bargain with an established union which loses its majority because of the employer's unfair labor practices. In Franks Bros. Co. v. NLRB, [321 U.S. 702 (1944)], the Supreme Court upheld a Board order that a company guilty of an unfair labor practice must bargain with the incumbent union even though the union had lost its majority status not directly as a result of the illegal act of the company but due to normal labor turnover occurring during the adjudication of the company's wrongdoing. The Court noted the Board's fear that requiring a union to maintain its majority "during delays incident to hearings would result in permitting employers to profit from their own wrongful refusal to bargain." 321 U.S. at 704.

Underlying Board compulsory bargaining orders is an eminently reasonable principle: those workers who have voted for a representative should not have their choice cancelled out by an employer's unfair labor practice. If a union loses its majority because some workers were coerced or because the company wrongfully refused to bargain with it, restoration of the status quo calls for Board recognition of the Union. A compulsory bargaining order in such circumstances is merely a recognition of the earlier vote of the workers, which is reasonably presumed to represent a more accurate reflection of their sentiments than the later vote, colored if not distorted by the company's illegal conduct. If the union majority is lost after an unfair labor practice because of a normal labor turnover during the period of the subsequent litigation, only slightly different considerations are involved. The Board may reasonably conclude that the employer's prior illegal act could similarly discourage union membership of new workers entering the bargaining unit.

The crucial element in all these cases is that the interest being protected is the freedom of choice of the workers in a bargaining unit. The compulsory bargaining order is intended to put into effect what these workers had voted. Even when the majority of the plant vote against the union after an unfair labor practice and the swing votes are cast by new workers, a substantial number of the workers still in the unit had opted for the union when free to do so; there is, moreover, the additional factor that the later vote may have been tainted by the company's unfair labor practices. The suggestion in *Franks*, supra, that the Board could remove from the employer the benefit of its illegal act was merely the other side of the coin of making the injured employees whole.

The right to choose a union and have that union operate in a climate free of coercion, which is the goal of Board compulsory bargaining orders, is a cornerstone of the [NLRA]; equally protected by the Act with the right of the workers to choose that representative is the right to have none. Yet the remedy . . . in this case imposes on the Florida workers a bargaining representative without reference to their choice. Such an infringement of the Florida employees' §7 rights might be justified if some rights of the New York workers depended on that balancing or if for some other valid reason the Board considered it necessary to promote industrial peace.

The Board, however, justified its order only as being necessary to remove from the Employer the benefits of its wrongdoing. The hard question presented to us is whether this, standing alone and without relationship to redressing grievances of the New York workers, who suffered the violation of their statutory rights, is enough to justify infringing fundamental rights of comparable magnitude vested by law in the Florida workers.

The Board does not claim the bargaining order will restore to the New York workers their lost rights but, on the contrary, premised its remedial order on the assumption that few if any New York workers would accept reinstatement in Florida and, refusing to order the company to return to New York, decided that the New York workers would have to find their redress in back pay. The Board did not predicate its remedy on any finding that the unfair labor practices in New York precluded a free and untainted vote by the Florida workers.

There is one "boilerplate" clause in the Board decision referring to "the continuing coercive effects of [Garwin's] unfair labor practices." It is not clear whether the Board meant by this a continuing effect which would inhibit the New York workers from moving to Florida or an effect on the new employees in Florida. Even assuming the latter was intended, the remedy could not stand, for there is nothing in the record suggesting that the Florida workers were aware of what had occurred in New York. This is a different situation from that presented by new workers entering a bargaining unit at the original site — or near it — which still contains discriminatees. Secondly, the thrust of the Board's reference to the "continuing coercive effects" was not concern for those feeling the coercion but rather concern that Garwin would be successful in its flight from the union. This is putting the cart before the horse.

. . . [W]hen, as in this case, the Board has acted to redress the New York workers' grievances and plans no further reparation for them, we find it difficult to see justification for a remedy which deprives Florida workers of a basic right without genuinely benefiting the injured workers in New York. Once it has been assumed that the New York workers will not migrate to Florida, the Board cannot fairly describe its action as a balancing of their rights against those of the Florida workers; at this point the New York workers are out of the picture, and denial of basic rights of the Florida workers simply does not effectuate the policies of the Act.

That the Board has deprived Florida workers of freedom of choice for only one year[t] rather than two or three is hardly an answer if the right of choice is acknowledged.

The dissent views the deprivation of the rights of Florida workers as

___

[t][The Board's order had curtailed the normal contract bar by providing that any contract resulting from the bargaining order would bar an election for only one year. See Garwin Corp., 153 N.L.R.B. 664 (1965). — Eds.]

related to the purposes of the Act by the nexus of the Employers' "success-fully evading their duty to bargain with the union." This seems to rest on an acceptance of the Board's power to "punish" the Employer by means which invade guaranteed rights of Florida workers and fails to accord freedom of choice its proper place. It also fails to insist on a proper balancing of rights. Nowhere does the dissent meet the point that "restoration of the status quo" means redress to the injured workers, not punishment of errant employers.

The remedy at issue is not entirely new; the Board has applied it to "runaways" where the move was of such a short distance that the Board could assume that, absent the unfair labor practices, workers would have followed the employer to the new site. In these cases, the Board has required the company to bargain even if a substantial number does not follow the Em-ployer. However, even though the Board has thus limited its application, this remedy has met with divided judicial response. The Ninth Circuit has upheld the Board's order that a company which had failed to bargain about a twelve-mile move must deal with the union as the workers' representative even if the union does not have a majority at the new location. NLRB v. Lewis, 246 F.2d 886 (9th Cir. 1957). But the Second Circuit refused, more recently, to enforce this remedy since the "Union does not appear to represent any of the employees in the [new] plant." NLRB v. Rapid Bindery, Inc., 293 F.2d 170, 177 (2d Cir. 1961). We consider this the sound view, at least as applied to the facts of this case.

The Board seeks to distinguish *Rapid Bindery* from the instant case by arguing that there was no hostility to the union shown in *Rapid Bindery*, as there is here. We are not told, however, in what way the motivation for an unfair labor practice is relevant to a remedy which strikes at workers in order to inflict pain on an employer unless the Board is trying to punish an employer for his unlawful intent. If the Board is suggesting that this remedy is suitable because the Company has been hostile, it is making out a case that the order is not remedial but punitive. That is not a valid basis for an order. The Board's attempted distinction also overlooks the fact that Employer animosity toward the union was present in *Rapid Bindery*, although the Court concluded that the record did not support the Board's finding that this was the preponderant motive for the move. Finally, there was no hostility to the union in *Lewis*, supra, where the Ninth Circuit affirmed the remedy. Employer motivation or attitudes toward the union hardly seem to be the touchstone of judicial response.

As final argument, the Board urges here that the remedy is necessary to deter other employers from fleeing union relationships and thus to protect statutory rights of employees generally. . . . It has been established, how-ever, that the purpose of Board remedies is to rectify the harm done the injured workers, not to provide punitive measures against errant employers. "[T]he power to command affirmative action is remedial, not punitive." Republic Steel Corp. v. NLRB, 311 U.S. 7, 12 (1940). Deterrence alone is not a proper basis for a remedy. Ibid. The Board argues that the order is permitted by §10(a), which allows the Board "to prevent any person from engaging in any unfair labor practice." But it seems quite clear that this means the Board may stop an actively continuing unfair labor practice that has been discovered and adjudicated, as distinguished from a general deterrence of unfair labor practices. . . .

In our view the Board should not seek to "discipline" the Employer at the expense of the new Florida employees.[22] Such a remedy is, on its face, arbitrary; the Board ought not rob Peter to punish Paul.

We remand the record to the Board for further consideration of this aspect of its remedy, in light of this opinion. In all other respects, the Board's order will be enforced.

McGOWAN, J. (concurring in part and dissenting in part). . . . The order prevents petitioners from successfully evading their duty to bargain with the union. I cannot agree with the majority that that conclusion was so misplaced as to warrant the substitution of judicial judgment. The remedy here prescribed is not, in its precise factual context, a "patent attempt to achieve ends other than those which can fairly be said to effectuate the policies of the Act." Fibreboard Paper Products Corp. v. NLRB, supra, 379 U.S. at 216. . . .

It seems equally clear that the order has not been fashioned in such disregard for the circumstances of this case as to be oppressive. . . . The Board has weighed the interests of the new Florida employees in being free from a bargaining representative not of their choosing. In deference to this interest and to accommodate the conflicting policies of the statute, the Board relaxed its customary contract bar rules. Petitioners argue that the Board's order unduly interferes with the rights of their new employees. But the Board, as the agency entrusted with the task of permanently protecting these rights, is perhaps in a better position to assess the impact of this temporary limitation than an employer who relies on those rights to preserve the benefits of its unfair labor practices. . . .

---

[22] If the Board wishes to redress injury suffered by the Union as such it might well consider, for example, assessment on the Employer of an amount directed at reimbursing the Union for its loss represented by organizational expenses invested in the New York local; and if the Union seeks to organize the new Florida workers, the expense of a campaign there will be substantial. We are not told whether the Board has statutory authority to make such a monetary assessment against the Employer.

That the Board, in striking a balance between the need to protect a collective bargaining relationship and the interests of new employees in being free to select their own bargaining agent, has determined to give precedence to the former is, in my view, a judgment consistent with its statutory responsibilities. "It is not for us to weigh [the] . . . countervailing considerations." NLRB v. Seven-Up Bottling Co., supra, 344 U.S. at 348.

NOTES

1. Would *Gissel* support the bargaining order in *Garwin Corp.?* Is the risk that the union would lack majority support when the order was issued greater in *Garwin Corp.* than in situations that did not involve plant relocation but did involve employees who supported the union and left their jobs following the employer's refusal to bargain and his unfair labor practices? Should a bargaining order affecting a "run-away plant" be withheld unless the "chill-elsewhere" tests of *Darlington* are satisfied?

2. A collective bargaining agreement for a three-year term, expiring December 31, 1984, provides: "The Company recognizes the Union as the exclusive representative, for collective bargaining, of all the Company's production and maintenance (P&M) employees employed in the Company's plant in Roslindale, Mass." In January of 1984, the company, learning that its lease would not be renewed, notified the union of a planned move to Brockton, Mass., 17 miles away. The company also advised the employees and the union that the existing agreement would not cover Brockton and that the company would not recognize the union there unless a majority of the Brockton employees expressed a desire for such representation. When the company completed its move, it employed 26 of its 64 Roslindale employees, and 36 new hires. The Brockton and Roslindale plants were essentially the same, using the same supervisors and machinery to make the same products. Upon the company's refusal to recognize the union as the representative of the Brockton P & M employees, or to apply the existing agreement there, the union filed unfair labor practice charges. What result?

Would your answer be affected by any of the following facts: (a) The collective agreement had expired prior to the move to Brockton; (b) The Brockton plant made substantially different products; (c) The new location was 50 miles from Roslindale; (d) The company owned another Massachusetts plant, four miles from Roslindale, and both those plants, because of centralized operations and management, had been part of a single bargaining unit, voluntarily recognized by the company; but the new Brockton plant, by contrast, is to be substantially autonomous because of lower-cost labor there and the company's present opinion that the prior management structure had been top heavy. See NLRB v. Marine Optical Inc., 671 F.2d 11 (1st Cir. 1982). See also the materials on accretion, supra p. 408, the materials on the duty to bargain in Chapter 9, and the successorship problems in Chapter 10.

CHAPTER 7

THE REGULATION OF COLLECTIVE ACTION BY LABOR ORGANIZATIONS

A. ANTI-INJUNCTION LEGISLATION

For an overview of the Norris-LaGuardia Act, students might now usefully review Chapter 1(C)(2), then read the provisions of the Act in the Appendix.

Jacksonville Bulk Terminals, Inc. v. International Longshoremen's Assn.
457 U.S. 702 (1982)

[Following the Soviet intervention in Afghanistan, President Carter, on January 4, 1980, imposed an embargo on grain shipments to the Soviet Union. On January 9, the ILA announced that its members would not handle any cargo going to or coming from the Soviet Union or carried on Russian ships. Thereupon, an ILA local refused to load superphosphoric acid, used in agricultural fertilizers, onto three ships that had arrived at the terminal operated by Jacksonville Bulk Terminals, Inc. (JBT). The collective agreement between the union and JBT contained a broad no-strike clause banning "any strike of any kind" and channelled all disputes through a grievance procedure culminating in arbitration. JBT sued, under LMRA §301, alleging a violation of the no-strike pledge and requesting an order against the union compelling arbitration, injunctive relief against the stoppage pending arbitration, and damages. The Fifth Circuit affirmed the district court's arbitration order but reversed its grant of injunctive relief. It rejected the district court's conclusion that the Norris-LaGuardia Act is inapplicable to politically motivated strikers, but held that an injunction pending arbitration was not warranted because the underlying dispute was not arbitrable. The Supreme Court affirmed.]

Marshall, J. . . .

II

. . . Congress adopted this broad prohibition [Norris-LaGuardia Act, §4(a)] to remedy the growing tendency of federal courts to enjoin strikes by narrowly construing the Clayton Act's labor exemption from the Sherman Act's prohibition against conspiracies to restrain trade. . . . This Court has consistently given the anti-injunction provisions of the Norris-LaGuardia Act a broad interpretation, recognizing exceptions only in limited situations where necessary to accommodate the Act to specific federal legislation or paramount congressional policy. . . .

The *Boys Markets* exception, as refined in Buffalo Forge Co. v. Steelworkers, 428 U.S. 397 (1976), is relevant to our decision today. In *Boys Markets*, this Court re-examined Sinclair Refining Co. v. Atkinson, 370 U.S. 195 (1962), which held that the Norris-LaGuardia Act precludes a federal district court from enjoining a strike in breach of a collective-bargaining agreement, even where that agreement contains provisions for binding arbitration of the grievance concerning which the strike was called. 398 U.S., at 237-238. The Court overruled *Sinclair* and held that, in order to accommodate the anti-injunction provisions of Norris-LaGuardia to the subsequently enacted provisions of §301(a) and the strong federal policy favoring arbitration, it was essential to recognize an exception to the anti-injunction provisions for cases in which the employer sought to enforce the union's contractual obligation to arbitrate grievances rather than to strike over them. 398 U.S., at 249-253.

. . . In *Buffalo Forge*, the Court resolved [a] conflict [among courts of appeals] and held that the *Boys Markets* exception [to the Norris-LaGuardia Act] does not apply when only the question whether the strike violates the no-strike pledge, and not the dispute that precipitated the strike, is arbitrable under the parties' collective-bargaining agreement.[8] . . .

III

. . . [W]e must [first] determine whether this is a "case involving or growing out of any labor dispute" within the meaning of §4 of the Norris-LaGuardia

---

[8]In *Buffalo Forge*, . . . at issue was a sympathy strike in support of sister unions negotiating with the employer. The Court reasoned that there was no need to accommodate the policies of the Norris-LaGuardia Act to §301 and to the federal policy favoring arbitration when a strike is not called over an arbitrable dispute, because such a strike does not directly frustrate the arbitration process by denying or evading the union's promise to arbitrate. 428 U.S., at 407-412.

[Students will find the discussion of the applicability and soundness of *Buffalo Forge* clearer after they have examined the material in Chapter 10(B)(1) and (3) on specific enforcement, under §301, of no-strike and other provisions of collective agreements. — EDS.]

Act. Section 13(c) . . . broadly defines the term "labor dispute" to include "any controversy concerning terms or conditions of employment."

The Employer argues that the existence of political motives takes this work stoppage controversy outside the broad scope of this definition. This argument, however, has no basis in the plain statutory language of the Norris-LaGuardia Act or in our prior interpretations of that Act. Furthermore, the argument is contradicted by the legislative history of not only the Norris-LaGuardia Act but also the 1947 amendments to the [NLRA].

A

An action brought by an employer against the union representing its employees to enforce a no-strike pledge generally involves two controversies. First, there is the "underlying dispute," which is the event or condition that triggers the work stoppage. This dispute may or may not be political, and it may or may not be arbitrable under the parties' collective-bargaining agreement. Second, there is the parties' dispute over whether the no-strike pledge prohibits the work stoppage at issue. This second dispute can always form the basis for federal-court jurisdiction, because §301(a) gives federal courts jurisdiction over "[s]uits for violation of contracts between an employer and a labor organization."

It is beyond cavil that the second form of dispute — whether the collective-bargaining agreement either forbids or permits the union to refuse to perform certain work — is a "controversy concerning the terms or conditions of employment." [§13(c).] This §301 action was brought to resolve just such a controversy. . . . [T]he Employer did not seek to enjoin the intervention of the Soviet Union in Afghanistan, nor did it ask the District Court to decide whether the Union was justified in expressing disapproval of the Soviet Union's actions. Instead, the Employer sought to enjoin the Union's decision not to provide labor, a decision which the Employer believed violated the terms of the collective-bargaining agreement. It is this contract dispute, and not the political dispute, that the arbitrator will resolve, and on which the courts are asked to rule.

The language of the Norris-LaGuardia Act does not except labor disputes having their genesis in political protests. Nor is there any basis in the statutory language for the argument that the Act requires that *each* dispute relevant to the case be a labor dispute. The Act merely requires that the case involve "any" labor dispute. Therefore, the plain terms of §4(a) and §13 . . . deprive the federal courts of the power to enjoin the Union's work stoppage in this §301 action, without regard to whether the Union also has a nonlabor dispute with another entity.

The conclusion that this case involves a labor dispute within the mean-

ing of the Norris-LaGuardia Act comports with this Court's consistent interpretation of that Act. Our decisions have recognized that the term "labor
dispute" must not be narrowly construed because the statutory definition
itself is extremely broad and because Congress deliberately included a broad
definition to overrule judicial decisions that had unduly restricted the Clayton Act's labor exemption from the antitrust laws. . . .

The critical element in determining whether the provisions of [Norris-
LaGuardia] apply is whether "the employer-employee relationship [is] the
matrix of the controversy." Columbia River Packers Assn., Inc. v. Hinton,
315 U.S. 143, 147 (1942). In this case, the Employer and the Union
representing its employees are the disputants, and their dispute concerns the
interpretation of the labor contract that defines their relationship.[12] Thus, the
employer-employee relationship is the matrix of this controversy.

Nevertheless, the Employer argues that a "labor dispute" exists only
when the Union's action is taken in its own "economic self-interest." The
Employer cites Musicians v. Carroll, 391 U.S. 99 (1968), and Columbia
River Packers Assn., supra, for this proposition. In these cases, however, the
Court addressed the very different question whether the relevant parties were
"labor'" groups involved in a labor dispute for the purpose of determining
whether their actions were exempt from the antitrust laws. These cases do not
hold that a union's noneconomic motive inevitably takes the dispute out of
the Norris-LaGuardia Act, but only that the protections of that Act do not
extend to labor organizations when they cease to act as labor groups or when
they enter into illegal combinations with nonlabor groups in restraint of
trade.[14] Here, there is no question that the Union is a labor group, representing its own interests in a dispute with the Employer over the employees'
obligation to provide labor.

Even in cases where the disputants did not stand in the relationship of
employer and employee, this Court has held that the existence of noneconomic motives does not make the Norris-LaGuardia Act inapplicable. For
example, in New Negro Alliance v. Sanitary Grocery Co., 303 U.S. 552
(1938), this Court held that the Norris-LaGuardia Act prohibited an injunc-

---

[12] A labor dispute might be present under the facts of this case even in the absence of the
dispute over the scope of the no-strike clause. Regardless of the political nature of the Union's
objections to handling Soviet-bound cargo, these objections were expressed in a work stoppage by employees against their employer, which focused on particular work assignments.
Thus, apart from the collective-bargaining agreement, the employer-employee relationship
would be the matrix of the controversy. We need not decide this question, however, because
this case does involve a dispute over the interpretation of the parties' collective-bargaining
agreement.

[14] The Employer's economic-motive analysis also leads to the untenable result that
strikes in protest of unreasonably unsafe conditions and some sympathy strikes are not "labor
disputes."

tion against picketing by members of a civic group, which was aimed at inducing a store to employ Negro employees. In determining that the group and its members were "persons interested in a labor dispute" within the meaning of §13, the Court found it immaterial that the picketers, who were neither union organizers nor store employees, were not asserting economic interests commonly associated with labor unions — e.g., terms and conditions of employment in the narrower sense of wages, hours, unionization, or betterment of working conditions. Id., at 560. Although the lower courts found Norris-LaGuardia inapplicable because the picketing was motivated by the group's "political" or "social" goals of improving the position of Negroes generally, and not by the desire to improve specific conditions of employment, this Court reasoned: "The Act does not concern itself with the background or the motives of the dispute." Id., at 561.[a]

B

The Employer's argument that the Union's motivation for engaging in a work stoppage determines whether the Norris-LaGuardia Act applies is also contrary to the legislative history of that Act. The Act was enacted in response to federal-court intervention on behalf of employers through the use of injunctive powers against unions and other associations of employees. This intervention had caused the federal judiciary to fall into disrepute among large segments of this Nation's population. See generally S. Rep. No. 163, 72d Cong., 1st Sess., 8, 16-18 (1932); 75 Cong. Rec. 4915 (1932) (remarks of Sen. Wagner).

Apart from the procedural unfairness of many labor injunctions, one of the greatest evils associated with them was the use of tort-law doctrines, which often made the lawfulness of a strike depend upon judicial views of social and economic policy. . . . In debating the Act, its supporters repeatedly expressed disapproval of this Court's interpretations of the Clayton Act's labor exemption — interpretations which permitted a federal judge to find the Act inapplicable based on his or her appraisal of the "legitimacy" of the union's objectives. See, e.g., 75 Cong. Rec. 4916 (1932). . . . The legisla-

---

[a] [The Court in New Negro Alliance continued: "The desire for fair and equitable conditions of employment on the part of persons of any race, color, or persuasion, and the removal of discriminations against them by reason of their race or religious beliefs is quite as important to those concerned as fairness and equity in terms and conditions of employment can be to trade or craft unions or any form of labor organization or association. Race discrimination by an employer may reasonably be deemed more unfair and less excusable than discrimination against workers on the ground of union affiliation. There is no justification in the apparent purposes or the express terms of the Act for limiting its definition of labor disputes and cases arising therefrom by excluding those which arise with respect to discrimination in terms and conditions of employment based upon differences of race or color." See 303 U.S. at 561. — EDS.]

tive history is replete with criticisms of the ability of powerful employers to use federal judges as "strike-breaking" agencies; by virtue of their almost unbridled "equitable discretion," federal judges could enter injunctions based on their disapproval of the employees' objectives, or on the theory that these objectives or actions, although lawful if pursued by a single employee, became unlawful when pursued through the "conspiracy" of concerted activity. See, e.g., 75 Cong. Rec., at 4928-4938, 5466-5468, 5478-5481, 5487-5490.

Furthermore, the question whether the Norris-LaGuardia Act would apply to politically motivated strikes was brought to the attention of the 72nd Congress when it passed the Act. Opponents criticized the definition of "labor dispute" in §13(c) on the ground that it would cover politically motivated strikes. Representative Beck argued that federal courts should have jurisdiction to enjoin political strikes like those threatened by labor unions in Europe. Id., at 5471-5473 (discussing threatened strike by British unions protesting the cancellation of leases held by Communist Party members, and threatened strikes by Belgian unions protesting a decision to supply military aid to Poland). In response, Representative Oliver argued that the federal courts should not have the power to enjoin such strikes. Id., at 5480-5481. Finally, Representative Beck offered an amendment . . . that would have permitted federal courts to enjoin strikes called for ulterior purposes, including political motives. This amendment was defeated soundly. See id., at 5507.

Further support for our conclusion that Congress believed that the Norris-LaGuardia Act applies to work stoppages instituted for political reasons can be found in the legislative history of the 1947 amendments to the NLRA. That history reveals that Congress rejected a proposal to repeal the Norris-LaGuardia Act with respect to one broad category of political strikes.[17] The House bill included definitions of various kinds of labor disputes. . . . Section 2(13) defined a "sympathy" strike as a strike "called or conducted not by reason of any dispute between the employer and the employees on strike or participating in such concerted interference, but rather by reason of either (A) a dispute involving another employer or other employees of the same employer, or (B) *disagreement with some governmen-*

---

[17] In relying on this history, we do not argue that congressional rejection of a broad repeal of the Norris-LaGuardia Act precludes accommodation of that Act to the LMRA. See Sinclair Refining Co. v. Atkinson, 370 U.S. 195, 204-210 (1962). In Boys Markets, Inc. v. Retail Clerks, 398 U.S., at 249, this Court put that argument to rest. Rather, we rely on this legislative history because it demonstrates that Congress believed that the Norris-LaGuardia Act did apply to controversies concerning politically motivated work stoppages. Furthermore, in this case, unlike Boys Markets, we are not asked to accommodate the Norris-LaGuardia Act to a specific federal Act or to the strong policy favoring arbitration.

tal policy," H.R. 3020, §2(13), 1 Leg. Hist. 168 (emphasis added). Section 12 of the House bill made this kind of strike "unlawful concerted activity," and "it remove[d] the immunities that the present laws confer upon persons who engage in them." H.R. Rep. No. 245, supra, at 23, 1 Leg. Hist. 314. In particular, the Norris-LaGuardia Act would not apply to suits brought by private parties to enjoin such activity, and damages could be recovered. See H.R. Rep. No. 245, supra, at 23-24, 43-44, 1 Leg. Hist. 314-315, 334-335. In explaining these provisions, the House Report stated that strikes "against a policy of national or local government, which the employer cannot change," should be made unlawful, and that "[t]he bill makes inapplicable in such suits the Norris-LaGuardia Act, which heretofore has protected parties to industrial strife from the consequences of their lawlessness." H.R. Rep. No. 245, supra, at 24, 44, 1 Leg. Hist. 315, 335.

The Conference Committee accepted the Senate version, which had eliminated these provisions of the House bill. The House Managers' statement accompanying the Conference Report explained that its recommendation did not go as far as the House bill, that §8(b) prohibits jurisdictional strikes and illegal secondary boycotts, and that the Board, *not private parties*, may petition a district court under §10(k) or §10(*l*) to enjoin these activities notwithstanding the provisions of the Norris-LaGuardia Act. H.R. Conf. Rep. No. 510, 80th Cong., 1st Sess., 36, 42-43, 57, 58-59 (1947), 1 Leg. Hist. 540, 546-547, 561, 562-563. In short, Congress declined in 1947 to adopt a broad "political motivation" exception to the Norris-LaGuardia Act for strikes in protest of some governmental policy. Instead, if a strike of this nature takes the form of a secondary boycott prohibited by §8(b), Congress chose to give the Board, not private parties, the power to petition a federal district court for an injunction. . . . Cf. Longshoremen v. Allied International, Inc., 456 U.S. 212 (1982).

C

This case . . . involves a "labor dispute" within any common-sense meaning of that term. Were we to ignore this plain interpretation and hold that the political motivation underlying the work stoppage removes this controversy from the prohibitions of the Norris-LaGuardia Act, we would embroil federal judges in the very scrutiny of "legitimate objectives" that Congress intended to prevent. . . . The applicability not only of §4, but also of all of the procedural protections embodied in that Act, would turn on a single federal judge's perception of the motivation underlying the concerted activity.[19] The

---

[19] This proposed exception does not limit the judge's discretion to consideration of specified external conduct or of provisions in a collective-bargaining agreement, as does the *Boys Markets* exception. It provides no guidance to judges in dealing with concerted activity

Employer's interpretation is simply inconsistent with the need, expressed by Congress when it enacted the Norris-LaGuardia Act, for clear "mileposts for judges to follow." 75 Cong. Rec. 4935 (1932) (remarks of Sen. Bratton).

In essence, the Employer asks us to disregard the legislative history of the Act and to distort the definition of a labor dispute in order to reach what it believes to be an "equitable" result. The Employer's real complaint, however, is not with the Union's political objections to the conduct of the Soviet Union, but with what the Employer views as the Union's breach of contract. The Employer's frustration with this alleged breach of contract should not be remedied by characterizing it as other than a labor dispute. We will not adopt by judicial fiat an interpretation that Congress specifically rejected when it enacted the 1947 amendments to the NLRA. See generally n. 17, supra. In the past, we have consistently declined to constrict Norris-LaGuardia's broad prohibitions except in narrowly defined situations where accommodation of that Act to specific congressional policy is necessary. We refuse to deviate from that path today.

IV

Alternatively, the Employer argues that the Union's work stoppage may be enjoined under the rationale of [Boys Markets] and [Buffalo Forge], because the dispute underlying the work stoppage is arbitrable under the collective-bargaining agreement. . . . [T]he employer [thus] disavows its earlier argument that the underlying dispute is purely political, and asserts that the Union's work stoppage was motivated by a disagreement with the Employer over the management-rights clause in the collective-bargaining agreement. The Solicitor General, in an amicus brief . . . agrees with the Employer that the work stoppage may be enjoined pending arbitration. He contends that in addition to the political dispute, disputes concerning both the management-rights clause and the work-conditions clause underlie the work stoppage, and that at least one of these disputes is arguably arbitrable.[20]

---

arguably designed to achieve both political and labor-related goals. Such mixed-motivation cases are bound to arise. For example, in United States Steel Corp. v. United Mine Workers, 519 F.2d 1236 (CA5 1975), miners picketed another employer for importing coal from South Africa. The Court of Appeals held that the Norris-LaGuardia Act applied, and that the Boys Markets exception was not available, because "the miners' action was not aimed at [their employer] at all, but rather at the national policy of this country's permitting the importation of South African coal." 519 F.2d, at 1247 (footnote omitted). Under the political-motivation exception, even if the miners had picketed because slave labor was employed to mine the imported coal, the Norris-LaGuardia Act might not apply. Minor variations in the facts would endow the courts with, or divest them of, jurisdiction to issue an injunction, and would create difficult line-drawing problems.

[20] The management-rights clause provides: "The Management of the Employer's business and the direction of the work force in the operation of the business are exclusively vested

We disagree. *Buffalo Forge* makes it clear that a *Boys Markets* injunction pending arbitration should not issue unless the dispute underlying the work stoppage is arbitrable. The rationale of *Buffalo Forge* compels the conclusion that the Union's work stoppage, called to protest the invasion of Afghanistan by the Soviet Union, may not be enjoined pending the arbitrator's decision on whether the work stoppage violates the no-strike clause in the collective-bargaining agreement. The underlying dispute, whether viewed as an expression of the Union's "moral outrage" at Soviet military policy or as an expression of sympathy for the people of Afghanistan, is plainly not arbitrable under the collective-bargaining agreement.

. . . The "underlying" disputes concerning the management-rights clause or the work-conditions clause simply did not trigger the work stoppage. To the contrary, the applicability of these clauses to the dispute, if any, was triggered by the work stoppage itself. Consideration of whether the strike intruded on the management-rights clause or was permitted by the work-conditions clause may inform the arbitrator's ultimate decision on whether the strike violates the no-strike clause. Indeed, the question whether striking over a nonarbitrable issue violates other provisions of the collective-bargaining agreement may itself be an arbitrable dispute. The fact remains, however, that the strike itself was not over an arbitrable dispute and therefore may not be enjoined pending the arbitrator's ruling on the legality of the strike under the collective-bargaining agreement.

The weaknesses in the analysis of the Employer and the Solicitor General can perhaps best be demonstrated by applying it to a pure sympathy strike, which clearly cannot be enjoined pending arbitration under the rationale of *Buffalo Forge*. If this work stoppage were a pure sympathy strike, it could be characterized alternatively as a dispute over the Employer's right to choose to do business with the employer embroiled in a dispute with a sister union, as a dispute over management's right to assign and direct work, or as a dispute over whether requiring the union to handle goods of the employer whose employees are on strike is an unreasonable work condition. None of these characterizations, however, alters the fact, essential to the rationale of *Buffalo Forge*, that the strike was not over an arbitrable issue and therefore did not directly frustrate the arbitration process. . . .

---

in the Employer as functions of Management. Except as specifically provided in the Agreement, all of the rights, powers, and authority Employer had prior to signing of this Agreement are retained by the Employer."

The work-conditions clause provides: "Where hardship is claimed by the Union because of unreasonable or burdensome conditions or where work methods or operations materially change in the future, the problem shall first be discussed between the local and management involved." [If disagreement persisted, arbitration could ultimately be invoked.]

V

. . . [W]e hold that an employer's §301 action to enforce the provisions of a collective-bargaining agreement allegedly violated by a union's work stoppage involves a "labor dispute" within the meaning of the Norris-LaGuardia Act, without regard to the motivation underlying the union's decision not to provide labor. Under our decisions in *Boys Markets* and *Buffalo Forge*, when the underlying dispute is not arbitrable, the employer may not obtain injunctive relief pending the arbitrator's ruling on the legality of the strike under the collective-bargaining agreement. Accordingly, the decision of the Court of Appeals is Affirmed.

[The opinion of O'Connor, J., concurring in the judgment, is omitted.]

BURGER, C. J., with whom POWELL, J., joins, dissenting.

I

This case in no sense involves or grows out of a [§13(c)] labor dispute. . . . The dispute . . . is a political dispute and has no relation to any controversy concerning terms or conditions of employment. If Congress had intended to bar federal courts from issuing injunctions in political disputes, it could have simply prohibited federal courts from enjoining strikes rather than limiting its prohibition to controversies concerning terms or conditions of employment. Accordingly, I disagree with the Court's conclusion that [Norris-LaGuardia] bars a federal court from enjoining this politically motivated work stoppage.

. . . No one has suggested that the union's action is actually motivated to obtain concessions concerning employment conditions. . . . Thus the plain meaning of §13(c) leads to the conclusion that this case does not involve or grow out of a labor dispute because the union members are not seeking to change their terms or conditions of employment.

As the Court recognizes, we have held that the test of whether [Norris-LaGuardia] applies is whether "the employer-employee relationship [is] the matrix of the controversy." Columbia River Packers Assn., Inc. v. Hinton, 315 U.S. 143, 147 (1942). Federal Courts of Appeals have stated that unions are protected by [that] Act when they act to advance the economic interests of their members. See, e.g., Brotherhood of Railroad Trainmen v. Atlantic Coast Line R. Co., 362 F.2d 649, 654 (CA5 1966). These cases illustrate the plain meaning of §13(c)'s [protection of] union organizational efforts and efforts to improve working conditions.

The Court errs gravely in finding that the matrix of this controversy is the union's relationship with the petitioners. The union's dispute with the petitioners merely flows from its decision to demonstrate its opposition to the invasion of Afghanistan. No economic interests of union members are involved; indeed, the union's policy is contrary to its members' economic interests since it reduces the amount of available work.[2] Thus, the cases generally explicating the meaning of §13(c) lend no support to the notion that this case involves a labor dispute.

The federal courts have consistently recognized that [Norris-LaGuardia] does not apply to politically motivated work stoppages concerning subjects over which employers have no control. These courts, in cases which are for all practical purposes indistinguishable from this case, . . . , properly concluded that the Act only applies to economic disputes.[3] This Court has never before held, as it holds here, that [Norris-LaGuardia] protects strikes resulting from political disputes rather than from labor disputes. Since the meaning of the words of the statute is plain, and since the applicable precedent supports the conclusion that this is not a labor dispute, we ought to conclude that politically motivated strikes are outside the coverage of the Norris-LaGuardia Act.[4]

Finally, the Court argues that a common-sense interpretation of the

[2] The Court's reliance on New Negro Alliance v. Sanitary Grocery Co., 303 U.S. 552 (1938), is misplaced. The picketers in that case might not have been seeking to better their own personal economic position, but their purpose was to affect the terms and conditions of employment of the picketed store, since their object was to persuade the store to employ Negroes. Section 13(c) explicitly states that the coverage of the Act does not depend on whether "the disputants stand in the proximate relation of employer and employee."

[3] See Khedivial Line, S.A.E. v. Seafarers International Union, 278 F.2d 49, 50-51 (CA2 1960) (politically motivated blacklist of Egyptian ships to retaliate for Egyptian blacklist of American ships that dealt with Israel is not "labor dispute" triggering Norris-LaGuardia); West Gulf Maritime Assn. v. International Longshoremen's Assn., 413 F. Supp. 372 (SD Tex. 1975), *summarily aff'd*, 531 F.2d 574 (CA5 1976) (union's refusal, on political grounds, in violation of a no-strike agreement, to load grain on a ship bound for the Soviet Union does not present a "labor dispute").

[4] The excerpts from the legislative history relied upon by the Court fall short of the clear evidence required to overcome the plain language of §13(c). . . . In 1947, Congress declined to amend the federal labor laws so that strikes protesting "disagreement with some governmental policy" would not be protected by [Norris-LaGuardia]. H. R. 3020, 80th Cong., 1st Sess., §2(13)(B)(1947), 1 Legislative History of the LMRA 168 (1947); ante, at 717. However, the language of the rejected House version of the amendment was quite broad. There are cases in which unions might disagree with governmental policy and properly take collective action protesting it in order to advance the legitimate economic interests of union members if the terms or conditions of their employment would be affected. Congress might have rejected the House version because of fear that its broad reach would render legitimate union activity unprotected.

In 1932, Congress rejected an amendment which would have permitted federal courts to enjoin acts "performed or threatened for an unlawful purpose or with an unlawful intent. . . ." 75 Cong. Rec. 5507 (1932). This amendment would have swept more broadly than the plain language of §13(c) as adopted. Indeed, Representative Beck's amendment could have rendered the Norris-LaGuardia Act a nullity, since federal judges in the 1930's would have been able to enjoin a strike merely by finding it motivated by an "unlawful purpose." . . .

meaning of the term "labor dispute" supports its conclusion. But the "common-sense" meaning of a term is not controlling when Congress has provided . . . an explicit definition of a labor dispute. "Common sense" and legislative history ought not change the meaning of the unambiguous words of a statute. . . .

II

This case, together with our recent decision in Longshoremen v. Allied International, Inc., 456 U.S. 212 (1982), illustrates the inherent flaw . . . in [*Buffalo Forge*]. If the Court cannot give to ordinary words their ordinary meaning and grasp that the dispute in this case is a purely political dispute rather than having any relation to a labor dispute, it should overrule *Buffalo Forge*. . . .

   In *Allied International* this union was found liable for damages [under LMRA §303] caused to a party with which it had no such agreement. Here, however, despite the no-strike agreement . . . , the Court holds that the union's illegal acts may not be enjoined.

   To reach this strange result, the Court first decides that this case involves a labor dispute rather than a political dispute, and therefore is within the scope of the Norris-LaGuardia Act. The Court then contradicts itself and concludes that, since the dispute is really a political protest over Soviet aggression, it may not be enjoined under the *Buffalo Forge* exception to the rule of [*Boys Markets*], since a federal court cannot resolve the actual dispute. This case, together with *Allied International*, persuades me that the artificial *Buffalo Forge* exception should be abolished. Rather than continuing to engage in mechanical and contradictory analyses as to the character of disputes such as this one, we should hold that a federal court may enjoin a strike pending arbitration when the striking union has agreed to a contract with a no-strike clause such as the one agreed to by petitioners and the ILA. That is what we seemed to hold in *Boys Markets*, and we should not have tinkered with that holding in *Buffalo Forge*. . . .

   [The separate dissenting opinions of Powell, J., and Stevens, J., are omitted.]

   NOTES

   1. Did the majority give adequate weight to the preambles of the Norris-LaGuardia and the Taft-Hartley Acts?
   2. The majority concedes that Norris-LaGuardia applies only when the "employer-employee relationship is the matrix of the controversy." Does

the majority undercut that concession by finding that the strike, although a protest over Soviet military action, meets that test? Wouldn't any strike that leads to an action for an injunction meet the majority's test?

3. Is *New Negro Alliance* fairly distinguishable from the principal case?

4. Assume that a union in a state in which corporate political contributions are legal solicits an employer for a contribution to a gubernatorial candidate who has promised to increase jobs in the pertinent industry. When the employer refuses, the union, which represents his employees, induces them to strike in support of its request. Would an injunction against the strike be barred by a state counterpart of the Norris-LaGuardia Act, interpreted as the federal act has been? What if the requested contribution would be unlawful?

5. The Court invokes the traditional wisdom regarding procedural abuses and class-based judicial policy-making that surrounded the use of labor injunctions before the enactment of Norris-LaGuardia. See F. Frankfurter & N. Greene, The Labor Injunction (1930); Winter, Labor Injunctions and Judge-made Labor Law: The Contemporary Role of Norris-LaGuardia, 70 Yale L.J. 70 (1960).

6. As the majority indicates in *Jacksonville Terminal*, the Court, without explicit legislative authorization, has limited the sweeping language of the Norris-LaGuardia Act in order to enforce other elements of federal labor regulation by granting injunctions sought by private parties. These accommodations are dealt with in Chapter 10. Furthermore, the Taft-Hartley Act enforced its proscription of union unfair labor practices through final and interim injunctive orders issued, as the Court notes, at the request of the NLRB, and not private parties. Section 2(13) of the NLRA, added in 1947, also relaxed, for the purposes of the NLRA, the strict standards for union vicarious responsibility embodied in §6 of Norris-LaGuardia. Finally, the contemporary significance of Norris-LaGuardia has been diminished by decisions that have read the NLRA, as amended, as conferring on the NLRB exclusive or primary jurisdiction over labor relations. See Chapter 8(C).

Brotherhood of R.R. Trainmen v. Toledo, P. & W. R.R., 321 U.S. 50 (1944). A long-continued dispute about working conditions and pay rates persisted despite negotiations and mediation. The mediator assigned by the National Mediation Board proposed arbitration pursuant to §5, First (b) of the Railway Labor Act (RLA). Both parties refused, and the Board terminated its services on November 21, 1941. After the bombing of Pearl Harbor on December 7, 1941, the Board again urged arbitration. The union, which, at the Board's request, had postponed an authorized strike, then agreed to arbitration; but the railroad persisted in its refusal and continued to urge the appointment of an emergency board. After the statutory waiting period expired, the railroad unilaterally changed working conditions, and the union called a strike. The company sought to maintain operations, and violence against the railroad's employees and property occurred. The district court found that the violence was substantial and that the protection afforded by local authorities was inadequate. The court granted an ex parte restraining order and, after a hearing, a temporary injunction against the defendants' interference with the company's operations. The court of appeals, one judge dissenting, affirmed, 132 F.2d 265 (7th Cir. 1942), but was reversed. The Supreme Court held that §8 of Norris-LaGuardia had deprived the district court of jurisdiction to grant injunctive relief since the railroad's refusal to arbitrate had constituted a failure, within the meaning of that section, "to make every reasonable effort to settle such dispute either by negotiation or with the aid of any available governmental machinery of mediation or voluntary arbitration."

Rutledge, J., speaking for a unanimous Court, declared: "It is wholly inconsistent with the section's language and purpose to construe it, as have the respondent and the lower courts, to require reasonable effort by only one conciliatory device when others are available. The explicit terms demand 'every reasonable effort' to settle the dispute." The quoted phrase, the Court added, excluded the company's argument based on the use of "either . . . or" in §8.

NOTES

1. Did the Court in *Toledo* give adequate weight to §7, First, of the RLA, which refers to arbitration by "agreement of the parties"? See Elgin, J. & E. Ry. v. Brotherhood of R.R. Trainmen, 302 F.2d 540, 544 (7th Cir.), *cert. denied*, 371 U.S. 823 (1962). Do you agree with *Toledo*, as a matter of statutory construction? As a matter of policy? The dubious basis for the *Toledo* doctrine may explain its having been limited for not altogether convincing reasons. See Bonanno Linen Serv. v. McCarthy, 532 F.2d 189 (1st Cir. 1976); Atlanta & W. Pt. R.R. v. U.T.W., 439 F.2d 73 (5th Cir. 1971); Washington Post Co. v. Local 6, 92 L.R.R.M. 2961, 2974 (D.C. Super. Ct. 1976).

2. In United States v. UMW, 330 U.S. 258 (1947), the Norris-LaGuardia Act was held (in a 5-4 decision) inapplicable to strikes by "government employees," during a dispute following governmental seizure of coal mines under the War Labor Disputes Act.

3. Some states enacted counterparts of the anti-injunction provisions of

the Clayton Act or the Norris-LaGuardia Act. Although the constitutionality of such statutes was generally upheld, invalidity was sometimes predicated on denial of equal protection or legislative encroachment on judicial power, under state constitutions. See Comment, 47 Yale L.J. 1136 (1938). State interpretations of such statutes have reflected considerable diversity. In Opera on Tour, Inc. v. Weber, 285 N.Y. 348, 34 N.E.2d 349 (1941), the court declared: "Unless the objective of the defendant-union is a lawful one, this controversy is not a labor dispute in the sense of Section 876-a of the Civil Practice Act" (the New York "baby" Norris-LaGuardia Act). In contrast with this eviscerating interpretation is the expansive approach of Krystad v. Lau, 65 Wash. 827, 400 P.2d 72 (1965), holding that employees discharged because of their union membership were entitled to lost pay, reinstatement, and an injunction against further reprisal by the employer. The court relied primarily on a declaration of public policy in the state statute substantially the same as that embodied in §2 of the Norris-LaGuardia Act. See generally Peck, Judicial Creativity and State Labor Law, 40 Wash. L. Rev. 743 (1965).

Do *Opera on Tour* and *Krystad* ignore the underlying purpose of statutes modeled on Norris-LaGuardia? Would *Krystad* be consistent with a state counterpart incorporating §4 of Norris-LaGuardia?

B. CONSTITUTIONAL LIMITATIONS

Thornhill v. Alabama
310 U.S. 88 (1940)

[Petitioner was convicted and sentenced, ultimately, to 73 days in prison upon nonpayment of a $100 fine for violation of §3448 of the Alabama code, which provided as follows:

> Loitering or picketing forbidden. — Any person or persons, who, without a just cause or legal excuse therefor, go near to or loiter about the premises or place of business of any other person, firm, corporation, or association of people, engaged in a lawful business, for the purpose, or with the intent of influencing, or inducing other persons not to trade with, buy from, sell to, have business dealings with, or be employed by such persons, firm, corporation, or association, or who picket the works or place of business of such other persons, firms, corporations, or associations of persons, for the purpose of hindering, delaying, or interfering with or injuring any lawful business or enterprise of another, shall be guilty of a misdemeanor; but nothing herein shall prevent any person from soliciting trade or business for a competitive business.

The petitioner had participated in a picket line of six or eight other men that was maintained at the plant entrance 24 hours a day following a strike order by a union to which 96 of the plant's 100 employees belonged. Almost all the employees lived on company property, where they received mail and the union had held meetings. The pickets had not been requested to keep off company property. No evidence had been introduced regarding the nature of the underlying dispute.

The Supreme Court invalidated the conviction as violative of the First Amendment.]

MURPHY, J. . . . The section in question must be judged upon its face. The finding against petitioner was a general one. It did not specify the testimony upon which it rested. The charges were framed in the words of the statute and so must be given a like construction. The courts below expressed no intention of narrowing the construction put upon the statute by prior state decisions. . . .

There is a further reason for testing the section on its face. Proof of an abuse of power in the particular case has never been deemed a requisite for attack on the constitutionality of a statute purporting to license the dissemination of ideas. Schneider v. State, 308 U.S. 147, 162-165; Hague v. C.I.O., 307 U.S. 496, 516; Lovell v. Griffin, 303 U.S. 444, 451. The cases . . . indicate that the rule is not based upon any assumption that application for the license would be refused or would result in the imposition of other unlawful regulations: Rather it derives from an appreciation of the character of the evil inherent in a licensing system. . . . It is not merely the sporadic abuse of power by the censor but the pervasive threat inherent in its very existence that constitutes the danger to freedom of discussion. See Near v. Minnesota, 283 U.S. 697, 713. One who might have had a license for the asking may therefore call into question the whole scheme of licensing when he is prosecuted for failure to procure it. . . . A like threat is inherent in a penal statute, like that in question here, which does not aim specifically at evils within the allowable area of state control but, on the contrary, sweeps within its ambit other activities that in ordinary circumstances constitute an exercise of freedom of speech or of the press. The existence of such a statute, which readily lends itself to harsh and discriminatory enforcement by local prosecuting officials, against particular groups deemed to merit their displeasure, results in a continuous and pervasive restraint on all freedom of discussion that might reasonably be regarded as within its purview. . . .

Section 3448 has been applied by the state courts so as to prohibit a single individual from walking slowly and peacefully back and forth on the public sidewalk in front of the premises of an employer, without speaking to anyone, carrying a sign or placard . . . stating only the fact that the employer did not employ union men affiliated with the American Federation of Labor;[13] the purpose of the described activity was concededly to advise customers and prospective customers of the relationship existing between the employer and its employees and thereby to induce such customers not to patronize the employer. O'Rourke v. Birmingham, 27 Ala. App. 133; 168 So. 206, *cert. denied*, 232 Ala. 355; 168 So. 209. The statute as thus authoritatively construed and applied leaves room for no exceptions based upon either the number of persons engaged in the proscribed activity, the peaceful character of their demeanor, the nature of their dispute with an employer, or the restrained character and the accurateness of the terminology used in notifying the public of the facts of the dispute. . . .

. . . [O]ne or the other of the offenses [proscribed by §3448] comprehends every practicable method whereby the facts of a labor dispute may be publicized in the vicinity of the place of business of an employer. The phrase "without just cause or legal excuse" does not in any effective manner restrict the breadth of the regulation; the words themselves have no ascertainable meaning either inherent or historical. . . . The courses of action, listed under the first offense, which an accused — including an employee — may not urge others to take, comprehends those which in many instances would normally result from merely publicizing, without annoyance or threat of any kind, the facts of a labor dispute. An intention to hinder, delay or interfere with a lawful business, which is an element of the second offense, likewise can be proved merely by showing that others reacted in a way normally expectable of some upon learning the facts of a dispute.[17] The vague contours of the term "picket" are nowhere delineated.[18] Employees or others, accordingly,

[13] The employer in fact had locked out its union stagehands and was working others not regularly employed as stagehands in admitted violation of the National Industrial Recovery Act.

[17] The only direct evidence . . . to show that the activity of petitioner was accompanied by the necessary intent or purpose is the fact that one other employee, after talking with petitioner, refrained from reporting for work as planned. There is evidence here that the other employee was acquainted with the facts prior to his conversation wth petitioner. The State concedes, however, that under §3448 everyone must be deemed to intend the natural and probable consequences of his acts . . . .

[18] See Hellerstein, Picketing Legislation and the Courts (1931), 10 No. Car. L. Rev. 158, 186n.: "A picketer may: (1) Merely observe workers or customers. (2) Communicate information, e.g., that a strike is in progress, making either true, untrue or libelous statements. (3) Persuade employees or customers not to engage in relations with the employer: (a) through the use of banners, without speaking, carrying true, untrue or libelous legends; (b) by speaking, (i) in a calm, dispassionate manner, (ii) in a heated, hostile manner, (iii) using abusive epithets and profanity, (iv) yelling loudly, (v) by persisting in making arguments when employees or customers refuse to listen; (c) by offering money or similar inducements to strike breakers. (4) Threaten employees or customers: (a) by the mere presence of the picketer; the presence may be a threat of, (i) physical violence, (ii) social ostracism, being branded in the

may be found to be within the purview of the term and convicted for engaging in activities identical with those proscribed by the first offense. In sum, whatever the means used to publicize the facts of a labor dispute, whether by printed sign, by pamphlet, by word of mouth or otherwise, all such activity without exception is within the inclusive prohibition of the statute so long as it occurs in the vicinity of the scene of the dispute.

. . . We think that §3448 is invalid on its face.

The freedom of speech and of the press guaranteed by the Constitution embraces at the least the liberty to discuss publicly and truthfully all matters of public concern without previous restraint or fear of subsequent punishment. . . . Freedom of discussion, if it would fulfill its historic function in this nation, must embrace all issues about which information is needed or appropriate to enable the members of society to cope with the exigencies of their period.

In the circumstances of our times the dissemination of information concerning the facts of a labor dispute must be regarded as within that area of free discussion that is guaranteed by the Constitution. Hague v. C.I.O., 307 U.S. 496; Schneider v. State, 308 U.S. 147, 155, 162-63. See Senn v. Tile Layers Union, 301 U.S. 467, 478. . . . [S]atisfactory hours and wages and working conditions . . . and a bargaining position which makes these possible have an importance which is not less than the interests of those in the business or industry directly concerned. . . . Free discussion concerning the conditions in industry and the causes of labor disputes appears to us indispensable to the effective and intelligent use of the processes of popular government to shape the destiny of modern industrial society. The issues raised by regulations, such as are challenged here, infringing upon the right of employees effectively to inform the public of the facts of a labor dispute are part of this larger problem. We concur in the observation of Mr. Justice Brandeis, speaking for the Court in Senn's case (301 U.S. at 478): "Members of a union might, without special statutory authorization by a State, make known the facts of a labor dispute, for freedom of speech is guaranteed by the Federal Constitution."

It is true that the rights of employers and employees to conduct their economic affairs and to compete with others for a share in the products of

community as a "scab," (iii) a trade or employees' boycott, i.e., preventing workers from securing employment and refusing to trade with customers, (iv) threatening injury to property; (b) by verbal threats. (5) Assaults and use of violence. (6) Destruction of property. (7) Blocking of entrances and interference with traffic.

"The picketer may engage in a combination of any of the types of conduct enumerated above. The picketing may be carried on singly or in groups; it may be directed to employees alone or to customers alone or to both. It may involve persons who have contracts with the employer or those who have not or both."

industry are subject to modification or qualification in the interests of the society in which they exist. This is but an instance of the power of the State to set the limits of permissible contest open to industrial combatants. See Mr. Justice Brandeis in 254 U.S. at 488. It does not follow that the State in dealing with the evils arising from industrial disputes may impair the effective exercise of the right to discuss freely industrial relations which are matters of public concern. A contrary conclusion could be used to support abridgment of freedom of speech and of the press concerning almost every matter of importance to society. . . .

It may be that effective exercise of the means of advancing public knowledge may persuade some of those reached to refrain from entering into advantageous relations with the business establishment which is the scene of the dispute. Every expression of opinion on matters that are important has the potentiality of inducing action in the interests of one rather than another group in society. But the group in power at any moment may not impose penal sanctions on peaceful and truthful discussion of matters of public interest merely on a showing that others may thereby be persuaded to take action inconsistent with its interests. Abridgment of the liberty of such discussion can be justified only where the clear danger of substantive evils arises under circumstances affording no opportunity to test the merits of ideas by competition for acceptance in the market of public opinion. We hold that the danger of injury to an industrial concern is neither so serious nor so imminent as to justify the sweeping proscription of freedom of discussion embodied in §3448. . . .

Reversed.

[Justice McReynolds would have affirmed the judgment below.]

Teamsters, Local 695 v. Vogt, Inc.
354 U.S. 284 (1957)

FRANKFURTER, J. This is one more in the long series of cases in which this Court has been required to consider the limits imposed by the Fourteenth Amendment on the power of a State to enjoin picketing. The case was heard below on the pleadings and affidavits, the parties stipulating that the record contained "all of the facts and evidence that would be adduced upon a trial on the merits. . . ." Respondent owns and operates a gravel pit in Oconomowoc, Wisconsin, where it employs 15 to 20 men. Petitioner unions sought unsuccessfully to induce some of respondent's employees to join the unions and commenced to picket the entrance to respondent's place of business with signs reading, "The men on this job are not 100% affiliated with the AFL." "In consequence," drivers of several trucking companies refused to deliver and haul goods to and from respondent's plant, causing substantial damage to respondent. Respondent thereupon sought an injunction to restrain the picketing.

The trial court did not make the finding, requested by respondent:

> That the picketing of plaintiff's premises has been engaged in for the purpose of coercing, intimidating and inducing the employer to force, compel, or induce its employees to become members of defendant labor organizations, and for the purpose of injuring the plaintiff in its business because of its refusal to in any way interfere with the rights of its employees to join or not to join a labor organization.

It nevertheless held that by virtue of Wis. Stat. §103.535, prohibiting picketing in the absence of a "labor dispute," the petitioners must be enjoined from maintaining any pickets near respondent's place of business, from displaying at any place near respondent's place of business signs indicating that there was a labor dispute between respondent and its employees or between respondent and any of the petitioners, and from inducing others to decline to transport goods to and from respondent's business establishment.

On appeal, the Wisconsin Supreme Court at first reversed, relying largely on AFL v. Swing, 312 U.S. 321, to hold §103.535 unconstitutional, on the ground that picketing could not constitutionally be enjoined merely because of the absence of a "labor dispute." 270 Wis. 315, 71 N.W. 2d 359.

Upon reargument, however, the court withdrew its original opinion. Although the trial court had refused to make the finding requested by respondent, the Supreme Court, noting that the facts as to which the request was made were undisputed, drew the inference from the undisputed facts and itself made the finding. It canvassed the whole circumstances surrounding the picketing and held that "One would be credulous, indeed, to believe under the circumstances that the union had no thought of coercing the employer to interfere with its employees in their right to join or refuse to join the defendant union." Such picketing, the court held, was for "an unlawful purpose," since Wis. Stat. §111.06(2)(b) made it an unfair labor practice for an employee individually or in concert with others to "coerce, intimidate or induce any employer to interfere with any of his employes in the enjoyment of their legal rights . . . or to engage in any practice with regard to his employes which would constitute an unfair labor practice if undertaken by him on his own initiative." Relying on Building Service Employees v. Gazzam, 339 U.S. 532, and Pappas v. Stacey, 151 Me. 36, 116 A.2d 497, the Wisconsin Supreme Court therefore affirmed the granting of the injunction . . . 270 Wis. 321a, 74 N.W. 2d 749. . . .

It is inherent in the concept embodied in the Due Process Clause that its scope be determined by a "gradual process of judicial inclusion and exclusion," Davidson v. New Orleans, 96 U.S. 97, 104. Inevitably, therefore, the doctrine of a particular case "is not allowed to end with its enunciation and . . . an expression in an opinion yields later to the impact of facts unforeseen." Jaybird Mining Co. v. Weir, 271 U.S. 609, 619 (Brandeis, J., dissenting). It is not too surprising that the response of States — legislative and judicial — to use of the injunction in labor controversies should have given rise to a series of adjudications in this Court relating to the limitations on state action contained in the provisions of the Due Process Clause of the Fourteenth Amendment. It is also not too surprising that examination of these adjudications should disclose an evolving, not a static, course of decision.

The series begins with Truax v. Corrigan, 257 U.S. 312, in which a closely divided Court found it to be violative of the Equal Protection Clause — not of the Due Process Clause — for a State to deny use of the injunction in the special class of cases arising out of labor conflicts. The considerations that underlay that case soon had to yield, through legislation and later through litigation, to the persuasiveness of undermining facts. Thus, to remedy the abusive use of the injunction in the federal courts (see Frankfurter and Greene, The Labor Injunction), the Norris-LaGuardia Act withdrew, subject to qualifications, jurisdiction from the federal courts to issue injunctions in labor disputes to prohibit certain acts. Its example was widely followed by state enactments.

Apart from remedying the abuses of the injunction in this general type of litigation, legislatures and courts began to find in one of the aims of picketing an aspect of communication. This view came to the fore in Senn v. Tile Layers Union, 301 U.S. 468, where the Court held that the Fourteenth Amendment did not prohibit Wisconsin from authorizing peaceful stranger picketing by a union that was attempting to unionize a shop and to induce an employer to refrain from working in his business as a laborer.

Although the Court had been closely divided in the Senn case, three years later, in passing on a restrictive instead of a permissive state statute, the Court made sweeping pronouncements about the right to picket in holding unconstitutional a statute that had been applied to ban all picketing, with "no exceptions based upon either the number of persons engaged in the proscribed activity, the peaceful character of their demeanor, the nature of their dispute with an employer, or the restrained character and the accurateness of the terminology used in notifying the public of the facts of the dispute." Thornhill v. Alabama, 310 U.S. 88, 99. As the statute dealt at large with all picketing, so the Court broadly assimilated peaceful picketing in general to freedom of speech, and as such protected against abridgment by the Four-teenth Amendment.

The principles were applied by the Court in AFL v. Swing, 312 U.S. 321, to hold unconstitutional an injunction against peaceful picketing, based on a State's common-law policy against picketing when there was no imme-diate dispute between employer and employee. On the same day, however, the Court upheld a generalized injunction against picketing where there had been violence because "it could justifiably be concluded that the momentum of fear generated by past violence would survive even though future picket-ing might be wholly peaceful." Milk Wagon Drivers Union v. Meadowmoor Dairies, 312 U.S. 287, 294.

Soon, however, the Court came to realize that the broad pronounce-ments, but not the specific holding, of *Thornhill* had to yield "to the impact of facts unforeseen," or at least not sufficiently appreciated. . . . Cases reached the Court in which a State had designed a remedy to meet a specific situation or to accomplish a particular social policy. These cases made mani-fest that picketing, even though "peaceful," involved more than just com-munication of ideas and could not be immune from all state regulation. "Picketing by an organized group is more than free speech, since it involves patrol of a particular locality and since the very presence of a picket line may induce action of one kind or another, quite irrespective of the nature of the ideas which are being disseminated." Bakery Drivers Local v. Wohl, 315 U.S. 769, 776 (concurring opinion); see Carpenters Union v. Ritter's Cafe, 315 U.S. 722, 725-728.

These latter two cases required the Court to review a choice made by two States between the competing interests of unions, employers, their employees, and the public at large. In the *Ritter's Cafe* case, Texas had enjoined as a violation of its antitrust law picketing of a restaurant by unions to bring pressure on its owner with respect to use of nonunion labor by a contractor of the restaurant owner in the construction of a building having nothing to do with the restaurant. The Court held that Texas could, consis-tent with the Fourteenth Amendment, insulate from the dispute a neutral establishment that industrially had no connection with it. This type of picket-ing certainly involved little, if any "communication."

In Bakery Drivers Local v. Wohl, 315 U.S. 769, in a very narrowly restricted decision, the Court held that because of the impossibility of other-wise publicizing a legitimate grievance and because of the slight effect on "strangers" to the dispute, a State could not constitutionally prohibit a union from picketing bakeries in its efforts to have independent peddlers, buying from bakers and selling to small stores, conform to certain union requests. Although the Court in *Ritter's Cafe* and *Wohl* did not question the holding of *Thornhill*, the strong reliance on the particular facts in each case demonstrated a growing awareness that these cases involved not so much questions of free speech as review of the balance struck by a State between picketing that involved more than "publicity" and competing interests of state policy. (See also Cafeteria Union v. Angelos, 320 U.S. 293, where the Court reviewed a New York injunction against picketing by a union of a restaurant that was run by the owners without employees. The New York court appeared to have justified an injunction on the alternate grounds that there was no "labor dispute" under the New York statute or that use of untruthful placards justified the injunction. We held, in a brief opinion, that the abuses alleged did not justify an injunction against all picketing and that AFL v. Swing governed the alternate ground for decision.)

The implied reassessments of the broad language of the *Thornhill* case were finally generalized in a series of cases sustaining injunctions against peaceful picketing, even when arising in the course of a labor controversy, when such picketing was counter to valid state policy in a domain open to state regulation. The decisive reconsideration came in Giboney v. Empire Storage & Ice Co., 336 U.S. 490. A union, seeking to organize peddlers, picketed a wholesale dealer to induce it to refrain from selling to nonunion peddlers. The state courts, finding that such an agreement would constitute a conspiracy in restraint of trade in violation of the state antitrust laws, enjoined the picketing. This Court affirmed unanimously.

> It is contended that the injunction against picketing adjacent to Empire's place of business is an unconstitutional abridgment of free speech because the picketers were attempting peacefully to publicize truthful facts about a labor dispute. . . . But the record here does not permit this publicizing to be treated in isolation. . . . [T]he sole immediate object of the publicizing adjacent to the premises of Empire, as well as the other activities of the appellants and their allies, was to compel Empire to agree to stop selling ice to nonunion peddlers. Thus all of appellants' activities . . . constituted a single and integrated course of conduct, which was in violation of Missouri's valid law. In this situation, the injunction did no more than enjoin an offense against Missouri law, a felony.

Id., at 497-498. The Court therefore concluded that it was "clear that appellants were doing more than exercising a right of free speech or press. . . . They were exercising their economic power together with that of their allies to compel Empire to abide by union rather than by state regulation of trade." Id., at 503.

The following Term, the Court decided a group of cases applying and elaborating on the theory of *Giboney*. In Hughes v. Superior Court, 339

U.S. 460, the Court held that the Fourteenth Amendment did not bar use of the injunction to prohibit picketing of a place of business solely to secure compliance with a demand that its employees be hired in percentage to the racial origin of its customers. "We cannot construe the Due Process Clause as precluding California from securing respect for its policy against involuntary employment on racial lines by prohibiting systematic picketing that would subvert such policy." Id., at 466. The Court also found it immaterial that the state policy had been expressed by the judiciary rather than by the legislature.

On the same day, the Court decided Teamsters Union v. Hanke, 339 U.S. 470, holding that a State was not restrained by the Fourteenth Amendment from enjoining picketing of a business, conducted by the owner himself without employees, in order to secure compliance with a demand to become a union shop. . . . [Hanke] was another instance of the affirmance of an injunction against picketing because directed against a valid public policy of the State.

A third case, Building Service Employees v. Gazzam, 339 U.S. 532, was decided the same day. Following an unsuccessful attempt at unionization of a small hotel and refusal by the owner to sign a contract with the union as bargaining agent, the union began to picket the hotel wth signs stating that the owner was unfair to organized labor. The State, finding that the object of the picketing was in violation of its statutory policy against employer coercion of employees' choice of bargaining representative, enjoined picketing for such purpose. This Court affirmed, rejecting the argument that

> the Swing case, supra, is controlling . . . . In that case this Court struck down the State's restraint of picketing based solely on the absence of an employer-employee relationship. An adequate basis for the instant decree is the unlawful objective of the picketing, namely, coercion by the employer of the employee's selection of a bargaining representative. Peaceful picketing for any lawful purpose is not prohibited by the decree under review.

Id., at 539.

A similar problem was involved in Plumbers Union v. Graham, 345 U.S. 192, where a state court had enjoined, as a violation of its "Right to Work" law, picketing that advertised that nonunion men were being employed on a building job. This Court found that there was evidence in the record supporting a conclusion that a substantial purpose of the picketing was to put pressure on the general contractor to eliminate nonunion men from the job and, on the reasoning of the cases that we have just discussed, held that the injunction was not in conflict with the Fourteenth Amendment.

This series of cases, then, established a broad field in which a State, in enforcing some public policy, whether of its criminal or its civil law, and whether announced by its legislature or its courts, could constitutionally enjoin peaceful picketing aimed at preventing effectuation of that policy.

In the light of this background, the Maine Supreme Judicial Court in 1955 decided, on an agreed statement of facts, the case of Pappas v. Stacey, 151 Me. 36, 116 A.2d 497. From the statement, it appeared that three union employees went on strike and picketed a restaurant peacefully "for the sole purpose of seeking to organize other employees of the Plaintiff, ultimately to have the Plaintiff enter into collective bargaining and negotiations with the Union. . . . " Maine had a statute providing that workers should have full liberty of self-organization, free from restraint by employers or other persons. The Maine Supreme Judicial Court drew the inference from the agreed statement of facts that

> there is a steady and exacting pressure upon the employer to interfere with the free choice of the employees in the matter of organization. To say that the picketing is not designed to bring about such action is to forget an obvious purpose of picketing — to cause economic loss to the business during non-compliance by the employees with the request of the union.

151 Me., at 42, 116 A.2d, at 500. It therefore enjoined the picketing, and an appeal was taken to this Court.

The whole series of cases discussed above allowing, as they did, wide discretion to a State in the formulation of domestic policy, and not involving a curtailment of free speech in its obvious and accepted scope, led this Court, without the need of further argument, to grant appellee's motion to dismiss the appeal in that it no longer presented a substantial federal question. 350 U.S. 870.

The *Stacey* case is this case. As in *Stacey*, the present case was tried without oral testimony. As in *Stacey*, the highest state court drew the inference from the facts that the picketing was to coerce the employer to put pressure on his employees to join the union, in violation of the declared policy of the state. (For a declaration of similar congressional policy, see §8 of the [NLRA].) The cases discussed above all hold that, consistent with the Fourteenth Amendment, a State may enjoin such conduct.

Of course, the mere fact that there is "picketing" does not automatically justify its restraint without an investigation into its conduct and purposes. State courts, no more than state legislatures, cannot enact blanket prohibitions against picketing. Thornhill v. Alabama and AFL v. Swing, supra. The series of cases following *Thornhill* and *Swing* demonstrate that the policy of Wisconsin enforced by the prohibition of this picketing is a valid one. In this case, the circumstances set forth in the opinion of the Wisconsin Supreme

Court afford a rational basis for the inference it drew concerning the purpose of the picketing. No question was raised here concerning the breadth of the injunction, but of course its terms must be read in the light of the opinion of the Wisconsin Supreme Court, which justified it on the ground that the picketing was for the purpose of coercing the employer to coerce his employees. "If astuteness may discover argumentative excess in the scope of the [injunction] beyond what we constitutionally justify by this opinion, it will be open to petitioners to raise the matter, which they have not raised here, when the [case] on remand [reaches] the [Wisconsin] court." Teamsters Union v. Hanke, 339 U.S., at 480-481. . . .

Affirmed.

Whittaker, J. took no part in the consideration or decision of this case.

DOUGLAS, J. with whom the CHIEF JUSTICE and BLACK, J., concur, dissenting.

The Court has now come full circle. In [*Thornhill*], we struck down a state ban on picketing on the ground that "the dissemination of information concerning the facts of a labor dispute must be regarded as within that area of free discussion that is guaranteed by the Constitution." Less than one year later, we held that the First Amendment protected organizational picketing on a factual record which cannot be distinguished from the one now before us. AFL v. Swing, 312 U.S. 321. Of course, we have always recognized that picketing has aspects which make it more than speech. Bakery Drivers Local v. Wohl, 315 U.S. 769, 776-777 (concurring opinion). That difference underlies our decision in Giboney v. Empire Storage & Ice Co., 336 U.S. 490. There, picketing was an essential part of "a single and integrated course of conduct, which was in violation of Missouri's valid law." Id., at 498. . . . We emphasized that "there was clear danger, imminent and immediate, that unless restrained, appellants would succeed in making [the state] policy a dead letter. . . ." 336 U.S., at 503. Speech there was enjoined because it was an inseparable part of conduct which the State constitutionally could and did regulate.

But where, as here, there is no rioting, no mass picketing, no violence, no disorder, no fisticuffs, no coercion — indeed nothing but speech — the principles announced in *Thornhill* and *Swing* should give the advocacy of one side of a dispute First Amendment protection.

The retreat began when, in Teamsters Union v. Hanke, 339 U.S. 470, four members of the Court announced that all picketing could be prohibited if a state court decided that that picketing violated the State's public policy. The retreat became a rout in Plumbers Union v. Graham, 345 U.S. 192. It was only the "purpose" of the picketing which was relevant. The state court's characterization of the picketers' "purpose" had been made well-nigh conclusive. Considerations of the proximity of picketing to conduct which the State could control or prevent were abandoned, and no longer was it necessary for the state court's decree to be narrowly drawn to prescribe a specific evil. Id., at 201-205 (dissenting opinion).

Today, the Court signs the formal surrender. State courts and state legislatures cannot fashion blanket prohibitions on all picketing. But, for practical purposes, the situation now is as it was when Senn v. Tile Layers Union, 301 U.S. 468, was decided. State courts and state legislatures are free to decide whether to permit or suppress any particular picket line for any reason other than a blanket policy against all picketing. I would adhere to the principle announced in *Thornhill*. I would adhere to the result reached in *Swing*. I would return to the test enunciated in *Giboney* — that this form of expression can be regulated or prohibited only to the extent that it forms an essential part of a course of conduct which the State can regulate or prohibit. I would reverse the judgment below.

NOTES

1. Under *Vogt* and antecedent decisions, labor picketing appears to have been treated as a form of economic pressure subject to regulation tested under a due process analysis rather than a First Amendment analysis. What is the rationale for that approach? The proper constitutional treatment of labor picketing is the subject of an extensive literature. See, e.g., St. Antoine, Free Speech or Economic Weapon? The Persisting Problem of Picketing, 16 Suffolk U. L. Rev. 883 (1982); C. Gregory & H. Katz, Labor and the Law ch. XI (3d ed. 1979); Farmer & Williamson, Picketing and the Injunctive Power of State Courts — from *Thornhill* to *Vogt*, 35 U. Det. J. Urb. L. 431 (1958). For earlier discussions, see Jaffe, In Defense of the Supreme Court's Picketing Doctrine, 41 Mich. L. Rev. 1037 (1943); Teller, Picketing and Free Speech, 56 Harv. L. Rev. 180 (1942); Dodd, Picketing and Free Speech: A Dissent, 56 Harv. L. Rev. 513 (1943); Teller, Picketing and Free Speech: A Reply, 56 Harv. L. Rev. 532 (1943). Cf. Gregory, Constitutional Limitations on the Regulation of Union and Employer Conduct, 49 Mich. L. Rev. 191 (1950); Jones, Free Speech: Pickets on the Grass, Alas! Amidst Confusion A Consistent Principle, 29 S. Cal. L. Rev. 137 (1956) (a comparison of picketing and nonpicketing cases).

2. Should picketing directed at consumers automatically have greater constitutional protection than picketing directed at employees at their work sites? Should the effect of consumer picketing on values that Congress has decided to protect, such as employee self-determination, limit the scope of

constitutional protection? Suppose that the Furniture Workers Union, seeking to organize a Wisconsin furniture store, did not picket but instead placed the store on the local labor council's "Do Not Patronize" list, which was widely circulated through union newspapers, etc. Would an injunction against the union's action be constitutional? Would your answer be affected by the fact that the store's business sharply declined as a result of those activities or by the fact that the Wisconsin statute granted protection to self-determination by employees substantially the same as that provided by the NLRA? Would the resolution of the constitutional issue be affected if the union implemented its campaign by distributing "Do Not Patronize" fliers at the store's entrance? By picketing at that entrance with "Do Not Patronize" placards? See NLRB v. IAM, 263 F.2d 796, 799-800 (9th Cir. 1959); cf. Capital Serv. v. NLRB, 204 F.2d 848 (9th Cir. 1953), aff'd on other grounds, 347 U.S. 501 (1954); NLRB v. Fruit Packers, infra, p. 582.

See Cox, The Supreme Court, 1979 Term, Foreword: Freedom of Expression in the Burger Court, 94 Harv. L. Rev. 1, 36-39 (1980); but cf. Note, Labor Picketing and Commercial Speech: Free Enterprise Values in the Doctrine of Free Speech, 91 Yale L.J. 938 (1982).

3. Does the constitutional protection of picketing arising from labor disputes extend to picketing at places physically remote from the establishment involved in the dispute, e.g., at the residence of the owner or chief executive of the employer or the school attended by his child? See Carey v. Brown, 447 U.S. 455 (1980) (Illinois statute prohibiting residential picketing but exempting "peaceful picketing of a place of employment involved in a labor dispute" declared invalid on equal protection grounds; the Court noted, "We are not to be understood to imply, however, that residential picketing is beyond the reach of uniform and non-discriminatory regulation." 477 U.S. at 470.). See Arnolds & Seng, Picketing and Privacy: Can I Patrol on the Street Where You Live?, 1982 S. Ill. U.L.J. 463.

4. Does the First Amendment bar an injunction against picketing with libelous placards during a labor dispute? Against a union's distribution of libelous leaflets to pedestrians adjacent to an employer's premises? See Montgomery Ward & Co. v. United Retail Employees, 400 Ill. 38, 79 N.E.2d 46 (1948). Consider also the issue of federal preemption covered in Chapter 8 (C), infra.

Hudgens v. NLRB
424 U.S. 507 (1976)

Stewart, J. . . . . [L]abor union members who engaged in peaceful primary picketing within the confines of a privately owned shopping center were threatened by an agent of the owner with arrest for criminal trespass if they did not depart. The question presented is whether this threat violated the [NLRA]. The [Board] concluded that it did, 205 N.L.R.B. 628, and . . . the Fifth Circuit agreed. 501 F.2d 161. . . .

I

The petitioner, Scott Hudgens, is the owner of the North DeKalb Shopping Center, located in suburban Atlanta, Ga. The center consists of a single large building with an enclosed mall. Surrounding the building is a parking area which can accommodate 2,640 automobiles. The shopping center houses 60 retail stores leased to various businesses. One of the lessees is the Butler Shoe Co. Most of the stores, including Butler's, can be entered only from the interior mall.

In January 1971, warehouse employees of the Butler Shoe Co. went on strike to protest the company's failure to agree to demands made by their union in contract negotiations. The strikers decided to picket not only Butler's warehouse but its nine retail stores in the Atlanta area as well, including the store in the North DeKalb Shopping Center. On January 22, 1971, four of the striking warehouse employees entered the center's enclosed mall carrying placards which read: "Butler Shoe Warehouse on Strike, AFL-CIO, Local 315." The general manager of the shopping center informed the employees that they could not picket within the mall or on the parking lot and threatened them with arrest if they did not leave. The employees departed but returned a short time later and began picketing in an area of the mall immediately adjacent to the entrances of the Butler store. After the picketing had continued for approximately 30 minutes, the shopping center manager again informed the pickets that if they did not leave they would be arrested for trespassing. The pickets departed. . . .

[The court of appeals had upheld the NLRB's decision that Hudgens had violated §8(a)(1).[3] It was, however, uncertain whether the decisions below had rested solely on §7 of the NLRA independently of any constitutional right of access to private property (including certain shopping centers) classified as "quasi public." As the Court's present opinion showed, its prior decisions had recognized such a right but the status of those decisions had been placed in doubt by later decisions rendered during the instant litigation.]

[3] [This note is relocated in the opinion. — EDS.] . . . Section 8(a)(1) makes it an unfair labor practice for "an employer" to "restrain, or coerce employees" in the exercise of their §7 rights. While Hudgens was not the employer of the employees involved in this case, it seems to be undisputed that he was an employer engaged in commerce within the meaning of §§2(6) and (7) of the Act. The Board has held that a statutory "employer" may violate §8(a)(1) with respect to employees other than his own. See Austin Co., 101 N.L.R.B. 1257, 1258-1259. See also §2(13) of the Act.

II

. . . In the present posture of the case the most basic question is whether the respective rights and liabilities of the parties are to be decided under the criteria of the [NLRA] alone, under a First Amendment standard or under some combination of the two. . . .

It is , of course, a commonplace that the constitutional guarantee of free speech is a guarantee only against abridgment by government, federal or state. . . . Thus, while statutory or common law may in some situations extend protection or provide redress against a private corporation or person who seeks to abridge the free expression of others, no such protection or redress is provided by the Constitution itself.

This elementary proposition is little more than a truism. But even truisms are not always unexceptionably true, and an exception to this one was recognized almost 30 years ago in Marsh v. Alabama, 326 U.S. 501. In *Marsh*, a Jehovah's Witness who had distributed literature without a license on a sidewalk in Chickasaw, Ala., was convicted of criminal trespass. Chickasaw was a so-called company town, wholly owned by the Gulf Shipbuilding Corp. It was described in the Court's opinion as follows:

> Except for [ownership by a private corporation] it has all the characteristics of any other American town. The property consists of residential buildings, streets, a system of sewers, a sewage disposal plant and a "business block" on which business places are situated. A deputy of the Mobile County Sheriff, paid by the company, serves as the town's policeman. Merchants and service establishments have rented the stores and business places on the business block and the United States uses one of the places as a post office. . . . The town and the surrounding neighborhood . . . are thickly settled, and according to all indications the residents use the business block as their regular shopping center. . . . In short the town and its shopping district are accessible to and freely used by the public in general and there is nothing to distinguish them from any other town and shopping center except the fact that the title to the property belongs to a private corporation.

Id., at 502-503.

The Court pointed out that if the "title" to Chickasaw had "belonged not to a private but to a municipal corporation and had appellant been arrested for violating a municipal ordinance rather than a ruling by those appointed by the corporation to manage a company town it would have been clear that appellant's conviction must be reversed." Id., at 504. Concluding that Gulf's "property interests" should not be allowed to lead to a different result in Chickasaw, which did "not function differently from any other town," id., at 506-508, the Court invoked the First and Fourteenth Amendments to reverse the appellant's conviction.

It was the *Marsh* case that in 1968 provided the foundation for the Court's decision in Amalgamated Food Employees Union v. Logan Valley Plaza, 391 U.S. 308. That case involved peaceful picketing within a large shopping center near Altoona, Pa. One of the tenants of the shopping center was a retail store that employed a wholly nonunion staff. Members of a local union picketed the store carrying signs proclaiming that it was nonunion and that its employees were not receiving union wages or other union benefits. The picketing took place on the shopping center's property in the immediate vicinity of the store. A Pennsylvania court issued an injunction that required all picketing to be confined to public areas outside the shopping center, and the Supreme Court of Pennsylvania affirmed the issuance of this injunction. This Court held that the doctrine of the *Marsh* case required reversal of that judgment.

The Court's opinion pointed out that the First and Fourteenth Amendments would clearly have protected the picketing if it had taken place on a public sidewalk: "It is clear that if the shopping center premises were not privately owned but instead constituted the business area of a municipality, which they to a large extent resemble, petitioners could not be barred from exercising their First Amendment rights there on the sole ground that title to the property was in the municipality. . . . " 391 U.S., at 315.

The Court's opinion then . . . emphasized the similarities between the business block in Chickasaw, Ala., and the Logan Valley shopping center, and unambiguously concluded: "The shopping center here is clearly the functional equivalent of the business district of Chickasaw involved in *Marsh*." 391 U.S., at 318. Upon the basis of that conclusion, the Court held that the First and Fourteenth Amendments required reversal of the judgment of the Pennsylvania Supreme Court.

There were three dissenting opinions in the *Logan Valley* case, one of them by the author of the Court's opinion in *Marsh*, Mr. Justice Black. His disagreement with the Court's reasoning was total:

"The question is, Under what circumstances can private property be treated as though it were public? The answer that *Marsh* gives is when that property has taken on *all* the attributes of a town, i.e., 'residential buildings, streets, a system of sewers, a sewage disposal plant and a "business block" on which business places are situated.' 326 U.S., at 502. I can find nothing in *Marsh* which indicates that if one of these features is present, e.g., a business district, this is sufficient for the Court to confiscate a part of an owner's private property and give its use to people who want to picket on it." Id., at 332.

"To hold that store owners are compelled by law to supply picketing areas for pickets to drive store customers away is to create a court-made law wholly disregarding the constitutional basis on which private ownership of property rests in this country. . . . " Id., at 332-333.

Four years later the Court had occasion to reconsider the *Logan Valley* doctrine in Lloyd Corp. v. Tanner, 407 U.S. 551. That case involved a shopping center covering some 50 acres in downtown Portland, Ore. On a November day in 1968 five young people entered the mall of the shopping center and distributed handbills protesting the then ongoing American military operations in Vietnam. Security guards told them to leave, and they did so, "to avoid arrest." Id., at 556. They subsequently brought suit in a Federal District Court, seeking declaratory and injunctive relief. The trial court ruled in their favor, holding that the distribution of handbills on the shopping center's property was protected by the First and Fourteenth Amendments. . . . [T]he Ninth Circuit affirmed the judgment, 446 F.2d 545, expressly relying on this Court's *Marsh* and *Logan Valley* decisions. This Court reversed. . . .

The Court in its *Lloyd* opinion did not say that it was overruling the *Logan Valley* decision. Indeed, a substantial portion of the Court's opinion in *Lloyd* was devoted to pointing out the differences between the two cases, noting particularly that, in contrast to the handbilling in *Lloyd*, the picketing in *Logan Valley* had been specifically directed to a store in the shopping center and the pickets had had no other reasonable opportunity to reach their intended audience. 407 U.S., at 561-567.[5] But the fact is that the reasoning of the Court's opinion in *Lloyd* cannot be squared with the reasoning of the Court's opinion in *Logan Valley*.

It matters not that some Members of the Court may continue to believe that the *Logan Valley* case was rightly decided. Our institutional duty is to follow until changed the law as it now is, not as some Members of the Court might wish it to be. And in the performance of that duty we make clear now, if it was not clear before, that the rationale of *Logan Valley* did not survive the Court's decision in the *Lloyd* case.[7] Not only did the *Lloyd* opinion incorporate lengthy excerpts from two of the dissenting opinions in *Logan Valley*, 407 U.S., at 562-563, 565; the ultimate holding in *Lloyd* amounted to a total rejection of the holding in *Logan Valley*: . . .

"Respondents contend . . . that the property of a large shopping center is 'open to the public,' serves the same purposes as a 'business district' of a municipality, and therefore has been dedicated to certain types of public use. The argument is that such a center has sidewalks, streets, and parking areas which are functionally similar to facilities customarily provided by municipalities. It is then asserted that all members of the public, whether invited as customers or not, have the same right of free speech as they would have on the similar public facilities in the streets of a city or town.

[5] Insofar as the two shopping centers differed as such, the one in *Lloyd* more closely resembled the business section in Chickasaw, Ala. . . .

[7] This was the entire thrust of Mr. Justice Marshall's dissenting opinion in the *Lloyd* case. See id., at 584.

"The argument reaches too far. The Constitution by no means requires such an attenuated doctrine of dedication of private property to public use. The closest decision in theory, Marsh v. Alabama, supra, involved the assumption by a private enterprise of all the attributes of a state-created municipality and the exercise by that enterprise of semiofficial municipal functions as a delegate of the State. In effect, the owner of the company town was performing the full spectrum of municipal powers. . . . In the instant case there is no comparable assumption or exercise of municipal functions or power." Id., at 568-569.

"We hold that there has been no such dedication of Lloyd's privately owned and operated shopping center to public use as to entitle respondents to exercise therein the asserted First Amendment rights. . . ." Id., at 570.

If a large self-contained shopping center *is* the functional equivalent of a municipality, as *Logan Valley* held, then the First and Fourteenth Amendments would not permit control of speech within such a center to depend upon the speech's content. . . . It conversely follows, therefore, that if the respondents in the *Lloyd* case did not have a First Amendment right to enter that shopping center to distribute handbills concerning Vietnam, then the pickets in the present case did not have a First Amendment right to enter this shopping center for the purpose of advertising their strike against the Butler Shoe Co.

We conclude, in short, that under the present state of the law the constitutional guarantee of free expression has no part to play in a case such as this.

III

. . . The rights and liabilities of the parties . . . are dependent exclusively upon the [NLRA]. Under the Act the task of the Board, subject to review by the courts, is to resolve conflicts between §7 rights and private property rights, "and to seek a proper accommodation between the two." Central Hardware Co. v. NLRB, 407 U.S., at 543. What is "a proper accommodation" in any situation may largely depend upon the content and the context of the §7 rights being asserted. . . .

. . . Accommodation [by the NLRB] between employees' §7 rights and employers' property rights, the Court said in *Babock & Wilcox*, "must be obtained with as little destruction of one as is consistent with the maintenance of the other." 351 U.S., at 112.

Both *Central Hardware* and *Babcock & Wilcox* involved organizational activity carried on by nonemployees on the employers' property.[10] The

---

[10] A wholly different balance was struck when the organizational activity was carried on by employees already rightfully on the employer's property, since the employer's management interests rather than his property interests were there involved. Republic Aviation Corp.

context of the §7 activity in the present case was different in several respects which may or may not be relevant in striking the proper balance. First, it involved lawful economic strike activity rather than organizational activity. . . . Second, the §7 activity here was carried on by Butler's employees (albeit not employees of its shopping center store), not by outsiders. See NLRB v. Babcock & Wilcox Co., supra, at 111-113. Third, the property interests impinged upon in this case were not those of the employer against whom the §7 activity was directed, but of another.

The *Babcock & Wilcox* opinion established the basic objective under the Act: accommodation of §7 rights and private property rights "with as little destruction of one as is consistent with the maintenance of the other." The locus of that accommodation, however, may fall at differing points along the spectrum depending on the nature and strength of the respective §7 rights and private property rights asserted in any given context. In each generic situation, the primary responsibility for making this accommodation must rest with the Board in the first instance. See NLRB v. Babcock & Wilcox, supra, at 112; cf. NLRB v. Erie Resistor Corp., 373 U.S. at 235-236; NLRB v. Truckdrivers Union, 353 U.S. 87, 97. . . .

. . . [T]he judgment is vacated and the case is remanded to the Court of Appeals with directions to remand to the [NLRB], so that the case may be there considered under the statutory criteria of the [NLRA] alone.

[Powell, J., with whom Burger, C. J., joined, concurred in the Court's opinion, but noted that *Tanner* had not overruled *Logan Valley*, and expressed a preference for such overruling rather than resort to the Court's distinctions based on "attenuated factual differences." White, J., concurred only in result. He too maintained that *Logan Valley* had not been overruled but would have distinguished it from *Hudgens* in that the *Hudgens* pickets were not communicating about the store being picketed. Stevens, J., did not participate.]

MARSHALL, J., with whom BRENNAN, J., joins, dissenting. . . . In explaining why it addresses any constitutional issue at all, the Court observes simply that the history of the litigation has been one of "shifting positions on the part of the litigants, the Board, and the Court of Appeals," ante, at 512, as to whether relief was being sought, or granted, under the First Amendment, under §7 of the Act, or under some combination of the two. On my reading, the Court of Appeals' decision and, even more clearly, the Board's decision here for review, were based solely on §7, not on the First Amendment; and this Court ought initially consider the statutory question without reference to

---

v. NLRB, 324 U.S. 793. This difference is "one of substance." NLRB v. Babcock & Wilcox Co., 351 U.S. 105, 113.

the First Amendment — the question on which the Court remands. But even under the Court's reading of the opinions of the Board and the Court of Appeals, the statutory question on which it remands is now before the Court. By bypassing that question and reaching out to overrule a constitutionally based decision, the Court surely departs from traditional modes of adjudication.

I would affirm . . . the Court of Appeals on purely statutory grounds. And on the merits of the only question that the Court decides, I dissent from the overruling of *Logan Valley.* . . .

The Court adopts the view that *Marsh* has no bearing on this case because the privately owned property in *Marsh* involved all the characteristics of a typical town. But there is nothing in *Marsh* to suggest that its general approach was limited to the particular facts of that case. The underlying concern in *Marsh* was that traditional public channels of communication remain free, regardless of the incidence of ownership. Given that concern, the crucial fact in *Marsh* was that the company owned the traditional forums essential for effective communication. . . .

In *Logan Valley* we recognized what the Court today refuses to recognize — that the owner of the modern shopping center complex, by dedicating his property to public use as a business district, to some extent displaces the "State" from control of historical First Amendment forums, and may acquire a virtual monopoly of places suitable for effective communication. The roadways, parking lots, and walkways of the modern shopping center may be as essential for effective speech as the streets and sidewalks in the municipal or company-owned town. . . .

. . . [T]he *Lloyd* Court remained responsive in its own way to the concerns underlying *Marsh*. *Lloyd* retained the availability of First Amendment protection when the picketing is related to the function of the shopping center, and when there is no other reasonable opportunity to convey the message to the intended audience. Preserving *Logan Valley* subject to *Lloyd*'s two related criteria guaranteed that the First Amendment would have application in those situations in which the shopping center owner had most clearly monopolized the forums essential for effective communication. . . .

The Court's only apparent objection to this analysis is that it makes the applicability of the First Amendment turn to some degree on the subject matter of the speech. But that in itself is no objection, and the cases cited by the Court to the effect that government may not "restrict expression because of its message, its ideas, its subject matter, or its content," Police Dept. of Chicago v. Mosley, 408 U.S. 92, 95 (1972), are simply inapposite. In those cases, it was clearly the government that was acting, and the First Amendment's bar against infringing speech was unquestionably applicable; the

Court simply held that the government, faced with a general command to permit speech, cannot choose to forbid some speech because of its message. The shopping center cases are quite different; in these cases the primary regulator is a private entity whose property has "assume[d] to some significant degree the functional attributes of public property devoted to public use." Central Hardware Co. v. NLRB, 407 U.S., at 547. The very question in these cases is whether, and under what circumstances, the First Amendment has any application at all. The answer to that question, under the view of *Marsh* described above, depends to some extent on the subject of the speech the private entity seeks to regulate, because the degree to which the private entity monopolizes the effective channels of communication may depend upon what subject is involved.

[On remand, the Board in Scott Hudgens, 230 N.L.R.B. 414 (1977), reaffirmed its finding of a violation of §8(a)(1), declaring:]
. . . We conclude that the three factual differences [between the instant case and *Central Hardware* and *Babcock & Wilcox*, noted by the Supreme Court] do not preclude our finding that Hudgens violated §8(a)(1).
Concerning the first distinction . . . , that the instant case involves economic strike activity rather than organizational activity, . . . both types of activity are protected by §7. . . . [T]he fact that the picketing here was in support of an economic strike does not warrant denying it the same measure of protection afforded to organizational picketing.
With respect to the Court's second distinguishing factor, that the picketers were employees of the company whose store they were picketing rather than nonemployees, . . . it is basic that §7 . . . was intended to protect the rights of employees rather than those of nonemployees. . . . [T]he employee status of the pickets here entitled them to at least as much protection as would be afforded to nonemployee organizers such as those in *Babcock & Wilcox*.
However, the fact that economic rather than organizational picketing is involved . . . may require a different application of the accommodation principle. . . . It is clear that the §7 rights involved in *Babcock & Wilcox*, as in *Central Hardware*, are those of the employees rather than those of the nonemployees seeking to organize them. That is to say, if the employees are beyond the reach of reasonable union efforts to communicate with them, it is the employees' right to receive information on the right to organize that is abrogated when an employer denies nonemployee union organizers access to the employer's property. Similarly, where, as here, economic strike picketing is involved, the §7 rights at issue are those of employees, i.e., the pickets' right to communicate their message both to persons who would do business with

the struck employer and to those employees of the struck employer who have not joined the strike.

One difference between organizational campaigns as opposed to economic strike situations is that in the former the §7 rights being protected are those of the intended audience (the employees sought to be organized), and in the latter the §7 rights are those of the persons attempting to communicate with *their* intended audience, the public as well as the employees. A further distinction between organizational and economic strike activity becomes apparent when the focus shifts to the characteristics of the audience at which the §7 activity in question is directed. In an organizational campaign, the group of employees whose support the union seeks is specific and often is accessible by means of communication other than direct entry of the union organizers onto the employer's property. . . .

Here, the pickets' intended audience comprised two distinct groups: (1) those members of the buying public who might, when seeing Butler's window display inside the Mall, think of doing business with that one employer, and (2) the employees at the Butler store. Although the non-striking employees at the Butler store were obviously a clearly defined group, the potential customers (the more important component of the intended audience) became established as such only when individual shoppers decide to enter the store.

Hudgens contends that *Babcock & Wilcox* should be read to require that, if television, radio, and newspaper advertising is available, the picketers' §7 rights must yield to property rights regardless of the expense involved. . . . [T]he [ALJ] found, and we agree, that the mass media . . . are not "reasonable" means of communication for employee pickets seeking to publicize their labor dispute with a single store in the Mall. . . . As to Hudgens' suggestion that the pickets could have used public streets and sidewalks, the [ALJ noted] that Butler is only one of 60 stores fronting on the same common inside walkways, that the closest public area — i.e., not privately owned — is 500 feet away from the store, and that a message announced orally or by picket sign at such a distance from the focal point would be too greatly diluted to be meaningful. Further, . . . safety considerations, the likelihood of enmeshing neutral employers, and the fact that many people become members of the pickets' intended audience on impulse all weigh against requiring the pickets to remove to public property or even to the sidewalks surrounding the Mall.

As for the third consideration . . . , that "the property rights impinged upon . . . were not those of the employer against whom the §7 activity was directed, but of another," we find that . . . Hudgen's property right to exclude certain types of activity on his Mall must yield to the §7 right of lawful primary economic picketing directed against an employer doing business on that Mall. The walkways on the common areas . . . near the Butler store, although privately owned, are, during business hours, essentially open to the public and . . . are the equivalent of sidewalks for the people who come to the Center. . . .

Further, we find no merit to Hudgens' assertion that he is a completely neutral bystander. . . . Although Hudgens is neutral in the sense that he is not the primary employer and is, therefore, not a party to the labor dispute, he is nonetheless financially interested in the success of each of the businesses in his Center inasmuch as he receives a percentage of their gross sales as part of his rental arrangement. . . . To the extent that the businesses on the Mall have delegated to Hudgens responsibility for the maintenance of an environment that maximizes the shoppers' peace of mind, and therefore sales, those doing business at the Center are protecting their own interests through Hudgens. [Under] the lease, part of the rent they pay Hudgens is for such protection. . . .

NOTES

1. Would it be material if the picketers in *Hudgens* were not striking employees but had been hired by the union to serve as pickets?

2. In Giant Food Markets, Inc. v. NLRB, 633 F.2d 18 (6th Cir. 1980), lawful "area standards" picketing occurred about 250 feet from a shopping center's entrance, next to a nonunion food store that had replaced a unionized store in the center without hiring any of its employees. The picketed store, its sublessor department store, and the center's owner demanded that the pickets and handbillers leave the property; that demand was not honored, and picketing continued until enjoined by a state court. The Board found that the property rights involved must yield to the interests served by the picketing and held that the demands for the departure of the pickets — but not the petition for an injunction — violated §8(a)(1). 241 N.L.R.B. 727 (1979). The court, applying the *Babcock & Wilcox* tests, could not find sufficient evidence to support the Board's balance of the conflicting rights. Remanding, the court directed the Board to "take further evidence" on whether picketing away from the food store, at the entrance to the center's parking lot, would have (1) diluted the union's message and (2) tended to enmesh neutral employees. How is the Board to acquire the evidence the court asks for?

3. Even after *Tanner*, the "quasi-public" doctrine was used to support access by outsiders to residential labor camps for migrant agricultural workers. See, e.g., Illinois Migrant Council v. Campbell Soup Co., 519 F.2d

391 (7th Cir. 1975), where counsel, federally financed in part, seeking to tell workers about federal and state services, was denied entry to a camp described as follows in the counsel's complaint seeking to compel the defendant-owner to grant access: a residential community for 150 persons, supplying a work place, residences, a store, a cafeteria, and recreational buildings; and subject to a no-trespass policy. The reviewing court found that "a company town" had been alleged and that, under the First Amendment, dismissal of the complaint had been error, without regard to whether alternative methods of communication existed. But cf. Asociacion de Trabajadores v. Green Giant Co., 518 F.2d 130 (3d Cir. 1975) (denying union organizers right of entry to a more elaborate worker-residential complex). What impact does *Hudgens* have on the right of access by outsiders to such labor camps?

The grounds on which such entry rights have been granted are discussed in Note, 61 Cornell L. Rev. 560 (1976); Note, 29 Rutgers L. Rev. 972 (1976). The constitutionality of California's statutory requirement of access by union organizers to farm workers on growers' land was upheld by the California Supreme Court. Agricultural Lab. Rel. Bd. v. Superior Court, 16 Cal. 3d 392, 546 P.2d 687, 128 Cal. Rptr. 183 (1976). The Supreme Court has refused to invalidate state legislation that denies to unions seeking to organize agricultural workers (a group excluded from the NLRA) rights of access as great as those conferred by the NLRA. See Babbitt v. United Farm Workers, 442 U.S. 289 (1979).

Courts have rejected claims that the Constitution guarantees the right to strike in the private as well as the public sector. See United Federation of Postal Clerks v. Blount, 325 F. Supp. 879 (D.D.C. 1971), *aff'd*, 404 U.S. 802 (1971); Meltzer & Sunstein, Public Employee Strikes, Executive Discretion and the Air Traffic Controllers, 50 U. Chi. L. Rev. 731, 778-781 (1983); Cox, Strikes, Picketing, and the Constitution, 4 Vand. L. Rev. 574 (1951).

C. ORGANIZATIONAL PICKETING

As suggested by the *Vogt* case, supra p. 487, recognitional picketing involves tensions between the principles of employee self-determination and majority rule embodied in the Wagner Act. Furthermore, such picketing by a union that lacks majority support confronts an employer with a dilemma. If he capitulates and recognizes a minority union, he violates the law. If he obeys the law and withholds recognition, he risks loss to, and sometimes destruction of, his enterprise.

The Taft-Hartley amendments were ultimately read as not providing any relief from the foregoing difficulties. These amendments did expressly provide that employees were to have the same freedom to reject, as to accept, a would-be representative. Compare §7 of the NLRA, as amended, with §1, as amended; see also the *Savair* case, supra p. 144. There was, however, a substantial gap between that principle and the operative statutory provisions. Section 8(b)(4)(C) provided only limited protection for the integrity of the Board's election machinery, by proscribing recognitional picketing only when another union had been certified by the Board. Section 8(b)(1)(A), moreover, at first reached only cruder pressures, such as actual or threatened violence and threatened economic reprisals, by which unions sought to conscript unwilling employees. It was not until ten years after the enactment of the Taft-Hartley Act that the Board ruled that §8(b)(1) barred all recognition picketing by a minority union. See Teamsters Union (Curtis Bros.), 119 N.L.R.B. 232, 256 (1957). That ruling reached the Supreme Court only after the Landrum-Griffin Act (1959) had added §8(b)(7) to the NLRA. The Court relied on that section, inter alia, in rejecting the Board's ruling in *Curtis Bros*. See NLRB v. Drivers Local 639, 362 U.S. 274 (1960).

The NLRB, although frequently divided, at first gave generous scope to §8(b)(7). But, after two appointments by President Kennedy, the Board reconsidered and reversed some of its initial decisions or modified its reasoning. Those changes, which progressively narrowed the scope of §8(b)(7) as well as §8(b)(4)(C), are reflected in the materials below. See generally Meltzer, Organizational Picketing and the NLRB: Five on a Seesaw, 30 U. Chi. L. Rev. 78 (1962). For a review of subsequent developments, see Modjeska, Recognition Picketing Under the NLRA, 35 U. Fla. L. Rev. 633 (1983).

International Hod Carriers, Local 840 (Blinne Constr.)

135 N.L.R.B. 1153 (1962), supplementing 130 N.L.R.B. 587 (1961)

[On February 20, 1961, the Board, in a divided opinion, concluded that the respondent union had violated §8(b)(7)(C). The Board later granted the union's motion for reconsideration.]

. . . [I]t is essential to note the interplay of the several subsections of §8(b)(7), of which subparagraph (C) is only a constituent part.

The section as a whole, as is apparent from its opening phrases, prescribes limitations only on picketing for an object of "recognition" or "bargaining" (both of which terms will hereinafter be subsumed under the single term "recognition") or for an object of organization. Picketing for other objects is not proscribed by this section. Moreover, not all picketing for recognition or organization is proscribed. A "currently certified" union may picket for recognition or organization of employees for whom it is certified. And even a union which is not certified is barred from recognition or organization picketing only in three general areas. The first area, defined in subparagraph (A) of §8(b)(7), relates to situations where another union has been lawfully recognized and a question concerning representation cannot appropriately be raised.[5] The second area, defined in subparagraph (B), relates to situations where, within the preceding 12 months, a "valid election" has been held.

The intent of subparagraphs (A) and (B) is fairly clear. Congress concluded that where a union has been lawfully recognized and a question concerning representation cannot appropriately be raised, or where the employees within the preceding 12 months have made known their views concerning representation, both the employer and employees are entitled to immunity from recognition or organization picketing for prescribed periods.

. . . Deeply concerned with other abuses, most particularly "blackmail" picketing, Congress concluded that it would be salutary to impose even further limitations on picketing for recognition or organization. Accordingly, subparagraph (C) provides that even where such picketing is not barred by the provisions of (A) or (B) so that picketing for recognition or organization would otherwise be permissible, such picketing is limited to a reasonable period not to exceed 30 days unless a representation petition is filed prior to the expiration of that period. Absent the filing of such a timely petition, continuation of the picketing beyond the reasonable period becomes an unfair labor practice. On the other hand, the filing of a timely petition stays the limitation and picketing may continue pending the processing of the petition. Even here, however, Congress by the addition of the first proviso to subparagraph (C) made it possible to foreshorten the period of permissible picketing by directing the holding of an expedited election pursuant to the representation petition.

The expedited election procedure is applicable, of course, only in a §8(b)(7)(C) proceeding, i.e., where an 8(b)(7)(C) unfair labor practice charge has been filed. Congress rejected efforts to amend the provisions of §9(c) . . . so as to dispense generally with preelection hearings. Thus, in the absence of an 8(b)(7)(C) unfair labor practice charge, a union will not be

[5] . . . Subparagraph (A) represents a substantial enlargement upon the prohibition already embodied in §8(b)(4)(C) of the Taft-Hartley Act which merely insulates certified unions from proscribed "raiding" by rival labor organizations. Subparagraph (A) affords protection to lawfully recognized unions which do not have certified status, and also incorporates, in effect, the Board's contract-bar rules relating to the existence of a question concerning representation.

enabled to obtain an expedited election by the mere device of engaging in recognition or organization picketing and filing a representation petition.[10] And on the other hand, a picketing union which files a representation petition pursuant to the mandate of §8(b)(7)(C) and to avoid its sanctions will not be propelled into an expedited election, which it may not desire, merely because it has filed such a petition. In both the above situations, the normal representation procedures are applicable; the showing of a substantial interest will be required, and the preelection hearing directed in §9(c)(1) will be held.

This . . . puts the expedited election procedure prescribed in the first proviso to subparagraph (C) in its proper and intended focus. That procedure was devised to shield aggrieved employers and employees from the adverse effects of prolonged recognition or organizational picketing. Absent such a grievance, it was not designed either to benefit or to handicap picketing activity. . . .

Subparagraphs (B) and (C) serve different purposes. But it is especially significant to note their interrelationship. Congress was particularly concerned, even where picketing for recognition or organization was otherwise permissible, that the question concerning representation which gave rise to the picketing be resolved as quickly as possible. It was for this reason that it provided for the filing of a petition pursuant to which the Board could direct an expedited election in which the employees could freely indicate their desires as to representation. If, in the free exercise of their choice, they designate the picketing union as their bargaining representative, that union will be certified and it will by the express terms of §8(b)(7) be exonerated from the strictures of that section. If, conversely, the employees reject the picketing union, that union will be barred from picketing for 12 months thereafter under the provisions of subparagraph (B).

The scheme which Congress thus devised represents what that legislative body deemed a practical accommodation between the right of a union to engage in legitimate picketing for recognition or organization and abuse of that right. One caveat must be noted. . . . The congressional scheme is, perforce, based on the premise that the election to be conducted under the first proviso to subparagraph (C) represents the free and uncoerced choice of the employee electorate. Absent such a free and uncoerced choice, the underlying question concerning representation is not resolved and, more particularly, subparagraph (B) which turns on the holding of a "valid election" does not become operative.

There remains to be considered only the second proviso to subpara-

---

[10] Congress plainly did not intend such a result. See Congressman Barden's statement (105 Daily Cong. Rec., A8062, September 2, 1959; 2 Legis. Hist. 1813). And the Board has ruled further that a charge filed by a picketing union or a person "fronting" for it may not be utilized to invoke an expedited election.

graph (C). In sum, that proviso removes the time limitation imposed upon, and preserves the legality of, recognition or oganization picketing falling within the ambit of subparagraph (C), where that picketing merely advises the public that an employer does not employ members of, or have a contract with, a union unless an effect of such picketing is to halt pickups or deliveries, or the performance of services. Needless to add, picketing which meets the requirements of the proviso also renders the expedited election procedure inapplicable.

Except for the final clause in §8(b)(7) which provides that nothing in that section shall be construed to permit any act otherwise proscribed under §8(b) of the Act, the foregoing sums up the limitations imposed upon recognition or organization picketing by the Landrum-Griffin amendments. However, . . . it is important to note that structurally, as well as grammatically, subparagraphs (A), (B), and (C) are subordinate to and controlled by the opening phrases of §8(b)(7). In other words, the thrust of all the §8(b)(7) provisions is only upon picketing for an object of recognition or organization, and not upon picketing for other objects. Similarly, both structurally and grammatically, the two provisos in subparagraph (C) appertain only to the situation defined in the principal clause of that subparagraph. . . .

[W]e . . . turn to a consideration of the instant case which presents issues going to the heart of [§8(b)(7)(C)].

. . . On February 2, 1960, all three common laborers employed by Blinne at the Fort Leonard Wood jobsite signed cards designating the Union to represent them for purposes of collective bargaining. The next day the Union demanded that Blinne recognize the Union as the bargaining agent for the three laborers. Blinne not only refused recognition but told the Union it would transfer one of the laborers, Wann, in order to destroy the Union's majority. Blinne carried out this threat and transferred Wann 5 days later, on February 8. Following this refusal to recognize the Union and the transfer of Wann the Union started picketing at Fort Wood. The picketing, which began on February 8, immediately following the transfer of Wann, had three announced objectives: (1) recognition of the Union; (2) payment of the Davis-Bacon scale of wages; and (3) protest against Blinne's unfair labor practices in refusing to recognize the Union and in threatening to transfer and transferring Wann.

The picketing continued, with interruptions due to bad weather, until at least March 11, 1960, a period of more than 30 days from the date the picketing commenced.[15] The picketing was peaceful, only one picket was on duty, and the picket sign he carried read "C.A. Blinne Construction Com-

[15] Subsequently, on April 5, 1960, upon application of the Regional Director, a temporary injunction restraining further picketing [was issued].

pany, unfair." The three laborers on the job (one was the replacement for Wann) struck when the picketing started.

The Union, of course, was not the certified bargaining representative of the employees. Moreover, no representation petition was filed during the more than 30 days in which picketing was taking place. On March 1, however, about 3 weeks after the picketing commenced and well within the statutory 30-day period, the Union filed unfair labor practice charges against Blinne, alleging violations of §8(a)(1), (2), (3), and (5). On March 22, the Regional Director dismissed the 8(a)(2) and (5) charges, whereupon the Union forthwith filed a representation petition under §9(c). . . . Subsequently, on April 20, the Regional Director approved a unilateral settlement agreement with Blinne with respect to the §8(a)(1) and (3) charges which had not been dismissed. In the settlement agreement, Blinne neither admitted nor denied that it had committed unfair labor practices.[17]

General Counsel argues that a violation of §8(b)(7)(C) has occurred within the literal terms of that provision because (1) the Union's picketing was concededly for an object of obtaining recognition; (2) the Union was not currently certified as the representative of the employees involved; and (3) no petition for representation was filed within 30 days of the commencement of the picketing. Inasmuch as the Union made no contention that its recognition picketing was "informational" within the meaning of the second proviso to subparagraph (C) or that it otherwise comported with the strictures of that proviso, General Counsel contends that a finding of unfair labor practice is required.

Respondent Union . . . points to the manifest inequity of such a finding and argues that Congress could not have intended so incongruous a result. In essence, its position is that it was entitled to recognition because it represented all the employees in the appropriate unit, that Blinne by a series of unfair labor practices deprived the Union and the employees it sought to represent of fundamental rights guaranteed by the Act, and that the impact of a finding adverse to the Union would be to punish the innocent and reward the wrongdoer. More specifically, Respondent argues that §8(b)(7)(C) was not intended to apply to picketing by a majority union and that, in any event, Blinne's unfair labor practices exonerated it from the statutory requirement of filing a timely representation petition.

The Trial Examiner found . . . that the Union represented all the employees in what he "assumed" in the absence of adequate evidence to be an appropriate unit. He found further that Blinne "not only rejected the

---

[17] [The union's representation petition filed on March 22] was dismissed on April 26, 1960, [because] "the unit sought appears . . . inappropriate and is . . . expected to go out of existence within about 4 months."

principle of collective bargaining but was willing to and did engage in further unfair labor practices to insure that his obligations under the statute would not be met." Notwithstanding that, in this frame of reference, "the equities . . . so obviously rest with the picketing union," the Trial Examiner "reluctantly" concluded that §8(b)(7) deprived employees of rights considered fundamental under other provisions of the Act. Accordingly, he found that Respondent Union had violated §8(b)(7)(C). . . .

In our view, the Trial Examiner has set up a false dichotomy. We do not believe that §8(b)(7) denies, or that Congress intended it to deny, fundamental rights theretofore guaranteed by the Act and still embodied in its provisions. We believe rather that the Trial Examiner's dilemma arose from his misconception of the structure of §8(b)(7), its operational interrelationship with the other provisions of the Act, and settled decisional law thereunder. . . .

Respondent, urging the self-evident proposition that a statute should be read as a whole, argues that §8(b)(7)(C) was not designed to prohibit picketing for recognition by a union enjoying majority status in an appropriate unit. Such picketing is for a lawful purpose inasmuch as §8(a)(5) and 9(a) of the Act specifically impose upon an employer the duty to recognize and bargain with a union which enjoys that status. Accordingly, Respondent contends, absent express language requiring such a result, §8(b)(7)(C) should not be read in derogation of the duty so imposed.

There is grave doubt that the argument here made is apposite in this case.[18] But, assuming its relevance, we find it to be without merit. To be sure, the legislative history is replete with references that Congress in framing the 1959 amendments was primarily concerned with "blackmail" picketing where the picketing union represented none or few of the employees whose allegiance it sought. Legislative references susceptible to an interpretation that Congress was concerned with the evils of majority picketing are sparse. Yet it cannot be gainsaid that §8(b)(7) by its explicit language exempts only "currently certified" unions from its proscriptions. Cautious as we should be to avoid a mechanical reading of statutory terms in involved legislative enactments, it is difficult to avoid giving the quoted words, essentially words of art, their natural construction. Moreover, such a construction is consonant with the underlying statutory scheme which is to resolve disputed issues of majority status, whenever possible, by the machinery of a Board election.

---

[18] The argument here is based, as it must be, on the premise that Respondent not only represented a majority of the employees but that this majority status was in an appropriate unit. The latter proposition is by no means established. The Trial Examiner "assumed" existence of an appropriate unit for purposes of his analysis. The dismissal of the 8(a)(5) charge and, particularly, the subsequent dismissal of the representation petition and the reason given therefor tend to invalidate his assumption.

Absent unfair labor practices or preelection misconduct warranting the setting aside of the election, majority unions will presumably not be prejudiced by such resolution. On the other hand, the admitted difficulties of determining majority status without such an election are obviated by this construction. . . .

We turn now to the second issue, namely, whether employer unfair labor practices are a defense to an 8(b)(7)(C) violation. . . . [T]he Union argues that Blinne was engaged in unfair labor practices within the meaning of §8(a)(1) and (3) . . . ; that it filed appropriate unfair labor practice charges against Blinne within a reasonable period of time after the commencement of the picketing; that it filed a representation petition as soon as the 8(a)(2) and (5) allegations of the charges were dismissed; that the 8(a)(1) and (3) allegations were in effect sustained and a settlement agreement was subsequently entered into with the approval of the Board; and that, therefore, this sequence of events should satisfy the requirements of §8(b)(7)(C).

The majority of the Board in the original Decision and Order rejected this argument. Pointing out that the representation petition was concededly filed more than 30 days after the commencement of the picketing, the majority concluded that the clear terms of §8(b)(7)(C) had been violated.

The majority also addressed itself specifically to the Union's contention that §8(b)(7)(C) could not have been intended by Congress to apply where an employer unfair labor practice had occurred. Its opinion alludes to the fact that the then Senator, now President, Kennedy had proposed statutory language to the effect that any employer unfair labor practice would be a defense to a charge of an 8(b)(7) violation both with respect to an application to the courts for a temporary restraining order and with respect to the unfair labor practice proceeding itself. The majority noted that the Congress did not adopt this proposal but instead limited itself merely to the insertion of a proviso in §10(1) prohibiting the application for a restraining order under §8(b)(7)(C) if there was reason to believe that a §8(a)(2) violation existed. Accordingly, the majority concluded that Congress had specifically rejected the very contention which Respondent urged.

The dissenting member in the original Decision . . . took sharp issue with the majority. In his view, the majority failed to "look to the provisions of the whole law and its object and policy" [citing Mastro Plastics Corp. v. NLRB, 350 U.S. 270, 285]. Conceding that §8(b)(7)(C) in terms outlawed recognition picketing for more than 30 days unless a representation petition was filed, he emphasized that the cited section also provided for an expedited election if such a petition was filed. The purpose of the election is to obtain a free and uncoerced expression of the employees' desires to their representation. Where unfair labor practices have taken place, however, such a free and uncoerced expression is precluded and the filing of a representation petition would be a futility. Indeed, consistent Board practice, presumably known to Congress, is to stay representation proceedings and elections thereunder until the effect of existing unremedied unfair labor practices is dissipated. Accordingly, the dissenting member concluded that the failure of a picketing union to file a timely petition in the face of employer unfair labor practices should not be made the basis for a finding of a violation under §8(b)(7)(C). . . .

The dissenting opinion likewise did not find the majority's reliance upon the proviso to §10(1) persuasive. On the basis of the relevant legislative history, the dissent concluded that this proviso was intended merely to implement §8(b)(7)(A) . . . , that is, to insure that a union which was the beneficiary of a "sweetheart agreement" with an employer could not derive the benefit of injunctive relief that would otherwise be accorded by virtue of the provisions of subparagraph (A).[22] . . .

Fortified by . . . deliberation as to the ramifications of the majority and minority opinions, we are now of the view that neither opinion affords a complete answer to the question here presented. It seems fair to say that Congress was unwilling to write an exemption into §8(b)(7)(C) dispensing with the necessity for filing a representation petition wherever employer unfair labor practices were alleged. . . . [T]hat the bill as ultimately enacted . . . did not contain the amendment to §10(1) which the Senate had adopted in S.1555 (see footnote 22, supra) cogently establishes that this reluctance was not due to oversight. On the other hand, it strains credulity to believe that Congress proposed to make the rights of unions and employees turn upon the results of an election which, because of the existence of unremedied unfair labor practices, is unlikely to reflect the true wishes of the employees.

We do not find ourselves impaled on the horns of this dilemma. Upon careful reappraisal of the statutory scheme we are satisfied that Congress meant to require, and did require, in an 8(b)(7)(C) situation, that a representation petition be filed within a reasonable period, not to exceed 30 days. By this device machinery can quickly be set in motion to resolve by a free and fair election the underlying question concerning representation out of which the picketing arises. This is the normal situation, and the situation which it is basically designed to serve.

There is legitimate concern, however, with the abnormal situation, that

[22] . . . [T]he dissent cites Cox, The Landrum-Griffin Amendments of the National Labor Relations Acts, 44 Minn. Law Rev. 257, 264-265 (1959). This acknowledged authority in the field, who was also close to the deliberations resulting in the Landrum-Griffin amendments, draws a like conclusion as to the 10(1) proviso.

is, the situation where because of unremedied unfair labor practices a free and fair election cannot be held. We believe Congress anticipated this contingency also. Thus, we find no mandate in the legislative scheme to compel the holding of an election pursuant to a representation petition where, because of unremedied unfair labor practices or for other valid reason, a free and uncoerced election cannot be held. On the contrary, the interrelated provisions of subparagraphs (B) and (C), by their respective references to a "valid election" and to a "certif[ication of] results" presuppose that Congress contemplated only a fair and free election. Only after such an election could the Board certify the results and only after such an election could the salutary provisions of subparagraph (B) become operative.

In our view, therefore, Congress intended that, except to the limited extent set forth in the first proviso, the Board in 8(b)(7)(C) cases follow the tried and familiar procedures it typically follows in representation cases where unfair labor practice charges are filed. That procedure, as already set forth, is to hold the representation case in abeyance and refrain from holding an election pending the resolution of the unfair labor practice charges. Thus, the fears that the statutory requirement for filing a timely petition will compel a union which has been the victim of unfair labor practices to undergo a coerced election are groundless. No action will be taken on that petition while unfair labor practice charges are pending, and until a valid election is held pursuant to that petition, the union's right to picket under the statutory scheme is unimpaired.

On the other side of the coin, it may safely be assumed that groundless unfair labor practice charges in this area, because of the statutory priority accorded §8(b)(7) violations, will be quickly dismissed. Following such dismissal an election can be directed forthwith upon the subsisting petition, thereby effectuating the congressional purpose. Moreover, . . . a timely petition . . . on file will protect the innocent union, which through a mistake of fact or law has filed a groundless unfair labor practice charge, from a finding of an 8(b)(7)(C) violation. Thus, the policy of the entire Act is effectuated and all rights guaranteed by its several provisions are appropriately safeguarded. . . .

The facts of the instant case may be utilized to demonstrate the practical operation of the legislative scheme. Here the union had filed unfair labor practice charges alleging violations by the employer of §§8(a)(1), (2), (3), and (5). . . . General Counsel found the allegations of 8(a)(2) and (5) violations groundless. Hence had these allegations stood alone and had a timely petition been on file, an election could have been directed forthwith and the underlying question concerning representation out of which the picketing arose could have been resolved pursuant to the statutory scheme. The failure to file a timely petition frustrated that scheme.[24]

On the other hand, the §8(a)(1) and (3) charges were found meritorious. Under these circumstances, and again consistent with uniform practice, no election would have been directed notwithstanding the currency of a timely petition; the petition would be held in abeyance pending a satisfactory resolution of the unfair labor practice charges.[25] The aggrieved union's right to picket would not be abated in the interim and the sole prejudice to the employer would be the delay engendered by its own unfair labor practices.[26] The absence of a timely petition, however, precludes disposition of the

[24] We would, however, have had a much different case here if the §8(a)(5) charge had been found meritorious so as to warrant issuance of a complaint. A representation petition assumes an unresolved question concerning representation. A §8(a)(5) charge, on the other hand, presupposes that no such question exists and that the employer is wrongfully refusing to recognize or bargain with a statutory bargaining representative. Because of this basic inconsistency, the Board has over the years uniformly refused to entertain representation petitions where a meritorious charge of refusal to bargain has been filed and, indeed, has dismissed any representation petition which may already have been on file. The same considerations apply where a meritorious §8(a)(5) charge is filed in a §8(b)(7)(C) context. Congressional acquiescence in the Board's long-standing practice prior to the enactment of §8(b)(7)(C) imports, in our view, congressional approval of a continuation of that practice thereafter. . . . Accordingly, where a meritorious 8(a)(5) charge was filed in an 8(b)(7)(C) situation, the Board dismissed the representation petition. See Robert P. Scott, Inc. v. Rothman, 46 L.R.R.M. 2793 (D.C.D.C.); Colony Materials, Inc. v. Rothman, 46 L.R.R.M. 2794 (D.C.D.C.). So here, if a meritorious 8(a)(5) charge had been filed, a petition for representation would not have been required.

But this situation . . . is not presented in the instant case and is footnoted here only to mark the boundaries of our holding in the situation which is presented. It is regrettable, therefore, that in respect to the *only* substantive matter discussed in their separate opinion our respected colleagues, Members Rodgers and Leedom, have focused their attention upon this fringe issue. Nevertheless, they do not persuade us even in this regard. We assert, to be sure, that the filing of a representation petition will not be required of a union when it has filed a meritorious 8(a)(5) charge, but will be required where it has filed other 8(a) charges. This point of the distinction — a point which our colleagues inexplicably ignore — is simply this: a meritorious 8(a)(5) case moots the question concerning representation which the petition is designed to resolve; other 8(a) charges merely delay the time when that unresolved question can be submitted to a free election by the employees. Indeed, our colleagues concede . . . that an 8(a)(5) charge, found meritorious after investigation, dictates a dismissal of a pending representation petition, and, hence, on their own analysis, to require the union to file a petition in such circumstances is to require the union to perform a futile act. [What is the impact, if any, of *Bernel Foam*, supra p. 441, on the foregoing reasoning? — EDS.]

[25] The Board's practice of declining to entertain, or dismissing, representation petitions does not apply to situations involving unlawful interference or unlawful discrimination. The inconsistency latent in the refusal-to-bargain situation is not present in the latter situations and uniform practice has been merely to hold such petitions in abeyance.

[26] . . . [W]e would not permit a union to benefit by itself committing unfair labor practices to delay the holding of an election and thereby stay the sanctions of §8(b)(7).

underlying question concerning representation which thus remains unresolved even after the §8(a)(1) and (3) charges are satisfactorily disposed of. Accordingly, to condone the refusal to file a timely petition in such situations would be to condone the flouting of a legislative judgment. Moreover, and most important, to impose a lesser requirement would fly in the face of the public interest which prompted that judgment.

Because we read §8(b)(7)(C) as requiring in the instant case the filing of a timely petition and because such a petition was admittedly not filed until more than 30 days after the commencement of the picketing, we find that Respondent violated §8(b)(7)(C). . . . As previously noted, it is undisputed that "an object" of the picketing was for recognition. It affords Respondent no comfort that its picketing was also in protest against the discriminatory transfer of an employee and against payment of wages at a rate lower than that prescribed by law. Had Respondent confined its picketing to these objectives rather than, as it did, include a demand for recognition, we believe none of the provisions of §8(b)(7) would be applicable.[29] Under the circumstances here, however, §8(b)(7)(C) is applicable.

Accordingly, having concluded as in the original decision herein that a

[29] As noted at the outset, §8(b)(7) is directed only at recognition and organization picketing and not at picketing for other objects including so-called protest picketing against unfair labor practices. . . . Absent other evidence (such as is present in this case) of an organizational, recognition, or bargaining objective it is clear that Congress did not consider picketing against unfair labor practices as such to be also for proscribed objectives and, hence, outlawed. Parenthetically, it follows that a cease-and-desist order issued against picketing in violation of §8(b)(7) will enjoin only picketing for recognition, bargaining, or organization and will not be a bar to protest picketing against unfair labor practices.

We are aware that this analysis runs counter to what the majority of the Board had held in Lewis Food Company, 115 N.L.R.B. 890, namely, that a strike to compel reinstatement of a discharged employee was necessarily a strike to force or require the employer "to recognize and bargain" with the union as to such matter. Implicit in that holding was the broader proposition that any strike or picketing in support of a demand which could be made through the process of collective bargaining was a strike or picketing for recognition or bargaining. Included in this category, presumably, would be picketing against substandard wages or working conditions in a competing plant, or a strike in support of an economic demand at a bargaining table where neither recognition nor willingness to bargain are really in issue but only the reluctance of the employer to grant the particular economic demand. Cf. Cartage [130 N.L.R.B. 558], a companion case to the instant case . . . which presents a closely related issue but in which a majority of the Board (Chairman McCulloch and Member Brown dissenting) voted to deny reconsideration. We might well concede that in the long view all union activity, including strikes and picketing, has the ultimate economic objective of organization and bargaining. But we deal here not with abstract economic ideology. Congress itself has drawn a sharp distinction between recognition and organization picketing and other forms of picketing, thereby recognizing, as we recognize, that a real distinction does exist. The Lewis Food issue and its ramifications are not crucial in this case. Moreover, the Lewis Food case itself has now been reversed in any event. Local 259, International Union United Automobile, etc. (Fanelli Ford Sales, Inc.), 133 N.L.R.B. 1468. . . .

violation of §8(b)(7)(C) has occurred, albeit for differing reasons, we reaffirm the Order entered therein.

Members Rodgers and Leedom, in separate opinions, adhered to the majority opinion originally issued herein, and Member Fanning concurred in part and dissented in part.

NOTES

1. In assessing the NLRB's claim that through its approach "the policy of the entire act is effectuated and all rights guaranteed by its several provisions are appropriately safeguarded," consider the following:

(a) A union's charge that a discharge violates §8(a)(3) leads to a complaint ultimately dismissed by the Board. While the Board's machinery is operating, picketing may lawfully take place; the employer, despite the ultimate dismissal of that complaint, has no remedy for the economic loss involved. Is picketing an appropriate extrastatutory remedy for merely plausible, or, indeed, meritorious unfair labor practice charges? Is such picketing conducted in connection with organizational activity likely to supersede the election machinery and majority rule where economically weak employers are involved?

(b) Does §8(b)(7) limit picketing during an organizational campaign, in protest against a discharge that is manifestly for good cause and that is not even alleged to be an unfair labor practice?

(c) A union pickets for both recognition and in protest against allegedly coercive interrogation by the employer and files an election petition as well as an unfair labor practice charge within a "reasonable period" after the picketing began. The Board issues a complaint. Would it be desirable to condition the Board's suspension of the election machinery, pending disposition of that complaint, on the union's abandonment of recognitional picketing after a "reasonable period"?

2. Which of the following activities by union agents constitute "picketing" under §8(b)(7): (a) handbilling persons approaching an employer's premises (see Teamsters Local 688 (Levitz Furniture Co.), 205 N.L.R.B. 1131 (1973)); (b) affixing signs to trees and retiring to adjacent cars while remaining visible to passersby and speaking to those approaching an employer's premises (see NLRB v. Furniture Workers, 337 F.2d 936 (2d Cir. 1964)); (c) skywriting "unfair" over an employer's premises; (d) announcing "unfair" over a sound truck operating close to an employer's premises?

3. After a bargaining deadlock over the terms of a renewal agreement, the union, which had majority support, struck. A week later, the employer

permanently replaced all strikers and, alleging a good-faith doubt of the union's majority status, terminated negotiations. The union's 8(a)(5) charge was dismissed. The union continued to picket for three months after the beginning of the strike, without filing a petition for an election. In dismissing the complaint based on §8(b)(7)(C), the Board relied on the concern about the evils of "blackmail picketing" reflected in the legislative history and on statements therein that the proposed 1959 legislation would not impair the right to strike and picket for better conditions. See Warehouse Emp., Local 570, 149 N.L.R.B. 731 (1964). But cf. Penello v. Warehouse Employees, Local 570, 230 F. Supp. 892, 898-899 (D. Md. 1964).

4. A union seeking to represent guards began to picket and simultaneously filed an election petition even though §9(b)(3) foreclosed certification because the union admitted into membership other employees as well as guards. That petition was dismissed five days after filing, but the union continued to picket for ten more days. Should the filing of a petition that does not raise a question of representation be a nullity under §8(b)(7)(C), and should picketing by a noncertifiable union violate §8(b)(7)(C) or (B), ab initio? The Board answered "yes" to both questions. See Teamsters Local 71 (Wells Fargo), 221 N.L.R.B. 1240 (1975), enforced, 553 F.2d 1368 (D.C. Cir. 1977). Consider the possible effect of this approach on picketing by unions deemed ineligible for a Board election under the standards considered in Chapter 6.

5. A union, bypassing the National Mediation Board, pickets a firm subject to the Railway Labor Act, for recognition. The picketing continues for 15 days, and employees of other firms refuse to cross the picket line. The picketed firm sues for an injunction in a federal district court. What result? Cf. Summit Airlines v. Teamsters Local 295, 628 F.2d 787 (2d Cir. 1980); Brotherhood of R.R. Trainmen v. Jacksonville Terminal Co., infra p. 754.

Smitley v. NLRB
327 F.2d 351 (9th Cir. 1964)

[The unions picketed a cafeteria for more than 30 days before filing a representation petition under §9(c). . . . An object of the picketing was to secure recognition. The purpose of the picketing was truthfully to advise the public that petitioners employed nonunion employees or had no contract with the unions. The picketing did not induce any stoppage of deliveries or services to the cafeteria by employees of any other employer. The Board first concluded (3 to 2) that the picketing did violate §8(b)(7)(C) (Hotel & Restaurant Employees Local 681 (Crown Cafeteria), 130 N.L.R.B. 570

(1961)), and then, following a change in membership, upheld (3 to 2) the picketing (135 N.L.R.B. 1183 (1964)). The court affirmed the Board's second decision.]

DUNIWAY, J. . . . The Board states its interpretation of the section . . . as follows:

> Congress framed a general rule covering all organizational or recognitional picketing carried on for more than 30 days without the filing of a representation petition. Then, Congress excepted from that rule picketing which, although it had an organizational or recognitional objective, was addressed primarily to the public, was truthful in nature, and did not interfere to any significant extent with deliveries or the rendition of services by the employees of any other employer.

We think that this is the correct interpretation. . . . Subdivision (7) of subsection (b), §8, quoted above, starts with the general prohibition of picketing "where an object thereof is forcing or requiring an employer to recognize or bargain with a labor organization" (This is often called recognitional picketing) " . . . or forcing or requiring the employees of an employer to accept or select such labor organization. . . . " (This is often called organizational picketing)," . . . unless such labor organization is currently certified as the representative of such employees: . . . . " This is followed by three subparagraphs, (A), (B) and (C). . . . (C), with which we are concerned, refers to a situation "where" there has been no petition for an election under §9(c) filed within a reasonable period of time, not to exceed thirty days, from the commencement of the picketing. Thus, §8(b)(7) does not purport to prohibit all picketing having the named "object" of recognitional or organizational picketing. It limits the prohibition of such picketing to three specific situations.

There are no exceptions or provisos in subparagraphs (A) and (B), which describe two of those situations. There are, however, two provisos in subparagraph (C). The first sets up a special procedure for an expedited election under §9(c). The second is the one with which we are concerned. It is an exception to the prohibition of "such picketing," i.e., recognitional or organizational picketing, being a proviso to a prohibition of such picketing "where" certain conditions exist. It can only mean, indeed, it says, that "such picketing," which otherwise falls within subparagraph (C), is not prohibited if it falls within the terms of the proviso. That proviso says that subparagraph (C) is not to be construed to prohibit "any picketing" for "the purpose" of truthfully advising the public (including consumers) that an employer does not employ members of, or have a contract with, a labor organization. To this exception there is an exception, stated in the last "unless" clause, namely, that "such picketing," i.e., picketing where "an object" is recognitional or organizational, but which has "the" excepting "purpose," would still be illegal if an effect were to induce any individual employee of other persons not to pick up, deliver, or transport any goods, or not to perform any services. Admittedly, the picketing here does not fall within the "unless" clause in the second proviso to subparagraph (C). It does however, fall within the proviso, since it does have "the purpose" that brings it within the proviso. It also has "an object" that brings it within the first sentence of subsection (b) and the first clause of subdivision (7), and within the circumstances stated in the opening clause of subparagraph (C). If it did not have "an object" bringing it within subdivision (7), it would not be prohibited at all. Moreover, if it did have that "object," it still would not be prohibited at all, unless it occurred in circumstances described in subparagraph (A), (B) or (C). Here, neither (A) or (B) applies; (C) does. But, unlike (A) or (B), it has an excepting proviso. Unless that proviso refers to picketing having as "an object" either recognition or organization, it can have no meaning, for it would not be an exception or proviso to anything. It would be referring to conduct not prohibited in section 8(b) at all.

Petitioners urge that if the picketing has as "an object" recognition or organization, then it is still illegal, even though it has "the purpose" of truthfully advising the public, etc., within the meaning of the second proviso to subparagraph (C). It seems to us, as it did to the Board, that to so construe the statute would make the proviso meaningless. The hard realities of union-employer relations are such that it is difficult, indeed almost impossible, for us to conceive of picketing falling within the terms of the proviso that did not also have as "an object" obtaining a contract with the employer. This is normally the ultimate objective of any union in relation to an employer who has employees whose jobs fall within the categories of employment that are within the jurisdiction of the union, which is admittedly the situation here.

. . . [T]he Second Circuit has reached a similar conclusion. In NLRB v. Local 3, International Bhd. Electrical Workers, 2d Cir., 1963, 317 F.2d 193, that court . . . said:

> It seems, however, much more realistic to suppose that Congress framed a general rule covering the field of recognitional and organizational picketing, conducted under alternate sets of circumstances described in subparagraphs (A), (B), and (C), and then excepted from the operation of the rule, as it applied to the circumstances set forth in subparagraph (C), a comparatively innocuous species of picketing having the immediate purpose of informing or advising the public, even though its ultimate object was success in recognition and organization. . . .

One of the principal difficulties in construing and applying subparagraph

(C) is that §8(b)(7) contains the partially synonymous words, "object" and "purpose," used in two distinct contexts but to which much of the same evidence is relevant. These are: "where an object thereof is forcing or requiring an employer to recognize or bargain . . . " and "for the purpose of truthfully advising the public. . . . " It does not necessarily follow that, where an object of the picketing is forcing or requiring an employer to recognize or bargain, the purpose of the picketing, in the context of the second proviso, is not truthfully to advise the public, etc. The union may legitimately have a long range or strategic objective of getting the employer to bargain with or recognize the union and still the picketing may be permissive. This proviso gives the union freedom to appeal to the unorganized public for spontaneous popular pressure upon an employer; it is intended, however, to exclude the invocation of pressure by organized labor groups or members of unions, as such.

The permissible picketing is, therefore, that which through the dissemination of certain allowed representations, is designed to influence members of the unorganized public, as individuals, because the impact upon the employer by way of such individuals is weaker, more indirect and less coercive. . . .

Both sides have reviewed legislative history. We think this unnecessary, because we think that the meaning of the statute is clear. We also find the history inconclusive, but it seems to us to point somewhat more strongly toward the view that we here adopt than to the contrary view. Petitioners rely on language used by Senator Kennedy, who was one of the sponsors of the bill in the Senate and one of the Senate Conferees, in which he referred to the second proviso as permitting "purely informational" picketing. Counsel for petitioners frankly conceded, however, at oral argument, that most of the legislative history is against the view that he urged, and we agree. A discussion of legislative history appears in the dissent to the Board's first opinion (130 N.L.R.B. 576-577) and we therefore do not repeat it here. We think that even Senator Kennedy's comment, upon which petitioners most heavily rely, taken in context, was not intended to have the limiting effect which petitioners would give it. Senator Kennedy was more concerned, on the one hand, with the economic pressure involved in recognitional and organizational picketing, and on the other hand, with the right of labor truthfully to advise the public that the employer was nonunion, or that the employer did not have a contract with the union, than he was with whether or not, in addition to having an informational purpose described in the proviso, there was also a recognitional or organizational object. See 105 Cong. Rec. 17,898 (1959). See also Cox, The Landrum-Griffin Amendments to the National Labor Relations Act, 44 Minn. L. Rev. 258, 267. Mr. Cox, now the Solicitor General, was then Senator Kennedy's chief advisor on the bill.

We think that, in substance, the effect of the second proviso to subparagraph (C) is to allow recognitional or organizational picketing to continue if it meets two important restrictions: (1) it must be addressed to the public and be truthful and (2) it must not induce other unions to stop deliveries or services. The picketing here met those criteria. . . .

NOTES

1. In determining whether informational picketing is protected by the second proviso of §8(b)(7)(C), the NLRB, at least in the case of retail firms, has considered the "actual impact" on the business and has rejected a "quantitative" test based solely on the number of deliveries aborted or services withheld. See Retail Clerks, 138 N.L.R.B. 478 (1962), aff'd 328 F.2d 431 (9th Cir. 1964). (The union picketed eighteen stores for about twelve weeks and took steps to insure no interruption of services. The Board held that three delivery stoppages, two work delays, and several delivery delays did not constitute the "effect" contemplated by the proviso, absent any evidence as to their impact on the employer's business.) Cf. San Diego County Waiters & Bartenders Union, Local 500, 138 N.L.R.B. 470 (1962) (failure of all trucks to deliver constituted sufficient "effect" to make the second proviso inapplicable, even though employers obtained supplies from warehouses and from trucks several blocks from the restaurant).

2. When recognitional picketing is not protected by the second proviso of §8(b)(7)(C), and when a petition has been filed, the employer may secure an expedited election by filing a charge even though he does so at the beginning of the "reasonable period" provided for in that section. The Board will dismiss the charge and hold the election. What considerations will be relevant to an employer's decision to seek an expedited election by filing a charge and petition?

3. If recognitional picketing continues for more than 30 days without the filing of a petition, can an expedited election be secured? If not, what action can be taken to stop the picketing? See §10(l) of the Act.

4. Five construction unions, each taking turns for less than 30 days, picketed a nonunion building contractor employing crafts within their respective jurisdictions. Although finding that this "relay picketing" resulted from the unions' common understanding, a Board majority held that the evidence failed to show that the unions had been engaged in a "joint enterprise," and, accordingly, held that their picketing was not to be aggregated for the purpose of the 30-day limitation in §8(b)(7)(C). The Board was, however, unanimous in aggregating intermittent picketing during an eight-week period by one of the participating unions even though that union had not picketed continuously for 30 days. Operating Engrs., Local 4, 193 N.L.R.B. 632 (1971).

5. Several employees participated in picketing found by the NLRB to be in violation of §8(b)(7)(B). Several other employees struck, but did not picket, for the same recognitional purpose. The Board (2 to 1) held that the pickets, but not the strikers, could be lawfully discharged. See Local 707, Motor Freight Drivers (Claremont Polychem. Corp.), 196 N.L.R.B. 613 (1972).

Is the distinction between strikers and pickets consistent with footnote 7 of *Local 1229*, supra p. 230? Should participation in illegal activity, regardless of the uncertainty of the governing law and of the failure of the employer to warn the offending employees that they are risking their jobs, automatically justify discharge?

International Hod Carriers, Local 41 (Calumet Contractors Assn.), 133 N.L.R.B. 512 (1961), supplementing 130 N.L.R.B. 78 (1961). Several months after another union had been certified as the bargaining representative for employees in a multiemployer unit, the Hod Carriers' local picketed the employees' entrance of a member of that unit, for the stated purpose of forcing it, as well as the larger unit, to pay prevailing wages. Although the local disclaimed any interest in representation, it had intervened, along with other craft unions, in the prior election in order to contest the appropriate unit. Initially the Board, by a unanimous three-member panel, found that the picketing had been designed to force bargaining or recognition by the employer, in violation of §8(b)(4)(C). After reconsideration, the full Board dismissed the complaint and declared:

"We hold that Respondent's admitted objective to require the Association and DeJong to conform standards of employment to those prevailing in the area, is not tantamount to, nor does it have an objective of, recognition or bargaining. A union may legitimately be concerned that a particular employer is undermining area standards of employment by maintaining lower standards. It may be willing to forgo recognition and bargaining provided subnormal working conditions are eliminated from area considerations. We are of the opinion that §8(b)(4)(C) does not forbid such an objective.

"It may be argued — with some justification — that picketing by an outside union when another union has newly won Board certification is an unwarranted harassment of the picketed employer. But this is an argument that must be addressed to Congress. §8(b)(4)(C), as we read it, does not contain a broad proscription against all types of picketing. It forbids only picketing with the objective of obtaining recognition and bargaining. On the record before us, Respondent clearly disclaimed such an objective and sought only to eliminate subnormal working conditions from area considerations. As this objective could be achieved without the Employer either bargaining with or recognizing Respondent, we cannot reasonably conclude that Respondent's objective in picketing DeJong was to obtain recognition or bargaining. Accordingly, we find no violation of §8(b)(4)(C) . . . in the circumstances of this case. . . ."

Members Rodgers and Leedom, dissenting: "We do not agree with our colleagues that Respondent's picketing did not have as an objective 'recognition or bargaining' with the Association and DeJong. . . . [D]espite the disclaimer of interest in recognition or bargaining by the Respondent, picketing for a change in the prevailing rates of pay and conditions of employment agreed upon between a certified bargaining agent and an employer constitutes an attempt to obtain conditions and concessions normally resulting from collective bargaining. Thus, Respondent's picketing clearly was an attempt by Respondent to force itself upon the employees as their bargaining agent, for, under the circumstances in this case, Respondent's picketing must necessarily have had as its ultimate end the substitution of Respondent for the certified bargaining agent. Such an objective is clearly proscribed by §8(b)(4)(C). . . ."

NOTES

1. Is the supplemental decision compatible with the employer's duty to bargain and with the certified union's exclusive bargaining rights? Could the picketed employer, during the term of his agreement with the incumbent union, have lawfully conformed to "area standards" without prior bargaining and agreement with that union? See J.I. Case Co. v. NLRB, infra p. 799, and NLRB v. Katz, infra p. 838.

2. A union, without demanding recognition from an unorganized employer, pickets against "substandard wages" for more than 30 days without filing a petition; the employees of truckers and other secondary employers respect the picket line; and "substantial interference" with the picketed employer's operations results from the picketing. Has the union violated §8(b)(7)(C)? See Houston Bldg. Council, 136 N.L.R.B. 321 (1962).

3. A union, disclaiming any recognitional objective, picketed with placards protesting the employer's failure to meet area standards. Would it be material to a charge of an 8(b)(7) violation: (a) that the union demanded employee benefits substantially the same as those in the union agreement; (b) that the union had failed to investigate the employer's labor costs; or (c) disregarded his offer to eliminate any difference? See Retail Clerks, Local 899, 166 N.L.R.B. 818 (1967), enforced per curiam, 404 F.2d 855 (9th Cir. 1968); Teamsters Union (Alpha Beta Acme Mkts.), 205 N.L.R.B. 462

(1973). See generally Rosen, Area Standards Picketing, 23 Lab. L.J. 67 (1972); Note, 1968 Duke L.J. 767.

4. A union pickets a general construction contractor, for a clause limiting his subcontracting to unionized subcontractors. Does the requested clause evidence a recognitional objective? Would it be material that the general contractor never uses his own employees to perform work of the kind to be covered by the subcontracting clause? See North Central Montana Bldg. & Constr. Trades Council, 222 N.L.R.B. 176 (1976) (supplemental decision). What if the general contractor had not recognized any other union?

Cf. *Connell Constr. Co.*, infra p. 664.

D.   VIOLENCE AND COERCION

Violence in American labor relations has a long history, with many controversies about the comparative guilt of labor and management for the "small wars" that sometimes broke out. See Taft & Ross, American Labor Violence: Its Causes, Character, and Outcome, in 1 Violence in America: Historical and Comparative Perspectives 221 (H. Graham & T. Gurr eds. 1969); A. Thieblot, Jr. & T. Haggard, Union Violence: The Record and the Response by Courts, Legislatures, and the NLRB, ch. II (1984) (reviewing NLRB cases).

Section 8(b)(1) is the provision of the Act most directly aimed at union violence, although violence may accompany union violations of other provisions of the Act and may also influence remedies for employer misconduct, such as violations of §8(a)(5).

This section will seek to introduce only three issues: first, the general scope of §8(b)(1)(A); second, the standards established by the Act for vicarious responsibility of labor organizations for violence; and, finally, the propriety of the NLRB's refusal, in general, to order back pay for employees deterred from working by union violence, actual or threatened.

United Furniture Workers of America
81 N.L.R.B. 886 (1949)

1. We find, as did the Trial Examiner, that the following conduct attributable to the Respondents or their agents . . . constituted restraint

and coercion within the meaning of §8(b)(1)(A): (1) the carrying of sticks by the pickets on the picket line; (2) the open piling of bricks for use by the pickets; (3) the blocking of plant entrances by (a) railroad ties, (b) automobiles, (c) raised gutter plates, and (d) tacks; (4) the threat of violence to the nonstriking employees over the loudspeaker; (5) the threats of bodily harm to [four] nonstriking employees [named]; (6) the intimidation of and threats of violence to nonstriking employees, including specifically Walter Hilton, Milt Trinkle, Ralph Dobbins, Mabel Asher,[2] and Mirel Mount, as they sought to enter the plant; (7) the warning given nonstriking employee Albert Holt that "when we get in with the Union you old fellows won't have a job";[3] (8) the placing of pickets in such a manner as to prevent nonstriking employees from performing their work during the boxcar incidents; (9) the "goon squad" mass assaults upon various nonstriking employees, and the overturning of the automobile belonging to employee James Hyde on that occasion; (10) the assaults committed upon nonstriking employees Hobart Walton, Homer Williams, and Walter Brickey, and upon nonstriking employee Rowe White and his family; (11) the damage to the automobile of White during the aforesaid assault; (12) the barring from the plant of Superintendent Simpson and Foreman McKinney by force and intimidation; (13) the assaults upon Superintendent Simpson; and (14) the attempt to upset Foreman McKinney's automobile as he sought to enter the plant, and the damage thereto as McKinney later drove past the plant.

The Respondents contend that (1) inasmuch as the Company's refusal to bargain precipitated the strike the Board should not "lend" its support to the Company by processing this complaint, (2) that their activity herein was and is protected by the 1st and 5th Amendments to the Constitution and that §8 (b)(1)(A) is unconstitutional and void insofar as it proscribes that activity,

---

[2] Asher sought to enter the plant merely for the purpose of getting her tools. The illegality of the conduct which prevented her from doing so lies therefore, not in the interference with an employee's right to work in the face of a strike, . . . but in the effort to coerce her into joining the Unions or participating in the concerted activity.

[3] The majority finds this statement to be coercive because it is a threat of loss of employment reasonably calculated to have an effect on the listener without regard to the question of the Unions' ability to carry out the threat.

Chairman Herzog and Member Houston do not rely upon this statement in finding a violation of §8(b)(1)(A). . . . They find that the threat of loss of employment inherent in this remark was not reasonably calculated to restrain or coerce employee Holt, because the Unions, even if eventually successful in gaining recognition, were powerless, under the amended Act, to affect Holt's employment status with the Company (unless, of course, a union-shop contract was then properly executed and Holt refused to become a union member or was unwilling to pay union initiation fees or periodic dues). In these circumstances they view such a declaration, the implementation of which is deferred, and conditioned upon a circumstance not certain to happen in the first place, and impossible of accomplishment in any event, as falling within the protection of §8(c). . . .

and (3) that the above acts, even if committed, do not constitute restraint or coercion for the reasons that (a) they failed to accomplish their purpose of deterring the employees from working during the course of the strike, and (b) the interference with the right to work in the face of a strike is not, in any event, a violation of the Act.

. . . [W]e find these contentions to be without merit. With respect to the first contention, we have heretofore held that the single issue in cases of this type is whether or not the Respondent has unlawfully restrained and coerced *employees* by its activities during the course of a strike, and that employer practices which prompted the calling of the strike are not material to the resolution of that issue.[6] We therefore find it unnecessary to consider, as did the Trial Examiner, the propriety of the Company's refusal to recognize and bargain with the Unions. The second contention raises a constitutional question which we leave to the courts, it being inappropriate for us to pass upon the validity of congressional enactments. As to the issues raised by the third contention, we hold, as we did in the *Sunset* case, (1) that to constitute restraint and coercion within the meaning of the Act, it is immaterial that the acts in question, which we find were calculated to restrain and coerce employees in the exercise of rights guaranteed by §7 . . . , failed to accomplish that purpose, and (2) that the interdependent guarantees of §8(b)(1)(A) and §7 . . . include the protected right of employees to work in the face of a strike.

The Respondents further argue that the Board is not warranted in finding that the acts directed against the Company's supervisors violated §8(b)(1)(A) because that Section protects "employees" only. However, . . . with respect to the incidents involving Superintendent Simpson and Foreman McKinley, adverted to above, . . . nonstriking employees witnessed them, or were in the immediate vicinity at the time of their occurrence . . . We find . . . that these employees might have reasonably regarded these incidents as a reliable indication of what would befall them if they sought to work during the strike. The coercive effect of such conduct on "employees" within the meaning of the Act is therefore clear. And inasmuch as the illegality of coercive activity directed against supervisors is found to depend upon its commission in the presence of nonstriking employees or under such circumstances as to insure that these employees would hear of it, we shall reject the Trial Examiner's findings with respect to the threats to company officials which were not made in such a context. Accordingly, we do not find, as did the Trial Examiner, that §8(b)(1)(A) was violated by Burger's warnings to the Company's president and vice president

[6] Matter of Sunset Line and Twine Company, 79 N.L.R.B. 1487.

that there would be "trouble" if they attempted to bring cars into the plant, and that the windshields of such cars would be smashed.

2. We do not agree with the Trial Examiner's findings that the statement by Burger to employee Mount, who was voicing objection to using the Company's lumber for picketing purposes, that he Burger, "knowed where . . . [Mount] live[d]," violated the Act. Under the circumstances, we regard this statement as too vague to constitute restraint and coercion within the meaning of the Act.

3. We [conclude] that both the Local and the International should be charged with responsibility for the various acts of restraint and coercion. . . . We have considered the facts herein in the light of the common law rule of agency, controlling in cases of this type, that a principal may be responsible for the act of his agent within the scope of the agent's authority, even though the principal has not specifically authorized or, indeed, may have specifically forbidden the act in question.

. . . [T]he several individuals named as Respondents, as well as George Little and Oscar Spurgeon, assumed leading roles in the calling of the strike and in the conduct thereof, and either personally engaged in the unlawful strike activity or directed and incited the others who took part therein. . . .

That these individuals had the authority to bind the Unions is established unequivocally by the record. Thus, during all time material herein Fulford was not only the International's Regional Director of District 6, which encompassed the Company's plant in Indiana, but also its International representative and its district representative on the General Executive Board. During this same period, Quimby was one of four International representatives serving under Fulford. Fulford, in his capacities as International representative and district representative, and Quimby, as an International representative, were members of the International's organizational department, and both operated under the general direction of the International's director of organization. The International paid Quimby's entire salary, 50 percent of Fulford's salary, and all the latter's expenses.

The other individual Respondents, as well as George Little and Oscar Spurgeon, were the principal officers of the Local and the members of its Executive Board which, during the strike meeting, was authorized by the membership to take such action as it deemed necessary to "get the Company to recognize the Union." This delegation of power included the authority to call the strike and to direct the manner in which the strike was conducted. Burger, Mays, Smedley, Gorman, and Jackson were also members of the Local's strike committee which was created at the strike meeting, and Harmon also had occasion to serve thereon.

In view of the foregoing, and based upon the entire record,[15] we find that the officials of the International and the local referred to above were acting as agents of their respective organizations while engaged in the calling of the strike, and in the strike activity which we have found to be unlawful. It is equally plain that these individuals were acting within the scope of their authority on these occasions, for the strike was admittedly precipitated by the Company's refusal to bargain with the International or the Local, and the strike activity which we have characterized as unlawful was obviously designed to make a success of the strike by hampering the Company's operations for the purpose of forcing it into granting recognition. We therefore conclude and find that the acts of restraint and coercion which they committed, directed, or incited became, at the least, the acts of their respective principals, the Unions herein, and that each Union thereby violated §8(b)(1)(A). . . . It is additionally clear from the foregoing that the International and the Local, charged as they are with the acts of their agents herein, did not act independently of one another in calling the strike and in the strike activity, but that their participation therein was in the nature of a joint venture. We find further, therefore, that the International and the Local are responsible, as found above, not only for the acts committed and directed by their respective agents, but that both the Unions are responsible for all the acts which we have attributed to either of them.[16]

4. We agree with the Trial Examiner that the individuals named as Respondents also violated the Act. However, we do not, under the circumstances of this case, thereby adopt the Trial Examiner's subsidiary findings (a) that the pickets on the picket line were agents of the individual Respondents, and (b) that each individual Respondent is chargeable with the unlawful acts of any one of them. Rather we rest our finding solely upon the fact that each of the individual Respondents, by participating in acts of restraint and coercion as an agent of the Unions in furtherance of the purposes of the strike thereby individually violated the Act.

THE REMEDY

Although the Trial Examiner finds, as do we, that the Unions as well as the individual Respondents violated §8(b)(1)(A) of the Act, his recommended

---

[15] . . . Of consequence herein . . . is Fulford's testimony that he "assumes" (1) that he recommended a strike to the Local, (2) that he consulted the International "before going into anything as serious as a strike," and (3) that the International in accordance with its policy, was consulted by the Local before the strike was called.

[16] In so concluding, we find it unnecessary to adopt the Trial Examiner's finding that the Unions' act of setting up a picket line at the Company's plant entrances raised a presumption in law that the individuals on the picket line were their agents with authority to act for, and bind, them as principals.

order is not coextensive with that finding in that it is directed against the Unions alone. We shall accordingly correct this apparent inadvertence and include these individuals within the scope of our order herein.

Transportation Union, Local 1023
187 N.L.R.B. 406 (1970)

MILLER, Chairman, dissenting in part: . . . The incidents in question occurred at the Washington and Philadelphia bus terminals owned or operated by Safeway or its subsidiaries and utilized by Capitol Bus in its operations. Two incidents occurred at the Washington terminal. In one, McGuire, the president of Capitol who was riding on a Capitol bus, told pickets that they should stop annoying customers and intimidating employees with their remarks and indicated he would get an injunction to stop such activity if necessary. There was credited testimony that King, one of the pickets replied that "we will put 50 people on the sidewalk without picket signs to take care of you" and to "keep Capitol out." The second Washington incident occurred on June 13, 1969, when picket Hawkins approached Van Atta, Capitol's vice president and told him to tell McGuire that "I am going to punch him in the nose, that I'm captain of this picket line." The same picket cursed Van Atta in obscene terms a few days later and threatened to mop up the sidewalk with him. The picket later apologized to Van Atta for this latter conversation.

There were three separate incidents at the Philadelphia terminal on August 21, 1969, when Capitol buses driven by supervisors were prevented for 5 to 10 minutes from entering the terminal by pickets who massed in front of the buses. Special policemen stationed at the terminal during the course of the strike were called upon to remove the pickets so the buses could enter.

The Trial Examiner recommended dismissing these incidents on the ground, inter alia, that responsibility of the Respondent could not be inferred for the conduct since no representative or agent of Respondent was at the scene when the unlawful conduct took place, and there was no showing that the Respondent Union adopted or ratified the pickets' misconduct. This rationale, in my opinion, leads to condonation of picket line misconduct in many §8(b)(4) situations and overlooks the realities involved, particularly in this case. Contrary to my colleagues and the Trial Examiner, I have no difficulty concluding that Respondent was responsible for the conduct in which its pickets engaged and the record supports such a conclusion.

Thus, Respondent has admitted that it authorized the strike against

Safeway and that it established these picket lines at places where it was aware that other employers did business. Additionally, in Washington, the Respondent was in close touch with its picket lines — so close in fact that its union hall was just across the street and two doors down from the terminal where the pickets were engaged in their picket duties. Not only did the Union vice chairman visit the picket line daily, but individuals in charge of the union hall visited the picket line hourly. The union officials scheduled pickets for picket duty, the pickets were paid to picket by the Respondent, and the pickets were wearing authorized picket signs. Apparently, the situation was the same at Philadelphia, except that the Respondent's strike headquarters were in a restaurant near the terminal, and picket captains were on the picket line at times. Furthermore, the record establishes that buses were blocked in Philadelphia on enough occasions that it became necessary to have a labor policeman constantly stationed at that terminal. Inasmuch as the unlawful activity did recur, it is reasonable to infer that the Union would have to have had some knowledge of the activity on its picket line there.

All of the above factors lead me to conclude, as my colleagues did, in adopting the Trial Examiner's Decision in *Pellitteri Trucking*,[4] that "a union which calls a strike and authorizes picketing must retain control over the pickets in whatever manner it deems necessary, in order to insure that they do not act improperly. If a union is unwilling, or unable, to take the necessary steps to control its pickets, it must then bear the responsibility for their misconduct." This is especially true in situations where neutrals are involved and innocent persons become the victims of the union's unlawful conduct.[5]

NOTE

Union responsibility for violence and other conduct in a variety of contexts is discussed in Evans, The Law of Agency and the National Union, 49 Ky. L.J. 295 (1961); Note, 63 Harv. L. Rev. 1035 (1950); Parker, The Liability of Labor Unions for Picket Line Assaults, 21 U.C.L.A. L. Rev. 600 (1973). See also Chapter 7(H), infra.

---

[4] Drivers, Salesman, Warehousemen, Cannery, [Dairy Employees and Helpers Union], Local 695, IBT, and its agents Donald Eaton and Eugene Machkovitz . . . , 174 N.L.R.B. No. 115.

[5] This view of union responsibility for results of actions which it sets in motion would appear to be supported by the plain words of §2(13) of the Act. . . .

Union de Tronquistas de Puerto Rico, Local 901 (Lock Joint Pipe & Co. of Puerto Rico)
202 N.L.R.B. 399 (1973)

. . . The [NLRB] has considered the record and the [ALJ's] Decision in light of the exceptions and briefs and has decided to affirm the ALJ's rulings, findings, and conclusions and to adopt his recommended Order, as modified below.

We agree with the ALJ that Respondent Union violated §8(b)(1)(A) by engaging in threats and picket line violence at the Lock Joint Plant in Puerto Rico beginning on August 9, 1971.

We do not, however, agree with his further recommendation that the proper remedy in this case, contrary to Board precedent, is an order directing the Union to give backpay to all employees who did not work as a result of these unfair labor practices. From the very earliest days of the Taft-Hartley Act the desirability of such a remedy has been argued to the Board. . . . The Board has refused to enlarge the scope of its traditional remedies for picket line misconduct. The latest Board decision, Long Construction Company, 145 NLRB 554, involved physical injury to employees attempting to cross the picket line. The Board reiterated its view that a backpay order was not appropriate where the union's unfair labor practices involved solely interference with an employee's right of ingress to his place of employment.

These important decisions have stood the test of 24 years of court litigation and Congressional scrutiny. They have not been reversed or nullified and we do not believe the time has come for the Board itself to take that step. National Cash Register Co., et al. v. NLRB, 466 F.2d 945, on which our dissenting colleagues rely, stands only for the well-established principle that where an employer unlawfully prevents an employee from working at the insistence of a union both are jointly and severally liable for the employee's loss of pay.

In exercising its broad discretionary powers under §10(c) of the Act the Board has always been careful to balance the effectiveness of a particular remedy against its consequences. Thus, the Board has refrained from directing an otherwise appropriate remedy where practical and economic considerations dictated a lesser deterrent. . . . The extension of backpay liability to a situation where, as here, only picket line misconduct has occurred involves important considerations going to the heart of the right to strike under §§7 and 13. . . . Those sections of the Act have been called the safety valves of labor management relations. Emotions run high among those for and those against the union. Regrettably, sometimes there is violence and the threat of violence. This we deplore and in no way condone. However, adequate remedies under the Act other than backpay exist to prevent the occurrence of violence without interfering with the right to strike.[5] Where union agents, including pickets, engage in conduct violative of §8(b)(1)(A) the Board enjoins the continuation of such conduct and may, if warranted, seek an immediate court injunction under §10(j). . . . If such judicially directed injunctive relief is ignored effective contempt action is available. Finally, when a union resorts to or encourages the use of violent tactics to enforce its representation rights the Board may decline to issue a bargaining order to remedy an employer's unfair labor practices and instead may direct an election to determine whether or not the union is the recognized representative.[6]

To do more, in our opinion, runs the risk of inhibiting the right of employees to strike to such an extent as to substantially diminish that right. For the misconduct of a few pickets may be sufficient to find the union in violation of §8(b)(1)(A) and enough to intimidate many employees. The Board would then be required, under the logic of our dissenting colleagues, to seek backpay for all intimidated employees. Faced with this financial responsibility, few unions would be in a position to establish a picket line. In our opinion, union misconduct of this nature, while serious, does not warrant the adoption of a remedy so severe as to risk the diminution of the right to strike, a fundamental right guaranteed by §§7 and 13. . . .

Chairman MILLER and Member KENNEDY, dissenting in part. . . . We are unable to perceive the basis of our colleagues' conclusion that a backpay remedy herein would unnecessarily "risk the diminution of the right to strike," and their reliance on the existence of "adequate remedies . . . other than backpay . . . to prevent the occurrence of violence without interfering with the right to strike." Section 10(c)'s concern is not with preventing or deterring violence but with eliminating and remedying [its] effects. Hence, any incidental deterrent or penal effect of backpay is irrelevant in our determination of an adequate remedy for the violation found herein. Indeed, it is difficult to comprehend how making an employee whole for loss of wages suffered because of the union's unlawful activity in preventing employees from working is any less remedial or any more punitive or

---

[5] . . . [T]he lack of a . . . backpay [order] to employees unable to work because of injuries resulting from a union's unlawful conduct will not leave such employees without redress against those responsible for their injuries. These individuals will still have available those private remedies traditionally used [against] another's tortious conduct. In fact they may be better served by pursuing such remedies as the employee's pay may be only a small part of the total required to make him whole, such as medical expenses as well as compensation for physical injury and pain and suffering.

[6] Allou Distributors, Inc., 201 NLRB No. 4; Laura Modes Company, 144 N.L.R.B. 1592.

deterrent in effect than making an employee whole for loss of wages suffered when the employer would not allow him to work because of the union's unlawful activity.

. . . [A] backpay order herein is no more penal or deterring . . . than any other backpay order issued by the Board. Indeed, a backpay remedy [here] is necessary to remove the effect of the Union's unlawful conduct and thereby effectuate the policies of the Act. . . .

While the *Long* decision acknowledges Colonial Hardwood [84 N.L.R.B. 563] and related Board decisions cited by our colleagues as denying backpay when a union violates §8(b)(1)(A) by interfering with an employee's right of ingress to his place of employment, the Board in *Long* expressly refused to decide whether the result of those decisions is or is not required by any lack of statutory authority. Rather, the Board relied entirely on reasons of policy in denying backpay in *Long*. Obviously, therefore, *Colonial Hardwood* can no longer be considered controlling on the issue of the Board's authority to render such a backpay award;[10] the Board's rationale in *Long*, instead, makes the denial of backpay in cases involving such violations dependent only on certain policy considerations. The reasons of policy set forth in *Long*,[11] however, in themselves distinguish that case from the facts before us.

---

[10] The past failure of the Board to prescribe such a remedy is not controlling. Acknowledging the Board's authority to fashion a new remedy (the *Woolworth* formula for computing backpay, 90 N.L.R.B. 289), the Supreme Court stated in NLRB v. Seven-Up Bottling Company of Miami, Inc., 344 U.S. 344 (1953): "[Section 10(c)] charges the Board with the task of devising remedies to effectuate the policies of the Act. . . . In fashioning remedies to undo the effects of violations of the Act, the Board must draw on enlightenment gained from experience." And in NLRB v. Local 138, International Union of Operating Engineers, AFL-CIO, 380 F.2d 244 (C.A. 2), the court, upholding the Board's right to include interest in backpay awards . . . noted that the Board has broad discretion in determining what will effectuate the policies of the Act and held that the Board "is not bound by its prior precedent not to grant interest if it decides that an award of interest is consonant with the broad remedial purposes of the Act."

[11] The Board in *Long* declined to award backpay for the following reasons:

(1) The cease-and-desist order, in conjunction with the utilization of the contempt procedures provided in the Act, is well designed to prevent the recurrence of the unfair labor practices and to vindicate public rights; (2) to the extent that the Board has power to award backpay to employees injured by Respondent's violent conduct, such power derives from the effect of such conduct on the employee's employment relationship; yet the employee's loss of pay may be only a small part of the total required to make him whole, which total may well include medical expenses as well as compensation for physical injury and pain and suffering; (3) to the extent that satisfaction of individual claims which are primarily private in nature may also serve to further the public interest in obtaining the peaceful resolution of labor disputes, such interest is equally well served by the individual's resort to those remedies traditionally used to process claims resulting from another's tortious conduct; (4) the numerous and complicated factual

Obviously the Board's primary concern in *Long* was the existence of damages other than the loss of wages. But the fact that the loss of wages was only a small part of the total required to make the employees whole in that case is clearly nonexistent here. Therefore, the policy reasons for denying backpay — the necessity of private actions to fully recover damages, complicated factual questions outside the Board's expertise, and the existence of state interest in remedying tortious conduct — are manifestly irrelevant in determining whether or not a backpay remedy herein would effectuate the policies of the Act.

The Board's authority to issue a backpay order to remedy union conduct found to be a violation of 8(b)(1)(A) . . . recently received . . . approval from . . . the Sixth Circuit in National Cash Register Co., et al. v. NLRB, 466 F.2d 945. The court there enforced the Board's backpay order against a union to remedy picket line restraint and coercion of employees found to be a violation of §8(b)(1)(A) of the Act. The Board did not find the 8(b)(2) violation alleged in the complaint in that case. . . . The court expressly rejected the contention that it is necessary to find a violation of §8(b)(2) . . . for a backpay order . . . against a union. . . . [I]n the case before us — where the Union has flagrantly violated §8(b)(1)(A) . . . and where the only losses suffered by the employees are wages — the Board should exercise its discretion . . . and award backpay in order to remedy the Union's unfair labor practices.

NOTES

1. In Union Nacional de Trabajadores (Huelga de Catalytic), 219 N.L.R.B. 414 (1975), *enforced*, 540 F.2d 1 (1st Cir. 1976), *cert. denied*, 429 U.S. 1039 (1977), the Union told an employee seeking to cross a picket line to reach work: "This is Union Nacional and we kill people. So leave." Dissenting again from a denial of back pay, Member Kennedy noted (1) that this case and others showed that serious violence against employees was part of the Union's standard operating procedure, and (2) that the Union's violence had continued in violation of a federal district court's restraining order

---

questions involved in settling such claims are not such questions as fall within the Board's special expertise, but do fall within the special competence of judge and jury; and (5) in our opinion, our exercise of such authority as may reside in the Board to award compensatory relief might well exert an inhibitory effect on the exercise of State authority, and would, in any event, complicate and confuse the issue, to the possible detriment of the employees whose rights we seek to protect. [145 N.L.R.B. at 556.]

against secondary picketing. Should recidivism of the offending union be material in deciding whether to grant a back pay remedy?

2. Which opinion in *Lock Joint Pipe* is more persuasive? Would it be appropriate for a court, disapproving of the Board's established policy, to overturn it? See Drobena v. NLRB, 612 F.2d 1095, 1096 (8th Cir.), *cert. denied*, 449 U.S. 821 (1980) (upholding a Board order not requiring back pay from the union, the court noted that it "[does] not think highly of the Board's policy," but declared that it was not the court's function to make policy and therefore declined to disturb the Board's longstanding position). See Comment, Strike Violence: The NLRB's Reluctance to Wield its Broad Remedial Power, 50 Fordham L. Rev. 1371, 1388, 1397 (1982). If the Board is to grant employees back pay for violations of §8(b)(1)(A), what of orders granting lost profits to employers resulting from union violations of §8(b)(1)(B)? Cf. LMRA, §303. Does the explicit provision in §303 for damage awards against a union that violates §8(b)(4) imply that Congress "intended" that a damage remedy for violations of other sections of the Act not be granted by the Board?

3. In UAW v. Russell, 356 U.S. 634 (1958), the Court (two justices strongly dissenting) upheld state authority to grant individual employees compensatory and punitive damages against a union guilty of intimidation and threats of violence against employees. Notwithstanding contrary Board precedents, the Court assumed, arguendo, that §10(c) authorizes the Board to award lost pay to an employee whose access to the plant was blocked by pickets threatening to turn over his car if he attempted to cross the picket line. Does the existence of state jurisdiction obviate the need for NLRB grants of back pay remedies to employees who lose pay because of union violence in violation of §8(b)(1)?

4. In United Bhd. of Carpenters & Joiners, Local 610 v. Scott, 103 S. Ct. 3352 (1983), the Court considered whether labor union violence was actionable in a federal court under the "Ku Klux Klan Act," 42 U.S.C. §1985(3), which provides a remedy to persons injured by conspiracies formed "for the purpose of depriving, either directly or indirectly, any person or class of persons of the equal protection of the laws, or of equal privileges and immunities under the laws." The Court denied relief to two employees who had been beaten by a mob, and to their employer, whose construction equipment the mob had destroyed. The mob had been organized or encouraged by a local construction trade's council protesting the employer's hiring of nonunion personnel for a construction project. The Court (1) held that §1985(3) does not reach wholly private conspiracies to abridge rights of association conferred by the First Amendment, and (2) reversed the lower court's decision on the "dispositive ground" that the Act did not apply to

conspiracies motivated by economic or commercial animus, as distinguished from racial bias. Four justices dissented.

5. Violence under the Hobbs Anti-Racketeering Act is considered in Chapter 7(H), infra.

E. SECONDARY PRESSURES

1. The "Primary-Secondary" Distinction

Although "secondary boycotts" were generally illegal at common law, that term was ill defined. See C. Gregory & H. Katz, Labor and the Law 39-51, 120-157 (3d ed. 1979); Barnard & Graham, Labor and the Secondary Boycott, 15 Wash. L. Rev. 137 (1940). Its core meaning was, however, reflected in a standard definition appearing in F. Frankfurter & N. Greene, The Labor Injunction 43 (1930): "a combination to influence A by exerting some sort of economic or social pressure against persons who deal with A. . . . " The proscription of secondary boycotts by unions was designed to bar the deliberate extension of labor's pressures, such as strikes and picketing, beyond the employer with whom a union had a dispute (the primary employer) to other firms doing business with the primary employer but unable directly to settle the primary dispute.

Unions had resorted to secondary pressures to achieve recognition or to enforce bargaining demands. In the recognitional context, a union denied recognition by a primary employer (R-1) could sometimes cause a strike by the employees of a secondary employer (R-2), who was purchasing R-1's goods, or could otherwise interfere with R-2's production or sales. By exerting pressures on R-2, the union could indirectly exert pressure on R-1, the primary target of the union's demands. In the pre-Wagner Act period, unions were relatively weak, and the law generally did not prohibit employers' use of economic power to avert or destroy organization through yellow-dog contracts or discriminatory hiring and firing. Accordingly, pressure against R-2 as a lever against R-1 had considerably more justification than was subsequently the case. After the enactment of the Wagner Act, secondary pressures might not only involve secondary employers in labor disputes for which they had no direct responsibility, but could also threaten the statutory principles of free choice and majority rule.

When an incumbent union called a strike to enforce its bargaining demands, the problems raised by secondary pressures against, for example,

R-2, a customer of the struck employer, were quite different. A completely successful strike against R-1 would stop production; apart from goods in inventory or in the pipeline, R-2 would not be able to buy goods from R-1. Accordingly, in the bargaining context, a completely successful strike, by stopping R-1's production, would in time obviate the need for direct pressures designed to compel secondary employers to boycott R-1. But where R-1, despite a strike, maintained production, direct pressure against R-2 could serve as an auxiliary strike weapon and might achieve the result that would flow from a successful strike, i.e., the cessation of mutually advantageous dealing between R-1 and R-2. In short, secondary pressure sometimes enabled a union otherwise weak in relation to a struck employer to achieve the result ordinarily associated with a successful strike against the primary employer.

Section 8(b)(4)(A) of the Taft-Hartley Act did not use the term "secondary boycotts,"[b] but its legislative history showed that Congress' purpose had been to reinstate union liabilities for such boycotts similar to those that had been imposed under the Sherman Act — until the Supreme Court in 1941 virtually eliminated those liabilities by ruling that the Norris-LaGuardia Act immunized unions against antitrust liability, criminal and civil, for secondary boycotts. See United States v. Hutcheson, infra p. 627.

Sections 8(b)(4)(A) and (B) have spawned a complex, unstable, and far from coherent body of regulation. One underlying difficulty, already noticed, is the absence of a clear-cut rationale for insulating a secondary employer or, for that matter, a primary one, from the injury that would have resulted from a completely effective strike against the primary employer. A second and related difficulty arises from the diverse spatial, functional, and property relations among suppliers — producers, distributors, and service units — whose relationships do not fit neatly into the core primary-secondary categories highlighted in the pertinent legislative history. Finally, Congress, despite its 1959 amendments expressly exempting a "primary strike or primary picketing" from the ban of §8(b)(4)(B), did not clarify the basis for distinguishing between "primary" and "secondary" pressures. The materials below will explore the resultant difficulties.

See generally R. Dereshinsky, A. Berkowitz, & P. Miscimarra, The NLRB and Secondary Boycotts (rev. ed. 1981); Goetz, Secondary Boycotts

---

[b] The principal prohibition was contained in §8(b)(4)(A). Under the 1959 amendments, that section (with minor modifications) became §8(b)(4)(B). Accordingly, in the opinions below that refer to §8(b)(4), as enacted by Taft-Hartley in 1947, the references to §8(b)(4)(A) involve provisions now in §8(b)(4)(B) of the NLRA, as amended.

and the LMRA: A Path Through the Swamp, 19 U. Kan. L. Rev. 651 (1971); St. Antoine, What Makes Secondary Boycotts Secondary?, Southwestern Legal Found., 11th Ann. Inst. on Labor Law 5 (1964).

a. "Allies"; Common Ownership and Control

NLRB v. Business Machine, Local 459 (Royal Typewriter Co.)

228 F.2d 553 (2d Cir. 1955), *cert. denied*, 351 U.S. 962 (1956)

LUMBARD, J. . . . The [NLRB] now seeks enforcement of an order directing the Union to cease and desist from certain picketing. . . .

The findings of the Board . . . disclose the following [virtually undisputed] facts. On about March 23, 1954, the Union, being unable to reach agreement with Royal on the terms of a contract, called the Royal service personnel out on strike. The service employees customarily repair typewriters either at Royal's branch offices or at its customers' premises. Royal has several arrangements under which it is obligated to render service to its customers. First, Royal's warranty on each new machine obligates it to provide free inspection and repair for one year. Second, for a fixed periodic fee Royal contracts to service machines not under warranty. Finally, Royal is committed to repairing typewriters rented from it or loaned by it to replace machines undergoing repair. Of course, in addition Royal provides repair services on call by noncontract users.

During the strike Royal differentiated between calls from customers to whom it owed a repair obligation and others. Royal's office personnel were instructed to tell the latter to call some independent repair company listed in the telephone directory. Contract customers, however, were advised to select such an independent from the directory, to have the repair made, and to send a receipted invoice to Royal for reimbursement for reasonable repairs within their agreement with Royal. Consequently many of Royal's contract customers had repair services performed by various independent repair companies. In most instances the customer sent Royal the unpaid repair bill and Royal paid the independent company directly. Among the independent companies paid directly by Royal for repairs made for such customers were Typewriter Maintenance and Sales Company and Tytell Typewriter Company. . . .

. . . [T]he Union picketed some of Royal's larger customers whom it had reason to believe were having independent companies do repair work on

Royal contract machines. This picketing continued until restrained on June 15,1954 by a temporary injunction issued by the District Court for the Southern District of New York, 122 F. Supp. 43. . . .

[T]he Board found that the picketing of these companies took place before entrances "commonly used by members of the public, by employees of the picketed firm, and by employees of any other tenants of the building, and also by deliverymen making light deliveries." There was no evidence that the picketing took place at entrances used exclusively by employees. . . .

From April 13th until April 23rd, . . . the pickets carried signs reading . . . (with the picketed customer's name inserted):

Royal Business Machines In
N.Y. Life Ins. Co.
are being repaired by
Scab Labor
Local 459, IUE-CIO

Sometime after April 23rd the words "Notice to the Public Only" were added to the signs in large letters at the top. This was on advice of counsel after a conference with representatives of the Board who suggested that the picketing was unlawful. The picketing was carried on during ordinary business hours and during the time when at least some employees would be going to lunch. In at least one instance picketing began before the start of employees' working hours.

One of the picketed customers, Charles Pfizer, did agree to discontinue doing business with Royal and the Union withdrew its pickets. There is no evidence to indicate that this came about through any pressure on or from any of Pfizer's employees.

The Board found, and it is conceded, that an object of the picketing of Royal's customers was to induce the customers to cease doing business with Royal. The Union contended that it sought to do this only by embarrassing the firms picketed and bringing its grievance to the attention of the customers of those firms and the general public. The Trial Examiner found that the picketing constituted inducement and encouragement of employees, that the Union's professed intent not to influence employees was no defense, and that the picketing was therefore unlawful. These findings the Board adopted.

During May 1954 the Union also picketed four independent typewriter repair companies who had been doing work covered by Royal's contracts pursuant to the arrangement described above. The Board found this picketing unlawful with respect to Typewriter Maintenance and Tytell. . . . In each instance the picketing, which was peaceful and orderly, took place before entrances used in common by employees, deliverymen and the general public. The signs read substantially as follows (with the appropriate repair company name inserted):

Notice To The Public Only
Employees Of Royal Typewriter Co.
On Strike
Tytell Typewriter Company Employees
Are Being Used As Strikebreakers

Business Machine & Office Appliance
Mechanics Union, Local 459, IUE-CIO

Both before and after this picketing, . . . Tytell and Typewriter Maintenance did work on Royal accounts and received payment directly from Royal. . . . [E]ach independent serviced various of Royal's customers on numerous occasions and received payment directly from Royal.

With one exception there was no evidence that the picketing of either the customers or the repair companies resulted in a strike or refusal to work by any employee. . . . [N]o employee ceased work or refused to operate any Royal typewriter or other machine. . . .

. . . [T]he Trial Examiner and the Board found that both the customer picketing and the repair company picketing violated §8(b)(4) . . . which provides: It shall be an unfair labor practice for a labor organization or its agents ". . . to induce or encourage the employees of any employer to engage in a strike or a concerted refusal in the course of their employment . . . to perform any services, where an object thereof is: (A) forcing or requiring . . . any employer . . . to cease doing business with any other person; . . ." . . . [T]he Board's finding with respect to the repair company picketing cannot be sustained. The independent repair companies were so allied with Royal that the Union's picketing of their premises was not prohibited by §8(b)(4)(A).

We approve the "ally" doctrine which had its origin in a well reasoned opinion by Judge Rifkind in the Ebasco case, Douds v. Metropolitan Federation of Architects, Engineers, Chemists & Technicians, Local 231, D.C.S.D.N.Y. 1948, 75 F. Supp. 672, 676. Ebasco, a corporation engaged in the business of providing engineering services, had a close business relationship with Project, a firm providing similar services. Ebasco subcontracted some of its work to Project and when it did so Ebasco supervised the work of Project's employees and paid Project for the time spent by Project's employees on Ebasco's work plus a factor for overhead and profit. When Ebasco's employees went on strike, Ebasco transferred a greater percentage of its work to Project, including some jobs that had already been started by Ebasco's employees. When Project refused to heed the Union's request to stop doing Ebasco's work, the Union picketed Project and induced some of Project's employees to cease work. On these facts Judge Rifkind found that Project was not "doing business" with Ebasco within the meaning of §8(b)(4)(A) and that the Union had therefore not committed an unfair labor practice under that section. He reached this result by looking to the legislative history of the Taft-Hartley Act and to the history of the secondary boycotts which it sought to outlaw. He determined that Project was not a person " 'wholly unconcerned in the disagreement between an employer and his employees' " such as §8(b)(4)(A) was designed to protect. This result has been described as a proper interpretation of the Act by its principal sponsor, Senator Taft, 95 Cong. Rec. (1949) 8709,ᶜ and President Eisenhower in his January 1954 recommendations to Congress for revision of the Act included a suggestion which would make this rule explicit.

Here there was evidence of only one instance where Royal contacted an independent (Manhattan Typewriter Service, not named in the complaint) to see whether it could handle some of Royal's calls. Apart from that incident there is no evidence that Royal made any arrangement with an independent directly. It is obvious, however, that what the independents did would inevitably tend to break the strike. As Judge Rifkind pointed out in the Ebasco case: "The economic effect upon Ebasco's employees was precisely that which would flow from Ebasco's hiring strikebreakers to work on its own premises." And at 95 Cong. Rec. (1949) page 8709 Senator Taft said: "The spirit of the Act is not intended to protect a man who . . . is cooperating with a primary employer and taking his work and doing the work which he is unable to do because of the strike."

President Eisenhower's recommendation referred to above was to make it explicit "that concerted action against (1) an employer who is performing 'farmed-out' work for the account of another employer whose employees are

---

ᶜ[Two statements by Senator Taft regarding §8(b)(4) have been prominent in discussions of its legislative history. The first, relied on in *Ebasco* and made during legislative consideration of §8(b)(4), is:

This provision makes it unlawful to resort to a secondary boycott to injure the business of a third person who is *wholly unconcerned* in the disagreement between an employer and his employees. [Emphasis supplied. 93 Cong. Rec. 4323 (1947), II NLRB, Leg. Hist. 1106 (1947).]

The second, made after enactment of §8(b)(4), is:

. . . the secondary boycott ban is merely intended to prevent a union from injuring a third person who is [not] involved in any way in the dispute or strike. . . . It is not intended to apply to a case where the third party is, in effect, in cahoots with or acting as a part of the primary employer. [95 Cong. Rec. 8709 (1949).] — EDS.]

on strike . . . will not be treated as a secondary boycott." Text of President's Message to Congress on Taft-Hartley Amendments, January 11, 1954. At least one commentator has suggested that the enactment of this change would add nothing to existing law. Cushman, Secondary Boycotts and the Taft-Hartley Law, 6 Syracuse L. Rev. 109, 121 (1954). Moreover, there is evidence that the secondary strikes and boycotts sought to be outlawed by §8(b)(4)(A) were only those which had been unlawful at common law. 93 Cong. Rec. (1947) 3950, 4323 (Senator Taft), 2 Legislative History of the Labor-Management Relations Act, 1947, pp. 1006, 1106. And although secondary boycotts were generally unlawful, it has been held that the common law does not proscribe union activity designed to prevent employers from doing the farmed-out work of a struck employer. Iron Molders Union No. 125 of Milwaukee, Wis. v. Allis-Chalmers Co., 7th Cir., 1908, 166 F. 45, 51. Thus the picketing of the independent typewriter companies was not the kind of secondary activity which §8(b)(4)(A) of the Taft-Hartley Act was designed to outlaw. Where an employer is attempting to avoid the economic impact of a strike by securing the services of others to do his work, the striking union obviously has a great interest, and we think a proper interest, in preventing those services from being rendered. This interest is more fundamental than the interest in bringing pressure on customers of the primary employer. Nor are those who render such services completely uninvolved in the primary strike. By doing the work of the primary employer they secure benefits themselves at the time that they aid the primary employer. The ally employer may easily extricate himself from the dispute and insulate himself from picketing by refusing to do that work. A case may arise where the ally employer is unable to determine that the work he is doing is "farmed-out." We need not decide whether the picketing of such an employer would be lawful, for that is not the situation here. The existence of the strike, the receipt of checks from Royal, and the picketing itself certainly put the independents on notice that some of the work they were doing might be work farmed-out by Royal. Wherever they worked on new Royal machines they were probably aware that such machines were covered by a Royal warranty. But in any event, before working on a Royal machine they could have inquired of the customer whether it was covered by a Royal contract and refused to work on it if it was. There is no indication that they made any effort to avoid doing Royal's work. The Union was justified in picketing them in order to induce them to make such an effort. We therefore hold that an employer is not within the protection of §8(b)(4)(A) when he knowingly does work which would otherwise be done by the striking employees of the primary employer and where this work is paid for by the primary employer pursuant to an arrangement devised and originated by him to enable him to meet his contractual obligations. The result must be the same whether or not the primary employer makes any direct arrangement with the employers providing the services. . . .

Enforcement of the Board's order is therefore in all respects denied.

HAND, J., (concurring). . . . [I]t seems to me that both "independents" had so far associated themselves with Royal in the controversy with its employees as to forfeit their privilege as neutrals. After the picketing began both necessarily knew of the strike against Royal; indeed, the Union's representative spoke to each of them. I altogether agree that they were nevertheless entitled to do work for Royal's customers. One does not make oneself a party to the dispute with a primary employer by taking over the business that the strike has prevented him from doing. On the other hand if a secondary employer, knowing of the strike, not only accepts the customer of the primary employer but takes his pay, not from the customer but from the primary employer, I do not see any relevant difference in doing so from accepting a subcontract from the primary employer, which would certainly forfeit the exemption. As I understand §8(b)(4)(A), it is meant to protect from industrial pressure employers, who have not made common cause with the primary employer. The theory is that they should be free to carry on their businesses without being subject to sanctions that are reasonable between parties to the dispute. When, however, a secondary employer accepts business for which the primary employer pays him, although it is not an inevitable inference that, but for the strike, the primary employer would have done the business himself, I see no reason why he should not be compelled to prove that the primary employer would not have done it, if he could have. Therefore I think that, even though the Union meant to induce a strike of the "independents'" employees, it was within its rights.

[The concurring opinion of Medina, J., is omitted.]

NOTES

1. (a) If Royal had told its customers only that it would honor its warranty and would pay them directly the fair costs of repairs covered by the warranty, would the union have been privileged to induce a strike against independent companies doing repair work for Royal's customers? Would it be material whether Royal volunteered that information or disclosed it only to inquiring customers? Whether the repairers were aware of the strike or the continued applicability of Royal's warranty and the company's intention to honor it by direct payments to its own customers?

(b) Suppose that Royal's customers had set off against their liabilities to Royal the amounts they paid to independent repairers for work covered by Royal's warranty. Would the union have violated the Act by picketing the employee entrances of the independents making repairs only for such customers?

(c) Suppose Royal's products had not been warranted but that Royal, like distributors of Ford cars, supplied repair services to its customers. Would independents who, during a strike against Royal, performed repair work for Royal's customers be covered by the "ally" doctrine?

2. In Irwin-Lyons Lumber Co., 87 N.L.R.B. 54 (1949), R-1, a logging and sawmill operator, also maintained a ship to transport the mill's lumber. R-2, a public utility with an exclusive franchise covering the transport of logs along a 30-mile stretch of river at regulated rates, transported R-1's logs to the mill. Both companies were owned and controlled by substantially the same individuals. When a labor dispute arose at R-1's dock over the crew hired for the ship that hauled the lumber from the mill, the unions, in addition to picketing all of R-1's work sites, picketed the bridge used by both R-1's and R-2's employees to get to their jobs. (The Trial Examiner found that all of the logs held by R-2 when the picketing began were R-1's logs.) The Board held that R-2 was not a "neutral . . . within the meaning of §8(b)(4)(A)," and that the unions could lawfully picket R-2.

In Bachman Machine Co. v. NLRB, 121 N.L.R.B. 1229 (1958), rev'd, 266 F.2d 599 (8th Cir. 1959), the Board dismissed a complaint against a union that, during an economic strike against Plastics Molding Co., posted pickets next to the Bachman Machine Co. plant. The pickets bore placards urging the Bachman employees, who were represented by a different union, to strike. Plastic and Bachman were separate legal entities and produced different lines of products on plant sites that were physically separate but within 650 feet of each other. The officers, directors, and shareholders of both companies were members of the Bachman family; W. Bachman was president and principal stockholder of both companies and, the Board found, controlled their labor relations. The companies had only one common employee; they operated as separate enterprises but purchased substantial amounts of goods from each other. The court reversed, rejecting the Board's view that evidence of common ownership and control warranted treating the two companies as "allies" or as a single enterprise under §8(b)(4). A different problem would have resulted, the court said, if, as in Irwin-Lyons Lumber, the two companies were engaged in an "integrated operation." Cf., Local 46, Miami Newspapers Printing Pressmen, 138 N.L.R.B. 1346 (1962), enforced, 322 F.2d 405 (D.C. Cir. 1963): The Miami Herald and the Detroit Free Press were owned by Knight Newspapers, Inc. and had common officers and directors. Each paper was, however, operated independently under separate managers. The union, after a bargaining strike against the Miami Herald, picketed the Detroit Free Press. The NLRB, observing that those papers were not a "single integrated operation," concluded that they enjoyed the protection of §8(b)(4)(B). The union had also urged that the picketing had not been prompted by the purpose of causing a cessation of business, which was de minimis, between the papers and that, accordingly, the object proscribed by §8(b)(4)(B) had not been accomplished. The Board found that object in the union's purpose of forcing the Free Press to cease doing business with its customers and suppliers.

Why should the factors mentioned above, including various degrees of vertical integration (a "straight-line" operation), be relevant in determining whether different parts of a commonly-owned business structure are "allies" or "neutrals"?

3. In the application of §8(b)(4), should it matter whether commonly-owned operations are conducted by separate corporations rather than separate divisions of the same corporation? See Teamsters Local 391 v. NLRB (Chattanooga Div., Vulcan Materials Co.), 543 F.2d 1373 (D.C. Cir. 1976), cert. denied, 430 U.S. 967 (1977); Siegel, Conglomerates, Subsidiaries, Divisions and the Secondary Boycott, 9 Ga. L. Rev. 329 (1975); Levin, "Wholly Unconcerned": The Scope and Meaning of the Ally Doctrine Under Section 8(b)(4) of the NLRA, 119 U. Pa. L. Rev. 283 (1970).

4. Hospital A, after getting timely notice of an impending strike, transfers its critically ill patients to Hospital B, and other patients to Hospital C. The Union strikes A and pickets B and C. Has §8(b)(4) been violated? Cf. §8(d) of the NLRA, as amended in 1974, and NLRB General Counsel Advice Memorandum in United Nurses Assn. of Cal., Case Nos. 31-CC-820 and 821, 31-CG-7 and 8 (Sept. 2, 1977), finding no "ally" relationship from transfer of intensive care patients and indicating that the union seeking to picket the transferee hospital for accepting "struck work" would have to show that transferred patients were not "critically ill."

b. Common Situs Problems

Sailors' Union of the Pacific and Moore Dry Dock
92 N.L.R.B. 547 (1950)

[Samsoc, a Greek-controlled corporation, entered into a six-year contract to carry gypsum from Mexico to Kaiser plants in California. This agreement contemplated that an American ship, previously operated by a Kaiser subsidiary under a contract with the respondent union, would be replaced by a Samsoc ship, S.S. Phopho. Samsoc arranged with Moore Dry Dock to perform the major work required to convert that ship into a gypsum carrier and for the right to place a crew on board for training two weeks before the completion of the work. After Samsoc had hired a predominantly Greek crew at approximately one-half the union scale, the union requested but was denied bargaining rights with respect to the ship's crew. The union's petition for an election, filed on February 24, 1950, was dismissed because a foreign ship was involved. Meanwhile, on February 17, 1950, the union had stationed pickets at the shipyard's entrance after having been denied permission to picket immediately adjacent to the dock where the Phopho was located. The union also advised various unions representing Moore's employees that the Phopho was "hot" and requested their cooperation. On February 21, Moore's employees stopped work on the Phopho but continued all other work throughout the picketing.]

Section 8(b)(4)(A) is aimed at secondary boycotts and secondary strike activities. It was not intended to proscribe primary action by a union having a legitimate labor dispute with an employer. Picketing at the premises of a primary employer is traditionally recognized as primary action even though it is "necessarily designed to induce and encourage third persons to cease doing business with the picketed employer." . . . Hence, if Samsoc, the owner of the S.S. Phopho, had had a dock of its own in California to which the Phopho had been tied up while undergoing conversion by Moore Dry Dock employees, picketing by the Respondent at the dock site would unquestionably have constituted *primary* action, even though the Respondent might have expected that the picketing would be more effective in persuading Moore employees not to work on the ship than to persuade the seamen aboard the Phopho to quit that vessel. The difficulty in the present case arises therefore, not because of any difference in picketing objectives,[5] but from the fact that the Phopho was not tied up at its own dock, but at that of Moore, while the picketing was going on in front of the Moore premises.

In the usual case, the situs of a labor dispute is the premises of the primary employer. Picketing of the premises is also picketing of the situs. . . . But in some cases the situs of the dispute may not be limited to a fixed location; it may be ambulatory. Thus in the *Schultz* case, . . . the Board held that the truck upon which a truck driver worked was the situs of a labor dispute between him and the owner of the truck. Similarly, we

---

[5] "Plainly, the object of all picketing at all times is to influence third persons to withhold their business or services from the struck employer. In this respect there is no distinction between lawful primary picketing and unlawful secondary picketing proscribed by §8(b)(4)(A)." International Brotherhood of Teamsters, etc. (Schultz Refrigerated Service, Inc.) [87 N.L.R.B. 502, 505 (1949)].

hold . . . that, as the Phopho was the place of employment of the seamen, it was the situs of the dispute between Samsoc and the Respondent over working conditions aboard that vessel.

When the situs is ambulatory, it may come to rest temporarily at the premises of another employer. The perplexing question is: Does the right to picket follow the situs while it is stationed at the premises of a secondary employer, when the only way to picket that situs is in front of the secondary employer's premises? Admittedly, no easy answer is possible. Essentially the problem is one of balancing the right of a union to picket at the site of its dispute as against the right of a secondary employer to be free from picketing in a controversy in which it is not directly involved.

When a secondary employer is harboring the situs of a dispute between a union and a primary employer, the right of neither the union to picket nor of the secondary employer to be free from picketing can be absolute. The enmeshing of premises and situs qualifies both rights. . . . [W]e believe that picketing of the premises of a secondary employer is primary if it meets the following conditions: (a) The picketing is strictly limited to times when the situs of dispute is located on the secondary employer's premises; (b) at the time of the picketing the primary employer is engaged in its normal business at the situs; (c) the picketing is limited to places reasonably close to the location of the situs; and (d) the picketing discloses clearly that the dispute is with the primary employer. All these conditions were met in the present case.

(a) During the entire period of the picketing the Phopho was tied up at a dock in the Moore shipyard.

(b) Under its contract with Samsoc, Moore agreed to permit the former to put a crew on board the Phopho for training purposes during the last 2 weeks before the vessel's delivery to Samsoc. At the time the picketing started on February 17, . . . 90 percent of the conversion job had been completed, practically the entire crew had been hired, the ship's oil bunkers had been filled, and other stores were shortly to be put aboard. The various members of the crew commenced work as soon as they reported aboard the Phopho. Those in the deck department did painting and cleaning up; those in the steward's department, cooking and cleaning up; and those in the engine department, oiling and cleaning up. The crew were thus getting the ship ready for sea. They were on board to serve the purposes of Samsoc, the Phopho's owners, and not Moore. The normal business of a ship does not only begin with its departure on a scheduled voyage. The multitudinous steps of preparation, including hiring and training a crew and putting stores aboard, are as much a part of the normal business of a ship as the voyage itself. We find, therefore, that during the entire period of the picketing, the Phopho was engaged in its normal business.

(c) Before placing its pickets outside the entrance to the Moore shipyard, the Respondent Union asked, but was refused, permission to place its pickets at the dock where the Phopho was tied up. The Respondent therefore posted its pickets at the yard entrance which, as the parties stipulated, was as close to the Phopho as they could get under the circumstances.

(d) Finally, by its picketing and other conduct the Respondent was scrupulously careful to indicate that its dispute was solely with the primary employer, the owners of the Phopho. Thus the signs carried by the pickets said only that the Phopho was unfair to the Respondent. The Phopho and not Moore was declared "hot." Similarly, in asking cooperation of other unions, the Respondent clearly revealed that its dispute was with the Phopho. Finally, Moore's own witnesses admitted that no attempt was made to interfere with other work in progress in the Moore yard.

We believe that our dissenting colleagues' expressions of alarm are based on a misunderstanding of our decision. We are not holding, as the dissenters seem to think, that a union which has a dispute with a shipowner over working conditions of seamen aboard a ship may lawfully picket the premises of an independent shipyard to which the shipowner has delivered his vessel for overhaul and repair. We are only holding that, if a shipyard permits the owner of a vessel to use its dock for the purpose of readying the ship for its regular voyage by hiring and training a crew and putting stores aboard ship, a union representing seamen may then, within the careful limitations laid down in this decision, lawfully picket in front of the shipyard premises to advertise its dispute with the shipowner.

It is true, of course, that the Phopho was delivered to the Moore yard for conversion into a bulk gypsum carrier. But Moore in its contract agreed that "During the last two weeks, . . . [the Phopho's] Owner shall have the right to put a crew on board the vessel for training purposes, provided, however, that such crew shall not interfere in any way with the work of conversion." Samsoc (the Phopho's owner) availed itself of this contract privilege. When it did, Moore and Samsoc were simultaneously engaged in their separate businesses in the Moore yard.

The dissent finds it "logically" difficult to believe in this duality. We find no such difficulty. Nor did Moore, apparently, when it included the above clause in its contract. Indeed, from a practical standpoint, there was a strong reason why Samsoc should ready the ship for sea while the conversion work was still going on. A laid-up ship does not earn money. By completing training and preparation for sea while the ship was still undergoing conversion, the lay-up time was reduced, with a consequent money saving to owner Samsoc.

We . . . find that the picketing practice followed by the Respondent

was primary and not secondary and therefore did not violate §8(b)
(4)(A). . . .

[The dissenting opinion by Members Reynolds and Murdock is
omitted.]

**Sales Drivers, Helpers, & Bldg. Constr. Drivers (Assoc. Gen.
Contractors),** 110 N.L.R.B. 2192 (1954). Campbell Coal sells ready-
mixed concrete. It delivers the ready-mix by employing truck drivers, who
operate the unloading mechanism so as to place the materials at areas designated by construction contractors and who spend about 50 percent of their
time at the construction sites, 25 percent enroute, and 25 percent at Campbell's plants.

After a strike against Campbell, prompted by the discharge of several
truck drivers, Campbell continued to operate. The union picketed the company's two ready-mix plants and also followed the company's trucks deliver-
ing to construction sites. The union asked each contractor to refuse delivery
and picketed the construction sites of noncomplying contractors. The picketing took place in the immediate area of the trucks or as close thereto as the
pickets could get without trespassing on private property. The pickets' signs
stated that Campbell's employees were on strike to protest the discharge of
some union employees but did not otherwise communicate with employees
working at the construction sites. Some of those employees quit work for the
duration of the picketing, attributing their stoppage to the presence of the
pickets.

The NLRB, although conceding that the picketing met the *Moore Dry
Dock* criteria, held it to be a violation of §8(b)(4)(A), urging that "effective"
picketing could have been carried on at the primary employer's situs and that
the picketing, accordingly, was unlawful under the doctrine of Washington
Coca-Cola, 107 N.L.R.B. 299 (1953), *enforced*, Brewery Drivers, Local 67
v. NLRB, 220 F.2d 380 (D.C. Cir. 1955).

The D.C. Circuit reversed and remanded, holding that the "rigid rule"
of *Washington Coca-Cola* was not supported by the statutory language.

> Section 8(b)(4)(A) does not contain a provision which condemns concerted
> activity of employees with respect to their own employer merely because it
> occurs at a place where it comes to the attention of and incidentally affects
> employees of another, even where the activity could be carried on at a place
> where the primary employer alone does business. [Sales Drivers, Local 859 v.
> NLRB, 229 F.2d 514, 517 (D.C. Cir. 1955).]

On remand, the Board again found a violation (116 N.L.R.B. 1020
(1956)), emphasizing that picketing had occurred only at the sites of contractors who, contrary to the union's request, had accepted delivery of the

ready-mix. In affirming (2-1), the court ruled that the Board could properly rely on that fact, as well as on the union's failure to advise the contractors' striking employees that the picket line was not aimed at the secondary employers, as evidence that the picketing had been for an object proscribed by §8(b)(4)(A). See Truck Drivers v. NLRB (Campbell Coal Co.), 249 F.2d 512 (D.C. Cir. 1957), cert. denied, 355 U.S. 958 (1958).

(The Board subsequently repudiated the "rigid [*Washington Coca-Cola*] rule" and stated that the accessibility of a primary employer's business situs to the union's picketing was only one of the relevant circumstances; it echoed the caveat in the *General Electric* case (infra p. 558) against mechanical application of the *Moore Dry Dock* criteria. See Local 861 Elec. Wkrs. (Plauche Elec.), 135 N.L.R.B. 250 (1962).)

NOTES

1. Where R-1 may be picketed at his fixed situs, is picketing at a secondary situs, conforming to the *Moore Dry Dock* criteria, permitted because it is deemed lawful for the union to induce secondary employees at the secondary situs to refuse to handle materials coming from, or destined for, the primary employer? Cf. Teamsters Local 807 (Schultz Refrigerated Serv.), 87 N.L.R.B. 502 (1949) (R-1 moved his headquarters from New York City to New Jersey, replaced members of Local 807 with drivers from a New Jersey local, then continued to service the N.Y.C. delivery area; the Board held that picketing of Schultz's trucks (driven by members of the rival local) at delivery points in N.Y.C. was "primary" picketing because N.Y.C. was "the scene of the labor dispute.").

2. Would ambulatory picketing, notwithstanding its compliance with *Moore Dry Dock* and requests by the picketing union that the secondary employees continue all work except that involving the primary employer, become illegal if the secondary employees refused to do any work of any kind while the picketing continued? Compare Seafarers Intl. Union v. NLRB, 265 F.2d 585 (D.C. Cir. 1959), with Superior Derrick Corp. v. NLRB, 273 F.2d 891 (5th Cir.), cert. denied, 364 U.S. 816 (1960). Would it be material that R-1 could be easily picketed at a fixed situs?

NLRB v. Denver Bldg. & Constr. Trades Council
341 U.S. 675 (1951)

BURTON, J. The principal question here is whether a labor organization committed an unfair labor practice, within the meaning of §8(b)(4)(A),

. . . by engaging in a strike, an object of which was to force the general contractor on a construction project to terminate its contract with a certain subcontractor on that project. . . . [W]e hold that such an unfair labor practice was committed.

. . . Doose & Lintner was the general contractor for the construction of a commercial building. . . . It awarded a subcontract for electrical work . . . , in an estimated amount of $2,300, to Gould & Preisner, a firm which for 20 years had employed nonunion workmen on construction work. . . . The latter's employees proved to be the only nonunion workmen on the project. Those of the general contractor and of the other subcontractors were members of unions affiliated with the respondent Denver Building and Construction Trades Council. . . . A representative of one of those unions told Gould that he did not see how the job could progress with Gould's nonunion men on it. Gould insisted that they would complete the electrical work unless bodily put off. The representative replied that the situation would be difficult for both Gould & Preisner and Doose & Lintner.

January 8, 1948, the [Council] instructed [its] representative "to place a picket on the job stating that the job was unfair" to it. In keeping with the Council's practice, each affiliate was notified of that decision. That notice was a signal in the nature of an order to the members of the affiliated unions to leave the job and remain away until otherwise ordered. Representatives of the Council and each of the respondent unions visited the project and reminded the contractor that Gould & Preisner employed nonunion workmen and said that union men could not work on the job with nonunion men. They further advised that if Gould & Preisner's men did work on the job, the Council and its affiliates would put a picket on it to notify their members that nonunion men were working on it and that the job was unfair. All parties stood their ground.

January 9, the Council posted a picket at the project carrying a placard stating "This Job Unfair to Denver Building and Construction Trades Council." He was paid by the Council and his picketing continued from January 9 through January 22. During that time the only persons who reported for work were the nonunion electricians of Gould & Preisner. January 22, before Gould & Preisner had completed its subcontract, the general contractor notified it to get off the job so that Doose & Lintner could continue with the project. January 23, the Council removed its picket and shortly thereafter the union employees resumed work on the project. Gould & Preisner protested this treatment but its workmen were denied entrance to the job. . . .

[The court of appeals rejected the Board's finding that the respondents' activity was secondary and denied enforcement of the Board's order.]

While §8(b)(4) does not expressly mention "primary" or "secondary" disputes, strikes or boycotts, that section often is referred to in the Act's legislative history as one of the Act's "secondary boycott sections." The other is §303, which uses the same language in defining the basis for private actions for damages caused by these proscribed activities.

Senator Taft, who was the sponsor of the bill in the Senate and was the Chairman of the Senate Committee on Labor and Public Welfare in charge of the bill, said:

> . . . under . . . the Norris-LaGuardia Act, it became impossible to stop a secondary boycott or any other kind of a strike, no matter how unlawful it may have been at common law. All this provision . . . does is to reverse the effect of the law as to secondary boycotts. It has been set forth that there are good secondary boycotts and bad secondary boycotts. Our committee heard evidence for weeks and never succeeded in having anyone tell us any difference between different kinds of secondary boycotts. So we have so broadened the provision dealing with secondary boycotts as to make them an unfair labor practice.

93 Cong. Rec. 4198. . . .

At the same time that §§7 and 13 safeguard collective bargaining, concerted activities and strikes between the primary parties to a labor dispute, §8(b)(4) restricts a labor organization and its agents in the use of economic pressure where an object of it is to force an employer or other person to boycott someone else.

A. We must first determine whether the strike in this case had a proscribed object. The conduct which the Board here condemned is readily distinguishable from that which it declined to condemn in the *Rice Milling* case [346 U.S. 665]. There the accused union sought merely to obtain its own recognition by the operator of a mill, and the union's pickets near the mill sought to influence two employees of a customer of the mill not to cross the picket line. . . . [W]e supported the Board in its conclusion that such conduct was no more than was traditional and permissible in a primary strike. The union did not engage in a strike against the customer. It did not encourage concerted action by the customer's employees to force the customer to boycott the mill. It did not commit any unfair labor practice proscribed by §8(b)(4).[d]

---

[d] [The rationale in *Rice Milling* was that the union's encouragement of the men on the truck had not constituted the "concerted action" necessary for a violation of §8(b)(4)(A) prior to its being amended in 1959. Hence, even though the union had sought to force the mill's customer to cease doing business with the mill, a violation had not been made out because of

. . . [Here] there was a long-standing labor dispute between the Council and Gould & Preisner due to the latter's practice of employing nonunion workmen on construction jobs in Denver. The respondent labor organizations contend that they engaged in a primary dispute with Doose & Lintner alone, and that they sought simply to force Doose & Lintner to make the project an all-union job. If there had been no contract between Doose & Lintner and Gould & Preisner there might be substance in their contention that the dispute involved no boycott. If, for example, Doose & Lintner had been doing all the electrical work on this project through its own nonunion employees, it could have replaced them with union men and thus disposed of the dispute.[e] However, the existence of the Gould & Preisner subcontract presented a materially different situation. The nonunion employees were employees of Gould & Preisner. The only way that respondents could attain their purpose was to force Gould & Preisner itself off the job. This, in turn, could be done only through Doose & Lintner's termination of Gould & Preisner's subcontract. The result is that the Council's strike, in order to attain its ultimate purpose, must have included among its objects that of forcing Doose & Lintner to terminate that subcontract. On that point, the Board adopted the following finding: "That *an* object, if not the only object, of what transpired with respect to . . . Doose & Lintner was to force or require them to cease doing business with Gould & Preisner seems scarcely open to question, in view of all of the facts. And it is clear at least as to Doose & Lintner, that that purpose was achieved." (Emphasis supplied.) 82 N.L.R.B. at 1212.

We accept this crucial finding. . . .

B. We hold also that a strike with such an object was an unfair labor practice within the meaning of §8(b)(4)(A).

It is not necessary to find that the *sole* object of the strike was that of forcing the contractor to terminate the subcontractor's contract. . . .

We agree with the Board . . . that the fact that the contractor and subcontractor were engaged on the same construction project, and that the contractor had some supervision over the subcontractor's work, did not eliminate the status of each as an independent contractor or make the em-

---

the absence of the proscribed means. The Court's opinion also stated that the proximity of the picketing to the primary employer had been significant but not necessarily conclusive. The basic rationale with respect to "concerted activities" raised a question as to whether §8(b)(4) would be violated by picketing at a secondary employer's premises, aimed at his employees or the employees of his suppliers. The Court in the principal case and in IBEW v. NLRB, 341 U.S. 694 (1951), decided the same day, made clear the important differences between picketing at the premises of the primary employer and elsewhere. — EDS.]

  [e][Would such replacement by the employer have violated any provisions of the NLRA? — EDS.]

ployees of one the employees of the other. The business relationship between independent contractors is too well established in the law to be overridden without clear language doing so. The Board found that the relationship between Doose & Lintner and Gould & Preisner was one of "doing business" and we find no adequate reason for upsetting that conclusion.

Finally, §8(c) safeguarding freedom of speech has no significant application to the picket's placard in this case. Section 8(c) does not apply to a mere signal by a labor organization to its members, or to the members of its affiliates, to engage in an unfair labor practice such as a strike proscribed by §8(b)(4)(A). That the placard was merely such a signal, tantamount to a direction to strike, was found by the Board.

> . . . [T]he issues in this case turn upon acts by labor organizations which are tantamount to directions and instructions to their members to engage in strike action. The protection afforded by §8(c) . . . to the expression of "any views, argument or opinion" does not pertain where, as here, the issues raised under §8(b)(4)(A) turn on official directions or instructions to a union's own members.

82 N.L.R.B. at 1213 . . .

The judgment of the Court of Appeals accordingly is reversed and the case is remanded to it for procedure not inconsistent with this opinion.

Jackson, J., would affirm the judgment of the Court of Appeals.

Douglas, J., with whom Reed, J., joins, dissenting. The employment of union and nonunion men on the same job is a basic protest in trade union history. That was the protest here. The union was not out to destroy the contractor because of his antiunion attitude. The union was not pursuing the contractor to other jobs. All the union asked was that union men not be compelled to work alongside nonunion men on the same job. As Judge Rifkind stated in an analogous case, "the union was not extending its activity to a front remote from the immediate dispute but to one intimately and indeed inextricably united to it." [Ebasco, 75 F. Supp. 672, 677.]

The picketing would undoubtedly have been legal if there had been no subcontractor involved — if the general contractor had put nonunion men on the job. The presence of a subcontractor does not alter one whit the realities of the situation; the protest of the union is precisely the same. In each the union was trying to protect a job on which union men were employed. If that is forbidden, the Taft-Hartley Act makes the right to strike, guaranteed by §13, dependent on fortuitous business arrangements that have no significance so far as the evils of the secondary boycott are concerned. I would give scope to both §8(b)(4) and §13 by reading the restrictions of §8(b)(4) to reach the case where an industrial dispute spreads from the job to another front.

NOTES

1. Could the union in the principal case have achieved its purpose, without violating §8(b)(4)(A), by changing the language of its placards? See Ramey Constr. v. Local 544 Painters, 472 F.2d 1127 (5th Cir. 1973).

2. In connection with the legality of inducements to secondary employees to respect an organizational picket line, is the proviso immediately following §8(b)(4)(D) relevant? That proviso has been called "the puzzling proviso." What is the puzzle? See Petro, "Primary" and "Secondary" Labor Action, 1 Lab. L.J. 339 (1950), and Taft-Hartley and the "Secondary Boycott," 1 Lab. L.J. 835 (1950); but cf. Tower, The Puzzling Proviso, 1 Lab. L.J. 1019 (1950).

Local 761, Intl. Union of Elec., Radio, & Mach. Wkrs. v. NLRB (General Electric)
366 U.S. 667 (1961)

FRANKFURTER, J. . . . . General Electric Corporation operates a plant outside of Louisville, Kentucky, where it manufactures washers, dryers, and other electrical household appliances. The square-shaped, thousand-acre, unfenced plant is known as Appliance Park. A large drainage ditch makes ingress and egress impossible except over five roadways across culverts, designated as gates.

Since 1954, General Electric sought to confine the employees of independent contractors, described hereafter, who work on the premises of the Park, to the use of Gate 3-A and confine its use to them. The undisputed reason for doing so was to insulate General Electric employees from the frequent labor disputes in which the contractors were involved. Gate 3-A is 550 feet away from the nearest entrance available for General Electric employees, suppliers, and deliverymen. Although anyone can pass the gate without challenge,[1] the roadway leads to a guardhouse where identification must be presented. Vehicle stickers of various shapes and colors enable a guard to check on sight whether a vehicle is authorized to use Gate 3-A. Since January 1958, a prominent sign has been posted at the gate which states: "GATE 3-A FOR EMPLOYEES OF CONTRACTORS ONLY — G.E. EMPLOYEES USE OTHER GATES." On rare occasions, it appears, a General Electric employee was allowed to pass the guardhouse, but such occurrence was in

---

[1] During the strike in question a guard was stationed at the gate.

violation of company instructions. There was no proof of any unauthorized attempts to pass the gate during the strike in question.[f]

The independent contractors are utilized for a great variety of tasks on the Appliance Park premises. Some do construction work on new buildings; some install and repair ventilating and heating equipment; some engage in retooling and rearranging operations necessary to the manufacture of new models; others do "general maintenance work." These services are contracted to outside employers either because the company's employees lack the necessary skill or manpower, or because the work can be done more economically by independent contractors. The latter reason determined the contracting of maintenance work for which the Central Maintenance department of the company bid competitively with the contractors. While some of the work done by these contractors had on occasion been previously performed by Central Maintenance, the findings do not disclose the number of employees of independent contractors who were performing these routine maintenance services, as compared with those who were doing specialized work of a capital-improvement nature.

The Union, petitioner here, is the certified bargaining representative for the production and maintenance workers who constitute approximately 7,600 of the 10,500 employees of General Electric at Appliance Park. On July 27, 1958, the Union called a strike because of 24 unsettled grievances with the company. Picketing occurred at all the gates, including Gate 3-A, and continued until August 9 when an injunction was issued by a Federal District Court. The signs carried by the pickets at all gates read: "LOCAL 761 ON STRIKE G.E. UNFAIR." Because of the picketing, almost all of the employees of independent contractors refused to enter the company premises.

Neither the legality of the strike or of the picketing at any of the gates except 3-A nor the peaceful nature of the picketing is in dispute. The sole claim is that the picketing before the gate exclusively used by employees of independent contractors was conduct proscribed by §8(b)(4)(A).

The Trial Examiner . . . concluded that the limitations on picketing which the Board had prescribed in so-called "common situs" cases were not applicable to the situation before him, in that the picketing at Gate 3-A represented traditional primary action which necessarily had a secondary effect of inconveniencing those who did business with the struck employer. He reasoned that if a primary employer could limit the area of picketing around his own premises by constructing a separate gate for employees of

[f][More than 2,000 General Electric employees in the bargaining unit, as well as nonunit employees, worked during the strike. See Local 761, Intl. Union of Elec., Radio & Mach. Wkrs., 123 N.L.R.B. 1547, 1556 (1959). — EDS.]

independent contractors, such a device could also be used to isolate employees of his suppliers and customers, and that such action could not relevantly be distinguished from oral appeals made to secondary employees not to cross a picket line where only a single gate existed.

The Board rejected the Trial Examiner's conclusion, 123 N.L.R.B. 1547. It held that, since only the employees of the independent contractors were allowed to use Gate 3-A, the Union's object in picketing there was "to enmesh these employees of the neutral employers in its dispute with the Company," thereby constituting a violation of §8(b)(4)(A) because the independent employees were encouraged to engage in a concerted refusal to work "with an object of forcing the independent contractors to cease doing business with the Company."

The Court of Appeals . . . granted enforcement of the Board's order, 278 F.2d 282. . . . [I]t concluded that the Board was correct in finding that the objective of the Gate 3-A picketing was to encourage the independent-contractor employees to engage in a concerted refusal to perform services for their employers in order to bring pressure on General Electric. . . .

I

Section 8(b)(4)(A) . . . provides that it shall be an unfair labor practice for a labor organization

> . . . to engage in, or to induce or encourage the employees of any employer to engage in, a strike or a concerted refusal in the course of their employment to use, manufacture, process, transport, or otherwise handle or work on any goods, articles, materials, or commodities or to perform any services, where an object thereof is: (A) forcing or requiring . . . any employer or other person . . . to cease doing business with any other person. . . .

This provision could not be literally construed; otherwise it would ban most strikes historically considered to be lawful, so-called primary activity. "While §8(b)(4) does not expressly mention 'primary' or 'secondary' disputes, strikes or boycotts, that section often is referred to in the Act's legislative history as one of the Act's 'secondary boycott sections.'" Labor Board v. Denver Building Council, 341 U.S. 675, 686. "Congress did not seek, by §8(b)(4), to interfere with the ordinary strike. . . ." Labor Board v. International Rice Milling Co., 341 U.S. 665, 672. The impact of the section was directed toward what is known as the secondary boycott whose "sanctions bear, not upon the employer who alone is a party to the dispute, but upon some third party who has no concern in it." Electrical Workers v. Labor Board, 181 F.2d 34, 37. Thus the section left a striking labor organization free to use persuasion, including picketing, not only on the primary employer and his employees but on numerous others. Among these were secondary employers who were customers or suppliers of the primary employer and persons dealing with them . . . and even employees of secondary employers so long as the labor organization did not . . . "induce or encourage the employees of any employer to engage in a strike or a concerted refusal in the course of their employment". . . .

Labor Board v. Local 294, Teamsters, 284 F.2d 887, 889.

But not all so-called secondary boycotts were outlawed in §8(b)(4)(A).

The section does not speak generally of secondary boycotts. It describes and condemns specific union conduct directed to specific objectives. . . . Employees must be induced; they must be induced to engage in a strike or concerted refusal; an object must be to force or require their employer or another person to cease doing business with a third person. Thus, much that might argumentatively be found to fall within the broad and somewhat vague concept of secondary boycott is not in terms prohibited.

Local 1976, United Brotherhood of Carpenters v. Labor Board, 357 U.S. 93, 98. . . .

Important as is the distinction between legitimate "primary activity" and banned "secondary activity," it does not present a glaringly bright line. The objectives of any picketing include a desire to influence others from withholding from the employer their services or trade. See [Moore Dry Dock], 92 N.L.R.B. 547. "[I]ntended or not, sought for or not, aimed for or not, employees of neutral employers do take action sympathetic with strikers and do put pressure on their own employers." Seafarers International Union v. Labor Board, 265 F.2d 585, 590. . . . But picketing which induces secondary employees to respect a picket line is not the equivalent of picketing which has an object of inducing those employees to engage in concerted conduct against their employer in order to force him to refuse to deal with the struck employer. [Rice Milling], supra.

However difficult the drawing of lines more nice than obvious, the statute compels the task. Accordingly, the Board and the courts have attempted to devise reasonable criteria drawing heavily upon the means to which a union resorts in promoting its cause. Although "[n]o rigid rule which would make . . . [a] few factors conclusive is contained in or deducible from the statute," Sales Drivers v. Labor Board, 229 F.2d 514, 517, "[i]n the absence of admissions by the union of an illegal intent, the nature of acts performed shows the intent." Seafarers International Union, supra, at 591. . . .

II

The early decisions of the Board following the Taft-Hartley amendments involved activity which took place around the secondary employer's premises. For example, in *Wadsworth Building Co.* [81 N.L.R.B. 802-805], the union set up a picket line around the situs of a builder who had contracted to purchase prefabricated houses from the primary employer. The Board found this to be illegal secondary activity. . . . In contrast, when picketing took place around the premises of the primary employer, the Board regarded this as valid primary activity. In [Pure Oil Co.], 84 N.L.R.B. 315, Pure had used Standard's dock and employees for loading its oil onto ships. The companies had contracted that, in case of a strike against Standard, Pure employees would take over the loading of Pure oil. The union struck against Standard and picketed the dock, and Pure employees refused to cross the picket line. The Board held this to be a primary activity, although the union's action induced the Pure employees to engage in a concerted refusal to handle Pure products at the dock. The fact that the picketing was confined to the vicinity of the Standard premises influenced the Board not to find that an object of the activity was to force Pure to cease doing business with Standard, even if such was a secondary effect.

> A strike, by its very nature, inconveniences those who customarily do business with the struck employer. Moreover, any accompanying picketing of the employer's premises is necessarily designed to induce and encourage third persons to cease doing business with the picketed employer. It does not follow, however, that such picketing is therefore proscribed by §8(b)(4)(A) of the Act.

84 N.L.R.B., at 318. . . .

   In [Ryan Construction Corp.], 85 N.L.R.B. 417, Ryan had contracted to perform construction work on a building adjacent to the Bucyrus plant and inside its fence. A separate gate was cut through the fence for Ryan's employees which no employee of Bucyrus ever used. The Board concluded that the union — on strike against Bucyrus — could picket the Ryan gate, even though an object of the picketing was to enlist the aid of Ryan employees, since Congress did not intend to outlaw primary picketing.

> When picketing is wholly at the premises of the employer with whom the union is engaged in a labor dispute, it cannot be called "secondary" even though, as is virtually always the case, an object of the picketing is to dissuade all persons from entering such premises for business reasons. It makes no difference whether 1 or 100 other employees wish to enter the premises. It follows in this case that the picketing of Bucyrus premises, which was primary because in support of a labor dispute with Bucyrus, did not lose its character

and become "secondary" at the so-called Ryan gate because Ryan employees were the only persons regularly entering Bucyrus premises at that gate.

85 N.L.R.B., at 418. . . . Thus, the Board eliminated picketing which took place around the situs of the primary employer — regardless of the special circumstances involved — from being held invalid secondary activity under §8(b)(4)(A).

However, the impact of the new situations made the Board conscious of the complexity of the problem by reason of the protean forms in which it appeared. This became clear in the "common situs" cases — situations where two employers were performing separate tasks on common premises. The *Moore Dry Dock* case laid out the Board's new standards in this area. These tests were widely accepted by reviewing federal courts. . . .

As is too often the way of law or, at least, of adjudications, soon the *Dry Dock* tests were mechanically applied so that a violation of one of the standards was taken to be presumptive of illegal activity. For example, failure of picket signs clearly to designate the employer against whom the strike was directed was held to be violative of §8(b)(4)(A).[4]

In Local 55 (PBM), 108 N.L.R.B. 363, the Board for the first time applied the *Dry Dock* test, although the picketing occurred at premises owned by the primary employer. There, an insurance company owned a tract of land that it was developing, and also served as the general contractor. A neutral subcontractor was also doing work at the site. The union, engaged in a strike against the insurance company, picketed the entire premises, characterizing the entire job as unfair, and the employees of the subcontractor walked off. . . . [T]he Tenth Circuit enforced the Board's order which found the picketing to be illegal on the ground that the picket signs did not measure up to the *Dry Dock* standard that they clearly disclose that the picketing was directed against the struck employer only. 218 F.2d 226.

The Board's application of the *Dry Dock* standards to picketing at the premises of the struck employer was made more explicit in Retail Fruit & Vegetable Clerks (Crystal Palace Market), 116 N.L.R.B. 856. The owner of a large common market operated some of the shops within, and leased out others to independent sellers. The union, although given permission to picket the owner's individual stands, chose to picket outside the entire market. The Board held that this action was violative of §8(b)(4)(A) in that the union did not attempt to minimize the effect of its picketing, as required in a common-situs case, on the operations of the neutral employers utilizing the

---

[4]The *Dry Dock* criteria had perhaps their widest application in the trucking industry. There, unions on strike against truckers often staged picketing demonstrations at the places of pickup and delivery. . . .

market. "We believe . . . that the foregoing principles should apply to all common situs picketing, including cases where, as here, the picketed premises are owned by the primary employer." 116 N.L.R.B., at 859. The *Ryan* case, supra, was overruled to the extent it implied the contrary. . . . [T]he Ninth Circuit, in enforcing the Board's order, specifically approved its disavowance of an ownership test. 249 F.2d 591. . . .

In rejecting the ownership test in situations where two employers were performing work upon a common site, the Board was naturally guided by this Court's opinion in *Rice Milling*, in which we indicated that the location of the picketing at the primary employer's premises was "not necessarily conclusive" of its legality. 341 U.S., at 671. Where the work done by the secondary employees is unrelated to the normal operations of the primary employer, it is difficult to perceive how the pressure of picketing the entire situs is any less on the neutral employer merely because the picketing takes place at property owned by the struck employer. The application of the *Dry Dock* tests to limit the picketing effects to the employees of the employer against whom the dispute is directed carries out the "dual congressional objectives of preserving the right of labor organizations to bring pressure to bear on offending employers in primary labor disputes and of shielding unoffending employers and others from pressures in controversies not their own." Labor Board v. Denver Building Council, supra, at 692.

III

From this necessary survey of the course of the Board's treatment of our problem, the precise nature of the issue before us emerges. . . . [T]he question is whether the Board may apply the *Dry Dock* criteria so as to make unlawful picketing at a gate utilized exclusively by employees of independent contractors who work on the struck employer's premises. The effect of such a holding would not bar the union from picketing at all gates used by the employees, suppliers, and customers of the struck employer. Of course an employer may not, by removing all his employees from the situs of the strike, bar the union from publicizing its cause. . . . The basis of the Board's decision in this case would not remotely have that effect, nor any such tendency for the future.

The Union claims that, if the Board's ruling is upheld, employers will be free to erect separate gates for deliveries, customers, and replacement workers which will be immunized from picketing. This fear is baseless. The key to the problem is found in the type of work that is being performed by those who use the separate gate. It is significant that the Board has since applied its rationale, first stated in the present case, only to situations where the independent workers were performing tasks unconnected to the normal operations of the struck employer — usually construction work on his buildings. In such situations, the indicated limitations on picketing activity respect the balance of competing interests that Congress has required the Board to enforce. On the other hand, if a separate gate were devised for regular plant deliveries, the barring of picketing at that location would make a clear invasion on traditional primary activity of appealing to neutral employees whose tasks aid the employer's everyday operations. The 1959 Amendments . . . , which removed the word "concerted" from the boycott provisions, included a proviso that "nothing contained in this clause (B) shall be construed to make unlawful, where not otherwise unlawful, any primary strike or primary picketing." . . . The proviso was directed against the fear that the removal of "concerted" from the statute might be interpreted so that "the picketing at the factory violates §8(b)(4)(A) because the pickets induce the truck drivers employed by the trucker not to perform their usual services where an object is to compel the trucking firm not to do business with the . . . manufacturer during the strike." . . . 105 Cong. Rec. 16589.

In a case similar to the one now before us, . . . the Second Circuit sustained the Board in its application of §8(b)(4)(A) to a separate-gate situation. "There must be a separate gate marked and set apart from other gates; the work done by the men who use the gate must be unrelated to the normal operations of the employer and the work must be of a kind that would not, if done when the plant were engaged in its regular operations, necessitate curtailing those operations." United Steelworkers v. Labor Board, 289 F.2d 591, 595, decided May 3, 1961.[g] These seem to us controlling considerations.

IV

The foregoing course of reasoning would require that the judgment below sustaining the Board's order be affirmed but for one consideration, even

[g] [The Second Circuit had also declared in *Steelworkers*: ". . . [T]he contractors . . . were truly neutral and were not the alter ego of the employer, taking over its ordinary business and benefiting from the strike. They were not an 'ally' of the struck employer hired to do its everyday business in an effort to preserve its good will and perhaps its profits. Compare NLRB v. Business Machine and Office Appliance Workers, etc., 228 F.2d 553 (2d Cir. 1955). Nor was the work they were engaged in of a kind that would have necessitated closing down or curtailing the activity at the plant so that by hiring them after the strike began or in anticipation of it, the employer was escaping from or mitigating the economic effect of the strike. . . . On the contrary, the contractors were constructing a capital improvement, and their work had gone on for several weeks before the strike without curtailing the ordinary plant operations." — EDS.]

though this consideration may turn out not to affect the result. The legal path by which the Board and the Court of Appeals reached their decisions did not take into account that if Gate 3-A was . . . used by employees of independent contractors who performed conventional maintenance work necessary to the normal operations of General Electric, the use of the gate would have been a mingled one outside the bar of §8(b)(4)(A). In short, such mixed use of this portion of the struck employer's premises would not bar picketing rights of the striking employees. While the record shows some such mingled use, it sheds no light on its extent. It may well turn out to be that the instances of these maintenance tasks were so insubstantial as to be treated by the Board as de minimis. We cannot here guess at the quantitative aspect of this problem. It calls for Board determination. For determination of the questions thus raised, the case must be remanded by the Court of Appeals to the Board.

Reversed.

The Chief Justice and Black, J., concur in the result.

[Douglas, J., concluded that the decision below fell within the court of appeal's authority under *Universal Camera* and, finding no "egregious error," would not have reversed.

Upon remand of the *General Electric* case, the Trial Examiner recommended dismissal of the complaint, reasoning that the work of rearranging and enlarging the conveyor system in two appliance departments was "related to GE's normal operation" since the conveyor system was essential for the resumption of production of finished products. The Board rejected this reasoning but not the result; it relied not on the conveyor work but on the installation of showers and miscellaneous repairs and alterations performed by subcontractors, which involved a total cost of approximately $15,000, and which, the Board emphasized, had in the past been done by GE's employees. It concluded that these jobs were "necessarily related to GE's normal operations" and that the picketing had, accordingly, been "primary." See 138 N.L.R.B. 342 (1962).]

NOTES

1. For a valuable study of the maze described in *General Electric*, see Lesnick, The Gravamen of the Secondary Boycott, 62 Colum. L. Rev. 1363 (1962); see also Zimmerman, Secondary Picketing and the Reserved Gate: The General Electric Doctrine, 47 Va. L. Rev. 1164 (1961). For a survey of post-GE cases, see Cantor, Separate Gates, Related Work, and Secondary Boycotts, 27 Rutgers L. Rev. 613 (1974).

2. Assume that the primary dispute had been between the contractor

and his employees, and that GE had set up separate gates for its employees and the contractor's employees, respectively. Could the union have lawfully picketed next to the gates reserved for GE's employees?

Markwell & Hartz, Inc. v. NLRB
387 F.2d 79 (5th Cir. 1967), *cert. denied,* 391 U.S. 914 (1968)

[Markwell and Hartz (M & H), the general contractor for a construction project, entered into a recognition agreement with the UMW, before beginning the work involved. M & H subcontracted about 20 percent of the work, including the pile driving to Binnings and the electrical work to Barnes. The subcontractors' employees were represented by the Building and Construction Trades Council. The Council, seeking recognition as the representative of M & H's employees, began picketing the gates to the job site on October 17, 1963. By November 16, M & H had clearly marked one gate for the exclusive use of its own employees and suppliers, and three gates for the exclusive use of the subcontractors and of their suppliers.

The Council, until enjoined by a federal district court, continued to picket all these gates even though employees used the gates as marked. Binnings' and Barnes' employees honored the picket lines, and M & H recalled its employees (who had previously been withdrawn from the site) to complete the pile driving. The Board held (3 to 2) that the picketing of the gates reserved for the subcontractors' employees had violated §8(b)(4)(B). The majority, although conceding that the subcontractors' work was "in a sense related to M & H's normal operations," concluded that the principles of *Moore Dry Dock,* and not those of *General Electric,* governed common situs picketing in the construction industry.

The court of appeals enforced the Board's order, (2 to 1), with the two judges in the majority relying on different rationales.]

CONNALLY, J. Three years [after the *General Electric* decision] in *Carrier* [376 U.S. 492 (1964)] the Court, again without dissent, rejected the theory that ownership or control of the site of the picketing was controlling. There Carrier was engaged in a dispute with its employees, at its own plant. The picketing in question took place at a railroad spur track, owned by the railroad and used exclusively by the railroad and its employees, but located immediately adjacent to Carrier's plant and used for the delivery of supplies and removal of the manufactured products of Carrier. Approving and reaffirming the test of *General Electric,* the Court in *Carrier* held that the ownership of the railroad spur was immaterial, and that it was in fact, no more than another gate to the Carrier plant; hence the picketing at such gate to inform the railroad and its employees who were suppliers of Carrier of the existence of the dispute was primary and protected activity.

Thus the question posed here is whether the work of subcontractors Binnings and Barnes was "related to the normal operations" of Markwell and Hartz (as, for example, ordinary maintenance as in *General Electric*), in which event the picketing is primary; or whether it is unrelated to the normal operations (as of a capital improvement nature).

While it would seem clear from a statement of this test that the work of Binnings and Barnes, consisting of specialized work for which Markwell and Hartz was unequipped and unable to perform itself, was of the unrelated variety, we need not speculate upon the answer to this question. It is answered authoritatively in *Denver*. That case involved a construction project common situs where employees of the general and the subcontractors worked side by side. In a dispute with the subcontractor, picketing was likewise directed at the employees of the prime. There, as here, it was found that an object of such picketing was to force or require the cessation of business, one with the other, and to force a termination of the subcontract. . . .

The Trades Council argues that there is a conflict between *Denver*, on the one hand, and *General Electric* and *Carrier*, on the other. We find no such conflict. *Denver* is cited with approval in *General Electric*.

The Council further argues that *Denver* should be limited to its precise facts, that is, where the dispute is with a subcontractor and the general contractor is a neutral. Such a position is supported by neither logic nor authority. The statute, in condemning the secondary boycott, makes no such distinction and we are unable to say that it is less an unfair labor practice to bring economic pressure on a subcontractor to induce him to breach his contract and cease doing business with the prime, rather than where the parties are reversed. . . .

Holding as we do that the subcontractors here were entitled to protection from the . . . picketing, the Trades Council was obliged to restrict its picketing in conformity with the *Moore Dry Dock* criteria.

RIVES, J. [(specially concurring), found that the work of the subcontractors and of M & H was "related," noting that M & H's employees had completed the pile driving after Binnings' employees had left the job. Excerpts from his opinion follow.]

When the work done by the secondary employees is related to the normal operations of the primary employer there remains a distinction between picketing at the situs of the primary employer and picketing at a common situs where two or more employers are performing separate tasks on common premises. It seems to me that the opinion in *General Electric* clearly recognizes that distinction and approves the four *Moore Dry Dock* standards as applicable to common situs picketing. . . .

I agree that *General Electric* and *Carrier* are not inconsistent with *Denver*. *Denver* relates to common situs picketing. *General Electric* and *Carrier* involve illegal picketing at the premises of a struck manufacturer. Except for this difference in reasoning, I concur fully with Judge Connally.

WISDOM, J. [dissented at length:] The Board attempts to distinguish away *General Electric* and *Carrier* on the ground that they were the product of the "lenient treatment . . . given to strike action taking place at the separate premises of a struck employer." Those decisions, so the Board and the Court here say, were not intended to upset the traditional approach to common situs problems in the construction industry. Relying therefore on *Denver* (although *Denver* did not involve a separate gate) and on the *Moore Dry Dock* criteria, the Board found that the timing and the picketing at the reserved gates were not intended to reach the employees of Markwell and Hartz but had the unlawful *object* of inducing strike action by the employees of neutral Binnings and Barnes.

General Electric and *Carrier* cannot be brushed off lightly. They represent an attempt to show in what circumstances picketing of a secondary employer is permissible. Under *General Electric*, not all independent contractors are neutrals: They lose their neutral status when their work is related ("necessary") to the normal or day-to-day operations of the primary employer.

Here the board apparently limited the use of the term "common situs" to situations where the primary and secondary employers are engaged in operations on premises owned by a third person or by a secondary employer. But the Supreme Court in *General Electric* used the term "common situs" to refer to any location where both the primary and the secondary employers were present. 366 U.S. at 676. The Board itself, in Crystal Palace Market, 116 N.L.R.B. 856, 859 (1956) stated: "[*Moore Dry Dock*] principles should apply to all common situs picketing, including cases where, as here, the picketed premises are owned by the primary employer. We can see no logical reasons why the legality of such picketing should depend on title to property." The effect of the Board's decision is to apply more rigid standards to the construction industry than to the manufacturing industry. Any prime contractor would be able to frustrate the purposes of picketing by opening gates reserved for his subcontractors.

The Board assumes that if the related-work standard is applied to common construction situs, *General Electric* must be considered as having overruled *Denver* sub silentio. In *Denver*, however, the Court focused on the point that contractors and subcontractors on a construction project are not *necessarily* so interconnected that they should all be regarded as one entity. The Court did not hold that as a matter of law all independent contractors on a common situs must be considered as neutrals. . . . The touchstone furnished by *Carrier* as well as by *General Electric* is relatedness of work. To the extent that the conclusions in *Denver* were arrived at independent of any consideration of relatedness, those conclusions must be considered as modified by application of the relatedness standard set down in *General Electric*. Here, therefore, the Board should have made a finding on the issue of relatedness. An unlawful object under §8(b)(4) cannot be inferred simply from the fact that the union has picketed at a gate reserved for the subcontractors' employees.

Since the Board has considered *General Electric* inapposite and has not made any finding on the issue of relatedness of work, the case should be remanded to the Board for such a finding. . . .

The dissenting members of the Board would apply the "related work" standard only where the dispute is with the general contractor. I agree with the majority on this point: "The plain logic of their position is equally applicable where the primary dispute is with a building subcontractor whose employees are working closely with employees of other subcontractors or those of the general contractor."

The statute, in condemning the secondary boycott, makes no such distinction and we are unable to say that it is less an unfair labor practice to bring economic pressure on a subcontractor to induce him to breach his contract and cease doing business with the prime, rather than where the parties are reversed. . . .

NOTES

1. In Carpenters Local 470 (Mueller-Anderson, Inc.), 224 N.L.R.B. 315 (1976), *enforced*, 564 F.2d 1360 (9th Cir. 1977), the Board (3 to 2), applied *Markwell & Hartz* even though the general contractor (the primary employer) owned the land being developed. For the purposes of §8(b)(4), is there any reason that the primary employer's ownership of the building site should be material? Is a separate gate economically important because it facilitates a lawful appeal by the pickets to employees of suppliers of the primary employer?

2. A general contractor let out all work on a construction site to union subcontractors, except for the plumbing and heating work, which went to Roberts, Inc., a nonunion firm. When Roberts and another plumber began work on the site, the plumbers' local began picketing with a placard stating

that Roberts' rates were substandard and that the picketing was not "intended to cause any employees to strike the employer or to refuse to deliver any goods." This picketing began when only Roberts' employees were on the site. When other employees were to appear, the general contractor and Roberts arranged to have the plumbers work only after 4:30 p.m. and on weekends, when no other employees were to be on the site, and so advised the plumbers' union. Nevertheless, the union continued to picket during regular working hours. The general contractor asked the union what would happen if another plumbing contractor were engaged; the union replied that it would stop picketing Roberts. Thereafter the union attorney advised the general contractor that only Roberts was being picketed, that the picketing was informational and was "specifically not intended to cause Roberts to lose his contract with you." Nevertheless, the general contractor cancelled that contract, and work on the site proceeded. The Board found a violation of §8(b)(4)(B). See Plumbers Local 519, 171 N.L.R.B. 251 (1968), *enforced*, 416 F.2d 1120, 1125 (D.C. Cir. 1969) (no real distinction between "separate gates and separate hours"). But cf. Local 901, Teamsters v. NLRB, 293 F.2d 881 (D.C. Cir. 1961). The Board has distinguished situations where picketing continued during "temporary or sporadic" absences of the primary employees. See International Bhd. of Elec. Wkrs., Local 861, 135 N.L.R.B. 250 (1962); International Bhd. of Elec. Wkrs., Local 861, 145 N.L.R.B. 1163 (1964).

c. "Political" Boycotts

International Longshoremen's Assn. v. Allied International, Inc.
456 U.S. 212 (1982)

POWELL, J. The question . . . is whether a refusal by an American longshoremen's union to unload cargoes shipped from the Soviet Union is an illegal secondary boycott under §8(b)(4). . . .

I

On January 9, 1980, Thomas Gleason, president of the International Longshoremen's Association (ILA), ordered ILA members to stop handling cargoes arriving from or destined for the Soviet Union. Gleason took this action to protest the Russian invasion of Afghanistan. In obedience to the order, longshoremen up and down the east and gulf coasts refused to service ships carrying Russian cargoes.

Respondent Allied International, Inc. (Allied), is an American company that imports Russian wood products for resale in the United States. Allied contracts with Waterman Steamship Lines (Waterman), an American corporation operating ships of United States registry, for shipment of the wood from Leningrad to ports on the east and gulf coasts of the United States. Waterman, in turn, employs the stevedoring company of John T. Clark & Son of Boston, Inc. (Clark), to unload its ships docking in Boston. Under the terms of the collective-bargaining agreement between ILA Local 799 and the Boston Shipping Association, of which Clark is a member, Clark obtains its longshoring employees through the union hiring hall.

As a result of the boycott, Allied's shipments were disrupted completely. Ultimately, Allied was forced to renegotiate its Russian contracts, substantially reducing its purchases and jeopardizing its ability to supply its own customers. On March 31, 1980, after union officials informed Allied that ILA members would continue to refuse to unload any Russian cargo, Allied brought this action in the United States District Court. . . . Claiming that the boycott violated the prohibition against secondary boycotts in §8(b) (4) . . . , Allied sued for damages under [LMRA] §303, which creates a private damages remedy for the victims of secondary boycotts.[6] At about the same time, Allied filed an unfair labor practice charge with the [NLRB].[7]

. . . [T]he District Court dismissed Allied's complaint. 492 F. Supp. 334 (1980). The court characterized the ILA boycott as a purely political, primary boycott of Russian goods . . . not within the scope of §8(b)(4).

. . . [T]he First Circuit reversed the dismissal of Allied's complaint and remanded for further proceedings. 640 F.2d 1368 (1981). As an initial matter, . . . the court found that the effects of the ILA boycott were "in commerce" within the meaning of the NLRA as interpreted by a long line of decisions of this Court. The court held further that the ILA boycott . . . was within §8(b)(4)'s prohibition of secondary boycotts, despite its political purpose, and that resort to such behavior was not protected activity under the First Amendment. . . . We affirm.

[6] Allied also alleged that the ILA boycott violated the Sherman Act, 15 U.S.C. §1, and amounted to a tortious interference with Allied's business relationships in violation of admiralty law. The Court of Appeals affirmed the District Court's dismissal of these claims, and they are not before us now. See 640 F.2d 1368, 1379-1382 (CA1 1981).

[7] [T]he Regional Director issued an unfair labor practice complaint against the ILA and filed a request for a preliminary injunction in Federal District Court. Finding that the ILA boycott was a political dispute outside the scope of §8(b)(4)(B), the District Court denied the request for a preliminary injunction. . . . The Court of Appeals affirmed on a different theory. Walsh v. International Longshoremen's Assn., 630 F.2d 864 (CA1 1980). It found that the denial of the Board's earlier request for injunctive relief against the boycott in Baldovin v. International Longshoremen's Assn., Civ. No. 80-259 (SD Tex. Feb. 15, 1980), aff'd, 626 F.2d 445 (CA5 1980), had preclusive effect.

II

Our starting point . . . must be the language of the statute. By its exact terms the secondary boycott provisions of §8(b)(4)(B) . . . would appear to be aimed precisely at the sort of activities alleged in this case. Section 8(b) (4)(B) governs activities designed to influence individuals employed by "any person engaged in commerce or in an industry affecting commerce." Certainly Allied, Waterman, and Clark were engaged "in commerce," and Allied alleges that the effect of the ILA action was to obstruct commerce. . . . Just as plainly, it would appear that the ILA boycott fell within §8(b)(4)(B)'s prohibition of secondary boycotts. Allied alleges that by inducing members of the union to refuse to handle Russian cargoes, the ILA boycott was designed to force Allied, Waterman, and Clark "to cease doing business" with one another and "to cease using, selling, handling, transporting, or otherwise dealing in" Russian products.

[The Court rejected petitioners' arguments that their conduct was not "in commerce" and, alternatively, was not the sort of secondary boycott Congress intended to proscribe. The union, the ship, and the importer were, the Court reasoned, all American. Hence, this case was distinguishable from cases holding the NLRA inapplicable to labor disputes concerning foreign crews of foreign flag ships (and, accordingly, not preemptive of state jurisdiction over such disputes). Holding the boycott not "in commerce" could lead to inconsistent state decisions, as well as denial of NLRB jurisdiction over this national boycott, even though (according to the State Department) it "conflicted with significant U.S. foreign policy interests."]

B

The secondary boycott provisions in §8(b)(4)(B) prohibit a union from inducing employees to refuse to handle goods with the object of forcing any person to cease doing business with any other person. By its terms the statutory prohibition applies to the undisputed facts of this case. The ILA has no dispute with Allied, Waterman, or Clark. It does not seek any labor objective from these employers. Its sole complaint is with the foreign and military policy of the Soviet Union. As understandable and even commendable as the ILA's ultimate objectives may be, the certain effect of its action is to impose a heavy burden on neutral employers. And it is just such a burden, as well as widening of industrial strife, that the secondary boycott provisions were designed to prevent. As the NLRB explained in ruling upon the Regional Director's complaint against the ILA:

> . . . Here, the Union's sole dispute is with the USSR over its invasion of Afghanistan. Allied, Waterman, and Clark have nothing to do with this dis-

pute. Yet the Union's actions in furtherance of its disagreement with Soviet foreign policy have brought direct economic pressure on all three parties and have resulted in a substantial cessation of business. Thus, the conduct alleged in this case is precisely the type of conduct Congress intended the [NLRA] to regulate.

257 N.L.R.B. [1075, 1078-1079]. . . .

Nor can it be argued that the ILA's action was outside of the prohibition on secondary boycotts because its object was not to halt business between Allied, Clark, and Waterman with respect to Russian goods, but simply to free ILA members from the morally repugnant duty of handling Russian goods. Such an argument misses the point. Undoubtedly many secondary boycotts have the object of freeing employees from handling goods from an objectionable source. Nonetheless, when a purely secondary boycott "reasonably can be expected to threaten neutral parties with ruin or substantial loss," NLRB v. Retail Store Employees, 447 U.S. 607, 614 (1980), the pressure on secondary parties must be viewed as at least one of the objects of the boycott or the statutory prohibition would be rendered meaningless. The union must take responsibility for the "foreseeable consequences" of its conduct. Id., at 614, n.9. . . . Here the union was fully aware of the losses it was inflicting upon Allied. It is undisputed that Allied officials endeavored to persuade ILA leaders to allow it to fulfill its Russian contracts. On the basis of the record before it, the Court of Appeals correctly concluded that Allied had alleged a violation of §8(b)(4).

Neither is it a defense to the application of §8(b)(4) that the reason for the ILA boycott was not a labor dispute with a primary employer but a political dispute with a foreign nation. Section 8(b)(4) contains no such limitation. In the plainest of language it prohibits "forcing . . . any person to cease . . . handling . . . the products of any other producer . . . or to cease doing business with any other person." The legislative history does not indicate that political disputes should be excluded from the scope of §8(b)(4). The prohibition was drafted broadly to protect neutral parties, "the helpless victims of quarrels that do not concern them at all." H. R. Rep. No. 245, 80th Cong., 1st Sess., 23 (1947). Despite criticism from President Truman as well as from some legislators that the secondary boycott provision was too sweeping, the Congress refused to narrow its scope. Recognizing that "[i]llegal boycotts take many forms," id., at 24, Congress intended its prohibition to reach broadly.[h]

We would create a large and undefinable exception to the statute if we

_____

[h] [Is this statement consistent with the Court's prior approach to interpretation of §8(b)(4)? — Eds.]

accepted the argument that "political" boycotts are exempt from the secondary boycott provision. The distinction between labor and political objectives would be difficult to draw in many cases. In the absence of any limiting language in the statute or legislative history, we find no reason to conclude that Congress intended such a potentially expansive exception to a statutory provision purposefully drafted in broadest terms.

We agree with the Court of Appeals that it is "more rather than less objectionable that a national labor union has chosen to marshal against neutral parties the considerable powers derived by its locals and itself under the federal labor laws in aid of a random political objective far removed from what has traditionally been thought to be the realm of legitimate union activity." 640 F.2d, at 1378. In light of the statutory language and purpose, we decline to create a far-reaching exemption from the statutory provision for "political" secondary boycotts.

III

Application of §8(b)(4) to the ILA's activity in this case will not infringe upon the First Amendment rights of the ILA and its members. We have consistently rejected the claim that secondary picketing by labor unions in violation of §8(b)(4) is protected activity under the First Amendment. See, e.g., NLRB v. Retail Store Employees, supra, at 616. . . . Cf. NLRB v. Fruit Packers, 377 U.S. 58, 63 (1964).[25] It would seem even clearer that conduct designed not to communicate but to coerce merits still less consideration under the First Amendment.[26] The labor laws reflect a careful balancing of interests. See NLRB v. Retail Store Employees, 447 U.S., at 617 (Blackmun, J., concurring). There are many ways in which a union and its individual members may express their opposition to Russian foreign policy without infringing upon the rights of others.

Affirmed.

---

[25] In Electrical Workers v. NLRB, 341 U.S. 694, 705 (1951), the Court held: "The prohibition of inducement or encouragement of secondary pressure by §8(b)(4)(A) carries no unconstitutional abridgement of free speech. The inducement or encouragement in the instant case took the form of picketing. . . . [W]e recently have recognized the constitutional right of states to proscribe picketing in furtherance of comparably unlawful objectives. There is no reason why Congress may not do likewise" (footnote omitted).

[26] Cf. NLRB v. Retail Store Employees, 447 U.S. 607, 619 (1980) ("The statutory ban in this case affects only that aspect of the union's efforts to communicate its views that calls for an automatic response to a signal, rather than a reasoned response to an idea") (Stevens, J., concurring); United States v. O'Brien, 391 U.S. 367, 376 (1968) ("This Court has held that when 'speech' and 'nonspeech' elements are combined in the same course of conduct, a sufficiently important governmental interest in regulating the nonspeech element can justify incidental limitations on First Amendment freedoms").

NOTE

In light of the exemption from the Sherman Act for union action during a "labor dispute" (see infra p. 624), would the acceptance of the union's defense, under LMRA §303, that the dispute was "political" have prejudiced the union's claim of a Sherman Act exemption? Cf. Missouri v. National Organization for Women, Inc. (NOW), 620 F.2d 1301 (8th Cir.), cert. denied, 449 U.S. 842 (1980) (immunizing from Sherman Act NOW's campaign encouraging ERA supporters to withhold convention business from nonratifying states); but see Kennedy, Political Boycotts, The Sherman Act, and the First Amendment, 55 S. Cal. L. Rev. 983 (1982) (opposing a blanket political-boycott immunity from the Sherman Act, but proposing a "rule-of-reason" approach).

2.   Appeals to Customers of Secondary Employers

The 1959 amendments to §8(b)(4) were designed to plug certain loopholes in the Act's secondary boycott provisions and to shelter from §8(b)(4) certain union appeals to prospective customers of secondary employers. Before turning to the legal status of such appeals, it may be helpful to identify the loopholes targeted by those amendments: (1) The statutory definitions of "employee" (§2(3)) and "employer" (§2(2)) had been so limited that unions could lawfully induce stoppages both by supervisors in companies covered by the NLRA and by employees of firms excluded from the Act, including railroads, nonprofit hospitals, farms, and governmental agencies. (2) Section 8(b)(4) had proscribed only inducements to strikes or concerted withholding of services by statutory employees. Accordingly, no violation occurred unless a union's inducement was aimed at two or more employees. (3) Finally, threats of picketing and strikes directed at secondary employers had been held not to be proscribed. See NLRB v. Servette, 377 U.S. 46, 51-52 (1964). See also §8(b)(4) ("Hot Cargo" clauses), infra p. 598.

Edward J. DeBartolo Corp. v. NLRB
103 S. Ct. 2926 (1983)

STEVENS, J. As a result of a labor dispute between respondent union and the H.J. High Construction Company (High), the union passed out handbills urging consumers not to trade with a group of employers who had no business relationship of any kind with High. The question presented is whether that handbilling is exempted from the prohibition against secondary boycotts contained in §8(b)(4), as amended, by what is known as the "publicity proviso" to that section.

High is a general building contractor retained by the H. M. Wilson Company (Wilson) to construct a department store in a shopping center in Tampa, Florida. Petitioner, the Edward J. DeBartolo Company (DeBartolo) owns and operates the center. Most of the 85 tenants in the mall signed a standard lease with DeBartolo providing for a minimum rent (which increases whenever a large new department store opens for business) plus a percentage of gross sales, and requiring the tenant to pay a proportionate share of the costs of maintaining the mall's common areas, to pay dues to a merchants' association, and to take part in four joint advertising brochures. Wilson signed a slightly different land lease agreement, but he also promised to pay dues to the merchants' association and to share in the costs of maintaining the common areas. Under the terms of Wilson's lease, neither DeBartolo nor any of the other tenants had any right to control the manner in which High discharged its contractual obligation to Wilson.

The union conducted its handbilling at all four entrances to the shopping center for about three weeks, while the new Wilson store was under construction. Without identifying High by name, the handbill stated that the contractors building Wilson's Department Store were paying substandard wages, and asked the readers not to patronize any of the stores in the mall until DeBartolo publicly promised that all construction at the mall would be done by contractors who pay their employees fair wages and fringe benefits. The handbilling was conducted in an orderly manner, and was not accompanied by any picketing or patrolling. DeBartolo advised the union that it would not oppose this handbilling if the union modified its message to make clear that the dispute did not involve DeBartolo or any of Wilson's co-tenants, and if it limited its activities to the immediate vicinity of Wilson's. When the union persisted in distributing handbills to all patrons of the shopping center, DeBartolo filed a trespass action in the state court and an unfair labor practice charge. . . . The Board's General Counsel issued a complaint.

The complaint recited the dispute between the union and High, and noted the absence of any labor dispute between the union and DeBartolo, Wilson, or any of the other tenants of the East Lake Mall. The complaint then alleged that in furtherance of its primary dispute with High, the union "has threatened, coerced or restrained, and is threatening, coercing or restraining, various tenant Employers who are engaged in business at East Lake Square Mall, and who lease space from DeBartolo in East Lake Square Mall, by handbilling the general public not to do business with the above-described tenant Employers. . . ."

The complaint alleged that the object of the handbilling "was and is, to force or require the aforesaid tenant Employers in East Lake Square Mall . . . to cease using, handling, transporting, or otherwise dealing in products and/or services of, and to cease doing business with DeBartolo, in order to force DeBartolo and/or Wilson's not to do business with High.". . .

. . . Without deciding whether the handbilling constituted a form of "coercion" or "restraint" proscribed by §8(b)(4), the Board concluded that it was exempted from the Act by the "publicity proviso" and dismissed the complaint. [252 N.L.R.B. 702 (1980)]. The Board reasoned that there was a "symbiotic" relationship between DeBartolo and its tenants, including Wilson, and that they all would derive a substantial benefit from the "product" that High was constructing, namely Wilson's new store. The Board did not expressly state that DeBartolo and the other tenants could be said to be distributors of that product, but concluded that High's status as a producer brought a total consumer boycott of the shopping center within the publicity proviso.

The Court of Appeals agreed. [662 F.2d 264 (CA4 1981)]. It observed that our decision in NLRB v. Servette, Inc., 377 U.S. 46 (1964), had rejected a narrow reading of the proviso and that the Board had consistently construed it in an expansive manner. Finding the Board's interpretation consistent with the rationale of the [Act], it held that High was a producer and that DeBartolo and the other tenants were distributors within the meaning of the proviso. This holding reflected the court's belief that in response to the union's consumer handbilling, DeBartolo and the storekeepers would be able "in turn, to apply pressure on Wilson's and High." 662 F.2d, at 271. Because the decision conflicts with that of the . . . Eighth Circuit in Pet, Inc. v. NLRB, 641 F.2d 545 (CA8 1981), we granted certiorari. . . .[i]

The Board and the union correctly point out that DeBartolo cannot obtain relief in this proceeding unless it prevails on three separate issues. It must prove that the union did "threaten, coerce, or restrain" a person engaged in commerce, with the object of "forcing or requiring" someone to cease doing business with someone else—that is to say, it must prove a violation of §8(b)(4)(ii)(B). It must also overcome both the union's defense based on the publicity proviso and the union's claim that its conduct was protected by the First Amendment. Neither the Board nor the Court of Appeals considered whether the handbilling in this case was covered by §8(b)(4)(ii)(B) or protected by the First Amendment, because both found that it fell within the proviso. We therefore limit our attention to that issue.

[i][Despite a state court injunction against the handbilling, issued in DeBartolo's trespass action, the Court rejected a mootness claim because the union asserted a right to engage in comparable handbilling at other shopping centers owned by DeBartolo. — Eds.]

The publicity proviso applies to communications "other than picketing," that are "truthful," and that do not produce either an interference with deliveries or a work stoppage by employees of any person other than the firm engaged in the primary labor dispute. The Board and the Court of Appeals found that these three conditions were met, and these findings are not now challenged. The only question is whether the handbilling "advis[ed] the public . . . that a product or products are being produced by an employer with whom the labor organization has a primary dispute and are distributed by another employer." . . .

We have analyzed the producer-distributor requirement in only one case, NLRB v. Servette, Inc., 377 U.S. 46 (1964). *Servette* involved a primary dispute between a union and a wholesale distributor of candy and certain other specialty items sold to the public by supermarkets. The union passed out handbills in front of some of the chain stores urging consumers not to buy any products purchased by the store from Servette. We held that even though Servette did not actually manufacture the items that it distributed, it should still be regarded as a "producer" within the meaning of the proviso. We thus concluded that the handbills advised the public that the products were produced by an employer with whom the union had a primary dispute (Servette) and were being distributed by another employer (the supermarket).

In reaching that conclusion, we looked to the legislative history of the [LMRDA] of 1959, . . . which had simultaneously strengthened the secondary boycott prohibition and added the publicity proviso. We noted that a principal source of congressional concern had been the secondary boycott activities of the Teamsters Union, which for the most part represented employees of motor carriers who did not "produce" goods in the technical sense of the verb. The Teamsters' activities were plainly intended to be covered by the new prohibitions in §8(b)(4)(ii)(B), and we declined to hold that Congress, in using the word "produced," had intended to exclude the Teamsters entirely from the offsetting protections of the proviso. "There is nothing in the legislative history which suggests that the protection of the proviso was intended to be any narrower in coverage than the prohibition to which it is an exception, and we see no basis for attributing such an incongruous purpose to Congress." 377 U.S., at 55. The focus of the analysis in *Servette* was on the meaning of the term "producer." In this case, DeBartolo is willing to concede that Wilson distributes products that are "produced" by High within the meaning of the statute. This would mean that construction workers, like truck drivers, may perform services that are essential to the production and distribution of consumer goods. We may therefore assume in this case that High, the primary employer, is a producer within the meaning of the proviso.[6] Indeed, we may assume here that the proviso's "coverage" — the types of primary disputes it allows to be publicized — is broad enough to include almost any primary dispute that might result in prohibited secondary activity.[7]

We reject, however, the Board's interpretation of the extent of the secondary activity that the proviso permits. The only publicity exempted from the prohibition is publicity intended to inform the public that the primary employer's product is "distributed by" the secondary employer. We are persuaded that Congress included that requirement to reflect the concern that motivates all of §8(b)(4): "shielding . . . unoffending employers and others from pressures in controversies not their own." N.L.R.B. v. Denver Building and Construction Trades Council, 341 U.S. 675, 692 (1951).[8]

. . . [T]he Board did not find that any product produced by High was being distributed by DeBartolo or any of Wilson's cotenants. Instead, it relied on the theory that there was a symbiotic relationship between them and Wilson, and that DeBartolo and Wilson's cotenants would derive substantial benefit from High's work. That form of analysis would almost strip the distribution requirement of its limiting effect. It diverts the inquiry away from the relationship between the primary and secondary employers and toward the relationship between two secondary employers. It then tests that relationship by a standard so generous that it will be satisfied by virtually any secondary employer that a union might want consumers to boycott. Yet if Congress had intended all peaceful, truthful handbilling that informs the public of a primary dispute to fall within the proviso, the statute would not have contained a distribution requirement.

. . . DeBartolo is willing to assume that Wilson distributes products that are "produced" by High within the meaning of the statute. Wilson contracted with High to receive the construction services that are the subject of the primary dispute, and the cost of those services will presumably be reflected in the prices of the products sold by Wilson. But the handbills at issue in this case did not merely call for a boycott of Wilson's products; they also called for a boycott of the products being sold by Wilson's cotenants.

---

[6] Cf. Local 712, IBEW (Goldendorm Foods), 134 N.L.R.B. 812 (1961) (electrical and refrigeration work); Plumbers & Pipefitters, Local 142 (Shop-Rite Foods), 133 N.L.R.B. 307 (1961) (refrigeration work).

[7] As the Board stated in International Brotherhood of Teamsters, Local 537 (Lohman Sales Co.), 132 N.L.R.B. 901, 907 (1961), "there is no suggestion either in the statute itself or in the legislative history that Congress intended the words 'product' and 'produced' to be words of special limitation."

[8] See also International Longshoremen's Association, AFL-CIO v. Allied International, Inc., 456 U.S. 212, 223 (1982). . . .

Neither DeBartolo nor any of the cotenants has any business relationship with High. Nor do they sell any products whose chain of production can reasonably be said to include High. Since there is no justification for treating the products that the cotenants distribute to the public as products produced by High, the Board erred in concluding that the handbills came within the protection of the publicity proviso.

Stressing . . . that this case arises out of an entirely peaceful and orderly distribution of a written message, rather than picketing, the union argues that its handbilling is a form of speech protected by the First Amendment. The Board, without completely endorsing the union's constitutional argument, contends that it has sufficient force to invoke the Court's prudential policy of construing acts of Congress so as to avoid the unnecessary decision of serious constitutional questions. That doctrine, however, serves only to authorize the construction of a statute in a manner that is "fairly possible." Crowell v. Benson, 285 U.S. 22, 62 (1932). We do not believe that the Board's expansive reading of the proviso meets that standard.

Nevertheless, we do not reach the constitutional issue in this case. For, as we noted at the outset, the Board has not yet decided whether the handbilling in this case was proscribed by the Act. It rested its decision entirely on the publicity proviso and never considered whether, apart from that proviso, the union's conduct fell within the terms of §8(b)(4)(ii)(B). Until the statutory question is decided, review of the constitutional issue is premature.

The judgment of the Court of Appeals is vacated and the case is remanded for further proceedings consistent with this opinion. . . .

NOTES

1. The Court purported not to decide whether the union's handbilling was covered by §8(b)(4)(ii)(B) or whether it was protected by the First Amendment. Does the Court imply an answer to the first question by its reasoning in *DeBartolo* and particularly by its argument in *Servette* (repeated in *DeBartolo*) that the scope of the proviso should be coextensive with the scope of the proscription it limits?

2. In *Servette*, the Supreme Court rejected the Board's distinction between a union's inducement of "low level" supervisors (forbidden) and of "high level" supervisors (permissible). The Court held that subsection (i) of §8(b)(4) applies when the union appeals to supervisors to stop performing employment services, rather than to exercise their discretion not to buy from a primary employer.

NLRB v. Fruit & Vegetable Packers, Local 760 (Tree Fruits)
377 U.S. 58 (1964)

BRENNAN, J. The question . . . is whether the respondent unions violated [§8(b)(4)(ii)(B)] when they limited their secondary picketing of retail stores to an appeal to the customers of the stores not to buy the products of certain firms against which one of the respondents was on strike.

Respondent Local 760 called a strike against fruit packers and warehousemen doing business in Yakima, Washington.[2] The struck firms sold Washington State apples to the Safeway chain of retail stores in and about Seattle. . . . Local 760, aided by respondent Joint Council, instituted a consumer boycott against the apples in support of the strike. They placed pickets who walked back and forth before the customers' entrances of 46 Safeway stores in Seattle. The pickets — two at each of 45 stores and three at the 46th store — wore placards and distributed handbills which appealed to Safeway customers, and to the public generally, to refrain from buying Washington State apples, which were only one of numerous food products sold in the stores.[3] Before the pickets appeared at any store, a letter was delivered to the store manager informing him that the picketing was only an appeal to his customers not to buy Washington State apples, and that the pickets were being expressly instructed "to patrol peacefully in front of the

---

[2] The [24] firms . . . are members of the Tree Fruits Labor Relations Committee, Inc. [the members' collective bargaining agent]. . . . The strike was called in a dispute over the terms of the renewal of a collective bargaining agreement.

[3] The placard worn by each picket stated: "To the Consumer: Non-Union Washington State apples are being sold at this store. Please do not purchase such apples. Thank you. Teamsters Local 760, Yakima, Washington."

A typical handbill read:

DON'T BUY WASHINGTON STATE APPLES
The 1960 Crop of Washington State Apples Is Being Packed by Non-Union Firms
Included in this non-union operation are twenty-six firms in the Yakima Valley with which there is a labor dispute. These firms are charged with being
UNFAIR
by their employees who, with their union, are on strike and have been *replaced by non-union strike-breaking workers* employed under substandard wage scales and working conditions. In justice to these striking union workers who are attempting to protect their living standards and their right to engage in good-faith collective bargaining, we request that you
DON'T BUY WASHINGTON STATE APPLES
Teamsters Union Local 760
Yakima, Washington
This is not a strike against any store or market.
(P.S. — PACIFIC FRUIT & PRODUCE CO. is the only firm packing Washington State Apples under a union contract.)

customer entrances of the store, to stay away from the delivery entrances and not to interfere with the work of your employees, or with deliveries to or pickups from your store." A copy of written instructions to the pickets — which included the explicit statement that "you are also forbidden to request that the customers not patronize the store" — was enclosed with the letter. Since it was desired to assure Safeway employees that they were not to cease work, and to avoid any interference with pickups or deliveries, the pickets appeared after the stores opened for business and departed before the stores closed. At all times during the picketing, the store employees continued to work, and no deliveries or pickups were obstructed. Washington State apples were handled in normal courses by both Safeway employees and the employees of other employers involved. Ingress and egress by customers and others was not interfered with in any manner.

. . . The Board held . . . [that] consumer picketing in front of a secondary establishment is prohibited. 132 N.L.R.B. 1172, 1177. . . . [T]he Court of Appeals . . . set aside the Board's order and remanded. The court rejected the Board's construction and held that the statutory requirement of a showing that respondents' conduct would "threaten, coerce, or restrain" Safeway could only be satisfied by affirmative proof that a substantial economic impact on Safeway had occurred, or was likely to occur as a result of the conduct. . . .

The Board's reading of the statute — that the legislative history and the phrase "other than picketing" in the proviso reveal a congressional purpose to outlaw all picketing directed at customers at a secondary site — necessarily rested on the finding that Congress determined that such picketing always threatens, coerces or restrains the secondary employer. We therefore have a special responsibility to examine the legislative history for confirmation that Congress made that determination. Throughout the history of federal regulation of labor relations, Congress has consistently refused to prohibit peaceful picketing except where it is used as a means to achieve specific ends which experience has shown are undesirable. "In the sensitive area of peaceful picketing Congress has dealt explicitly with isolated evils which experience has established flow from such picketing." Labor Board v. Drivers Local Union, 362 U.S. 274, 284. We have recognized this congressional practice and have not ascribed to Congress a purpose to outlaw peaceful picketing unless "there is the clearest indication in the legislative history," ibid., that Congress intended to do so as regards the particular ends of the picketing under review. Both the congressional policy and our adherence to this principle of interpretation reflect concern that a broad ban against peaceful picketing might collide with the guarantees of the First Amendment.

We have examined the legislative history of the amendments to

§8(b)(4), and conclude that it does not reflect with the requisite clarity a congressional plan to proscribe all peaceful consumer picketing at secondary sites, and, particularly, any concern with peaceful picketing when it is limited, as here, to persuading Safeway customers not to buy Washington State apples when they traded in the Safeway stores. All that the legislative history shows in the way of an "isolated evil" believed to require proscription of peaceful consumer picketing at secondary sites, was its use to persuade the customers of the secondary employer to cease trading with him in order to force him to cease dealing with, or to put pressure upon, the primary employer. This narrow focus reflects the difference between such conduct and peaceful picketing at the secondary site directed only at the struck product. In the latter case, the union's appeal to the public is confined to its dispute with the primary employer, since the public is not asked to withhold its patronage from the secondary employer, but only to boycott the primary employer's goods. On the other hand, a union appeal to the public at the secondary site not to trade at all with the secondary employer goes beyond the goods of the primary employer, and seeks the public's assistance in forcing the secondary employer to cooperate with the union in its primary dispute.[7] This is not to say that this distinction was expressly alluded to in the debates. It is to say, however, that the consumer picketing carried on in this case is not attended by the abuses at which the statute was directed.

The story of the 1959 amendments, which we have detailed at greater length in our opinion filed today in Labor Board v. Servette, Inc., . . . begins with the original §8(b)(4). . . . . Its prohibition, in pertinent part, was confined to the inducing or encouraging of "the employees of any employer to engage in a strike or a concerted refusal . . . to . . . handle . . . any goods . . . " of a primary employer. This proved to be inept language. Three major loopholes were revealed. [Here the Court points to the "loopholes" described supra p. 576.]

Proposed amendments of §8(b)(4) offered [in 1958] by several Senators to fill the three loopholes were rejected. The Administration introduced such a bill, and it was supported by Senators Dirksen and Goldwater. Senator

---

[7] The distinction between picketing a secondary employer merely to "follow the struck goods," and picketing designed to result in a generalized loss of patronage, was well established in the state cases by 1940. The distinction was sometimes justified on the ground that the secondary employer, who was presumed to receive a competitive benefit from the primary employer's nonunion, and hence lower, wage scales, was in "unity of interest" with the primary employer, Goldfinger v. Feintuch, 276 N.Y. 281, 286, 11 N.E.2d 910, 913 . . . , and sometimes on the ground that picketing restricted to the primary employer's product is "a primary boycott against the merchandise." Chiate v. United Cannery Agricultural Packing & Allied Workers of America, 2 CCH Lab. Cas. 125, 126 (Cal. Super. Ct.). See I Teller, Labor Disputes and Collective Bargaining §123 (1940).

Goldwater, an insistent proponent of stiff boycott curbs, also proposed his own amendments. We think it is especially significant that neither Senator, nor the Secretary of Labor in testifying in support of the Administration's bill, referred to consumer picketing as making the amendments necessary.[10] Senator McClellan, who also offered a bill to curb boycotts, mentioned consumer picketing but only such as was "pressure in the form of dissuading customers *from dealing with* secondary employers." (Emphasis supplied.) It was the opponents of the amendments who, in expressing fear of their sweep, suggested that they might proscribe consumer picketing. . . .

The House history is similarly beclouded, but what appears confirms our conclusion. From the outset the House legislation included provisions concerning secondary boycotts. The Landrum-Griffin bill, which was ultimately passed by the House, embodied the Eisenhower Administration's proposals as to secondary boycotts. The initial statement of Congressman Griffin in introducing the bill which bears his name, contains no reference to consumer picketing in the list of abuses which he thought required the secondary boycott amendments. Later in the House debates he did discuss consumer picketing, but only in the context of its abuse when directed against shutting off the patronage of a secondary employer.

In the debates before passage of the House bill he stated that the amendments applied to consumer picketing of customer entrances to retail stores selling goods manufactured by a concern under strike, if the picketing were designed to "coerce or to restrain the employer of [the] second establishment, to get him not to do business with the manufacturer . . . ," and further that, "of course, this bill and any other bill is limited by the constitutional right of free speech. If the purpose of the picketing is to *coerce the retailer not to do business* with the manufacturer" — then such a boycott could be stopped. (Italics supplied.)

. . . There is thus nothing in the legislative history prior to the con-

---

[10] . . . It is true that Senator Goldwater referred to consumer picketing when the Conference bill was before the Senate. His full statement reads as follows: "the House bill . . . closed up every loophole in the boycott section of the law including the use of a secondary consumer picket line, an example of which the President gave on his nationwide TV program on August 6. . . ." 105 Cong. Rec. 17904, II Leg. Hist. 1437. The example given by the President was this: "The employees [of a furniture manufacturer] vote against joining a particular union. Instead of picketing the furniture plant itself, unscrupulous organizing officials . . . picket the stores which sell the furniture . . . How can anyone justify this kind of pressure against stores which are not involved in any dispute? . . . This kind of action is designed to make the stores bring pressure on the furniture plant and its employees. . . ." 105 Cong. Rec. 19954, II Leg. Hist. 1842. Senator Goldwater's own definition of what he meant by a secondary consumer boycott is even more clearly narrow in scope: "A secondary consumer, or customer, boycott involves the refusal of . . . customers to buy the products or services of one employer in order to force him to stop doing business with another employer." 105 Cong. Rec. 17674, II Leg. Hist. 1386.

vening of the Conference Committee which shows any congressional concern with consumer picketing beyond that with the "isolated evil" of its use to cut off the business of a secondary employer as a means of forcing him to stop doing business with the primary employer. When Congress meant to bar picketing per se, it made its meaning clear; for example, §8(b)(7) makes it an unfair labor practice, "to picket or cause to be picketed . . . any employer. . . ." In contrast, the prohibition of §8(b)(4) is keyed to the coercive nature of the conduct, whether it be picketing or otherwise.

Senator Kennedy presided over the Conference Committee. He and Congressman Thompson prepared a joint analysis of the Senate and House bills. This analysis pointed up the First Amendment implications of the broad language in the House revisions of §8(b)(4) stating,

> The prohibition [of the House bill] reaches not only picketing but leaflets, radio broadcasts, and newspaper advertisements, thereby interfering with freedom of speech. . . .
>
> [O]ne of the apparent purposes of the amendment is to prevent unions from appealing to the general public as consumers for assistance in a labor dispute. This is a basic infringement upon freedom of expression.

This analysis was the first step in the development of the publicity proviso, but nothing in the legislative history of the proviso alters our conclusion that Congress did not clearly express an intention that amended §8(b)(4) should prohibit all consumer picketing. Because of the sweeping language of the House bill, and its implications for freedom of speech, the Senate conferees refused to accede to the House proposal without safeguards for the right of unions to appeal to the public, even by some conduct which might be "coercive." The result was the addition of the proviso. But it does not follow from the fact that some coercive conduct was protected by the proviso, that the exception "other than picketing" indicates that Congress had determined that all consumer picketing was coercive.

No Conference Report was before the Senate when it passed the compromise bill, and it had the benefit only of Senator Kennedy's statement of the purpose of the proviso. He said that the proviso preserved

> the right to appeal to consumers by methods other than picketing asking them to refrain from buying goods made by nonunion labor *and* to refrain from trading with a retailer who sells such goods. . . . We were not able to persuade the House conferees to permit picketing in front of that secondary shop, but were able to persuade them to agree that the union shall be free to conduct informational activity short of picketing. In other words, the union can hand out handbills at the shop . . . and can carry on all publicity short of having ambulatory picketing. . . . (Italics supplied.)

This explanation does not compel the conclusion that the Conference Agreement contemplated prohibiting any consumer picketing at a secondary site beyond that which urges the public, in Senator Kennedy's words, to "refrain from trading with a retailer who sells such goods." To read into the Conference Agreement, on the basis of a single statement, an intention to prohibit all consumer picketing at a secondary site would depart from our practice of respecting the congressional policy not to prohibit peaceful picketing except to curb "isolated evils" spelled out by the Congress itself.

Peaceful consumer picketing to shut off all trade with the secondary employer unless he aids the union in its dispute with the primary employer, is poles apart from such picketing which only persuades his customers not to buy the struck product. The proviso indicates no more than that the Senate conferees' constitutional doubts led Congress to authorize publicity other than picketing which persuades the customers of a secondary employer to stop all trading with him, but not such publicity which has the effect of cutting off his deliveries or inducing his employees to cease work. On the other hand, picketing which persuades the customers of a secondary employer to stop all trading with him was also to be barred.

In sum, the legislative history does not support the Board's finding that Congress meant to prohibit all consumer picketing at a secondary site, having determined that such picketing necessarily threatened, coerced or restrained the secondary employer. Rather, the history shows that Congress was following its usual practice of legislating against peaceful picketing only to curb "isolated evils."

This distinction is opposed as "unrealistic" because, it is urged, all picketing automatically provokes the public to stay away from the picketed establishment. The public will, it is said, neither read the signs and handbills, nor note the explicit injunction that "This is not a strike against any store or market." Be that as it may, our holding today simply takes note of the fact that Congress has never adopted a broad condemnation of peaceful picketing, such as that urged upon us by petitioners, and an intention to do so is not revealed with that "clearest indication in the legislative history," which we require. Labor Board v. Drivers Local Union, supra.

We come then to the question whether the picketing in this case, confined as it was to persuading customers to cease buying the product of the primary employer, falls within the area of secondary consumer picketing which Congress did clearly indicate its intention to prohibit under §8(b)(4)(ii). We hold that it did not fall within that area, and therefore did not "threaten, coerce, or restrain" Safeway. While any diminution in Safeway's purchases of apples due to a drop in consumer demand might be said to be a result which causes respondents' picketing to fall literally within the statutory prohibition, "it is a familiar rule, that a thing may be within the letter of the statute and yet not within the statute, because not within its spirit, nor within the intention of its makers." Holy Trinity Church v. United States, 143 U.S. 457, 459. When consumer picketing is employed only to persuade customers not to buy the struck product, the union's appeal is closely confined to the primary dispute. The site of the appeal is expanded to include the premises of the secondary employer, but if the appeal succeeds, the secondary employer's purchases from the struck firms are decreased only because the public has diminished its purchases of the struck product. On the other hand, when consumer picketing is employed to persuade customers not to trade at all with the secondary employer, the latter stops buying the struck product, not because of a falling demand, but in response to pressure designed to inflict injury on his business generally. In such case, the union does more than merely follow the struck product; it creates a separate dispute with the secondary employer.

We disagree therefore with the Court of Appeals that the test of "to threaten, coerce, or restrain" for the purposes of this case is whether Safeway suffered or was likely to suffer economic loss. A violation of §8(b)(4)(ii)(B) would not be established, merely because respondents' picketing was effective to reduce Safeway's sales of Washington State apples, even if this led or might lead Safeway to drop the item as a poor seller.

The judgment of the Court of Appeals is vacated and the case is remanded with direction to enter judgment setting aside the Board's order.

Douglas J., took no part in the consideration or decision of this case.

[Black, J., concurring, declared that §8(b)(4)(ii)(B) must be read as proscribing the consumer picketing in question but that that section so construed violated the First Amendment. He stated:]

In short, we have neither a case in which picketing is banned because the picketers are asking others to do something unlawful nor a case in which *all* picketing is, for reasons of public order, banned. Instead, we have a case in which picketing, otherwise lawful, is banned only when the picketers express particular views. The result is an abridgment of the freedom of these picketers to tell a part of the public their side of a labor controversy, a subject the free discussion of which is protected by the First Amendment.

I cannot accept my Brother Harlan's view that the abridgment of speech and press here does not violate the First Amendment because other methods of communication are left open. This reason for abridgment strikes me as being on a par with holding that governmental suppression of a newspaper in a city would not violate the First Amendment because there continue to be radio and television stations. First Amendment freedoms can no more validly be taken away by degrees than by one fell swoop.

HARLAN, J., whom STEWART, J., joins, dissenting. . . . Nothing in the statute lends support to the fine distinction which the Court draws between general and limited product picketing. The enactment speaks pervasively of threatening, coercing, or restraining any person; the proviso differentiates only between modes of expression, not between types of secondary consumer picketing. . . .

The difference to which the Court points between a secondary employer merely lowering his purchases of the struck product to the degree of decreased consumer demand and such an employer ceasing to purchase one product because of consumer refusal to buy any products, is surely too refined in the context of reality. It can hardly be supposed that in all, or even most, instances the result of the type of picketing involved here will be simply that suggested by the Court. Because of the very nature of picketing there may be numbers of persons who will refuse to buy at all from a picketed store, either out of economic or social conviction or because they prefer to shop where they need not brave a picket line. Moreover, the public can hardly be expected always to know or ascertain the precise scope of a particular picketing operation. Thus in cases like this, the effect on the secondary employer may not always be limited to a decrease in his sales of the struck product. And even when that is the effect, the employer may, rather than simply reducing purchases from the primary employer, deem it more expedient to turn to another producer whose product is approved by the union.

The distinction drawn by the majority becomes even more tenuous if a picketed retailer depends largely or entirely on sales of the struck product. If, for example, an independent gas station owner sells gasoline purchased from a struck gasoline company, one would not suppose he would feel less threatened, coerced, or restrained by picket signs which said "Do not buy X gasoline" than by signs which said "Do not patronize this gas station." To be sure Safeway is a multiple article seller, but it cannot well be gainsaid that the rule laid down by the Court would be unworkable if its applicability turned on a calculation of the relation between total income of the secondary employer and income from the struck product.

The Court informs us that "Peaceful consumer picketing to shut off all trade with the secondary employer unless he aids the union in its dispute with the primary employer, is poles apart from such picketing which only persuades his customers not to buy the struck product." The difference was, it is stated, "well established in the state cases by 1940," . . . that is, before the present federal enactment. In light of these assertions, it is indeed remarkable that the Court not only substantially acknowledges that the statutory language does not itself support this distinction . . . but cites no report of Congress, no statement of a legislator, not even the view of any of the many commentators in the area, in any way casting doubt on the applicability of §8(b)(4)(ii)(B) to picketing of the kind involved here.

The Court's distinction fares no better when the legislative history of §8(b)(4)(ii)(B) is examined. . . . Fairly assessed [the legislative and other background materials], in my opinion, belie Congress' having made the distinction upon which the Court's thesis rests. Nor can the Court find comfort in the generalization that " 'In the sensitive area of peaceful picketing Congress has dealt explicitly with isolated evils which experience has established flow from such picketing' " . . . ; in enacting the provisions in question Congress *was* addressing itself to a particular facet of secondary boycotting not dealt with in prior legislation, namely, peaceful secondary consumer picketing. I now turn to the materials which illuminate what Congress had in mind.

. . . [C]onsumer picketing in connection with secondary boycotting was at the forefront of the problems which led to the amending of the Taft-Hartley Act by the [LMRDA] of 1959. . . . During Senate debate before passage of the Kennedy-Ervin bill, Senator Humphrey criticized an amendment proposed by Senator Goldwater to §(8)(b)(4) of the Taft-Hartley Act, which reflected the position of the Administration and was incorporated in substance in the Landrum-Griffin bill passed by the House. He said:

> To distribute leaflets at the premises of a neutral employer to persuade customers not to buy a struck product is one form of consumer appeal. To peacefully picket the customer entrances, with a placard asking that the struck product not be bought, is another form. I fear that consumer picketing may also be the target of the words "coerce, or restrain." . . .

105 Cong. Rec. 6232, II Leg. Hist. 1037.

Reporting on the compromise reached by the Conference Committee on the Kennedy-Ervin and Landrum-Griffin bills, Senator Kennedy, who chaired the Conference Committee, stated:

> [T]he House bill prohibited the union from carrying on any kind of activity to disseminate informational material to secondary sites. They could not say that there was a strike in a primary plant. . . . Under the language of the conference [ultimately resulting in present §8(b)(4)(ii)(B)], we agreed there would not be picketing at a secondary site. What was permitted was the giving out of handbills or information through the radio, and so forth.

105 Cong. Rec. 17720, II Leg. Hist. 1389.

Senator Morse . . . explained quite explicitly his objection to the relevant portion of the bill reported out of the Conference Committee, of which he was a member:

. . . [This bill] also makes it illegal for a union to "coerce, or restrain." This prohibits consumer picketing. What is consumer picketing? A shoe manufacturer sells his product through a department store. The employees of the shoe manufacturer go on strike for higher wages. The employees, in addition to picketing the manufacturer, also picket at the premises of the department store with a sign saying, "Do not buy X shoes." This is consumer picketing, an appeal to the public not to buy the product of a struck manufacturer.

105 Cong. Rec. 17882, II Leg. Hist. 1426. . . .

The Court does not consider itself compelled by these remarks to conclude that the Conference Committee meant to prohibit *all* secondary consumer picketing. A fair reading of these comments, however, can hardly leave one seriously in doubt that Senator Kennedy believed this to be precisely what the Committee had done; the Court's added emphasis on the word "and" . . . is, I submit, simply grasping at straws, if indeed the phrase relied on does not equally well lend itself to a disjunctive reading. . . . The complicated role the Court assigns to the publicity proviso . . . makes even less understandable its failure to accord to the remarks of Senator Kennedy their proper due. The proviso, according to the Court's interpretation, is unnecessary in regard to picketing designed to effect a boycott of the primary product and comes into play only if a complete boycott of the secondary employer is sought. Had this ingenious interpretation been intended, would not Senator Kennedy, who was at pains to emphasize the scope of activities still left to unions, have used it to refute the criticisms of Senator Morse made only shortly before? . . .

The Court points out that the Senate had no Conference Report when it passed the compromise bill and that it had only Senator Kennedy's statement of the purpose of the proviso. . . . But I am wholly at a loss to understand how on that premise (particularly when Senator Kennedy's remarks are supplemented by the comments of one Senator (Morse) who thought the final bill too harsh and those of another (Goldwater) who believed the Senate bill too weak) one can conclude that the members of the Senate did not mean by their vote to outlaw all kinds of secondary consumer picketing.

A reading of proceedings in the House of Representatives leads to a similar conclusion regarding the intent of that body. In criticism of the Landrum-Griffin bill, Congressman Madden stated, "It would prohibit any union from advising the public that an employer is unfair to labor, pays substandard wages, or operates a sweatshop. . . ." 105 Cong. Rec. 15515, II Leg. Hist. 1552. Since the theory of the majority regarding the publicity proviso adopted by the Conference is that it is redundant in situations where the union seeks only a boycott of the struck product, the sweep of Congressman Madden's comment is plainly at odds with the Court's view of §8(b)(4)(ii)(B). . . .

The majority . . . relies on remarks made by Congressman Griffin, the bill's co-sponsor. When read in context what seems significant about them is that the Congressman nowhere suggests that there can be some kind of consumer picketing which does not coerce or restrain the secondary employer. Nor does he intimate any constitutional problem in prohibiting picketing that follows the struck product. . . .

In the light of the foregoing, I see no escape from the conclusion that §8(b)(4)(ii)(B) does prohibit *all* consumer picketing. . . .

Under my view of the statute the constitutional issue is therefore reached. Since the Court does not discuss it, I am content simply to state in summary form my reasons for believing that the prohibitions of §8(b)(4)(ii)(B), as applied here, do not run afoul of constitutional limitations. This Court has long recognized that picketing is "inseparably something more [than] and different" from simple communication. Hughes v. Superior Court, 339 U.S. 460, 464; see, e.g., Building Service Employees v. Gazzam, 339 U.S. 532, 537; Bakery Drivers v. Wohl, 315 U.S. 769, 776 (concurring opinion of Douglas, J.). Congress has given careful and continued consideration to the problems of labor-management relations, and its attempts to effect an accommodation between the right of unions to publicize their position and the social desirability of limiting a form of communication likely to have effects caused by something apart from the message communicated, are entitled to great deference. The decision of Congress to prohibit secondary consumer picketing during labor disputes is, I believe, not inconsistent with the protections of the First Amendment, particularly when, as here, other methods of communication are left open.

Contrary to my Brother Black, I think the fact that Congress in prohibiting secondary consumer picketing has acted with a discriminating eye is the very thing that renders this provision invulnerable to constitutional attack. That Congress has permitted other picketing which is likely to have effects beyond those resulting from the "communicative" aspect of picketing does not, of course, in any way lend itself to the conclusion that Congress here has aimed to "prevent dissemination of information about the facts of a labor dispute." . . . Even on the highly dubious assumption that the "non-speech" aspect of picketing is always the same whatever the particular context, the social consequences of the "non-communicative" aspect of picketing may certainly be thought desirable in the case of "primary" picketing and undesirable in the case of "secondary" picketing, a judgment Congress has indeed made in prohibiting secondary but not primary picketing.

I would enforce the Board's order.

NLRB v. Retail Store Employees Union, Local 1001 (Safeco Title Ins. Co.)
447 U.S. 607 (1980)

[Following a bargaining impasse, the union struck Safeco Title Insurance Company, which, however, maintained operations. In addition to Safeco's Seattle office, the union picketed five local title companies, whose sale of Safeco policies constituted over 90 percent of their business. The pickets' signs asked customers to cancel, or not to buy, Safeco policies. The Supreme Court, disagreeing with the court of appeals, upheld the Board's position that the picketing violated the Act.[j] Distinguishing *Tree Fruits*, the Court, through Powell, J., declared in part:]

Although *Tree Fruits* suggested that secondary picketing against a struck product and secondary picketing against a neutral party were "poles apart," id., at 70, the courts soon discovered that product picketing could have the same effect as an illegal secondary boycott. In Hoffman ex rel. NLRB v. Cement Masons Local 337, 468 F.2d 1187 (CA9 1972), *cert. denied*, 411 U.S. 986 (1973), for example, a union embroiled with a general contractor picketed the housing subdivision that he had constructed for a real estate developer. Pickets sought to persuade prospective purchasers not to buy the contractor's houses. The picketing was held illegal because purchasers "could reasonably expect that they were being asked not to transact any business whatsoever" with the neutral developer. 468 F.2d, at 1192. "[W]hen a union's interest in picketing a primary employer at a 'one product' site [directly conflicts] with the need to protect . . . neutral employers from the labor disputes of others," Congress has determined that the neutrals' interests should prevail. Id., at 1191.[7]

Cement Masons highlights the critical difference between the picketing

---

[j] [The union's handbilling was not in issue before the Court; nor was the court of appeals' holding that the local title companies were "neutral, secondary parties" despite Safeco's substantial stockholdings in them. — Eds.]

[7] The so-called merged product cases also involve situations where an attempt to follow the struck product inevitably encourages an illegal boycott of the neutral party. See K & K Construction Co. v. NLRB, 592 F.2d 1228, 1231-1234 (CA3 1979); American Bread Co. v. NLRB, 411 F.2d 147, 154-155 (CA6 1969); Honolulu Typographical Union No. 37 v. NLRB, 131 U.S. App. D.C. 1, 3-4, 401 F.2d 952, 954–955 (1968); Note, Consumer Picketing and the Single-Product Secondary Employer, 47 U. Chi. L. Rev. 112, 132–136 (1979).

[The dissenters in *Safeco* did not question that the merged-product doctrine applied to situations where the integration of the primary product with the secondary product precludes a clear identification and separation of the primary and secondary goods; a consumer boycott of the primary product would, in such situations, also encompass the secondary product. — Eds.]

in this case and . . . *Tree Fruits*. The product picketed in *Tree Fruits* was but one item among the many that made up the retailer's trade. 377 U.S., at 60. . . . In this case, . . . the title companies sell only the primary employer's product and perform the services associated with it. Secondary picketing against consumption of the primary product leaves responsive consumers no realistic option other than to boycott the title companies altogether. If the appeal succeeds, each company "stops buying the struck product, not because of a falling demand, but in response to pressure designed to inflict injury on [its] business generally." Thus, "the union does more than merely follow the struck product; it creates a separate dispute with the secondary employer." Id., at 72. . . .

As long as secondary picketing only discourages consumption of a struck product, incidental injury to the neutral is a natural consequence of an effective primary boycott. See id., at 72-73. But the Union's secondary appeal against the central product sold by the title companies in this case is "reasonably calculated to induce customers not to patronize the neutral parties at all." 226 N.L.R.B., at 757. The resulting injury to their businesses is distinctly different from the injury that the Court considered in *Tree Fruits*.[9] Product picketing that reasonably can be expected to threaten neutral parties with ruin or substantial loss simply does not square with the language or the purpose of §8(b)(4)(ii)(B). Since successful secondary picketing would put the title companies to a choice between their survival and the severance of their ties with Safeco, the picketing plainly violates the statutory ban on the coercion of neutrals with the object of "forcing or requiring [them] to cease . . . dealing in the [primary] produc[t] . . . or to cease doing business with" the primary employer. §8(b)(4)(ii)(B); see *Tree Fruits*, 377 U.S., at 68.[11]

The Court of Appeals suggested that application of §8(b)(4)(ii)(B) to the picketing . . . might violate the First Amendment. We think not. Although the Court recognized in *Tree Fruits* that the Constitution might not permit "a broad ban against peaceful picketing," the Court left no doubt that Congress may prohibit secondary picketing calculated "to persuade the

---

[9] The Union is responsible for the "foreseeable consequences" of its conduct. . . .

[11] The picketing in *Tree Fruits* and the picketing in this case are relatively extreme examples of the spectrum of conduct that the Board and the courts will encounter in complaints charging violations of §8(b)(4)(ii)(B). If secondary picketing were directed against a product representing a major portion of a neutral's business, but significantly less than that represented by a single dominant product, neither *Tree Fruits* nor today's decision necessarily would control. The critical question would be whether, by encouraging customers to reject the struck product, the secondary appeal is reasonably likely to threaten the neutral party with ruin or substanial loss. Resolution of the question in each case will be entrusted to the Board's expertise.

customers of the secondary employer to cease trading with him in order to force him to cease dealing with, or to put pressure upon, the primary employer." 377 U.S., at 63. Such picketing spreads labor discord by coercing a neutral party to join the fray. In Electrical Workers v. NLRB, 341 U.S. 694, 705 (1951), this Court expressly held that a prohibition on "picketing in furtherance of [such] unlawful objectives" did not offend the First Amendment. See American Radio Assn. v. Mobile S.S. Assn., 419 U.S. 215, 229-231 (1974); Teamsters v. Vogt, Inc., 354 U.S. 284 (1957). We perceive no reason to depart from that well-established understanding. As applied to picketing that predictably encourages consumers to boycott a secondary business, §8(b)(4)(ii)(B) imposes no impermissible restrictions upon constitutionally protected speech.

Accordingly, the judgment of the Court of Appeals is reversed, and the case is remanded with directions to enforce the [NLRB's] order.

[Blackmun and Stevens, JJ., in separate concurrences, objected to the Court's perfunctory rejection of the First Amendment claim. Blackmun, J., noted that he concurred in the result "only because I am reluctant to hold unconstitutional Congress' striking of the delicate balance between union freedom of expression and the ability of neutral employers, employees, and consumers to be free from coerced participation in industrial strife." Stevens, J., stated that picketing involves a mixture of conduct and communication; the First Amendment does not invalidate the statute, which bans only the union's conduct, that is, a signal calling for an automatic response, rather than a reasoned response to an idea.

Brennan, J., joined by White and Marshall, JJ., dissented on these grounds: The picketing, since it was directed only at primary goods, passed the *Tree Fruits* test. By contrast, picketing aimed at nonprimary goods imposes on a secondary employer risks beyond those "assumed by [his] handling the primary employer's product" and also injures the interests of firms supplying nonprimary goods to the picketed enterprise. The dissenters noted that "the conceptual underpinnings of [the Court's] new standard are seriously flawed": First, the harmfulness of a primary product boycott is not necessarily correlated with the percentage of the secondary firm's business represented by that product. Second, a single-product retailer always suffers some harm from a successful primary product boycott even though union activity is not focused on him; 8(b)(4)'s prohibition against coercion of neutral parties "is mismatched to the goal of averting that harm." Finally, because of the Court's imprecise standard, unions would no longer be able to shelter their secondary picketing by restricting their appeals to a boycott of the primary product. Unions will be forced to speculate about the ratio "sufficient . . . to trigger the displeasure of the courts or the . . . Board."

Moreover, the Court's reference to "ruin or substantial loss . . . leaves one wondering whether unions will . . . have to inspect balance sheets to determine whether the primary product they wish to picket is too profitable for the secondary firm."]

NOTES

1. Once the decision in *Tree Fruits* is accepted, can *Safeco* be fairly distinguished under the Act or the First Amendment?

2. Did the secondary picketing in *Safeco* impose on the picketed firms losses no greater than those which would flow from a successful primary strike? Is an affirmative answer to that question controlling under the Act? Should it be, as a matter of policy?

3. In *DeBartolo*, the owner of the shopping center conceded arguendo, and the Court assumed, that the department store "distributes" products "produced" by the nonunion general contractor and that the publicity proviso would have sheltered handbilling pinpointed at the department store premises. In light of the merged-product doctrine applied to picketing, what should the result be if the department store charged that such handbilling, unaccompanied by picketing, violated §8(b)(4)(B)? Cf. Sheet Metal Wkrs., Local Union No. 54 (Sakowitz), 174 N.L.R.B. 362 (1969) (publicity proviso permits handbilling asking for complete boycott of retailer who has leased space in a shopping center being constructed in part by nonunion subcontractors); Central Ind. Bldg. & Constr. Trades Council (K-Mart), 257 N.L.R.B. 86, 89 (1981). Under the Act and the First Amendment, is there any basis for distinguishing between an enterprise boycott implemented by handbilling and one implemented by picketing, when in either event the injury to secondary employers is assumed to be the same?

4. Delta Air Lines replaced a unionized janitorial contractor with a nonunion firm; as a result, the terminated firm laid off five of the six employees who had serviced Delta's offices at Los Angeles International Airport. A year later, the union handbilled at both Delta's Los Angeles ticket offices and the airport. One handbill, without identifying the primary dispute, asked the public not to fly Delta because it was "unfair" and did not provide "AFL-CIO" employment standards. The handbill's other side warned that "It takes more than money to fly Delta. It takes nerve," and included information from federal agencies on Delta's record of flight safety and customers' complaints. The union's two newspapers published this handbill, as well as an advertisement: "Don't Fly Delta." A second handbill identified the nature of the union's primary dispute on one side, but also included the statistical information on flight safety and consumer complaints

on side two. In a NLRB proceeding, the parties stipulated that the union's conduct did not cause Delta's employees or other employees to withhold their services; apparently no mention was made of the amount of business losses, if any, suffered by Delta.

Does any part (or parts) of the union's campaign violate §8(b)(4)? Would a Board cease and desist order against any element (or elements) of that campaign be invalid under the First Amendment? Should the Board decide that issue? Should constitutional considerations influence the Board's interpretation of the scope of the publicity proviso? See Hospital & Serv. Employees Union, Local 399 (Delta Air Lines), 263 N.L.R.B. 996 (1982); cf. Eastex, Inc. v. NLRB, supra p. 214.

NAACP v. Claiborne Hardware Co., 458 U.S. 886 (1982). Following unsatisfactory responses to demands for racial equality and desegregation that were submitted by blacks to business and civic leaders (some of whom were local white merchants), the blacks instituted a consumer boycott of those merchants. The Mississippi Supreme Court, holding the boycott to be tortious because it had been implemented by violence, actual or threatened, against non-cooperative blacks, upheld an injunction and a damage award consisting of all business losses resulting from the boycott.

The United States Supreme Court unanimously struck down the damage award. Justice Stevens, writing for seven members of the Court (Justice Rehnquist concurred in result; Justice Marshall took no part in the consideration or decision of the case), stated: The First Amendment protected the boycott insofar as it was nonviolent. The record showed only "isolated acts of violence" insufficient to taint the entire collective effort; thus liability could be constitutionally imposed only on those defendants who had engaged in or threatened violent acts, or who had authorized or ratified the threats or the acts. Because of the "strong governmental interest in certain forms of economic regulation," secondary labor boycotts and picketing could be constitutionally prohibited as part of "Congress' striking of the delicate balance between union freedom of expression and the ability of neutral employers, employees, and consumers to remain free from coerced participation in industrial strife" (quoting from Justice Blackmun's concurrence in *Safeco* and citing ILA v. Allied International, supra p. 571); government does not, however, have "a comparable right to prohibit peaceful political activity" such as the consumer boycott in this case, "a major purpose of [which] . . . was to influence governmental action." 458 U.S. at 912-914.

Justice Stevens purported to distinguish Hughes v. Superior Court, 339 U.S. 460 (1950): "Nor are we presented with a boycott designed to secure aims that are themselves prohibited by a valid state law." 458 U.S. at 915 n.49. (But cf. the Court's statement in *Hughes* that the California court could constitutionally enjoin the picketing even though California did "not forbid the employer to adopt such a quota system of his own free will." 460 U.S. at 468.) For a discussion of the tensions between *Claiborne* and the regulation of labor picketing intended to evoke a consumer boycott, see Harper, The Consumer's Emerging Right to Boycott: NAACP v. Claiborne Hardware and Its Implications for American Labor Law, 93 Yale L.J. 409, 442-454 (1984). See also Comment, Political Boycott Activity and the First Amendment, 91 Harv. L. Rev. 659 (1978); cf. Note, Labor Picketing and Commercial Speech: Free Enterprise Values in the Doctrine of Free Speech, 91 Yale L.J. 938 (1982).

3.   *"Hot Cargo" Clauses*

National Woodwork Mfg. Assn. v. NLRB
386 U.S. 612 (1967)

BRENNAN, J. The questions here are whether . . . the Metropolitan District Council of Philadelphia and Vicinity of the United Brotherhood of Carpenters and Joiners of America, AFL-CIO (hereafter the Union), [violated] §§8(e) and 8(b)(4)(B).

Frouge Corporation, a Bridgeport, Connecticut, concern, was the general contractor on a housing project in Philadelphia. Frouge had a collective bargaining agreement with the Carpenters' International Union under which Frouge agreed to be bound by the rules and regulations agreed upon by local unions with contractors in areas in which Frouge had jobs. Frouge was therefore subject to the provisions of a collective bargaining agreement between the Union and an organization of Philadelphia contractors, the General Building Contractors Association, Inc. A sentence in a provision of that agreement entitled Rule 17 provides that " . . . No member of this District Council will handle . . . any doors . . . which have been fitted prior to being furnished on the job. . . . "[2] Frouge's Philadelphia project

---

[2] The full text of Rule 17 is as follows:

"No employee shall work on any job on which cabinet work, fixtures, millwork, sash, doors, trim or other detailed millwork is used unless the same is Union-made and bears the Union Label of the United Brotherhood of Carpenters and Joiners of America. No member of this District Council will handle material coming from a mill where cutting out and fitting has been done for butts, locks, letter plates, or hardware of any description, nor any doors or transoms which have been fitted prior to being furnished on job, including base, chair, rail, picture moulding, which has been previously fitted. This section to exempt partition work furnished in sections." The [NLRB] determined that the first sentence violated §8(e), 149 N.L.R.B. 646, 655-656, and the Union did not seek judicial review of that determination.

called for 3,600 doors. Customarily, before the doors could be hung on such projects, "blank" or "blind" doors would be mortised for the knob, routed for the hinges, and beveled to make them fit between jambs. These are tasks traditionally performed in the Philadelphia area by the carpenters employed on the jobsite. However, precut and prefitted doors ready to hang may be purchased from door manufacturers. Although Frouge's contract and job specifications did not call for premachined doors, and "blank" or "blind" doors could have been ordered, Frouge contracted for the purchase of premachined doors from a Pennsylvania door manufacturer which is a member of the National Woodwork Manufacturers Association, petitioner in No. 110 and respondent in No. 111. The Union ordered its carpenter members not to hang the doors when they arrived at the jobsite. Frouge thereupon withdrew the prefabricated doors and substituted "blank" doors which were fitted and cut by its carpenters on the jobsite.

The National Woodwork Manufacturers Association and another [charged] . . . that by including the "will not handle" sentence of Rule 17 in the collective bargaining agreement the Union [violated] §8(e) [by] entering into an "agreement . . . whereby [the] employer . . . agrees to cease or refrain from handling . . . any of the products of any other employer . . . ," and [also charged] that in enforcing the sentence against Frouge, the Union [violated] §8(b)(4)(B) [by] "forcing or requiring any person to cease using . . . the products of any other . . . manufacturer. . . . " The [NLRB] dismissed the charges, 149 N.L.R.B. 646. The Board [concluded] that the "will not handle" sentence in Rule 17 was language used by the parties to protect and preserve cutting out and fitting as unit work to be performed by the jobsite carpenters. The Board also [concluded] that both the sentence of Rule 17 itself and its maintenance against Frouge were therefore "primary" activity outside the prohibition of §§8(e) and 8(b)(4)(B). . . .

[The Court, reversing the Seventh Circuit, upheld the Board's position.]

I

Even on the doubtful premise that the words of §8(e) unambiguously embrace the sentence of Rule 17,[4] this does not end inquiry into Congress'

---

[4]The statutory language of §8(e) is far from unambiguous. It prohibits agreements to "cease . . . from handling . . . any of the products *of any other employer*. . . ." (Emphasis supplied.) Since both the product and its source are mentioned, the provision might be read not to prohibit an agreement relating solely to the nature of the product itself, such as a work-preservation agreement, but only to prohibit one arising from an objection to the other employers or a definable group of employers who are the source of the product, for example, their nonunion status.

purpose in enacting the section. It is a "familiar rule, that a thing may be within the letter of the statute and yet not within the statute, because not within its spirit, nor within the intention of its makers." Holy Trinity Church v. United States, 143 U.S. 457, 459. That principle has particular application in the construction of labor legislation which is "to a marked degree, the result of conflict and compromise between strong contending forces and deeply held views on the role of organized labor in the free economic life of the Nation and the appropriate balance to be struck between the uncontrolled power of management and labor to further their respective interests." Local 1976, United Brotherhood of Carpenters v. Labor Board (Sand Door), 357 U.S. 93, 99-100. . . .

Strongly held opposing views have invariably marked the controversy over labor's use of the boycott to further its aims by involving an employer in disputes not his own. But congressional action to deal with such conduct has stopped short of proscribing identical activity having the object of pressuring the employer for agreements regulating relations between him and his own employees. That Congress meant §§8(e) and 8(b)(4)(B) to prohibit only "secondary" objectives clearly appears from an examination of the history of congressional action on the subject; we may, by such an examination, "reconstitute the gamut of values current at the time when the words were uttered."

[The Court surveyed the status of secondary pressures under the Sherman Act, Clayton Act, Norris-LaGuardia Act, and the Taft-Hartley Act, as amended, and stressed that the 1947 ban against "secondary boycotts" (now embodied in §8(b)(4)(B)) was aimed at pressures calculated to induce neutrals to stop doing business with the primary employer.]

Despite this virtually overwhelming support for the limited reading of §8(b)(4)(A) [in the Court's prior decisions], the Woodwork Manufacturers Association relies on Allen Bradley Co. v. Local Union No. 3, 325 U.S. 797, [reproduced infra p. 633], as requiring that the successor section, §8(b)(4)(B), be read as proscribing the District Council's conduct in enforcing the "will not handle" sentence of Rule 17 against Frouge. The Association points to the references to *Allen Bradley* in the legislative debates leading to the enactment of the predecessor §8(b)(4)(A). We think that this is an erroneous reading of the legislative history. *Allen Bradley* held violative of the antitrust laws a combination between Local 3 of the International Brotherhood of Electrical Workers and both electrical contractors and manufacturers of electrical fixtures in New York City to restrain the bringing in of such equipment from outside the city. The contractors obligated themselves to confine their purchases to local manufacturers, who in turn obligated themselves to confine their New York City sales to contractors employing members of the local, and this scheme was supported by threat of boycott by the contractors' employees. While recognizing that the union might have had an immunity for its contribution to the trade boycott had it acted alone, citing *Hutcheson*, supra, the Court held immunity was not intended by the Clayton or Norris-LaGuardia Acts in cases in which the union's activity was part of a larger conspiracy to abet contractors and manufacturers to create a monopoly.

The argument that the references to *Allen Bradley* in the debates over §8(b)(4)(A) have broader significance in the determination of the reach of that section is that there was no intent on Local 3's part to influence the internal labor policies of the boycotted out-of-state manufacturers of electrical equipment. There are three answers to this argument: First, the boycott of out-of-state electrical equipment by the electrical contractors' employees was not in pursuance of any objective relating to pressuring their employers in the matter of *their* wages, hours, and working conditions; there was no work preservation or other primary objective related to the union employees' relations with their contractor employers. On the contrary, the object of the boycott was to secure benefits for the New York City electrical manufacturers and their employees. "This is a secondary object because the cessation of business was being used tactically, with an eye to its effect on conditions elsewhere."[17] Second, and of even greater significance on the question of the inferences to be drawn from the references to *Allen Bradley*, Senator Taft regarded the Local 3 boycott as in effect saying, "We will not permit any material made by any other union or by any nonunion workers to come into New York City and be put into any building in New York City." 93 Cong. Rec. 4199, II 1947 Leg. Hist. 1107. This clearly shows that the Senator viewed the pressures applied by Local 3 on the employers of its members as having solely a secondary objective. The Senate Committee Report echoes the same view: "[It is] an unfair labor practice for a union to engage in the type of secondary boycott that has been conducted in New York City by local No. 3 of the IBEW, whereby electricians have refused to install electrical products of manufacturers employing electricians who are members of *some labor organization other than local No. 3*." S. Rep. No. 105, 80th Cong., 1st Sess., 22, I 1947 Leg. Hist. 428. (Emphasis supplied.)

---

[17] Lesnick, Job Security and Secondary Boycotts: The Reach of NLRA §§8(b)(4) and 8(e), 113 U. Pa. L. Rev. 1000, 1017-1018 (1965).

It is suggested that the boycott in *Allen Bradley* is indistinguishable from the activity today held protected in Houston Insulation Contractors Association v. Labor Board, post, p. 664. The crucial distinction is that in *Houston Insulation Contractors Association* the boycott was being carried out to affect the labor policies of the employer of the boycotting employees, the primary employer, and not, as in *Allen Bradley*, for its effect elsewhere.

. . . Third, even on the premise that Congress meant to prohibit boycotts such as that in *Allen Bradley* without regard to whether they were carried on to affect labor conditions elsewhere, the fact is that the boycott in *Allen Bradley* was carried on, not as a shield to preserve the jobs of Local 3 members, traditionally a primary labor activity, but as a sword, to reach out and monopolize all the manufacturing job tasks for Local 3 members. It is arguable that Congress may have viewed the use of the boycott as a sword as different from labor's traditional concerns with wages, hours, and working conditions. But the boycott in the present cases was not used as a sword; it was a shield carried solely to preserve the members' jobs. We therefore have no occasion today to decide the questions which might arise where the workers carry on a boycott to reach out to monopolize jobs or acquire new job tasks when their own jobs are not threatened by the boycotted product.[19]

It is true that the House bill proposed to amend the Clayton Act to narrow labor's immunity from the antitrust laws. H.R. 3020, §301(b), I 1947 Leg. Hist. 220. This was omitted from the Conference agreement. It is suggested that this history evidences that Congress meant §8(b)(4)(A) to reach all product boycotts with work preservation motives. The argument is premised on a statement by the House Managers in the House Conference Report that "[s]ince the matters dealt with in this section have to a large measure been effectuated through the use of boycotts, and since the conference agreement contains effective provisions directly dealing with boycotts themselves, this provision is omitted from the conference agreement." H.R. Conf. Rep. No. 510, 80th Cong., 1st Sess., 65, I 1947 Leg. Hist. 569. The statement is hardly probative that §8(b)(4)(A) enacted a broad prohibition in face of the overwhelming evidence that its Senate sponsors intended the narrower reach. Actually the statement at best reflects that the House may have receded from a broader position and accepted that of the Senate. For §8(b)(4)(A) constituted the "effective provisions" referred to, and the House Managers' understanding of and agreement with the reach of the section as intended by its Senate sponsors is expressed at page 43 of the same Report, I 1947 Leg. Hist. 547:

> . . . Thus [under §8(b)(4)(A)] it was made an unfair labor practice for a union to engage in a strike against employer A for the purpose of forcing that employer to cease doing business with employer B. Similarly it would not be lawful for a union to boycott employer A because employer A uses or otherwise deals in the goods of, or does business with, employer B.

---

[19]We likewise do not have before us [here], and express no view upon, the antitrust limitations, if any, upon union-employer work-preservation or work-extension agreements. See [UMW] v. Pennington, 381 U.S. 657, 662–665.

In effect Congress, in . . . §8(b)(4)(A), . . . returned to the regime of *Duplex Printing Press Co.* and *Bedford Cut Stone Co.*, . . . and barred as a secondary boycott union activity directed against a neutral employer, including the immediate employer when in fact the activity directed against him was carried on for its effect elsewhere.

Indeed, Congress in rewriting §8(b)(4)(A) as §8(b)(4)(B) took pains to confirm the limited application of the section to such "secondary" conduct. The word "concerted" in former §8(b)(4) was deleted to reach secondary conduct directed to only one individual. This was in response to the Court's holding in Labor Board v. International Rice Milling Co., 341 U.S. 665, that "concerted" required proof of inducement of two or more employees. But to make clear that the deletion was not to be read as supporting a construction of the statute as prohibiting the incidental effects of traditional primary activity, Congress added the proviso that nothing in the amended section "shall be construed to make unlawful, where not otherwise unlawful, any primary strike or primary picketing." Many statements and examples proffered in the 1959 debates confirm this congressional acceptance of the distinction between primary and secondary activity.

II

The Landrum-Griffin Act amendments in 1959 were adopted only to close various loopholes in the application of §8(b)(4)(A). . . .

Section 8(e) simply closed still another loophole. In Local 1976, United Brotherhood of Carpenters v. Labor Board (Sand Door), 357 U.S. 93, the Court held that it was no defense to an unfair labor practice charge under §8(b)(4)(A) that the struck employer had agreed, in a contract with the union, not to handle nonunion material. However, the Court emphasized that the mere execution of such a contract provision (known as a "hot cargo" clause because of its prevalence in Teamsters Union contracts), or its voluntary observance by the employer, was not unlawful under §8(b)(4)(A).[k] Section 8(e) was designed to plug this gap in the legislation by making the "hot cargo" clause itself unlawful. The *Sand Door* decision was believed by Congress not only to create the possibility of damage actions against employers for breaches of "hot cargo" clauses, but also to create a situation in which such clauses might be employed to exert subtle pressures upon employers to engage in "voluntary" boycotts. Hearings in late 1958 before the Senate Select Committee explored seven cases of "hot cargo" clauses in Teamsters Union

---

[k] [*Sand Door* deserves careful attention because it looms large, not only in the legislative history, but also in the Court's interpretation of §8(e) and its provisos. — Eds.]

contracts, the use of which the Committee found conscripted neutral employers in Teamsters organizational campaigns.

This loophole-closing measure likewise did not expand the type of conduct which §8(b)(4)(A) condemned. Although the language of §8(e) is sweeping, it closely tracks that of §8(b)(4)(A), and just as the latter and its successor §8(b)(4)(B) did not reach employees' activity to pressure their employer to preserve for themselves work traditionally done by them, §8(e) does not prohibit agreements made and maintained for that purpose.

The legislative history of §8(e) confirms this conclusion. The Kennedy-Ervin bill as originally reported proposed no remedy for abuses of the "hot cargo" clauses revealed at the hearings of the Select Committee. Senators Goldwater and Dirksen filed a minority report urging that a prohibition against "hot cargo" clauses should be enacted to close that loophole. Their statement expressly acknowledged their acceptance of the reading of §8(b)(4)(A) as applicable only "to protect genuinely neutral employers and their employees, not themselves involved in a labor dispute, against economic coercion designed to give a labor union victory in a dispute with some other employer." They argued that a prohibition against "hot cargo" clauses was necessary to further that objective. They were joined by Senator McClellan, Chairman of the Select Committee, in their proposal to add such a provision. Their statements in support consistently defined the evil to be prevented in terms of agreements which obligated neutral employers not to do business with other employers involved in labor disputes with the union. Senator Gore initially proposed, and the Senate first passed, a "hot cargo" amendment to the Kennedy-Ervin bill which outlawed such agreements only for "common carriers subject to Part II of the Interstate Commerce Act." This reflected the testimony at the Select Committee hearings which attributed abuses of such clauses primarily to the Teamsters Union. Significantly, such alleged abuses by the Teamsters invariably involved uses of the clause to pressure neutral trucking employers not to handle goods of other employers involved in disputes with the Teamsters Union.

The House Labor Committee first reported out a bill containing a provision substantially identical to the Gore amendment. The House Report expressly noted that since that proposal tracked the language of §8(b)(4)(A) "it preserved the established distinction between primary activities and secondary boycotts." The substitute Landrum-Griffin bill, however, expanded the proposal to cover all industry and not common carriers alone.

. . . In describing the substitute bill, Representative Landrum pointedly spoke of the situation "where the union, in a dispute with one employer, puts pressure upon another employer or his employees, in order to force the second employer or his employees, to stop doing business with the first employer, and 'bend his knee to the union's will.'" Ibid. . . . . In Conference Committee, the Landrum-Griffin application to all industry, and not just to common carriers, was adopted.

However, provisos were added to §8(e) to preserve the status quo in the construction industry, and exempt the garment industry from the prohibitions of §§8(e) and 8(b)(4)(B). This action of the Congress is strong confirmation that Congress meant that both §§8(e) and 8(b)(4)(B) reach only secondary pressures. If the body of §8(e) applies only to secondary activity, the garment industry proviso is a justifiable exception which allows what the legislative history shows it was designed to allow, secondary pressures to counteract the effects of sweatshop conditions in an industry with a highly integrated process of production between jobbers, manufacturers, contractors and subcontractors. First, this motivation for the proviso sheds light on the central theme of the body of §8(e), to which the proviso is an exception. Second, if the body of that provision and §8(b)(4)(B) were construed to prohibit primary agreements and their maintenance, such as those concerning work preservation, the proviso would have the highly unlikely effect, unjustified in any of the statute's history, of permitting garment workers, but garment workers only, to preserve their jobs against subcontracting or prefabrication by such agreements and by strikes and boycotts to enforce them. Similarly, the construction industry proviso, which permits "hot cargo" agreements only for jobsite work, would have the curious and unsupported result of allowing the construction worker to make agreements preserving his traditional tasks against jobsite prefabrication and subcontracting, but not against nonjobsite prefabrication and subcontracting. On the other hand, if the heart of §8(e) is construed to be directed only to secondary activities, the construction proviso becomes, as it was intended to be, a measure designed to allow agreements pertaining to certain secondary activities on the construction site because of the close community of interests there, but to ban secondary-objective agreements concerning nonjobsite work, in which respect the construction industry is no different from any other. The provisos are therefore substantial probative support that primary work preservation agreements were not to be within the ban of §8(e).

The only mention of a broader reach for §8(e) appears in isolated statements by opponents of that provision, expressing fears that work preservation agreements would be banned. These statements have scant probative value against the backdrop of the strong evidence to the contrary. Too, "we have often cautioned against the danger, when interpreting a statute, of reliance upon the views of its legislative opponents. In their zeal to defeat a bill, they understandably tend to overstate its reach." Labor Board v. Fruit & Vegetable Packers, 377 U.S. 58, 66. . . .

In addition . . . "[t]he silence of the sponsors of [the] amendments is pregnant with significance. . . ." Labor Board v. Fruit & Vegetable Packers [ibid]. Before we may say that Congress meant to strike from workers' hands the economic weapons traditionally used against their employers' efforts to abolish their jobs, that meaning should plainly appear.

> [I]n this era of automation and onrushing technological change, no problems in the domestic economy are of greater concern than those involving job security and employment stability. Because of the potentially cruel impact upon the lives and fortunes of the working men and women of the Nation, these problems have understandably engaged the solicitous attention of government, of responsible private business, and particularly of organized labor.

Fibreboard Paper Products Corp. v. Labor Board, 379 U.S. 203, 225 (concurring opinion of Stewart, J.) [reproduced infra p. 860]. We would expect that legislation curtailing the ability of management and labor voluntarily to negotiate for solutions to these significant and difficult problems would be preceded by extensive congressional study and debate, and consideration of voluminous economic, scientific, and statistical data. The silence regarding such matters in the Eighty-sixth Congress is itself evidence that Congress, in enacting §8(e), had no thought of prohibiting agreements directed to work preservation. . . .

Moreover, our decision in *Fibreboard Paper Products Corp.*, supra, implicitly recognizes the legitimacy of work preservation clauses like that involved here. Indeed, in the circumstances presented in *Fibreboard*, we held that bargaining on the subject was made mandatory by §8(a)(5) of the Act, concerning as it does "terms and conditions of employment," §8(d). *Fibreboard* involved an alleged refusal to bargain with respect to the contracting-out of plant maintenance work previously performed by employees in the bargaining unit. . . . It would therefore be incongruous to interpret §8(e) to invalidate clauses over which the parties may be mandated to bargain and which have been successfully incorporated through collective bargaining in many of this Nation's major labor agreements.

Finally, important parts of the historic accommodation by Congress of the powers of labor and management are §§7 and 13 of the [NLRA]. . . . Section 13 preserves the right to strike, of which the boycott is a form, except as specifically provided in the Act. In the absence of clear indicia of congressional intent to the contrary, these provisions caution against reading statutory prohibitions as embracing employee activities to pressure their own employers into improving the employees' wages, hours, and working conditions. . . .

The Woodwork Manufacturers Association and amici who support its position advance several reasons, grounded in economic and technological factors, why "will not handle" clauses should be invalid in all circumstances. Those arguments are addressed to the wrong branch of government. . . .

III

The determination whether the "will not handle" sentence of Rule 17 and its enforcement violated §8(e) and §8(b)(4)(B) cannot be made without an inquiry into whether, under all the surrounding circumstances,[38] the Union's objective was preservation of work for Frouge's employees, or whether the agreements and boycott were tactically calculated to satisfy union objectives elsewhere. Were the latter the case, Frouge, the boycotting employer, would be a neutral bystander, and the agreement or boycott would . . . become secondary. There need not be an actual dispute with the boycotted employer, here the door manufacturer, for the activity to fall within this category, so long as the tactical object of the agreement and its maintenance is that employer, or benefits to other than the boycotting employees or other employees of the primary employer thus making the agreement or boycott secondary in its aim. The touchstone is whether the agreement or its maintenance is addressed to the labor relations of the contracting employer vis-à-vis his own employees. This will not always be a simple test to apply. But "[h]owever difficult the drawing of lines more nice than obvious, the statute compels the task." Local 761, Electrical Workers v. Labor Board, 366 U.S. 667, 674.

That the "will not handle" provision was not an unfair labor practice in these cases is clear. The finding of the Trial Examiner, adopted by the Board, was that the objective of the sentence was preservation of work traditionally performed by the jobsite carpenters. This finding is supported by substantial evidence, and therefore the Union's making of the "will not handle" agreement was not a violation of §8(e).

Similarly, the Union's maintenance of the provision was not a violation of §8(b)(4)(B). The Union refused to hang prefabricated doors whether or not they bore a union label, and even refused to install prefabricated doors manufactured off the jobsite by members of the Union. This and other substantial evidence supported the finding that the conduct of the Union on the Frouge jobsite related solely to preservation of the traditional tasks of the jobsite carpenters. . . .

---

[38] As a general proposition, such circumstances might include the remoteness of the threat of displacement by the banned product or services, the history of labor relations between the union and the employers who would be boycotted, and the economic personality of the industry. See Comment, 62 Mich. L. Rev. 1176, 1185 et seq. (1964).

[The Appendix to the Court's opinion and the concurring memorandum of Harlan, J., are omitted.]

STEWART, J., whom BLACK, DOUGLAS, and CLARK, JJ., join, dissenting. . . .

. . . As the Court points out, a typical form of secondary boycott is the visitation of sanctions on Employer A, with whom the union has no dispute, in order to force him to cease doing business with Employer B, with whom the union does have a dispute. But this is not the only form of secondary boycott that §8(b)(4) was intended to reach. The Court overlooks the fact that a product boycott for work preservation purposes has consistently been regarded by the courts, and by the Congress that passed the Taft-Hartley Act, as a proscribed "secondary boycott." . . .

A proper understanding of the purpose of Congress in enacting §8(b)(4) . . . requires an appreciation of the impact of this Court's 1945 decision in Allen Bradley Co. v. Local Union No. 3, 325 U.S. 797. . . . As part of a conspiracy between the manufacturers, the contractors and the union, union members refused to install any electrical equipment manufactured outside the city. The Union's interest in this scheme is plainly set forth in the Court's opinion; it was to obtain "work for its own members." 325 U.S., at 799. "The business of New York City manufacturers had a phenomenal growth, thereby multiplying the jobs available for the Local's members." 325 U.S., at 800. Just as in the cases before us, the union enforced the product boycott to protect the work opportunities of its members.[6] The Court found the antitrust laws applicable to the union's role in the scheme, but solely on the ground that the union had conspired with the manufacturers and contractors. Significantly for present purposes, the Court stated that "had there been no union-contractor-manufacturer combination the union's actions here . . . would not have been violations of the Sherman Act." 325 U.S., at 807. The Court further indicated that, by itself, a bargaining agreement authorizing the product boycott in question would not transgress the antitrust laws. 325 U.S., at 809. In conclusion, the Court recognized that allowing unions to effect product boycotts might offend sound public policy, but indicated that the remedy lay in the hands of the legislature. . . . 325 U.S., at 810.

Congress responded when it enacted the Taft-Hartley Act. Although there have been differing views within the Court as to the scope of labor

---

[6] The present cases, in which the boycotting employees were protecting their own work opportunities, cannot be distinguished from *Allen Bradley* on the ground that there the boycotting employees were protecting the work opportunities of other members of their union. For today in Houston Insulation Contractors Assn. v. Labor Board, post, p. 664, the Court applies its holding in the present cases to validate a boycott by employees to protect the work opportunities of other workers who were not even members of their union.

unions' exemption from the antitrust laws, the Court in *Allen Bradley* had plainly stated that a work preservation product boycott by a union acting alone fell within that exemption. Two years after the *Allen Bradley* decision, the 80th Congress prohibited such product boycotts, but did so through the Taft-Hartley Act rather than by changing the antitrust laws. The Senate report on §8(b)(4)(A) of the bill that became law clearly indicates that Congress intended to proscribe not only the Employer A — Employer B model of secondary boycott, but also product boycotts like that involved in *Allen Bradley* and in the cases before us:

> . . . This paragraph [§8(b)(4)(A)] also makes it an unfair labor practice for a union to engage in the type of secondary boycott that has been conducted in New York City by local No. 3 of the IBEW, whereby electricians have refused to install electrical products of manufacturers employing electricians who are members of some labor organization other than local No. 3. (See . . . Allen Bradley Co. v. Local Union No. 3, I.B.E.W., 325 U.S. 797.)

. . . It is entirely understandable that Congress should have sought to prohibit product boycotts having a work preservation purpose. Unlike most strikes and boycotts, which are temporary tactical maneuvers in a particular labor dispute, work preservation product boycotts are likely to be permanent, and the restraint on the free flow of goods in commerce is direct and pervasive, not limited to goods manufactured by a particular employer with whom the union may have a given dispute.

Although it was deeply concerned with the extensive restraints on trade caused by product boycotts, the 80th Congress specifically declined to amend the antitrust laws to reach the *Allen Bradley* type of secondary boycott because it correctly understood that such practices were already directly covered by §8(b)(4) of the 1947 Act. The House Conference Report explained why a provision in the House draft that would have amended "the Clayton Act so as to withdraw the exemption of labor organizations under the antitrust laws when such organizations engaged in combinations or conspiracies . . . [to] impose restrictions or conditions upon the purchase, sale, or use of any product, material, machine, or equipment . . ." was dropped in the conference that agreed on the Taft-Hartley Act. It stated that "Since the matters dealt with in this section have to a large measure been effectuated through the use of boycotts, and since the conference agreement contains effective provisions directly dealing with boycotts themselves, this provision is omitted from the conference agreement."

The Court seeks to avoid the thrust of this legislative history . . . by suggesting that in the present cases, the product boycott was used to preserve work opportunities traditionally performed by the Union, whereas in *Allen*

Bradley the boycott was originally designed to create new job opportunities. But it is misleading to state that the union in *Allen Bradley* used the product boycott as a "sword." The record in that case establishes that the boycott was undertaken for the defensive purpose of restoring job opportunities lost in the depression. Moreover, the Court is unable to cite anything in *Allen Bradley*, or in the Taft-Hartley Act and its legislative history, to support a distinction in the applicability of §8(b)(4) based on the origin of the job opportunities sought to be preserved by a product boycott. The Court creates its sword and shield distinction out of thin air; nothing could more clearly indicate that the Court is simply substituting its own concepts of desirable labor policy for the scheme enacted by Congress.

The courts and the . . . Board fully recognized that Congress had intended to ban product boycotts along with other forms of the secondary boycott, and that it had not distinguished between "good" and "bad" secondary boycotts. In a 1949 decision involving §8(b)(4), the Board stated that "Congress considered the 'product boycott' one of the precise evils which that provision was designed to curb."[13] . . . In Joliet Contractors Assn. v. Labor Board, 202 F.2d 606, *cert. denied*, 346 U.S. 824, . . . the Seventh Circuit held that a glaziers' union boycott of preglazed sashes to preserve work they had traditionally performed was an unfair labor practice under §8(b)(4). . . . There were no court decisions to the contrary prior to the 1959 amendments to the [NLRA]. Although it made extensive other changes in §8 at that time, Congress did not disturb the law firmly established by these decisions. The conclusion is inescapable that the Union's boycott of the prefitted doors in these cases clearly violated §8(b)(4)(B).

In 1959 Congress enacted §8(e) to ensure that §8(b)(4)'s ban on boycotts would not be circumvented by unions that obtained management's agreement to practices which would give rise to a §8(b)(4) violation if the union attempted unilaterally to enforce their observance. In the *Sand Door* decision in 1958, the Court had indicated that the execution of a union-employer agreement authorizing a secondary boycott, and the employer's observance of that agreement, did not constitute an unfair labor practice. Section 8(e) was the congressional response. Congress also added a new paragraph (A) to §8(b)(4), proscribing union pressure on an employer to force him to execute an agreement banned by §8(e). It is thus evident that §§8(b)(4)(A), 8(b)(4)(B) and 8(e) must be construed in harmony as prohibiting various union methods of implementing the type of boycotts that Congress sought to prohibit in the Taft-Hartley Act. As the Court observes, the sweep of §8(e) is no greater than that of §8(b)(4). By the same logic, it is no

---

[13] United Brotherhood of Carpenters, 81 N.L.R.B. 802, 806, *enforced*, 184 F.2d 60 [10th Cir. 1950].

narrower. The relation between the two sections was set forth in Ohio Valley Carpenters, 136 N.L.R.B. 977, 987:

> [T]he validity of a restrictive agreement challenged under 8(e) must be considered in terms of whether that agreement, if enforced by prohibited means, would result in an unfair labor practice under Section 8(b)(4)(B). Clearly, there is little point and no logic in declaring an agreement lawful under 8(e), but in finding its enforcement condemned under 8(b)(4)(B). . . .

Since, as has been shown, the product boycott enforced by the union in the cases before us violates §8(b)(4)(B), it follows that Rule 17, the provision in the collective bargaining agreement applied to authorize this same boycott by agreement, equally violates §8(e). . . .

The content of the construction industry proviso to §8(e) is also persuasive of that section's principal scope. That proviso exempts only construction industry agreements "relating to the contracting or subcontracting of work to be done at the site of the construction. . . ." The logical inference from this language is that boycotts of products shipped from outside the worksite are prohibited by §8(e), and that inference is confirmed by the House Conference Report [H.R. Conf. Rep. No. 1147, 86th Cong., 1st Sess. 39, I 1959 Leg. Hist. 943.]:

The Court indeed recognizes that the §8(e) construction industry proviso does not immunize product boycotts from the reach of that section. By a curious inversion of logic, the Court purports to deduce from this fact the proposition that product boycotts are not covered by §8(e). But if §8(e) and its legislative history are approached without preconceptions, it is evident that Congress intended to bar the use of any provisions in a collective agreement to authorize the product boycott involved in the cases before us.

Finally, the Court's reliance on [*Fibreboard*], 379 U.S. 203, is wholly misplaced. . . . The circumscribed nature of the decision is established by the Court's careful observation that

> The Company's decision to contract out the maintenance work did not alter the Company's basic operation. The maintenance work still had to be performed in the plant . . . the Company merely replaced existing employees with those of an independent contractor to do the same work under similar conditions of employment. Therefore, to require the employer to bargain about the matter would not significantly abridge his freedom to manage the business.

379 U.S., at 213. An employer's decision as to the products he wishes to buy presents entirely different issues. That decision has traditionally been re-

garded as one within management's discretion, and Fibreboard does not indicate that it is a mandatory subject of collective bargaining, much less a permissible basis for a product boycott made illegal by federal labor law.

The relevant legislative history confirms and reinforces the plain meaning of the statute and establishes that the Union's product boycott in these cases and the agreement authorizing it were both unfair labor practices. In deciding to the contrary, the Court has substituted its own notions of sound labor policy for the word of Congress. . . .

NOTES

1. In a companion case, Houston Insulation Contractors Assn. v. NLRB, 386 U.S. 664 (1967), the employer had purchased precut asbestos fittings in violation of its agreement with Local 22, requiring cutting at the employer's Houston shop. Coemployees, members of a sister local, refused to install the precut fittings at another location in Texas. The Court, affirming the NLRB's dismissal of a complaint under §8(b)(4)(B), reasoned that action supporting coemployees is not secondary even though the economic interests of the sympathetic employees are not directly involved; the Court did not mention "straight-line" or control relationships between the employer's operations. Cf. the ownership and control branch of the "ally" doctrine, supra p. 547.

2. Is there any basis for distinguishing a union signatory clause (like that in the first sentence of Rule 17) from a clause that restricts subcontracting to employers under contract with "labor unions having jurisdiction over the type of services performed"? Will the practical effect of those two types of clauses be different? See Meat & Highway Drivers v. NLRB, 335 F.2d 709, 715-717 (D.C. Cir. 1964), involving a manufacturer employing his own truck drivers but occasionally engaging other trucking companies, including nonunion ones, to deliver his products. The union representing the manufacturer's employees requested the following clause in a renewal agreement: "If the employer does not have sufficient equipment to make all deliveries itself, it may contract with any cartage company whose truck drivers enjoy the same or greater wages and other benefits as provided in this agreement for employees making deliveries."

In determining the circumstances under which such a clause would be compatible with §8(e), consider also footnote 38 in *National Woodwork*.

3. Suppose Frouge's employees had not previously done the work of finishing doors, but the union, in order to counteract a decline in employ-

ment or to provide work for more members, strikes for and secures a clause assigning such work to the bargaining unit. Has the union violated §8(b)(4)(A) or §8(e)? Is there anything in those statutory provisions or the policy of protecting "neutrals" that warrants a distinction between work preservation and work acquisition? Does that distinction rest on a fear that work acquisition would cause undue friction, or on a desire to limit resistance to technological change, especially in the construction trades where new technology has been needed to make "decent housing" available to lower-income groups? Are those considerations material, under the controlling statutory provisions?

4. Under the distinction between work preservation and work acquisition, legality of an agreement under §8(e) may turn on whether the disputed work is defined as that performed in the bargaining unit before the use of new technology, rather than as work performed outside the bargaining unit as a result of technological innovation. The difficulties involved are illustrated by the labor-management disputes and extensive litigation arising from the increased use of maritime containers — large reusable metal receptacles that can hold tons of cargo and can be loaded or unloaded away from the pier, thus making the movement of cargo much more economical but cutting into the jobs of longshoremen, who formerly handled cargo piece by piece at piers. This development led to the ILA "Rules for Containers," providing essentially that if containers owned or leased by shipping companies were to be stuffed (loaded) or stripped (unloaded) within a radius of less than 50 miles of a local port area by anyone other than the employees of the cargo's beneficial owner, the work was to be done at the pier by ILA labor. The Rules also provided for "liquidated damages" for containers violative of the rules, and for royalty payments on any container passing over a pier intact.

The NLRB invalidated these collectively bargained rules, under §8(e), as well as union action to enforce them, under §8(b)(4)(B), finding that unlawful work acquisition was involved. See, e.g., International Longshoremen's Assn. (Dolphin Forwarding Inc.), 236 N.L.R.B. 525 (1978), *enforcement denied*, 613 F.2d 890 (D.C. Cir. 1979). Resolving intercircuit conflicts, the Supreme Court (5-4) rejected the Board's definition of the disputed work, vacated its orders, and remanded the case to the Board. See NLRB v. International Longshoremen's Assn., 447 U.S. 490 (1980). The Court observed that the Board had ignored whether the disputed work was the functional equivalent of work traditionally done by longshoremen. Similarly, the Court emphasized that the Board must focus on the work of the bargaining unit employees, not on the work of other employees who may be doing the same or similar work, and must decide "whether the historical and functional relationship" between the traditional work and the work reserved for the bargaining unit "can support the conclusion that the objective of the agreement was work-preservation rather than the satisfaction of union goals elsewhere." The Court noted that "the question is not whether the rules represent the most rational or efficient response to innovation but whether they are a legally permissible effort to preserve jobs."

On remand and consolidation of other cases, the NLRB in general upheld the Rules on Containers as having an overall work preservation objective, under the Supreme Court's approach. Nonetheless, the Board found an unlawful objective and invalidated the Rules in the two respects in which they had sought to reserve for longshoremen work made superfluous by the new technology. International Longshoremen's Assn. (N.Y. Shipping Assn.), 266 N.L.R.B. No. 54, 112 L.R.R.M. 1305 (1983). On appeal, the Fourth Circuit rejected the Board's findings and upheld the Rules in their entirety, concluding that a work-acquisition label may not properly be attached to work preserved in a collective agreement merely because the disputed work is duplicative and rendered unnecessary and uneconomic by technological change. The court also upheld the Board's determination that the union had met the other requirement recognized by the Supreme Court, namely, that the shipping companies involved possessed "the right of control" over the disputed work. See American Trucking Assn. v. NLRB, 734 F.2d 966 (1984). Cf. Chapter 7(H).

5. When the work sought to be acquired or, indeed, to be protected, would require the employer to procure new capital equipment, would the union's insistence on performance of such work by bargaining unit employees violate §8(b)(3)? Cf. Fibreboard Paper Products Corp. v. NLRB, infra p. 860.

6. In applying the rationale of *National Woodwork*, should recapture of work formerly done be treated as "work preservation" or "work acquisition"? See American Boiler Mfrs. Assn. v. NLRB, 404 F.2d 547 (8th Cir. 1968), *cert. denied*, 398 U.S. 960 (1970), upholding a clause banning use of prefabricated material that had reduced bargaining unit work by 60 to 85 percent and indicating that "work preservation" includes "recapture," at least where employees had not lost all the work before the disputed clause had been negotiated. See also Retail Clerks Local 1288 v. NLRB, 390 F.2d 858, 861 (D.C. Cir. 1968) ("fairly claimable" work may lawfully be recaptured).

7. A collective agreement provided that the owner and operator of American flag ships should not sell a vessel without giving prior notice to the union and without securing from the transferee an agreement to observe all provisions of the agreement. The Board found that that provision violated §8(e) and declined to defer to an arbitration award enforcing it against a

transferee. Concluding that maritime buyers and sellers are "doing business" within the meaning of §8(e), the Board noted that sales of United States flag vessels (about 200 annually) are "fairly common." The Board rejected the union's defense of lawful work preservation, and noted that after a sale the clause did not require the retention of the existing crew but only that replacements belong to the signatory union. See NMU (Commerce Tankers Corp.), 196 N.L.R.B. 110 (1972), *enforced*, 486 F.2d 907 (2d Cir. 1973), *cert. denied*, 416 U.S. 970 (1974). Cf. Operating Engrs. Local 701 (Tru-Mix Constr. Co.), 221 N.L.R.B. 751 (1975), distinguishing *Commerce Tankers* and upholding the provision of a collective agreement extending the agreement to purchasers of the entire business. For the antitrust issues involved, see Commerce Tankers v. NMU, 553 F.2d 793 (2d Cir.), *cert. denied*, 434 U.S. 923 (1977). Cf. also Chapter 10(B)(2) on "successorship."

NLRB v. Enterprise Assn. of Steam Pipefitters, 429 U.S. 507 (1977). Austin, the general contractor for the construction of a home for the aged, awarded a subcontract to Hudik for heating, ventilation and air conditioning work. That contract specified that Austin should buy and install climate control units manufactured by the Slant/Fin Company, and that the manufacturer should cut and thread the internal piping in these units. Those specifications conflicted with Rule IX of the collective agreement between Hudik and Enterprise Association (the union for the steamfitters employed by Hudik), which required the threading and cutting to be done on the job site. When the prethreaded units arrived there, the union steamfitters refused to install them; the union representative told Austin that the factory installation of the internal piping violated the union's agreement with Hudik. Austin's charge ultimately brought the dispute to the NLRB. The Board conceded that the union's refusal had been based on a valid work-preservation clause covering work traditionally performed by Hudik's employees. It stressed, however, that Hudik did not control the assignment of this work; accordingly, an object of the union's pressure was either forcing Hudik to terminate its subcontract with Austin, or forcing Austin to change its manner of doing business. That pressure, according to the Board, was exerted on Hudik for its effect on other employers and was, accordingly, secondary and violative of §8(b)(4)(B). A divided court of appeals set aside the Board's order, reasoning that a strike to compel an employer to honor a lawful work-preservation agreement made for their benefit is not against a "neutral," but is "primary." The Supreme Court reversed (6 to 3) and held that there was no adequate basis for the conclusion below that the Board's distinction "is erroneous as a matter of law." The Court added that under *Sand*

Door, which had been approved by Congress and not disturbed by the Court, even a valid work-preservation agreement does not provide a defense against a §8(b)(4) charge.

Brennan, J., joined by Stewart, J. (who had dissented in *National Woodwork*), and Marshall, J., dissented, on these grounds: Under *National Woodwork*, Rule IX (requiring on-the-site threading) had been "primary" because it had been designed to benefit Hudik's own employees and not to affect another employer's personnel policies. Accordingly, the union's pressure to get, or to enforce, such a clause was also "primary." It was inconsistent with *National Woodwork* to hold that because Austin, not Hudik, had the right to control the assignment of the disputed work, Austin was the target of the union's pressure. Hudik was not a neutral even after his contract with Austin, which he knew conflicted with his contract with the union, since Hudik could have negotiated with the union over premium pay or other substitutes for the lost work. Furthermore, *Sand Door* was distinguishable since the provision there barred the use of doors from nonunion suppliers and was secondary. Accordingly, despite the legality of the secondary clause in *Sand Door* (under the law then in effect), pressure to enforce it was illegal. By contrast, the *Enterprise* clause was primary as well as lawful, as was the pressure to enforce it.

NOTES

1. Suppose that in *Enterprise* the union had given Hudik the option of installing the prethreaded units, provided that the steamfitters received premium pay for that work, and upon the employer's rejection of that option, the union had refused to allow the steamfitters to install those units. Any difference in result? Cf. Carpenters, Local 742 (J.L. Simmons Co.), 237 N.L.R.B. 564 (1978).

2. If a union is barred from picketing a construction subcontractor who lacks "control," may it lawfully picket the general contractor for the purpose of requiring changed specifications designed to increase work for the subcontractor? What if the general contractor were already unionized?

3. In connection with the materials on unions and the Sherman Act (Chapter 7(F), infra), consider whether work-preservation clauses are exempt from the Sherman Act and whether it is material for that purpose whether a subcontractor who enters into a collective agreement barring prefabricated materials has "the right to control" the materials chosen. See Leslie, Right to Control: A Study in Secondary Boycotts and Labor Antitrust, 89 Harv. L. Rev. 904 (1976); Note, A Rational Approach to Secondary Boycotts and Work Preservation, 57 Va. L. Rev. 1280 (1971).

Note: Refusals to Cross Picket Lines — Contractual and Statutory Protection

Various contractual clauses dealing with the honoring of picket lines, struck work, and related matters have tested the outer limits of §8(e). The Board and courts have typically invalidated clauses that would authorize the application of secondary pressures, e.g., clauses sheltering from discipline employees who refuse to cross secondary picket lines. Regarding the distinction between "primary" and "secondary," see, e.g., Truck Drivers Local 413 v. NLRB, 334 F.2d 539 (D.C. Cir.), cert. denied, 379 U.S. 916 (1964). The Board has also upheld clauses protecting refusals to cross picket lines that fall within the second proviso to §8(b)(4).

Should the invalidity of contractual clauses designed to shelter employees from discipline for respecting specified picket lines automatically divest the employees of the statutory protection against discipline?

In the absence of a collective agreement specifically covering employee refusals to cross picket lines, the extent to which the NLRA limits employer discipline or countermeasures is not clear. The extent of such limitation will depend, in part, on whether the picket line is located at the employee's own work place or at firms doing business with his employer. In addition, determining the extent of such limitation involves considerations reflected in *Elk Lumber*, supra p. 224, *Local 1229*, supra p. 228, *Mackay*, supra p. 301, and *Great Dane*, supra p. 334, as well as the policies behind §§7 and 8(b)(4)(B).

Consider the following situations:

(1) A union representing R's production and maintenance workers is picketing R's premises in support of a strike for higher wages. Employee Solidarity, an R office clerical outside the bargaining unit, honors the picket line, "as a matter of principle." Employee Timidity, another nonunit R employee, also respects the picket line, but only because he is afraid — reasonably or unreasonably — of violence.

Would R's discharge of either of these employees violate the Act? Compare Ashtabula Forge, Div. of ABS Co., 269 N.L.R.B. No. 138, 115 L.R.R.M. 1295 (1984), with NLRB v. Union Carbide Corp., 440 F.2d 54 (4th Cir.), cert. denied, 404 U.S. 826 (1971). Would your answer change if the picketing were by an outside union protesting R's substandard wages and benefits? If the picketing were by an outside union attempting to compel R to stop doing business with a supplier struck by that union?

(2) Transport, Inc., a trucker, generally serves Motors, Inc., whose P & M employees are represented by the UAW. Those employees are picketing Motors in connection with a lawful economic strike. Employee Driver,

dispatched by Transport to make a delivery to Motors, is threatened with violence as he approaches the picket line and fails to complete the delivery. The next day, disobeying a direct order from his supervisor, he again declines to cross the Motors picket line. At the same time, Transport employee Hayward declines, "on principle," to deliver to a second Motors plant, which is part of the bargaining unit and is being picketed. Motors, which is operating with replacements, is insisting on deliveries from Transport.

Would Transport violate the NLRA if it discharged Driver or Hayward, or replaced either of them permanently? Would it be material if the discharges occurred even though Transport could not hire replacements willing to cross the picket line, or if other Transport employees were willing to make the deliveries declined by Driver and Hayward? See NLRB v. Browning-Ferris Industries, 700 F.2d 385 (7th Cir. 1983); Overnite Transportation Co., 212 N.L.R.B. 515 (1974).

Presumably, an employee replaced in the foregoing situations enjoys, as a minimum, the right of preferential employment spelled out in *Laidlaw*, supra p. 314. But would properly drafted contractual provisions protect such employees against permanent replacement? What of the following provision?

> It shall not be a violation of this Agreement and it shall not be cause for discharge or disciplinary action [if] an employee refuses to enter upon any property involved in a labor dispute or refuses to go through or work behind any picket line at the place of business of any employer party to this Agreement.

Does this clause waive an employer's right to replace permanently employees who refuse to cross picket lines? The NLRB said "no" in Butterworth-Manning-Ashmore Mortuary, 270 N.L.R.B. No. 148, 116 L.R.R.M. 1193 (1984), after having said "yes" in Torrington Constr. Co., 235 N.L.R.B. 1540 (1978). Should the Board's customary test of a "clear and unmistakable" waiver apply in this context? Compare Note 5, infra p. 1050. If the contractual language "discharge or disciplinary action" does not affect an employer's right to hire replacements, does the picket line clause set out above grant employees any protections not already enjoyed under NLRA §7?

On the problems generated by respect of picket lines, see C. Morris, 2 The Developing Labor Law 1202 (2d ed. 1983); Haggard, Picket Line Observance As A Protected Concerted Activity, 53 N.C.L. Rev. 43 (1974); Note, Picket Line Observance: The Board and Balance of Interests, 79 Yale L.J. 1369 (1970).

Note: The Industry-Wide Provisos to §8(e)

The garment and construction industries differed in their structure and history, and in the obstacles they presented to union organization. These differences help account for differences in the scope of the exemptions from the prohibitions of §8(e) applicable to those two industries.

The garment industry proviso is the broader one; it embodies an exemption from §8(b)(4)(B), as well as from §8(e), and provides that the NLRA shall not be a bar to enforcement of hot cargo clauses by strikes or other economic pressures. This broader scope is attributable to the structure of the garment industry and the organizing weapons unions used there. Garment manufacturers, seeking to avoid unionization, became "jobbers," farming out manufacturing work to contractors. The intense competition among the latter was linked to the low wages they paid. Faced with practical difficulties in reaching contractors' employees directly, unions pressured jobbers and manufacturers to do business only with unionized contractors. The legislative history indicates that Congress intended the garment industry proviso to continue to permit unions to use those organizational weapons. See Danielson v. Joint Board of Coat, Suit & Allied Garment Workers' Union (Hazantown), 494 F.2d 1230, 1234-1236 (2d Cir. 1974), holding that §8(b)(7) is not applicable to picketing of a jobber to secure a "standard jobbers agreement" that comprehensively regulated contractors' employment terms but excluded coverage of a jobber's employees on his premises.

The scope of the construction industry proviso is dealt with in *Connell Construction* (an antitrust case), infra p. 664, and *Woelke & Romero* (a case arising under §8(e)), noted infra p. 673. Those materials might usefully be examined at this point.

NOTES

In light of §8(b)(2), §8(a)(3), and §8(b)(7), the two provisos to §8(e) and §8(b)(4), consider the following questions involving the construction industry proviso:

1. The lawfulness of a strike to obtain a clause sheltered by that proviso (the question reserved in *Woelke*). Would it be material that compliance with such a clause would require the contracting employer to sever preexisting arrangements with a nonunion contractor? Cf. Los Angeles Bldg. & Constr. Trades Council (Gasket Mfg. Co.), 175 N.L.R.B. 242 (1969).

2. W is a construction subcontractor whose employees are represented

by the United Steelworkers. In order to secure jobs in an area where general contractors are required by their collective agreements to use subs who employ members of an AFL-CIO building trade union, W incorporates the Y company, which engages primarily in bridge construction and which uses AFL-CIO hiring halls. The Operating Engineers Union considers such "double-breasted" employers a threat and strikes the Y company for these provisions: (1) No employee would be required to operate equipment owned by a company with whom the union does not have an agreement, provided that union equipment is available in the area. (2) No signatory employer should rent or supply unmanned equipment to construction firms not under agreement with the union. (3) No employee would be required to operate equipment for any employer with an interest in a construction company that does not have a contract with the union. Has the union committed any unfair labor practices? Would it be material if the suppliers of the equipment had employees on the job site? Cf. NLRB v. Operating Engrs., Local 542 (York County Bridge, Inc.), 532 F.2d 902 (3d Cir. 1976), cert. denied, 429 U.S. 1072 (1977).

3. A collective bargaining agreement between a construction union and a construction subcontractor provides for premium pay for installation of prefabricated climate-control units on a construction job, regardless of whether the subcontractor has the "right to control" the decision to use such units. Is that agreement sheltered by the construction industry proviso?

Note: Hot Cargo Remedies

Violations of §§8(e) and 8(b)(7), unlike those of §8(b)(4), are not subject to the damage remedy established by the LMRA §303. Is that disparity warranted as a matter of policy?

Shepard v. NLRB, 459 U.S. 344 (1983), involves §10(c) of the Act as a possible basis for monetary relief for §8(e) violations. The master agreement, covering San Diego building contractors and a Teamsters local, barred the contractors from using nonunion dump truck operators for hauling to and from construction sites. The builders were to use only signatory brokers, and the latter were to hire only unionized truck operators for such hauling. After this agreement was executed, Shepard's broker (Terra), with Shepard's authorization, deducted from Shepard's earnings payments made to the union's "fringe benefit funds." The union later advised Terra not to deal with seven nonunion operators, including Shepard, who had previously contracted for Terra's services. As a result, Terra told Shepard to join the union or find a new broker. Shepard joined under protest and paid initiation fees and dues to the Teamsters. The Board upheld the ALJ's finding that the dump truck operators were independent contractors and that, accordingly, the master agreement violated §8(e). The Board, however, rejected his recommendation of a reimbursement order covering the union initiation fees, dues, and the fringe benefits paid by the owner-operators involved, stating:

> The Board has on one occasion adopted without comment an [ALJ's] recommended order containing such a remedy. Local 814, International Brotherhood of Teamsters, Chauffeurs, Warehousemen and Helpers of America (Santini Brothers, Inc.), 208 N.L.R.B. 184, 201 (1974). In the present case, however, there is insufficient evidence in the record with respect to alleged losses directly attributable to actual coercion by Respondents. Furthermore, we find a reimbursement order, typically used to "make whole" *employees* for violations of the Act, to be generally overbroad and inappropriate in the context of 8(e) violations. We note that aggrieved owner-operators engaged in business as independent contractors may pursue a damage claim under §303 of the Act. For the foregoing reasons, we find that the reimbursement of owner-operators ordered by the [ALJ] would not effectuate the remedial policies of the Act. See [Carpenters Local 60] v. NLRB, 365 U.S. 651 (1961). 249 N.L.R.B. 386, n.2, (1980).

The Supreme Court, through Rehnquist, J., agreed with the D.C. Circuit that the Board's decision should be affirmed, reasoning as follows: The Ninth Circuit's position that the Board should order a refund of money collected illegally, unless there is a rational ground for not making such an order, involved too limited a view of the Board's discretion under §10(c). Although the Board's explanation for denying reimbursement was vague, it was reasonable for the Board to order reimbursement only where Congress had permitted damages. For, quoting from UAW v. Russell, 356 U.S. 634, 642-643 (1958), the Board's "power to order affirmative relief under §10(c) is merely incidental to the primary purpose of Congress to stop and to prevent unfair labor practices. Congress did not establish a remedial scheme authorizing the Board to award full compensatory damages for injuries caused by wrongful conduct." Justice O'Connor agreed that the Board had discretion to deny reimbursement to Shepard but dissented from the Court's conclusion that the Board had adequately explained its decision; accordingly, she would have remanded for the Board's determination of whether reimbursement of any or all the funds paid by Shepard to the union was necessary to effectuate the purposes of the hot cargo prohibition.

NOTES

1. Is Justice O'Connor's dissent well-founded?

2. Does the Court indicate that the issuance of a reimbursement order would have been within the Board's discretion?

3. Why should §10(c) be read as permitting the Board (a) to grant a remedy only when a link between an invalid hot cargo clause and "coercion" violative of §8(b)(4)(B) activates a duplicative §303 remedy, and (b) to deny a remedy in the only situation where it would make a difference — i.e., when §303 (and assumably other legislation) does not provide a remedy? On the other hand, should the failure of §303 to cover hot cargo violations be read as denying the Board discretion to issue make-whole remedies for such violations?

4. For the interaction of §8(e) and the Sherman Act as a basis for imposing treble damage liability on the parties to unlawful hot cargo provisions, see Chapter 7(F), which follows below.

F.   THE ANTITRUST LAWS AS LIMITATIONS ON COLLECTIVE ACTION [1]

Even before many union activities were exempted from the Sherman Act, that Act, as applied by the Supreme Court,[11] was not directed at the existence of union "monopoly" in the labor market or at efforts by a union to organize substantially all of the workers producing for a given market. The Act was essentially a proscription against bad practices, such as union-instigated boycotts implemented through consumers or employees of secondary employers.[12] In proscribing boycotts, the Court had not explicitly attached any importance to union efforts to extend unionization, together with the closed shop, over an entire industry. Indeed, the Court appeared to have recognized the legality of industry-wide unions even before they had apparently been legitimized by Section 6 of the Clayton Act. Nor did the Court explicitly concern itself with the quantitative impact of particular boycotts on supply

---

[1][The following introductory section draws on Meltzer, Labor Unions, Collective Bargaining and the Antitrust Laws, 32 U. Chi. L. Rev. 659, 661–668 (1965). — EDS.]

[11] Loewe v. Lawlor, 208 U.S. 274 (1908), the first Supreme Court case applying the Act to union activities, was decided before the enactment of the Clayton Act in 1914.

[12] See Duplex Printing Press Co. v. Deering, 254 U.S. 443 (1921); Bedford Cut Stone Co. v. Stone Cutters Assn., 274 U.S. 37 (1927).

and price in interstate markets; the union-sponsored boycott was unlawful so long as it was aimed at interstate trade.

The Court's treatment of strikes that obstructed the production of goods for interstate shipment contrasted sharply with its condemnation of boycotts that interfered with the sale of goods at their destination rather than at their point of origin. Such strikes generally did not fall within the Sherman Act. So long as the union's primary objective was found to have been the resolution of a "local" labor controversy, even strikes that interfered with (and were expected to do so) the production of goods destined for interstate commerce were held not to be a "direct," i.e., unlawful, restraint on such commerce.[16]

In Coronado Coal Co. v. UMW (*Coronado II*),[17] a unanimous Court indicated, however, that a "local" strike would be unlawful if it could be established that the union's specific purpose was to prevent "local" nonunion goods from competing with union goods in interstate commerce. This approach in *Coronado II* rested on a plainly unmanageable distinction, i.e. between local labor purposes and the purpose of sheltering union goods against nonunion competition. Those purposes were inextricably connected since local labor purposes could be achieved only by protecting the local unionized sector against the pressure of nonunion goods originating elsewhere.

Furthermore, the consideration it deemed decisive was irrelevant to the general objectives of both the Sherman Act and the union movement. Plainly, where strikes reduced output destined for interstate markets, the consequences for supply, price and the union involved were not affected by determinations as to whether the union's dominant purpose was to protect a local unionized sector or to reduce nonunion output destined for interstate commerce. Whatever the union's dominant purpose, preservation of benefits from organization in the unionized sector was dependent on spreading unionization or on choking off the flow of competitive nonunion goods by the use of economic pressure.

The Court's distinction between legal strikes and illegal boycotts was also irrelevant to the preservation of competition. That distinction depended on whether interstate commerce was pinched at its origin or at its destination. The effect on trade obviously was, however, a function of the effectiveness of the union pressure rather than the point at which it was exerted. Further-

---

[16]See United Leather Workers v. Herkert & Meisel Trunk Co., 265 U.S. 457 (1924); UMW v. Coronado Coal Co., 259 U.S. 344 (1922). These opinions emphasized the narrow concept of interstate commerce that prevailed prior to 1937 and linked the constitutional question to the existence of a specific intent to restrain trade, as distinguished from an intent to settle a local labor controversy.

[17]Coronado Coal Co. v. UMW, 268 U.S. 295 (1925).

more, strikes and boycotts were frequently alternative methods for achieving the same union objectives. We have already seen that where a union could mount an effective strike, there was no need for the union to organize a boycott. Indeed, resort to boycotts to break a bargaining impasse was typically a sign of weakness rather than of strength. Hence, the unfavorable treatment of boycotts, compared to strikes, seemed perverse in relation to any general objective of limiting private economic power.

In these decisions antedating the Wagner Act, the Court had eviscerated the vague labor clauses of the Clayton Act. By ruling that §6 of that act did not exempt union departures from "normal and legitimate objects," the Court had preserved controversial and uncertain judicial regulation of "union purposes." It had restricted the application of §20 to the parties to a dispute concerning their own employment, present, past, or prospective, thereby rendering that section inapplicable to secondary activities initiated by immediate parties but implemented by affiliated or sympathetic unions. Thus, notwithstanding the Clayton Act, classic weapons of organization and collective bargaining remained subject to the Sherman Act.

The legislation of the thirties (such as the Norris-LaGuardia and Wagner Acts) was, however, designed to promote the use of those weapons and to curtail the role of the courts in the formulation of labor policy. But that legislation had not integrated the new freedoms with the old restrictions; indeed, the new statutes had not even mentioned the Sherman Act and, hence, had not eliminated the threat of criminal and treble damage actions based on the characterization of boycotts or organizational efforts as "direct" attacks on interstate commerce.

In Apex Hosiery Co. v. Leader (310 U.S. 469 (1940)) the Court moved toward harmonizing the antitrust laws with the freedoms conferred by labor legislation. In Apex, a union, after organizing eight of the 2,500 employees of a Philadelphia hosiery manufacturer, unsuccessfully sought a closed shop. Thereupon, the union stopped production for about three months, occupied the plant, and refused to permit the shipment of existing goods to out-of-state customers. The Supreme Court, dismissing the union's violence as irrelevant, held that its conduct had not violated the Sherman Act. The Court announced (at 512) that the Act did not apply to strikes or other obstructions to interstate commerce unless they had an effect, or were intended to have an effect, on prices. The Court stated (at 502-504):

> A combination of employees necessarily restrains competition among themselves in the sale of their services to the employer; yet such a combination was not considered an illegal restraint of trade at common law when the Sherman Act was adopted, either because it was not thought to be unreasonable or because it was not deemed a "restraint of trade." Since the enactment

of the declaration in §6 of the Clayton Act that "the labor of a human being is not a commodity or article of commerce . . . nor shall such [labor] organizations, or the members thereof, be held or construed to be illegal combinations or conspiracies in the restraint of trade under the antitrust laws," it would seem plain that restraints on the sale of the employee's services to the employer, however much they curtail the competition among employees, are not in themselves combinations or conspiracies in restraint of trade or commerce under the Sherman Act. . . . Since, in order to render a labor combination effective it must eliminate the competition from non-union made goods, see American Steel Foundries v. Tri-City Central Trades Council, 257 U.S. 184, 209, an elimination of price competition based on differences in labor standards is the objective of any national labor organization. But this effect on competition has not been considered to be the kind of curtailment of price competition prohibited by the Sherman Act. . . . And in any case, the restraint here is . . . of a different kind and has not been shown to have any actual or intended effect on price or price competition. . . .

This passage plainly suggested that industry-wide or market-wide unionization, whatever its effect on product competition or prices, was privileged and that strikes, at least for conventional objectives, such as higher wages, were lawful without regard to their impact on price and competition in the product market.

That implication, was, however, muddied because the Court emphasized that the union's obstructions to interstate commerce had not affected price and had not been so intended. Thus the possibility remained that a strike, or other obstructions to commerce that eliminated enough output to affect price, violated the Sherman Act. But to apply the Act to such strikes would have been contrary to both the basic premises behind labor legislation and the dominant thrust of the Apex opinion. Such an application would have converted the Act into an antistrike weapon protecting only larger enterprises, since the elimination of their output, or indeed their unionization under strike pressure, might have affected the price of goods. But one of the declared objectives of the labor statutes was the protection of labor organization in order to balance the power of large business combinations. Plainly, strike protection confined to large enterprises would have been a perverse response to that objective. Furthermore, industry-wide unionization sanctioned by the Court could scarcely have achieved labor's purposes in the labor market without strikes that might have affected price by withdrawing a substantial volume of output for substantial periods. Those considerations suggested that the Court's emphasis, in Apex, on the absence of price effects, was a convenient ad hoc expedient rather than a formulation of a general principle condemning union activity producing such effects. That conclusion was, moreover, reinforced by language throughout the opinion, implying that the statute was directed solely at business combinations and trusts.

Although *Apex* thus seemed to foreshadow substantial union emancipation from the Sherman Act, it did not articulate an exemption for unions. Nor did the Court purport to overrule the secondary boycott cases, such as *Bedford Stone* or *Duplex Printing Press*, but stressed (at 506) that those cases had involved union activities directed at control of the market and were so widespread as substantially to affect it. The Court declared (at 495) that the Act would continue to apply to union activities that affected or restrained "commercial competition." But the illustrations of restraints on such competition, drawn as they were from cases involving business combinations (see 497-498), provided scant guidance as to whether and how the Act should be applied to a variety of controversial union activities, such as secondary boycotts, restraints on the use of new technology or of new products, the exclusion of certain enterprises (whether or not unionized) from particular markets, or the restriction of supply through control of production schedules. Plainly, such restrictions, even though designed for the sole benefit of union members, could significantly affect the character of competition and could adversely affect consumers. Furthermore, even if *Apex* is read as immunizing union restraints on the "labor market" but not the "product market," the line between those two markets is not easily drawn. In any event, the impact of wage costs on supply and price inextricably links the two markets. In short, there was a basic conflict between the purposes of the Sherman Act and the protection accorded by the Wagner Act to "concerted activities" by employees.

Assistant Attorney General Thurman Arnold in 1939, seeking to mediate that conflict, proposed that the Sherman Act be used against certain "unreasonable restraints" by unions, including "jurisdictional strikes" and strikes and boycotts directed at preventing the use of "economical and standardized building material, in order to compel persons in need of low-cost housing to hire unnecessary labor." See T. Arnold, The Bottlenecks of Business 249-253 (1940). This program led to (and was aborted by) the *Hutcheson* case, infra, which exempted some union activities from the Sherman Act.

The materials below will invite consideration of:

1. the interaction of the labor statutes and the Sherman Act in determining both the scope of the "labor exemption" and the basis for liability under the Sherman Act for nonexempt union activities or labor-management arrangements; and

2. whether the labor statutes may be properly read (or should be amended) to foreclose any Sherman Act remedy for union conduct that is

protected, permitted, or proscribed by the Taft-Hartley Act, as amended.

See generally Cox, Labor and the Antitrust Laws—A Preliminary Analysis, 104 U. Pa. L. Rev. 252 (1955); Cox, Labor and the Antitrust Laws: Pennington and Jewel Tea, 46 B.U.L. Rev. 317 (1966); Meltzer, Labor Unions, Collective Bargaining, and the Antitrust Laws, 32 U. Chi. L. Rev. 659 (1965); Winter, Collective Bargaining and Competition: The Application of Antitrust Standards to Union Activities, 73 Yale L.J. 14 (1963); E. B. Miller, Antitrust Laws and Employee Relations: An Analysis of Their Impact on Management and Union Policies (1984).

United States v. Hutcheson
312 U.S. 219 (1941)

FRANKFURTER, J. . . . Anheuser-Busch, Inc., operating a large plant in St. Louis, contracted with Borsari Tank Corporation for the erection of an additional facility. The Gaylord Container Corporation, a lessee of adjacent property from Anheuser-Busch made a similar contract for a new building with the Stocker Company. Anheuser-Busch obtained the materials for its brewing and other operations and sold its finished products largely through interstate shipments. The Gaylord Corporation was equally dependent on interstate commerce for marketing its goods, as were the construction companies for their building materials. Among the employees of Anheuser-Busch were members of the United Brotherhood of Carpenters . . . and of the International Association of Machinists. The conflicting claims of these two organizations, affiliated with the [AFL], in regard to the erection and dismantling of machinery had long been a source of controversy between them. Anheuser-Busch had had agreements with both organizations whereby the Machinists were given the disputed jobs and the Carpenters agreed to submit all disputes to arbitration. But in 1939 the president of the Carpenters, their general representative, and two officials of the Carpenters' local organization, the four men under indictment, stood on the claims of the Carpenters for the jobs. Rejection by the employer of the Carpenters' demand and the refusal of the latter to submit to arbitration were followed by a strike of the Carpenters, called by the defendants against Anheuser-Busch and the construction companies, a picketing of Anheuser-Busch and its tenant, and a request through circular letters and the official publication of the Carpenters that union members and their friends refrain from buying Anheuser-Busch beer.

These activities on behalf of the Carpenters formed the charge of the indictment as a criminal combination and conspiracy in violation of the Sherman Law. Demurrers denying that what was charged constituted a violation of the laws of the United States were sustained, 32 F. Supp. 600, and the case came here under the Criminal Appeals Act. 18 U.S.C. §682. . . .

Section 1 of the Sherman Law on which the indictment rested is as follows: "Every contract, combination in the form of trust or otherwise, or conspiracy, in restraint of trade or commerce among the several States, or with foreign nations, is hereby declared to be illegal." The controversies engendered by its application to trade union activities and the efforts to secure legislative relief from its consequences are familiar history. The Clayton Act of 1914 was the result. "This statute was the fruit of unceasing agitation, which extended over more than twenty years and was designed to equalize before the law the position of workingmen and employer as industrial combatants." Duplex Co. v. Deering, 254 U.S. 443, 484. Section 20 of that Act . . . withdrew from the general interdict of the Sherman Law specifically enumerated practices of labor unions by prohibiting injunctions against them — since the use of the injunction had been the major source of dissatisfaction — and also relieved such practices of all illegal taint by the catch-all provision, "nor shall any of the acts specified in this paragraph be considered or held to be violations of any law of the United States." The Clayton Act gave rise to new litigation and to renewed controversy in and out of Congress regarding the status of trade unions. By the generality of its terms the Sherman Law had necessarily compelled the courts to work out its meaning from case to case. It was widely believed that into the Clayton Act courts read the very beliefs which that Act was designed to remove. Specifically the courts restricted the scope of §20 to trade union activities directed against an employer by his own employees. Duplex Co. v. Deering, supra. Such a view it was urged, both by powerful judicial dissents and informed lay opinion, misconceived the area of economic conflict that had best be left to economic forces and the pressure of public opinion and not subjected to the judgment of courts. Ibid., pp. 485-486. Agitation again led to legislation and in 1932 Congress wrote the Norris-LaGuardia Act. . . .

The Norris-LaGuardia Act removed the fetters upon trade union activities, which according to judicial construction §20 of the Clayton Act had left untouched, by still further narrowing the circumstances under which the federal courts could grant injunctions in labor disputes. More especially, the Act explicitly formulated the "public policy of the United States" in regard to the industrial conflict, and by its light established that the allowable area of union activity was not to be restricted, as it had been in the Duplex case, to an immediate employer-employee relation. Therefore, whether trade union conduct constitutes a violation of the Sherman Law is to be determined only by reading the Sherman Law and §20 of the Clayton Act and the Norris-La-Guardia Act as a harmonizing text of outlawry of labor conduct.

Were, then, the acts charged against the defendants prohibited, or permitted, by these three interlacing statutes? If the facts laid in the indictment come within the conduct enumerated in §20 of the Clayton Act they do not constitute a crime within the general terms of the Sherman Law because of the explicit command of that section that such conduct shall not be "considered or held to be violations of any law of the United States." So long as a union acts in its self-interest and does not combine with nonlabor groups,[3] the licit and the illicit under §20 are not to be distinguished by any judgment regarding the wisdom or unwisdom, the rightness or wrongness, the selfishness or unselfishness of the end of which the particular union activities are the means. There is nothing remotely within the terms of §20 that differentiates between trade union conduct directed against an employer because of a controversy arising in the relation between employer and employee, as such, and conduct similarly directed but ultimately due to an internecine struggle between two unions seeking the favor of the same employer. Such strife between competing unions has been an obdurate conflict in the evolution of so-called craft unionism and has undoubtedly been one of the potent forces in the modern development of industrial unions. These conflicts have intensified industrial tension but there is not the slightest warrant for saying that Congress has made §20 inapplicable to trade union conduct resulting from them. . . .

It is at once apparent that the acts with which the defendants are charged are the kind of acts protected by §20 of the Clayton Act. The refusal of the Carpenters to work for Anheuser-Busch or on construction work being done for it and its adjoining tenant, and the peaceful attempt to get members of other unions similarly to refuse to work, are plainly within the free scope accorded to workers by §20 for "terminating any relation of employment," or "ceasing to perform any work of labor," or "recommending, advising, or persuading others by peaceful means so to do." The picketing of Anheuser-Busch premises with signs to indicate that Anheuser-Busch was unfair to organized labor, a familiar practice in these situations, comes within the language "attending at any place where any such person or persons may lawfully be, for the purpose of peacefully obtaining or communicating information, or from peacefully persuading any person to work or to abstain from working." Finally, the recommendation to union members and their friends

---

[3] Cf. United States v. Brims, 272 U.S. 549, involving a conspiracy of mill work manufacturers, building contractors and union carpenters.

not to buy or use the product of Anheuser-Busch, is explicitly covered by "ceasing to patronize . . . any party to such dispute, or from recommending, advising, or persuading others by peaceful and lawful means so to do."

Clearly, then, the facts here charged constitute lawful conduct under the Clayton Act unless the defendants cannot invoke that Act because outsiders to the immediate dispute also shared in the conduct. But we need not determine whether the conduct is legal within the restrictions which Duplex Co. v. Deering gave to the immunities of §20 of the Clayton Act. Congress in the Norris-LaGuardia Act has expressed the public policy of the United States and defined its conception of a "labor dispute" in terms that no longer leave room for doubt. Milk Wagon Drivers' Union v. Lake Valley Farm Products, 311 U.S. 91. This was done, as we recently said, in order to "obviate the results of the judicial construction" theretofore given the Clayton Act. New Negro Alliance v. Sanitary Grocery Co., 303 U.S. 552, 562; see Apex Hosiery Co. v. Leader, 310 U.S. 469, 507, n.26. Such a dispute, §13(c) provides, "includes any controversy concerning terms or conditions of employment, or concerning the association or representation of persons in negotiating, fixing, maintaining, changing, or seeking to arrange terms or conditions of employment, regardless of whether or not the disputants stand in the proximate relation of employer and employee." And under §13(b) a person is "participating or interested in a labor dispute" if he "is engaged in the same industry, trade, craft, or occupation, in which such dispute occurs, or has a direct or indirect interest therein, or is a member, officer, or agent of any association composed in whole or in part of employers or employees engaged in such industry, trade, craft, or occupation."

To be sure, Congress expressed this national policy and determined the bounds of a labor dispute in an act explicitly dealing with the further withdrawal of injunctions in labor controversies. But to argue, as it was urged before us, that the *Duplex* case still governs for purposes of a criminal prosecution is to say that that which on the equity side of the court is allowable conduct may in a criminal proceeding become the road to prison. It would be strange indeed that although neither the Government nor Anheuser-Busch could have sought an injunction against the acts here challenged, the elaborate efforts to permit such conduct failed to prevent criminal liability punishable with imprisonment and heavy fines. That is not the way to read the will of Congress, particularly when expressed by a statute which, as we have already indicated, is practically and historically one of a series of enactments touching one of the most sensitive national problems. Such legislation must not be read in a spirit of mutilating narrowness. . . .

The relation of the Norris-LaGuardia Act to the Clayton Act is not that of a tightly drawn amendment to a technically phrased tax provision. The underlying aim of the Norris-LaGuardia Act was to restore the broad purpose which Congress thought it had formulated in the Clayton Act but which was frustrated, so Congress believed, by unduly restrictive judicial construction. This was authoritatively stated by the House Committee on the Judiciary. "The purpose of the bill is to protect the rights of labor in the same manner the Congress intended when it enacted the Clayton Act, October 15, 1914, which act, by reason of its construction and application by the Federal courts, is ineffectual to accomplish the congressional intent." H.R. Rep. No. 669, 72d Congress, 1st Session, p. 3. The Norris-LaGuardia Act was a disapproval of Duplex Printing Press Co. v. Deering, supra, and Bedford Cut Stone Co. v. Journeymen Stone Cutters' Assn., 274 U.S. 37, as the authoritative interpretation of §20 of the Clayton Act, for Congress now placed its own meaning upon that section. The Norris-LaGuardia Act reasserted the original purpose of the Clayton Act by infusing into it the immunized trade union activities as redefined by the later Act. In this light §20 removes all such allowable conduct from the taint of being a "violation of any law of the United States," including the Sherman Law. . . .

Affirmed.

Murphy, J., took no part in the disposition of this case.

STONE, J., concurring. As I think it clear that the indictment fails to charge an offense under the Sherman Act, as it has been interpreted and applied by this Court, I find no occasion to consider the impact of the Norris-LaGuardia Act on the definition of participants in a labor dispute in the Clayton Act, as construed by this Court in Duplex Printing Press Co. v. Deering, 254 U.S. 443 — an application of the Norris-LaGuardia Act which is not free from doubt and which some of my brethren sharply challenge. . . .

ROBERTS, J., dissenting. . . . In 1908 this court held a secondary boycott [affecting interstate commerce], instigated to enforce the demands of a labor union against an employer, was a violation of the Sherman Act and could be restrained at the suit of the employer [Loewe v. Lawlor, 208 U.S. 274]. . . . As a result of continual agitation the Clayton Act was adopted. . . . The contention was made that the Clayton Act exempted labor organizations from suits [to restrain secondary boycotts]. That contention was not sustained. Upon the fullest consideration, this court reached the conclusion that the provisions of §20 of the Clayton Act governed not the substantive rights of persons and organizations but merely regulated the practice according to which, and the conditions under which, equitable relief might be granted in suits of this character. Section 6 has no bearing on the offense charged in this case. . . .

. . . [A]gitation for complete exemption of labor unions from the provisions of the antitrust laws persisted. Instead of granting the complete exemption desired, Congress adopted, March 23, 1932, the Norris-LaGuardia Act. The title and the contents of that Act, as well as its legislative history, demonstrate beyond question that its purpose was to define and to limit the jurisdiction of federal courts sitting in equity. The Act broadens the scope of labor disputes as theretofore understood. . . . [A] reading of the Act makes letter clear, that the jurisdiction of actions for damages authorized by the Sherman Act, and of the criminal offenses denounced by that Act, are not touched by the Norris-LaGuardia Act.

By a process of construction never, as I think, heretofore indulged by this court, it is now found that, because Congress forbade the issuing of injunctions to restrain certain conduct, it intended to repeal the provisions of the Sherman Act authorizing actions at law and criminal prosecutions for the commission of torts and crimes defined by the antitrust laws. The doctrine now announced seems to be that an indication of a change of policy in an Act as respects one specific item in a general field of the law, covered by an earlier Act, justifies this court in spelling out an implied repeal of the whole of the earlier statute as applied to conduct of the sort here involved. I venture to say that no court has ever undertaken so radically to legislate where Congress has refused so to do.

. . . [T]o attribute to Congress an intent to repeal legislation which has had a definite and well understood scope and effect for decades past, by resurrecting a rejected construction of the Clayton Act and extending a policy strictly limited by the Congress itself in the Norris-LaGuardia Act, seems to me a usurpation by the courts of the function of the Congress not only novel but fraught, as well, with the most serious dangers to our constitutional system of division of powers.

The Chief Justice joins in this opinion.

NOTES

1. Cf. F. Frankfurter & N. Greene, The Labor Injunction 220 (1930): "[T]he proposed bill [referring to a bill substantially similar to the Norris-LaGuardia Act] . . . explicitly applies only to the authority of the United States courts 'to issue any restraining order or injunction.' All other remedies in federal courts and all remedies in state courts remain available." See also id. at 215 and Kadish, Labor and the Law, in Mendelson, Felix Frankfurter: The Judge 171-172 n.92 (1964), explaining why Frankfurter had resisted a proposed provision that conduct unenjoinable under §4 should not be "unlawful."

2. For contemporaneous discussions of the *Hutcheson* case, see Steffen, Labor Activities in Restraint of Trade: The Hutcheson Case, 36 Ill. L. Rev. 1 (1941); Gregory, The New Sherman-Clayton-Norris-LaGuardia Act, 8 U. Chi. L. Rev. 503 (1941); Nathanson & Wirtz, The Hutcheson Case: Another View, 36 Ill. L. Rev. 41 (1941).

3. Does the labor exemption from the Sherman Act apply equally to agricultural unions even though they are excluded from NLRA coverage? See Bodine Produce, Inc. v. United Farm Workers Organizing Comm., 494 F.2d 541, 554-555 (9th Cir. 1974).

Allen Bradley Co. v. Local 3, IBEW
325 U.S. 797 (1945)

BLACK, J. . . . [Petitioners, manufacturers of electrical equipment outside of New York City and, for the most part, outside of New York State as well, brought this action because they had been excluded from the New York City market, through activities of respondents and others.]

Respondents are a labor union, its officials and its members. The union, Local No. 3 of the International Brotherhood of Electrical Workers, has jurisdiction only over the metropolitan area of New York City. It is therefore impossible for the union to enter into a collective bargaining agreement with petitioners. Some of petitioners do have collective bargaining agreements with other unions, and in some cases even with other locals of the IBEW.

Some of the members of respondent union work for manufacturers who produce electrical equipment similar to that made by petitioners; other members of respondent union are employed by contractors and work on the installation of electrical equipment, rather than in its production.

The union's consistent aim for many years has been to expand its membership, to obtain shorter hours and increased wages, and to enlarge employment opportunities for its members. To achieve this latter goal — that is, to make more work for its own members — the union realized that local manufacturers, employers of the local members, must have the widest possible outlets for their product. The union therefore waged aggressive campaigns to obtain closed-shop agreements with all local electrical equipment manufacturers and contractors. Using conventional labor union methods, such as strikes and boycotts, it gradually obtained more and more closed-shop agreements in the New York City area. Under these agreements, contractors were obligated to purchase equipment from none but local manufacturers who also had closed-shop agreements with Local No. 3; manufacturers obligated themselves to confine their New York City sales to contractors employing the Local's members. In the course of time, this type of individual employer-employee agreement expanded into industry-wide understandings, looking not merely to terms and conditions of employment but also to price and market control. Agencies were set up composed of representatives of all three groups to boycott recalcitrant local contractors and manufacturers and to bar from the area equipment manufactured outside its boundaries. The combination among the three groups, union, contractors, and manufacturers, became highly successful from the standpoint of all of them. The business of New York City manufacturers had a phenomenal growth, thereby multiplying the jobs available for the Local's members. Wages went up, hours were shortened, and the New York electrical equipment prices soared, to the decided financial profit of local contractors and manufacturers. The success is illustrated by the fact that some New York manufacturers sold their goods in the protected city market at one price and sold identical goods outside of New York at a far lower price. All of this took place as the Circuit Court of Appeals declared, "through the stifling of competition," and because the three groups in combination as "copartners," achieved "a complete monopoly which they used to boycott the equipment manufactured by the plaintiffs." Interstate sale of various types of electrical equipment has, by this powerful combination, been wholly suppressed.

Quite obviously, this combination of business men has violated both §§1 and 2 of the Sherman Act, unless its conduct is immunized by the participation of the union. For it intended to and did restrain trade in and monopolize the supply of electrical equipment in the New York City area to the exclusion of equipment manufactured in and shipped from other states, and did also control its price and discriminate between its would-be customers. Apex Hosiery Co. v. Leader, 310 U.S. 469, 512-513. Our problem in this case is therefore a very narrow one — do labor unions violate the Sherman Act when, in order to further their own interests as wage earners, they aid and abet business men to do the precise things which that Act prohibits? . . .

[Here followed a summary of the Sherman, Clayton, Norris-LaGuardia, and Wagner Act(s) and of selected decisions, culminating in United States v. Hutcheson.]

The result of all this is that we have two declared congressional policies which it is our responsibility to try to reconcile. The one seeks to preserve a competitive business economy; the other to preserve the rights of labor to organize to better its conditions through the agency of collective bargaining. We must determine here how far Congress intended activities under one of these policies to neutralize the results envisioned by the other.

Aside from the fact the labor union here acted in combination with the contractors and manufacturers, the means it adopted to contribute to the combination's purpose fall squarely within the "specified acts" declared by §20 not to be violations of federal law.[12] For the union's contribution to the trade boycott was accomplished through threats that unless their employers bought their goods from local manufacturers the union laborers would terminate the "relation of employment" with them and cease to perform "work or labor" for them; and through their "recommending, advising, or persuading others by peaceful and lawful means" not to "patronize" sellers of the boycotted electrical equipment. Consequently, under our holding in the *Hutcheson* case and other cases which followed it, had there been no union-contractor-manufacturer combination the union's actions here, coming as they did within the exceptions of the Clayton and Norris-LaGuardia Acts, would not have been violations of the Sherman Act. We pass to the question of whether unions can with impunity aid and abet business men who are violating the Act.

    . . . [W]e think Congress never intended that unions could, consistently with the Sherman Act, aid nonlabor groups to create business monopolies and to control the marketing of goods and services. . . .

    [After quoting from §6 of the Clayton Act, the opinion stated]: But "the purpose of mutual help" can hardly be thought to cover activities for the purpose of "employer-help" in controlling markets and prices. . . .

    . . . It has been argued that [the immunity claimed by the defendants] can be inferred from a union's right to make bargaining agreements with its employer. Since union members can without violating the Sherman Act strike to enforce a union boycott of goods, it is said they may settle the strike by getting their employers to agree to refuse to buy the goods. Employers and the union did here make bargaining agreements in which the employers agreed not to buy goods manufactured by companies which did not employ the members of Local No. 3. We may assume that such an agreement standing alone would not have violated the Sherman Act. But it did not stand alone. It was but one element in a far larger program in which contractors and manufacturers united with one another to monopolize all the business in New York City, to bar all other business men from that area, and to charge the public prices above a competitive level. It is true that victory of the union in its disputes, even had the union acted alone, might have added to the cost of goods, or might have resulted in individual refusals of all of their employers to buy electrical equipment not made by Local No. 3. So far as the union might

_____

[12] It has been argued that no labor disputes existed. The argument is untenable. We do not have here, as we did in Columbia River Packers Assn. v. Hinton, 315 U.S. 143, a dispute between groups of business men revolving solely around the price at which one group would sell commodities to another group. On the contrary, Local No. 3 is a labor union and its spur to action related to wages and working conditions.

have achieved this result acting alone, it would have been the natural consequence of labor union activities exempted by the Clayton Act from the
coverage of the Sherman Act. Apex Hosiery Co. v. Leader, supra, 503. But
when the unions participated with a combination of business men who had
complete power to eliminate all competition among themselves and to prevent all competition from others, a situation was created not included within
the exemptions of the Clayton and Norris-LaGuardia Acts. . . .

      Our holding means that the same labor union activities may or may not
be in violation of the Sherman Act, dependent upon whether the union acts
alone or in combination with business groups. This, it is argued, brings about
a wholly undesirable result — one which leaves labor unions free to engage in
conduct which restrains trade. But the desirability of such an exemption of
labor unions is a question for the determination of Congress. . . . It is true
that many labor union activities do substantially interrupt the course of trade
and that these activities, lifted out of the prohibitions of the Sherman Act,
include substantially all, if not all, of the normal peaceful activities of labor
unions. It is also true that the Sherman Act "draws no distinction between the
restraints effected by violence and those achieved by peaceful . . . means,"
Apex Hosiery Co. v. Leader, supra, 513. . . . Congress evidently concluded . . . that the chief objective of Antitrust legislation, preservation of
business competition, could be accomplished by applying the legislation
primarily only to those business groups which are directly interested in
destroying competition. . . . We know that Congress feared the concentrated power of business organizations to dominate markets and prices. It
intended to outlaw business monopolies. A business monopoly is no less such
because a union participates, and such participation is a violation of the Act.

      . . . We cannot sustain the judgment or the injunction in the form in
which they were entered. The judgment and the injunction apply only to the
union, its members, and its agents, since they were the only parties against
whom relief was asked. . . .

      Respondents objected to the form of the injunction and specifically
requested that it be amended so as to enjoin only those prohibited activities in
which the union engaged in combination "with any person, firm or corporation which is a nonlabor group. . ." Without such a limitation, the injunction as issued runs directly counter to the Clayton and the Norris-LaGuardia
Acts. The district court's refusal so to limit it was error.

      The judgment of the Court of Appeals ordering the action dismissed is
accordingly reversed and the cause is remanded to the district court for
modification and clarification of the judgment and injunction, consistent
with this opinion.

      [Urging that the union had been the dynamic force behind the formation of the challenged agreements — a finding made by the trial court (41 F. Supp. 727, 750 (S.D.N.Y. 1941)) and not disturbed on appeal — Murphy, J., dissented; Roberts, J., concurred only in the Court's result.

After remand, the court of appeals explicitly directed that the injunction should be inapplicable if the union did not act in conjunction with nonlabor groups. See Allen Bradley v. Local 3, IBEW, 164 F.2d 71, 75 (2d Cir. 1947).]

NOTES

1. Was the injunction sanctioned in the principal case barred by a literal reading of §4 of the Norris-LaGuardia Act? If so, what basis, if any, was there for the injunction?

2. Was the Supreme Court's decision of any direct practical help in opening the New York market to the plaintiffs?

3. Given Local No. 3's control over the electrical contractors, was the local's development of, or acquiescence in, the market control schemes and sharing of monopoly gains by the New York manufacturers and contractors consistent with achieving maximum wages for the employees of the electrical contractors?

4. Would customers of the electrical contractors have been materially affected if the union had permitted active competition among the New York contractors, and between New York and other manufacturers, and had used its leverage solely to maximize the gains of the unionized employees of the New York contractors?

5. Suppose that the union and the contractors' association had agreed that the contractors would use only components bearing the Local 3 label and that no price fixing or other forms of market control had occurred. Under the hypothetical arrangement, would the contractors have been receiving any "monopoly benefits"? Would the hypothetical agreement have violated the Sherman Act?

6. Would the arrangements in Allen Bradley now constitute a violation of §8(b)(4) of the NLRA?

United Mine Workers v. Pennington
381 U.S. 657 (1965)

WHITE, J., delivered the opinion of the Court. This action began as a suit by the trustees of the United Mine Workers of America Welfare and

Retirement Fund against . . . Phillips Brothers Coal Company, . . . seeking to recover some $55,000 in royalty payments [allegedly] due under the trust provisions of the National Bituminous Coal Wage Agreement of 1950, as amended. . . . Phillips filed an answer and a cross claim against UMW, alleging in both that the trustees, the UMW and certain large coal operators had conspired to restrain and to monopolize interstate commerce in violation of §§1 and 2 of the Sherman Antitrust Act, as amended. Actual damages . . . of $100,000 were claimed for the period [from] February 14, 1954, [to] December 31, 1958.

[Phillips'] allegations were essentially as follows: Prior to the 1950 Wage Agreement between the operators and the union, severe controversy had existed in the industry, particularly over wages, the welfare fund and the union's efforts to control the working time of its members. Since 1950, however, relative peace has existed in the industry, all as the result of the 1950 Wage Agreement and its amendments and the additional understandings entered into between UMW and the large operators. Allegedly the parties considered overproduction to be the critical problem of the coal industry. The agreed solution was to be the elimination of the smaller companies, the larger companies thereby controlling the market. More specifically, the union abandoned its efforts to control the working time of the miners, agreed not to oppose the rapid mechanization of the mines which would substantially reduce mine employment, agreed to help finance such mechanization and agreed to impose the terms of the 1950 agreement on all operators without regard to their ability to pay. The benefit to the union was to be increased wages as productivity increased with mechanization, these increases to be demanded of the smaller companies whether mechanized or not. Royalty payments into the welfare fund were to be increased also, and the union was to have effective control over the fund's use. The union and large companies agreed upon other steps to exclude the marketing, production, and sale of nonunion coal. Thus the companies agreed not to lease coal lands to nonunion operators, and in 1958 agreed not to sell or buy coal from such companies. The companies and the union jointly and successfully approached the Secretary of Labor to obtain establishment under the Walsh-Healey Act, as amended, of a minimum wage for employees of contractors selling coal to the TVA, such minimum wage being much higher than in other industries and making it difficult for small companies to compete in the TVA term contract market. At a later time, at a meeting attended by both union and company representatives, the TVA was urged to curtail its spot market purchases, a substantial portion of which were exempt from the Walsh-Healey order. Thereafter four of the larger companies waged a destructive and collusive price-cutting campaign in the TVA spot market for coal, two of the companies, West Kentucky Coal Co. and its subsidiary

Nashville Coal Co., being those in which the union had large investments and over which it was in position to exercise control.

The complaint survived motions to dismiss and after a five-week trial before a jury, a verdict was returned in favor of Phillips and against the trustees and the union, the damages against the union being fixed in the amount of $90,000, to be trebled under 15 U.S.C. §15 (1958 ed.). The trial court set aside the verdict against the trustees but overruled the union's motion for judgment notwithstanding the verdict or in the alternative for a new trial. The Court of Appeals affirmed. 325 F.2d 804. . . . We reverse and remand the case for proceedings consistent with this opinion.

I

We first consider UMW's contention that the trial court erred in denying its motion for a directed verdict and for judgment notwithstanding the verdict, since a determination in UMW's favor on this issue would finally resolve the controversy. The question presented by this phase of the case is whether in the circumstances of this case the union is exempt from liability under the antitrust laws. We think the answer is clearly in the negative and that the union's motions were correctly denied.

The antitrust laws do not bar the existence and operation of labor unions as such. Moreover, §20 of the Clayton Act and §4 of the Norris-LaGuardia Act permit a union, acting alone, to engage in the conduct therein specified without violating the Sherman Act. United States v. Hutcheson. . . .

But neither §20 nor §4 expressly deals with arrangements or agreements between unions and employers. Neither section tells us whether any or all such arrangements or agreements are barred or permitted by the antitrust laws. Thus Hutcheson itself stated: "So long as a union acts in its self-interest *and does not combine with nonlabor groups*, the licit and the illicit under §20 are not to be distinguished by any judgment regarding the wisdom or unwisdom, the rightness or wrongness, the selfishness or unselfishness of the end of which the particular union activities are the means." 312 U.S., at 232. (Emphasis added.)

And in Allen Bradley Co. v. Union, 325 U.S. 797, this Court made explicit what had been merely a qualifying expression in *Hutcheson* and held that "when the unions participated with a combination of business men who had complete power to eliminate all competition among themselves and to prevent all competition from others, a situation was created not included within the exemptions of the Clayton and Norris-LaGuardia Acts." Id., at 809. . . . Subsequent cases have applied the *Allen Bradley* doctrine to such combinations without regard to whether they found expression in a collective bargaining agreement, Brotherhood of Carpenters v. United States [330 U.S. 395]; see Teamsters Union v. Oliver, 358 U.S. 283, 296, and even though the mechanism for effectuating the purpose of the combination was an agreement on wages . . . or on hours of work. . . .

If the UMW in this case, in order to protect its wage scale by maintaining employer income, had presented a set of prices at which the mine operators would be required to sell their coal, the union and the employers who happened to agree could not successfully defend this contract provision if it were challenged under the antitrust laws by the United States or by some party injured by the arrangement. Cf. Allen Bradley Co. v. Union, 325 U.S. 797. . . . In such a case, the restraint on the product market is direct and immediate, is of the type characteristically deemed unreasonable under the Sherman Act and the union gets from the promise nothing more concrete than a hope for better wages to come.

Likewise, if as is alleged in this case, the union became a party to a collusive bidding arrangement designed to drive Phillips and others from the TVA spot market, we think any claim to exemption from antitrust liability would be frivolous at best. For this reason alone the motions of the unions were properly denied.

A major part of *Phillips* case, however, was that the union entered into a conspiracy with the large operators to impose the agreed-upon wage and royalty scales upon the smaller, nonunion operators, regardless of their ability to pay and regardless of whether or not the union represented the employees of these companies, all for the purpose of eliminating them from the industry, limiting production and preempting the market for the large, unionized operators. The UMW urges that since such an agreement concerned wage standards, it is exempt from the antitrust laws.

It is true that wages lie at the very heart of those subjects about which employers and unions must bargain and the law contemplates agreements on wages not only between individual employers and a union but agreements between the union and employers in a multiemployer bargaining unit. Labor Board v. Truck Drivers Union, 353 U.S. 87, 94-96. The union benefit from the wage scale agreed upon is direct and concrete and the effect on the product market, though clearly present, results from the elimination of competition based on wages among the employers in the bargaining unit, which is not the kind of restraint Congress intended the Sherman Act to proscribe. Apex Hosiery Co. v. Leader, 310 U.S. 469, 503-504. . . . We think it beyond question that a union may conclude a wage agreement with the multiemployer bargaining unit without violating the antitrust laws and that it may as a matter of its own policy, and not by agreement with all or part of the employers of that unit, seek the same wages from other employers.

This is not to say that an agreement resulting from union-employer negotiations is automatically exempt from Sherman Act scrutiny simply because the negotiations involve a compulsory subject of bargaining, regardless of the subject or the form and content of the agreement. Unquestionably the Board's demarcation of the bounds of the duty to bargain has great relevance to any consideration of the sweep of labor's antitrust immunity, for we are concerned here with harmonizing the Sherman Act with the national policy expressed in the National Labor Relations Act of promoting "the peaceful settlement of industrial disputes by subjecting labor-management controversies to the mediatory influence of negotiation," [*Fibreboard*], 379 U.S. 203, 211. But there are limits to what a union or an employer may offer or extract in the name of wages, and because they must bargain does not mean that the agreement reached may disregard other laws. Teamsters Union v. Oliver, 358 U.S. 283, 296. . . .

We have said that a union may make wage agreements with a multiemployer bargaining unit and may in pursuance of its own union interests seek to obtain the same terms from other employers. No case under the antitrust laws could be made out on evidence limited to such union behavior.[2] But we think a union forfeits its exemption from the antitrust laws when it is clearly shown that it has agreed with one set of employers to impose a certain wage scale on other bargaining units. One group of employers may not conspire to eliminate competitors from the industry and the union is liable with the employers if it becomes a party to the conspiracy. This is true even though the union's part in the scheme is an undertaking to secure the same wages, hours or other conditions of employment from the remaining employers in the industry.

We do not find anything in the national labor policy that conflicts with this conclusion. This Court has recognized that a legitimate aim of any national labor organization is to obtain uniformity of labor standards and that a consequence of such union activity may be to eliminate competition based on differences in such standards. Apex Hosiery Co. v. Leader, 310 U.S. 469, 503. But there is nothing in the labor policy indicating that the union and the employers in one bargaining unit are free to bargain about the wages, hours and working conditions of other bargaining units or to attempt to settle these matters for the entire industry. On the contrary, the duty to bargain unit by unit leads to a quite different conclusion. The union's obligation to its members would seem best served if the union retained the ability to respond to each bargaining situation as the individual circumstances might warrant,

---

[2] Unilaterally, and without agreement with any employer group to do so, a union may adopt a uniform wage policy and seek vigorously to implement it even though it may suspect that some employers cannot effectively compete if they are required to pay the wage scale demanded by the union. The union need not gear its wage demands to wages which the weakest units in the industry can afford to pay. Such union conduct is not alone sufficient evidence to maintain a union-employer conspiracy charge under the Sherman Act. There must be additional direct or indirect evidence of the conspiracy. There was, of course, other evidence in this case, but we indicate no opinion as to its sufficiency.

without being strait-jacketed by some prior agreement with the favored employers.

So far as the employer is concerned it has long been the Board's view that an employer may not condition the signing of a collective bargaining agreement on the union's organization of a majority of the industry. American Range Lines, Inc., 13 N.L.R.B. 139, 147 (1939). . . . In such cases the obvious interest of the employer is to ensure that acceptance of the union's wage demands will not adversely affect his competitive position. . . . Such an employer condition, if upheld, would clearly reduce the extent of collective bargaining. . . . Permitting insistence on an agreement by the union to attempt to impose a similar contract on other employers would likewise seem to impose a restraining influence on the extent of collective bargaining, for the union could avoid an impasse only by surrendering its freedom to act in its own interest vis-à-vis other employers, something it will be unwilling to do in many instances. Once again, the employer's interest is a competitive interest rather than an interest in regulating its own labor relations, and the effect on the union of such an agreement would be to limit the free exercise of the employees' right to engage in concerted activities according to their own views of their self-interest. In sum, we cannot conclude that the national labor policy provides any support for such agreements.

On the other hand, the policy of the antitrust laws is clearly set against employer-union agreements seeking to prescribe labor standards outside the bargaining unit. One could hardly contend, for example, that one group of employers could lawfully demand that the union impose on other employers wages that were significantly higher than those paid by the requesting employers, or a system of computing wages that, because of differences in methods of production, would be more costly to one set of employers than to another. The anticompetitive potential of such a combination is obvious, but is little more severe than what is alleged to have been the purpose and effect of the conspiracy in this case to establish wages at a level that marginal producers could not pay so that they would be driven from the industry. And if the conspiracy presently under attack were declared exempt it would hardly be possible to deny exemption to such avowedly discriminatory schemes.

From the viewpoint of antitrust policy, moreover, all such agreements between a group of employers and a union that the union will seek specified labor standards outside the bargaining unit suffer from a more basic defect, without regard to predatory intention or effect in the particular case. For the salient characteristic of such agreements is that the union surrenders its freedom of action with respect to its bargaining policy. Prior to the agreement the union might seek uniform standards in its own self-interest but would be required to assess in each case the probable costs and gains of a strike or other collective action to that end and thus might conclude that the objective of uniform standards should temporarily give way. After the agreement the union's interest would be bound in each case to that of the favored employer group. It is just such restraints upon the freedom of economic units to act according to their own choice and discretion that run counter to antitrust policy. See, e.g., Associated Press v. United States, 326 U.S. 1, 19; Fashion Originators' Guild v. Federal Trade Commn., 312 U.S. 457, 465; Anderson v. Shipowners Assn., 272 U.S. 359, 364-365.

Thus the relevant labor and antitrust policies compel us to conclude that the alleged agreement between UMW and the large operators to secure uniform labor standards throughout the industry, if proved, was not exempt from the antitrust laws. . . .

[In Part II of this opinion, White, J., based reversal and remand on the following errors in the instructions to the jury: (1) noncompliance with Eastern R.R. Presidents Conference v. Noerr Motor Freight, Inc., 365 U.S. 127 (1961), which the Justice read as legalizing joint efforts to influence public officials even though such efforts are part of a larger scheme violative of the Sherman Act; (2) failure to exclude any damages that Phillips, who had not been claimed to be a coconspirator, might have suffered as a result of Walsh-Healey determinations by the Secretary of Labor.]

DOUGLAS, J., with whom BLACK and CLARK, JJ., agree, concurring. As we read the opinion of the Court, it reaffirms the principles of [Allen Bradley], 325 U.S. 797, and tells the trial judge:

First. On the new trial the jury should be instructed that if there were an industry-wide collective bargaining agreement whereby employees and the union agreed on a wage scale that exceeded the financial ability of some operators to pay and that if it was made for the purpose of forcing some employers out of business, the union as well as the employers who participated in the arrangement with the union should be found to have violated the antitrust laws.

Second. An industry-wide agreement containing those features is prima facie evidence of a violation.* . . .

Congress can design an oligopoly for our society, if it chooses. But business alone cannot do so as long as the antitrust laws are enforced. Nor should business and labor working hand-in-hand be allowed to make that basic change in the design of our so-called free enterprise system. . . .

---

*. . . . "[A]n unlawful conspiracy may be and often is formed without simultaneous action or agreement on the part of the conspirators. Schenck v. United States, 253 F. 212, 213, aff'd, 249 U.S. 47; Levey v. United States, 92 F.2d 688, 691. Acceptance by competitors, without previous agreement, of an invitation to participate in a plan, the necessary consequence of which, if carried out, is restraint of interstate commerce, is sufficient to establish an unlawful conspiracy under the Sherman Act." . . . Interstate Circuit v. United States, 306 U.S. 208, 227.

[Goldberg, J., in a lengthy opinion, joined by Harlan and Stewart, JJ., concurred in the reversal but dissented from the grounds relied on in the opinion by White, J.; excerpts from this concurring opinion appear at infra p. 653.]

NOTES

1. Assume that a union and a multiemployer group agree to wages that are likely to and do eliminate marginal producers who have not mechanized and whose wages constitute a larger percentage of total costs than do the wages of larger producers who dominate the multiemployer group. Is that agreement vulnerable under Justice Douglas' approach? Under Justice White's?

2. On remand in *Pennington*, the trial judge, after a bench trial, dismissed the complaint, noting that the Supreme Court's opinion requires "predatory intent to drive small coal operators out of business in order to hold the employer and the union for a violation of the Sherman Act." Lewis v. Pennington, 257 F. Supp. 815, 829 (E.D. Tenn. 1966), *aff'd* 400 F.2d 806, 814 (6th Cir. 1968), *cert. denied*, 393 U.S. 983 (1969).

In Ramsey v. UMW, 401 U.S. 302 (1971), which had involved proof similar to that presented in *Pennington*, the Court held (5 to 4) that the "clear proof" standard of §6 of Norris-LaGuardia applies only to the issue of the responsibility of persons or organizations for allegedly unlawful acts and not to the occurrence of such acts. On remand, the trial court, which had originally heard the case without a jury, concluded that there had been a failure of proof even under a preponderance test, despite the court's prior concession that the evidence had met that test but not a "clear evidence" test. See 344 F. Supp. 1029, 1033 (E.D. Tenn. 1972), *aff'd*, 481 F.2d 742 (6th Cir.), *cert. denied*, 414 U.S. 1067 (1973). In *Ramsey*, the district court (344 F. Supp. at 1033) suggested that the "proof of predatory intent" was unnecessary.

Other similarly situated coal companies were, however, successful in their actions against the UMW under the Sherman Act. See Tennessee Consol. Coal Co. v. UMW, 416 F.2d 1192 (6th Cir. 1969), *cert. denied*, 397 U.S. 964 (1970) (jury trial; damages (after reduction with plaintiff's consent and trebling) amounted to $1.4 million for one plaintiff plus $150,000 attorney fees and much less for another plaintiff); and South-East Coal Co. v. UMW and Consol. Coal Co., 434 F.2d 767 (6th Cir. 1970), *cert. denied*, 402 U.S. 983 (1971) (jury trial; treble damage award against company as well as UMW, amounting to $7.2 million plus counsel fees of $335,000).

3. In 1968, the parties rescinded the 1958 protective wage clause involved in *Pennington*, without apparently affecting the union's policy of uniformity. See Smitty Baker Coal Co. v. UMW, 620 F.2d 416 (4th Cir.), *cert. denied*, 449 U.S. 870 (1980).

4. (a) Do two or more unions lose their exemption when they agree to coordinate bargaining policy with respect to different bargaining units of the same employer or in the same industry?

(b) What of that exemption when two or more employers who are not part of a formal multiemployer unit agree to coordinate bargaining strategy or to lockout if one employer is struck?

5. A union and an employer (or an employers' association), accounting for 60 percent of the output of a given industry, enter into a collective bargaining agreement with the following "most favored nation" or "me-too" clause: "The union agrees that if it grants an employer competing with the signatory employer (or employers) lower wages or better terms or conditions than those prescribed herein, the union will immediately advise the signatory employer(s) and give them the benefit of such lower wages or more favorable terms and conditions." Would such an agreement be exempt from the Sherman Act under Justice White's approach? Under Justice Douglas'? Under the Sherman Act, should a "me-too" clause be treated differently from the "they-too" clause in *Pennington?* In Dolly Madison Indus., 182 N.L.R.B. 1037 (1970), the NLRB distinguished a "me-too" clause from a "they-too" clause and concluded that the former clause, in the absence of a "predatory purpose," would not violate the Sherman Act and was, accordingly, a mandatory subject of bargaining on which the employer could lawfully insist to the point of impasse. But cf. Associated Milk Dealers Inc. v. Milk Drivers, Local 753, 422 F.2d 546 (7th Cir. 1970) (union contended that the antitrust laws barred enforcement of a "me-too" clause).

6. In *Pennington*, do the provisions barring leases to, and sales to or purchases from, nonunion firms operate merely to preserve union standards and jobs for organized employees, or do those provisions provide monopoly benefits to the signatory employers, e.g., to those who sell more supplementary coal than they buy?

Local 189, Meat Cutters v. Jewel Tea Co.
381 U.S. 676 (1965)

WHITE, J., announced the judgment of the Court and delivered an opinion in which WARREN, C. J., and BRENNAN, J., join. . . . [This case] concerns the lawfulness of the following restriction on the operating hours of food store meat departments contained in a collective bargaining agreement

executed after joint multiemployer multiunion negotiations: "Market operating hours shall be 9:00 a.m. to 6:00 p.m. Monday through Saturday,
inclusive. No customer shall be served who comes into the market before or
after the hours set forth above."

This litigation arose out of the 1957 contract negotiations between the
representatives of 9,000 Chicago retailers of fresh meat and the seven union
petitioners, who are local affiliates of the Amalgamated Meat Cutters and
Butcher Workmen of North America, AFL-CIO, representing virtually all
butchers in the Chicago area. During the 1957 bargaining sessions the
employer group presented several requests for union consent to a relaxation
of the existing contract restriction on marketing hours for fresh meat, which
forbade the sale of meat before 9 a.m. and after 6 p.m. in both service and
self-service markets. The unions rejected all such suggestions, and their own
proposal retaining the marketing-hours restriction was ultimately accepted at
the final bargaining session by all but two of the employers, National Tea Co.
and Jewel Tea Co. (hereinafter "Jewel"). Associated Food Retailers of
Greater Chicago, a trade association having about 1,000 individual and
independent merchants as members and representing some 300 meat dealers
in the negotiations, was among those who accepted. Jewel, however, asked
the union negotiators to present to their membership, on behalf of it and
National Tea, a counter-offer that included provision for Friday night operations. At the same time Jewel voiced its belief, as it had midway through the
negotiations, that any marketing-hours restriction was illegal. On the recommendation of the union negotiators, the Jewel offer was rejected by the union
membership, and a strike was authorized. Under the duress of the strike vote,
Jewel decided to sign the contract previously approved by the rest of the
industry.

In July 1958 Jewel brought suit against the unions, . . . Associated,
and Charles H. Bromann, Secretary-Treasurer of Associated, seeking invalidation under §§1 and 2 of the Sherman Act of the contract provision that
prohibited night meat market operations. The gist of the complaint was that
the defendants and others had conspired together to prevent the retail sale of
fresh meat before 9 a.m. and after 6 p.m. As evidence of the conspiracy Jewel
relied in part on the events during the 1957 contract negotiations — the
acceptance by Associated of the market-hours restriction and the unions'
imposition of the restriction on Jewel through a strike threat. Jewel also
alleged that it was a part of the conspiracy that the unions would neither
permit their members to work at times other than the hours specified nor
allow any grocery firm to sell meat, with or without employment of their
members, outside those hours; that the members of Associated, which had
joined only one of the 1957 employer proposals for extended marketing
hours, had agreed among themselves to insist on the inclusion of the market-

ing-hours limitation in all collective bargaining agreements between the unions and any food store operator; that Associated, its members and officers had agreed with the other defendants that no firm was to be permitted to operate self-service meat markets between 6 p.m. and 9 p.m.; and that the unions, their officers and members had acted as the enforcing agent of the conspiracy.

The complaint [alleged]: In recent years the prepackaged, self-service system of marketing meat had come into vogùe, that 174 of Jewel's 196 stores were equipped to vend meat in this manner, and a butcher need not be on duty in a self-service market at the time meat purchases were actually made. The prohibition of night meat marketing unlawfully impeded Jewel in the use of its property and adversely affected the general public in that many persons find it inconvenient to shop during the day. An injunction, treble damages and attorneys' fees were demanded.

The trial judge held the allegations of the complaint sufficient to withstand a motion to dismiss made on the grounds, inter alia, that (a) the alleged restraint was within the exclusive regulatory scope of the National Labor Relations Act and was therefore outside the jurisdiction of the Court and (b) the controversy was within the labor exemption to the antitrust laws. That ruling was sustained on appeal. Jewel Tea Co. v. Local Unions Nos. 189, etc., Amalgamated Meat Cutters, AFL-CIO, 274 F.2d 217 (C.A. 7th Cir. 1960), *cert. denied*, 362 U.S. 936. After trial, however, the District Judge ruled the "record was devoid of any evidence to support a finding of conspiracy" between Associated and the unions to force the restrictive provision on Jewel. 215 F. Supp. 839, 845. Testing the unions' action standing alone, the trial court found that even in self-service markets removal of the limitation on marketing hours either would inaugurate longer hours and night work for the butchers or would result in butchers' work being done by others unskilled in the trade. Thus, the court concluded, the unions had imposed the marketing-hours limitation to serve their own interests respecting conditions of employment, and such action was clearly within the labor exemption of the Sherman Act established by Hunt v. Crumboch, 325 U.S. 821; United States v. Hutcheson, 312 U.S. 219; United States v. American Federation of Musicians, 318 U.S. 741. Alternatively, the District Court ruled that the arrangement did not amount to an unreasonable restraint of trade in violation of the Sherman Act.

The Court of Appeals reversed the dismissal of the complaint as to both the unions and Associated. Without disturbing the District Court's finding that, apart from the contractual provision itself, there was no evidence of conspiracy, the Court of Appeals concluded that a conspiracy in restraint of trade had been shown. The court noted that "[t]he rest of the Industry agreed with the Defendant Local Unions to continue the ban on night operations," while plaintiff resisted, and concluded that Associated and the unions "entered into a combination or agreement, which constituted a conspiracy, as charged in the complaint . . . [w]hether it be called an agreement, a contract or a conspiracy, is immaterial." 331 F.2d 547, 551.

Similarly, the Court of Appeals did not find it necessary to review the lower court's finding that night marketing would affect either the butchers' working hours or their jurisdiction, for the court held that an employer-union contract respecting working hours would be unlawful.

> One of the proprietary functions is the determination of what days a week and what hours of the day the business will be open to supply its customers. . . . As long as all rights of employees are recognized and duly observed by the employer, including the number of hours per day that any one shall be required to work, any agreement by a labor union, acting in concert with business competitors of the employer, designed to interfere with his operation of a retail business . . . is a violation of the Sherman Act. . . . [T]he furnishing of a place and advantageous hours of employment for the butchers to supply meat to customers are the prerogatives of the employer.

331 F.2d 547, 549.

We . . . now reverse the Court of Appeals.

[Part I (reflecting the Court's unanimous position) rejected the union's contention that the case was within the NLRB's "primary and exclusive jurisdiction." The Court suggested, first, that a characterization of the disputed clause as an item of mandatory bargaining would not have controlled the Sherman Act claim. Second, the Board's machinery would not be available when, for example, an agreement challenged under the Sherman Act had been reached without insistent bargaining.]

II

Here, as in United Mine Workers v. Pennington, the claim is made that the agreement under attack is exempt from the antitrust laws. We agree, but not on the broad grounds urged by the union.

It is well at the outset to emphasize that this case comes to us stripped of any claim of a union-employer conspiracy against Jewel. The trial court found no evidence to sustain Jewel's conspiracy claim and this finding was not disturbed by the Court of Appeals. We therefore have a situation where the unions, having obtained a marketing-hours agreement from one group of employers, have successfully sought the same terms from a single employer, Jewel, not as a result of a bargain between the unions and some employers directed against other employers, but pursuant to what the unions deemed to be in their own labor union interests.

Jewel does not allege that it has been injured by the elimination of competition among the other employers within the unit with respect to marketing hours; Jewel complains only of the unions' action in forcing it to accept the same restriction, the unions acting not at the behest of any employer group but in pursuit of their own policies. It might be argued that absent any union-employer conspiracy against Jewel and absent any agreement between Jewel and any other employer, the union-Jewel contract cannot be a violation of the Sherman Act. But the issue before us is not the broad substantive one of a violation of the antitrust laws — was there a conspiracy or combination which unreasonably restrained trade or an attempt to monopolize and was Jewel damaged in its business? — but whether the agreement is immune from attack by reason of the labor exemption from the antitrust laws. . . . The fact that the parties to the agreement are but a single employer and the unions representing its employees does not compel immunity for the agreement. We must consider the subject matter of the agreement in the light of the national labor policy. . . .

We pointed out in *Pennington* that exemption for union-employer agreements is very much a matter of accommodating the coverage of the Sherman Act to the policy of the labor laws. Employers and unions are required to bargain about wages, hours and working conditions, and this fact weighs heavily in favor of antitrust exemption for agreements on these subjects. But neither party need bargain about other matters and either party commits an unfair labor practice if it conditions its bargaining upon discussions of a nonmandatory subject. Labor Board v. Borg-Warner Corp., 356 U.S. 342. Jewel, for example, need not have bargained about or agreed to a schedule of prices at which its meat would be sold and the unions could not legally have insisted that it do so. But if the unions had made such a demand, Jewel had agreed and the United States or an injured party had challenged the agreement under the antitrust laws, we seriously doubt that either the unions or Jewel could claim immunity by reason of the labor exemption, whatever substantive questions of violation there might be.

Thus the issue in this case is whether the marketing-hours restriction, like wages, and unlike prices, is so intimately related to wages, hours and working conditions that the unions' successful attempt to obtain that provision through bona fide, arm's-length bargaining in pursuit of their own labor union policies, and not at the behest of or in combination with nonlabor groups, falls within the protection of the national labor policy and is therefore exempt from the Sherman Act.[5] We think that it is.

The Court of Appeals would classify the marketing-hours restriction

---

[5] The crucial determinant is not the form of the agreement — e.g., prices or wages — but its relative impact on the product market and the interests of union members. Thus in Teamsters Union v. Oliver [infra p. 732], we held that federal labor policy precluded

with the product-pricing provision and place both within the reach of the Sherman Act. In its view, labor has a legitimate interest in the number of hours it must work but no interest in whether the hours fall in the daytime, in the nighttime or on Sundays. "[T]he furnishing of a place and advantageous hours of employment for the butchers to supply meat to customers are the prerogatives of the employer." 331 F.2d 547, 549. That reasoning would invalidate with respect to both service and self-service markets the 1957 provision that "eight hours shall constitute the basic work day, Monday through Saturday; *work to begin at 9:00 a.m. and stop at 6:00 p.m.* . . ." as well as the marketing-hours restriction.

Contrary to the Court of Appeals, we think that the particular hours of the day and the particular days of the week during which employees shall be required to work are subjects well within the realm of "wages, hours, and other terms and conditions of employment" about which employers and unions must bargain. National Labor Relations Act, §8(d); see Timken Roller Bearing Co., 70 N.L.R.B. 500, 504, 515-516, 521 (1946), *rev'd on other grounds*, 161 F.2d 949 (C.A. 6th Cir. 1947) (employer's unilateral imposition of Sunday work was refusal to bargain); Massey Gin & Machine Works, Inc., 78 N.L.R.B. 189, 195, 199 (1948) (change in starting and quitting time); Camp & McInnes, Inc., 100 N.L.R.B. 524, 532 (1952) (reduction of lunch hour and advancement of quitting time). And, although the effect on competition is apparent and real, perhaps more so than in the case of the wage agreement, the concern of union members is immediate and direct. Weighing the respective interests involved, we think the national labor policy expressed in the National Labor Relations Act places beyond the reach of the Sherman Act union-employer agreements on when, as well as how long, employees must work. An agreement on these subjects between the union and the employers in a bargaining unit is not illegal under the Sherman Act, nor is the union's unilateral demand for the same contract of other employers in the industry.

Disposing of the case, as it did, on the broad grounds we have indicated,

---

application of state antitrust laws to an employer-union agreement that when leased trucks were driven by their owners, such owner-drivers should receive, in addition to the union wage, not less than a prescribed minimum rental. Though in form a scheme fixing prices for the supply of leased vehicles, the agreement was designed "to protect the negotiated wage scale against the possible undermining through diminution of the owner's wages for driving which might result from a rental which did not cover his operating costs." Id., at 293-294. As the agreement did not embody a "'remote and indirect approach to the subject of wages' . . . but a direct frontal attack upon a problem thought to threaten the maintenance of the basic wage structure established by the collective bargaining contract," id., at 294, the paramount federal policy of encouraging collective bargaining proscribed application of the state law. See also Meat Drivers v. United States, 371 U.S. 94, 98; Milk Wagon Drivers' Union, Local No. 753 v. Lake Valley Farm Products, Inc., 311 U.S. 91.

the Court of Appeals did not deal separately with the marketing-hours provision, as distinguished from hours of work, in connection with either service or self-service markets. The dispute here pertains principally to self-service markets. . . .

If it were true that self-service markets could actually operate without butchers, at least for a few hours after 6 p.m., that no encroachment on butchers' work would result and that the workload of butchers during normal working hours would not be substantially increased, Jewel's position would have considerable merit. For then the obvious restraint on the product market — the exclusion of self-service stores from the evening market for meat — would stand alone, unmitigated and unjustified by the vital interests of the union butchers which are relied upon in this case. In such event the limitation imposed by the unions might well be reduced to nothing but an effort by the unions to protect one group of employers from competition by another, which is conduct that is not exempt from the Sherman Act. Whether there would be a violation of §§1 and 2 would then depend on whether the elements of a conspiracy in restraint of trade or an attempt to monopolize had been proved.[6]

Thus the dispute between Jewel and the unions essentially concerns a narrow factual question: Are night operations without butchers, and without infringement of butchers' interests, feasible? The District Court resolved this

[6]One issue, for example, would be whether the restraint was unreasonable. Judicial pronouncements regarding the reasonableness of restraints on hours of business are relatively few. Some cases appear to have viewed such restraints as tantamount to limits on hours of work and thus reasonable, even though contained in agreements among competitors. Thus in Chicago Board of Trade v. United States, 246 U.S. 231, the Court upheld a rule of grain exchange that had the form of a restriction on prices of transactions outside regular trading hours but was characterized by the Court as a rule designed to shift transactions to the regular trading period, i.e., to limit hours of operation. The Court, per Mr. Justice Brandeis, stated: "Every board of trade and nearly every trade organization imposes some restraint upon the conduct of business by its members. Those relating to the hours in which business may be done are common; and they make a special appeal where, as here, *they tend to shorten the working day* or, at least, limit the period of most exacting activity." 246 U.S., at 241. (Emphasis added.) . . .

Other cases have upheld operating-hours restraints in factual circumstances that make it seem likely that the agreement affected hours of operation and hours of work in equal measure but without stressing that fact. See Dunkel Oil Corp. v. Anich, 1944-1945 Trade Cas., ¶57,306 (D.C.E.D. Ill. 1944); Baker v. Retail Clerks Assn., 313 Ill. App. 432, 40 N.E.2d 571 (1942); Stovall v. McCutchen, 107 Ky. 577, 54 S.W. 969 (1900).

Kold Kist, Inc. v. Amalgamated Meat Cutters, Local No. 421, 99 Cal. App. 2d 191, 221 P.2d 724 (1950), held unreasonable a union-employer agreement limiting night sales of frozen poultry, which had previously been obtained from the plaintiff distributor. The plaintiff alleged, however, that it had been severely affected, since many stores had stopped carrying its products entirely due to the lack of storage facilities in which to keep the poultry during hours in which sale was prohibited, and such effects may be atypical.

The decided cases thus do not appear to offer any easy answer to the question whether in a particular case an operating-hours restraint is unreasonable.

factual dispute in favor of the unions. It found that "in stores where meat is sold at night it is impractical to operate without either butchers or other employees. Someone must arrange, replenish and clean the counters and supply customer services." Operating without butchers would mean that "their work would be done by others unskilled in the trade," and "would involve an increase in workload in preparing for the night work and cleaning the next morning." 215 F. Supp., at 846. Those findings were not disturbed by the Court of Appeals, which, as previously noted, proceeded on a broader ground. Our function is limited to reviewing the record to satisfy ourselves that the trial judge's findings are not clearly erroneous. Fed. R. Civ. P. 52(a).

The trial court had before it evidence concerning the history of the unions' opposition to night work, the development of the provisions respecting night work and night operations, the course of collective bargaining negotiations in 1957, 1959, and 1961[7] with regard to those provisions, and the characteristics of meat marketing insofar as they bore on the feasibility of night operations without butchers. . . .

Concomitant with the unions' concern with the working hours of butchers was their interest in the hours during which customers might be served. The 1920 agreement provided that "no customers will be served who come into the market after 6 p.m. and 9 p.m. on Saturdays and on days preceding holidays. . . ." That provision was continued until 1947, when it was superseded by the formulation presently in effect and here claimed to be unlawful.

During the 1957 negotiations numerous proposals for relaxation of the operating-hours restriction were presented by the employer group. Each of these proposals, including that submitted separately by Jewel for consideration at the unions' ratification meetings, combined a provision for night operations with a provision for a more flexible workday that would permit night employment of butchers. Such juxtaposition of the two provisions could, of course, only serve to reinforce the unions' fears that night operations meant night work. Jewel did allege in its complaint, filed in July 1958, that night operations were possible without butchers, but even in the 1959 bargaining sessions Jewel failed to put forth any plan for night operations that did not also include night work. Finally, toward the end of the 1961 negotiations, Jewel did make such a suggestion, but, as the trial judge remarked, the "unions questioned the seriousness of that proposal under the circumstances." 215 F. Supp., at 843.

The unions' evidence with regard to the practicability of night opera-

---

[7]In 1959, and again in 1961, new collective bargaining agreements containing the challenged provision were executed. In each instance, Jewel reserved its position with respect to this litigation.

tions without butchers was accurately summarized by the trial judge as follows:

> [I]n most of plaintiff's stores outside Chicago, where night operations exist, meat cutters are on duty whenever a meat department is open after 6 p.m. . . . . Even in self-service departments, ostensibly operated without employees on duty after 6 p.m., there was evidence that requisite customer services in connection with meat sales were performed by grocery clerks. In the same vein, defendants adduced evidence that in the sale of delicatessen items, which could be made after 6 p.m. from self-service cases under the contract, "practically" always during the time the market was open the manager, or other employees, would be rearranging and restocking the cases. There was also evidence that even if it were practical to operate a self-service meat market after 6 p.m. without employees, the night operations would add to the workload in getting the meats prepared for night sales and in putting the counters in order the next day.

215 F. Supp., at 844.

Jewel challenges the unions' evidence on each of these points — arguing, for example, that its preference to have butchers on duty at night, where possible under the union contract, is not probative of the feasibility of not having butchers on duty and that the evidence that grocery clerks performed customer services within the butchers' jurisdiction was based on a single instance resulting from "entrapment" by union agents. But Jewel's argument — when considered against the historical background of union concern with working hours and operating hours and the virtually uniform recognition by employers of the intimate relationship between the two subjects, as manifested by bargaining proposals in 1957, 1959, and 1961 — falls far short of a showing that the trial judge's ultimate findings were clearly erroneous.

Reversed.

GOLDBERG, J., with whom HARLAN and STEWART, JJ., join, dissenting from the opinion but concurring in the reversal in *Pennington* and concurring in the judgment of the Court in *Jewel Tea*. . . .

I

Pennington presents a case of a union negotiating with the employers in the industry for wages, fringe benefits, and working conditions. Despite allegations of conspiracy, which connotes clandestine activities, it is no secret that the United Mine Workers, acting to further what it considers to be the best interests of its members, espouses a philosophy of achieving uniform high wages, fringe benefits, and good working conditions. As the quid pro quo for this, the Union is willing to accept the burdens and consequences of automation. Further, it acts upon the view that the existence of marginal operators who cannot afford these high wages, fringe benefits, and good working conditions does not serve the best interests of the working miner but, on the contrary, depresses wage standards and perpetuates undesirable conditions. This has been the articulated policy of the Union since 1933. . . . The Mine Workers has openly stated its preference, if need be, for a reduced working force in the industry, with those employed working at high wages, rather than for greater total employment at lesser wage rates. Ibid. . . .

Jewel Tea presents another and different aspect of collective bargaining philosophy. . . . While it is claimed by Jewel Tea, a large operator of automated self-service markets, that it can operate beyond the set hours without increasing the work of butchers or having others do butchers' work —a claim rejected by the trial court and the majority of this Court—it is conceded, on this record, that the small, independent service operators cannot do so. Therefore to the extent that the Union's uniform policy limiting hours of selling fresh meat has the effect of aiding one group of employers at the expense of another, here the union policy, unlike that in *Pennington*, aids the small employers at the expense of the large. . . .

[Here the opinion reviewed the history of labor and the antitrust laws through *Allen Bradley*.]

In my view, this history shows a consistent congressional purpose to limit severely judicial intervention in collective bargaining under cover of the wide umbrella of the antitrust laws, and, rather, to deal with what Congress deemed to be specific abuses on the part of labor unions by specific proscriptions in the labor statutes. I believe that the Court should respect this history of congressional purpose and should reaffirm the Court's holdings in *Apex* and *Hutcheson*. . . . [T]he Court should hold that, in order to effectuate congressional intent, collective bargaining activity concerning mandatory subjects of bargaining under the Labor Act is not subject to the antitrust laws. This rule flows directly from the *Hutcheson* holding that a union acting as a union, in the interests of its members, and not acting to fix prices or allocate markets in aid of an employer conspiracy to accomplish these objects, with only indirect union benefits, is not subject to challenge under the antitrust laws. To hold that mandatory collective bargaining is completely protected would effectuate the congressional policies of encouraging free collective bargaining subject only to specific restrictions contained in the labor laws, and of limiting judicial intervention in labor matters via the antitrust route— an intervention which necessarily under the Sherman Act places on judges and juries the determination of "what public policy in regard to the industrial struggle demands." Duplex Co. v. Deering, supra, at 485 (dissenting opinion of Brandeis, J.). See Winter, Collective Bargaining and Competition:

The Application of Antitrust Standards to Union Activities, 73 Yale L.J. 14 (1963). . . .

The Court in *Pennington* today ignores this history of the discredited judicial attempt to apply the antitrust laws to legitimate collective bargaining activity, and it flouts the clearly expressed congressional intent that, since "[t]he labor of a human being is not a commodity or article of commerce," the antitrust laws do not proscribe, and the national labor policy affirmatively promotes, the "elimination of price competition based on differences in labor standards," Apex Hosiery Co. v. Leader, [310 U.S. 469 (1940)], at 503. While purporting to recognize the indisputable fact that the elimination of employer competition based on substandard labor conditions is a proper labor union objective endorsed by our national labor policy and that, therefore, "a union may make wage agreements with a multiemployer bargaining unit and may in pursuance of its own union interests seek to obtain the same terms from other employers," *Pennington*, ante, at 665, the Court holds that "a union forfeits its exemption from the antitrust laws when it is clearly shown that it has agreed with one set of employers to impose a certain wage scale on other bargaining units." Ibid.

This rule seems to me clearly contrary to the congressional purpose manifested by the labor statutes, and it will severely restrict free collective bargaining. Since collective bargaining inevitably involves and requires discussion of the impact of the wage agreement reached with a particular employer or group of employers upon competing employers, the effect of the Court's decision will be to bar a basic element of collective bargaining from the conference room. If a union and employer are prevented from discussing and agreeing upon issues which are, in the great majority of cases, at the central core of bargaining, unilateral force will inevitably be substituted for rational discussion and agreement. Plainly and simply, the Court would subject both unions and employers to antitrust sanctions, criminal as well as civil, if in collective bargaining they concluded a wage agreement and, as part of the agreement, the union has undertaken to use its best efforts to have this wage accepted by other employers in the industry. Indeed, the decision today even goes beyond this. Under settled antitrust principles which are accepted by the Court as appropriate and applicable, which were the basis for jury instructions in *Pennington*, and which will govern it upon remand, there need not be direct evidence of an express agreement. Rather the existence of such agreement, express or implied, may be inferred from the conduct of the parties. . . . Or, as my Brother Douglas, concurring in *Pennington*, would have it, conduct of the parties could be prima facie evidence of an illegal agreement. . . . As the facts of *Pennington* illustrate, the jury is therefore at liberty to infer such an agreement from "clear" evidence that a union's philosophy that high wages and mechanization are desirable has been accepted by a group of employers and that the union has attempted to achieve like acceptance from other employers. . . .

Furthermore, in order to determine whether, under the Court's standard, a union is acting unilaterally or pursuant to an agreement with employers, judges and juries will inevitably be drawn to try to determine the purpose and motive of union and employer collective bargaining activities. The history I have set out, however, makes clear that Congress intended to foreclose judges and juries from roaming at large in the area of collective bargaining, under cover of the antitrust laws, by inquiry into the purpose and motive of the employer and union bargaining on mandatory subjects. . . .

In *Pennington*, central to the alleged conspiracy is the claim that hourly wage rates and fringe benefits were set at a level designed to eliminate the competition of the smaller nonunion companies by making the labor costs too high for them to pay. Indeed, the trial judge charged that there was no violation of the Sherman Act in the establishing of wages and welfare payments through the national contract, "provided" the mine workers and the major coal producers had not agreed to fix "high" rates "in order to drive the small coal operators out of business." Under such an instruction, if the jury found the wage scale too "high" it could impute to the union the unlawful purpose of putting the nonunion operators out of business. It is clear that the effect of the instruction therefore, was to invite 12 jurymen to become arbiters of the economic desirability of the wage scale in the Nation's coal industry. The Court would sustain the judgment based on this charge and thereby put its stamp of approval on this role for courts and juries. . . . It is clear, as experience shows, that judges and juries neither have the aptitude nor possess the criteria for making this kind of judgment. . . .

. . . Moreover, an attempted inquiry into the motives of employers or unions for entering into collective bargaining agreements on subjects of mandatory bargaining is totally artificial. It is precisely in this area of wages, hours, and other working conditions that Congress has recognized that unions have a substantial, direct, and basic interest of their own to advance. . . . To allow a court or a jury to infer an illegal agreement from collective bargaining conduct inevitably requires courts and juries to analyze the terms of collective bargaining agreements and the purposes and motives of unions and employers in agreeing upon them. Moreover, the evidence most often available to sustain antitrust liability under the Court's theory would show, as it did in *Pennington*, simply that the motives of the union and employer coincide — the union seeking high wages and protection from low-wage, nonunion competition, and the employer who pays high wages seeking protection from competitors who pay lower wages. When there is this coincidence of motive, does the illegality of the "conspiracy" turn on whether the Union pursued its goal of a uniform wage policy through strikes and not negotiations? As I read the Court's opinion this is precisely what the result turns on and thus unions are forced, in order to show that they have not illegally "agreed" with employers, to pursue their aims through strikes and not negotiations. Yet, it is clear that such a result was precisely what the [NLRA] was designed to prevent. The only alternative to resolution of collective bargaining issues by force available to the parties under the Court's holding is the encouragement of fraud and deceit. An employer will be forced to take a public stand against a union's wage demands, even if he is willing to accept them, lest a too ready acceptance be used by a jury to infer an agreement between the union and employer that the same wages will be sought from other employers. . . .

[L]abor contracts establishing more or less standardized wages, hours, and other terms and conditions of employment in a given industry or market area are often secured either through bargaining with multiemployer associations or through bargaining with market leaders that sets a "pattern" for agreements on labor standards with other employers. These are two similar systems used to achieve the identical result of fostering labor peace through the negotiation of uniform labor standards in an industry. Yet the Court makes antitrust liability for both unions and employers turn on which of these two systems is used. It states that uniform wage agreements may be made with multiemployer units but an agreement cannot be made to affect employers outside the formal bargaining unit. I do not believe that the Court understands the effect of its ruling in terms of the practical realities of the automobile, steel, rubber, shipbuilding, and numerous other industries which follow the policy of pattern collective bargaining. See Chamberlain, Collective Bargaining 259-263 (1951). . . . I also do not understand why antitrust liability should turn on the form of unit determination rather than the substance of the collective bargaining impact on the industry. . . .

The judicial expressions in *Jewel Tea* represent another example of the reluctance of judges to give full effect to congressional purpose in this area and the substitution by judges of their views for those of Congress as to how free collective bargaining should operate. In this case the Court of Appeals would have held the Union subject to the Sherman Act's criminal and civil penalties because in the court's social and economic judgment, the determination of the hours at which meat is to be sold is a "proprietary" matter within the exclusive control of management and thus the Union had no legitimate interest in bargaining over it. My Brother Douglas, joined by Mr. Justice

Black and Mr. Justice Clark, would affirm this judgment apparently because the agreement was reached through a multiemployer bargaining unit. But, as I have demonstrated above, there is nothing even remotely illegal about such bargaining. Even if an independent conspiracy test were applicable to the *Jewel Tea* situation, the simple fact is that multiemployer bargaining conducted at arm's length does not constitute union abetment of a business combination. It is often a self-defensive form of employer bargaining designed to match union strength. . . .

. . . My Brother White recognizes that the issue of the hours of sale of meat concerns a mandatory subject of bargaining based on the trial court's findings that it directly affected the hours of work of the butchers in the self-service markets, and therefore, since there was a finding that the Union was not abetting an independent employer conspiracy, he joins in reversing the Court of Appeals. In doing so, however, he apparently draws lines among mandatory subjects of bargaining, presumably based on a judicial determination of their importance to the worker, and states that not all agreements resulting from collective bargaining based on mandatory subjects of bargaining are immune from the antitrust laws, even absent evidence of union abetment of an independent conspiracy of employers. Following this reasoning, my Brother White indicates that he would sustain a judgment here, even absent evidence of union abetment of an independent conspiracy of employers, if the trial court had found "that self-service markets could actually operate without butchers, at least for a few hours after 6 p.m., that no encroachment on butchers' work would result and that the workload of butchers during normal working hours would not be substantially increased. . . ." . . . Such a view seems to me to be unsupportable. It represents a narrow, confining view of what labor unions have a legitimate interest in preserving and thus bargaining about. Even if the self-service markets could operate after 6 p.m., without their butchers and without increasing the work of their butchers at other times, the result of such operation can reasonably be expected to be either that the small, independent service markets would have to remain open in order to compete, thus requiring their union butchers to work at night, or that the small, independent service markets would not be able to operate at night and thus would be put at a competitive disadvantage. Since it is clear that the large, automated self-service markets employ fewer butchers per volume of sales than service markets do, the Union certainly has a legitimate interest in keeping service markets competitive so as to preserve jobs. Job security of this kind has been recognized to be a legitimate subject of union interest. See Telegraphers v. Chicago & N.W.R. Co., 362 U.S. 330; Teamsters Union v. Oliver, 358 U.S. 283, 362 U.S. 605. . . . The direct interest of the union in not working undesirable hours by curtailing all business at those hours is, of course, a far cry from the indirect "interest" in *Allen Bradley* in fixing prices and allocating markets solely to increase the profits of favored employers.

Indeed, if the Union in *Jewel Tea* were attempting to aid the small service butcher shops and thus save total employment against automation, perhaps at a necessarily reduced wage scale, the case would present the exact opposite union philosophy from that of the Mine Workers in *Pennington*. Putting the opinion of the Court in *Pennington* together with the opinions of my Brothers Douglas and White in *Jewel Tea*, it would seem that unions are damned if their collective bargaining philosophy involves acceptance of automation (*Pennington*) and are equally damned if their collective bargaining philosophy involves resistance to automation (*Jewel Tea*). Again, the wisdom of a union adopting either philosophy is not for judicial determination. . . .

My view that Congress intended that collective bargaining activity on mandatory subjects of bargaining under the Labor Act not be subject to the antitrust laws does not mean that I believe that Congress intended that activity involving all nonmandatory subjects of bargaining be similarly exempt. The direct and overriding interest of unions in such subjects as wages, hours, and other working conditions, which Congress has recognized in making them subjects of mandatory bargaining, is clearly lacking where the subject of the agreement is price-fixing and market allocation. Moreover, such activities are at the core of the type of anticompetitive commercial restraint at which the antitrust laws are directed. . . .

DOUGLAS, J., with whom BLACK and CLARK, JJ., concur, dissenting. If we followed Allen Bradley Co. v. Union, 325 U.S. 797, we would hold with the Court of Appeals that this multiemployer agreement with the union not to sell meat between 6 p.m. and 9 a.m. was not immunized from the antitrust laws and that respondent's evidence made out a prima facie case that it was in fact a violation of the Sherman Act.

If, in the present case, the employers alone agreed not to sell meat from 6 p.m. to 9 a.m., they would be guilty of an anticompetitive practice, barred by the antitrust laws. Absent an agreement or conspiracy, a proprietor can keep his establishment open for such hours as he chooses. . . .

At the conclusion of respondent's case, the District Court dismissed Associated and Bromann from the action, which was tried without a jury, on the ground that there was no evidence of a conspiracy between Associated and the unions. But in the circumstances of this case the collective bargaining agreement itself, of which the District Court said there was clear proof, was evidence of a conspiracy among the employers with the unions to impose the marketing-hours restriction on Jewel via a strike threat by the unions. This tended to take from the merchants who agreed among themselves their freedom to work their own hours and to subject all who, like Jewel, wanted to sell meat after 6 p.m. to the coercion of threatened strikes, all of which if done in concert only by businessmen would violate the antitrust laws. See Fashion Guild v. Federal Trade Commn., 312 U.S. 457, 465.

In saying that there was no conspiracy, the District Court failed to give any weight to the collective bargaining agreement itself as evidence of a conspiracy and to the context in which it was written. This Court makes the same mistake. . . . Here the contract of the unions with a large number of employers shows it was planned and designed not merely to control but entirely to prohibit "the marketing of goods and services" from 6 p.m. until 9 a.m. the next day. Some merchants relied chiefly on price competition to draw trade; others employed courtesy, quick service, and keeping their doors open long hours to meet the convenience of customers. The unions here induced a large group of merchants to use their collective strength to hurt others who wanted the competitive advantage of selling meat after 6 p.m. Unless *Allen Bradley* is either overruled or greatly impaired, the unions can no more aid a group of businessmen to force their competitors to follow uniform store marketing hours than to force them to sell at fixed prices. Both practices take away the freedom of traders to carry on their business in their own competitive fashion. . . .

NOTE

In formulating the issue in *Jewel Tea*, Justice White ignored the trial court's finding that the collective bargaining agreement provided that "the unions agree not to enter into a contract with any other employer designating lower wages, or longer hours, or more favorable conditions of employment." See Jewel Tea Co. v. Local Unions 189, et al., 215 F. Supp. 839, 842 (N.D. Ill. 1963). In the light of the Justice's emphasis on extraunit bargaining in *Pennington*, consider whether the presence of this clause should have affected his approach to the exemption issue.

American Federation of Musicians v. Carroll, 391 U.S. 99 (1968). In an action based on the Sherman Act, orchestra leaders complained primarily about the unions' regulation of so-called "club dates" or one-time musical engagements, which are to be contrasted with so-called "steady [longer term] engagements." The latter engagements were usually governed by collective bargaining agreements, with the purchaser of the music treated as the employer. By contrast, club dates were governed by regulations unilaterally adopted by the unions, which, inter alia:

(1) enforced a closed shop;

(2) required orchestra leaders to engage a minimum number of sidemen;

(3) prescribed minimum prices for local engagements consisting of (a) a minimum scale for sidemen, (b) a "leader's fee," which was twice the sidemen's scale in orchestras of at least four, and (c) an additional eight percent for social security, unemployment insurance, and other expenses; furthermore, if a leader did not appear but designated a subleader and four or more musicians performed, the leader was required to pay the subleader 1.5 times the sidemen's scale, from his leader's fee;

(4) prescribed higher minimum prices for travelling orchestras; and

(5) barred leaders from accepting engagements from, or making payment to, caterers and permitted leaders to deal only with booking agents licensed by the unions.

The plaintiffs contended, inter alia, that the AFM and its New York local, through those unilateral rules, violated the Sherman Act by (1) pressuring the leaders into union membership; (2) fixing prices; (3) failing to bargain with the leaders; and (4) monopolizing the music industry. Agreeing with the lower courts and upholding dismissal of this action, the Supreme Court found that the leaders, although "employers" and "independent contractors," were a "labor group" and exempt. Relying on Teamsters Local 24 v. Oliver (infra p. 732), footnote 5 of *Jewel Tea*, and Los Angeles Meat & Provisions Drivers v. United States (infra p. 662), Brennan, J. (for the Court) declared:

> [T]he price floors, including the minimums for leaders, are simply a means for coping with the job and wage competition of the leaders to protect the wage scales of musicians who (plaintiffs) concede are employees on club-dates, namely, sidemen and subleaders. [The foregoing reasons] embrace the provision fixing the minimum price for a club-date engagement when the orchestra leader does not perform and does not displace an employee-musician. . . . There was evidence that when the leader does not collect from the purchaser of the music an amount sufficient to make up the total of his out-of-pocket expenses, including the sum of his wage-scale wages and the scale wages of the sidemen, he will, in fact, not pay the sidemen the prescribed scale. In other words, the price of the product — here the price for an orchestra for a club-date — represents almost entirely the scale wages of the sidemen and the leader. Unlike most industries, except for the 8% charge, there are no other costs contributing to the price. Therefore, if leaders cut prices, inevitably wages must be cut.

The Court also upheld the restrictions on caterers and booking agents, reasoning that those restrictions were as intimately related to wages as the price floors because the booking agents had charged orchestra leaders exorbitant fees, and caterers had received kick-backs from leaders whom they had recommended.

White, J., joined by Black, J., dissented, urging that price floors could be lawfully prescribed for leaders only when they actually lead, in order to insure that they are not in effect working below scale by failing to charge enough to cover administrative costs, entrepreneurial profit, etc. He maintained, however, that only entrepreneurial concerns were generated by engagements where the leaders do not themselves lead or by those leaders who never lead. He stated: . . .

> The union has of course a full right to impose on this leader, who is in effect an employer, its minimum scale for work by sidemen and subleaders. The musicians union, however, goes further. It requires that, for an engagement of four or more musicians, the leader charge his customer not less than the sideman's scale times the number of musicians (including the subleader), plus double the sideman's scale to compensate the leader, of which one-fourth — plus the sideman's scale — goes to the subleader. The union is clearly requiring that the leader charge his customer more than the total of the leader's wage bill, even though the leader himself does no "labor group" work.

In these circumstances, he urged, the interest in price competition outweighs the union's interest in selling prices, and, under *Jewel Tea*, the union's price-fixing should not be exempt from the Sherman Act.

NOTES

1. Los Angeles Meat & Provisions Drivers v. United States, 371 U.S. 94 (1962), on which the Court, in *Carroll*, relied, involved the following situation: Grease processors in Los Angeles obtained waste grease (1) by direct purchases from restaurants and pickup by the processors' own employee drivers and (2) by purchases from peddlers who acted as intermediaries between the various sources of supply and the processors. After unionization of the peddlers, the union fixed the peddlers' purchase and selling prices, allocated accounts and territories, eliminated recalcitrant peddlers by (in effect) blacklisting them with processors, and enforced its total program by strikes and boycotts. At the trial stage, the union, having stipulated that those practices had occurred and were enjoinable as violations of the Sherman Act, had contested only an order terminating the union membership of the peddlers. In sustaining that order as compatible with the

Clayton and Norris LaGuardia Acts, the Supreme Court (at 98) emphasized the absence of any "showing of actual or potential wage or job competition, or of any other economic interrelationship between the grease peddlers and the other members of the union." The Court relied on a finding below that no such competition had existed—a finding based on a stipulation that no processor had ever substituted peddlers for employee drivers or had threatened to do so. That stipulation, as Justice Douglas urged in dissent, scarcely warranted that finding. In any event, the Court's emphasis implied that if the missing economic interrelationship had been found to exist (e.g., if the peddlers had been directly substitutable for the unionized employees), it would have been permissible for the union to cartelize the peddlers even though they had been properly characterized as "independent contractors" rather than employees.

(a) Was the result implied by the grease peddlers' case consistent with the policy reflected in §8(b)(4)(A) of the NLRA, as amended? With the policies of the Sherman Act? Could the peddlers, without the intervention of the union, have lawfully fixed prices? Assume the existence of an "economic interrelationship" between the peddlers and other union members. How would one determine whether the union's organization of the peddlers operated to protect the peddlers as workers, the employee drivers, or the peddlers as businessmen seeking monopoly profits? Or are these questions irrelevant once an "economic interrelationship" is found between conventional employees and independent contractors who superficially appear to have fixed prices? Would the NLRB's characterization of the individuals be controlling for antitrust purposes? Cf. Bernstein v. Universal Pictures, Inc., 517 F.2d 976 (2d Cir. 1975).

(b) A Teamsters local picketed the grease processors for recognition as the peddlers' representative in determining the terms on which the peddlers sold grease to the processors. Truck drivers observed the picket line. Although the picketing continued for more than 30 days, the General Counsel of the NLRB declined to issue a complaint on the processors' charge of a violation of §8(b)(7)(C). A processor sued under the Sherman Act for an injunction against the picketing. Several years earlier the plaintiff had transferred his own employee drivers to other work and had replaced them with peddlers. What additional information would you want in evaluating the plaintiff's claim? Cf. Columbia River Packers Assn. v. Hinton, 315 U.S. 143 (1942); Scott Paper Co. v. Gulf Post Pulpwood Assn., 85 L.R.R.M. 2978 (S.D. Ala. 1973), aff'd, 491 F.2d 119 (5th Cir. 1974).

2. Is Carroll at odds with Goldfarb v. Virginia State Bar, 421 U.S. 773 (1975) (bar association's minimum fee schedules violate Sherman Act where attorneys refused to quote lower fees for title search)?

3. Actors' Equity negotiated "scale" (minimum wages) with theatrical

producers, for actors and actresses ("performers"). Equity also unilaterally imposed "regulations" (later modified somewhat in negotiations) for arrangements between performers and their theatrical agents. These regulations banned commissions to agents for securing jobs paying only scale and required agents to pay Equity franchise and annual fees. Equity members using unfranchised agents were subject to union discipline. In an action under the Sherman Act challenging these regulations, the Supreme Court, in the main, upheld the dismissal of the complaint. H.A. Artists & Associates, Inc. v. Actors' Equity Assn., 451 U.S. 704 (1981). The Court noted that the industry had a "peculiar structure" because of its intermittent work; because the agents were the customary, if not essential, source of work; and their fees were a percentage of performers' wages. The Court stressed that Equity could not defend the integrity of its negotiated wage scale for performers without regulating the fees they paid to agents. Consequently, the agents were "a labor group" under the antitrust exemption. But (with three justices dissenting) the Court invalidated the fees imposed by Equity on would-be franchisees, concluding that even if the fees covered only the costs of the regulatory system, Equity's justification was inadequate.

Could Equity lawfully fix maximum prices payable by its members to firms supplying them with training or costumes? What information would you want before answering that question?

Connell Construction Co. v. Plumbers, Local 100
421 U.S. 616 (1975)

PowELL, J. . . .

I

Local 100 is the bargaining representative for workers in the plumbing and mechanical trades in Dallas. When this litigation began, it was party to a multiemployer bargaining agreement with the Mechanical Contractors Association of Dallas, a group of about 75 mechanical contractors. That contract contained a "most favored nation" clause, by which the union agreed that if it granted a more favorable contract to any other employer it would extend the same terms to all members of the Association.

Connell Construction Co. is a general building contractor in Dallas. It obtains jobs by competitive bidding and subcontracts all plumbing and mechanical work. Connell has followed a policy of awarding these subcontracts on the basis of competitive bids, and it has done business with both union and nonunion subcontractors. Connell's employees are represented by various building trade unions. Local 100 has never sought to represent them or to bargain with Connell on their behalf.

In November 1970, Local 100 asked Connell to agree that it would subcontract mechanical work only to firms that had a current contract with the union. . . .

When Connell refused to sign this agreement, Local 100 stationed a single picket at one of Connell's major construction sites. About 150 workers walked off the job, and construction halted. Connell filed suit in state court to enjoin the picketing as a violation of Texas antitrust laws. Local 100 removed the case to federal court. Connell then signed the subcontracting agreement under protest. It amended its complaint to claim that the agreement violated §§1 and 2 of the Sherman Act and was therefore invalid. Connell sought a declaration to this effect and an injunction against any further efforts to force it to sign such an agreement.

By the time the case went to trial, Local 100 had submitted identical agreements to a number of other general contractors in Dallas. Five others had signed, and the union was waging a selective picketing campaign against those who resisted.

The District Court held that the subcontracting agreement was exempt from federal antitrust laws because it was authorized by the construction industry proviso to §8(e). . . . The court also held that federal labor legislation preempted the State's antitrust laws. . . . [T]he Fifth Circuit affirmed, 483 F.2d 1154 (1973), with one judge dissenting. It held that Local 100's goal of organizing nonunion subcontractors was a legitimate union interest and that its efforts toward that goal were therefore exempt from federal antitrust laws. . . . We reverse on the question of federal antitrust immunity and affirm the ruling on state law preemption.

II

The basic sources of organized labor's exemption from federal antitrust laws are §§6 and 20 of the Clayton Act, . . . and the Norris-LaGuardia Act. . . . These statutes declare that labor unions are not combinations or conspiracies in restraint of trade, and exempt specific union activities, including secondary picketing and boycotts, from the operation of the antitrust laws. See United States v. Hutcheson, 312 U.S. 219 (1941). They do not exempt concerted action or agreements between unions and nonlabor parties. Mine Workers v. Pennington, 381 U.S. 657, 662 (1965). The Court has recognized, however, that a proper accommodation between the congressional policy favoring collective bargaining under the NLRA and the congressional policy favoring free competition in business markets requires that some union-employer agreements be accorded a limited nonstatutory exemption from antitrust sanctions. Meat Cutters v. Jewel Tea Co., 381 U.S. 676 (1965).

The nonstatutory exemption has its source in the strong labor policy favoring the association of employees to eliminate competition over wages and working conditions. Union success in organizing workers and standardizing wages ultimately will affect price competition among employers, but the goals of federal labor law never could be achieved if this effect on business competition were held a violation of the antitrust laws. The Court therefore has acknowledged that labor policy requires tolerance for the lessening of business competition based on differences in wages and working conditions. See Mine Workers v. Pennington, supra, at 666; Jewel Tea, supra, at 692-693 (opinion of White, J.). Labor policy clearly does not require, however, that a union have freedom to impose direct restraints on competition among those who employ its members. Thus, while the statutory exemption allows unions to accomplish some restraints by acting unilaterally, e.g., Federation of Musicians v. Carroll, 391 U.S. 99 (1968), the nonstatutory exemption offers no similar protection when a union and a nonlabor party agree to restrain competition in a business market. See Allen Bradley Co. v. Electrical Workers, 325 U.S. 797, 806-811 (1945); Cox, Labor and the Antitrust Laws — A Preliminary Analysis, 104 U. Pa. L. Rev. 252 (1955); Meltzer, Labor Unions, Collective Bargaining, and the Antitrust Laws, 32 U. Chi. L. Rev. 659 (1965).

In this case Local 100 used direct restraints on the business market to support its organizing campaign. The agreements with Connell and other general contractors indiscriminately excluded nonunion subcontractors from a portion of the market, even if their competitive advantages were not derived from substandard wages and working conditions but rather from more efficient operating methods. Curtailment of competition based on efficiency is neither a goal of federal labor policy nor a necessary effect of the elimination of competition among workers. Moreover, competition based on efficiency is a positive value that the antitrust laws strive to protect.

The multiemployer bargaining agreement between Local 100 and the Association, though not challenged in this suit, is relevant in determining the effect that the agreement between Local 100 and Connell would have on the business market. The "most favored nation" clause in the multiemployer agreement promised to eliminate competition between members of the Association and any other subcontractors that Local 100 might organize. By giving members of the Association a contractual right to insist on terms as favorable as those given any competitor, it guaranteed that the union would make no agreement that would give an unaffiliated contractor a competitive advantage over members of the Association. Subcontractors in the Association thus stood to benefit from any extension of Local 100's organization, but the method Local 100 chose also had the effect of sheltering them from outside competition in that portion of the market covered by subcontracting agreements between general contractors and Local 100. In that portion of the market, the restriction on subcontracting would eliminate competition on all subjects covered by the multiemployer agreement, even on subjects unrelated to wages, hours, and working conditions.

Success in exacting agreements from general contractors would also give Local 100 power to control access to the market for mechanical subcontracting work. The agreements with general contractors did not simply prohibit subcontracting to any nonunion firm; they prohibited subcontracting to any firm that did not have a contract with Local 100. The union thus had complete control over subcontract work offered by general contractors that had signed these agreements. Such control could result in significant adverse effects on the market and on consumers — effects unrelated to the union's legitimate goals of organizing workers and standardizing working conditions. For example, if the union thought the interests of its members would be served by having fewer subcontractors competing for the available work, it could refuse to sign collective bargaining agreements with marginal firms. Cf. Mine Workers v. Pennington, supra. Or, since Local 100 has a well-defined geographical jurisdiction, it could exclude "traveling" subcontractors by refusing to deal with them. Local 100 thus might be able to create a geographical enclave for local contractors, similar to the closed market in *Allen Bradley*, supra.

This record contains no evidence that the union's goal was anything other than organizing as many subcontractors as possible.[2] This goal was legal, even though a successful organizing campaign ultimately would reduce the competition that unionized employers face from nonunion firms. But the methods the union chose are not immune from antitrust sanctions simply because the goal is legal. Here Local 100, by agreement with several contractors, made nonunion subcontractors ineligible to compete for a portion of the available work. This kind of direct restraint on the business market has substantial anticompetitive effects, both actual and potential, that would not follow naturally from the elimination of competition over wages and

---

[2] There was no evidence that Local 100's organizing campaign was connected with any agreement with members of the multiemployer bargaining unit, and the only evidence of agreement among those subcontractors was the "most favored nation" clause in the collective bargaining agreement. In fact, Connell has not argued the case on a theory of conspiracy between the union and unionized subcontractors. It has simply relied on the multiemployer agreement as a factor enhancing the restraint of trade implicit in the subcontracting agreement it signed.

working conditions. It contravenes antitrust policies to a degree not justified by congressional labor policy, and therefore cannot claim a nonstatutory exemption from the antitrust laws.

There can be no argument in this case, whatever its force in other contexts, that a restraint of this magnitude might be entitled to an antitrust exemption if it were included in a lawful collective bargaining agreement. Cf. Mine Workers v. Pennington, 381 U.S., at 664-665; Jewel Tea, 381 U.S., at 689-690 (opinion of White, J.); id., at 709-713, 732-733 (opinion of Goldberg, J.). In this case, Local 100 had no interest in representing Connell's employees. The federal policy favoring collective bargaining therefore can offer no shelter for the union's coercive action against Connell or its campaign to exclude nonunion firms from the subcontracting market.

III

Local 100 nonetheless contends that the kind of agreement it obtained from Connell is explicitly allowed by the construction-industry proviso to §8(e) and that antitrust policy therefore must defer to the NLRA. The majority in the Court of Appeals declined to decide this issue, holding that it was subject to the "exclusive jurisdiction" of the NLRB. 483 F.2d, at 1174. This Court has held, however, that the federal courts may decide labor law questions that emerge as collateral issues in suits brought under independent federal remedies, including the antitrust laws. We conclude that §8(e) does not allow this type of agreement. . . .

Section 8(e) was part of a legislative program designed to plug technical loopholes in §8(b)(4)'s general prohibition of secondary activities. In §8(e) Congress broadly proscribed using contractual agreements to achieve the economic coercion prohibited by §8(b)(4). See National Woodwork Mfrs. Assn., supra, at 634. The provisos exempting the construction and garment industries were added by the Conference Committee in an apparent compromise between the House bill, which prohibited all "hot cargo" agreements, and the Senate bill, which prohibited them only in the trucking industry. Although the garment-industry proviso was supported by detailed explanations in both Houses, the construction-industry proviso was explained only by bare references to "the pattern of collective bargaining" in the industry. It seems, however, to have been adopted as a partial substitute for an attempt to overrule this Court's decision in NLRB v. Denver Building & Construction Trades Council, 341 U.S. 675 (1951). Discussion of "special problems" in the construction industry, applicable to both the §8(e) proviso and the attempt to overrule *Denver Building Trades*, focused on the problems of picketing a single nonunion subcontractor on a multiemployer building project, and the close relationship between contractors and subcontractors at the jobsite. Congress limited the construction-industry proviso to that single situation, allowing subcontracting agreements only in relation to work done on a jobsite. In contrast to the latitude it provided in the garment-industry proviso, Congress did not afford construction unions an exemption from §8(b)(4)(B) or otherwise indicate that they were free to use subcontracting agreements as a broad organizational weapon. In keeping with these limitations, the Court has interpreted the construction-industry proviso as "a measure designed to allow agreements pertaining to certain secondary activities on the construction site because of the close community of interests there, but to ban secondary-objective agreements concerning nonjobsite work, in which respect the construction industry is no different from any other." National Woodwork Mfrs. Assn., 386 U.S., at 638-639. . . . Other courts have suggested that it serves an even narrower function: "[T]he purpose of the §8(e) proviso was to alleviate the frictions that may arise when union men work continuously alongside nonunion men on the same construction site." Drivers Local 695 v. NLRB, 361 F.2d 547, 553 (1966). . . .

Local 100 does not suggest that its subcontracting agreement is related to any of these policies. . . . The union admits that it sought the agreement solely as a way of pressuring mechanical subcontractors in the Dallas area to recognize it as the representative of their employees.

If we agreed with Local 100 that the construction-industry proviso authorizes subcontracting agreements with "stranger" contractors, not limited to any particular jobsite, our ruling would give construction unions an almost unlimited organizational weapon.[10] The unions would be free to enlist any general contractor to bring economic pressure on nonunion subcontractors, as long as the agreement recited that it only covered work to be performed on some jobsite somewhere. The proviso's jobsite restriction then

---

[10] Local 100 contends, unsoundly we think, that the NLRB has decided this issue in its favor. It cites Los Angeles Building & Construction Trades Council (B & J Investment Co.), 214 N.L.R.B. No. 86, 87 L.R.R.M. 1424 (1974), and a memorandum from the General Counsel explaining his decision not to file unfair labor practice charges in a similar case, Plumbers Local 100 (Hagler Construction Co.), No. 16-CC-447 (May 1, 1974). In B & J Investment the Board approved, without comment, an administrative law judge's conclusion that the §8(e) proviso authorized a subcontracting agreement between the Council and a general contractor who used none of his own employees in the particular construction project. The agreement in question may have been a prehire contract under §8(f), and it is not clear that the contractor argued that it was invalid for lack of a collective bargaining relationship. The General Counsel's memorandum in Hagler Construction is plainly addressed to a different argument — that a subcontracting clause should be allowed only if there is a preexisting collective bargaining relationship with the general contractor or if the general contractor has employees who perform the kind of work covered by the agreement.

would serve only to prohibit agreements relating to subcontractors that deliver their work complete to the jobsite.

It is highly improbable that Congress intended such a result. One of the major aims of the 1959 Act was to limit "top-down" organizing campaigns, in which unions used economic weapons to force recognition from an employer regardless of the wishes of his employees. . . . The only special consideration given [construction unions] in organizational campaigns is §8(f), which allows "prehire" agreements in the construction industry, but only under careful safeguards preserving workers' rights to decline union representation. The legislative history accompanying §8(f) also suggests that Congress may not have intended that strikes or picketing could be used to extract prehire agreements from unwilling employers.[12]

These careful limits on the economic pressure unions may use in aid of their organizational campaigns would be undermined seriously if the proviso to §8(e) were construed to allow unions to seek subcontracting agreements, at large, from any general contractor vulnerable to picketing. Absent a clear indication that Congress intended to leave such a glaring loophole in its restrictions on "top-down" organizing, we are unwilling to read the construction industry proviso as broadly as Local 100 suggests. Instead, we think its authorization extends only to agreements in the context of collective bargaining relationships and, in light of congressional references to the *Denver Building Trades* problem, possibly to common-situs relationships on particular jobsites as well.

Finally, Local 100 contends that even if the subcontracting agreement is not sanctioned by the construction-industry proviso and therefore is illegal under §8(e), it cannot be the basis for antitrust liability because the remedies in the NLRA are exclusive. This argument is grounded in the legislative history of the 1947 Taft-Hartley amendments. Congress rejected attempts to regulate secondary activities by repealing the antitrust exemptions in the Clayton and Norris-LaGuardia Acts, and created special remedies under the labor law instead. It made secondary activities unfair labor practices under §8(b)(4), and drafted special provisions for preliminary injunctions at the suit of the NLRB and for recovery of actual damages in the district courts. Sections 10(1), 303. . . . But whatever significance this legislative choice has for antitrust suits based on those secondary activities prohibited by §8(b)(4), it has no relevance to the question whether Congress meant to preclude antitrust suits based on the "hot-cargo" agreements that it outlawed in 1959. There is no legislative history in the 1959 Congress suggesting that labor-law remedies for §8(e) violations were intended to be exclusive, or that

---

[12]. . . . The NLRB has taken this view. Operating Engineers Local 542, 142 N.L.R.B. 1132 (1963), *enforced*, 331 F.2d 99 (3rd Cir.), *cert. denied*, 379 U.S. 889 (1964).

Congress thought allowing antitrust remedies in cases like the present one would be inconsistent with the remedial scheme of the NLRA.[16]

We therefore hold that this agreement, which is outside the context of a collective bargaining relationship and not restricted to a particular jobsite, but which nonetheless obligates Connell to subcontract work only to firms that have a contract with Local 100, may be the basis of a federal antitrust suit because it has a potential for restraining competition in the business market in ways that would not follow naturally from elimination of competition over wages and working conditions. . . .

IV

. . . Congress and this Court have carefully tailored the antitrust statutes to avoid conflict with the labor policy favoring lawful employee organization, not only by delineating exemptions from antitrust coverage but also by adjusting the scope of the antitrust remedies themselves. State antitrust laws generally have not been subjected to this process of accommodation. . . . Permitting state antitrust law to operate in this field could frustrate the basic federal policies favoring employee organization and allowing elimination of competition among wage earners, and interfere with the detailed system Congress has created for regulating organizational techniques.

Because employee organization is central to federal labor policy and regulation of organizational procedures is comprehensive, federal law does not admit the use of state antitrust law to regulate union activity that is closely related to organizational goals. Of course, other agreements between unions and nonlabor parties may yet be subject to state antitrust laws. See Teamsters v. Oliver, supra, at 295-297. The governing factor is the risk of conflict with the NLRA or with federal labor policy.

V

Neither the District Court nor the Court of Appeals decided whether the agreement between Local 100 and Connell, if subject to the antitrust laws, would constitute an agreement that restrains trade within the meaning of the

---

[16][The Court found unpersuasive the dissent's argument that the legislative history supported the exclusivity of §303 as a remedy for violations of §8(e), observing:] Congress did not amend §303 expressly to provide a remedy for violations of §8(e). . . . The House in 1959 did reject proposals . . . to repeal labor's antitrust immunity. . . . The Hiestand-Alger proposal would have repealed antitrust immunity for any action in concert by two or more labor organizations. The Hoffman proposal apparently intended to repeal labor's antitrust immunity entirely. That the Congress rejected these extravagant proposals hardly furnishes proof that it intended to extend labor's antitrust immunity to include agreements with nonlabor parties, or that it thought antitrust liability under the existing statutes would be inconsistent with the NLRA. . . .

Sherman Act. The issue was not briefed and argued fully in this Court. Accordingly, we remand for consideration whether the agreement violated the Sherman Act.[19]

Reversed in part and remanded.

DOUGLAS, J., dissenting. . . . Throughout this litigation, Connell has maintained only that Local 100 coerced it into signing the subcontracting agreement. With the complaint so drawn, I have no difficulty in concluding that the union's conduct is regulated solely by the labor laws. The question of antitrust immunity would be far different, however, if it were alleged that Local 100 had conspired with mechanical subcontractors to force nonunion subcontractors from the market by entering into exclusionary agreements with general contractors like Connell. An arrangement of that character was condemned in Allen Bradley Co. v. Electrical Workers, 325 U.S. 797 (1945). . . . Were such a conspiracy alleged, the multiemployer bargaining agreement between Local 100 and the mechanical subcontractors would unquestionably be relevant. See Mine Workers v. Pennington, 381 U.S. 657, 673 (1965) (concurring opinion); Meat Cutters v. Jewel Tea Co., 381 U.S. 676, 737 (1965) (dissenting opinion). . . .

[Stewart, J., joined by Brennan and Marshall, JJ., dissented on the following grounds: The LMRA was the only source of remedies for the petitioner. In 1947, Congress had rejected a provision that would have subjected secondary boycotts to customary antitrust remedies. In 1959 Congress had rejected similar proposals, in enacting §8(e) and in extending §303 to provide a damage remedy for secondary pressures designed to force an employer to sign an "illegal 'hot cargo' clause." On the other hand, if the disputed subcontracting agreement were valid, picketing to secure it should also be valid under decisions by the NLRB and the reviewing courts. Finally, activity "authorized" under the NLRA should not, by itself, be a basis for antitrust liability. The dissent concluded]:

---

[19] In addition to seeking a declaratory judgment that the agreement with Local 100 violated the antitrust laws, Connell sought a permanent injunction against further picketing to coerce execution of the contract in litigation. Connell obtained a temporary restraining order against the picketing on January 21, 1971, and thereafter executed the contract — under protest — with Local 100 on March 28, 1971. So far as the record in this case reveals, there has been no further picketing at Connell's construction sites. Accordingly, there is no occasion for us to consider whether the Norris-LaGuardia Act forbids such an injunction where the specific agreement sought by the union is illegal, or to determine whether, within the meaning of the Norris-LaGuardia Act, there was a "labor dispute" between these parties. If the Norris-LaGuardia Act were applicable to this picketing, injunctive relief would not be available under the antitrust laws. See United States v. Hutcheson, 312 U.S. 219 (1941). If the agreement in question is held on remand to be invalid under federal antitrust laws, we cannot anticipate that Local 100 will resume picketing to obtain or enforce an illegal agreement.

[T]he legislative history of the 1947 and 1959 amendments and additions to national labor law clearly demonstrates that Congress did not intend to restore antitrust sanctions for secondary boycott activity such as that engaged in by Local 100 in this case, but rather intended to subject such activity only to regulation under the [NLRA] and §303 of the [LMRA].

NOTES

1. In Woelke & Romero Framing, Inc. v. NLRB, 456 U.S. 645 (1982), a unanimous Court, upholding the Board's position, held that the construction proviso to §8(e) validates union signatory clauses arising from a collective bargaining relationship even though they are not confined to jobsites where both union and nonunion workers are employed. Concluding that the issue had not been properly raised below, the Court declined to review the court of appeals' decision agreeing with the Board and upholding the legality of picketing to obtain a subcontracting clause valid under the construction industry proviso.

Does the existence of a collective bargaining relationship in Woelke necessarily affect the anticompetitive impact of union signatory clauses such as those involved in that case and in Connell, or their usefulness as a top-down organizing technique? The Court did not identify any such difference in these two cases. Does that failure imply that Connell may be ripe for overruling?

2. Under Justice Stewart's dissent in Connell would the LMRA provide the only remedies against secondary pressures even if they were of a kind proscribed under the Sherman Act before the LMRA was enacted? What, for instance, does the dissent imply with respect to the union's antitrust liability for the activities condemned in Allen Bradley?

See generally St. Antoine, Connell: Antitrust Law at the Expense of Labor Law, 62 Va. L. Rev. 603 (1976); Note, 17 B.C. Ind. & Com. L. Rev. 217 (1976).

3. Long John Silver's, Inc. (Silver's), a restaurant chain, engaged Muko, a nonunion builder, to build two restaurants in the Pittsburgh area. While Muko was building the first one, the local Building Trades Councils, picketed the site. When the building was completed, handbills were distributed, urging customers not to patronize because Silver's contractors undercut prevailing wages. Upon the completion of the first restaurant, Silver's told Muko that it would give him more construction work if his competitive prices and his good quality work continued. But Silver's, informed that the

handbills were reducing patronage, later advised the Councils of the chain's intention to use only union contractors in the future and of the importance of Silver's facilities not being subjected to informational picketing. Silver's later employed only union general contractors, whom, however, it left free to use nonunion subs. Muko, having advised Silver's, in reply to its inquiry, of his unwillingness to bid on construction as a union firm, did not get any more construction work from Silver's.

Muko, in an action against Silver's and the Councils for damages under the Sherman Act, alleged that the defendants had entered into an agreement that only union contractors were to get contracts for the construction of Silver's restaurants in the Pittsburgh area, and thereby had engaged in unreasonable restraint of trade. After trial, the jury's special verdicts were that: (1) Silver's and the Councils had entered into an agreement or combination to withhold construction contracts from nonunion firms, including Muko; (2) that agreement did impose a "restraint of free competition beyond that which would follow from the elimination of competition based on wages, rates and working conditions;" and (3) that agreement did not constitute an "unreasonable restraint of trade." The trial judge thereupon entered judgment for the defendant. Muko appeals, urging, inter alia, error in the judge's instructing the jury to apply "the rule of reason rather than a per se standard" to the disputed agreement.

What should be the disposition of Muko's contention? Any difference in result if Muko had sued, under the Sherman Act, only for an injunction or if the signatory firm had been the largest builder in the state accounting for approximately 20 percent of the total home building? What considerations might a union urge under a "rule of reason" test for the legality of nonexempt activity that would not have been urged in support of the union's exemption claim? Cf. Larry V. Muko, Inc. v. Southwestern Pa. Bldg. & Constr. Trades Council, 670 F.2d 421 (3d Cir.), *cert. denied*, 103 S. Ct. 229 (1982); Adams Constr. Co. v. Georgia Power Co., 116 L.R.R.M. 2553 (11th Cir. 1984); Handler & Zifchak, Collective Bargaining and the Antitrust Laws: The Emasculation of the Labor Exemption, 81 Colum. L. Rev. 459, 511 (1981), with which cf. Leslie, Principles of Labor Antitrust, 66 Va. L. Rev. 1183, 1222-1224 (1980). Antitrust commentators have complained of the uncertainties generated by "the rule of reason" even without the additional complication of union involvement. See, e.g., R. Posner & F. Easterbrook, Antitrust Cases, Economic Notes and Other Materials 258-262 (2d ed. 1981).

4. Sometimes unions or employees, reversing the usual roles, have sued employers under the Sherman Act. See, e.g., Anderson v. Shipowners Assn. of the Pacific Coast, 272 U.S. 359 (1926) (claim under Sherman Act

alleged that association members agreed (not in the context of collective bargaining) to hire only seamen referred by Association hiring offices, at wages fixed by the Association). Professional athletes have frequently brought such actions, challenging employer restraints on player mobility, and courts sometimes have given new twists to the labor exemption invoked by employers. See, e.g., Mackey v. National Football League, 543 F.2d 606, 616 (8th Cir. 1976) ("Rozelle rule" not exempt because "no bona fide arms-length bargaining over rule" had preceded execution of collective agreements). Cf. McCourt v. California Sports, Inc., 460 F. Supp. 904 (E.D. Mich. 1978), rev'd, 600 F.2d 1193 (6th Cir. 1979).

(a) Would such judicial inquiry into antecedent bargaining be consistent with the NLRA policy against detailed regulation of the bargaining process or the NLRB's primary jurisdiction over issues arising under §8(a)(5)? See generally Weistart, Judicial Review of Sports Agreements: Lessons from the Sports Industry, 44 Law & Contemp. Probs. 109 (1981).

(b) Assume that a construction union, suing for treble damages under §4 of the Clayton Act, alleges these violations of the antitrust laws: An association of construction firms, despite their long-established collective bargaining relationships with construction unions, agreed among themselves and with other construction firms to boycott union-signatory subcontractors, to maintain nonunion divisions, to breach their collective bargaining agreements with the unions, and to encourage and coerce land owners to engage nonunion contractors. The "purpose and effect of these activities" was to "weaken . . . and restrain the trade of certain [unionized] contractors." Consequently, the union suffered (unspecified) injuries in its business activities. The defendants move to dismiss. What result? Cf. Associated General Contractors of California, Inc. v. California State Council of Carpenters, 103 S. Ct. 897 (1983) (declaring, through Stevens, J., that similar allegations might violate the antitrust laws, but holding that the union lacked standing to maintain a treble damage action under §4 of the Clayton Act, and reversing the Ninth Circuit's holding that the complaint was sufficient; the Court did not consider the defendants' claim of a "labor exemption").

For a discussion of the possible use by labor of the antitrust laws "as a sword," see Altman, Antitrust as a Tool for Labor, 131 U. Pa. L. Rev. 127 (1982); but cf. Jerry & Knebel, Antitrust and Employer Restraints in Labor Markets, 6 Ind. Rel. L.J. 173 (1984).

5. Recently, antitrust questions have arisen from the placing of union representatives on the boards of directors of companies with which an international union or its local bargains. A well-known example is the membership on Chrysler's board of Douglas A. Fraser, then President of the UAW. See Note, Labor Unions in the Boardroom: An Antitrust Dilemma, 92 Yale L.J.

106 (1983); Note, Employee Representative on the Corporate Board of Directors: Implications Under Labor, Antitrust, and Corporate Law, 27 Wayne L. Rev. 367, 382-387 (1980).

G.   WORK-ASSIGNMENT DISPUTES

"Jurisdictional disputes" is used loosely to describe two types of interunion disputes. The first involves disputes over which of several unions should represent a group of employees performing a defined task. For example, should patternmakers be represented by a craft or by an industrial union? Such disputes concern representation, rather than job rights, and can be resolved under §9 of the Act. The second type of dispute concerns which of two or more competing groups of workers, organized or not, should be assigned a given job. For example, should plumbers or carpenters install wooden pipes? Regardless of which union prevails in such a dispute, each group of employees would generally continue to have the same representation. The winning union would get more work for its constituents but not a new group of constituents — at least in the short run. The foregoing distinction is, however, sometimes blurred because representational and job interests overlap. See, e.g., Carey v. Westinghouse Elec. Corp., infra p. 1081.

Work-assignment disputes have for many years created thorny problems. At common law, courts disagreed over the legality of strikes and picketing to secure the assignment of work. See, e.g., Pickett v. Walsh and related materials, Chapter 1(B), supra, and 1 L. Teller, Labor Disputes and Collective Bargaining §131 (1940). Later, the *Hutcheson* case, supra p. 627, precluded the use of the Sherman Act against such stoppages. After World War II ended, such disputes proliferated, and Congress in 1947, by enacting §§8(b)(4)(D), 10(k), 10(1), and 303, sought to promote orderly resolution of the underlying disputes and to avert resultant work stoppages.

The materials below will explore the effect and the interplay of those sections (as amended in 1959).

See generally Leslie, The Role of the NLRB and the Courts in Resolving Union Jurisdictional Disputes, 75 Colum. L. Rev. 1470 (1975); Player, Work Assignment Disputes Under Section 10(k): Putting the Substantive Cart Before the Procedural Horse, 52 Tex. L. Rev. 417 (1974); Farmer & Powers, The Role of the National Labor Relations Board in Resolving Jurisdictional Disputes, 46 Va. L. Rev. 660 (1960); Mann & Husband, Private and Governmental Plans for the Adjustment of Interunion Disputes, 13 Stan. L. Rev. 5 (1960).

NLRB v. Plasterers' Local Union No. 79
404 U.S. 116 (1971)

WHITE, J. When a charge is filed under §8(b)(4)(D) . . . , the provision banning so-called jurisdictional disputes, the Board must under §10(k) "hear and determine the dispute out of which [the] unfair labor practice shall have arisen, unless . . . the parties to such dispute" adjust or agree upon a method for the voluntary adjustment of the dispute. The issue here is whether an employer, picketed to force reassignment of work, is a "party" to the "dispute" for purposes of §10(k). When the two unions involved, but not the employer, have agreed upon a method of settlement, must the Board dismiss the §10(k) proceedings or must it proceed to determine the dispute with the employer being afforded a chance to participate?

I

Texas State Tile & Terrazzo Co. (Texas State) and Martini Tile & Terrazzo Co. (Martini) are contractors in Houston, Texas, engaged in the business of installing tile and terrazzo. Both have collective-bargaining agreements with the [Tile Setters Local Union No. 20] and have characteristically used members of the Tile Setters union for laying tile and also for work described in the collective-bargaining contract as applying "a coat or coats of mortar, prepared to proper tolerance to receive tile on floors, walls and ceiling regardless of whether the mortar coat is wet or dry at the time the tile is applied to it."

This case arose when [Plasterers' Local Union No. 79] picketed the job sites of Texas State and Martini claiming that the work of applying the mortar to receive tile was the work of the Plasterers' union and not of the Tile Setters.[4] Neither Texas State nor Martini had a collective-bargaining contract with the Plasterers or regularly employed workers represented by that union.

Before the Texas State picketing began, the Plasterers submitted their claim to the disputed work to the National Joint Board for Settlement of Jurisdictional Disputes (Joint Board), a body established by the Building Trades Department, AFL-CIO, and by certain employer groups.[5] Both the

---

[4]This dispute grew out of a new method of applying tile that was developed in the mid-1950's.

[5]The National Joint Board for the Settlement of Jurisdictional Disputes is an arbitration panel established by a 1948 agreement between the Building and Construction Trades Department, AFL-CIO, and the Associated General Contractors of America and several specialty contractors' associations. The Joint Board consists of an equal number of representatives of employers and unions and a neutral chairman. An employer may become a party to a Joint Board proceeding by signing a stipulation agreeing to be bound by the results of the proceeding. Art. III, §7, AFL-CIO, Bldg. & Constr. Trades Dept., Plan for Settling Jurisdic-

Plasterers' and the Tile Setters' locals were bound by Joint Board decisions because their international unions were members of the AFL-CIO's Building Trades Department. Neither Texas State nor Martini had agreed to be bound by Joint Board procedures and decisions, however. The Joint Board found the work in dispute to be covered by an agreement of August 1917, between the two international unions, and awarded the work to the Plasterers.[6] When Texas State and the Tile Setters refused to acquiesce in the Joint Board decision and change the work assignment, the Plasterers began the picketing of Texas State which formed the basis for the §8(b)(4)(D) charges. The Plasterers also picketed a jobsite where Martini employees, members of the Tile Setters, were installing tile, although this dispute had not been submitted to the Joint Board.

Martini and Southwestern Construction Co., the general contractor that had hired Texas State, filed §8(b)(4)(D) . . . charges against the Plasterers, and the NLRB's Regional Director noticed a consolidated §10(k) hearing to determine the dispute. Southwestern, Texas State, Martini, and the two unions participated in the hearing. A panel of the Board noted that the Tile Setters admitted being bound by Joint Board procedures, but deemed the Joint Board decision to lack controlling weight, and "after taking into account and balancing all relevant factors" awarded the work to the Tile Setters.[9] When the Plasterers refused to indicate that they would abide by the

---

tional Disputes Nationally and Locally 10 (1970). Member unions of the AFL-CIO's Building Trades Department do not have to agree formally to abide by Joint Board decisions, because they are bound by virtue of provisions contained in their constitutions. AFL-CIO, Bldg. & Constr. Trades Dept., Procedural Rules and Regulations of the National Joint Board 2 (1970). See generally K. Strand, Jurisdictional Disputes in Construction: The Causes, the Joint Board, and the NLRB 89-104 (1961). In the cases here, both the Tile Setters and the Plasterers were members of the Building Trades Department.

[6] In the Texas State case, the Joint Board on November 9, 1966, awarded all of the disputed work to the Plasterers except "any coat to be applied wet the same day under tile." The Tile Setters refused to give up the work of laying the plaster undercoat to which the dry mortar was applied, claiming that the Joint Board decision gave this work to them. The Plasterers established a picket line on January 24, 1967; on March 15, 1967, the Joint Board issued a clarification of its decision, stating that the final smooth plaster coat was to be done by the Plasterers unless it was laid the same day as the tile and dry-set mortar were applied, in which case it was to be done by the Tile Setters.

[9] The NLRB considered the collective-bargaining agreements among the parties, industry and area practice, relative skills and efficiency of operation, past practices of the employers, agreements between the Plasterers and the Tile Setters, the Joint Board award (the NLRB refused to give this controlling weight because of its "ambiguous nature") and concluded:

"Tile setters are at least as skilled in the performance of the work as plasterers, and both Texas Tile and Martini, which assigned them to the work, have been satisfied with both the quality of their work and the cost of employing them. Moreover, the instant assignments of the disputed work to tile setters are consistent with the explicit provisions of the collective-bargaining agreement between the Tile Setters and Texas Tile and Martini, are consistent with

Board's award, a §8(b)(4)(D) complaint was issued against them, and they were found to have committed an unfair labor practice by picketing to force Texas State and Martini to assign the disputed work to them.[10] In making both the §10(k) and §8(b)(4)(D) decisions, the Board rejected the Plasterers' contention that even though the employer had not agreed to be bound by the Joint Board decision, the provisions of §10(k) precluded a subsequent Board decision because the competing unions had agreed upon a voluntary method of adjustment.

On petition to review by the Plasterers and cross petition to enforce by the Board, a divided panel of the Court of Appeals set aside the order of the Board.[11] It held that: "It is not the employer but the rival unions (or other employee groups) who are the parties to the jurisdictional dispute contesting which employees are entitled to seek the work in question."[12] It concluded that the Board may not make a §10(k) determination of a jurisdictional dispute where the opposing unions have agreed to settle their differences through binding arbitration. Both the Board and the employers petitioned for certiorari, and we granted the petitions.

II

Section 8(b)(4)(D) makes it an unfair labor practice for a labor organization to strike or threaten or coerce an employer or other person in order to force or require an employer to assign particular work to one group of employees rather than to another, unless the employer is refusing to honor a representation order of the Board. On its face, the section would appear to cover any

---

the past practice of the Employers, and are not inconsistent with area or industry practice. . . . " The Board's decision in the §10(k) proceeding is reported at 167 N.L.R.B. 185 (1967) and its decision and order in the unfair labor practice proceeding are reported at 172 N.L.R.B. Nos. 70, 72 (1968).

[10] The §10(k) determination is not binding as such even on the striking union. If that union continues to picket despite an adverse §10(k) decision, the Board must prove the union guilty of a §8(b)(4)(D) violation before a cease-and-desist order can issue. The findings and conclusions in a §10(k) proceeding are not *res judicata* on the unfair labor practice issue in the later §8(b)(4)(D) determination. International Typographical Union, 125 N.L.R.B. 759, 761 (1959). Both parties may put in new evidence at the §8(b)(4)(D) stage, although often, as in the present cases, the parties agree to stipulate the record of the §10(k) hearing as a basis for the Board's determination of the unfair labor practice. Finally, to exercise its powers under §10(k), the Board need only find that there is reasonable cause to believe that a §8(b)(4)(D) violation has occurred, while in the §8(b)(4)(D) proceeding itself the Board must find by a preponderance of the evidence that the picketing union has violated §8(b)(4)(D). International Typographical Union, supra, at 761 n. 5 (1959).

[11] 142 U.S. App. D.C. 146, 440 F.2d 174 (1970).

[12] Id., at 152, 440 F.2d, at 180. Although the dispute at the Martini worksite had not been submitted to the Joint Board, the Court of Appeals nevertheless held that, because the two unions had agreed to be bound by the procedures and decisions of the Joint Board, the NLRB was precluded from hearing and determining the Martini dispute under §10(k).

union challenge to an employer work assignment where the prohibited means are employed. NLRB v. Radio & Television Broadcast Engineers Union, Local 1212, 364 U.S. 573, 576 (1961) (hereinafter CBS). As the charging or intervening party, the employer would normally be a party to any proceedings under that section. Section 8(b)(4)(D), however, must be read in light of §10(k) with which it is interlocked. CBS, supra, at 576. When a §8(b)(4)(D) charge is filed and there is reasonable cause to believe that an unfair labor practice has been committed, issuance of the complaint is withheld until the provisions of §10(k) have been satisfied. That section directs the Board to "hear and determine" the dispute out of which the alleged unfair labor practice arose; the Board is required to decide which union or group of employees is entitled to the disputed work in accordance with acceptable, Board-developed standards, unless the parties to the underlying dispute settle the case or agree upon a method for settlement. Whether the §8(b)(4)(D) charge will be sustained or dismissed is thus dependent on the outcome of the §10(k) proceeding. The Board allows an employer to fully participate in a §10(k) proceeding as a party. If the employer prefers the employees to whom he has assigned the work, his right to later relief against the other union's picketing is conditioned upon his ability to convince the Board in the §10(k) proceeding that his original assignment is valid under the criteria employed by the Board.

The alleged unfair labor practice in this cause was the picketing of the jobsites by the Plasterers, and the dispute giving rise to this picketing was the disagreement over whether Plasterers or Tile Setters were to lay the final plaster coat. This dispute was a three-cornered one. The Plasterers made demands on both Texas State and the Tile Setters and on both Martini and the Tile Setters. In both cases, the employers' refusal to accede to the Plasterers' demands inevitably and inextricably involved them with the Tile Setters against the Plasterers. It was this triangular dispute that the §10(k) proceeding was intended to resolve.

It may be that in some cases employers have no stake in how a jurisdictional dispute is settled and are interested only in prompt settlement. Other employers, as shown by this cause, are not neutral and have substantial economic interests in the outcome of the §10(k) proceeding. A change in work assignment may result in different terms or conditions of employment, a new union to bargain with, higher wages or costs, and lower efficiency or quality of work. In the construction industry, in particular, where employers frequently calculate bids on very narrow margins, small cost differences are likely to be extremely important.[15] In the present cause, both employers had

---

[15] See Comment, The Employer as a Necessary Party to Voluntary Settlement of Work Assignment Disputes Under Section 10(k) of the NLRA, 38 U. Chi. L. Rev. 389, 400 (1971).

collective-bargaining contracts with the Tile Setters specifically covering the work at issue; neither had contracts with the Plasterers nor employed Plasterers regularly. Both employers determined it to be in their best interests to participate vigorously in the Board's §10(k) proceeding. The employers contended it was more efficient and less costly to use the same craft for applying the last coat of plaster, putting on the bonding coat, and laying the tile and that it was more consistent with industry practice to use the Tile Setters as they did. Both companies claimed that their costs would be substantially increased if the award went to the Plasterers, and that without collective-bargaining contracts with the Plasterers, they would lose 30%-40% of their work to plastering contractors. . . .

The phrase "parties to the dispute" giving rise to the picketing must be given its commonsense meaning corresponding to the actual interests involved here. . . . Section 10(k) does not expressly or impliedly deny party status to an employer, and since the section's adoption in 1947, the Board has regularly accorded party status to the employer and has refused to dismiss the proceeding when the unions, but not the employer, have agreed to settle.

The Court of Appeals rejected this construction of §10(k). Its reasoning, which we find unpersuasive, was that because the employer is not bound by the §10(k) decision, he sould have no right to insist upon participation. But the §10(k) decision standing alone, binds no one. No cease-and-desist order against either union or employer results from such a proceeding; the impact of the §10(k) decision is felt in the §8(b)(4)(D) hearing because for all practical purposes the Board's award determines who will prevail in the unfair labor practice proceeding. If the picketing union persists in its conduct despite a §10(k) decision against it, a §8(b)(4)(D) complaint issues and the union will likely be found guilty of an unfair labor practice and be ordered to cease and desist. On the other hand, if that union wins the §10(k) decision and the employer does not comply, the employer's §8(b)(4)(D) case evaporates and the charges he filed against the picketing union will be dismissed.[19] Neither the employer nor the employees to whom he has assigned the work are legally bound to observe the §10(k) decision, but both will lose their §8(b)(4)(D) protection against the picketing which may, as it did here, shut

[19] This dismissal will not be pursuant to the language of §10(k) directing dismissal upon "compliance by the parties . . . with the [Board's] decision" but, rather, under §8(b)(4)(D) because the "employer is failing to conform to an order or certification of the Board determining the bargaining representative for employees performing such work." Apparently, the Board construes this language to include disregarding a §10(k) decision. . . . The Board's regulations now provide that "if the Board determination is that employees represented by a charged union are entitled to perform the work in dispute, the regional director shall dismiss the charge as to that union irrespective of whether the employer has complied with that determination." 36 Fed. Reg. 9133 (1971).

down the job. The employer will be under intense pressure, practically, to conform to the Board's decision. This is the design of the Act; Congress provided no other way to implement the Board's §10(k) decision. . . .

[The Court here examined the legislative history and did not find that it required a different conclusion.]

. . . It is clear that Congress intended to protect employers and the public from the detrimental economic impact of "indefensible"[25] jurisdictional strikes. It would therefore be myopic to transform a procedure that was meant to protect employer interests into a device that could injure them. . . . We conclude, therefore, that these sections were enacted to protect employers who are partisan in a jurisdictional dispute as well as those who are neutral.

Nothing in *CBS*, supra, mandates a different conclusion. Until that case, the Board's practice had been to decide against the striking or picketing union unless it was entitled to the work pursuant to a Board certification or a collective-bargaining contract. The Court found the Board to have taken too narrow a view of its task and held that the Board, employing broader, more inclusive criteria with respect to entitlement, must make an affirmative award to one union or the other. In the course of its opinion, the Court referred to §10(k)'s phrase "the dispute out of which such unfair labor practice shall have arisen" as having "no other meaning except a jurisdictional dispute under §8(b)(4)(D) which is a dispute between two or more groups of employees over which is entitled to do certain work for an employer." 364 U.S., at 579. Again, we have no quarrel with the view that §10(k) is designed to decide which union is entitled to the work. But the issue before us is whether the employer is also a party to that dispute and to the proceeding that decides that question. The Court in *CBS* did not have before it a case in which the employer was particularly interested in which union did the work, since it had collective-bargaining contracts with both unions and since both unions were able to do the disputed work with equal skill, expense, and efficiency. The Court recognized that there, *"as in most instances"* the quarrel was of "so little interest to the employer that he seems perfectly willing to assign work to either [union] if the other will just let him alone." Ibid. (Emphasis added.) We have no doubt, therefore, that the Court had no intention of deciding the case now before us.

If employers must be considered parties to the dispute that the Board must decide under §10(k), absent private agreement, they must also be deemed parties to the adjustment or agreement to settle that will abort the §10(k) proceedings. It is insisted that so holding will encourage employers to

---

[25] President Truman, 1947 State of the Union Message, 93 Cong. Rec. 136.

avoid private arbitration, whereas holding union agreement alone sufficient to foreclose Board action will pressure employers to become part of private settlement mechanisms productive of sound result and much swifter decision.

The difficulties with this argument are several. First of all, if union agreements to arbitrate are sufficient to terminate §10(k) proceedings, there is no assurance that these private procedures will always be open to employer participation, that an employer will be afforded a meaningful chance to participate, or that all relevant factors will be properly considered.[26]

Second, the argument for regarding the employer as a dispensable neutral is reminiscent of the position taken by the Board and rejected by the Court in the *CBS* case. There, the Board sought to justify a narrow view of its function and its failure to make affirmative awards as generating pressure to settle or arbitrate privately. As §10(k) passed the Senate, it directed the Board to decide the dispute *or* to order arbitration, but the arbitration alternative was deleted in Conference, and the amended bill was passed by the Senate over the strenuous objections of Senator Morse and others.[27] By this amendment, the Court in *CBS* held that Congress had expressed a clear preference for Board decision as compared with compelled arbitration, and that this policy preference must be respected. 364 U.S., at 581-582. . . .

There remains the matter of the so-called *Safeway* rule announced by

---

[26] The Board has stated its guidelines for resolving jurisdictional disputes:

"The Board will consider all relevant factors in determining who is entitled to the work in dispute, e.g., the skills and work involved, certifications by the Board, company and industry practice, agreements between unions and between employers and unions, awards of arbitrators, joint boards, and the AFL-CIO in the same or related cases, the assignment made by the employer, and the efficient operation of the employer's business. This list of factors is not meant to be exclusive, but is by way of illustration. . . . Every decision will have to be an act of judgment based on common sense and experience rather than on precedent." Intl. Assn. of Machinists, Lodge 1743 (J.A. Jones Construction Co.), 135 N.L.R.B. 1402, 1410-1411 (1962).

The Joint Board award in this case was based solely on the Joint Board's interpretation of a 1917 agreement between the two international unions and a 1924 decision interpreting that agreement. . . . At the time of the dispute, the criteria used by the Joint Board in making awards were: "Decisions and agreements of record as set forth in the Green Book [the Building Trades Department's book of precedents], valid agreements between affected International Unions attested by the Chairman of the Joint Board, established trade practice and prevailing practice in the locality." Art. III, §1(a), AFL-CIO Bldg. & Constr. Trades Dept., Plan for Settling Jurisdictional Disputes Nationally and Locally (1965). These criteria were broadened in 1970 by the addition of Art. III, §1(f), which provides: "Because efficiency, cost and good management are essential to the well-being of the industry, the Joint Board should not ignore the interests of the consumer in settling jurisdictional disputes." AFL-CIO Bldg. & Constr. Trades Dept., Plan for Settling Jurisdictional Disputes Nationally and Locally 8 (1970).

[27] 93 Cong. Rec. 6452-6453; 93 Cong. Rec. 6519 (remarks of Sen. Pepper).

the Board in 1962[28] and followed since.[29] Under this rule, the Board has held that if one of the unions claiming work effectively renounces its claim, §10(k) proceedings are aborted despite legitimate interests an employer may have in securing a Board decision. It is urged that if union agreement prevents a §10(k) decision in such a situation, the employer cannot be considered a party to the §10(k) dispute when the unions but not the employer have *agreed* upon a method of settlement. As we understand the *Safeway* doctrine, however, when one union disclaims the work, §10(k) proceedings terminate, not because all "parties" to the dispute have settled or agreed to settle within the meaning of the statute, but on the ground that, in the words of the Board's brief in this case, "the Board has power, under Section 10(k), only to hear and determine the merits of a jurisdictional dispute and . . . by definition, such a dispute cannot exist unless there are rival claims to the work. . . ." A §10(k) hearing is a comparative proceeding aimed at determining which union is entitled to perform certain tasks. Its function evaporates when one of the unions renounces and refuses the work. Similarly, the applicability of §8(b)(4)(D) is premised on conflicting claims of unions or groups of employees for the same job; absent such an actual conflict, it would be futile to proceed under that section unless the employer replaces the disclaiming employees by a new third group of employees when they reject the work assignment, and the disfavored union resumes picketing.

If union settlement followed by disclaimer ends the §10(k) case, some of the argument about the employer's party status becomes academic; for whether the employer is a party or not, the two unions alone can prevent a Board decision. . . .

[T]he Board's *Safeway* rule applies only where the inter-union conflict is effectively settled and the employer no longer faces conflicting claims to the work. As this case demonstrates, the Board does not apply the *Safeway* rule to unimplemented agreements to arbitrate between the unions alone, and it does not consider it applicable where employees continue on the job after their international union loses an arbitration proceeding and renounces the work.[31] These *de facto* disputes are real, and they deserve Board resolution if the purposes of §10(k) are to be achieved. Cf. *CBS,* supra, at 579-580.

[28] Highway Truckdrivers, Local 107 (Safeway Stores, Inc.), 134 N.L.R.B. 1320 (1961).
[29] Intl. Assn. of Bridge Workers, Local 678 (W.R. Aldrich & Co.), 145 N.L.R.B. 943 (1964). . . .
[31] Carpenters Local 1849 v. C.J. Montag & Sons, Inc., 335 F.2d 216, 221 (CA9 1964); Bldg. and Construction Trades Council of Las Vegas, Local 525 (Charles J. Dorfman), 173 N.L.R.B. 1339 (1968). The Board has also held that a union cannot avoid a §10(k) determination by a disclaimer of interest in presently representing the employees in question, United Mine Workers (Turman Construction Co.), 136 N.L.R.B. 1068 (1962), and it has ignored explicit disclaimers when it has questioned a representative's authority to disclaim work, Millwrights' Local 1113 (Brogdex Co.), 157 N.L.R.B. 996, 1002 (1966). . . .

The Court of Appeals would extend the *Safeway* rule to foreclose Board decision where the two unions, but not the employer, have agreed to arbitrate; inter-union agreement was deemed equivalent to effective disclaimer by one of the unions. This view ignores the narrow view the Board has taken of the *Safeway* rule. It also fails to recognize the problem arising where a local union or group of employees continues to do work assigned by the employer despite agreement or disclaimer by their parent body. It makes little difference to the picketing union that there has been a "settlement" or an agreed-upon method of deciding the dispute as long as it is barred from enjoying the results of such a theoretical resolution.

Reversed.

NOTES

1. In ITT v. Local 134, IBEW, 419 U.S. 428 (1975), the Court ruled that a §10(k) determination is not a "final disposition," an "order," or an "agency process for the formulation" of a §8(b)(4)(D) order, and, hence, is not an "adjudication" governed by §5 of the Administrative Procedure Act, which prohibits the commingling of prosecutorial and adjudicatory functions. Accordingly, an NLRB attorney who had acted as a hearing examiner in a §10(k) proceeding was not disqualified from representing the NLRB's General Counsel in the subsequent and related §8(b)(4)(D) proceeding. This decision in effect upheld the Board's procedures under which a field examiner from a regional office takes evidence in a §10(k) proceeding and transmits the record to the Board in Washington without making a recommendation. See 29 CFR §101.34 (1975).

Is the rationale of *ITT* consistent with the rationale of *Plasterers* for dismissing a §8(b)(4)(D) charge upon the employer's noncompliance with a §10(k) award, namely, that such an award is an "order," as that term is used in the final clause of §8(b)(4)(D)?

2. The Board's approach to §10(k) determinations set forth in Machinists, Lodge 1743 (J.A. Jones Constr.) (see *Plasterers*, footnote 26), was issued after extensive consideration and discussion with union leaders and employers following the *CBS* decision. Subsequently, the Board retained its case-by-case approach, adding to the relevant factors "safety" and, in connection with the introduction of new technology, the issue of whether employees previously performing the given function would be displaced. See Laborers District Council (Anjo Constr.), 265 N.L.R.B. 186 (1982); Philadelphia Typographical Union, Local 2, 142 N.L.R.B. 36 (1963).

3. In approximately 95 percent of the decisions during the three years

after the *CBS* decision (1961), the Board upheld the employer's assignment of the disputed work. Given the Board's 10(k) criteria, is this tendency surprising? Is it desirable? See Supp. Report of the Special "10(k)" Committee, ABA Lab. Rel. Section 437, 438 (1964). The Special "10(k)" Committee unanimously recommended that the Board be divested of its power "to hear and determine." The committee urged that unions believed that the Board was not qualified to deal with complex questions of union jurisdiction and that employers were concerned that the Board's awards would disrupt established bargaining relationships and would improperly encroach on managerial judgments. The committee divided, however, on whether Congress should also establish new tripartite industry committees for the resolution of work-assignment disputes. See also Sussman, Section 10(k): Mandate for Change, 47 B.U.L. Rev. 201 (1967).

Reviewing courts have generally upheld the Board's 10(k) awards, but not without criticism of its lack of standards for weighing the pertinent factors and its failure to follow its own precedents. See NLRB v. Teamsters Local 584, 535 F.2d 205, 207-208 (2d Cir. 1976).

4. Suppose that the contending unions and the employer have agreed to arbitration for resolving work-assignment disputes. One union either strikes in the face of an adverse arbitral award or repudiates the arbitral machinery and strikes before any award is rendered. Upon the filing of a charge, should the Board issue a complaint under §8(b)(4)(D) without a hearing or determination under §10(k)? See Wood, Wire & Metal Lathers, 119 N.L.R.B. 1345 (1958); Laborers, Local 423 (V & C Brickcleaning Co.), 203 N.L.R.B. 1015 (1973). See generally Note, The NLRB as Arbiter of Work Assignment Disputes Under 10(k), 50 Geo. L.J. 121 (1961). For problems arising when the voluntary machinery, after awarding the disputed work, becomes inoperative and cannot police its awards, see Modern Acoustics, 260 N.L.R.B. 883 (1982).

Note: The Relation Between Sections 8(b)(4)(D) and 10(k) and Other Statutory Provisions

In *CBS*, the Supreme Court, in rejecting the Board's contention that requiring the Board affirmatively to assign disputed work would be inconsistent with the Act, stated:

The first such inconsistency urged is with §§8(a)(3) and 8(b)(2) of the Act on the ground that the determination of jurisdictional disputes on their merits by the Board might somehow enable unions to compel employers to discriminate in regard to employment in order to encourage union membership. The argument here, which is based upon the fact that §10(k), like §8(b)(4)(D), extends to jurisdictional disputes between unions and unorganized groups as well as to disputes between two or more unions, appears to be that groups represented by unions would almost always prevail over nonunion groups in such a determination because their claim to the work would probably have more basis in custom and tradition than that of unorganized groups. No such danger is present here, however, for both groups of employees are represented by unions. Moreover, we feel entirely confident that the Board, with its many years of experience in guarding against and redressing violations of §§8(a)(3) and 8(b)(2), will devise means of discharging its duties under §10(k) in a manner entirely harmonious with those sections. A second inconsistency is urged with §303(a)(4) of the Taft-Hartley Act, which authorizes suits for damages suffered because of jurisdictional strikes. The argument here is that since §303(a)(4) does not permit a union to establish, as a defense to an action for damages under that section, that it is entitled to the work struck for on the basis of such factors as practice or custom, a similar result is required here in order to preserve "the substantive symmetry" between §303(a)(4) on the one hand and §§8(b)(4)(D) and 10(k) on the other. This argument ignores [this Court's recognition of] the separate and distinct nature of these two approaches to the problem of handling jurisdictional strikes [citing International Longshoremen's Union v. Juneau Spruce Corp., 342 U.S. 237 (1952)]. Since we do not require a "substantive symmetry" between the two, we need not and do not decide what effect a decision of the Board under §10(k) might have on actions under §303(a)(4).

The Board has sought to avoid tensions with §§8(a)(3) and 8(b)(2) by awarding disputed work to employees represented by the winning union and not to that union or to its members as such. See e.g., Operative Plasterers Local 179 (Bertolini Bros. Co.), 194 N.L.R.B. 403, 405 (1971). Nevertheless, compliance with a 10(k) award may result in discharge of, or failure to hire members of, the losing union because of a strike, actual or threatened, by the prevailing union, thereby raising acute questions under §§8(a)(3) and 8(b). The Board has, however, held that when the actions of all parties, including discharges, are part and parcel of a bona fide work-assignment dispute, §§10(k) and 8(b)(4)(D) are the exclusive remedies. See Brady-Hamilton Stevedore Co., 198 N.L.R.B. 147 (1972), *review denied sub nom.* Operating Engrs. Local 701 v. NLRB, 504 F.2d 1222 (9th Cir. 1974), *cert. denied*, 420 U.S. 973 (1975). Accordingly, even when an employer unilaterally changes work practices, discharges the employees favored by the §10(k) award, and assigns the work to members of another union, §§8(a)(3), 8(b)(2), and 8(a)(5) are not applicable. One court has, however, expressed doubt as to the continued vitality of the Brady-Hamilton decision. See Metromedia, Inc. v. NLRB, 586 F.2d 1182, 1190 n.4 (8th Cir. 1978).

The *Plasterers* case declared that a union would not violate §8(b)(4)(D) by picketing in order to enforce a 10(k) award. But what of liability under §303(a) for damages caused by a strike or picketing by the prevailing union before it was awarded the work in a 10(k) proceeding or, indeed, thereafter? Cf. Local 714 v. Sullivan Transfer, Inc., 650 F.2d 669 (5th Cir. 1981).

Teamsters Local 839 (Shurtleff & Andrews Contractors), 249 N.L.R.B. 176 (1980). One employee represented by the Operating Engineers had been assigned to operate cranes used to pull floats and trailers on the job site. The Teamsters local picketed the employer to compel its hiring a Teamster as part of a composite crew, to consist of one operating engineer working the crane and one Teamster doing hook-up, guiding and signalling work. After the employer had filed 8(b)(4)(D) charges, as well as 8(b)(6) charges, the Board issued a notice of a 10(k) hearing. Both unions moved to quash, urging that neither union was doing or seeking each other's work. The employer claimed that only an engineer should be used even when a crane or similar equipment pulls a trailer. The Board (2-1), finding no "substantial evidence" that two groups of employees were contending for the work involved, concluded that there was no jurisdictional dispute cognizable under §10(k) and "quashed" the notice of hearing — after the hearing had been held.

The employer appealed this quashing order, and, in Foley-Wismer & Becker v. NLRB, 682 F.2d 770 (9th Cir. 1982) (en banc), the court held that the Board's order quashing the notice of hearing was appealable. The court acknowledged that other circuits had reached a contrary result. Nevertheless, the Ninth Circuit distinguished such orders from work-assignment awards under §10(k): unlike such awards, quashing orders prevented the statutory machinery from operating. Five dissenting judges noted that §10(k) operates to set the statutory machinery in motion and that an 8(b)(4)(D) charge would not issue until the provisions of §10(k) were satisfied. Accordingly, the dissenters analogized a quashing order to the General Counsel's refusal to issue a complaint and urged that the order should be equally unreviewable.

NOTES

1. Is the court's distinguishing of other nonappealable orders from those quashing 10(k) hearings convincing? Do other nonappealable orders sometimes erroneously deny an aggrieved party, as well as the public, the benefit of the Act?

2. In Foley-Wismer & Becker v. NLRB, 695 F.2d 424 (9th Cir.

1982), the court upheld the Board's finding that no jurisdictional dispute existed under §10(k), since the Teamsters and the Operating Engineers were not competing for the same work, and, indeed, the latter union's members had never performed or requested the disputed work.

3. In Local 1291, ILA (Pocahontas Steamship Co.), 152 N.L.R.B. 676 (1965), *enforced*, 368 F.2d 107 (3d Cir. 1966), *cert. denied*, 386 U.S. 1033 (1967), seamen opened and closed ship hatches in less than one half hour, in accordance with a steamship company's contract with the National Maritime Union (NMU). One Coslett under a cost-plus contract employed ILA Longshoremen for loading ships. The ILA picketed the pier in order to force Coslett to hire six-man hatch-and-beam gangs to open and close those hatches. The NMU expressly disclaimed any interest in the disputed work, but the seamen continued to do it on request. The NLRB held that the purported disclaimer was ineffective "to defeat a dispute between two unions or group of employees"; that a jurisdictional dispute existed; and, pursuant to §10(k), awarded the work to the seamen. Later, the Board found that the ILA's noncompliance had violated §8(b)(4)(D).

Are the Board's decisions in *Pocahontas* and *Shurtleff*, supra, distinguishable?

4. A company owns three plants, I, II, and II; the employees of each plant are represented by different locals of the same international union, and the company has had long-standing collective bargaining relationships with each local. The company transfers work done for five years by employees of Plant I to the employees of Plant II. The Plant I local pickets that plant for a reallocation of the work. Is there a "jurisdictional dispute" covered by §8(b)(4)(D)? See Highway & Truck Drivers Local 107 (Safeway Stores, Inc.), 134 N.L.R.B. 1320 (1961). Suppose that the same company transfers work previously done by employees of Plant III to employees of Plant II, and that the employees of Plant I picket for that work. Is a "jurisdictional dispute" involved? Cf. Teamsters Local 680 (Kraft, Inc.), 265 N.L.R.B. 915 (1982).

5. Picketing by a union for the reinstatement of economic strikers replaced by the employer does not involve a "jurisdictional dispute." See Sheet Metal Workers Intl. Assn., Local 99, 90 N.L.R.B. 1015 (1950).

Do economic strikers and their replacements compete for the same work? How do you explain the Board's result? Would such picketing violate §8(b)(2) of the Act?

The Board has also held summarily that a strike designed "to get all the strikers back to work, in preference to the replacements" is "clearly a legitimate bargaining demand." See Portland Stereotypers' and Electrotypers' Union No.48, 137 N.L.R.B. 782, 786 n.6 (1962) (strike clearly economic; replacements presumably "permanent").

Is it at least fairly arguable that employers' capitulation to union pressure for reinstatement of economic strikers in preference to their permanent replacements violates §8(a)(3) and that such union pressure violates §8(b)(2)? What practical difficulties would arise from accepting that argument? What interpretive difficulties under §8(a)(3)?

H. "FEATHERBEDDING"

"Featherbedding" refers to practices such as make-work rules, excessive manning, production quotas, and resistance to technological improvements. Such practices, like limitations on subcontracting and work-assignment disputes, reflect the desire of employees for job security or increased employment and of unions for institutional survival and growth. Unions, on health and safety grounds, may genuinely or pretextually support rules challenged as featherbedding.

Featherbedding is an old phenomenon and has not been confined to the unionized sector. But the power of organization can institutionalize obstructions to efficiency and shield them against the pressure of market forces for considerably longer periods.[m]

The classic view — to which most union spokesmen have paid at least lip service — is that featherbedding, since it inhibits productivity and a rising standard of living, is contrary to the public interest.[n] That assessment led many courts, at common law, to condemn as unlawful and enjoinable strikes to impose make-work practices. See Haverhill Strand Theater v. Gillen, 229 Mass. 413, 118 N.E. 671 (1918) (union enjoined from enforcing rule requiring the hiring of a minimum of five musicians where employer desired services of single musician); Opera on Tour v. Weber, 285 N.Y. 348, 34 N.E.2d 349, cert. denied, 314 U.S. 615 (1941) (despite state counterpart of Norris-LaGuardia Act, injunction upheld against stagehands' strike inspired by musicians in protest against use by travelling opera company of recorded music rather than live orchestra). But cf. Bayer v. Bhd. of Painters, 108 N.J.

---

[m] The union impact on efficiency may, of course, be positive not only through improvement of morale but also through direct contributions to increased productivity, particularly when jobs are threatened by the competition of other suppliers or other products.

[n] There are substantial obstacles to a reliable quantitative estimate of the costs of union-made featherbedding rules. See Rees, The Effects of Unions on Resource Allocation, 6 J. Law & Econ. 69, 76 (1963). The literature suggests that much of the total cost has been concentrated in a few industries, especially railroads, printing, longshoring, entertainment, and building construction.

Eq. 257, Ct. Err. & App., 154 A. 759 (1931). See Teller, Focal Problems in American Labor Law — Opera on Tour, Inc. v. Weber, 28 Va. L. Rev. 727 (1942).

The classic condemnation has been challenged by suggestions, revived in the 1960s by "automation" and more recently by "robotics," that work will wither away and the productive apparatus will be manned by a small fraction of the population. But such alarms ignore important considerations: the low median family income; the increasing importance of the personal services sector where productivity increases are difficult to achieve; the massive demands on resources resulting from heightened concerns about pollution, urban decay, mass transportation, and the increasing proportion of the population consisting of nonproductive senior citizens. See L. Ulman, Automation in Perspective (Reprint No. 305, Univ. of Calif., Berkeley) (1967). In any event, there appears to be no basis for the contention that there is a connection between rapid technological change and high unemployment. See Solow, Technology and Unemployment, 1 The Public Interest 17, 18-19 (1965); but cf. H. Rothwell & W. Zegveld, Technical Change and Employment, esp. ch. 7 (1979).

Technological change may impose special burdens on particular workers, who may suffer not only unemployment but the obsolescence of hard-earned skills and the concomitant loss of earning power and of a sense of status. There is a general consensus that such burdens should be reduced by public and private measures, such as severance pay, retraining, relocation, or similar cushions.° See Automation and the Workplace, Selected Labor, Education and Training Issues, A Technical Memorandum, U.S. Congress, Office of Technology Assessment, ch. 3 (March 1983); Killingsworth, Cooperative Approaches to Problems of Technological Change, in G. Somers, E. Cushman, & N. Weinberg, Adjusting to Technological Change 61 (1963). Furthermore, concern has been expressed recently about allegedly increased worker alienation that is attributed to technology. See Work in America, Rep. of Special Task Force to the Secretary of HEW, 93d Cong., 1st Sess. (1973), critically reviewed by I. Kristol, Wall St. J., Jan. 18, 1973, at 12, col. 4.

In the materials immediately following, our primary concern is with legal proscriptions aimed at various efforts by unions to resist change or to make work for employees whom they represent. See Aaron, Governmental Restraints on Featherbedding, 5 Stan. L. Rev. 680 (1953).

°See G. Somers, ed., Adjusting to Technological Change (1963). There are, of course, difficulties in distinguishing "technological" unemployment from other forms of unemployment. A broad range of public and private measures is directed at unemployment, whatever its source. See J. P. Goldberg, et al., Federal Policies and Worker Status Since the Thirties (Industrial Rel. Res. Assn. (1976)), esp. ch. 6.

NLRB v. Gamble Enterprises, Inc.
345 U.S. 117 (1953)

BURTON, J. For generations professional musicians have faced a short-age in the local employment needed to yield them a livelihood. They have been confronted with the competition of military bands, traveling bands, foreign musicians on tour, local amateur organizations and, more recently, technological developments in reproduction and broadcasting. To help them conserve local sources of employment, they developed local protective socie-ties. Since 1896, they also have organized and maintained on a national scale the American Federation of Musicians, affiliated with the American Federa-tion of Labor. By 1943, practically all professional instrumental performers and conductors in the United States had joined the Federation, establishing a membership of over 200,000, with 10,000 more in Canada.

The Federation uses its nationwide control of professional talent to help individual members and local unions. It insists that traveling band contracts be subject to its rules, laws and regulations. Article 18, §4, of its By-Laws provides: "Traveling members cannot, without the consent of a Local, play any presentation performances in its jurisdiction unless a local house orches-tra is also employed."

. . . For more than 12 years the Palace Theater in Akron, Ohio, has been one of an interstate chain of theaters managed by respondent, Gamble Enterprises, Inc. . . . Before the decline of vaudeville and until about 1940, respondent employed a local orchestra of nine union musicians to play for stage acts at that theater. When a traveling band occupied the stage, the local orchestra played from the pit for the vaudeville acts and, at times, augmented the performance of the traveling band.

Since 1940, respondent has used the Palace for showing motion pic-tures with occasional appearances of traveling bands. Between 1940 and 1947, the local musicians, no longer employed on a regular basis, held periodic rehearsals at the theater and were available when required. When a traveling band appeared there, respondent paid the members of the local orchestra a sum equal to the minimum union wages for a similar engagement but they played no music.

The Taft-Hartley Act, containing §8(b)(6) . . . took effect August 22. Between July 2 and November 12, seven performances of traveling bands were presented on the Palace stage. Local musicians were neither used nor paid on those occasions. They raised no objections and made no demands for "stand-by" payments. However, in October, 1947, the American Federation of Musicians, Local No. 24, of Akron, Ohio . . . opened negotiations with respondent for the latter's employment of a pit orchestra of local musicians whenever a traveling band performed on the stage. The pit orchestra was to play overtures, "intermissions" and "chasers" (the latter while patrons were leaving the theater). The union required acceptance of this proposal as a condition of its consent to local appearances of traveling bands. Respondent declined the offer and a traveling band scheduled to appear November 20 canceled its engagement on learning that the union had withheld its consent.

May 8, 1949, the union made a new proposal. It sought a guaranty that a local orchestra would be employed by respondent on some number of occasions having a relation to the number of traveling band appearances. This and similar proposals were declined on the ground that the local orchestra was neither necessary nor desired. Accordingly, in July, 1949, the union again declined to consent to the appearance of a traveling band desired by respondent and the band did not appear.

[The Board, with one dissent, dismissed a complaint of the union's violation of §8(b)(6) but was reversed by the court of appeals.]

We accept the finding of the Board . . . that the union was seeking actual employment for its members and not mere "stand-by" pay. . . . [The union] has . . . consistently negotiated for actual employment in connection with traveling band and vaudeville appearances. It has suggested various ways in which a local orchestra could earn pay for performing competent work and, upon those terms, it has offered to consent to the appearance of traveling bands which are Federation-controlled. . . .

Since we and the Board treat the union's proposals as in good faith contemplating the performance of actual services, we agree that the union has not, on this record, engaged in a practice proscribed by §8(b)(6). It has remained for respondent to accept or reject the union's offers on their merits in the light of all material circumstances. We do not find it necessary to determine also whether such offers were "in the nature of an exaction." We are not dealing here with offers of mere "token" or nominal services. The proposals before us were appropriately treated by the Board as offers in good faith and substantial performances by competent musicians. There is no reason to think that sham can be substituted for substance under §8(b)(6) any more than under any other statute. Payments for "standing-by," or for the substantial equivalent of "standing-by," are not payments for services performed, but when an employer receives a bona fide offer of competent performance of relevant services, it remains for the employer, through free and fair negotiation, to determine whether such offer shall be accepted and what compensation shall be paid for the work done.[5]

[5] In addition to the legislative history cited in the *American Newspaper* case, the following explanation by Senator Ball emphasizes the point that §8(b)(6) proscribes *only* payments where *no work is done*. As a member of the Senate Committee on Labor and Public Welfare,

The judgment of the Court of Appeals, accordingly, is reversed and the cause is remanded to it.

JACKSON, J., dissenting. . . . Granting that Congress failed to reach all "featherbedding" practices, [§8(b)(6)] should not be interpreted to have no practical effect beyond requiring a change in the form of an exaction.

Accepting the result in No. 53, American Newspaper Publishers Association v. Labor Board, [345 U.S. 100, summarized infra, Note 3], I think that differences in this case require a contrary result.

In both cases, the payments complained of obviously were caused by the respective unions. In both, the work performed was unwanted by the employer and its cost burdened the industry and contributed nothing to it. But here resemblance ceases. The Typographical Union is adhering to an old custom which mutual consent established and for years maintained and to which other terms of employment have long since been adjusted. In this case the union has substituted for the practice specifically condemned by the statute a new device for achieving the same result. The two cases may exemplify the same economic benefits and detriments from made work, but superfluous effort which long and voluntary usage recognized as a fair adjustment of service conditions between employer and employee in the printing industry is "exacted" for the first time in the entertainment field in order to evade the law.

That the payments involved in this case constitute a union "exaction" within the statute would seem hard to deny, whatever may be thought of the printers' case. As the Court says, the American Federation of Musicians has established a "nationwide control of professional talent." No artist or organization can perform without its approval. The respondent is in the entertainment business but can get no talent to exhibit unless it makes these payments. The "service" tendered for the payments is not wanted or useful. What the Court speaks of as "free and fair negotiation, to determine whether such offer shall be accepted" is actually only freedom to pay or go out of business with all its attendant losses. If that does not amount to an exaction, language has lost all integrity of meaning.

---

and as one who had served as a Senate conferee, he made it on the floor of the Senate immediately preceding the passage of the bill, over the President's veto, June 23, 1947:

"There is not a word in that [§8(b)(6)], Mr. President, about 'featherbedding.' It says that it is an unfair practice for a union to force an employer to pay for *work which is not performed*. In the colloquy on this floor between the Senator from Florida [Mr. Pepper] and the Senator from Ohio [Mr. Taft], before the bill was passed, it was made abundantly clear that it did not apply to rest periods, it did not apply to speed-ups or safety provisions, or to anything of that nature; it applied *only* to situations, for instance, where the Musicians' Federation forces an employer to hire one orchestra and then to pay for another *stand-by orchestra, which does no work at all*." (Emphasis supplied.) 93 Cong. Rec. 7529.

But the Court holds that so long as some exertion is performed or offered by the employees, no matter how useless or unwanted, it can never be said that there is an exaction "for services which are not performed or not to be performed." This language undoubtedly presents difficulties of interpretation, but I am not persuaded that it is so meaningless and empty in practice as the Court would make it. Congress surely did not enact a prohibition whose practical application would be restricted to those without sufficient imagination to invent some "work."

Before this Act, the union was compelling the theatre to pay for no work. When this was forbidden, it sought to accomplish the same result by compelling it to pay for useless and unwanted work. This is not continuation of an old usage that long practice has incorporated into the industry but is a new expedient devised to perpetuate a union policy in the face of its congressional condemnation. Such subterfuge should not be condoned.

CLARK, J., with whom the CHIEF JUSTICE joins, dissenting. The Chief Justice and I dissent on the basis of our dissenting opinion in American Newspaper Publishers Association v. Labor Board. . . . We cannot perceive a tenable distinction between this and the printers' "featherbedding" case. . . . True, the employees there "work" on the keyboard of a Linotype, and here on the keys of a musical instrument. But, realistically viewed, one enterprise is as bogus as the other; both are boondoggles which the employer "does not want, does not need, and is not even willing to accept." The statute, moreover, does not distinguish between modern make-work gimmicks and featherbedding techniques encrusted in an industry's lore. . . .

NOTES

1. Cf. §302, especially §302(b)(2), of the LMRA.

2. Could the AFM have lawfully promoted jobs for local musicians by imposing higher rates for the services of traveling bands when a local band was not also employed? If the Supreme Court had condemned the arrangement challenged in the *Gamble* case, would the alternative just suggested also be illegal? What considerations are likely to impel a union to impose unneeded employees rather than to secure higher rates for a reduced complement?

3. In American Newspaper Pub. Assn. v. NLRB, 345 U.S. 100 (1953), a companion case to *Gamble Enterprises*, the Court, agreeing with the Board, held that §8(b)(6) did not prohibit the ITU's practice of setting "bogus" type. That practice had begun with the introduction of the linotype

machine in 1890, which had permitted one newspaper to set type for a given advertisement and to produce a mat that other papers could use to print the same advertisement. In order to avoid the loss of work for compositors, the ITU had secured the agreement of newspaper publishers to permit their compositors, at their regular rates of pay, to set type for a bogus copy of an advertisement despite the use of a mat. The bogus work, done during slack time, took from two to five percent of a printer's time. Some employees have expressed distaste for bogus work. See P. Jacobs, The State of the Unions, Dead Horse and the Featherbird 197 (1963). Nevertheless, after an international convention supported repeal of the union law requiring the resetting of type when matrices had been supplied, the membership (by a vote of 41,090 to 30,863) refused to ratify that change even though it was strongly supported by their national leaders, who urged that the practice was regarded as featherbedding and that it hurt the union. See N.Y. Times, Nov. 2, 1960, at 39, cols. 2-3. Subsequently, the New York City local of the typographical union agreed with the leading local newspapers to the elimination of "bogus" and the reduction of "featherbedding" in exchange for what was described as a "lifetime guarantee of employment"; this agreement was ratified by an overwhelming majority of the members. See 86 L.R.R. 327 (1974).

4. Lathers Local 46 (Expanded Metal Eng. Co.), 207 N.L.R.B. 631 (1973), is one of the Board's rare holdings of a §8(b)(6) violation. Some manufacturing had been done by a unit employee represented by the Teamsters, which had a collective agreement with the employer. The lathers' local, despite the employer's statement that he had no work for a lather, forced the employer to hire a lather who was paid $400 per week but did no lathering. As suggested by the local's business agent, that employee was assigned odd office jobs, some of which he could not perform and others of which he rejected as "demeaning." The Board concluded that the union's demand had not been, in the language of the *American Newspaper* case, "a *bona fide* offer of competent performance of *relevant* services." See also Teamsters Local 456 (J.R. Stevenson Corp.), 212 N.L.R.B. 968 (1974) (construction contractor's $20,000-a-year employee serving as union's agent in checking union cards of incoming truck drivers had not provided the "relevant services" to employer required under §8(b)(6)).

Are situations where a union insists on unwanted employees (such as musical groups) whose services are allegedly "irrelevant" to the employer's enterprise distinguishable?

5. A play that does not call for any music has been running in a Chicago theater for forty weeks. The theater has agreed with the AFM to guarantee six musicians forty-six weeks of work so long as they perform in accordance with the theater's directions. Pursuant to that agreement, the theater has paid

the musicians a weekly stipend even though they have not performed or even appeared at the theater while the play has been running. The individual musicians have telephoned the theater each week and offered to perform but have been told that their services are not needed. Has the union violated §8(b)(6)? Would your answer be affected if the Chicago agreement had been executed after the New York cast, which was to perform in Chicago, had, without any music, played to capacity crowds for two years in New York?

6. The Hobbs Act, 18 U.S.C. 1951, has been construed to make it a criminal offense for individuals by violence, actual or threatened, to compel wage payments for "imposed, unwanted, superfluous and fictitious services." See United States v. Green, 350 U.S. 415 (1956). Cf. United States v. Enmons, 410 U.S. 396 (1976) (a 5 to 4 decision), holding the Act inapplicable to deliberate and serious physical destruction of an employer's property in an otherwise lawful strike for higher wages. On the applicability of the Hobbs Act to improper means used by management to secure employees' agreement to reduction of collectively bargained benefits, see United States v. Russo, 708 F.2d 209 (6th Cir.), *cert. denied*, 104 S. Ct. 487 (1983).

For discussion of the tension between construction of §8(b)(6) of the NLRA and of the Hobbs Act, see Note, Featherbedding and the Federal Anti-Racketeering Act, 26 U. Chi. L. Rev. 150 (1958); Note, Labor Violence and the Hobbs Act: A Judicial Dilemma, 67 Yale L.J. 325 (1957).

CHAPTER 8

NATIONAL REGULATION AND PREEMPTION OF STATE AUTHORITY

Under §§10(a) and 9(c)(1) of the NLRA, as amended, the NLRB's jurisdiction extends to cases "affecting commerce," as that term is defined in §2(7) of the Act. In upholding the constitutionality of the Wagner Act, the Supreme Court announced that the Board's statutory jurisdiction was coextensive with the power of Congress under the commerce clause. See NLRB v. Jones & Laughlin Steel Corp., 301 U.S. 1 (1937); Stern, The Commerce Clause and the National Economy, 1933-1946, 59 Harv. L. Rev. 645, 674-682 (1946). Although subsequently in Polish National Alliance v. NLRB, 322 U.S. 643 (1944), the Court warned against "scholastic reasoning" that would subject all activities to the commerce power, subsequent decisions suggest that the commerce power and the Board's jurisdiction extend to "small" and "local" enterprises. See NLRB v. Reliance Fuel Oil Corp., 371 U.S. 224 (1963); Amalgamated Meat Cutters v. Fairlawn Meats, Inc., 353 U.S. 20 (1957); NLRB v. Denver Building & Constr. Trades Council, 341 U.S. 675 (1951); Heart of Atlanta Motel, Inc. v. United States, 379 U.S. 241 (1964). The Board, through its policy of jurisdictional self-limitation, has in general avoided serious tests of the limits that might be imposed on the reach of the commerce power. If such tests should arise, the Supreme Court would probably give expansive scope to the Board's jurisdiction.

A. THE NLRB'S JURISDICTIONAL SELF-LIMITATION

The Board at first exercised its policy of self-limitation case by case, declining jurisdiction over cases it deemed to have an insignificant effect on interstate commerce. In 1950, the Board, in order to conserve its resources and to reduce the confusion of litigants and its own staff, began to publish "jurisdictional yardsticks," which prescribed various monetary minima for the exercise of jurisdiction. These yardsticks were revised in 1954 and again in 1958, with a view to expanding the Board's effective jurisdiction and, concomitantly, reducing the no-man's-land in which state authority was inoperative even though the Board declined to act. See Siemons Mailing Serv., 122 N.L.R.B. 81 (1958); 23 N.L.R.B. Ann. Rep. 7-8 (1959). The Board has generally formulated new standards in the course of adjudication, rather than by exercising the rule-making authority conferred by NLRA, §6. This practice has generated extensive and critical discussion. See, e.g., Bernstein, The NLRB's Adjudication-Rule Making Dilemma Under the Administrative Procedure Act, 79 Yale L. J. 571 (1970). See also Peck, The Atrophied Rule Making Powers of the National Labor Relations Board, 70 Yale L.J. 729 (1961).

The 1958 standards, set forth (but not promulgated) in a press release (R-576, Oct. 2, 1958), included the following:

1. *Nonretail:* $50,000 outflow or inflow, direct or indirect.
2. *Office Buildings:* Gross revenue of $100,000, of which $25,000 or more is derived from organizations which meet any of the new standards.
3. *Retail concerns:* $500,000 gross volume of business.
4. *Instrumentalities, links, and channels of interstate commerce:* $50,000 from interstate (or linkage) part of enterprise, or from services performed for employers in commerce.
5. *Public utilities:* $250,000 gross volume, or meet standard 1 (nonretail).
6. *Transit system:* $250,000 gross volume. (Except taxicabs, to which the retail test ($500,000 gross volume of business) shall apply.)
7. *Newspapers and communication systems:* Radio, television, telegraph, and telephone: $100,000 gross volume. Newspapers: $200,000 gross volume.
8. *National defense:* Substantial impact on national defense.
9. *Business in the Territories and District of Columbia:* D.C.— Plenary. Territories — Standards apply.
10. *Associations:* Regarded as single employer.

Direct outflow refers to goods shipped or services furnished by the employer outside the State. Indirect outflow includes sales within the State to users meeting any standard except solely an indirect inflow or indirect outflow standard. Direct inflow refers to goods or services furnished directly to the employer from outside the State in which the employer is located.

Indirect inflow refers to the purchase of goods or services which originated outside the employer's State but which he purchased from a seller within the State. Direct and indirect outflow may be combined, and direct and indirect inflow may also be combined, to meet the $50,000 requirement. However, outflow and inflow may not be combined.

NOTES

1. Selected post-1958 developments in the Board's jurisdictional standards illustrate the steady expansion of Board jurisdiction through the exercise of its discretionary authority — despite its crowded docket. That docket has increased not only by virtue of direct Congressional mandates, but also because of the indirect impact of inflation. See §14(c) of the Act; Meltzer & La Londe, Inflation and the NLRB: A Case of Fortuitous Regulatory Expansion, 4 Reg., Sept.-Oct. 1980, at 43. The Board will exercise jurisdiction over entities meeting these standards:

(a) Private nonprofit colleges or universities with a gross annual revenue of at least $1 million for operating expenses, excluding contributions restricted by the donor against such use. See 35 Fed. Reg. 18370 (1970), 29 C.F.R. §103.1. (This standard was estimated to cover 80 percent of private colleges and universities. Id., at 18371.) The Board, in an about-face, first asserted jurisdiction over a private, nonprofit university in Cornell Univ., 183 N.L.R.B. 329 (1970). Then, exercising its rulemaking authority for the first time to establish a jurisdictional standard, the Board subsequently promulgated §103.1.

(b) Secular private secondary and elementary schools with an annual gross volume of at least $1 million. (See Windsor School, 200 N.L.R.B. 991 (1972)).

In NLRB v. Catholic Bishop of Chicago, 440 U.S. 490 (1979), the Court, in an opinion by Burger, C.J., joined by Stewart, Powell, Rehnquist and Stevens, JJ., held that the Board lacked jurisdiction over teachers in church-operated schools regardless of whether they are "completely religious" or "merely religiously associated." The Court reasoned that since the Board's exercise of jurisdiction would implicate the guarantees of the religion clauses of the First Amendment, its jurisdiction should be denied because Congress had not clearly conferred it.

Brennan, J., with whom White, Marshall, and Blackmun, JJ., concurred, dissented, disagreeing with the Court's reading of the legislative history and objecting that the Court had not distinguished Associated Press v. NLRB, 301 U.S. 103 (1937) (rejecting claim that the First Amendment barred application of Act to editorial employees of nonprofit newsgathering organization).

(c) Proprietary hospitals with at least $250,000 gross annual revenue, and proprietary nursing homes with at least $100,000 gross annual revenue.

Butte Medical Properties, 168 N.L.R.B. 266 (1967); University Nursing Home, 168 N.L.R.B. 263 (1967).

After the 1974 amendments to the NLRA brought nonprofit hospitals under the Act, the Board applied the $250,000 standard to such hospitals and eliminated for jurisdictional purposes the distinction between profit and nonprofit institutions. See 40 N.L.R.B. Ann. Rep. 37-38 (1976); Rhode Island Catholic Orphan Asylum, 224 N.L.R.B. 1344 (1976). Despite the 1974 health-care amendments, the Board (4 to 1) held that hospital interns, residents, and clinical fellows (comprising a medical center's house staff, who had filed an election petition) were primarily "students" rather than "employees" and, accordingly, were not covered by the NLRA. Cedars-Sinai Medical Center, 223 N.L.R.B. 251 (1976); Physicians House Staff Assn. v. Fanning, 642 F.2d 492 (D.C. Cir. 1980) (en banc), cert. denied, 450 U.S. 917 (1981) (no jurisdiction under Leedom v. Kyne, supra p. 434, to review Board's dismissal of election petitions by house staffs, despite probability that house staffs could not otherwise secure judicial review, e.g., in an unfair labor practice proceeding).

(d) Symphony orchestras with a gross annual revenue of at least $1 million (excluding contributions barred by donor from use for operating expenses). See 38 Fed. Reg. 6177 (1973), 29 C.F.R. §103.2, overturning prior policy of declining jurisdiction.

(e) Law firms and legal assistance programs with gross annual revenues of at least $250,000. See Camden Regional Legal Servs., 231 N.L.R.B. 224 (1977); Kleinberg, Kaplan, Wolff, Cohen & Burrows, P.C., 253 N.L.R.B. 450 (1980). The Board had previously declined jurisdiction over law firms (see Bodle, Fogel, Julber, Reinhardt & Rothschild, 206 N.L.R.B. 512 (1973)), but in Foley, Hoag & Eliot, 229 N.L.R.B. 456 (1977), it overturned that policy and reinstated the petition of a union seeking to represent file clerks and messengers. See Comment, NLRB Asserts Jurisdiction over Law Firms: Has the Door Been Opened to Lawyer Unionization? 27 Buffalo L. Rev. 361 (1978).

2. The Board may exercise jurisdiction even though its customary standards are not met and, "absent extraordinary circumstances," or abuse by the Board of its discretion, courts will not interfere. See NLRB v. Erlich's 814, Inc., 577 F.2d 68 (8th Cir. 1978); Clark & Hinojosa, 247 N.L.R.B. 710 (1980) (jurisdiction may be exercised over both §8(a)(4) charge that employee was denied promised post-termination pay after threatening to complain to NLRB and closely related §8(a)(1) charge, so long as record is "sufficient to demonstrate the presence of legal jurisdiction beyond de minimis limits").

Office Employees, Local 11 v. NLRB, 353 U.S. 313 (1957). The Board declined to take jurisdiction over unfair labor practice complaints arising from an organizational campaign among the office employees of Teamsters locals. The Board conceded that the locals were "employers" under the Act but, noting their nonprofit character, declared: "Labor organizations, which, when engaged in their primary function of advancing employee welfare, are institutions unto themselves within the framework of this country's economic scheme, should [not] be made subject to any of the standards originated for business organizations." 113 N.L.R.B. at 991. The Supreme Court, rejecting the Board's position, concluded that the unambiguous and specific inclusion in NLRA §2(2) of a labor organization when "acting as an employer" precluded "such an arbitrary blanket exclusion of union employers as a class . . ." without even an inquiry whether their operations were local in character. The Court distinguished, without approving or disapproving, Board declinations based on a particularized finding that the statutory policies would not be effectuated by an assertion of jurisdiction over local operations. Four justices dissented from what they deemed to be the Court's position that the Board lacked authority to decline jurisdiction over labor unions as a class even when the Board has determined for proper reasons that the policies of the Act would not be effectuated by its assertion of jurisdiction. Finding that the grounds relied upon by the Board were not "proper reasons," the dissenters would have remanded for Board reconsideration.

NOTES

1. In 1959, §14(c) was added to the NLRA in order to eliminate the no-man's-land created by Guss v. Utah Labor Relations Board, 353 U.S. 1 (1957), and to clarify and restrict the Board's authority to decline jurisdiction. Thereafter, the Board, at the request of a party to a state proceeding or a state tribunal, began to render advisory opinions as to whether its jurisdictional standards had been met. See 29 C.F.R. §102.98 (1975); Jemcon Broadcasting Co., 135 N.L.R.B. 362 (1962).

2. Questions about the effect of §14(c) on state and national jurisdiction are suggested below:

(a) If the Board has not issued, or has not been requested to issue, an advisory opinion, it is not wholly clear whether and under what circumstances states have jurisdiction to determine their own jurisdiction. See, e.g., Stryjewski v. Local 830, Brewery Drivers, 426 Pa. 512, 233 A.2d 264 (1967) (state court lacks jurisdiction unless the Board has in fact declined to exercise jurisdiction, despite employer's showing that "in all probability" the Board's jurisdictional yardsticks are not satisfied). In this connection, a complication results from the Board's occasional exercise of jurisdiction despite the failure to satisfy its jurisdictional standards (see NLRB v. WGOK, Inc., 384 F.2d 500 (5th Cir. 1967)), and from the shifting character of those standards. Nevertheless, the position of the Pennsylvania Supreme Court would re-create the no-man's-land and has been properly rejected elsewhere. See Russell v. IBEW, Local 569, 64 Cal. 2d 22, 48 Cal. Rptr. 702, 409 P.2d 926 (1966), and authorities cited therein.

(b) It is not clear whether an advisory opinion is binding on state tribunals.

(c) Congress did not specify the law governing state proceedings in the area of Board-declined jurisdiction. Although that question has evoked extensive commentary, the legislative history of §14(c) suggests that states were to be free to apply their own law, and state courts have so ruled. See McCoid, Notes on a "G-String": A Study of the "No-Man's-Land" of Labor Law, 44 Minn. L. Rev. 205, 240-242 (1959); Cooper v. Nutley Sun Printing Co., 36 N.J. 189, 175 A.2d 639 (1961); Kempf v. Carpenters' Local 1273, 229 Ore. 337, 367 P.2d 436 (1961). But see Hanley, Federal-State Jurisdiction in Labor's No-Man's-Land: 1960, 48 Geo. L.J. 709, 721-735 (1960).

(d) Section 103.3 of the Board's Rules and Regulations, promulgated in 1973, provides that the Board will not exercise jurisdiction in the horse and dog racing industry. Before promulgating §103.3, the Board made findings about the extensive state control over, and financial reliance on, this industry; the infrequency of its labor disputes; and the administrative difficulties arising from its pattern of short-term and sporadic employment. The Board also noted its own heavy workload. The Board did not, however, inquire extensively into either the industry's impact on interstate commerce or into the character of the industry's labor relations.

B.   EXCLUSIONS FROM THE NLRA

The most important express exclusions cover agricultural laborers; domestics; employees of federal, state, and local governments, including wholly owned government corporations; railroads and airlines subject to the Railway Labor Act; "independent contractors"; and "supervisors."[a]

The 1947 amendments expressly excluded "independent contractors" and "supervisors" from the Act's coverage. Determining whether borderline

[a]See §§2(2), 2(3), 2(11), and 14(a) of the Act.

personnel fell within those excluded categories — or within categories covered by implied exclusions — has raised difficult issues regarding both the interpretation of rubbery terms and the proper relationship among Congress, the Board, and the courts — issues to be explored in the materials below.

1. Independent Contractors

NLRB v. Hearst Publications, Inc.
322 U.S. 111 (1944)

RUTLEDGE, J. These cases arise from the refusal of respondents, publishers of four . . . daily newspapers, to bargain collectively with a union representing newsboys who distribute their papers on the streets of [Los Angeles]. . . . [The newsboys] may be "bootjackers," selling to the general public at places other than established corners, or they may sell at fixed "spots." They may sell only casually or part-time, or full-time; and they may be employed regularly and continuously or only temporarily. The units which the Board determined to be appropriate are composed of those who sell full-time at established spots. Those vendors, misnamed boys, are generally mature men, dependent upon the proceeds of their sales for their sustenance, and frequently supporters of families. Working thus as news vendors on a regular basis, often for a number of years, they form a stable group with relatively little turnover, in contrast to schoolboys and others who sell as bootjackers, temporary and casual distributors. . . .

The principal question is whether the newsboys are "employees." Because Congress did not explicitly define the term, respondents say its meaning must be determined by reference to common-law standards. In their view "common-law standards" are those the courts have applied in distinguishing between "employees" and "independent contractors" when working out various problems unrelated to the Wagner Act's purposes and provisions.

The argument assumes that there is some simple, uniform and easily applicable test which the courts have used . . . to determine whether persons doing work for others fall in one class or the other. Unfortunately this is not true. Only by a long and tortuous history was the simple formulation worked out which has been stated most frequently as "the test" for deciding whether one who hires another is responsible in tort for his wrongdoing.[19]

[19] The so-called "control test" with which common-law judges have wrestled to secure precise and ready applications did not escape the difficulties encountered in borderland cases by its reformulation in the Restatement of the Law of Agency §220. . . . [E]ven at the common law the control test and the complex of incidents evolved in applying it to distinguish an "employee" from an "independent contractor," for purposes of vicarious liability in tort, did not necessarily have the same significance in other contexts. . . .

But this formula has been by no means exclusively controlling in the solution of other problems. And its simplicity has been illusory because it is more largely simplicity of formulation than of application. Few problems in the law have given greater variety of application and conflict in results than the cases arising in the borderland between what is clearly an employer-employee relationship and what is clearly one of independent, entrepreneurial dealing. This is true within the limited field of determining vicarious liability in tort. It becomes more so when the field is expanded to include all of the possible applications of the distinction. . . . .

Whether, given the intended national uniformity, the term "employee" includes such workers as these newsboys must be answered primarily from the history, terms and purposes of the legislation. The word "is not treated by Congress as a word of art having a definite meaning. . . . " Rather "it takes color from its surroundings . . . [in] the statute where it appears," . . . and derives meaning from the context of that statute, which "must be read in the light of the mischief to be corrected and the end to be attained." South Chicago Coal & Dock Co. v. Bassett, 309 U.S. 251, 259. . . .

Congress was not seeking to solve the nationally harassing problems with which the statute deals by solutions only partially effective. It rather sought to find a broad solution, one that would bring industrial peace by substituting, so far as its power could reach, the rights of workers to self-organization and collective bargaining for the industrial strife which prevails where these rights are not effectively established. Yet only partial solutions would be provided if large segments of workers about whose technical legal position such local differences exist should be wholly excluded from coverage by reason of such differences. Yet that result could not be avoided, if choice must be made among them and controlled by them in deciding who are "employees" within the Act's meaning. Enmeshed in such distinctions, the administration of the statute soon might become encumbered by the same sort of technical legal refinement as has characterized the long evolution of the employee-independent contractor dichotomy in the courts for other purposes. The consequences would be ultimately to defeat, in part at least, the achievement of the statute's objectives. Congress no more intended to import this mass of technicality as a controlling "standard" for uniform national application than to refer decision of the question outright to the local law. . . .

The mischief at which the Act is aimed and the remedies it offers are not confined exclusively to "employees" within the traditional legal distinctions separating them from "independent contractors." . . . Unless the common-law tests are to be imported and made exclusively controlling, without regard to the statute's purposes, it cannot be irrelevant that the particular workers in these cases are subject, as a matter of economic fact, to the evils the statute was designed to eradicate and that the remedies it affords are appropriate for preventing them or curing their harmful effects in the special situation. Interruption of commerce through strikes and unrest may stem as well from labor disputes between some who, for other purposes, are technically "independent contractors" and their employers as from disputes between persons who, for those purposes, are "employees" and their employers. Cf. Drivers' Union v. Lake Valley Co., 311 U.S. 91. Inequality of bargaining power in controversies over wages, hours and working conditions may as well characterize the status of the one group as of the other. The former, when acting alone, may be as "helpless in dealing with an employer," as "dependent . . . on his daily wage" and as "unable to leave the employ and to resist arbitrary and unfair treatment" as the latter. For each, "union . . . [maybe] essential to give . . . opportunity to deal on equality with their employer." And for each, collective bargaining may be appropriate and effective for the "friendly adjustment of industrial disputes arising out of differences as to wages, hours, or other working conditions." In short, when the particular situation of employment combines these characteristics, so that the economic facts of the relation make it more nearly one of employment than of independent business enterprise with respect to the ends sought to be accomplished by the legislation, those characteristics may outweigh technical legal classification for purposes unrelated to the statute's objectives and bring the relation within its protections. . . .

It is not necessary in this case to make a completely definitive limitation around the term "employee." That task has been assigned primarily to the agency created by Congress to administer the Act. Determination of "where all the conditions of the relation require protection" involves inquiries for the Board charged with this duty. Everyday experience in the administration of the statute gives it familiarity with the circumstances and backgrounds of employment relationships in various industries, with the abilities and needs of the workers for self-organization and collective action, and with the adaptability of collective bargaining for the peaceful settlement of their disputes with their employers. The experience thus acquired must be brought frequently to bear on the question who is an employee under the Act. . . .

In making [the Board's] determinations as to the facts in these matters conclusive, if supported by evidence, Congress entrusted to it primarily the decision whether the evidence establishes the material facts. Hence in reviewing the Board's ultimate conclusions, it is not the court's function to substitute its own inferences of fact for the Board's, when the latter have support in the record. . . . Undoubtedly questions of statutory interpretation . . . are for the courts to resolve, giving appropriate weight to the judgment of those whose special duty is to administer the questioned statute. But where the question is one of specific application of a broad statutory term in a proceeding in which the agency administering the statute must determine it initially, the reviewing court's function is limited. . . .

In this case the Board found that the designated newsboys work continuously and regularly, rely upon their earnings for the support of themselves and their families, and have their total wages influenced in large measure by the publishers, who dictate their buying and selling prices, fix their markets and control their supply of papers. Their hours of work and their efforts on the job are supervised and to some extent prescribed by the publishers or their agents. Much of their sales equipment and advertising materials is furnished by the publishers with the intention that it be used for the publisher's benefit. Stating that "the primary consideration in the determination of the applicability of the statutory definition is whether effectuation of the declared policy and purposes of the Act comprehend securing to the individual the rights guaranteed and protection afforded by the Act," the Board concluded that the newsboys are employees. The record sustains the Board's findings and there is ample basis in the law for its conclusion.

The judgments are reversed and the causes are remanded for further proceedings not inconsistent with this opinion.

[Reed, J., concurred in the result; the dissenting opinion of Roberts, J., is omitted.[b]]

House of Representatives Report No. 245
80th Cong., 1st Sess., on H.R. 3020, at 18 (1947)

. . . [I]n . . . [NLRB] v. Hearst Publications, Inc., the Board expanded the definition of the term "employee" beyond anything that it ever had included before, and the Supreme Court, relying upon the theoretic "expertness" of the Board, upheld the Board. In this case the Board held independent merchants who bought newspapers from the publisher and hired people to sell them to be "employees." The people the merchants hired

---

[b][Similar characterization problems have, of course, arisen under other statutes whose applicability may turn on the existence of an employment relationship. See, e.g., Broden, General Rules Determining the Employment Relationship under Social Security Laws, 33 Temp. L.Q. 307, 381 (1960); Annot., 37 A.L.R. Fed. 95 (1978) (Fed. Insurance Contributions Act & Fed. Unemployment Tax Act); Annot., 51 A.L.R. Fed. 702 (1981) (Fair Labor Standards Act). — Eds.]

to sell the papers were "employees" of the merchants, but holding the merchants to be "employees" of the publisher of the papers was most far reaching. . . . [W]hen Congress passed the Labor Act, it intended words it used to have the meanings that they had when Congress passed the act, not new meanings that, nine years later, the Labor Board might think up. In the law, there always has been a difference, and a big difference, between "employees" and "independent contractors." "Employees" work for wages or salaries under direct supervision. "Independent contractors" undertake to do a job for a price, decide how the work will be done, usually hire others to do the work, and depend for their income not upon wages, but upon the difference between what they pay for goods, materials, and labor and what they receive for the end result, that is, upon profits. . . . To correct what the Board has done, and what the Supreme Court, putting misplaced reliance upon the Board's expertness, has approved, the bill excludes "independent contractors" from the definition of "employee."

NOTES

1. Despite congressional condemnation of the *Hearst* decision, the NLRB subsequently characterized as "employees" of a newspaper publisher all dealers who distributed the newspapers to carrier boys, retail stores, and vending racks; who maintained their own distribution facilities; and who hired and fired the carrier boys. The Board has announced a "right of control test, which turns essentially on whether the person for whom the services are performed retains the right to control the *manner* and *means* by which the result is to be accomplished or whether he controls only the result." In applying that test to newsdealers, the Board has subordinated the question of whether the publisher controlled the manner of distribution to questions of the control exercised by the publisher over matters such as wholesale and retail prices, the number of newspapers received by the dealer, and other restrictions on the dealer's freedom of action as a businessman. See El Mundo, Inc., 167 N.L.R.B. 760 (1967). But cf. F. H. Snow Canning Co., 156 N.L.R.B. 1075 (1966), and Denver Post, Inc., 196 N.L.R.B. 1162 (1972). The Board's characterizations of newspaper deliverers as "employees" on the basis of direction and control by the publishers have generally been upheld on review. See, e.g., Herald Co. v. NLRB, 444 F.2d 430 (2d Cir. 1971), *cert. denied*, 404 U.S. 990 (1971); News-Journal Co. v. NLRB, 447 F.2d 65 (3d Cir. 1971), *cert. denied*, 404 U.S. 1016 (1972). But cf. Brown v. NLRB, 462 F.2d 699 (9th Cir.), *cert. denied*, 409 U.S. 1008 (1972).

2. If "dealers" functioning as they did in *El Mundo* are not "independent contractors," are they nonetheless excluded from the Act's coverage as "supervisors"? For the NLRB's oscillation on this question, see Oakland Press, 249 N.L.R.B. 1081 (1980), *aff'd*, Teamster's Local 372 v. NLRB (Oakland Press), 116 L.R.R.M. 2584 (6th Cir. 1984).

NLRB v. United Insurance Co.
390 U.S. 254 (1968)

[The company contended that approximately 3,300 debit agents, who primarily collected premiums, prevented lapsing of policies, and sold new insurance, were independent contractors; it refused to recognize a union certified by the Board as the agents' representative. The court of appeals, agreeing with the company, declined to enforce the Board's bargaining order. The Supreme Court reversed.]

BLACK, J. [after mentioning Congress' adverse reaction to the *Hearst* decision, stated in part:] . . . On the one hand these debit agents perform their work primarily away from the company's offices and fix their own hours of work and work days; and clearly they are not as obviously employees as are production workers in a factory. On the other hand, however, they do not have the independence, nor are they allowed the initiative and decision-making authority, normally associated with an independent contractor. In such a situation as this there is no shorthand formula or magic phrase that can be applied to find the answer, but all of the incidents of the relationship must be assessed and weighed with no one factor being decisive. What is important is that the total factual context is assessed in light of the pertinent common-law agency principles. When this is done, the decisive factors in these cases become the following: the agents do not operate their own independent businesses, but perform functions that are an essential part of the company's normal operations; they need not have any prior training or experience, but are trained by company supervisory personnel; they do business in the company's name with considerable assistance and guidance from the company and its managerial personnel and ordinarily sell only the company's policies; the "Agent's Commission Plan" that contains the terms and conditions under which they operate is promulgated and changed unilaterally by the company; the agents account to the company for the funds they collect under an elaborate and regular reporting procedure; the agents receive the benefits of the company's vacation plan and group insurance and pension fund; and the agents have a permanent working arrangement with the company under which they may continue as long as their performance is satisfactory. Probably the best summation of what these factors mean in the reality of the actual working relationship was given by the chairman of the board of respondent company in a letter to debit agents about the time this unfair labor practice proceeding arose:

> if any agent believes he has the power to make his own rules and plan of handling the company's business, then that agent should hand in his resignation at once, and if we learn that said agent is not going to operate in accordance with the company's plan, then the company will be forced to make the agents final [sic]. . . .

The Board examined all of these facts and found that they showed the debit agents to be employees. This was not a purely factual finding by the Board, but involved the application of law to facts — what do the facts establish under the common law of agency: employee or independent contractor? . . . [S]uch a determination of pure agency law involved no special administrative expertise that a court does not possess. On the other hand, the Board's determination was a judgment made after a hearing with witnesses and oral argument . . . and on the basis of written briefs. Such a determination should not be set aside just because a court would, as an original matter, decide the case the other way. As we said in Universal Camera Corp. v. NLRB, 340 U.S. 474, "Nor does it [the requirement for canvassing the whole record] mean that even as to matters not requiring expertise a court may displace the Board's choice between two fairly conflicting views, even though the court would justifiably have made a different choice had the matter been before it *de novo*." 340 U.S., at 488. Here the least that can be said for the Board's decision is that it made a choice between two fairly conflicting views, and under these circumstances the Court of Appeals should have enforced the Board's order.

Brennan and Marshall, JJ., took no part in the consideration or decision of these cases.

NOTES

1. Is the judicial self-limitation prescribed by the Court consistent with the excerpt from H.R. Rep. No. 245, supra p. 708? With the Court's approach in *Babcock & Wilcox*, supra p. 161?

2. For the flip side of the problem of judicial deference to Board determinations, see Yellow Taxi Co. of Minneapolis v. NLRB, 721 F.2d

366 (D.C. Cir. 1983), in which Judge MacKinnon admonished the Board
"to halt its apparently *willful* defiance of long established, controlling judicial
precedent in independent contractor cases involving lessee cab drivers" and
threatened "measures more direct than refusing to enforce [the Board's]
orders" if the practice continued. Id. at 383. Judge Bork restricted his criticism to the Board's "somewhat disingenuous" treatment of the particular
facts involved; Judge Wright expressly dissociated himself from Judge
MacKinnon's criticism.

The Board's duty to formulate and apply a uniform national policy
seems to collide with its duty to respect decisions by the courts of appeals,
which are authorized by Congress to review its work. How should this
conflict, which pervades the entire Act and indeed the administrative process
generally, be resolved?

3. Another express exemption, for states and their political subdivisions
(see §§2(3) and 2(2)), has produced difficulties when a statutory employer
claims exemption on the ground that most of its employees provide services
to an exempt governmental entity. For fluctuations in the Board's views, see
National Transportation Service, 240 N.L.R.B. 565 (1979) (statutory employer exempted when exempt entity exercises such extensive control over
compensation and personnel policies as to preclude effective bargaining by
statutory employer). See generally Comment, The Political Subdivision
Exemption of the NLRA and the Board's Discretionary Authority, 1982
Duke L.J. 733.

2. Supervisors;[c] Managerial and Confidential Personnel

The 1947 exclusion of "supervisors" was designed to protect management
from the "divided loyalty" of its "agents," and thereby to remedy the loss of
productivity associated with both the unionization of foremen during World
War II and Board decisions granting protection to supervisors under the
Wagner Act. See H.R. Rep. No. 245, 80th Cong., 1st Sess. on H. 3020,
13-17 (1947), I Legis. History 304-308. The legislative history of Taft-Hartley also raised questions as to whether similar exclusions from some or all the
protections of the Act were implied for other workers said to be allied with
management, such as "confidential" and "managerial" personnel. These
and related questions are explored in the materials below.

---

[c]See generally Larrowe, Meteor on the Industrial Relations Horizon: The Foreman's
Association of America, 2 Labor History 259 (1961); Levinson, Foremen's Unions and the
Law, 1950 Wis. L. Rev. 79.

NLRB v. Hendricks County Rural Elec. Membership Corp.
454 U.S. 170 (1981)

BRENNAN, J. . . .

I

We have before us two cases. . . .

THE HENDRICKS CASE

Mary Weatherman was the personal secretary to the general manager and chief executive officer of respondent Hendricks County Rural Electric Membership Corp., a rural electric membership cooperative. She had been employed by the cooperative for nine years. In May 1977 she signed a petition seeking reinstatement of a close friend and fellow employee, who had lost his arm in the course of employment with Hendricks, and had been dismissed. Several days later she was discharged.

Weatherman filed an unfair labor practice charge . . . , alleging that the discharge violated §8(a)(1). . . . Hendricks' defense, *inter alia*, was that Weatherman . . . , as a "confidential" secretary . . . was impliedly excluded from the Act's definition of "employee" in §2(3). The . . . (ALJ) rejected this argument. He noted that the Board's decisions had excluded from bargaining units only those "confidential employees . . . [']who assist and act in a confidential capacity to persons who formulate, determine, and effectuate management policies in the field of labor relations.'" 236 N.L.R.B. 1616, 1619 (1978), quoting B. F. Goodrich Co., 115 N.L.R.B. 722, 724 (1956). Applying this "labor nexus" test, the ALJ found that Weatherman was not in any event such a "confidential employee." He also determined that Hendricks had discharged Weatherman for activity — signing the petition — protected by §7. . . . The Board affirmed . . . the [ALJ] and ordered that Weatherman be reinstated with back pay. 236 N.L.R.B., at 1616.

. . . A divided panel of the [Seventh Circuit] reversed and remanded . . . , 603 F.2d 25 (1979). Although the majority agreed with the Board's factual finding that Weatherman did not "assist in a confidential capacity with respect to labor relations policies," id., at 28, the majority, relying on language in a footnote to NLRB v. Bell Aerospace Co., 416 U.S. 267, 284, n. 12 (1974), held that "*all* secretaries working in a confidential capacity, without regard to labor relations, [must] be excluded from the Act." 603 F.2d, at 30. The Court of Appeals therefore remanded for a determination whether Weatherman came within this substantially broader definition of confidential secretary.

On remand, the Board found that Weatherman was not privy to the confidences of her employer and thus concluded that she did not fall within [that] broader definition of confidential secretary. . . . 247 N.L.R.B. No. 68 (1980).[5] . . . The Court of Appeals, by a divided panel, denied enforcement. 627 F.2d 766 (1980). The majority held that the Board had "actually reapplie[d] the old standard incorporating the labor nexus," and that the evidence in the record failed to support a finding that Weatherman did not come within the court's broader definition of confidential secretary. Id., at 770.

THE MALLEABLE CASE

. . . [T]he Union sought certification . . . for a unit of office clerical, technical, and professional personnel employed at the respondent's [Malleable's] facility in Beaver Dam, Wisconsin. . . .

Malleable challenged the inclusion of 18 employees in the unit on the ground that they had access to confidential business information. The Regional Director rejected Malleable's objection, concluding that none of the challenged 18 employees was a confidential employee under the Board's "labor nexus" test. . . . Malleable . . . refused to bargain with the Union [after it won the election and was certified]. . . . The Board found that Malleable [had] violated §§8(a)(5) and (1) . . . and issued a bargaining order. 244 N.L.R.B. 485 (1979).

. . . In an unreported opinion, a divided panel of the [Seventh Circuit] denied enforcement. . . . The majority noted that the Regional Director, in determining that none of the 18 individuals was a confidential employee, had applied the Board's labor-nexus test which the Seventh Circuit had rejected in . . . *Hendricks*. . . .

We granted . . . certiorari in both cases to resolve the conflict . . .

---

[5] The Board stated in part:

"Although Weatherman typed all of [general manager] Dillon's letters, this correspondence apparently did not relate to labor relations or personnel matters other than occasional letters referring to the dates of negotiating meetings with a union. Nor is there any evidence that it concerned confidential matters of any description. Weatherman generally did not place Dillon's telephone calls, nor did she keep a record of his appointments. Weatherman did share a partitioned office with Dillon, but no personnel records or confidential records of any type were kept there, excluding Dillon's testimony that he kept some papers concerning labor negotiations in a file behind his desk. Weatherman did not attend meetings of Respondent's board of directors or other management meetings. However, she did type minutes of meetings of the board of directors and the agenda for such meetings. While these meetings apparently occasionally involved personnel matters, there is no indication that such matters, or any other issues discussed during them, were confidential. Weatherman did not type internal memoranda regarding labor relations or personnel or employment matters. Finally, and most significantly, Dillon conceded at the hearing that the Respondent did not maintain secret or classified papers or documents." 247 N.L.R.B., at 498-499 (footnotes omitted).

respecting the propriety of the Board's practice of excluding from collective-bargaining units only those confidential employees with a "labor nexus," while rejecting any claim that all employees with access to confidential information are beyond the reach of §2(3)'s definition of "employee." . . . We hold that there is a reasonable basis in law for the Board's use of the "labor nexus" test. . . .

II

. . . Under a literal reading of the phrase "any employee," the workers in question are "employees." But for over 40 years, the NLRB, while rejecting any claim that the definition of "employee" in §2(3) excludes confidential employees, has excluded from . . . units determined under the Act those confidential employees satisfying the Board's labor-nexus test. Respondents Hendricks and Malleable argue that . . . all employees who may have access to confidential business information are impliedly excluded from the definition of employee in §2(3).

In assessing the respondents' argument, we must be mindful of the canon that "the construction of a statute by those charged with its execution should be followed unless there are compelling indications that it is wrong, especially where Congress has refused to alter the administrative construction." Red Lion Broadcasting Co. v. FCC, 395 U.S. 367, 381 (1969); . . . see NLRB v. Bell Aerospace Co., 416 U.S., at 274-275. . . .

A

. . . Although the [Wagner] Act's express exclusions did not embrace confidential employees, the Board was soon faced with the argument that all individuals who had access to confidential information of their employers should be excluded, as a policy matter, from the definition of "employee." The Board rejected such an implied exclusion, finding it to have "no warrant under the Act." Bull Dog Electric Products Co., 22 N.L.R.B. 1043, 1046 (1940). . . . But in [determining] appropriate bargaining units under §9, . . . the Board adopted special treatment for the narrow group of employees with access to confidential, labor-relations information of the employer. The Board excluded these individuals from bargaining units composed of rank-and-file workers.[10] See, e.g., Brooklyn Daily Eagle, 13 N.L.R.B. 974, 986 (1939). . . . The Board's rationale was that "management should not be required to handle labor relations matters through em-

---

[10] Although the early decisions did not explicitly preclude the Board from certifying a bargaining unit composed solely of confidential employees, that possibility was apparently foreclosed in Hoover Co., 55 N.L.R.B. 1321, 1322-1323 (1944), . . . thereby excluding confidential employees, as defined by the Board, from collective-bargaining units.

ployees who are represented by the union with which the [c]ompany is required to deal and who in the normal performance of their duties may obtain advance information of the [c]ompany's position with regard to contract negotiations, the disposition of grievances, and other labor relations matters." Hoover Co., 55 N.L.R.B. 1321, 1323 (1944).

Following its formulation, through 1946, the Board routinely applied the labor-nexus test in numerous decisions to identify those individuals who were to be excluded from bargaining units because of their access to confidential information. And in at least one instance . . . , the [labor-nexus] test was upheld. NLRB v. Poultrymen's Service Corp., 138 F.2d 204, 210-211 (CA3 1943). . . .

[The Court described the Board's approach, which was to exclude from rank and file bargaining units employees with access to the employer's confidential labor relations information. In 1946, in Ford Motor, 66 N.L.R.B. 1317, 1322, the Board narrowed that exclusion.] "Henceforth," the Board announced, it intended "to limit the term 'confidential' so as to embrace only those employees who assist and act in a confidential capacity to persons who exercise 'managerial' functions in the field of labor relations." This was the state of the law in 1947 when Congress [enacted] . . . the Taft-Hartley Act.

B

Although the text of the Taft-Hartley Act also makes no explicit reference to confidential employees, when Congress addressed the scope of the NLRA's coverage, the status of confidential employees was discussed. But nothing in that legislative discussion supports any inference . . . that Congress intended to alter the Board's pre-1947 determinations that only confidential employees with a "labor nexus" should be excluded from bargaining units. Indeed, the contrary appears.

The Taft-Hartley Act was in part a response to the Court's decision in Packard Motor Car Co. v. NLRB, 330 U.S. 485 (1947), which upheld the Board's certification of a bargaining unit composed of plant foremen. . . . Although the House and Senate initially passed differing bills, both Houses explicitly excluded "supervisors" from the definition of "employee" in the NLRA. H.R. 3020, 80th Cong., 1st Sess., §2(3) (1947); S. 1126, 80th Cong., 1st Sess., §2(3) (1947). In defining the term "supervisor," however, the bills differed substantially. The House bill defined "supervisor" to include . . . the confidential employee, broadly defined as one "who by the nature of his duties is given by the employer information that is of a confidential nature, and that is not available to the public, to competitors, or to employees generally, for use in the interest of the employer." The Senate, on

the other hand, did not include the confidential employee within its definition of "supervisor."

. . . In [the Conference Committee], the Senate definition of "supervisor," with no reference to confidential employees, prevailed. As described
in the statement of the House Managers, appended to the Conference
Report:

> The conference agreement, in the definition of "supervisor," limits such
> term to those individuals treated as supervisors under the Senate amendment.
> In the case of persons working in the labor relations, personnel and employ-
> ment departments, it was not thought necessary to make specific provision, as
> was done in the House bill, since the Board has treated, and presumably will
> continue to treat, such persons as outside the scope of the act. This is the
> prevailing Board practice with respect to such people as confidential secre-
> taries as well, and it was not the intention of the conferees to alter this practice
> in any respect.

H.R. Conf. Rep. No. 510, 80th Cong., 1st Sess., 35 (1947). With this
understanding, both Houses adopted the Conference Report. . . .

The Court of Appeals interpreted the legislative history of Congress'
exclusion of "supervisors" from the definition of "employees" as warranting
an implied exclusion for all workers who may have access to confidential
business information of their employer. That interpretation must be rejected.
It is flatly belied by the Conference Committee's rejection of the House
proposal of an exclusion of all confidential employees — for obviously the
House conceded on this issue to the Senate.

Indeed, the Taft-Hartley Act's express inclusion of "professional employees" under the Act's coverage negates any reading of the legislative
history as excluding confidential employees generally from the definition of
employee in §2(3). The definition of professional employees was intended to
cover "such persons as legal, engineering, scientific and medical personnel
together with their junior professional assistants." H.R. Conf. Rep. No. 510,
80th Cong., 1st Sess., 36 (1947). But surely almost all such persons would
likely be privy to confidential business information and thus would fall within
the broad definition of confidential employee excluded under the House bill.
It would therefore be extraordinary to read an implied exclusion for confidential employees into the statute that would swallow up and displace almost
the entirety of the professional-employee inclusion.

Plainly, too, nothing in the legislative history of the Taft-Hartley Act
provides any support for the argument that Congress disapproved the Board's
prior practice of applying a labor-nexus test to identify confidential employees whom the Board excluded from bargaining units. To the contrary,

the House Managers' statement accompanying the Conference Committee Report indicates that Congress intended to leave the Board's historic practice undisturbed.[19]

III

The Court of Appeals, and the respondents here, rely on dictum in a footnote to NLRB v. Bell Aerospace Co., 416 U.S. 267 (1974), to suggest that the 80th Congress believed that all employees with access to confidential business information of their employers had been excluded from the Wagner Act by prior NLRB decisions and that Congress intended to freeze that interpretation of the Wagner Act into law. The *Bell Aerospace* dictum is:

> In 1946 in Ford Motor Co., 66 N.L.R.B. 1317, 1322, the Board had narrowed its definition of "confidential employees" to embrace only those who exercised "'managerial' functions in the field of labor relations." The discussion of "confidential employees" in both the House and Conference Committee Reports, however, unmistakably refers to that term as defined in the House bill, which was not limited just to those in "labor relations." Thus, although Congress may have misconstrued recent Board practice, it clearly thought that the Act did not cover "confidential employees" even under a broad definition of that term.

Id., at 284, n. 12.

Obviously this statement was unnecessary to the determination whether *managerial* employees are excluded from the Act, which was the question decided in *Bell Aerospace*. In any event, the statement that Congress "clearly thought that the Act did not cover 'confidential employees,' even under a broad definition of that term," is error. The error is clear in light of our analysis above of the legislative history of the Taft-Hartley Act pertinent to

---

[19] It is true that the Conference Committee Report, in stating that the Board had treated confidential employees as "outside the scope of" the Wagner Act, could suggest that Congress failed to discern the Board's actual practice of excluding confidential employees, as defined by the labor-nexus test, from bargaining units, but still affording them the other protections of the Act. See, e.g., Bethlehem Steel Co., 63 N.L.R.B. 1230, 1232, and n. 2 (1945); Southern Colorado Power Co., 13 N.L.R.B. 699, 710 (1939), enf'd, 111 F. 2d 539 (CA10 1940). Whether Congress' use of that phrase indicates that it misperceived the state of the law in this respect is not clear since the Board itself, in several instances, had used a similarly imprecise shorthand description of its practice with respect to confidential employees. See General Motors Corp., 53 N.L.R.B., at 1098 (1943). . . .

Justice Powell, in dissent, relying in part on the conferees' use of the phrase "outside the scope of," criticizes the Board's practice of allowing "labor nexus" employees some protections under the Act. Because we hold that the Board properly determined that neither the secretary in *Hendricks* nor the 18 workers in *Malleable* were "labor nexus" employees, we have no occasion in this case to decide the propriety of this aspect of the Board's practice. . . .

the question. Moreover, the footnote erroneously implies that Ford Motor Co., 66 N.L.R.B. 1317 (1946), marked a major departure from the Board's prior practice. To the contrary, that Board decision introduced only a slight refinement of the labor-nexus test which the Board had applied in numerous decisions from 1941 to 1946. Certainly the Conference Committee, in approving the Board's "prevailing practice," was aware of the Board's line of decisions.[20] . . .

Thus the only plausible interpretation of the Report is that, in describing the Board's prevailing practice of denying certain employees the full benefits of the Wagner Act, the Report referred only to employees involved in labor relations, personnel and employment functions, and confidential secretaries *to such persons*. For that, in essence, is where the Board law as of 1947 stood. It follows that the dictum in *Bell Aerospace*, and the Court of Appeals' reliance upon it, cannot be squared with congressional intent, and should be "recede[d] from" now that the issue of the status of confidential employees is "squarely presented." NLRB v. Boeing Co., 412 U.S. 67, 72 (1973). . . .

[Following its reaffirmation in *B.F. Goodrich*, 115 N.L.R.B. 722 (1956), of the labor-nexus test formulated in *Ford Motor*], the Board has deviated from its stated intention [to apply that test] in only one major respect: it has . . . on occasion, consistent with the underlying purpose of the labor-nexus test . . . designated as confidential employees persons who, although not assisting persons exercising managerial functions in the labor-relations area, "regularly have access to confidential information concerning anticipated changes which may result from collective-bargaining negotiations." Pullman Standard Division of Pullman, Inc., 214 N.L.R.B. 762, 762-763 (1974). . . .

---

[20] Indeed, the Board's labor-nexus test had been brought to the attention of the Congress through the NLRB's annual reports. See, *e.g.*, 10 N.L.R.B. Ann. Rep. 34, and n. 92 (1945). . . .

Citing two *1941* NLRB decisions, E. P. Dutton & Co., Inc., 33 N.L.R.B. 761 (1941); Montgomery Ward & Co., 36 N.L.R.B. 69 (1941), Justice Powell finds "support in the case law" for his assertion that it was Congress' understanding that the Board had previously excluded from the Act all secretaries with access to confidential information, without regard to labor nexus. Post, at 5, n. 7. The significance he would give these two cases is clearly unwarranted. *E. P. Dutton* rested explicitly on the seminal labor-nexus decision in Brooklyn Daily Eagle, 13 N.L.R.B. 974 (1939), to exclude three secretaries from a bargaining unit. 33 N.L.R.B., at 767-768, n. 8. And in Montgomery Ward & Co., supra, the Board relied in turn on *E. P. Dutton*. See Montgomery Ward & Co., supra, at 73, n. 6, citing *E. P. Dutton*. But whatever support Justice Powell may find in these two decisions for his understanding of Board law *in 1941*, his reading of Congressional awareness is plainly erroneous; it entirely ignores Congressional acceptance of the countless Board decisions between 1941 and 1947 in which the NLRB, in determining whether individuals were confidential employees excludable from bargaining units, *consistently and explicitly* required a labor nexus.

In sum, our review of the Board's decisions indicates that the Board has never followed a practice of depriving all employees who have access to confidential business information from the full panoply of rights afforded by the Act. Rather, for over 40 years, the Board, while declining to create any implied exclusion from the definition of "employee" for confidential employees, has applied a labor-nexus test in identifying those employees who should be excluded from bargaining units because of access to confidential business information. We cannot ignore this consistent, longstanding interpretation of the NLRA by the Board. . . .

IV

The Court's ultimate task here is, of course, to determine whether the Board's "labor nexus" limitation on the class of confidential employees who, although within the definition of "employee" under §2(3), may be denied inclusion in bargaining units has "a reasonable basis in law." . . .

Clearly the NLRB's longstanding practice of excluding from bargaining units only those confidential employees satisfying the Board's labor-nexus test, rooted firmly in the Board's understanding of the nature of the collective-bargaining process, and Congress' acceptance of that practice, fairly demonstrates that the Board's treatment of confidential employees does indeed have "a reasonable basis in law." We therefore return finally to the disposition of the cases before us.

HENDRICKS

. . . [The Court of Appeals had affirmed the finding that Weatherman "did not act 'in a confidential capacity' with respect to labor relations matters." Nevertheless, it] denied enforcement . . . on the basis that the evidence failed to support the Board's additional finding, required by the Court of Appeals, that Weatherman had no access to confidential *non*-labor-related information. In approving the Board's limited labor-nexus exclusion, we have held that such a finding is irrelevant to the determination of whether the secretary was a confidential employee. . . .

Because there is . . . no dispute in this respect [that Weatherman meets the Board's labor-nexus test], and in any event no suggestion that the Board's finding regarding labor nexus was not supported by substantial evidence, we conclude that the Court of Appeals erred in holding that the record did not support the Board's determination that Weatherman was not a confidential employee with a labor nexus.[23] We therefore reverse the judg-

---

[23] We do not suggest that personal secretaries to the chief executive officers of corporations will ordinarily not constitute confidential employees. *Hendricks* is an unusual case, inasmuch as Weatherman's tasks were "deliberately restricted so as to preclude her from"

ment of the Court of Appeals in *Hendricks* . . . and remand with directions to enter an order enforcing the Board's order.

MALLEABLE

. . . [T]he respondent makes no argument that the 18 employees in question satisfy the labor-nexus test. . . . Rather, Malleable argues, and the Court of Appeals held, that the Board should have applied a broader definition of confidential employee to include all employees in possession of confidential business information. Having rejected the broad exclusion on which the Court of Appeals' judgment relies, we reverse that judgment. But because the Court of Appeals has not yet addressed Malleable's contentions that some of the 18 employees should have been excluded from the bargaining unit for reasons entirely unrelated to whether they are confidential employees, we remand *Malleable* for further proceedings consistent with this opinion.

POWELL, J., with whom The CHIEF JUSTICE, REHNQUIST, and O'CONNOR, JJ., join, concurring in part and dissenting in part.

I concur in the Court's holding that employees in the possession of proprietary or nonpublic business information are not for that reason excluded from the NLRA as "confidential" employees. . . . But because the majority's decision "tends to obliterate the line between management and labor,"[1] a line which Congress insisted be observed by enacting the Taft-Hartley Act, I dissent from the conclusion that the confidential secretary in this case is not a confidential employee excluded from the Act.

I . . .

The "confidential employee" exclusion and the labor nexus which the Board insists upon must be viewed as part of this larger effort to keep the line between management and labor distinct. . . . [U]seful as it may be in identifying employees who are allied to management, the "labor nexus" test is but a means to this end. By its rigid insistence on the labor nexus in the case

---

gaining access to confidential information concerning labor relations. 236 N.L.R.B. 1616, 1619 (1978). . . .

[1]Packard Motor Car Co. v. NLRB, 330 U.S. 485, 494 (1947) (Douglas, J., dissenting). . . . As Justice Douglas explained in his dissent in *Packard*, supra:

"The present decision [by the Court] . . . tends to obliterate the line between management and labor. It lends the sanctions of federal law to unionization at all levels of the industrial hierarchy. It tends to emphasize that the basic opposing forces in industry are not management and labor but the operating group on the one hand and the stockholder and bondholder group on the other. . . . [I]f Congress, when it enacted the [NLRA], had in mind such a basic change in industrial philosophy, it would have left some clear and unmistakable trace of that purpose. But I find none." Id. at 494-495. [Relocated from n. 4 of Justice Powell's dissent.— ED.]

of confidential secretaries, the Board, and now this Court, have lost sight of the basic purpose of the labor-nexus test itself and of the fundamental theory of our labor laws. Thus, it makes little sense to exclude "expediters," "assistant buyers," and "employment interviewers" as managerial but include within the rank and file confidential secretaries who are privy to the most sensitive details of management decisionmaking, who work closely with managers on a personal and daily basis, and who occupy a position of trust incompatible with labor-management strife. To include employees so clearly allied to management within the ranks of labor does a disservice to management and labor alike.[6]

II

The Court's decision . . . conflicts with explicit expressions of congressional intent on this subject. Congress only forbore from including an explicit provision in the Taft-Hartley Act excluding confidential secretaries because of its belief that the Board had been treating, and would continue to treat, such employees as allied to management. In discussing a proposed exclusion for confidential employees, the House Report stated:

> Most of the people who would qualify as "confidential" employees are executives and are excluded from the act in any event.
> The Board, itself, normally excludes from bargaining units *confidential clerks and secretaries to such people as these.*

H.R. Rep. No. 245, 80th Cong., 1st Sess., 23 (1947) (emphasis added). The Conference Report indicated a similar belief. . . . It was in light of these statements . . . that we felt confident in *Bell Aerospace* that "'Congress could not have supposed that, while "confidential secretaries" could not be organized, their bosses could be.'" 416 U.S., at 284, quoting Bell Aerospace Co. v. NLRB, 475 F.2d 485, 491-492 (CA2 1973).

   The Court's opinion argues that the foregoing explicit legislative history is to be ignored because the express exclusion in the House bill of confidential secretaries was omitted in Conference. But it is clear from the language in the Reports italicized above that the omission was prompted by an understanding that the Board itself consistently had excluded "such people as confidential secretaries." Indeed, the Members of Congress had no reason to believe that

---

[6]Just as management opposes the creation of conflicts of loyalty within its midst, neither does labor wish to represent employees who are allied to management. . . . See, e.g., Stroock & Stroock & Lavan, 253 N.L.R.B. 447, 448 (1980) ("the Employer argues the secretaries to the firm's executive committee are not confidential employees and should be included in the unit. The [union] counters that the Employer must have some confidential employees . . . "). . . .

it could be argued seriously that confidential secretaries to management officials were not among the "individuals allied with management." Swift & Co., 115 N.L.R.B. 752, 754 (1956). The "labor nexus," as increasingly narrowed by the Board and now accepted by this Court, is antithetical to any common-sense view or understanding of the role of confidential secretaries.

III

. . . I would reject the Board's position that confidential employees are not excluded from the Act as a whole but only from collective bargaining. The Board urges the Court to hold that even if the secretary in this case was conceded to be a confidential employee, indeed, *even if she had a labor nexus*, the company still could not have dismissed her without incurring liability under the Act.

The Court wisely declines the Board's invitation. See, ante, at 186, n. 19. Such a holding would be a major departure from the basic philosophy of the Act. See Packard Motor Car Co. v. NLRB, 330 U.S. 485 (1947). Under such an interpretation confidential employees *with* a labor nexus might do anything in furtherance of their allegiance to labor except join the union, and the company would be powerless to protect itself. Confidential employees might join picket lines, sign petitions advocating the cause of labor, speak out against management at employee meetings, and engage in all manner of concerted activity. Even in the midst of labor-management strife, the confidential secretaries to the top managers of the company, with daily access to the company's bargaining positions, might convey confidential information as to these positions to the union, as well as take their place on the picket lines. The company would be unable to dismiss them or demote them, at least without the risk of an unfair labor practice charge. . . . The Board developed the labor-nexus test because it recognized that "management should not be required to handle labor relations matters through employees who are represented by the union." Hoover Co., 55 N.L.R.B. 1321, 1323 (1944). Neither should management be required to expose its flank to confidential employees who are overtly committed to the union or the cause of labor in all but actual membership.

The legislative history of the Act contains no support whatever for the Board's position. To the contrary, the Congress repeatedly stated its belief that in addition to supervisors certain other employees would be excluded from the Act. . . .

. . . The majority accepts [the] holding [in *Bell Aerospace*]. Yet if managerial employees are excluded from the Act in its entirety I see no principled reason why confidential employees with a labor nexus should be treated differently. . . .

IV

After today's decision, labor must accept into its ranks confidential secretaries who are properly allied to management. And these confidential employees, who are privy to the daily affairs of management, who have access to confidential information, and who are essential to management's operation may be subjected to conflicts of loyalty when the essence of their working relationship requires undivided loyalty. The basic philosophy of the labor relations laws, the expressed intent of Congress, and the joint desire of labor and management for undivided loyalty all counsel against such a result.

NLRB v. Yeshiva University, 444 U.S. 672 (1980). The Court (5-4), through Powell, J., affirmed the denial of enforcement to a Board bargaining order based on the university's refusal to bargain with a Board-certified representative of a unit composed largely of full-time faculty members. The Court highlighted the following considerations: The faculty fell within the "judicially implied exclusion for 'managerial employees'" and therefore were beyond the Board's jurisdiction. The NLRB had failed to make relevant findings of fact; by contrast, the court of appeals had examined the record and found that the NLRB had ignored the faculty's extensive control over academic and personnel decisions and over the central policies of the university. (Justice Powell indicated that faculty lacking such effective influence might be subject to the NLRB's jurisdiction and that at Yeshiva itself "[i]t may be that a rational line could be drawn between tenured and untenured faculty. . . .") Justice Brennan, for the dissenters, urged that the university's administration, not the faculty, managed the university; that the faculty's influence arose from its collective expertise and not from any managerial prerogatives; and that the administration's interests and decisions did not always coincide with the faculty's — indeed, on subjects such as wages, hours, and other terms and conditions of employment, their interests "are often diametrically opposed."

NOTES

1. For the convincing suggestion that the terms "manager" and "supervisor" usually are not helpful designations of either university faculty or university administrators, see Sussman, University Governance Through a Rose-Colored Lens: NLRB v. Yeshiva, 1980 Sup. Ct. Rev. 27.

2. Does *Yeshiva* bar a state from ordering a university to bargain with respect to faculty who would be beyond the NLRB's jurisdiction?

3. The issue of whether particular personnel should be classified as "supervisors" has produced much litigation and often inconsistent results. One potential source of such inconsistency is that labor and management, as well as any "non-neutral" Board members, will prefer an expansive or narrow scope for the definition of "supervisors," depending on the context. For example, a worker classified as an "employee" is protected against discharge for his prounion activities; therefore, in a discharge case, a union would prefer that "supervisor" be read narrowly, while the employer would argue for a broader reading. On the other hand, in unit determination, if certain fringe workers are considered pro-management, the union might prefer an expansive view of "supervisor," which would exclude that group from the unit. For a context-based analysis, see Comment, The NLRB and Supervisory Status: An Explanation of Inconsistent Results, 94 Harv. L. Rev. 1713 (1981) (arguing that "[t]he Board applies the definition of supervisor that most widens the coverage of the Act . . . that maximizes both the number of unfair labor practice findings it makes and the number of unions it certifies").

In NLRB v. Res-Care, Inc., 705 F.2d 1461 (7th Cir. 1983) (with which cf. NLRB v. American Medical Services, Inc., 705 F.2d 1472 (7th Cir. 1983)), the court, upholding the Board's classification of practical nurses as "employees," rather than "supervisors," and enforcing the Board's bargaining order, made these points: First, the Board's finding was entitled to some judicial deference but less than if the Board had exercised its rule-making powers with respect to the medical context involved. Second, the seven practical nurses (a third of the nursing home's staff) would have constituted a high ratio of supervisors to rank and file. (But cf. Aladdin Hotel, 270 N.L.R.B. No. 122, 116 L.R.R.M. 1155 (1984), classifying as "supervisors" personnel occasionally but regularly exercising "supervisory functions" at gambling tables even though almost all personnel at those tables were consequently "supervisors.") Third, a person is not a "supervisor" merely because he directs another person's work but must also have authority over another's job tenure or employment conditions. Thus, professionals, e.g., lawyers (granted bargaining rights under §§2(12), 9(b)), are not "supervisors" merely because they give directions to a secretary. Fourth, if the practical nurses were held protected by the Act, "the employer will [not] be helplessly overmatched, lose control of the work force, have no loyal cadre of supervisors" (705 F.2d at 1468).

What are the yardsticks for determining whether an employer would be "overmatched" as a result of a particular classification? Should personnel be held to be covered by, or excluded from, the Act according to some sense of relative power in a particular case rather than the particular responsibilities of the personnel involved? What effect would an affirmative answer to that question have on the nature and length of records in Board proceedings? Finally, what basis, if any, is there for the court's suggestion that a Board finding resting on a rule promulgated under the Board's rule-making authority, under §6 of the Act, is entitled to more deference than a Board finding based directly on the Act?

Even when a particular category of personnel is excluded in general from statutory coverage, employer or union action against such personnel may bring the Act into play — as the following case illustrates.

Parker-Robb Chevrolet, Inc.
262 N.L.R.B. 402 (1982)

[On April 8 or 9, 1980, two supervisors, Doss and Langley, attended a union organizational meeting. Doss noted at the meeting that the union's representation of Parker-Robb's salesmen would be difficult, even with majority support. When a question arose about the supervisors' eligibility for inclusion in the unit, they were told they were ineligible. On April 9, the union claimed majority support and requested recognition. Almost immediately, the employer fired six of the 13 salesmen who had signed union authorization cards, including Berger and Mitchell. When Doss asked Used Car Sales Manager Parsons why Mitchell, "one of [our] best men," was being fired, Parsons replied that the company needed to cut back. When Doss asked New Car Sales Manager Greenberg about the discharge, he received the same explanation. (The ALJ, however, found on the basis of undisputed evidence that Greenberg, in a sales meeting earlier that day, had said business was good and the company was not contemplating cut-backs.) When Doss lost his temper and used obscenities during discussion of the discharges, Greenberg fired him too. The Board rejected the ALJ's conclusion that the firing of Doss violated the Act, but agreed with his findings that the employer's serious unfair labor practices had undermined the union's majority status and tainted the election, and, accordingly, entered a bargaining order.]

The [ALJ] . . . found that Respondent, "as part of its overall plan to discourage its employees' support of the Union," violated §8(a)(1) . . . by discharging . . . Doss, an admitted supervisor. We disagree.

Whether and under what circumstances the discharge of a supervisor will violate the Act has been a recurring issue . . . which has divided the Board and has produced sometimes confusing and inconsistent decisions. As noted above, the [ALJ] relied on DRW Corporation [248 N.L.R.B. 828

(1980)], where a panel of the Board found that the respondent violated §8(a)(1) by discharging a supervisor as part of "a pattern of conduct aimed at coercing employees in the exercise of their §7 rights." . . . [W]e conclude that the so-called "integral part" or "pattern of conduct" line of cases, as typified by *DRW Corporation*, . . . misread the intent of Congress when it amended the Act to exclude specifically "any individual employed as a supervisor" from the definition of . . . "employee." Accordingly, we have determined to overrule *DRW* and similar cases. . . . [W]e wish to emphasize that in certain circumstances the discharge of a supervisor may violate §8(a)(1). . . . [T]he practical effect of the amendments [excluding supervisors] was to free "employers to discharge supervisors without violating the Act's restraints against discharges on account of labor union membership." Beasley v. Food Fair of North Carolina, 416 U.S. 653, 654-655 (1974). Indeed, down through the years the Board has consistently held that a supervisor may be discharged for union activity.

Notwithstanding the general exclusion of supervisors from coverage . . . , the discharge of a supervisor may violate §8(a)(1) in certain circumstances, none of which are present here. Thus, an employer may not discharge a supervisor for giving testimony adverse to an employer's interest either at an NLRB proceeding or during the processing of an employee's grievance under the collective-bargaining agreement. Similarly, an employer may not discharge a supervisor for refusing to commit unfair labor practices, or because the supervisor fails to prevent unionization. In all these situations, . . . the protection afforded supervisors stems not from any statutory protection inuring to them, but rather from the need to vindicate employees' exercise of their §7 rights.

We are in full agreement that the discharge of a supervisor in the circumstances described above violates §8(a)(1) . . . because such discharge interferes with the exercise of employees' §7 rights. However, the "integral part" or "pattern of conduct" line of cases unduly extends these circumstances. . . . [T]his line of cases . . . [differs] from the other categories of supervisory discharge cases in several respects. Supervisors in the "integral part" or "pattern of conduct" cases were, themselves, active for the union or participated in the concerted activity. Other than the fact that the supervisors were discharged contemporaneously with rank-and-file employees, it is difficult to distinguish these cases from those in which the Board has found that the discharge of a supervisor does not violate the Act. The "integral part" or "pattern of conduct" line of cases has produced inconsistent decisions which cannot be reconciled with the statute, so that all concerned — employers, unions, and, indeed, supervisors, themselves — have no clear guidelines as to when supervisors may be lawfully discharged.

The confusion in this area . . . stems from extension of the rationale of the seminal *Pioneer Drilling* case[11] to . . . situations in which the only common denominator was a "pattern of pervasive unfair labor practices." In *Pioneer*, it was customary . . . in the drilling industry for rank-and-file employees to depend on the continued employment of the drillers who had hired and supervised them. Thus, it was reasonable . . . to find the discharge of the supervisors to be a mechanism to effectuate the employer's efforts to rid itself of union adherents in general, and to find it necessary to reinstate the driller, along with the employees, as an effective remedy.[12] [In] the cases after *Pioneer Drilling*, . . . the . . . situation in *Pioneer Drilling* has been unduly extended to apply the Act's protection to supervisors who merely join with rank-and-file employee protected activity and who are then subjected to the same discharge or other disciplinary treatment unlawfully meted out to those employees. No matter how appealing from an equitable standpoint, the "integral part" or "pattern of conduct" line of cases disregards . . . that *employees*, but not *supervisors*, are protected against discharge for engaging in . . . concerted activity. The results must be the same under the Act whether the supervisors engage in union or concerted activity by themselves or along with employees.

In a number of decisions, the Board has suggested that employer motivation in discharging a supervisor controls. That is, there is no violation if a supervisory discharge is motivated by disloyalty, but a supervisor's discharge is found to be unlawful if it is motivated by a desire to thwart organizational activity among employees. However, the justification for finding a violation and reinstating a supervisor who would otherwise be [outside] the Act is grounded upon the view that the discharge itself severely impinged on the employees' §7 rights. . . . In contrast, although we recognize that the discharge of a supervisor for engaging in union or concerted activity almost invariably has a secondary or incidental effect on employees, . . . when a supervisor is discharged either because he . . . engaged in union or concerted activity or because the discharge is contemporaneous with the unlawful discharge of statutory employees, or both, this incidental or secondary effect on the employees is insufficient to warrant an exception to the general statutory provision excluding supervisors from the protection of the Act. Thus, it is irrelevant that an employer may have hoped, or even expected,

---

[11] Pioneer Drilling Co., Inc., 162 N.L.R.B. 918 (1967), *enfd. in pertinent part*, 391 F.2d 961, 962-963 (10th Cir. 1968).

[12] Because of its novel . . . situation, we do not believe that the *Pioneer Drilling* rationale can or should be applied generally to supervisory discharge cases. In reaching the result herein, Chairman Van de Water finds it unnecessary to pass on the merits of the rationale expressed in *Pioneer Drilling*.

that its decision to terminate a supervisor for his union or concerted activity would cause employees to reconsider, and perhaps abandon, their own concerted or union activity. No matter what the employer's subjective hope or expectation, that circumstance cannot change the character of its otherwise lawful conduct.

In the final analysis, the instant case, and indeed all supervisory discharge cases, may be resolved by this analysis: The discharge of supervisors is unlawful when it interferes with the right of employees to exercise their §7 rights . . . , as when they give testimony adverse to their employer's interest or when they refuse to commit unfair labor practices. The discharge of supervisors as a result of their participation in union or concerted activity — either by themselves or when allied with rank-and-file employees — is *not* unlawful for the simple reason that employees, but not supervisors, have rights protected by the Act. When this test is applied to the situation present here, we are unable to conclude that the discharge of . . . Doss interfered with the right of employees to exercise their §7 rights or that his reinstatement is necessary to convey to employees the extent to which the Act protects these rights. . . .

[The concurring opinion of Member Jenkins is omitted.]

[In Automobile Salesmen's Union, Local 1095 v. NLRB, 711 F.2d 383 (D.C. Cir. 1983), the court, noting its limited review, upheld the Board's overruling of the "pattern of conduct cases," in *Parker-Robb*, as "consistent with the structure of the Act, [with] a reasonable basis in law, and certainly defensible." The court also observed that the lack of any evidence that Doss was fired for protesting the unfair labor practices committed against employees weighed in favor of affirmance. See Comment, Discharge of Supervisors Held Lawful Regardless of Intended Effect on Employee Rights: *Parker-Robb* Overrules Pattern of Conduct Theory, 32 Buffalo L. Rev. 317 (1983); cf. Brod, The NLRB Changes Its Policy On the Legality of an Employer's Discharge of a Disloyal Supervisor, 34 Lab. L.J. 13 (1983).]

NOTES

1. Member Jenkins, although concurring in the result, urged that the Board, in cases involving discharge of supervisors, should follow its usual approach to the significance of the employer's motive under §§8(a)(1) and 8(a)(3). Should that contention be accepted, given the policy behind excluding supervisors? How should situations involving dual motivations be handled? Cf. *Transportation Management*, supra p. 268. Would application of the "dominant motive" test, previously applied by some courts to the dis-

charge of employees, be compatible with the majority's approach in *Parker-Robb?* Preferable to it?

2. An employer rejects his employee's bid for promotion to supervisor solely because of the employee's vigorous participation in concerted activity. Has the employer violated the Act? If so, is the employee entitled to a Board-ordered promotion as well as an award of the salary differential? See NLRB v. Ford Motor Co., 683 F.2d 156 (6th Cir. 1982), accepted as law of the case, Ford Motor Co., 266 N.L.R.B. No. 115, 113 L.R.R.M. 1006 (1983). Cf. Hishon v. King & Spalding, 104 S. Ct. 2229 (1984) (Title VII's anti-discrimination provisions apply to selection of a law firm associate for partnership, at least where opportunity to become a partner was part and parcel of associate's status as employee).

Would the result be different if a new employer rejected the same individual's application for employment as a supervisor solely because of the applicant's protected activities in his previous employment? Cf. Ace Machine Co., 249 N.L.R.B. 623 (1980), permitting employer to interrogate nonemployee applicant for supervisory position about his attitudes towards unions; and declaring that such individuals may properly be treated as "supervisors," even though the individual is subsequently hired as a rank-and-file employee. Does that result square with the language of the Act?

3. See also Chapter 12(B) for materials on the legality of union fines against supervisors under various circumstances, and Paper Mill Workers, Local 962, 215 N.L.R.B. 414 (1974), *enforced*, 510 F.2d 1364 (9th Cir. 1975). (On remand, the Board reaffirmed earlier back pay award to a supervisor terminated because of union's violation of §8(b)(1)(B), urging need for that remedy to protect the employer's right to uncoerced and loyal representatives.)

4. The validity of state restrictions on concerted activities by, or on behalf of supervisors, is treated infra Chapter 8(C).

C. THE IMPACT OF NATIONAL REGULATION ON STATE JURISDICTION

For over three decades, the Court has struggled to formulate workable guidelines for state jurisdiction over labor relations. It has had little success. The Court has generally been divided; furthermore, individual justices and the Court itself have shifted emphasis from case to case.

The dominant theme comes, of course, from the supremacy clause:

The Court must strike down state regulation that "conflicts" with national laws. But whether invalidating conflict exists is typically a difficult issue. The decisive consideration, as the Court has reiterated, is Congress' intention concerning the kinds of actual and potential conflict to be avoided. However, with respect to labor-management disputes, Congress has in the main failed to provide any clear guidance. The customary difficulties created by the absence of legislative guidance were aggravated by two considerations: first, continuing divisions in the community over the adequacy of the national regulation; and, second, unions generally argued for (while employers opposed) preemption of state authority. Consequently, courts and ultimately the Supreme Court and the Justices individually seemed to be choosing not only between the merits of state and federal regulation, but also between one interest or the other. Such choices involved obvious tensions with an objective of the Norris-LaGuardia Act — limiting judicial policy making.

The nature and pervasiveness of state regulation impinging on labor relations has also complicated the Court's task. The states have not developed a discrete body of such regulation. Instead, they have applied to labor disputes both statutes tailor-made for such disputes and statutory and common laws of general application, such as laws against violence, defamation, trespass, restraint of trade, and racial discrimination in employment.

In seeking to accommodate such regulation to the national arrangements, the Court has delineated several potential sources of impermissible conflict. First, such conflict would arise if conduct federally protected against employer encroachments were proscribed by a state. Second, the states, by duplicating or supplementing federal prohibitions, and bringing state procedures and attitudes to bear on the conduct in question, could also create "conflict" with the federal scheme. Third, even though conduct was not federally protected or prohibited, state regulation filling what seemed to be a gap in federal regulation might nevertheless be "conflicting." This type of conflict occurs because Congressional failure to regulate certain conduct could sometimes be read as a mandate that such conduct should be free from all regulation, state as well as federal. Congress had, in the familiar phrase, "occupied the field," thereby telling the states to keep out. If that were the case, it would not be important to determine whether the NLRB or the state courts should first classify the conduct in question as "protected" or "prohibited" under the NLRA; regardless of how the conduct were classified, the states were preempted from dealing with it. Where, however, the existence of state power turned on whether the activities were neither federally protected nor prohibited, the issue arose as to whether states could be permitted to make the initial characterization.

Further complications arose from the Court's conviction that some state interests were so strong or traditional, and the competing federal interest so "peripheral," that Congress did not "intend" to foreclose state jurisdiction. It followed that state jurisdiction was preserved and could be exercised even though the NLRB had not previously decided whether the conduct in question was protected, prohibited, or ungoverned by the federal law. Such exercises of state jurisdiction plainly involved the risk that a state would restrict "protected" activity, or would devise remedies overlapping with, duplicating, or supplementing federal remedies — consequences that the general body of preemption doctrine was designed to avoid. But under the balance struck between state and federal interests in these exceptional classes of cases, such risks became acceptable.

In developing both general approaches to the preemption of state authority and exceptions to the general approach, the Court's concern went far beyond questions of process, i.e., whether a party aggrieved was to be relegated to a federal or state forum, or whether the state might be able to act after the NLRB's primary jurisdiction had been exercised. Frequently, only a state forum could provide speedy relief, comprehensive relief, or, indeed, any relief at all. The interest in providing effective relief for breaches of social norms plainly clashed with the interest in preserving a national, uniform, centralized regulatory system for labor relations.

For consideration of the Court's initial efforts, see Cox, Federalism in the Law of Labor Relations, 67 Harv. L. Rev. 1297 (1954); Meltzer, The Supreme Court, Congress, and State Jurisdiction over Labor Relations, 59 Colum. L. Rev. 6, 269, pts. 1-2 (1959).

Local 24, Teamsters v. Oliver
358 U.S. 283 (1959)

BRENNAN, J. As the result of multiemployer, multistate collective bargaining with the Central States Drivers Council, comprising local unions of truck drivers affiliated with [the Teamsters], a collective bargaining agreement, . . . effective February 1, 1955, and expiring January 31, 1961, was entered into by the locals and motor carriers in interstate commerce who operate under the authority of the Interstate Commerce Commission in twelve midwestern States, including Ohio. Article XXXII of this . . . agreement prescribes terms and conditions which regulate the minimum rental and certain other terms of lease when a motor vehicle is leased to a carrier by an owner who drives his vehicle in the carrier's service. The Ohio courts enjoined the petitioner, . . . Teamsters Local 24 and its president, and the respondent carriers, A.C.E. Transportation Company, Inc., and

Interstate Truck Service, Inc., Ohio employers, from giving effect to the provisions of Article XXXII. The Ohio courts held that the Article violates the Ohio antitrust law. . . .

No claim is made that Article XXXII violates any provision of federal law. . . . The respondent, Revel Oliver, a member of the union, is the owner of motor equipment which, at the time the collective bargaining agreement was negotiated, was subject to written lease agreements with the carrier respondents, A.C.E. Transportation Company, Inc., and Interstate Truck Service, Inc. The terms and conditions of the leases, particularly in regard to rental compensation, differ substantially from those provided in Article XXXII.

At the trial the respondent carriers joined with Oliver in making the attack on the Article. The petitioners defended on the ground that the State could not lawfully . . . apply its antitrust law to cause a forfeiture of the product . . . of federally sanctioned collective bargaining rights. . . . The Court of Common Pleas held . . . that the [NLRA] could not "be reasonably construed to permit this remote and indirect approach to the subject of wages," and that Article XXXII [violated] the State's antitrust law because "there are restrictions and restraints imposed upon articles [the leased vehicles] that are widely used in trade and commerce. . . . [and that] preclude an owner of property from reasonable freedom of action in dealing with it." Ohio's Ninth Judicial District Court of Appeals . . . heard the case de novo and affirmed the judgment of the Court of Common Pleas, adopting its opinion. The Court of Appeals entered a permanent injunction perpetually restraining the petitioners and the respondent carriers (1) "from entering into any agreements . . . or carrying out the . . . requirements . . . of any such agreement, which will require the alteration" of Revel Oliver's "existing lease or leasing agreement"; (2) "from entering into any . . . agreement or stipulation in the future, or the negotiation therefor, the . . . tendency of which is to . . . determine in any manner the rate to be charged for the use of" Revel Oliver's equipment; (3) "from giving force and effect to Section 32 [sic] of the Contract . . . or any modification . . . thereof, the . . . tendency of which shall attempt to fix the rates" for the use of Revel Oliver's equipment. . . .

First. The Ohio courts rejected the petitioners' contention that the evidence conclusively established that Article XXXII dealt with subject matter within the scope of [federally sanctioned] "collective bargaining". . . . The state courts rested their judgments principally on the minimum rental regulations of §12 of the Article. . . . These regulations were held to constitute the Article a price-fixing arrangement violating the Ohio antitrust law in that they evidenced "concerted action of the Union combining with a nonla-

bor third party in a formal contract. . . . [the] effect [of which] is to oppress
and destroy competition. . . . [and] preclude an owner of property from
reasonable freedom of action in dealing with it."

. . . [I]n considering whether the Article deals with a subject matter
within the scope of collective bargaining as defined by federal law the Ohio
courts did not give proper significance to the Article's narrowly restricted
application to the times when the owner drives his leased vehicle for the
carrier, and to the adverse effects upon the negotiated wage scale which
might result when the rental for the use of the leased vehicle was unregulated
at these times. Since no claim was presented to the Ohio courts that the
petitioners sought to apply these regulations to Revel Oliver's arrangements
with the respondent carriers except on the very infrequent and irregular
occasions when Oliver drove one of his vehicles for a carrier, we take it that
the Ohio courts' opinions and judgments relate only to the validity of the
Article as applied at such times. . . .

In the light of the Article's history and purpose, we cannot agree with
the Court of Common Pleas that its regulations constitute a "remote and
indirect approach to the subject of wages," outside the range of matters on
which the federal law requires the parties to bargain. The . . . Article and
its unchallenged history show that its objective is to protect the negotiated
wage scale against the possible undermining through diminution of the
owner's wages for driving which might result from a rental which did not
cover his operating costs. . . . Looked at in this light, . . . the point of the
Article is obviously not price fixing but wages. The regulations embody not
the "remote and indirect approach to the subject of wages" perceived by the
Court of Common Pleas but a direct frontal attack upon a problem thought to
threaten the maintenance of the basic wage structure established by the
collective bargaining contract. The inadequacy of a rental which means that
the owner makes up his excess costs from his driver's wages not only clearly
bears a close relation to labor's efforts to improve working conditions but is in
fact of vital concern to the carrier's employed drivers; an inadequate rental
might mean the progressive curtailment of jobs through withdrawal of more
and more carrier-owned vehicles from service. . . . It is not necessary to
attempt to set precise outside limits to the subject matter properly included
within the scope of mandatory collective bargaining, cf. Labor Board v.
Borg-Warner Corp., 356 U.S. 342, to hold, as we do, that the obligation
under §8(d) on the carriers and their employees to bargain collectively "with
respect to wages, hours, and other terms and conditions of employment" and
to embody their understanding in "a written contract incorporating any
agreement reached," found an expression in the subject matter of Article
XXXII. . . . And certainly bargaining on this subject through their representatives was a right of the employees protected by §7 of the Act.

Second. We must decide whether Ohio's antitrust law may be applied to prevent the contracting parties from carrying out their agreement upon a subject matter as to which federal law directs them to bargain. Little extended discussion is necessary to show that Ohio law cannot be so applied. We need not concern ourselves today with a contractual provision dealing with a subject matter that the parties were under no obligation to discuss. . . . Within the area in which collective bargaining was required, Congress was not concerned with the substantive terms upon which the parties agreed. . . . The purposes of the Acts are served by bringing the parties together and establishing conditions under which they are to work out their agreement themselves. To allow the application of the Ohio antitrust law here would wholly defeat the full realization of the congressional purpose. The application would frustrate the parties' solution of a problem which Congress has required them to negotiate in good faith toward solving, and in the solution of which it imposed no limitations relevant here. Federal law here created the duty upon the parties to bargain collectively; Congress has provided for a system of federal law applicable to the agreement the parties made in response to that duty, Textile Workers Union v. Lincoln Mills, 353 U.S. 448; and federal law sets some outside limits (not contended to be exceeded here) on what their agreement may provide, see Allen Bradley Co. v. Local Union, 325 U.S. 797. . . . [T]here is no room in this scheme for the application here of this state policy limiting the solutions that the parties' agreement can provide to the problems of wages and working conditions. . . . Since the federal law operates here, in an area where its authority is paramount, to leave the parties free, the inconsistent application of state law is necessarily outside the power of the State. Hill v. Florida, 325 U.S. 538, 542-544. Cf. International Union v. O'Brien, 339 U.S. 454, 457; Amalgamated Assn. v. Wisconsin Employment Relations Board, 340 U.S. 383. . . . The solution worked out by the parties was not one of a sort which Congress has indicated may be left to prohibition by the several States. Of course, the paramount force of the federal law remains even though it is expressed in the details of a contract federal law empowers the parties to make, rather than in terms in an enactment of Congress. See Railway Employes' Dept. v. Hanson, 351 U.S. 225, 232. Clearly it is immaterial that the conflict is between federal labor law and the application of what the State characterizes as an antitrust law. ". . . Congress has sufficiently expressed its purpose to . . . exclude state prohibition, even though that with which the federal law is concerned as a matter of labor relations be related by the State to the more inclusive area of restraint of trade." Weber v. Anheuser-Busch, Inc., 348 U.S. 468, 481. We have not here a case of a collective bargaining agreement in conflict with a local health or safety regulation; the conflict here is between the federally sanctioned agreement and state policy which seeks specifically to adjust relationships in the world of commerce. . . .

Reversed.

The Chief Justice, Frankfurter, J., and Stewart, J., took no part in the consideration or decision of this case.

WHITTAKER, J., believing that respondent Oliver, while driving his own tractor in the performance of his independent contract with the respondent carriers, was not an employee of those carriers, but was an independent contractor, and that, as such, he was expressly excluded from the coverage of the [NLRA], . . . would affirm the judgment of the [Ohio] Court of Appeals. . . .

NOTES

1. A collective bargaining agreement, enforceable under §301, bars discharges without "just cause" and provides that all claims of improper discharge be channelled through the grievance-arbitration procedure. An employee subject to that agreement brings a state court damage action and alleges that he was fired because he disobeyed his supervisor's order to deliver spoiled milk and, instead, notified the health department, which condemned the milk. Count I alleged defendant's termination of the plaintiff's employment in bad faith, and wrongful and intentional infliction of emotional distress, all in violation of the state's public policy. Count II alleged that the termination was a breach of both the collective agreement and the plaintiff's individual agreement with the company. The company moved to dismiss both counts. What result? Would it be material if, before the plaintiff had filed his action, an arbitrator, acting under the collective agreement, had denied the plaintiff's grievance? Cf. Garibaldi v. Lucky Food Stores, 726 F.2d 1367 (9th Cir. 1984); see also Alexander v. Gardner Denver Co., reproduced infra p. 1104.

2. California requires that employers pay for prorated vacation time to employees who are discharged or leave their employers before becoming eligible for vacation pay. An employer has a collective bargaining agreement that bars prorating for employees who do not meet the contractual eligibility provisions. An employee entitled to proration under the California statute, but not under the collective agreement, brings a state court action against the employer. The employer moves to dismiss. What result? Cf. California Hospital Assn. v. Henning, 569 F. Supp. 1544 (C.D. Cal. 1983).

The effect of ERISA, and to some extent of *Oliver*, on state regulation of pensions and other items frequently covered in collective agreements is considered in Malone v. White Motor Corp., 435 U.S. 497 (1978).

3. In *Oliver*, the use of state antitrust law as a basis for outlawing the disputed provision of the collective agreement depended on the presence of concerted activity. One purpose of the federal labor acts was to protect activities from invalidation merely because they were concerted. Does respect for that purpose require the expansive language in *Oliver* validating arrangements, otherwise unlawful under state law, merely because they are the product of "concerted activity," i.e., "mandatory bargaining"? Was that sweeping language necessary to the decision in *Oliver?*

4. A state legislature enacts a law requiring a business planning to relocate outside the state to notify in writing its employees and designated officers of the municipality where the plant is located, at least 90 days prior to the relocation. Noncomplying firms are subject to penalties as high as $50,000. Prior to the enactment or even the introduction of this law, Mobile, Inc., had entered into a collective bargaining agreement with an NLRB-certified union, expressly providing that Mobile had the unrestricted right to relocate its business, subject only to specified severance pay obligations to its employees. Would *Oliver* bar the state from enforcing that law against Mobile? What if the statute had been enacted before Mobile had negotiated its collective agreement?

San Diego Building Trades Council v. Garmon
359 U.S. 236 (1959)

FRANKFURTER, J. This case is before us for the second time. The present litigation began with a dispute between the petitioning unions and respondents, copartners in the business of selling lumber and other materials in California. Respondents began an action in the Superior Court for the County of San Diego, asking for an injunction and damages. . . . [T]he trial court found the following facts. In March of 1953 the unions sought from respondents an agreement to retain in their employ only those workers who were already members of the unions, or who applied for membership within thirty days. Respondents refused, claiming that none of their employees had shown a desire to join a union, and that, in any event, they could not accept such an arrangement until one of the unions had been designated by the employees as a collective bargaining agent. The unions began at once peacefully to picket the respondents' place of business, and to exert pressure on customers and suppliers in order to persuade them to stop dealing with respondents. The sole purpose of these pressures was to compel execution of the proposed contract. The unions contested this finding, claiming that the only purpose of their activities was to educate the workers and persuade them to become members. On the basis of its findings, the court enjoined the unions from picketing and from the use of other pressures to force an agreement, until one of them had been properly designated as a collective bargaining agent. The court also awarded $1,000 damages for losses found to have been sustained.

At the time the suit in the state court was started, respondents had begun a representation proceeding before the [NLRB]. The Regional Director declined jurisdiction, presumably because the amount of interstate commerce involved did not meet the Board's monetary standards. . . .

. . . [T]he California Supreme Court [affirmed] the Superior Court, holding that, since the [NLRB] had declined to exercise its jurisdiction, the California courts had power over the dispute. They further decided that the conduct of the union [had violated] §8(b)(2) . . . , and hence was not privileged under California law. . . . [T]his decision did not specify what law, state or federal, was the basis of the relief granted. . . .

We . . . decided the case together with Guss v. Utah Labor Relations Board, 353 U.S. 1, and Amalgamated Meat Cutters v. Fairlawn Meats, Inc., 353 U.S. 20. In those cases, we held that the refusal of the [NLRB] to assert jurisdiction did not leave with the States power over activities they otherwise would be preempted from regulating. Both *Guss* and *Fairlawn* involved relief of an equitable nature. In vacating and remanding the judgment of the California court in this case, we pointed out that those cases controlled this one, "in its major aspects," 353 U.S., at 28. However, since it was not clear whether the judgment for damages would be sustained under California law, we remanded to the state court for consideration of that local law issue. The federal question, namely, whether the [NLRA] precluded California from granting an award for damages arising out of the conduct in question, could not be appropriately decided until the antecedent state law was decided by the state court.

On remand, the California court . . . set aside the injunction, but sustained the award of damages. Garmon v. San Diego Bldg. Trades Council, 49 Cal. 2d 595 (three judges dissenting). After deciding that California had jurisdiction to award damages for injuries caused by the union's activities, the California court held that those activities constituted a tort based on an unfair labor practice under state law. In so holding the court relied on general tort provisions of the California Civil Code, §§1677, 1708, as well as state enactments dealing specifically with labor relations. . . .

We again granted certiorari to determine whether the California court had jurisdiction to award damages arising out of peaceful union activity which it could not enjoin. . . .

. . . We have necessarily been concerned with the potential conflict of two law-enforcing authorities, with the disharmonies inherent in two systems, one federal the other state, of inconsistent standards of substantive law and differing remedial schemes. But the unifying consideration of our decisions has been regard to the fact that Congress has entrusted administration of the labor policy for the Nation to a centralized administrative agency, armed with its own procedures, and equipped with its specialized knowledge and cumulative experience. . . .

Administration is more than a means of regulation; administration is regulation. We have been concerned with conflict in its broadest sense; conflict with a complex and interrelated federal scheme of law, remedy, and administration. Thus, judicial concern has necessarily focused on the nature of the activities which the States have sought to regulate, rather than on the method of regulation adopted. When the exercise of state power over a particular area of activity threatened interference with the clearly indicated policy of industrial relations, it has been judicially necessary to preclude the States from acting. However, due regard for the presuppositions of our embracing federal system, including the principle of diffusion of power not as a matter of doctrinaire localism but as a promoter of democracy, has required us not to find withdrawal from the States of power to regulate where the activity regulated was a merely peripheral concern of the Labor Management Relations Act. See Machinists v. Gonzales, 356 U.S. 617. Or where the regulated conduct touched interests so deeply rooted in local feeling and responsibility that, in the absence of compelling congressional direction, we could not infer that Congress had deprived the States of the power to act.

When it is clear or may fairly be assumed that the activities which a State purports to regulate are protected by §7 of the [NLRA], or constitute an unfair labor practice under §8, due regard for the federal enactment requires that state jurisdiction must yield. To leave the States free to regulate conduct so plainly within the central aim of federal regulation involves too great a danger of conflict between power asserted by Congress and requirements imposed by state law. Nor has it mattered whether the States have acted through laws of broad general application rather than laws specifically directed towards the governance of industrial relations.[3] Regardless of the mode adopted, to allow the States to control conduct which is the subject of national regulation would create potential frustration of national purposes.

At times it has not been clear whether the particular activity regulated by the States was governed by §7 or §8 or was, perhaps, outside both these

---

[3] See Weber v. Anheuser-Busch, Inc., 348 U.S. 468, in which it was pointed out that the state court had relied on a general restraint of trade statute. . . . The case before us involves both tort law of general application and specialized labor relations statutes.

sections. But courts are not primary tribunals to adjudicate such issues. It is essential to the administration of the Act that these determinations be left in the first instance to the [NLRB]. What is outside the scope of this Court's authority cannot remain within a State's power and state jurisdiction too must yield to the exclusive primary competence of the Board. See, e.g., Garner v. Teamsters Union, 346 U.S. 485, especially at 489-491. . . .

The case before us is such a case. The adjudication in California has throughout been based on the assumption that the behavior of the petitioning unions constituted an unfair labor practice. This conclusion was derived by the California courts from the facts as well as from their view of the Act. It is not for us to decide whether the [NLRB] would have, or should have, decided these questions in the same manner. When an activity is arguably subject to §7 or §8 of the Act, the States as well as the federal courts must defer to the exclusive competence of the [NLRB] if the danger of state interference with national policy is to be averted.

To require the States to yield to the primary jurisdiction of the National Board does not ensure Board adjudication of the status of a disputed activity. If the Board decides, subject to appropriate federal judicial review, that conduct is protected by §7, or prohibited by §8, then the matter is at an end, and the States are ousted of all jurisdiction. Or, the Board may decide that an activity is neither protected nor prohibited, and thereby raise the question whether such activity may be regulated by the States.[4] However, the Board may also fail to determine the status of the disputed conduct by declining to assert jurisdiction, or by refusal of the General Counsel to file a charge, or by adopting some other disposition which does not define the nature of the activity with unclouded legal significance. This was the basic problem underlying our decision in Guss v. Utah Labor Relations Board, 353 U.S. 1 [see supra p. 703]. . . . It follows that the failure of the Board to define the legal significance under the Act of a particular activity does not give the States the power to act. In the absence of the Board's clear determination that an activity is neither protected nor prohibited or of compelling precedent applied to essentially undisputed facts, it is not for this Court to decide whether such activities are subject to state jurisdiction. The withdrawal of this narrow area from possible state activity follows from our decisions in *Weber* and *Guss*. The governing consideration is that to allow the States to control activities that are potentially subject to federal regulation involves too great a danger of conflict with national labor policy.

[4]See Auto Workers v. Wisconsin Board [*Briggs Stratton*], 336 U.S. 245. The approach taken in that case, in which the Court undertook for itself to determine the status of the disputed activity, has not been followed in later decisions, and is no longer of general application.

In the light of these principles the case before us is clear. Since the [NLRB] has not adjudicated the status of the conduct for which the State of California seeks to give a remedy in damages, and since such activity is arguably within the compass of §7 or §8 of the Act, the State's jurisdiction is displaced.

Nor is it significant that California asserted its power to give damages rather than to enjoin what the Board may restrain though it could not compensate. Our concern is with delimiting areas of conduct which must be free from state regulation if national policy is to be left unhampered. Such regulation can be as effectively exerted through an award of damages as through some form of preventive relief. The obligation to pay compensation can be, indeed is designed to be, a potent method of governing conduct and controlling policy. Even the States' salutary effort to redress private wrongs or grant compensation for past harm cannot be exerted to regulate activities that are potentially subject to the exclusive federal regulatory scheme. See Garner v. Teamsters Union, 346 U.S. 485, 492-497. It may be that an award of damages in a particular situation will not, in fact, conflict with the active assertion of federal authority. The same may be true of the incidence of a particular state injunction. To sanction either involves a conflict with federal policy in that it involves allowing two law-making sources to govern. In fact, since remedies form an ingredient of any integrated scheme of regulation, to allow the State to grant a remedy here which has been withheld from the [NLRB] only accentuates the danger of conflict.

It is true that we have allowed the States to grant compensation for the consequences, as defined by the traditional law of torts, of conduct marked by violence and imminent threats to the public order. United Automobile Workers v. Russell, 356 U.S. 634; United Construction Workers v. Laburnum Corp., 347 U.S. 656. We have also allowed the States to enjoin such conduct. Youngdahl v. Rainfair, 355 U.S. 131; Auto Workers v. Wisconsin Board, 351 U.S. 266. State jurisdiction has prevailed in these situations because the compelling state interest, in the scheme of our federalism, in the maintenance of domestic peace is not overridden in the absence of clearly expressed congressional direction. We recognize that the opinion in United Construction Workers v. Laburnum Corp., 347 U.S. 656, found support in the fact that the state remedy had no federal counterpart. But that decision was determined, as is demonstrated by the question to which review was restricted, by the "type of conduct" involved, i.e., "intimidation and threats of violence." In the present case there is no such compelling state interest. [Reversed.]

[Harlan, J., joined by Whittaker and Stewart, JJ., concurred on "the narrow ground" that the union's activities could fairly be deemed protected.

Distinguishing between preventive procedures and damage awards, he expressed profound disagreement with the Court's foreclosure of state damage awards for conduct arguably or actually prohibited by the national scheme. He also observed that neither principle nor precedent supported the Court's intimation that the states lacked jurisdiction over conduct neither protected nor prohibited.]

Linn v. United Plant Guard Wkrs., Local 114, 383 U.S. 53 (1966). Relying on state law, Linn, a Pinkerton manager, sued the union, two of its officers, and a Pinkerton employee, alleging that during an organizational campaign among Pinkerton employees, the defendants' leaflets had willfully and falsely accused plaintiff and other managers of lying to the employees and subjecting them to other illegal and improper tactics. Prior to the filing of Linn's suit, the NLRB's Regional Director had declined to issue a §8(b)(1)(A) complaint, having found the union not responsible for the leaflet distribution. The district court dismissed Linn's action, reasoning that even if the union had been responsible, *Garmon* preempted the court's jurisdiction. The court of appeals affirmed, limiting its holding to an action for defamation growing out of, and relevant to, an organizational campaign among employees covered by the NLRA.

The Supreme Court reversed and remanded. Speaking through Clark, J., it noted several potential grounds for preemption. For example, the NLRB had granted protection to certain defamatory and false statements if made without "malice" ("a deliberate intention to falsify"). The Board had also protected epithets, such as "scab," "unfair," "liar," made during organizational campaigns. In addition, malicious defamation might constitute a basis for setting aside an election or finding a violation of §8.

Nevertheless, the Court found two related justifications for preserving state jurisdiction over certain defamatory statements made during labor disputes. First, redressing knowing and reckless defamation was "peripheral" to the jurisdiction of the NLRB, which could not remedy injury to the victim. On the other hand, concern for the victim was "deeply rooted in local feeling and responsibility" and, therefore, covered by the exception embodied in *Garmon*. Furthermore, the Court, in order to curb interference with the national act, imposed two special requirements for recovery under state law: (1) compliance with the "malice" test announced in New York Times v. Sullivan, 376 U.S. 254 (1964) (proof of defendant's knowledge of falsity or of his reckless indifference to falsity or truth); and (2) proof of compensable damages as a prerequisite for recovering punitive damages. Finally, the Court noted that it would reexamine its approach in light of experience in order to protect national policy against impairment.

Black, J., dissented, urging preemption, inter alia.

Fortas, J., joined by Warren, C.J., and Douglas, J., dissented, urging that libel suits arising from, and involving participants in, labor disputes, would disrupt the balance struck by Congress and that the outcome of libel suits was likely to reflect community attitudes toward unions rather than an appreciation of the forces underlying labor-management relations.

NOTES

1. A local union was seeking to sign up the handful of bargaining unit employees who were not members. Its monthly newsletter included one Austin in a "List of Scabs." He disclaimed knowing what a scab was but objected to being called one. The newsletter again printed his name (with 12 others) and added a pungent definition sometimes attributed to Jack London:

The Scab

After God had finished the rattlesnake, the toad, and the vampire, He had some awful substance left with which He made a *scab*.

A scab is a two-legged animal with a corkscrew soul, a water brain, a combination backbone of jelly and glue. Where others have hearts, he carries a tumor of rotten principles.

When a scab comes down the street, men turn their backs and Angels weep in Heaven, and the Devil shuts the gates of hell to keep him out.

No man (or woman) has a right to scab so long as there is a pool of water to drown his carcass in, or a rope long enough to hang his body with. Judas was a gentleman compared with a scab. For betraying his Master, he had character enough to hang himself. A scab has not.

Esau sold his birthright for a mess of pottage. Judas sold his Savior for thirty pieces of silver. Benedict Arnold sold his country for a promise of a commission in the British Army. *The scab sells his birthright, country, his wife, his children and his fellowmen for an unfulfilled promise from his employer.*

Esau was a traitor to himself; Judas was a traitor to his God; Benedict Arnold was a traitor to his country; a SCAB is a traitor to his God, his country, his family and his class.

Three employees listed as "scabs" in the newsletter brought a state action against the local for libel. The Supreme Court reversed state court awards of $10,000 (compensatory damages) and $45,000 (punitive damages) to each of three plaintiffs. The Court held that calling a nonmember a "scab" is protected by federal law, under the *New York Times* standard and, alternatively, that no defamation had occurred since the labor movement considers all nonmembers to be "scabs." Branch 496, Letter Carriers v. Austin, 418 U.S. 264 (1974).

2. The Anti-Injunction Act, 28 U.S.C. §2283 (1970), which limits federal injunctions against enforcement of state court proceedings, has blocked private litigants from enjoining the enforcement of state court decrees that contravene preemption doctrines. See Amalgamated Clothing Wkrs. v. Richman Bros. Co., 348 U.S. 511 (1955). The NLRB has, however, secured injunctions against such enforcement. See Capital Serv., Inc. v. NLRB, 347 U.S. 501 (1954); and NLRB v. Nash-Finch Co., 404 U.S. 138 (1971).

3. Delay in securing reversals of state court injunctions invalid under preemption doctrine may have influenced the Supreme Court's decisions summarized below.

(a) In re Green, 369 U.S. 689 (1962): A state court had issued an ex parte order restraining peaceful picketing defended as the union's protest against a refusal to bargain. The union's lawyer advised his client that the injunction was invalid because of preemption and the denial of a hearing required by state law, and recommended that the picketing be continued in order to secure a test of the state court's jurisdiction. In a contempt action against the lawyer, he was denied an opportunity to prove that the continuation of the picketing had been agreed to by opposing counsel, as well as by the judge, as a test of jurisdiction. Although that denial was emphasized in the opinion of the Court, by Douglas, J., that opinion also declared broadly (at 692): "[A] state court is without power to hold one in contempt for violating an injunction that the state court had no power to enter by reason of federal preemption." Harlan and Clark, JJ., although concurring in Green, dissented from that broad proposition on the ground that it was contrary to United States v. UMW, 330 U.S. 258, 289-295 (1947). See generally Cox, The Void Order and the Duty to Obey, 16 U. Chi. L. Rev. 87 (1948).

(b) Laborers, Local 438 v. Curry, 371 U.S. 542 (1963): Despite 28 U.S.C. §1257 (1970), which limits the Supreme Court's jurisdiction to the review of "final" state court judgments, the Court has jurisdiction to review the affirmance of a preliminary labor injunction by the highest state court, at least when a preemption question is presented. The Court defended that result as necessary to protect the right of appellate review and a hearing before the NLRB.

Brown v. Hotel & Restaurant Employees, Local 54, 104 S. Ct. 3179 (1984). The New Jersey Casino Control Act comprehensively regulates the state's gambling industry, because of its special vulnerability to infiltration by organized crime. Section 93 requires annual registration with the Casino Control Commission by unions seeking to represent employees in the casino industry, and provides, inter alia, that such a union may be prohibited from receiving dues because (1) its officers have been convicted of enumerated offenses, or (2) associated with certain offenders. Local 54, which represents 8,000 employees of Atlantic City casino hotels, registered with the Commission; that body initiated proceedings to determine whether §86 disqualified certain of the Local's officers. A federal district court declined to enjoin those proceedings. The Commission held several union officials disqualified under §86 and ordered that, if they were not removed, the Local would be barred from collecting dues from employees in the casino industry. The court of appeals held, however, that the NLRA preempted this order. The Supreme Court vacated that judgment and remanded to the district court, in an opinion by O'Connor, J., which included these considerations: Preemption resting on primary jurisdiction generally applies even when a state regulates conduct only arguably protected by federal law. Such preemption, however, "admits to exception when unusually 'deeply rooted' local interests are at stake." By contrast, if a state regulates conduct "actually protected by federal law," preemption follows "not as a matter of protecting primary jurisdiction but as a matter of substantive right" — regardless of the relative importance to the state of its own law.

The Court rejected the claim that the New Jersey law conflicts with employee self-determination guaranteed by §7 of the NLRA, reasoning this way: Title V of the LMRDA (1959), and §504(a) specifically, limit the policy of unrestricted employee free choice of bargaining representatives, by imposing restrictions on, and qualifications for, union officials — restrictions that result from conviction for various state crimes and presuppose lack of uniformity in state criminal laws. Furthermore, LMRDA §603(a) preserves state law and permits some state action concerning the qualifications of union officials. Congress also indicated a similar intent in approving the compact between New York and New Jersey that provisionally barred waterfront unions from collecting dues if its officers or agents had been convicted of a felony — a compact upheld against preemption claims in DeVeau v. Braisted, 363 U.S. 144 (1960). Consequently, in the absence of a more specific Congressional intent to the contrary, the New Jersey casino regulation does not conflict with §7 and is not preempted.

The Court declined to decide whether the dues-collection ban was preempted, noting that the courts below had not addressed the union's factual contentions that that ban would prevent the union from functioning as a collective representative and that the Commission maintained that it could enforce §93(b) by numerous other means. Accordingly, the Court directed that on remand the District Court should determine the unresolved factual issue.

White, J., joined by Powell and Stevens, JJ., agreed with the Court that federal law does not preempt state laws barring certain types of individuals from serving as union officials, and that direct New Jersey sanctions against such individuals would be valid. But those Justices dissented, urging that the dues-collection ban operates directly against the union and prevents it from functioning as a bargaining representative and thereby, as a matter of law, infringes on the federally protected right of employee free choice. Consequently, the Court's remand was unnecessary.

Brennan and Marshall, JJ., did not participate.

NOTES

1. Is the Court's opinion internally consistent?

2. Doesn't it seem likely that on remand the courts below will uphold the union's contention that it would be disabled by the dues-collection ban? If so, what point, if any, is there in the Court's result?

3. Suppose that New Jersey, as authorized by New Jersey law, enjoined all the newly-elected principal officials of a union in the casino industry from taking office on the ground of their felony convictions. Would that injunction interfere with §7 rights? Be preempted? Is the dissent in *Local 54* internally consistent?

Bill Johnson's Restaurants, Inc. v. NLRB, 461 U.S. 731 (1983). After the General Counsel issued a complaint on a charge by one Helton, a waitress, that the company had fired her because of her efforts to organize a union, Helton and others picketed the restaurant, carrying signs urging a customers' boycott. Despite the manager's threat "to get even," the group continued picketing and also distributed a leaflet reporting the Board's complaint and accusing management of "unwanted sexual advances" and of maintaining "filthy restrooms for women employees." The restaurant's owners sued Helton and the other demonstrators in a state court, alleging that the defendants had harassed customers, blocked access to the restaurant, and maliciously libelled the owners, and requesting compensatory damages and $500,000 in punitive damages. Helton thereupon filed a second NLRB charge, alleging that the lawsuit was in retaliation for both her initial NLRB charges and her protected activities and, accordingly, violated §§8(a)(1) and 8(a)(4). The ALJ, after a four-day hearing, found no reasonable basis for the state court action and concluded therefore that the retaliatory animus behind the lawsuit violated the Act. The Board agreed. Its prior position had been that a retaliatory lawsuit, regardless of its merit, violated the Act. See Power Systems, Inc., 239 N.L.R.B. 445, 449-50 (1978), *enforcement denied*, 601 F.2d 936 (7th Cir. 1979). The court of appeals enforced the Board's order requiring the restaurant owners to withdraw their state complaint and to pay defendants their resultant legal expenses.

Reversing and remanding, the Supreme Court acknowledged that a lawsuit might chill the employees' exercise of rights protected by the Act. But the Court pointed to these countervailing considerations: (1) the First Amendment right to petition the Government, hence the courts, for redress; and (2) the Court's continuing concern for the states' compelling interest in maintaining domestic peace — a concern that influenced its reading the NLRA as not preempting state civil remedies "for conduct touching interests deeply rooted in local feeling and responsibility." The Court, in light of these interests, rejected the Board's construction of the Act as untenable, even though "not irrational."

The Court announced these substantive rules: "The filing and prosecution of a well-founded lawsuit may not be enjoined as an unfair labor practice, even if it would not have been commenced but for the plaintiff's desire to retaliate against the defendant for exercising rights protected by the Act." But "it is an enjoinable unfair labor practice to prosecute a baseless lawsuit with the intent of retaliating against an employee for the exercise of rights protected by §7. . . ."

The Court laid down general rules governing the crucial procedural issue, i.e., the role of the Board and a state court in determining whether a state lawsuit had been baseless. (The Supreme Court held that in this case the ALJ had erred in holding a "de facto trial" on the factual issues — the only issues here in dispute.) Those rules involved a reverse twist on the NLRB's primary jurisdiction:

"Although the Board's reasonable basis inquiry need not be limited to the bare pleadings, if there is a genuine issue of material fact that turns on the credibility of witnesses or on the proper inferences to be drawn from undisputed facts, it cannot . . . be concluded that the suit should be enjoined. When a suit presents genuine factual issues, the state plaintiff's First Amendment interest in petitioning the state court for redress of his grievance, his interest in having the factual dispute resolved by a jury, and the State's interest in protecting the health and welfare of its citizens, lead us to construe the Act as not permitting the Board to usurp the traditional fact-finding function of the state-court jury or judge. Hence, we conclude that if a state plaintiff is able to present the Board with evidence that shows his lawsuit raises genuine issues of material fact, the Board should proceed no further with the §8(a)(1)-§8(a)(4) unfair labor practice proceedings but should stay those proceedings until the state-court suit has been concluded. . . .

"Just as the Board must refrain from deciding genuinely disputed material factual issues with respect to a state suit, it likewise must not deprive a litigant of his right to have genuine state-law legal questions [including mixed questions of law and fact] decided by the state judiciary. While the Board need not stay its hand if the plaintiff's position is plainly foreclosed as a matter of law or is otherwise frivolous, the Board should allow such issues to be decided by the state tribunals if there is any realistic chance that the plaintiff's legal theory might be adopted.

"In instances where the Board must allow the lawsuit to proceed, if the employer's case in the state court ultimately proves meritorious and he has judgment against the employees, the employer should also prevail before the Board, for the filing of a meritorious law suit, even for a retaliatory motive, is not an unfair labor practice. If judgment goes against the employer in the state court, however, or if his suit is withdrawn or is otherwise shown to be without merit, the employer has had its day in court, the interest of the state in providing a forum for its citizens has been vindicated, and the Board may then proceed to adjudicate the §8(a)(1) and 8(a)(4) unfair labor practice case. The employer's suit having proved unmeritorious, the Board would be warranted in taking that fact into account in determining whether the suit had been filed in retaliation for the exercise of the employees' §7 rights. If a violation is found, the Board may order the employer to reimburse the employees whom he had wrongfully sued for their attorneys' fees and other expenses. It may also order any other proper relief that would effectuate the policies of the Act. . . ."

NOTES

1. Are the Court's general rules compatible with §10(a) of the Act?

2. Assume that the union, seeking to organize Bill Johnson's restaurant, filed objections to an election, contending that "laboratory conditions" had been destroyed by the company's bringing baseless lawsuits after the union had filed its election petition. Would the NLRB be bound by the general rules announced in *Bill Johnson's*?

3. Under the NLRA, should threats to file lawsuits be treated differently from the actual filing of them?

Hanna Mining v. Marine Engineers
382 U.S. 181 (1965)

[District 2 Marine Engineers (MEBA) had represented the licensed engineers on Hanna's fleet, under a collective agreement terminating on July 15, 1962. According to Hanna, in August, during negotiations for a renewal agreement, a majority of the engineers informed the company by written petitions that they did not wish to be represented by MEBA.

Hanna then declined to negotiate until MEBA's majority status was established by a secret ballot. MEBA's response was to picket one of Hanna's ships unloading at a Duluth dock, with signs naming the ship and stating that Hanna had unfairly refused to negotiate and that MEBA had no dispute with any other employer. Because of the picketing, dock workers refused to unload the ship until shipping ended for the winter. MEBA also picketed Hanna's ships at other Great Lakes ports. The NLRB sustained a Regional Director's dismissal of Hanna's election petition (at the end of September), on the ground that the engineers were "supervisors" under the NLRA. That ground was also asserted for a Regional Director's dismissal of a §8(b)(7)(C) charge. Another Regional Director had previously dismissed Hanna's §8(b)(4)(B) charge, stating that MEBA's conduct at the various ports was lawful.

With the opening of the navigation season in Spring 1963, MEBA's picketing resumed. The Wisconsin courts denied Hanna's request for an injunction. The Wisconsin Supreme Court found an arguable violation of §§8(b)(4)(B) and 8(b)(7), and concluded that under *Garmon* its jurisdiction was preempted. The Supreme Court reversed and remanded.]

HARLAN, J. . . . [T]he Board's decision that Hanna engineers are supervisors removes from this case most of the opportunities for preemption.

When in 1947 the [NLRA] was amended to exclude supervisory workers from the critical definition of "employees," §2(3), it followed that many provisions of the Act employing that pivotal term would cease to operate where supervisors were the focus of concern. . . .

[Thus] activity designed to secure organization or recognition of supervisors is not protected by §7 of the Act, arguably or otherwise. . . . Correspondingly, the situations in which that same activity can be prohibited by the Act, even arguably, are fewer than . . . if employees were being organized or seeking recognition. There can be no breach of §8(b)(7), curtailing organizational or recognitional picketing, because there cannot exist the forbidden objective of requiring representation of "employees" by the picketing organization. . . .

Even though such efforts to unionize supervisors are not protected by the Act, or in the respects immediately relevant prohibited by it, the question arises whether Congress nonetheless desired that in their peaceful facets these efforts remain free from state regulation as well as Board authority. . . . Arguing that the States are indeed powerless in this respect, MEBA pitches its case chiefly on the 1947 amendment of the "employee" definition and on the concurrent enactment of §14(a) . . . , which provides in relevant part that "[n]othing herein shall prohibit any individual employed as a supervisor from becoming or remaining a member of a labor organization. . . ." It is contended that the amendment and this section signify a federal policy of laissez faire toward supervisors ousting state as well as Board authority and, more particularly, that to allow the Wisconsin injunction would obliterate the opportunity for supervisor unions that Congress expressly reserved.

This broad argument fails utterly in light of the legislative history, for the Committee reports reveal that Congress' propelling intention was to relieve employers from any compulsion under the Act and under state law to countenance or bargain with any union of supervisory employees. Whether the legislators fully realize that their method of achieving this result incidentally freed supervisors' unions from certain limitations under the newly enacted §8(b) is not wholly clear, but certainly Congress made no considered decision generally to exclude state limitations on supervisory organizing. As to the portion of §14(a) quoted above, some legislative history suggests that it was not meant to immunize any conduct at all but only to make it "clear that the amendments to the act do not prohibit supervisors from joining unions. . . ." S. Rep. No. 105, 80th Cong., 1st Sess., p. 28; H.R. Conf. Rep. No. 510, 80th Cong., 1st Sess., p. 60. . . .

The remaining question . . . is whether the supervisory status of Hanna's engineers has been settled "with unclouded legal significance," *Garmon*, 359 U.S., at 246, so as to preclude arguable application of the Act in the respects discussed. We hold that the Board's statement accompanying its refusal to order a representation election does resolve the question with the clarity necessary to avoid preemption. While MEBA does not contend that the Board erred in its determination, an abstract difficulty arises from the lack of a statutory channel for judicial review of such a Board decision. Compare Hotel Employees v. Leedom, 358 U.S. 99 (equity action to obtain election). However, the usual deference to Board expertise in applying statutory terms to particular facts assures that its decision would in any event be respected in a high percentage of instances, and so diminished a risk of interference with federal labor policy does not justify use of the preemption doctrine to thwart state regulation bound to be legitimate on this score in almost all cases.

A further basis for preemption, urged by MEBA . . . , is that the picketing at Superior exerted secondary pressure arguably violating §8(b)(4)(B). The argument appears to be that a state injunction banishing the pickets inevitably impinges upon the Board's authority to regulate facets of the picketing that might exceed "primary" picketing and violate §8(b)(4)(B) — facets never specified by MEBA but presumably those that ignore the Board's limitations on time, location, and manner of common situs picketing. See Sailors' Union of the Pacific (Moore Dry Dock), 92 N.L.R.B. 547. . . .

The Wisconsin Supreme Court refused to credit [the finding made by the Regional Director and the General Counsel in declining to issue a complaint under §8(b)(4)(B)] because of this Court's comment in *Garmon* that the "refusal of the General Counsel to file a charge" is one of those dispositions "which does not define the nature of the activity with unclouded legal significance." 359 U.S., at 245-246. This language allows more than one interpretation, but we take it not to apply to those refusals of the General Counsel which are illuminated by explanations that do squarely define the nature of the activity. The General Counsel has statutory "final authority, on behalf of the Board, in respect of the investigation of charges and issuance of complaints," §3(d) . . . , and his pronouncements in this context are entitled to great weight. The usual inability of the charging party to contest the General Counsel's adverse decision in the courts, see Hourihan v. Labor Board, 201 F.2d 187, does to be sure create a slight risk if the state courts may proceed on this basis, but in the context of this case we believe the risk is too minimal to deserve recognition.

[The Court explained why the Board's dismissal of §8(b)(4)(B) charges, based on the 1962 picketing, was equally applicable to the virtually identical 1963 picketing — according to Hanna's offer of proof.]

Additionally, even if a §8(b)(4)(B) violation were present, central interests served by the *Garmon* doctrine are not endangered by a state injunction when, in an instance such as this, the Board has established that the workers sought to be organized are outside the regime of the Act. Most importantly, the Board's decision on the supervisory question determines . . . that none of the conduct is arguably protected nor does it fall in some middle range impliedly withdrawn from state control. Consequently, there is wholly absent the greatest threat against which the *Garmon* doctrine guards, a State's prohibition of activity that the Act indicates must remain unhampered.

Nor is this a case in which the presence of arguably prohibited activity may permit the Board to afford complete protection to the legitimate interests advanced by the State. Since Hanna as the primary employer is present at the picketed situs, the primary picketing proviso of §8(b)(4)(B) severely inhibits the Board's use of that section to reach the volatile core of the conduct, the impact on secondary employers that follows from the mere presence of the pickets at a common situs. Section 8(b)(7) which might provide full relief is rendered inapplicable by the supervisor ruling. Thus, so far as *Garmon* may proceed on the view that the opportunity belongs to the Board whenever it and the State offer duplicate relief, it has limited application to the present facts.[16] . . .

[The concurring opinion of Brennan, J., is omitted.]

NOTES

1. Only "labor organizations" (see NLRA §2(5), as amended) or their "agents" are subject to the unfair labor practice provisions of §8. Suppose that a union local, seeking to represent only the supervisors working for a manufacturer, pickets the latter's customers in order to secure recognition from the manufacturer. Suppose also that the local represents "employees" of other companies. Is its picketing a violation of §8(b)(4)? In the absence of a characterization of the local's status by the NLRB, may state courts enjoin the picketing? How should the employer proceed in order to secure a characterization of the local that might serve as a foundation for a state court injunction? Consider the following passage from Marine Engrs. Beneficial Assn. v. Interlake S.S. Co., 370 U.S. 173, 179-182 (1962):

> . . . [T]he phrase "organization . . . in which employees participate" is far from self-explanatory. Several recurring questions stem from the fact that national or even local unions may represent both "employees" and "supervisors." For example, is employee participation in any part of a defendant national or local union sufficient, or must "employees" be involved in the immediate labor dispute? What percentage or degree of employee participation in the relevant unit is required? If an organization is open to "employees" or solicits their membership, must there be a showing that there are actually employee members? And, if a local union is not itself a "labor organization," are there conditions under which it may become subject to §8(b) as an agent of some other organization which is?

---

[16] In Marine Engineers v. Interlake Co., 370 U.S. 173, we overturned a state ban on picketing arguably violating §8(b)(4)(B); and to the counterargument that the picketing group was not a "labor organization" subject to §8(b), we pointed out that this decision was for the Board. Unlike the present case, in *Interlake* the §8(b)(4)(B) remedy had not been tried; but quite apart from that consideration, had the Board held the union a "labor organization" and also held those being organized to be "employees" — another point not recently decided by the Board — complete relief against the picketing might well have been available under §8(b)(7). See 370 U.S., at 182-183.

The considerations involved in answering these questions are largely of a kind most wisely entrusted initially to the agency charged with the day-to-day administration of the Act as a whole. The term "labor organization" appears in a number of sections of the Act [including] §§8(a)(2), 8(a)(3), and 9(c). . . . The policy considerations underlying these and other sections . . . and the relationship of a particular definitional approach under §8(b) to the meaning of the same term in the various sections, must obviously be taken into account if the statute is to operate as a coherent whole. A centralized adjudicatory process is also essential in working out a consistent approach to the status of the many separate unions which may represent interrelated occupations in a single industry. Moreover, . . . the Board should be free in the first instance to consider the whole spectrum of possible approaches to the question, ranging from a broad definition of "labor organization" in terms of an entire union to a narrow case-by-case consideration of the issue. Only the Board can knowledgeably weigh the effect of either choice upon the certainty and predictability of labor management relations, or assess the importance of simple administrative convenience in this area.

[T]he task of determining what is a "labor organization" in the context of §8(b) must in any doubtful case begin with the NLRB; the only workable way to assure this result is for the courts to concede that a union is a "labor organization" for §8(b) purposes whenever a reasonably arguable case is made to that effect.

2. The NLRB has held that, under §8(b)(1)(B), a union representing supervisors is a "labor organization" if it represents statutory employees of any employer and not necessarily the "employees" of the employer subject to the coercion banned by that section. See International Organization of Masters, Mates & Pilots, 197 N.L.R.B. 400 (1972), *enforced*, 486 F.2d 1271 (D.C. Cir. 1973), *cert. denied*, 416 U.S. 956 (1974) (union picketed purchaser in order to preserve jobs of supervisors displaced pursuant to prehire agreement with another union, made by purchaser of a vessel on which supervisors had worked prior to seller's bankruptcy).

3. A union pickets for the inclusion of store managers of a supermarket chain in a bargaining unit that includes "employees" represented by the union; the employer contends convincingly that the managers are supervisors.

(a) Would a state court have jurisdiction to enjoin such picketing?

(b) Should state jurisdiction depend on prior NLRB determination of the store managers' supervisory status?

Cf. Safeway Stores v. Retail Clerks Assn., 41 Cal. 2d 567, 261 P.2d 721 (1953).

4. Even if the NLRB determines that the managers are "supervisors," should state jurisdiction be preempted if §8(b)(3) is violated by union pres-

sure for a mixed unit that is a permissive rather than a "mandatory" subject of bargaining? Cf. NLRB v. Committee of Interns & Residents, 566 F.2d 810 (2d Cir. 1977), cert. denied, 435 U.S. 904 (1978) (state jurisdiction over staff physicians preempted by NLRB decision that they were not "employees" under the NLRA, coupled with NLRB's stated intention to preclude state regulation)]; Retail Clerks v. Schermerhorn, infra p. 1217.

5. Suppose that the store managers are discharged because of union membership and claim damages in a state court, urging that their discharge violated the state right-to-work law. The employer, invoking the LMRA, moves to dismiss. What result? Cf. Beasley v. Food Fair of North Carolina, Inc., 416 U.S. 653 (1974).

6. After the decision in Bell Aerospace, supra p. 718, would the results in the foregoing situations be the same if "managerial employees" were substituted for "supervisors"? Consider §14(a) and NLRB v. Committee of Interns & Residents, supra.

7. In Brotherhood of R.R. Trainmen v. Jacksonville Terminal Co., 394 U.S. 369 (1969), noted 48 Tex. L. Rev. 518 (1970), the Florida East Coast Ry. Co., after exhausting the machinery of the Railway Labor Act, unilaterally changed rates of pay and working conditions. The unions called a strike and picketed various locations where the railroad conducted operations, including a railroad terminal jointly owned by Florida East Coast and three other railroads. A Florida trial court found that the picketing constituted a secondary boycott illegal under state law and would cause serious economic damage to the entire state, and granted an injunction restraining the unions from picketing the terminal except at a gate purportedly reserved for employees of the struck railroad. The Supreme Court (4 to 3) reversed, ruling that the state court was not preempted of jurisdiction, but that picketing by a railway union — whether characterized as primary or secondary — was protected against state proscription. Douglas, J., joined by Black and Stewart, JJ., dissented. What arguments support each of the competing positions? How would you resolve this question?

Note: The Reaffirmation of *Garmon*

In Amalgamated Assn. of Street Employees v. Lockridge, 403 U.S. 274 (1971), the Court, although its primary focus was the "arguably prohibited" branch of *Garmon*, reaffirmed (5 to 4) both branches of that case. Harlan, J., who in *Garmon* had criticized the arguably prohibited approach, spoke for the majority.

The questions presented by the situation in *Lockridge* made it a surprising vehicle for the reaffirmation of *Garmon*. Lockridge, for 16 years a union member and Greyhound employee, had in September 1959 revoked his authorization to Greyhound to check off his union dues. Lockridge then failed to pay those monthly dues to the union. On November 2, the union suspended him from membership and immediately had him fired by Greyhound, under the following union security clause: "All present employees covered by this contract shall become members of the ASSOCIATION [Union] not later than thirty (30) days following its effective date and shall remain members as a condition precedent to continued employment. . . ."

On November 10, 1959, when Lockridge was on vacation, the union rejected a tender by Lockridge's wife of his delinquent October and November dues. Lockridge thereupon sued in the Idaho courts, alleging (Count 1) that the union's malicious and wrongful suspension of his membership had deprived him of his employment, and (Count 2) that the union had thereby violated the union's constitution, which formed a contract between the union and its membership. That constitution provided:

> All dues . . . of the members of this Association are due and payable on the first day of each month for that month. . . . They must be paid by the fifteenth of the month in order to continue the member in good standing. . . . A member in arrears for his dues . . . after the fifteenth day of the month is not in good standing . . . and where a member allows his arrearage . . . to run into the second month before paying the same, he shall be debarred from benefits for one month after payment. Where a member allows his arrearage . . . to run over the last day of the second month without payment, he does thereby suspend himself from membership in this Association. . . . Where agreements with employing companies provide that members must be in continuous good financial standing, the member in arrears one month may be suspended from membership and removed from employment, in compliance with the terms of the agreement. . . .

The Idaho Supreme Court, despite its conclusion that the union had violated §§8(b)(1)(A) and 8(b)(2) of the NLRA, relied on IAM v. Gonzales, 356 U.S. 617 (1958),[d] and upheld the breach of contract claim and the

---

[d]In *Gonzales*, the Supreme Court had upheld a California judgment against a union, ordering reinstatement of the plaintiff to membership, payment of damages to him for breach of the "contract" embodied in the union constitution, and other relief. The Court had acknowledged that a violation of §8(b)(2) might have been involved. Nevertheless, it rejected the preemption contention, reasoning this way: The NLRA did not protect union membership rights against arbitrary conduct by unions. Accordingly, the remote possibility of conflict with federal policy should not result in denying the plaintiff the comprehensive remedy that only the state courts could provide.

judgment ordering Lockridge's reinstatement into the union and compensation for his lost wages, among other relief. In explaining the Court's reversal of that judgment, Harlan, J., reaffirmed the general approach to state authority set forth in *Garmon*. *Lockridge* was, as already indicated, remote from the Board's plenary responsibilities, but close to the traditional concerns of state courts — the interpretation of union constitutions and the monitoring of internal union affairs. (See LMRDA §603, preserving state jurisdiction over such matters.) Furthermore, §14(b) of the NLRA, by authorizing the states to proscribe union security arrangements, rejected in that context both national substantive standards and plenary national enforcement.

In his dissent, Douglas, J., stressed the distinctive context involved and also repudiated his prior dissent in *Gonzales*, urging that experience under *Garmon* showed that it should not be applied to grievances of an individual employee against a union.

Justice White's dissent also objected to the undercutting of *Gonzales*. He listed the many exceptions to both the Board's primary jurisdiction and preemption of state jurisdiction: the NLRB's deference to arbitration; judicial enforcement of contractual claims overlapping with violations of the NLRA; judicial enforcement of the duty of fair representation; actions based on §303 of the LMRA; and claims based on violence. He urged that there were convincing reasons for an exception that would uphold Idaho's exercise of jurisdiction over the dispute between Lockridge and his union, even though the union's conduct was arguably or actually an unfair labor practice.

Turning to a more general difficulty that went well beyond union-employee disputes, White, J., also objected to the "arguably protected" branch of *Garmon*. He stressed that an employer frequently could not get an NLRB determination on whether the disputed conduct was actually protected — at least without committing an unfair labor practice. He called for reexamination of a doctrine that either denies the parties a hearing or promotes the commission of unfair labor practices as a means of securing a hearing. This theme would surface again. See Sears Roebuck & Co. v. San Diego County Dist. Council of Carpenters, infra p. 770.

NOTES

1. For assessments of the approaches and result in *Lockridge*, see Cox, Labor Law Preemption Revisited, 85 Harv. L. Rev. 1337 (1972); Lesnick, Preemption Reconsidered: The Apparent Reaffirmation of *Garmon*, 72 Colum. L. Rev. 469 (1972); Bryson, A Matter of Wooden Logic: Labor Law Preemption and Individual Rights, 51 Tex. L. Rev. 1037 (1973).

2. In Windward Shipping Ltd. v. American Radio Assn., 415 U.S. 104 (1974), owners of vessels of foreign registry sought injunctive relief against picketing in American ports. The picketers protested the substandard wages of the crews on such vessels and induced American port workers to decline to service those vessels. The Texas courts found their authority preempted, since the picketing was arguably protected or prohibited. The Supreme Court reversed (6 to 3), emphasized the need for comity in foreign trade, and concluded that the picketing was not "in commerce," as defined by the NLRA. In American Radio Assn. v. Mobile S.S. Assn. Inc., 419 U.S. 215 (1974), which involved substantially identical picketing, the plaintiffs, American companies seeking to service or load foreign ships, alleged that the defendants' secondary activities constituted tortious interference with the plaintiff's business. The Supreme Court (5 to 4), upheld Alabama's jurisdiction to enjoin the picketing, again finding that the American companies were not "affecting" or "in commerce" with respect to the foreign ships. The Court noted that the unions, having unsuccessfully urged in *Windward* that the picketing was "protected," now claimed that it was "prohibited." The Court also declared (at 225, n.10) that its decision "need cast no doubt on those cases which hold that the Board has jurisdiction under §8(b)(4) of domestic secondary activities which are in commerce even though the primary employer is located outside the United States."

Lodge 76, IAM v. Wisconsin Employment Rel. Commn.
427 U.S. 132 (1976)

BRENNAN, J. . . . The question . . . is whether federal labor policy preempts the authority of a state labor relations board to grant an employer covered by the [NLRA] an order enjoining a union and its members from continuing to refuse to work overtime pursuant to a union policy to put economic pressure on the employer in negotiations for renewal of an expired collective bargaining agreement.

A collective bargaining agreement between petitioner Local 76 (the Union) and respondent, Kearney and Trecker Corporation (the employer) was terminated by the employer pursuant to the terms of the agreement on June 19, 1971. Good-faith bargaining over the terms of a renewal agreement continued for over a year thereafter, finally resulting in the signing of a new agreement effective July 23, 1972. A particularly controverted issue during negotiations was the employer's demand that the provision of the expired agreement under which, as for the prior 17 years, the basic workday was seven and one-half hours, Monday through Friday, and the basic workweek was 37 1/2 hours, be replaced with a new provision providing a basic workday of eight hours and a basic workweek of 40 hours, and that the terms on which overtime rates of pay were payable be changed accordingly.

A few days after the old agreement was terminated the employer unilaterally began to make changes in some conditions of employment provided in the expired contract, e.g., eliminating the checkoff of Union dues, eliminating the Union's office in the plant and eliminating Union lost time. . . . [I]n March 1972, the employer announced that it would [also] unilaterally implement, as of March 13, 1972, its proposal for a 40-hour week and eight-hour day. [At] a membership meeting on March 7 . . . , strike action was authorized and a resolution was adopted binding union members to refuse to work any overtime, defined as work in excess of seven and one-half hours in any day or 37 1/2 hours in any week. Following the strike vote, the employer offered to "defer the implementation" of its workweek proposal if the Union would agree to call off the concerted refusal to work overtime. The Union, however, refused the offer and indicated its intent to continue the concerted ban on overtime. Thereafter, the employer did not make effective the proposed changes in the workday and workweek before the new agreement became effective on July 23, 1972. Although all but a very few employees complied with the Union's resolution against acceptance of overtime work during the negotiations, the employer did not discipline, or attempt to discipline, any employee for refusing to work overtime.

Instead, while negotiations continued, the employer filed a charge . . . that the Union's resolution violated §8(b)(3) of the [NLRA]. The Regional Director dismissed the charge on the ground that the "policy prohibiting overtime work by its member employees does not appear to be in violation of the Act" and therefore was not conduct cognizable by the Board under NLRB v. Insurance Agents Internl. Union, 361 U.S. 477 (1960). However, the employer also filed a complaint before the Wisconsin Employment Relations Commission charging that the refusal to work overtime constituted an unfair labor practice under state law. . . . [T]he Commission . . . [held] that "the concerted refusal to work overtime is not an activity which is arguably protected under §7 or arguably prohibited under §8 of the [NLRA] and . . . therefore the . . . Commission is not preempted from asserting its jurisdiction to regulate said conduct." The Commission also adopted the further Conclusion of Law that the Union "by authorizing . . . the concerted refusal to work overtime . . . engaged in a concerted effort to interfere with production . . . committed an unfair labor practice within the meaning of §111.06(2)(h) . . . ."[1] The Commission

---

[1] Wis. Stat. §111.06(2) provides:
  "It shall be an unfair labor practice for an employee individually or in concert with others: . . .

thereupon entered an order that the Union, inter alia, "[i]mmediately cease and desist from authorizing, encouraging or condoning any concerted refusal to accept overtime assignments. . . ." The Wisconsin Circuit Court entered judgment enforcing the Commission's order. The Wisconsin Supreme Court affirmed the Circuit Court. . . . We reverse.

I

Cases that have held state authority to be preempted by federal law tend to fall into one of two categories: (1) those that reflect the concern that "one forum would enjoin, as illegal, conduct which the other forum would find legal" and (2) those that reflect the concern "that the [application of state law by] state courts would restrict the exercise of rights guaranteed by the Federal Acts." Automobile Workers v. Russell, 356 U.S. 634, 644 (1958). "[I]n referring to decisions holding state laws preempted by the NLRA, care must be taken to distinguish preemption based on federal protection of the conduct in question . . . from that based predominantly on the primary jurisdiction of the [NLRB] . . . , although the two are often not easily separable." Brotherhood of Railroad Trainmen v. Jacksonville Terminal Co., 394 U.S. 369, 383 n.19 (1969). Each of these distinct aspects of labor law preemption has had its own history in our decisions to which we now turn.

We consider first preemption based predominantly on the primary jurisdiction of the Board. This line of preemption analysis was developed in [Garmon], 359 U.S. 236, and its history was recently summarized in [Lockridge], 403 U.S. 274, 290-291 (1971). . . .

However, a second line of preemption analysis has been developed in cases focusing upon the crucial inquiry whether Congress intended that the conduct involved be unregulated because left "to be controlled by the free play of economic forces." NLRB v. Nash-Finch Co., 404 U.S. 138, 144 (1971).[4] Concededly this inquiry was not made in 1949 in the so-called Briggs-Stratton case, Automobile Workers v. Wisconsin Board, 336 U.S. 245 (1949), the decision of this Court heavily relied upon by the court below

---

"(h) To take unauthorized possession of the property of the employer or to engage in any concerted effort to interfere with production except by leaving the premises in an orderly manner for the purpose of going on strike."

[4] See Cox, Labor Law Preemption Revisited, 85 Harv. L. Rev. 1337, 1352 (1972): "An appreciation of the true character of the national labor policy expressed in the NLRA and the LMRA indicates that in providing a legal framework for union organization, collective bargaining, and the conduct of labor disputes, Congress struck a balance of protection, prohibition, and laissez-faire in respect to union organization, collective bargaining, and labor disputes that would be upset if a state could enforce statutes or rules of decision resting upon its views concerning accommodation of the same interests." . . .

in reaching its decision that state regulation of the conduct at issue is not preempted by national labor law. . . .

However, the *Briggs-Stratton* holding that state power is not preempted as to peaceful conduct neither protected by §7 nor prohibited by §8 of the federal Act, a holding premised on the statement that "[t]his conduct is either governable by the State or it is entirely ungoverned," id., at 254, was undercut by subsequent decisions of this Court. For the Court soon recognized that a particular activity might be "protected" by federal law not only where it fell within §7, but also when it was an activity that Congress intended to be "unrestricted by *any* governmental power to regulate" because it was among the permissible "economic weapons in reserve . . . actual exercise [of which] on occasion by the parties is part and parcel of the system that the Wagner and Taft-Hartley Acts have recognized." NLRB v. Insurance Agents, 361 U.S., at 488, 489 (emphasis added) [infra p. 830]. "[T]he legislative purpose may . . . dictate that certain activity 'neither protected nor prohibited' be privileged against state regulation." Hanna Mining Co. v. Marine Engineers, 382 U.S., at 187.

II

Insurance Agents, supra, involved a charge of a refusal by the union to bargain in good faith in violation of §8(b)(3). . . . The charge was based on union activities that occurred during good-faith bargaining. . . . During the negotiations, the union directed concerted on-the-job activities by its members of a harassing nature designed to interfere with the conduct of the employer's business, for the avowed purpose of putting economic pressure on the employer to accede to the union's bargaining demands. . . .

We held that such tactics would not support a finding by NLRB that the union had failed to bargain in good faith as required by §8(b)(3) and rejected the per se rule applied by the Board that use of "economically harassing activities" alone sufficed to prove a violation of that section. The Court assumed "that the activities in question were not 'protected' under §7 of the Act," id., at 483 n.6, but held that the per se rule was beyond the authority of NLRB to apply. . . . We noted further that "Congress has been rather specific when it has come to outlaw particular economic weapons on the part of unions" and "the activities here involved have never been specifically outlawed by Congress." Id., at 498. Accordingly, the Board's claim "to power . . . to distinguish among various economic pressure tactics and brand the ones at bar inconsistent with good-faith collective bargaining," id., at 492, was simply inconsistent with the design of the federal scheme in which "the use of economic pressure by the parties to a labor dispute is . . . part and parcel of the process of collective bargaining." Id., at 495.

The Court had earlier recognized in preemption cases that Congress meant to leave some activities unregulated and to be controlled by the free play of economic forces. Garner v. Teamsters, 346 U.S. 485 [quoting the passage quoted in *Morton* below]. Moreover, [*Garmon*], 359 U.S. 236, expressly recognized "the Board may decide that an activity is neither protected nor prohibited, and thereby raise the question whether such activity may be regulated by the States." Id., at 245. . . .

. . . [T]he analysis of *Garner* and *Insurance Agents* came full bloom . . . in Local 20, Teamsters v. Morton, 377 U.S. 252 (1964), which held preempted the application of state law to award damages for peaceful union secondary picketing. Although *Morton* involved conduct neither "protected nor prohibited" by §7 or §8 . . . , we recognized the necessity of an inquiry whether " 'Congress occupied the field and closed it to state regulation.' " Id., at 258. Central to *Morton's* analysis was the observation that "[i]n selecting which forms of economic pressure should be prohibited . . . , Congress struck the 'balance . . . between the uncontrolled power of management and labor to further their respective interests,' " id., at 258-259 and that:

> This weapon of self-help, permitted by federal law, formed an integral part of the petitioner's effort to achieve its bargaining goals during negotiations. . . . Allowing its use is a part of the balance struck by Congress between the conflicting interests of the union, the employees, the employer and the community. . . . If the Ohio law of secondary boycott can be applied to proscribe the same type of conduct which Congress focused upon but did not proscribe when it enacted §303, the inevitable result would be to frustrate the congressional determination to leave this weapon of self-help available, and to upset the balance of power between labor and management expressed in our national labor policy. "For a state to impinge on the area of labor combat designed to be free is quite as much an obstruction of federal policy as if the state were to declare picketing free for purposes or by methods which the federal Act prohibits." Garner v. Teamsters Union, 346 U.S. 485, 500.

Morton, supra, at 259-260.

Although many of our past decisions concerning conduct left by Congress to the free play of economic forces address the question in the context of union and employee activities, self-help is of course also the prerogative of the employer because he too may properly employ economic weapons Congress meant to be unregulable. . . .

. . . Whether self-help economic activities are employed by employer or union, the crucial inquiry regarding preemption is the same: whether "the exercise of plenary state authority to curtail or entirely prohibit self-help would frustrate effective implementation of the Act's processes." Railroad Trainmen v. Jacksonville Terminal Co., 394 U.S., at 380.

III

There is simply no question that the Act's processes would be frustrated in the instant case were the State's ruling permitted to stand. The employer in this case invoked the Wisconsin law because unable to overcome the union tactic with its own economic self-help means. Although it did employ economic weapons putting pressure on the union when it terminated the previous agreement, it apparently lacked sufficient economic strength to secure its bargaining demands under "the balance of power between labor and management expressed in our national labor policy," Teamsters Union v. Morton, 377 U.S., at 260. But the economic weakness of the affected party cannot justify state aid contrary to federal law for, "as we have developed, the use of economic pressure by the parties to a labor dispute is not a grudging exception [under] . . . the [federal] Act; it is part and parcel of the process of collective bargaining." Insurance Agents, 361 U.S., at 495. . . .

Our decisions hold that Congress meant that these activities, whether of employer or employees, were not to be regulable by States any more than by the NLRB, for neither States nor the Board are "afforded flexibility in picking and choosing which economic devices of labor and management would be branded as unlawful." [Id. at 498.] . . . To sanction state regulation of such economic pressure deemed by the federal Act 'desirabl[y] . . . left for the free play of contending economic forces, . . . is not merely [to fill] a gap [by] outlaw[ing] what federal law fails to outlaw; it is denying to one party to an economic contest a weapon that Congress meant him to have available." Lesnick, Preemption Reconsidered: The Apparent Reaffirmation of Garmon, 72 Colum. L. Rev. 469, 478 (1972). Accordingly, such regulation by the State is impermissible because it "'stands as an obstacle to the accomplishment and execution of the full purposes and objectives of Congress.'" Hill v. Florida, 325 U.S. 538, 542 (1945).

IV

. . . [Garmon], 359 U.S., at 245 n.4, made clear that the Briggs-Stratton approach to preemption is "no longer of general application." We hold today that the ruling of Briggs-Stratton, permitting state regulation of partial strike activities such as are involved in this case is likewise "no longer of general application."

Briggs-Stratton assumed "management . . . would be disabled from any kind of self-help to cope with these coercive tactics of the union" and could not "take any steps to resist or combat them without incurring the sanctions of the Act." 336 U.S., at 264. But as Insurance Agents held, where the union activity complained of is "protected," not because it is within §7, but only because it is an activity Congress meant to leave unregulated, "the employer could have discharged or taken other appropriate disciplinary action against the employees participating." 361 U.S., at 493. Moreover, even were the activity presented in the instant case "protected" activity within the meaning of §7, economic weapons were available to counter the union's refusal to work overtime, e.g., a lockout, American Ship Building Co. v. NLRB, 380 U.S. 300, and the hiring of permanent replacements under NLRB v. Mackay Radio & Tel. Co., 304 U.S. 333 (1938). See Prince Lithograph Co., 205 N.L.R.B. 110, 115 (1973). . . .

Our decisions since *Briggs-Stratton* have made it abundantly clear that state attempts to influence the substantive terms of collective bargaining agreements are as inconsistent with the federal regulatory scheme as are such attempts by the NLRB. . . . And indubitably regulation, whether federal or State, of "the choice of economic weapons that may be used as part of collective bargaining [exerts] considerable influence upon the substantive terms on which the parties contract." NLRB v. Insurance Agents, supra, 361 U.S., at 490. The availability or not of economic weapons that federal law leaves the parties free to use cannot "depend upon the forum in which the [opponent] presses its claims." Howard Johnson Co., Inc. v. Hotel Employees, 417 U.S. 249, 256 (1974). . . .

V

Since *Briggs-Stratton* is today overruled, and as we hold further that the Union's refusal to work overtime is peaceful conduct constituting activity which must be free of regulation by the States if the congressional intent in enacting the comprehensive federal law of labor relations is not to be frustrated, the judgment of the Wisconsin Supreme Court is reversed.

POWELL, J., with whom THE CHIEF JUSTICE joins, concurring. . . . I write to make clear my understanding that the Court's opinion does not, however, preclude the States from enforcing, in the context of a labor dispute, "neutral" state statutes or rules of decision: state laws that are not directed toward altering the bargaining positions of employers or unions but which may have an incidental effect on relative bargaining strength. Except where Congress has specifically provided otherwise, the States generally should remain free to enforce, for example, their law of torts or of contracts, and other laws reflecting neutral public policy.* See Cox, Labor Law Preemption Revisited, 85 Harv. L. Rev. 1337, 1355-1356 (1972).

With this understanding, I join the opinion of the Court.

STEVENS, J., with whom STEWART and REHNQUIST, JJ., join, dissenting. . . .

---

* State laws should not be regarded as neutral if they reflect an accommodation of the special interests of employers, unions, or the public in areas such as employee self-organization, labor disputes, or collective bargaining.

If Congress had focused on the problems presented by partial strike activity, and enacted special legislation dealing with this subject matter, but left the form of the activity disclosed by this record unregulated, the Court's conclusion would be supported by Teamsters Union v. Morton, 377 U.S. 252. But this is not such a case. Despite the numerous statements in the Court's opinion about Congress' intent to leave partial strike activity wholly unregulated, I have found no legislative expression of any such intent nor any evidence that Congress has scrutinized such activity.

If this Court had previously *held* that the no-man's-land in which conduct is neither arguably protected nor arguably prohibited by federal law is nevertheless preempted by an unexpressed legislative intent, I would follow such a holding. But none of the cases reviewed in the Court's opinion so holds. Ever since 1949, when *Briggs-Stratton* was decided, the rule has been that partial strike activity within that area may be regulated by the States.

If adherence to the rule of *Briggs-Stratton* would permit the States substantially to disrupt the balance Congress has struck between union and employer, I would readily join in overruling it. But I am not persuaded that partial strike activity is so essential to the bargaining process that the States should not be free to make it illegal. . . .

NOTES

1. In the 1959 amendments to the NLRA, Congress dealt with recognitional picketing and secondary pressures but did not focus on "partial strikes" or the problem of jurisdiction in *Briggs-Stratton* situations. Are those considerations relevant in determining the extent of the "field" occupied by Congress? Since the corollary of such "occupation" is the exclusion of state jurisdiction from the field occupied, that metaphor could be used to oust the states completely from regulation of "labor relations." What are the relevant considerations in marking out the zone of occupation and in deciding whether that approach, rather than a primary jurisdiction approach, should govern?

2. Under either the *Garmon* guidelines or the occupation-of-the-field approach of *Lodge* 76, severe restrictions are imposed on state jurisdiction over strikes or lockouts that create acute problems for local communities but are too localized to activate the LMRA's national emergency procedures. See, e.g., Street Employees v. Wisconsin Emp. Rel. Bd., 340 U.S. 383 (1951); Division 1287, Street Elec. Ry. & Motor Coach Employees v. Missouri, 374 U.S. 74 (1963).

3. Local anti-strike breaking legislation has prohibited the following conduct by persons or firms involved in a strike or lockout:

(a) the "knowing" employment of an individual who regularly offers to serve as a replacement for striking or locked-out workers;

(b) soliciting persons to serve as such replacements without giving them adequate notice of that fact;

(c) doing any of the above, but only when replacements are to be employed for the purpose of interfering, by "force or threats," with peaceful picketing during a labor dispute.

Are these prohibitions preempted by the NLRA? Cf. U.S. Chamber of Commerce v. New Jersey, 89 N.J. 131, 445 A.2d 353 (1982); Michigan Chamber of Commerce v. Michigan, 115 L.R.R.M. 2887 (Mich. Cir. Ct. 1984).

Farmer, Admr. v. United Bhd. of Carpenters, Local 25, 430 U.S. 290 (1977). After plaintiff's election as a local's vice-president, his differences with other union officials over internal policies ultimately led to his complaint in a California court against the local and international unions and individual officers. Count II alleged that because of the defendants' intentional, outrageous, and intimidating conduct, plaintiff had suffered grievous emotional distress resulting in bodily injury. Three other counts claimed that, because of the plaintiff's dissident intraunion political activities, the unions had discriminated in employment referrals through the local's exclusive hiring hall for area carpenters, thereby violating both the multiemployer collective argreement and the plaintiff's membership contract. The trial judge restricted his jurisdiction to Count II. He instructed the jury, inter alia, that the plaintiff's recovery depended on proof that he had suffered severe emotional distress because of the defendants' intentional and outrageous conduct that had gone beyond mere insults to the infliction of substantial injury that "no reasonable man in a civilized society should be expected to endure." The judge denied an instruction barring the jury's consideration of employment discrimination. Judgment issued on the jury's award of $7,500 actual damages and $175,000 punitive damages. On appeal, California courts reversed on preemption grounds. The Supreme Court vacated that decision and remanded. It declared (per Powell, J.):

"Although cases like *Linn* and *Russell* involve state-law principles with only incidental application to conduct occurring in the course of a labor dispute, it is well settled that the general applicability of a state cause of action is not sufficient to exempt it from pre-emption. '[I]t [has not] mattered whether the States have acted through laws of broad general application rather than laws specifically directed towards the governance of industrial relations.'⁹ *Garmon*, 359 U.S., at 244. Instead, the cases reflect a balanced inquiry into such factors as the nature of the federal and state interests in regulation and the potential for interference with federal regulation. As was said in Vaca v. Sipes, 386 U.S., at 180, our cases 'demonstrate that the decision to pre-empt federal and state court jurisdiction over a given class of cases must depend upon the nature of the particular interests being asserted and the effect upon the administration of national labor policies of concurrent judicial and administrative remedies.'¹⁰

". . . In the context of Hill's [the original plaintiff who had died] other allegations of discrimination in hiring hall referrals, these allegations of tortious conduct might form the basis for unfair labor practice charges before the Board. On this basis a rigid application of the *Garmon* doctrine might support the conclusion of the California courts that Hill's entire action was preempted by federal law. Our cases indicate, however, that inflexible appli-

---

⁹In Plumbers v. Borden, 373 U.S. 690 (1963), an employee sued his union, which operated a hiring hall, claiming that the union had arbitrarily refused to refer him for employment on one particular occasion. He alleged that the union's conduct constituted both tortious interference with his right to contract for employment and breach of a promise, implicit in his membership arrangement with the union, not to discriminate unfairly against any member or deny him the right to work. Under these circumstances, concurrent state-court jurisdiction would have impaired significantly the functioning of the federal system. If unfair labor practice charges had been filed, the Board might have concluded that the refusal to refer Borden was due to a lawful hiring hall practice, see Teamsters v. NLRB, 365 U.S. 667 (1961). Board approval of various hiring hall practices would be meaningless if state courts could declare those procedures violative of the contractual rights implicit between a member and his union. Accordingly, the state cause of action was pre-empted under *Garmon*. Similar reasoning prompted the court to apply the *Garmon* rule in the companion case of Iron Workers v. Perko, 373 U.S. 701 (1963).

¹⁰Machinists v. Gonzales, 356 U.S. 617 (1958), established another exception to the general rule of pre-emption for state-law actions alleging expulsion from union membership in violation of the applicable union constitution and bylaws and seeking restoration to membership and damages due to the illegal expulsion. *Gonzales* was decided prior to this Court's adoption in *Garmon* of the current pre-emption test, and our decision in *Lockridge* makes it clear that "the full-blown rationale of *Gonzales* could not survive the rule of *Garmon*." *Lockridge*, 403 U.S., at 295. At the same time, we stated that "*Garmon* did not cast doubt upon the result reached in *Gonzales*," id., at 295, since *Garmon* cited *Gonzales* as an example of the nonapplicability of the normal pre-emption rule "where the activity regulated was a merely peripheral concern of the . . . Act." 359 U.S., at 243.

Although the *Lockridge* decision has been the subject of extensive criticism, [references, supra p. 756, are cited here], the instant case presents no occasion for us to reconsider the relationship between *Lockridge* and *Gonzales*. Whatever the scope of *Gonzales* after *Garmon* and *Lockridge*, the analysis used by the Court in those cases is consistent with the framework discussed in the text above. *Lockridge* held that the state-court action at issue involved a "real and immediate" potential for conflict with the federal scheme, 403 U.S., at 296, whereas the possibility that the state court in *Gonzales* "would directly and consciously implicate principles of federal law" was considered "at best tangential and remote." Ibid.

cation of the doctrine is to be avoided, especially where the state has a substantial interest in regulation of the conduct at issue and the state's interest is one that does not threaten undue interference with the federal regulatory scheme. With respect to Hill's claims of intentional infliction of emotional distress, we cannot conclude that Congress intended exclusive jurisdiction to lie in the Board. . . . Regardless of whether the operation of the hiring hall was lawful or unlawful under federal statutes, there is no federal protection for conduct on the part of union officers which is so outrageous that 'no reasonable man in a civilized society should be expected to endure it.' . . . Thus, as in Linn v. Plant Guard Workers, 383 U.S. 53 (1966), and Automobile Workers v. Russell, 356 U.S. 634 (1958), permitting the exercise of state jurisdiction over such complaints does not result in state regulation of federally protected conduct.

"The State, on the other hand, has a substantial interest in protecting its citizens from the kind of abuse of which Hill complained. That interest is no less worthy of recognition because it concerns protection from emotional distress caused by outrageous conduct, rather than protection from physical injury, as in *Russell*, or damage to reputation, as in *Linn*. . . .

"There is, to be sure, some risk that the state cause of action for infliction of emotional distress will touch on an area of primary federal concern. . . . In those counts of the complaint that the trial court dismissed, Hill alleged discrimination against him in hiring hall referrals, which were also alleged to be violations of both the collective bargaining agreement and the membership contract. These allegations if sufficiently supported before the [NLRB], would make out an unfair labor practice[11] and the Superior Court considered them preempted by the federal Act.[12] Even in count two of the complaint Hill made allegations of discrimination in 'job-dispatching procedures' and 'work assignments' which, standing alone, might well be preempted as the exclusive concern of the Board. The occurrence of the abusive conduct, with which the state tort action is concerned, in such a

---

[11] . . . Prior to the filing of this suit, Hill filed an unfair labor practice charge with the Board with respect to one specific instance of alleged discrimination. He alleged that the Union violated §§8(b)(1)(A) and 8(b)(2) by refusing to honor an employer's request that he be referred for employment on a particular construction job. The Board awarded Hill $2,517 in backpay.

[12] Whether a hiring hall practice is discriminatory and therefore violative of federal law is a determination Congress has entrusted to the Board. See Teamsters Local v. Labor Board, 365 U.S. 667 (1961). Whether there is federal preemption with respect to allegations of breach of a *contractual* obligation depends upon the nature of the obligation and the alleged breach. See Motor Coach Employees v. Lockridge, 403 U.S., at 292-297, 298-301. Casting a complaint in terms of breach of a *membership agreement* does not necessarily insulate a state court action from application of the preemption doctrine. . . .

context of federally prohibited discrimination suggests a potential for interference with the federal scheme of regulation.

"Viewed, however, in light of the discrete concerns of the federal scheme and the state tort law, that potential for interference is insufficient to counterbalance the legitimate and substantial interest of the State in protecting its citizens. If the charges in Hill's complaint were filed with the Board, the focus of any unfair labor practice proceeding would be on whether the statements or conduct on the part of union officials discriminated or threatened discrimination against him in employment referrals for reasons other than failure to pay union dues. Whether the statements or conduct of the respondents also caused Hill severe emotional distress and physical injury would play no role in the Board's disposition of the case, and the Board could not award Hill damages for pain, suffering, or medical expenses. Conversely, the state court tort action can be adjudicated without resolution of the 'merits' of the underlying labor dispute. Recovery for the tort of emotional distress under California law requires proof that the defendant intentionally engaged in outrageous conduct causing the plaintiff to sustain mental distress. . . . The state court need not consider, much less resolve, whether a union discriminated or threatened to discriminate against an employee in terms of employment opportunities. To the contrary, the tort action can be resolved without reference to any accommodation of the special interests of unions and members in the hiring hall context.

"On balance, we cannot conclude that Congress intended to oust state court jurisdiction over actions for tortious activity such as that alleged in this case. At the same time, we reiterate that concurrent state court jurisdiction cannot be permitted where there is a realistic threat of interference with the federal regulatory scheme. Union discrimination in employment opportunities cannot itself form the underlying 'outrageous' conduct on which the state court tort action is based; to hold otherwise would undermine the preemption principle. Nor can threats of such discrimination suffice to sustain state court jurisdiction. It may well be that the threat, or actuality, of employment discrimination will cause a union member considerable emotional distress and anxiety. But something more is required before concurrent state court jurisdiction can be permitted. Simply stated, it is essential that the state tort be either unrelated to employment discrimination or a function of the particularly abusive manner in which the discrimination is accomplished or threatened rather than a function of the actual or threatened discrimination itself.[13]

---

[13] In view of the potential for interference with the federal scheme of regulation, the trial court should be sensitive to the need to minimize the jury's exposure to evidence of employment discrimination in cases of this sort. Where evidence of discrimination is necessary to establish the context in which the state claim arose, the trial court should instruct the jury that

"Two further limitations deserve emphasis. Our decision rests in part on our understanding that California law permits recovery only for emotional distress sustained as a result of 'outrageous' conduct. The potential for undue interference with federal regulation would be intolerable if state tort recoveries could be based on the type of robust language and clash of strong personalities that may be commonplace in various labor contexts. We also repeat that state trial courts have the responsibility in cases of this kind to assure that the damages awarded are not excessive. See Linn v. Plant Guard Workers, 383 U.S., at 65-66.

"Although the second count of petitioner's complaint alleged the intentional infliction of emotional distress, it is clear from the record that the trial of that claim was not in accord with the standards discussed above. The evidence supporting the verdict in Hill's favor focuses less on the alleged campaign of harassment, public ridicule, and verbal abuse, than on the discriminatory refusal to dispatch him to any but the briefest and least desirable jobs; and no appropriate instruction distinguishing the two categories of evidence was given to the jury. The consequent risk that the jury verdict represented damages for employment discrimination rather than for instances of intentional infliction of emotional distress precludes reinstatement of the judgment of the Superior Court.

"The Judgment of the Court of Appeals is vacated, and the case is remanded to that court for further proceedings not inconsistent with this opinion."

NOTES

1. If the plaintiff had unequivocally alleged only a breach of the duty of fair representation, his claim presumably would not have been preempted. See Vaca v. Sipes, infra p. 1145.

2. If federal and state courts are entitled to resolve a claim of a breach of the duty of fair representation, how are such claims to be distinguished from preempted claims based on §§8(b)(1) and 8(b)(2) discrimination?

3. In IBEW v. Foust, infra p. 1167, the Supreme Court barred punitive damages against a union for unfair representation. Consider the effect of *Foust* and *Linn*, supra p. 742, on the continued availability of punitive damages when *Farmer's* requirements are met.

4. Given the "outrageous conduct" required by *Farmer* and the pliable

---

the fact of employment discrimination (as distinguished from attendant tortious conduct under state law) should not enter into the determination of liability or damages.

standards governing damage awards, is a jury instruction to disregard the "fact of employment discrimination" likely to be effective?

Sears, Roebuck & Co. v. San Diego County District Council of Carpenters
436 U.S. 180 (1978)

STEVENS, J. . . . The question . . . is whether the [NLRA] deprives a state court of the power to entertain an action by an employer to enforce state trespass laws against picketing which is arguably — but not definitely — prohibited or protected by federal law.

I

On October 24, 1973, two business representatives of respondent Union visited the department store operated by petitioner (Sears) in Chula Vista, Cal., and determined that certain carpentry work was being performed by men who had not been dispatched from the Union hiring hall. Later that day, the Union agents met with the store manager and requested that Sears either arrange to have the work performed by a contractor who employed dispatched carpenters or agree in writing to abide by the terms of the Union's master labor agreement with respect to the dispatch and use of carpenters. The Sears manager stated that he would consider the request, but he never accepted or rejected it.

Two days later the Union established picket lines on Sears' property. The store is located in the center of a large rectangular lot. The building is surrounded by walkways and a large parking area. A concrete wall at one end separates the lot from residential property; the other three sides adjoin public sidewalks which are adjacent to the public streets. The pickets patrolled either on the privately owned walkways next to the building or in the parking area a few feet away. They carried signs indicating that they were sanctioned by the "Carpenters Trade Union." The picketing was peaceful and orderly.

Sears' security manager demanded that the Union remove the pickets from Sears' property. The Union refused, stating that the pickets would not leave unless forced to do so by legal action. On October 29, Sears filed a verified complaint in the Superior Court of California seeking an injunction against the continuing trespass; the court entered a temporary restraining order enjoining the Union from picketing on Sears' property. The Union promptly removed the pickets to the public sidewalks. On November 21, 1973, after hearing argument on the question whether the Union's picketing on Sears' property was protected by state or federal law, the court entered a preliminary injunction. The California Court of Appeal affirmed. While acknowledging the [*Garmon*] preemption guidelines, the court held that the Union's continuing trespass fell within the longstanding exception for conduct which touched interests so deeply rooted in local feeling and responsibility that pre-emption could not be inferred in the absence of clear evidence of congressional intent.

The Supreme Court of California reversed. It concluded that the picketing was arguably protected by §7 of the Act, because it was intended to secure work for Union members and to publicize Sears' undercutting of the prevailing area standards. . . . The court reasoned that the trespassory character of the picketing did not disqualify it from arguable protection, but was merely a factor which the [NLRB] would consider in determining whether or not it was in fact protected. The court also considered it "arguable" that the Union had engaged in recognitional picketing subject to §8(b)(7)(C). . . . Because the picketing was both arguably protected by §7 and arguably prohibited by §8, the court held that state jurisdiction was pre-empted under [*Garmon*].

Since the Wagner Act was passed in 1935, this Court has not decided whether, or under what circumstances, a state court has power to enforce local trespass law against a union's peaceful picketing. The obvious importance of this problem led us to grant certiorari in this case. . . .

II

We start from the premise that the Union's picketing on Sears' property after the request to leave was a continuing trespass in violation of state law. We note, however, that the scope of the controversy in the state court was limited. Sears asserted no claim that the picketing itself violated any state or federal law. It sought simply to remove the pickets from its property to the public walkways, and the injunction issued by the state court was strictly confined to the relief sought. Thus, as a matter of state law, the location of the picketing was illegal but the picketing itself was unobjectionable.

As a matter of federal law, the legality of the picketing was unclear. Two separate theories would support an argument by Sears that the picketing was prohibited by §8 of the NLRA and a third theory would support an argument by the Union that the picketing was protected by §7. Under each of these theories the Union's purpose would be of critical importance.

If an object of the picketing was to force Sears into assigning the carpentry work away from its employees to Union members dispatched from the hiring hall, the picketing may have been prohibited by §8(b)(4)(D). Alternatively, if an object of the picketing was to coerce Sears into signing a prehire or members-only type agreement with the Union, the picketing was at least arguably subject to the prohibition on recognitional picketing contained in §8(b)(7)(C). Hence, if Sears had filed an unfair labor practice charge against the Union, the Board's concern would have been limited to the question whether the Union's picketing had an objective proscribed by the Act; the location of the picketing would have been irrelevant.

On the other hand, the Union contends that the sole objective of its action was to secure compliance by Sears with area standards, and therefore the picketing was protected by §7. Longshoremen v. Ariadne Shipping Co., 397 U.S. 195. Thus, if the Union had filed an unfair labor practice charge under §8(a)(1) when Sears made a demand that the pickets leave its property, it is at least arguable that the Board would have found Sears guilty of an unfair labor practice.

Our second premise, therefore, is that the picketing was both arguably prohibited and arguably protected by federal law. The case is not, however, one in which "it is clear or may fairly be assumed" that the subject matter which the state court sought to regulate — that is, the location of the picketing — is either prohibited or protected by the Federal Act.

III

In San Diego Building Trades Council v. Garmon, 359 U.S. 236, the Court made two statements which have come to be accepted as the general guidelines for deciphering the unexpressed intent of Congress regarding the permissible scope of state regulation of activity touching upon labor-management relations. The first related to activity which is clearly protected or prohibited by the federal statute. The second articulated a more sweeping prophylactic rule: "When an activity is arguably subject to §7 or §8 of the Act, the States as well as the federal courts must defer to the exclusive competence of the [NLRB] if the danger of state interference with national policy is to be averted." Id., at 245. . . .

[T]he Court has refused to apply the *Garmon* guidelines in a literal, mechanical fashion. This refusal demonstrates that "the decision to preempt . . . state court jurisdiction over a given class of cases must depend upon the nature of the particular interests being asserted and the effect upon the administration of national labor policies" of permitting the state court to proceed. Vaca v. Sipes, 386 U.S. 171, 180.

With this limitation in mind, we turn to the question whether preemption is justified in a case of this kind under either the arguably protected or the arguably prohibited branch of the *Garmon* doctrine. While the considerations underlying the two categories overlap, they differ in significant respects and therefore it is useful to review them separately. We therefore first consider whether the arguable illegality of the picketing as a matter of federal law should oust the state court of jurisdiction to enjoin its trespassory aspects. Thereafter, we consider whether the arguably protected character of the picketing should have that effect. . . .

IV

The leading case holding that when an employer grievance against a union may be presented to the [NLRB] it is not subject to litigation in a state tribunal is Garner v. Teamsters, 346 U.S. 485. *Garner* involved peaceful organizational picketing which arguably violated §8(b)(2). . . . A Pennsylvania equity court held that the picketing violated the Pennsylvania Labor Relations Act and therefore should be enjoined. The State Supreme Court reversed because the union conduct fell within the jurisdiction of the [NLRB] to prevent unfair labor practices.

  This Court affirmed because Congress had "taken in hand this particular type of controversy . . . [i]n language almost identical to parts of the Pennsylvania statute," 346 U.S. at 488. Accordingly, the State, through its courts, was without power to "adjudge the same controversy and extend its own form of relief." Id., at 489. This conclusion did not depend on any surmise as to "how the [NLRB] might have decided this controversy had petitioners presented it to that body." Ibid. The precise conduct in controversy was arguably prohibited by federal law and therefore state jurisdiction was pre-empted. The reason for preemption was clearly articulated:

> Congress evidently considered that centralized administration of specially designed procedures was necessary to obtain uniform application of its substantive rules and to avoid these diversities and conflicts likely to result from a variety of local procedures and attitudes. . . . A multiplicity of tribunals and a diversity of procedures are quite as apt to produce incompatible or conflicting adjudications as are different rules of substantive law. The same reasoning which prohibits federal courts from intervening in such cases, except by way of review or on application of the federal Board, precludes state courts from doing so. . . . The conflict lies in remedies. . . . [W]hen two separate remedies are brought to bear on the same activity, a conflict is imminent. Id., at 498-499.

  This reasoning has its greatest force when applied to state laws regulating the relations between employees, their union, and their employer. It may also apply to certain laws of general applicability which are occasionally invoked in connection with a labor dispute. Thus, a State's antitrust law may not be invoked to enjoin collective activity which is also arguably prohibited by the federal Act. Capital Service, Inc. v. NLRB, 347 U.S. 501; Weber v. Anheuser Busch, Inc., 348 U.S. 468. In each case, the pertinent inquiry is whether the two potentially conflicting statutes were "brought to bear on precisely the same conduct." Id., at 479.

On the other hand, the Court has allowed a State to enforce certain laws of general applicability even though aspects of the challenged conduct were arguably prohibited by §8 of the NLRA. Thus, for example, the Court has upheld state-court jurisdiction over conduct that touches "interests so deeply rooted in local feeling and responsibility that, in the absence of compelling congressional direction, we could not infer that Congress had deprived the States of the power to act." San Diego Building Trades Council v. Garmon, 359 U.S., at 244. . . .

[In *Farmer*, the] Court identified those factors which warranted a departure from the general pre-emption guidelines in the "local interest" cases. Two are relevant to the arguably *prohibited* branch of the *Garmon* doctrine. First, there existed a significant state interest in protecting the citizen from the challenged conduct. Second, although the challenged conduct occurred in the course of a labor dispute and an unfair labor practice charge could have been filed, the exercise of state jurisdiction over the tort claim entailed little risk of interference with the regulatory jurisdiction of the Labor Board. Although the arguable federal violation and the state tort arose in the same factual setting, the respective controversies presented to the state and federal forums would not have been the same.

The critical inquiry, therefore, is not whether the State is enforcing a law relating specifically to labor relations or one of general application but whether the controversy presented to the state court is identical to (as in *Garner*) or different from (as in *Farmer*) that which could have been, but was not, presented to the Labor Board. For it is only in the former situation that a state court's exercise of jurisdiction necessarily involves a risk of interference with the unfair labor practice jurisdiction of the Board which the arguably prohibited branch of the *Garmon* doctrine was designed to avoid.[27]

In the present case, the controversy which Sears might have presented to the Labor Board is not the same as the controversy presented to the state court. If Sears had filed a charge, the federal issue would have been whether the picketing had a recognitional or work-reassignment objective; decision of that issue would have entailed relatively complex factual and legal determinations completely unrelated to the simple question whether a trespass had

---

[27]While the distinction between a law of general applicability and a law expressly governing labor relations is . . . not dispositive for preemption purposes, it is of course apparent that the latter is more likely to involve the accommodation which Congress reserved to the Board. It is also evident that enforcement of a law of general applicability is less likely to generate rules or remedies which conflict with federal labor policy than the invocation of a special remedy under a state labor relations law.

occurred. Conversely, in the state action, Sears only challenged the location of the picketing; whether the picketing had an objective proscribed by federal law was irrelevant to the state claim. Accordingly, permitting the state court to adjudicate Sears' trespass claim could create no realistic risk of interference with the Labor Board's primary jurisdiction to enforce the statutory prohibition against unfair labor practices.

The reasons why pre-emption of state jurisdiction is normally appropriate when union activity is arguably prohibited by federal law plainly do not apply to this situation; they therefore are insufficient to preclude a State from exercising jurisdiction limited to the trespassory aspects of that activity.

V

The question whether the arguably protected character of the Union's trespassory picketing provides a sufficient justification for pre-emption of the state court's jurisdiction over Sears' trespass claim involves somewhat different considerations.

Apart from notions of "primary jurisdiction,"[29] there would be no objection to state courts' and the NLRB's exercising concurrent jurisdiction over conduct prohibited by the federal Act. But there is a constitutional objection to state-court interference with conduct actually protected by the Act. Considerations of federal supremacy, therefore, are implicated to a greater extent when labor-related activity is protected than when it is prohibited. Nevertheless, several considerations persuade us that the mere fact that the Union's trespass was *arguably* protected is insufficient to deprive the state court of jurisdiction in this case.

The first is the relative unimportance in the context of the "primary

---

[29] In this opinion, the term "primary jurisdiction" is used to refer to the various considerations articulated in *Garmon* and its progeny that militate in favor of pre-empting state-court jurisdiction over activity which is subject to the unfair labor practice jurisdiction of the federal Board. This use of the term should not be confused with the doctrine of primary jurisdiction, which has been described by Professor Davis as follows:

"The precise function of the doctrine of primary jurisdiction is to guide a court in determining whether the court should refrain from exercising its jurisdiction until after an administrative agency has determined some question or some aspect of some question arising in the proceeding before the court. The doctrine of primary jurisdiction does not necessarily allocate power between courts and agencies, for it governs only the question whether court or agency will *initially* decide a particular issue, not the question whether court or agency will *finally* decide the issue." 3 K. Davis, Administrative Law Treatise §19.01, p. 3 (1958) (emphasis in original).

While the considerations underlying *Garmon* are similar to those underlying the primary-jurisdiction doctrine, the consequences of the two doctrines are therefore different. Where applicable, the *Garmon* doctrine completely pre-empts state-court jurisdiction unless the Board determines that the disputed conduct is neither protected nor prohibited by the federal Act.

jurisdiction" rationale articulated in *Garmon*. In theory, of course, that rationale supports pre-emption regardless of which section of the NLRA is critical to resolving a controversy which may be subject to the regulatory jurisdiction of the NLRB. Indeed, at first blush, the primary-jurisdiction rationale provides stronger support for pre-emption in this case when the analysis is focused upon the arguably protected, rather than the arguably prohibited, character of the Union's conduct. For to the extent that the Union's picketing was arguably protected, there existed a potential overlap between the controversy presented to the state court and that which the Union might have brought before the NLRB. Prior to granting any relief from the Union's continuing trespass, the state court was obligated to decide that the trespass was not actually protected by federal law, a determination which might entail an accommodation of Sears' property rights and the Union's §7 rights. In an unfair labor practice proceeding initiated by the Union, the Board might have been required to make the same accommodation.

Although it was theoretically possible for the accommodation issue to be decided either by the state court or by the [NLRB], there was in fact no risk of overlapping jurisdiction in this case. The primary-jurisdiction rationale justifies pre-emption only in situations in which an aggrieved party has a reasonable opportunity either to invoke the Board's jurisdiction himself or else to induce his adversary to do so. In this case, Sears could not directly obtain a Board ruling on the question whether the Union's trespass was federally protected. Such a Board determination could have been obtained only if the Union had filed an unfair labor practice charge alleging that Sears had interfered with the Union's §7 right to engage in peaceful picketing on Sears' property. By demanding that the Union remove its pickets from the store's property, Sears in fact pursued a course of action which gave the Union the opportunity to file such a charge. But the Union's response to Sears' demand foreclosed the possibility of having the accommodation of §7 and property rights made by the [NLRB]; instead of filing a charge with the Board, the Union advised Sears that the pickets would only depart under compulsion of legal process.

In the face of the Union's intransigence, Sears had only three options: permit the pickets to remain on its property; forcefully evict the pickets; or seek the protection of the State's trespass laws. Since the Union's conduct violated state law, Sears legitimately rejected the first option. Since the second option involved a risk of violence, Sears surely had the right — perhaps even the duty — to reject it. Only by proceeding in state court, therefore, could Sears obtain an orderly resolution of the question whether the Union had a federal right to remain on its property.

The primary-jurisdiction rationale unquestionably requires that when the same controversy may be presented to the state court or the NLRB, it must be presented to the Board. But that rationale does not extend to cases in which an employer has no acceptable method of invoking, or inducing the Union to invoke, the jurisdiction of the Board. We are therefore persuaded that the primary-jurisdiction rationale does not provide a *sufficient* justification for pre-empting state jurisdiction over arguably protected conduct when the party who could have presented the protection issue to the Board has not done so and the other party to the dispute has no acceptable means of doing so.[34]

This conclusion does not, however, necessarily foreclose the possibility that pre-emption may be appropriate. The danger of state interference with federally protected conduct is the principal concern of the *Garmon* doctrine. To allow the exercise of state jurisdiction in certain contexts might create a significant risk of misinterpretation of federal law and the consequent prohibition of protected conduct. In those circumstances, it might be reasonable to infer that Congress preferred the costs inherent in a jurisdictional hiatus to the frustration of national labor policy which might accompany the exercise of state jurisdiction. Thus, the acceptability of "arguable protection" as a justification for preemption in a given class of cases is, at least in part, a function of the strength of the argument that §7 does in fact protect the disputed conduct.

The Court has held that state jurisdiction to enforce its laws prohibiting violence, defamation, the intentional infliction of emotional distress, or obstruction of access to property is not pre-empted by the NLRA. But none of those violations of state law involves protected conduct. In contrast,

---

[34] "If the [NLRA] provided an effective mechanism whereby an employer could obtain a determination from the [NLRB] as to whether picketing is protected or unprotected, I would agree that the fact that picketing is 'arguably' protected should require state courts to refrain from interfering in deference to the expertise and national uniformity of treatment offered by the NLRB. But an employer faced with 'arguably protected' picketing is given by the present federal law no adequate means of obtaining an evaluation of the picketing by the NLRB. The employer may not himself seek a determination from the Board and is left with the unsatisfactory remedy of using 'self-help' against the pickets to try to provoke the union to charge the employer with an unfair labor practice.

"So long as employers are effectively denied determinations by the NLRB as to whether 'arguably protected' picketing is actually protected except when an employer is willing to threaten or use force to deal with picketing, I would hold that only labor activity determined to be actually, rather than arguably, protected under federal law should be immune from state judicial control. To this extent San Diego Building Trades Council v. Garmon, 359 U.S. 236 (1959), should be reconsidered." Longshoremen v. Ariadne Shipping Co., 397 U.S. 195, 201-202 (White, J., concurring).

some violations of state trespass laws may be actually protected by §7 of the federal Act.

In NLRB v. Babcock & Wilcox Co., 351 U.S. 105, for example, the Court recognized that in certain circumstances nonemployee union organizers may have a limited right of access to an employer's premises for the purpose of engaging in organization solicitation. And the Court has indicated that *Babcock* extends to §7 rights other than organizational activity, though the "locus" of the "accommodation of §7 rights and private property rights . . . may fall at differing points along the spectrum depending on the nature and strength of the respective §7 rights and private property rights asserted in any given context." Hudgens v. NLRB, 424 U.S. 507, 522. . . .

The remaining question is whether under *Babcock* the trespassory nature of the picketing caused it to forfeit its protected status. Since it cannot be said with certainty that, if the Union had filed an unfair labor practice charge against Sears, the Board would have fixed the locus of the accommodation at the unprotected end of the spectrum, it is indeed "arguable" that the Union's peaceful picketing, though trespassory, was protected. Nevertheless, permitting state courts to evaluate the merits of an argument that certain trespassory activity is protected does not create an unacceptable risk of interference with conduct which the Board, and a court reviewing the Board's decision, would find protected. For while there are unquestionably examples of trespassory union activity in which the question whether it is protected is fairly debatable, experience under the Act teaches that such situations are rare and that a trespass is far more likely to be unprotected than protected.

Experience with trespassory organizational solicitation by nonemployees is instructive in this regard. While *Babcock* indicates that an employer may not always bar nonemployee union organizers from his property, his right to do so remains the general rule. To gain access, the union has the burden of showing that no other reasonable means of communicating its organizational message to the employees exists or that the employer's access rules discriminate against union solicitation. That the burden imposed on the union is a heavy one is evidenced by the fact that the balance struck by the Board and the courts under the *Babcock* accommodation principle has rarely been in favor of trespassory organizational activity.

Even on the assumption that picketing to enforce area standards is entitled to the same deference in the *Babcock* accommodation analysis as organizational solicitation,[42] it would be unprotected in most instances.

---

[42] This assumption, however, is subject to serious question. Indeed, several factors make the argument for protection of trespassory-area-standards picketing as a category of conduct less compelling than that for trespassory organizational solicitation. First, the right to organize

While there does exist some risk that state courts will on occasion enjoin a trespass that the Board would have protected, the significance of this risk is minimized by the fact that in the cases in which the argument in favor of protection is the strongest, the union is likely to invoke the Board's jurisdiction and thereby avoid the state forum. Whatever risk of an erroneous state-court adjudication does exist is outweighed by the anomalous consequence of a rule which would deny the employer access to any forum in which to litigate either the trespass issue or the protection issue in those cases in which the disputed conduct is least likely to be protected by §7.

If there is a strong argument that the trespass is protected in a particular case, a union can be expected to respond to an employer demand to depart by filing an unfair labor practice charge; the protection question would then be decided by the agency experienced in accommodating the §7 rights of unions and the property rights of employers in the context of a labor dispute. But if the argument for protection is so weak that it has virtually no chance of prevailing, a trespassing union would be well advised to avoid the jurisdiction of the Board and to argue that the protected character of its conduct deprives the state court of jurisdiction.

As long as the union has a fair opportunity to present the protection issue to the [NLRB], it retains meaningful protection against the risk of error in a state tribunal. In this case the Union failed to invoke the jurisdiction of the Labor Board, and Sears had no right to invoke that jurisdiction and could not even precipitate its exercise without resort to self-help. Because the assertion of state jurisdiction in a case of this kind does not create a significant risk of prohibition of protected conduct, we are unwilling to presume that Congress intended the arguably protected character of the Union's conduct to deprive the California courts of jurisdiction to entertain Sears' trespass action.[44]

---

is at the very core of the purpose for which the NLRA was enacted. Area-standards picketing, in contrast, has only recently been recognized as a §7 right. Hod Carriers Local 41 (Calumet Contractors Assn.), 133 N.L.R.B. 512 (1961). Second, *Babcock* makes clear that the interests being protected by according limited-access rights to nonemployee, union organizers are not those of the organizers but of the employees located on the employer's property. The Court indicated that "no . . . obligation is owed nonemployee organizers"; any right they may have to solicit on an employer's property is a derivative of the right of that employer's employees to exercise their organization rights effectively. Area-standards picketing, on the other hand, has no such vital link to the employees located on the employer's property. While such picketing may have a beneficial effect on the compensation of those employees, the rationale for protecting area-standards picketing is that a union has a legitimate interest in protecting the wage standards of its members who are employed by competitors of the picketed employer.

[44] The fact that Sears demanded that the Union discontinue the trespass before it initiated the trespass action is critical to our holding. While it appears that such a demand was a

The judgment of the Supreme Court of California is therefore reversed, and the case is remanded to that court for further proceedings not inconsistent with this opinion.

[Justice Blackmun's concurrence included two points. First, the corollary of the Court's reasoning is this: If after the employer asks the union to leave his property, the union files and expeditiously pursues an NLRB charge, state jurisdiction is preempted (and states should not act) until the General Counsel declines to issue a complaint or the Board dismisses the complaint and holds the picketing unprotected. Second, the likelihood of frequent state-court interference with protected activities will diminish if state courts provide an adversary hearing before restraining union picketing.

Powell, J., concurring separately, rejected Blackmun's corollary, stressing the slowness of the Board's processes, coupled with the risk of violence in situations where trespass has occurred.

Brennan, J., with whom Stewart and Marshall, JJ., joined in dissent, urged that the limitation of employer remedies by *Garmon* produces no social harm while averting the danger of state interference with national policy that "may seriously erode §7's protections. . . ." He continued:]

The present case illustrates both the necessity of this flat rule [the "arguably protected" branch of *Garmon*] and the danger of even the slightest deviation from it. . . . The question submitted to the state court was whether the Union had a protected right to locate peaceful nonobstructive pickets on the privately owned walkway adjacent to Sears' retail store or on the privately owned parking lot a few feet away.

That the trespass was arguably protected could scarcely be clearer. NLRB v. Babcock & Wilcox Co., 351 U.S., at 112, indicates that trespassory §7 activity is protected when "reasonable efforts . . . through other available channels" will not enable the union to reach its intended audience. This standard, which was developed in the context of a rather different factual situation, is but an application of more general principles. "[T]he basic objective under the Act [is the] accommodation of §7 rights and private

---

precondition to commencing a trespass action under California law, see 122 Cal. Rptr. 449 (1975), in order to avoid a valid claim of pre-emption it would have been required as a matter of federal law in any event.

The Board has taken the position that "a resort to court action . . . does not violate §8(a)(1)." NLRB v. Nash-Finch Co., supra, at 142. If the employer were not required to demand discontinuation of the trespass before proceeding in state court and the Board did not alter its position in cases of this kind, the union would be deprived of an opportunity to present the protection issue to the agency created by Congress to decide such questions. While the union's failure to invoke the Board's jurisdiction should not be a sufficient basis for pre-empting state jurisdiction, the employer should not be permitted to deprive the union of an opportunity to do so.

property rights 'with as little destruction of one as is consistent with the maintenance of the other.' The locus of that accommodation, however, may fall at differing points along the spectrum depending on the nature and strength of the respective §7 rights and private property rights asserted in any given context." Hudgens v. NLRB, 424 U.S., at 522, quoting NLRB v. Babcock & Wilcox Co., supra, at 112; see Scott Hudgens, 230 N.L.R.B., at 417.

Here, it can seriously be contended that the locus of the accommodation should be on the side of permitting the trespass. The §7 interest is strong: The object of the picketing was arguably protected on one of two theories — as "area standards" or as "recognitional" picketing — and the record suggests that the relocation of the picketing to the nearest public area — a public sidewalk 150 to 200 feet away — may have so diluted the picketing's impact as to make it virtually meaningless. The private property interest, in contrast, was exceedingly weak. The picketing was confined to a portion of Sears' property which was open to the public and on which Sears had permitted solicitations by other groups. Thus, while Sears to be sure owned the property, it resembled public property in many respects. Indeed, while Sears' legal position would have been quite different if the lot and walkways had been owned by the city of Chula Vista, it is doubtful that Sears would have been any less angered or upset by the picketing if the property had in fact been public.

But the Court refuses to follow the simple analysis that has been sanctioned by the decisions of the last 20 years. Its reasons for discarding prior teachings, apparently, is a belief that faithful application of *Garmon* to the generic situation presented by this case causes positive social harm. I disagree. . . .

[P]re-emption of state-court jurisdiction to deal with trespassory picketing has been largely, if not entirely, confined to situations such as presented in this case, i.e., in which the interest of the employer in preventing the picketing is weak, the §7 interest in picketing on the employer's property strong, and the picketing peaceful and nonobstructive. In this circumstance, I think the denial to the employer of a remedy is an entirely acceptable social cost for the benefits of a pre-emption rule that avoids the danger of state-court interference with national labor policy. The Court's arguments to the contrary are singularly unpersuasive. . . .

[T]he Court places no great reliance on the likelihood of violence. But the only other reason advanced for a conclusion that *Garmon* produces socially intolerable results is that it is "anomalous" to deny an employer a trespass remedy. Since the Act extensively regulates the conditions under which an employer's proprietary rights must yield to the exercise of §7 rights,

I am at a loss as to why the anomaly here is any greater than that which results from the pre-emption of state remedies against tortious conspiracies, compare §7 of the Act with Frankfurter & Greene 26-39, or from the pre-emption of state remedies against nonmalicious libels. See Linn v. Plant Guard Workers, 383 U.S. 53 (1966).

That this Court's departure from *Garmon* creates a great risk that protected picketing will be enjoined is amply illustrated by the facts of this case and by the task that was assigned to the California Superior Court. To decide whether the location of the Union's picketing rendered it unlawful, the state court here had to address a host of exceedingly complex labor law questions, which implicated nearly every aspect of the Union's labor dispute with Sears and which were uniquely within the province of the Board. Because it had to assess the "relative strength of the §7 right," see Hudgens v. NLRB, 424 U.S., at 522, its first task necessarily was to determine the nature of the Union's picketing. This picketing could have been characterized in one of three ways: as protected area-standards picketing . . . ; as prohibited picketing to compel a reassignment of work . . . ; or as recognitional picketing that is protected at the outset but prohibited if no petition for a representative election is filed within a reasonable time, not to exceed 30 days. . . . Notably, if the state court concluded that the picketing was prohibited by §8(b)(4) — or unprotected by §7 on any other theory — that determination would have been conclusive against respondent: Whether or not the state court agreed with the Union's contention that effective communication required that picketing be located on Sears' premises, the court would enjoin the trespassory picketing on the ground that no protected §7 interest was involved. Obviously, since even the Court admits that the characterization of the picketing "entail[s] relatively complex factual and legal determinations," . . . there is a substantial danger that the state court, lacking the Board's expertise and specialized sensitivity to labor relations matters, would err at the outset and effectively deny respondent the right to engage in any effective §7 communication.

But even if the state court correctly assesses the §7 interest, there are a host of other pitfalls. A myriad of factors are or could be relevant to determining whether §7 protected the trespass: e.g., whether and to what extent relocating the picketing on the nearest public property 150 feet away would have diluted its impact; whether the picketing was characterized as recognitional or area standards; whether or the extent to which Sears had opened the property up to the public or permitted similar solicitation on it; whether it mattered that the pickets did not work for Sears, etc. . . .

It simply cannot be seriously contended that the thousands of judges, state and federal, throughout the United States can be counted upon accurately to identify the relevant considerations and give each the proper weight in accommodating the respective rights. . . .

[The dissent here challenges the Court's conclusion that nonemployee trespasses would probably be "unprotected" and that unions, when there were strong reasons for finding their activity "protected," would probably avoid state interference by going to the NLRB.]

. . . [W]hat is far more disturbing than the specific holding in this case is its implications for different generic situations. Whatever the shortcomings of *Garmon*, none can deny the necessity for a rule in this complex area that is capable of uniform application by the lower courts. The Court's new exception to *Garmon* cannot be expected to be correctly applied by those courts and thus most inevitably will threaten erosion of the goal of uniform administration of the national labor laws. Even though the Court apparently intends to create only a very narrow exception to *Garmon* — largely if not entirely limited to situations in which the employer first requested the nonemployees engaged in area-standards picketing on the employer's property to remove the pickets from the employer's land and the union did not respond by filing §8(a)(1) unfair labor practice charges — the approach the Court today adopts cannot be so easily cabined and thus threatens intolerable disruption of national labor policy.

Because §8(b) only affords an employer a remedy against certain types of unprotected employee activity, there necessarily will be a myriad of circumstances in which an employer will be confronted with possibly unprotected employee or union conduct, and yet be unable directly to invoke the Board's processes to receive a determination of the protected character of the conduct. Today's decision certainly opens the door to a conclusion by state and federal courts that the Court's new exception applies in any situation where the employer has requested that the labor organization cease what the employer claims is unprotected conduct and the union has not responded by filing a §8(a)(1) charge. . . .

The burden that will be thrown upon this Court finally to decide, on an ad hoc, generic-situation-by-generic-situation basis, whether the employer had a "reasonable opportunity" to obtain a Board determination and, if not, whether the risk of interference outweighs the anomaly of denying the employer a remedy, should give us pause. Inconsistency and error in decisions below may compel review of an inordinate number of cases, lest lower court adjudications threaten irretrievable injury to interests protected by §7. . . .

[On remand, the California Supreme Court reversed the order granting a preliminary injunction, holding that the union's picketing on private property was both lawful under California law and protected from injunction by the state's anti-injunction statute. Sears, Roebuck & Co. v. San Diego County District Council of Carpenters, 25 Cal. 3d 317, 599 P.2d 676, 158 Cal. 3d 170 (1979).]

NOTES

1. Was the Supreme Court's approach to "arguably" protected activities restricted to trespassory conduct or does it have a broader application? Compare the Court's rationale for upholding state jurisdiction with that of the California Court of Appeals.

2. When a union, defendant in a state court action, has filed a charge with the NLRB, at what stage of the NLRB's proceeding — from the filing of the charge to a final judgment enforcing a Board order or affirming a dismissal — should the state court stay or dismiss the proceeding against the union or enter a judgment against it? Does the Supreme Court's approach in *Bill Johnson's Restaurants*, supra p. 746, cast any light on this question? Suppose that prior to a company's filing a state court action against the union, the union has filed a charge with the NLRB. What effect will the pendency of the prior charge have on the exercise of state jurisdiction?

3. How broad is the impact of *Sears* on the "arguably prohibited" branch of *Garmon?* How much difference between the essential elements of the state and federal claims will be sufficient to meet the Court's test for state jurisdiction? Will artful pleadings be decisive?

4. In secondary boycott cases, the location as well as the purpose of picketing may be material, although title to the picketed site usually is not. What effect, if any, are these considerations likely to have on the Court's approach to trespassory picketing that allegedly involves a violation of §8(b)(4)(B)?

5. Jones, after accepting the employer's offer of a supervisory job, worked for two days and then, by agreement, took an eight-day vacation. Upon his return, he was fired. Jones, who believed that the union had procured his discharge in retaliation for his having worked for a nonunion firm years ago, filed §§8(b)(1)(A) and (B) charges. The Regional Director informed Jones that he would not issue a complaint since (1) there was insufficient evidence to show that the union had caused the discharge or coerced the employer in the selection of its collective bargaining representative; and (2) Jones' discharge had apparently been a part of changes in the company's supervisory structure (and the union had only participated in discussions of such changes). Without appealing to the General Counsel, Jones brought a state suit against both the company and the union, alleging

the foregoing facts. Count I claimed that the union had interfered with his employment contract with the company, in that the union's business agent had maliciously and intentionally coerced and intimidated the company into breaching that contract. Jones sought lost wages, punitive damages, and counsel fees. Count II claimed that the union had interfered (non-coercively) with Jones' contractual relationship, and requested the same relief. Count III sought relief only against the company for breach of the employment contract. The defendants moved to dismiss all counts. Is the "identical controversies" approach of *Sears* applicable here? If so, what should be the disposition of that motion? Cf. Local 926, Operating Engrs. v. Jones, 460 U.S. 669 (1983). Would plaintiff's case against preemption have been stronger if he had brought his state suit before going to the NLRB? If the claim against the union is held preempted, must the claim against the company also be preempted?

New York Telephone Co. v. New York Dept. of Labor
440 U.S. 519 (1979)

[The Communications Workers, following a negotiating impasse, called a nationwide strike against Bell Telephone on July 14, 1971. For most workers the strike ended a week later. In New York, however, it lasted seven months. New York law normally authorizes payment of unemployment compensation after approximately one week of the claimant's unemployment. However, if unemployment is caused by a "strike, lockout, or other industrial controversy in the establishment in which [the claimant] was employed," there is an additional seven-week waiting period for benefits. During the ensuing five months, after the expiration of the waiting period, 33,000 strikers received more than $49 million in benefits, an average of almost $75 a week — approximately one-half of their average wages. Under New York's "experience rating," the company ultimately bore a substantial part of the cost of those benefits.

The company brought suit in a federal district court against the state administrators of the fund, requesting a declaratory judgment that the New York law (§591.1) conflicts with federal law and is invalid, an injunction against its enforcement, and an award of the increase in the company's taxes because of the benefits paid to the strikers. After a long trial, the district court granted the requested relief, finding that the availability of unemployment compensation was a substantial factor in prolonging strikes and that it conflicted with "the federal labor policy favoring the free play of economic forces in the collective bargaining process." The Second Circuit, without disturbing the trial court's finding, reversed. It inferred from the legislative history of the NLRA, Title IX of the Social Security Act, and subsequent developments, that Congress had intended to tolerate this conflict. The Supreme Court affirmed, also relying on the legislative history of those two federal statutes and also conceding that the New York law alters the economic balance between labor and management.]

STEVENS, J., announced the judgment of the Court in an opinion in which WHITE and REHNQUIST, JJ., joined.

. . . The differences between state laws regulating private conduct and the unemployment benefits program at issue here are important. . . . For a variety of reasons, they suggest an affinity between this case and others in which the Court has shown a reluctance to infer a pre-emptive congressional intent.

Section 591.1 is not a "State law regulating the relations between employees, their union and their employer," as to which the reasons underlying the pre-emption doctrine have their "greatest force." *Sears*, supra, at 193. Instead, as discussed below, the statute is a law of general applicability. Although that is not a sufficient reason to exempt it from pre-emption, Farmer v. Carpenters, 430 U.S. 290, 300, our cases have consistently recognized that a congressional intent to deprive the States of their power to enforce such general laws is more difficult to infer than an intent to pre-empt laws directed specifically at concerted activity. . . .

[P]ayments to the strikers implement a broad state policy that does not primarily concern labor-management relations, but is implicated whenever members of the labor force become unemployed. Unlike most States,[24] New York has concluded that the community interest in the security of persons directly affected by a strike outweighs the interest in avoiding any impact on a particular labor dispute.

New York's program . . . is structured to comply with a federal statute, and as a consequence is financed, in part, with federal funds. The federal subsidy mitigates the impact on the employer of any distribution of benefits [and] the federal statute authorizing the subsidy provides additional evidence of Congress' reluctance to limit the States' authority in this area. . . .

In this case, there is no evidence that the Congress that enacted the

---

[24] This may be an overstatement. It is true that only Rhode Island has a statutory provision like New York's that allows strikers to receive benefits after a waiting period of several weeks. See Grinnell Corp. v. Hackett, 475 F.2d 449, 457-459 (1st Cir. 1973). But most States provide benefits to striking employees who have been replaced by nonstriking employees, and many States, pursuant to the so-called "American rule," allow strikers to collect benefits so long as their activities have not substantially curtailed the productive operations of their employer. . . .

[NLRA] intended to deny the States the power to provide unemployment benefits for strikers. . . . Far from the compelling congressional direction [required for preemption here], the silence of Congress in 1935 actually supports the contrary inference that Congress intended to allow the States to make this policy determination for themselves.

New York was one of five States that had an unemployment insurance law before Congress passed the Social Security and the Wagner Acts in the summer of 1935. Although the New York law did not then assess taxes against employers on the basis of their individual experience, it did authorize the payment of benefits to strikers out of a general fund financed by assessments against all employers in the State. The junior Senator from New York, Robert Wagner, was a principal sponsor of both the [NLRA] and the Social Security Act, the two statutes were considered in Congress simultaneously and enacted into law within five weeks of one another; and the Senate Report on the Social Security Bill, in the midst of discussing the States' freedom of choice with regard to their unemployment compensation laws, expressly referred to the New York statute as a qualifying example. Even though that reference did not mention the subject of benefits for strikers, it is difficult to believe that Senator Wagner and his colleagues were unaware of such a controversial provision, particularly . . . when both unemployment and labor unrest were matters of vital national concern.

Difficulty becomes virtual impossibility when it is considered that the issue of public benefits for strikers became a matter of express congressional concern in 1935 during the hearings and debates on the Social Security Act. . . . [T]he scheme of the Social Security Act has always allowed the States great latitude in fashioning their own programs. From the beginning, however, the Act has contained a few specific requirements for federal approval. One of these provides that a State may not deny compensation to an otherwise qualified applicant because he had refused to accept work as a strikebreaker, or had refused to resign from a union as a condition of employment. By contrast, Congress rejected the suggestions of certain advisory members of the Roosevelt Administration as well as some representatives of citizens and business groups that the States be prohibited from providing benefits to strikers. . . .

Undeniably, Congress was aware of the possible impact of unemployment compensation on the bargaining process. The omission of any direction concerning payment to strikers in either the [NLRA] or the Social Security Act implies that Congress intended that the States be free to authorize, or to prohibit, such payments.

. . . On several occasions since the 1930s Congress has expressly addressed the question of paying benefits to strikers, and especially the effect of such payments on federal labor policy. On none of these occasions has it suggested that such payments were already prohibited by an implicit federal rule of law. Nor, on any of these occasions has it been willing to supply the prohibition. . . .

[Blackmun, J., with whom Marshall, J., concurred, questioned Stevens' suggestion that there should be a "compelling congressional direction" of preemption, as inconsistent with the position in *Lodge 76*, and called for preemption unless "there is evidence of congressional intent to tolerate the state practice."

Powell, J., with whom the Chief Justice and Stewart, J., joined, dissented; he urged that there was no evidence that Congress intended to permit New York to upset the balance reflected in national policy by cushioning the impact of long strikes on employees and by making employers pay for most of that cushion. For these reasons, he also rejected the plurality's categorization of the New York law as one of general applicability. More generally, he referred to the national policy in favor of free collective bargaining and to Congress' selectivity in regulating the use of economic weapons in support of bargaining demands. He added:]

The availability and usefulness of many [other economic weapons] depend entirely upon the relative economic strength of the parties.

What Congress left unregulated is as important as the regulations that it imposed. It sought to leave labor and management essentially free to bargain for an agreement to govern their relationship. Congress also intended, by its limited regulation, to establish a fair balance of bargaining power. That balance, once established, obviates the need for substantive regulation of the fairness of collective-bargaining agreements: whatever agreement emerges from bargaining between fairly matched parties is acceptable. Thus, the NLRA's regulations not only are limited in scope but also must be viewed as carefully chosen to create the congressionally desired balance in the bargaining relationship. . . .

A much more cautious approach to implied amendments of the NLRA is required if the Court is to give proper effect to the legislative judgments of the Congress. Having once resolved the balance to be struck in the collective-bargaining relationship, and having embodied that balance in the NLRA, Congress should not be expected by the Court to reaffirm the balance explicitly each time it later enacts legislation that may touch in some way on the collective-bargaining relationship. Absent explicit modification of the NLRA, or clear inconsistency between the terms of the NLRA and a subsequent statute, the Court should assume that Congress intended to leave the NLRA unaltered. This assumption is especially appropriate in considering the intent of Congress when it enacted the Social Security Act just five weeks after completing its deliberations on the NLRA. . . .

NOTES

1. Justice Stevens in footnote 15 of his opinion rejected the company's suggestion that the NLRA should be interpreted as at least forbidding state benefits to participants in strikes illegal under the NLRA (the Board had declared part of the telephone strike illegal), because such a rule would involve the state in ruling on the legality of strikes under §8. Is the corollary of his position that a state that now denies any compensation to strikers would not be authorized to provide for compensation, provided that a strike does not violate §8(b)?

2. Would that hypothetical state statute be distinguishable from a statute that grants unemployment compensation to employees who are locked out, but not to strikers? Cf. Kimbell, Inc. v. Employment Security Comm. of New Mexico, 429 U.S. 804 (1976) (dismissing for want of a substantial federal question an appeal from a state holding that federal law did not bar a retroactive post-strike award of unemployment benefits to strikers eligible only because their strike had not substantially curtailed their employer's operations).

3. Suppose a state provided for unemployment compensation from the first day of unemployment, including strike-caused unemployment. Would this statute involve a greater or lesser intrusion into the federal scheme? Would it more easily be classified as a statute of "general applicability" than the New York law? If both of your answers are "yes," what are their implications for the significance of such classifications in preemption analysis?

4. Kennan, in The Effect of Unemployment Insurance Payments on Strike Duration (Working Paper No. 79-26, Dept. of Econ., Brown Univ., May, 1980), cautiously and qualifiedly concluded that the settlement probability of New York strikes after the eight-week period is substantially and significantly less than elsewhere. On the other hand, the New York settlement probability, before the eight weeks have run, is substantially greater than that of the other states. That difference, which is greatest when the strike is very young, decreases with time, and, after the crossover on the 50th day, there is a difference in the other direction, which thereafter steadily widens. The author was quite cautious about any inferences regarding the cause (or causes) of these remarkable differences.

On the causation issue, should unemployment insurance payments to strikers be expected to prolong stoppages, or, instead, would the prospect of such payments be discounted and affect the parties' demands and sticking points?

Belknap, Inc. v. Hale
103 S. Ct. 3172 (1983)

[After unsuccessful negotiations for a renewal agreement, employees in the warehouse and maintenance unit struck Belknap, Inc., on February 1. The company immediately granted a wage increase, effective on that date, to employees who stayed on the job; it also advertised in local newspapers for permanent replacements for the strikers. A large number of candidates appeared, and the company hired many new employees. Each new employee signed a statement that he was a permanent replacement for a designated Belknap employee in a designated job classification. The union's March 7 charge that the employer's February unilateral wage increase violated the NLRA led to the issuance of a complaint in April. Following that charge and complaint, Belknap's letters reiterated to the employees: "You will continue to be permanent replacement employees so long as you conduct yourselves in accordance with the policies . . . in effect here at Belknap." Also, "we continue to meet and negotiate in good faith with the Union. . . . However, we have made it clear to the Union that we have no intention of getting rid of the permanent replacements just in order to provide jobs for the replaced strikers if and when the Union calls off the strike." Shortly before the unfair labor practice hearing in July, the Regional Director convened a conference and said that a settlement would lead him to agree to dismiss the charges and complaints against both parties. (The union had also been charged with an unfair labor practice.) The parties ultimately settled the one major unresolved issue — the recall of the strikers — by agreeing that the company would reinstate at least 35 strikers a week.

Replacements laid off to make room for returning strikers sued Belknap in a state court. They alleged that the company had represented that it was hiring permanent employees, knowing that the statement was false and that the plaintiffs would detrimentally rely on it. Alternatively, they claimed that Belknap's firing of them was a breach of contract. Each plaintiff sought $250,000 in compensatory damages and an equal amount in punitive damages. The Kentucky Court of Appeals reversed a summary judgment for Belknap, reasoning that Belknap had not committed any unfair labor practices and, additionally, that preemption was not warranted because the plaintiffs' claims were of only peripheral concern to the NLRA and were deeply rooted in local law. The Supreme Court, in a lengthy opinion by White, J., upheld Kentucky's jurisdiction.]

WHITE, J. . . . . We are unpersuaded [by the contention that Congress intended the Union's and Belknap's conduct "to be controlled by the free play of economic forces" (quoting from *Machinists*)]. We find unacceptable the notion that the federal law on the one hand insists on promises of permanent employment if the employer anticipates keeping the replacements in preference to returning strikers, but on the other hand forecloses damage suits for the employer's breach of these very promises. Even more mystifying is the suggestion that the federal law shields the employer from damages suits for misrepresentations that are made [while] securing permanent replacements and [that] are actionable under state law.

Arguments that entertaining suits by innocent third parties for breach of contract or for misrepresentation will "burden" the employer's right to hire permanent replacements are no more than arguments that "this is war", that "anything goes", and that promises of permanent employment that under federal law the employer is free to keep, if it so chooses, are essentially meaningless. It is one thing to hold that the federal law intended to leave the employer and the union free to use their economic weapons against one another, but is quite another to hold that either the employer or the union is also free to injure innocent third parties without regard to the normal rules of law governing those relationships. We cannot agree with the dissent that Congress intended such a lawless regime.

The argument that entertaining suits like this will interfere with the asserted policy of the federal law favoring settlement of labor disputes fares no better. This is just another way of asserting that the employer need not answer for its repeated assurances of permanent employment or for its otherwise actionable misrepresentations to secure permanent replacements. We do not think that the normal contractual rights and other usual legal interests of the replacements can be so easily disposed of by broad-brush assertions that no legal rights may accrue to them during a strike because the federal law has privileged the "permanent" hiring of replacements and encourages settlement. . . .

If serious detriment will result to the employer from conditioning offers so as to avoid a breach of contract if the employer is forced by Board order to reinstate strikers or if the employer settles on terms requiring such reinstatement, much the same result would follow from Belknap's and the Board's construction of the Act. Their view is that, as a matter of federal law, an employer may terminate replacements, without liability to them, in the event of settlement or Board decision that the strike is an unfair labor practice strike. Any offer of permanent employment to replacements is thus necessarily conditional and nonpermanent. This view of the law would inevitably become widely known and would deter honest employers from making promises that they know they are not legally obligated to keep. Also, many putative replacements would know that the proffered job is, in important respects, non-permanent and may not accept employment for that reason. It is doubtful, with respect to the employer's ability to hire, that there would be a substantial difference between the effect of the Board's preferred rule and a rule that would subject the employer to damages liability unless it suitably conditions its offers of employment made to replacements.

Belknap counters that conditioning offers in such manner will render replacements non-permanent employees subject to discharge to make way for strikers at the conclusion or settlement of a purely economic strike, which would not be the case if replacements had been hired on a "permanent" basis as the Board now understands that term. The balance of power would thus be distorted if the employer is forced to condition its offers for its own protection. Under Belknap's submission, however, which is to some extent supported by the Board, Belknap's promises, although in form assuring permanent employment, would as a matter of law be non-permanent to the same extent as they would be if expressly conditioned on the eventuality of settlement requiring reinstatement of strikers and on its obligation to reinstate unfair labor practice strikers. . . .

An employment contract with a replacement promising permanent employment, subject only to settlement with its employees' union and to a Board unfair labor practice order directing reinstatement of strikers, would not in itself render the replacement a temporary employee subject to displacement by a striker over the employer's objection during or at the end of what is proved to be a purely economic strike. The Board suggests that such a conditional offer "might" render the replacements only temporary hires that the employer would be required to discharge at the conclusion of a purely economic strike. . . . But the permanent-hiring requirement is designed to protect the strikers, who retain their employee status and are entitled to reinstatement unless they have been permanently replaced. That protection is unnecessary if the employer is ordered to reinstate them because of the commission of unfair labor practices. It is also meaningless if the employer settles with the union and agrees to reinstate strikers. But the protection is of great moment if the employer is not found guilty of unfair practices, does not settle with the union, or settles without a promise to reinstate. In that eventuality, the employer, although he has prevailed in the strike, may refuse reinstatement only if he has hired replacements on a permanent basis. If he has promised to keep the replacements on in such a situation, discharging them to make way for selected strikers whom he deems more experienced or more efficient would breach his contract with the replacements. Those contracts, it seems to us, create a sufficiently permanent arrangement to permit the prevailing employer to abide by its promises.[8]

We perceive no substantial impact on the availability of settlement of economic or unfair labor practice strikes if the employer is careful to protect itself against suits like this in the course of contracting with strike replacements.[9] Its risk of liability if it discharges replacements pursuant to a settlement or to a Board order would then be minimal. We fail to understand why in such circumstances the employer would be any less willing to settle the strike than it would be under the regime proposed by Belknap and the Board, which as a matter of law, would permit it to settle without liability for misrepresentation or for breach of contract.

. . . *Machinists* did not deal with solemn promises of permanent employment, made to innocent replacements, that the employer was free to make and keep under federal law. J. I. Case, Co. v. NLRB, 321 U.S. 332 (1944), suggests that individual contracts of employment must give way to otherwise valid provisions of the collective bargaining contract, id., at 336-339, but it was careful to say that the Board "has no power to adjudicate the validity or effect of such contracts except as to their effect on matters within its jurisdiction." . . . There, the cease-and-desist order, as modified, stated that the discontinuance of the individual contracts was "without prejudice to the assertion of any legal rights the employee may have acquired under such contract or to any defenses thereto by the employer." Id., at 342. . . .

It is said that respondent replacements are employees within the bargaining unit, that the Union is the bargaining representative of petitioner's employees, and the replacements are thus bound by the terms of the settle-

---

[8] The refusal to fire permanent replacements because of commitments made to them in the course of an economic strike satisfies the requirement of NLRB v. Fleetwood Trailer Co., 389 U.S. 375, 380 (1967), that the employer have a "legitimate and substantial justification" for his refusal to reinstate strikers. That the offer and promise of permanent employment are conditional does not render the hiring any less permanent if the conditions do not come to pass. All hirings are to some extent conditional. . . .

[9] If, as we hold, an employer may condition his offer to replacements and hence avoid conflicting obligations to strikers and replacements in the event of a settlement providing for reinstatement, the employer will very likely do so. Hence, there will be little occasion for replacements to bring suits for breach of contract or misrepresentation. The employer that nevertheless makes unconditional commitments to replacements and wants to discharge them after settlement with the union will be in much the same position as the employer in W. R. Grace & Co. v. Local 759, 103 S. Ct. 2177 (1983). There the employer signed a conciliation agreement with the EEOC that conflicted with its collective bargaining agreement with the union. We recognized the employer's dilemma, but because it was of the employer's own making we unanimously refused to relieve the employer of either obligation. 103 S. Ct., at 2184-2186.

ment negotiated between the employer and "their" representative.[10] The argument is not only that as a matter of federal law the employer cannot be foreclosed from discharging the replacements pursuant to a contract with a bargaining agent, but also that by virtue of the agreement with the Union it is relieved from responding in damages for its knowing breach of contract — that is, that the contracts are not only not specifically enforceable but also may be breached free from liability for damages. We need not address . . . the issue of specific performance since the respondents ask only damages. As to the damages issue, as we have said above, such an argument was rejected in *J.I. Case*.

If federal law forecloses this suit, more specific and persuasive reasons than those based on *Machinists* must be identified to support any such result. Belknap insists that the rationale of the *Garmon* decision, properly construed and applied, furnishes these reasons.

[The Regional Director's complaint alleged that Belknap's unilateral wage increase, on February 1, violated the Act and prolonged the strike. The Court, assuming proof of those allegations, examined the resulting legal situation.]

[T]he strike would have been an unfair labor practice strike almost from the very start. Belknap's [subsequent] advertised offers of permanent employment to replacements would arguably have been unfair labor practices since they could be viewed as threats to refuse to reinstate unfair labor practice strikers. See NLRB v. Laredo Coca Cola Bottling Co., 613 F.2d 1338, 1341 (CA5), *cert. denied*, 449 U.S. 889 (1980). Furthermore, if the strike had been an unfair labor practice strike, Belknap would have been forced to reinstate the strikers rather than keep replacements on the job. . . . Belknap submits that its offers of permanent employment to respondents were therefore arguably unfair labor practices, the adjudication of which were within the exclusive jurisdiction of the Board, and that discharging respondents to make way for strikers was protected activity since it was no more than the federal law required in the event the unfair labor practices were proved. . . .

Under *Garmon*, a state may regulate conduct that is of only peripheral concern to the Act or which is so deeply rooted in local law that the courts should not assume that Congress intended to preempt the application of state law. [The Court summarized *Linn*, *Farmer*, and *Sears Roebuck*.] In [*Sears Roebuck*] we emphasized that a critical inquiry in applying the *Garmon* rules, where the conduct at issue in the state litigation is said to be arguably

---

[10] The AFL-CIO disavows this argument. It suggests that replacements are bound only by those agreements that a union makes, as the exclusive bargaining agent for the struck employer's workers, regarding the terms and conditions of employment for the employer's workforce after the termination of the strike. . . .

prohibited by the Act and hence within the exclusive jurisdiction of the NLRB, is whether the controversy presented to the state court is identical with that which could be presented to the Board. . . .

. . . It is true that whether the strike was an unfair labor practice strike and whether the offer to replacements was the kind of offer forbidden during such a dispute were matters for the Board. The focus of these determinations, however, would be on whether the rights of strikers were being infringed. Neither controversy would have anything in common with the question whether Belknap made misrepresentations to replacements that were actionable under state law. . . . The strikers cannot secure reinstatement, or indeed any relief, by suing for misrepresentation in state court. The state courts in no way offer them an alternative forum for obtaining relief that the Board can provide. The same was true in *Sears* and *Farmer*. Hence, it appears to us that maintaining the misrepresentation action would not interfere with the Board's determination of matters within its jurisdiction and that such an action is of no more than peripheral concern to the Board and the federal law. At the same time, Kentucky surely has a substantial interest in protecting its citizens from misrepresentations that have caused them grievous harm. . . . The state interests involved in this case clearly outweigh any possible interference with the Board's function that may result from permitting the action for misrepresentation to proceed.

Neither can we accept the assertion that the breach of contract claim is preempted. . . .

[E]ven had there been no settlement and the Board had ordered reinstatement of what it held to be unfair labor practice strikers, the suit for damages for breach of contract could still be maintained without in any way prejudicing the jurisdiction of the Board or the interest of the federal law in insuring the replacement of strikers. The interests of the Board and the NLRA, on the one hand, and the interest of the state in providing a remedy to its citizens for breach of contract, on the other, are "discrete" concerns, cf. Farmer v. Carpenters, supra, 430 U.S., at 304. . . .

Because neither the misrepresentation nor the breach-of-contract cause of action is preempted under the *Garmon* or the *Machinists* [decisions], the decision of the Kentucky Court of Appeals is Affirmed.

Blackmun, J., concurred separately.

Brennan, J., joined by Marshall and Powell, JJ., dissented.

NOTE

What considerations and what precedents would you expect the dissent to emphasize?

CHAPTER 9

REGULATION OF THE BARGAINING PROCESS

Section 8(5) of the Wagner Act imposed on employers a duty to bargain, and §8(b)(3), added by the Taft-Hartley Act, imposed a corresponding obligation on unions. The objective of §8(5) — responsible and genuine negotiations between employers and the representatives of their employees — was central to the entire statutory scheme. However, the attempt to achieve that objective by the force of law involved substantial tensions with other objectives of labor policy, as well as many administrative difficulties.

Section 8(5) was read as requiring employers to negotiate in "good faith," but the determination of whether an employer had done so was frequently a delicate task, requiring a scrutiny of the employer's negotiating positions. Such scrutiny undermined another objective of national policy — the preservation of a system of private decision-making under which the parties were, in general, to be free to make their own bargain without governmental dictation as to content. They were also to be legally free to agree to disagree, although agreement was to be encouraged by the consideration that disagreement would trigger economic pressure, costly to both sides. Economic warfare, actual or prospective, was thus the motive power for the bargaining process while the duty to bargain was designed to foster responsible dialogue, fair terms of employment, and industrial peace. Yet there was an obvious conflict between the power component of bargaining and those goals. That conflict was likely to be especially sharp when a union, particularly a newly recognized one, because of its "weakness," could not achieve substantial gains or a "fair bargain."

Enforcing a duty to bargain was further complicated by the absence of manageable criteria for assessing the fairness of employment terms. Such criteria as were furnished by economic analysis or the "market" were of dubious help; it was precisely those criteria that the bargaining system fostered by the statute was to supplant or to supplement. An attempt by government to develop criteria of fairness would have involved formidable intellectual difficulties as well as serious tensions with "freedom of contract"

797

and the self-help protected or permitted by the statute. On the other hand, a complete disregard of an employer's bargaining posture threatened to convert the duty of recognition and bargaining into a sterile ritual.

The legislative history of the Wagner Act failed to provide clear guides for resolving these basic difficulties surrounding the effort to legislate "good faith" in the context of a private bargaining system. The changes made by the LMRA (§8(d)) not only failed to resolve those difficulties, but also raised as many new questions of detail as the old ones that they clarified.[a]

The continuing difficulty in this area is suggested by the persistence of a substantial number and percentage of annual §8(a)(5) charges — amounting to 34.5 percent of all charges filed against employers in 1968, 27.7 percent in 1975, and 31.4 percent (or nearly 10,000 charges) in 1981. See 33 N.L.R.B. Ann. Rep. 203 (1968); 40 N.L.R.B. Ann. Rep. 205 (1975); 46 N.L.R.B. Ann. Rep. 176 (1981). Although some charges of "bad faith" are essentially tactical maneuvers and some result from outright employer defiance of the law, many §8(a)(5) charges can fairly be attributed to instability in administration and adjudication.

In 1961, a distinguished group[b] of students declared: "[I]t is unrealistic to expect that, by legislation, 'good faith' can be brought to the bargaining table." That group concluded:

> The subjects to be covered by bargaining, the procedures to be followed, the nuances of strategy involving the timing of a "best offer," the question of whether to reopen a contract during its term — such matters as these are best left to the parties themselves. Indeed the work load of the National Labor Relations Board and of the parties could be substantially reduced by returning these issues to the door of the employer or union. [Labor Study Group, The Public Interest in National Labor Policy 82 (Comm. for Econ. Dev., 1961).]

For a contrary assessment, emphasizing "the critical significance of the duty to bargain to the scheme of the Act," see Ross, The Government as a Source of Union Power 263-265 (1965) (critically reviewed by Meltzer, 33 U. Chi. L. Rev. 166 (1965)).

Among many useful general discussions of the duty to bargain are Cox,

---

[a]For a discussion of the legislative background of the pertinent provisions of both statutes, see Duvin, The Duty to Bargain: Law in Search of Policy, 64 Colum. L. Rev. 248, 250-256 (1964); P. Ross, The Government as a Source of Union Power: The Role of Public Policy in Collective Bargaining 8-100 (1965). But cf. Smith, The Evolution of the Duty to Bargain, 39 Mich. L. Rev. 1065 (1941).

[b]The study group consisted of Clark Kerr, Douglas V. Brown, David L. Cole, John T. Dunlop, William Y. Elliott, Albert Rees, Robert M. Solow, Phillip Taft, and George W. Taylor. George P. Shultz was Staff Director.

The Duty to Bargain in Good Faith, 71 Harv. L. Rev. 1401 (1958); Feinsinger, The National Labor Relations Act and Collective Bargaining, 57 Mich. L. Rev. 807 (1959); Fleming, New Challenges for Collective Bargaining, 1964 Wis. L. Rev. 426.

A. EXCLUSIVE REPRESENTATION: AN OVERVIEW

J.I. Case Co. v. NLRB
321 U.S. 332 (1944)

JACKSON, J. . . . The petitioner, J.I. Case Company, . . . from 1937 offered each [plant] employee an individual contract of employment. The contracts were uniform and for a term of one year. The Company agreed to furnish employment as steadily as conditions permitted, to pay a specified rate, which the Company might redetermine if the job changed, and to maintain certain hospital facilities. The employee agreed to accept the provisions, to serve faithfully and honestly for the term, to comply with factory rules, and that defective work should not be paid for. About 75% of the employees accepted and worked under these agreements.

. . . [T]he execution of the contracts was not a condition of employment, nor was the status of individual employees affected by reason of signing or failing to sign the contracts. It is not found or contended that the agreements were coerced, obtained by any unfair labor practice, or that they were not valid under the circumstances in which they were made.

While the individual contracts executed August 1, 1941 were in effect, a CIO union petitioned the Board for certification as the exclusive bargaining representative of the production and maintenance employees. On December 17, 1941 a hearing was held, at which the Company urged the individual contracts as a bar to representation proceedings. The Board, however, directed an election, which was won by the union. The union was thereupon certified as the exclusive bargaining representative of the employees in question. . . .

The union then asked the Company to bargain. It refused, declaring that it could not deal with the union in any manner affecting rights and obligations under the individual contracts while they remained in effect. It offered to negotiate on matters which did not affect rights under the individual contracts, and said that upon the expiration of the contracts it would bargain as to all matters. Twice the Company sent circulars to its employees asserting the validity of the individual contracts and stating the position that it took before the Board in reference to them.

The Board held that the Company had refused to bargain collectively, in violation of [NLRA] §8(5) . . . ; and that the contracts had been utilized, by means of the circulars, to impede employees in the exercise of rights guaranteed by §7 . . . , with the result that the Company had engaged in unfair labor practices within the meaning of §8(1). . . .

Contract in labor law is a term the implications of which must be determined from the connection in which it appears. Collective bargaining between employer and the representatives of a unit, usually a union, results in an accord as to terms which will govern hiring and work and pay in that unit. The result is not, however, a contract of employment except in rare cases; no one has a job by reason of it and no obligation to any individual ordinarily comes into existence from it alone. The negotiations between union and management result in what often has been called a trade agreement, rather than in a contract of employment. Without pushing the analogy too far, the agreement may be likened to the tariffs established by a carrier, to standard provisions prescribed by supervising authorities for insurance policies, or to utility schedules of rates and rules for service, which do not of themselves establish any relationships but which do govern the terms of the shipper or insurer or customer relationship whenever and with whomever it may be established. . . .

After the collective trade agreement is made, the individuals who shall benefit by it are identified by individual hirings. The employer, except as restricted by the collective agreement itself and except that he must engage in no unfair labor practice or discrimination, is free to select those he will employ or discharge. But the terms of the employment already have been traded out. There is little left to individual agreement except the act of hiring. This hiring may be by writing or by word of mouth or may be implied from conduct. In the sense of contracts of hiring, individual contracts between the employer and employee are not forbidden, but indeed are necessitated by the collective bargaining procedure.

But, however engaged, an employee becomes entitled by virtue of the Labor Relations Act somewhat as a third party beneficiary to all benefits of the collective trade agreement, even if on his own he would yield to less favorable terms. The individual hiring contract is subsidiary to the terms of the trade agreement and may not waive any of its benefits, any more than a shipper can contract away the benefit of filed tariffs, the insurer the benefit of standard provisions, or the utility customer the benefit of legally established rates. . . .

Care has been taken in the opinions of the Court to reserve a field for the individual contract, even in industries covered by the [NLRA], not merely as an act or evidence of hiring, but also in the sense of a completely individually bargained contract setting out terms of employment, because there are circumstances in which it may legally be used, in fact, in which there is no alternative. Without limiting the possibilities, instances such as the following will occur: Men may continue work after a collective agreement expires and, despite negotiations in good faith, the negotiation may be deadlocked or delayed; in the interim express or implied individual agreements may be held to govern. The conditions for collective bargaining may not exist; thus a majority of the employees may refuse to join a union or to agree upon or designate bargaining representatives, or the majority may not be demonstrable by the means prescribed by the statute, or a previously existent majority may have been lost without unlawful interference by the employer and no new majority have been formed. As the employer in these circumstances may be under no legal obligation to bargain collectively, he may be free to enter into individual contracts.

Individual contracts, no matter what the circumstances that justify their execution or what their terms, may not be availed of to defeat or delay the procedures prescribed by the National Labor Relations Act looking to collective bargaining, nor to exclude the contracting employee from a duly ascertained bargaining unit; nor may they be used to forestall bargaining or to limit or condition the terms of the collective agreement. "The Board asserts a public right vested in it as a public body, charged in the public interest with the duty of preventing unfair labor practices." National Licorice Co. v. Labor Board, 309 U.S. 350, 364. Wherever private contracts conflict with its functions, they obviously must yield or the Act would be reduced to a futility.

It is equally clear [that] . . . the individual contract cannot be effective as a waiver of any benefit to which the employee otherwise would be entitled under the trade agreement. The very purpose of providing by statute for the collective agreement is to supersede the terms of separate agreements of employees with terms which reflect the strength and bargaining power and serve the welfare of the group. Its benefits and advantages are open to every employee of the represented unit, whatever the type or terms of his preexisting contract of employment.

But it is urged that some employees may lose by the collective agreement, that an individual workman may sometimes have, or be capable of getting, better terms than those obtainable by the group and that his freedom of contract must be respected on that account. We are not called upon to say that under no circumstances can an individual enforce an agreement more advantageous than a collective agreement, but we find the mere possibility that such agreements might be made no ground for holding generally that individual contracts may survive or surmount collective ones. The practice and philosophy of collective bargaining looks with suspicion on such individual advantages. Of course, where there is great variation in circumstances of employment or capacity of employees, it is possible for the collective bargain to prescribe only minimum rates or maximum hours or expressly to leave certain areas open to individual bargaining. But except as so provided, advantages to individuals may prove as disruptive of industrial peace as disadvantages. They are a fruitful way of interfering with organization and choice of representatives; increased compensation, if individually deserved, is often earned at the cost of breaking down some other standard thought to be for the welfare of the group, and always creates the suspicion of being paid at the long-range expense of the group as a whole. Such discriminations not infrequently amount to unfair labor practices. The workman is free, if he values his own bargaining position more than that of the group, to vote against representation; but the majority rules, and if it collectivizes the employment bargain, individual advantages or favors will generally in practice go in as a contribution to the collective result. We cannot except individual contracts generally from the operation of collective ones because some may be more individually advantageous. Individual contracts cannot subtract from collective ones, and whether under some circumstances they may add to them in matters covered by the collective bargain, we leave to be determined by appropriate forums under the laws of contracts applicable, and to the Labor Board if they constitute unfair labor practices.

It also is urged that such individual contracts may embody matters that are not necessarily included within the statutory scope of collective bargaining. . . . We know of nothing to prevent the employee's, because he is an employee, making any contract provided it is not inconsistent with a collective agreement or does not amount to or result from or is not part of an unfair labor practice. But in so doing the employer may not incidentally exact or obtain any diminution of his own obligation or any increase of those of employees in the matters covered by collective agreement.

Hence we find that the contentions of the Company that the individual contracts precluded a choice of representatives and warranted refusal to bargain during their duration were properly overruled. It follows that representation to the employees by circular letter that they had such legal effect was improper and could properly be prohibited by the Board.

[The Court modified the Board's order so as to make clear that the employer was barred only from invoking the individual agreements to forestall collective bargaining or to deter self-organization and not from entering into or enforcing individual agreements valid ab initio.

The dissenting opinion of Roberts, J., is omitted.]

NOTES

1. The doctrines of majority rule and exclusive representation are designed to reduce intraunion conflict, to facilitate the reconciliation of competing interests within a bargaining unit, and to blunt employer divide-and-conquer tactics. See Bok, Reflections on the Distinctive Character of American Labor Laws, 84 Harv. L. Rev. 1394, 1426-1427. As indicated by *Emporium Capwell*, supra p. 236, and *Shop Rite Foods*, supra p. 248, the exclusivity principle impinges on basic elements of the regulatory system, most notably the rights of employees under §§7 and 9(a). In this chapter (and the two that follow) the effects of exclusivity are examined in various contexts, ranging from the duty to bargain to the union's duty of fair representation. For useful general discussions, see Schatzki, Majority Rule, Exclusive Representation, and the Interests of Individual Workers: Should Exclusivity Be Abolished? 123 U. Pa. L. Rev. 897 (1975); Schreiber, The Origin of the Majority Rule and Simultaneous Development of Institutions to Protect the Minority, 25 Rutgers L. Rev. 237 (1971); Weyand, Majority Rule in Collective Bargaining, 45 Colum. L. Rev. 556 (1945).

2. An employer, in order to keep employee Jones, who had indicated that he might leave for a better-paying job, agreed with Jones to pay him more than the rate prescribed in the collective bargaining agreement. The union representative, upon learning of that increase, persuaded the employer to fire Jones. (a) Did the employer's negotiations with, or discharge of, Jones violate the Act? (b) Did the union violate the Act? (c) If the employer failed to perform on the individually negotiated agreement, does *J. I. Case* bar Jones from enforcing it by a legal action? Cf. Taft Broadcasting Co., 264 N.L.R.B. 185 (1982); International Assn. of Bridge, Structural & Ornamental Iron Workers, 128 N.L.R.B. 1379 (1960), *enforced*, 295 F.2d 808 (10th Cir. 1961).

B.   GOOD FAITH: BARGAINING POSITIONS AND PRACTICES

NLRB v. American National Insurance Co.
343 U.S. 395 (1952)

VINSON, C.J. . . . The Office Employees International Union, AFL Local 27, certified . . . as the exclusive bargaining representative of respondent's office employees, requested a meeting with respondent for the purpose of negotiating an agreement. . . . At the first meetings, beginning on November 30, 1948, the Union submitted a proposed contract covering wages, hours, promotions, vacations and other provisions commonly found in collective bargaining agreements, including a clause establishing a procedure for settling grievances arising under the contract by successive appeals to management with ultimate resort to an arbitrator.

On January 10, 1949, following a recess for study of the Union's contract proposals, respondent objected to the provisions calling for unlimited arbitration. To meet this objection, respondent proposed a so-called management functions clause listing matters such as promotions, discipline and work scheduling as the responsibility of management and excluding such matters from arbitration. The Union's representative took the position "as soon as [he] heard [the proposed clause]" that the Union would not agree to such a clause so long as it covered matters subject to the duty to bargain collectively under the Labor Act.

Several further bargaining sessions were held without reaching agreement on the Union's proposal or respondent's counterproposal to unlimited arbitration. As a result, the management functions clause was "by-passed" for bargaining on other terms of the Union's contract proposal. On January 17, 1949, respondent stated in writing its agreement with some of the terms proposed by the Union and, where there was disagreement, respondent offered counterproposals, including a clause entitled "Functions and Prerogatives of Management" along the lines suggested at the meeting of January 10th. The Union objected to the portion of the clause providing:

> The right to select and hire, to promote to a better position, to discharge, demote or discipline for cause, and to maintain discipline and efficiency of employees and to determine the schedules of work is recognized by both union and company as the proper responsibility and prerogative of management . . . , and while it is agreed that an employee feeling himself to have been aggrieved by any decision of the company in respect to such matters, or the union in his behalf, shall have the right to have such decision reviewed by top management officials . . . under the grievance machinery hereinafter set forth, it is further agreed that the final decision of the company made by such top management officials shall not be further reviewable by arbitration.

At this stage of the negotiations, the [NLRB] filed a complaint . . . based on the Union's charge that respondent had refused to bargain as required by the Labor Act and was thereby guilty of interfering with the rights of its employees guaranteed by §7 . . . and of unfair labor practices under §§8(a)(1) and 8(a)(5). . . . While the proceeding was pending, negotiations between the Union and respondent continued with the management functions clause remaining an obstacle to agreement. During the negotiations, respondent established new night shifts and introduced a new system of lunch hours without consulting the Union.

On May 19, 1949, a Union representative offered a second contract proposal which included a management functions clause containing much of the language found in respondent's second counterproposal, quoted above, with the vital difference that questions arising under the Union's proposed clause would be subject to arbitration as in the case of other grievances. Finally, on January 13, 1950, after the Trial Examiner had issued his report but before decision by the Board, an agreement between the Union and respondent was signed. The agreement contained a management functions clause that rendered nonarbitrable matters of discipline, work schedules and other matters covered by the clause. The subject of promotions and demotions was deleted from the clause and made the subject of a special clause establishing a union-management committee to pass upon promotion matters.

While these negotiations were in progress, the Board's Trial Examiner . . . held that respondent had a right to bargain for inclusion of a management functions clause in a contract. However, upon review of the entire negotiations, including respondent's unilateral action in changing working conditions during the bargaining, the Examiner found that from and after November 30, 1948, respondent had refused to bargain in a good faith effort to reach agreement. The Examiner recommended that respondent be ordered in general terms to bargain collectively with the Union. . . . [T]he Board rejected the Examiner's views on an employer's right to bargain for a management functions clause and held that respondent's action in bargaining for inclusion of any such clause "constituted, quite [apart from] Respondent's demonstrated bad faith, per se violations of §§8(a)(5) and (1)." Accordingly, the Board not only ordered respondent in general terms to bargain collectively with the Union (par. 2(a)), but also included in its order a paragraph designed to prohibit bargaining for any management functions clause covering a condition of employment. (Par. 1(a)). 89 N.L.R.B. 185. . . .

First. The [NLRA] is designed to promote industrial peace by encouraging the making of voluntary agreements governing relations between unions and employers. The Act does not compel any agreement whatsoever. . . . Nor does the Act regulate the substantive terms governing wages, hours and working conditions which are incorporated in an agreement. The theory of the Act is that the making of voluntary labor agreements is encouraged by protecting employees' rights to organize for collective bargaining and by imposing on labor and management the mutual obligation to bargain collectively.

Enforcement of the obligation to bargain collectively is crucial to the statutory scheme. And, as has long been recognized, performance of the duty to bargain requires more than a willingness to enter upon a sterile discussion of union-management differences. Before the [NLRA], it was held that the duty of an employer to bargain collectively required the employer "to negotiate in good faith with his employees' representatives; to match their proposals, if unacceptable, with counter-proposals; and to make every reasonable effort to reach an agreement."[9] The duty to bargain collectively, implicit in the Wagner Act as introduced in Congress, was made express by the insertion of the fifth employer unfair labor practice accompanied by an explanation of the purpose and meaning of the phrase "bargain collectively in a good faith effort to reach an agreement."[10] This understanding of the duty to bargain collectively has been accepted and applied throughout the administration of the Wagner Act by the [NLRB] and the Courts of Appeal.

In 1947, the fear was expressed in Congress that the Board "has gone very far, in the guise of determining whether or not employers had bargained in good faith, in setting itself up as the judge of what concessions an employer must make and of the proposals and counterproposals that he may or may not make."[12] Accordingly, the Hartley Bill, passed by the House, eliminated the good faith test and expressly provided that the duty to bargain collectively did not require submission of counterproposals. As amended in the Senate and passed as the Taft-Hartley Act, the good faith test of bargaining was retained and written into §8(d). . . . That Section contains the express provision

---

[9] Houde Engineering Corp., 1 N.L.R.B. (old) 35 (1934), decided by the National Labor Relations Board organized under 48 Stat. 1183 (1934).

[10] Before the addition of §8(5), now §8(a)(5), to the bill, Senator Wagner described the bill as imposing the duty to bargain in good faith, citing the *Houde Engineering* case, note 9, supra. Hearings before the Senate Committee on Education and Labor on S. 1958, 74th Cong., 1st Sess. 43 (1935). Section 8(5) was inserted at the suggestion of the Chairman of the Board that decided *Houde*. Id., at 79, 136-137. The insertion of §8(5) was described by the Senate Committee as follows:

"The committee wishes to dispel any possible false impression that this bill is designed to compel the making of agreements or to permit governmental supervision of their terms. . . . [T]he essence of collective bargaining is that either party shall be free to decide whether proposals made to it are satisfactory.

"But, after deliberation, the committee has concluded that this fifth unfair labor practice should be inserted in the bill. . . . [A] guarantee of the right of employees to bargain collectively through representatives of their own choosing is a mere delusion if it is not accompanied by the correlative duty on the part of the other party to recognize such representatives as they have been designated . . . and to negotiate with them in a bona fide effort to arrive at a collective agreement. . . ." S. Rep. No. 573, 74th Cong., 1st Sess. 12 (1935). . . .

[12] H. R. Rep. No. 245, 80th Cong., 1st Sess. 19 (1947).

that the obligation to bargain collectively does not compel either party to agree to a proposal or require the making of a concession.[14]

Thus it is now apparent from the statute itself that the Act does not encourage a party to engage in fruitless marathon discussions at the expense of frank statement and support of his position. And it is equally clear that the Board may not, either directly or indirectly, compel concessions or otherwise sit in judgment upon the substantive terms of collective bargaining agreements.

Second. The Board offers . . . before this Court a theory quite apart from the test of good faith bargaining prescribed in §8(d) . . . , a theory that respondent's bargaining for a management functions clause as a counterproposal to the Union's demand for unlimited arbitration was, "per se," a violation of the Act.

Counsel for the Board do not contend that a management functions clause covering some conditions of employment is an illegal contract term. As a matter of fact, a review of typical contract clauses collected for convenience in drafting labor agreements shows that management functions clauses similar in essential detail to the clause proposed by respondent have been included in contracts negotiated by national unions with many employers. . . . Without intimating any opinion as to the form of management functions clause proposed by respondent in this case or the desirability of including any such clause in a labor agreement, it is manifest that bargaining for management functions clauses is common collective bargaining practice.

If the Board is correct, an employer violates the Act by bargaining for a management functions clause touching any condition of employment without regard to the traditions of bargaining in the particular industry or such other evidence of good faith as the fact in this case that respondent's clause was offered as a counterproposal to the Union's demand for unlimited arbitration. The Board's argument is a technical one for it is conceded that respondent would not be guilty of an unfair labor practice if, instead of proposing a clause that removed some matters from arbitration, it simply refused in good faith to agree to the Union proposal for unlimited arbitration. The argument starts with a finding, not challenged by the court below or by respondent, that at least some of the matters covered by the management functions clause proposed by respondent are "conditions of employment" which are appropriate subjects of collective bargaining under §§8(a)(5), 8(d)

---

[14] The term "concession" was used in place of "counterproposal" at the suggestion of the Chairman of the Board that the statutory definition of collective bargaining should conform to the meaning of good faith bargaining as understood at the passage of the Wagner Act. S. Rep. No. 105, 80th Cong., 1st Sess. 24 (1947). . . .

and 9(a). . . . . The Board considers that employer bargaining for a clause under which management retains initial responsibility for work scheduling, a "condition of employment," for the duration of the contract is an unfair labor practice because it is "in derogation of" employees' statutory rights to bargain collectively as to conditions of employment.[22]

Conceding that there is nothing unlawful in including a management functions clause in a labor agreement, the Board would permit an employer to "propose" such a clause. But the Board would forbid bargaining for any such clause when the Union declines to accept the proposal, even where the clause is offered as a counterproposal to a Union demand for unlimited arbitration. Ignoring the nature of the Union's demand in this case, the Board takes the position that employers . . . must agree to include in any labor agreement provisions establishing fixed standards for work schedules or any other condition of employment. An employer would be permitted to bargain as to the content of the standard so long as he agrees to freeze a standard into a contract. Bargaining for more flexible treatment of such matters would be denied employers even though the result may be contrary to common collective bargaining practice in the industry. The Board was not empowered so to disrupt collective bargaining practices. . . .

Congress provided expressly that the Board should not pass upon the desirability of the substantive terms of labor agreements. Whether a contract should contain a clause fixing standards for such matters as work scheduling or should provide for more flexible treatment of such matters is an issue for determination across the bargaining table, not by the Board. If the latter approach is agreed upon, the extent of union and management participation in the administration of such matters is itself a condition of employment to be settled by bargaining.

Accordingly, we reject the Board's holding that bargaining for the management functions clause proposed by respondent was, per se, an unfair labor practice. Any fears the Board may entertain that use of management functions clauses will lead to evasion of an employer's duty to bargain collectively as to "rates of pay, wages, hours and conditions of employment" do not justify condemning all bargaining for management functions clauses covering any "condition of employment" as per se violations of the Act. The duty to bargain collectively is to be enforced by application of the good faith

---

[22] The Board's argument would seem to prevent an employer from bargaining for a "no-strike" clause, commonly found in labor agreements, requiring a union to forego for the duration of the contract the right to strike expressly granted by §7. . . . However, the Board has permitted an employer to bargain in good faith for such a clause. Shell Oil Co., 77 N.L.R.B. 1306 (1948). This result is explained by referring to the "salutary objective" of such a clause. Bethlehem Steel Co., 89 N.L.R.B. 341, 345 (1950).

bargaining standards of §8(d) to the facts of each case rather than by prohibiting all employers in every industry from bargaining for management functions clauses altogether.

Third. The court below correctly applied the statutory standard of good faith bargaining to the facts of this case. It held that the evidence, viewed as a whole, does not show that respondent refused to bargain in good faith by reason of its bargaining for a management functions clause as a counterproposal to the Union's demand for unlimited arbitration. Respondent's unilateral action in changing working conditions during bargaining, now admitted to be a departure from good faith bargaining, is the subject of an enforcement order issued by the court below and not challenged in this Court.

. . . [A] statutory standard such as "good faith" can have meaning only in its application to the particular facts of a particular case. Accepting as we do the finding of the court below that respondent bargained in good faith for the management functions clause proposed by it, we hold that respondent was not in that respect guilty of refusing to bargain collectively as required by the [Act]. . . .

Affirmed.

MINTON, J., with whom BLACK and DOUGLAS, JJ., join, dissenting. I do not see how this case is solved by telling the [NLRB] that since *some* "management functions" clauses are valid (which the Board freely admits), respondent was not guilty of an unfair labor practice *in this case*. The record is replete with evidence that respondent insisted on a clause which would classify the control over certain conditions of employment as a management prerogative, and that the insistence took the form of a refusal to reach a settlement unless the Union accepted the clause. The Court of Appeals agreed that respondent was "steadfast" in this demand. Therefore, *this case* is one where the employer came into the bargaining room with a demand that certain topics upon which it had a duty to bargain were to be removed from the agenda — that was the price the Union had to pay to gain a contract. . . . No one suggests that an employer is guilty of an unfair labor practice when it proposes that it be given unilateral control over certain working conditions and the union accepts the proposal in return for various other benefits. But where, as here, the employer tells the union that the only way to obtain a contract as to wages is to agree not to bargain about certain other working conditions, the employer has refused to bargain about those other working conditions. . . .

I need not and do not take issue with the Court of Appeals' conclusion that there was no absence of good faith. Where there is a refusal to bargain, the Act does not require an inquiry as to whether that refusal was in good faith or bad faith. . . . The majority seems to suggest that an employer could be found guilty of bad faith if it used a "management functions" clause to close off bargaining about all topics of discussion. Whether the employer closes off all bargaining or, as in this case, only a certain area of bargaining, he has refused to bargain as to whatever he has closed off, and any discussion of his good faith is pointless.

That portion of §8(d) . . . which declares that an employer need not agree to a proposal or make concessions does not dispose of this case. Certainly the Board lacks power to compel concessions as to the substantive terms of labor agreements. But the Board in this case was seeking to compel the employer to bargain about subjects properly within the scope of collective bargaining. . . .

An employer may not stake out an area which is a proper subject for bargaining and say, "As to this we will not bargain." To do so is a plain refusal to bargain in violation of §8(a)(5). . . . I would reverse.

NOTE

The company had extensive negotiations with the certified union, fully discussed its proposals, but maintained that the dynamic nature of its business required that it reserve unilateral control of virtually all aspects of employment relations, including wages, discharges, and promotions. The company offered the union a signed contract that provided for such control, excluded arbitration, and included a broad no-strike pledge. If the union refuses to sign and files unfair labor practice charges, will the company prevail under *American Natl. Ins.*? Compare White v. NLRB, 255 F.2d 564 (5th Cir. 1958), and Gulf States Mfrs. v. NLRB, 579 F.2d 1298 (5th Cir. 1978), with NLRB v. A-1 King Size Sandwiches, 732 F.2d 872 (11th Cir. 1984).

Borg-Warner Controls
198 N.L.R.B. 726 (1972)

. . . The General Counsel contends that Respondent's conduct during negotiations shows that [it] had no intention of reaching an agreement with the Union. Respondent contends that it was engaged in hard but lawful bargaining.

. . . [W]e note that no case involving an allegation of surface bargaining presents an easy issue to decide. . . . [S]uch cases present problems of great complexity and ordinarily, as is the present case, are not solvable by pointing to one or two instances during bargaining as proving an allegation that one of the parties was not bargaining in good faith. In fact, no two cases are alike and none can be determinative precedent for another, as good faith "can have meaning only in its application to the particular facts of a particular case." NLRB v. American National Insurance Co., 343 U.S. 395, 410. It is the total picture shown by the factual evidence that either supports the complaint or falls short of the quantum of affirmative proof required by law.

We have considered the following matters in evaluating Respondent's totality of conduct during the bargaining at issue herein.

I.   RESPONDENT'S PROPOSALS

. . . Respondent's initial set of proposals, which were submitted . . . [soon after the union's certification], substantially represented the existing terms and conditions of employment. In particular, the parties agreed that the wage ranges were the same. However, some of the Respondent's proposals represented less than the existing terms and conditions of employment. Specifically, these latter proposals . . . related to vacation pay, holiday pay, merit increases, rest periods, report pay, sick leave pay, and the grievance procedure. Finally, the record shows that Respondent's proposals involving certain areas not covered prior to the certification of the Union included a limited union-security provision; i.e., an agency shop with a grandfather clause.

Subsequent written proposals submitted by the Respondent . . . related almost entirely to peripheral matters. On August 5 (at the seventh meeting), Respondent submitted a proposal on plant visitation by union representatives. On October 8 (the 15th meeting), Respondent submitted new proposals related to seniority lists, probationary period, out of unit promotions, supervisors, and transfers (temporary and permanent), and re-stated earlier proposals on plant visitation, checkoff, and leadman. On October 22 (17th meeting), Respondent submitted a revised proposal related to the grievance procedure. On February 11 (19th meeting), Respondent presented a revised proposal on leave of absence. And finally, on February 18 (20th and final meeting), Respondent presented a document representing the Respondent's understanding as to what was agreed to and for those items not agreed to or partially agreed to, the Respondent's proposals.

After 8 months and 20 negotiation meetings, the agreements reached by the parties essentially represented obligations imposed by law, established employment practices, and formalities of contract, minor matters, and defini-tions. The parties also agreed to a no-strike and no-lockout clause. On the other hand, the record shows that no agreement was reached on any of the major economic issues; namely, wages, standby pay, callback pay, report pay, shift premiums, vacations, Good Friday, sick leave, group insurance, merit increases, pensions, cost-of-living allowances, pay differentials for leadman, and wage progressions. Similarly, the record shows that no agreement was reached on any of the major noneconomic issues; namely, union-security and union checkoff, investigation and presentation of grievances, subcontracting, and plant visitation by union representatives.

The court's language in NLRB v. Herman Sausage Co., Inc., 275 F.2d 229 (5th Cir.), is particularly applicable: . . .

> The obligation of the employer to bargain in good faith does not require the yielding of positions fairly maintained. It does not permit the Board, under the guise of finding of bad faith, to require the employer to contract in a way the Board might deem proper. Nor may the Board ". . . directly or indirectly, compel concessions or otherwise sit in judgment upon the substantive terms of collective bargaining agreements . . . ," for the Act does not "regulate the substantive terms governing wages, hours and working conditions which are incorporated in an agreement." [Citation omitted.]

On the other hand while the employer is assured these valuable rights, he may not use them as a cloak. In approaching it from this vantage, one must recognize as well that bad faith is prohibited though done with sophistication and finesse. Consequently, to sit at a bargaining table, or to sit almost forever, or to make concessions here and there, could be the very means by which to conceal a purposeful strategy to make bargaining futile or fail. [275 F.2d at 231.]

Thus, we do not find, nor do we suggest, that Respondent's refusal to make concessions with regard to economic matters violates the Act. However, pursuant to the principles expressed in *Herman Sausage*, . . . Respondent's proposals and its approach to bargaining . . . may be taken into account in assessing its motivation. . . . Thus, rigid adherence to proposals, which are predictably unacceptable to the employee representative, may be considered in proper circumstances as evidencing a predetermination not to reach agreement.

A close examination of Respondent's proposals shows that Respondent maintained an inflexible attitude and position on all major issues, both economic and noneconomic, and made no real attempt to reconcile the differences between the parties. In particular, Respondent never altered any of its original economic proposals; rather, it took the position that its wages were fair and adequate and that it liked its existing benefit plans.[7] There was no real

---

[7] The record shows that the Union never asked Respondent for any financial statements of profits or losses of Respondent's business, since Respondent never stated that it could not afford a wage increase, just that it would not grant a wage increase. The record also shows that,

bargaining on major economic issues and the record does not show a genuine attempt by the Respondent to explain the basis for its assessment of its economic proposals.

Moreover, by providing, in a number of areas, for less than the existing terms and conditions of employment which may be viewed as *de minimis* when considered separately but which are significant in the context of whether Respondent bargained in good faith as required by the Act, while rigidly holding the line in all other areas, and by proposing limited union-security and plant visitation provisions, Respondent could only have anticipated that the Union would have great difficulty in accepting Respondent's proposals and reaching agreement.

Accordingly, we agree with the Trial Examiner that the Board's language in Sweeney & Co., Inc., [176 N.L.R.B. 208 (1969), *enforced in pertinent part*, 437 F.2d 1127 (5th Cir. 1971)] . . . applies equally to the instant case: . . . Respondent's position with respect to economic issues, considered in the light of the employment benefits enjoyed by its work force at the outset of negotiations, was generally lacking in concessions of value and is strongly suggestive of an intention on its part to engage in sterile discussions, accompanied by illusory and meaningless concessions, without real intention of engaging in the type of bargaining that could lead to . . . [a] contract. It would be unreasonable to assume that Respondent's attitude with respect to economic issues was taken without anticipating that communication of its views to the Union would create anything other than immediate stalemate. . . .

II. PROCEDURAL CONSIDERATIONS

A. NEGOTIATION MEETINGS

Respondent unilaterally decided, prior to the commencement of the negotiations, that no negotiation meetings were to be held during working hours. Soon after negotiations began, Respondent unilaterally decided that negotiations should be held only once a week. The record also shows that Respondent arranged for the location of the meetings. . . . [T]he Union capitulated and met with the Respondent when and where the Respondent chose to meet. However, the record is also clear that the Union sought to find other mutually satisfactory times and places for the meetings and to schedule

---

in an attempt to move bargaining off its stalemated course, the Union asked Madden, Respondent's chief negotiator, at the February 18 meeting, whether Respondent would consider a wage proposal if the Union would agree to Respondent's other proposals. Madden said he would not. This union proposal was repeated two more times later in the meeting and Madden finally said that Respondent would consider a new wage proposal. However, Madden withdrew this statement of intention at the end of the meeting.

additional meetings in order to stimulate progress in the negotiations. By contrast, Respondent refused to consider an alternative.

On February 22, 1971, the Union sent the Respondent a telegram requesting that the next negotiation meeting be held before 2 p.m. on any Monday through Friday. All the previous meetings were held after working hours. This request raised anew (Respondent had previously rejected several union offers to meet on Saturday) the question of discussing, considering, and agreeing upon a satisfactory time and place to meet. Rather than consider an alternative, Respondent simply reiterated its earlier position and insisted on meeting at the time and place it had unilaterally selected. Such conduct patently indicates an unusual reluctance to accommodate to the required bargaining relationship and is wholly inconsistent with a genuine desire to reach a mutual accommodation. . . .

C. REFUSAL TO RELEASE EMPLOYEES DURING WORKING HOURS

Throughout the negotiations, Respondent refused to release employees on the Union's negotiating committee from work in order to allow these employees to participate in bargaining sessions and bargaining-related meetings. While Respondent's position put a substantial burden on the employee negotiators, the Trial Examiner found that the inconvenience did not prevent bargaining and was not a sufficient detriment to the bargaining process to make unlawful Respondent's contention that the employees' working time was for work. We agree that this conduct did not per se constitute a violation of the Act. However, Respondent's refusal to even consider an accommodation, particularly when the record clearly shows that the employees were not such key employees that they could not have been replaced for the time needed for bargaining, and especially where the Respondent was not being asked to compensate these employees, supports a finding that Respondent was not interested in accommodating in good faith the bargaining process but rather was devising means to frustrate and prolong the bargaining in the hopes that the Union would either capitulate to its proposals or abandon the employees it represented. In these circumstances, and on the entire record, we conclude this conduct necessarily had a negative impact on the bargaining relationship and was part and parcel of Respondent's design not to engage in meaningful bargaining. . . .

D. REFUSAL TO MAKE NEGOTIATORS AVAILABLE DURING WORKING HOURS

The record shows that Respondent refused to make its negotiators available for negotiation meetings during working hours. The Trial Examiner did not find this action to be a per se violation of the Act because the Union never "specifically forced this question by demanding bargaining sessions during working hours without coupling that demand with its insistence that employees be given time off for negotiations." This reasoning by the Trial Examiner raises a conflict between the Respondent's right, under the facts herein, to deny employees on the bargaining committee time off during working hours for negotiations, and the Union's right freely to select its own negotiators. For, whenever a bargaining committee includes employees of the employer the union is bargaining with, as here, the union would be, ipso facto, unable to force the question of an employer's refusal to make its negotiators available during working hours. Consequently, we are not persuaded by the Trial Examiner's resolution of this issue. The Respondent's refusal to make its negotiators available during working hours is yet another example of the rigidity with which Respondent approached bargaining and further evidences its design to avoid bargaining.

RESPONDENT'S TOTALITY OF CONDUCT

. . . [T]his case does not present a simple case of whether the Respondent's actions constituted an outright refusal to bargain with the certified representative . . . , but rather whether the record establishes that the Respondent engaged in a lengthy series of bargaining conferences with no intention of reaching agreement with the Union.

The issue is not, as Respondent suggests, that Respondent did not make enough concessions. Rather, the issue is whether Respondent's approach to bargaining demonstrated an unyielding rigidity . . . which made collective bargaining a futility. Respondent's unyielding rigidity is clearly established both in terms of Respondent's substantive proposals and its conduct relative to the procedural considerations of bargaining. Accordingly, the totality of Respondent's conduct . . . compels the conclusion that Respondent only went through the elaborate motions of bargaining and adapted its tactics to its own ends with no sincere desire of reaching an agreement. . . .

[The Board ordered the employer to cease and desist from refusing to bargain in good faith and from interfering with §7 rights; to bargain upon request with the union; and to post a notice, advising employees of the substance of the Board's order.]

Chairman MILLER, dissenting: As stated . . . in NLRB v. American National Insurance Co., 343 U.S. 395, 404, "the Board may not, either directly or indirectly, compel concessions or otherwise sit in judgment upon the substantive terms of collective bargaining agreements." If we are to adhere to this injunction caution must be exercised to avoid findings of subjective bad faith based solely upon the view that an employer could have adopted what we might regard as a more reasonable stance at the bargaining table.

Here, the entire case against the Employer is predicated upon its lawfully held positions with respect to certain procedural matters and its failure to make economic concessions. There is no evidence of union *animus* or hostility to the bargaining process. The Employer engaged in no conduct independently violating §8(a)(5), nor is there any extraneous evidence suggesting an intention to avoid agreement.

Neither §§8(a)(5) nor 8(d) precludes an employer from engaging in hard bargaining of the type calculated to assure a favorable agreement. On this record, the evidence shows nothing more. To find, as does the majority, that the Employer was guilty of overall bad faith is to violate statutory and judicial limitations upon the Board's authority in this type of case through issuance of a remedy which in effect requires concessions of the Employer. Such a result conflicts with the statutory policy encouraging free collective bargaining by inviting labor organizations to indirectly seek through the Board's processes what cannot be obtained at the bargaining table. I would dismiss the complaint in its entirety.

NOTES

1. In NLRB v. Tomco Communications, 567 F.2d 871 (9th Cir. 1978), the court, reversing the Board, held that the employer's hard bargaining with a newly certified union, coupled with a post-impasse lockout, had not violated §8(a)(5). The court criticized the Board for resting its finding of bad faith on the following considerations, among others:

(a) The company's failure to offer "major economic improvements." (Although noting that the company's wages met area standards, the court added that the right to representation "does not imply the right to a better deal");

(b) The omission from the company's "last, best, and final offer" of certain concessions that the company had previously agreed to consider or had tentatively accepted. (The court noted in general that, "absent abuse not present here," it is legitimate for a party to withdraw a proposal before its acceptance; otherwise the parties would be handicapped in exploring their positions early in the negotiations);

(c) "No self-respecting union" could be expected to accept the company's terms. (The court renewed its prior criticism of this celebrated phrase, from NLRB v. Reed & Prince Mfg. Co., 205 F.2d 131, 139 (1st Cir.), *cert. denied*, 346 U.S. 887 (1953), as conclusory rather than analytically useful, and as focusing on what employees want rather than on the employer's economic position and the level of past benefits.)

See generally Comment, The Radical Potential of the Wagner Act: The Duty to Bargain Collectively, 129 U. Pa. L. Rev. 1392 (1981).

2. Suppose an employer that has recognized a union for fifteen years rejects any renewal agreement that would increase wages, urging that profits had substantially declined. The union points to inflation and to the high settlements secured by other unions and insists on a five percent wage increase. Both sides are adamant, and a long strike results. Have any unfair labor practices been committed?

3. Does the Board's order in *Borg-Warner* identify the company's misconduct with sufficient particularity to notify the company of the corrective action required in later bargaining and to lay the basis for contempt if such correction does not take place? See generally Gross, Cullen & Hanslowe, Good Faith in Labor Negotiations: Tests and Remedies, 53 Cornell L. Rev. 1009, 1020-1021 (1968).

4. The central problem of *Borg-Warner*, as well as the effect of §8(c), arose in NLRB v. General Electric Co., 418 F.2d 736 (2d Cir. 1969), *cert. denied*, 397 U.S. 965 (1970), a celebrated case that produced lengthy and divided opinions. See also J. P. Stevens & Co. v. NLRB, 623 F.2d 322 (4th Cir. 1980), *cert. denied*, 449 U.S 1077 (1981), where the court upheld the Board's finding that J. P. Stevens had violated the Act by employing on four separate occasions a bargaining strategy that included developing comprehensive improvements in company-wide fringe benefits, keeping the union in the dark on matters relevant to collective bargaining, and announcing or implementing changes at times that precluded "meaningful negotiations." This strategy, according to Board and court, confronted the union with a "Hobson's choice" of accepting or rejecting the predetermined modifications and denigrated the union's representative status, tactics that "go to the very heart of the Act and our national policy."

5. Consider the possible impact of "concessionary bargaining," noted in Chapter 1(A), on the disposition of contentions that an employer's hard-line insistence on reducing or not increasing labor costs is evidence of an absence of good faith bargaining.

See generally H. Raiffa, The Art and Science of Negotiation (1982).

NLRB v. Truitt Mfg. Co.
351 U.S. 149 (1956)

BLACK, J. . . . The question presented by this case is whether the [NLRB] may find that an employer has not bargained in good faith where the employer claims it cannot afford to pay higher wages but refuses requests to produce information substantiating its claim.

The dispute here arose when a union [representative] . . . asked for a wage increase of 10 cents per hour. The company answered that it could not afford to pay such an increase, it was undercapitalized, had never paid dividends, and that an increase of more than 2 1/2 cents per hour would put it out of business. The union asked the company to produce some evidence substantiating these statements, requesting permission to have a certified public accountant examine the company's books, financial data, etc. This request being denied, the union asked that the company submit "full and complete information with respect to its financial standing and profits," insisting that such information was pertinent and essential for the employees to determine whether or not they should continue to press their demand for a wage increase. A union official testified before the trial examiner that "[W]e were wanting anything relating to the Company's position, any records or what have you, books, accounting sheets, cost expenditures, what not, anything to back the Company's position that they were unable to give any more money." The company refused all the requests, relying solely on the statement that "the information . . . is not pertinent to this discussion and the company declines to give you such information; you have no legal right to such."

On the basis of these facts the [Board] found that the company had "failed to bargain in good faith with respect to wages in violation of §8(a)(5) of the Act." 110 N.L.R.B. 856. The Board ordered the company to supply the union with such information as would "substantiate the Respondent's position of its economic inability to pay the requested wage increase." The Court of Appeals refused to enforce the Board's order, agreeing with respondent that it could not be held guilty of an unfair labor practice because of its refusal to furnish the information requested by the union. 224 F.2d 869. . . .

The company raised no objection to the Board's order on the ground that the scope of information required was too broad or that disclosure would put an undue burden on the company. Its major argument throughout has been that the information requested was irrelevant to the bargaining process and related to matters exclusively within the province of management. Thus we lay to one side the suggestion by the company here that the Board's order might be unduly burdensome or injurious to its business. In any event, the Board has heretofore taken the position in cases such as this that "It is sufficient if the information is made available in a manner not so burdensome or time-consuming as to impede the process of bargaining." And in this case the Board has held substantiation of the company's position requires no more than "reasonable proof."

We think that in determining whether the obligation of good-faith bargaining has been met the Board has a right to consider an employer's refusal to give information about its financial status. While Congress did not compel agreement between employers and bargaining representatives, it did require collective bargaining in the hope that agreements would result. Section 204(a)(1) of the Act admonishes both employers and employees to "exert every reasonable effort to make and maintain agreements concerning rates of pay, hours, and working conditions. . . . " In their effort to reach an agreement here both the union and the company treated the company's ability to pay increased wages as highly relevant. The ability of an employer to increase wages without injury to his business is a commonly considered factor in wage negotiations. Claims for increased wages have sometimes been abandoned because of an employer's unsatisfactory business condition; employees have even voted to accept wage decreases because of such conditions.

Good-faith bargaining necessarily requires that claims made by either bargainer should be honest claims. This is true about an asserted inability to pay an increase in wages. If such an argument is important enough to present in the give and take of bargaining, it is important enough to require some sort of proof of its accuracy. And it would certainly not be farfetched for a trier of fact to reach the conclusion that bargaining lacks good faith when an employer mechanically repeats a claim of inability to pay without making the slightest effort to substantiate the claim. Such has been the holding of the Labor Board since shortly after the passage of the Wagner Act. . . . This was the position of the Board when the Taft-Hartley Act was passed in 1947 and has been its position ever since. We agree with the Board that a refusal to attempt to substantiate a claim of inability to pay increased wages may support a finding of a failure to bargain in good faith.

The Board concluded that under the facts and circumstances of this case the respondent was guilty of an unfair labor practice in failing to bargain in good faith. We see no reason to disturb the findings of the Board. We do not hold, however, that in every case in which economic inability is raised as an argument against increased wages it automatically follows that the employees are entitled to substantiating evidence. Each case must turn upon its particular facts. . . . Reversed.

FRANKFURTER, J., whom CLARK and HARLAN, JJ., join, concurring in part and dissenting in part. . . . "Good faith" means more than merely going through the motions of negotiating; it is inconsistent with a predetermined resolve not to budge from an initial position. But it is not necessarily incompatible with stubbornness or even with what to an outsider may seem unreasonableness. A determination of good faith or of want of good faith normally can rest only on an inference based upon more or less persuasive manifestations of another's state of mind. The previous relations of the parties, antecedent events explaining behavior at the bargaining table, and the course of negotiations constitute the raw facts for reaching such a determination. The appropriate inferences to be drawn from what is often confused and tangled testimony about all this makes a finding of absence of good faith one for the judgment of the Labor Board, unless the record as a whole leaves such judgment without reasonable foundation.

An examination of the Board's opinion and the position taken by its counsel here disclose that the Board did not so conceive the issue of good-faith bargaining in this case. The totality of the conduct of the negotiation was apparently deemed irrelevant to the question; one fact alone disposed of the case. "[I]t is settled law [the Board concluded], that when an employer seeks to justify the refusal of a wage increase upon an economic basis, as did the Respondent herein, good-faith bargaining under the Act requires that upon request the employer attempt to substantiate its economic position by reasonable proof." 110 N.L.R.B. 856.

This is to make a rule of law out of one item—even if a weighty item—of the evidence. There is no warrant for this. . . .

Since the Board applied the wrong standard here, by ruling that Truitt's failure to supply financial information to the union constituted per se a refusal to bargain in good faith, the case should be returned to the Board. There is substantial evidence in the record which indicates that Truitt tried to reach an agreement. It offered a 2 1/2-cent wage increase, it expressed willingness to discuss with the union "at any time the problem of how our wages compare with those of our competition," and it continued throughout to meet and discuss the controversy with the union. . . . I would return the case to the Board so that it may apply the relevant standard for determining "good faith."

NOTES

1. An employer rejects the union's wage demand saying "the business couldn't stay competitive" if the demand were granted. Would *Truitt* require the employer to comply with a request for substantiating information? See, e.g., NLRB v. Pacific Grinding Wheel Co., 572 F.2d 1343, 1348 (9th Cir. 1978).

2. Following the employer's plea of "inability to pay," the union asked to see the firm's profit and loss statement. Does *Truitt* require the employer to comply? See, e.g., C-B Buick, Inc. v. NLRB, 506 F.2d 1086 (3d Cir. 1974). Should the employer be required to comply with the union's request for data about the salary and expense accounts of executives, or depreciation and maintenance charges against earnings? Cf. Metlox Mfg. v. NLRB, 378 F.2d 728 (9th Cir. 1967), *cert. denied*, 389 U.S. 1037 (1968). Would it be material if the agreement provided for profit sharing by employees?

3. Information on the wage rates and job classifications of unit em-

ployees is usually treated as "presumptively relevant"; it must be furnished on request unless the employer proves a lack of relevance. Curtiss-Wright Corp., 145 N.L.R.B. 152 (1963), *enforced*, 347 F.2d 61 (3d Cir. 1965). Apart from wage and related data, the scope of the presumptive relevance doctrine is unclear. Under *Truitt's* rationale, should any information pertaining to mandatory subjects of bargaining be presumptively relevant? The standard for determining relevance is commonly said to be "a liberal one, [like] that applied in discovery proceedings." Local 13, Detroit Newspaper Printing & Graphic Communications Union v. NLRB, 598 F.2d 267, 271 (D.C. Cir. 1979) (§8(b)(3) violated by a union's refusal, during negotiations, to supply information regarding availability of straight-time substitutes requested by an employer convinced that its overtime costs were excessive because of the union's failure to refer straight-time help).

4. A showing of prior misuse of disclosed information has been held to rebut any presumption of relevance. See NLRB v. A.S. Abell Co., 624 F.2d 506 (4th Cir. 1980). Similarly, justifiable fears of harassment of employees have been held to qualify an employer's duty to provide relevant information — e.g., the names and addresses of employees, requested following a strike marked by violence. See Shell Oil Co. v. NLRB, 457 F.2d 615 (9th Cir. 1972), summarized in *Detroit Edison* (footnote 14), the principal case immediately following. Decisions involving the so-called clear and present danger defense to disclosure requests are collected in Soule Glass and Glazing Co., 652 F.2d 1055 (1st Cir. 1981).

5. Disclosure demands have produced considerable litigation. See generally Shedlin, Regulation of Disclosure of Economic and Financial Data and the Impact on the American System of Labor-Management Relations, 41 Ohio St. L.J. 441 (1980); J. O'Reilly, Unions' Rights to Company Information (1980).

Detroit Edison Co. v. NLRB
440 U.S. 301 (1979)

STEWART, J. . . . This is apparently the first case in which the Board has held that an employer's duty to provide relevant information to the employees' bargaining representative includes the duty to disclose tests and test scores achieved by named employees in a statistically validated psychological aptitude testing program administered by the employer. [The Court had noted earlier that the employer had supplied the union with much of the information it had requested.] Psychological aptitude testing is a widely used employee selection and promotion device in both private industry and government. Test secrecy is concededly critical to the validity of any such program, and confidentiality of scores is undeniably important to the examinees. The underlying question is whether the Board's order, enforced without modification by the Court of Appeals, adequately accommodated these concerns.

I

. . . At the time of the hearing in this case, one of the units represented by the Union was a unit of operating and maintenance employees at the Company's plant in Monroe, Mich. The Union was certified as the exclusive bargaining agent for employees in that unit in 1971, and it was agreed that these employees would be covered by a pre-existing collective-bargaining agreement, one of the provisions of which specified that promotions within a given unit were to be based on seniority "whenever the reasonable qualifications and abilities of the employee being considered are not significantly different." Management decisions to bypass employees with greater seniority were subject to the collective agreement's grievance machinery, including ultimate arbitration, whenever a claim was made that the bypass had been arbitrary or discriminatory.

The aptitude tests at issue were used by the Company to screen applicants for the job classification of "Instrument Man B." . . . The position of Instrument Man B, although at the lowest starting grade under the contract and usually requiring on the job training, was regarded by the Company as a critical job because it involved activities vital to the operation of the plant.

The Company has used aptitude tests as a means of predicting job performance since the late 1920s or early 1930s. In the late 1950s, the Company first began to use a set of standardized tests (test battery) as a predictor of performance on the Instrument Man B job. The battery, which had been "validated" for this job classification[4] consisted of the Wunderlich Personnel Test, the Minnesota Paper Form Board (MPFB), and portions of the Engineering and Physical Science Aptitude Test (EPSAT). All employees who applied for acceptance into the Instrument Man classification were required to take this battery. . . .

In the late 1960s, the technical engineers responsible for the Company's instrumentation department complained that the test battery was not an accurate screening device. The Company's industrial psychologists, accordingly, performed a revalidation study of the tests. As a result, the Personnel Test was dropped, and the scoring system was changed. . . .

---

[4] . . . Incumbents were given the preselected tests, and their scores were then compared with the supervisory ratings. A statistically significant correlation between the scores and the ratings was demonstrated. . . .

The Company administered the tests to applicants with the express commitment that each applicant's test score would remain confidential. Test and test scores were kept in the offices of the Company's industrial psychologists who, as members of the American Psychological Association, deemed themselves ethically bound not to disclose test information to unauthorized persons. Under this policy, the Company's psychologists did not reveal the tests or report actual test numerical scores to management or to employee representatives. The psychologists would, however, if an individual examinee so requested, review the test questions and answers with that individual.

The present dispute had its beginnings in 1971 when the Company invited bids from employees to fill six Instrument Man B openings at the Monroe plant. Ten Monroe unit employees applied. None received a score designated as "acceptable," and all were on that basis rejected. The jobs were eventually filled by applicants from outside the Monroe plant bargaining unit.

The Union filed a grievance on behalf of the Monroe applicants, claiming that the new testing procedure was unfair and that the Company had bypassed senior employees in violation of the collective-bargaining agreement. The grievance was rejected by the Company at all levels. . . . In preparation for arbitration, the Union requested the Company to turn over various materials related to the Instrument Man B testing program. The Company furnished the Union with copies of test validation studies performed by its industrial psychologists and with a report by an outside consultant on the Company's entire testing program. It refused, however, to release the actual test battery, the applicants' test papers, and their scores, maintaining that complete confidentiality of these materials was necessary in order to insure the future integrity of the tests and to protect the privacy interests of the examinees.

The Union then filed . . . the unfair labor practice charge involved in this case. The charge alleged that the information withheld by the Company was relevant and necessary to the arbitration of the grievance, "including the ascertainment of promotion criteria, the veracity of the scoring and grading of the examination, and the testing procedures, and the job relatedness of the test(s) to the Instrument Man B classification."

After filing this unfair labor practice charge, the Union asked the Arbitrator to order the Company to furnish the materials at issue. He declined on the ground that he was without authority to do so. In view of the pendency of the charges before the Board, the parties proceeded with the arbitration on the express understanding that the Union could reopen the case should it ultimately prevail in its claims. During the course of the arbitration, however, the Company did disclose the raw scores of those who had taken the test, with the names of the examinees deleted. In addition, it provided the Union with sample questions indicative of the types of questions appearing on the test battery and with detailed information about its scoring procedures. It also offered to turn over the scores of any employee who would sign a waiver releasing the Company psychologist from his pledge of confidentiality. The Union declined to seek such releases.

The Arbitrator's decision found that the Company was free under the collective agreement to establish minimum reasonable qualifications for the job of Instrument Man and to use aptitude tests as a measure of those qualifications; that the Instrument Man B test battery was a reliable and fair test in the sense that its administration and scoring had been standardized; and that the test had a "high degree of validity" as a predictor of performance in the job classification for which it was developed. . . . [He] expressed the view that the Union's position in the arbitration had not been impaired because of lack of access to the actual test battery.

Several months later the Board issued a complaint based on the Union's unfair labor practice charge. At the outset of the hearing before the [ALJ] the Company offered to turn over the test battery and answer sheets to an industrial psychologist selected by the Union for an independent evaluation, stating that disclosure to an intermediary obligated to preserve test secrecy would satisfy its concern that direct disclosure to the Union would inevitably result in dissemination of the questions. The Union rejected this compromise.

The [ALJ] found that notwithstanding the conceded statistical validity of the test battery, the tests and scores would be of probable relevant help to the Union in the performance of its duties as collective-bargaining agent. He reasoned that the Union, having had no access to the tests, had been "deprived of any occasion to check the tests for built-in bias, or discriminatory tendency, or any opportunity to argue that the tests or test questions are not well suited to protect the employees' rights, or to check the accuracy of the scoring." The Company's claim that employees' privacy might be abused by disclosure to the Union of the scores he rejected as insubstantial. Accordingly, he recommended that the Company be ordered to turn over the test scores directly to the Union. He did, however, accept the Company's suggestion that the test battery and answer sheets be disclosed to an expert intermediary. Disclosure of these materials to lay Union representatives, he reasoned, would not be likely to produce constructive results, since the tests could be properly analyzed only by professionals. The Union was to be given "the right to see and study the tests," and to use the information therein "to the extent necessary to process and arbitrate the grievances," but not to disclose the information to third parties other than the Arbitrator.

The Company specifically requested the Board "to adopt that part of the order which requires that tests be turned over to a qualified psychologist," but excepted to the requirement that the employee-linked scores be given to the Union. It contended that the only reason asserted by the Union in support of its request for the scores — to check their arithmetical accuracy — was not sufficient to overcome the principle of confidentiality that underlay its psychological testing program. The Union filed a cross-exception to the requirement that it select a psychologist, arguing that it should not be forced to "employ an outsider for what is normal grievance and Labor-Management work."

The Board, and the . . . Sixth Circuit in its decision enforcing the Board's order, ordered the Company to turn over all the material directly to the Union. They concluded that the Union should be able to determine for itself whether it needed a psychologist to interpret the test battery and answer sheets. Both recognized the Company's interest in maintaining the security of the tests, but both reasoned that appropriate restrictions on the Union's use of the materials would protect this interest.[9] Neither was receptive to the Company's claim that employee privacy and the professional obligations of the Company's industrial psychologists should outweigh the Union request for the employee-linked scores. . . .

A

We turn first to the question whether the Board abused its remedial discretion when it ordered the Company to deliver directly to the Union the copies of the test battery and answer sheets. The Company's position, stripped of the argument that it had no duty at all to disclose these materials, is as follows: It urges that disclosure directly to the Union would carry with it a substantial risk that the test questions would be disseminated. Since it spent considerable time and money validating the Instrument Man B tests and since its tests depend for reliability upon the Examinee's lack of advance preparation, it contends that the harm of dissemination would not be trivial. The future validity of the tests is tied to secrecy, and disclosure to employees would not

---

[9] The Board, although it ordered the Company to supply the tests and answer sheets directly to the Union, incorporated by reference the [ALJ's] restrictions on the Union's use of the materials. Under those restrictions, the Union was given the right "to use the tests and the information contained therein to the extent necessary to process and arbitrate the grievances, but not to copy the tests, or otherwise use them, for the purpose of disclosing the tests or the questions to employees who have in the past, or who may in the future take these tests, or to anyone (other than the arbitrator) who may advise the employees of the contents of the tests."

After the conclusion of the arbitration, the Union was required to return "all copies of the battery of tests" to the Company. The Court of Appeals . . . stated that the "restrictions on use of the materials and obligation to return them to Detroit Edison are part of the decision and order which we enforce." 560 F.2d 722, 726.

only threaten the Company's investment but would also leave the Company with no valid means of measuring employee aptitude. The Company also maintains that its interest in preserving the security of its tests is consistent with the federal policy favoring the use of validated, standardized and non-discriminatory employee selection procedures reflected in the Civil Rights Act of 1964.

. . . [T]he Solicitor General has acknowledged the existence of a strong public policy against disclosure of employment aptitude tests and, at least in the context of civil service testing, has conceded that "governmental recruitment would be seriously disputed and public confidence eroded if the integrity of . . . tests were compromised." Indeed, he has also acknowledged that the United States Civil Service Commission has "been zealous to guard against undue disclosure and has successfully contended for protective orders which limit exposure of the tests to attorneys and professional psychologists with restrictions on copying or disseminating test materials." He urges, however, that the Board's order can be justified on the grounds that the Union's institutional interests militate against improper disclosure, and that the specific protective provisions in the Board's order will safeguard the integrity of the tests. . . . We do not find these justifications persuasive.

A union's bare assertion that it needs information to process a grievance does not automatically oblige the employer to supply all the information in the manner requested. The duty to supply information under §8(a)(5) turns upon "the circumstances of the particular case," NLRB v. Truitt Mfg. Co., 351 U.S. 149, 153, and much the same may be said for the type of disclosure that will satisfy that duty. See, e.g., American Cyanamid Co., 129 N.L.R.B. 683, 684 (1960). . . . [T]he reasonableness of the Company's concern for test secrecy has been essentially conceded. The finding by the Board that this concern did not outweigh the Union's interest in exploring the fairness of the Company's criteria for promotion did not carry with it any suggestion that the concern itself was not legitimate and substantial. Indeed, . . . the strength of the Company's concern has been abundantly demonstrated. The Board has cited no principle of national labor policy to warrant a remedy that would unnecessarily disserve this interest, and we are unable to identify one.

It is obvious that the remedy selected by the Board does not adequately protect the security of the tests. The restrictions barring the Union from taking any action that might cause the tests to fall into the hands of employees who have taken or are likely to take them are only as effective as the sanctions available to enforce them. In this instance, there is substantial doubt whether the Union would be subject to a contempt citation were it to ignore the restrictions. It was not a party to the enforcement proceeding in the Court of Appeals. . . . Further, the Board's regulations contemplate a contempt sanction only against a respondent, . . . and the initiation of contempt proceedings is entirely within the discretion of the Board's General Counsel. . . . Effective sanctions at the Board level are similarly problematic. To be sure, the Board's General Counsel could theoretically bring a separate unfair labor practice charge against the Union, but he could also in his unreviewable discretion refuse to issue such a complaint. . . . Moreover, the Union clearly would not be accountable in either contempt or unfair labor practice proceedings for the most realistic vice inherent in the Board's remedy — the danger of inadvertent leaks. . . .

The Board in this case having identified no justification for a remedy granting such scant protection to the Company's undisputed and important interests in test secrecy, we hold that the Board abused its discretion in ordering the Company to turn over the test battery and answer sheets directly to the Union.

B

The dispute over Union access to the actual scores received by named employees is in a somewhat different procedural posture, since the Company did on this issue preserve its objections to the basic finding that it had violated its duty under §8(a)(5) when it refused disclosure. The Company argues that even if the scores were relevant to the Union's grievance (which it vigorously disputes), the Union's need for the information was not sufficiently weighty to require breach of the promise of its industrial psychologists' code of professional ethics, and potential embarrassment and harassment of at least some of the examinees. The Board responds that this information does satisfy the appropriate standard of "relevance," see NLRB v. Acme Industrial Inc., 385 U.S. 432, and that the Company having "unilaterally" chosen to make a promise of confidentiality to the examinees, cannot rely on that promise to defend against a request for relevant information. The professional obligations of the Company's psychologists, it argues, must give way to paramount federal law. Finally, it dismisses as speculative the contention that employees with low scores might be embarrassed or harassed.

We may accept for the sake of this discussion the finding that the employee scores were of potential relevance to the Union's grievance, as well as the position of the Board that the federal statutory duty to disclose relevant information cannot be defeated by the ethical standards of a private group. . . . Nevertheless we agree with the Company that its willingness to disclose these scores only upon receipt of consents from the examinees satisfied its statutory obligations under §8(a)(5).

The Board's position appears to rest on the proposition that union interests in arguably relevant information must always predominate over all other interests, however legitimate. But such an absolute rule has never been established,[14] and we decline to adopt such a rule here. There are situations in which an employer's conditional offer to disclose may be warranted. . . .

The sensitivity of any human being to disclosure of information that may be taken to bear on his or her basic competence is sufficiently well known to be an appropriate subject of judicial notice. There is nothing in this record to suggest that the Company promised the examinees that their scores would remain confidential in order to further parochial concerns or to frustrate subsequent union attempts to process employee grievances. And it has not been suggested at any point in this proceeding that the Company's unilateral promise of confidentiality was in itself violative of the terms of the collective-bargaining agreement. Indeed, the Company presented evidence that disclosure of individual scores had in the past resulted in the harassment of some lower scoring examinees who had, as a result, left the Company.

Under these circumstances, any possible impairment of the function of the Union in processing the grievances of employees is more than justified by the interests served in conditioning the disclosure of the test scores upon the consent of the very employees whose grievance is being processed. . . .

In light of the sensitive nature of testing information, the minimal burden that compliance with the Company's offer would have placed on the Union, and the total absence of evidence that the Company had fabricated concern for employee confidentiality only to frustrate the Union in the discharge of its responsibilities, we are unable to sustain the Board in its conclusion that the Company in resisting an unconsented-to disclosure of individual test results violated the statutory obligation to bargain in good faith. . . . Accordingly, we hold that the order requiring the Company unconditionally to disclose the employee scores to the Union was erroneous.

The judgment is vacated and the case remanded to the Court of Appeals . . . for further proceedings consistent with this opinion.

[Stevens, J., agreed with the Court's requiring the consent of individual employees to the release of their test scores and also agreed with the dissent's

---

[14] See Emeryville Research Center, Shell Development Co. v. NLRB, 441 F.2d 880 (CA9 1971) (refusal to supply relevant salary information in precise form demanded did not constitute violation of §8(a)(5) when company's proposed alternatives were responsive to union's need); Shell Oil Co. v. NLRB, 457 F.2d 615 (9th Cir. 1975) (refusal to supply employee names without employee consent not unlawful when company had well-founded fear that non-striking employees would be harassed); cf. Kroger Co. v. NLRB, 399 F.2d 455 (6th Cir. 1958) (no disclosure of operating ratio data when, under circumstances, interests of employer predominated); United Aircraft Corp., 192 N.L.R.B. 382, 390 (employer acted reasonably in refusing to honor generalized request for employee medical records without employee's permission), modified on other grounds, Lodges 743 and 1746 v. United Aircraft Corp., 534 F.2d 422 (2nd Cir. 1975).

insistence that the Board's broad remedial authority should have been upheld with respect to the test questions and the answers.

White, J., with whom Brennan, and Marshall, JJ., joined in dissent, emphasized that, official sanctions aside, the union would probably have honored the conditions imposed on disclosure of the tests and answers because of the union's long relationship with the employer and its concern about the NLRB's and the employees' negative reaction to a breach. The dissenters urged that channelling disclosure through a psychologist, whose services might be unneeded, diluted the union's primary responsibility for grievance evaluation. With respect to individual test scores, the dissenters noted that confidentiality had already been compromised by disclosures during arbitration and that the employer had not justified its opposition to the additional disclosure deemed appropriate by the Board for the union's discharge of its statutory responsibility, including, perhaps, determination of whether "demographic and occupational characteristics" indicated "bias in the operation of the tests."]

NOTES

1. T, employed in the bargaining unit, was involved in an altercation with K, a nonunit employee. Both were discharged for violating the employer's plant-wide (and valid) rule prohibiting fighting. T asserted his innocence, contending that he had been assaulted by K without provocation. In preparing for arbitration of T's grievance, the union, alleging disparate application of the rule in question, requested the employer to furnish K's work record as well as documents pertaining to other employees disciplined for fighting during the preceding three years. The employer denied the request. In addition to contesting the relevance of the information sought, the employer, asserting a general claim that "employees' work records should be confidential," conditioned disclosure of K's work record on K's consent. Has the employer satisfied its §8(a)(5) obligations? Compare Pfizer, Inc., 268 N.L.R.B. No. 126, 115 L.R.R.M. 1105 (1984), with New Jersey Bell Tel. Co. v. NLRB, 720 F.2d 789 (3d Cir. 1983). See also NLRB v. Acme Indus., infra p. 1080.

2. The NLRB has generally rejected employer claims that relevant information should be withheld as "confidential." See, e.g., Oil, Chem. & Atomic Wkrs., Local No. 5-114 v. NLRB, 711 F.2d 348 (D.C. Cir. 1983) (enforcing order requiring employers to bargain with unions over conditions for disclosing "trade secrets" in relevant health and safety information); General Elec. Co. v. NLRB, 466 F.2d 1177 (6th Cir. 1972) (employer must

disclose wage data collected from specific companies under a pledge of confidentiality). Cf. American Cyanamid Co., 129 N.L.R.B. 683 (1960) (employer's concededly relevant wage data interwoven with confidential technological information; rejection of union's demand to copy such information not a violation of the Act, because union precluded a test of employer's willingness to compromise the conflicting interests). Should *Detroit Edison* be read as suggesting that it is not practicable to grant unions access to confidential data subject to a pledge of confidentiality? Did the Court exaggerate the difficulty of devising remedies for breach of such a pledge?

3. Incumbent unions have, through §8(a)(5), secured information about the racial and sexual composition of the employer's work force and about employees' complaints of invidious discrimination. See, e.g., Safeway Stores v. NLRB, 691 F.2d 953 (10th Cir. 1982). But cf. Electrical Workers v. NLRB (Westinghouse Elec. Corp.), 648 F.2d 18 (D.C. Cir. 1980) (refusing to compel disclosure of employer's entire affirmative action plan, with its candid self-criticism, absent a particularized showing of relevance).

NLRB v. Insurance Agents' Intl. Union
361 U.S. 477 (1960)

Brennan, J. . . . The precise question is whether the Board may find that a union, which confers with an employer with the desire of reaching agreement on contract terms, has nevertheless refused to bargain collectively, thus violating [§8(b)(3)], solely and simply because during the negotiations it seeks to put economic pressure on the employer to yield to its bargaining demands by sponsoring on-the-job conduct designed to interfere with the carrying on of the employer's business.

Since 1949 the respondent Insurance Agents' International Union and the Prudential Insurance Company have negotiated collective bargaining agreements covering district agents employed by Prudential in thirty-five States and the District of Columbia. The principal duties of a Prudential district agent are to collect premiums and to solicit new business in an assigned locality known in the trade as his "debit." He has no fixed or regular working hours except that he must report at his district office two mornings a week and remain for two or three hours to deposit his collections, prepare and submit reports, and attend meetings to receive sales and other instructions. He is paid commissions on collections made and on new policies written; his only fixed compensation is a weekly payment of $4.50 intended primarily to cover his expenses.

In January 1956 Prudential and the union began the negotiation of a new contract to replace an agreement expiring in the following March.

Bargaining was carried on continuously for six months before the terms of the new contract were agreed upon on July 17, 1956. It is not questioned that, if it stood alone, the record of negotiations would establish that the union conferred in good faith for the purpose and with the desire of reaching agreement with Prudential on a contract.

However, in April 1956, Prudential filed a §8(b)(3) charge of refusal to bargain collectively against the union. The charge was based upon actions of the union and its members outside the conference room, occurring after the old contract expired in March. The union had announced in February that if agreement on the terms of the new contract was not reached when the old contract expired, the union members would then participate in a "Work Without a Contract" program — which meant that they would engage in certain planned, concerted on-the-job activities designed to harass the company.

A complaint of violation of §8(b)(3) issued on the charge and hearings began before the bargaining was concluded. [The evidence showed] that the union's harassing tactics involved activities by the member agents such as these: refusal for a time to solicit new business, and refusal (after the writing of new business was resumed) to comply with the company's reporting procedures; refusal to participate in the company's "May Policyholders' Month Campaign"; reporting late at district offices the days the agents were scheduled to attend them, and refusing to perform customary duties at the offices, instead engaging there in "sit-in-mornings," "doing what comes naturally" and leaving at noon as a group; absenting themselves from special business conferences arranged by the company; picketing and distributing leaflets outside the various offices of the company on specified days and hours as directed by the union; distributing leaflets each day to policyholders and others and soliciting policyholders' signatures on petitions directed to the company; and presenting the signed policyholders' petitions to the company at its home office while simultaneously engaging in mass demonstrations there.

[The Board, rejecting the Trial Examiner's recommendation that the complaint be dismissed, found a refusal to bargain and entered a cease and desist order against the union. 119 N.L.R.B. 768. The Court of Appeals set aside that order. 260 F.2d 736.]

. . . The Board's opinion answers flatly "we do not agree" [with the Trial Examiner's conclusion] and proceeds to say

> . . . the Respondent's reliance upon harassing tactics during the course of negotiations for the avowed purpose of compelling the Company to capitulate to its terms is the antithesis of reasoned discussion it was duty-bound to follow. Indeed, it clearly revealed an unwillingness to submit its demands to the

consideration of the bargaining table where argument, persuasion, and the free interchange of views could take place. In such circumstances, the fact that the Respondent continued to confer with the Company and was desirous of concluding an agreement does not *alone* establish that it fulfilled its obligation to bargain in good faith. . . .

119 N.L.R.B., at 769, 770-771. Thus the Board's view is that irrespective of the union's good faith in conferring with the employer at the bargaining table for the purpose and with the desire of reaching agreement on contract terms, its tactics during the course of the negotiations constituted per se a violation of §8(b)(3). Accordingly, as is said in the Board's brief, "The issue here . . . comes down to whether the Board is authorized under the Act to hold that such tactics, which the Act does not specifically forbid but §7 does not protect, support a finding of a failure to bargain in good faith as required by §8(b)(3)."

First . . . [T]he nature of the duty to bargain in good faith imposed upon employers by §8(5) of the original Act was not sweepingly conceived. The Chairman of the Senate Committee declared:

When the employees have chosen their organization, when they have selected their representatives, all the bill proposes to do is to escort them to the door of their employer and say, "Here they are, the legal representatives of your employees." What happens behind those doors is not inquired into, and the bill does not seek to inquire into it.[9]

The limitation implied by the last sentence has not been in practice maintained — practically, it could hardly have been — but the underlying purpose of the remark has remained the most basic purpose of the statutory provision. That purpose is the making effective of the duty of management to extend recognition to the union; the duty of management to bargain in good faith is essentially a corollary of its duty to recognize the union. Decisions under this provision reflect this. For example, an employer's unilateral wage increase during the bargaining processes tends to subvert the union's position as the representative of the employees in matters of this nature, and hence has been condemned as a practice violative of this statutory provision. See Labor Board v. Crompton-Highland Mills, Inc., 337 U.S. 217. . . . Collective bargaining, then, is not simply an occasion for purely formal meetings between management and labor, while each maintains an attitude of "take it or leave it"; it presupposes a desire to reach ultimate agreement, to enter into a

[9] Senator Walsh, at 79 Cong. Rec. 7660.

collective bargaining contract. See Heinz Co. v. Labor Board, 311 U.S. 514. . . .

But at the same time, Congress was generally not concerned with the substantive terms on which the parties contracted. Cf. Terminal Railroad Assn. v. Brotherhood of Railroad Trainmen, 318 U.S. 1, 6. Obviously there is tension between the principle that the parties need not contract on any specific terms and a practical enforcement of the principle that they are bound to deal with each other in a serious attempt to resolve differences and reach a common ground. And in fact criticism of the Board's application of the "good-faith" test arose from the belief that it was forcing employers to yield to union demands if they were to avoid a successful charge of unfair labor practice. Thus, in 1947 in Congress the fear was expressed that the Board had "gone very far, in the guise of determining whether or not employers had bargained in good faith, in setting itself up as the judge of what concessions an employer must make and of the proposals and counterproposals that he may or may not make." H.R. Rep. No. 245, 80th Cong., 1st Sess., p. 19. Since the Board was not viewed by Congress as an agency which should exercise its powers to arbitrate the parties' substantive solutions of the issues in their bargaining, a check on this apprehended trend was provided by writing the good-faith test of bargaining into §8(d) of the Act. . . .

Second. At the same time as it was statutorily defining the duty to bargain collectively, Congress, by adding §8(b)(3) . . . through the Taft-Hartley amendments, imposed that duty on labor organizations. Unions obviously are formed for the very purpose of bargaining collectively; but the legislative history makes it plain that Congress was wary of the position of some unions, and wanted to ensure that they would approach the bargaining table with the same attitude of willingness to reach an agreement as had been enjoined on management earlier. It intended to prevent employee representatives from putting forth the same "take it or leave it" attitude that had been condemned in management. 93 Cong. Rec. 4135, 4363, 5005.

Third. It is apparent from the legislative history of the whole Act that the policy of Congress is to impose a mutual duty upon the parties to confer in good faith with a desire to reach agreement, in the belief that such an approach from both sides of the table promotes the over-all design of achieving industrial peace. Discussion conducted under that standard of good faith may narrow the issues, making the real demands of the parties clearer to each other, and perhaps to themselves, and may encourage an attitude of settlement through give and take. The mainstream of cases before the Board and in the courts reviewing its orders, under the provisions fixing the duty to bargain collectively, is concerned with insuring that the parties approach the bargaining table with this attitude. But apart from this essential standard of conduct,

Congress intended that the parties should have wide latitude in their negotiations, unrestricted by any governmental power to regulate the substantive solution of their differences. See Teamsters Union v. Oliver, 358 U.S. at 295.

We believe that the Board's approach in this case — unless it can be defended, in terms of §8(b)(3), as resting on some unique character of the union tactics involved here — must be taken as proceeding from an erroneous view of collective bargaining. It must be realized that collective bargaining, under a system where the Government does not attempt to control the results of negotiations, cannot be equated with an academic collective search for truth — or even with what might be thought to be the ideal of one. The parties — even granting the modification of views that may come from a realization of economic interdependence — still proceed from contrary and to an extent antagonistic viewpoints and concepts of self-interest. The system has not reached the ideal of the philosophic notion that perfect understanding among people would lead to perfect agreement among them on values. The presence of economic weapons in reserve, and their actual exercise on occasion by the parties, is part and parcel of the system that the Wagner and Taft-Hartley Acts have recognized. Abstract logical analysis might find inconsistency between the command of the statute to negotiate toward an agreement in good faith and the legitimacy of the use of economic weapons, frequently having the most serious effect upon individual workers and productive enterprises, to induce one party to come to the terms desired by the other. But the truth of the matter is that at the present statutory stage of our national labor relations policy, the two factors — necessity for good-faith bargaining between parties, and the availability of economic pressure devices to each to make the other party incline to agree on one's terms — exist side by side. . . . Doubtless one factor influences the other; there may be less need to apply economic pressure if the areas of controversy have been defined through discussion; and at the same time, negotiation positions are apt to be weak or strong in accordance with the degree of economic power the parties possess. . . .

For similar reasons, we think the Board's approach involves an intrusion into the substantive aspects of the bargaining process — again, unless there is some specific warrant for its condemnation of the precise tactics involved here. The scope of §8(b)(3) and the limitations on Board power which were the design of §8(d) are exceeded, we hold, by inferring a lack of good faith not from any deficiencies of the union's performance at the bargaining table by reason of its attempted use of economic pressure, but solely and simply because tactics designed to exert economic pressure were employed during the course of the good-faith negotiations. Thus the Board in the guise of determining good or bad faith in negotiations could regulate what economic weapons a party might summon to its aid. And if the Board could regulate the choice of economic weapons that may be used as part of collective bargaining, it would be in a position to exercise considerable influence upon the substantive terms on which the parties contract. As the parties' own devices became more limited, the Government might have to enter even more directly into the negotiation of collective agreements. Our labor policy is not presently erected on a foundation of government control of the results of negotiations. . . . Nor does it contain a charter for the [NLRB] to act at large in equalizing disparities of bargaining power between employer and union.

Fourth. The use of economic pressure . . . is of itself not at all inconsistent with the duty of bargaining in good faith. But in three cases in recent years, the Board has assumed the power to label particular union economic weapons inconsistent with that duty. See the *Personal Products* case,[15] 108 N.L.R.B. 743, *set aside,* 227 F.2d 409; the *Boone County* case, United Mine Workers, 117 N.L.R.B. 1095, *set aside,* 257 F.2d 211; and the present case. The Board freely (and we think correctly) conceded here that a "total" strike called by the union would not have subjected it to sanctions under §8(b)(3), at least if it were called after the old contract, with its no-strike clause, had expired. Cf. *United Mine Workers,* supra. The Board's opinion in the instant case is not so unequivocal as this concession (and therefore perhaps more logical). But in the light of it and the principles we have enunciated, we must evaluate the claim of the Board to power, under §8(b)(3), to distinguish among various economic pressure tactics and brand the ones at bar inconsistent with good-faith collective bargaining. We conclude its claim is without foundation.

(a) The Board contends that the distinction between a total strike and the conduct at bar is that a total strike is a concerted activity protected against employer interference by §§7 and 8(a)(1) of the Act, while the activity at bar is not a protected concerted activity. We may agree arguendo with the Board that this Court's decision in the *Briggs-Stratton* case, Automobile Workers v. Wisconsin Board, 336 U.S. 245, establishes that the employee conduct here was not a protected concerted activity. On this assumption the employer could have discharged or taken other appropriate disciplinary action against

---

[15] The facts in *Personal Products* did, in the Board's view, present the case of a union which was using economic pressure against an employer . . . without identifying what its bargaining demands were—a matter which can be viewed quite differently [under] §8(b)(3) . . . from the present case. The Board's decision in *Personal Products* may have turned on this to some extent, see 108 N.L.R.B., at 746; but its decision in the instant case seems to view *Personal Products* as turning on the same point as does the present case.

the employees participating in these "slow-down," "sit-in," and arguably unprotected disloyal tactics. See Labor Board v. Fansteel Metallurgical Corp., 306 U.S. 240; Labor Board v. Electrical Workers, 346 U.S. 464. But surely that a union activity is not protected against disciplinary action does not mean that it constitutes a refusal to bargain in good faith. The reason why the ordinary economic strike is not evidence of a failure to bargain in good faith is not that it constitutes a protected activity but that, as we have developed, there is simply no inconsistency between the application of economic pressure and good-faith collective bargaining. The Board suggests that since (on the assumption we make) the union members' activities here were unprotected, and they could have been discharged, the activities should also be deemed unfair labor practices, since thus the remedy of a cease-and-desist order, milder than mass discharges of personnel and less disruptive of commerce, would be available. The argument is not persuasive. There is little logic in assuming that because Congress was willing to allow employers to use self-help against union tactics, if they were willing to face the economic consequences of its use, it also impliedly declared these tactics unlawful as a matter of federal law. Our problem remains that of construing §8(b)(3)'s terms, and we do not see how the availability of self-help to the employer has anything to do with the matter.

(b) The Board contends that because an orthodox "total" strike is "traditional" its use must be taken as being consistent with §8(b)(3); but since the tactics here are not "traditional" or "normal," they need not be so viewed. Further, the Board cites what it conceives to be the public's moral condemnation of the sort of employee tactics involved here. But again we cannot see how these distinctions can be made under a statute which simply enjoins a duty to bargain in good faith. Again, these are relevant arguments when the question is the scope of the concerted activities given affirmative protection by the Act. But as we have developed, the use of economic pressure by the parties to a labor dispute is not a grudging exception to some policy of completely academic discussion enjoined by the Act; it is part and parcel of the process of collective bargaining. On this basis, we fail to see the relevance of whether the practice in question is time-honored or whether its exercise is generally supported by public opinion. It may be that the tactics used here deserve condemnation, but this would not justify attempting to pour that condemnation into a vessel not designed to hold it. The same may be said for the Board's contention that these activities, as opposed to a "normal" strike, are inconsistent with §8(b)(3) because they offer maximum pressure on the employer at minimum economic cost to the union. One may doubt whether this was so here, but the matter does not turn on that. Surely it cannot be said that the only economic weapons consistent with good-faith bargaining are those which minimize the pressure on the other party or maximize the disadvantage to the party using them. The catalog of union and employer weapons that might thus fall under ban would be most extensive.

Fifth. These distinctions essayed by the Board here, and the lack of relationship to the statutory standard inherent in them, confirm us in our conclusion that the judgment of the Court of Appeals, setting aside the order of the Board, must be affirmed. For they make clear to us that when the Board moves in this area, with only §8(b)(3) for support, it is functioning as an arbiter of the sort of economic weapons the parties can use in seeking to gain acceptance of their bargaining demands. It has sought to introduce some standard of properly "balanced" bargaining power, or some new distinction of justifiable and unjustifiable, proper and "abusive" economic weapons into the collective bargaining duty imposed by the Act. The Board's assertion of power under §8(b)(3) allows it to sit in judgment upon every economic weapon the parties to a labor contract negotiation employ, judging it on the very general standard of that section, not drafted with reference to specific forms of economic pressure. We have expressed our belief that this amounts to the Board's entrance into the substantive aspects of the bargaining process to an extent Congress has not countenanced. . . .

Congress has been rather specific when it has come to outlaw particular economic weapons on the part of unions. See §8(b)(4) . . . , as added by the Taft-Hartley Act and as supplemented by the Labor-Management Reporting and Disclosure Act of 1959; §8(b)(7), as added by the latter Act. But the activities here involved have never been specifically outlawed by Congress. To be sure, the express prohibitions of the Act are not exclusive — if there were any questions of a stratagem or device to evade the policies of the Act, the Board hardly would be powerless. Phelps Dodge Corp. v. Labor Board, 313 U.S. 177, 194. But it is clear to us that the Board needs a more specific charter than §8(b)(3) before it can add to the Act's prohibitions here. . . . Affirmed.

[Frankfurter, J., with whom Harlan and Whittaker, JJ., concurred, agreed that the union's conduct did not per se violate §8(b)(3) but urged that harassing tactics, as well as other action outside the bargaining room, such as violence, might be evidence of bad faith. Accordingly, those Justices would have remanded the case to the Board.]

NOTE

Is there any tension between the approach in *Truitt* and in *Insurance Agents*? If so, which approach seems preferable?

NLRB v. Katz
369 U.S. 736 (1962)

BRENNAN, J. Is it a violation of the duty "to bargain collectively" . . . for an employer, without first consulting a union with which it is carrying on bona fide contract negotiations, to institute changes regarding matters which are subjects of mandatory bargaining under §8(d) and which are in fact under discussion? The [NLRB] answered the question affirmatively in this case, in a decision which expressly disclaimed any finding that the totality of the respondents' conduct manifested bad faith in the pending negotiations. 126 N.L.R.B. 288. . . . [T]he Second Circuit denied enforcement of the Board's [order], finding in our decision in Labor Board v. Insurance Agents' Union, 361 U.S. 477, a broad rule that the statutory duty to bargain cannot be held to be violated, when bargaining is in fact being carried on, without a finding of the respondent's subjective bad faith in negotiating. 289 F.2d 700. . . . We find nothing in the Board's decision inconsistent with *Insurance Agents* and hold that the Court of Appeals erred in refusing to enforce the Board's order. . . .

. . . As amended and amplified at the hearing and construed by the Board, the complaint's charge of unfair labor practices particularly referred to three acts by the company: unilaterally granting numerous merit increases in October 1956 and January 1957; unilaterally announcing a change in sick-leave policy in March 1957; and unilaterally instituting a new system of automatic wage increases during April 1957. . . . [T]he company has defended against the charges along two fronts: First, it asserts that the unilateral changes occurred after a bargaining impasse had developed through the union's fault in adopting obstructive tactics.[7] According to the Board, however, "the evidence is clear that the Respondent undertook its unilateral actions before negotiations were discontinued in May 1957, or before, as we find on the record, the existence of any possible impasse." 126 N.L.R.B., at 289-290. There is ample support in the record considered as a whole for this finding of fact, . . . which the Court of Appeals did not question.

The second line of defense was that the Board could not hinge a conclusion that §8(a)(5) had been violated on unilateral actions alone, with-

---

[7]The Examiner rejected the company's offer to prove union-instigated slowdowns. But such proof would not have justified the company's refusal to bargain. Since, as we held in Labor Board v. Insurance Agents' Union, 361 U.S. 477, the Board may not brand partial strike activity as illegitimate and forbid its use in support of bargaining, an *employer* cannot be free to refuse to negotiate when the union resorts to such tactics. Engaging in partial strikes is not inherently inconsistent with a continued willingness to negotiate; and as long as there is such willingness and no impasse has developed, the employer's obligation continues.

out making a finding of the employer's subjective bad faith at the bargaining table; and that the unilateral actions were merely evidence relevant to the issue of subjective good faith. This argument prevailed in the Court of Appeals which remanded the cases to the Board. . . .

The duty "to bargain collectively" enjoined by §8(a)(5) is defined by §8(d) as the duty to "meet . . . and confer in good faith with respect to wages, hours, and other terms and conditions of employment." Clearly, the duty thus defined may be violated without a general failure of subjective good faith; for there is no occasion to consider the issue of good faith if a party has refused even to negotiate *in fact* — "to meet . . . and confer" — about any of the mandatory subjects. A refusal to negotiate *in fact* as to any subject which is within §8(d), and about which the union seeks to negotiate, violates §8(a)(5) though the employer has every desire to reach agreement with the union upon an over-all collective agreement and earnestly and in all good faith bargains to that end. We hold that an employer's unilateral change in conditions of employment under negotiation is similarly a violation of §8(a)(5), for it is a circumvention of the duty to negotiate which frustrates the objectives of §8(a)(5) much as does a flat refusal.[11]

The unilateral actions of the respondent illustrate the policy and practical considerations which support our conclusion.

We consider first the matter of sick leave. A sick-leave plan had been in effect since May 1956, under which employees were allowed ten paid sick-leave days annually and could accumulate half the unused days, or up to five days each year. Changes in the plan were sought and proposals and counter-proposals had come up at three bargaining conferences. In March 1957, the company, without first notifying or consulting the union, announced changes in the plan, which reduced from ten to five the number of paid sick-leave days per year, but allowed accumulation of twice the unused days, thus increasing to ten the number of days which might be carried over. This action plainly frustrated the statutory objective of establishing working conditions through bargaining. Some employees might view the change to be a diminution of benefits. Others, more interested in accumulating sick-leave days, might regard the change as an improvement. If one view or the other clearly prevailed among the employees, the unilateral action might well mean that the employer had either uselessly dissipated trading material or aggravated the sick-leave issue. On the other hand, if the employees were more evenly divided on the merits of the company's changes the union

---

[11] . . . *Crompton-Highland Mills* [337 U.S. 217] sustained the Board's conclusion that the employer's unilateral grant of a wage increase substantially greater than any it had offered to the union during negotiations which had ended in impasse clearly manifested bad faith and violated the employer's duty to bargain.

negotiators, beset by conflicting factions, might be led to adopt a protective vagueness on the issue of sick leave, which also would inhibit the useful discussion contemplated by Congress in imposing the specific obligation to bargain collectively.

Other considerations appear from consideration of the respondents' unilateral action in increasing wages. At the April 4, 1957, meeting the employers offered, and the union rejected, a three-year contract with an immediate across-the-board increase of $7.50 per week, to be followed at the end of the first year and again at the end of the second by further increases of $5 for employees earning less than $90 at those times. Shortly thereafter, without having advised or consulted with the union, the company announced a new system of automatic wage increases whereby there would be an increase of $5 every three months up to $74.99 per week; an increase of $5 every six months between $75 and $90 per week; and a merit review every six months for employees earning over $90 per week. It is clear at a glance that the automatic wage increase system which was instituted unilaterally was considerably more generous than that which had shortly theretofore been offered to and rejected by the union. Such action conclusively manifested bad faith in the negotiations, Labor Board v. Crompton-Highland Mills, 337 U.S. 217, and so would have violated §8(a)(5) even on the Court of Appeals' interpretation, though no additional evidence of bad faith appeared. An employer is not required to lead with his best offer; he is free to bargain. But even after an impasse is reached he has no license to grant wage increases greater than any he has ever offered the union at the bargaining table, for such action is necessarily inconsistent with a sincere desire to conclude an agreement with the union.

The respondents' third unilateral action related to merit increases, which are also a subject of mandatory bargaining. Labor Board v. Allison & Co., 165 F.2d 766. The matter of merit increases had been raised at three of the conferences during 1956 but no final understanding had been reached. In January 1957, the company, without notice to the union, granted merit increases to 20 employees out of the approximately 50 in the unit, the increases ranging between $2 and $10. This action too must be viewed as tantamount to an outright refusal to negotiate on that subject, and therefore as a violation of §8(a)(5), unless the fact that the January raises were in line with the company's long-standing practice of granting quarterly or semiannual merit reviews — in effect, were a mere continuation of the status quo — differentiates them from the wage increases and the changes in the sick-leave plan. We do not think it does. Whatever might be the case as to so-called "merit raises" which are in fact simply automatic increases to which the employer has already committed himself, the raises here in question were in no sense automatic, but were informed by a large measure of discretion.

There simply is no way in such case for a union to know whether or not there has been a substantial departure from practice, and therefore the union may properly insist that the company negotiate as to the procedures and criteria for determining such increases.

It is apparent from what we have said why we see nothing in *Insurance Agents* contrary to the Board's decision. The union in that case had not in any way whatever foreclosed discussion of any issue, by unilateral actions or otherwise. . . . We held that Congress had not, in §8(b)(3), the counterpart of §8(a)(5), empowered the Board to pass judgment on the legitimacy of any particular economic weapon used in support of genuine negotiations. But the Board *is* authorized to order the cessation of behavior which is in effect a refusal to negotiate, or which directly obstructs or inhibits the actual process of discussion, or which reflects a cast of mind against reaching agreement. Unilateral action by an employer without prior discussion with the union does amount to a refusal to negotiate about the affected conditions of employment under negotiation and must of necessity obstruct bargaining, contrary to the congressional policy. It will often disclose an unwillingness to agree with the union. It will rarely be justified by any reason of substance. It follows that the Board may hold such unilateral action to be an unfair labor practice in violation of §8(a)(5), without also finding the employer guilty of overall subjective bad faith. While we do not foreclose the possibility that there might be circumstances which the Board could or should accept as excusing or justifying unilateral action, no such case is presented here.

[Reversed and remanded with direction to the court of appeals to enforce the Board's order.]

Frankfurter [and White, JJ.] took no part in the decision of this case.

NOTES

1. *Crompton-Highland Mills* (see footnote 11 of the principal case) did not expressly require an "impasse" as a condition for an employer's lawful institution of benefits previously rejected by the bargaining representative. The NLRB added the impasse requirement (see Bradley Washfountain Co., 89 N.L.R.B. 1662 (1950), *enforcement denied*, 192 F.2d 144 (7th Cir. 1951); it remains the accepted rule. See, e.g., Atlas Metal Parts Co. v. NLRB, 660 F.2d 304 (7th Cir. 1981). Once a genuine impasse is reached, the Board takes the view that the duty to bargain about the subject matter of the impasse becomes dormant "until changed circumstances indicate that an agreement may be possible." Providence Medical Center, 243 N.L.R.B. 714 (1979).

In view of the employer's interest in a satisfied work force, equity for employees, and the desirability of avoiding contrived "impasses," should an "impasse" be decisive where wages or other benefits are improved during bargaining? Would it be preferable to require only that the union be given a fair opportunity to agree to an interim wage increase without prejudice to further negotiations? Is it possible to make a valid generalization about the impact of such interim increases on the employees' willingness to strike? Should the Board be concerned with that consideration? See generally Stewart & Engeman, Impasse, Collective Bargaining, and Action, 39 U. Cin. L. Rev. 233 (1970).

2. Prior to *Katz*, the Board had held that slowdowns, or strikes in the face of a no-strike clause (whether or not sponsored by the union), suspend the employer's duty to bargain and justify unilateral action. See, e.g., Valley City Furniture Co., 110 N.L.R.B. 1589, 1592 (1954). Does footnote 7 of the *Katz* opinion repudiate those decisions? Does that footnote rest on the premise that only prohibited, as distinguished from unprotected, activity suspends the duty to bargain? Is that premise sound? In any event, the NLRB, without mentioning *Katz*, has held that an employer's duty to bargain is suspended during a strike unprotected because in violation of an interim no-strike pledge. See Arundel Corp., 210 N.L.R.B. 525 (1974).

3. An expired collective bargaining agreement continues, in general, to govern the employment relationship. Despite the expiration of an agreement §§8(a)(5) and 8(d) impose an obligation to bargain to impasse prior to alteration of existing, contractually-established wages and working conditions (i.e., mandatory subjects of bargaining). Thus, notwithstanding LMRA §302(c)(5), an employer's unilateral ceasing of payments into a health and welfare fund, absent express contract language authorizing such action, violates §8(a)(5). See, e.g., Cauthorne Trucking, 256 N.L.R.B. 721 (1981), *enforcement granted in part and denied in part*, 691 F.2d 1023 (D.C. Cir. 1982). However, not all contractual obligations survive the terminated agreement. An employer who may not implement a preimpasse change in wages has been permitted, without prior bargaining, to suspend such items as union shop and checkoff provisions. See NLRB v. Cone Mills Corp., 373 F.2d 595 (4th Cir. 1967); Marine and Shipbuilding Wkrs. v. NLRB, 320 F.2d 615 (3d Cir. 1963), *cert. denied*, 375 U.S. 984 (1964). These exceptions to the general obligation to maintain contract provisions on mandatory subjects are said to rest on a distinction between terms governing the "employer-employee" relationship and those governing the "employer-union" relationship. See Gordon L. Rayner & Frank H. Clark, d/b/a Bay Area Sealers, 251 N.L.R.B. 89, 90 (1980), *enforced as modified*, 665 F.2d 970, 977 (9th Cir. 1982). How should contract provisions granting superseniority for union officials be classified?

4. Should the employer's promise to arbitrate grievances survive contract expiration? In 1970, the Board formulated the following guidelines for grievance adjustment during a contract hiatus: An employer is not required either to adhere to the arbitration procedure of an expired agreement or to bargain to an impasse over the suspension of that procedure. Such a requirement would run counter to the essentially consensual nature of arbitration. The parties are, however, under a statutory duty to confer about grievances arising after the expiration of their contract, and they may not abandon established grievance procedures (short of arbitration) — even though such procedures had their genesis in the contract. Hilton-Davis Chem. Co., 185 N.L.R.B. 241 (1970).

A decade later, in American Sink Top & Cabinet Co., 242 N.L.R.B. 408 (1979), the Board concluded that the Supreme Court's decision in Nolde Bros. v. Local 358, Bakery Wkrs., infra p. 1068, required abandonment of the *Hilton-Davis* analysis and result. Accordingly, a §8(a)(5) violation was found where the employer refused to arbitrate a grievance over a discharge that occurred after the contract had expired. The grievance was "at least arguably" based on the expired contract, and there was "no reason to conclude that the parties had intended the arbitration provisions to end with the contract's terms." Subsequently, two Reagan appointees indicated that *Nolde Bros.* does not warrant the application of an arbitration clause to discharges based entirely on conduct occurring after the expiration of the collective agreement and implied that *American Sink* should be limited accordingly. See Digmor Equipment & Engineering Co., 261 N.L.R.B. 1175 (1982) (Chairman Van de Water concurring); Southwest Security Equipment Corp., 262 N.L.R.B. 665 (1982) (Member Hunter concurring).

Do you agree with the proposed limitation on *American Sink?* If an arbitration clause applies to discharges based solely on conduct occurring after contract expiration, under what circumstances should a no-strike clause also be enforced after contract expiration? Consider the relevance of the view that an arbitration clause is the quid pro quo for a no-strike clause; and see *Goya Foods*, referred to infra p. 1069.

5. Different issues arise when unilateral reductions in employee benefits are made in order either to meet business problems caused by fruitless negotiations or to exert bargaining pressure. Consider these situations:

(a) An employer and the union, after ten bargaining sessions over a two-month period following the expiration of their agreement, remain far apart on wages and other money items. The employer's salesmen are experiencing increasing difficulty in getting orders because of customers' fears that a strike will delay deliveries. The employer accordingly advises the union and his employees as follows: In order to expedite bargaining and to meet the increased costs of doing business resulting from the bargaining deadlock, he has put into effect a 10 percent wage cut, pending the execution of a new agreement. Has the employer violated §8(a)(5)? What if bargaining had reached an "impasse" and the employer's wage cut was prompted solely by the desire to exert bargaining pressure on the union and its employees?

(b) Despite substantial negotiations, the parties were deadlocked over wages, paid holidays, and retirement provisions. After the union called a strike and established picket lines, the employer sought to hire temporary replacements at the wage rate previously offered to the union but was unable to recruit enough workers to permit the resumption of operations. The employer thereupon improved that rate by 5 percent (which was less than the union's demand), hired enough replacements to resume operations, and advised the replacements that they would be replaced upon settlement of the current dispute with the union. Has the employer violated the statute? Would it be material if the replacements were offered "permanent" jobs? If the employer refused to engage his regular workers who offered to work at the higher rate?

Have the employers in these situations engaged in unlawful "harassment" or "discrimination"? Consider *Erie Resistor Corp.*, supra p. 305, *American Ship Bldg. Co.*, supra p. 316, and *Insurance Agents' Intl.*, supra p. 830. See also Midstate Tel. Corp. v. NLRB, 706 F.2d 401 (2d Cir. 1983).

See generally Schatzki, The Employer's Unilateral Act: A Per Se Violation — Sometimes, 44 Tex. L. Rev. 470 (1966).

C. REMEDIES FOR REFUSAL TO BARGAIN

H.K. Porter Co. v. NLRB
397 U.S. 99 (1970)

BLACK, J. After an election respondent United Steelworkers Union was, on October 5, 1961, certified . . . as the bargaining agent for certain employees at the Danville, Virginia, plant of the petitioner, H.K. Porter Co. Thereafter negotiations commenced for a collective-bargaining agreement. Since that time the controversy has seesawed between the Board, the [D.C. Cir.] Court of Appeals, and this Court. This delay of over eight years is not because the case is exceedingly complex, but appears to have occurred chiefly because of the skill of the company's negotiators in taking advantage of every opportunity for delay in an act more noticeable for its generality than for its precise prescriptions. The entire lengthy dispute mainly revolves around the union's desire to have the company agree to "check off" the dues owed to the union by its members, that is, to deduct those dues periodically from the company's wage payments to the employees. The record shows, as the Board found, that the company's objection to a checkoff was not due to any general principle or policy against making deductions from employees' wages. The company does deduct charges for things like insurance, taxes, and contributions to charities, and at some other plants it has a checkoff arrangement for union dues. The evidence shows, and the court below found, that the company's objection was not because of inconvenience, but solely on the ground that the company was "not going to aid and comfort the union." Efforts by the union to obtain some kind of compromise on the checkoff request were all met with the same staccato response to the effect that the collection of union dues was the "union's business" and the company was not going to provide any assistance. Based on this and other evidence the Board found, and the Court of Appeals approved the finding, that the refusal of the company to bargain about the checkoff was not made in good faith, but was done solely to frustrate the making of any collective bargaining agreement. In May 1966, the Court of Appeals upheld the Board's order requiring the company to cease and desist from refusing to bargain in good faith and directing it to engage in further collective bargaining, if requested by the union to do so, over the checkoff. United Steelworkers v. NLRB, 363 F.2d 272, *cert. denied*, 385 U.S. 851.

. . . [T]he Court of Appeals intimated that the Board conceivably might have required petitioner to agree to a checkoff provision as a remedy for the prior bad-faith bargaining, although the order enforced at that time did not contain any such provision. 363 F.2d, at 275-276, and n.16. In the ensuing negotiations the company offered to discuss alternative arrangements for modification. Because of this disagreement over the proper interpretation of the court's opinion, the union, in February 1967, filed a motion for clarification of the 1966 opinion. The motion was denied by the court on March 22, 1967, in an order suggesting that contempt proceedings by the Board would be the proper avenue for testing the employer's compliance with the original order. A request for the institution of such proceedings was made by the union, and, in June 1967, the Regional Director . . . declined to prosecute a contempt charge, finding that the employer had "satisfactorily complied with the affirmative requirements of the Order." . . . The union then filed in the Court of Appeals a motion for reconsideration of the earlier motion to clarify the 1966 opinion. The court granted that motion and issued a new opinion in which it held that in certain circumstances a "checkoff may be imposed as a remedy for bad faith bargaining." United Steelworkers v. NLRB, 389 F.2d 295, 298 (1967). The case was then remanded to the

Board and on July 3, 1968, the Board issued a supplemental order requiring the petitioner to "[g]rant to the Union a contract clause providing for the checkoff of union dues." 172 N.L.R.B. No. 72. The Court of Appeals affirmed this order, H.K. Porter Co. v. NLRB, 414 F.2d 1123 (1969). . . . For reasons to be stated we hold that while the Board does have power under the [NLRA] . . . to require employers and employees to negotiate, it is without power to compel a company or a union to agree to any substantive contractual provision of a collective bargaining agreement. . . .

The object of [the Wagner] Act was not to allow governmental regulation of the terms and conditions of employment, but rather to ensure that employers and their employees could work together to establish mutually satisfactory conditions. The basic theme of the Act was that through collective bargaining the passions, arguments, and struggles of prior years would be channeled into constructive, open discussions leading, it was hoped, to mutual agreement. But it was recognized from the beginning that agreement might in some cases be impossible, and it was never intended that the Government would in such cases step in, become a party to the negotiations and impose its own views of a desirable settlement. . . .

The Act was passed at a time in our Nation's history when there was considerable legal debate over the constitutionality of any law that required employers to conform their business behavior to any governmentally imposed standards. It was seriously contended that Congress could not constitutionally compel an employer to recognize a union and allow his employees to participate in setting the terms and conditions of employment. In NLRB v. Jones & Laughlin Steel Corp., 301 U.S. 1 (1937), this Court, in a 5 to 4 decision, held that Congress was within the limits of its constitutional powers in passing the Act. In the course of that decision the Court said [at p. 45]:

> The Act does not compel agreements between employers and employees. It does not compel any agreement whatever. . . . The theory of the Act is that free opportunity for negotiation with accredited representatives of employees is likely to promote industrial peace and may bring about the adjustments and agreements which the Act in itself does not attempt to compel.

In 1947 Congress reviewed the experience under the Act and concluded that certain amendments were in order. In the House committee report accompanying what eventually became the [LMRA], the committee referred to the above-quoted language in *Jones & Laughlin* and said:

> Notwithstanding this language of the Court, the present Board has gone very far, in the guise of determining whether or not employers had bargained

in good faith, in setting itself up as the judge of what concessions an employer must make and of the proposals and counterproposals that he may or may not make. . . . [U]nless Congress writes into the law guides for the Board to follow, the Board may attempt to carry this process still further and seek to control more and more the terms of collective bargaining agreements.[3]

Accordingly Congress amended the provisions defining unfair labor practices and said in §8(d) that: ". . . *such obligation* [to bargain collectively] *does not compel either party to agree to a proposal or require the making of a concession* [emphasis added by the Court]."

In discussing the effect of that amendment, this Court said it is "clear that the Board may not, either directly or indirectly, compel concessions or otherwise sit in judgment upon the substantive terms of collective bargaining agreements." NLRB v. American Ins. Co., 343 U.S. 395, 404 (1952). Later this Court affirmed that view stating that "it remains clear that §8(d) was an attempt by Congress to prevent the Board from controlling the settling of the terms of collective bargaining agreements." NLRB v. Insurance Agents, 361 U.S. 477, 487 (1960). The parties to the instant case are agreed that this is the first time in the 35-year history of the Act that the Board has ordered either an employer or a union to agree to a substantive term of a collective bargaining agreement.

Recognizing the fundamental principle "that the [NLRA] is grounded on the premise of freedom of contract," 389 F.2d, at 300, the Court of Appeals . . . concluded that nevertheless in the circumstances presented here the Board could properly compel the employer to agree to a proposed checkoff clause. The Board had found that the refusal was based on a desire to frustrate agreement and not on any legitimate business reason. On the basis of that finding the Court of Appeals approved the further finding that the employer had not bargained in good faith, and the validity of that finding is not now before us. Where the record thus revealed repeated refusals by the employer to bargain in good faith on this issue, the Court of Appeals concluded that ordering agreement to the checkoff clause "may be the only means of assuring the Board, and the court, that [the employer] no longer harbors an illegal intent." 389 F.2d, at 299.

In reaching this conclusion the Court of Appeals held that §8(d) did not forbid the Board from compelling agreement. That court felt that "§8(d) defines collective bargaining and relates to a determination of whether a . . . violation has occurred and not to the scope of the remedy which may be necessary to cure violations which have already occurred." 389 F.2d, at

---

[3] H.R. Rep. No. 245, 80th Cong., 1st Sess., 19-20 (1947).

299. We may agree with the Court of Appeals that as a matter of strict, literal interpretation that section refers only to deciding when a violation has occurred, but we do not agree that that observation justifies the conclusion that the remedial powers of the Board are not also limited by the same considerations that led Congress to enact §8(d). It is implicit in the entire structure of the Act that the Board acts to oversee and referee the process of collective bargaining, leaving the results of the contest to the bargaining strengths of the parties. It would be anomalous indeed to hold that while §8(d) prohibits the Board from relying on a refusal to agree as the sole evidence of bad-faith bargaining, the Act permits the Board to compel agreement in that same dispute. The Board's remedial powers under §10 of the Act are broad, but they are limited to carrying out the policies of the Act itself. One of these fundamental policies is freedom of contract. While the parties' freedom of contract is not absolute under the Act, allowing the Board to compel agreement when the parties themselves are unable to agree would violate the fundamental premise on which the Act is based — private bargaining under governmental supervision of the procedure alone, without any official compulsion over the actual terms of the contract.

In reaching its decision the Court of Appeals relied extensively on the equally important policy of the Act that workers' rights to collective bargaining are to be secured. In this case the court apparently felt that the employer was trying effectively to destroy the union by refusing to agree to what the union may have considered its most important demand. Perhaps the court, fearing that the parties might resort to economic combat, was also trying to maintain the industrial peace that the Act is designed to further. But the Act as presently drawn does not contemplate that unions will always be secure and able to achieve agreement even when their economic position is weak, or that strikes and lockouts will never result from a bargaining impasse. It cannot be said that the Act forbids an employer or a union to rely ultimately on its economic strength to try to secure what it cannot obtain through bargaining. . . .

[Reversed and remanded to the Court of Appeals for further action consistent with this opinion.]

White, J., took no part in the decision of this case.

Marshall, J., took no part in the consideration or decision of this case.

[The concurring opinion of Harlan, J., is omitted.]

Douglas, J., with whom Stewart, J., concurs, dissenting. . . . Here the employer did not refuse the checkoff for any business reason, whether cost, inconvenience, or what not. Nor did the employer refuse the checkoff as a factor in its bargaining strategy, hoping that delay and denial might bring it in exchange favorable terms and conditions. Its reason was a resolve to avoid reaching any agreement with the union.

In those narrow and specialized circumstances, I see no answer to the power of the Board in its discretion to impose the checkoff as "affirmative action" necessary to remedy the flagrant refusal of the employer to bargain in good faith.

The case is rare, if not unique. . . . I realize that any principle once announced may in time gain a momentum not warranted by the exigencies of its creation. But once there is any business consideration that leads to a denial of a demand or any consideration of bargaining strategy that explains the refusal, the Board has no power to act. Its power is narrowly restricted to the clear case where the refusal is aimed solely at avoidance of any agreement. Such is the present case. . . .

NOTES

1. Is the approach in *H.K. Porter* likely to inhibit regulation of the details of negotiations? See Comment, The H.K. Porter Experiment in Bargaining Remedies: A Study in Black and Wright, 56 Va. L. Rev. 530 (1970).

2. What reasons, if any, could an employer in negotiations urge against a checkoff without running a substantial risk of a §8(a)(5) violation? Cf. Church Point Wholesale Grocery, 215 N.L.R.B. 500 (1974), *enforced sub nom.* Chemical Wkrs. Union v. NLRB, 538 F.2d 1199 (5th Cir. 1976). Would your answer be affected if the union (a) was newly certified or (b) had, for some time, entered into agreements with the employer without a checkoff provision?

3. An employer, otherwise in compliance with §8(a)(5), rejects the union's demand for a union-security clause (a mandatory subject of bargaining) urging that (a) the recruitment of members or the securing of financial support should be the union's own business; (b) compulsory unionism is repugnant to the employer's principles; (c) compulsory unionism destroys employee morale; (d) compulsory unionism would give the union excessive power; and (e) that he, as the champion of the nonunion employees in the unit, had to resist that demand.

In each case, has the employer satisfied the Act's bargaining requirements? Cf. Atlas Metal Parts Co. v. NLRB, 660 F.2d 304, 308 (7th Cir. 1981). Would it be material that the parties, for a considerable time, had entered into agreements not containing a union-security clause? Or that the union had just been certified, after an extremely close election preceded by vigorous antiunion propaganda from the employer, and had failed to secure a collective agreement?

Note: Extraordinary Remedies for Refusals to Bargain

The NLRB's conventional remedies for §8(a)(5) violations have long been criticized as inadequate. See, e.g., McCulloch, Past, Present and Future Remedies Under §8(a)(5) of the NLRA, 19 Lab. L.J. 131 (1968); D. McDowell & K. Huhn, NLRB Remedies for Unfair Labor Practices (1976). In Ex-Cell-O Corp., 185 N.L.R.B. 107 (1970), the Board ruled (3-2) that it lacked authority to issue an order making the employees whole for the benefits they would have received but for the employer's unlawful failure to bargain. The Board was upheld by the court of appeals on the ground that the employer's objections to the union's certification (and defense in the resulting §8(a)(5) proceeding) — specifically, that the union's misrepresentations had tainted the election — were "fairly debatable" rather than "frivolous" or in "bad faith." See Ex-Cell-O Corp. v. NLRB, 449 F.2d 1058, 1064-1065 (D.C. Cir. 1971).

A year later, the Board, although acknowledging its authority to issue a make-whole order as the "law of the case" (as declared by the court of appeals in its remand), unanimously declined to do so, even though the employer's violation had been "clear and flagrant." The Board rested its declination in part on the ground that it could not determine what the parties would have agreed to. See Tiidee Products, Inc., 194 N.L.R.B. 1234, 1235 (1972). The Board, however, did require the employer (a) to mail copies of the NLRB notice of violation to each employee's home, (b) to give the union reasonable access to company bulletin boards, (c) to supply the union with (and to update for a year) the names and addresses of the company's employees, and (d) to reimburse the union and the NLRB for litigation expenses, including counsel fees. Although the court of appeals accepted the Board's position on the make-whole remedy, it modified the award of attorney fees, first, by denying reimbursement for the NLRB's litigation expenditures (on the ground that the employer had not been an habitual offender) and, second, by limiting the union's recovery to litigation expenses incurred prior to the NLRB's initial order (on the ground that subsequent litigation had not been frivolous but had, on the contrary, supported the NLRB's position against the novel make-whole remedy). Electrical Wkrs. v. NLRB (Tiidee Products), 502 F.2d 349 (D.C. Cir. 1974), cert. denied, 421 U.S. 991 (1975).

For a review of Board policy on the award of organization, litigation, or negotiation expenses as extraordinary remedies for bad faith refusals to bargain, see Autoprod, Inc., 265 N.L.R.B. 331 (1982); J.P. Stevens & Co., 244 N.L.R.B. 407 (1979), enforced, 668 F.2d 767 (4th Cir. 1982). See also Morris, The Role of the NLRB and the Courts in the Collective Bargaining Process: A Fresh Look at the Conventional Wisdom and Unconventional Remedies, 30 Vand. L. Rev. 661 (1977). The unavailability of a make-whole remedy, along with the slowness of NLRB procedures, has been a factor in proposals for greater use of §10(j) injunctions. See Note, The Use of Section 10(j) of the Labor Management Relations Act in Employer Refusal to Bargain Cases, 1976 Ill. L.F. 845.

Would a make-whole remedy be consistent with H.K. Porter? With the Act? The proposed Labor Reform Act of 1978 provided for a make-whole remedy from an employer that had unlawfully refused to bargain over a first collective agreement. A make-whole remedy was authorized by the California Agricultural Labor Relations Act. See Adam Dairy, 4 A.L.R.B. No. 24 (1978); Comment, Make-Whole Under the Agricultural Labor Relations Act: Its Applicability and Scope, 13 U.S.F. L. Rev. 971 (1979).

D.   THE SUBJECTS OF "MANDATORY BARGAINING"

Collective bargaining is increasingly viewed not merely as an alternative to individual bargaining but as a process for achieving a measure of joint determination of the rules and decisions shaping the employment relationship. Although an incumbent union's standing with respect to matters encompassed by the terms "wages" and "hours" is undisputed, controversy and uncertainty exist concerning a union's right to participate in decisions that affect the existence of jobs rather than their terms and conditions — e.g., plant expansion or contraction, the contracting out of work, or automation. In responding to such issues, the NLRB has tended to enlarge the bargaining duty, an approach upheld as appropriate nearly four decades ago in a celebrated case that spoke of the need to meet "new conditions." See Inland Steel Co. v. NLRB, 170 F.2d 247, 254 (7th Cir. 1948). cert. denied, 336 U.S. 960 (1949).

These "new conditions" include the progressive expansion of collective agreements into areas once left for managerial discretion. That expansion has frequently occurred, independently of direct legal compulsion, as a result of changing technology, changes in the parties' views as to what subjects should be open to bargain, and the determination of unions to exert economic power to enlarge the area governed by jointly formulated standards. Decisions under the NLRA have both reflected and reinforced those institutional tendencies.

Those decisions have involved a cluster of issues, including the following:

1. What is the test for characterizing a given subject as falling within or beyond the scope of mandatory bargaining?

2. In making such characterizations, how and on what basis is a balance to be struck between the interest of management in speedy innovation and employee interests in participating in decisions that may significantly affect their economic lives and in moderating or cushioning change?

3. What are, and what should be, the respective roles of the law and of economic power in determining the area of negotiation and of jointly determined standards?

4. What is the proper sphere of the NLRB, the courts, and Congress, in making and changing the principles for adjusting the competing interests involved?

For useful perspectives on the foregoing problems, see N. Chamberlain, The Union Challenge to Management Control (1948); Cox & Dunlop, Regulation of Collective Bargaining by the NLRB, 63 Harv. L. Rev. 389 (1950).

Outside the United States, other forms of participation have proliferated since World War II, including systems of "codetermination" under which workers' representatives join stockholders' representatives on directorial boards. See 2 G. Murg & J. Fox, Labor Relations Law: Canada, Mexico and Western Europe, ch. 8 (1978), for a treatment of "codetermination" in West Germany. But cf. Fraser, Worker Participation in Corporate Government: The UAW-Chrysler Experience, 58 Chi.-Kent L. Rev. 949 (1982), for a description by the ex-president of the UAW of the best known American arrangement for service by a union president on a corporate board; Comment, Serving Two Masters: Union Representation on Corporate Boards of Directors, 81 Colum. L. Rev. 639 (1981); Davies, Employee Representation on Company Boards and Participation in Corporate Planning, 38 Mod. L. Rev. 254 (1975); Vagts, Reforming The "Modern" Corporation, Perspectives from the German, 80 Harv. L. Rev. 23, 64 (1966). Occasional suggestions for similar arrangements for firms in the United States have not generated much support from either labor or management. See Winpisinger, An American Unionist Looks at Co-Determination, 2 Employee Relations L.J. 133 (1976).

NLRB v. Wooster Div. of Borg-Warner Corp.
356 U.S. 342 (1958)

BURTON, J. . . . [A]n employer insisted that its collective bargaining contract . . . include: (1) a "ballot" clause calling for a prestrike secret vote of [the] employees (union and nonunion) as to the employer's last offer, and (2) a "recognition" clause which excluded, as a party to the contract, the

International Union which has been certified by the [NLRB] as the employees' exclusive bargaining agent, and substituted for it the agent's uncertified local affiliate. The Board held that the employer's insistence upon either of such clauses amounted to a . . . violation of §8(a)(5). . . . The issue turns on whether either of these clauses comes within the scope of mandatory collective bargaining as defined in §8(d). . . . [W]e agree with the Board that neither clause comes within that definition. . . .

Late in 1952, the International Union, United Automobile, Aircraft and Agricultural Implement Workers of America, CIO (here called International) was certified by the Board to the Wooster (Ohio) Division of the Borg-Warner Corporation (here called the company) as the elected representative of an appropriate unit of the company's employees. Shortly thereafter, International chartered Local No. 1239, UAW-CIO (here called the Local). Together the unions presented the company with a comprehensive collective bargaining agreement. In the "recognition" clause, the unions described themselves as both the "International Union, United Automobile, Aircraft and Agricultural Implement Workers of America and its Local Union No. 1239, UAW-CIO. . . ."

The company submitted a counterproposal which recognized as the sole representative of the employees "Local Union 1239, affiliated with the International Union, United Automobile, Aircraft and Agricultural Implement Workers of America (UAW-CIO)." The unions' negotiators objected because such a clause disregarded the Board's certification of International as the employees' representative. The negotiators declared that the employees would accept no agreement which excluded International as a party.

The company's counterproposal also contained the "ballot" clause. . . . [T]his clause provided that, as to all nonarbitrable issues (which eventually included modification, amendment or termination of the contract), there would be a 30-day negotiation period after which, before the union could strike, there would have to be a secret ballot taken among all employees in the unit (union and nonunion) on the company's last offer. In the event a majority of the employees rejected the company's last offer, the company would have an opportunity, within 72 hours, of making a new proposal and having a vote on it prior to any strike. The unions' negotiators announced they would not accept this clause "under any conditions."

. . . The company's representatives made it equally clear that no agreement would be entered into by it unless the agreement contained both clauses. In view of this impasse, there was little further discussion of the clauses, although the parties continued to bargain as to other matters. The company submitted a "package" proposal covering economic issues but made the offer contingent upon the satisfactory settlement of "all other issues. . . ." The "package" included both of the controversial clauses. On March 15, 1953, the unions rejected that proposal and the membership voted to strike on March 20 unless a settlement were reached by then. None was reached and the unions struck. Negotiations, nevertheless, continued. . . . Finally, on May 5, the Local, upon the recommendation of International, gave in and entered into an agreement containing both controversial clauses. . . .

Read together, [§§8(a)(5) and 8(d)] . . . establish the obligation of the employer and the representative of its employees to bargain with each other in good faith with respect to "wages, hours, and other terms and conditions of employment. . . ." The duty is limited to those subjects, and within that area neither party is legally obligated to yield. Labor Board v. American Insurance Co., 343 U.S. 395. As to other matters, however, each party is free to bargain or not to bargain, and to agree or not to agree.

The company's good faith has met the requirements of the statute as to the subjects of mandatory bargaining. But that good faith does not license the employer to refuse to enter into agreements on the ground that they do not include some proposal which is not a mandatory subject of bargaining. We agree with the Board that such conduct is, in substance, a refusal to bargain about the subjects that are within the scope of mandatory bargaining. This does not mean that bargaining is to be confined to the statutory subjects. Each of the two controversial clauses is lawful in itself. Each would be enforceable if agreed to by the unions. But it does not follow that, because the company may propose these clauses, it can lawfully insist upon them as a condition to any agreement.

Since it is lawful to insist upon matters within the scope of mandatory bargaining and unlawful to insist upon matters without, the issue here is whether either the "ballot" or the "recognition" clause is a subject within the phrase "wages, hours, and other terms and conditions of employment" which defines mandatory bargaining. The "ballot" clause is not within that definition. It relates only to the procedure to be followed by the employees among themselves before their representative may call a strike or refuse a final offer. It settles no term or condition of employment — it merely calls for an advisory vote of the employees. It is not a partial "no-strike" clause. A "no-strike" clause prohibits the employees from striking during the life of the contract. It regulates the relations between the employer and the employees. See Labor Board v. American Insurance Co., supra, at 408, n.22. The "ballot" clause, on the other hand, deals only with relations between the employees and their unions. It substantially modifies the collective bargaining system provided for in the statute by weakening the independence of the "representative" chosen by the employees. It enables the employer, in effect, to deal with its employees rather than with their statutory representative.

The "recognition" clause likewise does not come within the definition of mandatory bargaining. The statute requires the company to bargain with the certified representative of its employees. It is an evasion of that duty to insist that the certified agent not be a party to the collective bargaining contract. The Act does not prohibit the voluntary addition of a party, but that does not authorize the employer to exclude the certified representative from the contract. . . .

FRANKFURTER, J., joins this opinion insofar as it holds that insistence by the company on the "recognition" clause, in conflict with the provisions of the Act requiring an employer to bargain with the representative of his employees, constituted an unfair labor practice. He agrees with the views of Harlan, J., regarding the "ballot" clause. The subject matter of that clause is not so clearly outside the reasonable range of industrial bargaining as to establish a refusal to bargain in good faith, and is not prohibited simply because not deemed to be within the rather vague scope of the obligatory provisions of §8(d).

HARLAN, J., whom CLARK and WHITTAKER, JJ., join, concurring in part and dissenting in part. . . . [I]n light of the finding below that the company bargained in "good faith," I dissent from the view that its insistence on the "ballot" clause can support the charge of an unfair labor practice.

Preliminarily, I must state that I am unable to grasp a concept of "bargaining" which enables one to "propose" a particular point, but not to "insist" on it as a condition to agreement. The right to bargain becomes illusory if one is not free to press a proposal in good faith to the point of insistence. Surely adoption of so inherently vague and fluid a standard is apt to inhibit the entire bargaining process because of a party's fear that strenuous argument might shade into forbidden insistence and thereby produce a charge of an unfair labor practice. This watered-down notion of "bargaining" which the Court imports into the Act with reference to matters not within the scope of §8(d) appears as foreign to the labor field as it would be to the commercial world. To me all of this adds up to saying that the Act limits *effective* "bargaining" to subjects within the three fields referred to in §8(d), that is "wages, hours, and other terms and conditions of employment," even though the Court expressly disclaims so holding. . . .

. . . I question the Court's conclusion that the "ballot" clause does not come within the "other terms and conditions of employment" provision of §8(d). The phrase is inherently vague and prior to this decision has been accorded by the Board and courts an expansive rather than a grudging interpretation. Many matters which might have been thought to be the sole concern of management are now dealt with as compulsory bargaining topics. E.g., Labor Board v. J. H. Allison & Co., 165 F.2d 766 (merit increases). And since a "no-strike" clause is something about which an employer can concededly bargain to the point of insistence, see Shell Oil Co., 77 N.L.R.B. 1306, I find it difficult to understand even under the Court's analysis of this problem why the "ballot" clause should not be considered within the area of bargaining described in §8(d). It affects the employer-employee relationship in much the same way, in that it may determine the timing of strikes or even whether a strike will occur by requiring a vote to ascertain the employees' sentiment prior to the union's decision.

Nonetheless I shall accept the Court's holding that this clause is not a condition of employment, for even though the union would accordingly not be *obliged* under §8(d) to bargain over it, in my view it does not follow that the company was *prohibited* from insisting on its inclusion in the collective bargaining agreement. In other words, I think the clause was a permissible, even if not an obligatory, subject of good faith bargaining.

The legislative history behind the Wagner and Taft-Hartley Acts persuasively indicates that the Board was never intended to have power to prevent good faith bargaining as to any subject not violative of the provision or policies of those Acts. [Senator Walsh's statement, reproduced in *Insurance Agents*, supra p. 832, is quoted here. — EDS.]. . . .

The decision of this Court in 1952 in Labor Board v. American National Insurance Co., supra, was fully in accord with this legislative background in holding that the Board lacked power to order an employer to cease bargaining over a particular clause because such bargaining under the Board's view, entirely apart from a showing of bad faith, constituted per se an unfair labor practice. . . .

The most cursory view of decisions of the Board and the circuit courts under the [Act] reveals the unsettled and evolving character of collective bargaining agreements. Provisions which two decades ago might have been thought to be the exclusive concern of labor or management are today commonplace in such agreements. The bargaining process should be left fluid, free from intervention of the Board leading to premature crystallization of labor agreements into any one pattern of contract provisions, so that these agreements can be adapted through collective bargaining to the changing needs of our society and to the changing concepts of the responsibilities of labor and management. What the Court does today may impede this evolutionary process. Under the facts of this case, an employer is precluded from attempting to limit the likelihood of a strike. But by the same token it would seem to follow that unions which bargain in good faith would be precluded from insisting upon contract clauses which might not be deemed statutory subjects within §8(d).

As unqualifiedly stated in Labor Board v. American National Insurance Co., supra, p. 357, it is through the "good faith" requirement of §8(d) that the

Board is to enforce the bargaining provisions of §8. A determination that a party bargained as to statutory or nonstatutory subjects in good or bad faith must depend upon an evaluation of the total circumstances surrounding any given situation. I do not deny that there may be instances where unyielding insistence on a particular item may be a relevant consideration in the over-all picture in determining "good faith," for the demands of a party might in the context of a particular industry be so extreme as to constitute some evidence of an unwillingness to bargain. But no such situation is presented in this instance by the "ballot" clause. "No-strike" clauses, and other provisions analogous to the "ballot" clause limiting the right to strike, are hardly novel to labor agreements. And in any event the uncontested finding of "good faith" by the Trial Examiner forecloses that issue here.

Of course an employer or union cannot insist upon a clause which would be illegal under the Act's provisions, Labor Board v. National Maritime Union, 175 F.2d 686, or conduct itself so as to contravene specific requirements of the Act. Medo Photo Supply Corp. v. Labor Board, 321 U.S. 678. But here the Court recognizes, as it must, that the clause is lawful under the Act, and I think it clear that the company's insistence upon it violated no statutory duty to which it was subject. . . .

The company's insistence on the "recognition" clause, which had the effect of excluding the International Union as a party signatory to agreement and making Local 1239 the sole contracting party on the union side, presents a different problem. In my opinion the company's action in this regard did constitute an unfair labor practice since it contravened specific requirements of the Act.

. . . I think it hardly debatable that this language [of §9(c) and §8(d)] must be read to require the company, if so requested, to sign any agreement reached with the same representative with which it is required to bargain. By conditioning agreement upon a change in signatory from the certified exclusive bargaining representative, the company here in effect violated this duty.

I would affirm the judgment of the Court of Appeals. . . .

NOTES

1. Would it have been material if (a) the company had denied any wage increase unless the union agreed to the ballot clause or (b) the company had offered a larger increase if it secured that clause?

2. Since under *Borg-Warner* the parties are not required to make a "concession" even with respect to "mandatory" matters, what are the practical results of classifying demands that are not illegal as involving "manda-

tory" or "permissive" subjects? Does the mandatory-permissive distinction encourage bad faith posturing in negotiations?

3. Payment to employee members of the union's negotiating committee for time spent on negotiations has been held a mandatory subject of bargaining. Axelson, Inc., 234 N.L.R.B. 414 (1978), *enforced*, 599 F.2d 91 (5th Cir. 1979). What is the basis for concluding that reimbursement of negotiators' lost wages affects "the relations between the employer and the employees" within the meaning of *Borg-Warner*? Cf. Bartlett-Collins Co., 237 N.L.R.B. 770 (1978), *enforced*, 639 F.2d 652 (10th Cir. 1981), where the Board, overruling prior decisions, held that the presence of a court reporter (or a recording device) at negotiations was not a mandatory item of bargaining. Accordingly, an employer's insistence to impasse on a reporter's presence was a per se violation, despite the employer's good faith belief that a transcript would protect him from again being held to have violated §8(a)(5) on the basis of what had been said during negotiations. Does the recording of bargaining sessions involve considerations that go beyond the question of a significant relationship to terms or conditions of employment?

4. The Board has held that demands for indemnity bonds or security deposits to insure performance of contractual obligations are outside the area of mandatory bargaining. See Radiator Specialty Co. v. NLRB, 336 F.2d 495 (4th Cir. 1964) (employer's demand for bond covering union liability under no-strike clause); Carpenters' Dist. Council, 145 N.L.R.B. 663 (1963) (union's demand for money deposit to secure wage obligations). Is "remoteness" from the employment relationship sufficient to explain these decisions?

5. Since the 1930s the parties, following the custom in the newspaper printing industry, had agreed that any issues unresolved by negotiations would be submitted for determination by an arbitrator. Their contract, which expired in 1970, contained a clause for such "interest arbitration." During negotiations for a renewal agreement, the employer requested the deletion of that clause; the union declined. That issue was submitted to an arbitrator, who decided that the interest arbitration clause should be continued in the 1970 contract, which ran for three years. Upon expiration of the 1970-1973 agreement, the parties agreed on all matters, except for their disagreement as to whether their renewal agreement should contain the provision for interest arbitration. The employer urged that the demand for interest arbitration fell outside the area of "mandatory bargaining" and that, accordingly, the union was required, under §8(b)(3), to sign a written agreement embodying the parties' settlement of all other matters. The union countered by seeking to initiate an arbitration proceeding under the prior agreement, to resolve the parties' deadlock regarding the continuation of the interest arbitration clause.

The employer filed a timely §8(b)(3) charge; the union filed a §8(a)(5) charge. How should these disputed issues be resolved? See NLRB v. Columbus Printing Pressmen, 543 F.2d 1161 (5th Cir. 1976); N.L.R.B. Gen. Coun. Advice Mem. No. 18-CB-1347, in Sheet Metal Wkrs., Local 263, 115 L.R.R.M. 1007 (1983); Sheet Metal Wkrs., Local 14 v. Aldrich Air Conditioning, 717 F.2d 456 (8th Cir. 1983).

Ford Motor Co. v. NLRB, 441 U.S. 488 (1979). The Court, affirming the Seventh Circuit's enforcement of a Board order, deferred to the NLRB's view that when an employer provides in-plant eating facilities for employees, food prices and services are "terms and conditions of employment" and therefore mandatory subjects of bargaining. The Court noted, without endorsing, the court of appeals' emphasis on the employee's lack of reasonable eating alternatives. (The lunch period was 30 minutes and the few nearby restaurants were more than a mile away.) On Ford's argument that it would be unduly disruptive to require negotiation on issues as minor as the price of a soft drink, the Court accepted the Board's position that the bargaining duty is satisfied if management honors a specific union request for bargaining about changes that have been made or are to be made (in prices and presumably in services), but reserved the issue of whether a demand for the institution of food services, when they are not being provided, is a mandatory item. That a third-party supplier set vending machine and cafeteria prices at the plant was held not to affect the bargaining duty, because Ford had by contract retained a right to control the supplier's food services and prices.

Blackmun, J., concurring, expressed concern about the Court's "implications," first, that the company's control over prices in this case was irrelevant to the "mandatory subject" inquiry and, second, that an employer must bargain over prices even when he lacks any actual control over them, for example, when he rents space to a restaurant and keeps "hands off" the operation.

Railroad Telegraphers v. Chicago & Nw. Ry., 362 U.S. 330 (1960). The Court held (5 to 4) that the Norris-LaGuardia Act barred a permanent injunction against a threatened strike in support of a demand that the railroad should not abolish preexisting jobs without the incumbent union's consent. (The railroad had refused to negotiate on the union's proposal, contending that it was not a proper subject for bargaining under the RLA.) Among those jobs were some that would have been eliminated by the realignment of obsolete and wasteful station services, pursuant to authorizations granted by state regulatory agencies. The Court's majority found that the union's demand fell within bargainable subjects listed in RLA §2, First ("rates of pay, rules, and working conditions"), and stated:

> The change desired . . . plainly referred to "conditions of employment" of the railroad's employees who are represented by the union. The employment of many of these station agents inescapably hangs on the number of railroad stations that will be either completely abandoned or consolidated with other stations. And, in the collective bargaining world today, there is nothing strange about agreements that affect the permanency of employment. . . . We cannot agree with the Court of Appeals that the union's effort to negotiate about the job security of its members represents an attempt to usurp legitimate managerial prerogative in the exercise of business judgment with respect to the most economical and efficient conduct of its operations. . . . [T]he whole idea of what is bargainable has been greatly affected by the practices and customs of the railroads and their employees. . . . It is too late now to argue that employees can have no collective voice to influence railroads to act in a way that will preserve the interests of the employees [and the railroad] . . . and the public at large. . . . It would stretch credulity too far to say that the [RLA], designed to protect . . . workers, was somehow violated by the union acting . . . to obtain stability and permanence in employment for workers.

NOTE

Should the Court's approach to mandatory bargaining under the RLA necessarily be followed under the NLRA? Are the RLA terms, "rates of pay, rules, and working conditions," different in nature or scope from "wages, hours, and other terms and conditions of employment" in §8(d)? Should the fact that there is no administrative agency to enforce the bargaining duty under the RLA affect the scope of mandatory bargaining under that statute compared to the NLRA? Consider First National Maintenance Corp. v. NLRB, infra p. 873, and particularly footnote 23 of that opinion, p. 880.

See generally Meltzer, The Chicago and North Western Case: Judicial Workmanship and Collective Bargaining, 1960 Sup. Ct. Rev. 113.

Fibreboard Paper Products Corp. v. NLRB
379 U.S. 203 (1964)

WARREN, C.J. . . . The primary issue is whether the "contracting out" of work being performed by employees in the bargaining unit is a statutory subject of collective bargaining under [§§8(a)(5), 8(d) and 9(a)].

. . . Since 1937 the [Union] has been the exclusive bargaining representative for a unit of the Company's maintenance employees. In September 1958, the Union and the Company entered the latest of a series of collective bargaining agreements which was to expire on July 31, 1959. The agreement provided for automatic renewal for another year unless one of the contracting parties gave 60 days' notice of a desire to modify or terminate the contract. On May 26, 1959, the Union gave timely notice of its desire to modify the contract and sought to arrange a bargaining session. . . . On June 2, the Company acknowledged receipt of the Union's notice and stated: "We will contact you at a later date regarding a meeting for this purpose." As required by the contract, the Union sent a list of proposed modifications on June 15. Efforts by the Union to schedule a bargaining session met with no success until July 27, four days before the expiration of the contract, when the Company notified the Union of its desire to meet.

The Company, concerned with the high cost of its maintenance operation, had undertaken a study of the possibility of effecting cost savings by engaging an independent contractor to do the maintenance work. At the July 27 meeting, the Company informed the Union that it had determined that substantial savings could be effected by contracting out the work. . . . The Company delivered to the [Union] a letter which stated in pertinent part: "For some time we had been seriously considering the question of letting out our Emeryville maintenance work . . . , and have now reached a definite decision to do so effective August 1, 1959. In these circumstances, we are sure you will realize that negotiation of a new contract would be pointless. However, if you have any questions, we will be glad to discuss them with you." After some discussion . . . , the meeting concluded with the understanding that the parties would meet again on July 30.

By July 30, the Company had selected Fluor Maintenance, Inc., to do the maintenance work. Fluor had assured the Company that maintenance costs could be curtailed by reducing the work force, decreasing fringe benefits and overtime payments, and by preplanning and scheduling the services to be performed. The contract provided that Fluor would:

> . . . furnish all labor, supervision and office help required for the performance of maintenance work . . . at the Emeryville plant of Owner as Owner shall from time to time assign to Contractor during the period of this contract; and shall also furnish such tools, supplies and equipment in connection therewith as Owner shall order from Contractor, it being understood however that Owner shall ordinarily do its own purchasing of tools, supplies and equipment.

The contract further provided that the Company would pay Fluor the costs of the operation plus a fixed fee of $2,250 per month.

At the July 30 meeting, the Company's representative, in explaining the decision to contract out the maintenance work, remarked that during bargaining negotiations in previous years the Company had endeavored to point out . . . "just how expensive and costly our maintenance work was and how it was creating quite a terrific burden upon the Emeryville plant." He further stated that unions representing other Company employees "had joined hands with management in an effort to bring about an economical and efficient operation," but "we had not been able to attain that in our discussions with this particular Local." The Company also distributed a letter stating that "since we will have no employees in the bargaining unit covered by our present Agreement, negotiation of a new or renewed Agreement would appear to us to be pointless." On July 31, the employment of the maintenance employees represented by the Union was terminated and Fluor employees took over. That evening the Union established a picket line at the Company's plant.

The Union filed . . . charges against the Company, alleging violations of §§8(a)(1), 8(a)(3) and 8(a)(5). . . . The Board . . . adhered to the Trial Examiner's finding that the Company's motive . . . was economic rather than antiunion but [ultimately] found nonetheless that the Company's "failure to negotiate with . . . [the Union] concerning its decision to subcontract its maintenance work constituted a violation of §8(a)(5). . . ." This ruling was based upon . . . Town & Country Mfg. Co., 136 N.L.R.B. 1022, 1027, *enforcement granted*, 316 F.2d 846 (C.A. 5th Cir. 1963), [holding] that contracting out work, "albeit for economic reasons, is a matter within the statutory phrase 'other terms and conditions of employment' . . . ."

The Board ordered the Company to reinstitute the maintenance operation . . . , to reinstate the employees to their former or substantially equivalent positions with back pay computed from the date of the Board's supplemental decision, and to fulfill its statutory obligation to bargain. . . . [T]he District of Columbia Circuit granted the Board's petition for enforcement. 322 F.2d 411. . . .

I

. . . Because of the limited grant of certiorari, we are concerned here only with whether the subject upon which the employer allegedly refused to bargain — contracting out of plant maintenance work previously performed by employees in the bargaining unit, which the employees were capable of continuing to perform — is covered by the phrase "terms and conditions of employment" within the meaning of §8(d).

The subject matter of the present dispute is well within the literal meaning of the phrase "terms and conditions of employment." See Order of Railroad Telegraphers v. Chicago & N.W.R. Co., 362 U.S. 330. A stipulation with respect to the contracting out of work performed by members of the bargaining unit might appropriately be called a "condition of employment." The words even more plainly cover termination of employment which, as the facts of this case indicate, necessarily results from the contracting out of work performed by members of the established bargaining unit.

The inclusion of "contracting out" within the statutory scope of collective bargaining also seems well designed to effectuate the purposes of the [NLRA]. . . . The Act was framed with an awareness that refusals to confer and negotiate had been one of the most prolific causes of industrial strife. . . . To hold, as the Board has done, that contracting out is a mandatory subject of collective bargaining would promote the fundamental purpose of the Act by bringing a problem of vital concern to labor and management within the framework established by Congress as most conducive to industrial peace.

The conclusion that "contracting out" is a statutory subject of collective bargaining is further reinforced by industrial practices in this country. While not determinative, it is appropriate to look to industrial bargaining practices in appraising the propriety of including a particular subject within the scope of mandatory bargaining. Labor Board v. American Natl. Ins. Co., 343 U.S. 395, 408. Industrial experience is not only reflective of the interests of labor and management in the subject matter but is also indicative of the amenability of such subjects to the collective bargaining process. Experience illustrates that contracting out in one form or another has been brought, widely and successfully, within the collective bargaining framework. Provisions relating to contracting out exist in numerous collective bargaining agreements, and "[c]ontracting out work is the basis of many grievances; and that type of claim is grist in the mills of the arbitrators." United Steelworkers v. Warrior & Gulf Nav. Co., 363 U.S. 574, 584. . . .

[The Court here referred to its approach and decision in Local 24, Teamsters v. Oliver, supra p. 732.]

The facts of the present case illustrate the propriety of submitting the dispute to collective negotiation. The Company's decision to contract out the maintenance work did not alter the Company's basic operation. The maintenance work still had to be performed in the plant. No capital investment was contemplated; the Company merely replaced existing employees with those of an independent contractor to do the same work under similar conditions of employment. Therefore, to require the employer to bargain about the matter would not significantly abridge his freedom to manage the business.

The Company was concerned with the high cost of its maintenance operation. It was induced to contract out the work by assurances from independent contractors that economies could be derived by reducing the work force, decreasing fringe benefits, and eliminating overtime payments. These have long been regarded as matters peculiarly suitable for resolution within the collective bargaining framework. . . . Yet, it is contended that when an employer can effect cost savings in these respects by contracting the work out, there is no need to attempt to achieve similar economies through negotiation with existing employees or to provide them with an opportunity to negotiate a mutually acceptable alternative. The short answer is that, although it is not possible to say whether a satisfactory solution could be reached, national labor policy is founded upon the congressional determination that the chances are good enough to warrant subjecting such issues to the process of collective negotiation.

The appropriateness of the collective bargaining process for resolving such issues was apparently recognized by the Company. In explaining its decision to contract out the maintenance work, the Company pointed out that in the same plant other unions "had joined hands with management in an effort to bring about an economical and efficient operation," but "we had not been able to attain that in our discussions with this particular Local." Accordingly, based on past bargaining experience with this union, the Company unilaterally contracted out the work. While "the Act does not encourage a party to engage in fruitless marathon discussions at the expense of frank statement and support of his position," Labor Board v. American Natl. Ins. Co., 343 U.S. 395, 404, it at least demands that the issue be submitted to the mediatory influence of collective negotiations. . . .

We are thus not expanding the scope of mandatory bargaining to hold, as we do now, that the type of "contracting out" involved in this case — the replacement of employees in the existing bargaining unit with those of an independent contractor to do the same work under similar conditions of employment — is a statutory subject of collective bargaining under §8(d). Our decision need not and does not encompass other forms of "contracting out" or "subcontracting" which arise daily in our complex economy.[8]

II

The only question remaining is whether, upon a finding that the Company had refused to bargain about a . . . statutory subject of collective bargain-

---

[8] As the Solicitor General points out, the terms "contracting out" and "subcontracting" have no precise meaning. These are used to describe a variety of business arrangements altogether different from that involved in this case. . . .

ing, the Board was empowered to order the resumption of maintenance operations and reinstatement with back pay. We believe that it was so empowered.

. . . [Section 10(c)] "charges the Board with the task of devising remedies to effectuate the policies of the Act." Labor Board v. Seven-Up Bottling Co., 344 U.S. 344, 346. The Board's power is a broad discretionary one, subject to limited judicial review. Ibid. "[T]he relation of remedy to policy is peculiarly a matter for administrative competence. . . ." Phelps Dodge Corp. v. Labor Board, 313 U.S. 177, 194. . . . The Board's order will not be disturbed "unless it can be shown that the order is a patent attempt to achieve ends other than those which can fairly be said to effectuate the policies of the Act." Virginia Elec. & Power Co. v. Labor Board, 319 U.S. 533, 540. . . .

There has been no showing that the Board's order restoring the status quo ante to insure meaningful bargaining is not well designed to promote the policies of the Act. Nor is there evidence which would justify disturbing the Board's conclusion that the order would not impose an undue or unfair burden on the Company.[10] . . .

The judgment of the Court of Appeals is Affirmed.

Goldberg, J., took no part in the consideration or decision of this case.

Stewart, J., with whom Douglas and Harlan, JJ., join, concurring. Viewed broadly, the question before us stirs large issues. The Court purports to limit its decision to "the facts of this case." But the Court's opinion radiates implications of such disturbing breadth that I am persuaded to file this separate statement of my own views. . . . The question posed is whether the particular decision sought to be made unilaterally by the employer in this case is a subject of mandatory collective bargaining. . . . That is all the Court decides. The Court most assuredly does not decide that every managerial decision which necessarily terminates an individual's employment is subject to the duty to bargain. Nor does the Court decide that subcontracting decisions are as a general matter subject to that duty. The Court holds no more than that this employer's decision to subcontract this work, involving "the replacement of employees in the existing bargaining unit with those of an independent contractor to do the same work under similar conditions of employment," is subject to the duty to bargain collectively. Within the narrow limitations implicit in the specific facts of this case, I agree with the Court's decision. . . .

[10] The Board stated: ". . . The record shows that the maintenance operation is still being performed in much the same manner as it was prior to the subcontracting arrangement. Respondent has a continuing need for the services of maintenance employees; and Respondent's subcontract is terminable at any time upon 60 days' notice." 138 N.L.R.B., at 555, n.19.

. . . It is true, as the Court's opinion points out, that industrial experience may be useful in determining the proper scope of the duty to bargain. . . . But data showing that many labor contracts refer to subcontracting or that subcontracting grievances are frequently referred to arbitrators under collective bargaining agreements, while not wholly irrelevant, do not have much real bearing, for such data may indicate no more than that the parties have often considered it mutually advantageous to bargain over these issues on a permissive basis. In any event, the ultimate question is the scope of the duty to bargain defined by the statutory language.

It is important to note that the words of the statute are words of limitation. The [Act] does not say that the employer and employees are bound to confer upon any subject which interests either of them; the specification of wages, hours, and other terms and conditions of employment defines a limited category of issues subject to compulsory bargaining. The limiting purpose of the statute's language is made clear by the legislative history of the present Act. As originally passed, the Wagner Act contained no definition of the duty to bargain collectively. In the 1947 revision of the Act, the House bill contained a detailed but limited list of subjects of the duty to bargain, excluding all others.[4] In conference the present language was substituted for the House's detailed specification. While the language thus incorporated in the 1947 legislation as enacted is not so stringent as that contained in the House bill, it nonetheless adopts the same basic approach in seeking to define a limited class of bargainable issues.

The phrase "conditions of employment" is no doubt susceptible of diverse interpretations. At the extreme, the phrase could be construed to apply to any subject which is insisted upon as a prerequisite for continued employment. Such an interpretation . . . would be contrary to the intent of Congress, as reflected in this legislative history. Yet there are passages in the Court's opinion today which suggest just such an expansive interpretation, for the Court's opinion seems to imply that any issue which may reasonably divide an employer and his employees must be the subject of compulsory collective bargaining.

Only a narrower concept of "conditions of employment" will serve the statutory purpose of delineating a limited category of issues which are subject to the duty to bargain collectively. Seeking to effect this purpose, at least seven circuits have interpreted the statutory language to exclude various kinds of management decisions from the scope of the duty to bargain. In

---

[4] H.R. 3020, 80th Cong., 1st Sess., §2(11)(B)(vi) (1947), in I Legislative History of the Labor Management Relations Act, 1947, at 166-167 (1948). (Hereinafter LMRA.)

common parlance, the conditions of a person's employment are most obviously the various physical dimensions of his working environment. What one's hours are to be, what amount of work is expected during those hours, what periods of relief are available, what safety practices are observed, would all seem conditions of one's employment. There are other less tangible but no less important characteristics of a person's employment which might also be deemed "conditions" — most prominently the characteristic involved in this case, the security of one's employment. On one view of the matter, it can be argued that the question whether there is to be a job is not a condition of employment; the question is not one of imposing conditions on employment, but the more fundamental question whether there is to be employment at all. However, it is clear that the Board and the courts have on numerous occasions recognized that union demands for provisions limiting an employer's power to discharge employees are mandatorily bargainable. Thus, freedom from discriminatory discharge, seniority rights, the imposition of a compulsory retirement age, have been recognized as subjects upon which an employer must bargain, although all of these concern the very existence of the employment itself.

While employment security has thus properly been recognized in various circumstances as a condition of employment, it surely does not follow that every decision which may affect job security is a subject of compulsory collective bargaining. Many decisions made by management affect the job security of employees. Decisions concerning the volume and kind of advertising expenditures, product design, the manner of financing, and sales, all may bear upon the security of the workers' jobs. Yet it is hardly conceivable that such decisions so involve "conditions of employment" that they must be negotiated with the employees' bargaining representative.

In many of these areas the impact of a particular management decision upon job security may be extremely indirect and uncertain, and this alone may be sufficient reason to conclude that such decisions are not "with respect to . . . conditions of employment." Yet there are other areas where decisions by management may quite clearly imperil job security, or indeed terminate employment entirely. An enterprise may decide to invest in labor-saving machinery. Another may resolve to liquidate its assets and go out of business. Nothing the Court holds today should be understood as imposing a duty to bargain collectively regarding such managerial decisions, which lie at the core of entrepreneurial control. Decisions concerning the commitment of investment capital and the basic scope of the enterprise are not in themselves primarily about conditions of employment though the effect of the decision may be necessarily to terminate employment. If, as I think clear, the purpose of §8(d) is to describe a limited area subject to the duty of collective bargaining, those management decisions which are fundamental to the basic direction of a corporate enterprise or which impinge only indirectly upon employment security should be excluded from that area.

Applying these concepts to the case at hand, I do not believe that an employer's subcontracting practices are, as a general matter, in themselves conditions of employment. Upon any definition of the statutory terms short of the most expansive, such practices are not conditions — tangible or intangible — of any person's employment. The question remains whether this particular kind of subcontracting decision comes within the employer's duty to bargain. On the facts of this case, I join the Court's judgment, because all that is involved is the substitution of one group of workers for another to perform the same task in the same plant under the ultimate control of the same employer. The question whether the employer may discharge one group of workers and substitute another for them is closely analogous to many other situations within the traditional framework of collective bargaining. . . .

Analytically, this case is not far from that which would be presented if the employer had merely discharged all its employees and replaced them with other workers willing to work on the same job in the same plant without the various fringe benefits so costly to the company. While such a situation might well be considered a §8(a)(3) violation upon a finding that the employer discriminated against the discharged employees because of their union affiliation, it would be equally possible to regard the employer's action as a unilateral act frustrating negotiation on the underlying questions of work scheduling and remuneration, and so an evasion of its duty to bargain on these questions, which are concededly subject to compulsory collective bargaining. Similarly, had the employer in this case chosen to bargain with the union about the proposed subcontract, negotiations would have inevitably turned to the underlying questions of cost, which prompted the subcontracting. Insofar as the employer frustrated collective bargaining with respect to these concededly bargaining issues by its unilateral act of subcontracting this work, it can properly be found to have violated its statutory duty under §8(a)(5). . . .

I am fully aware that in this era of automation and onrushing technological change, no problems in the domestic economy are of greater concern than those involving job security and employment stability. Because of the potentially cruel impact upon the lives and fortunes of the working men and women of the Nation, these problems have understandably engaged the solicitous attention of government, of responsible private business, and particularly of organized labor. It is possible that in meeting these problems Congress may eventually decide to give organized labor or government a far heavier hand in controlling what until now have been considered the prerogatives of private business management. That path would mark a sharp departure from the traditional principles of a free enterprise economy. Whether we should follow it is, within constitutional limitations, for Congress to choose. But it is a path which Congress certainly did not choose when it enacted the Taft-Hartley Act.

Goldberg, Management's Reserved Rights: A Labor View, Ninth Ann. Proc., Natl. Acad. of Arbitrators 123 (1956): "Management determines the product, the machine to be used, the manufacturing method, the price, the plant layout, the plant organization, and innumerable other questions. These are reserved rights, inherent rights, exclusive rights which are not diminished or modified by collective bargaining as it exists in industries such as steel. It is of great importance that this be generally understood and accepted by all parties. Mature, cooperative bargaining relationships require reliance on acceptance of the rights of each party by the other. A company has the right to know it can develop a product and get it turned out; develop a machine and have it manned and operated; devise a way to improve a product and have that improvement made effective; establish prices, build plants, create supervisory forces and not thereby become embroiled in a labor dispute."

Wallen, How Issues of Subcontracting and Plant Removal Are Handled by Arbitrators, 19 Ind. & Lab. Rel. Rev. 265, 266 (1966): "Business is often a conservative force on social questions. But when it comes to production, it is as radical as it can be. To the enterpriser feeling the sting of the competitive lash, there is no such thing as the status quo in technology or in the organization of production. He hunts feverishly for new materials, for new machines, for new ways of organizing work. When he finds them, he does not hesitate to uproot the established way of making or doing things in order to replace it with a better way.

"On the other hand, trade unionists and trade unions are often the pioneers, the radicals, in changing social institutions. But they tend to be the conservatives in their approach to changes in the methods of production. The status quo represents, they think, job security and certainty; change, presented in terms of the promise of a glowing long-run future, is often accompanied by an uncomfortable, if not menacing, tomorrow.

"It is these feelings and attitudes which make the subject of discussion so sensitive and contentious. The employer fights for retention of his right to innovation and change. The worker and his union cherish and seek to protect their hold on certainty and security."

NOTE

In *Fibreboard*, the NLRB's back pay order amounted to approximately $334,000. It was calculated on the basis of the wage formula embodied in the agreement in effect immediately prior to the subcontracting, even though the union had agreed to a lower rate when the employees subsequently returned to work. Back pay had been ordered only from September 13, 1962, the date of the Board's supplemental decision. In 1959, severance payments had been made to the terminated employees. The Board held that under the established policy of computing back pay on a quarterly basis, there was no back pay liability against which the severance payments could be offset. Fibreboard Paper Products Corp., 180 N.L.R.B. 142 (1969), *enforced*, 436 F.2d 908 (D.C. Cir. 1970).

Westinghouse Electric Corp., 150 N.L.R.B. 1574 (1965). For years, the company, without notice to the union, had regularly engaged in extensive subcontracting. The union had sought contract restrictions on that practice, but the union always dropped this demand during bargaining, and ensuing agreements were silent on the issue. In the period covered by the present §8(a)(5) proceeding, the company had awarded over 7,000 subcontracts involving work its own employees could have performed. The Board declared:

". . . [We] find merit in Respondent's contention that it was not obligated to notify and bargain with the Union before letting each contract involving unit work. . . .

"In the *Fibreboard* line of cases, where the Board has found unilateral contracting out of unit work to be violative of §§8(a)(5) and (1), it has invariably appeared that the contracting out involved a departure from previously established operating practices, effected a change in conditions of employment, or resulted in a significant impairment of job tenure, employment security, or reasonably anticipated work opportunities for those in the bargaining unit. . . .

". . . [B]earing in mind particularly that the recurrent contracting out of work here in question was motivated solely by economic considerations; that it comported with the [Respondent's] traditional methods . . . ; that it did not during the period here in question vary significantly in kind or degree from what had been customary under past established practice; that it had no demonstrable adverse impact on employees in the unit; and that the Union had the opportunity to bargain about changes in existing subcontracting practices at general negotiating meetings—for all these reasons cumulatively, we conclude that Respondent did not violate its statutory bargaining obligation by failing to invite union participation in individual subcontracting decisions."

NOTES

1. Is an employer required to bargain before deciding to terminate his business completely, for economic reasons? Cf. Textile Wkrs. v. Darlington, supra p. 294. Suppose a closing prompted by economic considerations is partial rather than complete. In various circumstances, the NLRB in the 1960s read *Darlington, Fibreboard*, and *Chicago & North Western* (supra p. 859) as calling for bargaining prior to the partial termination decision — notwithstanding the rejection of that position by some circuit courts. See, e.g., Ozark Trailers, 161 N.L.R.B. 561, 564-570 (1966). But see NLRB v. Adams Dairy, 350 F.2d 108 (8th Cir. 1965), *cert. denied*, 382 U.S. 1011 (1966). Moreover, during this period the NLRB required employers to bargain on a variety of business decisions affecting employment interests — decisions previously thought to be a management right and thus not bargainable. See, e.g., Renton News, 36 N.L.R.B. 1294 (1962) (installation of new machinery); Dixie-Ohio Exp. Co. 167 N.L.R.B. 573 (1967), *enforcement denied*, 409 F.2d 10 (6th Cir. 1969) (operational changes); Weltronic Co., 173 N.L.R.B. 235 (1968), *enforced*, 419 F.2d 1120 (6th Cir. 1969), *cert. denied*, 398 U.S. 938 (1970) (transfer of portion of work to nearby, "under-one-roof" location).

Since an employer need not agree to a union's proposals regarding a bargainable subject, what is the argument against classifying the foregoing decisions as mandatory subjects of bargaining? For illustrations of the often formidable remedial problems that result once changes have occurred without prior bargaining, see *Renton News*, supra, and Apex Linen Serv., 151 N.L.R.B. 305 (1965). See also Local 57, Garment Wkrs. v. NLRB (Garwin Corp.), supra p. 462.

2. Beginning in the early 1970s, the Board, on the basis of not altogether satisfying distinctions, appears to have limited its earlier position requiring employers to bargain over closings and similar decisions. Two cases attracted particular attention:

(a) General Motors Corp., 191 N.L.R.B. 951 (1971), *petition for review denied*, 470 F.2d 422 (D.C. Cir. 1972): GM, after taking over a franchised dealer, had operated a retail outlet in Houston for the sale and servicing of GM trucks and parts. Subsequently GM reestablished a dealership by "selling" certain of the outlet's assets and subleasing its premises under an agreement permitting cancellation of the sublease by either party and the transfer of the assets to GM if the buyer ceased to be a GM franchised truck dealer. GM had rejected the incumbent union's request for bargaining over the proposed "sale" while sale negotiations were in progress. The Board (3 to 2) characterized the transaction as a "sale," rather than as "subcontracting," and ruled that *Fibreboard* was not controlling. The majority appeared to acquiesce in court decisions rejecting the NLRB's position that the duty to bargain encompassed employer decisions concerning plant closings and removals and distinguishing those matters from "subcontracting." The majority extended the rationale of those decisions to sales by an employer involving significant investment or withdrawal of capital, urging that such matters are essentially managerial and financial, go to the core of entrepreneurial control, and frequently call for secret and quick action based on considerations probably unfamiliar to employees and their representatives. It concluded that such matters do not fall within "rates of pay . . . or other conditions of employment" and that an employer was not required to bargain over such decisions, as distinguished from their effects.

The dissenters, treating the transaction as "subcontracting," urged that the principles developed in *Ozark Trailers* should be applied, notwithstanding contrary judicial views; that meaningful bargaining over effects is not possible within the framework of an unalterable employer decision; and that Board cases requiring bargaining over a decision to terminate a portion of a business should be followed.

(b) Summit Tooling Co., 195 N.L.R.B. 479 (1972), *enforced,* 474 F.2d 1352 (7th Cir. 1973): An employer is not under a duty to bargain over a decision to end his manufacture of tooling products even though that decision could be viewed as "a partial plant closing." The Board emphasized that the employer's remaining operations had little relationship to the discontinued operations and did not utilize the skills of the employees involved in the latter operations. But cf. Royal Typewriter Co., 209 N.L.R.B. 1006 (1974), *enforced,* 533 F.2d 1030 (8th Cir. 1976) (an employer operating two or more plants required to bargain over a decision to close one of them; *Summit Tooling* distinguished on the ground that *Royal* did not involve "the prerogative of an employer . . . to eliminate itself as an employer").

What relevance, if any, should the factors emphasized by the Board in the foregoing decisions have on the scope of the bargaining duty?

3. Post-*Fibreboard* developments evoked extensive commentary. See, e.g., P. Miscimaira, The NLRB and Managerial Discretion: Plant Closings, Relocations, Subcontracting and Automation (1983); Note, Mandatory Bargaining and the Disposition of Closed Plants, 95 Harv. L. Rev. 1896 (1982); Rabin, The Decline and Fall of *Fibreboard,* N.Y.U. 24th Ann. Conf. on Labor 237 (1972); R. Swift, NLRB and Management Decision Making (1974).

First National Maintenance Corp. v. NLRB
452 U.S. 666 (1981)

BLACKMUN, J. Must an employer, under its duty to bargain in good faith "with respect to wages, hours, and other terms and conditions of employment," [§§8(d) and 8(a)(5)], negotiate with the certified representative of its employees over its decision to close a part of its business? In this case, the [NLRB] imposed such a duty on petitioner with respect to its decision to terminate a contract with a customer, and the . . . Court of Appeals, although differing over the appropriate rationale, enforced its order.

I

Petitioner, First National Maintenance Corporation (FNM) . . . [provides] housekeeping, cleaning, maintenance, and related services for commercial customers in the New York City area. It supplies each of its customers, at the customer's premises, contracted-for labor force and supervision in return for reimbursement of its labor costs (gross salaries, FICA and FUTA taxes, and insurance) and payment of a set fee. It contracts for and hires personnel separately for each customer, and it does not transfer employees between locations.

During the Spring of 1977, petitioner was performing maintenance work for the Greenpark Care Center, a nursing home in Brooklyn. Its written agreement dated April 28, 1976, with Greenpark specified that Greenpark "shall furnish all tools, equiptment [sic], materials, and supplies," and would pay petitioner weekly "the sum of five hundred dollars plus the gross weekly payroll and fringe benefits." Its weekly fee, however, had been reduced to $250 effective November 1, 1976. The contract prohibited Greenpark from hiring any of petitioner's employees during the term of the contract and for 90 days thereafter. Petitioner employed approximately 35 workers in its Greenpark operation.

Petitioner's business relationship with Greenpark, seemingly, was not very remunerative or smooth. In March 1977, Greenpark gave petitioner the 30 days' written notice of cancellation specified by the contract, because of "lack of efficiency." This cancellation did not become effective, for FNB's work continued after the expiration of that 30-day period. Petitioner, however, became aware that it was losing money at Greenpark. On June 30, by telephone, it asked that its weekly fee be restored at the $500 figure and, on July 6, it informed Greenpark in writing that it would discontinue its operations there on August 1 unless the increase were granted. By telegram on July 25, petitioner gave final notice of termination.

While FNM was experiencing these difficulties, District 1199, National Union of Hospital and Health Care Employees, Retail, Wholesale and Department Store Union, AFL-CIO (the union), was conducting an organization campaign among petitioner's Greenpark employees. On March 31, 1977, at a Board-conducted election, a majority of the employees selected the union as their bargaining agent. On July 12, the union's vice president, Edward Wecker, wrote petitioner, notifying it of the certification and of the union's right to bargain, and stating: "We look forward to meeting with you or your representative for that purpose. Please advise when it will be convenient." Petitioner neither responded nor sought to consult with the union.

On July 28, petitioner notified its Greenpark employees that they would be discharged 3 days later. Wecker immediately telephoned petitioner's secretary-treasurer, Leonard Marsh, to request a delay for the purpose of bargaining. Marsh refused the offer to bargain and told Wecker that the termination of the Greenpark operation was purely a matter of money, and final, and that the 30-days' notice provision of the Greenpark contract made staying on beyond August 1 prohibitively expensive. Wecker discussed the matter with Greenpark's management that same day, but was unable to obtain a waiver of the notice provision. Greenpark also was unwilling itself to hire the FNM employees because of the contract's 90-day limitation on hiring. With nothing but perfunctory further discussion, petitioner on July 31 discontinued its Greenpark operation and discharged the employees.

. . . Relying on Ozark Trailers, Inc., 161 N.L.R.B. 561 (1966), [the ALJ] ruled that petitioner had failed to satisfy its duty to bargain concerning both the decision to terminate the Greenpark contract and the effect of that change upon the unit employees. . . . [The] Board adopted the [ALJ's] findings without further analysis. . . .

The . . . Second Circuit, with one judge dissenting in part, enforced the Board's order, although it adopted an analysis different from that espoused by the Board. 627 F.2d 596 (1980). The Court of Appeals reasoned that no per se rule could be formulated to govern an employer's decision to close part of its business. Rather, the court said, §8(d) creates a *presumption* in favor of mandatory bargaining over such a decision, a presumption that is rebuttable "by showing that the purposes of the statute would not be furthered by imposition of a duty to bargain," for example, by demonstrating that "bargaining over the decision would be futile," or that the decision was due to "emergency financial circumstances," or that the "custom of the industry, shown by the absence of such an obligation from typical collective bargaining agreements, is not to bargain over such decisions." Id., at 601-602.

The Court of Appeals' decision in this case appears to be at odds with decisions of other Courts of Appeals,[7] some of which decline to require bargaining over any management decision involving "a major commitment of capital investment" or a "basic operational change" in the scope or direction of an enterprise, and some of which indicate that bargaining is not mandated unless a violation of §8(a)(3) (a partial closing motivated by antiunion animus) is involved. . . . The Board itself has not been fully consistent in its rulings applicable to this type of management decision.[10]

Because of the importance of the issue and the continuing disagreement between and among the Board and the Courts of Appeals, we granted certiorari.

II

. . . [I]n establishing what issues must be submitted to the process of bargaining, Congress had no expectation that the elected union representative would become an equal partner in the running of the business enterprise. . . . [T]here is an undeniable limit to the subjects about which bargaining must take place. . . .

Some management decisions, such as choice of advertising and promotion, product type and design, and financing arrangements, have only an indirect and attenuated impact on the employment relationship. See *Fibreboard*, 379 U.S., at 223 (Stewart, J., concurring). Other management decisions, such as the order of succession of layoffs and recalls, production quotas, and work rules, are almost exclusively, "an aspect of the relationship" be-

---

[7] The Court of Appeals in this case, for example, agreed, 627 F.2d at 601, with the Third Circuit in Brockway Motor Trucks, Etc. v. NLRB, 582 F.2d 720 (1978), that a presumption in favor of bargaining was to be established, but it analyzed differently how that presumption would be rebutted. The Third Circuit had decided that the competing interests of the employer and the employees, under the particular circumstances, must be weighed, and it had remanded the case before it to the Board for factfinding into the circumstances behind the partial closing. See also Equitable Gas Co. v. NLRB, 637 F.2d 980 (CA3 1981) (subcontracting). . . .

[10] Compare National Car Rental System, Inc., 252 N.L.R.B. No. 27, p. 15 (1980) (employer's decision to terminate car leasing operations at one location not a mandatory subject because " 'essentially financial and managerial in nature,' involving a 'significant investment or withdrawal of capital, affecting the scope and ultimate direction of an enterprise,' " quoting from General Motors Corp., GMC Truck & Coach Div., 191 N.L.R.B., at 952), and Summit Tooling Co., 195 N.L.R.B. 479, 480 (1972) (decision to close a subsidiary not a mandatory subject because "its practical effect was to take the Respondent out of the business of manufacturing tool and tooling products"), with Ozark Trailers, Inc., 161 N.L.R.B. 561, 567, 568 (1966) (employer's decision to shut down one of multiple plants was a mandatory subject because it was "a decision directly affecting terms and conditions of employment" and "interests of employees are of sufficient importance that their representatives ought to be consulted in matters affecting them"). . . .

tween employer and employee. *Chemical Workers*, 404 U.S., at 178. The present case concerns a third type of management decision, one that had a direct impact on employment, since jobs were inexorably eliminated by the termination, but had as its focus only the economic profitability of the contract with Greenpark, a concern under these facts wholly apart from the employment relationship. This decision, involving a change in the scope and direction of the enterprise, is akin to the decision whether to be in business at all, "not in [itself] primarily about conditions of employment, though the effect of the decision may be necessarily to terminate employment." *Fibreboard*, 379 U.S., at 223 (Stewart, J., concurring). Cf. Textile Workers v. Darlington Co., 380 U.S. 263, 268 (1965) ("an employer has the absolute right to terminate his entire business for any reason he pleases"). At the same time, this decision touches on a matter of central and pressing concern to the union and its member employees: the possibility of continued employment and the retention of the employees' very jobs. . . .

Petitioner contends it had no duty to bargain about its decision to terminate its operations at Greenpark. This contention requires that we determine whether the decision itself should be considered part of petitioner's retained freedom to manage its affairs unrelated to employment. The aim of labeling a matter a mandatory subject of bargaining, rather than simply permitting, but not requiring, bargaining, is to "promote the fundamental purpose of the Act by bringing a problem of vital concern to labor and management within the framework established by Congress as most conducive to industrial peace," *Fibreboard*, 379 U.S., at 211. The concept of mandatory bargaining is premised on the belief that collective discussions backed by the parties' economic weapons will result in decisions that are better for both management and labor and for society as a whole. . . . This will be true, however, only if the subject proposed for discussion is amenable to resolution through the bargaining process. Management must be free from the constraints of the bargaining process to the extent essential for the running of a profitable business. It also must have some degree of certainty beforehand as to when it may proceed to reach decisions without fear of later evaluations labeling its conduct an unfair labor practice. Congress did not explicitly state what issues of mutual concern to union and management it intended to exclude from mandatory bargaining. Nonetheless, in view of an employer's need for unencumbered decisionmaking, bargaining over management decisions that have a substantial impact on the continued availability of employment should be required only if the benefit, for labor-management relations and the collective bargaining process, outweighs the burden placed on the conduct of the business.

The Court in *Fibreboard* implicitly engaged in this analysis with regard to a decision to subcontract for maintenance work previously done by unit employees. Holding the employer's decision a subject of mandatory bargaining, the Court relied not only on the "literal meaning" of the statutory words, but also reasoned:

> The Company's decision to contract out the maintenance work did not alter the Company's basic operation. The maintenance work still had to be performed in the plant. No capital investment was contemplated; the Company merely replaced existing employees with those of an independent contractor to do the same work under similar conditions of employment. Therefore, to require the employer to bargain about the matter would not significantly abridge his freedom to manage the business.

379 U.S., at 213. The Court also emphasized that a desire to reduce labor costs, which it considered a matter "peculiarly suitable for resolution within the collective bargaining framework," id., at 214, was at the base of the employer's decision to subcontract. . . . The prevalence of bargaining over "contracting out" as a matter of industrial practice generally was taken as further proof of the "amenability of such subjects to the collective bargaining process." Id., at 211.

With this approach in mind, we turn to the specific issue at hand: an economically-motivated decision to shut down part of a business.

III

A

Both union and management regard control of the decision to shut down an operation with the utmost seriousness. As has been noted, however, the Act is not intended to serve either party's individual interest, but to foster in a neutral manner a system in which the conflict between these interests may be resolved. It seems particularly important, therefore, to consider whether requiring bargaining over this sort of decision will advance the neutral purposes of the Act.

A union's interest in participating in the decision to close a particular facility or part of an employer's operations springs from its legitimate concern over job security. The Court has observed: "The words of [§8(d)] . . . plainly cover termination of employment which . . . necessarily results" from closing an operation. *Fibreboard*, 379 U.S., at 210. The union's practical purpose in participating, however, will be largely uniform: it will seek to delay or halt the closing. No doubt it will be impelled, in seeking these ends, to offer concessions, information, and alternatives that might be helpful to management or forestall or prevent the termination of jobs.[19] It is unlikely, however, that requiring bargaining over the decision itself, as well as its effects, will augment this flow of information and suggestions. There is no dispute that the union must be given a significant opportunity to bargain about these matters of job security as part of the "effects" bargaining mandated by §8(a)(5). . . . And, under §8(a)(5), bargaining over the effects of a decision must be conducted in a meaningful manner and at a meaningful time, and the Board may impose sanctions to insure its adequacy. A union, by pursuing such bargaining rights, may achieve valuable concessions from an employer engaged in a partial closing. It also may secure in contract negotiations provisions implementing rights to notice, information, and fair bargaining. . . .

Moreover, the union's legitimate interest in fair dealing is protected by §8(a)(3), which prohibits partial closings motivated by anti-union animus, when done to gain an unfair advantage. Textile Workers v. Darlington Co., 380 U.S. 263 (1965). . . . An employer may not simply shut down part of its business and mask its desire to weaken and circumvent the union by labeling its decision "purely economic."

Thus, although the union has a natural concern that a partial closing decision not be hastily or unnecessarily entered into, it has some control over the effects of the decision and indirectly may ensure that the decision itself is deliberately considered. It also has direct protection against a partial closing decision that is motivated by an intent to harm a union.

Management's interest in whether it should discuss a decision of this kind is much more complex and varies with the particular circumstances. If labor costs are an important factor in a failing operation and the decision to close, management will have an incentive to confer voluntarily with the union to seek concessions that may make continuing the business profitable. Cf. U.S. News & World Report, Feb. 9, 1981, p. 74; BNA, Labor Relations Yearbook-1979, p. 5 (UAW agreement with Chrysler Corp. to make concessions on wages and fringe benefits). At other times, management may have great need for speed, flexibility, and secrecy in meeting business opportunities and exigencies. It may face significant tax or securities consequences that hinge on confidentiality, the timing of a plant closing, or a reorganization of the corporate structure. The publicity incident to the normal process of bargaining may injure the possibility of a successful transition or increase the

[19] We are aware of past instances where unions have aided employers in saving failing businesses by lending technical assistance, reducing wages and benefits or increasing production, and even loaning part of earned wages to forestall closures. . . . These have come about without the intervention of the Board enforcing a statutory requirement to bargain.

economic damage to the business. The employer also may have no feasible alternative to the closing, and even good-faith bargaining over it may be both futile and cause the employer additional loss.

There is an important difference, also, between permitted bargaining and mandated bargaining. Labeling this type of decision mandatory could afford a union a powerful tool for achieving delay, a power that might be used to thwart management's intentions in a manner unrelated to any feasible solution the union might propose. See Comment, Partial Terminations and Economic Efficiency, 14 U.C.L.A. L. Rev. 1089, 1103-1105 (1967). In addition, many of the cases before the Board have involved, as this one did, not simply a refusal to bargain over the decision, but a refusal to bargain at all, often coupled with other unfair labor practices. See, e.g., Electrical Products Div. of Midland-Ross Corp. v. NLRB, 617 F.2d 977 (CA3 1980), *cert. denied,* — U.S. — (1981). . . . In these cases, the employer's action gave the Board reason to order remedial relief apart from access to the decision-making process. It is not clear that a union would be equally dissatisfied if an employer performed all its bargaining obligations apart from the additional remedy sought here.

While evidence of current labor practice is only an indication of what is feasible through collective bargaining, and not a binding guide, see *Chemical Workers,* 404 U.S., at 176, that evidence supports the apparent imbalance weighing against mandatory bargaining. We note that provisions giving unions a right to participate in the decisionmaking process concerning alteration of the scope of an enterprise appear to be relatively rare. Provisions concerning notice and "effects" bargaining are more prevalent. . . .

Further, the presumption analysis adopted by the Court of Appeals seems ill suited to advance harmonious relations between employer and employee. An employer would have difficulty determining beforehand whether it was faced with a situation requiring bargaining or one that involved economic necessity sufficiently compelling to obviate the duty to bargain. If it should decide to risk not bargaining, it might be faced ultimately with harsh remedies forcing it to pay large amounts of backpay to employees who likely would have been discharged regardless of bargaining, or even to consider reopening a failing operation. . . . Also, labor costs may not be a crucial circumstance in a particular economically-based partial termination. . . . And in those cases, the Board's traditional remedies may well be futile. See ABC Trans-National Transport, Inc. v. NLRB, 642 F.2d 675 (CA3 1981) (although employer violated its "duty" to bargain about freight terminal closing, court refused to enforce order to bargain). If the employer intended to try to fulfill a court's direction to bargain, it would have difficulty determining exactly at what stage of its deliberations the duty to bargain would arise and what amount of bargaining would suffice before it could implement its decision. . . . If an employer engaged in some discussion, but did not yield to the union's demands, the Board might conclude that the employer had engaged in "surface bargaining," a violation of its good faith. See NLRB v. Reed & Prince Mfg. Co., 205 F.2d 131 (CA1), *cert. denied*, 346 U.S. 887 (1953). A union, too, would have difficulty determining the limits of its prerogatives, whether and when it could use its economic powers to try to alter an employer's decision, or whether, in doing so, it would trigger sanctions from the Board. . . .

We conclude that the harm likely to be done to an employer's need to operate freely in deciding whether to shut down part of its business purely for economic reasons outweighs the incremental benefit that might be gained through the union's participation in making the decision,[22] and we hold that the decision itself is *not* part of §8(d)'s "terms and conditions," over which Congress has mandated bargaining.[23]

B

In order to illustrate the limits of our holding, we turn again to the specific facts of this case. First, we note that when petitioner decided to terminate its Greenpark contract, it had no intention to replace the discharged employees or to move that operation elsewhere. Petitioner's sole purpose was to reduce its economic loss, and the union made no claim of anti-union animus. In addition, petitioner's dispute with Greenpark was solely over the size of the management fee Greenpark was willing to pay. The union had no control or authority over that fee. The most that the union could have offered would have been advice and concessions that Greenpark, the third party upon whom rested the success or failure of the contract, had no duty even to consider. These facts in particular distinguish this case from the subcontract-

---

[22] In this opinion we of course intimate no view as to other types of management decisions, such as plant relocations, sales, other kinds of subcontracting, automation, etc., which are to be considered on their particular facts. . . .

[23] Despite the contentions of *amicus* AFL-CIO our decision in Order of Railroad Telegraphers v. Chicago & N.W.R. Co., 362 U.S. 330 (1960), [summarized supra p. 859], does not require that we find bargaining over this partial closing decision mandatory. . . . Although the Court in part relied on an expansive interpretation of §2, First, which requires railroads to "exert every reasonable effort to make and maintain agreements concerning rates of pay, rules, and working conditions," and §13(c) of the Norris-LaGuardia Act, defining "labor dispute" as "any controversy concerning terms or conditions of employment," its decision also rested on the particular aims of the Railway Labor Act and national transportation policy. See 362 U.S., at 336-338. The mandatory scope of bargaining under the Railway Labor Act and the extent of the prohibition against injunctive relief contained in Norris-LaGuardia are not coextensive with the [NLRA] and the Board's jurisdiction over unfair labor practices. . . .

ing issue presented in *Fibreboard*. Further, the union was not selected as the bargaining representative or certified until well after petitioner's economic difficulties at Greenpark had begun. We thus are not faced with an employer's abrogation of ongoing negotiations or an existing bargaining agreement. Finally, while petitioner's business enterprise did not involve the investment of large amounts of capital in single locations, we do not believe that the absence of "significant investment or withdrawal of capital," General Motors Corp., GMC Truck & Coach Div., 191 N.L.R.B., at 952, is crucial. The decision to halt work at this specific location represented a significant change in petitioner's operations, a change not unlike opening a new line of business or going out of business entirely.

The judgment of the Court of Appeals, accordingly, is reversed and the case is remanded to that court for further proceedings consistent with this opinion.

BRENNAN, J., with whom MARSHALL, J., joins, dissenting. . . . [T]he words "terms and conditions of employment" plainly cover termination of employment resulting from a management decision to close an operation. Fibreboard Paper Products Corp. v. NLRB, 379 U.S. 203, 210 (1964). As the Court today admits, the decision to close an operation "touches on a matter of central and pressing concern to the union and its member employees." Ante, at 11. Moreover, as the Court today further concedes,· Congress deliberately left the words "terms and conditions of employment" indefinite, so that the NLRB would be able to give content to those terms in light of changing industrial conditions. Id., at 9, 9-10, n.14. . . . [T]he Board has determined that an employer's decision to close part of its operations affects the "terms and conditions of employment" within the meaning of the Act, and is thus a mandatory subject for collective bargaining. Ozark Trailers, Inc., 161 N.L.R.B. 561 (1966). Nonetheless, the Court today declines to defer to the Board's decision on this sensitive question of industrial relations, and on the basis of pure speculation reverses the judgment of the Board and of the Court of Appeals. I respectfully dissent.

The Court bases its decision on a balancing test. It states that "bargaining over management decisions that have a substantial impact on the continued availability of employment should be required only if the benefit, for labor-management relations and the collective-bargaining process, outweighs the burden placed on the conduct of the business." I cannot agree with this test, because it takes into account only the interests of *management*; it fails to consider the legitimate employment interests of the workers and their Union. . . . This one-sided approach hardly serves "to foster in a neutral manner" a system for resolution of these serious, two-sided controversies.

Even if the Court's statement of the test were accurate, I could not join in its application, which is based solely on speculation. Apparently, the Court concludes that the benefit to labor-management relations and the collective-bargaining process from negotiation over partial closings is minimal, but it provides no evidence to that effect. The Court acknowledges that the Union might be able to offer concessions, information, and alternatives that might obviate or forestall the closing, but it then asserts that "[i]t is unlikely, however, that requiring bargaining over the decision . . . will augment this flow of information and suggestions." Id., at 15. Recent experience, however, suggests the contrary. Most conspicuous, perhaps, were the negotiations between Chrysler Corporation and the United Auto Workers, which led to significant adjustments in compensation and benefits, contributing to Chrysler's ability to remain afloat. See Wall St. Journal, Oct. 26, 1979, at 3, col. 1. Even where labor costs are not the direct cause of a company's financial difficulties, employee concessions can often enable the company to continue in operation — if the employees have the opportunity to offer such concessions.*

The Court further presumes that management's need for "speed, flexibility, and secrecy" in making partial closing decisions would be frustrated by a requirement to bargain. In some cases the Court might be correct. In others, however, the decision will be made openly and deliberately, and considerations of "speed, flexibility, and secrecy" will be inapposite. Indeed, in view of management's admitted duty to bargain over the effects of a closing . . . it is difficult to understand why additional bargaining over the closing itself would necessarily unduly delay or publicize the decision.

I am not in a position to judge whether mandatory bargaining over partial closings *in all cases* is consistent with our national labor policy, and neither is the Court. The primary responsibility to determine the scope of the statutory duty to bargain has been entrusted to the NLRB, which should not be reversed by the courts merely because they might prefer another view of the statute. . . . I therefore agree with the Court of Appeals that employers presumptively have a duty to bargain over a decision to close an operation, and that this presumption can be rebutted by a showing that bargaining would be futile, that the closing was due to emergency financial circumstances, or

---

*Indeed, in this case, the Court of Appeals found: "On the record, . . . there is sufficient reason to believe that, given the opportunity, the union might have made concessions, by accepting reduction in wages or benefits (take-backs) or a reduction in the work force, which would in part or in whole have enabled FNM an increased management fee. At least, if FNM had bargained over its decision to close, that possibility would have been tested, and management would still have been free to close the Greenpark operation if bargaining did not produce a solution." 627 F.2d 596, 602 (CA2 1980).

that, for some other reason, bargaining would not further the purposes of the National Labor Relations Act. 627 F.2d 596, 601 (CA2 1980). I believe that this approach is amply supported by recent decisions of the Board. . . . With respect to the individual facts of this case, however, I would vacate the judgment of the Court of Appeals, and remand to the Board for further examination of the evidence. See SEC v. Chenery Corp., 318 U.S. 80, 94-95 (1943).

NOTES

1. Is the Court's refusal to defer to the decisions of the Board and the court of appeals based on "pure speculation," as Justice Brennan contends?

2. After *First Natl. Maintenance*, are all economically motivated decisions to close part of a business nonmandatory subjects? Or is factual similarity with *First Natl.* itself the pivotal consideration?

3. A company that operated five plants closed its only unionized plant and terminated the affected employees, refusing to bargain with the incumbent union over its decision. The closing decision was, in part, for the purpose of chilling union activities in the company's other plants, and, in the circumstances, such a chilling effect was reasonably foreseeable.

(a) Under *First Natl. Maintenance*, has the company violated §8(a)(5)?

(b) If the NLRB should find that the partial closing was based both on anti-union reasons and on legitimate economic reasons, and the company establishes that it would have made the same decision even absent union animus, would the Board, applying *First Natl. Maintenance*, find a violation of §8(a)(5)? Cf. Weather Tamer, Inc. v. NLRB, 676 F.2d 483 (11th Cir. 1982); Electrical Prods. Div. of Midland-Ross Corp. v. NLRB, 617 F.2d 977 (3d Cir. 1980), *cert. denied*, 449 U.S. 871 (1981).

4. Presumably, the "other types of management decisions" expressly left open in *First Natl. Maintenance* (footnote 22) are subject to the cost-benefit analysis approved by the Court. Which of those decisions ("plant relocations, sales, other kinds of subcontracting, automation"), if any, are distinguishable from a partial closing decision, for the purposes of §8(a)(5)? If only some of the managerial decisions mentioned in footnote 22 are properly treated like partial closings (and thus brought within the rule of *First Natl.*), what is the rationale for the law's approach to identifying bargaining duties when employment is affected?

The NLRB addressed relocation issues in *Otis Elevator II* (Otis Elevator Co., 269 N.L.R.B. No. 162, 115 L.R.R.M. 1281 (1984), reversing 255

N.L.R.B. 235 (1981)), and ruling that there was no obligation to bargain over a decision to transfer and consolidate New Jersey research and development operations into a Connecticut location. The consolidation was motivated not by labor costs, but by the unsuitability of the New Jersey facility for the company's research and development needs and by the company's determination that technological advances would accrue from housing all such operations in an expanded Connecticut facility. The Board's plurality opinion (by Chairman Dotson and Member Hunter) concluded:

> Despite the evident effect on employees, the critical factor to a determination whether the decision is subject to mandatory bargaining is the essence of the decision itself, i.e., whether it turns upon a change in the nature or direction of the business, or turns upon labor costs; *not* its effect on employees nor a union's ability to offer alternatives. The decision . . . here clearly turned upon a fundamental change in the nature and direction of the business . . .

That opinion, elaborating on footnote 22 of *First Natl. Maintenance*, further declared: ". . . [E]xcluded from §8(d) . . . are decisions which affect the scope, direction, or nature of the business. . . . Included within §8(d), however, . . . are all decisions which turn upon a reduction of labor costs. This is true whether the decision may be characterized as subcontracting, reorganization, consolidation, or relocation . . ."

Members Dennis and Zimmerman, in separate opinions, joined in the result but rejected the plurality's reasoning. Is the plurality opinion faithful to *Fibreboard* and *First Natl. Maintenance*? Consider *Milwaukee Spring II*, infra p. 901. Should "all decisions which turn upon a reduction of labor costs" be bargainable without regard to other considerations?

5. Should regulation focus on preventing displacement of workers or on cushioning worker dislocation caused by business closings? For example, under legislation recently proposed in Congress (the "National Employment Priorities Act"), certain businesses would be required both to give advance notice of changes in operations that produce layoffs and to provide, e.g., severance pay, transfer rights, and continued health and pension benefits. See 114 L.R.R. 125 (1983). What are the issues raised by such legislation? Should it be enacted?

6. For criticism of the principal case, see Harper, Leveling the Road from *Borg-Warner* to *First National Maintenance*: The Scope of Mandatory Bargaining, 68 Va. L. Rev. 1447 (1982). See also Kohler, Distinctions Without Differences: Effects Bargaining in Light of *First National Maintenance*, 5 Indus. Rel. L.J. 402 (1983) (arguing that retention of duty to bargain over effects of partial closings gives unions a substantial role in those decisions). For an economist's perspective, see Alchian, Decision Sharing

and Expropriable Specific Quasi-Rents: A Theory of First National Maintenance Corporation v. NLRB, 1 Sup. Ct. Econ. Rev. 235 (1982).

7. The impact of the Multiemployer Pension Plan Amendments Act of
1980 on plant closings was noted in Chapter 6, p. 425.

Allied Chemical & Alkali Workers v. Pittsburgh Plate Glass Co.
404 U.S. 157 (1971)

BRENNAN, J. . . . The [NLRB] . . . held that changes in retired employees' retirement benefits are embraced by the bargaining obligation and
that an employer's unilateral modification of them constitutes an unfair labor
practice in violation of §§8(a)(5) and (1) of the Act. 177 N.L.R.B. 911
(1969). The Court of Appeals for the Sixth Circuit disagreed . . . 427
F.2d 936 (1970). . . . We affirm the order of the Court of Appeals.

I

Since 1949, Local 1 [Allied Chemical Workers] . . . has been the exclusive bargaining representative for the employees "working" on hourly rates
of pay at the Barberton, Ohio, facilities of respondent Pittsburgh Plate Glass
Company. In 1950, the Union and the Company negotiated an employee
group health insurance plan, in which, it was orally agreed, retired employees
could participate by contributing the required premiums, to be deducted
from their pension benefits. This program continued unchanged until 1962,
except for an improvement unilaterally instituted by the Company in 1954
and another improvement negotiated in 1959.

In 1962 the Company agreed to contribute two dollars per month
toward the cost of insurance premiums of employees who retired in the
future and elected to participate in the medical plan. The parties also agreed
at this time to make 65 the mandatory retirement age. In 1964 insurance
benefits were again negotiated, and the Company agreed to increase its
monthly contribution from two to four dollars, applicable to employees
retiring after that date and also to pensioners who had retired since the
effective date of the 1962 contract. It was agreed, however, that the Company might discontinue paying the two-dollar increase if Congress enacted a
national health program.

In November 1965, Medicare, a national health program, was enacted. . . . The 1964 contract was still in effect, and the Union sought
mid-term bargaining to renegotiate insurance benefits for retired employees.
The Company responded in March 1966 that, in its view, Medicare ren-

dered the health insurance program useless because of a non-duplication-of-benefits provision in the Company's insurance policy, and stated, without negotiating any change, that it was planning to (a) reclaim the additional two-dollar monthly contribution as of the effective date of Medicare; (b) cancel the program for retirees; and (c) substitute the payment of the three-dollar monthly subscription fee for supplemental Medicare coverage for each retired employee.[5]

The Union acknowledged that the Company had the contractual right to reduce its monthly contribution, but challenged its proposal unilaterally to substitute supplemental Medicare coverage for the negotiated health plan. The Company, as it had done during the 1959 negotiations without pressing the point, disputed the Union's right to bargain in behalf of retired employees, but advised the Union that upon further consideration it had decided not to terminate the health plan for pensioners. The Company stated instead that it would write each retired employee, offering to pay the supplemental Medicare premium if the employee would withdraw from the negotiated plan. Despite the Union's objections the Company did circulate its proposal to the retired employees, and 15 of 190 retirees elected to accept it. The Union thereupon filed unfair labor practice charges. . . .

II

. . . This obligation [to bargain, arising from §§1, 8(a)(5), 8(d) and 9(a)] extends only to the "terms and conditions of employment" of the employer's "employees" in the "unit appropriate for such purposes" which the union represents. . . . The Board found that benefits of already retired employees fell within these constraints on alternative theories. First, it held that pensioners are themselves "employees" and members of the bargaining unit, so that their benefits are a "term and condition" of their employment. . . .

First. . . . [W]e hold that the Board's decision is not supported by the law. The Act, . . . as §1 makes clear, is concerned with the disruption to commerce that arises from interference with the . . . rights of "workers" — not those who have retired from the work force. The inequality of bargaining power that Congress sought to remedy was that of the "working" man, and the labor disputes that it ordered to be subjected to collective bargaining were those of employers and their active employees. Nowhere in the history of the [Act] is there any evidence that retired workers are to be considered as within the ambit of the collective bargaining obligations of the statute.

---

[5] Hospital benefits under Medicare are provided automatically to any social security annuitant 65 or over. Medical benefits are optional and, at the relevant time period, required a monthly three-dollar payment per person.

To the contrary, the legislative history of §2(3) itself indicates that the term "employee" is not to be stretched beyond its plain meaning embracing only those who work for another for hire. . . . Congress reacted [to the *Hearst* decision] by specifically excluding from the definition of "employee" "any individual having the status of an independent contractor." [The Court here quoted (with immaterial deletions) the passage from H.R. Rep. No. 245, 80th Cong., 1st Sess. on H.R. 3020 (1947), which is set forth supra p. 708.] . . .

The 1947 Taft-Hartley revision made clear that general agency principles could not be ignored in distinguishing "employees" from independent contractors. Although *Hearst Publications* was thus repudiated, we do not think its approach has been totally discredited. In doubtful cases resort must still be had to economic and policy considerations to infuse §2(3) with meaning. . . . [T]his is not a doubtful case. The ordinary meaning of "employee" does not include retired workers; retired employees have ceased to work for another for hire.

The decisions on which the Board relied in construing §2(3) to the contrary are wide of the mark. The Board enumerated

unfair labor practice situations where the statute has been applied to persons who have not been initially hired by an employer or whose employment has terminated. Illustrative are cases in which the Board has held that applicants for employment and registrants at hiring halls — who have never been hired in the first place — as well as persons who have quit or whose employers have gone out of business are "employees" embraced by the policies of the Act.

177 N.L.R.B., at 913. . . . Yet all of these cases involved people who, unlike the pensioners here, were members of the active work force available for hire and at least in that sense could be identified as "employees." No decision under the Act is cited, and none to our knowledge exists, in which an individual who has ceased work without expectation of further employment has been held to be an "employee."

The Board also found support for its position in decisions arising under [LMRA] §302(c)(5). . . . Section 302 prohibits, inter alia, any payment by an employer to any representative of any of his employees. Subsection (c)(5) provides an exemption for payments to an employee trust fund established "for the sole and exclusive benefit of the employees of such employer" and administered by equal numbers of representatives of the employer and employees. The word "employee," as used in that provision, has been construed to include "current employees and persons who were . . . current employees but are now retired." Blassie v. Kroger Co., 345 F.2d 58, 70 (CA 8th 1965). The Board considered that it would be anomalous to hold that retired employees are not "employees" whose ongoing benefits are fit subjects of bargaining under §8(a)(5), while under [§302(c)] they are "employees" for the purpose of administering the same health insurance benefits. It would create the further anomaly that a union would not be entitled to act as the representative of retired employees under §8(a)(5), while subject to an explicit statutory duty to act as their representative under [§302(c)].

177 N.L.R.B., at 915.

Yet the rationale of *Blassie* is not at all in point. The question there was simply whether under §302(c)(5) retirees remain eligible for benefits of trust funds established during their active employment. The conclusion that they do was compelled by the fact that the contrary reading of the statute would have made illegal contributions to pension plans, which the statute expressly contemplates in subsections (A) and (C). No comparable situation exists in this case. Furthermore, there is no anomaly in the conclusion that retired workers are "employees" within §302(c)(5) entitled to the benefits negotiated while they were active employees, but are not "employees" whose ongoing benefits are embraced by the bargaining obligation of §8(a)(5). Contrary to the Board's assertion, the union's role in the administration of the fund is of a far different order from its duties as collective bargaining agent. . . .

Second. Section 9(a) . . . accords representative status only to the labor organization selected or designated by the majority of employees in a "unit appropriate" "for the purposes of collective bargaining." . . . [W]e hold that [pensioners] were not and could not be "employees" included in the bargaining unit. The unit determined by the Board to be appropriate was composed of "employees of the Employer's plant . . . working on hourly rates, including group leaders who work on hourly rates of pay. . . ." . . . Although those terms may include persons on temporary or limited absence from work, such as employees on military duty, it would utterly destroy the function of language to read them as embracing those whose work has ceased with no expectation of return. . . .

Here, even if, as the Board found, active and retired employees have a common concern in assuring that the latter's benefits remain adequate, they plainly do not share a community of interests broad enough to justify inclusion of the retirees in the bargaining unit. Pensioners' interests extend only to retirement benefits, to the exclusion of wage rates, hours, working conditions, and all other terms of active employment. Incorporation of such a limited-purpose constituency in the bargaining unit would create the potential for severe internal conflicts that would impair the unit's ability to function and would disrupt the processes of collective bargaining. Moreover, the risk cannot be overlooked that union representatives on occasion might see fit to bargain for improved wages or other conditions favoring active employees at the expense of retirees' benefits.[12] . . .

Third. The Board found that bargaining over pensioners' rights has become an established industrial practice. But industrial practice cannot alter the conclusions that retirees are neither "employees" nor bargaining unit members. The parties dispute whether a practice of bargaining over pensioners' benefits exists and, if so, whether it reflects the views of labor and management that the subject is not merely a convenient but a mandatory topic of negotiation. But even if industry commonly regards retirees' benefits as a statutory subject of bargaining, that would at most, as we suggested in Fibreboard Corp. v. NLRB, 379 U.S. 203, 211 (1964), reflect the interests of employers and employees in the subject matter as well as its amenability to the collective bargaining process; it would not be determinative. . . .

III

Even if pensioners are not bargaining unit "employees," are their benefits, nonetheless, a mandatory subject of collective bargaining as "terms and conditions of employment" of the active employees who remain in the unit? The Board held, alternatively, that they are, on the ground that they "vitally" affect the "terms and conditions of employment" of active employees principally by influencing the value of both their current and future benefits. 177 N.L.R.B., at 915. . . .

Section 8(d) . . . does not immutably fix a list of subjects for mandatory bargaining. . . . But it does establish a limitation against which proposed topics must be measured. In general terms, the limitation includes only issues that settle an aspect of the relationship between the employer and the employee. See, e.g., NLRB v. Borg-Warner Corp., 356 U.S. 342 (1958). Although normally matters involving individuals outside the employment relationship do not fall within that category, they are not wholly excluded. Without determining [in Teamsters v. Oliver, 358 U.S. 283 (1959),] whether the owner-drivers were themselves "employees," we held that the minimum rental was a mandatory subject of bargaining, and hence immune from state antitrust laws, because the term "was integral to the establishment

---

[12] The Board argues in its brief that retirees will be at a greater disadvantage if they are required to bargain individually with the employer than if they are represented by the union. The argument assumes that collective bargaining over the benefits of already retired employees would be a one-way street in their favor. The assumption, however, is not free from doubt, as the Board itself recognized in its opinion, see 177 N.L.R.B., at 917, in declining to take a position on the question. . . . In any event, in representing retirees in the negotiation of retirement benefits, the union would be bound to balance the interests of all its constituents, with the result that the interests of active employees might at times be preferred to those of retirees. . . .

of a stable wage structure for clearly covered employee-drivers." . . . Similarly, in *Fibreboard*, we held that "the type of 'contracting out' involved in this case — the replacement of employees in the existing bargaining unit with those of an independent contractor to do the same work under similar conditions of employment — is a statutory subject of collective bargaining. . . ." . . .

The Board urges that *Oliver* and *Fibreboard* provide the principle governing this case. The Company . . . would distinguish those decisions on the ground that the unions there sought to protect employees from outside threats, not to represent the interests of third parties. We agree with the Board that the principle of *Oliver* and *Fibreboard* is relevant here; in each case the question is not whether the third-party concern is antagonistic to or compatible with the interests of bargaining-unit employees, but whether it vitally affects the "terms and conditions" of their employment. But we disagree with the Board's assessment of the significance of a change in retirees' benefits to the "terms and conditions of employment" of active employees.

The benefits that active workers may reap by including retired employees under the same health insurance contract are speculative and insubstantial at best. . . . [T]he relationship between the inclusion of retirees and the overall insurance rate is uncertain. Adding individuals increases the group experience and thereby generally tends to lower the rate, but including pensioners, who are likely to have higher medical expenses, may more than offset that effect. In any event, the impact one way or the other on the "terms and conditions of employment" of active employees is hardly comparable to the loss of jobs threatened in *Oliver* and *Fibreboard*. . . . The inclusion of retirees in the same insurance contract surely has even less impact on the "terms and conditions of employment" of active employees than some of the contracting activities that we excepted from our holding in *Fibreboard*.

The mitigation of future uncertainty and the facilitation of agreement on active employees' retirement plans, which the Board said would follow from the union's representation of pensioners, are equally problematical. To be sure, the future retirement benefits of active workers are part and parcel of their overall compensation and hence a well-established statutory subject of bargaining. Moreover, provisions of those plans to guard against future contingencies are equally subsumed under the collective bargaining obligation. Under the Board's theory, active employees undertake to represent pensioners in order to protect their own retirement benefits, just as if they were bargaining for, say, a cost-of-living escalation clause. But there is a crucial difference. Having once found it advantageous to bargain for improvements in pensioners' benefits, active workers are not forever thereafter bound to that view or obliged to negotiate in behalf of retirees again. To the contrary, they are free to decide, for example, that current income is preferable to greater certainty in their own retirement benefits or, indeed, to their retirement benefits altogether. By advancing pensioners' interests now, active employees, therefore, have no assurance that they will be the beneficiaries of similar representation when they retire. . . .

We recognize that "classification of bargaining subjects as 'terms (and) conditions of employment' is a matter concerning which the Board has special expertise." Meat Cutters v. Jewel Tea, 381 U.S. 676, 685-686 (1965). The Board's holding in this cause, however, depends on the application of law to facts, and the legal standard to be applied is ultimately for the courts to decide and enforce. We think that in holding the "terms and conditions of employment" of active employees to be *vitally* affected by pensioners' benefits, the Board here simply neglected to give the adverb its ordinary meaning. . . .

IV

The question remains whether the Company committed an unfair labor practice by offering retirees an exchange for their withdrawal from the already negotiated health insurance plan. . . . The Board [concluded] . . . that there were several possible ways of adjusting the negotiated plan to the Medicare provisions and the Company "modified" the contract by unilaterally choosing one of them. . . . We need not resolve, however, whether there was a "modification" within the meaning of §8(d), because we hold that even if there was, a "modification" is a prohibited unfair labor practice only when it changes a term that is a mandatory rather than a permissive subject of bargaining.

Paragraph (4) of §8(d) . . . requires that a party proposing a modification continue "in full force and effect . . . all the terms and conditions of the existing contract" until its expiration. Viewed in isolation from the rest of the provision, that language would preclude any distinction between contract obligations that are "terms and conditions of employment" and those that are not. But in construing §8(d), " 'we must not be guided by a single sentence or member of a sentence, but look to the provisions of the whole law, and to its object and policy.'" Mastro Plastics Corp. v. NLRB, 350 U.S. 270, 285 (1956). . . . Seen in that light, §8(d) embraces only mandatory topics of bargaining. The provision begins by defining "to bargain collectively" as meeting and conferring "with respect to wages, hours, and other terms and conditions of employment." It then goes on to state that "the duty to bargain collectively shall also mean" that mid-term unilateral modifications and terminations are prohibited. Although this part of the section is introduced by a "proviso" clause, . . . it quite plainly is to be construed *in pari materia*

with the preceding definition. Accordingly, just as §8(d) defines the obligation to bargain to be with respect to mandatory terms alone, so it prescribes
the duty to maintain only mandatory terms without unilateral modification
for the duration of the collective bargaining agreement.[22] . . .

The structure and language of §8(d) point to a more specialized purpose
than merely promoting general contract compliance. The conditions
. . . set out in paragraphs (1) through (4) plainly are designed to regulate
modifications and terminations so as to facilitate agreement in place of
economic warfare. . . .

If that is correct, the distinction that we draw between mandatory and
permissive terms of bargaining fits the statutory purpose. By once bargaining
and agreeing on a permissive subject, the parties, naturally, do not make the
subject a mandatory topic of future bargaining. When a proposed modification is to a permissive term, therefore, the purpose of facilitating accord on
the proposal is not at all in point, since the parties are not required under the
statute to bargain with respect to it. The irrelevance of the purpose is demonstrated by the irrelevance of the procedures themselves of §8(d). Paragraph
(2), for example, requires an offer "to meet and confer with the other party
for the purpose of negotiating a new contract or a contract containing the
proposed modifications." But such an offer is meaningless if a party is
statutorily free to refuse to negotiate on the proposed change to the permissive term. The notification to mediation and conciliation services referred to
in paragraph (3) would be equally meaningless, if required at all.[23] We think it
would be no less beside the point to read paragraph (4) of §8(d) as requiring
continued adherence to permissive as well as mandatory terms. The remedy
for a unilateral mid-term modification to a permissive term lies in an action
for breach of contract, . . . not in an unfair-labor-practice proceeding.

As a unilateral mid-term modification of a permissive term such as
retirees' benefits does not, therefore, violate §8(d), the judgment of the Court
of Appeals is affirmed.

Douglas, J., dissents.

---

[22] In coming to a contrary conclusion, the trial examiner mistakenly relied on Brotherhood of Painters, Local Union No. 1385, 143 N.L.R.B. 678 (1963), where the Board held
that a union violated §8(d) by refusing to execute a written contract containing a permissive
term to which it had previously agreed. . . . The union was required to sign the contract at
the employer's request not because §8(d) reaches permissive terms, but because the union's
refusal obstructed execution of an agreement on mandatory terms.

[23] The notification required by paragraph (3) is "of the existence of a dispute." Section
2(9) of the Act defines "labor dispute" to include "any controversy concerning terms, tenure
or conditions of employment, or concerning the association or representation of persons in
negotiating, fixing, maintaining, changing, or seeking to arrange terms or conditions of
employment. . . ." . . . Since controversies over permissive terms are excluded from the
definition, a paragraph (3) notice might not be required in the case of a proposed modification
to such a term even if §8(d) applied.

NOTES

1. Does the principal case mean that employers are privileged unilaterally to abrogate contractual clauses governing matters beyond the scope of mandatory bargaining, even though such clauses directly affect "employees" in the unit? Does such an approach promote stability in the parties' relationship? Is it compatible with the parties' expectancies and with the likelihood that negotiations involved trade-offs between "mandatory" and "nonmandatory" items?

2. Despite the classification of retirees' benefits as a nonmandatory item, there continues to be extensive voluntary bargaining on such matters by employers and unions. See, e.g., Simison, Pension Levels for Those Already Retired are a Thorny Issue in Auto Negotiations, Wall St. J., Aug. 29, 1979, at 34, col. 1. Such bargaining — indeed, the entire subject of employee benefit plans — has been affected by the 1974 enactment of the Employee Retirement Income Security Act (ERISA). See Fillion & Trebilock, The Duty to Bargain Under ERISA, 17 Wm. & Mary L. Rev. 251 (1975).

E. MIDTERM BARGAINING OVER MODIFICATIONS

Jacobs Mfg. Co.
94 N.L.R.B. 1214 (1951)

. . . In July 1948, the Respondent and the Union executed a 2-year bargaining contract which, by its terms, could be reopened one year after its execution date for discussion of "wage rates." In July 1949 the Union invoked the reopening clause . . . and thereafter gave the Respondent written notice of its "wage demands." In addition to a request for a wage increase, these demands included a request that the Respondent undertake the entire cost of an existing group insurance program, and another request for the establishment of a pension plan for the Respondent's employees. When the parties met thereafter to consider the Union's demands, the Respondent refused to discuss the Union's pension and insurance requests on the ground that they were not appropriate items of discussion under the reopening clause of the 1948 contract.

The group insurance program to which the Union alluded in its demands was established by the Respondent before 1948. It was underwritten by an insurance company, and provided life, accident, health, surgical, and hospital protection. All the Respondent's employees were eligible to participate in the program, and the employees shared its costs with the Respondent.

When the 1948 contract was being negotiated, the Respondent and the Union had discussed changes in this *insurance program*, and had agreed to increase certain of the benefits as well as the costs. However, neither the changes thereby effected, nor the insurance program itself, was mentioned in the 1948 contract.

As indicated by the Union's request, there was no *pension* plan for the Respondent's employees in existence in 1949. The subject of pensions, moreover, had not been discussed during the 1948 negotiations; and, like insurance, that subject is not mentioned in the 1948 contract.

a. For the reasons stated below, Chairman Herzog and Members Houston and Styles agree with the Trial Examiner's conclusion that the Respondent violated §8(a)(5) . . . by refusing to discuss the matter of *pensions* with the Union. . . .

We are satisfied . . . that the 1948 contract did not in itself impose on the Respondent any obligation to discuss pensions or insurance. The reopening clause of that contract refers to *wage rates*, and thus its intention appears to have been narrowly limited to matters directly related to the amount and manner of compensation for work. . . .

On the other hand, a majority of the Board believes that, regardless of the character of the reopening clause, the Act itself imposed upon the Respondent the duty to discuss *pensions* with the Union during the period in question.

It is now established . . . [that] . . . pensions [fall] within the area where the statute requires bargaining. And, as noted above, the 1948 contract between the Respondent and the Union was silent with respect to the subject of pensions; indeed, the matter had never been raised or discussed by the parties. The issue raised, therefore, is whether the Respondent was absolved of the obligation to discuss pensions because of the [§8(d)] limitation . . . dealing with the duty to discuss or agree to the modification of an existing bargaining contract. . . .   Section 8(d) does not itself license a party . . . to refuse, during the life of the contract, to discuss a bargainable subject unless it has been made a part of the agreement itself. . . . [T]herefore, the *Tide Water* [85 N.L.R.B. 1096 (1949)] construction of §8(d) means that the Respondent was obligated to discuss the Union's pension demand.

Members Houston and Styles have carefully reexamined the Board's construction of §8(d) in the *Tide Water* case, and are persuaded that the view the Board adopted [there] best effectuates the declared policy of the Act. Chairman Herzog, while joining in the result with respect to the obligation to bargain here concerning pensions — never previously discussed by the parties — joins in the rationale herein *only* to the extent that it is consistent with his views separately recited below, concerning the insurance program.

By making mandatory the discussion of bargainable subjects not already covered by a contract, the parties to the contract are encouraged to arrive at joint decisions with respect to bargainable matters, that, at least to the party requesting discussion, appear at the time to be of some importance. The Act's policy of "encouraging the practice and procedure of collective bargaining" is consequently furthered. A different construction of §8(d) in the circumstances — one that would permit a party to a bargaining contract to avoid discussion when it was sought on subject matters not contained in the contract — would serve, at its best, only to dissipate whatever the good will that had been engendered by the previous bargaining negotiations that led to the execution of a bargaining contract; at its worst, it could bring about the industrial strife and the production interruptions that . . . the Act also seeks to avert.

The significance of this point cannot be overemphasized. It goes to the heart of our disagreement with our dissenting colleague, Member Reynolds. His dissent stresses the need for "contract stability," and asserts that the furtherance of sound collective bargaining requires that the collective bargaining agreement be viewed as fixing, for the term of the contract, all aspects of the employer-employee relationship, and as absolving either party of the obligation to discuss, during that term, even those matters which had never been raised, or discussed in the past. We could hardly take issue with the virtue of "contract stability," at least in the abstract, and we would certainly agree that everyone is better off when, in negotiating an agreement, the parties have been able to foresee what all the future problems may be, to discuss those problems, and either to embody a resolution of them in the contract, or to provide that they may not be raised again during the contract. But we are here concerned with the kind of case in which . . . this has *not* been done, and the question is what best effectuates the policies of the Act in *such* a case.

In this connection we cannot ignore the fact that to say that a party to an agreement is absolved by §8(d) of an obligation to discuss a subject not contained in a contract does not mean that the other party is prohibited from taking economic action to compel bargaining on that subject. The portion of §8(d) we are here considering does no more than provide a *defense* to a charge of a refusal to bargain under §§8(a)(5) or 8(b)(3). . . . It does not render unlawful economic action aimed at securing lawful objectives.[10] That

---

[10] . . . [C]ontrary to the assertion of Member Reynolds, . . . nothing in this decision is to be construed as a determination of the issue of whether a union may strike to compel bargaining on a modification of a contract which seeks to add a matter not contained in the contract without complying with the procedural requirements of §8(d). Our decision here is limited to a construction of the language "modification of the terms and conditions *contained* in a contract." The issue raised by our dissenting colleague is not before us . . . and we in no way pass upon it.

being so, the view urged by Member Reynolds achieves "contract stability" but only at the price of industrial strife. . . . The basic policy of this Act to further collective bargaining is founded on the proposition — amply demonstrated by experience — that collective bargaining provides an escape valve for the pressures which otherwise result in industrial strife. With this policy in mind, we are loath to narrow the area of mandatory bargaining, except where the amended statute, in the clearest terms, requires that we do so.

The construction of §8(d) adopted . . . in the *Tide Water* case serves also to simplify, and thus to speed, the bargaining process. It eliminates the pressure upon the parties at the time when a contract is being negotiated to raise those subjects that may not then be of controlling importance, but which might in the future assume a more significant status. It also assures to both unions and employers that, if future conditions require some agreement as to matters about which the parties have not sought, or have not been able to obtain agreement, then some discussion of those matters will be forthcoming when necessary.

We cannot believe that Congress was unaware of the foregoing considerations when it amended the Act by inserting §8(d), or that it sought, by the provision in question, to freeze the bargaining relationship by eliminating any mandatory discussion that might lead to the addition of new subject matter to an existing contract.[11] What §8(d) does is to reject the pronouncements contained in some pre-1947 Board and court decisions . . . to the effect that the duty to bargain continues even as to those matters upon which the parties have reached agreement and which are set forth in the terms of a

---

[11] Unlike Member Reynolds we find little in the legislative history that sheds any real light on the meaning of that portion of §8(d) involved in this case. Even were we to assume, as our dissenting colleague asserts, that the provision in question had its origin in the House bill, it is significant that the provision in the House bill referred broadly to "modifications of an agreement," and did not contain the language finally enacted, i.e., "modification of the terms and conditions *contained in* a contract." In that posture we find no basis for our dissenting colleague's reliance on the *House* report, which correctly notes that the *House bill* language did "not require bargaining *on any matter* during the term of a collective bargaining contract."

The most pertinent reference to the relevant portion of §8(d) as enacted is the following statement by Senator Taft: "The amendment . . . providing that the duty to bargain collectively should not be construed as requiring either party to discuss or agree to any modification of the terms of a contract if such modification is to become effective before the contract may be reopened has been construed on the floor to mean 'Parties will be bound by contract without an opportunity for further collective bargaining.' The provision has no such effect. It merely provides that either party to a contract may refuse to change its terms or discuss such a change to take effect during the life thereof without being guilty of an unfair labor practice. Parties may meet and discuss the meaning of the terms of their contract and may agree to modification on change of circumstances, but it is not mandatory that they do so." 93 Cong. Rec. 7002; Legislative History of the [LMRA], 1947, p. 1625.

written contract. But we believe it does no more. Those bargainable issues which have never been discussed by the parties, and which are in no way treated in the contract, remain matters which both the union and the employer are obliged to discuss at any time.

. . . [I]f the parties originally desire to avoid later discussion with respect to matters not specifically covered in the terms of an executed contract, they need only so specify in the terms of the contract itself. Nothing in our construction of §8(d) precludes such an agreement, entered into in good faith, from foreclosing future discussion of matters not contained in the agreement.

b. Chairman Herzog . . . believes that — unlike the pensions issue — the Respondent was under no obligation to bargain concerning the *group insurance program.*

However, Members Houston and Styles — a minority of the Board on this issue — are of the further opinion that the considerations discussed above leading to the conclusion that the Respondent was obligated to discuss the matter of pensions, also impel the conclusion that the Respondent was obligated to discuss the Union's group insurance demand. Like pensions, the matter of group insurance benefits is a subject which has been held to be within the area of compulsory bargaining; and like pensions, the Respondent's group insurance program was not mentioned in the terms of the 1948 contract. Members Houston and Styles therefore believe that so far as the controlling facts are concerned, the ultimate issues presented by the Union's pension and group insurance demands are identical. . . .

Members Houston and Styles believe, moreover, that the view adopted by Chairman Herzog on the insurance issue is subject to the same basic criticism as is the view of Member Reynolds — it exalts "contract stability" over industrial peace; it eliminates mandatory collective bargaining on subjects about which one of the parties now wants discussion, and concerning which it may well be willing to take economic action if discussion is denied, solely because the matter has once been discussed in a manner which may warrant an inference that the failure to mention that subject in the contract was part of the bargain. Members Houston and Styles are constrained to reject the view of Chairman Herzog for the further reason that it would establish a rule which is administratively unworkable, and would inject dangerous uncertainty into the process of collective bargaining. Apart from the extremely difficult problems of proof — illustrated in this very case — which would constantly confront the Board in cases of this type, the parties to collective bargaining negotiations would always be faced with this question after a subject has been *discussed* — "Have we really *negotiated*, or are we under an obligation to discuss the subject further if asked to"? To this query the rule of the *Tide Water* case gives a clear and concise answer: "You are obligated to discuss any bargainable subject upon request unless you have reduced your agreement on that subject to writing or unless you have agreed in writing not to bargain about it during the term of the contract." Members Houston and Styles would apply that rule without deviation. . . .

[Chairman Herzog, concurring and dissenting, in part, urged the following considerations: After the union had advanced the disputed insurance proposal during the prior negotiations, the respondent had rejected it but had improved the insurance benefits outside the written contract. Hence, rejection of the insurance proposal had been part of "the bargain." Without regard to nice construction of §8(d), imposition of a bargaining duty in such situations would be inequitable and unwise.]

Member REYNOLDS, concurring separately and dissenting in part: . . . Reconsideration of the question which this case raises leads me to the conclusion that in the *Allied Mills* and *Tide Water* cases, the Board placed an erroneous interpretation on the language of the §8(d) proviso insofar as it refers to the requirements of collective bargaining during a contract term. Those cases interpret the pertinent language of the proviso to mean that a request during the term of a contract to bargain collectively on subjects which have not been reduced to writing and integrated in the contract is not a request to modify the contract. It logically follows, notwithstanding my colleagues' summary statement that they are not deciding the issue, that since no *modification* of the contract is contemplated, the party making such a request to bargain is relieved of the obligation to comply with certain procedural duties prescribed in §8(d). Where, as in this case, a union makes the request, the union would not then have to observe, among other things, the 60-day no-strike, or "cooling off," period, and could enforce its request by "quickie strike," precisely the practice which the Board has found §8(d) seeks to eliminate. . . .

. . . [W]e are left with the fact that the relevant language of the §8(d) proviso appears to have had its genesis in the original House bill, and that the report accompanying that bill explained the language as not requiring "bargaining on any matter during the term of a collective bargaining agreement, except as the express terms of the agreement permit." There is nothing in the Conference Report which indicates that such a construction would not be a reasonable construction with respect to the language of §8(d) in question. Indeed a statement by Senator Taft during debate on the Conference Agreement supports the conclusion that this is the proper construction. Senator Morse, after a lengthy analysis of §8(d), stated "the parties will be bound by the contract, without an opportunity for further collective bargaining in regard to it." . . . [Here the opinion quotes from Senator Taft's statement set forth in footnote 11 of the lead opinion.] Thus Senator Taft clearly interpreted §8(d) as stating that the parties are not bound to discuss changes to take place during the life of the contract.[36]

On the basis of the foregoing, it is my opinion that §8(d) imposes no obligation on either party to a contract to bargain on any matter during the term of the contract except as the express provisions of the contract may demand. This is a result reasonably compatible with the particular §8(d) language involved, as well as with §8(d) as a whole. Moreover, not only does the result accord stability and dignity to collective bargaining agreements, but it also gives substance to the practice and procedure of collective bargaining. . . . Contractually stabilized industrial relations enable employers, because of fixed labor costs, to engage in sound long-range production planning, and employees, because of fixed wage, seniority, promotion, and grievance provisions, to anticipate secure employment tenure. . . .

That a collective bargaining agreement stabilizes all rights and conditions of employment is consonant with the generally accepted concept of the nature of such an agreement. The basic terms and conditions of employment existing at the time the collective bargaining agreement is executed, and which are not specifically altered by, or mentioned in, the agreement, are part of the status quo which the parties, by implication, consider as being adopted as an essential element of the agreement. This view is termed "reasonable and logical," and its widespread endorsement as sound industrial relations practice makes it a general rule followed in the arbitration of disputes arising during the term of a contract. . . . Many items are not mentioned in a collective bargaining agreement either because of concessions at the bargaining table or because one of the parties may have considered it propitious to forego raising one subject in the hope of securing a more advantageous deal on another. Subjects traded off or foregone should, under these circumstances, be as irrevocably settled as those specifically covered and settled by the agreement. To require bargaining on such subjects during midterm debases initial contract negotiations. [The opinion of Member Murdock, dissenting in part, is omitted.]

---

[36] The Board's reliance on this statement of Senator Taft's to support the result reached in the *Allied Mills* and *Tide Water* cases appears erroneous. Professors Cox and Dunlop, in The Duty to Bargain Collectively During the Term of an Existing Agreement, 63 Harv. L. Rev. 1097 (1950), share this view, [stating at p. 1129]: "This statement [of Taft], in answer to the charge that §8(d) froze the terms of employment contained in a collective bargaining agreement, pointed out that the parties might voluntarily discuss proposed modification and change their contract but that 'it is not mandatory that they do so.' This was the thrust of the paragraph and [Taft] seems to have had no other thought in mind. Nothing in the passage suggests the NLRB [*Allied Mills* and *Tide Water*] distinction nor can we discover any basis for it in the other legislative explanations of §8(d)."

NOTES

1. The Board's view that §8(d) does not relieve an employer of the duty to bargain over subjects neither discussed in negotiations nor incorporated as terms of the agreement was affirmed in NLRB v. Jacobs Mfg. Co., 196 F.2d 680 (2d Cir. 1952). Although that court found it unnecessary to determine whether "discussion" of an item during negotiations relieves the employer of a midterm duty to bargain about inclusion of a provision on the item, subsequent Board and court decisions make clear that only discussions constituting a "waiver" will have that effect. See, e.g., N L Industries, 220 N.L.R.B. 41, 43 (1975), enforced, 536 F.2d 786 (8th Cir. 1976). The Board's customary "clear and unmistakable" test of waiver is applicable; thus, the item in issue must have been "fully discussed" or "consciously explored," and the union must have "consciously yielded or relinquished" in the "give and take" of negotiations. See Rockwell Intl. Corp., 260 N.L.R.B. 1346, 1347 (1982); Angelus Block Co., 250 N.L.R.B. 868, 877 (1980). See also Pepsi-Cola Distrib. Co., 241 N.L.R.B. 869, 870 (1979) (what is said during negotiations must "put the union on notice that its failure to include a provision would preclude it from future bargaining on the subject"). Does this approach sometimes impel an employer to raise and discuss matters that both sides would prefer to lie dormant?

2. The *Jacobs* case stimulated extensive use of so-called zipper clauses, such as the following (which, incidentally, is popular in collective agreements — e.g., NLRB v. C & C Plywood Corp., infra p. 1075):

> The parties acknowledge that during the negotiations which resulted in this Agreement, each had the unlimited right and opportunity to make demands and proposals with respect to any subject or matter . . . , and that the understanding and agreements arrived at by the parties . . . are set forth in this Agreement. Therefore, the Company and the Union, for the life of this Agreement, each voluntarily and unqualifiedly waives the right, and each agrees that the other shall not be obligated to bargain collectively with respect to any subject or matter referred to, or covered in this Agreement, or with respect to any subject or matter not specifically referred to or covered by this Agreement even though such subject or matter may not have been within the knowledge or contemplation of either or both of the parties at the time they negotiated or signed this Agreement.

It appears settled that "general" zipper clauses constitute only a waiver of the union's right to insist on bargaining over its proposals to add new terms and do not relieve the employer of its duty to bargain before initiating unilateral changes in existing conditions of employment. To avoid the latter duty, contract language (perhaps supported by bargaining history) must manifest a "clear and unmistakable" relinquishment of the union's bargaining rights with respect to the particular matter involved. Compare Radioear Corp., 214 N.L.R.B. 362 (1974), with Unit Drop Div., Eaton, Yale & Towne, 171 N.L.R.B. 600 (1968), *enforced in relevant part*, 412 F.2d 108 (7th Cir. 1969), and NLRB v. Auto Crane Co., 536 F.2d 310 (10th Cir. 1975).

(a) An employer, who suffered large losses, unilaterally discontinued a long-standing practice (not mentioned in the collective agreement) of giving all personnel a large turkey at Christmas. Does the above-quoted zipper clause protect the employer against an 8(a)(5) charge based on the employer's failure to bargain with the incumbent union over this action? Would it be material if the union in bargaining for the current agreement had made, but dropped, a request for a maintenance-of-benefits clause, without, however, mentioning the turkeys to the employer? Cf. Aeronca, Inc. v. NLRB, 650 F.2d 501 (4th Cir. 1981). But cf. Columbus & Southern Ohio Elec. Co., 270 N.L.R.B. No. 95, 116 L.R.R.M. 1148 (1984); Benchmark Indus., 270 N.L.R.B. No. 8, 116 L.R.R.M. 1032 (1984).

(b) Suppose the incumbent union makes a midterm request that the employer, for the first time, give each of his employees a Christmas turkey. Would the zipper clause justify the employer's refusal to discuss that request? Is it justifiable to distinguish between (i) unilateral action by a party to a contract that changes the status quo and (ii) his rejection, without discussion, of proposals for a midterm change in the status quo?

See generally Nelson & Howard, The Duty to Bargain During the Term of an Existing Agreement, 27 Lab. L.J. 573 (1976); Note, Mid-term Modification of Terms and Conditions of Employment, 1972 Duke L.J. 813.

3. Is the foregoing zipper clause a subject of bargaining upon which a party may insist to the point of impasse? Was this question answered by the Supreme Court's ruling on the management rights clause at issue in *American Natl. Ins.* (supra p. 803)? See NLRB v. Tomco Communications, Inc., 567 F.2d 871 (9th Cir. 1978).

Milwaukee Spring Div. of Illinois Coil Spring Co.
268 N.L.R.B. No. 87, 115 L.R.R.M. 1065 (1984)

[In *Milwaukee Spring I*, 265 N.L.R.B. 206 (1982), the Board (3-0) had held that respondent violated §§8(a)(1), (3) and (5) by deciding—during the term of a collective bargaining agreement and without the union's consent —to transfer its assembly operations from its unionized Milwaukee Spring facility to its unorganized McHenry Spring facility. While review was pending in the Seventh Circuit, that court — after a major change in the Board's membership — granted a Board motion for reconsideration of the case. Thereafter, the Board (3-1), with three Reagan appointees making up a new majority, reversed its original decision.]

I

. . . Illinois Coil Spring Company consists of three divisions — Holly Spring, McHenry Spring, and Respondent (Milwaukee Spring). . . . [A]lthough collectively the four entities are a single employer, each location constitutes a separate bargaining unit. Respondent . . . employed about 99 bargaining unit employees . . . in eight departments, including [assembly operations and molding operations].

The Union has represented Respondent's bargaining unit employees for a number of years. The most recent contract became effective on 1 April 1980, and remained in effect until at least 31 March 1983. The contract contains specific wage and benefits provisions. The contract also provides that the Company "recognizes the Union as the sole and exclusive collective bargaining agent for all production and maintenance employees in the Company's plant at Milwaukee, Wisconsin."

On 26 January 1982 Respondent asked the Union to forgo a scheduled wage increase and to grant other contract concessions. In March, because Respondent lost a major customer, it proposed to the Union relocating its assembly operations to the nonunionized McHenry facility, located in McHenry, Illinois, to obtain relief from the comparatively higher assembly labor costs at Milwaukee Spring. Respondent also advised the Union that it needed wage and benefit concessions to keep its molding operations in Milwaukee viable. On 23 March the Union rejected the proposed reduction in wages and benefits. On 29 March Respondent submitted to the Union a document entitled "Terms Upon Which Milwaukee Assembly Operations Will Be Retained in Milwaukee." On 4 April the Union rejected the Company's proposal for alternatives to relocation and declined to bargain further over the Company's decision to transfer its assembly operations. The Company then announced its decision to relocate the Milwaukee assembly operations to the McHenry facility.

The parties stipulated that the relocation decision was economically motivated and was not the result of union animus . . . [and] that Respondent has satisfied its obligation to bargain with the Union over the decision . . . and has been willing to engage in effects bargaining with the Union.[5]

---

[5] The parties' stipulation and the manner in which they briefed this case treat Respondent's relocation decision as a mandatory subject of bargaining. The dissent nevertheless insists on discussing at length what it terms the "threshold issue" of whether Respondent had a

II

A

. . . Generally, an employer may not unilaterally institute changes regarding mandatory subjects before reaching a good-faith impasse in bargaining.[6] Section 8(d) imposes an additional requirement when a collective-bargaining agreement is in effect and an employer seeks to "modif[y] . . . the terms and conditions contained in" the contract: the employer must obtain the union's consent before implementing the change. If the employment conditions the employer seeks to change are not "contained in" the contract, however, the employer's obligation remains the general one of bargaining in good faith to impasse over the subject before instituting the proposed change.

Applying these principles . . . , before the Board may hold that Respondent violated §8(d), the Board first must identify a specific term "contained in" the contract that the Company's decision to relocate modified. . . . [W]e have searched the contract in vain for a provision requiring bargaining unit work to remain in Milwaukee.

Milwaukee Spring I suggests, however, that the Board may have concluded that Respondent's relocation decision, because it was motivated by a desire to obtain relief from the Milwaukee contract's labor costs, modified that contract's wage and benefits provisions. We believe this reasoning is flawed. While it is true that the Company proposed modifying the wage and benefits provisions of the contract, the Union rejected the proposals. Following its failure to obtain the Union's consent, Respondent, in accord with §8(d), abandoned the proposals to modify the contract's wage and benefits provisions. Instead, Respondent decided to transfer the assembly operations to a different plant where different workers (who were not subject to the contract) would perform the work. In short, Respondent did not disturb the wages and benefits at its Milwaukee facility, and consequently did not violate §8(d) by modifying, without the Union's consent, the wage and benefits provisions contained in the contract.

Nor do we find that Respondent's relocation decision modified the contract's recognition clause. In two previous cases, the Board construed recognition clauses to encompass the duties performed by bargaining unit employees and held that employers' reassignment of work modified those clauses. In both instances, reviewing courts found no basis for reading jurisdictional rights into standard clauses that merely recognized the contracts'

---

duty to bargain over its decision. Based on the facts before us, we find no reason to enter this discussion. We do not find it necessary to decide whether the work relocation here was a mandatory subject of bargaining under the Supreme Court's decision in First National Maintenance Corp. v. NLRB, 452 U.S. 666 (1981).

[6]See NLRB v. Katz, 369 U.S. 736 (1962).

coverage of specified employees. Boeing Co., 230 N.L.R.B. 696 (1977), *enf. denied* 581 F.2d 793 (9th Cir. 1978); University of Chicago, 210 N.L.R.B. 190 (1974), *enf. denied* 514 F.2d 942 (7th Cir. 1975). We agree with the courts' reasoning.

Language recognizing the Union as the bargaining agent "for all production and maintenance employees in the Company's plant at Milwaukee, Wisconsin," does not state that the functions that the unit performs must remain in Milwaukee. No doubt parties could draft such a clause; indeed, work-preservation clauses are commonplace. It is not for the Board, however, to create an implied work-preservation clause in every American labor agreement based on wage and benefits or recognition provisions, and we expressly decline to do so.[10]

In sum, we find . . . that neither wage and benefits provisions nor the recognition clause . . . preserves bargaining unit work at the Milwaukee facility for the duration of the contract, and that Respondent did not modify these contract terms when it decided to relocate its assembly operations. Further, we find that no other term contained in the contract restricts Respondent's decision-making regarding relocation.

B[11]

Our dissenting colleague and the decision in *Milwaukee Spring I* fail to recognize that decision's substantial departure from NLRB textbook law that an employer need not obtain a union's consent on a matter not contained in the body of a collective-bargaining agreement even though the subject is a mandatory subject of bargaining.[12] See, e.g., Ozark Trailers, 161 N.L.R.B. 561 (1966). Although the Board found a violation in *Ozark*, it did so grounded on the employer's failure to bargain over its decision to close a part

---

[10] In *Boeing*, the court stated:

Since the purpose of the Act is to encourage labor/management peace by resolving differences through collective-bargaining and to stabilize *agreed upon* conditions during the term of a [contract], Steelworkers v. Warrior and Gulf Co., 363 U.S. 574, 578 . . . (1960), a rejection of the Board's position here would seem to further the purpose of the Act. Rather than stretching the meaning of a Recognition Clause "impliedly," "implicitly," or "in effect" to cover "functions" (as did the Board), a decision against the Board would encourage the parties affirmatively to negotiate an explicit "Jurisdictional Clause" to be included in the next [contract]. [581 F.2d at 798. Emphasis in original.]

[11] In agreeing with her colleagues that *Milwaukee Spring I* represented a substantial departure from well-established Board precedent, Member Dennis relies on part III of the decision, and finds it unnecessary to reach the matters discussed in part II,B.

[12] For a comprehensive review of prior decisions in this area, including cogent criticism of inconsistency and ambiguities, see Philip A. Miscimarra, The NLRB and Managerial Discretion: Plant Closings, Relocations, Subcontracting, and Automation. The Wharton School, University of Pennsylvania (1983) pp. 204-215.

of its operation during the collective-bargaining agreement, transfer equipment to another of its plants, and subcontract out work which had been performed at the Ozark plant. Even though the Board's ultimate conclusion in that case may not here survive the Supreme Court's analysis in *First National Maintenance*, it is instructive to note the Board's recognition that the employer's obligation, absent a specific provision in the contract restricting its rights, was to *bargain* with the union over its decision:

> . . . [A]n employer's obligation to bargain does not include the obligation to agree, . . . [and if] such efforts fail, the employer is wholly free to make and effectuate his decision. [161 NLRB at 568. Footnote omitted.]

In *Ozark* the company closed its plant midterm of the collective-bargaining agreement, transferred the equipment, and contracted out the manufacture of truck bodies formerly performed at the Ozark plant primarily for labor cost reasons. There was no contention that the employer's action in closing the plant violated any contractual provision since the contract itself did not prohibit the closing. . . .

. . . [I]n *Ozark* the Board recognized that it was common practice for unions and employers to negotiate concerning work relocation, subcontracting, contracting out, etc., and that such negotiations had resulted in contractual language in some contracts which restricted the employer's right to contract out unit work. Consequently, the General Counsel's assertion at oral argument and the implication of our dissenting colleague that to reverse *Milwaukee Spring I* would change the whole course of collective bargaining set forth throughout the years of the [NLRA] is not accurate. Rather, it was *Milwaukee Spring I* which was a radical departure. . . .

The rationale of our dissenting colleague adds to the collective-bargaining agreement terms not agreed to by the parties and forecloses the exercise of rational economic discussion and decision-making which ultimately accrue to the benefit of all parties.

C

Accordingly, we conclude that Respondent's decision to relocate did not modify the collective-bargaining agreement in violation of §8(d). In view of the parties' stipulation that Respondent satisfied its obligation to bargain over the decision, we also conclude that Respondent did not violate §8(a)(5).[13]

---

[13] The dissent's references to "contract avoidance" and "do[ing] indirectly what cannot be done directly" are misleading and deflect the reader's attention from the language of §8(d). . . .

. . . [B]ecause we can identify no term or condition contained in the contract that Respondent modified, we characterize Respondent's conduct as doing directly what lawfully

III

. . . *Milwaukee Spring I* relied on Los Angeles Marine Hardware Co., 235 N.L.R.B. 720 (1978), *enfd.* 602 F.2d 1302 (9th Cir. 1979) . . . , [which,] however, misapplied then current Board law. In holding that, after bargaining to impasse, the respondent was not free to relocate work from one location to another location during the contract term without union consent, *Los Angeles Marine* relied on *Boeing*, which in turn cited *University of Chicago*.

In finding an unlawful midterm modification in *University of Chicago*, the Board relied on the [continued performance of] the reassigned work at the same location by another group of the respondent's employees. The Board stated:

> It is well established that an employer may, after the necessary bargaining, terminate work done by the union's members at a particular location and . . . transfer it elsewhere . . . even though such action is taken during the contract term. . . . [210 N.L.R.B. at 190. Footnotes omitted.]

Thus, the Board's *University of Chicago* decision did not support *Los Angeles Marine*, because it viewed *relocations* differently from *reassignments*, and treated only the latter as requiring the union's consent during the term of a contract. Even if we were merely to correct *Los Angeles Marine*'s misapplication of then current Board law, we would find it "well established," in the words of the Board's *University of Chicago* decision, that a midterm relocation such as the one at issue is not a midterm modification within the meaning of §8(d).

As we stated in part II, A, of this decision, however, we agree with the appellate courts, and not the Board, in the *University of Chicago* and *Boeing* cases. We are also not persuaded that work reassignment decisions and relocation decisions should be treated differently for purposes of determining whether there has been a midcontract modification within the meaning of §8(d). Rather, we believe that the same standard applies in both instances, and that the Seventh Circuit correctly stated the governing principles in *University of Chicago*, as follows:

---

can be done directly, i.e., deciding to relocate unit work after bargaining with the Union in good faith to impasse.

The dissent claims that Respondent's work relocation decision would indirectly modify contractual wage rates. Thus, the dissent would imply a work-preservation clause from the mere fact that an employer and a union have agreed on a wage scale. . . . An agreed-upon wage scale, standing by itself, means only that the employer will pay the stated wages to the extent that the employer assigns work to the covered employees.

[U]nless transfers are specifically prohibited by the bargaining agreement, an employer is free to transfer work out of the bargaining unit if: (1) the employer complies with Fibreboard Paper Products v. NLRB, 379 U.S. 203 . . . (1964), by bargaining in good faith to impasse; and (2) the employer is not motivated by antiunion animus, Textile Workers v. Darlington Mfg. Co., 380 U.S. 263 . . . (1965). [514 F.2d at 949.][14]

Consistent with our decision today, we hereby overrule *University of Chicago, Boeing,* and the portion of *Los Angeles Marine* that held that the respondent's transfer of work from one location to another location violated §§8(a)(5) and 8(d).

IV

In *Milwaukee Spring I,* the Board also found that Respondent's laying off employees as a consequence of its relocation decision violated §8(a)(3) notwithstanding that the parties stipulated there was no union animus. Invoking the "inherently destructive" doctrine of *Great Dane Trailers,* the Board apparently held that the 8(a)(3) violation flowed from the finding that the relocation decision violated §8(a)(5). Accepting this logic for the purposes of our decision only, we conclude that, having found that Respondent complied with its [§8(a)(5)] statutory obligation before deciding to relocate . . . , there is no factual or legal basis for finding that the consequent layoff of employees violated §8(a)(3).

V

Los Angeles Marine and *Milwaukee Spring I* discourage truthful midterm bargaining over decisions to transfer unit work. Under those decisions, an employer contemplating a plant relocation for several reasons, one of which is labor costs, would be likely to admit only the reasons unrelated to labor costs in order to avoid granting the union veto power over the decision. The union, unaware that labor costs were a factor in the employer's decision, would be unlikely to volunteer wage or other appropriate concessions. Even if the union offered to consider wage concessions, the employer might hesitate to discuss such suggestions for fear that bargaining with the union over the union's proposals would be used as evidence that labor costs had motivated the relocation decision.

---

[14]The Seventh Circuit decided *University of Chicago* before the Supreme Court decided *First National Maintenance Corp.* We do not here consider the effect of *First National Maintenance* on *Fibreboard.* See fn. 5, supra.

Member Hunter agrees to overrule the Board's 8(d) and 8(a)(5) holdings of *Los Angeles Marine, Boeing,* and *University of Chicago,* but does so for the reasons stated in part II, and finds it unnecessary to reach the matters discussed in part III.

We believe our holding today avoids this dilemma and will encourage the realistic and meaningful collective bargaining that the Act contemplates. Under our decision, an employer does not risk giving a union veto power over its decision regarding relocation and should therefore be willing to disclose all factors affecting its decision. Consequently, the union will be in a better position to evaluate whether to make concessions. Because both parties will no longer have an incentive to refrain from frank bargaining, the likelihood that they will be able to resolve their differences is greatly enhanced.[16]

Accordingly, for all of the foregoing reasons, we reverse our original Decision and Order and dismiss the complaint.

Member ZIMMERMAN, dissenting. . . . [T]wo issues . . . must be decided in each plant relocation case. The first issue is whether an employer has a duty to bargain with a union over its relocation decision, or, in other words, whether the relocation decision is a mandatory subject of bargaining. . . . I would find such decision to be mandatory where the decision is amenable to resolution through collective bargaining. Here, I would find Respondent's decision to relocate its assembly work . . . amenable to resolution through bargaining and thus a mandatory subject of bargaining. The second issue is whether under §8(d) an employer may implement its relocation decision after an impasse in bargaining during the term of the collective-bargaining agreement. . . . I would find that §8(d) prohibits such a relocation of bargaining unit work in the absence of an agreement with the union, but only where the employer's relocation decision is motivated solely or predominantly by a desire to avoid terms of the collective-bargaining agreement. My colleagues and I apparently agree that if a collective-bargaining agreement contains an applicable work-preservation clause, §8(d) requires the employer to obtain the union's consent prior to any transfer of work regardless of the reasons underlying the transfer. The difference . . . between [us] is that I find §8(d) applicable to other contractual terms. Here, as Respondent's decision was motivated solely by its desire to avoid the wage provisions of the contract, I would find that Respondent is prohibited from implementing its decision without the Union's consent during the term of the collective-bargaining agreement. . . .

. . . Although the Supreme Court in *Fibreboard* and *First National Maintenance* did not deal directly with the issue presented here, . . . those decisions strongly suggest that . . . Respondent's decision to relocate its assembly work . . . was a mandatory subject of bargaining.

---

[16] The dissent misreads our decision. In part II, we hold that the relevant portion of §8(d) mandates that we identify a term or condition contained in a contract before finding that an employer modified a contract without union consent. In this part, we point out that our interpretation of §8(d) is consistent with the Act's policy, set forth in §1, of "encouraging the practice and procedure of collective bargaining." . . .

The common thread of both . . . decisions is that bargaining is required where the subject matter is amenable to resolution through the bargaining process. Where, as in *First National Maintenance*, the employer's decision to alter its operation is motivated by "a concern . . . wholly apart from the employment relationship," then bargaining is not required as the union has no control over or authority to affect the employer's concern. . . . [A]s the Court pointed out in *First National Maintenance*, all that a union can do in such cases is to offer advice. Under these circumstances, bargaining would be futile. But where, as in *Fibreboard*, the reasons for an employer's decision are "peculiarly suitable for resolution within the collective bargaining framework," bargaining is required. Thus, the Board in each case must analyze the employer's decision and the reasons underlying it to determine whether the decision is amenable to the resolution through collective bargaining or, in the words of [*First National Maintenance*], whether "the benefit, for labor-management relations and the collective-bargaining process, outweighs the burden placed on the conduct of the business."

I find . . . the instant relocation of work more analogous to the subcontracting decision in *Fibreboard* than the partial closing decision in *First National Maintenance*. . . .

. . . First, as in *Fibreboard*, Respondent's decision to relocate the assembly work would not alter Respondent's basic operation. Respondent would still perform the same amount of assembly work in the same manner. The only change in Respondent's operation would be the location of the work being performed and the employees performing it. Rather than continuing to perform the work in Milwaukee by employees represented by the Union, Respondent would have the work performed in McHenry by nonunion employees. Indeed, Respondent's decision contemplated even less of an alteration of its operation than was present in *Fibreboard* since Respondent, after the relocation, would still retain complete control over the employees performing the assembly work as contrasted with a subcontracting situation where the employees doing the work would be controlled by an altogether different employer. Second, relatively little capital investment was contemplated by Respondent in relocating the work. The only apparent expenditure of funds resulting from Respondent's relocation decision involved the relocation of some equipment from Milwaukee to McHenry, but the record contains no estimate of the cost involved.

Moreover, Respondent's decision to relocate the assembly work would not result in the shutting down of the Milwaukee plant or the sale of Respondent's assets at the Milwaukee plant. The assembly work represented only approximately one-third of the bargaining unit work performed at the Milwaukee plant, and Respondent intended to perform the remainder of the work at Milwaukee. . . . I do not find that Respondent's decision to relocate the valve work involved "a significant investment or withdrawal of capital [which] will affect the scope and ultimate direction of an enterprise." General Motors Corp., 191 N.L.R.B. 951, 952 (1971).

As in *Fibreboard*, Respondent's reasons for relocating the valve work are "peculiarly suitable for resolution within the collective-bargaining framework." The parties stipulated that Respondent's decision to relocate assembly work was motivated solely because of the comparatively higher labor costs at Milwaukee than McHenry. The Supreme Court in both *Fibreboard* and *First National Maintenance* emphasized that a desire to reduce labor costs was amenable to resolution through bargaining. . . . Where, as here, the factors predominantly involved are amenable to collective bargaining, requiring Respondent to bargain over its decision to relocate its valve operation provides benefits for labor-management relations and the collective-bargaining process which outweigh the burden placed on the conduct of its business. Accordingly, I find the decision to be a mandatory subject of bargaining.

I turn now to the issue of whether Respondent is free unilaterally to implement its relocation decision during the term of the collective-bargaining agreement without the Union's consent after bargaining to impasse with the Union. Strong policy arguments lie on both sides of this issue. However, . . . I am persuaded that Congress intended the Act to prohibit such midterm relocations where the employer's relocation decision was motivated solely or predominantly by a desire to avoid terms of a collective-bargaining agreement.

. . . It is well settled, and my colleagues agree, that an employer acts in derogation of its bargaining obligations under §8(d), and thereby violates §8(a)(5), when it makes any midterm change in the contractual wage rate even though the employer's action is compelled by economic necessity[9] or the employer has offered to bargain with the union over the change and the union has refused.[10] Obviously then, my colleagues and I would agree that had Respondent in this case decided to reduce the wages paid to the assembly employees while continuing to perform the assembly work at Milwaukee, Respondent's decision would violate §8(a)(5). Respondent's decision to relocate the assembly work to McHenry would achieve the same result, albeit indirectly: its employees would continue to perform assembly work but at reduced wage rates. . . .

. . . I find that Respondent's midterm relocation decision was proscribed under §8(d). . . . Respondent voluntarily obligated itself to pay a

[9]Oak Cliff-Golman Baking Co., 207 N.L.R.B. 1063 (1973), *enfd.* 505 F.2d 1302 (5th Cir. 1974), *cert. denied* 423 U.S. 826 (1975).
[10]C&S Industries, 158 N.L.R.B. 454 (1966).

certain amount of wages to employees performing assembly work during the term of the contract, and it cannot avoid this obligation merely by unilaterally relocating the work to another of its facilities, just as it could not by unilaterally reducing the wage rate. It is disingenuous to argue . . . that Respondent's relocation decision did not disturb the contractual wages and benefits at the Milwaukee facility. If Respondent had implemented its decision, there would be no assembly employees at the Milwaukee facility to receive the contractual wages and benefits. Rather, all assembly work would be performed at McHenry where Respondent would pay its employees less for the same work. Under these circumstances, my colleagues' conclusion that Respondent left the wage and benefit provisions "intact" at Milwaukee is illogical and without legal significance.

Similarly, their claim that my affirmation of the §8(d) mandate implies a work-preservation clause in virtually every labor contract is equally unfounded. Although a valid work-preservation clause could serve to bar a relocation of bargaining unit work motivated for reasons other than avoidance of contractual terms, that circumstance is unrelated to the instant case. Here, Respondent does seek to modify the contractual wage provision, a result that is prohibited by §8(d) itself and is not dependent on any work-preservation clause. It is hardly "revolutionary," as my colleagues assert, simply to apply the contractual terms to which the parties voluntarily agreed.

. . . [M]y views of the narrow reach of §8(d) bring me into partial agreement with my colleagues in this case. . . . I [too] would not endorse the approach utilized by the Board in its *University of Chicago* and *Boeing* decisions that employer midterm transfers of work abrogate the contractual recognition clause. Such clauses are "merely the parties' descriptive recitation of the physical location of the facilities at the time of the negotiations,"[18] and do not create an implied prohibition against the transfer or relocation of work away from the bargaining unit regardless of the employer's motivation.

Neither do I endorse the Board's decisions in *University of Chicago* and *Boeing* to the extent that the Board found that an employer's midterm relocation decision motivated by reasons unrelated to a desire to avoid the contractual wage rates is proscribed by §8(d). As the motivation for the employers' action in those cases was a desire to increase productivity, I concur in the court opinions in those cases that the employers' actions did not violate §8(d).[19]

---

[18] Los Angeles Marine Hardware Co., 602 F.2d at 1306.

[19] My colleagues' criticism that I have ignored the Board's decision in Ozark Trailers, 161 N.L.R.B. 561 (1966), reveals a misunderstanding of my position. In my view, even if the employer's proposed decision is amenable to resolution through collective bargaining and thus constitutes a subject of mandatory bargaining, an 8(d) violation is not established merely

Eer motive is key!

In my view the determinative factor in deciding whether an employer's midterm relocation decision is proscribed under §8(d) is the employer's motive.[20] Where, as here, the decision is controlled by a desire to avoid a contractual term with regard to a mandatory subject of bargaining, such as wages, then the decision [violates] §§8(d) and 8(a)(5), and the employer may not implement the decision during the term of the contract without the union's consent. But where the decision is motivated by reasons unrelated to contract avoidance, then the employer may unilaterally implement its decision after bargaining to impasse wth the union.[21]

My colleagues claim that this approach encourages employers to deny that a relocation decision is motivated by a desire to reduce labor costs. I disagree. An employer considering relocation to reduce labor costs has substantial incentive to tell the union why it needs relief and how much relief it needs: relocation will usually involve the transfer of equipment and management personnel, as well as the training of new employees to perform the relocated work. An employer who can avoid these kinds of disruption to production by bargaining with the union for contract concessions will likely do so. See [*First National Maintenance*], 442 U.S. at 682. Indeed, Respondent's actions illustrate this point. Respondent, whose relocation decision was admittedly motivated by its desire to reduce labor costs, informed the Union of its plan and its reasons, and engaged in concessions bargaining, which, if successful, would have resulted in the assembly operations remaining in Milwaukee.

Moreover, even assuming that my colleagues' prediction would prove

---

because the reasons underlying the employer's decision are economic; rather, the reasons must amount to the avoidance of a contractual term. Since *Ozark* was not litigated under an 8(d) theory, it is irrelevant to a discussion of the application of §8(d). In any event, it is difficult, if not impossible, to attempt to ascertain some 20 years later whether the employer's decision to close the Ozark plant and subcontract the work was motivated by a desire to avoid any contractual term. The employer's asserted reasons for its action were that "excessive man hours were required for the production of custom refrigerated truck bodies; the truck bodies produced and sold would not perform properly because of defective workmanship, necessitating a return of the bodies to the plant at disastrous expense to Respondents; and the plant facilities were not efficiently laid out." 161 N.L.R.B. at 567-568. Assuming none of these reasons related to a specific contractual term which the employer sought to avoid, the employer would be free to implement its decision after satisfying its bargaining obligations.

[20] See O'Keefe and Tuohey, Economically Motivated Relocations of Work and an Employer's Duties under Section 8(d) of the National Labor Relations Act: A Three-Step Analysis, Fordham Urban Law Journal 795, 842-843 (1982-83). As shown above, motive is also crucial in determining whether an employer's decision is a mandatory subject of bargaining.

[21] Where the employer's decision involves reasons both related to contract avoidance and unrelated to contract avoidance, I would find the decision proscribed by §8(d) only where the reasons related to contract avoidance are predominant.

to be accurate on some occasions under the limited application §8(d) I find in this case, the Board cannot use this reasoning to avoid the application of that section. Before the enactment of §8(d) in 1947, an employer was under a duty, upon request, to bargain with a union over terms and conditions of employment regardless of whether or not an existing collective-bargaining agreement bound the parties as to the terms and conditions to be discussed. See NLRB v. Sands Mfg. Co., 306 U.S. 332, 342 (1938). However, Congress, desiring to end this continuous bargaining, enacted the 8(d) proscription against midterm contract modifications to achieve "peaceful industrial relations" through stable collective-bargaining agreements which guard "the right of either party to a contract to hold firm to the . . . terms or conditions of employment specifically provided for in writing." Equitable Life Insurance Co., 133 N.L.R.B. 1675, 1689 (1961). . . . Under these circumstances, the Board may not undermine the statutory scheme merely because some violators of the Act may not be brought to justice. . . .

NOTES

1. Suppose that Milwaukee Spring had transferred the disputed work to another division of its Milwaukee plant and that otherwise the hypothetical and actual cases were the same. Would a majority of the Board, as then constituted, have necessarily reached the same result in both cases?

2. Do you expect *Milwaukee Spring II* substantially to increase the number of work preservation clauses in collective agreements? Consider footnote 11 of the majority opinion and the Board's subsequent treatment of work relocation in *Otis Elevator II*, supra p. 883.

3. Suppose that the union had invoked the collective agreement (which provided ultimately for arbitration of all questions arising under the agreement) and contended in arbitration that the company had violated an implied provision of the collective agreement. What arbitral award is likely? See *Allis-Chalmers Mfg. Co.*, infra p. 935; Teamsters Local 115 v. DeSoto, Inc., 725 F.2d 931 (3d Cir. 1984). Where the arbitration provision of a collective agreement covers the disputed relocation (and thus statutory and contract issues overlap), the NLRB may defer to arbitration. The Board's deferral doctrines are considered in Chapter 10(C).

4. Is there any justification for finding an implied prohibition against work relocation only when (as Member Zimmerman, dissenting, suggests) the relocation is motivated solely or predominantly by a desire to avoid the terms of the agreement? When relocation is prompted solely by cost savings, consisting primarily of lower labor costs, would the forbidden motive be

present? Is that motive germane under §8(d) rather than §8(a)(3)? Is the employer's motive of immediate interest to the displaced employees? In the longer term, might it chill their "concerted activity"?

5. Assume that the Milwaukee Spring operation was profitable but McHenry was experiencing severe financial difficulties, caused in part by a chronic lack of work. If Milwaukee Spring had bargained to impasse and then transferred the assembly work to McHenry in order to relieve its financial situation, would §8(d) have been violated under the majority's view? Under Zimmerman's view?

6. Did Milwaukee Spring's actions constitute a "repudiation" of its agreement with the union? If not, is it for the reason that the contract itself was not sufficiently clear to avoid a genuine dispute over its treatment of work relocations? Where the basic dispute can fairly be characterized as one of contract interpretation (i.e., no specific and unambiguous provision covers the matter), the NLRB generally would not treat an alleged breach as a "modification" of an agreement and thus a statutory unfair labor practice. Compare Coppus Eng. Corp., 195 N.L.R.B. 595 (1972), and United Tel. Co., 112 N.L.R.B. 779 (1955), with Century Papers, Inc., 155 N.L.R.B. 358 (1965). See also C & S Indus., Inc., 158 N.L.R.B. 454, 458 (1966) ("the breadth of §8(d) is not such as to make any default in a contract obligation an unfair labor practice, for [§8(d)] . . . is in terms confined to the 'modification' . . . of a contract"). Is this approach a sufficient justification for *Milwaukee Spring II?*

7. An employer who bargains to an impasse over a mandatory subject not contained in the contract must ordinarily comply with the notice and waiting periods prescribed by §8(d) before instituting changes. See Huttig Sash & Door Co., 154 N.L.R.B. 811 (1965), *enforced*, 377 F.2d 964 (8th Cir. 1967) (involving reduction of premium wages allegedly in violation of the agreement, which also made wage disputes arbitrable).

8. For consideration of the status of collective agreements in bankruptcy proceedings, see Chapter 10(B)(2).

NLRB v. Lion Oil Co.
352 U.S. 282 (1957)

WARREN, C. J. . . . The sole question [is whether] the requirement of [§8(d)] is satisfied where a contract provides for negotiation and adoption of modifications at an intermediate date during its term, and a strike in support of modification demands occurs after the date on which such modifications may become effective — and after the 60-day notice period has elapsed — but prior to the terminal date of the contract.

On October 23, 1950, respondent Lion Oil Co. and the Oil Workers International Union, CIO, entered into a contract which provided:

This agreement shall remain in full force and effect for the period beginning October 23, 1950, and ending October 23, 1951, and thereafter until canceled in the manner hereinafter in this Article provided.

This agreement may be canceled and terminated by the Company or the Union as of a date subsequent to October 23, 1951, by compliance with the following procedure:

(a) If either party to this agreement desires to amend the terms of this agreement, it shall notify the other party in writing of its desire to that effect, by registered mail. No such notice shall be given prior to August 24, 1951. Within the period of 60 days, immediately following the date of the receipt of said notice by the party to which notice is so delivered, the Company and the Union shall attempt to agree as to the desired amendments to this agreement.

(b) If an agreement with respect to amendment of this agreement has not been reached within the 60-day period mentioned in the subsection immediately preceding, either party may terminate this agreement thereafter upon not less than sixty days' written notice to the other. Any such notice of termination shall state the date upon which the termination of this agreement shall be effective.

On August 24, 1951, the union served written notice on the company of its desire to modify the contract. Negotiations began on the contractual changes proposed by the union. The union members voted for a strike on February 14, 1952, but the strike, thrice postponed as negotiations continued, did not actually begin until April 30, 1952. The union never gave notice to terminate the contract as contemplated by the quoted contractual provision. Therefore, at all relevant times a collective bargaining agreement was in effect. On August 3, a new contract was executed, and the strikers began to return to work the following day. . . .

The Labor Board found that the company was guilty of unfair labor practices under §8(a)(1), (3) and (5) of the Act.[d] The company defended on the ground that the strike, because it occurred while the contract was in effect, was in violation of §8(d)(4). A majority of the Board rejected this defense, holding that "The term 'expiration date' as used in §8(d) (4) . . . has a twofold meaning; it connotes not only the terminal date of a bargaining contract, but also an agreed date in the course of its existence

[d] [The Board had found that the employer had insisted on a one-year no-strike pledge as a condition of accepting the union's settlement offer and that, upon the union's rejection of that condition, had reinstated only those strikers pledging not to strike. See 109 N.L.R.B. 680, 686-688 (1954). — EDS.]

when the parties can effect changes in its provisions." The Board held that since, under the contract in dispute, October 23, 1951, was such an "agreed date," the notice given August 24 followed by a wait of more than 60 days satisfied the statute. . . .

. . . The Court of Appeals set aside the Board's order. 221 F.2d 231. The court held that the "expiration date" of the contract was the date on which all rights and obligations under it would cease; that the second notice required to bring about this termination not having been given, the strike violated §8(d)(4) and the strikers therefore lost their status as employees entitled to the protection of the Act. . . .

. . . [The] ambiguity was recognized by the Joint Committee of Congress created by the very act of which §8(d) was a part to study the operation of the federal labor laws. Members of the [NLRB] . . . have expressed divergent views on the proper construction of §8(d)(4); none of them has taken the position adopted by the court below.[6] . . .

We find our guide to the general context of the statute in *Mastro Plastics*. In that case we recognized a "dual purpose" in the Taft-Hartley Act — to substitute collective bargaining for economic warfare and to protect the right of employees to engage in concerted activities for their own benefit. 350 U.S., at 284. A construction which serves neither of these aims is to be avoided unless the words Congress has chosen clearly compel it. The restriction on employees' concerted activities which would result from the construction placed upon §8(d)(4) by the Court of Appeals is obvious. [Cf. §13 of the Act.] Too, we think it would discourage the development of long-term bargaining relationships. Unions would be wary of entering into long-term contracts with machinery for reopening them for modification from time to time, if they thought the right to strike would be denied them for the entire term of such a contract, though they imposed no such limitations on themselves.

We do not believe that the language used by Congress requires any such result. Section 8(d)(1) provides that no party to an existing collective bargaining contract "shall terminate or modify such contract, unless the party desiring such termination or modification — (1) serves a written notice upon the other party to the contract of the proposed termination or modification sixty days prior to the expiration date thereof. . . ." The phrase "expiration date" is repeated in §8(d)(1) and again in the "whichever occurs later" clause

[6] The Board's original view in Wilson & Co., 89 N.L.R.B. 310, was that §8(d) permitted strikes in support of contract changes any time after 60 days' notice. Member Peterson, concurring specially in the present case, adhered to that view. Member Murdock dissented on the same ground on which he had concurred specially in *Wilson & Co.*, namely, that §8(d) applies only during the period around the termination of a contract.

of §8(d)(4) upon which this case turns. The use of the three words "termination," "modification" and "expiration" is significant. We conceive that a notice of desired modification would typically be served in advance of the date when the contract by its own terms was subject to modification. Notice of desired termination would ordinarily precede the date when the contract would come to an end by its terms or would be automatically renewed in the absence of notice to terminate. Therefore we conclude that Congress meant by "expiration date" in §8(d)(1) to encompass both situations, and the same phrase in §8(d)(4) must carry the same meaning. "Expiration" has no such fixed and settled meaning as to make this an unduly strained reading.

Our conclusion is buttressed by a provision of §8(d) which was added by the Conference Committee. "[T]he duties . . . imposed [by subsections (2), (3) and (4)] shall not be construed as requiring either party to discuss or agree to any modification of the terms and conditions contained in a contract for a fixed period, if such modification is to become effective before such terms and conditions can be reopened under the provisions of the contract." The negative implication seems clear: Congress recognized a duty to bargain over modifications when the contract itself contemplates such bargaining. It would be anomalous for Congress to recognize such a duty and at the same time deprive the union of the strike threat. . . .

The contemporary legislative history manifests no real recognition of the problem before us. . . . Significance must be given to the clause, "or until the expiration date of such contract, whichever occurs later." We believe our construction gives meaning to the congressional language which accords with the general purpose of the Act.

Applying that construction to the facts of this case, we hold that the notice and waiting requirements of §8(d) were fully satisfied. October 23, 1951, was the first date upon which the contract by its terms was subject to amendment. Notice of proposed amendments were served 60 days in advance. The strike did not occur until long afterward. The fact that on October 23 the contract became terminable upon further notice by either party is immaterial. One thing the most authoritative legislative gloss on §8(d), the report of the Senate Committee, makes clear is that the statutory notice requirement operates wholly independently of whatever notice requirement the parties have fixed for themselves. The situation here is not different, so far as the applicability of the statute is concerned, from that of a fixed-term contract with a clause providing for reopening at some specified time.

Nor can we accept respondents' alternative contention that, even apart from §8(d), the strike was in breach of contract and the strikers were for that reason not entitled to relief at the hand of the Board. Respondents rely upon Labor Board v. Sands Mfg. Co., 306 U.S. 332. In *Sands*, as in this case, the contract did not contain an express no-strike clause. Employees there refused in the course of the contract to continue work "in accordance with their contract." Id., at 344. The refusal occurred midway in a fixed-term contract which did not provide for modifications during its term. This Court sustained the propriety of the employer's action in discharging the employees. Here the strike occurred at a time when the parties were bargaining over modifications after notice and in accordance with the terms of the contract. Where there has been no express waiver of the right to strike, a waiver of the right during such a period is not to be inferred. We do not believe that the two-phase provision for terminating this contract means that it was not within the contemplation of the parties that economic weapons might be used to support demands for modification before the notice to terminate was given.

The judgment below is reversed and the case remanded for proceedings in conformity with this opinion.

Brennan, J., took no part in the consideration or decision of this case.

[The separate opinions of Frankfurter, J., and Harlan, J., each concurring in part and dissenting in part, are omitted.]

NOTES

1. Apart from the special problems raised by "mid-term modifications," the §8(d) requirements of notice and waiting periods have generated various questions. See, e.g., Fort Smith Chair Co., 143 N.L.R.B. 514 (1963), aff'd, 336 F.2d 738 (D.C. Cir. 1964) (upholding legality of discharge of strikers whose bargaining representative failed to give prescribed notices to mediation services). In light of Lion Oil, consider (a) which §8(d) requirements would have to be satisfied before a union in a Jacobs or a Milwaukee Spring situation could lawfully strike in support of its bargainable demands, and (b) whether such a strike during the term of the contract would violate a no-strike clause written along the lines of the one included in Article X of the sample agreement in the Statutory Appendix.

See generally Note, Untimely Notice Under Section 8(d)(3) of the Taft-Hartley Act, 47 Va. L. Rev. 490 (1961).

2. A union served a 60-day termination notice pursuant to §8(d)(1). Assume (a) that the union did not serve §8(d)(3) notices until 45 days later, or (b) did not serve them at all. Under §8(d) how long is the employer required to wait before instituting a lockout? In Hooker Chems. & Plastic Corp., 224 N.L.R.B. 1535 (1976), the NLRB held that a lockout within 30 days of a union's untimely filing of notice with the FMCS violates the Act since a 30-day mediation period prior to self-help by either party is statutorily prescribed. The Seventh Circuit denied enforcement, 573 F.2d 965 (1978),

noting that the lockout had occurred after the agreement's expiration and more than 60 days after the union's original §8(d)(1) notice. The court explained that the legislative history relied on by the Board does not support "contorting the plain language of the statute" so as to effectuate the policy — however desirable — of giving mediation services at least 30 days before permitting strikes or lockouts. The court acknowledged that its position barred a strike until 30 days after a union's service of a §8(d)(3) notice while upholding the employer's privilege to lockout earlier, i.e., upon the contract's expiration.

3. Assume that while negotiations are proceeding, the bargaining agreement expires on January 31, 1985. The union strikes, or the employer locks out, without serving the notice provided for by §8(d)(1). Has the Act been violated?

4. Special notice, waiting, and mediation provisions apply to health care institutions. See §§8(d)(4)(A-C), §213 (LMRA); Reed, The NLRA & Health Care Institutions: The Persistent Paradox, 4 Employer Relations L.J. (No.3) 357 (1978-1979). For a study concluding that the notice requirements in the 1974 health care amendments have not eliminated "eleventh hour negotiations" or a "crisis atmosphere," see L. Tanner, H. Weinstein, & A. Ahmuty, The Impact of the 1974 Health Care Amendments to the NLRA on Collective Bargaining in the Health Care Industry (1979). The problems regarding the statutory role of the FMCS in health care labor disputes are suggested by Sinai Hospital v. Scearce, 561 F.2d 547 (4th Cir. 1977); Affiliated Hospitals v. Scearce, 583 F.2d 1097 (9th Cir. 1978).

CHAPTER 10

THE ENFORCEMENT OF COLLECTIVE AGREEMENTS

A. GRIEVANCE-ARBITRATION MACHINERY

1. Introduction

Disputes about rights, duties, and expectancies under a collective agreement or under the practices that grow out of group activity are normal incidents of the workplace. Most such disputes are settled informally, but others involve formal machinery. Approximately 96 percent of collective bargaining agreements provide for the channeling of some, but not necessarily all, such disputes through the grievance-arbitration machinery.[a] Arbitration concerning rights under an existing collective agreement, "rights arbitration," is to be distinguished from a much less frequent type of arbitration, "interest arbitration," which involves the determination of some or all of the terms of a future agreement.

The drafting of contractual provisions establishing grievance-arbitration machinery is affected by the size and nature of the bargaining unit, the parties' total relationship, and their trust of each other and of the arbitration process. The variables caution against efforts to formulate "model clauses."

Nevertheless, there is a common set of problems that a careful draftsman will consider, including the following: (1) the definition of a "grievance"; (2) the standing of union officials and individual employees, jointly or separately, to initiate a grievance; (3) limitation periods for initiating grievances or for resolving them in the various steps of multistep grievance

---

[a] 2 Collective Bargaining Negotiations and Contracts (BNA) No. 879 at 51:5 (Feb. 9, 1979). Although grievance-arbitration procedures have been union innovations, unorganized firms have also established them, sometimes to avert unionization. See Rees, Some Non-Wage Aspects of Collective Bargaining, in The Public Stake in Union Power (P. Bradley ed. 1959). See also Yenney, In Defense of the Grievance Procedure in a Non-Union Setting, 2 Employee Rel. L.J. 434 (1977), replying to Epstein, The Grievance Procedure in the Non-Union Setting: Caveat Employer, 1 Employee Rel. L.J. 120 (1975).

procedures;[b] (4) limitation periods for initiating arbitration; (5) the scope of, and limitations on, the arbitrator's authority[c] with respect to subject matter or remedies; and (6) the appointment of, or the methods for selecting, the arbitrator(s). See the provisions of the illustrative agreement in the Statutory Appendix that accompanies this book.

Most collective agreements provide for ad hoc selection of a single arbitrator. If the parties cannot agree on the arbitrator, an outside agency, such as the Federal Mediation and Conciliation Service or the American Arbitration Association, may be authorized to appoint the arbitrator or to recommend a panel from which the parties choose by alternately striking names or by some other procedure.

Other agreements provide for a tripartite board, which acts by majority vote and which is composed of representatives of each side and a neutral who acts as chairman. This type of arrangement is sometimes viewed as contributing to mediation or informal settlement. The propensity of impartial chairmen to mediate is, however, quite variable. Tripartite boards may also avoid decisions unacceptable to both parties and may save the arbitrator from errors resulting from his lack of knowledge of the plant involved — a purpose that can also be served by a single arbitrator's use of tentative awards. Tripartism has been criticized on the ground that partisan adjudicators have no proper place in a quasi-judicial system and that the need for majority support sometimes forces an impartial arbitrator to agree to an award that he does not consider an appropriate resolution of the dispute. See, e.g., Publishers' Assn. of New York, 36 Lab. Arb. 706 (1961). Tripartite boards seem to be losing favor with the parties as well as arbitrators.

Professor Fuller (Collective Bargaining and the Arbitrator, 1963 Wis. L. Rev. 3, 36-38) suggested an alternative to tripartism, namely, using a single arbitrator but requiring him, before he issues a final award, to submit his proposed award to two persons designated in advance to represent each side and to confer with those designees. Under this alternative, would there be a greater likelihood that the neutral person would be more resistant to changing his award than if he had the other arbitrators' views before drafting a (tentative) award?

---

[b] Typically, grievances are to be considered, if need be, by progressively higher echelons of the union and management, thereby permitting reassessment and adjustment in the light of the different knowledge and perspectives involved in each step. To preserve that advantage and to avoid questions of arbitral jurisdiction, some arbitrators have sustained objections to the injection, during arbitration, of new issues not previously raised in the grievance procedure. See Borg-Warner, 27 Lab. Arb. 580, 584 (1956); but cf. Washington Motor Transport Assn., 28 Lab. Arb. 6 (1956).

[c] The arbitrator is usually restricted to issues arising under the agreement even though the grievance procedure may be open to any complaint without regard to whether it alleges a violation of the agreement.

Some agreements, particularly those applicable to large enterprises and multiemployer bargaining units, provide for a "permanent" umpire or impartial chairman appointed for a fixed term or for so long as neither party requests his removal. Such an arrangement avoids the delays involved in ad hoc selections, educates the umpire about the practices, personalities, and problems involved, and frequently promotes helpful mediation and counseling by the umpire. See generally Killingsworth & Wallen, Constraint and Variety in Arbitration Systems, Proc., 17th Ann. Meeting, Natl. Acad. of Arb. 56 (1964).

There is another arrangement that may reduce delays in ad hoc selection and may achieve to some extent the advantages of a permanent umpire; it consists of a panel of arbitrators who, subject to their availability and continuing acceptability, take cases in rotation. This arrangement has been used where the case load does not warrant a permanent arbitrator or where the parties are unwilling to put all their eggs in one basket even for a short time.

Arbitration proceedings are designed to be more informal than judicial proceedings and are not in general subject to the rules of evidence or the other procedural rules governing actions at law. Nevertheless, objections based on the rules of evidence, such as hearsay, are frequent. Normally arbitrators overrule such objections but indicate that they will "go to the weight." As in other nonjury proceedings, arbitral exclusion of relevant evidence on the basis of "technical" rules is more likely to lead to reversal than is free admission. See, e.g., Harvey Aluminum Inc. v. Steelworkers, 263 F. Supp. 488 (C.D. Cal. 1967) (exclusionary rulings denied a fair hearing). Despite the general consensus in favor of informal and relatively uninhibited hearings, criticism of delays and expense resulting from arbitral failure to keep hearings within bounds has increased.[d]

Among the cost-cutting measures that have developed is "expedited arbitration" for certain classes of disputes. Such procedures may dispense with recording of the proceedings, briefs, or arbitral opinions; they may also substantially shorten the time for taking a grievance to arbitration, scheduling a hearing, and issuing an award. See, e.g., Sandver, Blaine, & Woyar, Time and Cost Savings Through Expedited Arbitration Procedures, 36 Arb. J. 11 (1981), indicating that such procedures are suitable for relatively simple and unimportant issues not warranting a comprehensive opinion. In addition, a small but apparently increasing number of parties are providing for "mediation" as a prearbitral step, with a view to facilitating settlements. Grievance

---

[d]See, e.g., Goldberg, The Mediation of Grievances Under a Collective Bargaining Contract: An Alternative to Arbitration, 77 Nw. U.L. Rev. 270, 272-274 (1982) and Goldberg & Brett, infra p. 992.

mediation as an alternative or preliminary to arbitration is considered later in this chapter.

Arbitrators are drawn from a broad variety of occupations[e] and their competence, values, and styles are quite diverse. They are not bound by prior awards—not even, as a formal matter, those concerned with the same agreement.[f] Their awards are substantially immune from correction by reviewing courts.[g] An arbitrator's desire to preserve his acceptability may, to an uncertain extent, affect a particular decision. Finally, arbitrators, like other adjudicators, have divergent concepts of their role.

One concept is that the arbitrator is "essentially a judge," whose task is to do justice according to the rules imposed by the parties, letting the chips fall where they may. The rival concept is somewhat more elusive but, in general, suggests that the arbitrator will be less constrained by contractual provisions in seeking to achieve "industrial justice" and will also feel freer to mediate and to encourage or pressure the parties to hammer out an accommodation. See Fuller, Collective Bargaining and the Arbitrator, 1963 Wis. L. Rev. 3; Braden, The Function of the Arbitrator in Labor-Management Disputes, 4 Arb. J. (n.s.) 35, 36-37 (1949), summarizing the views of Professor Taylor, the most celebrated exponent of this view of the arbitrator as an "industrial physician." These concepts in practice tend to shade into each other. See Weiler, The Role of the Arbitrator: Alternative Versions, 19 U. Toronto L.J. 16-17 (1969). Plainly, selecting a judge as a model does not resolve the issue, for the arbitrator's model judge may pursue a passive or an active role. Cf. Weiler, Two Models of Judicial Decision Making, 46 Can. Bar Rev. 406 (1968). Furthermore, a sound judicial tradition stresses concern for context, purposes, needs, and consequences in resolving the ambiguities and the gaps that exist in all agreements. See Llewellyn, What Price Contract? An Essay in Perspective, 40 Yale L.J. 704, 722 (1931); Lewis v. Benedict Coal Corp., 361 U.S. 459, 475-476 (1960) (dissenting opinion). Perhaps, in the end, all that can be said in summary is that these two rival views reflect a difference in mood and emphasis with respect to the force to be attached to

---

[e] The majority of arbitrators have been lawyers.

[f] Except in unusual circumstances, an arbitrator will, however, follow an earlier award that involves the same parties and the same agreement and is in point. See Blaw-Knox Company, 50 Lab. Arb. 1086, 1087 et seq. (1968). Furthermore, many opinions cite and distinguish other awards involving other parties, just as judges cite other decisions.

[g] Arbitrators can also insulate their awards from detached professional criticism by not submitting them for publication. Only a small fraction of awards are published. It is, however, not clear whether that result is due to the parties' failure to give the required consent, the arbitrator's lack of interest in publication, or the unwillingness of publishers to reproduce awards that lack any general interest.

contractual provisions, as distinguished from plant practices, bargaining history, a sense of justice and other considerations not captured by contractual language.

In any event, grievance-arbitration machinery, as an adjunct to the collective agreement, has customarily been hailed as a major accomplishment of American industrial relations.[h] That machinery is extremely important to a worker's sense of independence and dignity and to his actual and perceived protection against arbitrary action by supervisors. When coupled with a no-strike clause, as it typically is, that machinery provides both a forum for orderly protest against managerial action and an alternative to strikes and other forms of disruption; it is a substitute not only for litigation but also, and more importantly, for economic warfare.

In addition to providing a channel for orderly protest, arbitration serves other purposes: (1) It frees unions from the need to repudiate the position of individual employees, and managements from the need to undercut supervisors. (2) It enables lower levels of supervision to obtain management's consideration of a problem when intermediate supervision blocks such consideration. (3) It may educate each party about the weaknesses of its own representatives, the erosion of formal rules by practice, the failure of communication within the enterprise or within the union or between the union and management, and the pressures and problems of the other side. (4) It serves as a channel for resolving problems not covered by the agreement. (5) It often gives able and articulate employees an opportunity to show their ability and qualifications for promotion within the union or the company.

The received wisdom about the virtues of grievance arbitration has, however, not gone unchallenged. The late Judge Paul Hays of the United States Court of Appeals for the Second Circuit, formerly an eminent arbitrator and law professor, indicted the entire system, principally on the grounds that most arbitrators are incompetent and that their dependence on the parties for their future employment is incompatible with a fair system of adjudication. See P. Hays, Labor Arbitration: A Dissenting View (1966). We will return to that indictment after presenting a few arbitration awards and related materials dealing with seniority, discharges, and other issues of job protection.

The literature on arbitration is extensive. Among the books relatively general in their approach are F. & E. Elkouri, How Arbitration Works (3d ed. 1973); O. Fairweather, Practice and Procedure in Labor Arbitration (2d ed. 1983); R. Fleming, The Labor Arbitration Process (1965); Arbitration in Practice (A. Zack ed. 1984).

[h] See, e.g., S. Slichter, Trade Unions in a Free Society 12 (1948).

2. Seniority and Job Allocation

"Competitive" seniority involves the use of length of service in a firm or a department in determining the rights of an employee relative to those of other workers in layoffs, recalls, transfers, or promotions. "Benefit" seniority is used in computing the amounts of fringe benefits, such as vacation pay or pensions, due from the employer. Competitive seniority generates considerably more problems in contract administration. In order to reduce such problems, an agreement should specify (1) the employment unit(s) in which seniority credits will accrue, (2) the job claims affected by such credits, and (3) the relative weight to be attached to seniority and other factors, such as ability. Statutes, such as Title VII of the Civil Rights Act of 1964, as amended, or the Military Selective Service Act of 1967, as amended, may of course limit the operation of contractual seniority provisions. Thus, as is true of any legislation significantly affecting employment matters, the parties, in negotiating a collective agreement or an agreement submitting an issue to arbitration, should consider whether to include specific provisions regarding arbitral authority to deal with statutory questions.

Industrial unions strongly rely on comprehensive seniority arrangements in order to reduce arbitrariness in job allocation and to protect employee expectancies. Craft unions controlling access to particular occupations have typically relied less on tight seniority arrangements than on the closed shop and the hiring hall. In such occupations, employees have looked more to the industry than to a particular employer for job security. See Meyers, The Analytic Meaning of Seniority, Proc., 18th Ann. Meeting, Indus. Rel. Research Assn. 194, 197-199 (1965) (suggesting that seniority rules were not invented by labor unions and represent a more general social norm — an "affirmative" expression of a quasi-"property" right — rather than what often constituted their "negative" formal justification, providing a shield against discrimination).

Laupahoehoe Sugar Co.
38 Lab. Arb. 404 (1961)

TSUKIYAMA, Arbitrator: — The issue submitted for arbitration is as follows: Did the Company violate §5-III-(a) of the collective bargaining agreement . . . by its selection of employee Lawrence Ignacio for promotion to the position of Motor Mechanic, Grade 7, over A__I__, an employee with greater length of service with the Company.

Section 5-III-(a) of the Agreement . . . reads: . . .

III. Promotions and Transfers — (a) In making promotions or transfers of employees to vacancies in regular jobs for which application is made, the qualifications of the applicants shall be determined by all relevant factors such as merit, experience, knowledge, ability, physical and mental fitness. If there is no material difference between qualifications of applicants, the one having the greater length of continuous service will be selected. If there is a material difference between qualifications of applicants, the best qualified applicant will be selected.

"Where seniority is qualified by skill and ability, the determination of employee ability is one of the thorniest problems in the application of contract terminology." (Howard — "The Role of the Arbitrator in Determination of Ability" — 12 Arb. J. 14.) This is so because to the union seniority is synonymous with job security for senior employees, whereas management's objective is to secure maximum productive efficiency in its direction of the workforce. Umpire Harry Shulman observed that unions are prone to overstress seniority and minimize merit and ability; conversely, management tends to overemphasize its responsibility to determine merit and ability in subordination of seniority (Ford Motor Co. 1 ALAA ¶67, 269; 2 LA 374). . . . In such instances . . . the ideal role of the arbitrator in reviewing the determination, as . . . expressed by Mr. Howard, . . . should be as follows:

. . . Regard for productive efficiency need not embody disregard for job security; indeed, in individual instances the one may go hand in hand with the other. Within the limits of his interpretive authority, therefore, the arbitrator's role in determining ability should be that of simultaneously resolving the goals of efficiency and security by laying down principles and procedures which assure proper consideration for each objective. . . .

"Seniority" is wholly a creature of agreement; thus, the extent of this "right" must be ascertained from the Agreement. . . .

While the Company may, as a matter of strict law, ignore years of service of applicants during its determination under this Agreement, nevertheless, as a practical matter, the Company would be prudent when making promotions to keep a wary eye focused on the element of seniority, especially where many years separate the junior from the senior, as its determination must be fairly, carefully, objectively and competently made and manifest a "material difference" in favor of the junior that will solidly withstand the test of possible subsequent grievance and arbitration. . . .

Each side attempted to heap the ultimate burden of proof in this matter upon the other. Aside from the Agreement (Sec. 23) which requires the complainant "to present a prima facie case," numerous arbitration decisions may be found to place the burden on one side or the other in this type of hearing. . . . Mr. Howard . . . finds:

> Two widely different schools of thought are found in arbitrator's opinions on this issue: that which would upset company determination only if it had been proved to be arbitrary, capricious, or discriminatory; and that which would demand proof on the part of the Company that the action they took was justifiable.

The first school of thought is based largely on the presumption that management has correctly measured the ability of employees (thus the Union has the burden of proving the Company wrong) whereas the underlying philosophy of the second school is that the senior applicant possesses the necessary ability for the promotion (thus the Company must prove the junior to be superior). To the author, the "burden-on-the-company" position appears to be the more sound but for different reasons, viz., (1) grievance procedure is a method to challenge the correctness of managerial action rather than its bad faith, (2) the burden of defending the determination is placed on that party which can best improve and sharpen the tools of selection, and (3) the arbitrator's authority extends to finding contract violations on other issues, not limited to review for arbitrary, capricious or discriminatory action.

In this case, the Arbitrator cannot place the burden of proof solely on one party or the other. Neither party comes into this arbitration with any presumption in its favor. Under the instant Agreement, each side has its own particular issue to prove if it is to prevail. The Union must prove there was "no material difference" if the Grievant is to prevail; conversely, the Company must prove there was a "material difference" in favor of the junior if its promotion is to be sustained. If at the hearing, the Union puts on a "prima facie case" that the applicants were more or less equal in qualifications, by the very nature of things, it becomes incumbent upon the Company, if it is to ultimately prevail, to clearly justify its determination by proof showing a "material difference" in favor of its promotee. Irrespective of whether it is labelled "burden of proof" or a "shifting burden," in hearings under §5-III-(a) of this Agreement, each side has a duty to establish the truth of its own particular and crucial issue, otherwise it succumbs.

The parties differed as to what the words "material difference" were intended to mean as used in the Agreement, citing dictionary definitions of "material." The Company's observation, that the definition of "material" can be as different as each of the authorities chosen, is well taken. Arbitration decisions on the matter reveal the use of such words as "definite superiority," "visible to the naked eye," "clear, measurable, substantial" (as well as the "head and shoulders" test cited by the Union) in assessing the proper measure of difference, but none of these spring from the exact phraseology found in our Agreement. The wording of our Agreement is rather unique [sic]. . . . The Arbitrator feels that when the parties phrased §5-III-(a) in terms of "material difference in qualifications," it was their intent that the Company was obligated to select for promotion *the best qualified applicant, showing a material difference in qualifications over other applicants*, otherwise, it could not bypass the senior applicant. If the parties intended that seniority would prevail if the relative qualifications of applicants were only "equal," or "substantially equal," they should have so worded it. . . .

A. *Union's Case*. The Union's case rides on the shoulders of witnesses Fujisawa and De Mattos. Both were senior Journeymen Grade 9 mechanics, both were familiar with the job specs for Grade 5 and Grade 7 work, and both had supervised Grievant and Ignacio at Grade 5 work. The witnesses concluded that based on the factors set forth in the Agreement (plus others), the Grievant was more or less equal to Ignacio as to qualifications excepting that Grievant held the edge in physical fitness and experience, and that Grievant could perform the Grade 7 job just as well as Ignacio. This was their opinion notwithstanding Ignacio's technical school training which they found was apparent in his work. Witness Masaki, also a Journeyman Grade 9, did not have Ignacio work under him so no comparative opinion was possible. Grievant himself also testified, but no significant weight can be given to his own assertions of competency for the promotion.

. . . [T]he Union's case for Grievant could have been improved with some specific illustrative requirements of the Grade 7 job but what was offered was ample. The testimony came from immediate superiors, both of whom worked several years as Grade 7 mechanics and were familiar with the job requirements, and they testified there was not much difference between Grade 7 and Grade 5 (the job both applicants were observed in). . . . All of the factors listed in the Agreement ("merit, experience, etc.") were covered in their opinion. They had supervised both applicants from periods of 1 1/2 to 3 years giving them adequate basis for observation and a firm foundation for their opinion; they were more intimately acquainted with the relative qualifications of the applicants than the Arbitrator ever would be. Their testimony is unrefuted. . . .

The Company did show that Ignacio generally had better high school grades than Grievant, although it is clear that scholastic records are not basic indicia of "knowledge" and "mental fitness," particularly as related to the requirements of Grade 7 work. Grievant obviously did not have the benefit of 2 years technical school training as did Ignacio but acquired his "experience" in the shop "the hard way" over 2 1/2 years. This point was the factual crux of this case. Evidence of a single reprimand of minor nature registered against Grievant before he entered the garage should not be considered of weighty negative import here. A more serious consideration is whether Grievant's refusal to participate in a "demonstration of ability" based on the Union's objection to nonbargained for piecemeal "testing," should be held against Grievant. . . . [A] "demonstration" offered by the Company at the fourth step of grievance and after the selection is made comes, as a practical matter, "too little, too late." . . . [S]uch "demonstration" should have been incorporated as part of the Company's initial process of selection. The Arbitrator definitely disagrees with the Company wherein it states on page 6 of its Answering Brief: "The Company, under its contract with the Union, cannot insist on any employee participating in such an outside demonstration of ability, nor are we permitted to make testing a prerequisite for applications for job openings." As will be more specifically discussed hereafter, *the Company is entitled to employ any method in its determination of relative ability* as long as the method (including testing) is reasonable, fair, sufficiently related to job requirements and administered without discrimination. Since it is the Company's sole right to judge ability initially, *its use of testing techniques does not require Union concurrence* . . . and *an applicant who refuses to participate in a test of ability forfeits his right to be considered for the vacancy.*

A "prima facie case" is defined as "one which is established by sufficient evidence, and can be overthrown only by rebutting evidence adduced on the other side" (Black's Law Dictionary (3rd Ed.) p. 1414). When it rested, the Union had made out such a "prima facie case" to the extent that the Arbitrator found there was no material difference between the qualifications of the Grievant and Ignacio in March 1961 for the Grade 7 vacancy.

B. *Company's Case.* . . . Section 5-III-(a) does not specify *how* the Company is to determine qualifications of applicants. In the absence of any contract provision specifying how ability is to be determined, since it is incumbent upon the Company to determine the relative abilities of applicants in some manner, the Company may use any method or methods of determination it chooses, so long as it is not unfair or discriminatory and does not ignore factors relevant to the job in question. . . . The following have been upheld as proper methods employed by management in discharging their obligation to judge relative abilities of applicants: (1) Tests or Examinations. . . . (2) Trial or Break-In Periods. . . . (3) Performance or Merit Rating. . . . (4) Supervisory Opinion. . . .

The foregoing methods are by no means exclusive, but the authorities indicate them to be the methods most relied upon by management in determining ability.

The Arbitrator had difficulty in following the Company's theory of the case, primarily because no evidence was put in the record as to *how* the Company made its determination of promotability in the first instance. As previously discussed, the Company proposed a "demonstration of ability," but this came during the grievance procedure and was not a part of the initial selection process. In June 1961, the Company instituted a performance rating system in the Garage where all Grade 5 mechanics were rated by 5 supervisors. When the recapitulated rating sheet prepared by the Company for grievant and Ignacio only was denied admission as not meeting the rule of "best evidence," the Company declined to produce the original rating sheets or to call the 5 supervisors to testify on grounds that the rating results were "confidential." Even if this evidence came in, it would have to be given little weight because *the ratings were made 3 months after the selection of Ignacio and were not relied upon in comparing the applicants in March 1961. . . .*

In response to the Arbitrator's inquiry, the official conducting the Company's case stated that the final selection of Ignacio was made by the Garage Superintendent upon advice of his supervisors. But neither the Superintendent nor any of the garage supervisors appeared or testified at the hearing at all! The only person who appeared from the Company was its Industrial Relations Director. A review of his testimony shows that he himself did not make the determination to promote Ignacio nor did he state how the determination was made on behalf of the Company and what factors were considered. In summary, then, *the record in this hearing does not show what method or procedure was used or relied on by the Company in March 1961 in selecting Ignacio for the promotion or that the Company attempted to comply with the provisions of Section 5-III-(a) of the Agreement in making the promotion. . . .*

Since this record shows little or no evidence as to *who* made the selection, *how* it was made, and *what factors* were considered by that person in making the selection (other than Ignacio's vocational training), the promotion of Ignacio must be set aside.

The Company argues that the "who-how-what" aspects of determining promotability are not relevant or material in this hearing, as indicated in its Answering Brief: . . .

> The Company made no particular effort to put into the record the procedures followed in making the selection on March 20, nor was any particular effort made by the Company to isolate the factors which were considered at that time. It is the Company's position that there is only one question before the arbitrator — was or was not Mr. Ignacio sufficiently better qualified — not what the Company used in making their determination. . . .

With this position the Arbitrator cannot agree. . . . All of the authorities reviewed speak in terms of *a review of management's determination* by the arbitrator. The arbitrator's function is thus explained:

> In such cases (where the Company's judgment is attacked) the arbitrator's function is to decide whether the means or method used by the Company in arriving at its judgment was fair and objective. Generally, this requires a showing: (1) That the Company's judgment, made through its supervisory staff with knowledge of the facts, was based upon definitive and objective standards and criteria; (2) That these standards and criteria were fairly evaluated, fairly considered and equally applied in the case of each applicant; and (3) That the judgment was arrived at without bias, prejudice or discrimination. (Imperial Paper & Color Corp., 4 ALAA 68, 817.)

The arbitrator himself, then, does not hear the case "de novo," weigh the relative qualifications of applicants and determine promotability; nor is he authorized to substitute his own judgment for that previously made by the management. . . .

While arbitration may be the last step in the grievance under our Agreement, the rule in arbitration is clear that qualifications of applicants are to be determined prior to the promotion. . . .

Finally, it was quite apparent the Company was attempting to show that it relied heavily (almost exclusively it appeared) on Ignacio's technical school training in deciding he was the superior applicant. Mr. Pittman and Mr. Carter were called in to show, among other things, "the full value of a technical school education" and "to support the Company's position by outside, impartial witnesses." . . . Even the Union conceded that Ignacio's training probably accounted for his rapid rise through training stages to the Grade 5 level. The critical question which both intrigues and plagues the Arbitrator here is whether, after rapidly ascending to the Grade 5 level, the "law of diminishing returns" had set in as to Ignacio's vocational training (as the Union contends), or that the benefits of such training are still manifest in his work performance so that he will continue to ascend with facility to higher levels of the trade series (as the Company contends). But these "outside" witnesses were not familiar with operations of a sugar plantation garage and were in no position to answer this question and to state that Ignacio's training *in fact* rendered him better qualified than Grievant to perform the specific requirements called for by the Grade 7 job at this Company. In the Arbitrator's opinion, only an "inside" witness, i.e., someone from the Company Garage, who observed the applicants at work and who knew the requirements of Grade 7 work, could have competently and authoritatively evaluated the effect of Ignacio's training as correlated to the job to be filled. . . .

The only direct correlation between Ignacio's training and the requirements of the Grade 7 job was made in the Company's second Reply Brief after the hearing. The Brief itemized the important requirements of the Grade 7 job and then indicated that Ignacio was trained at technical school in those same subjects. . . . [I]t was an excellent job of equating technical training to the job itself. Unfortunately, this was done by final argument and not as proof in evidence. Post-hearing briefs are designed to invite argument on the evidence; its contents do not constitute evidence itself. Had this training-to-job correlation come from the lips of the Garage Superintendent and placed in the record as evidence, the Arbitrator would have had no difficulty in upholding the promotion of Ignacio. The Company may insist that both the jobs specs for Grade 7 and Ignacio's Training Record are in evidence and comparison may be made therefrom. But it is not for this Arbitrator, an utter layman on the subject of mechanics who never set foot inside the Company Garage, to forge that connecting link between the training record and the job itself on the basis of these two documents alone. . . .

It is hoped that this decision will not be regarded as an overly "technical" one. The relaxing of technical rules of evidence authorized by §23 of the Agreement does not permit the Arbitrator to overlook the omission of evidence which is basic to a case. In the very next line of §23, the Arbitrator is mandated *to decide the case in the light of the whole record and upon the weight of all substantial evidence presented.* Accordingly, the Arbitrator finds that the Company failed to show that there was a material difference between the qualifications of the applicants in favor of Ignacio, therefore, the promotion of Ignacio to Motor Mechanic Grade 7 must be set aside and the Grievant be promoted to said position on the basis of his greater seniority.

C. *Back Pay.* The Union requests that the Grievant be awarded back pay retroactive to the date of selection if it prevails here. . . . The general theory of damages is to "make whole" a party who has been injured as a result of contract violations (International Harvester Co. 15 LA 1). The company should realize that a promotion not made in accordance with the contract involves a risk of financial loss. On the other hand some decisions have denied back pay where the company acted in good faith and made an honest effort to comply with the contract. . . . [T]here is also a duty upon the employee to render damages as light as possible. The Company protested for the record that the arbitration was heard 130 days after the arbitrator was appointed whereas the Agreement requires the hearing to be fixed within 30 days after such appointment. . . . It has been the customary practice for attorneys for both industry and labor to set a hearing date with concurrence of the arbitrator even though the date exceeded the 30-day limitations. The hearing date is adjusted to a considerable backlog of pending arbitrations between the same attorneys. The Union here had assumed that an attorney would represent the Company which is usually the case, but it was not until October 3, 1961 thereabouts that the Union learned that the Company was not employing an attorney to handle this case. The Company representative at this time raised the jurisdictional point that the Union had waived its right to arbitrate due to the long delay. At a prehearing conference with the Arbitrator, the parties mutually agreed that the delay would not constitute a bar to the hearing, but this lapse of time does bear upon the determination of back pay. Where misunderstandings such as herein involved delay an arbitration, it is difficult to lay fault exclusively at the door of one party only. The Company should have objected as soon as the 30 days had lapsed and not waited until the eve of arbitration to protest. The Union, representing the complaining party, should make every effort to conclude arbitrations promptly and to mitigate damages. The Arbitrator is mindful of the Union's letter dated July 7, 1959 exhorting all arbitrators to conclude arbitrations expeditiously. Considering all circumstances, the Arbitrator will make an award of partial back pay and require the Company to pay Grievant the difference between the Grade 5 and Grade 7 . . . pay rates computed from the date Grievant filed this grievance until July 10, 1961 (. . . 30 days after notice of the arbitrator's appointment).

NOTES

1. Did the arbitrator in the principal case reflect a clear understanding of the function served by allocating the burden of persuasion? In an extremely close case, is such an allocation avoidable? Even in such cases, arbitrators are reluctant to confront the allocation problem. In light of the considerations normally underlying the allocation of that burden and the arbitrator's need for acceptability, do you have an explanation for that reluctance?

2. Even though contract language attempts to give substantial weight to ability, is there something about the nature of seniority that virtually assures its securing great, and possibly excessive, weight in arbitration? Would deference to seniority tend to be even stronger if the senior grievant appears in the arbitration proceeding while the junior competitor does not? In a society strongly committed to productivity because, e.g., of increased fears of foreign competition, is it likely that seniority would get less weight?

3. Assume that a junior employee grieves to the union that his qualifications were materially superior to those of a senior employee designated for

promotion by the employer. Under an agreement like that in the principal case, what obligations, if any, have the employer and union, respectively, to the grievant? Cf. Belanger v. Matteson, 115 R.I. 332, 346 A.2d 124 (1975); Smith v. Hussman Refrigerator Co., noted infra p. 1161. See also Newspaper Guild, Local 35 (Communication Workers), 239 N.L.R.B. 1321 (1979) (union, without seeking views of junior employee, may lawfully interpret clause requiring promotions primarily by seniority where "qualifications are relatively equal" as giving controlling effect to seniority when both applicants are "minimally qualified").

4. One arbitral battleground is whether tests selected unilaterally by an employer to assess relative ability are sufficiently job-related. See Rollins Environmental Services, 75 Lab. Arb. 655 (1980). Questions also arise regarding the union's rights to participate in choosing a test, administering it, or evaluating its results. See, e.g., Lovejoy, Inc., 74 Lab. Arb. 811 (1980). As noted earlier, employer obligations in this context flow from §8(a)(5) as well as from the agreement. See Detroit Edison Co. v. NLRB, supra p. 821. Similarly, Title VII of the Civil Rights Act of 1964 has restricted the use of tests that have a disparate impact on members of groups accorded special protection under that Act.

The overlap of contractual and statutory issues raises a more general question implicated throughout this chapter — that is, the relevance of external law to arbitration under collective agreements. See especially Chapter 10(C).

Allis-Chalmers Mfg. Co.
39 Lab. Arb. 1213 (1962)

SMITH, Arbitrator: — . . . [T]he Union protests the contracting out of certain work. Grievance No. 1802-59-B concerns the use of an outside contractor to perform certain janitorial work. . . . Grievance No. 1183-262-A concerns two "subcontracts" for production work. One was for the manufacture of certain "operating mechanisms," which were components of power transformers. The other was for the manufacture of certain "stationary contacts," which were components of electrical equipment.

With respect to Grievance No. 1802-59-B, the parties stipulated as follows at the hearing: . . . "[O]n October 29 and 30, 1960, the Company called in an outside contractor, Don's Window Cleaning Company, to have janitorial work performed in the plant. . . . This work was normally and customarily performed by employees in the bargaining unit. At [that] time . . . there were employees from the bargaining unit on layoff."

The outside contractor used some 35 employees to perform this work, totaling approximately 435 man hours, of which 40% to 50% consisted of floor cleaning. . . . [This work] was performed on the second and third floors of the main office building. A number of office areas were being moved or relocated. . . . These moves were determined upon a week or ten days prior to the weekend of October 29 and 30. Involved in connection with the moves were the relocation of partitions, partition washing, floor scrubbing, light cleaning, the washing of partition windows and the inside of "outside" windows, and the moving of furniture, file cabinets, and drawing tables. It was necessary to coordinate the floor cleaning with the movement of the partitions and the various items of furniture and other equipment.

With respect to Grievance No. 1183-262-A, the parties stipulated as follows at the hearing: . . .

> [T]he manufacture of operating mechanisms was previously performed by unit employees. In connection with this subcontract, the Company furnished the subcontractor with jigs, perishable tools and fixtures or funds for the manufacture, modification or procurement of tools which the Company would have manufactured, modified or procured had it done the work in its own shops.
>
> The stationary contacts . . . included those fabricating operations which had previously been done regularly by unit employees in connection with this subcontract. The Company furnished the subcontractor with tools, including perishable tools, fixtures, and funds for the manufacture of tools, some of which the Company would have had available if the work had been done in its shops. . . . [A]t the times stated . . . there were unit employees on layoff or transfer out of the departments involved.

. . . The "operating mechanisms" operate the tap changing mechanism of a power transformer. In August, 1961, the mechanism was redesigned, and the first nine required thereafter were manufactured in the Company's shops in November or December, 1961. The next required lot consisted of 33 mechanisms. Outside bids were obtained for their manufacture, exclusive of the steel castings which were to be purchased by the Company from an outside source, as in the past, but including some tooling to be supplied by the Company, and a contract for the work was let to Kramer Industries. Kramer's bid was $175 each for the work it was to do. Taking into account the cost of the castings and of the tooling, the Company thus acquired the mechanisms for a cost of $197.90 each, as compared with a cost of $490 each for the nine mechanisms which had been manufactured in the Company's shops.

. . . Prior to the protested ["stationary contacts"] subcontract, the

Company had performed certain preliminary operations on the contacts, then contracted out the assembly and brazing . . . , and thereafter had completed the forming operation in the Company's shops. The total time consumed in the operation was at least 120 days. It was decided to have the parts made complete by the outside contractor. Procurement time was reduced to a 60-day cycle (and later to 30 days), and the average cost was reduced from $3.37 per piece to $2.02 per piece. The outside contractor was Fansteel Metallurgical Corporation. . . .

The initial question . . . is whether, as the Company contends, the . . . grievances fall outside the jurisdictional authority of the Referee. The Company relies upon Paragraph 167 of the Agreement, which provided as follows:

> The jurisdictional authority of the Impartial Referee is defined as and limited to the determination of any grievance which is a controversy between the parties or between the Company and employees covered by this agreement concerning compliance with any provision of this agreement and is submitted to him consistent with the provisions of this agreement.

The Company notes that the first step of the grievance procedure contemplates that an employee may present "any grievance concerning his employment," but asserts that this provision is much broader than the "arbitration clause" above quoted in that the latter limits arbitrable grievances to those which allege a violation of some express provision or provisions of the Agreement. The Company reasons that, inasmuch as the claim of the Union does not rest on any specific provision of the Agreement relating to the matter of subcontracting (or, more accurately, contracting out) of work encompassed by the defined bargaining unit, but, instead, rests on alleged implications derived from a composite of provisions (the definition of the bargaining unit, specified wage rates, seniority, etc.), the Referee has no jurisdiction.

This contention . . . is without merit and must be rejected. Without elaborating the point, it seems . . . that the Company is reading into Paragraph 167 a limitation which is not there. The Paragraph does not state that a grievance must concern and involve a "provision" which explicitly touches the subject matter of the grievance. It simply says, in effect, that the grievance must involve a controversy concerning compliance with "any provision" of the Agreement. This language does not foreclose the consideration of a claim based on the theory that one or more cited provisions of the Agreement give rise to an implied limitation or restriction on managerial action. There can be no doubt that in the area of contractual obligations generally it is frequently necessary, in order to give effect to the intent of the parties, to determine whether the specific provisions of the agreement, fairly and properly construed, import obligations not specifically stated. This is true at least as much in the case of labor agreements as in the case of other kinds of contracts.

The Referee therefore concludes that the instant grievances present claims which are within his jurisdiction to decide. The basic issue is whether, from the provisions defining the bargaining unit, specifying the wage structure, providing seniority rights, and otherwise providing rights and benefits to employees, there arises an implied prohibition upon the contracting out of work of kinds normally and customarily done by employees in the bargaining unit. This is a contention which involves a controversy concerning compliance with a provision of the Agreement alleged to be implicit in the specified provisions.

Insofar as the Union's case is predicated . . . on the broad proposition that the labor agreement, taken as a whole or in the light of the specific provisions cited, gives rise to an implied absolute and unqualified prohibition upon the contracting out of work normally and customarily performed by employees in the bargaining unit, the contention must be dismissed as untenable. The Referee . . . in Referee Case No. 8, Springfield Works, . . . stated:

> The Referee . . . is unable to accept as sound the broad proposition asserted by the Union that an absolute prohibition upon the contracting out of work done by bargaining unit employees can properly be implied from the "recognition," "wage" and "seniority" provisions of the contract. None of these provisions literally, historically, or in context is a guarantee to employees in the defined bargaining unit that the work which was there when the unit was first recognized will continue to be there. Rather, they assure that, insofar as persons are employed by the Company to perform work of the kinds which are included within the defined unit, there will be recognition by the Company of the Union as the bargaining representative of such persons, and that such persons will be entitled to the benefits of the wage, seniority, and other provisions of the labor agreement.

The Referee adheres to this position. Insofar as UAW v. Webster Electric Company, 299 F.2d 195, held otherwise, the Referee, with deference, disagrees. . . . The Court in that case predicated its ruling on what it conceived to be the import of the "union shop" provision of the labor agreement. . . . [A]n absolute prohibition on contracting out cannot properly be implied from such a provision. Moreover, the decision there reached was based upon the Court's interpretation of the agreement which was before it, an interpretation with which other federal and state courts, by the way, have disagreed. See, for example, Amalgamated Assn. of Street, Electric Railway and Motor Coach Employees, Division 1326 v. Greyhound Corporation, 231 F.2d 585. For a discussion of the judicial decisions on this subject, see 57 Am. Law Reports, Annotated, 2d series, p. 1399. It is there stated:

It has been generally held, that, at least in the absence of bad faith on the part of the employer, a collective labor agreement which contains no express prohibition against an employer's hiring an independent contractor for the performance of work formerly done by employees covered by the contract does not preclude the employer from hiring an independent contractor to do such work.

On a question of contract interpretation of this kind, . . . no fundamental rule or principle of federal law is involved, which becomes binding upon an arbitrator. The parties in the *Webster* case, as in the other cases cited, sought the aid of a judge in the interpretation of their respective labor agreements. This they received. In an arbitration case the parties seek the interpretation of their agreement by an arbitrator. So long, at least, as the issue is not resolved at the highest judicial level (by the United States Supreme Court) on the basis that some rule of federal substantive law requires a certain interpretation of certain provisions of the labor agreement, the arbitrator (no more and no less a judge) is entitled and expected to make his own determination concerning the issue of contract interpretation which is presented to him for decision. . . .

Little would be gained by attempting, here, to analyze the reported decisions. . . . As Bethlehem Steel Company Umpire Ralph T. Seward stated in 30 LA 678 . . . :

Beyond revealing that other companies and unions have faced this same question of implied obligations — have presented similar arguments and voiced similar fears — the cases show little uniformity of either theoretical argument or ultimate decision. . . . Within each group of decisions, moreover, there are conflicts of principle and approach. The Umpire has returned from his exploration of the cases a sadder — if not a wiser — man. . . .

The present Referee, while rejecting the Union's view that there exists an absolute (implied) prohibition on the contracting out of work of kinds regularly and normally performed by bargaining unit employees, likewise rejects the Company's view that it has complete freedom in this respect. In the *Springfield* case he indicated that "a standard of 'good faith' may be applicable, difficult of definition as this may be." Upon further reflection, he is prepared now to say that he thinks this standard is implicit in the union-management relationship represented by the parties' Agreement, in view of the quite legitimate interests and expectations which the employees and the Union have in protecting the fruits of their negotiations with the Company.

"Past practice" in subcontracting for services and for the manufacturing of components may properly be taken into account as a factor negating the existence of any broad, implied limitation on subcontracting, but not as eliminating the restriction altogether. Moreover, an unsuccessful Union attempt to negotiate into the contract specific restrictions on subcontracting, as was the case in the parties' negotiations of their 1959-1961 Agreement, is likewise a fact which may help to support the claim that the parties have recognized that the Company has substantial latitude in the matter of sub-contracting. Yet it would be unrealistic to interpret futile bargaining efforts as meaning the parties were in agreement that the Agreement implies no restriction at all. Parties frequently try to solidify through bargaining a posi-tion which they could otherwise take, or to broaden rights which otherwise might arguably exist. Thus, the Referee does not find either in the evidence of past practice, here adduced or in the history of the negotiations of the 1959-1961 Agreement, a satisfactory basis for concluding that the Company has complete, untrammeled freedom in the matter of subcontracting. Nor, incidentally, does he attach any special significance to the decisions of the [NLRB] holding that the matter of subcontracting is a "bargainable" issue under the [NLRA]. The parties did bargain on this subject without reaching agreement on any specific provision for inclusion in their Agreement. The question here is whether the Agreement they reached may properly be said to imply some kind of limitation on the Company's freedom to subcontract. In the Referee's judgment, some limitation may properly be implied, narrow though it may be.

Real difficulty arises, however, in attempting to lay down a set of specific criteria to be used in determining whether, in a subcontracting situation, an employer has acted in bad faith. . . . In general, it seems . . . that "good faith" is present when the managerial decision to contract out work is made on the basis of a rational consideration of factors related to the conduct of an efficient, economical operation, and with some regard for the interests and expectations of the employees affected by the decision, and that "bad faith" is present when the decision is arbitrary (i.e., lacks any rational basis) or fails to take into account at all the interests and expectations of employees affected. Without attempting anything like a complete "catalog," the following would appear, at least prima facie, to be instances of bad faith: (1) To negotiate a collective agreement . . . covering classifications of work while withhold-ing from the Union the fact that the employer contemplates, in the immedi-ate future, a major change in operations which will eliminate such work; (2) entering into a "subcontracting" arrangement which is a subterfuge, in the sense that the "employees" of the ostensible "subcontractor" become in substance the employees of the employer; (3) the commingling of employees of a subcontractor, working under a different set of wages or other working conditions, regularly and continuously with employees of the employer performing the same kinds of work; (4) contracting out work for the specific purpose of undermining or weakening the Union or depriving employees of employment opportunities. On the other hand, the Referee does not consider that it is per se arbitrary, unreasonable, or an act of bad faith to contract out work primarily to reduce production costs. After all, a prime managerial obligation is to conduct an efficient and profitable enterprise, and doing so serves, in the long run, the best interests of employees as well as stockholders.

The observations made above do not resolve cases. The facts of the particular case must be examined, especially in relation to the considerations underlying the managerial decision to contract out the work in question. Of necessity, the Referee, having taken the position that the managerial discretion is subject to the implied limitation that it must be exercised in good faith, cannot escape the necessity and responsibility for making a judgment on this matter. As a matter of procedure, it seems evident that management should explain *why* it made the decision, and that it is then appropriate for the Union to attempt either to show that the considerations motivating the decision, as disclosed by management, indicate bad faith, or else that other considerations of a kind indicating bad faith in fact motivated the decision.

PARTICULAR GRIEVANCES

(1) *The "janitorial" work.* The only part of [this] work . . . protested is floor cleaning. Company testimony is to the effect that this work (in addition to other work) was "let" to the outside contractor, rather than assigned at least in part to bargaining unit employees, on an overtime basis, because of these considerations: (1) The necessity of insuring that the work would be completed over the weekend; (2) lack of certainty as to when the floor washing would take place; (3) lack of certainty as to how many people would be required to do such work; (4) the difficulty of getting unit personnel to come in "on emergencies" or on overtime; (5) the inability of some of the unit personnel to handle "scrubbing machines"; (6) the necessity of coordinating the floor cleaning with the moving and other operations involved; (7) the limitations, under State law, of the number of hours which women could be required to work consecutively; and (8) safety factors. Economic considerations, such as the overtime premium payments which would have been required, were not, apparently, involved in the determination.

The Union does not claim that these considerations were not the factors motivating the decision. Its claim is that the Company judgment concerning some of them (e.g., the difficulty of coordinating the work of Company employees with the work of employees of the outside contractor) was unsound. It seems to the Referee, however, that the factors which management took into account were within the range of considerations which could rationally be taken into account, and that there is no evidence that the total judgment reached was either arbitrary or unreasonable, or failed to take into account the natural desires of unit personnel to avail themselves of an overtime opportunity. On the whole, the conclusion must be that there is no evidence of bad faith.

(2) *The contracting out of work on components.* . . . Company testimony indicates that the primary reason for the subcontracting to Kramer Company was economic — i.e., the fact that the price for the component as bid by the contractor, taken together with other applicable cost factors, would be substantially lower than the costs previously experienced by the Company in manufacturing the mechanism. Another consideration was apparently the fact that, according to the Company, planned time schedules were not met in connection with its earlier manufacture of this component.

. . . Company testimony is to the effect that the primary consideration motivating the decision to have Fansteel Metallurgical Company process the components, complete, was the shorter procurement cycle which would and did result, namely, 60 days as compared with 120 days under the prior practice. In addition, according to the Company, the unit cost was reduced from $3.37 to $2.02.

The Union does not contend that these considerations did not, in fact, motivate the decisions to contract out the work in question. . . .

As in the case of the janitorial work, the Referee concludes that the considerations which management took into account, although in these instances primarily or partially economic, indicate that its decisions were not arbitrary or unreasonable, and were not taken in bad faith. No ulterior purpose is indicated in terms either of the status of the Union or of employees in the bargaining unit, nor is there any showing, if this has relevance, that the effect of such subcontracting was to curtail bargaining unit jobs in any substantial way. The Referee repeats that, in his view, cost considerations as a basis for subcontracting, do not of themselves, necessarily indicate bad faith. Manufacturing operations commonly involve some contracting out or purchasing of components, or work thereon, and considerable flexibility in this regard is to be expected in the interest of an efficient and economically sound enterprise. It may fairly be presumed, indeed, that the Company on occasion takes contracts to supply components, or to perform work on components, for other manufacturing concerns. The existence of a substantial degree of managerial discretion, therefore, does not necessarily harm the employees. . . . They may actually gain thereby, rather than lose, in their over-all employment opportunities.

NOTES

1. Could the union in the principal case have secured any relief from the NLRB because of the employer's contracting out?

2. In a subcontracting case in which the employer's actions resulted in a loss of unit jobs, the arbitrator declared: ". . . [C]ontracting out of unit work merely because someone else will do it cheaper constitutes an improper evasion of contractual obligations and, in that sense, it does not matter whether the company acted in good faith or bad faith since the result is the same." Mead Corp., 75 Lab. Arb. 665, 667 (1980). Can this view be reconciled with the *Allis-Chalmers* analysis?

3. When the *Steelworkers* trilogy is reached (infra pp. 976-990), consider further Arbitrator Smith's view on the effect of judicial precedents on an arbitrator's autonomy.

4. The reasoning behind implied restrictions on contracting out is challenged in American Sugar Refining Co., 37 Lab. Arb. 334, 337 (1961). See also Sears, Roebuck & Co. v. Teamsters Local 243, 507 F. Supp. 658 (E.D. Mich. 1981) (specific contractual coverage of subcontracting bars an arbitrator from adding an implied condition that the employer's cost reduction must be weighed against the adverse impact on the bargaining unit).

5. An arbitrator faces the question of whether an employer has the right to transfer production from an obsolescent plant in New York to a more efficient plant in North Carolina, with resultant layoffs in New York. The collective agreement covering the New York plant is silent with respect to work transfers but contains a recognition clause, a clause barring discharge without just cause, and a clause barring layoffs "except for lack of work." (a) What award? (b) Would it be material if the employer was in financial distress? (c) Would your answer be affected if the employer terminated the New York operation and did not transfer the work, or if the transfer occurred soon after collective negotiations that did not mention transfer? Cf. Kenton Mfg. Co., 76 Lab. Arb. 817 (1981). Consider also *Milwaukee Spring II*, supra p. 901.

6. Developments in the arbitration of subcontracting disputes are traced in Sinicropi, Revisiting an Old Battleground: The Subcontracting Dispute, Proc., 32d Ann. Meeting, Natl. Acad. of Arb. 125 (1979).

3. Discharge and Discipline

Grief Bros. Cooperage Corp.
42 Lab. Arb. 555 (1964)

DAUGHERTY, Arbitrator: — . . . "Did the Company have just and proper cause for discharging grievant X___ on December 13, 1963? If not, what remedy is appropriate"?

On December 13, . . . the young [grievant], classified as a machine operator and . . . the Union [steward] in his department, . . . was capping Ro-Con fiber drums with metal tops. He capped several hundred that day. The operation involved tapping the top on to the fiber body with a wooden mallet and fastening the top with attached metal clips.

That afternoon his foreman, one Little, observed that two of said tops had been damaged by unduly hard blows from the mallet and that grievant X__ had kicked or shoved with his foot, with some force, one of the drums, producing a mark and some damage thereto. The foreman made no further investigation on the spot, told X__ that he was fired, ordered him to the foreman's office, and after an interval went to get the local Union president. In Little's office X__ asked for grievance forms to take with him and was told they were Company property. After some discussion, not harmonious, an altercation developed during which Little manhandled X__ until the president intervened. X__ finally clocked out.

It appears also from the record that the foreman had not warned X__ on December 13 not to hit the caps so hard, but X__ knew how to do the job properly. There is no evidence on which to base a firm conclusion either that X__ inadvertently damaged the two tops with too hard a mallet-blow or that he did same with willful and deliberate intent. But he did damage them.

It appears further that, after one of X__'s more recent earlier offenses, higher management wished to discharge X__, but the foreman intervened in X__'s behalf and induced management to give him another chance to develop his potential.

The Arbitrator finds from the uncontroverted facts of record that X__'s record had been unfavorable, although he was a fast and competent employee with considerable potential. Out of a number of incidents he had received several oral warnings and had twice been suspended, once for a portion of a day and once for three days.

The above-stated issue in this case of protested disciplinary action requires a definition of "just and proper cause." Since the Parties' Agreement contains no such definition, the Arbitrator will here apply to the above-summarized facts the guide lines or questions that are to be found in the document appended to this decision. [See questions, infra.]

. . . [T]he Arbitrator now finds as follows: (1) Young X__ knew that in effect he was on probation. He had been warned and penalized on previous offenses, but none was like the one involved here. It may not be said that he was specifically aware that to damage two or three drums out of several hundred, in the manner he did, would result in his discharge. Nevertheless, he knew that he would have to "watch his step." The answer to Question 1 must be "yes." (2) The Company's requirement of careful work was reasonable. The answer to Question 2 is "yes." (3) Foreman Little thought he had the evidence of his eyes in respect to X__'s damaging actions when Little told X⎯ he was fired. Little, however, made no effort, through conversation with X⎯, to discover whether Little's eyes had conveyed a correct impression. Little's announced disciplinary decision must be held to have been hasty. The visual evidence may well have been correct and a proper reason for discipline; but Little should have checked said evidence out for verification and for the purpose of learning whether X⎯'s behavior had justification. . . . [T]he answer to Question 3 must be "no." (4) Similarly the answer to Question 4 must be "no," and for the same reasons. (5) The same answer must be given to Question 5, for the same reasons. There was no proper predischarge investigation. (6) The answer to Question 6 must be "yes," because the record contains no probative evidence that the Company discriminated against X⎯. (7) If the aggrieved's guilt had been properly established by a fair predischarge investigation, so that Questions 3, 4, and 5 could have been answered "yes," then X⎯'s discharge would have to be upheld. The reason: Although his proven offense, as such might not have been serious enough to warrant dismissal if the offense had been a first one, X⎯'s record was poor; even a proven minor offense would have been enough to justify his discharge.

Given all the above answers to the seven tests or questions, the Arbitrator finds further as follows: (1) Little's behavior, including his post-discharge manhandling of X⎯, makes it impossible for the Arbitrator to rule that the discharge must "stick." That is, even though the "no" answers to Questions 3, 4, and 5 might appear to have been made on technical grounds, said answers have great weight in any discipline case. Every accused employee in an industrial democracy has the right of "due process of law" and the right to be heard before discipline is administered. These rights are precious to all free men and are not lightly or hastily to be disregarded or denied. The Arbitrator is fully mindful of the Company's need for equity in, and right to require careful, safe, efficient performance by its employees. But before the Company can discipline an employee for failure to meet said requirement, the Company must take the pains to establish such failure. Maybe X⎯ was guilty as hell; maybe also there are many gangsters who go free because of legal technicalities. And this is doubtless unfortunate. But company and government prosecutors must understand that the legal technicalities exist also to protect the innocent from unjust, unwarranted punishment. Society is willing to let the presumably guilty go free on technical grounds in order that free, innocent men can be secure from arbitrary, capricious action. (2) The Arbitrator then has only two alternatives: (a) reinstate X⎯ with pay for all time lost; and (b) reinstate him without such pay. (3) . . . [T]he proper decision here is to reinstate X⎯ as of the date of his discharge but without back pay. . . .

Grievant X— is to be reinstated as of discharge date, all rights unimpaired, but with no pay for time lost.

[ELEMENTS OF "JUST CAUSE" FOR EMPLOYEE DISCIPLINE]

Few if any union-management agreements contain a definition of "just cause." Nevertheless, over the years the opinions of arbitrators in innumerable discipline cases have developed a sort of "common law" definition thereof. This definition consists of a set of guide lines or criteria that are to be applied to the facts of any one case, and said criteria are set forth below in the form of questions.

A "no" answer to any one or more of the following questions normally signifies that just and proper cause did not exist. . . .

1. Did the company give to the employee forewarning or foreknowledge of the possible or probable disciplinary consequences of the employee's conduct?

Note 1: Said forewarning or foreknowledge may properly have been given orally by management or in writing through the medium of typed or printed sheets or books of shop rules and of penalties for violation thereof.

Note 2: There must have been actual oral or written communication of the rules and penalties to the employee.

Note 3: A finding of lack of such communication does not in all cases require a "no" answer to Question No. 1. This is because certain offenses such as insubordination, coming to work intoxicated, drinking intoxicating beverages on the job, or theft of the property of the company or of fellow employees are so serious that any employee in the industrial society may properly be expected to know already that such conduct is offensive and heavily punishable.

Note 4: Absent any contractual prohibition or restriction, the company has the right unilaterally to promulgate reasonable rules and give reasonable orders; and same need not have been negotiated with the union.

2. Was the company's rule or managerial order reasonably related to the orderly, efficient, and safe operation of the Company's business?

Note: If an employee believes that said rule or order is unreasonable, he must nevertheless obey same (in which case he may file a grievance thereover) unless he sincerely feels that to obey the rule or order would seriously and immediately jeopardize his personal safety and/or integrity. Given a firm finding to the latter effect, the employee may properly be said to have had justification for his disobedience.

3. Did the company, before administering discipline to an employee, make an effort to discover whether the employee did in fact violate or disobey a rule or order of management?

Note 1: This is the employee's "day in court" principle. An employee has the right to know with reasonable precision the offense with which he is being charged and to defend his behavior.

Note 2: The company's investigation must normally be made *before* its disciplinary decision is made. If the company fails to do so, its failure may not normally be excused on the ground that the employee will get his day in court through the grievance procedure after the exaction of discipline. By that time there has usually been too much hardening of positions.

Note 3: There may of course be circumstances under which management must react immediately to the employee's behavior. In such cases the normally proper action is to suspend the employee pending investigation, with the understanding that (a) the final disciplinary decision will be made after the investigation and (b) if the employee is found innocent after the investigation, he will be restored to his job with full pay for time lost.

4. Was the Company's investigation conducted fairly and objectively?

Note: At said investigation the management official may be both "prosecutor" and "judge," but he may not also be a witness against the employee.

5. At the investigation did the "judge" obtain substantial evidence or proof that the employee was guilty as charged?

Note: It is not required that the evidence be preponderant, conclusive or "beyond reasonable doubt." But the evidence must be truly substantial and not flimsy.

6. Has the company applied its rules, orders, and penalties evenhandedly and without discrimination to all employees?

Note 1: A "no" answer to this question requires a finding of discrimination and warrants negation or modification of the discipline imposed.

Note 2: If the company has been lax in enforcing its rules and orders and decides henceforth to apply them rigorously, the company may avoid a finding of discrimination by telling all employees beforehand of its intent to enforce hereafter all rules as written.

7. Was the degree of discipline administered by the company in a particular case reasonably related to (a) the seriousness of the employee's proven offense and (b) the record of the employee in his service with the company?

Note 1: A trivial proven offense does not merit harsh discipline unless the employee has properly been found guilty of the same or other offenses a number of times in the past. (There is no rule as to what number of previous offenses constitutes a "good," a "fair," or a "bad" record. Reasonable judgment thereon must be used.)

Note 2: An employee's record of previous offenses may never be used to discover whether he was guilty of the immediate or latest one. The only proper use of his record is to help determine the severity of discipline once he has properly been found guilty of the immediate offense.

Note 3: Given the same proven offense for two or more employees, their respective records provide the only proper basis for "discriminating" among them in the administration of discipline for said offense. Thus, if employee A's record is significantly better than those of employees B, C, and D, the company may properly give A a lighter punishment than it gives the others for the same offense: and this does not constitute true discrimination.

[The American Arbitration Association has accepted Arbitrator Daugherty's foregoing tests for determining "just cause" in discipline cases. See Indianapolis Rubber Co., 79 Lab. Arb. 529, 534 (1982).]

NOTES

1. Is it arbitrator Daugherty's position that an employee, before being discharged, is entitled to notice and a hearing from his employer regardless of whether the agreement provides therefor and regardless of the strength of proof of serious misconduct by the employee? If so, what is the basis for that right and how formal or extensive must that hearing be? What of a hearing prior to suspensions and lesser discipline than discharge? For consideration of similar problems in the public sector, see Loudermill v. Cleveland Bd. of Education, 721 F.2d 550 (6th Cir. 1983), *cert. granted*, 104 Sup. Ct. 2384 (1984).

2. For an employee's statutory right to union representation in an interview that an employee fears will lead to discipline, see NLRB v. J. Weingarten, infra p. 1181.

3. In light of the arbitrator's conclusion in *Grief Bros.* that there was not "just cause" for the discharge, how is the "split award" to be explained?

4. Judicial decisions on implied "just cause" restrictions in labor contracts are collected in Smith v. Kerrville Bus. Co., 709 F.2d 914, 917 (5th Cir. 1983), where the court suggests that "the provisions of a labor contract may be more readily expanded by implication than . . . contracts memorializing other [types of] transactions." What is the justification for "implying" away management's historic right to discharge or discipline employees?

For differing views on the extent to which courts should adopt the body of procedural law ("industrial due process") fashioned by labor arbitrators, see, e.g., Scott v. Riley, 645 F.2d 565 (7th Cir. 1981), and Teamsters Local 878 v. Coca-Cola Bottling Co., 613 F.2d 716 (8th Cir. 1980).

Ross, Comments on Kadish, The Criminal Law and Industrial Discipline as Sanctioning Systems: Some Comparative Observations

Proceedings, National Academy of Arbitrators, 17th Annual Meeting 144 (M. Kahn ed. 1964)

The assumption that industrial discipline and criminal law are first cousins is deeply embedded in the parlance of arbitration. It was not more than a month ago that a union representative exclaimed to me in a discharge hearing: "Mr. Arbiter, this man may have committed a mischievous demeanor, but that doesn't justify capital punishment." Arbitrators as well as their clients are wedded to the analogy. This accounts for some remarkable decisions based on burden of proof, degree of proof, etc. In cases of discharge for sleeping on the job, for example, it is well established that the only reliable means of substantiating guilt beyond a reasonable doubt is to lift the grievant from the chair in which he has been snoring and bounce him off the floor until he opens his eyes, blinks in confusion, and angrily inquires, "What's the big idea waking me up in the middle of a shift?" Otherwise the grievant may successfully claim that he was momentarily resting his eyes or that he was deep in meditation concerning the problems of the job. . . . I want to express sincere admiration for Mr. Kadish's paper because he has gotten more mileage from the analogy between industrial discipline and criminal law than I would have considered possible. He applies the principal theories of crime and punishment to common disciplinary practices with much insight and imagination, and in so doing raises significant questions about the purpose and rationality of these practices. His discussion of how punishment has evolved from the original stage of unlimited terror or massive retaliation, through an intermediate stage of mechanically doling out the prescribed penalty for each particular offense, to the present stage of individual treatment in search of rehabilitation and correction, is particularly valuable. . . .

. . . [T]he analogy between industrial discipline and criminal law has useful applications. At the same time I am persuaded that it has severe limitations and that it collapses and falls to the ground if we push it too hard. . . .

. . . [T]he relationship between the state and its citizens is not the same as the relationship between an employer and his employees. The thrust of criminal law is primarily negative or prohibitive, although there are exceptions such as the affirmative duty to support one's children, pay one's taxes, and register for the draft.

But the employee is involved in a commercial transaction with his employer, an exchange of services for wages. Though the terms of the bargain are notoriously ill-defined in many respects, nevertheless the bargain is there. The employers' obligations are enforced through the collective agreement and the grievance procedure. The employee's obligations are enforced through a system of inducements and sanctions including those we call industrial discipline. The thrust of industrial discipline is prohibitive to some extent: thou shalt not lift company property, thou shalt not slug the foreman, etc. But the affirmative commands are more prominent and more significant. They include dependability, diligence, collaboration, conformity, and all the other requirements for efficient production in a complex organization.

A *disciplined* worker, therefore, is not merely one who keeps out of fights, refrains from smoking in the washroom, and otherwise obeys the rules of comportment. He also makes a positive contribution more or less equivalent to what was contemplated when the employment relationship was originally sealed. He makes out; he cuts the mustard; or if he should be unready, unwilling, or unable to do so, the lapse is only temporary. I submit that we arbitrators are looking for evidence of discipline in this augmented sense when we confront the usual discharge case.

For this reason, Mr. Kadish's discussion of the issue of culpability must be regarded as one of the less successful portions of his paper. He points out that strict criminal liability, i.e., punishment in the absence of fault, "is, with some notable exceptions, foreign to the central tradition of the criminal law." Since he considers discharge as a form of punishment, he forces himself to wrestle with the problem of how an employer can discharge a worker lacking in mens rea, the guilty mind—for example, the worker who tries hard but is just incompetent. He adopts a terminological solution by suggesting that such discharges are exceptional: they "are not punishment sanctions but efforts at self-protection comparable to the civil commitment to the potentially dangerous mentally ill."

A much better solution becomes obvious once we pierce the veil of analogy and confront the realities of industrial discipline in their own right. Discharge, catastrophic as it may be, does not constitute punishment. Concededly it is sacrilegious to oppose such time-honored locutions as "the ultimate sanction," "the final penalty," and "industrial capital punishment." But the fact is that a worker is fired because the employer has decided, rightly or wrongly, that he is not getting what he bargained for and that he wants to close out the employment relationship. When we reinstate the worker, we commonly intone that "some penalty may have been justified but the ultimate sanction of discharge was too severe." In my opinion, however, we are really expressing our disagreement with the employer's judgment and our conviction that a viable relationship can be reconstructed.

If I am correct, it follows that the question of culpability is largely irrelevant in the arbitration of discharge cases. Assume the employer can show that the grievant has been chronically absent, for periods of one to three days at a time, over the course of several years. Finding replacements has been difficult, production has suffered, and his fellow workers have been unfairly burdened. There have been numerous conferences, warning notices, and so on. Is the grievant's state of mind really material? Perhaps he doesn't give a damn. Perhaps he gets drunk every weekend and suffers prolonged hangovers. Perhaps he is a hypochondriac. Perhaps he has some incurable physical ailment. I submit that the case looks essentially the same regardless of these gross differences in culpability.

Or take the following discharge case which I decided some years ago. A young man was hired by an oil company to deliver gasoline around the Los Angeles area, driving 5,000-gallon tank trucks weighing up to 30 tons when fully loaded. For a while all went well, but then he suffered a series of four mishaps within a ten-month period. While filling a storage tank, he cut off the flow of gasoline too late and flooded the pavement. Backing his rig up to a loading platform, he failed to notice that one of the elevators had not been raised sufficiently to permit his truck to clear it. On another occasion he forgot to disconnect the downspout while driving his truck off the platform, so that the spout and the dome cover of the truck were broken. Finally, he drove into the rear end of a passenger car which he had been trailing by only eighteen feet. This was enough for me, although the union argued that the monetary damage was relatively small, that the grievant had previously driven a mayonnaise truck without difficulty, and that accidents can happen to anyone. Since the line between negligence and incompetence is often difficult to locate, I was not prepared to say that the grievant was culpable. Was it important?

The analogy between criminal law and industrial discipline breaks down in another important respect. Unlike a criminal trial, the typical discharge arbitration is not a means of determining the guilt or innocence of the accused. On the contrary, it is a review of the reasonableness of management's action in a state of facts which, after the jousting and sparring are over, can be seen to be essentially uncontroverted. Some cases, it is true, actually turn on contested issues of fact. Did the grievant steal the screwdriver? Did he strike the first blow? Did he take command of the illegal walkout? But these cases are distinctly in the minority. More often the basic circumstances are clear enough (although any skillful advocate is capable of miring the hearing in endless confusion over trivial or peripheral details). Our real task is to decide whether these circumstances constituted just and proper cause for terminating the employment relationship in the face of the grievant's seniority and associated job property rights. If they did not, we reinstate the grievant. His state of mind and degree of guilt then become secondary problems which can be resolved by cutting or withholding back pay and by sternly admonishing him in the opinion — which, in all likelihood, he will never read.

As arbitrators we are frequently criticized on the ground that we substitute our judgment for that of the employer. In the whole lexicon of arbitration clichés, that one is the most overworked. If our task is officially to review the employer's judgment, obviously we must be ready to substitute our own if we find that his was unreasonable. What else are we there for? It is no answer to say that we should uphold the termination unless it was arbitrary and capricious. Let us face it, in most discharge cases the grievants are not model employees. There is generally *some* cause for discharge; the real problem is whether it was *sufficient* cause. We are not brought in to try the facts, but to review the employer's judgment.

In deciding whether to sustain or to reverse a disciplinary discharge, we consider numerous circumstances which really have little or nothing to do with guilt, innocence, mitigation, extenuation, or other criteria of criminal law. One of these circumstances is seniority. Long service creates a presumption that the employee is capable of satisfactory performance, so that stronger evidence is needed before the contrary is established. Moreover, the senior employee has developed a greater equity in his job, which is thought of as a species of property right. He has more to lose when he is terminated and finds it more difficult to get readjusted. We therefore tend to feel that an employer must be willing to put up with more from a long-service employee.

Another important circumstance is nature of the employment. Can a worker use rough language? It depends on his job. Likewise, there are great differences in the extent to which dependable teamwork, punctilious honesty, etc., are essential if one is to make out as an employee. A friend of mine arbitrated a case in which a salesgirl in a dress shop had been terminated for using improper language to a customer. It appears that the customer tried on a dress and inquired, "Do you think it does anything for me?" The grievant amiably responded, "Dearie, if I had a fat rump like yours I wouldn't go near that dress." My friend reinstated the grievant (without back pay) but remarked that if the incident had occurred in one of the really fashionable shops, the result could have been otherwise.

Once I upheld the discharge of an insurance agent whose job it was to sell industrial life policies to people of modest means. He had been a model employee in almost every way. He had been frequently praised by his superiors and his clients, and was the recipient of countless certificates, plaques, ribbons, and similar awards. He had an exemplary war record, a lovely wife, and several children. Out of good-heartedness he made one mistake. One of his customers was an elderly man who had carried a $500.00 term insurance policy for many years. Although the agent knew that this man had recently been refused a larger policy on the ground of high blood pressure, he accepted a renewal of the $500.00 policy. There was no commission on the transaction. Through a freakish combination of circumstances, this dereliction came to the attention of the regional officer and the agent was promptly discharged. Understandably, I felt as if I were hanging a man for stealing a sheep. But this was a situation in which the company was intrinsically vulnerable to any connivance between agents and customers. The problem had been fairly serious; numerous cases had been taken to arbitration; there was no leeway at all. If the situation had been different, an arbitrator would have been strongly tempted to find extenuating circumstances and to hold that although serious punishment was fully warranted, the ultimate sanction was a little too severe.

Mr. Kadish discusses the question of whether employees can be punished for misbehavior outside the job. Once again you will not find the answer by comparing the intrinsic culpability of different grievants. The celebrated infidelities of a movie star enormously increase her value as an employee; in fact the grateful studio even gives her husband $500,000 for being a good sport. But let us construct a hypothetical case of an instructor in a private girls' school operated by a devout religious group. He becomes involved in a juicy scandal and 25 percent of the girls are withdrawn by their parents. Have the employer's interests been sufficiently impaired that he is entitled to break off the employment relationship? I tried this out on my friend Jesse Friedin, a redoubtable champion of intellectual honesty. He accused me of being a mealy-mouthed hypocrite for espousing a double standard. But suppose that 50 percent or 75 percent of the pupils were withdrawn?

In discussing the philosophy of corrective discipline, Mr. Kadish points out that there are dramatic and paradoxical departures in cases of theft, immorality, negligence resulting in serious injury, and other so-called capital offenses. He observes that "the seriousness of the harm done or the moral gravity of the behavior do not themselves demonstrate the hopelessness of trying to correct the offender"; that "there is no infallible or even probable relation between the seriousness of the offense and the risk of repetition"; and that discharge cuts off the possibility of rehabilitation. The missing clue to the paradox, in my belief, is that we are speaking about a work situation in which people of limited capacity are supposed to work together effectively despite all the human failings which make this a difficult undertaking even under the best of circumstances. Even if there is no substantial risk that the grievant would slug his boss a second time, reinstatement might well entail so much embarrassment, resentment, and strain as to be impracticable. The true capital offense is one which destroys the viability of the employment relationship. I should add that there is a real danger of underestimating the capacity of supervisors and workers to let bygones be bygones and to live with other imperfect people.

The most interesting discipline cases are those which present a poignant picture of employees and supervisors attempting to live with each other's imperfections in the confining space of the work environment and the stringent imperatives of the production process. We try to analyze such cases in the language of crime, guilt, and punishment, but these concepts are frequently not very helpful. I want to illustrate this point and conclude my comments by relating an inspiring saga of the unquenchable human spirit which, for reasons that will be evident, I have called "The Unsinkable Molly Brown."

Molly Brown was really her name. She had worked about eleven years at a San Jose cannery and during this period she had been in and out of a fair amount of trouble. The principal problem, as an analysis of warning notices revealed, was that she went to the rest room too often and stayed too long. She had received an ultimatum that if she left her machine without permission, discharge would follow.

On the "day in question," as we arbitrators like to call it, peaches were being canned and a temporary forelady was in charge of Molly's group. As the forelady passed down the line, Molly beckoned her and said, "Dearie, I've got to go." The forelady responded, "You'll have to wait your turn, honey. There's five girls ahead of you waiting for the relief girl." Molly waited. Thirty-five minutes later, although seven girls had had relief, Molly's turn had still not arrived.

At this point the forelady was up on a ramp inspecting some peaches. Suddenly a piece of fruit hit her on the back of the head. It is stipulated that this was a half peach, unpeeled and uncooked but without the pit. Wheeling around, she saw Molly Brown down at the floor level, about twelve feet away, for it was Molly who had thrown the peach. There were sharp conflicts in testimony as to her motive and manner in so doing. The union asserted that she had tossed it lightly, expecting it to land on the conveyor belt next to the forelady, and thus attract her attention. The employer maintained, on the contrary, that she had viciously hurled this dangerous missile in a fit of uncontrollable anger.

When the forelady turned around, Molly flapped her arms and called out, "I gotta go, I tell you; I gotta go!" Once again the testimony is in conflict, this time as to the forelady's reply. According to the union, the forelady extended her palms and shouted, "OK, OK, OK!" This version is flatly contradicted by the employer, according to whom the forelady stated, "Wait, wait! It's not your turn yet!"

Molly did not wait. She proceeded to the ladies' room. Members of supervision followed her there, took her to Labor Relations and made out the discharge papers. She was terminated on three counts, to wit: gross insubordination, leaving her machine without permission, and assaulting a member of supervision.

Since my award has not been published, perhaps I should tell you the decision. I concluded that although Molly's misbehavior could not be condoned, there were mitigating factors, and the ultimate sanction of discharge was too severe.

NOTES

1. Employers have attempted to combat absenteeism through "no fault" plans (i.e., rules that prescribe automatic penalties, including discharge, when a stated number of absences have occurred, regardless of the reasons for them or mitigating circumstances). For such plans that have survived arbitration after being challenged under a "just cause" provision, see Scott & Taylor, An Analysis of Absenteeism Cases Taken to Arbitration: 1975-1981, 38 Arb. J. 61 (1983); Block & Mittenthal, Absenteeism, Proc., Natl. Acad. of Arbitrators,— Annual Meeting — (1984).

2. Would analysis of absenteeism plans be affected if greater weight were given to Ross' view that discipline is not a penalty for the employee's moral failures but is essentially a judgment that the employer has not received the consideration that he bargained for?

3. Absenteeism, which appears to have increased markedly in the last 30 years, imposes significant costs on American industry. Economists have suggested that this increase is linked to the greater percentage of total compensation represented by fringe benefits, such as medical and pension benefits, the size of which is not affected by an employee's absences from work. See R. Flanagan, Labor Economics and Labor Relations 140-141 (1984). See also Allen, How Much Does Absenteeism Cost? 18 J. Human Resources 379 (1983). Are the general increase in absenteeism and its cost relevant to an arbitrator's appraisal of an employer's absenteeism plan? How would you get such considerations before the arbitrator without unduly prolonging the proceeding?

4. What impact, if any, would you expect unionization to have on absenteeism? See Allen, Trade Unions, Absenteeism and Exit Voice, 37 Ind. & Lab. Rel. Rev. 331 (1984) (concluding that union members are at

least 29 percent more likely to be absent and that the use of absenteeism as an "exit response," along with findings of greater job dissatisfaction among union members, requires further thought regarding the effectiveness of unions as voice institutions). See Freeman & Medoff, supra p. 48.

Note: Unjust Dismissal of "At Will" Employees

Statutes such as the NLRA and the Civil Rights Act have curbed the right of employers to decide whom they will hire, retain, and promote. In addition, in the 1970s, courts began to erode the common law doctrine of "at will" employment. For a useful survey of the rationales used for this purpose, see Report by the Committee on Labor and Employment Law of the Association of the Bar of the City of New York (Professor Samuel Estreicher and Beverly Wolff, authors), 36 Rec. A.B. City N.Y. 170 (1981). See also J. Steiber & J. Blackburn, Protecting Unorganized Employees Against Unjust Discharge (1983) (a comprehensive discussion of alternatives); Individual Rights in the Workplace: The Employment-At-Will Issue, 16 J.L. Reform 321 (1983). An influential earlier article was Blades, Employment At Will v. Individual Freedom: On Limiting the Abusive Exercise of Employer Power, 67 Colum. L. Rev. 1404 (1967), urging the recognition of the tort of "abusive discharge" — i.e., a discharge motivated by considerations not reasonably related to employment. See, e.g., Monge v. Beebe Rubber Co., 114 N.H. 130, 316 A.2d 549 (1974) (plaintiff harassed and ultimately fired for refusing to date her foreman). See also Note, Implied Contract Rights to Job Security, 26 Stan. L. Rev. 335 (1974) (employment relation, analyzed under ordinary contract principles, supports the implication of a promise to terminate only for "cause").

Although both tort and contract theories have provided a basis for judicially-created exceptions to the at will doctrine, the most successful technique appears to be a tort claim that employer discipline violates some "mandate of public policy." See, e.g., Palmateer v. International Harvester Co., 85 Ill. 2d 124, 421 N.E.2d 876 (1981) (employee stated cause of action for retaliatory discharge; the alleged discharge resulted from his advising law enforcement agency that coemployee might be violating state's criminal laws, from his agreeing to gather further evidence implicating coemployee, and from his intending to testify at any trial); Sheets v. Teddy's Frosted Foods, Inc., 179 Conn. 471, 427 A.2d 385 (1980) (employee stated cause of action in tort; he alleged that discharge resulted from his insistence on employer compliance with statute prohibiting sale of mislabeled food). But see Murphy v. American Home Products Corp., 58 N.Y. 293, 448 N.E.2d

86 (1983) (rejecting "emerging view" of *Palmateer* and *Sheets*; "such a significant change in our law is best left to the legislature").

Proposals for statutory protection against arbitrary or retaliatory discharge include use of arbitration under a just cause standard. See Summers, Individual Protection against Unjust Dismissal: Time for a Statute, 62 Va. L. Rev. 481 (1976); Note, Reforming At-Will Employment Law: A Model Statute, 16 J.L. Reform 389 (1983) (collecting state legislative and judicial developments). But the effectiveness of arbitration, without a union, has been questioned:

> . . . [T]he private aspects of labor arbitration — the private source of the rules being applied, the technique for selection and payment of arbitrators, the interrelationship of arbitration with the . . . grievance system, and the use of arbitration . . . for the application of economic pressure — are all rooted in its relation to collective bargaining. Proposals lacking these features would produce a type of arbitration almost indistinguishable from agency adjudication.

Getman, Labor Arbitration and Dispute Resolution, 88 Yale L.J. 916, 937-938 (1979). See also Catler, The Case Against Proposals to Eliminate the Employment At Will Rule, 5 Indus. Rel. L.J. 471 (1983). In addition, increasing attention has been focused on the economic costs of reform — regardless of how it is implemented — costs largely neglected in the initial scholarly enthusiasm for reform. See, e.g., Harrison, The "New" Terminable-at-Will Employment Contract: An Interest and Cost Incidence Analysis, 69 Iowa L. Rev. 327 (1984); Epstein, In Defense of the Contract At Will, 51 U. Chi. L. Rev. 947 (1984).

It would be timely to review the material, in Chapter 8, supra p. 736, treating the impact of doctrines of preemption on state jurisdiction over claims for wrongful discharge covered by a collective bargaining agreement.

Safeway Stores, Inc.
74 Lab. Arb. 1293 (1980)

DOYLE, Arbitrator: — [The grievant, H——, was employed as a Safeway food clerk in July of 1979. On January 8, 1980, company officials were "informed that a local newspaper had reported that a H—— had been convicted and sentenced for . . . a burglary." A company investigation revealed that H—— had participated with others in burglarizing a water bed store on August 19, and that when arrested the following day H—— had in his possession a vacuum cleaner which he admitted taking from the store. H——

had pleaded guilty to a charge of burglary, a "Class III" felony under Nebraska law, and on December 21, 1979, was sentenced to probation for three years. On the basis of this information, the company, on January 26, 1980, discharged H— for "proven dishonesty."]

Article 17.2 of the Agreement provides that the "Employer shall not discharge any employee without just cause." Article 17.4 deals specifically with discharge. It provides:

> An employee shall have at least two (2) written warning notices of the specific complaint against the employee before discharge *except in cases of proven dishonesty*, drunkenness, gross insubordination, or falsification of application for employment (discharge for falsification of application for employment must be within sixty (60) days from date of hire). A copy of all written notices shall be given to the employee and a copy to the Union. Warning notices shall be void after six (6) months from date of issue. (Emphasis Supplied).

The gist of the Union's case is that "proven dishonesty", as that term is employed in Article 17.4, means an act of dishonesty related to the grievant's employment, such as a theft of Company property, or the mishandling of Company or customer's funds in the course of employment. Since the act of dishonesty involved here occurred off Company premises, after scheduled hours of work, and was unrelated to the grievant's job it did not fall within the meaning of Article 17.4. Therefore, in the absence of two written warning notices of the specific complaint against the employee, he could not be discharged. It further argues that there is no evidence that the grievant's conviction has harmed the Company's reputation or adversely affected sales at the store where the grievant was employed. The Company has failed to show, it also contends, that the act has affected the grievant's competence to perform the duties of his job. . . .

. . . The grievant admitted the [burglary]. It was a willful act, committed with force. Such an act, wherever committed, reflects seriously upon the honesty and integrity of the individual, and raises serious doubts as to his trustworthiness in a work environment involving the constant temptation associated with the handling of the employer's money and its merchandise. Honesty and complete trustworthiness are recognized as important qualifications for such a job. The evidence establishes that an applicant for employment previously convicted of burglary or larceny would not be employed by the Company. Previous conviction of a serious crime is a matter explored in interviewing and screening of applicants for jobs with the Company. The discharge of employees for theft of Company property or mishandling of Company funds is the established policy. Theft of another's property is universally regarded as a serious offense, and generally recognized by arbitrators, and by labor agreements, as just cause for summary discharge. No further discussion of the justness of the Company's action . . . would be necessary if it were not for the insistence of the Union that proven dishonesty, as that term is used in Article 17.4, was intended to be limited to proven dishonesty in the course of the performance of the grievant's duties as an employee on Company premises. . . .

. . . [T]he Union's interpretation of [Article 17.4] is unsound and unsupported by the evidence. Proven dishonesty is perhaps the most serious of the offenses recognized in Article 17.4 as warranting summary discharge. This is particularly true with reference to occupations in a retail store involving the handling of money, and affording ready opportunity for pilferage and theft of its merchandise. The willful appropriation of another's property . . . evidences a character trait of a kind far different from an altercation between two employees off duty, or the observation of an employee under the influence of alcohol in an off duty setting. These are instances of conduct of a nature with little, if any, relation to the grievant's qualifications to perform his job, and which, it may reasonably be expected, would respond favorably to corrective discipline effected through prior warning notices. To contend, however, that in the cases of burglary and theft two prior warning notices of the same conduct are required before discharge is proper is beyond reasonable comprehension. The ease with which knowledgeable negotiators could express such a limitation dissuades one from reading it into the contract by implication. And there is no evidence of custom and practice supporting such a limitation. Such an offense as that committed by the grievant warranted discharge under the plain . . . words chosen by the parties to express their agreement.

. . . In Great Atlantic and Pacific Tea Co., Inc., 45 LA 495, the general test to be employed in resolving such cases is expressed as follows:

> There is a widely recognized principle in labor arbitration that what an employee does on his own time and outside the employer's premises is his own affair and that violation of the criminal laws is not per se just cause for disciplinary action. But there is another principle — equally well recognized — that where an employee's conviction of crime impairs his usefulness to the employer or is likely to affect adversely the employer's business, the employer is entitled to take cognizance of the conviction by way of suspension or discharge.

In NRM Corp., 51 LA 177, the discharge of an employee for association with others engaged in illegal activities, including theft and the receipt of stolen property, was sustained on the ground that he could no longer be considered trustworthy. In American Airlines, 71-2 Arb. Par. 8497, the discharge of a stewardess convicted of shoplifting was sustained on the ground that it was damaging to the image of the employer. In Robertshaw Controls Co., 64-2 Arb. Par. 8748, the discharge of an employee found guilty of socially reprehensible conduct, the sexual perversion of young boys, was upheld. The Arbitrator emphasized that such off duty conduct cannot be kept separate from the day-to-day working environment of the plant. Obtention [sic] of narcotics off duty through fraud was held to be off duty conduct of a character adversely affecting the work relationship warranting discharge in Chicago Pneumatic Tool Co., 38 LA 892.

The offense involved in this case was of such a nature that it raised serious doubt as to the future trustworthiness of the grievant in the . . . Company's retail store. The text of Article 17.4 does not specifically preclude its application to [such] off duty offenses. . . . [Grievance denied.]

NOTES

1. A truck driver, suspended by his employer after being indicted for manslaughter while driving, is acquitted. Should the acquittal necessarily require reinstatement and back pay to the employee for the period of his suspension? Cf. Kennecott Copper Co., 38 Lab. Arb. 93 (1962); Lucky Stores, Inc., 50 Lab. Arb. 559 (1972). Should the back pay question turn on whether the suspension was proper when imposed? Consider, for example, acquittals that appear to have resulted from the exclusion of illegally acquired evidence.

2. A discharge gives rise to both an unemployment compensation proceeding and an arbitration under a bargaining agreement. The company offers into evidence at the arbitration the findings and conclusions of the hearing officer in the unemployment compensation case. Should the arbitrator admit this evidence? If so, what weight should it receive? See, e.g., St. Joe's Minerals Corp., 70 Lab. Arb. 1110 (1978).

3. For discussions of the extent to which the privilege against self-incrimination, the right of confrontation, and the rules excluding illegally acquired evidence should be observed in arbitration, see Note, 20 Vand. L. Rev. 81, 103-115 (1966); Problems of Proof in Arbitration, Proc., 19th Ann. Meeting, Natl. Acad. of Arb. 135, 136, 202, 232 (1966); O. Fairweather, Practice and Procedure in Labor Arbitration 312-348 (2d ed. 1983); United States Government Printing Office, 82 Lab. Arb. 78 (1984).

4. Plant rules providing for discharge of convicted employees may

constitute violations of Title VII of the Civil Rights Act of 1964, as amended. The EEOC has reasoned that since minorities constitute a disproportionately high percentage of those convicted of "serious" crimes, it is discriminatory to treat all such convictions as cause for termination, without regard to "job-relatedness" and the employee's recent employment history. See CCH EEOC Decisions No. 72-1460 ¶6341 (1972) and No. 72-1497 ¶6352 (1972). Regarding arrests and convictions as a basis for decisions to hire, see generally B. Schlei & P. Grossman, Employment Discrimination Law 173-184 (2d ed. 1983).

Diamond Gardner Corp., 32 Lab. Arb. 581 (1959). On March 28, another employee (Santel) told the foreman that the grievant had deliberately caused a machine to jam. The grievant admitted the jamming to the foreman but claimed (as he previously had claimed to the accusing employee) that it had been accidental. The foreman gave the grievant "a verbal warning" and threatened disciplinary action "if this happened again." A few days later, several employees charged in writing that they had seen the grievant deliberately jam the machine on March 28 and on March 19, 1958. On April 18, 1958, the foreman in the presence of a steward advised the grievant that he was being laid off for a week because of new evidence concerning the March 28 incident. That evidence, which the foreman had refused to disclose at that time, was disclosed in the grievance procedure.

Arbitrator Russell Smith, having found that the evidence supported a finding of deliberate jamming by the grievant on March 28, rejected the union's claim of "double jeopardy" and dismissed the grievance, stating:

". . . The basis for the legal rule against double jeopardy in criminal proceedings is doubtless the feeling of the community that to permit a person charged with a crime to be tried, and then retried, for the same offense, would be an oppressive exercise of the power of the state against the individual, and thus offensive to our notions of fairness.

"Whether these underlying considerations apply to industrial disciplinary proceedings is not entirely clear. As Mr. Justice Cardozo . . . said in a double jeopardy case, 'The tyranny of labels must not lead us to leap to a conclusion that a word which in one set of facts may stand for oppression or enormity is of like effect in every other case' (Palko v. Connecticut, 302 U.S. 319). Without attempting any final conclusions on the subject, in general, the Arbitrator is convinced that the rule may not properly be invoked in the instant case. At the very least, the rule presupposes that something in the nature of a formal charge and hearing and final disposition of the merits has been held. Foreman Stegmaier's action on the night of March 28 was not of this character. He made a summary investigation, which consisted simply of confronting grievant with the claim made by Santel. Upon grievant's denial, Stegmaier in effect elected, at that point, to do nothing further. He used language which could perhaps be construed literally as amounting to disciplinary action in the form of a 'verbal reprimand,' but this did not go on grievant's official personnel record and under the circumstances was not, in fact, disciplinary action which could be held against him in weighing subsequent penalties. A more realistic interpretation of the foreman's remarks is that he was not, on March 28, making any finding at all, and was simply reminding grievant that the alleged offense was serious in nature and, if committed in the future, would lead to disciplinary action. This, of course, was true in any event in view of the Shop Rules. The Foreman would have been well-advised to use somewhat different language in dealing with grievant that night, but his action could not reasonably be interpreted as the kind of investigation, charge, and hearing, resulting in a final disposition, such as to preclude any further action in the case on the part of the Company. Under the circumstances, it was not unfair or oppressive for the Company to consider and take action based on evidence which came to light the following week." [See also General Services Admin., 75 Lab. Arb. 1158, 1160 (1980): "In grievance-arbitration, . . . 'double jeopardy' has been held to mean 'that once discipline for a given offense has been imposed and accepted it cannot be increased.'"]

Gold Kist, Inc.
70 Lab. Arb. 342 (1978)

MORRIS, Arbitrator:— . . . The issue is whether the suspension of W— was for just cause. . . .

W— was suspended from work without pay for two weeks on April 6, 1977, based on a charge of misconduct involving vilification of the Company and its employees. This action followed the production and distribution of a leaflet, presumably for employees of the Durham plant of the Company on April 1, 1977, primarily by the Grievant. W— had received a written warning on March 31, 1977, on the basis of charges of misconduct for committing "such acts as encouraging assault on visitors to our plant." A leaflet had been produced on March 21, 1977, with primary participation by [W—] which made certain remarks about a future visit by the Union Vice-President to the plant. Over a period of several years W— had been active in producing leaflets and distributing them primarily to employees which were extremely critical of the Company and the Union. No action had been taken about the earlier leaflets, ostensibly . . . because the Company was not sure that they were primarily the product of W—. She had been suspended twice on earlier occasions for apparently unrelated violations.

. . . [T]he Company [charged] violation of facility rules and particularly Rule 1 which states as follows:

> Most people like to work in an orderly, clean and safe facility. Most people like to be treated with respect. In a small organization, rules usually do not need to be written. In a large organization such as Gold Kist certain rules and regulations must be published and understood by all employees. For the good of all employees, it is obvious that these rules must be followed. Appropriate disciplinary action will be taken for failure to abide by facility rules. The Gold Kist rules are:
>
> 1. You know the difference from right and wrong, therefore, you are to follow the rules of common decency in your dealing with others.

The Agreement . . . provides for disciplinary authority:

Article IX — Management Rights

> The rights of management shall be limited only to the extent necessary to carry out the terms and conditions set out in this agreement. The management of the Company and its operations and the direction of its working force, including the right to hire, promote, suspend or discharge employees for just cause and the maintenance of efficiency, are vested exclusively in the Company. The Company may, in its judgment, increase or decrease operations, remove or install machinery or appliances, determine work processes and procedures, maintain discipline and enact reasonable Company policies and plant rules and regulations which are not in conflict with the provisions of this agreement or legal rights of employees.

. . . The Union and the grievant . . . contend that the Company "did not have the right or just cause to discipline the grievant in any manner." It is asserted that the conduct of W___ was protected activity under the laws and Constitution of the United States. In any event, it is maintained the grievant's conduct was not in violation of the March 31, 1977, warning nor did it "adversely affect production, morale or productivity of the Company." Claim is that in any event proper disciplinary steps were not followed and the disciplinary action was too harsh. . . .

The record is clear that W___ was primarily responsible for producing and distributing leaflets over the years which were extremely critical of the Company and the Union and which, at least by inference, suggested a slowdown and violence. The activity of the grievant which is at issue here is that involved in the production and distributions of leaflets issued on March 21 and April 1, 1977, but the record of past derogatory comments and charges is relevant in understanding the meaning and purpose of the conduct of W ___. Prior suspensions for violations unrelated to the present issue are not considered as relevant to the question of just cause for this suspension.

In evaluation of the claim that because of First Amendment protection the suspension was not for just cause, the nature of the Company business must be considered. This is clearly a private sector industrial activity and the facts that the plant has government contracts and food inspectors does [sic] not support a determination that "state action" is involved. The extent of government involvement in the essential decision-making process of production and distribution and costing and pricing is not significant enough to uphold a charge that constitutional rights have been violated. . . . W ___ has the right to her opinions and to express them but she does not have the right to impair morale and efficiency in the plant by making slanderous and unproven charges against the Company or to infer [sic] that violence be employed in the plant against a visitor who happens to be a Union official.

In the same sense the evidence does not provide a sound basis for judging that the action of W ___ constituted protected activity under federal labor laws. . . . [E]mployees have the right to speak out on activities involved in labor relations. . . . These rights include organizing unions, bargaining collectively and expressing opinions on these subjects. Members of unions are also protected by the Union "bill of rights" under federal legislation. Orderly channels are generally available to express views, and they exist in this plant and in this local union, and there is no supportable evidence that the grievant was restricted in using these channels. . . . If the grievant felt that the Union was in collusion with the Company and was not properly representing the plant employees, for example, a decertification election could have been petitioned. The federal labor agency and the courts are available to provide protection of employee activities relating to collective bargaining and it is noted that charges by the grievant and others of violations by the Company and the Union were considered and not upheld.

The leaflets involved here went beyond mere expression but encouraged violence. Despite the absence of quantitative proof there can be little question that they had the potential to be seriously disruptive of morale and efficiency, properly the concern of the Company. It may well be that slanderous comments or drawings of big fish eating small fish are not taken seriously by employees but the encouragement of assault made in the leaflets at issue are certainly not protected activities. The Company also had reason to be aware earlier that the grievant was a very active participant in the production and distribution of the leaflets. . . . It is, therefore, noteworthy that no action was taken by the Company against W ___ until the issuance of leaflets which encouraged assault, which would have constituted an interference with the bargaining relationships of the parties and assuredly interfered with efficiency and sound working relationships in the plant.

It may be argued that the comments made in the leaflets were vaguely couched and should not be taken as serious suggestions for violent action. The March 21 and April 1 leaflets however were not only part of a pattern of disruptive suggestions, but they went beyond in terms of agitational impact. Even though Work Rule 1 is expressed in broad terms which reduce its effectiveness as a guide to making judgments about specific violations, there is no doubt that the grievant's behavior ran counter to its purpose.

Aside from violation of a work rule, however, it is found that the clear encouragement of violence in the plant represented off-duty behavior which had a significantly high potential for interfering with order and efficiency in the plant. The "apology" in the April 1 leaflet cannot be judged to be a retraction but rather was a continuation of behavior for which the grievant was issued a written warning. It is relevant that the written warning was not grieved and therefore must stand in the record. The conclusion is that just cause did exist for suspension of W___.

There is a legitimate question, however, of whether suspension for two weeks was a justifiable penalty. The question is not one of whether there is merit in the Company claim that discharge could have been justified and that a penalty of two weeks suspension was relatively mild. The record speaks clearly that the Company employs a system of progressive discipline starting with oral warnings and moving to written warnings, three-day suspension and then discharge. While the system is not carved in stone, it is established practice in this plant. Issuance of unusual punishments, such as a two-week suspension, therefore, should be justified by special circumstances or run the risk of being judged as arbitrary or discriminatory.

Persuasive support for a special form of penalty . . . is not provided in the record and it is found that the customary three-day suspension for similar infractions after a written warning would have served the purposes of the progressive disciplinary system. . . .

. . . [I]t is ruled that just cause existed for suspension. The proper penalty . . . , however, was a three-day rather than a two-week suspension. W___ will be paid for the seven-day excess penalty at the rates then prevailing in the plant and the records will be changed to reflect the revised penalty.

NOTES

1. Would the employer's case have been strengthened had the suspension been based on "disloyalty"? See NLRB v. Local 1229, IBEW, supra p. 228.

2. Under an agreement giving management sole discretion to discipline "any and all employees" who distribute leaflets in work areas during

working time, management fires half of the employees who in fact violated the rule on a certain day; all violators positively identified were discharged. Has management failed to administer discipline evenhandedly? Cf. Mac-Millan Bloedel Products, Inc., 55 Lab. Arb. 667 (1970).

3. In the criminal law system, disparity in sentences is notorious. There is, moreover, disagreement on the desirability of exemplary punishment. See, e.g., N. Morris, Madness and the Criminal Law 180, 200, 209 (1982). Is the inability of formally-trained judges to eliminate sentencing disparities relevant to the latitude to be given to administrators of employee discipline under the "equality" requirement? Are there reasons for upholding "example" punishment by judges but not by employers? Suppose that an employer has enforced rules leniently, but that, because of financial losses or new supervision, he decides to tighten up. Would his unilateral announcement of a tougher policy for the unexpired term of the agreement and enforcement of that policy constitute improper unequal treatment? A violation of §8(a)(5)?

4. Ten employees are guilty of breach of the no-strike clause; all ten could properly be discharged under the agreement. The employer needs their production to fill an urgent order but does not wish to overlook completely their breach of contract. He proposes to draw one of the ten names out of a hat and to discharge the employee whose name is drawn. Advise the employer whether that discharge would violate the agreement's just cause provision.

B. JUDICIAL ENFORCEMENT

Senate Report No. 105
80th Cong., 1st Sess. 15-18 (1947)

. . . [B]reaches of collective agreement have become so numerous that it is not sufficient to allow the parties to invoke the processes of the National Labor Relations Board when such breaches occur (as the bill proposes to do in title I). . . . [T]he aggrieved party should also have a right of action in the Federal courts. . . .

The laws of many States make it difficult to sue effectively and to recover a judgment against an unincorporated labor union. It is difficult to reach the funds of a union to satisfy a judgment against it. In some States it is necessary to serve all the members before an action can be maintained against the union. This is an almost impossible process. Despite these practical difficulties in the collection of a judgment against a union, the [NLRB] has held it an unfair labor practice for an employer to insist that a union incorporate or post a bond to establish some sort of legal responsibility under a collective agreement. . . .

. . . The chief advantage which an employer can reasonably expect from a collective labor agreement is assurance of uninterrupted operation during the term of the agreement. Without some effective method of assuring freedom from economic warfare for the term of the agreement, there is little reason why an employer would desire to sign such a contract.

Consequently, to encourage the making of agreements and to promote industrial peace through faithful performance by the parties, collective agreements affecting interstate commerce should be enforceable in the Federal courts. Our amendment would provide for suits by unions as legal entities and against unions as legal entities in the Federal courts in disputes affecting commerce.

The amendment specifically provides that only the assets of the union can be attached to satisfy a money judgment against it; the property of the individual members of the organization would not be subject to any liability under such a judgment. . . .

The initial obstacle in enforcing the terms of a collective agreement against a union . . . is the difficulty of subjecting the union to process. The great majority of labor unions are unincorporated associations. At common law voluntary associations are not suable as such. As a consequence the rule in most jurisdictions, in the absence of statute, is that unincorporated labor unions cannot be sued in their common name. Accordingly, the difficulty or impossibility of enforcing the terms of a collective agreement in a suit at law against a union arises from the fact that each individual member of the union must be named and made a party to the suit.

[The report here summarizes the divergent responses of various jurisdictions to the impediments to recovery from a union for its breach of agreement.]

Statutory recognition of the collective agreement as a valid, binding, and enforceable contract is a logical and necessary step. It will promote a higher degree of responsibility upon the parties to such agreements, and will thereby promote industrial peace.

NOTES

1. Although a collective agreement is a "contract," the opinions in this chapter make explicit a proposition suggested earlier (e.g., J.I. Case Co. v. NLRB, supra p. 799): "a collective agreement is not an ordinary contract." Accordingly, a recurring theme of the materials that follow is the relationship of general contract law to collective bargaining agreements. Prior to the

passage of the LMRA, several rationales had emerged for treating collective agreements as a direct source of judicially enforceable rights and obligations. See Summers, Collective Agreements and the Law of Contracts, 78 Yale L.J. 525, 538-548 (1969); Cox, The Legal Nature of Collective Bargaining Agreements, 57 Mich. L. Rev. 1, 19-21 (1958); Gregory, The Collective Bargaining Agreement: Its Nature and Scope, 1949 Wash. U.L.Q. 3. For differing views regarding the desirability of judicial enforceability, compare Shulman, Reason, Contract, and Law in Labor Relations, 68 Harv. L. Rev. 999 (1955), with Cox, Some Aspects of the Labor Management Relations Act, 1947, 61 Harv. L. Rev. 274, 313 (1948).

2. Although United Mine Workers v. Coronado Coal Co., 259 U.S. 344 (1922), held only that unions could be sued in their common name in federal courts in civil actions based on the Sherman Act, the Court's rationale warranted the treatment of unions as legal entities in all federal cases based on federal question jurisdiction. See id. at 383-385, 387, 388-390; and United Steelworkers v. Bouligny, 382 U.S. 145, 153 (1965). That approach was embodied in Rule 17(b) of the Federal Rules of Civil Procedure. Cf. United States v. White, 322 U.S. 694 (1944) (union books, like corporate books, are not protected by the privilege against self-incrimination). In *Bouligny*, supra, the Court, although acknowledging the force of the argument for also treating unions as entities in diversity jurisdiction, declined to do so, urging that such a change should be made by Congress. See generally Kamin, The Union as Litigant: Personality, Pre-Emption, and Propaganda, 1966 Sup. Ct. Rev. 253-269; Note, 66 Yale L.J. 712 (1957).

1. Arbitration and the Courts—A General Framework

Textile Workers Union v. Lincoln Mills of Alabama
353 U.S. 448 (1957)

DOUGLAS, J. . . . The agreement [in question] provided that there would be no strikes or work stoppages and that grievances would be handled pursuant to a specified procedure. The last step in the grievance procedure —a step that could be taken by either party—was arbitration.

This controversy involves several grievances that concern work loads and work assignments. The grievances were processed through the various steps in the grievance procedure and were finally denied by the employer. The union requested arbitration, and the employer refused. Thereupon the union brought this suit in the District Court to compel arbitration.

The District Court concluded that it had jurisdiction and ordered the employer to comply with the grievance arbitration provisions of the collective bargaining agreement. The Court of Appeals reversed by a divided vote. 230 F.2d 81. It held that, although the District Court had jurisdiction to entertain the suit, the court had no authority founded either in federal or state law to grant the relief. . . .

The starting point of our inquiry is §301 of the [LMRA] of 1947. . . .

There has been considerable litigation involving §301 and courts have construed it differently. There is one view that §301(a) merely gives federal district courts jurisdiction in controversies that involve labor organizations in industries affecting commerce, without regard to diversity of citizenship or the amount in controversy. Under that view §301(a) would not be the source of substantive law; it would neither supply federal law to resolve these controversies nor turn the federal judges to state law for answers to the questions. Other courts — the overwhelming number of them — hold that §301(a) is more than jurisdictional — that it authorizes federal courts to fashion a body of federal law for the enforcement of these collective bargaining agreements and includes within that federal law specific performance of promises to arbitrate grievances under collective bargaining agreements. Perhaps the leading decision representing that point of view is the one rendered by Judge Wyzanski in Textile Workers Union v. American Thread Co., 113 F. Supp. 137. That is our construction of §301(a), which means that the agreement to arbitrate grievance disputes, contained in this collective bargaining agreement, should be specifically enforced.

From the face of the Act it is apparent that §301(a) and §301(b) supplement one another. Section 301(b) makes it possible for a labor organization, representing employees in an industry affecting commerce, to sue and be sued as an entity in the federal courts. Section 301(b) in other words provides the procedural remedy lacking at common law. Section 301(a) certainly does something more than that. Plainly, it supplies the basis upon which the federal district courts may take jurisdiction and apply the procedural rule of §301(b). The question is whether §301(a) is more than jurisdictional.

The legislative history of §301 is somewhat cloudy and confusing. But there are a few shafts of light that illuminate our problem.

The bills, as they passed the House and the Senate, contained provisions which would have made the failure to abide by an agreement to arbitrate an unfair labor practice. S. Rep. No. 105, 80th Cong., 1st Sess., pp. 20-21, 23; H.R. Rep. No. 245, 80th Cong., 1st Sess., p. 21. This feature of the law was dropped in Conference. As the Conference Report stated, "Once parties have made a collective bargaining contract the enforcement of that contract should be left to the usual processes of the law and not to the National Labor Relations Board." H.R. Conf. Rep. No. 510, 80th Cong., 1st Sess., p. 42.

Both the Senate and the House took pains to provide for "the usual processes of the law" by provisions which were the substantial equivalent of §301(a) in its present form. Both the Senate Report and the House Report indicate a primary concern that unions as well as employees should be bound to collective bargaining contracts. But there was also a broader concern — a concern with a procedure for making such agreements enforceable in the courts by either party. At one point the Senate Report states,

> We feel that the aggrieved party should also have a right of action in the Federal courts. Such a policy is completely in accord with the purpose of the Wagner Act which the Supreme Court declared was "to compel employers to bargain collectively with their employees to the end that an employment contract, binding on both parties, should be made. . . ."

Congress was also interested in promoting collective bargaining that ended with agreements not to strike. . . .

Thus collective bargaining contracts were made "equally binding and enforceable on both parties." Id., p. 15. As stated in the House Report, the new provision "makes labor organizations equally responsible with employers for contract violations and provides for suit by either against the other in the United States district courts." To repeat, the Senate Report, p. 17, summed up the philosophy of §301 as follows: "Statutory recognition of the collective agreement as a valid, binding, and enforceable contract is a logical and necessary step. It will promote a higher degree of responsibility upon the parties to such agreements, and will thereby promote industrial peace."

Plainly the agreement to arbitrate grievance disputes is the *quid pro quo* for an agreement not to strike. Viewed in this light, the legislation does more than confer jurisdiction in the federal courts over labor organizations. It expresses a federal policy that federal courts should enforce these agreements on behalf of or against labor organizations and that industrial peace can be best obtained only in that way.

To be sure, there is a great medley of ideas reflected in the hearings, reports, and debates on this Act. Yet, to repeat, the entire tenor of the history indicates that the agreement to arbitrate grievance disputes was considered as *quid pro quo* of a no-strike agreement. And when in the House the debate narrowed to the question whether §301 was more than jurisdictional, it became abundantly clear that the purpose of the section was to provide the necessary legal remedies. Section 302 of the House bill, the substantial equivalent of the present §301, was being described by Mr. Hartley, the sponsor of the bill in the House:

> Mr. Barden. Mr. Chairman, . . . I want it understood that [my ques-

tion] is intended to make a part of the record that may hereafter be referred to as history of the legislation.

It is my understanding that §302, the section dealing with equal responsibility under collective bargaining contracts in strike actions and proceedings in district courts contemplates not only the ordinary lawsuits for damages but also such other remedial proceedings, both legal and equitable, as might be appropriate in the circumstances; in other words, proceedings could, for example, be brought by the employers, the labor organizations, or interested individual employees under the Declaratory Judgments Act in order to secure declarations from the Court of legal rights under the contract.

MR. HARTLEY. The interpretation the gentleman has just given of that section is absolutely correct.

93 Cong. Rec. 3656-3657.

It seems, therefore, clear to us that Congress adopted a policy which placed sanctions behind agreements to arbitrate grievance disputes,[6] by implication rejecting the common-law rule, discussed in Red Cross Line v. Atlantic Fruit Co., 264 U.S. 109, against enforcement of executory agreements to arbitrate. We would undercut the Act and defeat its policy if we read §301 narrowly as only conferring jurisdiction over labor organizations.

The question then is, what is the substantive law to be applied in suits under §301(a)? We conclude that the substantive law to apply . . . is federal law, which the courts must fashion from the policy of our national labor laws. The [LMRA] expressly furnishes some substantive law. It points out what the parties may or may not do in certain situations. Other problems will lie in the penumbra of express statutory mandates. Some will lack express statutory sanction but will be solved by looking at the policy of the legislation and fashioning a remedy that will effectuate that policy. The range of judicial inventiveness will be determined by the nature of the problem. Federal interpretation of the federal law will govern, not state law. But state law, if compatible with the purpose of §301, may be resorted to in order to find the rule that will best effectuate the federal policy. Any state law applied, however, will be absorbed as federal law and will not be an independent source of private rights.

It is not uncommon for federal courts to fashion federal law where federal rights are concerned. See Clearfield Trust Co. v. United States, 318 U.S. 363, 366-367. . . . Congress has indicated by §301(a) the purpose to

---

[6] Assn. of Westinghouse Employees v. Westinghouse Electric Corp., 348 U.S. 437, is quite a different case. There the union sued to recover unpaid wages on behalf of some 4,000 employees. The basic question concerned the standing of the union to sue and recover on those individual employment contracts. The question here concerns the right of the union to enforce the agreement to arbitrate which it has made with the employer.

follow that course here. There is no constitutional difficulty. Article III, §2, extends the judicial power to cases "arising under . . . the Laws of the United States. . . ." The power of Congress to regulate these labor-management controversies under the Commerce Clause is plain. A case or controversy arising under §301(a) is, therefore, one within the purview of judicial power as defined in Article III.

The question remains whether jurisdiction to compel arbitration of grievance disputes is withdrawn by [Norris-LaGuardia]. . . . Section 7 of that Act prescribes stiff procedural requirements for issuing an injunction in a labor dispute. The kinds of acts which had given rise to abuse of the power to enjoin are listed in §4. The failure to arbitrate was not a part and parcel of the abuses against which the Act was aimed. Section 8 of [Norris-LaGuardia] does, indeed, indicate a congressional policy toward settlement of labor disputes by arbitration, for it denies injunctive relief to any person who has failed to make "every reasonable effort" to settle the dispute by negotiation, mediation, or "voluntary arbitration." Though a literal reading might bring the dispute within the terms of the Act (see Cox, Grievance Arbitration in the Federal Courts, 67 Harv. L. Rev. 591, 602-604), we see no justification in policy for restricting §301(a) to damage suits, leaving specific performance of a contract to arbitrate grievance disputes to the inapposite procedural requirements of that Act. Moreover, we held in Virginian R. Co. v. System Federation, 300 U.S. 515, and in Graham v. Brotherhood of Firemen, 338 U.S. 232, 237, that the Norris-LaGuardia Act does not deprive federal courts of jurisdiction to compel compliance with the mandates of the Railway Labor Act. The mandates there involved concerned racial discrimination. Yet those decisions were not based on any peculiarities of the Railway Labor Act. We followed the same course in Syres v. Oil Workers International Union, 350 U.S. 892, which was governed by the [NLRA]. There an injunction was sought against racial discrimination in application of a collective bargaining agreement; and we allowed the injunction to issue. The congressional policy in favor of the enforcement of agreements to arbitrate grievance disputes being clear, there is no reason to submit them to the requirements of §7 of the Norris-LaGuardia Act.

The judgment of the Court of Appeals is reversed and the cause is remanded to that court for proceedings in conformity with this opinion.

[Burton, J., joined by Harlan, J., concurred separately. They found federal power to fashion an "appropriate federal remedy," i.e., specific performance, in §301 itself and in inherent equitable powers "nurtured by a congressional policy to encourage and enforce labor arbitration in industries affecting commerce." Their crucial difference with the majority lay in their conclusion that the federal courts should apply state substantive law and should look to federal law only in connection with remedial questions. They surmounted Article III problems by approving a concept of "protective jurisdiction."[i]

Frankfurter, J., in a lengthy dissent, urged that the Court's transformation of a plainly procedural or jurisdictional section into a mandate for the invention of a body of substantive federal law ignored both the language of §301 and its legislative history. He urged also that even if such a mandate were inferred, the relevant federal law, namely, the United States Arbitration Act, excluded specific enforcement of arbitration clauses in collective bargaining agreements. Finally, he rejected the applicability of a protective jurisdiction concept to this case. He concluded that §301, as an exclusively jurisdictional provision that was to operate in the absence of diversity of citizenship or a federal question, was beyond the federal judicial power conferred by Article III of the Constitution.]

NOTES

1. Among the most interesting of the many discussions of the principal case are Bickel & Wellington, Legislative Purpose and the Judicial Process: The Lincoln Mills Case, 71 Harv. L. Rev. 1 (1957); Feinsinger, Enforcement of Labor Agreements — A New Era in Collective Bargaining, 43 Va. L. Rev. 261 (1957); Gregory, The Law of the Collective Agreement, 57 Mich. L. Rev. 635 (1959).

2. After *Lincoln Mills*, the Supreme Court, in a series of cases involving federal preemption, the NLRB's primary jurisdiction in the contractual context, and the reach of §301, ruled:

(a) State courts have concurrent jurisdiction over actions within the ambit of §301 but are required to apply federal law. Local 174, Teamsters v. Lucas Flour Co., 369 U.S. 95 (1962). In *Lucas*, the Court also ruled that federal and state courts have jurisdiction over actions involving an alleged violation of a collective agreement, even though the conduct involved might be prohibited or protected by the NLRA. See 369 U.S. at 101, n.9. In Smith v. Evening News Assn., 371 U.S. 195 (1962), the Court, recognizing that its

---

[i][That concept has been invoked to sustain the jurisdiction of federal courts to apply state law in actions involving federally-created instrumentalities. See 353 U.S. at 473-477 (Frankfurter, J., dissenting). Such jurisdiction has been defended in the context of labor relations as necessary for the protection of an extensive body of federal labor regulation. See Mendelsohn, Enforceability of Arbitration Agreements Under Taft-Hartley Section 301, 66 Yale L.J. 167, 191 (1956). Senator Taft, during the hearings on the proposed legislation, defended federal jurisdiction on grounds quite similar to this protective jurisdiction concept, although he did not invoke it by that name. See Hearings on S. 55 and S.J. Res. 22 Before the Senate Comm. on Labor and Public Welfare, 80th Cong., 1st Sess. 57 (1947). — EDS.]

statement in *Lucas* (that preemption doctrines were not "relevant") might require qualification, stated (at 197):

> The authority of the Board to deal with an unfair labor practice that also violates a collective bargaining contract is not displaced by §301, but it is not exclusive and does not destroy the jurisdiction of courts under §301. If there are situations in which serious problems will arise from both the courts and the Board having jurisdiction over acts which amount to an unfair labor practice, we shall face those cases when they arise.

(b) Section 301 grants federal courts jurisdiction over actions brought by an employee to enforce individual rights arising under a collective agreement. Such actions are also governed by federal law. See Humphrey v. Moore, 375 U.S. 335, 344 (1964).

(c) Section 301 covers actions on "other labor contracts besides collective bargaining agreements." Retail Clerks v. Lion Dry Goods, Inc., 369 U.S. 17 (1962). The agreement in question had settled a long strike and included the union's acknowledgment that it lacked majority support and therefore was not entitled to recognition. The agreement contained provisions typical of collective agreements, including a provision that the employers would maintain existing wages and other benefits, a ban on discharges without just cause, and an arbitration clause. The specific issue before the Court was whether §301 provided the basis for an order compelling the employers to comply with two arbitration awards involving the union's access to the employees' cafeteria and assignments given to two employees who had been reinstated. In holding that the petition for enforcement of those awards was cognizable by the district court under §301(a), the Court declared (at 29): "[I]f the federal court's jurisdiction under §301(a) required a preliminary determination of the representative status of the labor organization involved, potential conflict with the [NLRB] would be increased."

(d) A union constitution is a "contract between labor organizations" within the meaning of §301(a). Therefore, a suit brought by a local union against its parent international, alleging a violation of the international's constitution, is within §301 jurisdiction of the federal courts. United Assn. of Journeymen & Apprentices of Plumbers v. Local 334, 452 U.S. 615 (1981). Reserved was the question of the source of federal law to be applied in such cases, as was the question of §301 suits on union constitutions brought by individual members against a labor organization.

3. (a) An employer defends an action on a collective agreement on the ground that the agreement — which recognized the union as the exclusive representative for all employees in the unit — is illegal because the union lacked majority support when the agreement was negotiated. Is the court to decide the issue of majority support? To ignore it unless the NLRB has

invalidated the agreement? To retain jurisdiction but defer disposition until the NLRB has resolved that issue? See, e.g., Glaziers & Glassworkers Local Union 767 v. Custom Auto Glass Distribs., 689 F.2d 1339 (9th Cir. 1982).

(b) In an action brought by a union, the employer defends on the ground that the union is seeking to enforce a clause proscribed by §8(a)(3) or by §8(e) of the NLRA. Should the court pass on either of those defenses? See Kaiser Steel Corp. v. Mullins, 455 U.S. 72, 86 (1982) ("where a §8(e) defense is raised by a party which §8(e) was designed to protect, and where the defense is not directed to a collateral matter but to the portion of the contract for which enforcement is sought, a court must entertain the defense"). Cf. Burke v. French Equip. Rental, 687 F.2d 307, 311 (9th Cir. 1982) (finding error in trial court's considering §8(e) defense in pension trustees' suit against construction contractor for delinquent payments, which did not involve effort to enforce the allegedly illegal self-help clause, and declaring "we find no indication in *Kaiser* that the Court meant to sweep away the entire jurisprudence of judicial deference to the expertise of the NLRB").

Is there a basis for contending that the analysis of the primary jurisdiction question in §8(e) cases does not necessarily apply to other sections of the Act?

Does Sears, Roebuck & Co. v. San Diego County Dist. Council of Carpenters (supra p. 770) bear on the foregoing questions? For example, what if the party asserting the statutory claim or defense could still raise it by filing a timely unfair labor practice charge with the NLRB? See generally Sovern, Section 301 and the Primary Jurisdiction of the NLRB, 76 Harv. L. Rev. 529, 551-569 (1963).

4. A newspaper's collective agreement with Newspaper Guild Local 10 provides that (1) the agreement shall remain in effect during negotiations for a renewal agreement, (2) the employees shall not work for a competitor, and (3) contractual disputes shall be subject to arbitration. After fruitless negotiations for 30 days, Local 10 voted to strike the publisher. Thereupon, that local, the Guild International, and individual members of other newspaper locals, carrying out prestrike plans, started a competitive newspaper staffed by employees on strike against the publisher.

Following a refusal to arbitrate by Local 10, the employer, under §301, sues that local in a federal district court for breach of contract, and also sues the members of the other locals, the Guild International, and the competitive newspaper, claiming punitive damages for inducing breach of contract.

All defendants move to dismiss on jurisdictional grounds. What result? Cf. Wilkes-Barre Publishing Co. v. Newspaper Guild, 647 F.2d 2312 (3d Cir. 1981), with Loss v. Blankenship, 673 F.2d 942 (7th Cir. 1982); see also the preemption materials in Chapter 8(C), supra.

United Steelworkers of America v. American Mfg. Co.
363 U.S. 564 (1960)

Douglas, J. This suit was brought by petitioner union in the District Court to compel arbitration of a "grievance" that petitioner, acting for one Sparks, a union member, had filed with the respondent, Sparks' employer. The employer defended on the ground (1) that Sparks is estopped from making his claim because he had a few days previously settled a workmen's compensation claim against the company on the basis that he was permanently partially disabled, (2) that Sparks is not physically able to do the work, and (3) that this type of dispute is not arbitrable under the collective bargaining agreement in question.

The agreement provided that during its term there would be "no strike," unless the employer refused to abide by a decision of the arbitrator. The agreement sets out a detailed grievance procedure with a provision for arbitration (regarded as the standard form) of all disputes between the parties "as to the meaning, interpretation and application of the provisions of this agreement."[1]

The agreement reserves to the management power to suspend or discharge any employee "for cause."[2] It also contains a provision that the employer will employ and promote employees on the principle of seniority "where ability and efficiency are equal." Sparks left his work due to an injury and while off work brought an action for compensation benefits. The case was settled, Sparks' physician expressing the opinion that the injury had made him 25% "permanently partially disabled." That was on September 9. Two weeks later the union filed a grievance which charged that Sparks was entitled to return to his job by virtue of the seniority provision of the collective bargaining agreement. Respondent refused to arbitrate and this action was brought. The District Court held that Sparks, having accepted the settlement on the basis of permanent partial disability, was estopped to claim any senior-

---

[1] The relevant arbitration provisions read as follows:

"Any disputes, misunderstandings, differences or grievances arising between the parties as to the meaning, interpretation and application of the provisions of this agreement, which are not adjusted as herein provided, may be submitted to the Board of Arbitration for decision. . . .

"The arbitrator may interpret this agreement and apply it to the particular case under consideration but shall, however, have no authority to add to, subtract from, or modify the terms of the agreement. . . ."

[2] "The Management of the works, the direction of the working force, plant layout and routine of work, including the right to hire, suspend, transfer, discharge or otherwise discipline any employee for cause, such cause being: infraction of company rules, inefficiency, insubordination, contagious disease harmful to others, and any other ground or reason that would tend to reduce or impair the efficiency of plant operation; and to lay off employees because of lack of work, is reserved to the Company, provided it does not conflict with this agreement. . . ."

ity or employment rights and granted the motion for summary judgment. The Court of Appeals affirmed, 264 F.2d 624, for different reasons. After reviewing the evidence it held that the grievance is "a frivolous, patently baseless one, not subject to arbitration under the collective bargaining agreement." Id., at 628. . . .

. . . [The] policy [of LMRA, §203(d)] can be effectuated only if the means chosen by the parties for settlement of their differences under a collective bargaining agreement is given full play.

A state decision that held to the contrary announced a principle that could only have a crippling effect on grievance arbitration. The case was International Assn. of Machinists v. Cutler-Hammer, Inc., 271 App. Div. 917, 67 N.Y.S.2d 317, aff'd 297 N.Y. 519, 74 N.E.2d 464. It held that "If the meaning of the provision of the contract sought to be arbitrated is beyond dispute, there cannot be anything to arbitrate and the contract cannot be said to provide for arbitration." 271 App. Div., at 918, 67 N.Y.S.2d, at 318. The lower courts in the instant case had a like preoccupation with ordinary contract law. The collective agreement requires arbitration of claims that courts might be unwilling to entertain. In the context of the plant or industry the grievance may assume proportions of which judges are ignorant. Yet, the agreement is to submit all grievances to arbitration, not merely those that a court may deem to be meritorious. There is no exception in the "no strike" clause and none therefore should be read into the grievance clause, since one is the quid pro quo for the other. . . . The function of the court is very limited when the parties have agreed to submit all questions of contract interpretation to the arbitrator. It is confined to ascertaining whether the party seeking arbitration is making a claim which on its face is governed by the contract. Whether the moving party is right or wrong is a question of contract interpretation for the arbitrator. In these circumstances the moving party should not be deprived of the arbitrator's judgment, when it was his judgment and all that it connotes that was bargained for.

The courts, therefore, have no business weighing the merits of the grievance, considering whether there is equity in a particular claim, or determining whether there is particular language in the written instrument which will support the claim. The agreement is to submit all grievances to arbitration, not merely those which the court will deem meritorious. The processing of even frivolous claims may have therapeutic values of which those who are not a part of the plant environment may be quite unaware.

The union claimed in this case that the company had violated a specific provision of the contract. The company took the position that it had not violated that clause. There was, therefore, a dispute between the parties as to "the meaning, interpretation and application" of the collective bargaining agreement. Arbitration should have been ordered. . . .

Reversed.

[Frankfurter, and Whittaker, JJ., concurred in the result.]

Black, J., took no part in the consideration or decision of this case.

[Brennan, J., with whom Harlan J., joined, wrote a concurring opinion, which appears at p. 984, infra.]

NOTE

The preceding case and the two that follow, which are known as the "Steelworkers trilogy," evoked an extensive literature, including: Aaron, Arbitration in the Federal Courts: Aftermath of the Trilogy, 9 U.C.L.A. L. Rev. 360 (1962); Meltzer, The Supreme Court, Arbitrability and Collective Bargaining, 28 U. Chi. L. Rev. 464 (1960); Hays, The Supreme Court and Labor Law—October Term 1959, 60 Colum. L. Rev. 901 (1960); Symposium—Arbitration and the Courts, 58 Nw. U.L. Rev. 466 (1963).

United Steelworkers of America v. Warrior & Gulf Navigation Co.
363 U.S. 574 (1960)

Douglas, J. Respondent transports steel and steel products by barge and maintains a terminal at Chicksaw, Alabama, where it performs maintenance and repair work on its barges. The employees at that terminal constitute a bargaining unit covered by a collective bargaining agreement negotiated by petitioner union. Respondent between 1956 and 1958 laid off some employees, reducing the bargaining unit from 42 to 23 men. This reduction was due in part to respondent contracting maintenance work, previously done by its employees, to other companies. The latter used respondent's supervisors to lay out the work and hired some of [respondent's] laid-off employees (at reduced wages). Some were in fact assigned to work on respondent's barges. A number of employees signed a grievance which petitioner presented to respondent, the grievance reading:

> We are hereby protesting the Company's actions, of arbitrarily and unreasonably contracting out work to other concerns, that could and previously has been performed by Company employees.
>
> This practice becomes unreasonable, unjust and discriminatory in lieu [sic] of the fact that at present there are a number of employees that have been laid off for about 1 and 1/2 years or more for allegedly [sic] lack of work.
>
> Confronted with these facts we charge that the Company is in violation of

the contract by inducing a partial lockout, of a number of the employees who would otherwise be working were it not for this unfair practice.

The collective agreement had both a "no strike" and a "no lockout" provision. It also had a grievance procedure which provided in relevant part as follows:

> Issues which conflict with any Federal statute in its application as established by Court procedure or matters which are strictly a function of management shall not be subject to arbitration under this section.
>
> Should differences arise between the Company and the Union or its members employed by the Company as to the meaning and application of the provisions of this Agreement, or should any local trouble of any kind arise, there shall be no suspension of work on account of such differences but an earnest effort shall be made to settle such differences immediately in the following manner:
>
> A. For Maintenance Employees:
>
> First, between the aggrieved employees, and the Foreman involved;
>
> Second, between a member or members of the Grievance Committee designated by the Union, and the Foreman and Master Mechanic. . . .
>
> Fifth, if agreement has not been reached the matter shall be referred to an impartial umpire for decision. The parties shall meet to decide on an umpire acceptable to both. If no agreement on selection of an umpire is reached, the parties shall jointly petition the United States Conciliation Service for suggestion of a list of umpires from which selection will be made. The decision of the umpire shall be final.

Settlement of this grievance was not had and respondent refused arbitration. This suit was then commenced by the union to compel it.

The District Court granted respondent's motion to dismiss the complaint. 168 F. Supp. 702. It held after hearing evidence, much of which went to the merits of the grievance, that the agreement did not "confide in an arbitrator the right to review the defendant's business judgment in contracting out work." Id., at 705. It further held that "the contracting out of repair and maintenance work, as well as construction work, is strictly a function of management not limited in any respect by the labor agreement involved here." Ibid. The Court of Appeals affirmed by a divided vote, 269 F.2d 633, the majority holding that the collective agreement had withdrawn from the grievance procedure "matters which are strictly a function of management" and that contracting out fell in that exception. . . .

We held in [Lincoln Mills], 353 U.S. 448, that a grievance arbitration provision in a collective agreement could be enforced by reason of §301(a) of the [Act] and that the policy to be applied in enforcing this type of arbitration was that reflected in our national labor laws. Id., at 456-457. The present federal policy is to promote industrial stabilization through the collective bargaining agreement. Id., at 453-454. A major factor in achieving industrial peace is the inclusion of a provision for arbitration of grievances in the collective bargaining agreement.[4]

Thus the run of arbitration cases, illustrated by Wilko v. Swan, 346 U.S. 427, becomes irrelevant to our problem. There the choice is between the adjudication of cases or controversies in courts with established procedures or even special statutory safeguards on the one hand and the settlement of them in the more informal arbitration tribunal on the other. In the commercial case, arbitration is the substitute for litigation. Here arbitration is the substitute for industrial strife. Since arbitration of labor disputes has quite different functions from arbitration under an ordinary commercial agreement, the hostility evinced by courts toward arbitration of commercial agreements has no place here. For arbitration of labor disputes under collective bargaining agreements is part and parcel of the collective bargaining process itself.

The collective bargaining agreement states the rights and duties of the parties. It is more than a contract; it is a generalized code to govern a myriad of cases which the draftsmen cannot wholly anticipate. See Shulman, Reason, Contract, and Law in Labor Relations, 68 Harv. L. Rev. 999, 1004-1005. The collective agreement covers the whole employment relationship.[5] It calls into being a new common law — the common law of a particular industry or of a particular plant. As one observer has put it:[6]

> . . . [I]t is not unqualifiedly true that a collective bargaining agreement is simply a document by which the union and employees have imposed upon management limited, express restrictions of its otherwise absolute right to manage the enterprise, so that an employee's claim must fail unless he can

---

[4] Complete effectuation of the federal policy is achieved when the agreement contains both an arbitration provision for all unresolved grievances and an absolute prohibition of strikes, the arbitration agreement being the "quid pro quo" for the agreement not to strike. Textile Workers v. Lincoln Mills, 353 U.S. 448, 455.

[5] "Contracts which ban strikes often provide for lifting the ban under certain conditions. . . . [C]ertain *subjects* may be exempted from the scope of the pledge, or the pledge may be lifted after certain *procedures* are followed by the union. . . .

"Most frequent conditions for lifting no-strike pledges are: (1) The occurrence of a deadlock in wage reopening negotiations; and (2) violation of the contract, especially noncompliance with the grievance procedure and failure to abide by an arbitration award.

"No-strike pledges may also be lifted after compliance with specified procedures. Some contracts permit the union to strike after the grievance procedure has been exhausted without a settlement, and where arbitration is not prescribed as the final recourse. Other contracts permit a strike if mediation efforts fail, or after a specified cooling-off period." Collective Bargaining, Negotiations and Contracts, Bureau of National Affairs, Inc., 77:101.

[6] Cox, Reflections Upon Labor Arbitration, 72 Harv. L. Rev. 1482, 1498-1499 (1959).

point to a specific contract provision upon which the claim is founded. There are too many people, too many problems, too many unforeseeable contingencies to make the words of the contract the exclusive source of rights and duties. One cannot reduce all the rules governing a community like an industrial plant to fifteen or even fifty pages. Within the sphere of collective bargaining, the institutional characteristics and the governmental nature of the collective bargaining process demand a common law of the shop which implements and furnishes the context of the agreement. We must assume that intelligent negotiators acknowledged so plain a need unless they stated a contrary rule in plain words.

A collective bargaining agreement is an effort to erect a system of industrial self-government. When most parties enter into contractual relationship they do so voluntarily, in the sense that there is no real compulsion to deal with one another, as opposed to dealing with other parties. This is not true of the labor agreement. The choice is generally not between entering or refusing to enter into a relationship, for that in all probability preexists the negotiations. Rather it is between having that relationship governed by an agreed-upon rule of law or leaving each and every matter subject to a temporary resolution dependent solely upon the relative strength, at any given moment, of the contending forces. The mature labor agreement may attempt to regulate all aspects of the complicated relationship, from the most crucial to the most minute over an extended period of time. Because of the compulsion to reach agreement and the breadth of the matters covered, as well as the need for a fairly concise and readable instrument, the product of negotiations (the written document) is, in the words of the late Dean Shulman, "a compilation of diverse provisions: some provide objective criteria almost automatically applicable; some provide more or less specific standards which require reason and judgment in their application; and some do little more than leave problems to future consideration with an expression of hope and good faith." *Shulman*, supra, at 1005. Gaps may be left to be filled in by reference to the practices of the particular industry and of the various shops covered by the agreement. Many of the specific practices which underlie the agreement may be unknown, except in hazy form, even to the negotiators. Courts and arbitration in the context of most commercial contracts are resorted to because there has been a breakdown in the working relationship of the parties; such resort is the unwanted exception. But the grievance machinery under a collective bargaining agreement is at the very heart of the system of industrial self-government. Arbitration is the means of solving the unforeseeable by molding a system of private law for all the problems which may arise and to provide for their solution in a way which will generally accord with the variant needs and desires of the parties. The processing of disputes through the grievance machinery is actually a vehicle by which meaning and content are given to the collective bargaining agreement.

Apart from matters that the parties specifically exclude, all of the questions on which the parties disagree must therefore come within the scope of the grievance and arbitration provisions. . . . The grievance procedure is, in other words, a part of the continuous collective bargaining process. It, rather than a strike, is the terminal point of a disagreement.

The labor arbitrator performs functions which are not normal to the courts; the considerations which help him fashion judgments may indeed be foreign to the competence of courts.

> A proper conception of the arbitrator's function is basic. He is not a public tribunal imposed upon the parties by superior authority which the parties are obliged to accept. He has no general charter to administer justice for a community which transcends the parties. He is rather part of a system of self-government created by and confined to the parties. . . .

Shulman, supra, at 1016.

The labor arbitrator's source of law is not confined to the express provisions of the contract, as the industrial common law — the practices of the industry and the shop — is equally a part of the collective bargaining agreement although not expressed in it. The labor arbitrator is usually chosen because of the parties' confidence in his knowledge of the common law of the shop and their trust in his personal judgment to bring to bear considerations which are not expressed in the contract as criteria for judgment. The parties expect that his judgment of a particular grievance will reflect not only what the contract says but, insofar as the collective bargaining agreement permits, such factors as the effect upon productivity of a particular result, its consequence to the morale of the shop, his judgment whether tensions will be heightened or diminished. For the parties' objective in using the arbitration process is primarily to further their common goal of uninterrupted production under the agreement to make the agreement serve their specialized needs. The ablest judge cannot be expected to bring the same experience and competence to bear upon the determination of a grievance, because he cannot be similarly informed.

The Congress, however, has by §301 . . . assigned the courts the duty of determining whether the reluctant party has breached his promise to arbitrate. For arbitration is a matter of contract and a party cannot be required to submit to arbitration any dispute which he has not agreed so to submit. Yet, to be consistent with congressional policy in favor of settlement of disputes by the parties through the machinery of arbitration, the judicial inquiry under §301 must be strictly confined to the question whether the reluctant party did agree to arbitrate the grievance or did agree to give the arbitrator power to make the award he made. An order to arbitrate the particular grievance should not be denied unless it may be said with positive assurance that the arbitration clause is not susceptible of an interpretation that covers the asserted dispute. Doubts should be resolved in favor of coverage.[7]

We do not agree with the lower courts that contracting-out grievances were necessarily excepted from the grievance procedure of this agreement. To be sure, the agreement provides that "matters which are strictly a function of management shall not be subject to arbitration." But it goes on to say that if "differences" arise or if "any local trouble of any kind" arises, the grievance procedure shall be applicable.

Collective bargaining agreements regulate or restrict the exercise of management functions; they do not oust management from the performance of them. Management hires and fires, pays and promotes, supervises and plans. All these are part of its function, and absent a collective bargaining agreement, it may be exercised freely except as limited by public law and by the willingness of employees to work under the particular, unilaterally imposed conditions. A collective bargaining agreement may treat only with certain specific practices, leaving the rest to management but subject to the possibility of work stoppages. When, however, an absolute no-strike clause is included in the agreement, then in a very real sense everything that management does is subject to the agreement, for either management is prohibited or limited in the action it takes, or if not, it is protected from interference by strikes. This comprehensive reach of the collective bargaining agreement does not mean, however, that the language, "strictly a function of management," has no meaning.

"Strictly a function of management" might be thought to refer to any practice of management in which, under particular circumstances prescribed by the agreement, it is permitted to indulge. But if courts, in order to determine arbitrability, were allowed to determine what is permitted and what is not, the arbitration clause would be swallowed up by the exception. Every grievance in a sense involves a claim that management has violated some provision of the agreement.

Accordingly, "strictly a function of management" must be interpreted as referring only to that over which the contract gives management complete control and unfettered discretion. Respondent claims that the contracting out of work falls within this category. Contracting out work is the basis of many

---

[7]. . . Where the assertion by the claimant is that the parties excluded from court determination not merely the decision of the merits of the grievance but also the question of arbitrability, vesting the power to make both decisions in the arbitrator, the claimant must bear the burden of a clear demonstration of that purpose.

grievances; and that type of claim is grist in the mills of the arbitrators. A specific collective bargaining agreement may exclude contracting out from the grievance procedure. Or a written collateral agreement may make clear that contracting out was not a matter for arbitration. In such a case a grievance based solely on contracting out would not be arbitrable. Here, however, there is no such provision. Nor is there any showing that the parties designed the phrase "strictly a function of management" to encompass any and all forms of contracting out.[j] In the absence of any express provision excluding a particular grievance from arbitration, we think only the most forceful evidence of a purpose to exclude the claim from arbitration can prevail, particularly where, as here, the exclusion clause is vague and the arbitration clause quite broad. Since any attempt by a court to infer such a purpose necessarily comprehends the merits, the court should view with suspicion an attempt to persuade it to become entangled in the construction of the substantive provisions of a labor agreement, even through the back door of interpreting the arbitration clause, when the alternative is to utilize the services of an arbitrator.

The grievance alleged that the contracting out was a violation of the collective bargaining agreement. There was, therefore, a dispute "as to the meaning and application of the provisions of this Agreement" which the parties had agreed would be determined by arbitration. . . .

Reversed.

Frankfurter, J., concurs in the result.

Black, J., took no part in the consideration or decision of this case.

BRENNAN, J., with whom HARLAN, J., joins, concurring: While I join in the Court's opinion in Nos. 443 [the *Warrior* case, p. 978], 360 [the *American Manufacturing* case, p. 976], and 538 [the *Enterprise Wheel* case, p. 987], I add a word in Nos. 443 and 360.

. . . [T]he arbitration promise is itself a contract. The parties are free to make that promise as broad or as narrow as they wish, for there is no compulsion in law requiring them to include any such promises in their agreement. The meaning of the arbitration promise is not to be found simply by reference to the dictionary definitions of the words the parties use, or by reference to the interpretation of commercial arbitration clauses. Words in a collective bargaining agreement, rightly viewed by the Court to be the charter instrument of a system of industrial self-government, like words in a

---

[j][The management-rights clause in *Warrior*, 168 F. Supp. 702, 704 (S.D. Ala. 1958), provided: "The management of the Company and the direction of the working forces, including the right to hire, suspend or discharge for proper cause, or transfer, and the right to relieve employees from duty because of lack of work, or for other legitimate reasons, is vested exclusively in the Company, provided that this will not be used for purposes of discrimination against any member of the Union." — EDS.]

statute, are to be understood only by reference to the background which gave rise to their inclusion. The Court therefore avoids the prescription of inflexible rules for the enforcement of arbitration promises. Guidance is given by identifying the various considerations which a court should take into account when construing a particular clause — considerations of the milieu in which the clause is negotiated and of the national labor policy. It is particularly underscored that the arbitral process in collective bargaining presupposes that the parties wanted the informed judgment of an arbitrator, precisely for the reason that judges cannot provide it. Therefore, a court asked to enforce a promise to arbitrate should ordinarily refrain from involving itself in the interpretation of the substantive provisions of the contract. . . .

The issue in the *Warrior* case is essentially no different from that in *American*, that is, it is whether the company agreed to arbitrate a particular grievance. In contrast to *American*, however, the arbitration promise here excludes a particular area from arbitration — "matters which are strictly a function of management." Because the arbitration promise is different, the scope of the court's inquiry may be broader. Here, a court may be required to examine the substantive provisions of the contract to ascertain whether the parties have provided that contracting out shall be a "function of management." If a court may delve into the merits to the extent of inquiring whether the parties have expressly agreed whether or not contracting out was a "function of management," why was it error for the lower court here to evaluate the evidence of bargaining history for the same purpose? Neat logical distinctions do not provide the answer. The Court rightly concludes that appropriate regard for the national labor policy and the special factors relevant to the labor arbitral process, admonish that judicial inquiry into the merits of this grievance should be limited to the search for an explicit provision which brings the grievance under the cover of the exclusion clause since "the exclusion clause is vague and arbitration clause quite broad." The hazard of going further into the merits is amply demonstrated by what the courts below did. On the basis of inconclusive evidence, those courts found that Warrior was in no way limited by any implied covenants of good faith and fair dealing from contracting out as it pleased — which would necessarily mean that Warrior was free completely to destroy the collective bargaining agreement by contracting out all the work.

The very ambiguity of the *Warrior* exclusion clause suggests that the parties were generally more concerned with having an arbitrator render decisions as to the meaning of the contract than they were in restricting the arbitrator's jurisdiction. The case might of course be otherwise were the arbitration clause very narrow, or the exclusion clause quite specific, for the inference might then be permissible that the parties had manifested a greater interest in confining the arbitrator; the presumption of arbitrability would then not have the same force and the Court would be somewhat freer to examine into the merits.

The Court makes reference to an arbitration clause being the *quid pro quo* for a no-strike clause. I do not understand the Court to mean that the application of the principles announced today depends upon the presence of a no-strike clause in the agreement.

WHITTAKER, J., dissenting. [The dissent urged forcefully that the Court's general approach departed from its own decisions and the parties' contract and continued:]

. . . [T]he parties by their conduct over many years interpreted the contracting out of major repair work to be "strictly a function of management," and if, as the concurring opinion suggests, the words of the contract can "be understood only by reference to the background which gave rise to their inclusion," then the interpretation given by the parties over 19 years to the phrase "matters which are strictly a function of management" should logically have some significance here. By their contract, the parties agreed that "matters which are strictly a function of management shall not be subject to arbitration." The union over the course of many years repeatedly tried to induce the employer to agree to a covenant prohibiting the contracting out of work, but was never successful. The union again made such an effort in negotiating the very contract involved here, and, failing of success, signed the contract, knowing, of course, that it did not contain any such covenant, but that, to the contrary, it contained, just as had the former contracts, a covenant that "matters which are strictly a function of management shall not be subject to arbitration." Does not this show that, instead of signifying a willingness to submit to arbitration the matter of whether the employer might continue to contract out work, the parties fairly agreed to exclude at least that matter from arbitration? . . .

NOTES

1. Does *Warrior & Gulf* mean that a court is required to enforce the parties' agreement to arbitrate even when the subject of a grievance can fairly be said to be "arguably excluded" from the arbitration clause?

2. After the Court's decision in the principal case, would an arbitrator be barred from deciding that contracting out was "strictly a function of management" and that the grievance was, accordingly, not arbitrable? See Communication Wkrs. v. Pacific N.W. Bell Tel. Co., 337 F.2d 455, 459-460 (9th Cir. 1964); Smith & Jones, The Impact of the Emerging Federal Law of Grievance Arbitration on Judges, Arbitrators, and Parties, 52

Va. L. Rev. 831, 871-873 (1966). Courts have disagreed regarding the propriety of resorting to extrinsic evidence in judicial determinations of arbitrability. See Local 13, Professional Engrs. v. General Electric Co., 531 F.2d 1178, 1182-1184 (3d Cir. 1976). If bargaining history can affect the arbitrability issue as well as the merits, and if the arbitrator but not a court may consider such history, should an arbitrator be bound by a judicial determination of arbitrability? Does his being bound make any practical difference, given his authority over the merits? In *Warrior & Gulf*, for instance, could not the arbitrator properly find that even though contracting out was not strictly a function of management for purposes of arbitrability, the particular contracting out, on the merits, was not a violation of the agreement?

Subsequent to the Court's decision, the arbitrator in Warrior & Gulf Navigation Co., 36 Lab. Arb. 695 (1961), after ruling that the exclusion from arbitration of "matters . . . strictly a function of management" did not cover contracting out, rendered an award that recognized "implied limitations" on the company's right to subcontract but failed to specify the nature of such limitations and basically directed the parties "to resolve the problem to their own interests and satisfaction."

3. Suppose that the *Warrior & Gulf* agreement had also contained a management-rights clause providing that "the contracting out of work is understood to be a right reserved to the Company." Would a grievance alleging that the company's contracting out violated the seniority, wage, and recognition clauses have been arbitrable? See Machinists v. General Electric Co., 406 F.2d 1046 (2d Cir. 1969).

4. In Electrical Wkrs. v. General Electric Co., 407 F.2d 253, 259 (2d Cir. 1968), *cert. denied*, 395 U.S. 904 (1969), a contractual clause negating the *Warrior* presumption of arbitrability was said to raise "a substantial question whether 'national labor policy' may be so blithely diluted." But cf. H.K. Porter Co. v. NLRB, supra p. 844, and NLRB v. Burns Security Services, infra p. 1009.

United Steelworkers of America v. Enterprise Wheel & Car Corp.
363 U.S. 593 (1960)

Douglas, J. Petitioner union and respondent during the period relevant here had a collective bargaining agreement which provided that any differences "as to the meaning and application" of the agreement should be submitted to arbitration and that the arbitrator's decision "shall be final and binding on the parties." . . . The agreement [also] stated:

Should it be determined by the Company or by an arbitrator in accordance with the grievance procedure that the employee has been suspended unjustly or discharged in violation of the provisions of this Agreement, the Company shall reinstate the employee and pay full compensation at the employee's regular rate of pay for the time lost.

The agreement also provided: ". . . It is understood and agreed that neither party will institute *civil suits* or *legal proceedings* against the other for alleged violation of any of the provisions of this labor contract; instead all disputes will be settled in the manner outlined in this Article III—Adjustment of Grievances."

A group of employees left their jobs in protest against the discharge of one employee. A union official advised them at once to return to work. An official of respondent at their request gave them permission and then rescinded it. The next day they were told that they did not have a job any more "until this thing was settled one way or the other."

A grievance was filed; and when respondent finally refused to arbitrate, this suit was brought for specific enforcement of the arbitration provisions of the agreement. The District Court ordered arbitration. The arbitrator found that the discharge of the men was not justified, though their conduct, he said, was improper. In his view the facts warranted at most a suspension of the men for 10 days each. After their discharge and before the arbitration award the collective bargaining agreement had expired. The union, however, continued to represent the workers at the plant. The arbitrator rejected the contention that expiration of the agreement barred reinstatement of the employees. He held that the provision of the agreement above quoted imposed an unconditional obligation on the employer. He awarded reinstatement with back pay minus pay for a 10-day suspension and such sums as these employees received from other employment.

Respondent refused to comply with the award. Petitioner moved the District Court for enforcement. [It] directed respondent to comply. 168 F. Supp. 308. The Court of Appeals, while agreeing that the District Court had jurisdiction to enforce an arbitration award under a collective bargaining agreement, held that the failure of the award to specify the amounts to be deducted from the back pay rendered the award unenforceable. That defect, it agreed, could be remedied by requiring the parties to complete the arbitration. It went on to hold, however, that an award for back pay subsequent to the date of termination of the collective bargaining agreement could not be enforced. It also held that the requirement for reinstatement of the discharged employees was likewise unenforceable because the collective bargaining agreement had expired. 269 F.2d 327. . . .

The refusal of courts to review the merits of an arbitration award is the proper approach to arbitration under collective bargaining agreements. The federal policy of settling labor disputes by arbitration would be undermined if courts had the final say on the merits of the awards. As we stated in [*Warrior & Gulf Navigation*, 363 U.S. 574], decided this day, the arbitrators under these collective agreements are indispensable agencies in a continuous collective bargaining process. They sit to settle disputes at the plant level — disputes that require for their solution knowledge of the custom and practices of a particular factory or of a particular industry as reflected in particular agreements.[2]

When an arbitrator is commissioned to interpret and apply the collective bargaining agreement, he is to bring his informed judgment to bear in order to reach a fair solution of a problem. This is especially true when it comes to formulating remedies. There the need is for flexibility in meeting a wide variety of situations. The draftsmen may never have thought of what specific remedy should be awarded to meet a particular contingency. Nevertheless, an arbitrator is confined to interpretation and application of the collective bargaining agreement; he does not sit to dispense his own brand of industrial justice. He may of course look for guidance from many sources, yet his award is legitimate only so long as it draws its essence from the collective bargaining agreement. When the arbitrator's words manifest an infidelity to this obligation, courts have no choice but to refuse enforcement of the award.

The opinion of the arbitrator in this case, as it bears upon the award of back pay beyond the date of the agreement's expiration and reinstatement, is ambiguous. It may be read as based solely upon the arbitrator's view of the requirements of enacted legislation, which would mean that he exceeded the scope of the submission. Or it may be read as embodying a construction of the agreement itself, perhaps with the arbitrator looking to "the law" for help in determining the sense of the agreement. A mere ambiguity in the opinion accompanying an award, which permits the inference that the arbitrator may have exceeded his authority, is not a reason for refusing to enforce the award. Arbitrators have no obligation to the court to give their reasons for an award. To require opinions free of ambiguity may lead arbitrators to play it safe by writing no supporting opinions. This would be undesirable for a well-reasoned opinion tends to engender confidence in the integrity of the process

---

[2] "Persons unfamiliar with mills and factories — farmers or professors, for example — often remark upon visiting them that they seem like another world. This is particularly true if, as in the steel industry, both tradition and technology have strongly and uniquely molded the ways men think and act when at work. The newly hired employee, the 'green hand,' is gradually initiated into what amounts to a miniature society. There he finds himself in a strange environment that assaults his senses with unusual sounds and smells and often with different 'weather conditions' such as sudden drafts of heat, cold, or humidity. He discovers that the society of which he only gradually becomes a part has of course a formal government of its own — the rules which management and the union have laid down — but that it also differs from or parallels the world outside in social classes, folklore, ritual, and traditions. . . ." Walker, Life in the Automatic Factory, 36 Harv. Bus. Rev. 111, 117.

and aids in clarifying the underlying agreement. Moreover, we see no reason to assume that this arbitrator has abused the trust the parties confided in him and has not stayed within the areas marked out for his consideration. It is not apparent that he went beyond the submission. The Court of Appeals' opinion refusing to enforce the reinstatement and partial back pay portions of the award was not based upon any finding that the arbitrator did not premise his award on his construction of the contract. It merely disagreed with the arbitrator's construction of it.

The collective bargaining agreement could have provided that if any of the employees were wrongfully discharged, the remedy would be reinstatement and back pay up to the date they were returned to work. Respondent's major argument seems to be that by applying correct principles of law to the interpretation of the collective bargaining agreement it can be determined that the agreement did not so provide, and that therefore the arbitrator's decision was not based upon the contract. The acceptance of this view would require courts, even under the standard arbitration clause, to review the merits of every construction of the contract. This plenary review by a court of the merits would make meaningless the provisions that the arbitrator's decision is final, for in reality it would almost never be final. . . . [T]he question of interpretation of the collective bargaining agreement is a question for the arbitrator. It is the arbitrator's construction which was bargained for; and so far as the arbitrator's decision concerns construction of the contract, the courts have no business overruling him because their interpretation of the contract is different from his.

We agree with the Court of Appeals that the judgment of the District Court should be modified so that the amounts due the employees may be definitely determined by arbitration. In all other respects we think the judgment of the District Court should be affirmed. Accordingly, we reverse the judgment of the Court of Appeals, except for that modification, and remand the case to the District Court for proceedings in conformity with this opinion.

Frankfurter, J., concurs in the result.

Black, J., took no part in the consideration or decision of this case. . . . [The dissenting opinion of Whittaker, J., is omitted.]

NOTES

1. For consideration of the effect of expiration of the collective agreement on the duty to arbitrate, see Nolde Bros. v. Local 358, Bakery Wkrs., infra p. 1068.

2. Judge Paul R. Hays of the United States Court of Appeals for the Second Circuit, formerly an active and respected arbitrator, countered the

Court's eulogy of labor arbitration in the *Steelworkers* trilogy with the following indictment:

(1) "A proportion of arbitration awards . . . are decided not on the basis of the evidence or of the contract or other proper considerations," but in a way designed to preserve the arbitrator's employability. Regardless of the proportion of such awards, which is unknown, a system of adjudication in which the judge's income depends on pleasing those who engage him is per se a thoroughly undesirable system, wholly incompatible with the independence that a judicial officer should have.

(2) Some awards, though probably not a large number, are rigged.

(3) There is probably a "fairly widespread use" of "compromise awards," resulting from the desire of arbitrators to preserve their acceptability and from their failure to recognize that rules regarding the burden of persuasion are indispensable for any adversary proceeding.

(4) A large proportion of awards, "literally thousands of cases every year," are rendered by arbitrators "who do not have the requisite knowledge, training, skill, intelligence, and character."

(5) Some arbitrators engage in ambulance chasing and fee padding, prolong hearings by failing to control them, and delay decisions, thereby frustrating the quick and inexpensive adjudication that the system is supposed to provide.

(6) Arbitrators, in order to make themselves acceptable to unions, have introduced factors, such as the "common law" of the plant, extraneous to a proper construction of agreements, thereby increasing the power of unions. Labor Arbitration: A Dissenting View 49, 59, 61-70, 112 (1966).

Judge Hays proposed these remedies: Courts, if they are to enforce the duty to arbitrate and arbitral awards, should carefully scrutinize, instead of rubber stamping, awards. But the remedy Hays preferred is the withholding of any judicial assistance to the arbitration process. Finally, as a concession to believers in "special expertise" in those who adjudicate asserted contractual violations, he suggested the establishment of labor courts, based on European experience and employing simplified procedures, such as those used by small claims courts in this country. Id. at 79-80, 113, 116-117.

The immediate and widespread criticism of the Hays' assessment is described in Edwards, Advantages of Arbitration Over Litigation: Reflections of a Judge, Proc., 35th Ann. Meeting, Natl. Acad. of Arb. 16 (1982). See also Jones & Smith, Management and Labor Appraisals and Criticisms of the Arbitration Process: A Report with Comments, 62 Mich. L. Rev. 1115 (1964) (reporting, at 1116-1117, the parties' overwhelming preference for arbitration over courts or alternative methods of adjudication); Getman, The Debate Over the Calibre of Arbitrators: Judge Hays and His Critics, 44 Ind. L.J. 182 (1969).

Does it follow from the continued popularity of arbitration that Judge Hays was wrong? Are the parties to collective bargaining agreements likely to discontinue arbitration of contractual disputes if presented with compelling proofs that Judge Hays' criticisms of that system are well-founded?

3. At one extreme, the "rigged award" (referred to by Judge Hays, supra) involves the "farce" of an adversary hearing even though the union, the company, and the arbitrator have already agreed on the award. Such an arrangement involves "the crassest infringement of adjudicative integrity," as Professor Fuller put it in Collective Bargaining and the Arbitrator, 1963 Wis. L. Rev. 3, 20. Fuller also suggests circumstances presenting the agreed-upon award in "its most innocent form." Ibid. 20-21.

The Code of Professional Responsibility for Arbitrators of Labor-Management Disputes, of the National Academy of Arbitrators, the American Arbitration Association, and the Federal Mediation and Conciliation Service, Principle 2I (1974) provides as follows:

> 1. Prior to issuance of an award, the parties may jointly request the arbitrator to include in the award certain agreements between them, concerning some or all of the issues. If the arbitrator believes that a suggested award is proper, fair, sound, and lawful, it is consistent with professional responsibility to adopt it.
>
> a. *Before complying with such a request, an arbitrator must be certain that he or she understands the suggested settlement adequately in order to be able to appraise its terms. If it appears that pertinent facts or circumstances may not have been disclosed, the arbitrator should take the initiative to assure that all significant aspects of the case are fully understood. To this end, the arbitrator may request additional specific information and may question witnesses at a hearing.*

Prior to, or simultaneously with, the rendition of an award, agreed to in whole or in part by the parties, should the parties or the arbitrator be required to advise an individual grievant (or grievants) of those elements of the award agreed to by the parties? See Meltzer, Book Review, 34 U. Chi. L. Rev. 211, 216-217 (1966).

Goldberg & Brett, Grievance Mediation: An Alternative to Arbitration[k]

Labor arbitration has been criticized as being too expensive, slow and formal. The costs of arbitration — arbitrator's fee, transcript, and attorneys'

---

[k][We are grateful to Stephen B. Goldberg, Professor, Northwestern University Law School, and Jeanne M. Brett, Professor, Northwestern University Kellogg Graduate School

fees — frequently exceed $5,000, and the time required to obtain an arbitrator's decision is typically in excess of six months. Arbitration has also been criticized for its tendency to resolve grievances solely by reference to the contract, while slighting underlying labor relations problems.

An alternative procedure, grievance mediation, operates as follows:

1. After the final step of the internal grievance procedure, one or both parties, depending on the agreement, may take an unresolved grievance to mediation, rather than directly to arbitration. The mediation procedure is informal. The relevant facts are presented in a narrative fashion, rather than through examination of witnesses. The rules of evidence do not apply, and no record of the proceedings is made. All participants are encouraged to take an active role in the proceedings.

2. The mediator is an experienced arbitrator with mediatory skills. His or her primary effort is to help settle the grievance. If no settlement is possible, the mediator gives the parties an immediate oral advisory opinion, based on the bargaining agreement, as to how an arbitrator would decide the grievance.

3. The parties are not bound by that opinion and may go on to arbitration. The mediator may not serve as arbitrator, and nothing said or done during mediation can be used against a party at arbitration.

Because there is no transcript, briefs or written decision, mediation should be both faster and cheaper than arbitration. Because of the informal procedures for presenting the evidence, representation by lawyers is less necessary, and costs are likely to be cut substantially. Informality should make the parties more comfortable and more capable of focusing on their underlying problems. Since dealing with the real problem should lead to a real solution, outcomes should improve.

The central risk of grievance mediation is that it will not settle grievances. If most grievances are not settled, but go on to arbitration, mediation will add to the time and cost of dispute resolution. There is also the risk that, if mediation is speedy and inexpensive, a party will calculate that the chance of a mediated settlement that improves on the best offer in the prior steps of the grievance procedure will warrant the slight additional cost and delay involved. If mediation operates primarily to move settlements up one step in the grievance procedure, the total time and cost of dispute resolution would increase.

---

of Management, for these comments on mediation. For a fuller discussion of the theoretical issues involved, see Goldberg, The Mediation of Grievances Under a Collective Bargaining Contract: An Alternative to Arbitration, 77 N.W.U.L. Rev. 270 (1982). For an extensive report on the results of grievance mediation experiments, see Brett & Goldberg, Grievance Mediation in the Coal Industry: A Field Experiment, 37 Indus. & Labor Rel. Rev. 49 (October 1983). — Eds.]

We have been experimenting with grievance mediation since November 1980, primarily in the coal industry. A total of 494 grievances have been submitted to mediation, of which 415 (84 percent) were finally resolved without arbitration. The cost of mediation has averaged $300 per case, and the time from the request for mediation to the final resolution in mediation has been from 15 to 30 days. There has not been any substantial diminution in the rate at which the parties resolve grievances prior to mediation. The mediated settlements have frequently responded to the labor relations problem that triggered the grievance.

Mediation can succeed only if both the employer and the union engage in a good faith effort to settle grievances. If that effort is made, the available evidence indicates that it will result in resolving a high proportion of grievances more promptly, inexpensively and satisfactorily than would arbitration.

NOTE

For a valuable discussion of the different purposes and moralities of mediation and arbitration, including consideration of the risks of confusion of roles when an arbitrator seeks to perform both functions in relation to a single dispute, see Fuller, Collective Bargaining and the Arbitrator, 1963 Wis. L. Rev. 3, 24-42. On similar problems raised by pretrial settlement conferences conducted by trial judges, see Resnick, Managerial Judges, 96 Harv. L. Rev. 374 (1982).

Torrington Co. v. Metal Products Wkrs. Union, Local 1645, 362 F.2d 677 (2d Cir. 1966). The company had for 20 years maintained a unilaterally-established policy of granting employees paid time-off for voting, without incorporating it in a collective agreement. The company formally and publicly abrogated that policy about nine months before the expiration of the then current agreement. In negotiations for a renewal agreement, the company rejected the union's request (made during August or September 1963) for the reinstitution of the former policy. The renewal agreement, executed after a long strike during which nonstrikers had not been given paid time-off for voting, was silent about such pay. A grievance under the renewal agreement led to an arbitration award binding the company to the established practice until it was changed by mutual agreement. The trial court vacated the award, concluding that the arbitrator had exceeded his authority by going outside the terms of the contract and reading the election day benefit into the new contract even though the parties had negotiated on that issue without providing for it in the contract.

In affirming, the court of appeals, through Lumbard, J., declared:

". . . Torrington contends that the arbitrator exceeded his authority . . . by 'adding' the election day bonus to the terms of the January 1964 agreement. However, the arbitrator held that such a provision was implied by the prior practice of the parties. In some cases, it may be appropriate exercise of an arbitrator's authority to resolve ambiguities in the scope of a collective bargaining agreement on the basis of prior practice, since no agreement can reduce all aspects of the labor-management relationship to writing. However, while courts should be wary of rejecting the arbitrator's interpretation of the implications of the parties' prior practice, the mandate that the arbitrator stay within the confines of the collective bargaining agreement, . . . requires a reviewing court to pass upon whether the agreement authorizes the arbitrator to expand its express terms on the basis of the parties' prior practice. Therefore, we hold that the question of an arbitrator's authority is subject to judicial review, and that the arbitrator's decision that he has authority should not be accepted where the reviewing court can clearly perceive that he has derived that authority from sources outside the collective bargaining agreement at issue. See Textile Workers Union of America v. American Thread Co., 291 F.2d 894 (4 Cir. 1961).[6]

"Unfortunately, as the dissenting opinion illustrates, agreeing upon these general principles does not make this case any easier. Certain it is that Torrington's policy of paid time off to vote was well established by 1962. On this basis, the arbitrator ruled that the policy must continue during the 1964 agreement because Torrington did not negotiate a contrary policy into that agreement. To bolster his decision, the arbitrator noted that Torrington's written demands of September 26, 1963, constituted the first occasion on which either party did not expressly insist that its election day position be adopted. Therefore, he concluded, it was the company which removed this question 'from the table' and the company cannot complain if its policy under the old contract is now continued.

"We cannot accept this interpretation of the negotiations. . . . [L]abor contracts generally state affirmatively what conditions the parties agree to,

---

[6] . . . [I]t can be argued that our decision authorizes an impermissible review of the "merits" in a case where the principal issue was whether the arbitrator should find an implied substantive obligation in the contract, see Meltzer, The Supreme Court, Arbitrability, and Collective Bargaining, 28 U. Chi. L. Rev. 464, 484-85 (1961), but we think this position is contrary to Enterprise Wheel.

The question of the arbitrator's authority is really one of his contractual jurisdiction, and the courts cannot be expected to place their stamp of approval upon his action without making some examination of his jurisdiction to act. As stated above, we think more exhaustive judicial review of this question is appropriate after the award has been made than before the award in a suit to compel arbitration; in this way, the court receives the benefit of the arbitrator's interpretive skills as to the matter of his contractual authority. . . .

more specifically, what restraints the parties will place on management's freedom of action. While it may be appropriate to resolve a question never raised during negotiations on the basis of prior practice in the plant or industry, it is quite another thing to assume that the contract confers a specific benefit when that benefit was discussed during negotiations but omitted from the contract. . . .

"The arbitrator's primary justification for reading the election day benefit into the 1964 agreement was that such a benefit corresponded to the parties' prior practice. But in this the arbitrator completely ignored . . . that the company had revoked that policy almost ten months earlier, by newsletter to the employees in December 1962 and by formal notice to the Union in April 1963. It was within the employer's discretion to make such a change since the narrow arbitration clause in the previous collective bargaining agreement precluded resort to arbitration by the Union. And there was no showing that Torrington's announcement was merely a statement of bargaining position and was not a seriously intended change in policy.

"In light of this uncontroverted fact, and bearing in mind that the arbitrator has no jurisdiction to 'add to' the 1964 agreement, we do not think it was proper to place the 'burden' of securing an express contract provision in the 1964 contract on the company. At the start of negotiations, Torrington announced its intent to *continue* its previous change of election day policy. This was an express invitation to the Union to bargain with respect to this matter. After the Union failed to press for and receive a change in the 1964 agreement, the company was surely justified in applying in November 1964 a policy it had rightfully established in 1962, and had applied in November 1963 (during the strike).

". . . [T]he Union by pressing this grievance has attempted to have 'added' to the 1964 agreement a benefit which it did not think sufficiently vital to insist upon during negotiations for the contract which ended a long and costly strike. We find this sufficiently clear from the facts as found by the arbitrator to agree with the district court that the arbitrator exceeded his authority by ruling that such a benefit was implied in the terms of that agreement. . . ."

Feinberg, J. dissenting. . . . "[T]he new contract did not by its terms deal with the time off for voting issue. But the arbitrator reasoned that it was the company, not the union, that was trying to change the twenty-year old practice. It was the company that introduced the issue into the bargaining at the first negotiation meeting in August 1963, and insisted on a change in the practice. Thereafter, according to the arbitrator, the company 're-moved . . . [this demand] from the table. . . . Thus . . . both parties agreed that the old contract was to be continued except for certain changes among which was *not* a change in the practice of giving time off with pay for voting.'

"The arbitrator [correctly] assumed that a collective bargaining agreement can include terms or conditions not made explicit in the written contract. . . . In [*Warrior & Gulf Nav. Co.*], 363 U.S. 574, 580 (1960), the Supreme Court said: 'Gaps [in the "written document"] may be left to be filled in by reference to the practices of the particular industry and of the various shops covered by the agreement.' Moreover, the difference between the earlier (1961-1963) and the new contract in this case is most significant. The arbitration article in the earlier contract contained the following limitations on the arbitrator's power:

> The Company's decisions will stand and will not be over-ruled by any arbitrator unless the arbitrator can find that the Company misinterpreted or violated the express terms of the agreement. . . .
>
> No point not covered by this contract shall be subject to arbitration. . . .

"After a 16-week strike in which the scope of the arbitration clause was an important issue (which, in itself, is unusual), these limitations on the arbitrator's power were excluded in the new contract. This was a clear recognition by the parties that there can be 'implied' as well as 'express' terms in the agreement. In this case, the arbitrator held that pay for time off for voting was a benefit which was such 'an implied part of the contract.' If so, then, of course, the arbitrator did not 'add to, delete from, or modify, in any way, any of the provisions of this agreement' in violation of the arbitration clause.

"Thus, the arbitrator looked to prior practice, the conduct of the negotiation for the new contract and the agreement reached at the bargaining table to reach his conclusion that paid time off for voting was 'an implied part of the contract.' From all of this, I conclude that the arbitrator's award 'draws its essence from the collective bargaining agreement' and his words do not 'manifest an infidelity to this obligation.' Once that test is met, the inquiry ends. Whether the arbitrator's conclusion was correct is irrelevant because the parties agreed to abide by it, right or wrong. . . .'"

NOTES

1. There are two opposing views regarding the effect of past practices on obligations during the term of an agreement and thereafter: (a) the view usually advanced by employers, that, except for obligations set forth in the

agreement, the employer reserves full freedom of action; and (b) the competing view, usually urged by union spokesmen, that the written contract is supplemented by obligations implicit in "past practices," and that such practices can be changed only by mutual agreement. Is either view a wholly acceptable approach to the problem of balancing the interest in protecting the reasonable expectancies of employees and the interest in discretionary and experimental innovation? Given the wide range of practices, can the issue be resolved by a simple formula? See generally Phelps, Goldberg, and Chamberlain (three separate papers), Management's Reserved Rights, Proceedings of National Academy of Arbitrators, 9th Ann. Meeting, 102, 118, 138 (1956); Mittenthal, Past Practice, 59 Mich. L. Rev. 1017 (1961). Use of past practice to resolve ambiguous contractual provisions must be distinguished from its use to establish obligations concerning matters covered by clear provisions of the agreement or completely unregulated by the agreement.

2. Did the *Torrington* court obey the mandate of the *Steelworkers* trilogy? One critic of *Torrington* wrote:

> [The court's] performance squarely presents the question whether a court may review an arbitral determination for error. The assumption of that judicial role is fundamentally faulty. . . . Confiding decision to the arbitrator's final and binding determination means that the parties accept the risk of mistakes, however serious they may be. . . . If the loser in arbitration has even modest prospects of winning in court, litigation is encouraged, and this means not only *nisi prius* judicial intervention but appellate review as well. And prolongation of the controversy defeats the essence of arbitration — the conclusiveness of the award. The parties have agreed to "final and binding" arbitration. . . . They should be held to their word. [Dunau, Three Problems in Labor Arbitration, 55 Va. L. Rev. 427, 460-462 (1969).]

Do you agree that courts should have no responsibility for the merits of arbitration awards or for arbitral procedures? Would you defend the *Torrington* decision on the ground that there was no rational basis for the award in the agreement and that "final and binding" presupposes that the arbitrator not exceed his jurisdiction or deprive the parties of "due process"?

2. The Obligations of Successor Employers

The sale or transfer of a business gives rise to problems similar to those already explored in this chapter. How should the legitimate expectations of the employees affected be defined? How should those interests be balanced against the interest of firms and of the community in the transfer of resources to more productive uses? What are to be the roles of courts, the NLRB, and arbitrators (as well as Congress) in shaping the appropriate adjustments? Difficult problems are, of course, raised by fundamental business changes, regardless of whether a collective bargaining relationship is involved. But the presence of such a relationship introduces special problems. The extensive literature includes Benetar, Successorship Liability Under Labor Agreements, 1973 Wis. L. Rev. 1026; Goldberg, The Labor Law Obligations of a Successor Employer, 63 Nw. U.L. Rev. 735 (1969); Platt, The NLRB and the Arbitrator in Sale and Merger Situations, N.Y.U. 19th Ann. Conf. on Labor 375 (1967); Slicker, A Reconsideration of the Doctrine of Employer Successorship — A Step Toward a Rational Approach, 55 Minn. L. Rev. 1051 (1973).

John Wiley & Sons, Inc. v. Livingston
376 U.S. 543 (1964)

HARLAN, J. This is [a §301] action by a union . . . to compel arbitration under a collective bargaining agreement. The major questions presented are (1) whether a corporate employer must arbitrate with a union under a bargaining agreement between the union and another corporation which has merged with the employer, and, if so, (2) whether the courts or the arbitrator is the appropriate body to decide whether procedural prerequisites which, under the bargaining agreement, condition the duty to arbitrate have been met. . . . [W]e granted certiorari to review a judgment of the Court of Appeals directing arbitration in reversal of the District Court which had refused such relief. We affirm the judgment below, but with respect to the first question above, on grounds which may differ from those of the Court of Appeals, whose answer to that question is unclear.

I

District 65, Retail, Wholesale and Department Store Union, AFL-CIO, entered into a collective bargaining agreement with Interscience Publishers, Inc., a publishing firm, for a term expiring on January 31, 1962. The agreement did not contain an express provision making it binding on successors of Interscience. On October 2, 1961, Interscience [for genuine business reasons] merged with the petitioner, John Wiley & Sons, Inc., another publishing firm, and ceased to do business as a separate entity. . . .

At the time of the merger Interscience had about 80 employees, of whom 40 were represented by this Union. It had a single plant in New York City, and did an annual business of somewhat over $1,000,000. Wiley was a much larger concern, having separate office and warehouse facilities and about 300 employees, and doing an annual business of more than $9,000,000. None of Wiley's employees was represented by a union.

In discussions before and after the merger, . . . [t]he Union's position was that despite the merger it continued to represent the covered Interscience employees taken over by Wiley, and that Wiley was obligated to recognize certain rights of such employees which had "vested" under the Interscience bargaining agreement. Such rights . . . concerned matters typically covered by collective bargaining agreements, such as seniority status, severance pay, etc. The Union contended also that Wiley was required to make certain pension fund payments called for under the Interscience bargaining agreement.

Wiley, though recognizing for purposes of its own pension plan the Interscience service of the former Interscience employees, asserted that the merger terminated the bargaining agreement for all purposes. It refused to recognize the Union as bargaining agent or to accede to the Union's claims on behalf of Interscience employees. All such employees, except a few who ended their Wiley employment with severance pay and for whom no rights are asserted here, continued in Wiley's employ.

No satisfactory solution having been reached, the Union, one week before the expiration date of the Interscience bargaining agreement, commenced this action to compel arbitration.

II

The threshold question in this controversy is who shall decide whether the arbitration provisions of the collective bargaining agreement survived the Wiley-Interscience merger, so as to be operative against Wiley. Both parties urge that this question is for the courts. Past cases leave no doubt that this is correct. . . .

The problem in those cases was whether an employer, concededly party to and bound by a contract which contained an arbitration provision, had agreed to arbitrate disputes of a particular kind. Here, the question is whether Wiley, which did not itself sign the collective bargaining agreement on which the Union's claim to arbitration depends, is bound at all by the agreement's arbitration provision. The reason requiring the courts to determine the issue is the same in both situations. The duty to arbitrate being of contractual origin, a compulsory submission to arbitration cannot precede judicial determination that the collective bargaining agreement does in fact create such a duty. Thus, just as an employer has no obligation to arbitrate issues which it has not agreed to arbitrate, so a fortiori, it cannot be compelled to arbitrate if an arbitration clause does not bind it at all.

. . . Wiley, objecting to arbitration, argues that it never was a party to the collective bargaining agreement, and that, in any event, the Union lost its status as representative of the former Interscience employees when they were mingled in a larger Wiley unit of employees. The Union argues that Wiley, as successor to Interscience, is bound by the latter's agreement, at least sufficiently to require it to arbitrate. The Union relies on §90 of the N.Y. Stock Corporation Law, which provides, among other things, that no "claim or demand for any cause" against a constituent corporation shall be extinguished by a consolidation. Alternatively, the Union argues that, apart from §90, federal law requires that arbitration go forward, lest the policy favoring arbitration frequently be undermined by changes in corporate organization.

Federal law, fashioned "from the policy of our national labor laws," controls. [*Lincoln Mills*], 353 U.S. 448, 456. State law may be utilized so far as it is of aid in the development of correct principles or their application in a particular case, id., at 457, but the law which ultimately results is federal. We hold that the disappearance by merger of a corporate employer which has entered into a collective bargaining agreement with a union does not automatically terminate all rights of the employees covered by the agreement, and that, in appropriate circumstances, present here, the successor employer may be required to arbitrate with the union under the agreement.

This Court has in the past recognized the central role of arbitration in effectuating national labor policy. . . . It would derogate from "the federal policy of settling labor disputes by arbitration," United Steelworkers v. Enterprise Wheel & Car Corp., 363 U.S. 593, 596, if a change in the corporate structure or ownership of a business enterprise had the automatic consequence of removing a duty to arbitrate previously established; this is so as much in cases like the present, where the contracting employer disappears into another by merger, as in those in which one owner replaces another but the business entity remains the same.

Employees, and the union which represents them, ordinarily do not take part in negotiations leading to a change in corporate ownership. The negotiations will ordinarily not concern the well-being of the employees, whose advantage or disadvantage, potentially great, will inevitably be incidental to the main considerations. The objectives of national labor policy, reflected in established principles of federal law, require that the rightful prerogative of owners independently to rearrange their businesses and even eliminate themselves as employers be balanced by some protection to the employees from a sudden change in the employment relationship. The transition from one corporate organization to another will in most cases be eased and industrial strife avoided if employees' claims continue to be resolved by arbitration rather than by "the relative strength . . . of the contending forces," *Warrior & Gulf* [363 U.S. 574], at 580.

The preference of national labor policy for arbitration as a substitute for tests of strength between contending forces could be overcome only if other considerations compellingly so demanded. We find none. While the principles of law governing ordinary contracts would not bind to a contract an unconsenting successor to a contracting party,[3] a collective bargaining agreement is not an ordinary contract. ". . . [I]t is a generalized code to govern a myriad of cases which the draftsmen cannot wholly anticipate. . . . The collective agreement covers the whole employment relationship. It calls into being a new common law — the common law of a particular industry or of a particular plant." *Warrior & Gulf*, supra, at 578-579 (footnotes omitted). Central to the peculiar status and function of a collective bargaining agreement is the fact, dictated both by circumstance, see id., at 580, and by the requirements of the [NLRA], that it is not in any real sense the simple product of a consensual relationship. Therefore, although the duty to arbitrate . . . must be founded on a contract, the impressive policy considerations favoring arbitration are not wholly overborne by the fact that Wiley did not sign the contract being construed.[4] This case cannot readily be assimilated to the category of those in which there is no contract whatever, or none which is reasonably related to the party sought to be obligated. There was a contract, and Interscience, Wiley's predecessor, was party to it. We thus find Wiley's obligation to arbitrate this dispute in the Interscience contract construed in the context of a national labor policy.

We do not hold that in every case in which the ownership or corporate structure of an enterprise is changed the duty to arbitrate survives. . . . [T]here may be cases in which the lack of any substantial continuity of identity in the business enterprise before and after a change would make a duty to arbitrate something imposed from without, not reasonably to be found in the particular bargaining agreement and the acts of the parties involved. So, too, we do not rule out the possibility that a union might abandon its right to arbitration by failing to make its claims known. Neither of these situations is before the Court. Although Wiley was substantially larger than Interscience, relevant similarity and continuity of operation across the change in ownership is adequately evidenced by the wholesale transfer of Interscience employees to the Wiley plant, apparently without difficulty. The Union made its position known well before the merger and never departed from it. In addition, we do not suggest any view on the questions

---

[3] But cf. the general rule that in the case of a merger the corporation which survives is liable for the debts and contracts of the one which disappears. 15 Fletcher, Private Corporations (1961 rev. ed.), §7121.

[4] Compare the principle that when a contract is scrutinized for evidence of an intention to arbitrate a particular kind of dispute, *national labor policy* requires, within reason, that "an interpretation that covers the asserted dispute," *Warrior & Gulf*, supra, pp. 582-583, be favored.

surrounding a certified union's claim to continued representative status following a change in ownership. This Union does not assert that it has any bargaining rights independent of the Interscience agreement; it seeks to arbitrate claims based on that agreement, now expired, not to negotiate a new agreement.[5]

III

Beyond denying its obligation to arbitrate at all, Wiley urges that the Union's grievances are not within the scope of the arbitration clause. . . . [The Court here listed the issues the union sought to arbitrate: the status, after January 30, 1962, of the Interscience employees' seniority, pension, job security, vacation pay, and severance pay rights under the agreement. The Court also noted the agreement's broad arbitration clause, which encompassed "any differences, grievance or dispute . . . arising out of or relating to this agreement, or its interpretation or application, or enforcement."[6]]
. . . Had a dispute concerning any of these subjects, such as seniority rights or severance pay, arisen between the Union and Interscience prior to the merger, it would have been arbitrable. Wiley argues, however, that the Union's claims are plainly outside the scope of the arbitration clause: first,

---

[5] . . . [T]hat the Union does not represent a majority of an appropriate bargaining unit in *Wiley* does not prevent it from representing those employees who are covered by the agreement which is in dispute and out of which Wiley's duty to arbitrate arises. Retail Clerks Intl. Assn., Local Unions Nos. 128 & 633 v. Lion Dry Goods, Inc., 369 U.S. 17. There is no problem of conflict with another union, . . . since Wiley had no contract with any union covering the unit of employees which received the former Interscience employees. [When such potential conflict between different unions exists, courts have generally declined to order a putative successor to arbitrate with the union representing the predecessor's employees, because of the risk of pressing the successor to commit a violation of §8(a)(5) or of provoking industrial unrest. See, e.g., McGuire v. Humble Oil & Refining Co., 355 F.2d 352 (2d Cir. 1966), *cert. denied*, 384 U.S. 988 (1966). — EDS.]
    Problems might be created by an arbitral award which required Wiley to give special treatment to the former Interscience employees because of rights found to have accrued to them under the Interscience contract. But the mere possibility of such problems cannot cut off the Union's right to press the employees' claims in arbitration. While it would be premature at this stage to speculate on how to avoid such hypothetical problems, we have little doubt that within the flexible procedures of arbitration a solution can be reached which would avoid disturbing labor relations in the Wiley plant.
    [6] [There were a number of specific exclusions from arbitration, quoted by the Court in this relocated footnote. — EDS.] Section 16.5 provides:
    "It is agreed that, in addition to other provisions elsewhere contained in this agreement which expressly deny arbitration to specific events, situations or contract provisions, the following matters shall not be subject to the arbitration provisions of this agreement:
    "(1) the amendment or modification of the terms and provisions of this agreement;
    "(2) salary or minimum wage rates as set forth herein;
    "(3) matters not covered by this agreement; and
    "(4) any dispute arising out of any question pertaining to the renewal or extension of this agreement." . . .

because the agreement did not embrace post-merger claims, and, second, because the claims relate to a period beyond the limited term of the agreement.

In all probability, the situation created by the merger was one not expressly contemplated by the Union or Interscience when the agreement was made in 1960. Fairly taken, however, the Union's demands collectively raise the question which underlies the whole litigation: What is the effect of the merger on the rights of covered employees? It would be inconsistent with our holding that the obligation to arbitrate survived the merger were we to hold that the fact of the merger, without more, removed claims otherwise plainly arbitrable from the scope of the arbitration clause.

It is true that the Union has framed its issues to claim rights not only "now" — after the merger but during the term of the agreement — but also after the agreement expired by its terms. Claimed rights during the term of the agreement, at least, are unquestionably within the arbitration clause; we do not understand Wiley to urge that the Union's claims to all such rights have become moot by reason of the expiration of the agreement. As to claimed rights "after January 30, 1962," it is reasonable to read the claims as based solely on the Union's construction of the Interscience agreement in such a way that, had there been no merger, Interscience would have been required to discharge certain obligations notwithstanding the expiration of the agreement. We see no reason why parties could not if they so chose agree to the accrual of rights during the term of an agreement and their realization after the agreement had expired. Of course, the Union may not use arbitration to acquire new rights against Wiley any more than it could have used arbitration to negotiate a new contract with Interscience, had the existing contract expired and renewal negotiations broken down.

Whether or not the Union's demands have merit will be determined by the arbitrator in light of the fully developed facts. . . .

IV

Wiley's final objection to arbitration raises the question of so-called "procedural arbitrability." The Interscience agreement provides for arbitration as the third stage of the grievance procedure. "Step 1" provides for "a conference between the affected employee, a Union Steward and the Employer, officer or exempt supervisory person in charge of his department." In "Step 2," the grievance is submitted to "a conference between an officer of the Employer, or the Employer's representative designated for that purpose, the Union Shop Committee and/or a representative of the Union." Arbitration is reached under "Step 3" "in the event that the grievance shall not have been resolved or settled in 'Step 2.'" Wiley argues that since Steps 1 and 2 have not been followed, and since the duty to arbitrate arises only in Step 3, it has no duty to arbitrate this dispute.[11] Specifically, Wiley urges that the question whether "procedural" conditions to arbitration have been met must be decided by the court and not the arbitrator.[12]

We think that labor disputes of the kind involved here cannot be broken down so easily into their "substantive" and "procedural" aspects. Questions concerning the procedural prerequisites to arbitration do not arise in a vacuum; they develop in the context of an actual dispute about the rights of the parties to the contract or those covered by it. In this case, for example, the Union argues that Wiley's consistent refusal to recognize the Union's representative status after the merger made it "utterly futile—and a little bit ridiculous to follow the grievance steps as set forth in the contract." Brief, p. 41. In addition, the Union argues that time limitations in the grievance procedure are not controlling because Wiley's violations of the bargaining agreement were "continuing." These arguments in response to Wiley's "procedural" claim are meaningless unless set in the background of the merger and the negotiations surrounding it.

Doubt whether grievance procedures or some part of them apply to a particular dispute, whether such procedures have been followed or excused, or whether the unexcused failure to follow them avoids the duty to arbitrate cannot ordinarily be answered without consideration of the merits of the dispute which is presented for arbitration. In this case, one's view of the Union's responses to Wiley's "procedural" arguments depends to a large extent on how one answers questions bearing on the basic issue, the effect of the merger; e.g., whether or not the merger was a possibility considered by Interscience and the Union during the negotiation of the contract. It would be a curious rule which required that intertwined issues of "substance" and "procedure" growing out of a single dispute and raising the same questions on the same facts had to be carved up between two different forums, one deciding after the other. Neither logic nor considerations of policy compel such a result.

Once it is determined, as we have, that the parties are obligated to submit the subject matter of a dispute to arbitration, "procedural" questions which grow out of the dispute and bear on its final disposition should be left to the arbitrator. Even under a contrary rule, a court could deny arbitration only

---

[11] . . . Wiley [also] objects to the Union's asserted failure to comply with §16.6, which provides: "Notice of any grievance must be filed with the Employer and with the Union Shop Steward within four (4) weeks after its occurrence or latest existence. The failure by either party to file the grievance within this time limitation shall be construed and be deemed to be an abandonment of the grievance."

[12] The Courts of Appeals have disagreed on this issue. . . .

if it could confidently be said not only that a claim was strictly "procedural," and therefore within the purview of the court, but also that it should operate to bar arbitration altogether, and not merely limit or qualify an arbitral award. In view of the policies favoring arbitration and the parties' adoption of arbitration as the preferred means of settling disputes, such cases are likely to be rare indeed. In all other cases, those in which arbitration goes forward, the arbitrator would ordinarily remain free to reconsider the ground covered by the court insofar as it bore on the merits of the dispute, using the flexible approaches familiar to arbitration. Reservation of "procedural" issues for the courts would thus not only create the difficult task of separating related issues, but would also produce frequent duplication of effort.

In addition, the opportunities for deliberate delay and the possibility of well-intentioned but no less serious delay created by separation of the "procedural" and "substantive" elements of a dispute are clear. While the courts have the task of determining "substantive arbitrability," there will be cases in which arbitrability of the subject matter is unquestioned but a dispute arises over the procedures to be followed. In all of such cases, acceptance of Wiley's position would produce the delay attendant upon judicial proceedings preliminary to arbitration. As this case, commenced in January 1962 and not yet committed to arbitration, well illustrates, such delay may entirely eliminate the prospect of a speedy arbitrated settlement of the dispute, to the disadvantage of the parties (who, in addition, will have to bear increased costs) and contrary to the aims of national labor policy.

No justification for such a generally undesirable result is to be found in a presumed intention of the parties. Refusal to order arbitration of subjects which the parties have not agreed to arbitrate does not entail the fractionating of disputes about subjects which the parties do wish to have submitted. Although a party may resist arbitration once a grievance has arisen, as does Wiley here, we think it best accords with the usual purposes of an arbitration clause and with the policy behind federal labor law to regard procedural disagreements not as separate disputes but as aspects of the dispute which called the grievance procedures into play. . . . .

Affirmed.

Goldberg, J., took no part in the consideration or decision of this case.

NOTES

1. How do you explain the Court's refusal in *Wiley* to rely on the New York merger statute?

2. Why should the survival of the arbitration duty depend on a "sub-

stantial continuity in the business enterprise"? Does such continuity affect the need of the predecessor's employees for protection? Does it affect the probable suitability of the predecessor's agreement for the new employment relationship?

3. Under the Court's approach, an arbitrator is to determine (a) which substantive provisions of the predecessor's agreement survive, and (b) the merit of union claims based on those provisions. Are arbitrators specially equipped for the first task? Should arbitrators recognize a presumption that all provisions survive, subject to rebuttal by a showing that a particular provision is "unsuited" for the successor's operation? If not, how should arbitrators proceed?

4. In Interscience Encyclopedia, 55 Lab. Arb. 210, 225-226 (1970), the arbitrator for the *Wiley* dispute issued the following award:

> I. The five (5) issues submitted for determination pursuant to the terms of the collective bargaining agreement effective February 1, 1960, are arbitrable.
>
> II. (a) The seniority rights built up by the Interscience employees shall be accorded to said employees up to January 12, 1962, the date the Interscience employees were moved to the Wiley headquarters and when the continuity of their identity separate from the Wiley employees ceased.
>
> (b) . . . [T]he Company was not under any obligation to continue to make contributions to the District 65 Security Plan and District 65 Security Plan Pension Fund after September 30, 1971. [The arbitrator found an "accord and satisfaction."]
>
> (c) The job security and grievance provisions of the Interscience Agreement continued in full force and effect [only] up to January 12, 1962. . . .
>
> (d) The Company did not have any continued liability for severance pay under the Interscience Agreement.
>
> (e) The Company was not obligated to make the vacation payments under the Interscience Agreement after January 12, 1962. In accordance with this finding, [five] employees shall be compensated in the stated amounts for accrued vacation based upon the continuance of the Agreement until January 12, 1962, rather than October 2, 1961, the date of the merger. . . . [Six employees were awarded approximately $338 in the aggregate.]

Operating Engrs. Local 150 v. Flair Builders, 406 U.S. 487 (1972). An arbitration clause applied to "any difference" not settled within 48 hours of its occurrence and provided for a meeting of the arbitration board within six days. The union, which had ignored the collective agreement for almost five years, did not demand arbitration until three years after the employer's alleged breach. The Seventh Circuit, affirming the district court's dismissal of the union's complaint, distinguished *Wiley* as involving an "intrinsic" defense (i.e., one relating to contract terms). Here, the defense of laches was "extrinsic" to the agreement; accordingly, disposition by the district court was proper since neither interpretation of the contract, nor consideration of the merits of the underlying dispute, was involved. 440 F.2d 557, 559-560 (1971). The Supreme Court reversed, declaring: ". . . [W]e must conclude that the parties meant what they said — that 'any difference' . . . should be referred to the arbitrator for decision . . . , even if 'extrinsic.' . . ."

Powell, J., dissenting, emphasized that the employer initially had adopted a preexisting multiemployer agreement, that it had been extended without his knowledge, and held applicable to him by the trial court on the basis of the incorporation provision of the prior agreement. He declared (at 497): "The effect of the Court's decision also could be far reaching. . . . [T]he long-accepted jurisdiction of the courts may now be displaced whenever a collective bargaining agreement contains a general arbitration clause similar to that here involved. If in such circumstances the affirmative defense of laches can no longer be invoked in the courts, what of other affirmative defenses that go to the enforceability of a contract? Does the Court's opinion vest in arbitrators the historic jurisdiction of the courts to determine fraud or duress in the inception of a contract? It seems to me that the courts are far better qualified than any arbitrators to decide issues of this kind. These are not questions of 'labor law,' nor are they issues of fact that arbitrators are peculiarly well qualified to consider. They are issues within the traditional equity jurisdiction of courts of law and issues which the courts below appropriately resolved."

NOTES

1. Had the arbitration clause in *Flair Builders* been narrower, e.g., "all disputes as to the meaning, interpretation, or application of this agreement," would the laches issue have been assigned to the arbitrator? On what reasoning?

2. What does *Flair Builders* imply with respect to arbitral, rather than judicial, determination of employer claims that a union had "repudiated" an arbitration provision by a strike and that, accordingly, an alleged violation of the no-strike clause was not arbitrable despite a broad arbitration clause encompassing "any dispute . . . concerning the effect, interpretation, application; claim of breach or violation . . . or any other dispute which may arise. . . ."? See Controlled Sanitation Corp. v. Machinists, 524 F.2d 1324 (3d Cir. 1975), *cert. denied*, 424 U.S. 915 (1976), holding such a claim of

repudiation arbitrable. Rosenn, J., dissenting, emphasized that the union had denied the existence of a collective agreement with the company throughout the ten-month litigation and then, after the court's rejection of that defense, had sought to change the forum. He asked: "What does the arbitrator do if he determines there was repudiation or waiver — remand to the district court or decide the case under a repudiated or waived arbitration clause?" What is your answer?

3. Suppose equitable defenses against arbitration are based on alleged misconduct in a judicial action, e.g., evasive and dilatory action by the party seeking arbitration. Will the court, rather than the arbitrator, determine the merits of such defenses? See, e.g., California Trucking Assn. v. Teamsters, Local 70, 659 F.2d 977 (9th Cir. 1981).

4. Regarding the applicability of general doctrines of "material breach" and "repudiation" to §301 actions, see Chapter 10(B)(3), infra.

5. Given *Wiley*'s reasoning, does the customary *Enterprise Wheel* standard apply when an arbitrator's determination of "procedural" issues is challenged at the review stage? In Detroit Coil Co. v. Machinists, Lodge 82, 594 F.2d 575 (6th Cir. 1979), *cert. denied*, 444 U.S. 840 (1979), the court held that an arbitrator had exceeded his authority by ignoring clear contractual time limitations (on a union's requests for arbitration) in order to prevent a "deterioration of the good company-union relationship." Cf. Board of School Directors v. Tri-Town Teachers Assn., 412 A.2d 990 (Me. 1980) (". . . . *Detroit Coil* did not hold that questions of procedural timeliness were for the court"; rather, it held that the award does not "draw its essence from the agreement").

NLRB v. Burns Security Services
406 U.S. 272 (1972)

WHITE, J. . . . The issues . . . are whether Burns refused to bargain with a union representing a majority of employees in an appropriate unit and whether the [NLRB] could order Burns to observe the terms of a collective bargaining contract signed by the union and Wackenhut that Burns had not voluntarily assumed. Resolution turns to a great extent on the precise facts involved here.

I

The Wackenhut Corp. provided protection services at the Lockheed plant for five years before Burns took over this task. On February 28, 1967, a few months before the changeover of guard employers, a majority of the Wackenhut guards selected the union as their exclusive bargaining representative in a Board election after Wackenhut and the union had agreed that the Lockheed plant was the appropriate bargaining unit. On March 8, the Regional Director certified the union as the exclusive bargaining representative for these employees and, on April 29, Wackenhut and the union entered into a three-year collective bargaining contract.

Meanwhile, since Wackenhut's one-year service agreement to provide security protection was due to expire on June 30, Lockheed had called for bids from various companies supplying these services, and both Burns and Wackenhut submitted estimates. At a prebid conference attended by Burns on May 15, a representative of Lockheed informed the bidders that Wackenhut's guards were represented by the union, that the union had recently won a Board election and been certified, and that there was in existence a collective bargaining contract between Wackenhut and the union. . . . Lockheed then accepted Burns' bid, and on May 31 Wackenhut was notified that Burns would assume responsibility for protection services on July 1. Burns chose to retain 27 of the Wackenhut guards, and it brought in 15 of its own guards from other Burns locations.

During June, when Burns hired the 27 Wackenhut guards, it supplied them with membership cards of the American Federation of Guards (AFG), another union with which Burns had collective bargaining contracts at other locations, and informed them that they had to become AFG members to work for Burns, that they would not receive uniforms otherwise, and that Burns "could not live with" the existing contract between Wackenhut and the union. On June 29, Burns recognized the AFG on the theory that it had obtained a card majority. On July 12, however, the UPG demanded that Burns recognize it as the bargaining representative of Burns' employees at Lockheed and that Burns honor the collective bargaining agreement between it and Wackenhut. When Burns refused, the UPG filed unfair labor practice charges, and Burns responded by challenging the appropriateness of the unit and by denying its obligation to bargain.

The Board . . . found the Lockheed plant an appropriate unit and held that Burns had violated §§8(a)(2) and 8(a)(1) . . . by unlawfully recognizing and assisting the AFG . . . ; and that it had violated §§8(a)(5) and 8(a)(1) by failing to recognize and bargain with the UPG and by refusing to honor the collective bargaining agreement that had been negotiated between Wackenhut and UPG.

Burns did not challenge the §8(a)(2) unlawful assistance finding . . . but sought review of the unit determination and the order to bargain and observe the preexisting collective bargaining contract. The Court of Appeals accepted the Board's unit determination and enforced the

Board's order insofar as it related to the finding of unlawful assistance of a rival union and the refusal to bargain, but it held that the Board had exceeded its powers in ordering Burns to honor the contract executed by Wackenhut. Both Burns and the Board petitioned for certiorari, Burns challenging the unit determination and the bargaining order and the Board maintaining its position that Burns was bound by the Wackenhut contract, and we granted both petitions, though we declined to review the propriety of the bargaining unit. . . .

II

We address first Burns' alleged duty to bargain with the union. . . . Because the Act itself imposes a duty to bargain with the representative of a majority of the employees in an appropriate unit, the initial issue before the Board was whether the charging union was such a bargaining representative.

The trial examiner first found that the unit designated by the regional director was an appropriate unit for bargaining. . . . This determination was affirmed by the Board, accepted by the Court of Appeals, and is not at issue here because pretermitted by our limited grant of certiorari.

The trial examiner then found, inter alia, that Burns "had in its employ a majority of Wackenhut's former employees," and that these employees had already expressed their choice of a bargaining representative in an election held a short time before. Burns was therefore held to have a duty to bargain, which arose when it selected as its work force the employees of the previous employer to perform the same tasks at the same place they had worked in the past.

The Board, without revision, accepted the trial examiner's findings and conclusions with respect to the duty to bargain, and we see no basis for setting them aside. In an election held but a few months before, the union had been designated bargaining agent for the employees in the unit and a majority of these employees had been hired by Burns for work in the identical unit. It is undisputed that Burns knew all the relevant facts in this regard and was aware of the certification and of the existence of a collective bargaining contract. In these circumstances, it was not unreasonable for the Board to conclude that the union certified to represent all employees in the unit still represented a majority of the employees and that Burns could not reasonably have entertained a good-faith doubt about that fact. Burns' obligation to bargain with the union over terms and conditions of employment stemmed from its hiring of Wackenhut's employees and from the recent election and Board certification. It has been consistently held that a mere change of employers or of ownership in the employing industry is not such an "unusual circumstance" as to affect the force of the Board's certification within the normal operative period if a majority of employees after the change of ownership or management were employed by the preceding employer. [Citations omitted.]

. . . Burns was not entitled to upset what it should have accepted as an established union majority by soliciting representation cards for another union and thereby committing the unfair labor practice of which it was found guilty by the Board. That holding was not challenged here and makes it imperative that the situation be viewed as it was when Burns hired its employees for the guard unit, a majority of whom were represented by a Board-certified union. See NLRB v. Gissel Packing Co., 395 U.S. 575, 609, 610-616 (1969).

It would be a wholly different case if the Board had determined that because Burns' operational structure and practices differed from those of Wackenhut, the Lockheed bargaining unit was no longer an appropriate one. Likewise, it would be different if Burns had not hired employees already represented by a union certified as a bargaining agent,[5] and the Board recognized as much at oral argument.[6] But where the bargaining unit remains unchanged and a majority of the employees hired by the new employer are represented by a recently certified bargaining agent there is little basis for faulting the Board's implementation of the express mandates of §8(a)(5) and §9(a) by ordering the employer to bargain with the incumbent union. . . .

III

It does not follow, however, from Burns' duty to bargain that it was bound to observe the substantive terms of the collective bargaining contract the union had negotiated with Wackenhut and to which Burns had in no way agreed. . . .

Section 8(d) . . . was enacted in 1947 because Congress feared that

---

[5] The Board has never held that the [NLRA] itself requires that an employer who submits the winning bid for a service contract or who purchases the assets of a business be obligated to hire all of the employees of the predecessor though it is possible that such an obligation might be assumed by the employer. But cf. Chemrock Corp., 151 N.L.R.B. 1074 (1965). However, an employer who declines to hire employees solely because they are members of a union commits a §8(a)(3) unfair labor practice. . . . Further restrictions on the successor employer's choice of employees would seem to follow from the Board's instant decision that the employer must honor the preexisting collective bargaining contract. . . .

[6] "Q: But [counsel for the Union], when he argued, said that even if [Burns] hadn't taken over any [employees of Wackenhut], even if they hadn't taken over a single employee, the legal situation would be the same.

"Mr. Come [for the NLRB]:   We do not go that far. We don't think that you have to go that far in —.

"Q: Do you think it has to be a majority?

"Mr. Come: I wouldn't say that it has to be a majority, I think it has to be a substantial number. It has to be enough to give you a continuity of employment conditions in the bargaining unit." . . .

the present Board has gone very far, in the guise of determining whether or not employers had bargained in good faith, in setting itself up as the judge of what concessions an employer must make and of the proposals and counterproposals that he may or may not make. . . . [U]nless Congress writes into the law guides for the Board to follow, the Board may attempt to . . . control more and more the terms of collective bargaining agreements.

H.R. Rep. No. 245, 80th Cong., 1st Sess., 19-20 (1947).

This history was reviewed in detail and given controlling effect in H.K. Porter Co. v. NLRB, 397 U.S. 99 (1970). There this Court, while agreeing that the employer violated §8(a)(5) by adamantly refusing to agree to a dues checkoff, intending thereby to frustrate the consummation of any bargaining agreement, held that the Board had erred in ordering the employer to agree to such a provision:

> [W]hile the Board does have power . . . to require employers and employees to negotiate, it is without power to compel a company or a union to agree to any substantive contractual provision of a collective bargaining agreement. . . .
>
> It would be anomalous indeed to hold that while §8(d) prohibits the Board from relying on a refusal to agree as the sole evidence of bad-faith bargaining, the Act permits the Board to compel agreement in that same dispute. The Board's remedial powers under §10 . . . are broad, but they are limited to carrying out the policies of the Act itself. One of these fundamental policies is freedom of contract.

397 U.S., at 102, 108. . . .

These considerations . . . underlay the Board's prior decisions, which until now have consistently held that, although successor employers may be bound to recognize and bargain with the union, they are not bound by the substantive provisions of a . . . contract negotiated by their predecessors but not agreed to or assumed by them.[8] . . .

The Board, however, has now departed from this view and argues that the same policies that mandate a continuity of bargaining obligation also require that successor employers be bound to the terms of a predecessor's collective bargaining contract. It asserts that the stability of labor relations will

---

[8] When the union that has signed a collective bargaining contract is decertified, the succeeding union certified by the Board is not bound by the prior contract, need not administer it, and may demand negotiations for a new contract, even if the terms of the old contract have not yet expired. American Seating Co., 106 N.L.R.B. 250 (1953). . . . The Board has declined to overturn its "long standing" *American Seating* rule after *Burns*. General Dynamics Corp., 184 N.L.R.B. No. 71 (1970). [This footnote number has been relocated in the text above. — EDS.]

be jeopardized and that employees will face uncertainty and a gap in the bargained-for terms and conditions of employment, as well as the possible loss of advantages gained by prior negotiations, unless the new employer is held to have assumed, as a matter of federal labor law, the obligations under the contract entered into by the former employer. . . . [T]he Board notes that in John Wiley & Sons, Inc. v. Livingston, 376 U.S. 543, 550 (1964), the Court declared that "a collective bargaining agreement is not an ordinary contract" but is, rather, an outline of the common law of a particular plant or industry. . . . The Board contends that the same factors that the Court emphasized in *Wiley*, the peaceful settlement of industrial conflicts and "protection [of] the employees [against] a sudden change in the employment relationship," id., at 549, require that Burns be treated under the collective bargaining contract exactly as Wackenhut would have been if it had continued protecting the Lockheed plant.

We do not find *Wiley* controlling . . . here. *Wiley* arose in the context of a §301 suit to compel arbitration, not in the context of an unfair labor practice proceeding where the Board is expressly limited by the provisions of §8(d). That decision emphasized "[t]he preference of national labor policy for arbitration as a substitute for tests of strength before contending forces" and held only that the agreement to arbitrate, "construed in the context of a national labor policy," survived the merger and left to the arbitrator, subject to judicial review, the ultimate question of the extent to which, if any, the surviving company was bound by other provisions of the contract. Id., at 549, 551.

Wiley's limited accommodation between the legislative endorsement of freedom of contract and the judicial preference for peaceful arbitral settlement of labor disputes does not warrant the Board's holding that the employer commits an unfair labor practice unless he honors the substantive terms of the preexisting contract. The present case does not involve a §301 suit; nor does it involve the duty to arbitrate. Rather, the claim is that Burns must be held bound by the contract executed by Wackenhut, whether Burns has agreed to it or not and even though Burns made it perfectly clear that it had no intention of assuming that contract. *Wiley* suggests no such open-ended obligation. Its narrower holding dealt with a merger occurring against a background of state law that embodied the general rule that in merger situations the surviving corporation is liable for the obligations of the disappearing corporation. See N.Y. Stock Corp. Law §90 (1951); 15 W. Fletcher, Private Corporations §7121 (1961 rev. ed.). Here there was no merger or sale of assets, and there were no dealings whatsoever between Wackenhut and Burns. On the contrary, they were competitors for the same work, each bidding for the service contract at Lockheed. Burns purchased nothing from Wackenhut and became liable for none of its financial obligations. Burns merely hired enough of Wackenhut's employees to require it to bargain with the union as commanded by §8(a)(5) and §9(a). But this consideration is a wholly insufficient basis for implying either in fact or in law that Burns had agreed or must be held to have agreed to honor Wackenhut's collective bargaining contract.

. . . [T]he Board failed to heed the admonitions of the *H.K. Porter* case. Preventing industrial strife is an important aim of federal labor legislation, but Congress has not chosen to make the bargaining freedom of employers and unions totally subordinate to this goal. . . . This bargaining freedom means both that parties need not make any concessions as a result of Government compulsion and that they are free from having contract provisions imposed upon them against their will. . . .

. . . [H]olding either the union or the new employer bound to the substantive terms of an old collective bargaining contract may result in serious inequities. A potential employer may be willing to take over a moribund business only if he can make changes in corporate structure, composition of the labor force, work location, task assignment, and nature of supervision. Saddling such an employer with the terms and conditions of employment contained in the old collective bargaining contract may make these changes impossible and may discourage and inhibit the transfer of capital. On the other hand, a union may have made concessions to a small or failing employer that it would be unwilling to make to a large or economically successful firm. The congressional policy manifest in the Act is to enable the parties to negotiate for any protection either deems appropriate, but to allow the balance of bargaining advantage to be set by economic power realities. Strife is bound to occur if the concessions that must be honored do not correspond to the relative economic strength of the parties.

The Board's position would also raise new problems, for the successor employer would be circumscribed in exactly the same way as the predecessor under the collective bargaining contract. It would seemingly follow that employees of the predecessor would be deemed employees of the successor, dischargeable only in accordance with provisions of the contract and subject to the grievance and arbitration provisions thereof. Burns would not have been free to replace Wackenhut's guards with its own except as the contract permitted. Given the continuity of employment relationship, the preexisting contract's provisions with respect to wages, seniority rights, vacation privileges, pension and retirement fund benefits, job security provisions, work assignments and the like would devolve on the successor. Nor would the union commit a §8(b)(3) unfair labor practice if it refused to bargain for a modification of the agreement effective prior to the expiration date of the agreement. A successor employer might also be deemed to have inherited its predecessor's preexisting contractual obligations to the union that had accrued under past contracts and that had not been discharged when the business was transferred. "[A] successor may well acquire more liabilities as a result of *Burns* than appear on the face of a contract."[11] Finally, a successor will be bound to observe the contract despite good-faith doubts about the union's majority during the time that the contract is a bar to another representation election, Ranch-Way, Inc., 183 N.L.R.B. No. 116 (1970). For the above reasons, the Board itself has expressed doubts as to the general applicability of its *Burns* rule.[13]

In many cases, of course, successor employers will find it advantageous not only to recognize and bargain with the union but also to observe the preexisting contract rather than to face uncertainty and turmoil. Also, in a variety of circumstances involving a merger, stock acquisition, reorganization, or assets purchase, the Board might properly find as a matter of fact that the successor had assumed the obligations under the old contract. Cf. Oilfield Maintenance Co., 142 N.L.R.B. 1384 (1963). Such a duty does not, however, ensue as a matter of law from the mere fact that an employer is doing the same work in the same place with the same employees as his predecessor. . . . We accordingly set aside the Board's finding of a §8(a)(5) unfair labor practice insofar as it rested on a conclusion that Burns was required to but did not honor the collective bargaining contract executed by Wackenhut.

IV

It therefore follows that the Board's order requiring Burns to "give retroactive effect to all the clauses of said [Wackenhut] contract and, with interest of 6 percent, make whole its employees for any losses suffered by reason of Respondent's [Burns'] refusal to honor, adopt and enforce said contract"

---

[11] Doppelt, Successor Companies: The NLRB Limits the Options — and Raises Some Problems, 20 De Paul L. Rev. 176, 191 (1971).

[13] Emerald Maintenance, Inc., 188 N.L.R.B. No. 139 (1971). *Emerald* involved a civilian contractor who undertook to provide certain maintenance services at an Air Force base. During the preceding year, the same services had been performed by two other companies whose employees were represented by a union that had negotiated collective bargaining agreements that had not yet expired. The employer performed the work with substantially the same employee complement as had its predecessors. The Board held that the employer had a duty to recognize and bargain with the union but could not agree with the trial examiner that the employer was bound by the provisions of the contract, emphasizing in this respect the impact of the Service Contract Act of 1965, 79 Stat. 1034. The case was considered as presenting unusual circumstances justifying an exception to the *Burns* rule; the Board noted that "[t]his case suggests the hazards of enforcing the contracts of one employer against a successor where annual rebidding normally produces annual changes in contract identity. These circumstances might encourage less arm's-length collective bargaining whenever the employer had reason to expect that it would not be awarded the next succeeding annual service contract." An amicus strongly contends that the *Emerald* rule is inconsistent with *Burns* and is based on a misreading of the legislative history of the Service Contract Act of 1965. Brief for AFL-CIO as Amicus Curiae 23 n.2.

must be set aside. We note that the regional director's charge instituting this case asserted that "[o]n or about July 1, 1967, Respondent [Burns] unilaterally changed existing wage rates, hours of employment, overtime wage rates, differentials for swing shift and graveyard shift, and other terms and conditions of employment of the employees in the appropriate unit . . . ," . . . and that the Board's opinion stated that

> [t]he obligation to bargain imposed on a successor-employer includes the negative injunction to refrain from unilaterally changing wages and other benefits established by a prior collective bargaining agreement even though that agreement had expired. In this respect, the successor-employer's obligations are the same as those imposed upon employers generally during the period between collective bargaining agreements.

. . . This statement by the Board is consistent with its prior and subsequent cases that hold that whether or not a successor employer is bound by its predecessor's contract, it must not institute terms and conditions of employment different from those provided in its predecessor's contract, at least without first bargaining with the employees' representative. . . . Thus, if Burns, without bargaining to impasse with the union, had paid its employees on and after July 1 at a rate lower than Wackenhut had paid under its contract, or otherwise provided terms and conditions of employment different from those provided in the Wackenhut collective bargaining agreement, under the Board's view, Burns would have committed a §8(a)(5) unfair labor practice and would have been subject to an order to restore to employees what they had lost by this so-called unilateral change. . . .

Although Burns had an obligation to bargain with the union concerning wages and other conditions of employment when the union requested it to do so, this case is not like a §8(a)(5) violation where an employer unilaterally changes a condition of employment without consulting a bargaining representative. It is difficult to understand how Burns could be said to have *changed* unilaterally any preexisting term or condition of employment without bargaining when it had no previous relationship whatsoever to the bargaining unit and, prior to July 1, no outstanding terms and conditions of employment from which a change could be inferred. . . .

Although a successor employer is ordinarily free to set initial terms on which it will hire the employees of a predecessor, there will be instances in which it is perfectly clear that the new employer plans to retain all of the employees in the unit and in which it will be appropriate to have him initially consult with the employees' bargaining representative before he fixes terms. In other situations, however, it may not be clear until the successor employer has hired his full complement of employees that he has a duty to bargain with a union, since it will not be evident until then that the bargaining representative represents a majority of the employees in the unit. . . . Here, for example, Burns' obligation to bargain with the union did not mature until it had selected its force of guards late in June. The Board quite properly found that Burns refused to bargain on July 12 when it rejected the overtures of the union. It is true that the wages it paid when it began protecting the Lockheed plant on July 1 differed from those specified in the Wackenhut . . . agreement, but there is no evidence that Burns ever unilaterally changed the terms and conditions of employment it had offered to potential employees in June after its obligation to bargain . . . became apparent. If the union had made a request to bargain after Burns had completed its hiring and if Burns had negotiated in good faith and had made offers to the union which the union rejected, Burns could have unilaterally initiated such proposals as the opening terms and conditions of employment on July 1 without committing an unfair labor practice. Cf. NLRB v. Katz, 369 U.S. 736, 745 n.12 (1962) . . . The Board's order requiring Burns to make whole its employees for any losses suffered by reason of Burns' refusal to honor and enforce the contract, cannot therefore be sustained on the ground that Burns unilaterally changed existing terms and conditions of employment, thereby committing an unfair labor practice which required monetary restitution in these circumstances.

Affirmed.

REHNQUIST, J., with whom BURGER, C.J., BRENNAN and POWELL, JJ., join, concurring in No. 71-123 and dissenting in No. 71-198. . . . Because I believe that the Board and the Court of Appeals stretched [the successorship] concept beyond the limits of its proper application, I would enforce neither the Board's bargaining order nor its order imposing upon Burns the terms of the contract between the union and Wackenhut. . . .

[The dissent made two initial points: First, it was uncertain whether the union had been the choice of the majority of the 42 employees involved, for the record did not show how many of the 27 former Wackenhut employees had chosen the union as their bargaining representative. Second, the conclusion that Burns' employees at Lockheed were an appropriate unit had been based on a premise that rested solely on the doctrines of successorship — the applicability of which had been in question.]

Wiley, supra, speaks . . . of a change in the "ownership or corporate structure of an enterprise" as bringing into play the obligation of the successor employer to perform an obligation voluntarily undertaken by the predecessor employer. But while the principle enunciated in *Wiley* is by no means limited to the corporate merger situation present there, it cannot logically be extended to a mere naked shifting of a group of employees from one employer to another without totally disregarding the basis for the doctrine. The notion of a change in the "ownership or corporate structure of an enterprise" connotes at the very least that there is continuity in the enterprise, as well as change; and that that continuity be at least in part on the employer's side of the equation, rather than only on that of the employees. If we deal with the legitimate expectations of employees that the employer who agreed to the collective bargaining contract perform it, we can require another employing entity to perform the contract only when he has succeeded to some of the tangible or intangible assets by the use of which the employees might have expected the first employer to have performed his contract with them.

Phrased another way, the doctrine of successorship in the federal common law of labor relations accords to employees the same general protection against transfer of assets by an entity against which they have a claim as is accorded by other legal doctrines to nonlabor-related claimants against the same entity. Nonlabor-related claimants in such transfer situations may be protected not only by assumption agreements resulting from the self-interest of the contracting parties participating in a merger or sale of assets but also by state laws imposing upon the successor corporation of any merger the obligations of the merged corporation (see, e.g., §90 of the N.Y. Stock Corp. Law (1951), cited in *Wiley*, supra), and by bulk sales acts found in numerous States [Uniform Commercial Code §§6-101 to 6-111]. These latter are designed to give the nonlabor-related creditor of the predecessor entity some claim, either as a matter of contract right against the successor, or as a matter of property right to charge the assets that pass from the predecessor to the successor. The implication of *Wiley* is that the federal common law of labor relations accords the same general type and degree of protection to employees claiming under a collective bargaining contract. . . .

The rigid imposition of a prior-existing labor relations environment on a new employer whose only connection with the old employer is the hiring of some of the latter's employees and the performance of some of the work which was previously performed by the latter, might well tend to produce industrial peace of a sort. But industrial peace in such a case would be produced at a sacrifice of the determination by the Board of the appropriateness of bargaining agents and of the wishes of the majority of the employees which the Act was designed to preserve. These latter principles caution us against extending successorship, under the banner of industrial peace, step by step to a point where the only connection between the two employing entities is a naked transfer of employees. . . .

Burns acquired not a single asset, tangible or intangible, by negotiation or transfer from Wackenhut. It succeeded to the contractual rights and duties of the plant protection service contract with Lockheed, not by reason of Wackenhut's assignment or consent, but over Wackenhut's vigorous opposition. . . .

To conclude that Burns was a successor to Wackenhut in this situation, with its attendant consequences under the Board's order imposing a duty to bargain with the bargaining representative of Wackenhut's employees, would import unwarranted rigidity into labor-management relations. The fortunes of competing employers inevitably ebb and flow, and an employer who has currently gained production orders at the expense of another may well wish to hire employees away from that other. There is no reason to think that the best interests of the employees, the employers, and ultimately of the free market are not served by such movement. Yet inherent in the expanded doctrine of successorship that the Board urges in this case is the notion that somehow the "labor relations environment" comes with the new employees if the new employer has but obtained orders or business that previously belonged to the old employer. The fact that the employees in the instant case continued to perform their work at the same situs, while not irrelevant to analysis, cannot be deemed controlling. For the rigidity that would follow from the Board's application of successorship to this case would not only affect competition between Wackenhut and Burns, but would also affect Lockheed's operations. In effect, it would be saddled, as against its competitors, with the disadvantageous consequences of a collective bargaining contract unduly favorable to Wackenhut's employees, even though Lockheed's contract with Wackenhut was set to expire at a given time. By the same token, it would be benefited, at the expense of its competitors, as a result of a "sweetheart" contract negotiated between Wackenhut and its employees. From the viewpoint of the recipient of the services, dissatisfaction with the labor relations environment may stimulate a desire for change of contractors. Where the relation between the first employer and the second is as attenuated as it is here, and the reasonable expectations of the employees equally attenuated, the application of the successorship doctrine is not authorized by the [Act]. . . .

. . . [T]he Board, instead of [making its usual analysis of whether an added group of employees should constitute a separate bargaining unit or be "accreted" to a preexisting unit], concluded that because Burns was a "successor" it was absolutely bound to the mold that had been fashioned by Wackenhut and its employees at Lockheed. Burns was thereby precluded from challenging the designation of Lockheed as an appropriate bargaining unit for a year after the original certification. [Citing §9(c)(3) of the Act.] . . .

NOTES

1. The predecessor company ceased operations on June 1, laying off all 50 of its unionized employees. On June 25, a potential buyer for the closed

business was quoted (accurately, in a local newspaper) as stating: "If current negotiations with the [predecessor] are successful, we will purchase the plant, carry on the same business, and offer jobs to many [predecessor] employees." From July 1, the date of the purchase, to July 15, predecessor employees applied for jobs with the purchaser and were told that wages and benefits would be lower than the predecessor's. On July 20, the purchaser began operations, with 30 ex-employees of the predecessor. Shortly thereafter the union requested recognition; the purchaser declined, stating that it intended to expand the operation to "over 100 employees by October."

Any §8(a)(5) violations? Cf. Spitzer Akron, Inc., 219 N.L.R.B. 20 (1975); Spruce Up Corp., 209 N.L.R.B. 194 (1974); Premium Foods v. NLRB, 709 F.2d 623 (9th Cir. 1983). See generally Comment, The Bargaining Obligations of Successor Employers, 88 Harv. L. Rev. 759 (1975).

2. Assume that the purchaser in the foregoing situation was told that all of the predecessor's employees were members of the union. Assume further that the purchaser had been advised (truthfully) that poor union-management relations — referred to in the community as "the union problem" — had been the major cause of the predecessor's low productivity and eventual closing. Is the purchaser entitled to take such information into account in making hiring decisions? Specifically, is he entitled to reject all former employees on the ground that their prior experience in the plant has given them poor work habits? See, e.g., Spencer Foods, 268 N.L.R.B. No. 231, 115 L.R.R.M. 1251 (1984).

3. In Golden State Bottling Co. v. NLRB, 414 U.S. 168 (1973), the Court upheld the Board's authority to issue a back pay and reinstatement order against a bona fide "successor" who had bought a business, knowing of an NLRB back pay and reinstatement order against the seller and "its successors and assigns." The Court relied on *Wiley*, spoke as if its vitality were unimpaired by *Burns*, disclaimed any qualification of *Burns*, and reaffirmed the propriety of finding "successorship" without distinguishing among mergers, sales, etc. Id. at 182-183 n.5.

Howard Johnson Co. v. Hotel Employees, 417 U.S. 249 (1974). The Grissoms operated a motor lodge and a restaurant under a franchise from Howard Johnson (Johnson). Employees at both places were covered by collective agreements providing for arbitration and the application of the agreements to the employer's "successors . . . purchasers, lessees or transferees." The Grissoms sold Johnson the personal property used in the franchised operations and leased the realty to Johnson. The latter advised the union, as well as the Grissoms, that it would not assume the collective agreement and that it would not recognize the union. Later, Johnson hired 9 of Grissoms' 53 employees and began operations with 45 employees. The union sued to compel both the Grissoms and Johnson to arbitrate their obligations to the Grissoms' employees under the agreements signed by the Grissoms, including Johnson's obligation, under the "just cause" and seniority provisions, to employ former Grissom employees. The Grissoms conceded, but Johnson denied, a duty to do so. The Supreme Court (8 to 1) sided with Johnson and declared that under *Lincoln Mills*, §301 decisions must reflect the policy of national labor laws; consequently, the reasoning of *Burns* had to be considered in a §301 action. The Court, however, found it unnecessary "to decide . . . whether there is an irreconcilable conflict between *Wiley* and *Burns*." It distinguished *Wiley* from the instant case, in part on the ground that after the Wiley merger, the original employing entity had disappeared; hence, a remedy against Wiley, the surviving company, had been necessary for enforcing any surviving employment obligations of the merged corporation. "Even more important, in *Wiley* the surviving corporation hired *all* the employees of the disappearing corporation." In the instant case, the Court emphasized, (1) there had been a lack of "a substantial continuity of identity in the work force across the change in ownership," (2) the buyer had not assumed the agreement to arbitrate, and (3) the union had been seeking to require Johnson to hire all Grissom's employees, contrary to the *Burns* principle freeing a new employer from such a requirement. The Court also noted (i) that the question of whether an employer was a "successor" could not be answered "in the abstract," (ii) that the "real question" is, on the particular facts, what are the legal obligations of the new employer to the employees of the former employer or to their representative, and (iii) that "no single definition of 'successor' [can be] applicable in every legal context." Id. at 262-263 n.9. Accordingly, consideration had to be given to the competing interests involved and the "policies of the labor laws in light of the facts of each case and the particular legal obligation which is at issue, whether it be the duty to recognize and bargain with the union, the duty to remedy unfair labor practices, the duty to arbitrate, etc." Id.

Has *Wiley* survived *Howard Johnson?* See Note, 74 Mich. L. Rev. 555 (1976). See also Severson & Willcoxon, Successorship Under Howard Johnson: Short Order Justice for Employees, 64 Calif. L. Rev. 795 (1976).

NOTES

1. In Boeing Co. v. International Assn. of Machinists, 504 F.2d 307 (5th Cir. 1974), the court rejected any "majority" requirement for ordering a new employer to arbitrate under the predecessor's agreement, emphasizing

that the elements of the question of whether there was a substantial continuity in the identity of the work force varied according to whether the dispute involved a duty to arbitrate or to bargain. Thus, with respect to the duty to arbitrate, the percentage of the *predecessor's* employees who had moved to the putative successor would be significant. When, however, the duty to bargain was involved, the significant percentage would be that of the putative "successor's" employees who had come from the predecessor. The court, declining to require arbitration by the new employer, who had hired only 35 percent of his predecessor's work force, declared that where business is allocated through periodic bidding and where "successorship" depends "completely on the continuity of the employee complement, the continuity in the identity of the work force must be more substantially established than would be required were the relationship . . . one of merger, or purchase or sale." Do you find the foregoing distinctions justifiable? (Courts generally follow the *Boeing* approach to relevant percentages. See, e.g., NLRB v. Band-Age, Inc., 534 F.2d 1, 4 (1st Cir. 1976)).

2. In *Howard Johnson*, the Court, noting that arbitration against the Grissoms could encompass their alleged breach of the agreement's successorship clause, added that the union might have protected its interests by moving to enjoin the sale. 417 U.S. at 258 n.3. Consider the situation below in light of *Howard Johnson*, *Burns*, and *First Natl. Maintenance*, supra p. 873.

In June 1984, the Seller agreed to sell certain unprofitable supermarkets to the Purchaser. After completing that sale, the parties also agreed, on August 19, 1984, that the Purchaser would lease, and later buy, the Seller's warehouse, formerly serving those stores. The Seller promptly advised the president of a Teamsters local, which represented the warehouse employees, of that agreement, telling him to negotiate with the Purchaser.

The Seller's collective agreement with the local contains a broad arbitration clause and provides: "This Agreement shall be binding not only upon the parties hereto but upon their successors and assigns." During negotiations for the transfer of the warehouse, the Seller notified the Purchaser of that provision and of the other provisions of the collective agreement.

On August 20, 1984, the Purchaser advised the local and the employees that it would not strictly follow seniority in employing warehouse personnel. The Purchaser, after taking over the warehouse, hired 49 of the Seller's ex-employees (comprising 54 percent of the Seller's bargaining unit employees and all the employees hired by the Purchaser for that unit), and observed all provisions of the Seller's collective agreement, except for the seniority provisions regarding hiring (or layoffs).

The local filed timely grievances, claiming that the Seller violated the collective agreement (which expires on December 31, 1986) by failing to require the Purchaser to assume it. The local simultaneously filed grievances against the Purchaser based on the latter's alleged violation of the agreement's seniority provisions. Pursuant to a judicial direction, the arbitrator is to decide the merits of the grievances against the Seller and to advise the court on the proper disposition of the grievance against the Purchaser, including its arbitrability. What results? What additional facts would you need and why? Cf. Kroger Co., 78 Lab. Arb. 569 (1982). Would it be material if the collective agreement also required the employer "to make it a condition of a transfer that the successor or assign shall be bound by the terms of this agreement"? Does such a clause alone require the Seller to insist that every transferee assume the agreement, or is it also necessary that the transferee have the "continuity of operations" required for "a successor" under *Wiley* and related Supreme Court cases? If the buyer meets those requirements but, prior to hiring anyone, announces that he will not be bound by his predecessor's agreement, is he nonetheless required to do so? Cf. Sexton's Steak House, 76 Lab. Arb. 576 (1981); Comment, Successorship Clauses in Collective Bargaining Agreements, 1979 B.Y.U. L.Rev. 99, 100-103.

Notwithstanding the Norris-LaGuardia Act, some federal courts have issued status quo injunctions pending arbitration of a claim that a seller's failure to secure assumption of its collective agreement by the buyer violates a successorship clause. See Local Lodge 1266, IAM v. Panoramic Corp., 668 F.2d 276 (7th Cir. 1981). After you have examined *Buffalo Forge* and related notes, infra p. 1038, consider under what circumstances, if any, such injunctions are proper.

3. In Lone Star Steel Co. v. NLRB, 639 F.2d 545 (10th Cir. 1980), a successorship clause barring sale or transfer of an operation unless the transferee assumed the employer's obligations under the collective agreement was held (2-1) to be a mandatory subject of bargaining. In characterizing the clause as mandatory, the court, approving the Board's approach, applied the "vitally affects" test of *Allied Chemical Workers*, supra p. 885. Accordingly, the union could insist on the successorship clause to the point of impasse and could strike, free of §8(b)(3), to obtain it. Is there tension between this result and *Burns?*

4. The Board also has developed a union successorship doctrine requiring an employer to continue to recognize a union that is essentially the old union under a new name, e.g., when after fair notice a majority of union employees have voted to merge with another local. The Board, changing its policy, held (3-2) that an affiliation election is not valid unless all employees in the bargaining unit, whether they are union members, are permitted to vote. See Amoco Production Co., 262 N.L.R.B. 1240 (1982) (3-2 decision),

aff'd, Oil Workers Local 4-14 v. NLRB, 114 L.R.R.M. 3676 (5th Cir. 1983).

Note: Collective Bargaining Agreements and Bankruptcy

In NLRB v. Bildisco & Bildisco, 104 S. Ct. 1188 (1984), the Supreme Court ruled (9-0) that a collective bargaining agreement is an "executory contract" subject to rejection under §365(a) of the Bankruptcy Code in a reorganization proceeding filed under Chapter 11 of that Code. Ordinarily, rejection of an executory contract is permissible if the rejection is in the interests of the creditors. The Court, however, declared (at 1196-1197) that the special nature of collective agreements requires a "somewhat stricter standard" for permitting rejection:

> . . . [T]he Bankruptcy Court should permit rejection . . . if the debtor can show that the collective bargaining agreement burdens the estate, and that after careful scrutiny, the equities balance in favor of rejecting the labor contract. . . . [H]owever, the Bankruptcy Court should be persuaded that reasonable efforts to negotiate a voluntary modification have been made and are not likely to produce a prompt and satisfactory solution. The NLRA requires no less . . . [for] the debtor-in-possession [remains] under a [§8(a)(5)] duty to bargain with the union. . . . Since the policy of Chapter 11 is to permit successful rehabilitation of debtors, rejection should not be permitted without a finding that that policy would be served by such action.

Bildisco raised a second issue, the validity of the NLRB's finding of §§8(a)(5) and 8(d) violations because of the company's unilateral departure from the agreement before formal rejection by the Bankruptcy Court. The Supreme Court (now in a 5 to 4 vote) disagreed with the Board and held that the filing of a reorganization petition renders a collective agreement no longer enforceable under NLRA, §8(d). Accordingly, §8(d) does not bar an employer's departures from a bargaining agreement, occurring after the filing of the bankruptcy petition and before formal rejection of the agreement by the Bankruptcy Court. "Board enforcement of a claimed violation of §8(d) [once bankruptcy proceedings are initiated] would run directly counter to the express provisions of the Bankruptcy Code and to the Code's overall . . . [policies]." 104 S. Ct. at 1200. The Court indicated, however, that if the Bankruptcy Court did not approve the employer's unilateral rejection, the union's and employees' damage claims for breach of agreement would not be diminished by the employer's rejection of the agreement. In addition, upon that court's approval of the debtor's rejection of the collective agreement, the debtor must, under the NLRA, bargain with the employees' representative with respect to the terms of a new agreement. (The union had not made, and the Court did not rule on, the contention that §365(a), as distinguished from the NLRA, does not permit a debtor to reject a collective agreement before securing court approval to do so.)

Brennan, J., joined in dissent on the second issue by White, Marshall, and Blackmun, JJ., contended that accommodation of important NLRA policies required the collective agreement to be preserved until the Bankruptcy Court authorized its rejection.

With respect to collective agreements covered by the Railway Labor Act, Congress created an exception to the general grant of authority to reject executory agreements in bankruptcy. See §77(n) of the Bankruptcy Act, 11 U.S.C. §205(n), requiring compliance with the RLA's usual notice and bargaining provisions. Is this explicit exception relevant to the issue of statutory construction raised in *Bildisco*? As a matter of policy is there any justification for different treatment of collective agreements according to whether the RLA or the NLRA is applicable?

Following the *Bildisco* decision, bills were introduced in Congress that would establish a new framework for the treatment of collective bargaining agreements in bankruptcy proceedings involving firms subject to the NLRA. Such bills raise four important questions. (1) Should collective agreements be subject to disaffirmance in bankruptcy? If so: (2) What should be the substantive and procedural requirements? (3) What priority, if any, should claims for breach of collective agreements have? and (4) How should damages be computed?

These questions obviously involve both bankruptcy and labor law considerations. What special labor law considerations are involved? Is *Darlington*, supra p. 294, or *Burns* relevant here? See generally Bordewieck & Countryman, The Rejection of Collective Bargaining Agreements by Chapter 11 Debtors, 57 Am. Bank. L.J. 293 (1983); but cf. Pulliam, The Rejection of Collective Bargaining Agreements Under Section 365 of the Bankruptcy Code, 58 Am. Bank. L.J. 1 (1984).

(On July 10, 1984, President Reagan signed into law the Bankruptcy Amendments and Federal Judgeship Act of 1984, which included a labor provision (§1113) requiring court approval for rejection of a collective bargaining agreement. Under that provision, an employer who files for bankruptcy must, before applying for rejection, make a proposal to the union for contract modifications "necessary" to permit reorganization. A bankruptcy court may approve rejection only after finding that a qualifying proposal has been made, the union has refused to accept it "without good cause," and the balance of the equities "clearly favors" rejection. Does the requirement that the employer's proposal be "necessary" for reorganization stiffen *Bildisco*'s standard for rejection?)

3. No-Strike Obligations

Boys Markets, Inc. v. Retail Clerks Union, Local 770
398 U.S. 235 (1970)

BRENNAN, J. . . . [W]e reexamine the holding of Sinclair Refining Co. v. Atkinson, 370 U.S. 195 (1962), that the antiinjunction provisions of the Norris-LaGuardia Act preclude a federal district court from enjoining a strike in breach of a no-strike obligation under a collective bargaining agreement, even though that agreement contains provisions, enforceable under §301(a) . . . , for binding arbitration of the grievance dispute concerning which the strike was called. . . . [T]he Ninth Circuit, considering itself bound by *Sinclair*, reversed the grant . . . [of] injunctive relief. 416 F.2d 368 (1969). . . . Having concluded that *Sinclair* was erroneously decided and that subsequent events have undermined its continuing validity, we overrule that decision and reverse the judgment of the Court of Appeals.

I

. . . [P]etitioner and respondent were parties to a collective bargaining agreement which provided, inter alia, that all controversies concerning its interpretation or application should be resolved by adjustment and arbitration procedures set forth therein and that, during the life of the contract, there should be "no cessation or stoppage of work, lockout, picketing or boycotts. . . ." The dispute arose when petitioner's frozen foods supervisor and certain members of his crew who were not members of the bargaining unit began to rearrange merchandise in the frozen food cases of one of petitioner's supermarkets. A union representative insisted that the food cases be stripped of all merchandise and be restocked by union personnel. When petitioner did not accede to the union's demand, a strike was called and the union began to picket petitioner's establishment. Thereupon petitioner demanded that the union cease the work stoppage and picketing and sought to invoke the grievance and arbitration procedures specified in the contract.

The following day, since the strike had not been terminated, petitioner filed a complaint in California Superior Court seeking a temporary restraining order, a preliminary and permanent injunction, and specific performance of the contractual arbitration provision. The state court issued a temporary restraining order forbidding continuation of the strike and also an order to show cause why a preliminary injunction should not be granted. Shortly thereafter, the union removed the case to the Federal District Court and there made a motion to quash the state court's temporary restraining order. In opposition, petitioner moved for an order compelling arbitration and enjoining continuation of the strike. Concluding that the dispute was subject to arbitration under the collective bargaining agreement and that the strike was in violation of the contract, the District Court ordered the parties to arbitrate the underlying dispute and simultaneously enjoined the strike, all picketing in the vicinity of petitioner's supermarket, and any attempts by the union to induce the employees to strike or to refuse to perform their services.

II

At the outset, we are met with respondent's contention that *Sinclair* ought not to be disturbed because the decision turned on a question of statutory construction which Congress can alter at any time. Since Congress has not modified our conclusions in *Sinclair*, even though it has been urged to do so,[5] respondent argues that principles of stare decisis should govern the present case.

We do not agree that the doctrine of stare decisis bars a reexamination of *Sinclair* in the circumstances of this case. We fully recognize that important policy considerations militate in favor of continuity and predictability in the law. Nevertheless, as Mr. Justice Frankfurter wrote for the Court, "[S]tare decisis is a principle of policy and not a mechanical formula of adherence to the latest decision, however recent and questionable, when such adherence involves collision with a prior doctrine more embracing in its scope, intrinsically sounder, and verified by experience." Helvering v. Hallock, 309 U.S. 106, 119 (1940). . . . It is precisely because *Sinclair* stands as a significant departure from our otherwise consistent emphasis upon the congressional policy to promote the peaceful settlement of labor disputes through arbitration and our efforts to accommodate and harmonize this policy with those underlying the antiinjunction provisions of the Norris-LaGuardia Act that we believe *Sinclair* should be reconsidered. Furthermore, in light of developments subsequent to *Sinclair*, in particular our decision in Avco Corp. v. Aero Lodge 735, 390 U.S. 557 (1968), it has become clear that the *Sinclair* decision does not further but rather frustrates realization of an important goal of our national labor policy.

Nor can we agree that conclusive weight should be accorded to the failure of Congress to respond to *Sinclair* on the theory that congressional

[5] See, e.g., Report of Special Atkinson-Sinclair Committee, A.B.A. Labor Relations Law Section — Proceedings 226 (1963) [hereinafter cited as A.B.A. Sinclair Report].

silence should be interpreted as acceptance of the decision. The Court has cautioned that "[i]t is at best treacherous to find in congressional silence alone the adoption of a controlling rule of law." Girouard v. United States, 328 U.S. 61, 69 (1946). Therefore, in the absence of any persuasive circumstances evidencing a clear design that congressional inaction be taken as acceptance of *Sinclair*, the mere silence of Congress is not a sufficient reason for refusing to reconsider the decision. . . .

III

. . . *Lincoln Mills* held generally that "the substantive law to apply in suits under §301(a) is federal law, which the courts must fashion from the policy of our national labor laws," 353 U.S., at 456, and more specifically that a union can obtain specific performance of an employer's promise to arbitrate grievances. We rejected the contention that the antiinjunction proscriptions of [Norris-LaGuardia] prohibited this type of relief, noting that a refusal to arbitrate was not "part and parcel of the abuses against which the Act was aimed," id., at 458, and that the Act itself manifests a policy determination that arbitration should be encouraged. See [§8]. Subsequently in the *Steelworkers trilogy* we emphasized the importance of arbitration . . . and cautioned the lower courts against usurping the functions of the arbitrator.

Serious questions remained, however, concerning the role that state courts were to play in suits involving collective bargaining agreements. Confronted with some of these problems in Charles Dowd Box Co. v. Courtney, 368 U.S. 502 (1962), we held that Congress clearly intended *not* to disturb the preexisting jurisdiction of the state courts over suits for violations of collective bargaining agreements. . . .

Shortly after the decision in *Dowd Box*, we sustained, in Teamsters Local 174 v. Lucas Flour Co., 369 U.S. 95 (1962), an award of damages by a state court to an employer for a breach by the union of a no-strike provision in its contract. While emphasizing that "in enacting §301 Congress intended doctrines of federal labor law uniformly to prevail over inconsistent local rules," id., at 104, we did not consider the applicability of the Norris-LaGuardia Act to state court proceedings because the employer's prayer for relief sought only damages and not specific performance of a no-strike obligation.

Subsequent to the decision in *Sinclair*, we held in Avco Corp. v. Aero Lodge 735, supra, that §301(a) suits initially brought in state courts may be removed to the designated federal forum under the federal question removal jurisdiction delineated in 28 U.S.C. §1441. In so holding, however, the Court expressly left open the questions whether state courts are bound by the antiinjunction proscriptions of the Norris-LaGuardia Act and whether federal courts, after removal of a §301(a) action, are required to dissolve any injunctive relief previously granted by the state courts. See generally General Electric Co. v. Local Union 191, 413 F.2d 964 (C.A. 5th Cir. 1969) (dissolution of state injunction required). Three Justices who concurred expressed the view that *Sinclair* should be reconsidered "upon an appropriate future occasion." 390 U.S., at 562 (Stewart, J., concurring).[10]

The decision in *Avco*, viewed in the context of *Lincoln Mills* and its progeny, has produced an anomalous situation which, in our view, makes urgent the reconsideration of *Sinclair*. The principal practical effect of *Avco* and *Sinclair* taken together is nothing less than to oust state courts of jurisdiction in §301(a) suits where injunctive relief is sought for breach of a no-strike obligation. Union defendants can, as a matter of course, obtain removal to a federal court,[11] and there is obviously a compelling incentive for them to do so in order to gain the advantage of the strictures upon injunctive relief which *Sinclair* imposes on federal courts. The sanctioning of this practice, however, is wholly inconsistent with our conclusion in *Dowd Box* that the congressional purpose embodied in §301(a) was to *supplement*, and not to encroach upon, the preexisting jurisdiction of the state courts. It is ironic indeed that the very provision that Congress clearly intended to provide additional remedies for breach of collective bargaining agreements has been employed to displace previously existing state remedies. We are not at liberty thus to depart from the clearly expressed congressional policy to the contrary.

On the other hand, to the extent that widely disparate remedies theoretically remain available in state, as opposed to federal, courts, the federal policy of labor law uniformity elaborated in *Lucas Flour Co.*, is seriously offended. This policy, of course, could hardly require, as a practical matter, that labor law be administered identically in all courts, for undoubtedly a certain diversity exists among the state and federal systems in matters of procedural and remedial detail, a fact that Congress evidently took into account in deciding not to disturb the traditional jurisdiction of the States. The injunction, however, is so important a remedial device, particularly in the arbitration context, that its availability or nonavailability in various courts will not only produce rampant forum shopping and maneuvering from one court to another but

---

[10] Shortly after *Sinclair* was decided, an erosive process began to weaken its underpinnings. Various authorities suggested methods of mitigating the absolute rigor of the *Sinclair* rule. For example, the [Fifth Circuit] held that *Sinclair* does not prevent a federal district court from enforcing an arbitrator's order directing a union to terminate a work stoppage in violation of a no-strike clause. New Orleans Steamship Assn. v. General Longshore Workers, 389 F.2d 369, *cert. denied*, 393 U.S. 828 (1968).

[11] Section 301(a) suits require neither the existence of diversity of citizenship nor a minimum jurisdictional amount in controversy. All §301(a) suits may be removed pursuant to 28 U.S.C. §1441.

will also greatly frustrate any relative uniformity in the enforcement of arbitration agreements.

Furthermore, the existing scheme, with the injunction remedy technically available in the state courts but rendered inefficacious by the removal device, assigns to removal proceedings a total unintended function. While the underlying purposes of Congress in providing for federal question removal jurisdiction remain somewhat obscure, there has never been a serious contention that Congress intended that the removal mechanism be utilized to foreclose completely remedies otherwise available in the state courts. Although federal question removal jurisdiction may well have been intended to provide a forum for the protection of federal rights where such protection was deemed necessary or to encourage the development of expertise by the federal courts in the interpretation of federal law, there is no indication that Congress intended by the removal mechanism to effect a wholesale dislocation in the allocation of judicial business between the state and federal courts. . . .

It is undoubtedly true that each of the foregoing objections to *Sinclair-Avco* could be remedied either by overruling *Sinclair* or by extending that decision to the States. While some commentators have suggested that the solution to the present unsatisfactory situation does lie in the extension of the *Sinclair* prohibition to state court proceedings, we agree with Chief Justice Traynor of the California Supreme Court that "whether or not Congress could deprive state courts of the power to give such [injunctive] remedies when enforcing collective bargaining agreements, it has not attempted to do so either in the Norris-LaGuardia Act or §301." McCarroll v. Los Angeles County Dist. Council of Carpenters, 49 Cal. 2d 45, 63, 315 P.2d 322, 332 (1957), *cert. denied*, 355 U.S. 932 (1958). . . .

An additional reason for not resolving the existing dilemma by extending *Sinclair* to the States is the devastating implications for the enforceability of arbitration agreements and their accompanying no-strike obligations if equitable remedies were not available.[15] As we have previously indicated, a no-strike obligation, express or implied, is the *quid pro quo* for an undertaking by the employer to submit grievance disputes to the process of arbitration. See [*Lincoln Mills*], supra, at 455. Any incentive for employers to enter into such an arrangement is necessarily dissipated if the principal and most expeditious method by which the no-strike obligation can be enforced is elimi-

---

[15] It is true that about one-half of the States have enacted so-called "little Norris-LaGuardia Acts" that place various restrictions upon the granting of injunctions by state courts in labor disputes. However, because many States do not bar injunctive relief for violations of collective bargaining agreements, in only about 14 jurisdictions is there a significant Norris-LaGuardia-type prohibition against equitable remedies for breach of no-strike obligations.

nated. While it is of course true . . . that other avenues of redress, such as an action for damages, would remain open to an aggrieved employer, an award of damages after a dispute has been settled is no substitute for an immediate halt to an illegal strike. Furthermore, an action for damages prosecuted during or after a labor dispute would only tend to aggravate industrial strife and delay an early resolution of the difficulties between employer and union.

Even if management is not encouraged by the unavailability of the injunction remedy to resist arbitration agreements, the fact remains that the effectiveness of such agreements would be greatly reduced if injunctive relief were withheld. Indeed, the very purpose of arbitration procedures is to provide a mechanism for the expeditious settlement of industrial disputes without resort to strikes, lockouts, or other self-help measures. This basic purpose is obviously largely undercut if there is no immediate, effective remedy for those very tactics that arbitration is designed to obviate. Thus, because *Sinclair*, in the aftermath of *Avco*, casts serious doubts upon the effective enforcement of a vital element of stable labor-management relations — arbitration agreements with their attendant no-strike obligations — we conclude that *Sinclair* does not make a viable contribution to federal labor policy.

IV

We have also determined that the dissenting opinion in *Sinclair* states the correct principles concerning the accommodation necessary between the seemingly absolute terms of the Norris-LaGuardia Act and the policy considerations underlying §301(a). 370 U.S., at 215. Although we need not repeat all that was there said, a few points should be emphasized at this time.

The literal terms of §4 of the Norris-LaGuardia Act must be accommodated to the subsequently enacted provisions of §301(a) . . . and the purposes of arbitration. Statutory interpretation requires more than concentration upon isolated words; rather, consideration must be given to the total corpus of pertinent law and the policies that inspired ostensibly inconsistent provisions. See . . . Mastro Plastics Corp. v. NLRB, 350 U.S. 270, 285 (1956); United States v. Hutcheson, 312 U.S. 219, 235 (1941).

The Norris-LaGuardia Act was responsive to a situation totally different from that which exists today. In the early part of this century, the federal courts generally were regarded as allies of management in its attempt to prevent the organization and strengthening of labor unions; and in this industrial struggle the injunction became a potent weapon that was wielded against the activities of labor groups. The result was a large number of sweeping decrees, often issued ex parte, drawn on an ad hoc basis without regard to any systematic elaboration of national labor policy. . . .

[In omitted passages, the Court described the purposes behind the enactment of both Norris-LaGuardia and the Wagner Act.]

As labor organizations grew in strength and developed toward maturity, congressional emphasis shifted from protection of the nascent labor movement to the encouragement of collective bargaining and to administrative techniques for the peaceful resolution of industrial disputes. This shift in emphasis was accomplished, however, without extensive revision of many of the older enactments, including the antiinjunction section of the Norris-La-Guardia Act. Thus it became the task of the courts to accommodate, to reconcile the older statutes with the more recent ones.

A leading example of this accommodation process is Brotherhood of Railroad Trainmen v. Chicago River & Ind. R. Co., 353 U.S. 30 (1957). There we were confronted with a peaceful strike which violated the statutory duty to arbitrate imposed by the Railway Labor Act. The Court concluded that a strike in violation of a statutory arbitration duty was not the type of situation to which the Norris-LaGuardia Act was responsive, that an important federal policy was involved in the peaceful settlement of disputes through the statutorily mandated arbitration procedure, that this important policy was imperiled if equitable remedies were not available to implement it, and hence that Norris-LaGuardia's policy of nonintervention by the federal courts should yield to the overriding interest in the successful implementation of the arbitration process.

The principles elaborated in *Chicago River* are equally applicable to the present case. To be sure, *Chicago River* involved arbitration procedures established by statute. However, we have frequently noted, in such cases as *Lincoln Mills*, the *Steelworkers trilogy*, and *Lucas Flour*, the importance that Congress has attached generally to the voluntary settlement of labor disputes without resort to self-help and more particularly to arbitration as a means to this end. Indeed, it has been stated that *Lincoln Mills*, in its exposition of §301(a), "went a long way towards making arbitration the central institution in the administration of collective bargaining contracts."

The *Sinclair* decision, however, seriously undermined the effectiveness of the arbitration technique as a method peacefully to resolve industrial disputes. . . . Clearly employers will be wary of assuming obligations to arbitrate specifically enforceable against them when no similarly efficacious remedy is available to enforce the concomitant undertaking of the union to refrain from striking. On the other hand, the central purpose of the Norris-LaGuardia Act to foster the growth and viability of labor organizations is hardly retarded—if anything, this goal is advanced—by a remedial device that merely enforces the obligation that the union freely undertook under a specifically enforceable agreement to submit disputes to arbitration.[22] We conclude, therefore, that the unavailability of equitable relief in the arbitration context presents a serious impediment to the congressional policy favoring the voluntary establishment of a mechanism for the peaceful resolution of labor disputes, that the core purpose of the Norris-LaGuardia Act is not sacrificed by the limited use of equitable remedies to further this important policy, and consequently that the Norris-LaGuardia Act does not bar the granting of injunctive relief in the circumstances of the instant case.

V

Our holding . . . is a narrow one. We do not undermine the vitality of the Norris-LaGuardia Act. We deal only with the situation in which a collective bargaining contract contains a mandatory grievance adjustment or arbitration procedure. Nor does it follow from what we have said that injunctive relief is appropriate as a matter of course in every case of a strike over an arbitrable grievance. The dissenting opinion in *Sinclair* suggested the following principles for the guidance of the district courts in determining whether to grant injunctive relief—principles that we now adopt:

> A District Court entertaining an action under §301 may not grant injunctive relief against concerted activity unless and until it decides that the case is one in which an injunction would be appropriate despite the Norris-LaGuardia Act. When a strike is sought to be enjoined because it is over a grievance which both parties are contractually bound to arbitrate, the District Court may issue no injunctive order until it first holds that the contract *does* have that effect; and the employer should be ordered to arbitrate, as a condition of his obtaining an injunction against the strike. Beyond this, the District Court must, of course, consider whether issuance of an injunction would be warranted under ordinary principles of equity—whether breaches are occur-

---

[22] As well stated by the neutral members of the A.B.A. Sinclair committee: ". . . [T]he reasons behind the Norris-LaGuardia Act seem scarcely applicable to the situation . . . [in which a strike in violation of a collective bargaining agreement is enjoined]. The Act was passed primarily because of widespread dissatisfaction with the tendency of judges to enjoin concerted activities in accordance with 'doctrines of tort law which made the lawfulness of a strike depend upon judicial views of social and economic policy.' . . . Where an injunction is used against a strike in breach of contract, the union is not subjected in this fashion to judicially created limitations on its freedom of action but is simply compelled to comply with limitations to which it has previously agreed. Moreover, where the underlying dispute is arbitrable, the union is not deprived of any practicable means of pressing its claim but is only required to submit the dispute to the impartial tribunal that it has agreed to establish for this purpose." A.B.A. Sinclair Report 242.

> ring and will continue, or have been threatened and will be committed;
> whether they have caused or will cause irreparable injury to the employer; and
> whether the employer will suffer more from the denial of an injunction than
> will the union from its issuance.

370 U.S., at 228. (Emphasis in original.)

In the present case there is no dispute that the grievance in question was subject to adjustment and arbitration under the collective bargaining agreement and that the petitioner was ready to proceed with arbitration at the time an injunction against the strike was sought and obtained. The District Court also concluded that, by reason of respondent's violations of its no-strike obligation, petitioner "has suffered irreparable injury and will continue to suffer irreparable injury." Since we now overrule *Sinclair*, the holding of the Court of Appeals in reliance on *Sinclair* must be reversed. Accordingly, we reverse . . . and remand the case with directions to enter a judgment affirming the order of the District Court.

. . . Marshall, J., took no part in the decision of this case. [Stewart, J., concurring, acknowledged that the Court's decision in *Sinclair* to which he had subscribed, had been erroneous and had been undermined by later developments.]

BLACK, J., dissenting.[1] . . . Although Congress has been urged to overrule our holding in *Sinclair*, it has steadfastly refused to do so. Nothing in the language or history of the two Acts has changed. Nothing at all has changed, in fact, except the membership of the Court and the personal views of one Justice. I remain of the opinion that *Sinclair* was correctly decided, and, moreover, that the prohibition of the Norris-LaGuardia Act is close to the heart of the entire federal system of labor regulation. In my view *Sinclair* should control the disposition of this case.

Even if the majority were correct, however, in saying that *Sinclair* misinterpreted the Taft-Hartley and Norris-LaGuardia Acts, I should be compelled to dissent. I believe that both the making and the changing of laws

---

[1] [Justice Black's dissent will be better understood in light of his opinion for the majority in *Sinclair*. Maintaining that §301 had not limited the Norris-LaGuardia Act, he had urged (370 U.S. at 204-209): (a) The absence of any limiting language was especially significant, given (i) the express "repeal" in §301(e) of the Norris-LaGuardia provision regarding union-vicarious responsibility and (ii) the LMRA's express provisions for injunctions, at the instance of the NLRB, under §10, and, at the instance of the Attorney General, under the national emergency provisions, §208(b). (b) The legislative history demonstrated that Congress had deliberately declined to lift the Norris-LaGuardia restrictions in actions on collective agreements. (c) No basis existed for arguing that Congress, although itself declining to repeal those restrictions, authorized the courts to do so if they deemed repeal appropriate for promoting policies fashioned under §301. — EDS.]

which affect the substantial rights of the people are primarily for Congress, not this Court. Most especially is this so when the laws involved are the focus of strongly held views of powerful but antagonistic political and economic interests. . . .

When the Court implies that the doctrine called stare decisis rests solely on "important policy considerations . . . in favor of continuity and pre-dictability in the law," it does not tell the whole story. . . .

Altering the important provisions of a statute is a legislative function. And the Constitution states simply and unequivocally: "All legislative Powers herein granted shall be vested in a Congress of the United States. . . ." U.S. Const. Art. I. It is the Congress, not this Court, that responds to the pressures of political groups, pressures entirely proper in a free society. It is Congress, not this Court, that has the capacity to investigate the divergent considerations involved in the management of a complex national labor policy. And it is Congress, not this Court, that is elected by the people. This Court should, therefore, interject itself as little as possible into the law-making and law-changing process. Having given our view on the meaning of a statute, our task is concluded, absent extraordinary circum-stances. When the Court changes its mind years later, simply because the judges have changed, in my judgment, it takes upon itself the function of the legislature. . . .

. . . Even on statutory questions the appearance of new facts or changes in circumstances might warrant re-examination of past decisions in exceptional cases under exceptional circumstances. In the present situation there are no such circumstances. . . .

The only "subsequent event" to which the Court can point is our decision in [Avco], 390 U.S. 557 (1968). The Court must recognize that the holding of Avco is in no way inconsistent with Sinclair. . . .

Avco does make any effort to enforce a no-strike clause in a state court removable to a federal court, but it does not follow that the no-strike clause is unenforceable. Damages may be awarded; the union may be forced to arbitrate. And the employer may engage in self-help. The Court would have it that these techniques are less effective than an injunction. That is doubtless true. But the harshness and effectiveness of injunction relief — and opposi-tion to "government by injunction" — were the precise reasons for the congressional prohibition in the Norris-LaGuardia Act. The effect of the Avco decision is, indeed, to highlight the limited remedial powers of federal courts. But if the Congress is unhappy with these powers as this Court defined them, then the Congress may act; this Court should not. The members of the majority have simply decided that they are more sensitive to the "realization of an important goal of our national labor policy" than the Congress or their predecessors on this Court. . . .

[White, J., dissented "for the reasons stated in the majority opinion" in *Sinclair*.]

NOTES

1. A union's threatened strike to secure compliance with its interpretation of an award of the Railroad Adjustment Board was held enjoinable in Brotherhood of Locomotive Firemen v. L. & N. R.R., 373 U.S. 33 (1963). (The employee affected by the award was relegated to the judicial action authorized by the RLA.) Should a strike also be enjoinable under §301 when an agreement contains a no-strike clause and the strike is prompted by the employer's noncompliance with an arbitration award? Consider §8 of the Norris-LaGuardia Act; Narragansett Improvement Co. v. Local 251, Teamsters, 506 F.2d 715 (1st Cir. 1974). Cf. *Buffalo Forge*, the LMRA case below.

2. In Gateway Coal Co. v. UMW, 414 U.S. 368 (1974), the arbitration clause reached beyond disputes over interpretation to "any local trouble of any kind aris[ing] at the mine," but there was no express no-strike clause. The union, rejecting arbitration, struck to protest both allegedly unsafe conditions and the employer's retention of foremen who had falsified air flow records. The Court, reversing the court of appeals, found the underlying dispute clearly arbitrable and upheld an injunction barring the strike, ordering the union to arbitrate, and providing for suspension of the foremen, pending the arbitral award. Rejecting expressions of contrary views by the court below, the Court announced the following general rules: First, the usual presumption of arbitrability applies to a safety dispute; second, a union seeking to shelter a contractually prohibited strike, under §502, LMRA, must present objective evidence of abnormally dangerous working conditions, as distinguished from merely an honest, but unjustifiable, belief in their existence.

For a discussion of *Gateway Coal*, the appropriate standard under §502, and the possibility that OSHA may enlarge protection of employee self-help in the face of apparently hazardous working conditions, see Atleson, Threats to Health and Safety: Employee Self-Help Under the NLRA, 59 Minn. L. Rev. 647 (1975). See also Whirlpool Corp. v. Marshall, 445 U.S. 1 (1980).

3. A collective agreement provided that a no-strike and arbitration clause would be inoperative if the employer violated certain provisions of the

agreement. In the employer's action to enjoin a strike, the union urged that the duties to arbitrate and not to strike had been lifted by the employer's violations of the agreement. Should the *Steelworkers* presumption of arbitrability operate in this context? (Did *Gateway Coal* answer that question?) Should an injunction issue pending arbitral determination that the alleged employer violations have occurred?

4. A federal district court, enjoining a strike protesting a railroad's elimination of jobs and changed working hours, conditioned the injunction on the carrier's rescinding the job changes or paying the adversely affected employees the wages they would have otherwise received, pending a determination by the adjustment board to which the underlying dispute had been submitted. The Supreme Court upheld the trial court's discretion to impose that condition. Brotherhood of Locomotive Engrs. v. Missouri-Kansas-Texas R.R., 363 U.S. 528 (1962).

5. After a state court had issued a temporary restraining order against a strike allegedly in breach of an agreement, the defendants removed the action to a federal court. That court denied a motion to dissolve the state court order, noting that *Sinclair*, relied on by defendants, had been overruled by *Boys Markets*. Almost six months later, the union resumed its strike activity. Holding that contempt would not lie, the Court ruled that an ex parte temporary restraining order issued by a state court is effective, after removal, only as long as it would have been under state law and in no event longer than the period prescribed by Rule 65(b) of the Federal Rules of Civil Procedure, measured from the date of removal. Granny Goose Foods v. Teamsters Local 70, 415 U.S. 423 (1974). Absent controlling contract terms, a federal court's *Boys Markets* injunction does not terminate on issuance of the arbitrator's decision but continues in force pending review of the award. See Sea-Land Serv. v. ILA, 625 F.2d 38 (5th Cir. 1980).

Buffalo Forge Co. v. United Steelworkers of America
428 U.S. 397 (1976)

WHITE, J. . . . The issue . . . is whether a federal court may enjoin a sympathy strike pending the arbitrator's decision as to whether the strike is forbidden by the express no-strike clause contained in the collective bargaining contract to which the striking union is a party.

I

The Buffalo Forge Company . . . operates three separate plant and office facilities in the Buffalo, New York area. For some years production and maintenance (P&M) employees at the three locations have been represented by the United Steelworkers . . . and its Local Unions No. 1874 and No. 3732 (the Union). The United Steelworkers is a party to the two separate collective bargaining agreements between the locals and the employer. The contracts contain identical no-strike clauses,[1] as well as grievance and arbitration provisions for settling disputes over the interpretation and application of each contract. The latter provide:

> 26. Should differences arise between the [employer] and any employee covered by this Agreement as to the meaning and application of the provisions of this Agreement, or should any trouble of any kind arise in the plant, there shall be no suspension of work on account of such differences, but an earnest effort shall be made to settle such differences immediately [under the six-step grievance and arbitration procedure provided in sections 27 through 32.][2]

Shortly before this dispute arose, the United Steelworkers and two other locals not parties to this litigation were certified to represent the employer's "office clerical-technical" (O&T) employees at the same three locations. On November 16, 1974, after several months of negotiations looking toward their first collective bargaining agreement, the O&T employees struck and established picket lines at all three locations. On November 18, P&M employees at one plant refused to cross the O&T picket line for the day. Two days later, the employer learned that the P&M employees planned to stop work at all three plants the next morning. In telegrams to the Union, the employer stated its position that a strike by the P&M employees would violate the no-strike clause and offered to arbitrate any dispute which had led to the planned strike. The next day, at the Union's direction, the P&M employees honored the O&T picket line and stopped work at the three plants. They did not return to work until December 16, the first regular working day after the District Court denied the employer's prayer for a preliminary injunction.

The employer's complaint under §301(a) [filed] . . . on November 26, claimed the work stoppage was in violation of the no-strike clause. Contending in the alternative that the work strike was caused by a specific

---

[1] Section 14.b. of each agreement provides: "There shall be no strikes, work stoppages or interruption or impeding of work. No Officers or representatives of the Union shall authorize, instigate, aid or condone any such activities. No employee shall participate in any such activity. The Union recognizes its possible liabilities for violation of this provision and will use its influence to see that work stoppages are prevented. . . ."

[2] The final step in the six-part grievance procedure is provided for in §32: "In the event the grievance involves a question as to the meaning and application of the provisions of this Agreement, and has not been previously satisfactorily adjusted, it may be submitted to arbitration upon written notice of the Union or the Company." . . .

incident involving P&M truck drivers' refusal to follow a supervisor's instructions to cross the O&T picket line, and that the question whether the P&M employees' work stoppage violated the no-strike clause was itself arbitrable, the employer requested damages, a temporary restraining order and a preliminary injunction against the strike and an order compelling the parties to submit any "underlying dispute" to the contractual grievance and arbitration procedures. The Union's position was that the work stoppage did not violate the no-strike clause. It offered to submit that question to arbitration "on one day's notice," but opposed the prayer for injunctive relief.

After denying the temporary restraining order and finding that the P&M work stoppage was not the result of the specific refusal to cross the O&T picket line, the District Court concluded that the P&M employees were engaged in a sympathy action in support of the striking O&T employees. The District Court then held itself forbidden to issue an injunction by §4 of the Norris-LaGuardia Act because the P&M employees' strike was not over an "arbitrable grievance" and hence was not within the "narrow" exception to the Norris-LaGuardia Act established in [Boys Markets], 398 U.S. 235 (1970).

On the employer's appeal from the denial of a preliminary injunction, . . . the parties stipulated that the District Court's findings of fact were correct, that the Union had authorized and directed the P&M employees' work stoppage, that the O&T employees' strike and picket line were bona fide, primary and legal, and that the P&M employees' work stoppage, though ended, might "be resumed at any time in the near future at the direction of the International Union, or otherwise."

. . . The Court of Appeals affirmed. . . . [We] now affirm the judgment of the Court of Appeals.

II

. . . Whether the sympathy strike the Union called violated the no-strike clause, and the appropriate remedies if it did, are subject to the agreed-upon dispute-settlement procedures of the contract and are ultimately issues for the arbitrator. [Citing the *Steelworkers* trilogy.] The employer thus was entitled to invoke the arbitral process to determine the legality of the sympathy strike and to obtain a court order requiring the Union to arbitrate if the Union refused to do so. Furthermore, were the issue arbitrated and the strike found illegal, the relevant federal statutes as construed in our cases would permit an injunction to enforce the arbitral decision. [*Enterprise Wheel & Car Corp.*].

The issue in this case arises because the employer not only asked for an order directing the Union to arbitrate but prayed that the strike itself be enjoined pending arbitration and the arbitrator's decision whether the strike was permissible under the no-strike clause. . . .

The holding in *Boys Markets* was said to be a "narrow one," dealing only with the situation in which the collective bargaining contract contained mandatory grievance and arbitration procedures. 398 U.S., at 253. "[F]or the guidance of the district courts in determining whether to grant injunctive relief," the Court expressly adopted the principles enunciated in the dissent in Sinclair Refining Co. v. Atkinson, 370 U.S. 195, 228 (1962), including the proposition that:

> 'When a strike is sought to be enjoined because it is over a grievance which both parties are contractually bound to arbitrate, the District Court may issue no injunctive order until it first holds that the contract *does* have that effect; and the employer should be ordered to arbitrate as condition of his obtaining an injunction against the strike.'

398 U.S., at 254 (emphasis in *Sinclair*). The driving force behind *Boys Markets* was to implement the strong congressional preference for the private dispute settlement mechanisms agreed upon by the parties. Only to that extent was it held necessary to accommodate §4 of the Norris-LaGuardia Act to §301 of the [LMRA] and to lift the former's ban against the issuance of injunctions in labor disputes. . . . Otherwise, the employer would be deprived of his bargain and the policy of the labor statutes to implement private resolution of disputes in a manner agreed upon would seriously suffer.

Boys Markets plainly does not control this case. The District Court found, and it is not now disputed, that the strike was not *over* any dispute between the Union and the employer that was even remotely subject to the arbitration provisions of the contract. . . . The strike had neither the purpose nor the effect of denying or evading an obligation to arbitrate or of depriving the employer of his bargain. Thus, had the contract not contained a no-strike clause or had the clause expressly excluded sympathy strikes, there would have been no possible basis for implying from the existence of an arbitration clause a promise not to strike that could have been violated by the sympathy strike in this case. Gateway Coal Co. v. Mine Workers, supra, at 382.[10]

Nor was the injunction authorized solely because it was alleged that the sympathy strike called by the Union violated the express no-strike provision of the contract. Section 301 . . . assigns a major role to the courts in

---

[10]To the extent that the Court of Appeals, 517 F.2d, at 1211, and other courts . . . have assumed that a mandatory arbitration clause implies a commitment not to engage in sympathy strikes, they are wrong. . . .

enforcing collective bargaining agreements, but aside from the enforcement
of the arbitration provisions of such contracts, within the limits permitted by
Boys Markets, the Court has never indicated that the courts may enjoin
actual or threatened contract violations despite the Norris-LaGuardia Act. In
the course of enacting the Taft-Hartley Act, Congress rejected the proposal
that the Norris-LaGuardia Act's prohibition against labor-dispute injunctions be lifted to the extent necessary to make injunctive remedies available in
federal courts for the purpose of enforcing collective bargaining agreements. . . . As was stated in the *Sinclair* dissent embraced in *Boys Markets*:

> [T]here is no general federal antistrike policy; and although a suit may be
> brought under §301 against strikes which, while they are breaches of private
> contracts, do not threaten any additional public policy, in such cases the
> antiinjunction policy of Norris-LaGuardia should prevail.

Sinclair Refining Co. v. Atkinson, supra, at 225.

. . . Here the Union struck, and the parties were in dispute whether
the sympathy strike violated the Union's no-strike undertaking. Concededly,
that issue was arbitrable. . . . But the Union does not deny its duty to
arbitrate; in fact, it denies that the employer ever demanded arbitration.
However that may be, it does not follow that the District Court was empowered not only to order arbitration but to enjoin the strike pending the decision
of the arbitrator, despite the express prohibition of §4(a) of [Norris-LaGuar-
dia]. . . . If an injunction could issue against the strike in this case, so in
proper circumstances could a court enjoin any other alleged breach of contract pending the exhaustion of the applicable grievance and arbitration
provisions even though the injunction would otherwise violate one of the
express prohibitions of [§4]. The court in such cases would be permitted, if
the dispute was arbitrable, to hold hearings, make findings of fact, interpret
the applicable provisions of the contract and issue injunctions so as to restore
the status quo ante or to otherwise regulate the relationship of the parties
pending exhaustion of the arbitration process. This would cut deeply into the
policy of the Norris-LaGuardia Act and make the courts potential participants in a wide range of arbitrable disputes under the many existing and
future collective bargaining contracts,[12] not just for the purpose of enforcing
promises to arbitrate, which was the limit of *Boys Markets*, but for the

---

[12] This could embroil the district courts in massive preliminary injunction litigation. In
1972, the most recent year for which comprehensive data have been published, more than
21,000,000 workers in the United States were covered under more than 150,000 collective
bargaining agreements. Bureau of Labor Statistics, Directory of National Unions and Employee Assns. 87-88 (1973).

purpose of preliminarily dealing with the merits of the factual and legal issues that are subjects for the arbitrator and of issuing injunctions that would otherwise be forbidden by the Norris-LaGuardia Act.

This is not what the parties have bargained for. Surely it cannot be concluded here, as it was in *Boys Markets*, that such injunctions pending arbitration are essential to carry out promises to arbitrate and to implement the private arrangements for the administration of the contract. As is typical, the agreement in this case outlines the prearbitration settlement procedures and provides that if the grievance "has not been . . . satisfactorily adjusted," arbitration may be had. Nowhere does it provide for coercive action of any kind, let alone judicial injunctions, short of the terminal decision of the arbitrator. The parties have agreed to grieve and arbitrate, not to litigate. They have not contracted for a judicial preview of the facts and the law. Had they anticipated additional regulation of their relationships pending arbitration, it seems very doubtful that they would have resorted to litigation rather than to private arrangements.

The unmistakable policy of Congress [is] stated in [LMRA §203(d)]. . . . But the parties' agreement to adjust or to arbitrate their differences themselves would be eviscerated if the courts for all practical purposes were to try and decide contractual disputes at the preliminary injunction stage.

The dissent suggests that injunctions should be authorized in cases such as this at least where the violation, in the court's view, is clear and the court is sufficiently sure that the parties seeking the injunction will win before the arbitrator. But this would still involve hearings, findings and judicial interpretations of collective bargaining contracts. It is incredible to believe that the courts would always view the facts and the contract as the arbitrator would; and it is difficult to believe that the arbitrator would not be heavily influenced or wholly preempted by judicial views of the facts and the meaning of contracts if this procedure is to be permitted. Injunctions against strikes, even temporary injunctions, very often permanently settle the issue; and in other contexts time and expense would be discouraging factors to the losing party in court in considering whether to relitigate the issue before the arbitrator.

With these considerations in mind, we are far from concluding that the arbitration process will be frustrated unless the courts have the power to issue interlocutory injunctions pending arbitration in cases such as this or in others in which an arbitrable dispute awaits decision. We agree with the Court of Appeals that there is no necessity here, such as was found to be the case in *Boys Markets*, to accommodate the policies of the Norris-LaGuardia Act to the requirements of §301 by empowering the District Court to issue the injunction sought by the employer.

The judgment of the Court of Appeals is affirmed.

STEVENS, J., with whom BRENNAN, MARSHALL, and POWELL, JJ., join, dissenting. . . . The Court today holds that only a part of the union's *quid pro quo* is enforceable by injunction.[2] The principal bases for the [Court's] holding are (1) the Court's literal interpretation of the Norris-LaGuardia Act; and (2) its fear that the federal judiciary would otherwise make a "massive" entry into the business of contract interpretation heretofore reserved for arbitrators. The first argument has been rejected repeatedly in cases in which the central concerns of [Norris-LaGuardia] were not implicated. The second is wholly unrealistic[3] and was implicitly rejected in *Gateway Coal* when the Court held that "a substantial question of contractual interpretation" was a sufficient basis for federal equity jurisdiction. 414 U.S., at 384. That case held that an employer might enforce a somewhat ambiguous *quid pro quo*; today the Court holds that a portion of the *quid pro quo* is unenforceable no matter how unambiguous it may be. . . . I am persuaded that a correct application of the reasoning underlying . . . [*Boys Markets*] requires a different result. . . . [Here follows a reference to four key points in the rationale of *Boys Markets*; the final point is quoted below.]

Finally, *Boys Markets* emphasized the strong federal policy favoring settlement of labor disputes by arbitration. Since . . . [generally] this method of settling disputes is available only when authorized by agreement between the parties, the policy favoring arbitration equally favors the making of enforceable agreements to arbitrate. For that reason, *Boys Markets* also emphasized the importance of ensuring enforceability of the union's *quid pro quo* for the employer's agreement to submit grievance disputes to arbitration. . . . A sympathy strike in violation of a no-strike clause does not directly frustrate the arbitration process, but if the clause is not enforceable against such a strike, it does frustrate the more basic policy of motivating

---

[2] The enforceable part of the no-strike agreement is the part relating to a strike "over an arbitrable dispute." In *Gateway Coal*, however, my Brethren held that the district court had properly entered an injunction that not only terminated a strike pending an arbitrator's decision of an underlying safety dispute, but also "prospectively required both parties to abide by his resolution of the controversy." Id., at 373. A strike in defiance of an arbitrator's award would not be "over an arbitrable dispute"; nevertheless, the Court today recognizes the propriety of an injunction against such a strike.

[3] The Court's expressed concern that enforcing an unambiguous no-strike clause by enjoining a sympathy strike might "embroil the district courts in massive preliminary injunction litigation," is supposedly supported by the fact that 21 million American workers were covered by over 150,000 collective bargaining agreements in 1972. These figures give some idea of the potential number of grievances that may arise, each of which could lead to a strike which is plainly enjoinable under *Boys Markets*. These figures do not shed any light on the number of sympathy strikes which may violate an express no-strike commitment. In the past several years over a dozen such cases have arisen. Future litigation of this character would, of course, be minimized by clarifying amendments to existing no-strike clauses.

employers to agree to binding arbitration by giving them an effective "assurance of uninterrupted operation during the term of the agreement." This portion of *Boys Markets* is therefore not entirely applicable to the present case. Accordingly, it is essential to consider the importance of arbitration to the holding in *Boys Markets*. . . .

II

The *Boys Markets* decision protects the arbitration process. A court is authorized to enjoin a strike over a grievance which the parties are contractually bound to arbitrate, but that authority is conditioned upon a finding that the contract does so provide, that the strike is in violation of the agreement, and further that the issuance of an injunction is warranted by ordinary principles of equity. These conditions plainly stated in *Boys Markets* demonstrate that the interest in protecting the arbitration process is not simply an end in itself which exists at large and apart from other fundamental aspects of our national labor policy.

On the one hand, an absolute precondition of any *Boys Markets* injunction is a contractual obligation. . . . If the union reserves the right to resort to self-help at the conclusion of the arbitration process, that agreement must be respected. The court's power is limited by the contours of the agreement between the parties.[17]

On the other hand, the arbitration procedure . . . performs the important purpose of determining what the underlying agreement actually means as applied to a specific setting. If the parties have agreed to be bound by the arbitrator's decision, the reasons which justify an injunction against a strike that would impair his ability to reach a decision must equally justify an injunction requiring the parties to abide by a decision that a strike is in violation of the no-strike clause.[18] The arbitration mechanism would hardly retain its respect as a method of resolving disputes if the end product of the process had less significance than the process itself.

The net effect of the arbitration process is to remove completely any ambiguity in the agreement as it applies to an unforeseen, or undescribed, set of facts. But if the specific situation is foreseen and described in the contract itself with such precision that there is no need for interpretation by an arbitrator, it would be reasonable to give the same legal effect to such an agreement prior to the arbitrator's decision. In this case, the question whether the sympathy strike violates the no-strike clause is an arbitrable issue. If the

---

[17] In particular, an implied no-strike clause does not extend to sympathy strikes. See ante, n.10.

[18] The Court recognizes that an injunction may issue to enforce an arbitrator's decision that a strike is in violation of the no-strike clause. . . .

court had the benefit of an arbitrator's resolution of the issue in favor of the employer, it could enforce that decision just as it could require the parties to submit the issue to arbitration. And if the agreement were so plainly unambiguous that there could be no bona fide issue to submit to the arbitrator, there must be the same authority to enforce the parties' bargain pending the arbitrator's final decision.[20]

The Union advances three arguments against this conclusion: (1) that interpretation of the collective bargaining agreement is the exclusive province of the arbitrator; (2) that an injunction erroneously entered pending arbitration will effectively deprive the union of the right to strike before the arbitrator can render his decision; and (3) that it is the core purpose of the Norris-LaGuardia Act to eliminate the risk of an injunction against a lawful strike.[21] Although I acknowledge the force of these arguments, I think they are insufficient to take this case outside the rationale of *Boys Markets*.

The *Steelworkers* trilogy establishes that a collective bargaining agreement submitting all questions of contract interpretation to the arbitrator deprives the courts of almost all power to interpret the agreement to prevent submission of a dispute to arbitration or to refuse enforcement of an arbitrator's award. . . . And *Gateway Coal* held that an injunction may issue to protect the arbitration process even if a "substantial question of contractual interpretation" must be answered to determine whether the strike is over an arbitrable grievance. In each of these cases, however, the choice was between interpretation of the agreement by the court or interpretation by the arbitrator; a decision that the dispute was not arbitrable, or not properly arbitrated,

[20] . . . It is not necessary to hold that an injunction may issue if the scope of the no-strike clause is not a clearly arbitrable issue. If the agreement contains no arbitration clause whatsoever, enforcement of the no-strike clause would not promote arbitration by encouraging employers to agree to an arbitration clause in exchange for a no-strike clause. Furthermore, even if the agreement contains an arbitration clause, but the clause does not clearly extend to the question whether a strike violates the agreement, then the parties' commitment to enforcement of the no-strike clause through enforcement of the arbitrator's final decision also remains unclear.

[21] The Union also argues that an injunction should be barred because the party seeking arbitration is usually required to accept the condition of which he complains pending the decision of the arbitrator. The employer normally receives the benefit of this rule, since it is the union that initiates most grievances. The Union contends that fairness dictates that it receive the same benefit pending the outcome of employer grievances. However, the rule has its origins in the need for production to go forward under the employer's control pending clarification of the agreement through arbitration. See Feller, A General Theory of the Collective Bargaining Agreement, 61 Calif. L. Rev. 663, 737-740 (1973). This justification hardly supports, but rather undermines, the Union's position.

The Court advances the same argument as a threat of "massive preliminary injunction litigation" by both employers and unions over all arbitrable disputes. Ante, n.12. This argument simply ignores the special status of the no-strike clause as the quid pro quo of the arbitration clause.

would have precluded an interpretation of the agreement according to the contractual grievance procedure. In the present case, an interim determination of the no-strike question by the court neither usurps nor precludes a decision by the arbitrator. By definition, issuance of an injunction pending the arbitrator's decision does not supplant a decision that he otherwise would have made. Indeed, it is the ineffectiveness of the damage remedy for strikes pending arbitration that lends force to the employer's argument for an injunction. The court does not oust the arbitrator of his proper function but fulfills a role that he never served.

The Union's second point, however, is that the arbitrator will rarely render his decision quickly enough to prevent an erroneously issued injunction from effectively depriving the union of its right to strike. . . . But this argument demonstrates only that arbitration, to be effective, must be prompt, not that the federal courts must be deprived entirely of jurisdiction to grant equitable relief. Denial of an injunction when a strike violates the agreement may have effects just as devastating to an employer as the issuance of an injunction may have to the union when the strike does not violate the agreement. Furthermore, a sympathy strike does not directly further the economic interests of the members of the striking local or contribute to the resolution of any dispute between that local, or its members, and the employer. On the contrary, it is the source of a new dispute which, if the strike goes forward, will impose costs on the strikers, the employer, and the public without prospect of any direct benefit to any of these parties. A rule that authorizes postponement of a sympathy strike pending an arbitrator's clarification of the no-strike clause will not critically impair the vital interests of the striking local even if the right to strike is upheld, and will avoid the costs of interrupted production if the arbitrator concludes that the no-strike clause applies.

Finally, the Norris-LaGuardia Act cannot be interpreted to immunize the union from all risk of an erroneously issued injunction. *Boys Markets* itself subjected the union to the risk of an injunction entered upon a judge's erroneous conclusion that the dispute was arbitrable and that the strike was in violation of the no-strike clause. *Gateway Coal* subjected the union to a still greater risk, for the court there entered an injunction to enforce an implied no-strike clause despite the fact that the arbitrability of the dispute, and hence the legality of the strike over the dispute, presented a "substantial question of contractual interpretation." . . .

These considerations, however, do not support the conclusion that a sympathy strike should be temporarily enjoined whenever a collective bargaining agreement contains a no-strike clause and an arbitration clause. The accommodation between the Norris-LaGuardia Act and §301(a) . . .

allows the judge to apply "the usual processes of the law" but not to take the place of the arbitrator. Because of the risk that a federal judge, less expert in labor matters than an arbitrator, may misconstrue general contract language, I would agree that no injunction or temporary restraining order should issue without first giving the union an adequate opportunity to present evidence and argument, particularly upon the proper interpretation of the collective bargaining agreement; the judge should not issue an injunction without convincing evidence that the strike is clearly within the no-strike clause.[27] Furthermore, to protect the efficacy of arbitration, any such injunction should require the parties to submit the issue immediately to the contractual grievance procedure, and if the union so requests, at the last stage and upon an expedited schedule that assures a decision by the arbitrator as soon as practicable. Such stringent conditions would insure that only strikes in violation of the agreement would be enjoined and that the union's access to the arbitration process would not be foreclosed by the combined effect of a temporary injunction and protected grievance procedures. Finally, as in *Boys Markets*, the normal conditions of equitable relief would have to be met.

Like the decision in *Boys Markets*, this opinion reflects, on the one hand, my confidence that experience during the decades since the Norris-LaGuardia Act was passed has dissipated any legitimate concern about the impartiality of federal judges in disputes between labor and management, and on the other, my continued recognition . . . that judges have less familiarity and expertise than arbitrators and administrators who regularly work in this specialized area. The decision in *Boys Markets* requires an accommodation between the Norris-LaGuardia Act and the [LMRA]. I would hold only that the terms of that accommodation do not entirely deprive the federal courts of all power to grant any relief to an employer, threatened with irreparable injury from a sympathy strike clearly in violation of a collective bargaining agreement, regardless of the equities of his claim for injunctive relief pending arbitration. . . .

NOTES

1. Students could now profitably reexamine Jacksonville Bulk Terminals, Inc. v. International Longshoremen's Assn., supra p. 469. In general, see Gould, On Labor Injunctions Pending Arbitration: Recasting *Buffalo*

---

[27] Of course, it is possible that an arbitrator would disagree with the court even when the latter finds the strike to be clearly prohibited. But in that case, the arbitrator's determination would govern, provided it withstands the ordinary standard of review for arbitrator's awards. See United Steelworkers of America v. Enterprise Wheel & Car Corp., 363 U.S. 593, 597-599.

Forge, 30 Stan. L. Rev. 533 (1978); Smith, The Supreme Court, *Boys Markets* Labor Injunctions, and Sympathy Work Stoppages, 44 U. Chi. L. Rev. 321 (1977).

2. The *Buffalo Forge* majority asserts that it is generally unwise to permit courts, in sympathy strike situations, to engage in a preliminary interpretation of the agreement in the light of the facts. Once the *Buffalo Forge* limitation on *Boys Markets* is established, is a judicial interpretation of the parties' agreement — prior to any arbitration — inevitable? If it is, how is the judicial involvement necessitated by *Buffalo Forge* different from the "judicial preview of the facts and the law" found objectionable by the majority in that case?

3. The parties had disagreed as to whether the collective agreement permitted the employer unilaterally to institute planned changes in work cycles. The employer had agreed to the union's request for immediate arbitration but declined to defer the changes; the court of appeals, prior to *Buffalo Forge*, sustained a preliminary injunction against the institution of the changes pending arbitration. Amalgamated Transit Union v. Greyhound Lines, 529 F.2d 1073 (9th Cir. 1976). Is that result consistent with *Buffalo Forge*?

Upon remand of *Greyhound Lines* by the Supreme Court (429 U.S. 807 (1976)) for further consideration in light of *Buffalo Forge*, the court of appeals reversed the district court's injunction, reasoning that (a) there had been no basis for finding an implied promise by the company to preserve the status quo pending arbitration, and (b) generally a change in the status quo, unlike a strike, would not interfere with arbitration. Amalgamated Transit Union v. Greyhound Lines, 550 F.2d 1237 (9th Cir.), *cert. denied*, 434 U.S. 837 (1977). Does *Buffalo Forge* require the court's reversal of position? Suppose that the union in *Greyhound Lines*, instead of bringing an injunction action, had struck against the employer's changes in work cycles, and in the employer's action for an injunction had requested that any injunction issued be conditioned on the deferral of the changes pending arbitration? Cf. Note 4, supra p. 1038.

4. Despite an employer's willingness to arbitrate actions challenged by the union under the agreement (e.g., a transfer of work), courts have enjoined such actions, pending arbitration, when the prerequisites for injunctive relief adopted in *Boys Markets* have been satisfied. For example, the Fourth Circuit's test for issuance of an injunction in such cases is whether an employer's proposed actions "must be enjoined because the available arbitral process could not possibly restore the status quo ante in an acceptable form were that conduct to be found violative of contract rights. This would render the arbitration process a hollow formality and necessitate an injunction . . . pending arbitration." Columbia Local, Postal Wkrs. v. Bolger,

621 F.2d 615, 618 (4th Cir. 1980) (union challenging a merger of shifts within the same facility failed to show that an arbitrator's award could not satisfactorily restore the status quo ante). See also Aluminum Wkrs., Local 215 v. Consolidated Aluminum Corp., 696 F.2d 437, 444 (6th Cir. 1982) (no evidence that employer would be unable "to comply fully" with arbitrator's back pay and reinstatement award); United Steelworkers v. Fort Pitt Casting, 598 F.2d 1273 (3d Cir. 1979) (employer required to pay hospitalization and insurance premiums during strike despite dispute over employer's and union's obligations and despite employer's contention that union was not exposed to irreparable harm because only money damages involved). For the general applicability of the requirements and limitations of §§7, 8, and 9 of Norris-LaGuardia to prayers for injunctions against unions and employers, see United Parcel Service (New York) v. Local 804, Teamsters, 698 F.2d 100 (2d Cir. 1983); UAW v. Lester Engg. Co., 718 F.2d 818 (6th Cir. 1983). See also Axelrod, The Application of the *Boys Markets* Decision in the Federal Courts, 16 B.C. Ind. & Com. L. Rev. 893 (1975); Cantor, *Buffalo Forge* and Injunctions Against Employer Breaches of Collective Bargaining Agreements, 1980 Wis. L. Rev. 247.

5. Since sympathy strikes are generally protected under §7 of the NLRA (see, e.g., Chevron, U.S.A., Inc., 244 N.L.R.B. 1981 (1979)), an employer may not discipline employee participants unless the Act's protections have been contracted away. The NLRB, once again requiring "clear and unmistakable" evidence of intention, has held that general no-strike agreements will not support an inference of waiver of the protected right to engage in sympathy strikes. Rather, an express contract term surrendering that right or discussion in negotiations to that effect is required. Operating Engrs., Local 18 (Davis McKee, Inc.), 238 N.L.R.B. 652 (1978).

(a) Can that rule of interpretation be justified? Why shouldn't the rule be that unrestricted no-strike promises forbid even sympathy strikes, absent extrinsic evidence indicating otherwise? (b) Should the principle of "coterminous application" — i.e., that a no-strike clause normally encompasses only strikes over arbitrable disputes — operate in the discipline context? The Board apparently thinks it should; some courts disagree. See, e.g., United States Steel Corp. v. NLRB, 711 F.2d 772 (7th Cir. 1983); Pacemaker Yacht Co. v. NLRB, 663 F.2d 455 (3d Cir. 1981); Amcar Div., ACF Indus. v. NLRB, 641 F.2d 561 (8th Cir. 1981).

Carbon Fuel Co. v. United Mine Workers
444 U.S. 212 (1979)

BRENNAN, J. The question for decision . . . is whether an international union, which neither instigates, supports, ratifies, nor encourages "wildcat" strikes engaged in by local unions in violation of a collective-bargaining agreement, may be held liable in damages to an affected employer if the union did not use all reasonable means available to it to prevent the strikes or bring about their termination.

Petitioner, Carbon Fuel Co., and respondent United Mine Workers of America (UMWA) were parties to the National Bituminous Coal Wage Agreements of 1968 and 1971, collective-bargaining agreements covering, inter alia, workers at petitioner's several coal mines in southern West Virginia. Forty-eight unauthorized or "wildcat" strikes were engaged in by three local unions at petitioner's mines from 1969 to 1973. Efforts of District 17, a regional subdivision of UMWA, to persuade the miners not to strike and to return to work were uniformly unsuccessful.[1]

Petitioner brought this suit pursuant to §301. . . . UMWA, District 17, and the three local unions were named defendants. The complaint sought injunctive relief[2] and damages, alleging that the strikes were in violation of the two collective-bargaining agreements. . . . The trial judge found as a matter of law that the strikes violated the agreements. The trial judge also instructed the jury, over objection of UMWA and District 17, that those defendants might be found liable in damages to petitioner "[i]f you find from a preponderance of the evidence that the International and District Unions did not use all of the reasonable means available to them to prevent work stoppages or strikes from occurring in violation of the contract, or to terminate any such work stoppages or strikes after they began. . . ." Verdicts in different amounts were returned against UMWA, District 17, and the three local unions.

. . . [T]he Fourth Circuit vacated in part the judgments against the three local unions but otherwise affirmed those judgments.[3] However, the Court of Appeals vacated the judgments against UMWA and District 17, and remanded to the District Court with directions to dismiss the case against those defendants. 582 F.2d 1346 (1978). The court held that this result was required by its earlier decision in United Construction Workers v. Haislip Baking Co., 223 F.2d 872 (1955). 582 F.2d, at 1351. Haislip held as follows, 223 F.2d, at 877-878:

[1] . . . The District and International were promptly notified of each strike. In each instance a District representative arranged for a meeting of the striking local and directed the members to return to work. Often the representative advised the members that the International and the District could take disciplinary action against participants in illegal, unauthorized strikes. If the strike did not end after the first meeting a second meeting was called. Most strikes ended in the first one or two days. No strike lasted longer than six days. From concern that such action might only aggravate a bad situation, no disciplinary action was taken against the strikers. There is however no suggestion that the District's efforts to end the strikes were not in good faith.

[2] The contracts have expired, and the question of injunctive relief is out of the case.

[3] Review of the judgments against the locals was not sought here.

We have never held . . . that there is any responsibility on the part of a union for a strike with which it has had nothing to do; and there manifestly is no such liability. If [UMWA or District 17] had done nothing when [petitioner] called on them to help get the men back to work, there would have been no liability on the part of [UMWA or District 17]. This being true, defendants were not rendered liable by the efforts which [District 17] made to bring about an adjustment of the difficulty, even if they did not do everything that they might have done to that end. The question is not whether they did everything they might have done, but whether they adopted, encouraged or prolonged the continuance of the strike. There is no evidence of any sort that they did.

The Court of Appeals recognized that its conclusion was in conflict with the holding of the . . . Third Circuit in Eazor Express, Inc. v. International Brotherhood of Teamsters, 520 F.2d 951 (1975) (union liable under no-strike clause for failure to use best efforts to end unauthorized strikes). . . . We affirm. . . .

A

[T]he legislative history [of §301] is clear that Congress limited the responsibility of unions for strikes in breach of contract to cases when the union may be found responsible according to the common-law rule of agency.[5]

    . . . At the same time, Congress gave careful attention to the problem of strikes during the term of a collective-bargaining agreement, but stopped short of imposing liability upon a union for strikes not authorized, participated in, or ratified by it. Rather, to effectuate §301(a), the Taft-Hartley Act provided in §301(b) that a union "shall be bound by the acts of its agents," and in §301(e) provided that the common law of agency shall govern "in determining whether any person is acting as an 'agent' of another person." . . .

    Congress' reason for adopting the common-law agency test, and applying to unions the common-law doctrine of *respondeat superior*, follows . . . Coronado Coal Co. v. Mine Workers, 268 U.S. 295, 304 (1925), [that is,] that to find the union liable "it must be clearly shown . . . that what was done was done by their agents in accordance with their fundamental agreement of association." The common-law agency test replaced the very loose

---

[5] An international union, of course, is responsible under §301 for any authorized strike if such strike violates any term of the contract, whether express or implied. See, *e.g.*, Gateway Coal Co. v. Mine Workers, 414 U.S. 368 (1974); Boys Markets, Inc. v. Retail Clerks, 398 U.S. 235 (1970). Our holding in Part A of this opinion does not affect the *content*, as implied by law, of arbitration clauses. Rather, we are addressing the wholly different issue of whether an international or district union may be held legally responsible for locals' unilateral actions which are concededly in violation of the locals' responsibilities under the contract.

test of responsibility incorporated in §2(2) of the original 1935 [NLRA] under which the term "employer" included "any person acting in the interest of an employer. . . ." 49 Stat. 450.[6]

Petitioner makes the distinct argument that we should hold the International liable for its *own* failure to respond to the locals' strike. In the face of Congress' clear statement of the limits of an international union's legal responsibility for the acts of one of its local unions, it would be anomalous to hold that an international is nonetheless liable for its failure to take certain steps in response to actions of the local. Such a rule would pierce the shield that Congress took such care to construct. Accordingly, we reject petitioner's suggestion that Congress' policy in favor of arbitration extends to imposing an obligation on the respondents, which agreed to arbitrate grievances, to use reasonable means to try to control the locals' actions in contravention of that agreement.

The Court of Appeals stated: "There was no evidence presented in the district court that either the District or International Union instigated, supported, ratified, or encouraged any of the work stoppages. . . ." 582 F.2d, at 1351. Under . . . the UMWA constitution, the local unions lacked authority to strike without authorization from UMWA. Moreover, UMWA had repeatedly expressed its opposition to wildcat strikes. Petitioner thus failed to prove agency as required by §§301(b) and (e). . . .

B

We turn next to petitioner's argument that even if the no-strike obligation to be implied from the promise to resolve disputes by arbitration did not carry with it the further step of implying an obligation on UMWA and District 17 to use all reasonable efforts to end an unauthorized strike, that obligation should nevertheless be implied from the contract provision obligating UMWA and District 17 to "maintain the integrity of this contract." . . .

The bargaining history of the contracts completely answers petitioner's argument. The parties directly addressed the issue early in their bargaining history and, after first including such an obligation, specifically deleted it from their agreement. The first agreement between the parties, in 1941, contained an explicit no-strike clause. In order to avoid liability under §301 for contract breaches, UMWA negotiated the deletion of the no-strike provision from the 1947 contract. Instead, the coverage of the contract was limited to employees "able and willing to work," and the parties agreed that all

---

[6] At the same time, Congress applied to unions the common-law doctrine of *respondeat superior* rather than the more restrictive test of union responsibility under §6 of the Norris-LaGuardia Act, which requires "clear proof of *actual* participation in, or *actual* authorization of, such acts, or of ratification of such acts after *actual* knowledge thereof."

disagreements would be settled through arbitration or collective bargaining. In 1950 the contract was again rewritten. The "able and willing" provision was dropped and replaced by a promise "to maintain the integrity of this contract and *to exercise their best efforts through available disciplinary measures* to prevent stoppages of work by strike or lockout." (Emphasis supplied.)

Because the union did not want to surrender its freedom to decide what measures to take or not to take in dealing with unauthorized strikes, it negotiated the deletion of the "best efforts through available disciplinary measures" clause. . . . The new provision in the 1952 contract, which was carried forward into the 1968 and 1971 contracts essentially unchanged as to this issue, read as follows:

> The United Mine Workers of America and the Operators agree and affirm that they will maintain the integrity of this contract and that all disputes and claims which are not settled by agreement shall be settled by the machinery provided in the "Settlement of Local and District Disputes" section of the Agreement unless national in character in which event the parties shall settle such disputes by free collective bargaining as heretofore practiced in the industry, it being the purpose of this provision to provide for the settlement of all such disputes and claims through the machinery in this contract provided and by collective bargaining without recourse to the courts.

new provision

It makes no sense to assume that the parties thought the new language subsumed the deleted provision. Had that been their intention, there would have been no reason to alter the contract.

The inescapable conclusion to be drawn . . . is that, whatever the integrity clause may mean, the parties purposely decided not to impose on the union an obligation to take disciplinary or other actions to get unauthorized strikers back to work. It would do violence to the bargaining process and the national policy furthering free collective bargaining to impose by judicial implication a duty upon UMWA and District 17 that the parties in arm's-length bargaining first included and then purposely deleted. . . .

Affirmed.

NOTES

1. As the Court's opinion states (footnote 3), review of the judgments against the three locals, aggregating $722,347.43, was not sought in *Carbon Fuel*. The Fourth Circuit, affirming the district court's directed verdicts, had endorsed the "mass action" theory as the basis for holding the locals responsi-

ble for most of 31 wildcat strikes. (There was evidence, uncontradicted, that all the members of the locals, including officers, had participated in the strikes.) Quoting Eazor Express, Inc. v. Teamsters, 520 F.2d 951 (3d Cir. 1975), the court of appeals declared that this theory "represents a sensible and pragmatic approach" to the problem of defining a local union's responsibility for wildcat strikes:

> When all the members of a union employed by a given employer engage in a concerted strike not formally authorized by the union, . . . many courts hold the union responsible on the theory that mass action by union members must realistically be regarded as union action. The premise is that large groups of men do not act collectively without leadership and that a functioning union must be held responsible for the mass action of its members.

After *Carbon Fuel*, (a) Should a local union be held liable at all for damages resulting from a "mass action" unauthorized strike which its officers have not instigated, encouraged, supported, or ratified? (Conflicting decisions are collected in Consolidation Coal Co. v. UMW, Local 1261, 725 F.2d 1258 (10th Cir. 1984).) (b) Could a local union avoid damage liability under the "mass action" theory by demonstrating in court that its officers used all reasonable means to prevent and end wildcat activity? (c) Would such a showing avoid a *Boys Markets* injunction against the local?

2. When a collective agreement expressly requires a local union to use "best efforts" to halt unauthorized stoppages, what difficulties result from such efforts when a wildcat strike is directed in part against the union or when the union is torn by factionalism? Consider the impact of §101(a)(5) of LMRDA; but see Hackenburg v. Boilermakers, Local 101, 694 F.2d 1237 (10th Cir. 1982) (union's "benching" of members for 90 days for wildcat strike, pursuant to provision in bargaining agreement, is employment-related action and thus not "discipline" within meaning of §101(a)(5)). See generally Handsaker & Handsaker, Remedies and Penalties for Wildcat Strikes: How Arbitrators and Federal Courts Have Ruled, 22 Cath. U.L. Rev. 279 (1973).

3. The union called a one-day strike to protest the company's actions on a matter clearly not subject to arbitration under the parties' agreement. That agreement, however, included a broad no-strike clause. The company sued the union under §301 for $25,000 in business losses resulting from the stoppage. The union, invoking *Buffalo Forge* and the doctrine of "coterminous application," contended that no breach of contract had occurred because a no-strike clause is operative only with respect to strikes over arbitrable disputes. What is your evaluation of the union's defense? Cf. Ryder Truck Lines, Inc. v. Teamsters Local 480, 115 L.R.R.M. 2912 (6th

Cir. 1984) (en banc); Delaware Coca-Cola Bottling Co. v. Teamsters Local 326, 624 F.2d 1182 (3d Cir. 1981). Consider also Note 5, supra p. 1050.

Complete Auto Transit, Inc. v. Reis, 451 U.S. 401 (1981). The Court, addressing a question reserved in Atkinson v. Sinclair Refining Co., 370 U.S. 238 (1962), held that §301(a) is not a basis for recovering damages from individual employees for unauthorized strikes in violation of a no-strike clause. Brennan, J., for the Court, relied principally on the legislative history: "§301(b) by its terms forbids a money judgment entered against a union from being enforced against individual union members. See Atkinson v. Sinclair Refining Co. . . . It is a mistake to suppose that Congress thereby suggested by negative implication that employees should be held liable where their union is not liable for the strike. . . . [T]he legislative history of §301 clearly reveals Congress' intent to shield individual employees from liability for damages arising from their breach of the no-strike clause . . . , whether or not the union participated in or authorized the illegality. Indeed, Congress intended this result even though it might leave the employer unable to recover for his losses. . . . Congress deliberately chose to allow a damages remedy for breach of the no-strike provision of a collective-bargaining agreement only against *unions*, not *individuals*, and, as to unions, only when they participated in or authorized the strike. See Carbon Fuel Co. v. United Mine Workers, 444 U.S. 212. . . ."

Accordingly, employers confronted with wildcat strikes must turn to "the significant array of other remedies available . . . to achieve adherence to collective bargaining agreements."

Powell, J. (concurring in part and in the judgment), after reviewing management remedies, declared: "The Court plainly is unrealistic . . . when it suggests that employers have at their disposal a battery of alternate remedies for illegal strikes. The result of the absence of remedies is a lawless vacuum. . . . It is, of course, the province of Congress to set the Nation's labor policy. I do not suggest that authorizing a damages remedy against individual wildcat strikers would be desirable. I do believe, however, that the absence of an effective remedy leaves such strikes undeterred and the public interest unprotected. . . ."

Metropolitan Edison Co. v. NLRB
460 U.S. 693 (1983)

[The company was building a nuclear generating station at Three Mile Island. A series of bargaining agreements with the IBEW provided that "the

Brotherhood and its members agree that during the term of this agreement there shall be no strikes or walkouts." Between 1970 and 1974, union members participated in four work stoppages violating that provision. On each occasion the company disciplined participating union officers more severely than the other participants. Two resultant arbitration awards had upheld the company's disparate treatment. In both cases, the arbitrator determined that union officials have an "affirmative duty" to uphold the bargaining agreement, breach of which justifies greater discipline.

In August of 1977, IBEW members refused to cross another union's informational picket line at the construction site. The company "repeatedly" ordered the local IBEW president to cross the picket line in order to demonstrate to other employees the IBEW's compliance with the no-strike clause. He refused to do so, choosing instead to attempt to persuade the other union to remove the picket line. Within four hours, the IBEW president and vice-president had negotiated a settlement of the other union's dispute with the company, and the line was removed. The company imposed 5- to 10-day suspensions on all employees who had refused to cross the picket line. The local union president and vice-president, however, each received 25-day suspensions and warnings that future participation in any unlawful work stoppage would result in immediate discharge.

The NLRB ruled that selective discipline of union officials violates §§8(a)(1) and 8(a)(3). 252 N.L.R.B. 1030 (1980). The Third Circuit enforced the Board's order, holding that an employer may impose greater discipline on union officials only when the collective agreement expressly states that the officials have an "affirmative duty" to prevent work stoppages. 663 F.2d 478 (1981). The Supreme Court affirmed.]

POWELL, J. . . .

II

This case does not present the question whether an employer may impose stricter penalties on union officials who take a leadership role in an unlawful strike. The [ALJ] found that neither Light nor Lang [the local's president and vice-president] acted as a strike leader.[6] Nor does this case question the

---

[6] The Board has held that employees who instigate or provide leadership for unprotected strikes may be subject to more severe discipline than other employees. See Midwest Precision Castings Co., 244 N.L.R.B. 597, 598 (1979); Chrysler Corp., 232 N.L.R.B. 466, 474 (1977). In making this factual determination the Board has recognized that a remark made by a union official may have greater significance than one made by a rank-and-file member. See *Midwest Precision Castings*, supra, at 599.

In this case the Board accepted the [ALJ's] finding that Light and Lang were not strike leaders, and the Court of Appeals affirmed that finding. See 663 F.2d 478, 484 (1981). . . .

employer's right to discipline union officials who engage in unprotected activity. Neither the union nor the Board has argued that union officials who fail to honor a no-strike clause are immunized from being disciplined in the same manner as other strike participants. The narrow question presented is whether an employer unilaterally may define the actions a union official is required to take to enforce a no-strike clause and penalize him for his failure to comply.

Metropolitan Edison . . . contends first that its actions did not violate §8(a)(3) because a union official has a duty to ensure compliance with the terms of the collective bargaining agreement. Breach of this duty justifies the imposition of an additional penalty on union officials. Alternatively, the company contends that a union in effect may waive any statutory protection that otherwise would be accorded its officials by agreeing that they will undertake specific action to assure compliance with the no-strike clause. . . .

The Board has found that disciplining union officials more severely than other employees for participating in an unlawful work stoppage "is contrary to the plain meaning of §8(a)(3) and would frustrate the policies of the Act if allowed to stand." Precision Castings Co., 233 N.L.R.B., at 184. This conduct, in the Board's view, is "inherently destructive" of protected individual rights because it discriminates solely on the basis of union status. See Consolidation Coal Co., 263 N.L.R.B. 1306 (1982); Indiana & Michigan Electric Co., 237 N.L.R.B. 226 (1978), enf. denied, 599 F.2d 227 (CA7 1979). The Board has concluded that an employer's contractual right to be free of unauthorized strikes does not counterbalance the "discriminatory effects of singling out union officers for especially harsh treatment." Consolidation Coal Co., 263 N.L.R.B., at 1309. Disciplining union officials discriminatorily may have only an indirect effect on the rank and file's decision to strike, but it may well deter qualified employees from seeking union office. See ibid.

We defer to the Board's conclusion that conduct such as Metropolitan Edison's adversely affects protected employee interests. Section 8(a)(3) not only proscribes discrimination that affects union membership, it also makes unlawful discrimination against employees who participate in concerted activities protected by §7. . . . See Radio Officers' Union v. NLRB, 347 U.S. 17, 39-40 (1954). Holding union office clearly falls within the activities protected by §7, . . . and there can be little doubt that an employer's unilateral imposition of discipline on union officials inhibits qualified employees from holding office. . . .

Determining that such conduct adversely affects protected employee interests does not conclude the inquiry. If the employer comes forward with a legitimate explanation for its conduct, the Board must "strike the proper balance between the asserted business justifications and the invasion of employee rights." NLRB v. Great Dane Trailers, Inc., 388 U.S., at 33-34. In this case the company has argued that its actions were justified because there is an implied duty on the part of the union officials to uphold the terms of the collective-bargaining agreement. Unquestionably there is support for the proposition that union officials, as leaders of the rank and file, have a legal obligation to support the terms of the contract and to set a responsible example for their members. See Indiana & Michigan Electric Co. v. NLRB, 599 F.2d, at 230-232. And in view of the disruptive effects of wildcat strikes, the importance of ensuring compliance with no-strike clauses is self-evident. See Boys Market, Inc. v. Retail Clerks, 398 U.S. 235, 248-249, and n. 17; Complete Auto Transit, Inc. v. Reis, 451 U.S. 401, 418-419 (1981) (Powell, J., concurring in part and concurring in the judgment). But it does not follow that an employer may assume that a union official is required to attempt to enforce a no-strike clause by complying with the employer's directions and impose a penalty on the official for declining to comply. . . .

We think the Board's view is consistent with the policies served by the Act. . . . If, as the company urges, an employer could define unilaterally the actions that a union official is required to take, it would give the employer considerable leverage over the manner in which the official performs his union duties. Failure to comply with the employer's directions would place the official's job in jeopardy. But compliance might cause him to take actions that would diminish the respect and authority necessary to perform his job as a union official. This is the dilemma Congress sought to avoid. We believe the Board's decision furthers these policies and uphold its determination.

III

The company argues that even if §8(a)(3) would prohibit it from imposing a more severe penalty on union officials than on other employees, the union in effect has waived the [statutory] protection. . . . The substance of this contention is that, in this case, the prior arbitration awards and the union's acquiescence in the harsher sanctions imposed on its officials are sufficient to establish a corresponding contractual duty. . . . [T]he union's response [is] that the statutory right to be free from discrimination may never be waived. . . .

A

. . . [A] union may waive a member's statutorily protected rights, including "his right to strike during the contract term, and his right to refuse to cross a lawful picket line." NLRB v. Allis-Chalmers Manufacturing Co., 388 U.S.

175, 180 (1967). Such waivers are valid because they "rest on 'the premise of fair representation' and presuppose that the selection of the bargaining representative 'remains free.'" NLRB v. Magnavox Co., 415 U.S. 322, 325 (1974) (quoting Mastro Plastics Corp. v. NLRB, 350 U.S. 270, 280 (1956). . . . Waiver should not undermine these premises. Thus a union may bargain away its members' economic rights, but it may not surrender rights that impair the employees' choice of their bargaining representative. See NLRB v. Magnavox Co., 415 U.S., at 325.

We think a union's decision to bind its officials to take affirmative steps to end an unlawful work stoppage is consistent with "the premise of fair representation."[10] Such a waiver imposes no constraints on the employees' ability to choose which union will represent them. Imposition of this duty is more closely related to the economic decision a union makes when it waives its members' right to strike. It merely requires union officials to take steps that are ancillary to the union's promise not to strike and provides the employer with an additional means of enforcing this promise. . . .

No-strike provisions, central to national labor policy, often have proven difficult to enforce. See Boys Markets, Inc. v. Retail Clerks, 398 U.S., at 248-249, and n.17; Complete Auto Transit, Inc. v. Reis, 451 U.S., at 423-424, (Powell, J., concurring in part and concurring in the judgment). A union and an employer reasonably could choose to secure the integrity of a no-strike clause by requiring union officials to take affirmative steps to end unlawful work stoppages. Indeed, a union could choose to bargain away this statutory protection to secure gains it considers of more value to its members. Its decision to undertake such contractual obligations promotes labor peace and clearly falls within the range of reasonableness accorded bargaining representatives.

---

[10] The Board's position on this question has not been consistent. Compare Super Valu Xenia, 228 N.L.R.B. 1254, 1259 (1977) (upholding discipline of union officials where collective bargaining agreement expressly imposed higher duty on union officials), with Gould Corp., 237 N.L.R.B. 881, 881 (1978) (discharge of union steward not validated by contractually imposed duty), enf. denied, 612 F.2d 728 (CA3 1979). Recently, in Consolidation Coal Co., 263 N.L.R.B. No. 188 (1982), two Board members held that a contractual duty will not justify the imposition of more severe sanctions on union officials. (Members Fanning and Jenkins). Member Zimmerman would have allowed waiver where the duty was explicit. Two members would have found an affirmative duty even absent such waiver. (Chairman Van de Water . . . [and] Member Hunter, dissenting). To the extent Consolidation Coal provides any guidance as to the Board's present views, it suggests that a majority of the Board would find no statutory violation where the bargaining agreement imposes a specific duty on union officials. The Courts of Appeals that have considered this question have agreed that this statutory protection may be waived. See, e.g., NLRB v. South Central Bell, 688 F.2d, at 356; Fournelle v. NLRB, 670 F.2d 331, 340-341 (CADC 1982); Gould, Inc. v. NLRB, 612 F.2d 728, 733 (CA3 1979), cert. denied, 449 U.S. 890 (1980); C. H. Heist Corp. v. NLRB, 657 F.2d, at 183.

B

. . . [Applying *Mastro Plastics Corp.*], we will not infer from a general contractual provision that the parties intended to waive a statutorily protected right unless the undertaking is "explicitly stated."[12] . . .

. . . Metropolitan Edison does not contend that the general no-strike clause included in the bargaining agreement imposed any explicit duty on the union officials. Rather it argues that the union's failure to change the relevant contractual language in the face of two prior arbitration decisions constitutes an implicit contractual waiver. . . .

. . . [W]e do not doubt that prior arbitration decisions may be relevant — both to other arbitrators and to the Board — in interpreting bargaining agreements.[13] But to waive a statutory right the duty must be established clearly and unmistakably. Where prior arbitration decisions have been inconsistent, sporadic, or ambiguous, there would be little basis for determining that the parties intended to incorporate them in subsequent agreements. Assessing the clarity with which a party's duties have been defined of course will require consideration of the specific circumstances of each case. Cf. Carbon Fuel Co. v. Mine Workers, 444 U.S. 212, 221-222 (1979).

. . . [T]he company argues that when the prior bargaining agreement was renegotiated, the union's silence manifested a clear acceptance of the earlier arbitration decisions. During the history of collective bargaining between these two parties, however, . . . only two arbitration decisions . . . imposed a higher duty on union officials. We do not think that two arbitration awards establish a pattern of decisions clear enough to convert the union's silence into binding waiver. This is especially so in light of the provision in the bargaining agreement that "[a] decision [by an arbitrator] shall be binding . . . for the term of *this* agreement." (emphasis added). We conclude that there is no showing that the parties intended to incorporate the two prior arbitration decisions into the subsequent agreement.

[12] The Courts of Appeals have agreed that the waiver of a protected right must be expressed clearly and unmistakably. . . . The holding in Teamsters v. Lucas Flour Co., 369 U.S. 95 (1962), is not to the contrary. There the Court found that a contract provision establishing that a dispute shall be settled exclusively and finally by compulsory arbitration makes clear that the union may not strike over such a dispute. See id., at 105. *Lucas Flour* established that there does not have to be an express waiver of statutory rights, but waiver was implied in that situation only because of the unique conjunction between arbitration and no-strike clauses. Cf. Gateway Coal Co. v. Mine Workers, 414 U.S. 368, 382 (1974).

[13] An arbitration decision may be relevant to establishing waiver of this statutory right when the arbitrator has stated that the bargaining agreement itself clearly and unmistakably imposes an explicit duty on union officials to end unlawful work stoppages. Absent such a statement, the arbitration decision would not demonstrate that the union specifically intended to waive the statutory protection otherwise afforded its officials. In this case, however, the two arbitration decisions did not purport to determine the parties' specific intent. . . .

IV

We accept the Board's conclusion that the imposition of more severe sanctions on union officials for participating in an unlawful work stoppage violates §8(a)(3). While a union may waive this protection by clearly imposing contractual duties on its officials to ensure the integrity of no-strike clauses, we find that no waiver occurred here. . . . Affirmed.

NOTE

Justice Powell relies in part on the contractual provision that an arbitral decision "shall be binding . . . for the term of *this* agreement" (emphasis added). Is there an explanation of that provision that would undercut the force that the Justice gave it? Cf. *W.R. Grace*, infra p. 1116.

Drake Bakeries, Inc. v. American Bakery & Confectionery Wkrs. Local 50, 370 U.S. 254 (1962). In 1959-1960, since Christmas and New Year's Day fell on Fridays, the employer, a bakery, in order to maintain fresh supplies, sought to reschedule work to the Saturdays following the holidays instead of the preceding Thursdays. The employer asserted that this rescheduling was management's prerogative. The union asserted that it would violate the agreement. Under a compromise for December 26, the employer operated with a reduced complement; but lack of employees precluded production on January 2. The employer promptly sued for damages for breach of the agreement's no-strike clause, and the union secured a stay pending arbitration. The Supreme Court (with Harlan, J., dissenting) upheld this stay and distinguished Atkinson v. Sinclair Refining Co.[m] (referred to supra p. 1056) on these grounds: The adjustment procedure (in Article V of the agreement) applied not only to questions of interpretation or application of any clause but also to "all complaints, all disputes and all grievances involving any conduct . . . or any relation between the parties, directly or indirectly." Furthermore, the arbitration clause, embraced, rather than excluded, disputes and conduct falling within that "comprehensive language," which easily covered the employer's damage claim. The Court declared:

"The company further asserts that even if it agreed in the contract to

---

[m] [In *Atkinson*, decided the same day as *Drake Bakeries*, the Court found the grievance-arbitration procedure to be "employee-oriented" — i.e., it covered only employee grievances and excluded employer claims of breach of contract. Thus, the Court held that an employer's §301 damage action for breach of the no-strike clause would not be stayed pending arbitration of that claim.— Eds.]

arbitrate union violations of the no-strike clause, it is excused by the union's breach from pursuing the post-breach remedies called for in the contract. . . . [I]n its view, the union's violation of the no-strike clause is *sui generis* and so basic to what the employer bargained for in the contract and so inherently and fundamentally inconsistent with the grievance and arbitration procedures that the faithful observance of the no-strike clause by the union is a condition precedent to the employer's duty to arbitrate (even though he has promised to do so), or that the union must be deemed to have waived, or to be estopped from asserting, its right to arbitrate.

"However, this Court has prescribed no such inflexible rule rigidly linking no-strike and arbitration clauses of every collective bargaining contract in every situation. The company has not attempted, or claimed the right, either to terminate the entire contract or to extinguish permanently its obligations under the arbitration provisions. Instead, it has sued for damages for an alleged strike, and, as far as this record reveals, the contract continued in effect, as did the promises of the parties to arbitrate and the promise of the union not to strike. Moreover, in this case, under this contract, by agreeing to arbitrate all claims without excluding the case where the union struck over an arbitrable matter, the parties have negatived any intention to condition the duty to arbitrate upon the absence of strikes. They have thus cut the ground from under the argument that an alleged strike, automatically and regardless of the circumstances, is such a breach or repudiation of the arbitration clause by the union that the company is excused from arbitrating, upon theories of waiver, estoppel, or otherwise. Arbitration provisions, which themselves have not been repudiated, are meant to survive breaches of contract, in many contexts, even total breach; and in determining whether one party has so repudiated his promise to arbitrate that the other party is excused the circumstances of the claimed repudiation are critically important. . . .

"Under our federal labor policy . . . we have every reason to preserve the stabilizing influence of the collective bargaining contract in a situation such as this. We could enforce only the no-strike clause by refusing a stay in the suit for damages in the District Court. We can enforce both the no-strike clause and the agreement to arbitrate by granting a stay until the claim for damages is arbitrated. This we prefer to do. . . .

"We do not decide in this case that in no circumstances would a strike in violation of the no-strike clause contained in this or other contracts entitle the employer to rescind or abandon the entire contract or to declare its promise to arbitrate forever discharged or to refuse to arbitrate its damage claims against the union. We do decide that Article V of this contract obligates the company to arbitrate its claims for damages from forbidden strikes by the union and that there are no circumstances in this record which justify relieving the company of its duty to arbitrate the consequences of this one-day strike, intertwined as it is with the union's denials that there was any strike or any breach of contract at all. . . ."

Local 721, United Packinghouse Workers v. Needham Packing Co., 376 U.S. 247 (1964). Nearly 200 union members left work in protest against the discharge of another member. The company advised the strikers that the discharge would be handled in the grievance procedure and that they would be terminated if they did not return to work. When the union and the strikers ignored this direction, the company terminated the strikers and began hiring replacements. The union filed grievances over the initial and the subsequent discharges. The company thereupon wrote the union that it declined to process the grievances, added that the union and its members had "repudiated and terminated the labor agreement," and declared that it would no longer recognize or deal with the union.

The union sued in a state court, under §301, to compel arbitration of the discharges; the company, counterclaiming for damages, urged that the union's breach of the no-strike clause released it of all obligations under the contract, including arbitration. The Iowa appellate court affirmed the trial court's denial of arbitration, agreeing that the union "had waived its right to arbitrate the grievances by its walkout." The Supreme Court reversed and remanded, Harlan, J., writing:

". . . [W]e must answer the question whether acts of the union relieved Needham of its contractual obligation to arbitrate almost entirely on the basis of the agreement itself. . . . The no-strike clause provides: '. . . [D]uring the period of this agreement the employees shall not engage in and the Union shall not call or sanction any slow down, work stoppage or strike. . . .' The grievance provisions include typical procedures for the resolution of a dispute preliminary to arbitration. They then provide:

> In the event a dispute shall arise between the Company and the Union with reference to the proper interpretation or application of the provisions of this contract and such dispute cannot be settled by mutual agreement of the parties, such dispute shall be referred to a board of arbitration upon the request of the Union.

It is evident from the above as well as other provisions of the agreement[3] that

---

[3] For example, the agreement provides that grievances must be presented within 14 days "of the occurrence giving rise to such grievance" or within 14 days "of the time the Union has knowledge, or should have had knowledge of such grievance. . . ."

the grievance procedures were intended largely, if not wholly, for the benefit of the union. . . .

"The law which controls . . . is stated in [*Drake Bakeries*], 370 U.S. 254. . . . Continuance of the duty to arbitrate is, if anything, clearer here than it was in *Drake Bakeries*, where one of the issues was whether an alleged strike was within the intended scope of the arbitration clause. There is no question in this case that the union's claim of wrongful discharge is one which Needham agreed to arbitrate. Nothing in the agreement indicates an intention to except from Needham's agreement to arbitrate disputes concerning the 'interpretation or application' of the agreement any dispute which involves or follows an alleged breach of the no-strike clause. That the no-strike clause does not itself carry such an implication is the holding of *Drake Bakeries*.

"The fact that the collective bargaining agreement does not require Needham to submit its claim to arbitration, as the employer was required to do in *Drake Bakeries*, and indeed appears to confine the grievance procedures to grievances of the union, does not indicate a different result. Needham's claim is the subject of a counterclaim in the Iowa courts; nothing we have said here precludes it from prosecuting that claim and recovering damages. That Needham asserts by way of defense to the union's action to compel arbitration the same alleged breach of the no-strike clause which is the subject of the counterclaim does not convert the union's grievance into Needham's different one.

"Nor do we believe that this case can be distinguished from *Drake Bakeries* on the ground that that case involved only a "one-day strike," id., at 265. Whether a fundamental and long-lasting change in the relationship of the parties prior to the demand for arbitration would be a circumstance which, alone or among others, would release an employer from his promise to arbitrate we need not decide. . . . The passage of time resulting from Needham's refusal to arbitrate cannot, of course, be a basis for releasing it from its duty to arbitrate.

"Needham's allegations . . . that the union breached the no-strike clause, supported by such facts as were undisputed on the pleadings, did not release Needham from its duty to arbitrate the union's claim that employees had been wrongfully discharged. On that basis, we reverse and remand to the Iowa Supreme Court for further proceedings. . . ."

NOTES

1. Does §8 of the Norris-LaGuardia Act provide a defense against a union's action to compel arbitration when the union has breached its

no-strike pledge? Consider Brotherhood of R.R. Trainmen v. Toledo, Peoria & Western, supra p. 481, and the *Steelworkers* trilogy, supra pp. 976-990.

2. The arbitration clause in *Drake Bakeries* was read as covering disputes over union violations of the no-strike clause. Given this reading, could an employer convincingly argue that particular circumstances — e.g., a long and violent strike authorized by the union — justified his bypassing arbitration and suing for breach of the no-strike clause?

3. Do *Drake* and *Needham* involve a total rejection of standard contract doctrines permitting termination for "material" breach? When an agreement provides for arbitration, would such rejection be equally desirable — regardless of whether arbitration is sought for a union's claim, as in *Needham*, or an employer's claim for damages, as in *Drake*?

See generally Summers, Collective Agreements and the Law of Contracts, 78 Yale L.J. 525, 542-547 (1969); Feller, A General Theory of the Collective Bargaining Agreement, 61 Calif. L. Rev. 663, 792-799 (1973).

Note: Contract Doctrine and NLRA Rights and Duties

In order to conserve energy, the R company unilaterally changed work schedules, thereby reducing the employees' earnings. Under the collective agreement, strikes were banned prior to exhaustion of the multistep grievance procedure, but arbitration required the consent of both parties. On June 7, 1973, the employees struck before completing the fifth and final step of the grievance procedure. R, on July 23, advised the employees that it would begin hiring replacements on July 29. On August 9, R rescinded the collective agreement, and subsequently terminated the striking employees. Upon being advised by a majority of his employees that they no longer wished to be represented by the union, R withdrew recognition. The NLRB held that (a) the unilateral change in schedules was not warranted by the management rights' clause and violated §8(a)(5); (b) but since that violation had not been "serious" within the meaning of Arlan's Department Store of Michigan (see supra p. 256), the strike in violation of the no-strike clause had been unprotected ab initio; and that (c) R did not violate the NLRA by rescinding the agreement in response to the strike or by his discharges and subsequent withdrawal of recognition. 212 N.L.R.B. 333 (1974).

A Third Circuit panel refused to resolve the case "by simply pigeonholing it as within the rule of *Mastro Plastics* or of *Arlan's*." Instead, the court remanded to the Board for further consideration in the light of post-*Mastro Plastics* developments in the law of labor contracts (notably the

Steelworkers trilogy and *Boys Markets*). Although noting that arbitration was not mandatory under the parties' agreement, the court criticized the Board for denying protection to the strikers without considering the company's failure to seek a settlement before resorting to self-help. Finally, the court concluded that the "strict application" of the contractual doctrine of material breach is inconsistent with labor policy. See Steelworkers v. NLRB (Dow Chemical Co.), 530 F.2d 266 (3d Cir. 1976), *cert. denied*, 429 U.S. 834 (1976).

On remand, the Board held, on the same record, that the company's unilateral change of working schedules had been a "serious" unfair labor practice and that under *Mastro Plastics* the strike had not been a breach of contract but was protected activity. 244 N.L.R.B. 1060 (1979). Hence, the Board did not reach the question whether the company's self-help, albeit in response to a strike violating the agreement, had constituted an unfair labor practice.

Another panel of the Third Circuit, reversing, reasoned as follows: *Mastro Plastics* is a rule of contract interpretation rather than an unfair labor practice rule; hence, under §301, courts owe no special deference to the Board's view regarding that rule. *Mastro Plastics* itself presented a question as to whether a contract clause could validly bar a strike prompted by an employer's encroachment on employees' free choice. In *Dow*, by contrast, a contract clause permitting employer unilateral change in the shift would clearly have been valid. Where a contract permits several interpretations — each valid under the NLRA — the interpretive issue could lawfully be resolved in arbitration. To hold that the resolution of such issues against an employer (with the concomitant condemnation of his unilateral action as an unfair labor practice) warranted a strike would defeat the parties' probable intentions. Furthermore, where, as in this case, *Boys Markets* relief was not available, the court spoke favorably of the doctrine of *Marathon Electric* (106 N.L.R.B. 1171 (1953), *enforced sub nom.* United Electrical Radio & Machine Workers v. NLRB, 223 F.2d 338, *cert. denied*, 350 U.S. 981 (1956)), namely, that a union's material breach warranted an employer's unilateral cancellation of the whole agreement.

Declining to remand again, the court decided the question avoided by the Board, holding that Dow's termination of the agreement and discharge of the strikers were not unfair labor practices. See Dow Chemical Co. v. NLRB, 636 F.2d 1352 (3d Cir. 1980).

Given the court's reasoning, would the result in *Dow* have been different had the company, before or after the strike, refused to confer with the union, or entertain its grievances, concerning the changes in schedules? See Isla Verde Hotel Corp. v. NLRB, 702 F.2d 268 (1st Cir. 1983). Cf. NLRB

v. Keller-Crescent Co., 538 F.2d 1291 (7th Cir. 1976) (employees held under a duty to arbitrate whether they were privileged to respect picket line of sister union; hence, employer's suspension for employees' work stoppage lawful without regard to interpretation of no-strike provisions of the agreement).

Nolde Bros. v. Local 358, Bakery & Confectionery Workers, 430 U.S. 243 (1977). A 1970 agreement between the company and the local, applicable to the company's Norfolk, Virginia, plant, provided for, inter alia: (1) a broad no-strike clause and binding arbitration for "any grievance"; (2) upon permanent closing of the plant, severance pay for employees who had worked three or more years immediately before layoff; (3) vacation pay graduated according to length of service; and (4) the agreement to be effective until July 21, 1973, and, thereafter, until its termination, upon seven days written notice by either party. After several months of bargaining that went beyond July 21, 1973, the union duly served a termination notice, which became effective on August 31, when the company, threatened by an economic strike, closed the plant, after advising the union of its intent to do so. The company distributed accrued vacation pay but refused to make severance payments or to arbitrate the union's claim therefor. In the union's §301 action to compel arbitration of that claim, the district court granted the employer a summary judgment. The court of appeals reversed, ordering arbitration. The Court affirmed, Burger, C. J., declaring:

"Only the issue of arbitrability is before us. . . .[8] [B]oth the Union's claim for severance pay and Nolde's refusal to pay the same are based on their differing perceptions of a provision of the expired [agreement]. . . . The dispute therefore, although arising *after* the expiration of the . . . contract, clearly arises *under* that contract.

"The parties agreed to resolve *all* disputes by resort to the mandatory grievance-arbitration machinery. . . . [T]here is nothing in the arbitration clause that expressly excludes from its operation a dispute [of this nature]. . . . [I]n the absence of some contrary indication, there are strong reasons to conclude that the parties did not intend their arbitration duties to terminate automatically with the contract. . . . [They] clearly expressed their preference for an arbitral, rather than a judicial, interpretation of their

---

[8] Certiorari was neither sought, nor granted, on the question of the arbitrator's authority to consider arbitrability following referral, and we express no view on that matter. Similarly, we need not speculate as to the arbitrability of post-termination contractual claims which, unlike the one presently before us, are not asserted within a reasonable time after the contract's expiration. [This footnote has been relocated in the text. — EDS.]

[contract] obligations. . . . [Their] confidence in the arbitration process and an arbitrator's presumed special competence . . . does not terminate with the contract. . . . [T]he alternative remedy of a lawsuit is the very remedy the arbitration clause was designed to avoid. . . .

"The parties must be deemed to have been conscious of [the well-established federal labor policy favoring arbitration] when they agree to resolve their contractual differences through arbitration. . . . [W]here the dispute is over a provision of the expired agreement the presumptions favoring arbitrability must be negated expressly or by clear implication."

Stewart, J., joined by Rehnquist, J., dissented, contending in part: "[The usual assumptions favoring arbitration] are wholly inapplicable to this case. The closing of the bakery . . . necessarily meant that there was no continuing relationship to protect or preserve. Cf. John Wiley & Sons v. Livingston, 376 U.S. 543; Howard Johnson Co. v. Hotel Employees, 417 U.S. 249. And the Union's termination of the contract, thereby releasing it from its obligation not to strike, foreclosed any reason for implying a continuing duty on the part of the employer to arbitrate as a *quid pro quo* for the Union's offsetting, enforceable duty to negotiate rather than strike. See Boys Markets, Inc. v. Retail Clerks, 398 U.S. 235. . . ."

NOTES

1. The Court appears to treat the issue before it as one of "substantive arbitrability." Is it fairly arguable that the issue is one of "procedural arbitrability" under *Wiley*, to be resolved by the arbitrator?

2. Assume that the no-strike clause in *Nolde Bros.* had included this language: "The obligation not to strike shall end for all purposes on July 21, 1973, the expiration date of this agreement, whether or not a notice of termination is given." Would such a provision have had any effect on the company's duty to arbitrate the severance pay dispute?

3. Had the dissenters' position in *Nolde Bros.* prevailed, would the union or the employees have had a judicial remedy for the employer's (alleged) breach of agreement? If so, are the advantages customarily attributed to arbitration, compared to courts, applicable in the context of *Nolde Bros.?*

4. In Goya Foods, Inc., 238 N.L.R.B. 1465 (1978), a strike following the agreement's expiration had been prompted by discharges effected during the term of the agreement, which contained both a broad arbitration clause and a no-strike clause. The Board held that the strike violated the no-strike clause and was, accordingly, unprotected. It reasoned that the no-strike

clause and the employer's arbitration duty were coterminous and that *Nolde Bros.* had established the proposition that the presumption favoring arbitrability "must be negated expressly or by clear implication" where the dispute is over a provision of the expired contract. Noting the parties' arbitration of the initial discharges, despite the agreement's expiration, the Board concluded that the words "during the life of the agreement" contained in the no-strike clause did not expressly negate the continuation of the duty not to strike along with the arbitration clause. Since, the Board suggested, the agreement "lives on" in the duty to arbitrate, the duty not to strike should "live on to the extent of the duty to arbitrate over issues created by or arising out of the expired agreement."

Can the result here be reconciled with the Board's usual requirement that a waiver of statutory rights must be "clear and unmistakable"?

5. What if the strike in *Goya Foods* had been called solely to support the union's contract-renewal demands? What if the union's objects in striking had been both reinstatement of the discharged employees and economic pressure in support of bargaining demands? Cf. Steelworkers v. Fort Pitt Steel Casting, 635 F.2d 1071 (3d Cir. 1980) (parties intended that obligation not to strike or lockout would be coterminous with duty to arbitrate but that no-strike clause would not apply to the use of economic weapons in support of either's bargaining position; accordingly, union's post-contract economic strike did not violate no-strike clause, and there was no need to decide whether that clause survived contract termination to the same extent as arbitration duty; strike did not alter company's obligation to arbitrate union's grievances arising after contract termination). See also American Sink Top & Cabinet Co., supra p. 843, where the Board, invoking *Nolde Bros.*, held that an employer's unilateral disavowal of the post-contract operation of the grievance procedure violated §8(a)(5).

C. ARBITRATION AND EXTERNAL LAW

The provisions of a collective agreement may parallel, overlap, or conflict with the requirements of external law, such as the NLRA or Title VII of the Civil Rights Act of 1964. As a consequence, public tribunals, such as the NLRB or the courts, confront the question of the effect to be given to contractual machinery — more specifically, whether and when they should defer to the arbitration process or to a completed arbitration award. On the other hand, questions as to the role of the external law in arbitration arise when an arbitrator is asked to invalidate a contractual provision as repugnant to a statute, to enforce the statute, or to construe an ambiguous agreement so as to avoid any conflict with a statute. At the drafting stage, the parties will face a related problem, i.e., the extent to which they should expressly provide that various public laws should be enforceable in, or excluded from, the arbitration.

This section examines the coordination of such private remedies and public regulation and policies.

Feller, The Coming End of Arbitration's Golden Age
Proceedings, National Academy of Arbitrators, 29th Annual Meeting 97, 98-101, 108-112 (1976)

. . . The reason for this special deference to arbitrators is usually said to be their special competence. . . . [S]ome arbitrators do have some special insight into the ways of doing things in an industrial plant, but in many other cases they do not. Clearly, an ad hoc arbitrator, who comes in to decide a grievance in a particular shop that he has never seen before, and may never see again, has no special knowledge of the "common law" of that shop.

It is certainly not true that arbitrators have a competence in their special field that exceeds the competence of other specialized adjudicators in our legal system. We have many such specialized adjudicators, from the members of the [NLRB] to the Tax Court, to the Court of Customs and Patent Appeals, and on to the many specialized agencies which both state and federal law have established to adjudicate disputes arising under particular statutes. There are enormous areas which, as Meltzer said nine years ago . . . are "at least as complex and specialized as labor arbitration,"[2] in which we presumably have judges with special expertise and competence. Sometimes the reviewing courts do give, or purport to give, deference to the specialized expertise of these tribunals. But in almost every case—the NLRB is perhaps the classic example—the courts nevertheless insist on performing a reviewing function, ensuring that the specialized adjudicators adhere to the letter and the spirit of the law that they are interpreting. . . . But not so with arbitrators' decisions. To put it in Meltzer's words: "In no other area of adjudication are courts asked to exercise their powers while they are denied any responsibility for scrutinizing the results they are to enforce."

The basic attitude . . . is premised on a sometimes unstated but ever-present recognition that arbitration is not a substitute for judicial adjudica-

---

[2] Meltzer, Ruminations About Ideology, Law, and Labor Arbitration, in The Arbitrator, the NLRB, and the Courts, Proceedings of the 20th Ann. Meeting, National Academy of Arbitrators, Dallas L. Jones—ed. (1967) 1, 11. [34 U. Chi. L. Rev. 545 (1967).]

tion, but a method of resolving disputes over matters which, except for the collective agreement and its grievance machinery, would be subject to *no* governing adjudicative principle at all. . . . [A]rbitration is a substitute for the strike. . . .

Arbitration, if viewed as a substitute for the strike, without more, would imply decision without reference to agreed-upon standards. But we know that isn't so of grievance arbitration as it has developed in this country, principally since World War II. Grievance arbitration is precisely adjudication against standards: the standards set forth in the collective bargaining agreement. The accepted principle is that the arbitrator has power neither to add to nor detract from, nor to change any of the provisions of, the agreement, but can only determine their proper interpretation and application. Sometimes this restriction is set forth in the agreement; sometimes not. But it makes virtually no difference: That is the accepted rule.

There is a contradiction between that rule and the proposition that arbitration is the substitute for the strike, a contradiction that can be resolved only if we make one critical distinction: Grievance arbitration is an adjudication against standards, but the standards are not those which would be applied by a court charged with adjudicating a contractual dispute. To put the matter in other words, the parties to the collective bargaining process have substituted for the strike, as a method of resolving differences between them as to the proper application and interpretation of their agreement, a system of adjudication against the standards set forth in that agreement; but that system of adjudication, since it is not a substitute for litigation, is not the same, in principle, historical background, or effect, as the system of adjudication used by the courts to resolve controversies over the meaning and application of contracts.

This is just another way of saying what I have written elsewhere at great length.[6] The collective bargaining agreement is not a contract insofar as it establishes the rights of employers and employees, but is, rather, a set of rules governing their relationship — rules which are integral with and cannot be separated from the machinery that the parties have established to resolve disputes as to their meaning. . . .

[I]t could be said, . . . with substantial correctness, that the sole source of law in industries in which the grievance and arbitration machinery was well established was the collective agreement. The principal impact of state and federal legislation was upon those industries in which collective bargaining was not established, or at least not well established, and in which, therefore,

---

[6]Feller, A General Theory of the Collective Bargaining Agreement, 61 Calif. L. Rev. 663, 720 et seq. (1973).

the institution of labor arbitration was similarly, and consequently, not established.

This was, truly, the Golden Age of Arbitration. . . . The beginning of its end can be dated to the 1960s, when we began to have an increasing quantity of substantive federal regulations of the terms and conditions of employment. In 1963 we had the Equal Pay Act, in 1964 Title VII of the Civil Rights Act, in 1970 the Occupational Safety and Health Act and, as well, Title III of the Consumer Credit Protection Act limiting the right of an employer to discharge because of garnishment. In 1974, we had ERISA, the Employee Retirement and Income Security Act, and the problems created by the interrelationships between that act and collective bargaining agreements are just beginning to be felt. . . . At about the same time, we have had a new development under an old law: the *Collyer* doctrine, under which what are essentially public-law decisions are being referred to arbitrators. This last development may appear, on the surface, to enlarge rather than diminish the status of arbitration, but . . . it must in the end have the same effect as the new statutory law. And that effect is, inevitably, to signal the end of arbitration's Golden Age.

The statutory development must do so, in the simple sense, because the introduction of public law as a source of individual employee rights, and the existence of public adjudicative and remedial bodies to vindicate those rights, necessarily undermine the hegemony of the collective bargaining agreement and the unitary — or almost unitary — system of governance under the agreement of which the institution of arbitration and its special status are the products. Arbitration is not an independent force, but a dependent variable, and to the extent that the collective agreement is diminished as a source of employee rights, arbitration is equally diminished.

. . . Far greater is the problem created by two facts. One is that the questions arising under the public, external law and the questions arising under collective bargaining agreements, which it is the function of grievance arbitration to decide, cannot be separated into nicely segmented compartments. The second is that the parties, or one of them, anxious to maintain the hegemony of the collective agreement, may force into the arbitration process questions of adjudication under the public law, sometimes — as in the case of the NLRB — with the active assistance of the public agency charged with enforcement of that law. I perhaps should add a third factor: the tendency of some arbitrators to reach out, without agreement from the parties, to engage in the process of public-law adjudication, a tendency which in the end, I think, can only be fatal to the posture, and the pretensions, of the arbitration profession.

The last-mentioned factor was essentially what was involved in the controversy generated at the 1967 meeting of the Academy by the separate papers of Meltzer[19] and Howlett[20] and continued by them, and by a distinguished set of arbitrators and academicians, at subsequent meetings.[21] The question . . . was the extent to which arbitrators, in resolving grievances, should implement or follow the rules governing the employment relationship imposed by external law rather than the agreement where the two conflict. The answers ranged from never (Meltzer) to always (Howlett). The others were somewhere in the middle and are best typified by Mittenthal and Sovern. Mittenthal, echoing Cox's earlier view, took the position that an arbitrator should base his decision on the law rather than the agreement where the employer sought to justify action in violation of the agreement on the ground that it was required by law; but he should base his decision on the agreement rather than the law where the employer complied with the agreement but the claim was that he should, rather, have complied with the law.[22] Sovern occupied ground somewhat closer to Meltzer. He would permit arbitral decision based on the law only in some of the cases in which Mittenthal would: those in which the arbitrator was competent and in which the courts would not have primary jurisdiction.[23]

If what I have argued so far has any validity, Meltzer was clearly right if — and I emphasize the *if* because I'm not at all sure that in the end that result is either desirable or attainable — arbitration is to continue to maintain its special status. Meltzer was right because to the extent that the arbitrator decides disputed questions of external law, he necessarily relinquishes his right to claim immunity from review by the bodies that external law has established as the ultimate deciders of what that law means and how it is to be applied in particular situations. By applying the external law, the arbitrator ceases to be part of an autonomous adjudicatory system and transposes

[19] Meltzer, supra, note 2.

[20] Howlett, The Arbitrator, the NLRB, and the Courts, supra, n.2, at 67. [Howlett urged that "every agreement incorporates all applicable law" and that arbitrators "should render decisions . . . based on both contract language and law." Howlett, supra, n.2, at 67, 83, 85.—Eds.]

[21] Meltzer, The Role of Law in Arbitration: Rejoinder, in Developments in American and Foreign Arbitration, Proceedings of the 21st Ann. Meeting, National Academy of Arbitrators, Charles M. Rehmus—ed. (1968); 58 Howlett, The Role of Law in Arbitration: A Reprise, id., at 64; Mittenthal, The Role of Law in Arbitration, id., at 42; St. Antoine, Discussion, id., at 75; Sovern, When Should Arbitrators Follow Federal Law? in Arbitration and the Expanding Role of Neutrals, Proceedings of the 23rd Ann. Meeting, National Academy of Arbitrators, Gerald G. Somers and Barbara D. Dennis—eds. (1970); . . . The Role of Arbitration in State and National Labor Policy, in Arbitration and the Public Interest, Proceedings of the 24th Ann. Meeting, National Academy of Arbitrators, Gerald G. Somers and Barbara D. Dennis—eds. (1971), 42; Morris, Comment, id., at 65. See also, Platt, The Relationship Between Arbitration and Title VII of the Civil Rights Act of 1964, 3 Ga. L.R. 398 (1969).

[22] Mittenthal, supra, note 21.

[23] Sovern, supra, note 21.

himself into another kind of adjudicatory system. If you will allow me to push my previous analogy a bit further — his judgments are no longer entitled to "full faith and credit" because, rather than being an adjudicator in a foreign jurisdiction, the arbitrator becomes more like a lower court whose decisions are subject to review by higher courts. Further, it seems probable that once undertaken, review can scarcely be limited to decisions on the issues of external law.

. . . Deference to the arbitration process was and is difficult to achieve. . . . It will be impossible to maintain if arbitrators extend themselves and regard arbitration as encompassing anything more than the interpretation and application of the rules which the parties have adopted to govern their particular relationship.[27]

NOTE

A nonveteran is laid off and files a grievance requesting reemployment and back pay, urging that the employer violated the agreement that gave veterans only their plant seniority plus the seniority they would have accumulated had they not been drafted. Even though the nonveteran had more seniority, the employer supports his action on this ground: The Selective Service Act of 1940 required the layoff of nonveterans rather than veterans during the first year of the veteran's return from military service even though the veteran's seniority, including credit for military service, was less than the nonveteran's seniority. Assume that the employer's interpretation of the statute is valid. Should the arbitrator give it effect and dismiss the grievance?

A second grievance involves the same basic situation, except for this variation: The employer, relying on the agreement, laid off the *veteran*, who filed a grievance based on the statute requesting reinstatement (and displacement of the nonveteran) and back pay. How should the arbitrator dispose of this grievance?

Should the role of law in such cases turn on the nature of the employer's initial resolution of a conflict between the law and the agreement?

NLRB v. C & C Plywood Corp.
385 U.S. 421 (1967)

STEWART, J. . . . The respondent employer was brought before the [NLRB] to answer a complaint that its inauguration of a premium pay plan

---

[27] As Meltzer said in his speech nine years ago, "It runs against the grain of judicial tradition." Supra, note 2.

during the term of a collective agreement, without prior consultation with the [incumbent] union, . . . violated . . . §§8(a)(5) and (1). . . . The Board . . . [rejected] the claim that the respondent's action was authorized by the collective agreement.[2] . . . The agreement . . . contained the following provision:

Article XVII   Wages

A. A classified wage scale has been agreed upon by the Employer and Union, and has been signed by the parties and thereby made a part of the written agreement. The Employer reserves the right to pay a premium rate over and above the contractual classified wage rate to reward any particular employee for some special fitness, skill, aptitude or the like. The payment of such a premium rate shall not be considered a permanent increase in the rate of that position and may, at sole option of the Employer, be reduced to the contractual rate. . . .

The agreement also stipulated that wages should be "closed" during the period it was effective and that neither party should be obligated to bargain collectively with respect to any matter not specifically referred to in the contract.[4] Grievance machinery was established, but no ultimate arbitration of grievances or other disputes was provided.

Less than three weeks after this agreement was signed, the respondent posted a notice that all members of the "glue spreader" crews would be paid $2.50 per hour if their crews met specified biweekly (and later weekly) production standards, although under the "classified wage scale" referred to in the above quoted Art. XVII of the agreement, the members of these crews were to be paid hourly wages ranging from $2.15 to $2.29, depending upon their function within the crew. [The union] . . . immediately asked for a conference with the respondent. During the meetings between the parties . . . , the employer indicated a willingness to discuss the terms of the plan, but refused to rescind it pending those discussions.

___

[2] The NLRB's order directed respondent to bargain with the union upon the latter's request and similarly to rescind any payment plan which it had unilaterally instituted.

[4] "Article XIX. WAIVER OF DUTY TO BARGAIN. The parties acknowledge that during negotiations which resulted in this Agreement, each had the unlimited right and opportunity to make demands and proposals with respect to any subject or matter of collective bargaining, and that the understanding and agreements arrived at by the parties after the exercise of that right and opportunity are set forth in this Agreement. Therefore, the Employer and Union, for the life of this Agreement, each voluntarily and unqualifiedly waives the right and each agree that the other shall not be obligated to bargain collectively with respect to any subject matter not specifically referred to or covered in this Agreement, even though such subjects or matters may not have been within the knowledge or contemplation of either or both of the parties at the time they negotiated or signed this Agreement."

. . . [T]his refusal prompted the union to charge the respondent with . . . violation[s] of §§8(a)(5) and (1). The trial examiner found that the respondent had instituted the premium pay program in good-faith reliance upon the right reserved to it in the collective agreement. He, therefore, dismissed the complaint. The Board reversed. [Considering] the history of negotiations between the parties, as well as the express provisions of the collective agreement, the Board ruled the union had not ceded power to the employer unilaterally to change the wage system as it had. For while the agreement specified different hourly pay for different members of the glue spreader crews and allowed for merit increases for "particular employee[s]," the employer had placed all the members of these crews on the same wage scale and had made it a function of the production output of the crew as a whole.

. . . [T]he Court of Appeals did not decide that the premium pay provision of the labor agreement had been misinterpreted by the Board. Instead, it held the Board did not have jurisdiction to find the respondent had violated §8(a) . . . , because the "existence . . . of an unfair labor practice [did] not turn entirely upon the provisions of the Act, but arguably upon a good-faith dispute as to the correct meaning of the provisions of the collective bargaining agreement. . . ." 351 F.2d, at 228.

. . . The [respondent's] argument is . . . that since the contract contained a provision which *might* have allowed [it] to institute the wage plan in question, the Board was powerless to determine whether that provision *did* authorize the respondent's action, because the question was one for a state or federal court under §301 of the Act.

. . . [I]t is important first to point out that the collective bargaining agreement contained no arbitration clause. . . . Thus, the Board's action in this case was in no way inconsistent with its previous recognition of arbitration as "an instrument of national labor policy for composing contractual differences." International Harvester Co., 138 N.L.R.B. 923, 926 (1962), *aff'd sub nom.* Ramsey v. Labor Board, 327 F.2d 784 (C.A. 7th Cir.), *cert. denied*, 377 U.S. 1003.

The respondent's argument rests primarily upon the legislative history of the 1947 amendments to the [NLRA]. It is said that the rejection by Congress of a bill which would have given the Board unfair labor practice jurisdiction over all breaches of collective bargaining agreements shows that the Board is without power to decide any case involving the interpretation of a labor contract. We do not draw that inference from this legislative history.

When Congress determined that the Board should not have general jurisdiction over all alleged violations of collective bargaining agreements and that such matters should be placed within the jurisdiction of the courts, it was acting upon a principle which this Court had already recognized: "The Railway Labor Act, like the National Labor Relations Act, does not undertake governmental regulation of wages, hours, or working conditions. Instead it seeks to provide a means by which agreement may be reached with respect to them." Terminal Railroad Assn. v. Brotherhood of Railroad Trainmen, 318 U.S. 1, 6. To have conferred upon the [NLRB] generalized power to determine the rights of parties under all collective agreements would have been a step toward governmental regulation of the terms of those agreements. We view Congress' decision not to give the Board that broad power as a refusal to take this step.

But in this case the Board has not construed a labor agreement to determine the extent of the contractual rights which were given the union by the employer. It has not imposed its own view of what the terms and conditions of the labor agreement should be. It has done no more than merely enforce a statutory right which Congress considered necessary to allow labor and management to get on with the process of reaching fair terms and conditions of employment. . . . The Board's interpretation went only so far as was necessary to determine that the union did not agree to give up these statutory safeguards. Thus, the Board, in necessarily construing a labor agreement to decide this unfair labor practice case, has not exceeded the jurisdiction laid out for it by Congress.

This conclusion is reinforced by previous judicial recognition that a contractual defense does not divest the Labor Board of jurisdiction. For example, in Mastro Plastics Corp. v. Labor Board, 350 U.S. 270, the legality of an employer's refusal to reinstate strikers was based upon the Board's construction of a "no strike" clause in the labor agreement, which the employer contended allowed it to refuse to take back workers who had walked out in protest over its unfair labor practice. . . .

If the Board in a case like this had no jurisdiction to consider a collective agreement prior to an authoritative construction by the courts, labor organizations would face inordinate delays in obtaining vindication of their statutory rights. Where, as here, the parties have not provided for arbitration, the union would have to institute a court action to determine the applicability of the premium pay provision. . . . If it succeeded in court, the union would then have to go back to the Labor Board to begin an unfair labor practice proceeding. It is not unlikely that this would add years to the already lengthy period required to gain relief from the Board. Congress cannot have intended to place such obstacles in the way of the Board's effective enforcement of statutory duties. For in the labor field, as in few others, time is crucially important in obtaining relief. . . .

The legislative history of the Labor Act, the precedents interpreting it, and the interest of its efficient administration thus all lead to the conclusion that the Board had jurisdiction to deal with the unfair labor practice charge in this case. We hold that the Court of Appeals was in error in deciding to the contrary.

The remaining question, not reached by the Court of Appeals, is whether the Board was wrong in concluding that the contested provision in the collective agreement gave the respondent no unilateral right to institute its premium pay plan. . . . [T]he Board relied upon its experience with labor relations and the Act's clear emphasis upon the protection of free collective bargaining. We cannot disapprove of the Board's approach. For the law of labor agreements cannot be based upon abstract definitions unrelated to the context in which the parties bargained and the basic regulatory scheme underlying that context. . . . Nor can we say that the Board was wrong in holding that the union had not forgone its statutory right to bargain about the pay plan inaugurated by the respondent. For the disputed contract provision referred to increases for "particular employee[s]," not groups of workers. And there was nothing in it to suggest that the carefully worked out wage differentials for various members of the glue spreader crew could be invalidated by the respondent's decision to pay all members of the crew the same wage.

The judgment is accordingly reversed and the case is remanded to the Court of Appeals with directions to enforce the Board's order. . . .

NOTES

1. Is the Court's emphasis on the absence of an arbitration clause justifiable? What result if the agreement had contained such a clause? Cf. Capitol City Lumber Co. v. NLRB, 721 F.2d 546, 549 (D.C. Cir. 1983).

2. Suppose that bargaining over the disputed change had produced an impasse. Would the employer's subsequent institution of the change have violated the NLRA? The agreement? Consider Jacobs Mfg. Co., supra p. 893; *Milwaukee Spring II*, supra p. 901.

3. Suppose that a court had decided that under the collective agreement the employer had been entitled to make the disputed change but the NLRB thereafter held that the employer had violated §8(a)(5) by making that change without prior bargaining. Does the principal case suggest that the Board's order would be enforced?

4. A union, in flagrant violation of a no-strike clause, calls a strike to protest grievances plainly covered by the grievance arbitration clause of the agreement. Has the union violated §8(b)(3)? Cf. UMW v. NLRB, 257 F.2d 211, 215, 218 (D.C. Cir. 1958).

NLRB v. Acme Industrial Co., 385 U.S. 432 (1967). A collective agreement provided that if plant equipment was moved to another location, employees laid off or reduced in grade would have transfer rights unless the new location was covered by a collective agreement. The union asked about machinery being removed and was told that since a contract violation had not occurred, the employer was not obliged to answer. The union filed grievances and asked for pertinent information about the moved machinery. The employer disclaimed any disclosure obligation, urging that no layoffs or reductions in grade had occurred within the five-day limitation period for filing grievances. The NLRB held that the employer had refused to bargain in good faith, noting that the information requested was necessary for the union's assessment of the grievances and that the collective agreement had not waived the union's statutory right to such information. In upholding the Board's result, the Supreme Court reasoned: The bargaining duty operates during the term of an agreement; arbitration functions properly only if the grievance procedure sifts out unmeritorious claims; the NLRB need not wait for an arbitrator to determine the relevancy of requested information but may make "a threshold determination of the potential relevance"; the Board here had not made a binding determination of the agreement or encroached on the arbitrator's jurisdiction.

NOTES

1. Under *Acme*, will §8(a)(5) and §8(b)(3) be the basis for broad and mutual discovery with respect to the merits of grievance arbitration before, or after, arbitration is instituted? Would such discovery be desirable? In Anheuser-Busch, Inc., 237 N.L.R.B. 982 (1978), the Board, concerned about "diminish[ing] the integrity of the grievance-arbitration process," upheld an employer's refusal to furnish the union copies of witnesses' statements regarding the grievant, prior to arbitration of the grievant's suspension for an "altercation." Can such statements be distinguished from the type of information considered in *Acme*? Should the result have been different had the union shown that it lacked access to information needed to process the grievance through arbitration? Cf. Transport of New Jersey, 233 N.L.R.B. 694 (1977); Tool & Die Makers' Lodge 78 (Square D Co.), 224 N.L.R.B. 111 (1976). See also Cook Paint & Varnish Co. v. NLRB, 648 F.2d 712 (D.C. Cir. 1981) (Board erred in adopting per se rule that employer may never use threat of discipline to obtain information from an employee concerning a matter set for arbitration; an employer may conduct investigatory interview in preparation for arbitration, subject to limits imposed by §8(a)(1)).

2. On discovery in connection with the grievance procedure and arbitration, including discovery under §8(a)(5), see generally O. Fairweather, Practice and Procedure in Labor Arbitration 134-158 (2d ed. 1983).

Carey v. Westinghouse Electric Corp.
375 U.S. 261 (1964)

Douglas, J. . . . The petitioner union (IUE) and respondent employer (Westinghouse) entered into a collective bargaining agreement covering workers at several plants including one where the present dispute occurred. The agreement states that Westinghouse recognizes IUE and its locals as exclusive bargaining representatives for each of those units for which IUE or its locals have been certified . . . as the exclusive bargaining representative . . . [including] a unit of "all production and maintenance employees" at the plant where the controversy arose, "but excluding all salaried technical . . . employees." The agreement also contains a grievance procedure for the use of arbitration in case of unresolved disputes, including those involving the "interpretation, application or claimed violation" of the agreement.

IUE filed a grievance asserting that certain employees in the engineering laboratory at the plant in question, represented by another union, Federation, which had been certified as the exclusive bargaining representative for a unit of "all salaried, technical" employees, excluding "all production and maintenance" employees, were performing production and maintenance work. Westinghouse refused to arbitrate on the ground that the controversy presented a representation matter for the [NLRB]. IUE petitioned the Supreme Court of New York for an order compelling arbitration. That court refused. The Appellate Division affirmed, one judge dissenting, 15 App. Div. 2d 7, 221 N.Y.S.2d 303. The Court of Appeals affirmed, one judge dissenting, holding that the matter was within the exclusive jurisdiction of the Board since it involved a definition of bargaining units. 11 N.Y.2d 452, 230 N.Y.S.2d 703. . . .

We have here a so-called "jurisdictional" dispute involving two unions and the employer. But the term "jurisdictional" is not a word of a single meaning. In the setting of the present case this "jurisdictional" dispute could be one of two different, though related, species, either — (1) a controversy as to whether certain work should be performed by workers in one bargaining unit or those in another; or (2) a controversy as to which union should represent the employees doing particular work. If this controversy is considered to be the former, the [NLRA] . . . does not purport to cover all phases and stages of it. While §8(b)(4)(D) makes it an unfair labor practice for a union to strike to get an employer to assign work to a particular group of employees rather than to another, the Act does not deal with the controversy anterior to a strike nor provide any machinery for resolving such a dispute absent a strike. The Act and its remedies for "jurisdictional" controversies of that nature come into play only by a strike or a threat of a strike. Such conduct gives the Board authority under §10(k) to resolve the dispute.

Are we to assume that the regulatory scheme contains a hiatus, allowing no recourse to arbitration over work assignments between two unions but forcing the controversy into the strike stage before a remedy before the Board is available? The Board, as admonished by §10(k), has often given effect to private agreements to settle disputes of this character; and that is in accord with the purpose as stated even by the minority spokesman in Congress — "that full opportunity is given the parties to reach a voluntary accommodation without governmental intervention if they so desire." 93 Cong. Rec. 4035; 2 Leg. Hist. L.M.R.A. (1947) 1046. . . .

Grievance arbitration is one method of settling disputes over work assignments; and it is commonly used, we are told. To be sure, only one of the two unions involved in the controversy has moved the state courts to compel arbitration. So unless the other union intervenes, an adjudication of the arbiter might not put an end to the dispute. Yet the arbitration may as a practical matter end the controversy or put into movement forces that will resolve it. . . . Since §10(k) not only tolerates but actively encourages voluntary settlements of work assignment controversies between unions, we conclude that grievance procedures pursued to arbitration further the policies of the Act.

What we have said so far treats the case as if the grievance involves only a work assignment dispute. If, however, the controversy be a representational one, involving the duty of an employer to bargain collectively with the representative of the employees as provided in §8(a)(5), further considerations are necessary. Such a charge, made by a union against the employer, would, if proved, be an unfair labor practice. . . . Or the unions instead of filing such a charge might petition the Board under §9(c)(1) to obtain a clarification of the certificates they already have from the Board; and the employer might do the same. . . .

If this is truly a representation case, either IUE or Westinghouse can move to have the certificate clarified. But the existence of a remedy before the Board for an unfair labor practice does not bar individual employees from seeking damages for breach of a collective bargaining agreement in a state court, as we held in Smith v. Evening News Assn., 371 U.S. 195. We think the same policy considerations are applicable here; and that a suit either in the federal courts, as provided by §301(a) . . . (Textile Workers v. Lincoln Mills, 353 U.S. 448), or before such state tribunals as are authorized to act

(Charles Dowd Box Co. v. Courtney, 368 U.S. 502) . . . is proper, even though an alternative remedy before the Board is available, which, if invoked by the employer, will protect him.

The policy considerations behind Smith v. Evening News Assn., supra, are highlighted here by reason of the blurred line that often exists between work assignment disputes and controversies over which of two or more unions is the appropriate bargaining unit. It may be claimed that A and B, to whom work is assigned as "technical" employees, are in fact "production and maintenance" employees; and if that charge is made and sustained the Board, under the decisions already noted, clarifies the certificate. But IUE may claim that when the work was assigned to A and B, the collective agreement was violated because "production and maintenance" employees, not "technical" employees, were entitled to it. As noted, the Board clarifies certificates where a certified union seeks to represent additional employees; but it will not entertain a motion to clarify a certificate where the union merely seeks additional work for employees already within its unit. . . . The Board's description of the line between the two types of cases is as follows:

> . . . a Board certification in a representation proceeding is not a juris-dictional award; it is merely a determination that a majority of the employees in an appropriate unit have selected a particular labor organization as their representative for purposes of collective bargaining. It is true that such certifi-cation presupposes a determination that the group of employees involved constitute an appropriate unit for collective bargaining purposes, and that in making such determination the Board considers the general nature of the duties and work tasks of such employees. However, unlike a jurisdictional award, this determination by the Board does not freeze the duties or work tasks of the employees in the unit found appropriate. Thus, the Board's unit finding does not per se preclude the employer from adding to, or subtracting from, the employee's work assignments. While that finding may be determined by, it does not determine, job content; nor does it signify approval, in any respect, of any work task claims which the certified union may have made before this Board or elsewhere.

Plumbing Contractors Assn., 93 N.L.R.B. 1081, 1087.

As the Board's decisions indicate, disputes are often difficult to classify. In the present case the Solicitor General, who appears amicus, believes the controversy is essentially a representational one. So does Westinghouse. IUE on the other hand claims it is a work assignment dispute. Even if it is in form a representation problem, in substance it may involve problems of seniority when layoffs occur . . . or other aspects of work assignment disputes. If that is true, there is work for the arbiter whatever the Board may decide.

If by the time the dispute reaches the Board, arbitration has already taken place, the Board shows deference to the arbitral award, provided the procedure was a fair one and the results were not repugnant to the act. . . .

Should the Board disagree with the arbiter, by ruling, for example, that the employees involved in the controversy are members of one bargaining unit or another, the Board's ruling would, of course, take precedence; and if the employer's action had been in accord with that ruling, it would not be liable for damages under §301. But that is not peculiar to the present type of controversy. Arbitral awards construing a seniority provision (Carey v. General Electric Co., 315 F.2d 499, 509-510), or awards concerning unfair labor practices, may later end up in conflict with Board rulings. See International Association of Machinists, 116 N.L.R.B. 645; Monsanto Chemical Co., 97 N.L.R.B. 517. Yet, as we held in Smith v. Evening News Assn., supra, the possibility of conflict is no barrier to resort to a tribunal other than the Board.

However the dispute be considered — whether one involving work assignment or one concerning representation — we see no barrier to use of the arbitration procedure. If it is a work assignment dispute, arbitration conveniently fills a gap and avoids the necessity of a strike to bring the matter to the Board. If it is a representation matter, resort to arbitration may have a pervasive, curative effect even though one union is not a party.

By allowing the dispute to go to arbitration its fragmentation is avoided to a substantial extent; and those conciliatory measures which Congress deemed vital to "industrial peace" (Textile Workers v. Lincoln Mills, supra, at 455) and which may be dispositive of the entire dispute, are encouraged. The superior authority of the Board may be invoked at any time. Meanwhile the therapy of arbitration is brought to bear in a complicated and troubled area.

Reversed.

Goldberg, J., took no part in the consideration or decision of this case.

Harlan, J., concurring. . . . As is recognized by all, neither position in this case is without its difficulties. Lacking a clear-cut command in the statute itself, the choice in substance lies between a course which would altogether preclude any attempt at resolving disputes of this kind by arbitration, and one which at worst will expose those concerned to the hazard of duplicative proceedings. The undesirable consequences of the first alternative are inevitable, those of the second conjectural. As between the two, I think the Court at this early stage of experience in this area rightly chooses the latter.

Black, J., with whom Clark, J., joins, dissenting. . . . Stripped of obscurantist arguments, this controversy is a plain, garden-variety jurisdictional dispute between two unions. The Court today holds, however, that the [NLRA] not only permits but compels Westinghouse to arbitrate the dispute with only one of the two warring unions. Such an arbitration could not, of course, bring about the "final and binding arbitration of grievance[s] and disputes" that the Court says contributes to the congressional objectives in passing the Labor Act. Unless all the salutary safeguards of due process of law are to be dissipated and obliterated to further the cause of arbitration, the rights of employees belonging to the Federation should not, for "policy considerations," be sacrificed by an arbitration award in proceedings between IUE and Westinghouse alone. Although I do not find the Court's opinion so clear on the point as I would like, I infer that it is not holding that this misnamed "award" would be completely final and binding on the Federation and its members. What the Court does plainly hold, however — that "the weight of the arbitration award is likely to be considerable, if the Board is later required to rule on phases of the same dispute" — seems only a trifle less offensive to established due process concepts. And this means, I suppose, that this same award, ex parte as to Federation, must be given the same or greater weight in any judicial review of the Board's final order involving the same "phases of the same dispute." . . .

The result of all this is that the [NLRB], the agency created by Congress finally to settle labor disputes in the interest of industrial peace, is to be supplanted in part by so-called arbitration which in its very nature cannot achieve a final adjustment of those disputes. One of the main evils it had been hoped the Labor Act would abate was jurisdictional disputes between unions over which union members would do certain work. The Board can make final settlements of such disputes. Arbitration between some but not all the parties cannot. I fear that the Court's recently announced leanings to treat arbitration as an almost sure and certain solvent of all labor troubles has been carried so far in this case as unnecessarily to bring about great confusion and to delay final and binding settlements of jurisdictional disputes by the Labor Board, the agency which I think Congress intended to do that very job.

[After the Court's decision, Westinghouse petitioned the NLRB to clarify the two bargaining units. The Board deferred action pending arbitration. The arbitrator, concluding that a "representation issue" was involved, split the disputed jobs between the contending unions on the basis of the employees' wage rates. Thereafter, acting on Westinghouse's petitions, the NLRB clarified the unit so as to include all of the jobs in question within the unit represented by the Salaried Employees Assn. Explaining its failure to follow the arbitration award, the Board stated:

Here, [given the claim of the rival union] . . . , the ultimate issue of representation could not be decided by the Arbitrator on the basis of his interpreting the contract . . . , but could only be resolved by utilization of Board criteria for making unit determinations. In such cases the arbitrator's award must clearly reflect the use of, and be consonant with, Board standards.

In this case apparently not all the evidence concerning all these standards was available to the Arbitrator . . . , and his award reflects this deficiency. . . . Consequently, while we give some consideration to the award, it would [not] effectuate statutory policy to defer to it entirely. [Westinghouse Electric Corp., 162 N.L.R.B. 768 (1967).]]

NOTES

1. The American Recording and Broadcasting Association demanded arbitration of its claim that certain work should be "assigned to it" under its agreement with CBS. CBS, under another agreement, had already assigned the work to the Radio & Television Broadcast Engrs.' Union (Local 1212). CBS demanded arbitration with Local 1212 and consolidation of both arbitrations, and joined that local as a party defendant in CBS' action under §301 to compel arbitration with the Association. Each collective agreement had broad arbitration provisions that covered the subject matter of the dispute. The Association objected to consolidation and moved to dismiss the complaint for failure to state a claim and for lack of jurisdiction. The Association's jurisdictional argument stressed that Local 1212 was a stranger to the Association's agreement with CBS. Local 1212 was, however, willing to submit the dispute to an arbitrator of the Association's choosing.

You are the trial court's clerk; the judge advises you that the CBS position seems sensible and practical, and he asks you to consider whether the *Steelworkers* trilogy, the *Wiley* case, and Rule 42(a) of the Federal Rules of Civil Procedure would warrant the consolidation requested by CBS. (a) Advise the judge. Cf. CBS v. American Recording & Broadcasting Assn., 293 F. Supp. 1400 (S.D.N.Y. 1968), *aff'd*, 414 F.2d 1326 (2d Cir. 1969). (b) Would your advice be affected had Local 1212 not agreed to accept the arbitrator chosen by the association? See Bell Aerospace Co. v. Local 516, UAW, 50 F.2d 921, 923 (2d Cir. 1974).

On the enforceability of Railway Labor Act work-assignment awards when an affected union refuses to participate in NRAB proceedings initiated by another union (in accordance with the then prevailing policy of railroad unions and the NRAB's duty to resolve the entire trilateral dispute), see Transportation-Communication Employees Union v. Union Pacific R.R., 385 U.S. 157 (1966).

2. For a spirited exchange on the issue of compulsory trilateral arbitration of nonrailway grievances involving conflicting claims under several agreements, see Jones, An Arbitral Answer to a Judicial Dilemma, etc., 11

U.C.L.A. L. Rev. 327 (1964); Bernstein, Judging and Shoving All Parties to a Jurisdictional Dispute into Arbitration, etc., 78 Harv. L. Rev. 784 (1965); Jones, On Nudging and Shoving, etc., 79 Harv. L. Rev. 327 (1965).

United Technologies Corp.
268 N.L.R.B. No. 83, 115 L.R.R.M. 1049 (1984)

. . . The complaint alleges that the Respondent violated §8(a)(1) by threatening [to discipline] employee Sherfield . . . if she persisted in processing a grievance. . . . Respondent denied [that charge] . . . and argued that, in any event, . . . it should be resolved [through the parties' grievance-arbitration procedures, which applied]. Accordingly, the Respondent urged the Board to defer the exercise of its jurisdiction. . . . The [ALJ], relying on General American Transportation Corp., 228 N.L.R.B. 808 (1977), rejected [that] contention because . . . [an] alleged violation of §8(a)(1) [was involved]. The [ALJ] correctly applied Board precedent. . . . Because we have decided to overrule General American Transportation, however, we do not adopt the judge's recommendations.

On 6 November 1981 the Union filed a third-step grievance alleging that the Respondent, through its general foreman, Peterson, intimidated, coerced, and harassed shop steward Wilson and employee Sherfield at a first-step grievance meeting by threatening [to discipline] Sherfield if she appealed her grievance to the second step.[2] The remedy the Union sought was that "the Company immediately stop these contract violations and . . . Peterson be properly disciplined and reinstructed for his misuse, abuse, and violation of the contract." The Respondent denied the Union's grievance at the third step, and the Union withdrew it on 27 January 1982 "without prejudice." The next day, the Respondent filed its own grievance alleging that "[n]otwithstanding the union's mistake in its allegations con-

---

[2] The grievance that was the subject of the first-step meeting alleged that Sherfield had been "repeatedly harassed, intimidated, and discriminated against" by her foreman, Cote, and that Cote had engaged in an "act of aggression" against her . . . [i.e.,] Cote had responded to Sherfield's request for certain parts by allegedly tossing a bag of parts weighing approximately one-third of an ounce at her workbench. . . . [D]uring the first-step meeting, Cote apologized to Sherfield, whereupon General Foreman Peterson denied the grievance and urged everyone to return to work. Shop steward Wilson and Sherfield indicated that they would appeal the grievance to the second step. Peterson then told Sherfield that the Company had been nice to her and that they had not disciplined her in the past because of her rejects. Wilson stated that Peterson's statement could be construed as a threat. Peterson denied that he was threatening Sherfield; rather, he said he was merely telling Sherfield what could and would happen.

cerning General Foreman Peterson, it has refused to withdraw, with prejudice, its grievance." The Union denied the Respondent's grievance. . . .
Following [Respondent's appeal and] a fourth-step meeting, the Union again
denied the Respondent's grievance and refused the Respondent's request
[for] arbitration. Thereafter, the Union filed the charge in [this case].

   . . . Article VII of the [parties'] contract establishes a grievance procedure[3] that includes an oral step, four written steps, and . . . [culminates in]
final and binding arbitration.

   . . . [Labor arbitration] now occupies a respected and firmly established place in Federal labor policy. . . . [quoting §203(d) of the Act]. It is
this congressional mandate [referring to that section] on which the Supreme
Court has consistently relied in sanctioning arbitration as a preferred instrument for preserving industrial peace. [Citing *Steelworkers* trilogy.]

   Similarly, the concept of judicial and administrative deference to the
arbitral process and the notion that courts should support, rather than interfere with, this method of dispute resolution have become entrenched in
American jurisprudence. . . . [T]he Board has played a key role in fostering
a climate in which arbitration could flourish. Thus, as early as 1943[7] the
Board [expressed sympathy for] the concept of prospective deference to
contractual grievance machinery. . . .

   The Board [embraced this concept] with renewed vigor in the seminal
case of Collyer Insulated Wire,[8] [and] dismissed a complaint alleging unilateral changes in wages and working conditions in violation of §8(a)(5) in
deference to the parties' grievance-arbitration machinery. The *Collyer* majority articulated several factors favoring deferral: The dispute arose . . .
[during] a long and productive collective-bargaining relationship; there was
no claim of employer animosity to the employees' exercise of protected
rights; the parties' contract provided [broadly] for arbitration . . . ; the
arbitration clause clearly encompassed the dispute . . . ; the employer had
asserted its willingness to [arbitrate] the dispute; and [it] was eminently well
suited to resolution by arbitration. . . . [T]he *Collyer* majority was holding
the parties to their bargain by directing them to avoid substituting the Board's
processes for their own mutually agreed-upon method for dispute resolution.

   The experience under *Collyer* was extremely positive. The *Collyer*

---

[3] Art. VII, sec. 1, states in pertinent part,

In the event that a difference arises between the company, the union, or any employee
concerning the interpretation, application or compliance with the provisions of this
agreement, an earnest effort will be made to resolve such difference in accordance with
the following procedure which must be followed.

[7] Consolidated Aircraft Corp., 47 N.L.R.B. 694, 706 (1943), *enfd. in pertinent part* 141
F.2d 785 (9th Cir. 1944).
[8] 192 N.L.R.B. 837 (1971).

deferral doctrine was endorsed by the courts of appeals[9] and was quoted favorably by the Supreme Court.[10] . . . . In *National Radio*[11] the Board extended the deferral policy to cases involving 8(a)(3) allegations [in that case, the disciplinary suspension and discharge of an active union adherent]. . . . .

[Thereafter,] the Board routinely dismissed complaints alleging violations of §§8(a)(3) and (1) in deference to the arbitral forum. . . . .

. . . [H]owever, the Board in *General American Transportation* abruptly changed course. . . . Indeed, by deciding to decline to defer cases alleging violations of §§8(a)(1) and (3) and 8(b)(1)(A) and (2), the *General American Transportation* majority essentially emasculated the Board's deferral policy. . . . [Their] reasons . . . are largely unsupportable. *Collyer* worked well because it was premised on sound legal and pragmatic considerations. . . . [W]e believe it deserves to be . . . infused with renewed life.

. . . Where an employer and a union have voluntarily [created] dispute resolution machinery culminating in final and binding arbitration, it is contrary to the basic principles of the Act for the Board to jump into the fray prior to an honest attempt by the parties to resolve their disputes through that machinery. . . . [T]he statutory purpose of encouraging the practice and procedure of collective bargaining is ill-served by permitting the parties to ignore their agreement and to petition this Board in the first instance for remedial relief. . . . .

. . . [D]eferral is not akin to abdication. It is merely the prudent exercise of restraint, a postponement of the use of the Board's processes to give the parties' own dispute resolution machinery a chance to succeed. The Board's processes may always be invoked if the arbitral result is inconsistent with the standards of *Spielberg*.[18] As the Supreme Court noted in Carey v. Westinghouse Corp., 375 U.S. 261, 272 (1964):

> By allowing the dispute to go to arbitration its fragmentation is avoided to a substantial extent; and those conciliatory measures which Congress deemed vital to "industrial peace" . . . and which may be dispositive of the entire dispute, are encouraged. The superior authority of the Board may be invoked at any time. Meanwhile the therapy of arbitration is brought to bear. . . . .

The *Collyer* policy we embrace today . . . has been applied with the rule of reason. . . . [D]issenting in *General American Transportation*, supra, former Members Penello and Walther observed:

[9] See Columbus Printing Pressmen Union 252 (R.W. Page Corp.), 219 N.L.R.B. 268 (1975), for a list of court opinions approving *Collyer*.

[10] Arnold Co. v. Carpenters, 417 U.S. 12, 16-17 (1974).

[11] National Radio Co., 198 N.L.R.B. 527 (1972).

[18] Spielberg Mfg. Co., 112 N.L.R.B. 1080 (1955).

The Board has not deferred cases to arbitration [indiscriminately], nor has it been insensitive to the statutory rights of employees in deciding whether to defer and whether to give effect to an arbitration award. The standard it has used is reasonable belief that arbitration procedures would resolve the dispute in a manner consistent with the criteria of *Spielberg*. Thus, it has refused to defer where the interests of the union which might be expected to represent the employee filing the unfair labor practice charge are adverse to those of the employee, or where the respondent's conduct constitutes a rejection of the principles of collective bargaining. And where, after deferral, the respondent has refused to proceed to arbitration, the Board has rescinded the deferral and decided the case on the merits. Finally, if for any reason the arbitrator's award fails to meet the *Spielberg* standards, as for example, that it is repugnant to the policies of the Act, the Board will not give it effect.[19] [Citations omitted.]

We shall continue to be guided by these principles.

The facts of the instant case make it eminently well suited for deferral. The dispute centers on a statement a single foreman made to a single employee and a shop steward during . . . a routine first-step grievance meeting allegedly concerning possible adverse consequences . . . [from] the employee's [decision] to process her grievance to the next step. The statement is alleged to be a threat violative of §8(a)(1) [but it] is also . . . clearly cognizable under the broad grievance-arbitration provision of [the] . . . bargaining agreement.[20] Moreover, Respondent has expressed its willingness, indeed its eagerness, to arbitrate the dispute.[21]

. . . [W]e believe it would best effectuate the purposes and policies of the Act to defer this case to the arbitral forum . . . , under the principles of *Collyer* and *National Radio*.[22]

The complaint is dismissed, provided that: Jurisdiction . . . is hereby

[19] General American Transportation Corp., supra at 817.

[20] . . . [Article] IV of the contract states that "the company and the union recognize that employees covered by this agreement may not be discriminated against in violation of the [LMRA]. . . ." [Plainly] the parties contemplated that disputes such as the one here be resolved under the grievance-arbitration machinery.

[21] Although the instant dispute arose [during] the processing of another grievance, the alleged misconduct "does not appear . . . to render the use of [the grievance-arbitration] machinery unpromising or futile." United Aircraft Corp., 204 N.L.R.B. 879. Indeed, both the Respondent and the Union continued to file and process grievances. Thus the record "demonstrates full acceptance by the parties of the grievance and arbitration route to the resolution of disputes." Community Convalescent Hospital, 199 N.L.R.B. 840, 841 fn. 2 (1972), and "demonstrates the existence of a workable and freely resorted to grievance procedure," Postal Service, supra, 210 N.L.R.B. at 560 fn. 1. Accordingly, we find that Ram Construction Co., 228 N.L.R.B. 769 (1977), cited by the judge, and Joseph T. Ryerson & Sons, 199 N.L.R.B. 461 (1972), are not controlling.

[22] The Respondent must, of course, waive any timeliness provisions of the grievance-arbitration clauses of the collective-bargaining agreement so that the Union's grievance may be processed in accordance with the following Order.

retained for the limited purpose of entertaining an appropriate and timely motion for further consideration upon a proper showing that either (a) the dispute has not, with reasonable promptness after the issuance of this . . . Order, either been resolved . . . in the grievance procedure or submitted . . . to arbitration, or (b) the grievance or arbitration procedures have not been fair and regular or have reached a result . . . repugnant to the Act.

Member ZIMMERMAN, dissenting. . . . [He urged continued adherence to the views in former Chairman Murphy's concurrence in *General American Transportation*. He stressed that *Collyer* had contemplated a limited deferral doctrine applicable to §8(a)(5) cases involving contract interpretation issues about unilateral action, and that the *Collyer* plurality opinion had emphasized the special circumstances of that case. He continued:]

. . . Former Chairman Murphy explained in her determinative concurring opinion [in *General American Transportation*] the fundamental reasons for a pre-arbitral deferral policy which distinguishes between unfair labor practices involving disputes between contracting parties about their collective-bargaining agreement and unfair labor practices involving disputes about individual employees' statutory rights:

> [T]he Board should stay its processes in favor of the parties' grievance arbitration machinery only in those situations where the dispute is essentially between the contracting parties and where there is no alleged interference with individual employees' basic rights under §7 of the Act. Complaints alleging violations of §§8(a)(5) and 8(b)(3) fall squarely into this category, while complaints alleging violations of §§8(a)(3), (a)(1), (b)(1)(A), and (b)(2) clearly do not. . . . [I]n the former category the dispute is principally between the contracting parties — the employer and the union — while in the latter the dispute is between the employee on the one hand and the employer and/or the union on the other. In cases [under] §§8(a)(5) and 8(b)(3), based on conduct assertedly in derogation of the contract, the principal issue is whether the complained-of conduct is permitted by the parties' contract. Such issues are eminently suited to the arbitral process, and resolution of the contract issue by an arbitrator will, as a rule, dispose of the unfair labor practice issue. On the other hand, in cases [under] §§8(a)(1), (a)(3), (b)(1)(A), and (b)(2), although arguably also involving a contract violation, the determinative issue is not whether the conduct is permitted by the contract, but whether the conduct was unlawfully motivated or whether it otherwise interfered with, restrained, or coerced employees in the exercise of rights guaranteed them by §7. . . . In these situations, an arbitrator's resolution of the contract issue will not dispose of the unfair labor practice allegation. Nor is the arbitration process suited for resolving employee complaints of discrimination under §7. . . . [228 N.L.R.B. at 810-811.]

Now, after 6 years [under] . . . *General American Transportation*, without any intervening judicial criticism, the majority has overruled that case and has returned to *National Radio*. The majority cites no specific evidence that *General American Transportation* actually has had any adverse effect upon private grievance and arbitration systems. Instead, the majority justifies the Board's return to an overly broad pre-arbitral deferral policy by relying on three articles of faith. . . .

First, the majority overstates the case . . . when it [refers to the] "universal judicial acceptance of the *Collyer* doctrine." While there is judicial acceptance for the proposition that the Board has broad discretionary authority to defer cases to the arbitral process, there is, equally, judicial acceptance of the proposition that the Board has broad authority to decline to defer. . . .

Furthermore, judicial precedent strongly indicates that the Board's discretion to defer . . . is not unlimited. Especially in the area of individual statutory rights, there are signals from the judiciary that the Board will abuse its discretion by deferring unfair labor practice claims. . . . For instance, the [D.C.] Circuit approved the original *Collyer* rule in Electrical Workers IBEW Local 2188 v. NLRB, 494 F.2d 1087 (1974), but emphasized at 1091 that: "This congruence between the contractual dispute and the overlying unfair labor practice charge is significant. If it were not present, the Board's abstention might have constituted not deference, but abdication."

While the national labor policy . . . requires the Federal judiciary to give broad . . . deference to grievance and arbitration systems in the resolution of contract issues, the Supreme Court has made clear that the same degree of deference does not apply — indeed cannot be applied — to such systems by the Board (and reviewing courts) where statutory issues are at stake. In NLRB v. Acme Industrial Co., 385 U.S. 432 (1967), the Supreme Court clearly stated at 436-437, that the "relationship of the Board to the arbitration process is of a quite different order. . . . Thus, to view the *Steelworkers* decisions as automatically requiring the Board in this case to defer to the primary determination of an arbitrator is to overlook important distinctions between those cases and this one."

More recent decisions by the Court indicate that the most important distinction between judicial deferral to arbitration of contract disputes and Board deferral under *Collyer* involves the existence of noncontractual, statutory, individual rights which the Board expressly is required to protect. [The opinion here refers to Barrentine v. Arkansas-Best Freight System, infra p. 1114 and Alexander v. Gardner-Denver Co., infra p. 1104, in support of the proposition that the presumption in favor of arbitration does not alone place statutory rights under the arbitration process.]

Employees' §7 rights are public rights charged to the Board's protection.[7] . . . [B]y forcing employees to pursue the private adjudication of their public rights through [arbitration] rather than through . . . the Board, my colleagues are actually repudiating . . . the relevant judicial precedent.

. . . Implicit in [my colleagues'] reasoning is that an exclusive collective-bargaining representative may waive an individual employee's right to seek initial redress of interference with §7 rights before the Board.[8] A union *waivable* may, of course, agree to waive some individual statutory rights.[9] But in my view a union cannot waive an individual employee's right to choose a statutory forum in which to initiate and litigate an unfair labor practice issue. Even if it could, such a waiver would have to be a "clear and unmistakable" one. Here, however, the majority forces individual employees to litigate statutory rights in a contractual forum . . . without [determining] that there has been a "clear and unmistakable" waiver of the right to resort first and exclusively to the Board. My colleagues simply assume that the mere existence of a contractual grievance and arbitration procedure proves a waiver.

Finally, it is pure conceit that the deferral doctrine announced here is mere "prudent restraint" and that *Spielberg* is a catchall safety net for those individuals whose individual rights are not protected in grievance and arbitration. The arbitration process is not designed to and is not particularly adept at protecting employee statutory or public rights. First, a union, without breaching its duty of fair representation, might not vigorously support an employee's claim in arbitration inasmuch as the union, in balancing individual and collective interests, might trade off an employee's statutory right in favor of some other benefits for employees in the bargaining unit as a whole.[n] Second, because arbitrators' competency is primarily in "the law of the shop, not the law of the land,"[11] they may lack the competency to resolve the statutory issue(s) involved in the dispute. Third, even if the arbitrator is conversant with the Act, he is limited to determining the dispute in accordance with the parties' intent under the collective-bargaining agreement.

---

[7] Amalgamated Utility Workers v. Edison Co., 309 U.S. 261 (1940); National Licorice Co. v. NLRB, 309 U.S. 350 (1940).

[8] The majority erroneously states that its expansive application of *Collyer* neither waives nor even diminishes individual statutory rights. At the very least, however, an individual employee's right to elect the statutory forum first will be waived. Moreover, because Collyer-ized cases are subject to only a limited review under *Spielberg*, an individual's right to full de novo consideration of the statutory issue before the Board will also be waived.

[9] Metropolitan Edison Co. v. NLRB, 103 S. Ct. 1467 (1983) [reproduced supra p. 1056].

[n] [In light of the material in Chapter 11(A) on a union's duty of fair representation, consider whether trading off individual grievances for collective interests is proper. — EDS.]

[11] Barrentine v. Arkansas-Best Freight System, supra at 743.

Finally, because the arbitrator's function is to effectuate the parties' intent rather than to enforce the Act, he may issue a ruling that is inimical to the public policies underlying the Act, thereby depriving an employee of his protected statutory rights.

Although I endorse the *Spielberg* policy, it is not a catchall justification for withholding Board processes until a reviewable arbitration award has been made. . . . [T]he District of Columbia Circuit has stated:

> Our endorsement of the *Collyer* rule would be incomplete without one further comment. While the Board's promise to overrule arbitration awards which are irregular or repugnant to the Act is a necessary condition to the legality of pre-arbitral deferrals, it is not a sufficient one. . . . [T]hat any ultimate award must conform to the policies of the Act does not guarantee that deferral itself is consistent with the Act.[14]

Even [*Spielberg's*] limited guarantee . . . becomes less certain when the Board will no longer require the party seeking deferral to an arbitration award to prove that the unfair labor practice issue has been presented to and considered by the arbitrator. Yet that is exactly what the Board's postarbitral deferral policy will be under the new standard announced today in *Olin Corp.* [reproduced infra]. . . .

NOTES

1. The Board, dividing 3 to 2 in *Collyer*, remained divided over that doctrine until *United Technologies*. Despite changes in membership, for most of this period at least two members either rejected *Collyer* altogether or would have restricted it, generally to cases arising under §§8(a)(5) and 8(b)(3). The extensive literature evoked by *Collyer* is also divided. See, e.g., Simon-Rose, Deferral Under *Collyer* by the NLRB of Section 8(a)(3) Cases, 27 Lab. L.J. 201 (1976); Nash, Wilder, & Banov, The Development of the *Collyer* Deferral Doctrine, 27 Vand. L. Rev. 23 (1974); Isaacson & Zifchak, Agency Deferral to Private Arbitration of Employment Disputes, 73 Colum. L. Rev. 1383 (1973); Christensen, Private Judges of Public Rights: The Role of Arbitration in the Enforcement of the National Labor Relations Act, in The Future of Labor Arbitration in America (eds. J. Correge, V. Hughes, & M. Stone, 1976); Schatzki, NLRB Resolution of Contract Disputes Under §8(a)(5), 50 Tex. L. Rev. 225 (1972); Zimmer, Wired for *Collyer*: Rationalizing NLRB and Arbitration Jurisdiction, 48 Ind. L.J. 141 (1973). The last

---

[14]Electrical Workers IBEW Local 2188 v. NLRB, supra at 1091.

two articles evoked a critical response from Getman: Collyer Insulated Wire: A Case of Misplaced Modesty, 49 Ind. L.J. 57 (1973), and then rejoinders from Schatzki, id. at 76; and Zimmer, id. at 80.

2. *Collyer* involved an employer's unilateral changes in wages and working conditions during the term of an agreement; factually, the case was of the *C & C Plywood* variety. As *United Technologies* indicates, prior to *General American Transportation* the *Collyer* doctrine was applied primarily in two types of cases: (a) when the employer's unilateral change in working conditions was challenged as a violation of §8(a)(5) and was defended as compatible with the agreement; and (b) when an employer's discipline was challenged as a reprisal for protected activity and, therefore, as violating §8(a)(3) as well as a contractual "just cause" provision. Is Member Zimmerman convincing in arguing that these two types of cases should be treated differently under a deferral doctrine?

3. The majority in *United Technologies*, citing Articles VII (§1) and IV of the parties' agreement (see footnotes 3 and 20, supra), asserts that it is "manifest that the parties contemplated that disputes such as the one here be resolved under the grievance-arbitration machinery." Do you understand the majority to say that the parties expressly agreed to bypass the Board on all NLRA issues?

4. For an example of the risks involved in assigning NLRA issues to arbitrators, see NLRB v. Owners Maintenance Corp., 681 F.2d 44 (2d Cir. 1978).

5. On March 6, 1984, the NLRB's General Counsel issued to the Regional Offices a memorandum concerning *United Technologies* and the Board's extension of its *Collyer* policy to cases arising under §§8(a)(1) and (3), 8(b)(1)(A), and 8(b)(2). See 115 L.R.R. 334 (1984). See also Local 2188, IBEW v. NLRB, 494 F.2d 1087, 1091 (D.C. Cir.), *cert. denied*, 419 U.S. 835 (1974), suggesting a possible limitation on deferral imposing an undue financial burden on unions. But see Croation Fraternal Union of America, 232 N.L.R.B. 1010 (1977) (rejecting contention that deferral under *Collyer* is inappropriate where a union is financially unable to pay the costs of arbitration).

Olin Corp.
268 N.L.R.B. No. 86, 115 L.R.R.M. 1056 (1984)

. . . [T]he Union is the exclusive collective-bargaining representative of Respondent's approximately 260 production and maintenance employees. [Article XIV ("Strikes and Lockouts")] of the 1980-1983 collective-bargaining agreement [provided]:

During the life of the Agreement, the Company will not conduct a lockout at the Plant and neither the Local Union nor the International Union, nor any officer or representative of either, will cause or permit its members to cause any strike, slowdown or stoppage (total or partial) of work or any interference, directly or indirectly, with the full operation of the plant.

Employee Spatorico was president of the Union from 1976 until his termination in December 1980. On the morning of 17 December, Respondent suspended two pipefitters for refusing to perform a job that they felt was more appropriately millwright work. A "sick out" ensued during which approximately 43 employees left work that day with medical excuses. Respondent gave formal written reprimands to 39 of the [participants]. In a letter dated 29 December, Respondent notified Spatorico that he was discharged based on his entire record and in particular for threatening the sick out, participating in [it], and failing to prevent it.

Spatorico's discharge was grieved and arbitrated. . . . [T]he arbitrator found that a sick out had occurred . . . , that Spatorico "at least partially caused or participated" in it, and that he failed to try to stop it until after it had occurred. The arbitrator concluded that Spatorico's conduct contravened his obligation under article XIV . . . [and] stated, "Union officers implicitly have an affirmative duty not to cause strikes which are in violation of the clause, not to participate in such strikes and to try to stop them when they occur." Accordingly, the arbitrator found that Spatorico had been appropriately discharged.

Noting that the unfair labor practice charges had been referred to arbitration under Dubo Mfg. Corp.,° 142 N.L.R.B. 431 (1963), the arbitrator . . . found "no evidence that the company discharged the grievant for his legitimate Union activities." The arbitrator [reiterated] that Spatorico had been discharged for participating in and failing to stop the sick out because Spatorico "is a Union officer but the contract's no strike clause *specifically* prohibits such activity by Union officers." (Emphasis added.)

[The ALJ rejected deference on these grounds: the arbitrator's failure to consider the unfair labor practice "in a serious way"; his lack of competence to decide that issue because he was limited to contract interpretation; and, his failure to refer explicitly to the statutory right and waiver questions raised by the unfair labor practice charge.]

. . . On the merits, however, the judge agreed with the arbitrator's conclusion in that he found Spatorico's "participation in the strike was

°[Under *Dubo*, the Board defers processing of an unfair labor practice case when the dispute is already in the grievance-arbitration procedure and it is likely that that machinery will resolve it. — EDS.]

inconsistent with his manifest contractual obligation to attempt to stem the tide of unprotected activity." The judge concluded that article XIV . . . was sufficiently clear and unmistakable to waive, at the least, the sort of conduct in which Spatorico engaged, that, therefore, "Spatorico exposed himself to the greater liability permitted by the Supreme Court" in Metropolitan Edison Co. v. NLRB, 103 S. Ct. 1467 (1983), and that Respondent did not violate §§8(a)(3) and (1) . . . by discharging him while merely reprimanding other employees.

We agree with the judge that the complaint should be dismissed. We do so, however, without reaching the merits because we would defer to the arbitrator's award consistent with the standards set forth in Spielberg Mfg. Co. [112 N.L.R.B. 1080 (1955).] . . . [I]n Spielberg, the Board held that it would defer to an arbitration award where the proceedings appear to have been fair and regular, all parties have agreed to be bound, and the decision of the arbitrator is not clearly repugnant to the purposes and policies of the Act. The Board in Raytheon Co.[3] further conditioned deferral on the arbitrator's having considered the unfair labor practice issue. Consistent application of the *Raytheon* requirement has proven elusive, and as illustrated by . . . *Propoco*,[4] its scope has expanded considerably. Accordingly, in *Propoco*, Member Hunter [dissenting] proposed certain standards limiting the application of *Raytheon*. . . . [W]e adopt these standards which in our view more fully comport with the aims of the Act and American labor policy.

. . . [T]he *Propoco* majority . . . [formulated] a standard of review that arbitration awards are appropriate for deferral only when the Board determines on de novo consideration that the award disposes of the issues just as the Board would have. This approach of determining the merits *before* considering the appropriateness of deferral was applied here by the judge, and he predictably reached a decision not to defer. The judge's decision here, like so many other past decisions of this sort, [frustrates] the declared purpose of *Spielberg* to recognize the arbitration process as an important aspect of the national labor policy. . . .

Accordingly, we adopt the following standard for deferral to arbitration awards. We would find that an arbitrator has adequately considered the unfair labor practice if (1) the contractual issue is factually parallel to the unfair labor practice issue, and (2) the arbitrator was presented generally with the facts relevant to resolving the unfair labor practice.[6] In this respect, differences, if

[3]140 N.L.R.B. 883 (1963).

[4]Propoco, Inc., 263 N.L.R.B. 136 (1982), enf. with unpublished, nonprecedential opinion, Case No. 83-4058 (2d Cir. 1983). See also American Freight System, 264 N.L.R.B. No. 18 (1982).

[6]This approach is supported by Board precedent. See, e.g., Kansas City Star Co., 236 N.L.R.B. 866 (1978), and Atlantic Steel Co., 245 N.L.R.B. 814 (1979).

any, between the contractual and statutory standards of review should be weighed by the Board as part of its determination under the *Spielberg* standards of whether an award is "clearly repugnant" to the Act. And, with regard to the inquiry into the "clearly repugnant" standard, we would not require an arbitrator's award to be totally consistent with Board precedent. Unless the award is "palpably wrong,"[7] i.e., unless the arbitrator's decision is not susceptible to an interpretation consistent with the Act, we will defer.

Finally, . . . the party seeking to have the Board reject deferral and consider the merits of a given case [must] show that the above standards for deferral have not been met. Thus, the party seeking to have the Board ignore the determination of an arbitrator has the burden of affirmatively demonstrating the defects in the arbitral process or award.[8]

The dissent [asserts] . . . that we are depriving employees of their statutory forum. On the contrary, the Board . . . retains and fulfills its statutory obligation to determine whether employee rights have been protected by the arbitral proceeding by our commitment to determine . . . whether the arbitrator has adequately considered the facts which would constitute unfair labor practices and whether the arbitrator's decision is clearly repugnant to the Act. We differ with our dissenting colleague concerning the scope of the inquiry into the arbitrator's consideration of unfair labor practices because our clarifications of the *Spielberg* standards are, in our view, necessary to restrict the "overzealous dissection of [arbitrators'] opinions by the NLRB" decried . . . in Douglas Aircraft Co. v. NLRB, 609 F.2d 352, 355 (9th Cir. 1979). . . .

. . . [T]he [resultant] infrequent deferrals by the Board (and the General Counsel's concomitant failure to defer at the complaint stage) under the burdens [allocated] in Suburban Motor Freight, 247 N.L.R.B. 146 (1980), leads us to the conclusion that a different allocation of burdens is more consistent with the goals of national labor policy.[9] . . . Thus, if a respondent establishes that an arbitration concerning the matter before the Board has taken place, the burden of persuasion rests with the General Counsel to

---

[7] International Harvester Co., 138 N.L.R.B. 923, 929 (1962), *aff'd sub nom.* Ramsey v. NLRB, 327 F.2d 784 (7th Cir. 1964), *cert. denied*, 377 U.S. 1003 (1964), quoted in former Member Penello's dissenting opinion in Douglas Aircraft Co., 234 N.L.R.B. 578, 581 (1978), *enf. denied*, 609 F.2d 352 (9th Cir. 1979).

[8] To the extent that Suburban Motor Freight, 247 N.L.R.B. 146 (1980), provided for a different allocation of burdens in deferral cases, it is overruled.

[9] . . . [N]o party to this proceeding has placed in the record those statistics relied on by our dissenting colleague. The basis for the statistics and how they were compiled is unexplained. . . . [W]e find it inappropriate to base any decision on this equivocal material. . . . [The majority pointed to deficiencies in the statistics and observed that firm guidelines for the General Counsel were especially needed with respect to alleged discrimination against individuals, allegations once again made subject to deferral by *United Technologies.*—Eds.]

demonstrate . . . deficiencies in the arbitral process requiring the Board to
ignore the determination of the arbitrator and subject the case to de novo
review.[10]

. . . [W]e find [here] that the arbitral proceeding has met the *Spielberg*
standards for deferral, and that the arbitrator adequately considered the unfair
labor practice issue. First, . . . the contractual and statutory issues were
factually parallel. Indeed, the arbitrator noted that the factual questions
[before him] were "1) whether . . . there was a sick out and 2) whether the
grievant caused, participated in or failed to attempt to stop [it], i.e., whether
the grievant failed to meet the obligation imposed upon him by Article XIV."
These factual questions are coextensive with those that would be considered
by the Board in a decision on the statutory question — i.e., whether the
collective-bargaining agreement clearly and unmistakably proscribed the
behavior engaged in by . . . Spatorico on 17 December 1980.

Second, . . . the arbitrator was presented generally with the facts relevant to resolving the unfair labor practice. . . . [T]he General Counsel has
not shown that the arbitrator was lacking any evidence relevant to the determination . . . of the obligations imposed by the no-strike clause . . . and
to the determination of the nexus between that clause and Spatorico's conduct. Thus the evidence before the arbitrator was essentially the same evidence necessary for determination of the merits of the unfair labor practice
charge.

Finally, we turn to whether the arbitrator's award is clearly repugnant to
the purposes and policies of the Act. . . . [T]he Supreme Court in *Metropolitan Edison Co.*, supra, recently addressed the merits of the substantive
issue involved here. . . . [T]he Court found that the Union had not clearly
and explicitly waived the §7 rights of its employee officials, and accordingly
that the employer violated §§8(a)(3) and (1) . . . by disciplining the officials more severely than rank-and-file employees. The Court noted [at 1477],
however, that a "union and an employer reasonably could choose to secure
the integrity of a no-strike clause by requiring union officials to take affirmative steps to end unlawful work stoppages," and that a union lawfully may
bargain away the statutory protection accorded union officials in order to
secure gains it considers more valuable to its members. A union's "decision to
undertake such contractual obligations," the Court added, "promotes labor

---

[10]Contrary to the dissent's claim, we are not returning to Electronic Reproduction
Service, 213 N.L.R.B. 758 (1974), in its entirety. Rather, we agree only with that part of
Electronic Reproduction which placed on the General Counsel the burden of demonstrating
that the arbitration is unworthy of deferral. We do not resurrect that part of *Electronic
Reproduction* which required no more than an "opportunity" to present the unfair labor
practice issue to the arbitrator to warrant deferral. . . .

peace and clearly falls within the range of reasonableness accorded bargaining representatives."

Article XIV of the parties' contract here, in addition to a general no-strike/no-lockout obligation similar to the clause . . . in *Metropolitan Edison*, includes a proscription that "neither the Local Union nor the International Union, nor any officer or representattive [sic] of either, will cause or permit its members to cause any strike, slowdown or stoppage (total or partial) of work or any interference, directly or indirectly, with the full operation of the plant." Certainly, were we reviewing the merits, Board members might differ as to the standards of specificity required for contractual language waiving statutory rights and as to whether the above language meets those standards at least as applied to employee Spatorico. The question of waiver, however, is also a question of contract interpretation. An arbitrator's interpretation of the contract is what the parties here have bargained for. . . . Particularly in view of the additional proscriptions in the no-strike clause quoted above, the arbitrator here had a reasonable basis for finding . . . that the clause "specifically prohibits" union officers from engaging in activity of the sort engaged in by Spatorico. We find that the arbitrator's contractual interpretation is not clearly repugnant to either the letter or the spirit of . . . *Metropolitan Edison*. . . .

[Noting that the evidence failed to show noncompliance with its deference standard, the Board dismissed the complaint in toto.]

Member ZIMMERMAN, dissenting in part: I dissent from the overruling of Suburban Motor Freight, 247 N.L.R.B. 146 (1980), and Propoco, Inc., 263 N.L.R.B. 136 (1982). . . . [T]he majority have grossly mischaracterized and unjustifiably rejected a well-reasoned and judicially approved addition to the original *Spielberg* standard. . . .

. . . [T]here must be some minimal proof that an unfair labor practice issue has been resolved in arbitration before the Board can defer to an [award]. With such proof, the Board can reasonably evaluate the award according to the *Spielberg* standards and can accommodate and encourage the arbitral process by deferring to it when the award meets those standards. Without such proof, the Board cannot defer because it has no reasonable basis for determining whether the award fulfills the Board's obligation under §10(a) of the Act. . . .

. . . Under the [majority's] new standard . . . an arbitrator need no longer actually consider and pass upon the unfair labor practice issue before the Board defers to his award. Instead, the Board will now presume that the unfair labor practice issue has been "adequately considered" by the arbitrator, and it will defer to an arbitration award if (1) the contractual issue is factually parallel to the unfair labor practice issue and (2) the arbitrator was

presented generally with the facts relevant to resolving [that issue]. Moreover, it will now be the General Counsel's burden to rebut the presumption
that these criteria have been met. . . .

. . . If the contractual issue is factually parallel to the unfair labor
practice issue, then how can one possibly prove that the facts relevant to
resolving [that] issue have not been presented to the arbitrator unless one
proves the absurdity that even the facts relevant to the contract issue were not
presented? In reality, the majority's new test involves only one step. It will
presume that an arbitrator has considered both contract and unfair labor
practice issues unless the General Counsel can prove that there is no factual
parallel between the issues. The more broadly the Board construes the notion
of factual parallelism,[7] the more difficult the General Counsel's task becomes. . . .

. . . First, and most importantly, the new standard expands the Board's
deferral policy beyond permissible statutory bounds. For all the reasons stated
by the Board in the long line of cases upon which I rely, . . . the use of a
presumption here to justify deferral amounts to an abdication by this Board of
its obligation under §10(a) . . . to protect employees' rights and the public
interest by preventing and remedying unfair labor practices. Nowhere in the
Act itself, its legislative history, or in its judicial interpretation is there authority for the proposition that the Federal labor policy favoring arbitration
requires or permits the Board to abstain from effectuating the equally important Federal labor policy entrusted to the Board under §10(a).

Second, . . . the overwhelming weight of judicial precedent stands
for the proposition that the Board *has no authority to defer* if it does not have
some affirmative proof that an unfair labor practice issue was presented to and
considered by an arbitrator. Judicial rulings on this point stand in sharp
contrast to the general proposition that the Board has broad discretionary
authority to defer to the grievance and arbitration process. . . .

[Third,] the majority's new rule [involves] the inequity of requiring that
"the party seeking to have the Board reject deferral . . . show that the
above standards for deferral have not been met." . . . To invoke a presumption and shift the burden of disproving a naked defense claim to the
General Counsel amounts to an abuse of the Board's discretion. In effect,
once the existence of an arbitration award has been proved by a respondent,
the majority will transform an affirmative defense into part of the General
Counsel's prima facie case. . . . [R]ebutting the presumption will be diffi-

---

[7]Deferring to arbitration on the basis of factual parallelism, of course, is a broader
standard for deferral than deferring only when contract and statutory issues are identical. See,
e.g., *NLRB v. Motor Convoy*, supra.

cult enough in light of the doctrine of factual parallelism. Moreover, there appears to be no sound procedural basis . . . for imposing on the General Counsel—the one party in unfair labor practice litigation who is not in privity through a collective-bargaining agreement—the responsibility of producing evidence about arbitral proceedings under that agreement.

A fourth major criticism . . . involves the relationship of this [new] standard to the expansion of prearbitral deferral policy announced . . . today in *United Technologies*, supra. In that decision, my colleagues seek to temper the broadened "postponement of the use of the Board's processes" by noting that those processes "may always be invoked if the arbitral result is inconsistent with the standards of *Spielberg*." The majority's reversal of policy in this case, however, suggests that such postarbitral review will be of scant significance. This raises a broader question about my colleagues' assumption that the more the Board defers to arbitration awards —and it undoubtedly will defer more under the law announced today in this case and in *United Technologies*—the better it will serve the . . . policy favoring dispute resolution through grievance and arbitration proceedings. They do not articulate any rationale for this assumption nor do they refer to any particular administrative expertise which might warrant judicial deference to their view.

[The dissent here urged that the Board, by forcing parties to resolve unfair labor practice issues in arbitration, might impair the values of arbitration—speed, economy, and informality. In addition, such deferral might strain the resources of unions, employees, and employers, and in the end might lead to opposition to arbitration clauses in collective agreements.]

Fifth, the majority's attack against the purported infrequency of deferrals by the Board under the law overruled today is uninformed and contrary to the Agency's actual experience. It seems that the majority's perception has been distorted by the disposition of the handful of contested cases which present the most difficult issues under *Suburban Motor Freight* and *Spielberg* and are decided by the Board members themselves. A vast number of cases are disposed of through deferral accommodation procedures, however, before they ever reach the Board. The Agency's own statistics, officially maintained by the Data Systems Branch of our Division of Administration, indicate that at the end of December 1983 there were 2185 pending unfair labor practice cases which had been deferred to arbitration machinery under *Dubo* or *Collyer*. . . . Between 1 October 1981 and the end of December 1983, in excess of 3800 cases were deferred under *Collyer* and *Dubo*. During the same period, the General Counsel's application of *Suburban Motor Freight* and *Spielberg* standards resulted in the issuance of complaints in only 163 previously deferred cases. In sharp contrast, over 1700 previously deferred cases were dismissed (357), withdrawn (1159),[12] or settled (62). These statistics dramatically belie the majority's specious claim of infrequent deferrals.

[The dissent also made these points: A change in law was not necessary to justify deference to the instant award, which meets the standard of *Suburban Motor Freight*. The arbitrator had been presented with and had ruled on the statutory issue, finding that discharge had resulted from the grievant's violation of the no-strike clause that specifically bars union officials from causing work stoppages. Finally, the award is consistent with *Metropolitan Edison*, supra p. 1056.]

NOTES

1. As you reflect on the cases raising both contractual and statutory issues (e.g., *Milwaukee Spring II*, supra p. 901, *Metropolitan Edison*, supra p. 1056, *C & C Plywood*, supra p. 1075), can you tell whether those issues were "factually parallel" in a given case? Are the refusal-to-bargain cases more likely to present discrete statutory issues than the discrimination cases? See, e.g., Bakery, Confectionery & Tobacco Workers Union 25 v. NLRB, 730 F.2d 812 (D.C. Cir. 1984); American Freight System, Inc. v. NLRB, 722 F.2d 828 (D.C. Cir. 1983); Capitol City Lumber Co. v. NLRB, 721 F.2d 546 (6th Cir. 1983).

2. Given *United Technologies* and *Olin*, (a) what steps should be taken in arbitration by the employer and the arbitrator, with a view to avoiding relitigation before the NLRB concerning a discharge that might be attacked as prompted, in whole or in part, by the employee's protected activities? (b) What steps should be taken by union counsel with a view either to securing arbitral consideration of the claim of a pretextual discharge or to preserving the Board as a forum for resolving that claim? Consider also Alexander v. Gardner-Denver, 415 U.S. 36, n.21 (1974), infra.

3. Probably a majority of arbitrators disclaim authority to determine statutory questions that are not congruent with contractual questions. Thus an arbitrator, after NLRB deferral, declined to determine whether an employer's unilateral suspension of a stock purchase plan violated §8(a)(5) even though it did not violate the agreement. See Western Mass. Elec. Co., 65 Lab. Arb. 816 (1975). What effect should that arbitral attitude have on the *Collyer* doctrine and vice versa? Cf. General Tel. Co. of Pennsylvania, 71

[12] Cases classified as withdrawn include those numerous cases in which the General Counsel has formally notified the charging party that the case will be dismissed if not withdrawn.

Lab. Arb. 488 (1978) (declaring that resolution of both the contract and unfair labor practice issues is "made mandatory by the NLRB's referral pursuant to *Collyer*").

4. Under §10(a), the Board has power to set aside employer-union agreements settling unfair labor practice charges. See NLRB v. South Cent. Bell Tel. Co., 688 F.2d 345, 352-354 (5th Cir. 1982), *cert. denied*, 103 S. Ct. 1768 (1983). The Board apparently engages in a case-by-case review of nonarbitral settlements for "substantive adequacy" — e.g., whether the agreement calls for substantial remedial action and whether it safeguards the statutory rights of affected employees. See, e.g., Hotel Holiday Inn de Isla Verde v. NLRB, 723 F.2d 169 (1st Cir. 1983). Should the NLRB's policy of deferral to nonarbitral settlements be different from its approach to arbitral resolutions of labor disputes? For criticism of the Board on the ground of uneven application of its deferral practices respecting nonarbitral settlements, see O'Connor, J., joined by Powell and Rehnquist, JJ., dissenting from the denial of certiorari in Schaefer v. NLRB, 104 S. Ct. 362 (1983).

Alexander v. Gardner-Denver Co.
415 U.S. 36 (1974)

POWELL, J. . . . [W]e must decide under what circumstances, if any, an employee's statutory right to a trial de novo under Title VII [Civil Rights Act of 1964] may be foreclosed by prior submission of his claim to final arbitration under the nondiscrimination clause of a collective bargaining agreement.

I

In May 1966, petitioner Harrell Alexander, Sr., a black, was hired by respondent Gardner-Denver Co. to perform maintenance work at the company's plant in Denver, Colorado. In June 1968, petitioner was awarded a trainee position as a drill operator. He remained at that job until his discharge . . . on September 29, 1969, . . . [allegedly] for producing too many defective or unusable parts that had to be scrapped.

On October 1, 1969, petitioner filed a grievance under the collective bargaining agreement in force between the company and petitioner's union, [Steelworkers] Local No. 3029. The grievance stated: "I feel I have been unjustly discharged and ask that I be reinstated with full seniority and pay." No explicit claim of racial discrimination was made.

Under Art. 4 of the collective bargaining agreement, the company retained "the right to hire, suspend or discharge [employees] for proper cause." Article 5, §2, provided, however, that "there shall be no discrimination against any employee on account of race, color, religion, sex, national origin, or ancestry," and Art. 23, §6(a), stated that "[n]o employee will be discharged, suspended or given a written warning notice except for just cause." The agreement also contained a broad arbitration clause. . . . Disputes were to be submitted to a multistep grievance procedure. . . . If the dispute remained unresolved, it was to be remitted to compulsory arbitration. The company and the union were to select and pay the arbitrator, and his decision was to be "final and binding upon the Company, the Union, and any employee or employees involved." The agreement further provided that "[t]he arbitrator shall not amend, take away, add to, or change any of the provisions of this Agreement, and the arbitrator's decision must be based solely upon an interpretation of the provisions of this Agreement." The parties also agreed that there "shall be no suspension of work" over disputes covered by the grievance-arbitration clause.

The union processed petitioner's grievance through the above machinery. In the final prearbitration step, petitioner raised, apparently for the first time, the claim that his discharge resulted from racial discrimination. The company rejected all of petitioner's claims, and the grievance proceeded to arbitration. Prior to the arbitration hearing, however, petitioner filed a charge of racial discrimination with the Colorado Civil Rights Commission, which referred the complaint to the Equal Employment Opportunity Commission [EEOC] on November 5, 1969.

At the arbitration hearing on November 20, 1969, petitioner testified that his discharge was the result of racial discrimination and informed the arbitrator that he had filed a charge with the Colorado Commission because he "could not rely on the union." The union introduced a letter in which petitioner stated that he was "knowledgeable that in the same plant others have scrapped an equal amount and sometimes in excess, but by all logical reasoning I . . . have been the target of preferential discriminatory treatment." The union representative also testified that the company's usual practice was to transfer unsatisfactory trainee drill operators back to their former positions.

On December 30, 1969, the arbitrator ruled that petitioner had been "discharged for just cause." He made no reference to petitioner's claim of racial discrimination. The arbitrator stated that the union had failed to produce evidence of a practice of transferring rather than discharging trainee drill operators who accumulated excessive scrap, but he suggested that the company and the union confer on whether such an arrangement was feasible in the present case.

On July 25, 1970, the [EEOC] determined that there was not reasonable cause to believe that a violation of Title VII . . . had occurred. The Commission later notified petitioner of his right to institute a civil action in federal court within 30 days. Petitioner then filed the present action in the United States District Court . . . , alleging that his discharge resulted from a racially discriminatory employment practice in violation of §703(a)(1) of the Act.

The District Court granted respondent's motion for summary judgment and dismissed the action. 346 F. Supp. 1012 (1971). The court found that the claim of racial discrimination had been submitted to the arbitrator and resolved adversely to petitioner. It then held that petitioner, having voluntarily elected to pursue his grievance to final arbitration under the nondiscrimination clause of the collective bargaining agreement, was bound by the arbitral decision and thereby precluded from suing his employer under Title VII. . . . [T]he Tenth Circuit affirmed per curiam. . . .

II

. . . Congress created the [EEOC] and established a procedure whereby existing state and local equal employment opportunity agencies, as well as the Commission, would have an opportunity to settle disputes through conference, conciliation, and persuasion before the aggrieved party was permitted to file a lawsuit. In the Equal Employment Opportunity Act of 1972, Congress amended Title VII to provide the Commission with further authority to investigate individual charges of discrimination, to promote voluntary compliance with the requirements of Title VII, and to institute civil actions against employers or unions named in a discrimination charge.

Even in its amended form, however, Title VII does not provide the Commission with direct powers of enforcement. The Commission cannot adjudicate claims or impose administrative sanctions. Rather, final responsibility for enforcement of Title VII is vested with federal courts. The Act authorizes courts to issue injunctive relief and to order such affirmative action as may be appropriate to remedy the effects of unlawful employment practices. 42 U.S.C. §§2000e-5(f) and (g) (1970 ed., Supp. II). Courts retain these broad remedial powers despite a Commission finding of no reasonable cause to believe that the Act has been violated. McDonnell Douglas Corp. v. Green [411 U.S., at 798-799]. . . . [T]hese provisions make plain that federal courts have been assigned plenary powers to secure compliance with Title VII.

In addition to reposing ultimate authority in federal courts, Congress gave private individuals a significant role in the enforcement process of Title VII. Individual grievants usually initiate the Commission's investigatory and conciliatory procedures. And although the 1972 amendment to Title VII empowers the Commission to bring its own actions, the private right of action remains an essential means of obtaining judicial enforcement of Title VII. 42 U.S.C. §2000e-5(f)(1) (1970 ed., Supp. II). In such cases, the private litigant not only redresses his own injury but also vindicates the important congressional policy against discriminatory employment practices. . . .

Pursuant to this statutory scheme, petitioner initiated the present action for judicial consideration of his rights under Title VII. The District Court and the Court of Appeals held, however, that petitioner was bound by the prior arbitral decision and had no right to sue under Title VII. Both courts evidently thought that this result was dictated by notions of election of remedies and waiver and by the federal policy favoring arbitration of labor disputes, as enunciated by this Court in [*Lincoln Mills*], 353 U.S. 448 (1957), and the *Steelworkers trilogy*. . . .

III

Title VII does not speak expressly to the relationship between federal courts and the grievance-arbitration machinery of collective bargaining agreements. It does, however, vest federal courts with plenary powers to enforce the statutory requirements; and it specifies with precision the jurisdictional prerequisites that an individual must satisfy before he is entitled to institute a lawsuit. In the present case, these prerequisites were met when petitioner (1) filed timely a charge of employment discrimination with the Commission, and (2) received and acted upon the Commission's statutory notice of the right to sue. . . . There is no suggestion in the statutory scheme that a prior arbitral decision either forecloses an individual's right to sue or divests federal courts of jurisdiction.

In addition, legislative enactments in this area have long evinced a general intent to accord parallel or overlapping remedies against discrimination. In the Civil Rights Act of 1964 Congress indicated that it considered the policy against discrimination to be of the "highest priority." Newman v. Piggie Park Enterprises, [390 U.S.] at 402. Consistent with this view, Title VII provides for consideration of employment-discrimination claims in several forums. See 42 U.S.C. §2000e-5(b) (1970 ed., Supp. II) (EEOC); 42 U.S.C. §2000e-5(c) (1970 ed., Supp. II) (state and local agencies); 42 U.S.C. §2000e-5(f) (1970 ed., Supp. II) (federal courts). And, in general, submission of a claim to one forum does not preclude a later submission to another. See 42 U.S.C. §§2000e-5(b) and (f) (1970 ed., Supp. II); McDonnell Douglas Corp. v. Green, supra. Moreover, the legislative history of Title VII manifests a congressional intent to allow an individual to pursue independently his rights under both Title VII and other applicable state and federal statutes.[9] The clear inference is that Title VII was designed to supplement, rather than supplant, existing laws and institutions relating to employment discrimination. In sum, Title VII's purpose and procedures strongly suggest that an individual does not forfeit his private cause of action if he first pursues his grievance to final arbitration under the nondiscrimination clause of a collective bargaining agreement.

In reaching the opposite conclusion, the District Court relied in part on the doctrine of election of remedies. That doctrine, which refers to situations where an individual pursues remedies that are legally or factually inconsistent, has no application in the present context. In submitting his grievance to arbitration, an employee seeks to vindicate his contractual right. . . . By contrast, in filing a lawsuit under Title VII, an employee asserts independent statutory rights accorded by Congress. The distinctly separate nature of these contractual and statutory rights is not vitiated merely because both were violated as a result of the same factual occurrence. And certainly no inconsistency results from permitting both rights to be enforced in their respectively appropriate forums. The resulting scheme is somewhat analogous to the procedure under the [NLRA], where disputed transactions may implicate both contractual and statutory rights. Where the statutory right underlying a particular claim may not be abridged by contractual agreement, the Court has recognized that consideration of the claim by the arbitrator as a contractual dispute under the collective bargaining agreement does not preclude subsequent consideration of the claim by the [NLRB] as an unfair labor practice charge or as a petition for clarification of the union's representation certificate under the Act. Carey v. Westinghouse Corp., 375 U.S. 261 (1964). Cf. Smith v. Evening News Assn., 371 U.S. 195 (1962). There, as here, the relationship between the forums is complementary since consideration of the claim by both forums may promote the policies underlying each. Thus,

---

[9]For example, Senator Joseph Clark, one of the sponsors of the bill, introduced an interpretive memorandum which stated: "Nothing in Title VII or anywhere else in this bill affects rights and obligations under the NLRA and the Railway Labor Act. . . . [T]itle VII is not intended to and does not deny to any individual, rights and remedies which he may pursue under other Federal and State statutes. If a given action should violate both Title VII and the National Labor Relations Act, the [NLRB] would not be deprived of jurisdiction." 110 Cong. Rec. 7207 (1964). Moreover, the Senate defeated an amendment which would have made Title VII the exclusive federal remedy for most unlawful employment practices. 110 Cong. Rec. 13650-13652 (1964). And a similar amendment was rejected in connection with the Equal Employment Opportunity Act of 1972. See H.R. 9247, 92d Cong., 1st Sess. (1971). See H.R. Rep. No. 92-238 (1971). The report of the Senate Committee responsible for the 1972 Act explained that neither the "provisions regarding the individual's right to sue under Title VII, nor any of the other provisions of this bill, are meant to affect existing rights granted under other laws." S. Rep. No. 92-415, p. 24 (1971). . . .

the rationale behind the election-of-remedies doctrine cannot support the decision below.[14]

We are also unable to accept the proposition that petitioner waived his cause of action under Title VII. . . . [W]e think it clear that there can be no prospective waiver of an employee's rights under Title VII. It is true, of course, that a union may waive certain statutory rights related to collective activity, such as the right to strike. These rights are conferred on employees collectively to foster the processes of bargaining and properly may be exercised or relinquished by the union as collective bargaining agent to obtain economic benefits for unit members. Title VII, on the other hand, stands on plainly different ground; it concerns not majoritarian processes, but an individual's right to equal employment opportunities. Title VII's strictures are absolute and represent a congressional command that each employee be free from discriminatory practices. Of necessity, the rights conferred can form no part of the collective bargaining process since waiver of these rights would defeat the paramount congressional purpose behind Title VII. In these circumstances, an employee's rights under Title VII are not susceptible for prospective waiver. . . .

The actual submission of petitioner's grievance to arbitration in the present case does not alter the situation. Although presumably an employee may waive his cause of action under Title VII as part of a voluntary settlement,[15] mere resort to the arbitral forum to enforce contractual rights constitutes no such waiver. Since an employee's rights under Title VII may not be waived prospectively, existing contractual rights and remedies against discrimination must result from other concessions already made by the union as part of the economic bargain struck with the employer. It is settled law that no additional concession may be exacted from any employee as the price for enforcing those rights. J.I. Case Co. v. NLRB, 321 U.S. 332, 338-339 (1944).

Moreover, a contractual right to submit a claim to arbitration is not displaced simply because Congress also has provided a statutory right against discrimination. Both rights have legally independent origins and are equally

---

[14]Nor can it be maintained that election of remedies is required by the possibility of unjust enrichment through duplicative recoveries. Where, as here, the employer has prevailed at arbitration, there, of course, can be no duplicative recovery. But even in cases where the employee has first prevailed, judicial relief can be structured to avoid such windfall gains. . . . Furthermore, if the relief obtained by the employee at arbitration were fully equivalent to that obtainable under Title VII, there would be no further relief for the court to grant and hence no need for the employee to institute suit.

[15]. . . In determining the effectiveness of any such waiver, a court would have to determine at the outset that the employee's consent to the settlement was voluntary and knowing. . . .

available to the aggrieved employee. This point becomes apparent through consideration of the role of the arbitrator in the system of industrial self-government.[16] As the proctor of the bargain, the arbitrator's task is to effectuate the intent of the parties. His source of authority is the collective bargaining agreement, and he must interpret and apply that agreement in accordance with the "industrial common law of the shop" and the various needs and desires of the parties. The arbitrator, however, has no general authority to invoke public laws that conflict with the bargain between the parties:

> [A]n arbitrator is confined to interpretation and application of the collective bargaining agreement; . . . He may of course look for guidance from many sources, yet his award is legitimate only so long as it draws its essence from the collective bargaining agreement. When the arbitrator's words manifest an infidelity to this obligation, courts have no choice but to refuse enforcement of the award.

United Steelworkers of America v. Enterprise Wheel & Car Corp., 363 U.S. 593, 597 (1960). If an arbitral decision is based "solely upon the arbitrator's view of the requirements of enacted legislation," rather than on an interpretation of the collective bargaining agreement, the arbitrator has "exceeded the scope of the submission," and the award will not be enforced. Ibid. Thus the arbitrator has authority to resolve only questions of contractual rights, and this authority remains regardless of whether certain contractual rights are similar to, or duplicative of, the substantive rights secured by Title VII.

IV

The District Court and the Court of Appeals reasoned that to permit an employee to have his claim considered in both the arbitral and judicial forums would be unfair since this would mean that the employer, but not the employee, was bound by the arbitral award. In the District Court's words, it could not "accept a philosophy which gives the employee two strings to his

---

[16] See Meltzer, Labor Arbitration and Overlapping and Conflicting Remedies for Employment Discrimination, 39 U. Chi. L. Rev. 30, 32-35 (1971); Meltzer, Ruminations About Ideology, Law, and Labor Arbitration, 34 U. Chi. L. Rev. 545 (1967). As the late Dean Shulman stated:

"A proper conception of the arbitrator's function is basic. He is not a public tribunal imposed upon the parties by superior authority which the parties are obliged to accept. He has no general charter to administer justice for a community which transcends the parties. He is rather part of a system of self-government created by and confined to the parties. He serves their pleasure only, to administer the rule of law established by their collective agreement." Shulman, Reason, Contract, and Law in Labor Relations, 68 Harv. L. Rev. 999, 1016 (1955).

bow when the employer has only one." . . . This argument mistakes the effect of Title VII. Under the *Steelworkers trilogy*, an arbitral decision is final and binding on the employer and employee, and judicial review is limited as to both. But in instituting an action under Title VII, the employee is not seeking review of the arbitrator's decision. Rather, he is asserting a statutory right independent of the arbitration process. An employer does not have "two strings to his bow" with respect to an arbitral decision for the simple reason that Title VII does not provide employers with a cause of action against employees. An employer cannot be the victim of discriminatory employment practices. . . .

The District Court and the Court of Appeals also thought that to permit a later resort to the judicial forum would undermine substantially the employer's incentive to arbitrate and would "sound the death knell for arbitration clauses in labor contracts." . . . Again, we disagree. The primary incentive for an employer to enter into an arbitration agreement is the union's reciprocal promise not to strike. . . . It is not unreasonable to assume that most employers will regard the benefits derived from a no-strike pledge as outweighing whatever costs may result from according employees an arbitral remedy against discrimination in addition to their judicial remedy under Title VII. Indeed, the severe consequences of a strike may make an arbitration clause almost essential from both the employees' and the employer's perspective. Moreover, the grievance-arbitration machinery of the collective bargaining agreement remains a relatively inexpensive and expeditious means for resolving a wide range of disputes, including claims of discriminatory employment practices. Where the collective bargaining agreement contains a nondiscrimination clause similar to Title VII, and where arbitral procedures are fair and regular, arbitration may well produce a settlement satisfactory to both employer and employee. An employer thus has an incentive to make available the conciliatory and therapeutic processes of arbitration which may satisfy an employee's perceived need to resort to the judicial forum, thus saving the employer the expense and aggravation associated with a lawsuit. For similar reasons, the employee also has a strong incentive to arbitrate grievances, and arbitration may often eliminate those misunderstandings or discriminatory practices that might otherwise precipitate resort to the judicial forum.

V

Respondent contends that even if a preclusion rule is not adopted, federal courts should defer to arbitral decisions on discrimination claims where: (i) the claim was before the arbitrator; (ii) the collective bargaining agreement prohibited the form of discrimination charged in the suit under Title VII; and (iii) the arbitrator has authority to rule on the claim and to fashion a remedy.[17] Under respondent's proposed rule, a court would grant summary judgment and dismiss the employee's action if the above conditions were met. The rule's obvious consequence in the present case would be to deprive the petitioner of his statutory right to attempt to establish his claim in a federal court.

At the outset, it is apparent that a deferral rule would be subject to many of the objections applicable to a preclusion rule. The purpose and procedures of Title VII indicate that Congress intended federal courts to exercise final responsibility for enforcement of Title VII; deferral to arbitral decisions would be inconsistent with that goal. Furthermore, we have long recognized that "the choice of forums inevitably affects the scope of the substantive right to be vindicated." U.S. Bulk Carriers v. Arguelles, 400 U.S. 351, 359-360 (1971) (Harlan, J., concurring). Respondent's deferral rule is necessarily premised on the assumption that arbitral processes are commensurate with judicial processes and that Congress impliedly intended federal courts to defer to arbitral decisions on Title VII issues. We deem this supposition unlikely.

Arbitral procedures, while well suited to the resolution of contractual disputes, make arbitration a comparatively inappropriate forum for the final resolution of rights created by Title VII. This conclusion rests first on the special role of the arbitrator, whose task is to effectuate the intent of the parties rather than the requirements of enacted legislation. Where the collective bargaining agreement conflicts with Title VII, the arbitrator must follow the agreement. To be sure, the tension between contractual and statutory objectives may be mitigated where a collective bargaining agreement contains provisions facially similar to those of Title VII. But other facts may still render arbitral processes comparatively inferior to judicial processes in the protection of Title VII rights. Among these is the fact that the specialized competence of arbitrators pertains primarily to the law of the shop, not the law of the land. United Steelworkers of America v. Warrior & Gulf Navigation Co., 363 U.S. 574, 581-583 (1960).[18] Parties usually choose an arbitrator because they trust his knowledge and judgment concerning the

---

[17] Respondent's proposed rule is analogous to the NLRB's policy of deferring to arbitral decisions on statutory issues in certain cases. See Spielberg Mfg. Co., 112 N.L.R.B. 1080, 1082 (1955).

[18] See also Gould, Labor Arbitration of Grievances Involving Racial Discrimination, 118 U. Pa. L. Rev. 40, 47-48 (1969); Platt, The Relationship between Arbitration and Title VII of the Civil Rights Act of 1964, 3 Ga. L. Rev. 398 (1969). Significantly, a substantial proportion of labor arbitrators are not lawyers. See Note, The NLRB and Deference to Arbitration, 77 Yale L.J. 1191, 1194 n.28 (1968). . . .

demands and norms of industrial relations. On the other hand, the resolution of statutory or constitutional issues is a primary responsibility of courts, and judicial construction has proved especially necessary with respect to Title VII, whose broad language frequently can be given meaning only by reference to public law concepts.

Moreover, the factfinding process in arbitration usually is not equivalent to judicial factfinding. The record of the arbitration proceedings is not as complete; the usual rules of evidence do not apply; and rights and procedures common to civil trials, such as discovery, compulsory process, cross-examination, and testimony under oath, are often severely limited or unavailable. . . . And as this Court has recognized, "[a]rbitrators have no obligation to the court to give their reasons for an award." United Steelworkers of America v. Enterprise Wheel & Car Corp., 363 U.S., at 598. Indeed, it is the informality of arbitral procedure that enables it to function as an efficient, inexpensive, and expeditious means for dispute resolution. This same characteristic, however, makes arbitration a less appropriate forum for final resolution of Title VII issues than the federal courts.[19]

It is evident that respondent's proposed rule would not allay these concerns. Nor are we convinced that the solution lies in applying a more demanding deferral standard, such as that adopted by the Fifth Circuit in Rios v. Reynolds Metals Co., 467 F.2d 54 (1972).[20] As respondent points out, a standard that adequately insured effectuation of Title VII rights in the

---

[19] A further concern is the union's exclusive control over the manner and extent to which an individual grievance is presented. See Vaca v. Sipes, 386 U.S. 171 (1967); Republic Steel Corp. v. Maddox, 379 U.S. 650 (1965). In arbitration, as in the collective bargaining process, the interests of the individual employee may be subordinated to the collective interests of all employees in the bargaining unit. See J. I. Case Co. v. NLRB, 321 U.S. 332 (1944). Moreover, harmony of interest between the union and the individual employee cannot always be presumed, especially where a claim of racial discrimination is made. See, e.g., Steele v. Louisville & N. R. Co., 323 U.S. 192 (1944). . . . And a breach of the union's duty of fair representation may prove difficult to establish. . . . In this respect, it is noteworthy that Congress thought it necessary to afford the protections of Title VII against unions as well as employers. See 42 U.S.C. §2000e-2(c).

[20] In Rios, the court set forth the following deferral standard: "First, there may be no deference to the decision of the arbitrator unless the contractual right coincides with rights under Title VII. Second, it must be plain that the arbitrator's decision is in no way violative of the private rights guaranteed by Title VII, nor of the public policy which inheres in Title VII. In addition, before deferring, the district court must be satisfied that (1) the factual issues before it are identical to those decided by the arbitrator; (2) the arbitrator had power under the collective agreement to decide the ultimate issue of discrimination; (3) the evidence presented at the arbitral hearing dealt adequately with all factual issues; (4) the arbitrator actually decided the factual issues presented to the court; (5) the arbitration proceeding was fair and regular and free of procedural infirmities. The burden of proof in establishing these conditions of limitation will be upon the respondent as distinguished from the claimant." 467 F.2d, at 58.

arbitral forum would tend to make arbitration a procedurally complex, expensive, and time-consuming process. And judicial enforcement of such a standard would almost require courts to make de novo determinations of the employees' claims. It is uncertain whether any minimal savings in judicial time and expense would justify the risk to vindication of Title VII rights.

A deferral rule also might adversely affect the arbitration system as well as the enforcement scheme of Title VII. Fearing that the arbitral forum cannot adequately protect their rights under Title VII, some employees may elect to bypass arbitration and institute a lawsuit. The possibility of voluntary compliance or settlement of Title VII claims would thus be reduced, and the result could well be more litigation, not less.

We think, therefore, that the federal policy favoring arbitration of labor disputes and the federal policy against discriminatory employment practices can best be accommodated by permitting an employee to pursue fully both his remedy under the grievance-arbitration clause . . . and his cause of action under Title VII. The federal court should consider the employee's claim de novo. The arbitral decision may be admitted as evidence and accorded such weight as the court deems appropriate.[21]

The judgment of the Court of Appeals is Reversed.

[Alexander v. Gardner-Denver Co., 519 F.2d 503 (10th Cir. 1975), *cert. denied*, 423 U.S. 1058 (1976), affirmed the district court's holding, upon remand, that the discharge was nondiscriminatory.]

NOTES

1. In Barrentine v. Arkansas-Best Freight System, 450 U.S. 728 (1981), the Court held that an action based on the Fair Labor Standards Act was not foreclosed by the prior rejection of individual grievances, based on

---

[21]We adopt no standards as to the weight to be accorded an arbitral decision, since this must be determined in the court's discretion with regard to the facts and circumstances of each case. Relevant factors include the existence of provisions in the collective bargaining agreement that conform substantially with Title VII, the degree of procedural fairness in the arbitral forum, adequacy of the record with respect to the issue of discrimination, and the special competence of particular arbitrators. Where an arbitral determination gives full consideration to an employee's Title VII rights, a court may properly accord it great weight. This is especially true where the issue is solely one of fact, specifically addressed by the parties and decided by the arbitrator on the basis of an adequate record. But courts should ever be mindful that Congress, in enacting Title VII, thought it necessary to provide a judicial forum for the ultimate resolution of discriminatory employment claims. It is the duty of courts to assure the full availability of this forum.

the same transactions, by the joint committee authorized by the collective agreement to deal with "any controversy." The Chief Justice, joined by Rehnquist, J., dissented, urging that the considerations behind *Gardner-Denver*, on which the Court had relied, should not be controlling in the context of routine wage claims based on the FLSA.

Subsequently, declaring that its result was required by *Gardner-Denver* and *Barrentine*, the Court held unanimously that an adverse arbitration award pursuant to a public sector collective agreement does not bar a discharged police officer's subsequent suit in federal court under §1983. *McDonald v. City of West Branch, Michigan*, 104 S. Ct. 1799 (1984). The Court gave these reasons for concluding that arbitration may not adequately protect §1983 rights: (a) arbitrators may lack the expertise required to resolve complex §1983 questions; (b) arbitrators may not have the contractual authority to enforce §1983; (c) because of possible divergence between individual and union interests, an employee may suffer from a union's exclusive control over the grievance procedure; and (d) arbitral factfinding is generally not equivalent to judicial factfinding.

Are the limitations of arbitration recognized in *Gardner-Denver*, *Barrentine*, and *McDonald* not applicable to federal rights created by the NLRA?

2. Does a contractual "just cause" provision by itself bar discipline influenced by race, sex, or other factors banned by Title VII, regardless of whether the employer is covered by that title? Doesn't such a provision exclude race, for example, as a factor in the entire range of employment decisions? If so, should the "existence of provisions . . . that conform substantially with Title VII" (see footnote 21 of *Gardner-Denver*) be relevant in deciding the weight to be given in a Title VII action to an arbitrator's finding that race, for example, was not a factor in a discharge? Cf. *Olin Corp.*, supra p. 1095.

3. It has been suggested that collective agreements should grant arbitrators broad authority to invalidate specific provisions of the agreement, such as facially neutral seniority agreements, deemed by arbitrators to be invalid under Title VII. What are the potential costs and benefits of such clauses? See generally Edwards, Arbitration of Employment Discrimination Cases: A Proposal for Employer and Union Representatives, 27 Lab. L.J. 265 (1976); Meltzer, Labor Arbitration and Discrimination: The Parties' Process and the Public's Purposes, 43 U. Chi. L. Rev. 724 (1976).

4. In order to avoid the proliferation of forums sanctioned by *Gardner-Denver*, some employers have sought to contract out of their obligation to arbitrate grievances arising from allegations of discrimination. The EEOC has urged that such a contract provision would affect minorities and women

adversely, and, accordingly, would be unlawful. See generally Hill & Sinicropi, Excluding Discrimination Grievances from Grievance and Arbitration Procedures: A Legal Analysis, 33 Arb. J. 16, 18-19 (1978). For a
description of the opposite approach, i.e., establishing separate procedures
for the arbitration of employment discrimination issues, see Youngdahl,
Arbitration of Discrimination Grievances: A Novel Approach Under One
Collective Agreement, 31 Arb. J. 145 (1976).

W.R. Grace & Co. v. Local 759, Rubber Workers
421 U.S. 757 (1983)

BLACKMUN, J. Faced with the prospect of liability for violations of Title
VII of the Civil Rights Act of 1964, as amended, petitioner signed with the
Equal Employment Opportunity Commission (Commission or EEOC) a
conciliation agreement that was in conflict with its collective bargaining
agreement with respondent. Petitioner then obtained a court order, later
reversed on appeal, that the conciliation agreement should prevail. The issue
presented is whether the Court of Appeals was correct in enforcing an arbitral
award of backpay damages against petitioner under the collective bargaining
agreement for layoffs pursuant to the conciliation agreement.

I

A

In October 1973, . . . the EEOC's District Director determined that
there was reasonable cause to believe that petitioner W.R. Grace and Company (Company) had violated Title VII . . . , by discriminating in the
hiring of Negroes and women at its Corinth, Miss., plastics manufacturing
facility. In addition, the Director found that the departmental and plant-wide
seniority systems, mandated by the Company's collective bargaining agreement with respondent Local Union No. 759 (Union), were unlawful because they perpetuated the effects of the Company's past discrimination.
The Company was invited, pursuant to §706(b) of the Act, to conciliate the
dispute. . . . [T]he Union declined [the Commission's invitation to partici-
pate].

B

A collective bargaining agreement between petitioner and respondent expired in March 1974, and failed negotiations led to a strike. The Company
hired strike replacements, some of whom were women who took Company
jobs never before held by women. The strike was settled in May with the

signing of a new agreement that continued the plant seniority system specified by the expired agreement. The strikers returned to work, but the Company also retained the strike replacements. The women replacements were
assigned to positions in the Corinth plant ahead of men with greater seniority.
Specifically, the Company prevented men from exercising the shift preference seniority (to which they were entitled under the collective bargaining
agreement) to obtain positions held by the women strike replacements. The
men affected by this action filed grievances. . . .

The Company refused to join the ultimate arbitration. Instead, it filed
an action under §301 . . . , in the United States District Court. . . . The
Company sought an injunction prohibiting arbitration of the grievances
while the Company negotiated . . . with the Commission. The Union
counterclaimed to compel arbitration.

Before the District Court took any action, the Company and the Commission signed a conciliation agreement dated December 11, 1974. In addition to ratifying the Company's position with respect to the shift preference
dispute, the conciliation agreement provided that in the event of layoffs, the
Company would maintain the existing proportion of women in the plant's
bargaining unit. The Company then amended its §301 complaint to add the
Commission as a defendant and to request an injunction barring the arbitration of grievances seeking relief that conflicted with . . . the conciliation
agreement. The Commission cross-claimed against the Union and counterclaimed against the Company for a declaratory judgment that the conciliation
agreement prevailed. . . .

While cross-motions for summary judgment were under consideration,
the Company laid off employees pursuant to the conciliation agreement.
Several men affected by the layoff, who would have been protected under the
seniority provisions of the collective bargaining agreement, filed grievances.
In November 1975, with the Company still refusing to arbitrate, the District
Court granted summary judgment for the Commission and the Company. It
held that under Title VII the seniority provisions could be modified to
alleviate the effects of past discrimination. [403 F. Supp. 1183, 1188 (1975)].
The court declared that the terms of the conciliation agreement were binding
on all parties and that "all parties . . . shall abide thereby."[2] The Union
appealed, and no party sought a stay.

[2]The relevant text of the order is as follows:

"(1) The terms of the conciliation agreement executed on December 11, 1974, by the
plaintiff and the defendant, EEOC, are binding upon all the parties to this action; and

"(2) Where the provisions of the collective bargaining agreement executed by the
plaintiff and defendant, Local 759, conflict with the provisions of the conciliation agreement
executed by the plaintiff and defendant, EEOC, the provisions of the conciliation agreement
are controlling and all parties to this action shall abide thereby."

With the Union's appeal pending . . . , the Company, following the terms of the conciliation agreement, laid off more employees. Again, adversely affected male employees filed grievances. In January 1978, . . . the Court of Appeals reversed. [565 F.2d 913]. Applying Teamsters v. United States, 431 U.S. 324 (1977), which was decided after the District Court's decision, the Court of Appeals held that because the seniority system was not animated by a discriminatory purpose, it was lawful and could not be modified without the Union's consent. 565 F.2d, at 916. The court granted the Union's counterclaim, compelling the Company to arbitrate the grievances.

. . . [T]he Company reinstated the male employees to the positions to which they were entitled under the collective bargaining agreement. The pending grievances, seeking backpay, then proceeded to arbitration. The first to reach arbitration was that of a male employee who had been demoted while the District Court order was in effect. Arbitrator Anthony J. Sabella, in August 1978, concluded that although the grievant was entitled to an award under the collective bargaining agreement, it would be inequitable to penalize the Company for conduct that complied with an outstanding court order. He thus denied the grievance. Instead of filing an action to set aside that award, the Union chose to contest Sabella's reasoning in later arbitrations.

C

The next grievance . . . resulted in the award in dispute here. Arbitrator Gerald A. Barrett was presented with the complaints of two men who had been laid off. . . . Acknowledging that the Sabella arbitration resolved the same contractual issue, Barrett first considered whether the . . . agreement required him to follow the Sabella arbitration award. He concluded that it did not. The collective bargaining agreement limited the arbitrator's authority, Barrett found, to considering whether the express terms of the contract had been violated.[4] Because Sabella had considered the fairness of enforcing the terms of the contract, he had acted outside his contractually defined jurisdiction. . . .

Arbitrator Barrett then turned to the grievances before him. The Company did not dispute that it had violated the seniority provisions of the

---

[4] The 1974 collective bargaining agreement and the succeeding 1977 agreement each defined the arbitrator's jurisdiction as follows:

"The jurisdiction and authority of the Arbitrator of the grievance and his opinion and award shall be confined exclusively to the interpretation and application of the express provision or provisions of this Agreement at issue between the Union and the Company. He shall have no authority to add to, adjust, change, or modify any provision of this Agreement." Art. IV, §3.

collective bargaining agreement, and Barrett also accepted the Company's contention that it had acted in good faith in following the conciliation agreement. He found, however, that the collective bargaining agreement made no exception for good faith violations of the seniority provisions, and that the Company had acted at its own risk in breaching the agreement. The Company, he held, could not complain that the law ultimately had made this out to be an unfortunate decision. . . .

D

The Company then instituted another action under §301 . . . to overturn the award. The [District Court] entered summary judgment for the Company, finding that public policy prevented enforcement of the collective bargaining agreement during the period prior to the Court of Appeals' reversal. The [Fifth Circuit] reversed. 652 F.2d 1248 (1981). . . .

II

The sole issue . . . is whether the Barrett award should be enforced. . . . Unless the arbitral decision does not "dra[w] its essence from the collective bargaining agreement," [*Enterprise Wheel*, 363 U.S. at 597], a court is bound to enforce the award and is not entitled to review the merits of the contract dispute. . . .

Under this standard, the Court of Appeals was correct in enforcing the Barrett award. . . . Barrett's initial conclusion that he was not bound by the Sabella decision was based on his interpretation of the . . . agreement's provisions defining the arbitrator's jurisdiction and his perceived obligation to give a prior award a preclusive effect. Because the authority of arbitrators is a subject of collective bargaining, just as is any other contractual provision, the scope of the arbitrator's authority is itself a question of contract interpretation that the parties have delegated to the arbitrator. Barrett's conclusions that Sabella acted outside his jurisdiction and that this deprived the Sabella award of precedential force under the contract draw their "essence" from the provisions of the collective bargaining agreement. Regardless of what our view might be of the correctness of Barrett's contractual interpretation, the Company and the Union bargained for that interpretation. A federal court may not second-guess it. [*Enterprise Wheel*], 363 U.S., at 599.

Barrett's analysis of the merits of the grievances is entitled to the same deference. He found that the collective bargaining agreement provided no good faith defense to claims of violations of the seniority provisions, and gave him no authority to weigh in some other fashion the Company's good faith. Again, although conceivably we could reach a different result were we to interpret the contract ourselves,[8] we cannot say that the award does not draw its essence from the collective bargaining agreement.

III

As with any contract, however, a court may not enforce a collective bargaining agreement that is contrary to public policy. See Hurd v. Hodge, 334 U.S. 24, 34-35 (1948). Barrett's view of his own jurisdiction precluded his consideration of this question, and, in any event, the question of public policy is ultimately one for resolution by the courts. . . . Kaden, Judges and Arbitrators: Observations on the Scope of Judicial Review, 80 Colum. L. Rev. 267, 287 (1980). If the contract as interpreted by Barrett violates some explicit public policy, we are obliged to refrain from enforcing it. . . . Such a public policy, however, must be well defined and dominant, and is to be ascertained "by reference to the laws and legal precedents and not from general considerations of supposed public interests." Muschany v. United States, 324 U.S. 49, 66 (1945).

A

. . . [O]bedience to judicial orders is an important public policy. An injunction issued by a court acting within its jurisdiction must be obeyed until the injunction is vacated or withdrawn. [United States v. United Mine Workers, 330 U.S. 258, 293-294 (1947)]. . . . A contract provision the performance of which has been enjoined is unenforceable. See Restatement (Second) of Contracts §§261, 264 (1981). Here, however, enforcement of the collective bargaining agreement as interpreted by Barrett does not compromise this public policy.

Given the Company's desire to reduce its workforce, it is undeniable that the Company was faced with a dilemma: it could follow the conciliation agreement as mandated by the District Court and risk liability under the collective bargaining agreement, or it could follow the bargaining agreement and risk both a contempt citation and Title VII liability. The dilemma, however, was of the Company's own making. The Company committed

---

[8] The 1974 and 1977 collective bargaining agreements each contained a clause that provided: "In the event that any provision of this Agreement is found to be in conflict with any State or Federal Laws now existing or hereinafter enacted, it is agreed that such laws shall supersede the conflicting provisions without affecting the remainder of these provisions." Art. XIV, §7. [T]he Company argued that under this "legality" clause the seniority provision was superseded by the District Court's determination that the provision was illegal. The Court of Appeals responded that its decision reversing the District Court had retroactive effect because it declared the law as it always had existed. 652 F.2d, at 1255. It seems to us, however, that the Company's argument was that the court should interpret the legality clause itself, a privilege not permitted to federal courts in reviewing an arbitral award.

itself voluntarily to two conflicting contractual obligations. When the Union attempted to enforce its contractual rights, the Company sought a judicial declaration of its respective obligations under the contracts. During the course of this litigation, before the legal rights were finally determined, the Company again laid off employees and dishonored its contract with the Union. For these acts, the Company incurred liability for breach of contract. In effect, Barrett interpreted the collective bargaining agreement to allocate to the Company the losses caused by the Company's decision to follow the District Court order that proved to be erroneous.[10]

Even assuming that the District Court's order was a mandatory injunction, nothing in the collective bargaining agreement as interpreted by Barrett required the Company to violate that order. Barrett's award neither mandated layoffs[12] nor required that layoffs be conducted according to the collective bargaining agreement. The award simply held, retrospectively, that the employees were entitled to damages for the prior breach of the seniority provisions.

. . . [T]he Company actually complied with the District Court's order, and nothing we say here causes us to believe that it would disobey the

---

[10] Although Barrett could have considered the District Court order to cause impossibility of performance and thus to be a defense to the Company's breach, he did not do so. Impossibility is a doctrine of contract interpretation. See 18 W. Jaeger, Williston on Contracts §§1931-1979 (3d ed. 1978). For the reasons stated in the text, we cannot revise Barrett's implicit rejection of the impossibility defense. Even if we were to review the issue *de novo*, moreover, it is far from clear that the defense is available to the Company, whose own actions created the condition of impossibility. See id., §1939, p. 50; Uniform Commercial Code §2-615(a) and comment 10, 1A U.L.A. 335, 338 (1976); Lowenschuss v. Kane, 520 F.2d 255, 265 (CA2 1975).

[12] Economic necessity is not recognized as a commercial impracticability defense to a breach of contract claim. Uniform Commercial Code §2-615, comment 4, 1A U.L.A. 336 (1976) (increased cost of performance does not constitute impossibility). . . . Thus, while it may have been economic misfortune for the Company to postpone or forgo its layoff plans, its extant, conflicting, and voluntarily assumed contractual obligations exposed it to liability regardless of the layoff procedure it followed. In order to avoid liability under either contract, the Company, of course, could have accepted the economic losses of forgoing its reduction-in-force plans.

This is not to say that in the face of the economic necessity of the layoffs, the Company had no way whatsoever to avoid the injury. Prior to conducting the layoffs, the Company could have requested a stay from the District Court to permit it to follow the collective bargaining agreement pending review by the Court of Appeals. It was the Company, which had sought the declaration of rights and obligations, and which chose to act before the determination of its respective contractual obligations was final; the Union most likely would have preferred that no lay-offs occur at all. Although the Union could have requested a stay, there is no rule requiring a party to ask for prospective relief from a possible contractual breach. The Union justifiably relied on its right to backpay damages. Moreover, the Company, in future contract negotiations, may seek to bargain for a contract provision expressly allocating the loss to its employees in a case such as this one.

order if presented with the same dilemma in the future. Enforcement of Barrett's award will not create intolerable incentives to disobey court orders. Courts have sufficient contempt powers to protect their injunctions, even if the injunctions are issued erroneously. . . . In addition to contempt sanctions, the Company here was faced with possible Title VII liability if it departed from the conciliation agreement in conducting its layoffs. The Company was cornered by its own actions, and it cannot argue now that liability under the collective bargaining agreement violates public policy.

Nor is placing the Company in this position with respect to the court order so unfair as to violate public policy. Obeying injunctions often is a costly affair. Because of the Company's alleged prior discrimination against women, some readjustments and consequent losses were bound to occur. The issue is whether the Company or the Union members should bear the burden of those losses. As interpreted by Barrett, the collective bargaining agreement placed this unavoidable burden on the Company. By entering into the conflicting conciliation agreement, by seeking a court order to excuse it from performing the collective bargaining agreement, and by subsequently acting on its mistaken interpretation of its contractual obligations, the Company attempted to shift the loss to its male employees, who shared no responsibility for the sex discrimination. The Company voluntarily assumed its obligations under the collective bargaining agreement and the arbitrators' interpretations of it. No public policy is violated by holding the Company to those obligations, which bar the Company's attempted reallocation of the burden. . . .

[In concluding, the Court stressed these considerations: Even though voluntary compliance and EEOC conciliation are important under Title VII, enforcement of the Barrett award was not inappropriate. Conciliation is not coercive. Neither the EEOC nor the company could alter a collective agreement, without the union's consent, which was not given here.

The judgment of the Court of Appeals, enforcing the Barrett award, was affirmed.]

NOTES

1. Would the Court have upheld the Sabella award if it, rather than the Barrett award, had been the subject of an enforcement action? If so, is there any inconsistency in the view, first, that Arbitrator B may review and set aside the work of Arbitrator A, insofar as A laid down a rule for future employer conduct, and second, that courts, because of the limited scope of judicial review, may not vacate either A's award or B's?

Courts reviewing inconsistent arbitration awards usually hold that inconsistency alone is not enough to justify vacating an award; thus, neither award will be set aside where both draw their essence from the agreement. See, e.g., Bacardi Corp. v. Congreso de Uniones Industriales de Puerto Rico, 692 F.2d 210 (1st Cir. 1982). But cf. Connecticut Light & Power Co. v. Local 420, Electrical Workers, 718 F.2d 14 (2d Cir. 1983), where the court, reviewing only the first of two inconsistent awards, found it necessary to resolve the conflict (because of the first award's cease and desist order against the company). The court defined a two-step analysis for such cases: (a) Determine whether each award, viewed separately, survives the *Enterprise Wheel* test; (b) If each does, select that award which "most nearly conforms to the intent of the parties." Pursuing that approach, the court selected the second award as "better reasoned" and affirmed the district court's vacating of the first award.

2. In *W.R. Grace*, what difference in result, if any, had the union accepted the EEOC's invitation to conciliate and approved the conciliation agreement? Cf. Firefighters Local 1784 v. Stotts, 104 S. Ct. 2576 n.9 (1984); EEOC v. Safeway Stores, 714 F.2d 567 (5th Cir. 1983); Telephone Wkrs. v. New Jersey Bell Tel. Co., 450 F. Supp. 284 (D.N.J. 1977), *aff'd*, 584 F.2d 31 (3d Cir. 1978).

3. A §301 suit is brought to compel arbitration of a union steward's request for preferential overtime based on the agreement's superseniority clause. The employer had unilaterally abrogated that clause as unlawful under *Gulton Electro-Voice* (supra p. 292), and the NLRB Regional Director, also relying on *Gulton*, had withheld a complaint on charges filed by the union. Does the *Steelworkers* trilogy dictate that the court order arbitration? Should the court, before acting, require a showing that an arbitral award in favor of the grievant could be compatible with external law? Cf. Crescent City Lodge 37 v. Boland Marine & Mfg. Co., 591 F.2d 1184 (5th Cir. 1979).

4. The *W.R. Grace* opinion indicates (footnote 8) that an arbitrator is to interpret a "separability" or "legality" clause. Does it follow (as is often argued) that such clauses authorize an arbitrator to invalidate a term of the agreement in conflict with external law? Does the clause quoted in footnote 8 confer such authority? Cf. Hunter Eng. Co., 82 Lab. Arb. 483 (1984).

5. Arbitral awards of damages that are, on analysis, not compensatory but "punitive" have been denied enforcement on public policy grounds. Could the parties avoid such results by expressly authorizing punitive damages in the collective agreement? See United Elec. Wkrs. v. Litton Systems, 704 F.2d 393 (8th Cir. 1983); Westinghouse Elec. Corp. v. IBEW, 561 F.2d 521 (4th Cir. 1977), *cert. denied*, 434 U.S. 1036 (1978).

CHAPTER 11

THE INDIVIDUAL AND COLLECTIVE ACTION

Mr. Justice Jackson, dissenting in Wallace Corp. v. NLRB, 323 U.S. 248, 271, (1944),[a] stated:

> The labor movement in the United States is passing into a new phase. The struggle of the unions for recognition and rights to bargain and of workmen for the right to join without interference seems to be culminating in a victory for labor forces. We appear to be entering the phase of struggle to reconcile the rights of individuals and minorities with the power of those who control collective bargaining groups.

This need for reconciliation arises in both the making and the administration of the agreement and is sharpened by the power of the representative to bind all members of the bargaining unit, to exclude individual bargaining, and to shape and control the grievance-arbitration machinery.

In making an agreement, labor and management frequently must reconcile differences between the skilled and unskilled, the young and old, male and female, black and white, employees who want larger take-home pay and those who prefer higher pensions, and the "social reformers" and the exponents of "business unionism." Such clashes of interest and ideology, although typically less visible and dramatic than confrontations between unions and management, are important and persistent aspects of the bargaining process. A union's performance (indeed, survival) depends not only on its capacity to deal with the employer but also on its ability to resolve differences among those whom it represents. Such differences tend to become more acute as bargaining units increase in size, as fringe benefits represent an increasing share of labor costs, as the administration of unions becomes more centralized, and as local and part-time officials are displaced by full-time paid

---

[a] This case was decided the same day as Steele v. Louisville Nashville R.R., reproduced immediately after these introductory remarks.

staffs. Another dimension has been added to those familiar difficulties by the heightened racial consciousness of black workers, dissatisfied with the representation they have received, with the legacy of union racial discrimination, and with a disproportionately high white union leadership, and who are seeking to establish an independent power base within the union movement.[b] In any event, although a union, in making an agreement, must be given broad authority to strike a balance among conflicting interests within the bargaining unit, that authority must be limited in order to protect disfavored minorities and individuals against oppressive and arbitrary action.

Similar problems of balancing authority against individual interests arise in the administration of the agreement. An individual's claim under the agreement may, as in seniority disputes, collide with the interests of other individuals; with the general interest in good relations, and informal adjustments, with management; or with the union's desire to avoid expenditures for dubious arbitrations. A union may, however, exercise its power over grievances to promote more questionable ends: eliminating or silencing critics, mavericks, or leaders of rival factions; trading one meritorious grievance for another; or rewarding some employers and penalizing others.

The making and administration of agreements are interrelated and overlapping elements of a bargaining system rather than nicely separable processes. Administration may reveal gaps or deficiencies in the agreement and may lead to the development of new contractual standards for the omitted case, or the modification or ad hoc waiver of existing standards.

Nevertheless, the function of laying down the major rules for the future, which is performed by the agreement, is different from the function of interpretation and interstitial completion or modification that is performed by administration. Those processes are also procedurally distinct. Most union constitutions prescribe different methods for negotiating and ratifying an agreement, on the one hand, and administering it, on the other. Furthermore, the agreement itself, through arbitration clauses that typically seek to confine the arbitrator, reflects the differing functions of those two processes. Finally, contractually determined standards are usually public, whereas ad hoc adjustments may be isolated and secret and may submerge individual interests to what is deemed group welfare for reasons unrelated to the grievances at issue. See R. James & E. James, Hoffa and the Teamsters ch. 11 (1965). These considerations pose the question of whether the parties to a

---

[b]These factors have led to the formation of black groups that operate either as "black caucuses" within a union or as extraunion groups. For a brief description of such groups and of their relationship to union structure and bargaining, see Henle, Some Reflections on Organized Labor and the New Militants, 92 Monthly Lab. Rev. 20 (1969). See also Gould, Black Power in the Unions: The Impact upon Bargaining Relationships, 79 Yale L.J. 46 (1969).

collective agreement should have the same latitude in its administration as in its formation. The answer to that question may, in turn, depend on whether legal safeguards, such as the union's duty of fair representation, can provide effective protection against arbitrary or oppressive improvisation in contract administration.

The foregoing comments suggest three lines of inquiry for the first section of this chapter: (1) What limitations should, in general, be imposed on the union's authority to bind members of the bargaining unit, and what are the forums and the legal bases for enforcing such limitations? (2) Should special limitations be imposed on the union's plenary power as exclusive representative and on its control over the grievance-arbitration machinery when employee claims of rights under the agreement are involved? (3) Should some kinds of employee grievances, e.g., those involving discharge, be given extraordinary protection against the combined power of the parties to the agreement? For example, should an employee have an unrestricted right to take to arbitration his discharge alleged to be violative of a contractual just-cause provision? These issues involve the balance to be struck between individual and collective interests, between tightly regulated and discretionary judgments by unions, and between the risks of union abuses of authority and of over-regulation unduly interfering with union autonomy. For differing appraisals, see Cox, Rights Under a Labor Agreement, 69 Harv. L. Rev. 601 (1956), and Summers, Individual Rights in Collective Agreements and Arbitration, 37 N.Y.U. L. Rev. 362 (1962).

A. THE DUTY OF FAIR REPRESENTATION

1. *Early Judicial Development*

Steele v. Louisville & Nashville R.R.
323 U.S. 192 (1944)

STONE, C.J. . . . Petitioner, a Negro, is a locomotive fireman . . . , suing on his own behalf and that of his fellow employees who, like petitioner, are Negro firemen employed by the Railroad. Respondent Brotherhood, a labor organization, is, as provided under §2, Fourth of the Railway Labor Act [RLA], the exclusive bargaining representative of the craft of firemen employed by the Railroad. . . . The majority of the firemen . . . are white and are members of the Brotherhood, but a substantial minority are Negroes who, by the constitution and ritual of the Brotherhood, are excluded from its membership. As the membership of the Brotherhood constitutes a majority of all firemen employed on respondent Railroad, and as under §2, Fourth, the members because they are the majority have the right to choose and have chosen the Brotherhood to represent the craft, petitioner and other Negro firemen . . . have been required to accept the Brotherhood as their representative. . . .

On March 28, 1940, the Brotherhood, purporting to act as representative of the entire craft of firemen, without informing the Negro firemen or giving them opportunity to be heard, served a notice on respondent Railroad and on twenty other railroads operating principally in the southeastern part of the United States. The notice announced the Brotherhood's desire to amend the existing collective bargaining agreement [so] as ultimately to exclude all Negro firemen from the service. By established practice on the several railroads so notified only white firemen can be promoted to serve as engineers, and the notice proposed that only "promotable," i.e. white, men should be employed as firemen or assigned to new runs or jobs or permanent vacancies in established runs or jobs.

On February 18, 1941, the railroads and the Brotherhood, as representative of the craft, entered into a new agreement which provided that not more than 50% of the firemen in each class of service in each seniority district of a carrier should be Negroes; that until such percentage should be reached all new runs and all vacancies should be filled by white men; and that the agreement did not sanction the employment of Negroes in any seniority district in which they were not working. The agreement reserved the right of the Brotherhood to negotiate for further restrictions on the employment of Negro firemen. . . . On May 12, 1941, the Brotherhood entered into a supplemental agreement with respondent Railroad further controlling the seniority rights of Negro firemen and restricting their employment. The Negro firemen were not given notice or opportunity to be heard with respect to either of these agreements, which were put into effect before their existence was disclosed. . . .

Until April 8, 1941, petitioner was in a "passenger pool," to which one white and five Negro firemen were assigned. These jobs were highly desirable. . . . Petitioner had performed and was performing his work satisfactorily. Following a reduction in the mileage covered by the pool, all jobs in the pool were, about April 1, 1941, declared vacant. The Brotherhood and the Railroad, acting under the agreement, disqualified all the Negro firemen and replaced them with four white men, members of the Brotherhood, all junior in seniority to petitioner and no more competent or worthy. . . . [P]etitioner was deprived of employment for sixteen days and then was assigned to more arduous, longer, and less remunerative work in local freight service. . . . [H]e was later replaced by a Brotherhood member junior to him, and assigned work on a switch engine, which was still harder and less remunerative, until January 3, 1942. On that date, after the bill of complaint in the present suit had been filed, he was reassigned to passenger service. . . .

The Supreme Court of Alabama . . . held . . . that petitioner's complaint stated no cause of action. . . . It thought that the Brotherhood was empowered by the statute to enter into the agreement of February 18, 1941, and that by virtue of the statute the Brotherhood has power by agreement with the Railroad both to create the seniority rights of petitioner and his fellow Negro employees and to destroy them. It construed the statute . . . as conferring on the Brotherhood plenary authority to treat with the Railroad and enter into contracts fixing rates of pay and working conditions for the craft as a whole without any legal obligation or duty to protect the rights of minorities from discrimination or unfair treatment, however gross. Consequently it held that neither the Brotherhood nor the Railroad violated any rights of petitioner or his fellow Negro employees by negotiating the contracts discriminating against them.

If . . . the Act confers this power on the bargaining representative of a craft or class of employees without any commensurate statutory duty toward its members, constitutional questions arise. For the representative is clothed with power not unlike that of a legislature which is subject to constitutional limitations on its power to deny, restrict, destroy or discriminate against the rights of those for whom it legislates and which is also under an affirmative constitutional duty equally to protect those rights. If the Railway Labor Act purports to impose on petitioner and the other Negro members of the craft the legal duty to comply with the terms of a contract whereby the representative has discriminatorily restricted their employment for the benefit and advantage of the Brotherhood's own members, we must decide the constitutional questions which petitioner raises in his pleading.

But we think that Congress, in enacting the Railway Labor Act and authorizing a labor union, chosen by a majority of a craft, to represent the craft, did not intend to confer plenary power upon the union to sacrifice, for the benefit of its members, rights of the minority of the craft, without imposing on it any duty to protect the minority. Since petitioner and the other Negro members of the craft are not members of the Brotherhood or eligible for membership, the authority to act for them is derived not from their action or consent but wholly from the command of the Act. . . .

Section 2, Second, requiring carriers to bargain with the representative so chosen, operates to exclude any other from representing a craft. Virginian R. Co. v. System Federation, supra [300 U.S.] 545. The minority members of a craft are thus deprived by the statute of the right, which they would otherwise possess, to choose a representative of their own, and its members cannot bargain individually on behalf of themselves as to matters which are properly the subject of collective bargaining. Order of Railroad Telegraphers v. Railway Express Agency, 321 U.S. 342, and see under the like provisions of the [NLRA]. J.I. Case Co. v. Labor Board, 321 U.S. 332. . . .

Unless the labor union representing a craft owes some duty to represent nonunion members of the craft, at least to the extent of not discriminating against them as such in the contracts which it makes as their representative, the minority would be left with no means of protecting their interests. . . . While the majority of the craft chooses the bargaining representative, when chosen it represents . . . the craft or class, and not the majority. The fair interpretation of the statutory language is that the organization chosen to represent a craft is to represent all its members, the majority as well as the minority, and it is to act for and not against those whom it represents. It is a principle of general application that the exercise of a granted power to act in behalf of others involves the assumption toward them of a duty to exercise the power in their interest and behalf, and that such a grant of power will not be deemed to dispense with all duty toward those for whom it is exercised unless so expressed.

We think that the Railway Labor Act imposes upon the statutory representative of a craft at least as exacting a duty to protect equally the interests of the members of the craft as the Constitution imposes upon a legislature to give equal protection to the interests of those for whom it legislates. Congress has seen fit to clothe the bargaining representative with powers comparable to those possessed by a legislative body both to create and restrict the rights of those whom it represents, cf. J.I. Case Co. v. Labor Board, supra, 335, but it has also imposed on the representative a corresponding duty. We hold that the language of the Act . . . , read in the light of the purposes of the Act, expresses the aim of Congress to impose on the bargaining representative of a craft or class of employees the duty to exercise fairly the power conferred upon it in behalf of all those for whom it acts, without hostile discrimination against them.

This does not mean that the statutory representative of a craft is barred from making contracts which may have unfavorable effects on some of the members of the craft represented. Variations in the terms of the contract based on differences relevant to the authorized purposes of the contract in conditions to which they are to be applied, such as differences in seniority, the type of work performed, the competence and skill with which it is performed, are within the scope of the bargaining representation of a craft, all of whose members are not identical in their interest or merit. . . . Without attempting to mark the allowable limits . . . , it is enough for present purposes to say that the statutory power to represent a craft and to make contracts as to wages, hours and working conditions does not include the authority to make among members of the craft discriminations not based on such relevant differences. Here the discriminations based on race alone are obviously irrelevant and invidious. Congress plainly did not undertake to authorize the bargaining representative to make such discriminations. . . .

The representative which thus discriminates may be enjoined from so doing, and its members may be enjoined from taking the benefit of such discriminatory action. No more is the Railroad bound by or entitled to take the benefit of a contract which the bargaining representative is prohibited by the statute from making. In both cases the right asserted, which is derived from the duty imposed by the statute on the bargaining representative, is a federal right implied from the statute and the policy which it has adopted. It is the federal statute which condemns as unlawful the Brotherhood's conduct. . . .

So long as a labor union assumes to act as the statutory representative of a craft, it cannot rightly refuse to perform the duty, which is inseparable from the power of representation conferred upon it, to represent the entire membership of the craft. While the statute does not deny to such a bargaining labor organization the right to determine eligibility to its membership, it does require the union, in collective bargaining and in making contracts with the carrier, to represent nonunion or minority union members of the craft without hostile discrimination, fairly, impartially, and in good faith. Wherever necessary to that end, the union is required to consider requests of nonunion members of the craft and expressions of their views with respect to collective bargaining with the employer and to give to them notice of and opportunity for hearing upon its proposed action. . . .

Section 3, First (i), which provides for reference to the Adjustment Board of "disputes between an employee or group of employees and a carrier or carriers growing out of grievances or out of the interpretation or application of agreements," makes no reference to disputes between employees and their representative. Even though the dispute between the railroad and the petitioner were to be heard by the Adjustment Board, that Board could not give the entire relief here sought. The Adjustment Board has consistently declined in more than 400 cases to entertain grievance complaints by individual members of a craft represented by a labor organization. . . .

In the absence of any available administrative remedy, the right here asserted, to a remedy for breach of the statutory duty of the bargaining representative to represent and act for the members of a craft, is of judicial cognizance. That right would be sacrificed or obliterated if it were without the remedy which courts can give for breach of such a duty or obligation and which it is their duty to give in cases in which they have jurisdiction. . . .

We conclude that . . . the statute contemplates resort to the usual judicial remedies of injunction and award of damages when appropriate for breach of that duty.

The judgment is accordingly reversed and remanded for further proceedings not inconsistent with this opinion.

[Black, J., concurred in result. The concurring opinion of Murphy, J., is omitted.]

NOTES

1. Assume that a union has been recognized as the representative of, and has bargained for, a group of employees that is not covered by national legislation or by comparable state law — e.g., agricultural workers. Under state law, would the union be subject to a duty of fair representation? Cf. Lerma v. D'Arrigo Bros., 144 Cal. Rptr. 18, 77 Cal. App. 3d 836 (1978).

2. The Court in *Steele* expressly imposes a vague obligation on the incumbent union to consider, "where necessary," the requests of nonunion members with respect to the agreement that will cover them. Should such a right to be consulted extend also to union members of the bargaining unit? See Hyde, Democracy in Collective Bargaining, 93 Yale L.J. 793, 819 (1984).

3. Railway workers may not enforce their rights under collective agreements by means of court actions against their employers without first exhausting the RLA's procedures. See Andrews v. Louisville & Nashville R.R., 406 U.S. 320 (1972). However, Glover v. St. Louis-San Francisco Ry., 393 U.S. 324 (1969), indicates that where a claim of unfair representation coalesces with a claim of breach of agreement, the claimants may, at least in some circumstances, resort to the courts rather than the NRAB. In that case, eight blacks and five whites, in an action against both the railroad and the union representing car men, alleged the following: In order to avoid promoting blacks from car-men helpers to car men, the railroad, pursuant to a tacit understanding with the union, had hired apprentices, thereby violating the collective agreement. The plaintiffs had complained to both defendants and had requested the union to file a grievance, all to no avail. The processing of a grievance without the union's cooperation would have been futile, and recourse to the NRAB would have been time-consuming and useless since it is manned by paid representatives of the carriers and unions and since the defendants had a working arrangement. The defendants moved to dismiss for failure to exhaust the contractual procedure and the NRAB machinery. The grant of this motion was affirmed by the circuit court. The Supreme Court reversed and remanded the case for trial, on the ground that the remedy

provided by both the NRAB and the agreement is inadequate when both parties to the agreement are charged with collaboration in betraying the employees' interests and that the usual requirement of exhaustion of contractual and administrative remedies should be dispensed with since resort thereto would be futile. (The *Glover* exception to the exhaustion requirement is generally viewed as a narrow one. See, e.g., Rader v. United Transp. Union, 718 F.2d 1012 (11th Cir. 1983).)

4. Brotherhood of R.R. Trainmen v. Howard, 343 U.S. 768 (1952), applied the *Steele* doctrine against a union (the BRT) even though it was not the bargaining representative of the aggrieved employees. After years of pressure by the BRT (the representative of white brakemen), the carrier agreed, in effect, to discharge black "train porters" who had in fact functioned as brakemen. In upholding injunctive relief, the Court declared: "The Federal Act . . . prohibits bargaining agents from using their position and power to destroy black workers' jobs in order to bestow them on white workers. . . . Bargaining agents who enjoy the advantages of the Railway Labor Act's provisions must execute their trust without lawless invasions of the rights of other workers." Three justices dissented, urging that the porters were not brakemen and thus not entitled to fair representation by the BRT and that the challenged discrimination was private action not prohibited by federal law.

2. Unfair Representation and the NLRB

Miranda Fuel Co., 140 N.L.R.B. 181 (1962). A member of the union began an extended leave of absence three days early. The union, receiving complaints from other employees, pressed the employer to drop that employee to the bottom of the seniority list — a reduction not required by the collective agreement. A majority of the Board concluded that the union had violated §8(b)(1)(A) and §8(b)(2), reasoning as follows: The duty of fair representation is a corollary of the representative's exclusivity under §9(a) and is incorporated into §7. A bargaining agent's breach of that duty, regardless of whether it was influenced by an employee's union activities, violates §7 and §8(b)(1)(A). Furthermore, a bargaining representative's attempt to secure employer participation or acquiescence in such a violation constitutes a violation of §8(b)(2), and resultant arbitrary employer action is derivatively a violation of §§8(a)(1) and 8(a)(3). The reviewing court denied enforcement of the Board's order, in NLRB v. Miranda Fuel Co., 326 F.2d 172 (2d Cir. 1963). Only one member of the court, Judge Medina, adopted the view of the Board's dissenting members, that "discrimination for reasons wholly unrelated to 'union membership, loyalty . . . or the performance of union obligations,' is not sufficient to support findings of violations of §§8(a)(3), 8(a)(1), 8(b)(2) and 8(b)(1)(A) of the Act." Id. at 175. Judge Lumbard concurred in the result without reaching the question of whether a union's violation of the duty of fair representation constitutes per se a violation of §8(b)(1). Judge Friendly, dissenting, also passed over that question and the derivative question under §8(a)(1). He would, however, have sustained the Board's order on the basis of §§8(b)(2) and 8(a)(3). He read "discrimination" broadly — as encompassing any differential treatment based on invidious or arbitrary considerations — and concluded that the demonstration of union power to bring about such treatment would constitute "encouragement" and thereby complete a violation of §8(a)(3).

NOTES

1. Although enforcement was denied in Miranda Fuel Co., the Board has maintained that breach of the duty of fair representation constitutes an unfair labor practice, usually under §8(b)(1)(A). There is substantial judicial acceptance of that approach, dating from Rubber Workers Local 12 v. NLRB, 368 F.2d 12 (5th Cir. 1966), cert. denied, 389 U.S. 837 (1967); but the Supreme Court has yet to rule on that question. See DelCostello v. Teamsters, infra p. 1173.

2. Assume that Judge Friendly's definition of "discrimination" is operative and that an employer, organized or unorganized, discriminates in employment on racial, or on nonracial but invidious, grounds. Would the employer violate the NLRA? Cf. and consider carefully Judge Skelly Wright's novel formulation in United Packinghouse Food & Allied Workers v. NLRB, 416 F.2d 1126 (D.C. Cir.), cert. denied, 396 U.S. 903 (1969):

. . . [I]n the context of employer racial discrimination, the question reduces to whether that discrimination inhibits its victims from asserting themselves against their employer to improve their lot. . . .

This effect is twofold: (1) racial discrimination sets up an unjustified clash of interests between groups of workers which tends to reduce the likelihood and the effectiveness of their working in concert to achieve their legitimate goals under the Act; and (2) racial discrimination creates in its victims an apathy or docility which inhibits them from asserting their rights against the perpetrator of the discrimination. We find, that the confluence of these two factors sufficiently deters the exercise of Section 7 rights as to violate Section 8(a)(1).

If the foregoing views of Judge Friendly and Judge Wright are pushed to the limits of their logic, is the NLRA distinguishable from fair employment practices legislation?

3. In Pioneer Bus Co., 140 N.L.R.B. (1962), decided shortly before *Miranda*, the NLRB, invoking judicial decisions that had condemned governmental support of racially separate groupings, modified its previous toleration of "separate but equal status" for black unions and employees. Specifically, the Board declined to recognize, for contract bar purposes, separate contracts for black and white employees, respectively. Although the Board permitted the union involved to participate in the impending election, it announced that the execution of such contracts on the basis of race is "in patent derogation of the certification and would warrant revocation of certification."

4. On the eve of the passage of Title VII of the Civil Rights Act of 1964, in Independent Metal Workers Union, Local 1 (the "second" *Hughes Tool Co.* case), 147 N.L.R.B. 1573 (1964), the NLRB, after holding that a union's outright rejection of a grievance on racial grounds violated §§8(b)(1)(A), 8(b)(2) and 8(b)(3), explicitly overruled a series of prior decisions and declared that racial segregation in membership by a statutory bargaining representation "may violate §8(b)." This dictum was a response, in part, to the developing policy against racial discrimination that was to lead to the Civil Rights Act of 1964.

In this case, Chairman McCulloch and Member Fanning amplified their objections to the *Miranda* doctrine. They concurred in the majority's holding (1) that the union's certification should be revoked because the union had entered into a racially discriminatory agreement and (2) that the union had violated §8(b)(1)(A) by refusing to process a grievance filed by a black employee for the reason that he was a nonmember. They dissented, however, from the majority's reliance on the duty of fair representation, stating:

". . . [N]either §7 nor §8(b)(1)(A) mentions a duty of fair representation. The majority in the *Miranda* case, reaffirmed here, found a right to fair representation implied in §7 on the basis of the bargaining representative's implied duty of fair representation derived from its status as bargaining representative under §9.

"There are a number of reasons why this conclusion based on verbal logic does not . . . represent the intent of Congress. . . . Section 7 was part of the Wagner Act which in its unfair labor practice section was aimed only at employer conduct. The Wagner Act also contained the present §9(a). It hardly seems reasonable to infer, in these circumstances, that §7 contained a protected implied right to fair representation against the bargaining representative, when the entire Wagner Act did not make any conduct by a labor organization unlawful. Section 7 was continued substantially unchanged in the Taft-Hartley Act except for the addition of the "right to refrain" clause, which is not material [here]. . . . Although [Taft-Hartley] added union unfair labor practices . . . , neither the Act nor the legislative history contains any mention of the duty of fair representation, despite the fact that the *Steele* and *Wallace* decisions were well known. . . . Again, although in the interval between the dates of the Taft-Hartley and Landrum-Griffin Acts, there were additional court decisions and articles . . . in the law journals dealing with the legal problems of fair representation, Congress made no change in the wording of §7, and ignored the problem completely in adding a "Bill of Rights" section to [Landrum-Griffin]. If Congress had really intended that violation of the duty of fair representation should be an unfair labor practice, . . . the 1959 revision afforded it an opportunity to clear up the uncertainty. . . . We do not believe that realistically [Congress'] silence can be interpreted as . . . favorable to the contention that the right to fair representation is a protected §7 right. . . . [I]f there had been any contemporary understanding that the Act had made it an unfair labor practice for a union to fail in its duty of fair representation, the opposition would have been both strong and loud.

"There is another and more important reason why the Board should not undertake to police a union's administration of its duties without a clear mandate from Congress. The purpose of the Act is primarily to protect the organizational rights of employees. But apart from the obligation to bargain in good faith, 'Congress intended that the parties would have wide latitude in their negotiations, unrestricted by any governmental power to regulate the substantive solution of their differences.' [NLRB v. Insurance Agents' Intl. Union, 361 U.S. 477, 488.] Before *Miranda*, it was assumed that contract or grievance decisions by employers and unions were immune from examination by the Board unless they were influenced by union considerations. But, under the underlying reasoning of the *Miranda* majority . . . , the Board is now constituted a tribunal to which every employee . . . aggrieved by a bargaining representative's action, whether in contract negotiations or in grievance handling, may appeal, regardless of whether the decision has been influenced in whole or in part by considerations of union membership, loyalty, or activity. The Board must determine on such appeal, without statutory standards, whether the representative's decision was motivated by "unfair or irrelevant or invidious" considerations and therefore to be set aside, or was within the 'wide range of reasonableness . . . allowed a statutory representative in serving the unit it represents . . . ' [Ford Motor Company v. Huffman, 345 U.S. 330, 338] and to be sustained. Inevitably, the Board will have to sit in judgment on the substantive matters of collective bargaining, the very thing the Supreme Court has said the Board must not do, and in which it has no special experience or competence. This is not exaggeration. The duty of fair representation covers more than racial discrimination. *Miranda* itself did not involve a race issue and since *Miranda*, the Board has had to decide a number of other cases where allegations of violation of the duty of fair representation rested on other than racial grounds, with many more such cases disposed of at the regional level. *Miranda* means that the Board is embarking on a wholly new field of activity for which it has had no preparation, and which is likely seriously to interfere with its present activities that are already more than enough to keep it fully occupied.

"What we are confronted with is an important question of policy which should be resolved not by logomachy, but by a careful weighing of alternatives in the light of ends to be achieved. Where specific statutory rights or prohibitions are not involved, should enforcement of the duty of fair representation be left to the courts, to the Board, or both? In such circumstances, should cases of breach of this duty insofar as they involve race discrimination be treated differently from breaches involving nonracial factors? If a separate agency is created to handle the task of eliminating employment discrimination by unions and employers based on race, should the Board have a duty in this field? If so, what should it be? To ask these questions is to appreciate that the problem with which we are presented is legislative to be resolved by the Congress and not by an administrative body whose duty it is only to administer the law which Congress has written."

Is the foregoing reasoning persuasive? How is it affected by the NLRB's stated policy of revoking the certification of unions for discriminatory practices?

5. Early in negotiations, the employer stated flatly that the union's wage demands would result in the elimination of all the clerical jobs. The union, without advising the clericals whom it represented of the employer's prediction, insisted on and obtained the wage increase, and the employees ratified the proposed agreement. Thereafter, the employer terminated all the clericals. (a) Is the union's nondisclosure "unfair, irrelevant, or invidious" conduct, i.e., "arbitrary," under *Miranda*? (b) Would it be material if the union representatives, in reply to the employer's prediction, had said: "We didn't want those women in the first place"? (c) Would the union have a defense if it argues that it believed that the employer's statement was a bargaining ploy and that disclosing it to the employees would have made them anxious, dignified the employer's posturing, and weakened the employees' bargaining power? (d) Would the result be different if the §8(b)(1)(A) test of "restraint or coercion" of §7 rights, not the *Miranda*

formula, were controlling? Cf. Teamsters Local 860 v. NLRB, 652 F.2d 1022 (D.C. Cir. 1981); Local 299, Teamsters (McLean Trucking Co.), 270 N.L.R.B. No. 188, 116 L.R.R.M. 1287 (1984).

6. A collective agreement, with a view to cutting labor costs, provides that future employees should get substantially lower wages than those of current employees doing the same work. Does such a two-tier system violate the duty of fair representation? Would it be material if new entrants were preponderantly black? See generally Flax, Pay Cuts Before the Job Even Starts, 109 Fortune 75 (1984).

Barton Brands, Ltd. v. NLRB
529 F.2d 793 (7th Cir. 1976)

[On August 31, 1969, Glencoe sold all its assets to Barton. Glencoe then had only six active employees and more than twenty employees on layoff. Each company's employees comprised a separate bargaining unit, represented by the union.]

BAUER, J. . . . Shortly after the sale, Barton and the Union began negotiations regarding integration of the bargaining units at the two plants. At separate meetings for the Barton and Glencoe employees, Paul Kraus, Barton's Chief Operations Officer . . . , explained that Barton's business was expanding and that the firm, among other developments, planned to build a new bottling facility at the site of the Glencoe plant. He told the employees that he felt their best interests would be served if the two units were integrated and the employees' seniority dovetailed; i.e., former Glencoe employees would be given full credit for seniority accumulated at Glencoe and both groups of employees would be placed on one combined seniority list.[5] Both the Barton and Glencoe employees voted in favor of dovetailing and the collective bargaining agreement between Barton and the Union was amended to reflect the plan.

Barton did not build the new facility. Within a year of the purchase, engineering studies showed the site to be unfeasible for bottling. A plan to build on a different site was abandoned when Barton sold its Canadian Mist brand, which accounted for about one-third of its business. Following these events, Barton laid off some employees and other employees began to worry about their job security. One manifestation of this apprehension was a dissat-

---

[5] The dovetailing plan benefited the former Glencoe employees by greatly increasing their job security, including the return to work of the laid off employees, and benefited the Barton employees by providing them the opportunity to transfer to the proposed new plant, a right which they were told they would not have if the units remained separate.

isfaction among some Barton employees with the dovetailing of the former Glencoe employees, which they saw as causing employees to be laid off despite having worked at Barton longer than employees who had received credit for their time worked at Glencoe.

. . . [B]efore June, 1972, the expiration date of the Barton collective bargaining agreement, the Union leadership canvassed the unit employees requesting suggestions for contract changes. One of the suggestions received was a proposal that the former Glencoe employees be endtailed; i.e., that they be placed on the seniority list below all Barton employees who were hired before Barton's purchase of Glencoe.[7] The Union presented the proposal to Barton during negotiations. Although Barton first rejected it, expressing some doubts about its legality, the parties ultimately agreed that for the purposes of layoff and recall, the seniority of the former Glencoe employees would be calculated from September 1, 1969, the day Barton acquired the Glencoe site. For all other purposes, including choice of jobs while working, vacations, and other benefits, the dovetail provision remained in effect. The parties reached agreement on September 22, 1972, and the Union membership ratified the contract on October 12.

During the [negotiation-ratification] period . . . , an average of 223 active employees [were] on the Barton payroll, twelve of whom were former Glencoe employees. As a result of the endtailing provision . . . , twelve former Glencoe employees suffered layoffs that would not have occurred if they had been permitted to retain their seniority from Glencoe.

At the request of a laid off former Glencoe employee, the Board's General Counsel filed complaints against the Union and Barton charging them respectively with violations of §§8(b)(2) and 8(b)(1)(A) and §§8(a)(3) and 8(a)(1). . . . The Board, [reversing the ALJ, found] that the Union breached its duty of fair representation by effecting the reduction in seniority and the layoff of the former Glencoe employees "largely, if not solely, for the reason to advance the political cause of Union official Ken Cecil." 213 N.L.R.B. No. 71 at 5. They found Barton liable for acquiescing in the Union breach.

The Board reached its finding regarding the Union's motivation on evidence which indicated that Cecil, Vice-President of Local 23 and the highest Union officer at Barton . . . , attended a January 1972 meeting with an international vice-president of the Union at which some Barton

---

[7] Prior to this time, a group of original Barton employees had obtained an attorney's opinion which found the dovetailing agreement not binding since it was based on an unfulfilled condition precedent—the building of the new bottling plant. Rather than take immediate action to rescind the agreement, the attorney recommended that the employees eliminate it during the next regular contract negotiations.

employees discussed the elimination of the dovetailing agreement, was part of a group that obtained an attorney's opinion concerning the legality of eliminating the agreement, presented the endtailing proposal to the Union contract negotiating committee, and claimed responsibility for the proposal during the contract negotiations and during his successful campaign for reelection to his Union office in November and December, 1972, which immediately followed the signing of the new contract.

    . . . [T]he Union alleges that (1) there is not substantial evidence on the record to support the [Board's] finding that the Union changed the Glencoe employees' seniority in order to further Cecil's political ambitions, (2) the change in seniority could not have violated §8(b)(2) . . . since the Glencoe employees were not discriminated against on the basis of union membership or activity, and (3) even if the seniority change was illegal discrimination under §8(b)(2), the Union's good faith is a defense to the charge against it. . . .

II

. . . The Board's determination that Cecil championed the endtailing of the former Glencoe employees to curry favor with the majority of the Barton employees in order to enhance his candidacy in the upcoming election is sustained by the evidence, but the Board's reasoning that Cecil's efforts are chargeable to the Union as a whole and that the enhancement of the Cecil candidacy was the motivating factor behind the endtailing decision is not borne out by the evidence. . . . Cecil's actions, which the Board attributes to the Union, were not undertaken in his capacity as a union officer but were undertaken in his own behalf as a candidate for union office. The only activity which the Board cites that Cecil undertook in his capacity as an officer was the presenting of the endtailing proposal to the union negotiating committee, an innocent act in which he served as the conduit for a rank and file proposal previously formulated.

    Furthermore, the situation at bar is distinguishable from one involving the attribution of union officers' conduct since the Board here is using Cecil's conduct to determine the *reason* behind the Union's action rather than whether the action has occurred. Looking to officers' conduct in order to determine the *actus reus* of union misconduct is entirely appropriate. If officers' actions cannot be charged to the union, unfair labor practices would rarely be found since the union normally acts through its representatives. But to look to officers' conduct to determine the reasons for union action is not always appropriate since the officers' motivations are not always the same as the motivations of the union as a whole.

    The case at hand presents an example of such disparity in motivation.

The record clearly indicates that the endtailing proposal arose out of rank and file apprehension about job security, not out of a Union desire to reelect Cecil. . . .

The evidence of rank and file motivation for the endtailing is so strong that we cannot accept the Board finding that the Union acted primarily to further Cecil's political ambitions. Since this finding is the basis for the Board's order charging the Union and Barton with unfair labor practices, the entire order must fall.

III

This does not necessarily end the case. If we think the Board's order may be sustained on other grounds, we must remand. . . . S.E.C. v. Chenery Corp., 318 U.S. 80 (1943). In this case we think sufficient grounds do exist to support a Board order and we will outline them to justify our remand and to aid the Board in its reconsideration of the case.

The record suggests that the union acted soley on grounds of political expediency in reducing the former Glencoe employees' seniority.[14] While a union may make seniority decisions within "a wide range of reasonableness . . . in serving the [interests of the] unit it represents," Ford Motor Co. v. Huffman, 345 U.S. 330, 338 (1950), such decisions may not be made *solely* for the benefit of a stronger, more politically favored group over a minority group. To allow such arbitrary decisionmaking is contrary to the union's duty of fair representation. . . . Such conduct has been held to constitute an unfair labor practice, Truck Drivers and Helpers, Local Union 568, Teamsters v. NLRB (Red Ball Motor Freight), 379 F.2d 137, 142 (1967), or a breach of the union's duty of fair representation as developed by the courts independent of unfair labor practice proceedings. Gainey v. Brotherhood of Railway and Steamship Clerks, 313 F.2d 318, 324 (3d Cir. 1963). . . .

Contrary to the Union's contention that no unfair labor practice can be found here since the alleged discrimination was not based on union member-

[14]There is no merit to the argument raised by both the Union and Barton that the Glencoe employees received a "windfall" as a result of the initial dovetailing which could properly be revoked. Not only is the windfall characterization an exaggeration since the dovetailing caused Glencoe employees to by-pass other employment when they came to work for Barton, but the origingal Barton employees voted for the dovetailing to further their own self-interest. See n.5, supra.

The argument that the endtailing is proper since Barton's decision not to build a new bottling plant was a failure to fulfill a condition precedent to the initial dovetailing agreement also is without merit. There is no express condition precedent in the agreement itself and there is nothing in the record which suggests that the building of a new plant was an implied condition precedent.

ship or activity, the Board and the courts in recent years have consistently held that a union violates §8(b)(2) when it causes an employer to discriminate against employees on arbitrary, hostile or bad faith grounds since such conduct causes or tends to result in unlawful encouragement of union activity. . . . These holdings reflect "a recognition that the union's ability to effect this kind of discrimination is likely to have an intimidating effect on [other] workers . . . ," NLRB v. International Longshoremen's Assoc., Local 1581, [489 F.2d 635, 638 (5th Cir. 1974), *cert. denied*, 419 U.S. 1040]. Thus, "Section 8(b)(2) is not concerned solely with situations where the discrimination involved is between union members and nonmembers or between 'good' members and 'bad or indifferent' members. . . . It applies where the union has induced the employer to discriminate on the basis of any invidious or arbitrary classification. . . . " Id. at 637. See Radio Officers Union v. NLRB, 347 U.S. 17, 39-42.

. . . [P]roof of good faith on the part of a union is not a defense to a charge based on the duty of fair representation since arbitrary conduct without evidence of bad faith has been held by this Circuit to constitute a breach of the duty. . . .

Furthermore, the cases cited . . . for the proposition that the endtailing of employees from an acquired firm into a unit of employees from the acquiring firm is permissible are distinguishable from the case at bar. . . . [Those cases] all involved endtailing decisions made at the time of the initial acquisition rather than after the employees had been dovetailed into the acquiring firm's unit. In these cases the affected employees, unlike the employees in the case at bar, did not lose benefits they believed they were entitled to, nor were they prejudiced by relinquishing other employment opportunities in reliance on the dovetailing arrangement.

Associated Transport, Inc., 185 N.L.R.B. 631 (1970), involved the union revocation of a dovetailing arrangement, but unlike the case at bar, the employees did not lose expected benefits nor were they otherwise unduly prejudiced since the union never acquiesced in the initial dovetailing, which was instituted through a disputed arbitration proceeding.

The only federal case in point on endtailing which we have found is Hargrove v. Brotherhood of Locomotive Engineers, 116 F. Supp. 3 (D.D.C. 1953), which holds that a cause of action for a breach of the union's duty of fair representation lies when, three years after the acquisition of a firm, the union abolishes seniority rights previously given employees for preacquisition work with the acquired firm. This case squarely supports our conclusion that an unfair labor practice may have been committed here. . . .

In summary, since the established seniority rights of a minority of the

Barton employees have been abridged . . . for no apparent reason other than political expediency, there seem to be sufficient grounds . . . to support the Board order. We thus are remanding . . . for a determination whether the Union violated its duty of fair representation . . . by successfully negotiating for the endtailing proposal. In making its determination, the Board should consider that in order to be absolved of liability the Union must show some objective justification for its conduct beyond that of placating the desires of the majority of the unit employees at the expense of the minority.

IV

In addition to challenging the . . . finding that the Union had committed an unfair labor practice, Barton challenges the Board's order on . . . [the ground that the Board failed] to expressly find an improper motive for Barton's acquiescence in the endtailing. . . .

Since [*Radio Officers*, supra p. 279] the Supreme Court has attempted to delineate the types of discrimination for which specific proof of intent is not necessary. . . . In *Great Dane* [388 U.S. 26] the Supreme Court . . . came up with "several principles of controlling importance":

> First, if it can reasonably be concluded that the employer's discriminatory conduct was "inherently destructive" of important employee rights, no proof of an antiunion motivation is needed and the Board can find an unfair labor practice even if the employer introduces evidence that the conduct was motivated by business considerations. Second, if the adverse effect of the discriminatory conduct on employee rights is "comparatively slight," an antiunion motivation must be proved to sustain the charge if the employer has come forward with evidence of legitimate and substantial business justifications for the conduct. Thus, in either situation, once it has been proved that the employer engaged in discriminatory conduct which could have adversely affected employee rights to some extent, the burden is upon the employer to establish that he was motivated by legitimate objectives since proof of motivation is most accessible to him.

388 U.S. at 34.

Since there is adequate evidence on the record showing that the endtailing proposal is discriminatory conduct which has at least a "comparatively slight" effect on employee rights, the *Great Dane* analysis should be applied by the Board. . . .

Enforcement denied and case remanded.

[The NLRB, on remand, based its findings of violations of §§8(b)(1)(A), 8(b)(2), and 8(a)(3) on (1) the union's failure to show, as required by the court of appeals, "objective justification" for impairing the seniority rights arising from the "dovetailing" agreement; (2) the lack of merit in the contention that the dovetailing provision was to be effective only if a new plant were built; (3) the employer's failure to show that "legitimate objectives" had motivated its actions; and (4) the lack of merit in the employer's professed ignorance of the illegality of the union's conduct, since the union's "endtailing" proposal was unlawful under ordinary circumstances. See 228 N.L.R.B. 889 (1977).

According to the company's lawyer, the dispute was later settled by the company's paying $300,000 in back pay and reinstating 50 employees.]

NOTES

1. On remand of the principal case, the employer's derivative §8(a)(3) violation was based on its failure to carry the probative burdens imposed by *Great Dane*. Should *Great Dane* apply to arrangements collectively bargained, as distinguished from unilateral employer conduct?

Consider the following: A union official revoked prior union approval of an employee's temporary work assignment, without consulting the employee or attempting to accommodate her need to find a companion for her blind mother. This revocation was not based on the bargaining agreement or on union policy but on the union official's personal view that such temporary assignments should be limited to 30 days. The employer, relying honestly and reasonably on its interpretation of the agreement (and a related arbitration award), acquiesced in the union's actions, believing that, absent union approval, the agreement's overtime provisions would be applicable. The employer neither knew or had reason to know of the official's motivation for the revocation.

(a) Has the union violated its duty of fair representation? (b) Has the employer violated §8(a)(1) and 8(a)(3)? See NLRB v. Postal Wrks., 618 F.2d 1249 (8th Cir. 1980), and Note 2 following *Great Dane*, supra p. 340.

2. The collective agreement permitted the union to determine annually the employees' wishes as to whether days off should be on a fixed or a rotating basis. The union's referendum meeting on that question excluded nonunion unit employees and denied them the right to vote or be heard. Under *Barton Brands*, has the union breached its duty? Is this situation distinguishable from contract ratification, which generally may lawfully be restricted to union members? Cf. Branch 6000, National Assn. of Letter Carriers v. NLRB, 595 F.2d 808 (D.C. Cir. 1979).

3. Suppose that the union, after considering all factors, including the

expectancies of Barton's long-time employees, the wishes of the majority of employees, and the prospects for industrial peace, had originally rejected dovetailing; and the employer had agreed. Would the union have defaulted on its duty of fair representation? In the principal case, suppose that the union, after considering the changes in circumstances following the purchase and the other factors listed above, had recommended that dovetailing be superseded by endtailing and the employer had agreed. Would any unfair labor practices have been committed? See generally Ekas v. Carling Natl. Breweries, 602 F.2d 664 (4th Cir. 1979), *cert. denied,* 444 U.S. 1017 (1980); King v. Space Carriers, Inc., 608 F.2d 285 (8th Cir. 1979).

4. For consideration of the union's duty of fair representation in negotiating and administering a collective agreement, see Blumrosen, The Worker and Three Phases of Unionism: Administrative and Judicial Control of the Worker-Union Relationship, 61 Mich. L. Rev. 1435 (1963); Clark, The Duty of Fair Representation: A Theoretical Structure, 51 Tex. L. Rev. 1119 (1973); Finkin, The Limits of Majority Rule in Collective Bargaining, 64 Minn. L. Rev. 183 (1980) (including, at 196-236, discussion of a union's handling of seniority problems arising from mergers or other business changes); Leffler, Piercing the Duty of Fair Representation: The Dichotomy Between Negotiations and Grievance Handling, 1979 Ill. L.F. 35. See also Freed, Polsby & Spitzer, Unions, Fairness, and the Conundrums of Collective Choice, 56 S. Cal. L. Rev. 461 (1983) (maintaining that there exists no "intelligible general rule of distributive or procedural fairness that may be interposed by a court to overrule the discretionary decisions made by a union in bargaining for its constituents"); Hyde, Can Judges Identify Fair Bargaining Procedures?: A Comment on Freed, Polsby & Spitzer, 57 S. Cal. L. Rev. 415 (1984); Freed, Polsby & Spitzer, A Reply to Hyde, Can Judges Identify Fair Bargaining Procedures? 57 S. Cal. L. Rev. 425 (1984).

3. Collective Agreements, Fair Representation, and Individual Rights

Vaca v. Sipes
386 U.S. 171 (1967)

WHITE, J. On February 13, 1962, Benjamin Owens[c] filed this class action against petitioners, as officers and representatives of the National

---

[c] [After Owens' death, Sipes, his administrator, was substituted for him as appellant in an appeal from the trial court's setting aside of the jury verdict on the ground that state jurisdiction had been preempted. — EDS.]

Brotherhood of Packinghouse Workers' and of its Kansas City Local No. 12 (the Union), in [a Missouri court]. Owens, a Union member, alleged that he had been discharged from his employment at Swift & Company's (Swift) Kansas City [plant] in violation of the collective bargaining agreement . . . between Swift and the Union, and that the Union had "arbitrarily, capriciously and without just or reasonable reason or cause" refused to take his grievance with Swift to arbitration under the fifth step of the bargaining agreement's grievance procedures. . . .

I

In mid-1959, Owens, a long-time high blood pressure patient, . . . entered a hospital on sick leave from his employment with Swift. After a long rest . . . , Owens was certified by his family physician as fit to resume his heavy work. . . . However, Swift's company doctor examined Owens upon his return and concluded that his blood pressure was too high to permit reinstatement. After securing a second authorization from another outside doctor, Owens returned to the plant . . . on January 6, 1960. However, on January 8, when the doctor discovered Owens' return, he was permanently discharged on the ground of poor health.

   . . . Owens then sought the union's help in securing reinstatement, and a grievance was filed. . . . By mid-November 1960, the grievance had been processed through the third and into the fourth step of the grievance procedure. . . . Swift adhered to its position that Owens' poor health justified his discharge, rejecting numerous medical reports of [his] reduced blood pressure [as not being] based upon sufficiently thorough medical tests.

   On February 6, 1961, the Union sent Owens to a new doctor at Union expense "to see if we could get some better medical evidence so that we could go to arbitration. . . ." This examination did not support Owens' position. When the Union received the report, its executive board voted not to take the Owens grievance to arbitration. . . . Union officers suggested to Owens that he accept Swift's offer of referral to a rehabilitation center, and the grievance was suspended for that purpose. Owens rejected this alternative and demanded that the Union take his grievance to arbitration, but the Union refused. With his contractual remedies thus stalled at the fourth step, Owens brought this suit. The grievance was finally dismissed by the Union and Swift shortly before trial began in June 1964.[4]

   . . . [T]he trial judge instructed [the jury] that petitioners would be liable if Swift had wrongfully discharged Owens and if the Union had "arbitrarily . . . and without just cause or excuse . . . refused" to press

---

[4] No notice of the dismissal was given to Owens, who by that time had filed a second suit against Swift for breach of contract. The suit against Swift is still pending in a pretrial stage.

Owens' grievance to arbitration. Punitive damages could also be awarded, the trial judge charged, if the Union's conduct was "willful, wanton and malicious." However, the jury must return a verdict for the defendants, the judge instructed, "if you find and believe from the evidence that the union and its representatives acted reasonably and in good faith in the handling and processing of the grievance of the plaintiff." The jury then returned the general verdict for Owens which eventually was reinstated by the Missouri Supreme Court. . . .

II

[After finding that Owens' complaint stated a breach of the union's statutory duty of fair representation, the Court traced the career of *Miranda Fuel* and noted that Local 12, United Rubber Workers v. NLRB, 368 F.2d 12 (5th Cir. 1966), *cert. denied*, 389 U.S. 837 (1967), had upheld the Board's *Miranda* doctrine and had indicated that it would "preempt judicial cognizance of some fair representation suits." The Court in Part II (A) of its opinion then referred to exceptions to preemption, mentioned the NLRB's belated enforcement of fair representation, and questioned whether the Board is more expert than the judiciary with respect to such enforcement.]

   In addition to the above considerations, the unique interests served by the duty of fair representation doctrine have a profound effect . . . on the applicability of the preemption rule to this class of cases. . . . The collective bargaining system as encouraged by Congress and administered by the NLRB of necessity subordinates the interests of an individual employee to the collective interests of all employees in a bargaining unit. See, e.g., J.I. Case Co. v. Labor Board, 321 U.S. 332. This Court recognized in *Steele* that the congressional grant of power to a union to act as exclusive collective bargaining representative . . . would raise grave constitutional problems if unions were free to exercise this power to further racial discrimination. 323 U.S., at 198-199. . . . Were we to hold, as petitioners and the Government urge, that the courts are foreclosed by the NLRB's *Miranda Fuel* decision from this traditional supervisory jurisdiction, the individual employee injured by arbitrary or discriminatory union conduct could no longer be assured of impartial review of his complaint, since the Board's General Counsel has unreviewable discretion to refuse to institute an unfair labor practice complaint. The existence of even a small group of cases in which the Board would be unwilling or unable to remedy a union's breach of duty would frustrate the basic purposes underlying the duty of fair representation doctrine. For these reasons, we cannot assume from the NLRB's tardy assumption of jurisdiction in these cases that Congress, when it enacted NLRA §8(b) in 1947, intended to oust the courts of their traditional jurisdiction to curb arbitrary conduct by the individual employee's statutory representative.

There are also some intensely practical considerations which foreclose preemption of . . . fair representation duty suits, considerations which emerge from the intricate relationship between the duty of fair representation and the enforcement of collective bargaining contracts. For the fact is that the question of whether a union has breached its duty of fair representation will in many cases be a critical issue in a suit under §301 charging an employer with a breach of contract. To illustrate, let us assume a collective bargaining agreement that limits discharges to those for good cause and that contains no grievance, arbitration or other provisions purporting to restrict access to the courts. If an employee is discharged without cause, either the union or the employee may sue the employer under §301. Under this section, courts have jurisdiction . . . even though the conduct of the employer which is challenged as a breach of contract is also arguably an unfair labor practice within the jurisdiction of the NLRB. *Garmon* and like cases have no application to §301 suits. Smith v. Evening News Assn., 371 U.S. 195.

The rule is the same with regard to preemption where the bargaining agreement contains grievance and arbitration provisions which are intended to provide the exclusive remedy for breach of contract claims. If an employee is discharged without cause in violation of such an agreement, that the employer's conduct may be an unfair labor practice does not preclude a suit by the union against the employer to compel arbitration of the employee's grievance, the adjudication of the claim by the arbitrator, or a suit to enforce the resulting arbitration award.

However, if the wrongfully discharged employee himself resorts to the courts before the grievance procedures have been fully exhausted, the employer may well defend on the ground that the exclusive remedies provided by such a contract have not been exhausted. Since the employee's claim is based upon breach of the collective bargaining agreement, he is bound by terms of that agreement which govern the manner in which contractual rights may be enforced. For this reason, it is settled that the employee must at least attempt to exhaust exclusive grievance and arbitration procedures established by the bargaining agreement. Republic Steel Corp. v. Maddox, 379 U.S. 650. However, because these contractual remedies have been devised and are often controlled by the union and the employer, they may well prove unsatisfactory or unworkable for the individual grievant. The problem then is to determine under what circumstances the individual employee may obtain judicial review of his breach-of-contract claim despite his failure to secure relief through the contractual remedial procedures.

An obvious situation in which the employee should not be limited to the . . . procedures established by the contract occurs when the conduct of the employer amounts to a repudiation of those contractual procedures. Cf.

Drake Bakeries v. Bakery Workers, 370 U.S. 254, 260-263. . . . In such a situation (and there may of course be others), the employer is estopped by his own conduct to rely on the unexhausted grievance . . . procedures as a defense to the employee's cause of action.

. . . [A]nother situation when the employee may seek judicial enforcement of his contractual rights arises if, as is true here, the union has sole power under the contract to invoke the higher stages of the grievance procedure, *and* if, as is alleged here, the employee-plaintiff has been prevented from exhausting his contractual remedies by the union's *wrongful* refusal to process the grievance. It is true that the employer in such a situation may have done nothing to prevent exhaustion of the exclusive contractual remedies. . . . But the employer has committed a wrongful discharge in breach of that agreement, a breach which could be remedied through the grievance process to the employee-plaintiff's benefit were it not for the union's breach of its statutory duty of fair representation to the employee. To leave the employee remediless in such circumstances would . . . be a great injustice. We cannot believe that Congress . . . intended to confer upon unions such unlimited discretion to deprive injured employees of all remedies for breach of contract. Nor do we think that Congress intended to shield employers from the natural consequences of their breaches of bargaining agreements by wrongful union conduct in the enforcement of such agreements.

For these reasons, we think the wrongfully discharged employee may bring an action against his employer in the face of a defense based upon the failure to exhaust contractual remedies, provided the employee can prove that the union as bargaining agent breached its duty of fair representation in its handling of the employee's grievance. We may assume for present purposes that such a breach of duty by the union is an unfair labor practice, as the NLRB and the Fifth Circuit have held. The employee's suit against the employer, however, remains a §301 suit, and the jurisdiction of the courts is no more destroyed by the fact that the employee, as part and parcel of his §301 action, finds it necessary to prove an unfair labor practice by the union, than it is by the fact that the suit may involve an unfair labor practice by the employer himself. The court is free to determine whether the employee is barred by the actions of his union representative, and, if not, to proceed with the case. And if, to facilitate his case, the employee joins the union as a defendant, the situation is not substantially changed. The action is still a §301 suit, and the jurisdiction of the courts is not preempted under [*Garmon*]. . . . And, insofar as adjudication of the union's breach of duty is concerned, the result should be no different if the employee, as Owens did here, sues the employer and the union in separate actions. There would be very little to commend a rule which would permit the Missouri courts to adjudicate the Union's conduct in an action against Swift but not in an action against the Union itself.

. . . [I]t is obvious that the courts will be compelled to pass upon whether there has been a breach of the duty of fair representation in the context of many §301 breach-of-contract actions. If a breach of duty by the union and a breach of contract by the employer are proven, the court must fashion an appropriate remedy. Presumably, in at least some cases, the union's breach of duty will have enhanced or contributed to the employee's injury. What possible sense could there be in a rule which would permit a court that has litigated the fault of employer and union to fashion a remedy only with respect to the employer? Under such a rule, either the employer would be compelled by the court to pay for the union's wrong — slight deterrence, indeed, to future union misconduct — or the injured employee would be forced to go to two tribunals to repair a single injury. Moreover, the Board would be compelled in many cases either to remedy injuries arising out of a breach of contract, a task which Congress has not assigned to it, or to leave the individual employee without remedy for the union's wrong.[12] Given the strong reasons for not preempting duty of fair representation suits in general, and the fact that the courts in many §301 suits must adjudicate whether the union has breached its duty, we conclude that the courts may also fashion remedies for such a breach of duty. . . .

III

Petitioners contend . . . that Owens failed to prove that the Union breached its duty of fair representation in its handling of Owens' grievance. Petitioners also argue that the Supreme Court of Missouri, in rejecting this contention, applied a standard that is inconsistent with governing principles of federal law with respect to the Union's duty to an individual employee in its processing of grievances. . . . We agree with both contentions.

A

. . . [T]he question which the Missouri Supreme Court thought dispositive of the issue of liability was whether the evidence supported Owens' assertion

---

[12] Assuming for the moment that Swift breached the collective agreement in discharging Owens and that the Union breached its duty in handling Owens' grievance, this case illustrates the difficulties that would result from a rule preempting the courts from remedying the Union's breach of duty. If Swift did not "participate" in the Union's unfair labor practice, the Board would have no jurisdiction to remedy Swift's breach of contract. Yet a court might be equally unable to give Owens full relief in a §301 suit against Swift. Should the court award damages against Swift for Owens' full loss, even if it concludes that part of that loss was caused by the Union's breach of duty? Or should it award Owens only partial recovery hoping that the Board will make him whole? These remedy problems are difficult enough when one tribunal has all parties before it; they are impossible if two independent tribunals, with different procedures, time limitations, and remedial powers, must participate.

that he had been wrongfully discharged by Swift, regardless of the Union's good faith in reaching a contrary conclusion. This was also the major concern of the plaintiff at trial: the bulk of Owens' evidence was directed at whether he was medically fit at the time of discharge and whether he had performed heavy work after that discharge.

A breach of the statutory duty of fair representation occurs only when a union's conduct toward a member of the collective bargaining unit is arbitrary, discriminatory, or in bad faith. . . . There has been considerable debate over the extent of this duty in the context of a union's enforcement of the grievance and arbitration procedures in a collective bargaining agreement. . . . Some have suggested that every individual employee should have the right to have his grievance taken to arbitration.[13] . . .

Though we accept the proposition that a union may not arbitrarily ignore a meritorious grievance or process it in perfunctory fashion, we do not agree that the individual employee has an absolute right to have his grievance taken to arbitration regardless of the provisions of the applicable collective bargaining agreement. . . . [In giving] the union discretion to supervise the grievance machinery and to invoke arbitration, the employer and the union contemplate that each will endeavor in good faith to settle grievances short of arbitration. Through this settlement process, frivolous grievances are ended prior to the most costly and time-consuming step in the grievance procedures. Moreover, both sides are assured that similar complaints will be treated consistently, and major problem areas in the interpretation of the collective bargaining contract can be isolated and perhaps resolved. . . .

If the individual employee could compel arbitration of his grievance regardless of its merit, the settlement machinery provided by the contract would be substantially undermined, thus destroying the employer's confidence in the union's authority. . . . Moreover, under such a rule, a significantly greater number of grievances would proceed to arbitration. This would greatly increase the cost of the grievance machinery and could so overburden the arbitration process as to prevent it from functioning successfully. . . . It can well be doubted whether the parties to collective bargaining agreements would long continue to provide for . . . procedures of the kind encouraged by . . . §203(d), if their power to settle the majority of grievances short of the costlier and more time-consuming steps was limited by a rule permitting the grievant unilaterally to invoke arbitration. Nor do we see substantial danger to the interests of the individual employee if his statutory agent is given the contractual power honestly and in good faith to settle grievances short of arbitration. . . .

---

[13] See Donnelly v. United Fruit Co, 40 N.J. 61, 190 A.2d 825; . . . Murphy, The Duty of Fair Representation under Taft-Hartley, 30 Mo. L. Rev. 373, 389 (1965); Summers, Individual Rights in Collective Agreements and Arbitration, 37 N.Y.U.L. Rev. 362 (1962).

For these same reasons, the standard applied here by the Missouri Supreme Court cannot be sustained. For if a union's decision that a particular grievance lacks sufficient merit to justify arbitration would constitute a breach of the duty of fair representation because a judge or jury later found the grievance meritorious, the union's incentive to settle such grievances short of arbitration would be seriously reduced. The dampening effect on the entire grievance procedure . . . would surely be substantial. Since the union's statutory duty of fair representation protects the individual employee from arbitrary abuses of the settlement device by providing him with recourse against both employer (in a §301 suit) and union, this severe limitation on the power to settle grievances is neither necessary nor desirable. . . .

B

. . . [W]e cannot uphold the jury's award, for we conclude that as a matter of federal law the evidence does not support a verdict that the Union breached its duty of fair representation. . . .

In administering the grievance and arbitration machinery as statutory agent of the employees, a union must, in good faith and in a nonarbitrary manner, make decisions as to the merits of particular grievances. See Humphrey v. Moore, 375 U.S. 335, 349-350; Ford Motor Co. v. Huffman, 345 U.S. 330, 337-339. In a case such as this, when Owens supplied the Union with medical evidence supporting his position, the Union might well have breached its duty had it ignored Owens' complaint or had it processed the grievance in a perfunctory manner. . . . But here the Union processed the grievance into the fourth step, attempted to gather sufficient evidence to prove Owens' case, attempted to secure for Owens less vigorous work at the plant, and joined in the employer's efforts to have Owens rehabilitated. Only when these efforts all proved unsuccessful did the Union conclude both that arbitration would be fruitless and that the grievance should be dismissed. There was no evidence that any Union officer was personally hostile to Owens or that the Union acted at any time other than in good faith. Having concluded that the individual employee has no absolute right to have his grievance arbitrated under the collective bargaining agreement at issue, and that a breach of the duty of fair representation is not established merely by proof that the underlying grievance was meritorious, we must conclude that that duty was not breached here.

. . . [T]here is another important reason why the judgment of the Missouri Supreme Court cannot stand. Owens' suit against the Union was grounded on his claim that Swift had discharged him in violation of the applicable collective bargaining agreement. In his complaint, Owens alleged "that, as a direct result of said wrongful breach of said contract, by employer . . . Plaintiff was damaged in the sum of Six Thousand, Five

Hundred ($6,500) Dollars per year, continuing until the date of trial." For the Union's role in "preventing Plaintiff from completely exhausting administrative remedies," Owens requested, and the jury awarded, compensatory damages for the above-described breach of contract plus punitive damages of $3,000. . . . We hold that such damages are not recoverable from the Union in the circumstances of this case.

The appropriate remedy for a breach of a union's duty of fair representation must vary with the circumstances of the particular breach. In this case, the employee's complaint was that the Union wrongfully failed to afford him the arbitration remedy against his employer established by the collective bargaining agreement. But the damages sought by Owens were primarily those suffered because of the employer's alleged breach of contract. Assuming for the moment that Owens had been wrongfully discharged, Swift's only defense to a direct action for breach of contract would have been the Union's failure to resort to arbitration, compare Republic Steel Corp. v. Maddox, 379 U.S. 650, with Smith v. Evening News Assn., 371 U.S. 195, and if that failure was itself a violation of the Union's statutory duty to the employee, there is no reason to exempt the employer from contractual damages which he would otherwise have had to pay. The difficulty lies in fashioning an appropriate scheme of remedies.

Petitioners urge that an employee be restricted in such circumstances to a decree compelling the employer and the union to arbitrate the underlying grievance. It is true that the employee's action is based on the employer's alleged breach of contract plus the union's alleged wrongful failure to afford him his contractual remedy of arbitration. For this reason, an order compelling arbitration should be viewed as one of the available remedies when a breach of the union's duty is proved. But we see no reason inflexibly to require arbitration in all cases. In some cases, for example, at least part of the employee's damages may be attributable to the union's breach of duty, and an arbitrator may have no power under the bargaining agreement to award such damages against the union. In other cases, the arbitrable issues may be substantially resolved in the course of trying the fair representation controversy. In such situations, the court should be free to decide the contractual claim and to award the employee appropriate damages or equitable relief. . . .

The governing principle, then, is to apportion liability between the employer and the union according to the damage caused by the fault of each.[18] Thus, damages attributable solely to the employer's breach of con-

---

[18] We are not dealing here with situations where a union has affirmatively caused the employer to commit the alleged breach of contract. In cases of that sort where the union's conduct is found to be an unfair labor practice, the NLRB has found an unfair labor practice by the employer, too, and has held the union and the employer jointly and severally liable for

tract should not be charged to the union, but increases if any in those damages caused by the union's refusal to process the grievance should not be charged to the employer. In this case, even if the Union had breached its duty, all or almost all of Owens' damages would still be attributable to his allegedly wrongful discharge by Swift. For these reasons, even if the Union here had properly been found liable for a breach of duty, it is clear that the damage award was improper.

Reversed.

Rev'd

FORTAS, J., with whom the CHIEF JUSTICE and HARLAN, J., join, concurring in the result. . . . There is no basis for failure to apply the preemption principle in the present case, and . . . strong reason for its application. The relationship between the union and the individual employee with respect to the processing of claims to employment rights under the collective bargaining agreement is fundamental to the design and operation of federal labor law. . . . It "presents difficult problems of definition of status, problems which we have held are precisely 'of a kind most wisely entrusted initially to the agency charged with the day-to-day administration of the Act as a whole.'" Iron Workers v. Perko, supra, 373 U.S., at 706. Accordingly, the judgment of the Supreme Court of Missouri should be reversed and the complaint dismissed . . . on this basis. I agree, however, that if it were assumed that jurisdiction of the subject matter exists, the judgment would still have to be reversed because of the use by the Missouri court of an improper standard for measuring the union's duty. . . .

I regret the elaborate discussion in the Court's opinion of problems which are irrelevant. This is not an action by the employee against the employer, and the discussion of the requisites of such an action is, in my judgment, unnecessary. The Court argues that the employee could sue the employer under §301; and that to maintain such an action the employee would have to show that he has exhausted his remedies under the collective bargaining agreement, or alternatively that he was prevented from doing so because the union breached its duty to him by failure completely to process his claim. That may be; or maybe all he would have to show to maintain an action against the employer for wrongful discharge is that he demanded that the union process his claim to exhaustion of available remedies, and that it refused to do so.[3] I see no need for the Court to pass upon that question,

---

any back pay found owing to the particular employee who was the subject of their joint discrimination. E.g., Imparato Stevedoring Corp., 113 N.L.R.B. 883 (1955). Even if this approach would be appropriate for analogous §301 and breach-of-duty suits, it is not applicable here. Since the Union played no part in Swift's alleged breach of contract and since Swift took no part in the Union's alleged breach of duty, joint liability for either wrong would be unwarranted. [This footnote number has been relocated in the text. — EDS.]

[3] Cf. my Brother Black's dissenting opinion in this case. . . . The Court states that "To leave the employee remediless" when the union wrongfully refuses to process his grievance,

which is not presented here, and which, with all respect, lends no support to the Court's argument. The Court seems to use its discussion of the employee-employer litigation as somehow analogous to or supportive of its conclusion that the employee may maintain a court action against the union. But I do not believe that this follows. I agree that the NLRB's unfair labor practice jurisdiction does not preclude an action under §301 against the employer for wrongful discharge from employment. Smith v. Evening News Assn., 371 U.S. 195 (1962). Therefore, Owens might have maintained an action against his employer in the present case. This would be an action to enforce the collective bargaining agreement, and Congress has authorized the courts to entertain actions of this type. But his claim against the union is quite different in character. . . . The Court holds — and I think correctly if the issue is to be reached — that the union could not be required to pay damages measured by the breach of the employment contract, because it was not the union but the employer that breached the contract. I agree; but I suggest that this reveals the point for which I contend: that the employee's claim against the union is not a claim under the collective bargaining agreement, but a claim that the union has breached its statutory duty of fair representation. This claim, I submit, is a claim of unfair labor practice and it is within the exclusive jurisdiction of the NLRB. The Court agrees that "one of the available remedies [obtainable, the Court says, by court action] when a breach of the union's duty is proved" is "an order compelling arbitration." This is precisely and uniquely the kind of order which is within the province of the Board. Beyond this, the Court is exceedingly vague as to remedy. . . . The Court's difficulty, it seems to me, reflects the basic awkwardness of its position: It is attempting to force into the posture of a contract violation an alleged default of the union which is not a violation of the collective bargaining agreement but a breach of its separate and basic duty fairly to represent all employees in the unit. This is an unfair labor practice, and should be treated as such.

. . . If we look beyond logic and precedent to the policy of the labor relations design which Congress has provided, court jurisdiction of this type of action seems anomalous and ill-advised. We are not dealing here with the interpretation of a contract or with an alleged breach of an employment agreement. . . . [W]e are concerned with the subtleties of a union's statutory duty faithfully to represent employees in the unit, including those who may not be members of the union. . . . [T]his is precisely and especially the

---

"would . . . be a great injustice." I do not believe the Court relieves this injustice to any great extent by requiring the employee to prove an unfair labor practice as a prerequisite to judicial relief for the employer's breach of contract. Nor do I understand how giving the employee a cause of action against the *union* is an appropriate way to remedy the injustice which would exist if the union were allowed to foreclose relief against the *employer*.

kind of judgment that Congress intended to entrust to the Board and which is well within the preemption doctrine that this Court has prudently stated. See cases cited, supra, especially the *Perko* and *Borden* cases, the facts of which strongly parallel the situation in this case. . . . The nuances of union-employee and union-employer relationships are infinite and consequential, particularly when the issue is as amorphous as whether the union was proved guilty of "arbitrary or bad-faith conduct". . . . In all reason and in all good judgment, this jurisdiction should be left with the Board and not be placed in the courts, especially with the complex and necessarily confusing guidebook that the Court now publishes.

Accordingly, I join the judgment of reversal, but on the basis stated.

[Black, J., dissented on these grounds: Owens, despite a judicial determination that he was wrongfully discharged, is left remediless by the Court. He must prove the union's unfair representation in order to recover in his contract action against Swift. But the character of the union's conduct should not be relevant to the question of Swift's liability for its "unrelated breach of contract." Moreover, the Court's standard for unfair representation was derived from inapposite cases—those in which the employee's sole or fundamental complaint was against the union. Here the employee has an independent and more valuable claim against the employer. The union's good faith decision to forego arbitration, although it might properly shield the union, should not also shield the employer from contract liability. The merits of an employee's grievance should be determined by a jury or an arbitrator; but under the Court's decision it will never be determined by either. The Court's principal reason for granting the union "almost" unlimited discretion to deprive injured employees of contractual remedies appears to be to further the interests of the union as statutory agent. Yet, it is not clear how the union's legitimate interests are undermined by requiring it either to prosecute "all serious grievances to a conclusion" or to allow the employee to sue his employer, after he has given the union a chance to do so. By contrast, the Court's vague standard puts an enormous burden on an employee seeking to sue his employer for breach of the collective agreement.]

NOTES

1. Assume that the union's failure to pursue arbitration is a breach of duty. Does the Court in *Vaca* persuade you that the individual should not be restricted to an order compelling arbitration? Why should the union's breach create for employees something the NLRA does not expressly provide—a private damage remedy against unions? Moreover, why should the union's

breach deprive the employer of the arbitration prescribed by the agreement? If the union is not behind the employee, is arbitration of his claim likely to involve a specially flawed tribunal? Cf. Alexander v. Gardner-Denver, supra p. 1104. On the problems in requiring arbitration as the remedy for an unlawful failure to pursue an employee's grievance, see Port Drum Co., 180 N.L.R.B. 590 (1970); Local 396, Teamsters (United Parcel Service), 203 N.L.R.B. 799 (1973), *enforced*, 509 F.2d 1075 (9th Cir. 1975).

2. Assume that arbitration of an individual's grievance occurs pursuant to a court order secured by the individual following the union's refusal to take the grievance to arbitration. What difficulties might the union, the employee, or the employer experience (a) if the individual had the right to prosecute his grievance to arbitration, or (b) if the union remained in control, with the individual entitled to intervene? Do prospective difficulties of individual prosecution or intervention explain why the Court's ardor for arbitration, reflected in the *Steelworkers'* trilogy, seems to have cooled in *Vaca?*

Would it be prudent for the union to consent to separate representation for the individual grievant in an arbitration proceeding (e.g., a discharge case), even though the grievant is not entitled to it?

3. The RLA gives a railway worker the right to pursue his own grievance to an adjustment board. Consequently, the Supreme Court ruled that a union's authority to settle a grievance required actual authority, granted by the individual or derived from the union constitution or custom or usage. See Elgin, J., & E. Ry. Co. v. Burley, 325 U.S. 711 (1945), *opinion adhered to*, 327 U.S. 661 (1946). Subsequently, the Court, in *Steele*, recognized the duty of fair representation, and Congress, by a 1951 amendment to the RLA, authorized union-security agreements. Should these developments increase judicial willingness to find that a union was authorized to settle an individual's grievance? See Pyzynski v. N.Y. Cent. R.R. Co., 421 F.2d 854 (2d Cir. 1970), indicating that a greater settlement leeway for the union was justified, in part because the individual's "only protection generally lies in [his union's] negotiating skill and strength." But cf. Graf v. Elgin, Joliet & Eastern Ry. Co., 697 F.2d 771, 778-781 (7th Cir. 1983), suggesting that an individual employee's RLA right to prosecute his own grievance is an added reason for limiting a railway union's duty of fair representation. Which of these views seems more convincing?

For the individual grievant's position under the NLRA, consider also §9(a); J.I. Case Co. v. NLRB, supra p. 799; and the discussion of the §9(a) proviso in *Emporium Capwell*, footnote 12, supra p. 241. Cf. Dunau, Employee Participation in the Grievance Aspect of Collective Bargaining, 50 Colum. L. Rev. 731 (1950).

4. A collective agreement establishes a four-step grievance procedure

terminating in arbitration and provides as follows: (a) All employees shall be bound by agreements or settlements made by the union and the employer with respect to grievances. (b) Failure by the union to process a grievance to the next step of the grievance procedure or to arbitration, within the time limits for such action prescribed herein, shall constitute agreement by the union to the employer's prior disposition thereof. (c) No employee shall have the right to maintain a legal action on this agreement, except actions for accrued pay, vacation benefits, or vested pension rights. (d) No employee shall have a right to notice of arbitration proceedings or a right to intervene therein. In light of *Vaca*, would that agreement be valid insofar as it purports to foreclose individual actions on the agreement? See also Metropolitan Edison Co. v. NLRB, supra p. 1056.

5. For a valuable effort to develop a comprehensive theory of the collective bargaining agreement and the suggestion that rights under the agreement should not run to the individual, as distinguished from the union, see Feller, A General Theory of the Collective Bargaining Agreement, 61 Calif. L. Rev. 663, 774, 792, 811 (1973).

Hines v. Anchor Motor Freight, Inc., 424 U.S. 554 (1976). The company fired eight truck drivers, for padding overnight motel expenses. The union did not act on the drivers' suggestion that the motel be investigated; instead, the union reassured the drivers, stating that they should not hire their own lawyer for the joint area committee's hearing of their grievances. The company's strong documentary evidence presented at the hearing was contradicted only by the drivers' denials. After the area committee upheld the discharges, the drivers retained counsel and requested a rehearing based on the motel owner's concession that the motel clerk could have overcharged petitioners, doctored the records, and pocketed the overcharges. The committee denied a rehearing for lack of new evidence. After further implication of the clerk, the drivers sued the company and the union, alleging breach of the contract's "just cause" provision and of the union's duty of fair representation. In a deposition the clerk confessed to falsifying the records. Nevertheless, the district court granted summary judgment to the defendants, reasoning that the decision of the "arbitration" committee bound the employees and finding a failure to show the union's "bad faith, arbitrariness or perfunctoriness." The Sixth Circuit reversed the summary judgment as to the local union but not as to the employer. The Supreme Court, assuming the correctness of the reversal of the summary judgment for the union, reversed the summary judgment for the employer. White, J., for the Court, extending *Vaca*, declared that a breach of the duty of fair representation, "if it seriously undermines the integrity of the arbitral process[,] also removes the bar of the [contract's] finality provisions." He continued:

". . . Under the [Court of Appeals'] rule . . . , unless the employer is implicated in the Union's malfeasance or has otherwise caused the arbitral process to err, petitioners would have no remedy against Anchor even though they [prove] the Union's bad faith, the falsity of the charges against them and the breach of contract by Anchor by discharging without cause. This rule would apparently govern even . . . where it is shown that a union has manufactured the evidence and knows . . . that it is false; or even if, unbeknownst to the employer, the union has corrupted the arbitrator to the detriment of disfavored union members. As is the case where there has been a failure to exhaust, . . . we cannot believe that Congress intended to foreclose the employee from his §301 remedy otherwise available against the employer if the contractual processes have been seriously flawed by the union's breach of its duty to represent employees honestly and in good faith and without invidious discrimination or arbitrary conduct. . . .

"Petitioners are not entitled to relitigate their discharge merely because they offer newly discovered evidence that . . . they were fired without cause. The grievance processes cannot be expected to be error-free. The finality provision has sufficient force to surmount occasional instances of mistake. But it is quite another matter to suggest that erroneous arbitration decisions must stand even though the employee's representation by the union has been dishonest, in bad faith or discriminatory; for in that event error and injustice of the grossest sort would multiply. The contractual system would then cease to qualify as an adequate mechanism to secure individual redress for damaging failure of the employer to abide by the contract. . . . In our view, enforcement of the finality provision where the arbitrator has erred is conditioned upon the Union's having satisfied its statutory duty fairly to represent the employee in connection with the arbitration proceedings. . . .

"Petitioners, if they prove an erroneous discharge and the Union's breach of duty tainting the decision of the joint committee, are entitled to an appropriate remedy against the employer as well as the Union."

Stevens, J., did not participate.

The concurring opinion of Stewart, J., is summarized in the *Bowen* case, immediately below. Rehnquist, J., joined by Burger, C.J., dissented, urging that a remedy against the employer, who had acted in good faith, would be based on the union's ineffectiveness as counsel; would undermine the finality of arbitration awards; and, given the remedy against the union, was unnecessary.

NOTES

1. To what standard of performance should the bargaining representative be held throughout the grievance-arbitration process? How does requiring the employee to prove that the union's conduct was "arbitrary" or "perfunctory" differ from requiring proof of "bad faith" or "'intentional misconduct"? Can intentional misconduct be inferred from "simple negligence"? From "gross negligence"? From "perfunctory" handling of a grievant's case? Is a "callous and reckless disregard" test appropriate? Can the practical significance of these differences in formulation be assessed without regard for the factual context from which a formulation emerges?

2. In formulating a standard, should the primary focus be on whether the union adopted a "fair process" for determining the facts and the law implicated in a grievance, as distinguished from reaching a "fair" result with respect to either taking a grievance to arbitration or conducting an arbitration proceeding? Will the "fair process" approach provide a better and more manageable balance between individual and collective interests? Suppose, for example, that business agents, without consulting the union's lawyer, erroneously but in good faith fail to take a discharge grievance to arbitration, on the ground that "the grievance was a clear loser" and that the employer and the members were getting tired of spending money on "frivolous grievances." After the grievance is time-barred, a lawyer concludes that the odds of winning were only a little less than 40-60. Should the union's process be considered "fair"? Would the result necessarily be the same if a ten-day suspension were involved? Cf. Curth v. Farady, 401 F. Supp. 678 (E.D. Mich. 1975).

3. Employees covered by grievance-arbitration procedures present the following situations and ask for your advice about their rights:

(a) Smith, laid off for two weeks for fighting, complained to the union business agent that the employer had lacked "just cause" in that Smith had defended himself against an unprovoked attack by another employee. The business agent put the grievance in the glove compartment of his automobile and forgot about it until it was time-barred; it was dismissed by an arbitrator on that ground. Among the questions Smith asks is whether he should complain to the NLRB about the union or sue for damages. Compare Office & Professional Employees, Local 2, 268 N.L.R.B. No. 207, 115 L.R.R.M. 1169 (1984), with Hoffman v. Lonza, Inc., 658 F.2d 519 (7th Cir. 1981), and Ruzicka v. General Motors, 649 F.2d 1207 (6th Cir. 1981).

(b) Jones, a long-service employee, was fired for drunkenness; and Maverick, for fighting. Maverick was unpopular with both his coemployees and his supervisors because of his radical politics and general dogmatism. The union believed that these discharges were close cases, and that it would probably lose both of them in arbitration. The union and the employer agreed that Jones would be reinstated but that Maverick's discharge would stand. Cf. Local 13, Longshoremen Union v. Pacific Maritime Assn., 441 F.2d 1061, 1068 (9th Cir. 1971), cert. denied, 404 U.S. 1016 (1972); Harrison v. United Transp. Union, 530 F.2d 558 (4th Cir. 1975), cert. denied, 425 U.S. 958 (1976).

(c) A company suspected that employee dishonesty caused excessive costs at one of its lunch counters. The union initially rejected the company's suggestion that the crew be wholly or partially replaced. Later, the union, having inspected the company's books, agreed to an experimental withdrawal of five counter employees. Costs declined thereafter, and, pursuant to its prior agreement with the union, the company terminated all five. They complained that their termination violated the "just cause" provision of the collective agreement, but the union declined to process any of their grievances. See Union News Co. v. Hildreth, 295 F.2d 658 (6th Cir. 1961); Simmons v. Union News Co., 382 U.S. 884 (1965).

4. What is a union's duty to individuals or groups whose interests would be adversely affected by the adoption of the position urged by the union in arbitration? Consider Clark v. Hein-Werner Corp., 8 Wis. 2d 264, 99 N.W.2d 264 (1959). Production employees who had been promoted to supervisory jobs resumed production work after a reduction in force. In computing their seniority, the company credited them with the time they had spent as supervisors. The agreement defined "seniority" as "length of service with the company." The union's grievance against that computation was upheld by the arbitrator. In affirming an injunction against enforcement of the award, the court stated: "[W]here the interests of two groups of employees are diametrically opposed . . . and the union espouses the cause of one in arbitration, it follows as a matter of law that there has been no fair representation of the other group." The court also ruled that the failure to give the plaintiffs (the ex-supervisors) formal notice of the arbitration proceeding and an opportunity to intervene precluded their being bound by the award. Is the court's approach sound? Are the issues involved governed by federal or state law?

In Smith v. Hussman Refrigerator Co., 619 F.2d 1229 (8th Cir. 1980) (en banc), rehearing denied and opinion clarified, 633 F.2d 18 (1980), cert. denied, 449 U.S. 839 (1980), a collective agreement permitted promotion of a more able junior employee unless a senior employee was "substantially equal" in ability. After four promotions, the union processed the grievances of the four most senior employees (among 26 grievants) without comparing their ability with that of the successful juniors. The arbitrator sustained two of those grievances. The two junior incumbents were accordingly displaced. The latter sued for breach of the collective agreement by the employer and of the duty of fair representation by the union. Sustaining damage awards against both defendants, a panel of the court held that the union had breached its duty by supporting the senior employees before the arbitrator (i.e., failing to balance seniority against the ability of the successful junior bidders, in accordance with the agreement) and by failing to notify the plaintiffs of the arbitration proceeding while permitting the grievants to appear and testify. 100 L.R.R.M. 2238 (1979). The full court, with only three of the eight judges joining in the lead opinion, concluded that the union's arrangements with the company to arbitrate without notice to or representation of the plaintiffs would be sufficient to support a jury finding of unfair representation, but that the union's advocating promotion of the senior employees at the arbitration would not. What is the probable rationale for that distinction?

5. For discussion of the problems in defining fair representation in grievance administration and arbitration, see T. Boyce & R. Turner, Fair Representation, The NLRB, and the Courts, chs. III, IV (rev. ed. 1984); Cheit, Competing Models of Fair Representation: The Perfunctory Processing Cases, 24 B.C. L. Rev. 1 (1982); Lewis, Fair Representation in Grievance Administration: Vaca v. Sipes, 1967 Sup. Ct. Rev. 81; Rabin, The Impact of the Duty of Fair Representation Upon Labor Arbitration, 29 Syracuse L. Rev. 851 (1978); Summers, The Individual Employee's Rights Under the Collective Agreement: What Constitutes Fair Representation? 126 U. Pa. L. Rev. 251 (1977); Vandervelde, A Fair Process Model for the Union's Fair Representation Duty, 67 Minn. L. Rev. 1079 (1983).

Bowen v. United States Postal Service
459 U.S. 212 (1983)

POWELL, J. The issue is whether a union may be held primarily liable for that part of a wrongfully discharged employee's damages caused by his union's breach of its duty of fair representation.

I

[Bowen, after an altercation with a coemployee, was suspended and later fired. Bowen, a union member, filed a grievance pursuant to the collective agreement. After the union declined to take it to arbitration, he sued the union and the Postal Service in a federal district court, alleging that the Service had violated the "just cause" provision of the agreement, and the union, its duty of fair representation. Bowen showed at trial that the responsible union officers, at each grievance step, had recommended pursuing the grievance, but that the national office, for no apparent reason, would not go to arbitration.]

   . . . [T]he court gave the jury a series of questions to be answered as a special verdict. If the jury found that the Service had discharged Bowen wrongfully and that the Union had breached its duty of fair representation, it was instructed to determine the amount of compensatory damages to be awarded and to apportion the liability for the damages between the Service and the Union. . . . [T]he court instructed the jury that the [apportionment] issue was left primarily to its discretion. The court indicated, however, that the jury equitably could base apportionment on the date of a hypothetical arbitration decision — the date at which the Service would have reinstated Bowen if the Union had fulfilled its duty. The court suggested that the Service could be liable for damages before that date and the Union for damages thereafter. Although the Union objected to the instruction allowing the jury to find it liable for any compensatory damages, it did not object to the manner in which the court instructed the jury to apportion the damages in the event apportionment was proper.

   Upon return of a special verdict in favor of Bowen and against both defendants, the District Court entered judgment, holding that the Service had discharged Bowen without just cause and that the Union had handled his "apparently meritorious grievance . . . in an arbitrary and perfunctory manner. . . ." 470 F. Supp. 1127, 1129 (WD Va. 1979). In so doing, both the Union and the Service acted "in reckless and callous disregard of [Bowen's] rights." Ibid. The court found that Bowen could not have proceeded independently of the Union and that if the Union had arbitrated Bowen's grievance, he would have been reinstated. Ibid.

   The court ordered that Bowen be reimbursed $52,954 for lost benefits and wages. . . . [I]t observed that "this is a case in which both defendants, by their illegal acts, are liable to plaintiff. . . . The problem in this case is not one of liability but rather one of apportionment. . . ." Id., at 1130-1131. The jury had found that the Union was responsible for $30,000 of Bowen's damages. The court approved that apportionment, ordering the Service to pay the remaining $22,954.[6]

   . . . [T]he Fourth Circuit overturned the damage award against the

---

   [6] The District Court found as a fact that if Bowen's grievance had been arbitrated he would have been reinstated by August, 1977. Lost wages after that date were deemed the fault of the Union: "While the [Service] set this case in motion with its discharge, the [Union's] acts, upon which [Bowen] reasonably relied, delayed the reinstatement of [Bowen] and it is a proper apportionment to assign fault to the [Union] for approximately two-thirds of the period [Bowen] was unemployed up to the time of trial." 470 F. Supp., at 1131.

Union. 642 F.2d 79 (CA4 1981). It . . . held as a matter of law that, "[a]s Bowen's compensation was at all times payable only by the Service, reimbursement of his lost earnings continued to be the obligation of the Service exclusively. Hence, no portion of the deprivations . . . was chargeable to the Union. Cf. Vaca v. Sipes, 386 U.S. 171, 195 . . . (1967)." Id., at 82. The court did not alter the District Court's judgment in any other respect. . . . Indeed, the court accepted the District Court's apportionment of fault so completely that it refused to increase the $22,954 award against the Service to cover the whole of Bowen's injury. Bowen was left with only a $22,954 award, whereas the jury and the District Court had awarded him lost earnings and benefits of $52,954—the undisputed amount of his damages.

II

. . . The Court [in Vaca] explained that the award must be apportioned according to fault [and continued]:

> . . . Thus, damages attributable solely to the employer's breach of contract should not be charged to the union, but increases if any in those damages caused by the union's refusal to process the grievance should not be charged to the employer.

Id., at 197-198.

Although Vaca's governing principle is well established, its application has caused some uncertainty. The Union argues that the Court of Appeals correctly determined that it cannot be charged with any damages resulting from a wrongful discharge. . . . The Union views itself as liable only for Bowen's litigation expenses resulting from its breach of duty. . . . The Union contends that its unrelated breach of the duty of fair representation . . . merely lifts the bar to the employee's suit on the contract against his employer.

The difficulty with this argument is that it treats the relationship between the employer and employee, created by the collective-bargaining agreement, as if it were a simple contract of hire governed by traditional common law principles . . . [whereas] it is an agreement creating relationships and interests under the federal common law of labor policy.

A

. . . The interests . . . identified in Vaca provide a measure of its principle for apportioning damages. Of paramount importance is the right of the employee . . . to be made whole. In determining the degree to which the employer or the union should bear the employee's damages, the Court held that the employer should not be shielded from the "natural consequences" of its breach by wrongful union conduct. Id., at 186. The Court noted, however, that the employer may have done nothing to prevent exhaustion. Were it not for the union's failure to represent the employee fairly, the employer's breach "could [have been] remedied through the grievance process to the employee-plaintiff's benefit." The fault that justifies dropping the bar to the employee's suit for damages also requires the union to bear some responsibility for increases in the employee's damages resulting from its breach. To hold otherwise would make the employer alone liable for the consequences of the union's breach of duty.

Hines v. Anchor Motor Freight, Inc., 424 U.S. 554 (1976), presented an issue analogous to that in Vaca: whether proof of a breach of the duty of fair representation would remove the bar of finality from an arbitral decision. We held that it would, in part because a contrary rule would prevent the employee from recovering "even in circumstances where it is shown that a union has manufactured the evidence and knows from the start that it is false; or even if, unbeknownst to the employer, the union has corrupted the arbitrator to the detriment of disfavored union members." Id., at 570.

It would indeed be unjust to prevent the employee from recovering in such a situation. It would be equally unjust to require the employer to bear the increase in the damages caused by the union's wrongful conduct.[11] It is true that the employer discharged the employee wrongfully and remains liable for the employee's backpay. See Vaca, supra, at 197. The union's breach of its duty of fair representation, however, caused the grievance procedure to malfunction resulting in an increase in the employee's damages. Even though both the employer and the union have caused the damage suffered by the employee, the union is responsible for the increase in damages and, as between the two wrongdoers, should bear its portion of the damages.[12] . . .

B

In approving apportionment of damages . . . , Vaca did not apply principles of ordinary contract law. . . . Fundamental to federal labor policy is the grievance procedure. See John Wiley & Sons v. Livingston, 376 U.S. 543, 549 (1964); Warrior & Gulf Navigation Co., supra, at 578. . . .

. . . [T]he union plays a pivotal role in the [grievance] process since it assumes the responsibility of determining whether to press an employee's claims. The employer . . . must rely on the union's decision not to pursue

[11] We note that this is not a situation in which either the union or the employer has participated in the other's breach. See Vaca, at 197 n. 18.

[12] Although the union remains primarily responsible for the portion of the damages resulting from its default, Vaca made clear that the union's breach does not absolve the employer of liability. Thus if the petitioner in this case does not collect the damages apportioned against the Union, the Service remains secondarily liable for the full loss of backpay.

an employee's grievance. . . . Just as a nonorganized employer may accept an employee's waiver of any challenge to his discharge as a final resolution of the matter, so should an organized employer be able to rely on a comparable waiver by the employee's exclusive representative.

There is no unfairness to the union in this approach. By seeking and acquiring the exclusive right and power to speak for a group of employees, the union assumes a corresponding duty to discharge that responsibility faithfully—a duty which it owes to the employees whom it represents and on which the employer with whom it bargains may rely. When the union . . . waives arbitration or fails to seek review of an adverse decision, the employer should be in substantially the same position as if the employee had had the right to act on his own behalf and had done so. Indeed, if the employer could not rely on the union's decision, the grievance procedure would not provide the "uniform and exclusive method for [the] orderly settlement of employee grievances," which the Court has recognized is essential to the national labor policy."[15] See Clayton v. International Union Automobile, Aerospace & Agricultural Implement Workers, 451 U.S. 679, 686-687 (1981).

. . . *Vaca* reflects this allocation of responsibilities in the grievance procedure—a procedure that contemplates that both employer and union will perform their respective obligations. Is the absence of damages apportionment where the default of both parties contributes to the employee's injury, incentives to comply with the grievance procedure will be diminished. Indeed, imposing total liability solely on the employer could well affect the

---

[15] Under the dissent's analysis, the employer may not rely on the union's decision not to pursue a grievance. Rather it can prevent continued liability only by reinstating the discharged employee. This leaves the employer with a dubious option: it must either reinstate the employee promptly or leave itself exposed to open-ended liability. If this were the rule, the very purpose of the grievance procedure would be defeated. It is precisely to provide the exclusive means of resolving this kind of dispute that the parties agree to such a procedure and national labor policy strongly encourages its use. See Republic Steel, supra, at 653.

When the union has breached its duty of fair representation, the dissent justifies its rule by arguing that "only the employer ha[s] the continuing ability to right the wrong by reinstating" the employee, an ability that the union lacks. But an employer has no way of knowing that a failure to carry a grievance to arbitration constitutes a breach of duty. Rather than rehiring, as the dissent suggests, the employer reasonably could assume that the union had concluded the discharge was justified. The union would have the option, if it realized it had committed an arguable breach of duty, to bring its default to the employer's attention. Our holding today would not prevent a jury from taking such action into account.

Moreover, the rule urged by the dissenting opinion would allow the union and the employee, once the case goes to trial, to agree to a settlement pursuant to which the union would acknowledge a breach of its duty of fair representation in exchange for the employee's undertaking to look to his employer for his entire recovery. Although we may assume that this would not occur frequently, the incentive the dissent's rule would provide to agree to such a settlement demonstrates its unsoundness.

willingness of employers to agree to arbitration clauses as they are customarily written.

Nor will requiring the union to pay damages impose a burden on the union inconsistent with national labor policy.[16] It will provide an additional incentive for the union to process its members' claims where warranted. See Vaca, supra, at 187. This is wholly consistent with a union's interest. It is a duty owed to its members as well as consistent with the union's commitment to the employer under the arbitration clause. See Republic Steel, supra, at 653.

III

The Union contends that Czosek v. O'Mara, 397 U.S. 25 (1970), requires a different reading of Vaca and a different weighing of the interests our cases have developed. Czosek, however, is consistent with our holding today. In Czosek, employees of the Erie Lackawanna Railroad were placed on furlough and not recalled. They brought suit against the railroad for wrongful discharge and against their union for breaching its duty of fair representation. They alleged that the union had arbitrarily and capriciously refused to process their claims againt the railroad. See id., at 26. The District Court dismissed the claim against the railroad because the employees had not pursued the administrative remedies provided by the Railway Labor Act.[18] It dismissed the claim against the union because the employee's ability to pursue an administrative remedy on their own absolved the union of any duty. The Court of Appeals . . . affirmed the dismissal of the claim against the railroad but found that the employees had stated a claim against the union. Even though the employees had a right to seek full redress from an administrative board, the union still had a duty to represent them fairly. See Conley v. Gibson, 355 U.S. 41 (1957).

This Court affirmed. In so doing, it addressed the union's concern that if the railroad were not joined as a party, the union might be held responsible

---

[16] Requiring the union to pay its share of the damages is consistent with the interests recognized in International Brotherhood of Electrical Workers v. Foust, 442 U.S. 42 (1979). In Foust, we found that a union was not liable for punitive damages. The interest in deterring future breaches by the union was outweighed by the debilitating impact that "unpredictable and potentially substantial" awards of punitive damages would have on the union treasury and the union's exercise of discretion in deciding what claims to pursue. Id., at 50-52. An award of compensatory damages, however, normally will be limited and finite. Moreover, the union's exercise of discretion is shielded by the standard necessary to prove a breach of the duty of fair representation. Thus, the threat that was present in Foust is absent here.

[18] See 45 U.S.C. §153 First (i), (j). These sections provide that an employee who is unsuccessful at the grievance level can seek relief on his own from the National Railroad Adjustment Board. The Board is authorized to provide remedies similar to those available in a court suit. See Republic Steel, supra, at 657, n. 14.

for damages for which the railroad was wholly or partly responsible. The Court stated:

> [J]udgment against [the union] can in any event be had only for those damages that flowed from [its] own conduct. Assuming a wrongful discharge by the employer independent of any discriminatory conduct by the union and a subsequent discriminatory refusal by the union to process grievances based on the discharge, damages for the union are unrecoverable except to the extent that its refusal to handle the grievances added to the difficulty and expense of collecting from the employer.

397 U.S., at 29.

Although the statement is broadly phrased, it should not be divorced from the context in which it arose. The Railway Labor Act provided the employees in *Czosek* with an alternate remedy, which they could have pursued when the union refused to process their grievances. Because the union's actions did not deprive the employees of immediate access to a remedy, it did not increase the damages that the employer otherwise would have had to pay. The Court therefore stated that the only damages flowing from the union's conduct in this case were the added expenses the employees incurred. This is consistent with *Vaca's* recognition that each party should bear the damages attributable to its fault.

IV

. . . [T]he findings of the District Court, accepted by the Court of Appeals, establish that the damages sustained by petitioner were caused initially by the Service's unlawful discharge and increased by the Union's breach of its duty of fair representation. Accordingly, apportionment of the damages was required by *Vaca*.[19] We reverse the judgment of the Court of Appeals and remand for entry of judgment allocating damages against both the Service and the Union consistent with this opinion.

WHITE, J., with whom MARSHALL, BLACKMUN, and REHNQUIST (except as to part IV), JJ., join, concurring in part in the judgment and dissenting in part. The Court holds that an employer who wrongfully discharges an employee protected by a collective bargaining agreement with an arbitration clause is only responsible for backpay that accrues prior to the hypothetical date upon which an arbitrator would have issued an award had the em-

---

[19] We need not decide whether the District Court's instructions on apportionment of damages were proper. The Union objected to the instructions only on the ground that no back wages at all could be assessed against it. It did not object to the manner of apportionment if such damages were to be assessed. Nor is it necessary in this case to consider whether there were degrees of fault, as both the Service and the Union were found to have acted in "reckless and callous disregard of [Bowen's] rights."

ployee's union taken the matter to arbitration. All backpay damages that accrue after this time are the sole responsibility of the union, even where, as here, the union is in no way responsible for the employer's decision to terminate the employee. This rationale, which . . . has been rejected by every Court of Appeals that has squarely considered it, does not give due regard to our prior precedents, to equitable principles, or to the national labor policy. . . . I believe that the employer should be primarily liable for all backpay.

I

. . . *Vaca* made clear that, with respect to an *employer*, the only consequence of a union's breach of a fair-representation duty to an *employee* is that it provides the employee with the means of defeating the employer's "defense based upon the failure to exhaust contractual remedies." . . . The Court explicitly stated that the union's violation of its statutory duty in no way "exempt[ed] the employer from contractual damages which he would otherwise have had to pay," id., at 196, and that the employer could not "hide behind the union's wrongful failure to act." Id., at 197.

. . . The arbitrator [in Hines v. Anchor Motor Freight, Inc., 424 U.S. 554] had upheld the discharge as rightful. Nevertheless, the Court held that the employee might still maintain a §301 action *if* he could establish that his union had breached its duty of representing him fairly during the arbitral proceedings, even though the employer was in no way responsible for the alleged union malfeasance. Id., at 569. The employer protested that, since its conduct during the arbitration was blameless, it should be able to rely on the finality of the arbitral award. We rejected this argument, pointing out that the employer had "surely played its part in precipitating [the] dispute" by discharging the plaintiff-employee in the first place. Ibid. As in V*aca*, with respect to the employer, the only consequence of the union's breach was that it "remove[d] the bar" to the employee's right to bring a §301 action.[3] Id., at 567.

That the union is not primarily liable for backpay is readily apparent upon close inspection of the facts in V*aca*. The employee in that case had been discharged in January 1960. Sometime after February 1961, the union refused to take the matter to arbitration, and, in February 1962, the employee

---

[3] Justice Stewart['s] two-paragraph [concurrence] in *Hines* [stated] that the employer should not be liable for backpay accruing between the time of the "tainted" arbitral decision and a subsequent "untainted" determination that the discharges were, after all, wrongful. 424 U.S. at 572-573. No other member of the Court joined [those] observations, and his opinion was founded on the employer's good-faith reliance on a favorable arbitral decision. Here, the Court goes far beyond Justice Stewart and grants the employer the right to rely on a nonexistent arbitration, even though the union is by no means under a duty to the employer to take any grievances to arbitration.

filed suit, claiming that the union's refusal to go to arbitration violated his rights. The trial began in June 1964, and the matter was not finally adjudicated until this Court rendered its decision in February 1967. Had the union opted in favor of arbitration, an award almost certainly would have been forthcoming long before the judicial suit had even proceeded to trial.[4] Nevertheless, the Vaca Court commented that "all or almost all" of the employee's damages would be attributable to the employer, not the union. Id., at 198. . . .

. . . The damages that an employee may recover upon proof that his union has breached its duty to represent him fairly are simply of a different nature than those recoverable from the employer. This is why we found in Vaca that "damages attributable to the employer's breach of contract should not be charged to the union, but increases if any in those damages caused by the union's refusal to process the grievance should not be charged to the employer." 386 U.S., at 197-198.

What, then, is the proper measure of the union's damages in a hybrid §301/breach-of-duty suit? . . . [I]n Czosek v. O'Mara, 397 U.S. 25, 29 (1970), [we] concluded that, under the Vaca rule, the union is liable in damages to the extent that its misconduct "add[s] to the difficulty and expense of collecting from the employer."[5] Czosek reassured unions that they would not be forced to pay damages "for which the employer is wholly or partly responsible." Id., at 28-29 (emphasis added).

. . . [U]nder the Vaca-Czosek rule, the union may sometimes only have de minimis liability, and we unanimously acknowledged this fact in Electrical Workers v. Foust, 442 U.S. 42, 48, 50 (1979). "The damages a union will have to pay in a typical unfair representation suit are minimal; under Vaca's apportionment formula, the bulk of the award will be paid by the employer, the perpetrator of the wrongful discharge, in a parallel §301 action." Id., at 57 (BLACKMUN, J., concurring in result; joined by Burger, C.J., Rehnquist, and Stevens, JJ.). The Foust majority nevertheless reaf-

---

[4]Statistics developed by the Federal Mediation and Conciliation Service ("FMCS") show that, in 1981, the average time between the filing of a grievance and the rendering of an arbitral award was 230.26 days. For the years between 1972 and 1980, the average varied from a high of 268.3 in 1977 to a low of 223.5 in 1975 and 1978. FMCS, Thirty-Fourth Annual Report 39 (1981). . . .

[5]Czosek arose under the Railway Labor Act ("RLA"), which permits an employee whose union fails to process his grievance to press it himself. Id. §§153 First (i), (j). The Court seeks to limit Czosek to the RLA context, on the theory that, because the employee in Czosek could have filed a grievance without union assistance, the union's default in that case did not "increase the damages that the employer otherwise would have had to pay." Ante, at 15-17. However, the Czosek opinion nowhere suggests that this distinction is relevant, and it cites only Vaca in support of its finding on this point. We reaffirmed in Electrical Workers v. Foust, 442 U.S. 42, 50 n.13 (1979), that the Czosek rule was an application of "Vaca's apportionment principle."

firmed *Vaca* and, moreover, further insulated unions from liability by holding that punitive damages could not be assessed in an action for breach of the duty of fair representation. . . . [T]he Court relied on the policy of affording individual employees redress for injuries caused by union misconduct without compromising the collective interests of union members in protecting limited union funds. As in *Vaca*, considerations of deterrence were deemed insufficient to risk endangering union "financial stability." Id., at 50-51.[6]

II

. . . [U]nder the Court's new rule, the "bulk of the award" for backpay in a hybrid §301/breach-of-duty suit will have to be borne by the union. . . . In the present case, for example, the jury, which was instructed in accordance with the Court's new test, assessed $30,000 in compensatory damages against the union, and only $17,000 against the employer. . . . Because the hypothetical arbitration date will usually be less than one year after the discharge, see note 4 supra, it is readily apparent that . . . in many cases the union will be subject to large liability, far greater than that of the employer, the extent of which will not be in any way related to the union's comparative culpability. Nor will the union have any readily apparent way to limit its constantly increasing liability.

Bowen and the Postal Service argue that the employer is not the "cause" of an employee's lost earnings after the date on which an arbitral decision would have reinstated or otherwise compensated the employee. In the "but for" sense, . . . this is patently false, as the Court concedes. Ante, at 10. But for the employer's breach of contract, there would be no occasion for *anyone* to reimburse the plaintiff for lost wages accumulated either before or after a hypothetical arbitration. . . .

Thus, there is no reason why the matter should not be governed by the traditional rule of contract law that a breaching defendant must pay damages equivalent to the total harm suffered, "even though there were contributing factors other than his own conduct." 5A. Corbin, Corbin on Contracts §999 (1964). The plaintiff need not show the proportionate part played by the defendant's breach of contract among all the contributing factors causing the injury, and his loss need not be "segregated proportionately." Ibid. We followed this rule in *Czosek*, supra, when we determined that an employer must pay the damages if it is "wholly or partly" responsible for the plaintiff-employee's loss. 397 U.S., at 29. . . .

---

[6] Even though *Foust* requires that punitive damages not be assessed against a union, the *Vaca* rule nevertheless provides for a credible deterrent against wrongful union conduct. Attorney's fees and other litigation expenses have been assessed as damages against unions, because such damages measure the extent by which the union's breach of duty adds to the difficulty and expense of collecting from the employer. . . .

It bears re-emphasizing that both before and after the hypothetical arbitration date, the union did not in any way prevent the employer from reinstating Bowen, and that the employer could reinstate him. Under these circumstances, it is bizarre to hold, as the Court does, that the relatively impotent union is *exclusively* liable for the bulk of the backpay. . . . The employer's wrongful conduct clearly was the generating cause of Bowen's loss, and only the employer had the continuing ability to right the wrong and limit liability by reinstating Bowen. The employer has the sole duty to pay wages, and it should be responsible for all back wages to which Bowen is entitled. . . .

. . . [N]either the collective bargaining agreement nor the union's duty of fair representation provides any support for the Court's conclusion that the union has somehow committed itself to protect the employer, and that the employer has the right to rely on the union to cut off its liability. . . . It is a basic tenet of national labor policy that "when neither the collective bargaining process nor its end product violates any command of Congress, a federal court has no authority to modify the substantive terms of a collective bargaining agreement." Mine Workers Health & Retirement Funds v. Robinson, 455 U.S. 562, 576 (1982).

The Court also contends that its rule will better enable grievance procedures to provide the uniform and exclusive method for the orderly settlement of employee grievances, because a contrary rule "could well affect the willingness of employers to agree to arbitration clauses as they are customarily written." Why the Court's rule will not "affect the willingness" of *unions* to agree to such clauses is left unexplained. More importantly, since the practical consequence of today's holding is that unions will take many unmeritorious grievances to arbitration simply to avoid exposure to the new breach-of-duty liability, the Court's rule actually impairs the ability of the grievance machinery to provide for orderly dispute resolution. . . .

III

There are at least two situations in which a union should bear some liability for backpay. First, as recognized in *Vaca*, the union and the employer may be jointly and severally liable where the union has affirmatively induced the employer to commit the alleged breach of contract. 386 U.S., at 197 n. 18. Second, even in a case such as this one, in which the union is not responsible for the discharge, the union should be secondarily liable. That is, if, due to a breach of duty by his union, an employee is unable to collect the backpay to which he is entitled from his employer, the entity primarily liable, he should then be entitled to collect from the union. . . .

No such exception to the rule I would apply is applicable in this case.

The union did not incite Bowen's discharge, and Bowen is able to recover in full from the Postal Service. . . .

Accordingly, I would affirm the Court of Appeals' judgment that the union was not liable for backpay damages, but I would reverse the remainder of the judgment and remand the case with instructions that the District Court be directed to enter judgment against the Postal Service for the entire amount of Bowen's backpay loss.

[The dissenting opinion of Rehnquist, J., is omitted.]

NOTES

1. Was the dissent's formulation of the Court's holding warranted by either the letter or the implications of the Court's opinion?

2. If you represented a union in a *Bowen* situation, and the trial court gave the jury the *Bowen* charge on apportionment of damages, what steps could preserve for appeal the question whether that charge was correct? How should that question be answered — on the basis of the Court's pre-*Bowen* precedents? On the basis of principle?

3. In Northwest Airlines, Inc. v. Transport Wkrs., 451 U.S. 77 (1981), the employer who had been held liable to women because collectively bargained wage differentials violated the Equal Pay Act and Title VII of the Civil Rights Act of 1964 was denied a right to contribution from the union despite its significant responsibility for the unlawful differentials. Is there any policy reason for apportioning damages in *Bowen* but declining to do so in *Northwest Airlines?* If the answer is "no," what should be the solution in both situations?

DelCostello v. Teamsters, 103 S. Ct. 2281 (1983). The Court, returning to issues dealt with two years earlier in United Parcel Service, Inc. v. Mitchell, 451 U.S. 56 (1981), concluded that §10(b) of the NLRA should be the governing statute of limitations, against both the employer and the union, in *Vaca* and *Hines* suits. Brennan, J., stated in part:

". . . [W]e have available [in §10(b)] a federal statute of limitations actually designed to accommodate a balance of interests very similar to that at stake here — a statute that is, in fact, an analogy to the present lawsuit more apt than any of the suggested state-law parallels. . . .

"The NLRB has consistently held that all breaches of a union's duty of fair representation *are* in fact unfair labor practices. E.g., Miranda Fuel Co., 140 N.L.R.B. 181 (1962), *enforcement denied,* 326 F.2d 172 (CA2 1963).

We have twice declined to decide the correctness of the Board's position, and we need not address that question today. Even if not all breaches of the duty are unfair labor practices, however, the family resemblance is undeniable, and indeed there is a substantial overlap. Many fair representation claims . . . include allegations of discrimination based on membership status or dissident views, which would be unfair labor practices under §8(a)(1) or (2). Aside from these clear cases, duty-of-fair-representation claims are allegations of unfair, arbitrary, or discriminatory treatment of workers by unions — as are virtually all unfair labor practice charges made by workers against unions. . . . Similarly, it may be the case that alleged violations by an employer of a collective bargaining agreement will also amount to unfair labor practices. . . ."

Stevens and O'Connor, JJ., in separate dissents, urged that in worker-union disputes over the fairness of representation state statutes of limitations governing malpractice suits against attorneys should be borrowed. Both opinions referred to Justice Stevens' position, stated in his partial dissent in United Parcel Service, Inc. v. Mitchell, 451 U.S. 56, 71 n.4 (1981), that the determination that an employer did not breach the collective agreement, although relevant to the damages collectible from a union, would not necessarily control the threshold question of the union's breach of duty. Subsequently, courts have relied on Stevens' position in holding unions liable for unfair representation, without requiring a finding of employer culpability. See Foster v. Bowman Transportation Co., 116 L.R.R.M. 2606, 2613 (D.C.N.D. Ala. 1983) (union advised black grievant to reject dispatch with allegedly unsafe driver, stating that grievant would probably be fired but would be reinstated; then union allowed pending arbitration of discharge to languish for six months; court awarded attorney's fees to grievant and directed union to proceed to arbitration).

NOTES

1. The six-months limitation period prescribed by §10(b) applies when an employee's charge of a union's unfair representation is filed with the NLRB. Is there any reason for applying a different (presumably longer) period when an employee brings an action against a union? Is it relevant that public counsel is provided in a NLRB proceeding, whereas individual employees frequently have difficulties in finding and paying for private counsel in actions against unions?

2. Should the same limitations period apply to an employee's claim against an employer and a union, respectively, when that claim, in effect, seeks to override an arbitral award in favor of the employer? To an em-

ployee's claim that the union's misconduct antedating his discharge was an important factor in both his discharge and the union's breach of duty?

Clayton v. International Union, UAW
451 U.S. 679 (1981)

[Clayton sued under §301, claiming that his former employer had breached the collective agreement by discharging him without just cause and that his union had breached its duty of fair representation by failing to pursue his grievance past the third step, to arbitration. He sought reinstatement from the employer and monetary relief from both the employer and the union. The court of appeals affirmed the district court's dismissal of Clayton's suit against the union and reversed the dismissal of his suit against the employer, reasoning that Clayton's failure to exhaust internal union appeal procedures barred his suit against the union but not against the employer.]

BRENNAN, J. . . . We reverse the dismissal of Clayton's suit against the union and affirm the reversal of the dismissal of his suit against the employer. We hold that where an internal union appeals procedure cannot result in reactivation of the employee's grievance or an award of the complete relief sought in his §301 suit, exhaustion will not be required with respect to either the suit against the employer or the suit against the union.

II

. . . The contractual procedures we required the employee to exhaust in *Republic Steel* [379 U.S. 650 (1965)] are significantly different from the procedures at issue here. In this case, the Court is asked to require exhaustion of *internal* union procedures. These procedures are wholly a creation of the UAW Constitution. They were not bargained for by the employer and union and are nowhere mentioned in the collective-bargaining agreement that Clayton seeks to have judicially enforced. Nonetheless, Clayton's employer and union contend that exhaustion of the UAW procedures, like exhaustion of contractual grievance and arbitration procedures, will further national labor policy and should be required as a matter of federal common law. Their argument . . . is that an exhaustion requirement will enable unions to regulate their internal affairs without undue judicial interference and that it will also promote the broader goal of encouraging private resolution of disputes arising out of a collective-bargaining agreement.

We do not agree that the policy of forestalling judicial interference with internal union affairs is applicable to this case. This policy has been strictly limited to disputes arising over *internal* union matters such as those involving the interpretation and application of a union constitution. . . . Here, Clayton's dispute against his union is based upon an alleged breach of the union's duty of fair representation. This allegation raises issues rooted in statutory policies extending far beyond internal union interests. . . .

Our analysis, then, focuses on that aspect of national labor policy that encourages private rather than judicial resolution of disputes. . . . Concededly, a requirement that aggrieved employees exhaust internal remedies might lead to nonjudicial resolution of some contractual grievances. For example, an employee who exhausts internal union procedures might decide not to pursue his §301 action in court, either because the union offered him a favorable settlement, or because it demonstrated that his underlying contractual claim was without merit. However, we decline to impose a universal exhaustion requirement lest employees with meritorious §301 claims be forced to exhaust themselves and their resources by submitting their claims to potentially lengthy internal union procedures that may not be adequate to redress their underlying grievances.

. . . [C]ourts have discretion to decide whether to require exhaustion of internal union procedures. In exercising this discretion, at least three factors should be relevant: first, whether union officials are so hostile to the employee that he could not hope to obtain a fair hearing . . . ; second, whether the internal union appeals procedures would be inadequate either to reactivate the employee's grievance or to award him the full relief he seeks under §301; and third, whether exhaustion of internal procedures would unreasonably delay the employee's opportunity to obtain a judicial hearing on the merits of his claim. If any of these factors are found to exist, the court may properly excuse the employee's failure to exhaust.

Clayton has not challenged the finding of the lower courts that the UAW internal appeals procedures are fair and reasonable. He concedes that he could have received an impartial hearing on his claim had he exhausted the internal union procedures. . . . Accordingly, our inquiry turns to the second factor, whether the relief available through the union's internal appeals procedures is adequate.

In his suit under §301, Clayton seeks reinstatement from his employer and monetary relief from both his employer and his union. Although, the UAW Constitution does not indicate on its face what relief is available through the internal union appeals procedures, the parties have stipulated that the Public Review Board can award backpay in an appropriate case. . . . It is clear, then, that at least some monetary relief may be obtained through the internal appeals procedure.[17]

---

[17] The record does not indicate whether this monetary relief includes backpay only, or whether it also may include prospective monetary relief and incidental or punitive damages, relief that Clayton is apparently seeking in his §301 action.

It is equally clear that the union can neither reinstate Clayton in his job nor reactivate his grievance. Article IX of the collective-bargaining agreement between Local 509 and ITT Gilfillan provides that the union may obtain arbitration of a grievance only if it gives "notice . . . to the Company in writing within fifteen (15) working days after the date of the Company's decision at Step 3 of the Grievance Procedure." By the time Clayton learned of his union's decision not to pursue the grievance to arbitration, this 15-day time limit had expired. Accordingly, the union could not have demanded arbitration even if the internal appeal had shown Clayton's claim to be meritorious. . . . [W]e conclude that these restrictions on the relief available through the internal UAW procedures render those procedures inadequate.[19]

. . . [I]f the employee received the full relief he requested through internal procedures, his §301 action would become moot, and he would not be entitled to a judicial hearing. Similarly, if the employee obtained reactivation of his grievance through internal union procedures, the policies underlying *Republic Steel* would come into play,[20] and the employee would be required to submit his claim to the collectively-bargained dispute-resolution procedures.[21] In either case, exhaustion of internal remedies could result in final resolution of the employee's contractual grievance through private rather than judicial avenues.

By contrast, where an aggrieved employee cannot obtain either the substantive relief he seeks or reactivation of his grievance, national labor policy would not be served by requiring exhaustion of internal remedies. In such cases, exhaustion would be a useless gesture: it would delay judicial consideration of the employee's §301 action, but would not eliminate it. The employee would still be required to pursue judicial means to obtain the relief he seeks under §301. Moreover, exhaustion would not lead to significant

[19] Accordingly, we need not discuss the third factor, whether exhaustion of the union's otherwise adequate internal appeals procedures would unreasonably delay the employee's opportunity to obtain a judicial hearing on the merits of his claim.

[20] Allowing a defendant in a §301 action to demand exhaustion of internal union procedures when those procedures could lead to reactivation of a stalled grievance is wholly consistent with Republic Steel Corp. v. Maddox, 379 U.S. 650 (1965). In *Republic Steel*, we held that an employer may rely on a provision in a collective-bargaining agreement requiring its employees to submit all contractual grievances to arbitration prior to bringing suit under §301. If a provision in the collective-bargaining agreement also permits reactivation of a grievance after an internal union appeal, an employer or union should also be able to rely on that provision and thus defend the §301 suit on the ground that the employee failed to exhaust internal union procedures.

[21] In addition, by reactivating the grievance, the union might be able to rectify the very wrong of which the employee complains — a breach of the duty of fair representation caused by the union's refusal to seek arbitration — and the employee would then be unable to satisfy the precondition to a §301 suit against the employer.

savings in judicial resources, because regardless of the outcome of the internal appeal, the employee would be required to prove *de novo* in his §301 suit that the union breached its duty of fair representation and that the employer breached the collective-bargaining agreement.[23] . . .

In reliance upon the Court of Appeals' opinion in this case, the UAW contends that even if exhaustion is not required with respect to the employer, it should be required with respect to the union, because the relief Clayton seeks *against the union* in his §301 suit is available through internal union procedures. But cf. supra, n.17. We disagree. While this argument might have force where the employee has chosen to bring his §301 suit only against the union, the defense should not be available where, as here, the employee has filed suit against both the union and the employer. A trial court requiring exhaustion with respect to the suit against the union, but not with respect to the suit against the employer, would be faced with two undesirable alternatives. If it stayed the action against the employer pending resolution of the internal appeals procedures, it would effectively be requiring exhaustion with respect to the suit against the employer, a result we have held would violate national labor policy. Yet if it permitted the action against the employer to proceed, and tolled the running of the statute of limitation in the suit against the union until the internal procedures had been exhausted, it could very well find itself with two separate §301 suits, based on the same facts, proceeding at different paces in its courtroom. As we suggested in Vaca v. Sipes, . . . at 920, this is a result that should be avoided if possible. The preferable approach is for the court to permit the employee's §301 action to proceed against both defendants, despite the employee's failure to exhaust, unless the internal union procedures can reactivate the grievance or grant the relief that would be available in the employee's §301 suit against both defendants. . . .

In this case, the internal union appeals panels cannot reactivate Clayton's grievance and cannot grant Clayton the reinstatement relief he seeks under §301. We therefore hold that Clayton should not have been required to exhaust internal union appeals procedures prior to bringing suit against his union and employer under §301.

Affirmed in part, reversed in part.

POWELL, J., with whom BURGER, C.J., joins, dissenting. . . . The

---

[23] Even if the union admitted during the internal appeals procedure that it had breached its duty of fair representation, an admission the UAW has apparently made only once in the 20 years preceding 1977, see Klein, "Enforcement of the Right to Fair Representation: Alternative Forums," in The Duty of Fair Representation 103 (1977), the employee would still not be saved the time and expense of proving that breach in his §301 suit. While a union's admission that it breached its duty of fair representation is certainly evidence a court can consider, an employer defending a §301 suit would still be entitled to prove that no such breach had occurred. See Vaca v. Sipes, supra, 386 U.S., at 186-187. . . .

union has not made a final determination whether to pursue arbitration on Clayton's behalf. Clayton should not be able to claim a breach of duty by the union until the union has had a full opportunity to make this determination. No such opportunity exists until Clayton exhausts the procedures available for resolving that question. Thus, as Clayton cannot claim a breach of duty by the union, he cannot bring a breach of contract suit under §301 against his employer.

In my view, the asserted distinction in a tripartite case such as this one between contractual and internal union remedies . . . is immaterial. The situation presented in this case is well within the doctrine, underlying Republic Steel Corp. v. Maddox, that employees must pursue all procedures established for determining whether a union will go forward with a grievance. Employees must pursue available procedures even if the collective-bargaining agreement contains time limits that appear on their face to bar revival of the grievance. As the Court noted in John Wiley & Sons v. Livingston, 376 U.S. 543, . . . "[q]uestions concerning the procedural prerequisites to arbitration do not arise in a vacuum; they develop in the context of an actual dispute about the rights of the parties to the contract or those covered by it." Therefore, "it best accords with the usual purposes of an arbitration clause and with the policy behind federal labor law to regard procedural disagreements not as separate disputes but as aspects of the dispute which called the grievance procedures into play." Id., at 559. Thus, the question whether such time limits should be waived in a particular case is itself an arbitrable matter.

REHNQUIST, J., with whom BURGER, C.J., STEWART, and POWELL, JJ., join, dissenting. . . . The second prong of the Court's test is "whether the internal union appeals procedures would be inadequate either to reactivate the employee's grievance or to award him the full relief he seeks under §301. . . . " Exhaustion is not required in this case, the Court says, because the UAW's internal union appeals procedures cannot provide Clayton with reinstatement or reactivation of his grievance.

. . . The principal difficulty with the Court's opinion lies in its framing of this second criterion which reflects much too narrow a view of the purposes of the exhaustion defense and the benefits which will likely result from requiring exhaustion in a case where a union has established a means for reviewing the manner in which it has represented an employee during a grievance. . . .

The error in the Court's analysis results in part from its apparent belief that intraunion remedies must provide a complete substitute for either the courts or the contract grievance procedure in order to be deemed "adequate." The purpose of intraunion remedies, however, is quite different. These remedies are provided to facilitate or encourage the private resolution

of disputes, not to be a complete substitute for the courts. Intraunion remedies can serve this purpose so long as they have the capacity to address
whether the union wrongfully handled the grievance. Obviously, if a union
appeals procedure cannot address this question, exhaustion should not be
required.

An additional question which is also of great importance is whether a
union should ever be found to have breached its duty of fair representation
when a union member shuns an appeals procedure which is both mandated
by the union constitution and established for the purpose of allowing the
union to satisfy its duty of fair representation. It seems to me not at all
unreasonable to say that a union should have the right to require its members
to give it the first opportunity to correct its own mistakes. Responsible union
self-government demands a fair opportunity to function. This is especially
true in a situation such as here where exhaustion of the union remedies could
eliminate the need to litigate altogether. Congress has recognized the importance of these values in §101(a)(4) of [LMRDA]. This section provides in
part:

> No labor organization shall limit the right of any member thereof to
> institute an action in any court, or any proceeding before any administrative
> agency . . . *Provided,* That any such member may be required to exhaust
> reasonable hearing procedures (but not to exceed a four-month lapse of time)
> within such organization, before instituting legal or administrative proceed-
> ings against such organizations or any officer thereof. . . .

The language of §104(a)(4) also goes a long way to satisfy the third
prong of the test set forth by the Court today. Exhaustion of internal union
procedures should not be required where such would unreasonably delay an
employee's opportunity to obtain a judicial hearing on the merits of his claim.
Intraunion procedures which take years to complete serve no worthwhile
purpose in the overall scheme of promoting the prompt and private resolution of claims. But a requirement that an employee not be permitted to go to
court without first having pursued an intraunion appeal for at least 4 months
does substantially further this national labor policy without placing any unfair
burden on an employee.

NOTES

1. In appraising the divisions in *Clayton*, what significance would you
attach to the fact that a discharged employee may have to relocate to find a
job?

2. If the apportionment formula advanced by the trial court in *Bowen* is ultimately upheld, would you expect unions to be less willing to invoke the exhaustion defense in a hybrid action?

With the case below we turn from a focus on the standing and responsibility of individuals and their bargaining representatives after discipline has been imposed to problems of procedure and representation arising during investigatory interviews. Students will notice the relationship between these problems and those generated by Miranda v. Arizona, 384 U.S. 436 (1966).

NLRB v. J. Weingarten, Inc.
420 U.S. 251 (1975)

BRENNAN, J. . . . Respondent operates a chain of . . . retail stores with lunch counters at some, and so-called lobby food operations at others. . . . Respondent's sales personnel are represented . . . by Retail Clerks Union, Local 455. Leura Collins . . . worked at the lunch counter at Store No. 2 from 1961 to 1970 when she was transferred to the lobby operation at Store No. 98. Respondent maintains a companywide security department staffed by "Loss Prevention Specialists" who work undercover . . . to guard against . . . shoplifting and employee dishonesty. In June 1972, "Specialist" Hardy, without the knowledge of the store manager, spent two days observing the lobby operation at Store No. 98 investigating a report that Collins was taking money from a cash register. When Hardy's surveillance of Collins . . . turned up no evidence to support the report, Hardy disclosed his presence to the store manager and reported that he could find nothing wrong. The store manager then told him that a fellow lobby employee . . . had just reported that Collins had purchased a box of chicken that sold for $2.98, but had placed only $1 in the cash register. Collins was summoned to an interview with Specialist Hardy and the store manager, and Hardy questioned her. The Board found that several times during the questioning she asked the store manager to call the union shop steward or some other union representative to the interview, and that her requests were denied. Collins admitted that she had purchased some chicken, a loaf of bread, and some cake which she said she paid for and donated to her church for a church dinner. She explained that she purchased four pieces of chicken for which the price was $1, but that because the lobby department was out of the small-size boxes in which such purchases were usually packaged she put the chicken into the larger box normally used for packaging larger quantities. Specialist Hardy left the interview to check Collins' explanation with the fellow employee who had reported Collins. This employee confirmed that the lobby department had run out of small boxes and also said that she did not know how many pieces of chicken Collins had put in the larger box. Specialist Hardy returned to the interview, told Collins that her explanation had checked out, that he was sorry if he had inconvenienced her, and that the matter was closed.

Collins thereupon burst into tears and blurted out that the only thing she had ever gotten from the store without paying for it was her free lunch. . . . [T]he store manager and Specialist Hardy closely interrogated Collins about violations of the policy [against free lunches] in the lobby department at Store No. 98. Collins again asked that a shop steward be called to the interview, but the store manager denied her request. Based on her answers to his questions, Specialist Hardy prepared a written statement which included a computation that Collins owed the store approximately $160 for lunches. Collins refused to sign the statement. The Board found that Collins, as well as most, if not all, employees in the lobby department of Store No. 98, including the manager of that department, took lunch from the lobby without paying for it, apparently because no contrary policy was ever made known to them. Indeed, when company headquarters advised Specialist Hardy by telephone during the interview that headquarters itself was uncertain whether the policy against providing free lunches at lobby departments was in effect at Store No. 98, he terminated his interrogation of Collins. . . . [After Collins informed the union of this interview, this unfair labor practice proceeding was initiated. The NLRB held that the employer had violated §8(a)(1) by denying Collins' request for the presence of her union representative at an investigatory interview that the employee had reasonably believed might result in discipline. The Fifth Circuit denied enforcement.]

II

The Board's construction that §7 creates a statutory right in an employee to refuse to submit without union representation to an interview which he reasonably fears may result in his discipline was announced in its decision and order of January 28, 1972, in Quality Mfg. Co., 195 N.L.R.B. 197, considered in Garment Workers v. Quality Mfg. Co., post, p. 276. In its opinions in that case and in Mobil Oil Corp., 196 N.L.R.B. 1052, . . . three months later, the Board shaped the contours and limits of the statutory right.

First, the right inheres in §7's guarantee of the right of employees to act in concert for mutual aid and protection. In *Mobil Oil*, the Board stated:

> An employee's right to union representation upon request is based on §7 . . . which guarantees the right of employees to act in concert for "mutual aid and protection." The denial of this right has a reasonable tendency to

interfere with, restrain, and coerce employees in violation of §8(a)(l). . . . Thus, it is a serious violation of the employee's individual right to engage in concerted activity by seeking the assistance of his statutory representation if the employer denies the employee's request and compels the employee to appear unassisted at an interview which may put his job security in jeopardy. . . .

Second, the right arises only in situations where the employee requests representation. . . .

Third, the employee's right to request representation as a condition of participation in an interview is limited to situations where the employee reasonably believes the investigation will result in disciplinary action.[5] Thus the Board stated in *Quality*:

> We would not apply the rule to such run-of-the-mill shop-floor conversations as, for example, the giving of instructions or training or needed corrections of work techniques. In such cases there cannot normally be any reasonable basis for an employee to fear that any adverse impact may result from the interview. . . .

195 N.L.R.B., at 199.

Fourth, exercise of the right may not interfere with legitimate employer prerogatives. The employer has no obligation to justify his refusal to allow union representation, and despite refusal, the employer is free to carry on his inquiry without interviewing the employee, and thus leave to the employee the choice between having an interview unaccompanied by his representative, or having no interview and forgoing any benefits that might be derived from one. . . .

Fifth, the employer has no duty to bargain with any union representative who may be permitted to attend the investigatory interview. The Board said in *Mobil*, "we are not giving the Union any particular rights with respect to predisciplinary discussions which it otherwise was not able to secure during collective bargaining negotiations." 196 N.L.R.B., at 1052 n.3. The Board thus adhered to its decisions distinguishing between disciplinary and investigatory interviews, imposing a mandatory affirmative obligation to meet with the union representative only in the case of the disciplinary interview. . . . "The representative is present to assist the employee, and may attempt to

---

[5] The Board stated in *Quality*: "'Reasonable ground' will of course be measured, as here, by objective standards under all the circumstances of the case." 195 N.L.R.B. 197, 198 n.3. In NLRB v. Gissel Packing Co., 395 U.S. 575, 608 (1969), the Court announced that it would "reject any rule that requires a probe of an employee's subjective motivations as involving an endless and unreliable inquiry," and we reaffirm that view today as applicable also in the context of this case.

clarify the facts or suggest other employees who may have knowledge of them. The employer, however, is free to insist that he is only interested, at that time, in hearing the employee's own account of the matter under investigation." Brief for Petitioner 22.

III

The Board's holding is a permissible construction of "concerted activities for . . . mutual aid or protection" . . . , and should have been sustained.

The action of an employee in seeking to have the assistance of his union representative at a confrontation with his employer clearly falls within the literal wording of §7 that "[e]mployees shall have the right . . . to engage in . . . concerted activities for the purpose of . . . mutual aid or protection." This is true even though the employee alone may have an immediate stake in the outcome; he seeks "aid or protection" against a perceived threat to his employment security. The union representative whose participation he seeks is, however, safeguarding not only the particular employee's interest, but also the interests of the entire bargaining unit by exercising vigilance to make certain that the employer does not initiate or continue a practice of imposing punishment unjustly. The representative's presence is an assurance to other employees in the bargaining unit that they, too, can obtain his aid and protection if called upon to attend a like interview. Concerted activity for mutual aid or protection is therefore as present here as it was held to be in NLRB v. Peter Cailler Kohler Swiss Chocolates Co., 130 F.2d 503, 505-506 (CA 2d Cir. 1942), cited with approval by this Court in Houston Contractors Assn. v. NLRB, 386 U.S. 664, 668-669 (1967):

> When all the other workmen in a shop make common cause with a fellow workman over his separate grievance, and go out on strike in his support, they engage in a "concerted activity" for "mutual aid or protection," although the aggrieved workman is the only one of them who has any immediate stake in the outcome. The rest know that by their action each of them assures himself, in case his turn ever comes, of the support of the one whom they are all then helping; and the solidarity so established is "mutual aid" in the most literal sense, as nobody doubts.

The Board's construction plainly effectuates the most fundamental purposes of the Act [paraphrasing §1]. . . . Requiring a lone employee to attend an investigatory interview which he reasonably believes may result in the imposition of discipline perpetuates the inequality the Act was designed to eliminate, and bars recourse to the safeguards the Act provided "to redress the perceived imbalance of economic power between labor and management." American Ship Building Co. v. NLRB, 380 U.S. 300, 316 (1965).

Viewed in this light, the Board's recognition that §7 guarantees an employee's right to the presence of a union representative at an investigatory interview in which the risk of discipline reasonably inheres is within the protective ambit of the section "'read in the light of the mischief to be corrected and the end to be attained.'" NLRB v. Hearst Publications, Inc., 322 U.S. 111, 124 (1944).

The Board's construction also gives recognition to the right when it is most useful to both employee and employer. A single employee confronted by an employer investigating whether certain conduct deserves discipline may be too fearful or inarticulate to relate accurately the incident being investigated, or too ignorant to raise extenuating factors. A knowledgeable union representative could assist the employer by eliciting favorable facts, and save the employer production time by getting to the bottom of the incident occasioning the interview. Certainly his presence need not transform the interview into an adversary contest. Respondent suggests nonetheless that union representation at this stage is unnecessary because a decision as to employee culpability or disciplinary action can be corrected after the decision to impose discipline has become final. In other words, respondent would defer representation until the filing of a formal grievance challenging the employer's determination of guilt after the employee has been discharged or otherwise disciplined. At that point, however, it becomes increasingly difficult for the employee to vindicate himself, and the value of representation is correspondingly diminished. The employer may then be more concerned with justifying his actions than reexamining them.

IV

The Court of Appeals rejected the Board's construction as foreclosed by that court's decision four years earlier in Texaco, Inc., Houston Producing Division v. NLRB, 408 F.2d 142 (1969), and by "a long line of Board decisions, each of which indicates — either directly or indirectly — that no union representative need be present" at an investigatory interview. 485 F.2d, at 1137. . . .

    . . . [T]he Board asserts that even though some "may be read as reaching a contrary conclusion," they should not be treated as impairing the validity of the Board's construction, because "[t]hese decisions do not reflect a considered analysis of the issue." . . . In that circumstance, and in the light of significant developments in industrial life believed by the Board to have warranted a reappraisal of the question,[10] the Board argues that the case

---

[10] "There has been a recent growth in the use of sophisticated techniques — such as closed circuit television, undercover security agents, and lie detectors — to monitor and investigate the employees' conduct at their place of work. See, e.g., Warwick Electronics,

is one where "[t]he nature of the problem, as revealed by unfolding variant situations, inevitably involves an evolutionary process for its rational response, not a quick, definitive formula as a comprehensive answer. . . .

The responsibility to adapt the Act to changing patterns of industrial life is entrusted to the Board. The Court of Appeals impermissibly encroached upon the Board's function in determining for itself that an employee has no "need" for union assistance at an investigatory interview. . . . [T]he Board's construction here, while it may not be required by the Act, is at least permissible under it, and insofar as the Board's application of that meaning engages in the "difficult and delicate responsibility" of reconciling conflicting interests of labor and management, the balance struck by the Board is "subject to limited judicial review." NLRB v. Truck Drivers, 353 U.S. 87, 96 (1957).

The statutory right confirmed today is in full harmony with actual industrial practice. Many important collective bargaining agreements . . . accord employees rights of union representation at investigatory interviews. Even where such a right is not explicitly provided in the agreement a "well-established current of arbitral authority" sustains the right of union representation at investigatory interviews which the employee reasonably believes may result in disciplinary action against him. Chevron Chemical Co., 60 Lab. Arb. 1066, 1071 (1973).

The judgment is reversed and the case is remanded with direction to enter a judgment enforcing the Board's order. . . .

POWELL, J., joined by STEWART, J., dissenting. . . . The Court today construes that right [conferred by §7] to include union representation or the presence of another employee[1] at any interview the employee reasonably fears might result in disciplinary action. In my view, such an interview is not *concerted activity* within the intendment of the Act.

. . . [A]s late as 1964 — after almost 30 years of experience with §7 — the Board flatly rejected an employee's claim that she was entitled to union representation in a "discharge conversation" with the general manager, who

---

Inc., 46 L.A. 95, 97-98 (1966); Bowman Transportation, Inc., 56 L.A. 283, 286-292 (1972). These techniques increase not only the employees' feelings of apprehension, but also their need for experienced assistance in dealing with them. Thus, often, as here and in *Mobil*, supra, an investigative interview is conducted by security specialists; the employee does not confront a supervisor who is known or familiar to him, but a stranger trained in interrogation techniques. These developments in industrial life warrant a concomitant reappraisal by the Board of their impact on statutory rights. Cf. Boys Markets, Inc. v. Retail Clerks, Local 770, 398 U.S. 235, 250." Brief for Petitioner 27 n.22.

[1] While the Court speaks only of the right to insist on the presence of a union representative, it must be assumed that the §7 right today recognized, affording employees the right to act "in concert" in employer interviews, also exists in the absence of a recognized union. Cf. NLRB v. Washington Aluminum Co., 370 U.S. 9 (1962).

later admitted that he had already decided to fire her. . . . Dobbs Houses, Inc., 145 N.L.R.B. 1565, 1571 (1964). [The dissent denied that the changes in the Board's position reflected a logical evolution.]. . . .

The power to discipline or discharge employees has been recognized uniformly as one of the elemental prerogatives of management. Absent specific limitations imposed by statute or through the process of collective bargaining, management remains free to discharge employees at will. . . . An employer's need to consider and undertake disciplinary action will arise in a wide variety of unpredictable situations. The appropriate disciplinary response also will vary significantly, depending on the nature and severity of the employee's conduct. Likewise, the nature and amount of information required for determining the appropriateness of disciplinary action may vary with the severity of the possible sanction and the complexity of the problem. And in some instances, the employer's legitimate need to maintain discipline and security may require an immediate response.

This variety and complexity necessarily call for flexible and creative adjustment. . . . [T]he question of union participation in investigatory interviews is a standard topic of collective bargaining.[8] Many agreements incorporate provisions that grant and define such rights, and arbitration decisions increasingly have begun to recognize them as well. Rather than vindicate the Board's interpretation of §7, however, these developments suggest to me that union representation at investigatory interviews is a matter that Congress left to the bargaining process. . . . The type of personalized interview with which we are here concerned is simply not "concerted activity" within the meaning of the Act.

[The dissenting opinion of Burger, C.J., is omitted.]

NOTES

1. Justice Powell in dissent stated that the §7 right recognized by the Court extends to unrepresented employees who request the presence of a

---

[8]The history of a similar case, Mobil Oil, 196 N.L.R.B. 1052 (1972), *enforcement denied*, 482 F.2d 842 (CA 7th 1973), illustrates how the Board has substituted its judgment for that of the collective-bargaining process. During negotiations leading to the establishment of a collective-bargaining agreement in that case, the union advanced a demand that existing provisions governing suspension and discharge be amended to provide for company-union discussions prior to disciplinary action. The employer refused to accede to that demand and ultimately prevailed, only to find his efforts at the bargaining table voided by the Board's interpretation of the statute.

Chairman Miller subsequently suggested that the union can waive the employee's §7 right to the presence of a union representative. See Western Electric Co., 198 N.L.R.B. 82 (1972). The Court today provides no indication whether such waivers in the collective bargaining process are permissible. Cf. NLRB v. Magnavox Co., 415 U.S. 322 (1974).

coworker at an investigatory interview. Does *Weingarten's* reasoning compel that conclusion? Is there a policy consideration that would warrant, in this context, a distinction between represented and unrepresented employees? Compare E. I. DuPont de Nemours & Co. v. NLRB, 707 F.2d 1076 (9th Cir. 1983), with E. I. DuPont de Nemours & Co. v. NLRB, 724 F.2d 1061 (3d Cir. 1983), *vacated and remanded*, 733 F.2d 296 (1984). Is the NLRB's shift on "concertedness" (see Meyers Industries, Inc., supra p. 212) relevant on this question? Does *Weingarten* itself rest on a theory of implied or "constructive" concerted activity?

2. Is an employer required to advise an employee of his *Weingarten* rights? Would it be material if the employee had been "confused and frightened"? See Montgomery Ward & Co., Inc., 269 N.L.R.B. No. 156, 115 L.R.R.M. 1321 (1984); cf. the Ross excerpt, supra p. 949.

3. Two employees, seen fighting in the plant, were summoned to their supervisor's office. Management did not answer their questions about the purpose of the meeting. Each employee asked the union steward to accompany and represent him. The steward's request of management for a consultation with the employees, individually and together, before the meeting with the supervisor, was denied without explanation. Upon arriving at the supervisor's office, the steward was told that he would not be permitted to say anything during the interview. At the conclusion of the interview, the employees, who confessed to fighting, received two-week suspensions. Does the Court's opinion in *Weingarten* indicate whether the Act has been violated? Would it be material if the steward, after being told to be silent during management's interviewing, had at the conclusion of management's interrogation been invited to clarify facts or to name knowledgeable employees? On the foregoing questions, see NLRB v. S.W. Bell Telephone Co., 730 F.2d 166 (5th Cir. 1984); Pacific Tel. & Tel. Co. v. NLRB, 711 F.2d 134 (9th Cir. 1983); Climax Molybdenum Co. v. NLRB, 584 F.2d 360 (10th Cir. 1978).

4. What is an appropriate remedy when an employer conducts an unlawful investigatory interview and the employee whose rights are violated is later disciplined for conduct that was the subject of the interview? If the employee's conduct was "cause" for discipline, should an employer's *Weingarten* violation shield the employee from discipline? Would §10(c) preclude a Board order of reinstatement? Would it be material if the decision to discipline was not based on information or clues obtained during the interview? See, e.g., Kraft Foods, Inc., 251 N.L.R.B. 598 (1980); NLRB v. Illinois Bell Tel. Co., 674 F.2d 618 (7th Cir. 1982).

For discussion of *Weingarten* issues, see Dobranski, The Right of Union Representation in Employer Interviews: A Post-*Weingarten* Analysis, 26 St. Louis U.L.J. 295 (1982); Ginsburg, The Right to Union Representation at Disciplinary Interviews: Recent Developments Since *Weingarten*, 1981 Wis. L. Rev. 1303.

5. An employer, subject to a "just cause" provision of a collective agreement, has information that he considers (and is) sufficient to justify discharging an employee. Nevertheless, the employer summons the employee with a view to letting him react to the evidence against him. The employee asks for his steward to be present. The employer says, "Forget it; you're fired." Has the employer violated the NLRA? The agreement? See *Grief Bros.*, supra p. 943.

6. Both opinions in *Weingarten* contemplate that union representation at investigatory interviews may be treated in collective bargaining agreements. Is there any reason to bar a union's contractual waiver of employees' *Weingarten* rights? Does an employer violate the Act by insisting to the point of impasse on a clause requiring employees to participate in all interviews without the presence of a union representative?

B. "UNION SECURITY"

1. Introductory Note

"Union security" agreements require union membership or some form of financial support of the union by employees as a condition of initial or continued employment by the signatory employer. The principal forms of such agreements (without regard to their current legality under the NLRA or state law) have been the following:

(1) The closed shop — requiring membership in the union involved as a condition of both initial and continued employment.

(2) The union shop — permitting employment of nonmembers, but requiring employees to join the union within a specified period and to maintain their membership as a condition of continued employment.

(3) The agency shop — under which members of the bargaining unit pay initiation fees and dues without necessarily joining or having the right to join the union.

(4) Maintenance of membership — under which an employee is not required to join the union, but if he does or, having been a member, fails to resign during an escape period, he must remain a member for the duration of the agreement as a condition of continued employment. Such provisions often help overcome employers' reluctance to force nonunion employees to

join or to finance unions that many employees, with employer encouragement, may have opposed.

(5) Preferential hiring — union members are given preference in hiring, but the employer is permitted to hire nonunion personnel if the union fails to supply needed workers. Such arrangements have sometimes been coupled with union shop provisions.

Students should consider the impact of each arrangement on union control of entry into the occupation involved and on union power to create or intensify "labor shortages," to discriminate on racial or other invidious grounds, to stifle internal criticism and dissent as well as free debate on public issues, and to help maintain industrial discipline.

American unions, from their inception, have sought some form of union security. One popular explanation for such demands has stressed the especially bitter opposition of American business to labor organization. Other considerations appear to have been at least as important. Early American unions, like the guilds that preceded them, sought to preempt certain jobs for their members and to control the entry of new workers into their "job territories." In the precolonial period, the closed shop served as an important means of such control. See P. Sultan, Right-to-Work Laws 14 (1958). Thereafter, the closed shop, coupled with the closed union, was used in an effort to insulate certain crafts against the pressures of recession, immigration, and increased labor mobility. Union security arrangements were thus a shield not only against the antiunion employer but also against the insecurity of employment in a market system. Id., ch. 2. Furthermore, the distaste of unions and union members for "free riders" is largely independent of employers' attitudes concerning organization. Union demands for union security have not declined with legal protection of collective activity, with the growth of union power, and with the acceptance by many employers of the idea of unionization and collective bargaining. On the contrary, "both in the U.S.A. and in Britain it is precisely from those unions that are strongest that demands for closed-shop agreements emanate. It is where solidarity is greatest that one finds the closed-shop principle firmly established." See V. Allen, Power in Trade Unions 50 (1954).

For a comparative view, see Forde, The "Closed Shop" Case, 11 Indus. L.J. 1 (1982), discussing the case of Young, James, and Webster, European Court of Human Rights, Judgment of 13 Aug. 1981, Series A, Judgments and Decisions 44, which held that firing three incumbent British workers, pursuant to a collective bargaining agreement, for refusing to join a union violated Article 11 of the European Convention for the protection of Human Rights and Fundamental Freedoms, which protects the right to freedom of association.

At common law, the states divided on the legality of a closed shop, but

the trend of later decisions was to recognize its validity. See generally Newman, The Closed Union and the Right to Work, 43 Colum. L. Rev. 42
(1943). Some jurisdictions, while not invalidating a closed shop as such,
barred a union from maintaining both a closed shop and a closed union. See,
e.g., Williams v. International Bhd. of Boilermakers, 27 Cal. 2d 586, 165
P.2d 903 (1946).

Approximately 20 states have banned union security arrangements by
statutory or constitutional provisions that vary in scope and in enforcement.
(These states include Alabama, Arizona, Arkansas, Florida, Georgia, Iowa,
Kansas, Louisiana (which enacted a general right-to-work law in 1954,
repealed it in 1956, replacing it with one relating only to agricultural workers,
then in 1976 enacted a statute similar to the 1954 law), Mississippi, Nebraska, Nevada, North Carolina, North Dakota, South Carolina, South
Dakota, Tennessee, Texas, Utah, Virginia, and Wyoming.) These "right-
to-work" laws have generated a highly emotional debate. For a review of the
competing arguments, see P. Sultan, Right-to-Work Laws, ch. 5 (1958).
Studies of such laws have generally concluded that they have not had a
significant impact on labor relations or on union "power" and that bootleg
union security arrangements are in fact maintained in the states involved. See
Kuhlman, Right-to-Work Laws, The Virginia Experience, 6 Lab. L.J. 453
(1955); Meyers, Effects of "Right-to-Work" Laws: A Study of the Texas
Act, 9 Ind. & Lab. Rel. Rev. 77 (1955); econometric studies cited in R.
Flanagan, Labor Economics and Labor Relations 375 n.37 (1984). But see
Kuhn, Right-to-Work Laws, Symbols or Substance, 14 Ind. & Lab. Rel.
Rev. 587 (1961).

Despite the controversy generated by "compulsory unionism," there
has been, during the last 20 years, a substantial increase in both the percentage of major agreements (now 83 percent) containing union security provisions and the percentage of workers covered by such provisions (now 90
percent of the six million workers covered by major agreements). Similarly,
there has been a substantial increase in the percentage of major agreements
containing provisions for employer check-off of union dues. See Major
Collective Agreements: Union Security and Dues Check-off Provisions,
BLS Bull. 1425 (May 1982).

2. Federal Regulation and State Authority

Federal regulation of union security has fluctuated over time and across
industries. The Railway Labor Act (1934), which had been agreed to by
railway unions and employers, prohibited all forms of union security. See §2,
Fourth, Fifth, Eleventh. Unions accepted that prohibition, apparently be-

cause of their fears of "company unions." The Wagner Act exempted union security agreements, including closed shops, from the proscription of §8(3) when the union had majority support, but did not displace state prohibitions. In 1947, the Taft-Hartley Act imposed substantial restrictions on such agreements and expressly preserved state authority to prohibit them. See §§8(a)(3), 8(b)(1), 8(b)(5), 14(b) and 9(e)(1). The 1951 amendments to the RLA rejected some of the restrictions embodied in Taft-Hartley by permitting agreements (with unions enjoying majority support) that required payment of assessments as well as periodic dues and initiation fees, and by superseding contrary state laws. See §2, Eleventh.

In 1951, the Taft-Hartley requirement that a majority of the affected employees vote to authorize a union security arrangement prior to its becoming effective, was repealed after such elections had overwhelmingly favored such arrangements. 29 U.S.C. 158(a)(3). That change did not, however, affect the provisions for deauthorization elections embodied in §9(e)(1). Great A & P Tea Co., 100 N.L.R.B. 1494 (1952), held that an affirmative vote in such an election immediately invalidates a union security provision, regardless of the length of the unexpired term of the agreement. See generally T. Haggard, Compulsory Unionism, The NLRB and the Courts: A Legal Analysis of Union Security Agreements (1977); Cantor, Uses and Abuses of the Agency Shop, 59 Notre Dame Law. 61 (1983).

NLRB v. General Motors Corp.
373 U.S. 734 (1963)

WHITE, J. The issue here is whether an employer commits an unfair labor practice [under §8(a)(5)] when it refuses to bargain with a certified union over the union's proposal for the adoption of the "agency shop." More narrowly, since the employer is not obliged to bargain over a proposal that he commit an unfair labor practice, the question is whether the agency shop is an unfair labor practice under §8(a)(3) . . . or else is exempted from the prohibitions of that section by the proviso thereto. We have concluded that this type of arrangement does not constitute an unfair labor practice and that it is not prohibited by §8.

Respondent's employees are represented by the [UAW], in a single, multiplant, companywide unit. The 1958 agreement . . . provides for maintenance of membership and the union shop. These provisions were not operative, however, in such States as Indiana where state law prohibited making union membership a condition of employment.

In June 1959, the Indiana intermediate appellate court held that an agency shop arrangement would not violate the state right-to-work law.

Meade Elec. Co. v. Hagberg, 129 Ind. App. 631, 159 N.E.2d 408. As defined in that opinion, . . . "agency shop" applies to an arrangement under which all employees are required as a condition of employment to pay dues to the union and pay the union's initiation fee, but they need not actually become union members. The union thereafter [proposed] the negotiation of a contractual provision covering Indiana plants "generally similar to that set forth" in the *Meade* case. . . . The respondent . . . replied . . . that the proposed agreement would violate the [NLRA] and that respondent must therefore "respectfully decline" . . . to bargain over the proposal.

[After the union's 8(a)(5) charge and the usual proceedings, the Board found that] "the Union was not seeking to bargain over a clause requiring nonmember employees to pay sums equal to dues and fees as a condition of employment while at the same time maintaining a closed-union policy with respect to applicants for membership," since the proposal contemplated an arrangement in which "all employees are *given the option* of becoming, or refraining from becoming, members of the Union." . . . [T]he Board assessed the union's proposal as comporting fully with the congressional declaration of policy in favor of union-security contracts and therefore a mandatory subject as to which the Act obliged respondent to bargain in good faith. . . . [I]t also stated that it had "no doubt that an agency-shop agreement is a permissible form of union-security within the meaning of §§7 and 8(a)(3) . . ." Accordingly, the Board . . . ordered respondent to bargain. . . .

. . . The Court of Appeals set the order aside on the grounds that the Act tolerates only "an agreement requiring membership in a labor organization as a condition of employment" when such agreements do not violate state right-to-work laws, and that the Act does not authorize agreements requiring payment of membership dues to a union, in lieu of membership, as a condition of employment. It held that the proposed agency shop agreement would violate §§7, 8(a)(1), and 8(a)(3) . . . and that the employer was therefore not obliged to bargain over it. 303 F.2d 428 (C.A. 6th Cir.). We . . . now reverse [that decision].

Section 8(3) under the Wagner Act was the predecessor to §8(a)(3) of the present law. Like §8(a)(3), §8(3) forbade employers to discriminate against employees to compel them to join a union. Because it was feared that §8(3) and §7, if nothing were added to qualify them, might be held to outlaw union-security arrangements such as the closed shop, the proviso to §8(3) was added expressly declaring:

. . . *Provided*, That nothing in this Act . . . or in any other statute of the United States, shall preclude an employer from making an agreement with a labor organization . . . to require as a condition of employment membership therein, if such labor organization is the representative of the employees as provided in §9(a). . . .

The prevailing administrative and judicial view under the Wagner Act was or came to be that the proviso to §8(3) covered both the closed and union shop, as well as less onerous union-security arrangements, if they were otherwise legal. The [NLRB] construed the proviso as shielding from an unfair labor practice charge less severe forms of union-security arrangements than the closed or the union shop, including an arrangement in Public Service Co. of Colorado, 89 N.L.R.B. 418, requiring nonunion members to pay to the union $2 a month "for the support of the bargaining unit." And in Algoma Plywood Co. v. Wisconsin Board, 336 U.S. 301, 307, which involved a maintenance of membership agreement, the Court, in commenting on petitioner's contention that the proviso of §8(3) affirmatively protected arrangements within its scope, cf. Garner v. Teamsters Union, 346 U.S. 485, said of its purpose: "The short answer is that §8(3) merely disclaims a national policy hostile to the closed shop *or other forms of union-security agreement.*" (Emphasis added.) . . .

[The LMRA additions to the original proviso to §8(3)] were intended to accomplish twin purposes. On the one hand, the most serious abuses of compulsory unionism were eliminated by abolishing the closed shop. On the other hand, Congress recognized that in the absence of a union-security provision "many employees sharing the benefits of what unions are able to accomplish by collective bargaining will refuse to pay their share of the cost." S. Rep. No. 105, 80th Cong., 1st Sess., p. 6, 1 Leg. Hist. L.M.R.A. 412. Consequently, under the new law "employers would still be permitted to enter into agreements requiring all the employees in a given bargaining unit to become members 30 days after being hired," but "expulsion from a union cannot be a ground of compulsory discharge if the worker is not delinquent in paying his initiation fee or dues." S. Rep. No. 105, p. 7, 1 Leg. Hist. L.M.R.A. 413. . . . As far as the federal law was concerned, all employees could be required to pay their way. The bill "abolishes the closed shop but permits voluntary agreements[d] for requiring such forms of compulsory membership as the union shop or maintenance of membership. . . ." S. Rep. No. 105, p. 3, 1 Leg. Hist. L.M.R.A. 409.

We find nothing in the legislative history . . . indicating that Congress intended the amended proviso to §8(a)(3) to validate only the union

---

[d] [The pertinent House report, after also stating that "the agreement [permitted under §8(a)(3)] must be voluntary," continued: "Unions may not strike to compel employers to enter into such agreements. They are subject to loss of bargaining rights if they do." H.R. Rep. No. 245, 80th Cong., 1st Sess. 9 (1947), Leg. Hist. at 300.—Eds.]

shop and simultaneously to abolish . . . all other union-security arrangements permissible under state law. There is much to be said for the Board's view that, if Congress desired in the Wagner Act to permit a closed or union shop and in the Taft-Hartley Act the union shop, then it also intended to preserve the status of less vigorous, less compulsory contracts which demanded less adherence to the union.

Respondent, however, relies upon the express words of the proviso which allow employment to be conditioned upon "membership": since the union's proposal here does not require actual membership but demands only initiation fees and monthly dues, it is not saved by the proviso. This position, of course, would reject administrative decisions concerning the scope of §8(3) of the Wagner Act, e.g., Public Service Co. of Colorado, supra, reaffirmed by the Board under the Taft-Hartley amendments, American Seating Co., 98 N.L.R.B. 800. Moreover, the 1947 amendments not only abolished the closed shop but also made significant alterations in the meaning of "membership" for the purposes of union-security contracts. Under the second proviso to §8(a)(3), the burdens of membership upon which employment may be conditioned are expressly limited to the payment of initiation fees and monthly dues. It is permissible to condition employment upon membership, but membership, insofar as it has significance to employment rights, may in turn be conditioned only upon payment of fees and dues. "Membership" as a condition of employment is whittled down to its financial core. This Court has said as much before in Radio Officers' Union v. Labor Board, 347 U.S. 17, 41:

> . . . This legislative history clearly indicates that Congress intended to prevent utilization of union security agreements for any purpose other than to compel payment of union dues and fees. Thus Congress recognized the validity of unions' concern about "free riders," i.e., employees who receive the benefits of union representation but are unwilling to contribute their fair share of financial support to such union, and gave unions the power to contract to meet that problem while withholding from unions the power to cause the discharge of employees for any other reason. . . .

We are therefore confident that the proposal made by the union here conditioned employment upon the practical equivalent of union "membership," as Congress used that term in the proviso to §8(a)(3).[9] The proposal for

---

[9] Referring to the Canadian practice, Senator Taft stated that the rule adopted by the Conference Committee "is substantially the rule now in effect in Canada" which is that "the employee must, nevertheless, pay dues, even though he does not join the union" and that if he pays the dues without joining he has the right to be employed. 93 Cong. Rec. 4887, 2 Leg. Hist. L.R.M.A. 1422.

requiring the payment of dues and fees imposes no burdens not imposed by a permissible union shop contract and compels the performance of only those duties of membership which are enforceable by discharge under a union shop arrangement. If an employee in a union shop unit refuses to respect any union-imposed obligations other than the duty to pay dues and fees, and membership in the union is therefore denied or terminated, the condition of "membership" for §8(a)(3) purposes is nevertheless satisfied and the employee may not be discharged for nonmembership even though he is not a formal member.[10] Of course, if the union chooses to extend membership even though the employee will meet only the minimum financial burden, and refuses to support or "join" the union in any other affirmative way, the employee may have to become a "member" under a union shop contract, in the sense that the union may be able to place him on its rolls. The agency shop arrangement proposed here removes that choice from the union and places the option of membership in the employee while still requiring the same monetary support as does the union shop. Such a difference between the union and agency shop may be of great importance in some contexts, but for present purposes it is more formal than real. To the extent that it has any significance at all it serves, rather than violates, the desire of Congress to reduce the evils of compulsory unionism while allowing financial support for the bargaining agent.

In short, the employer categorically refused to bargain with the union over a proposal for an agreement within the proviso to §8(a)(3) and as such lawful for the purposes of this case. . . . We hold that the employer was not excused from his duty to bargain over the proposal on the theory that his acceding to it would necessarily involve him in an unfair labor practice. Whether a different result obtains in States which have declared such arrangements unlawful is an issue still to be resolved in Retail Clerks Assn. v. Schermerhorn, and one which is of no relevance here because Indiana law does not forbid the present contract proposal. . . .

Reversed and remanded.

Goldberg, J., took no part in the consideration or decision of this case.

NOTES

1. Does the legislative history of §8(a)(3) support the contention that a union security provision is not a mandatory item of bargaining and thus a strike for such a provision violates §8(b)(3)?

---

[10] Union Starch & Ref. Co. v. Labor Board, 186 F.2d 1008 (C.A. 7th Cir.). . . .

2. A bargaining agreement contains the following clause:

It shall be a condition of employment that all employees of the Employer covered by this agreement who are members of the Union in good standing on the effective date of this agreement shall remain members in good standing and those who are not members on the effective date of this agreement shall on the thirtieth day [or such longer period as the parties may specify] following the effective date of this agreement, become and remain members in good standing in the Union. It shall also be a condition of employment that all employees covered by this agreement and hired on or after its effective date shall, on the thirtieth day following the beginning of such employment [or such longer period as the parties may specify] become and remain members in good standing in the Union.

Does that clause fairly apprise employees of their rights and obligations under §8(a)(3)? Should a union security clause, coupled with failure to make clear in the agreement or otherwise that the requirement of membership has been "whittled down to its financial core," constitute an unfair labor practice by the union or the employer? Cf. Marden v. Machinists, 91 L.R.R.M. 2841 (S.D. Fla. 1976), *aff'd in part*, 576 F.2d 576 (5th Cir. 1978). Could a union member, fined for violating the union's constitution, effectively defend against the union's action to collect the fine on the ground that, if adequately informed, he would have avoided full membership and the resultant obligations under the union's constitution? Cf. NLRB v. Allis-Chalmers, infra p. 1262. See Mayer, Union Security and the Taft-Hartley Act, 1961 Duke L.J. 505; Rosenthal, The National Labor Relations Act and Compulsory Unionism, 1954 Wis. L. Rev. 53.

3. Before a union may lawfully seek to secure an employee's discharge for nonpayment of dues required under a union security agreement, the union must advise the employee of the amount owed and the basis for computation and give him an opportunity to make payment. See Macy & Co., 266 N.L.R.B. No. 157, 113 L.R.R.M. 1049, 1050 n.10 (1983). Suppose that the employer, after being advised by the union of the employee's nonpayment, complies with the union's request that the employee be discharged, even though the employee claims that he made a tender or that a mistake had been made. Has the employer violated the Act? See *Macy*, supra; Philadelphia Sheraton Corp., 136 N.L.R.B. 888, 893 n.12 (1962).

NLRB v. Local Union No. 103, Intl. Assn. of Bridge, Structural & Ornamental Iron Workers, 434 U.S. 335 (1978). Higdon Construction Co. and Local 103, whose collective bargaining relationship began in 1968, reached a prehire agreement in 1973, obliging Higdon to abide by an agreement between the local and a multiemployer association. That agreement did not contain a union security clause and was reached only after the local had declined to refer employees to Higdon during the latter's ongoing construction project. In 1973, Higdon's president formed Higdon *Contracting* Company to do construction work with nonunion labor. Local 103 picketed two projects of Higdon Contracting and bore placards stating that the company was violating its agreement with the local. Picketing at one project exceeded 30 days, without an election petition being filed. The local did not have majority support at either site picketed. The NLRB, although accepting the ALJ's finding that the two Higdon companies constituted only one employer, sustained Higdon Construction's claim that the picketing violated §8(b)(7)(C). The Supreme Court, reversing the court of appeals, upheld the Board's result, White, J., stating:

". . . Under the Board's view of §8(f), a prehire agreement does not entitle a minority union to be treated as the majority representative of the employees until and unless it attains majority support in the relevant unit. Until that time the prehire agreement is voidable and does not have the same stature as a collective-bargaining contract entered into with a union actually representing a majority of the employees and recognized as such by the employer. Accordingly, the Board holds . . . that picketing by a minority union to enforce a prehire agreement that the employer refuses to honor, effectively has the object of attaining recognition as the bargaining representative with majority support among the employees, and is consequently violative of §8(b)(7)(C). . . . We have concluded that the Board's construction of the Act, although perhaps not the only tenable one, is an acceptable reading of the statutory language and a reasonable implementation of the purposes of the relevant statutory sections. Although on its face, §8(b)(7)(C) would apply to any extended picketing by an uncertified union where recognition or bargaining is an object, the section has not been literally applied. The Board holds that an employer's refusal to honor a collective-bargaining contract executed with the union having majority support is a refusal to bargain and an unfair labor practice under §8(a)(5). Extended picketing by the union attempting to enforce the contract thus seeks to require bargaining, but as the Board applies the Act, §8(b)(7)(C) does not bar such picketing. Building & Construction Trades Council of Santa Barbara County (Sullivan Electric Co.), 146 N.L.R.B. 1086 (1964). . . . The prohibition of §8(b)(7)(C) against picketing with an object of forcing an employer 'to recognize or bargain with a labor organization' should not be read as encompassing two separate and unrelated terms, but was 'intended to proscribe picketing having as its target forcing or requiring an employer's initial acceptance of the union as the bargaining representative of his employees.' *Sullivan Electric*, supra, at 1087.

". . . [T]he *Sullivan Electric* rule does not [however] protect picketing to enforce a contract entered into pursuant to §8(f) where the union is not and has never been the chosen representative of a majority of the employees in a relevant unit. Neither will the Board issue a §8(a)(5) bargaining order against an employer refusing to abide by a §8(f) contract unless the complaining union can demonstrate its majority status in the unit. R. J. Smith Construction Co., 191 N.L.R.B. 693 (1971). . . .

". . . The execution of an agreement with a minority union, an act normally an unfair practice by both employer and union, is legitimated by §8(f) when the employer is in the construction industry. The exception is nevertheless of limited scope, for the usual rule protecting the union from inquiry into its majority status during the terms of a collective-bargaining contract does not apply to prehire agreements. A proviso to the section declares that a §8(f) contract, which would be invalid absent the section, 'shall not be a bar to a petition filed pursuant to section 9(c) or 9(e). . . . As viewed by the Board, a 'prehire agreement is merely a preliminary step that contemplates further action for the development of a full bargaining relationship.' Ruttmann Construction Co., 191 N.L.R.B. 701, 702 (1971). The employer's duty to bargain and honor the contract is contingent on the union's attaining majority support at the various construction sites. . . .

". . . §8(f) itself does not purport to authorize picketing to enforce prehire agreements where the union has not achieved majority support. Neither does it expand the duty of an employer under §8(a)(5), which is to bargain with a *majority* representative, to require the employer to bargain with a union with which he has executed a prehire agreement but which has failed to win majority support in the covered unit.

"As for §8(b)(7), which, along with §8(f), was added in 1959, its major purpose was to implement one of the Act's principal goals — to ensure that employees were free to make an uncoerced choice of bargaining agent. . . .

"Congressional concern about coerced designations of bargaining agents did not evaporate as the focus turned to the construction industry.[10]

---

[10] . . . Representative Barden, an important House floor leader on the bill and a conferee, introduced as an expression of legislative intent Senator Kennedy's explanation the year before of the voluntary nature of the prehire provision:

> Mr. Kennedy: I shall answer the Senator from Florida as follows—and it is my intention, by so answering, to establish the legislative history on this question: It was not the intention of the committee to require by section 604(a) the making of prehire agreements, but, rather, to permit them; nor was it the intention of the committee to authorize a labor organization to strike, picket, or otherwise coerce an employer to sign

Section 8(f) was, of course, motivated by an awareness of the unique situation in that industry. Because the Board had not asserted jurisdiction over the construction industry before 1947, the House Committee Report observed that concepts evoked by the Board had been 'developed without reference to the construction industry.' H.R. Rep. No. 741, 86th Cong., 1st Sess., 19 (1959); 1 Leg. Hist. 777. There were two aspects peculiar to the building trades that Congress apparently thought justified the use of prehire agreements with unions that did not then represent a majority of the employees: 'One reason . . . is that it is necessary for the employer to know his labor costs before making the estimate upon which his bid will be based. A second reason is that the employer must be able to have available a supply of skilled craftsmen ready for quick referral. Ibid.'

"The Senate Report also noted that '[r]epresentation elections in a large segment of the industry are not feasible to demonstrate . . . majority status due to the short periods of actual employment by specific employers.' S. Rep. No. 187, 86th Cong., 1st Sess., 55 (1959); 1 Leg. Hist. 541-542. . . .

"The Board's position does not, as respondents claim, render §8(f) meaningless.[11] Except for §8(f), neither the employer nor the union could execute prehire agreements without committing unfair labor practices. Neither has the Board challenged the voluntary observance of otherwise valid §8(f) contracts, which is the normal course of events. . . .

"The Union argues that the Board's position permitting an employer to repudiate a prehire agreement until the union attains majority support renders the contract for all practical purposes unenforceable, assertedly contrary to this Court's decision in Retail Clerks v. Lion Dry Goods, Inc., 369 U.S. 17 (1962). There, the Court's opinion recognized that §301 . . . confers jurisdiction on the federal courts to entertain suits on contracts between an employer and a minority union, as well as those with majority-designated collective-bargaining agents. Section 8(f) contracts were noted as being in this category. The Court was nevertheless speaking to an issue of jurisdiction. That a court has jurisdiction to consider a suit on a particular contract does not suggest that the contract is enforceable. It would not be inconsistent with *Lion Dry Goods* for a court to hold that the union's majority

---

a prehire agreement where the majority status of the union had not been established. The purpose of this section is to permit voluntary prehire agreements. 105 Cong. Rec. 18128 (1959); 2 Leg. Hist. 1715.

The House Conference Report similarly stressed that "Nothing in such provision is intended . . . to authorize the use of force, coercion, strikes, or picketing to compel any person to enter into such prehire agreements." H.R. Rep. No. 1147, 86th Cong., 1st Sess., 42 (1959); 1 Leg. Hist. 946.

[11] A comparable situation obtains concerning hot-cargo clauses, which are permitted in the construction industry by §8(e), but which cannot be enforced by picketing. . . .

standing is subject to litigation in a §301 suit to enforce a §8(f) contract, just as it is in a §8(a)(5) unfair labor practice proceeding, and that absent a showing that the union is the majority's chosen instrument, the contract is unenforceable. . . ."

Reversed.

Stewart, J., with whom Blackmun and Stevens, JJ., joined, dissenting, urged that §8(b)(7)(C) restricted picketing only if it sought the initial recognition of a union as a bargaining representative and thus did not cover picketing to enforce a preexisting §8(f) agreement. Accordingly, there was no justification for the Board's permitting an employer to nullify such an agreement, compliance with which would have been lawful.

NOTES

1. The general contractor on a construction site signed a prehire agreement with an Operating Engineers local. That agreement, which many area general contractors had also signed, (a) restricted work on the job site to subcontractors who had signed a labor contract with the Operating Engineers Union, and (b) required the subs' employees to join the union. McNeff, a subcontractor, began work on a job without having signed an agreement with the union; nor were his employees at the job site union members. The union advised McNeff that he could remain on the project only by signing an agreement like that signed by the general contractor. McNeff at first refused, but signed after the union representative returned with the general contractor who said the same thing. McNeff's employees signed union cards the same day. The agreement required McNeff to make monthly contributions to trust funds for each covered employee. McNeff falsified monthly reports so as to negative liability and failed to make the required payments. The trustees of the funds sued under §301 to recover those amounts.

(a) Relying on these uncontested facts, plaintiffs move for summary judgment. What result? Cf. McNeff, Inc. v. Todd, 103 S. Ct. 1753 (1983).

(b) Suppose that McNeff, after he signed the agreement and his employees signed the union cards, received a letter signed by all his employees stating that they did not wish to be represented by the union. Thereupon he told the union that he would not make any future fringe-benefit payments prescribed by the agreement. Is McNeff legally bound to carry out the agreement? Cf. Precision Stripping Co. v. NLRB, 642 F.2d 1144 (9th Cir. 1981).

(c) Would there be any basis for a claim by McNeff that the subcontracting clause violated §8(e) of the NLRA or the Sherman Act? Cf. Donald Schriver, Inc. v. NLRB, 635 F.2d 859 (D.C. Cir. 1980), cert. denied, 451

U.S. 976 (1981); A. L. Adams Constr. Co. v. Georgia Power Co., 557 F. Supp. 168 (S.D. Ga. 1983).

2. A construction firm filed a petition for a NLRB election after a construction union asked for a §8(f) agreement and threatened to picket to get it. The union moved to dismiss the election petition. How should the Board dispose of the motion? Cf. Albuquerque Insulation Contractor, Inc., 256 N.L.R.B. 61 (1981).

International Assn. of Machinists v. Street
367 U.S. 740 (1961)

BRENNAN, J. A group of labor organizations, appellants here, and the carriers comprising the Southern Railway System, entered into a union-shop agreement pursuant to the authority of §2, Eleventh of the [RLA]. The agreement requires each of the appellees, employees of the carriers, as a condition of continued employment, to pay the appellant union representing his particular class or craft the dues, initiation fees and assessments uniformly required as a condition of acquiring or retaining union membership. The appellees, in behalf of themselves and of employees similarly situated, brought this action in the Superior Court of [Georgia], alleging that the money each was thus compelled to pay to hold his job was in substantial part used to finance the campaigns of candidates for federal and state offices whom he opposed, and to promote the propagation of political and economic doctrines, concepts and ideologies with which he disagreed. The Superior Court . . . entered a judgment and decree enjoining the enforcement of the union-shop agreement on the ground that §2, Eleventh violates the Federal Constitution to the extent that it permits such use by the appellants of the funds exacted from employees. The Supreme Court of Georgia affirmed, 215 Ga. 27, 108 S.E.2d 796. . . .

I. THE HANSON DECISION

We held in Railway Employes' Dept. v. Hanson, 351 U.S. 225, that enactment of the provision of §2, Eleventh authorizing union-shop agreements between interstate railroads and unions of their employees was a valid exercise by Congress of its powers under the Commerce Clause and did not violate the First Amendment or the Due Process Clause of the Fifth Amendment. . . . [A]ll that was held in *Hanson* was that §2, Eleventh was constitutional in its bare authorization of union-shop contracts requiring workers to give "financial support" to unions. . . . We sustained this requirement—and only this requirement—embodied in the statutory authorization of agreements under which "all employees shall become members of the labor organization representing their craft or class." . . . [W]e passed neither upon forced association in any other aspect nor upon the issue of the use of exacted money for political causes which were opposed by the employees.

The record in this case is adequate . . . to present the constitutional questions reserved in *Hanson*. These are questions of the utmost gravity. . . . Each named appellee in this action has made known to the union . . . his dissent from the use of his money for political causes which he opposes. We have therefore examined the legislative history of §2, Eleventh in the context of the development of unionism in the railroad industry under the . . . [RLA] to determine whether a construction is "fairly possible" which denies the authority to a union, over the employee's objection, to spend his money for political causes which he opposes. We conclude that such a construction is not only "fairly possible" but entirely reasonable, and we therefore find it unnecessary to decide the correctness of the constitutional determinations made by the Georgia courts.

II. THE RAIL UNIONS AND UNION SECURITY

The history of union security in the railway industry is marked *first*, by a strong and long-standing tradition of voluntary unionism on the part of the standard rail unions; *second*, by the declaration in 1934 of a congressional policy of complete freedom of choice of employees to join or not to join a union; *third*, by the modification of the firm legislative policy against compulsion, but only as a specific response to the recognition of the expenses and burdens incurred by the unions in the administration of the complex scheme of the [RLA]. . . .

A primary purpose of the major revisions made in 1934 was to strengthen the position of the labor organizations vis-à-vis the carriers, to the end of furthering the . . . basic congressional policy of self-adjustment of the industry's labor problems. . . .

In sum, in prescribing collective bargaining as the method of settling railway disputes, in conferring upon the unions the status of exclusive representatives in the negotiation and administration of collective agreements, and in giving them representation on the statutory board to adjudicate grievances, Congress has given the unions a clearly defined . . . role to play in effectuating the basic congressional policy of stabilizing labor relations. . . .

Performance of these functions entails the expenditure of considerable funds. Moreover, . . . a union's status as exclusive bargaining representative carries with it the duty fairly and equitably to represent all employees of the craft or class, union and nonunion. Steele v. Louisville & N.R. Co., 323

U.S. 192. . . . . The principal argument made by the unions in 1950 was based on their role in this regulatory framework. They maintained that because of the expense of performing their duties . . . , fairness justified the spreading of the costs to all employees who benefited. They thus [urged] . . . the elimination of the "free riders" — those employees who obtained the benefits of the unions' participation in the machinery of the Act without financially supporting the unions. . . .

. . . These considerations overbore the arguments in favor of the earlier policy of complete individual freedom of choice. . . . The conclusion to which this history clearly points is that §2, Eleventh contemplated compulsory unionism to force employees to share the costs of negotiating and administering collective agreements, and the costs of the adjustment and settlement of disputes. One looks in vain for any suggestion that Congress also meant in §2, Eleventh to provide the unions with a means for forcing employees, over their objection, to support political causes which they oppose.

III.   THE SAFEGUARDING OF RIGHTS OF DISSENT

To the contrary, Congress incorporated safeguards . . . to protect dissenters' interests. Congress became concerned during the hearings and debates that the union shop might be used to abridge freedom of speech and beliefs. The original proposal for authorization of the union shop was qualified in only one respect. It provided "That no such agreement shall require such condition of employment with respect to employees to whom membership is not available upon the same terms and conditions as are generally applicable to any other member. . . ." This was primarily designed to prevent discharge of employees for nonmembership where the union did not admit the employee to membership on racial grounds. See House Hearings, p. 68; Senate Hearings, pp. 22-25. But it was strenuously protested that the proposal provided no protection for an employee who disagreed with union policies or leadership. It was argued, for example, that "the right of free speech is at stake. . . . A man could feel that he was no longer able freely to express himself because he could be dismissed on account of criticism of the union. . . ." House Hearings, p. 115; see also Senate Hearings, pp. 167-169, 320. Objections of this kind led the rail unions to propose an addition to the proviso to §2, Eleventh to prevent loss of job for lack of union membership "with respect to employees to whom membership was denied or terminated for any reason other than the failure of the employee to tender the periodic dues, fees, and assessments uniformly required as a condition of acquiring or retaining membership." House Hearings, p. 247. . . .

A congressional concern over possible impingements on the interests of individual dissenters from union policies is therefore discernible. It is true that opponents of the union shop urged that Congress should not allow it without explicitly regulating the amount of dues which might be exacted or prescribing the uses for which the dues might be expended. We may assume that Congress was also fully conversant with the long history of intensive involvement of the railroad unions in political activities. But it does not follow that §2, Eleventh places no restriction on the use of an employee's money, over his objection, to support political causes he opposes merely because Congress did not enact a comprehensive regulatory scheme governing expenditures. For it is abundantly clear that Congress did not completely abandon the policy of full freedom of choice embodied in the 1934 Act, but rather made inroads on it for the limited purpose of eliminating the problems created by the "free rider." That policy survives in §2, Eleventh in the safeguards intended to protect freedom of dissent. Congress was aware of the conflicting interests involved in the question of the union shop and sought to achieve their accommodation. . . . We are not called upon to delineate the precise limits of that power in this case. We have before us only the question whether the power is restricted to the extent of denying the unions the right, over the employee's objection, to use his money to support political causes which he opposes. Its use to support candidates for public office, and advance political programs, is not a use which helps defray the expenses of the negotiation or administration of collective agreements, or the expenses entailed in the adjustment of grievances and disputes. . . . [I]t is a use which falls clearly outside the reasons [justifying] . . . authority to make union-shop agreements. . . . [I]t is equally clear that it is a use to support activities within the area of dissenters' interests which Congress enacted the proviso to protect. We give §2, Eleventh the construction which achieves both congressional purposes when we hold . . . that §2, Eleventh is to be construed to deny the unions, over an employee's objection, the power to use his exacted funds to support political causes which he opposes.

   We express no view as to other union expenditures objected to by an employee and not made to meet the costs of [negotiating] collective agreements, or the adjustment and settlement of grievances and disputes. We do not understand . . . that there is before us the matter of expenditures for activities in the area between the costs which led directly to the complaint as to "free riders," and the expenditures to support union political activities. We are satisfied, however, that §2, Eleventh is to be interpreted to deny the unions the power claimed in this case. . . . Both by tradition and, from 1934 to 1951, by force of law, the rail unions did not rely upon the compulsion of union security agreements to exact money to support the political activities in which they engage. Our construction therefore involves no curtailment of the traditional political activities of the railroad unions. It means only that those unions must not support those activities, against the expressed wishes of a dissenting employee, with his exacted money.

IV.   The Appropriate Remedy

Under our view of the statute, however, the decision of the court below was erroneous and cannot stand. The appellees [have] . . . made known to their respective unions their objection to the use of their money for the support of political causes. In that circumstance, the respective unions were without power to use payments thereafter tendered by them for such political causes. However, the union-shop agreement itself is not unlawful. Railway Employes' Dept. v. Hanson, supra. . . . [A]ppellees' grievance stems from the spending of their funds for purposes not authorized by the Act in the face of their objection, not from the enforcement of the union-shop agreement by the mere collection of funds. If their money were used for purposes contemplated by §2, Eleventh, the appellees would have no grievance at all. We think that an injunction restraining enforcement of the union-shop agreement is therefore plainly not a remedy appropriate to the violation of the Act's restriction on expenditures. Restraining the collection of all funds from the appellees sweeps too broadly. . . . Moreover, restraining collection of the funds . . . might well interfere with the appellant unions' performance of those functions and duties which the [RLA] places upon them. . . . The complete shutoff of this source of income defeats the congressional plan to have all employees benefited share costs . . . and threatens the basic congressional policy of the [RLA] for self-adjustments. . . .

Since the case must therefore be remanded . . . , we think that it is appropriate to suggest the limits within which remedial discretion may be exercised. . . . [A]n injunction against enforcement of the union shop itself through the collection of funds is unwarranted. We also think that a blanket injunction against all expenditures of funds for the disputed purposes, even one conditioned on cessation of improper expenditures, would not be a proper exercise of equitable discretion. Nor would it be proper to issue an interim or temporary blanket injunction of this character pending a final adjudication. The Norris-LaGuardia Act expresses a basic policy against the injunction of activities of labor unions. We have held that the Act does not deprive the federal courts of jurisdiction to enjoin compliance with various mandates of the [RLA]. Virginian R. Co. v. System Federation, 300 U.S. 515; Graham v. Brotherhood of Locomotive Firemen & Enginemen, 338 U.S. 232. However, the policy of the Act suggests that the courts should hesitate to fix upon the injunctive remedy for breaches of duty owing under the labor laws unless that remedy alone can effectively guard the plaintiff's right. . . . Moreover, the fact that these expenditures are made for political activities is an additional reason for reluctance to impose such an injunctive remedy. Whatever may be the powers of Congress or the States to forbid unions altogether to make various types of political expenditures, as to which we express no opinion here,[21] many of the expenditures involved in the present case are made for the purpose of disseminating information as to candidates and programs and publicizing the positions of the unions on them. As to such expenditures an injunction would work a restraint on the expression of political ideas which might be offensive to the First Amendment. For the majority also has an interest in stating its views without being silenced by the dissenters. To attain the appropriate reconciliation between majority and dissenting interests in the area of political expression, we think the courts . . . should select remedies which protect both interests to the maximum extent possible without undue impingement of one on the other.

. . . [T]wo [possible remedies] may be enforced with a minimum of administrative difficulty and with little danger of encroachment on the legitimate activities or necessary functions of the unions. Any remedies, however, would properly be granted only to employees who have made known to the union officials that they do not desire their funds to be used for political causes to which they object. The safeguards of §2, Eleventh were added for the protection of dissenters' interest, but dissent is not to be presumed — it must affirmatively be made known to the union. . . .

One remedy would be an injunction against expenditure for political causes opposed by each complaining employee of a sum, from those moneys to be spent by the union for political purposes, which is so much of the moneys exacted from him as is the proportion of the union's total expenditures made for such political activities to the union's total budget. The union should not be in a position to make up such sum from money paid by a nondissenter, for this would shift a disproportionate share of the costs of collective bargaining to the dissenter and have the same effect of applying his money to support such political activities. A second remedy would be restitution to each individual employee of that portion of his money which the union expended, despite his notification, for the political causes to which he had advised the union he was opposed. There should be no necessity, however, for the employee to trace his money up to and including its expenditure; if the money goes into general funds and no separate accounts of receipts and expenditures of the funds of individual employees are maintained, the por-

---

[21] No contention was made below or here that any of the expenditures involved in this case [violated] the Federal Corrupt Practices Act, 18 U.S.C. §610, or any state corrupt practices legislation.

tion of his money the employee would be entitled to recover would be in the same proportion that the expenditures for political purposes which he had advised the union he disapproved bore to the total union budget.

The judgment is reversed and the case is remanded to the court below for proceedings not inconsistent with this opinion.

[The concurring opinion of Douglas, J., is omitted.

Whittaker, J., dissented only from Part IV of the Court's opinion. He approved the Georgia court's remedy, finding the Supreme Court's restitutionary remedy impractical because of the uncertainty of "proscribed activity" and the attendant accounting and proof problems.]

BLACK, J., dissenting. . . . Neither §2, Eleventh nor any other part of the Act contains any implication or even a hint that Congress wanted to limit the purposes for which a contracting union's dues should or could be spent. All the parties to this litigation have agreed from its beginning, and still agree, that there is no such limitation in the Act. The Court nevertheless, in order to avoid constitutional questions, interprets the Act itself as barring use of dues for political purposes. . . . [T]he Court is once more "carrying the doctrine of avoiding constitutional questions to a wholly unjustifiable extreme." . . . I think the Court is actually rewriting §2, Eleventh to make it mean exactly what Congress refused to make it mean. . . .

The end result . . . is to distort this statute so as to deprive unions of rights I think Congress tried to give them and at the same time, in the companion case of Lathrop v. Donohue, decided today, post, p. 820, leave itself free later to hold that integrated bar associations can constitutionally exercise the powers now denied to labor unions for fear of unconstitutionality. The constitutional question raised alike in this case and in *Lathrop* is bound to come back here soon with a record so meticulously perfect that the Court cannot escape deciding it. Should the Court then hold that lawyers and workers can constitutionally be compelled to pay for the support of views they are against, the result would be that the labor unions would have lost their case this year on a statutory-constitutional basis while the integrated bar would win its case next year or the year after on the ground that the constitutional part of the basis for the holding against the unions today was groundless. . . . I must consider this case on the basis of my belief as to the constitutionality of §2, Eleventh, interpreted so as to authorize compulsion of workers to pay dues to a union for use in advocating causes and political candidates that the protesting workers are against. . . .

There is, of course, no constitutional reason why a union or other private group may not spend its funds for political or ideological causes if its members voluntarily join it and can voluntarily get out of it. . . . But a different situation arises when a federal law steps in and authorizes such a group to carry on activities at the expense of persons who do not choose to be members of the group as well as those who do. Such a law, even though validly passed by Congress, cannot be used in a way that abridges the specifically defined freedoms of the First Amendment. And whether there is such abridgment depends not only on how the law is written but also on how it works.[13]

There can be no doubt that the federally sanctioned union-shop contract here, as it actually works, takes a part of the earnings of some men and turns it over to others, who spend a substantial part of the funds so received in efforts to thwart the political, economic and ideological hopes of those whose money has been forced from them under authority of law. This injects federal compulsion into the political and ideological processes, a result which I have supposed everyone would agree the First Amendment was particularly intended to prevent. And it makes no difference if . . . political and legislative activities are helpful adjuncts of collective bargaining. Doubtless employers could make the same arguments in favor of compulsory contributions to an association of employers for use in political and economic programs calculated to help collective bargaining on their side. But the argument is equally unappealing whoever makes it. The stark fact is that this Act of Congress is being used as a means to exact money from these employees to help get votes to win elections for parties and candidates and to support doctrines they are against. If this is constitutional the First Amendment is not the charter of political and religious liberty its sponsors believed it to be. . . .

In my view, §2, Eleventh can constitutionally authorize no more than to make a worker pay dues to a union for the sole purpose of defraying the cost of acting as his bargaining agent. Our Government has no more power to compel individuals to support union programs or union publications than it has to compel the support of political programs, employer programs or church programs. And the First Amendment, fairly construed, deprives the Government of all power to make any person pay out one single penny against his will to be used in any way to advocate doctrines or views he is against, whether economic, scientific, political, religious or any other. . . .

---

[13] We held in the *Hanson* case, with respect to this very same §2, Eleventh, that even though the statutory provision authorizing union shops is only permissive, that provision, "which expressly declares that state law is superseded," is "the source of the power and authority by which any private rights are lost or sacrificed" and therefore is "the governmental action on which the Constitution operates." 351 U.S., at 232. Even though §2, Eleventh is permissive in form, Congress was fully aware when enacting it that the almost certain result would be the establishment of union shops throughout the railroad industry. Witness after witness so testified during the hearings on the bill, and this testimony was never seriously disputed.

[Black urged that the remedy would be adequate if it forbade the use of the union-shop clause to bar employment of the six dissidents so long as the union continued to spend its funds to support causes or doctrines "political, economic or other," over the expressed opposition of those dissidents.]

The decree requires the union to refund dues, fees and assessments paid under protest by three of the complaining employees and exempts the six complaining employees from the payment of any union dues, fees or assessments so long as funds so received are used by the union to promote causes they are against. The state court found that these payments had been and would be made by these employees only because they had been compelled to join the union to save their jobs, despite their objections to paying the union so long as it used its funds for candidates, parties and ideologies contrary to these employees' wishes. The Court does not challenge this finding but nevertheless holds that relieving protesting workers of all payment of dues would somehow interfere with the union's statutory duty to act as a bargaining agent. . . . [T]his would interfere with the union's activities only to the extent that it bars compulsion of dues payments from protesting workers to be used in some unknown part for unconstitutional purposes, and I think it perfectly proper to hold that such payments cannot be compelled. Furthermore, I think the remedy suggested by the Court will work a far greater interference with the union's bargaining activities because it will impose much greater trial and accounting burdens on both unions and workers. The Court's remedy is to give the wronged employees a right to a refund limited either to "the proportion of the union's total expenditures made for such political activities" or to the "proportion . . . [of] expenditures for political purposes which he had advised the union he disapproved." It may be that courts and lawyers with sufficient skill in accounting, algebra, geometry, trigonometry and calculus will be able to extract the proper microscopic answer from the voluminous and complex accounting records of the local, national and international unions involved. It seems to me, however, that while the Court's remedy may prove very lucrative to special masters, accountants and lawyers, this formula, with its attendant trial burdens, promises little hope for financial recompense to the individual workers whose First Amendment freedoms have been flagrantly violated. Undoubtedly, at the conclusion of this long exploration of accounting intricacies, many courts could with plausibility dismiss the workers' claims as de minimis when measured only in dollars and cents.

. . . The three workers who paid under protest here were forced under authority of a federal statute to pay *all* current dues or lose their jobs. They should get back *all* they paid with interest. . . .

I would affirm the judgment of the Georgia Supreme Court, with the modifications I have suggested.

FRANKFURTER, J., whom HARLAN, J., joins, dissenting. . . . I cannot attribute to Congress that sub silentio it meant to bar railway unions under a union-shop agreement from expending their funds in their traditional manner. . . . The claim that these expenditures infringe the appellees' constitutional rights under the First Amendment must therefore be faced. . . .

One would suppose that *Hanson's* reasoning disposed of the present suit. The Georgia Supreme Court, however, . . . relied upon the following reservation in our opinion: "if the exaction of dues, initiation fees, or assessments is used as a cover for forcing ideological conformity or other action in contravention of the First Amendment, this judgment will not prejudice the decision in that case." 351 U.S., at 238. The use of union dues to promote relevant and effective means of realizing the purposes for which unions exist does not constitute a utilization of dues "as a cover for forcing ideological conformity" in any fair reading of those words. . . . "Cover" implies a disguise, some sham; "forcing . . . conformity" means coercing avowal of a belief not entertained. Plaintiffs here are in no way subjected to such suppression of their true beliefs or sponsorship of views they do not hold. Nor are they forced to join a sham organization which does not participate in collective bargaining functions, but only serves as a conduit of funds for ideological propaganda. . . . [T]he gist of the complaint here is that the expenditure of a portion of mandatory funds for political objectives denies free speech — the right to speak or to remain silent — to members who oppose, against the constituted authority of union desires, this use of their union dues. No one's desire or power to speak his mind is checked or curbed. The individual member may express his views in any public or private forum as freely as he could before the union collected his dues. Federal taxes also may diminish the vigor with which a citizen can give partisan support to a political belief, but as yet no one would place such an impediment to making one's views effective within the reach of constitutionally protected "free speech." This is too fine-spun a claim for constitutional recognition. . . .

But were we to assume, arguendo, that the plaintiffs have alleged a valid constitutional objection if Congress had specifically ordered the result, we must consider the difference between such compulsion and the absence of compulsion when Congress acts as platonically as it did, in a wholly noncoercive way. Congress has not commanded that the railroads shall employ only those workers who are members of authorized unions. Congress has only given leave to a bargaining representative, democratically elected by a majority of workers, to enter into a particular contractual provision arrived at under the give-and-take of duly safeguarded bargaining procedures. . . . When we speak of the Government "acting" in permitting the union shop, the scope and force of what Congress has done must be heeded. There is not a trace of compulsion involved — no exercise of restriction by Congress on the freedom of the carriers and the unions. On the contrary, Congress expanded their freedom of action. Congress lifted limitations upon free action by parties bargaining at arm's length.[13]

The plaintiffs have not been deprived of the right to participate in determining union policies or to assert their respective weight in defining the purposes for which union dues may be expended. Responsive to the actualities of our industrial society, in which unions as such play the role that they do, the law regards a union as a self-contained, legal personality exercising rights and subject to responsibilities wholly distinct from its individual members. See United Mine Workers of America v. Coronado Coal Co., 259 U.S. 344. It is a commonplace of all organizations that a minority of a legally recognized group may at times see an organization's funds used for promotion of ideas opposed by the minority. The analogies are numerous. On the largest scale, the Federal Government expends revenue collected from individual taxpayers to propagandize ideas which many taxpayers oppose. Or, as this Court noted in *Hanson*, many state laws compel membership in the integrated bar as a prerequisite to practicing law, and the bar association uses its funds to urge legislation of which individual members often disapprove. The present case is, as the Court in *Hanson* asserted, indistinguishable from the issues raised by those who find constitutional difficulties with the integrated bar. If our statement in *Hanson* carried any meaning, it was an unqualified recognition that legislation providing for an integrated bar, exercising familiar functions, is subject to no infirmity derived from the First Amendment. . . .

Nothing was further from congressional purpose than to be concerned with restrictions upon the right to speak. Its purpose was to eliminate "free riders" in the bargaining unit. . . .

For us to hold that these defendant unions may not expend their moneys for political and legislative purposes would be completely to ignore the long history of union conduct and its pervasive acceptance in our political life. American labor's initial role in shaping legislation dates back 130 years. With the coming of the AFL in 1886, labor on a national scale was committed not to act as a class party but to maintain a program of political action in furtherance of its industrial standards. British trade unions were supporting members of the House of Commons as early as 1867. The Canadian Trades Congress in 1894 debated whether political action should be the main objective of the labor force. And in a recent Australian case, the High Court upheld the right of a union to expel a member who refused to pay a political

---

[13] For an analysis of the 1951 Amendment leading to a narrow scope of its constitutional implications, see Wellington, The Constitution, the Labor Union, and "Governmental Action," 70 Yale L.J. 345, 352-60, 363-71.

levy. That Britain, Canada and Australia have no explicit First Amendment is beside the point. For one thing, the freedoms safeguarded in terms in the First Amendment are deeply rooted and respected in the British tradition, and are part of legal presuppositions in Canada and Australia. And in relation to our immediate concern, the British Commonwealth experience establishes the pertinence of political means for realizing basic trade-union interests. . . .

We are asked by union members who oppose these expenditures to protect their right to free speech — although they are as free to speak as ever — against governmental action which has permitted a union elected by democratic process to bargain for a union shop and to expend the funds thereby collected for purposes which are controlled by internal union choice. To do so would be to mutilate a scheme designed by Congress for the purpose of equitably sharing the cost of securing the benefit of union exertions; it would greatly embarrass, if not frustrate, conventional labor activities which have become institutionalized through time. To do so is to give constitutional sanction to doctrinaire views and to grant a minuscule claim constitutional recognition.

I would reverse and remand the case for dismissal in the Georgia courts.

Ellis v. Brotherhood of Ry., Airline & S.S. Clerks, 104 S. Ct. 1883 (1984). Departing from the implications of *Street* and Railway Clerks v. Allen, 373 U.S. 113 (1963), the Court invalidated the union's remedy for impermissible funding, namely, a rebate to an objector paid a year after all his dues had been collected. The Court reasoned that this remedy forced an objector to make an interest-free loan in the amount of the rebate. Less restrictive alternatives, such as advance reduction of dues or interest-bearing escrow accounts, would place only minimal burdens on the union.

The Court also announced that, in determining the activities that the Railway Labor Act authorized to be financed by compulsory dues, "the test must be whether the challenged expenditures are necessarily or reasonably incurred for the purpose of performing the duties of an exclusive representative of the employees in dealing with the employer on labor-management issues." The Court found that the following disputed activities passed this test (we use the numbers used by the Court to designate the activities described below):

1. The union's quadrennial national conventions, where officers are elected, bargaining goals established, and overall policy formulated — activities characterized by the Court as essential to the effective discharge of a bargaining agent's duties.

2. Social activities — .7 percent of Grand Lodge expenditures designated for refreshments for union business meetings and social activities. These activities were "formally open to nonmembers." Noting that these expenditures were "de minimis," the Court found that they promoted harmony and closer ties between employees and improved the atmosphere of union meetings.

3. Limited union publications. Under the union's own policy, involuntary payments were not to be used for that part of a publication concerned with "political causes," as distinguished from negotiations, social activities, and (apparently) recently proposed as well as enacted legislation. Thus the union rebated to dissenters the proportion of total publication expenses represented by the ratio of "political" linage to total linage. More generally, the Court declared: "If a union cannot spend dissenters' funds for a particular activity . . . spending their funds for writing about that activity [is unjustifiable]."

The Court, however, concluded that the RLA did not authorize use of dissenters' dues to finance the following activities:

4. Organizing employees either outside or within the bargaining unit.

5. Litigation not involving bargaining, grievances, or the duty of fair representation within the bargaining unit. For example, unless "the bargaining unit was directly concerned, objecting employees need not share the cost of the union's challenge to the legality of airlines' mutual aid pact; [or] of litigation seeking to protect the rights of airline employees generally during bankruptcy. . . ."

Finally, noting the union's decertification, the Court declined to pass on (6) the financing of the union's $300 death benefit to a beneficiary of a member (and apparently to that of a nonmember compelled to pay dues to the union). Since dissenting nonmembers had enjoyed the insurance protection, the equities did not call for a refund.

The Court also rejected a challenge based on the First Amendment, finding that the government's interest in industrial peace that had led to authorization of the union shop also justified the disputed expenditures that the Court had upheld under the statute.

Powell, J., dissented from the Court's disposition concerning BRAC's quadrennial convention, on these grounds: Five prominent politicians plus four congressmen had made major addresses at the 25th convention, which cost the union $1.8 million, in toto. The union had not identified the expenses for these "political activities," in sharp contrast to its handling of publication expenses. All expenses of the convention did not have the nexus with collective bargaining required under the Court's test.

Powell, J., also expressed disagreement with the Court's summary disposition of the First Amendment question raised by the political expenditures at the convention — a question that under his view of the RLA he did not need to address.

NOTES

   1. Do the line-drawing and accounting problems inherent in the Court's approach suggest that the protection granted to dissidents is either too broad or too narrow? Should the Court now reconsider *Machinists v. Street* and adopt the view advanced either by Justice Frankfurter or by Justice Black?

   2. A union that engages in "political activity" asks for your advice on how fully to comply with *Ellis*. What is your answer?

   3. A union, pursuant to a union security provision valid under §8(a)(3), instigated the discharge of an employee, a Seventh-Day Adventist, whose religion forbade contributing financial support to a labor union.

   The employee sued for damages, claiming a violation of the First Amendment. Under the Taft-Hartley Act, would the court be able (1) to rely on the same processes of statutory construction employed in *Street* in order to avoid constitutional questions, and (2) to find "governmental action," given §14(b) of that Act?

   The presence of §14(b) changes the nature of the argument, but does it provide a basis for distinguishing union security provisions under the RLA from those under the NLRA, with respect to the presence of "governmental action"? Specifically, is the unconditional and preemptive authorization by the RLA of private union security arrangements materially different from their conditional authorization in the NLRA (the state involved must fail to proscribe)? See Kolinske v. Lubbers, 712 F.2d 471, 474-480 (D.C. Cir. 1983): The court held that because neither the UAW's eligibility require-ments for strike pay nor the inclusion in the contract of an agency shop clause (authorized by §8(a)(3)) constituted "governmental action," the First Amendment does not support a claim against the union by a nonmember who paid the equivalent of union dues and honored a picket line, but who was denied strike benefits because he failed to participate in such strike-con-nected activities as picketing or kitchen duties, as the union's eligibility standards required. The court, noting the origin of the duty of fair representa-tion in a union's status as the exclusive bargaining agent under §9, held that duty inapplicable to an employee's "relationship with the union structure," as distinguished from his relationship with his employer.

   4. The Seventh Day Adventist described in Note 3 above offers to pay

the equivalent of union dues to a nonreligious nonunion charity. The union declines and instigates his discharge for nonpayment of dues. The employee sues the employer and the union for damages and reinstatement, under §§703 and 701(j) of Title VII of the Civil Rights Act of 1964 and the First Amendment. What result? What if the employee had, before discharge, expressed willingness to "contribute to the proportionate cost of peaceful collective bargaining" with the employer, with the remainder of regular dues going to a nonreligious charity? Cf. McDaniel v. Essex Intern, Inc., 696 F.2d 34 (6th Cir. 1982).

Cf. NLRA §19, enacted in 1974, and amended in 1980 by Public Law 96-953 (H.R. 4774), so as to accommodate "conscientious objectors" under union security agreements. Section 19, as amended, also provides that "if such employee who holds conscientious objections pursuant to this section" requests the use of the grievance arbitration procedure on his behalf, "the labor organization is authorized to charge the employee for the reasonable cost of using such procedure." The accompanying report, H.R. Rep. No. 496, 96th Cong., 1st Sess., states (at p. 2) that "the bill reflects the legislative determination that the alternative to the payment of dues . . . provided in the bill 'reasonably accommodate(s) . . . an employee . . . (sic) religious observance or practice without undue hardship.' Title VII, §701(8). . . ."

Suppose that a union and an employee disagree as to whether §19 covers the particular sect involved, and the union requests the employer to discharge that employee for nonpayment of dues under a union security provision. How should the employer proceed?

Is the "reasonable cost" the total additional cost of invoking the grievance arbitration process for the individual grievant? If not, how should the reasonable cost be calculated?

5. Radio and TV commentators, namely, William F. Buckley and M. Stanton Evans, were employed in a bargaining unit covered by a collective bargaining agreement that purported to condition their continued employment on their maintaining full-fledged union membership. These commentators, urging infringement of their First Amendment rights, bring an action against the union and their employer to enjoin the enforcement of that clause. The defendants move to dismiss the complaint. The trial judge asks for your recommendation regarding that motion. Advise him. Cf. Buckley v. AFTRA, 496 F.2d 305 (2nd Cir.), cert. denied, 419 U.S. 1093 (1974); AFTRA, 222 N.L.R.B. 197 (1976); Lewis v. AFTRA, 34 N.Y.2d 265, 313 N.E.2d 735, 357 N.Y.S.2d 419 (1974), cert. denied, 419 U.S. 1093 (1974). See Wellington, Mr. Buckley and the Unions: Of Union Discipline and Member Dissidence, in D. Lipsky, Union Power and Public Policy, 25 (1975).

6. In Abood v. Detroit Board of Education, 431 U.S. 209 (1977), the

Court upheld the constitutionality of a Michigan statute authorizing the negotiation of "agency shop" clauses requiring public employees to pay a service fee equal to regular union dues — provided that such compelled fees were used only for collective bargaining, contract administration, and grievance adjustment. The Court recognized the greater haziness in the public sector of the line between such collective bargaining activities and ideological activities unrelated to collective bargaining for which compelled fees could not lawfully be used. The Court held that a general objection to "ideological expenditures," without further specification, was sufficient to preserve the rights of dissenters.

Five Justices subscribed to three separate concurring opinions. Powell, J., with whom the Chief Justice and Blackmun, J., joined concurring, rejected the Court's premise that public employers are under no greater constitutional restraints than private sector employees.

7. Materials on unions' use of "voluntarily" contributed money in national elections appear in Chapter 12(E), infra.

Retail Clerks v. Schermerhorn
373 U.S. 746 (1963)

[The collective agreement required employees who elected not to join the union to pay to it, as a condition of employment, "service fees" equal to the regular initiation fee and monthly dues. The Florida Supreme Court upheld Florida's competence to pass on that "agency shop" provision, and invalidated it as contrary to Florida's right-to-work law, which provided: "The right of persons to work shall not be denied or abridged on account of membership or non-membership in any labor union. . . . "]

WHITE, J. The connection between the §8(a)(3) proviso and §14(b) is clear. Whether they are perfectly coincident, we need not now decide, but unquestionably they overlap. . . . At the very least, the agreements requiring "membership" in a labor union which are expressly permitted by the proviso are the same "membership" agreements expressly placed within the reach of state law by §14(b). It follows that the *General Motors* case rules this one, for we there held that the "agency shop" arrangement involved here — which imposes on employees the only membership obligation enforceable under §8(a)(3) by discharge, namely, the obligation to pay initiation fees and regular dues — is the "practical equivalent" of an "agreement requiring membership in a labor organization as a condition of employment." Whatever may be the status of less stringent union-security arrangements, the agency shop is within §14(b). . . .

Petitioners, belatedly, would now distinguish the contract involved here from the agency shop contract dealt with in the *General Motors* case on the basis of allegedly distinctive features which are said to require a different result. Article 19 provides for nonmember payments to the union "for the purpose of aiding the Union in defraying costs in connection with its legal obligations and responsibilities as the exclusive bargaining agent of the employees in the appropriate bargaining unit," a provision which petitioners say confines the use of nonmember payments to collective bargaining purposes alone and forbids their use by the union for institutional purposes unrelated to its exclusive agency functions, all in sharp contrast, it is argued, to the *General Motors* situation where the nonmember contributions are available to the union without restriction.

We are wholly unpersuaded. There is before us little more than a complaint with its exhibits. The agency shop clause of the contract is, at best, ambiguous on its face and it should not, in the present posture of the case, be construed against respondent to raise a substantial difference between this and the *General Motors* case. There is no ironclad restriction imposed upon the use of nonmembers fees, for the clause merely describes the payments as being for "the purpose of aiding the Union" in meeting collective bargaining expenses. The alleged restriction would not be breached if the service fee was used for both collective bargaining and other expenses, for the union would be "aided" in meeting its agency obligations, not only by the part spent for bargaining purposes but also by the part spent for institutional items, since an equivalent amount of other union income would thereby be freed to pay the costs of bargaining agency functions.

But even if all collections from nonmembers must be directly committed to paying bargaining costs, this fact is of bookkeeping significance only rather than a matter of real substance. It must be remembered that the service fee is admittedly the exact equal of membership initiation fees and monthly dues, . . . and that, as the union says in its brief, dues collected from members may be used for a "variety of purposes, in addition to meeting the union's costs of collective bargaining." Unions "rather typically" use their membership dues "to do those things which the members authorize the union to do in their interest and on their behalf." If the union's total budget is divided between collective bargaining and institutional expenses and if nonmember payments, equal to those of a member, go entirely for collective bargaining costs, the nonmember will pay more of these expenses than his pro rata share. The member will pay less and to that extent a portion of his fees and dues is available to pay institutional expenses. . . . By paying a larger share of collective bargaining costs the nonmember subsidizes the union's institutional activities. In over-all effect, economically, and we think for the purposes of §14(b), the contract here is the same as the General Motors agency shop arrangement. . . .

[The Court, although ruling that under §14(b) Florida law governed the challenged arrangement, set down for reargument the question of whether Florida's jurisdiction to grant a remedy had been preempted. If, under §14(b) (the Court reasoned) union security arrangements that violated state law also violated §8(a)(3) of the NLRA, the power of the NLRB to "enjoin" such arrangements obviously raised a question about concurrent state authority to do so.

After reargument, the Court recognized state power "to enforce their laws restricting the execution and enforcement of union-security agreements" (375 U.S. 96, 102 (1963)), including "state power to reinstate with back pay an employee discharged in violation of such state laws." Id. at 105. Emphasizing the overriding effect accorded by Congress to state policy concerning union security, the Court expressed its reluctance "to conclude that [state policy] is nonetheless enforceable by the federal agency in Washington." Id. at 103. Nevertheless, the Court also said (at p. 105):

". . . [P]icketing in order to get an employer to execute an agreement to hire all-union labor in violation of a state union-security statute lies exclusively in the federal domain (Local Union 429 v. Farnsworth & Chambers Co., 353 U.S. 969, and Local No. 438 v. Curry, 371 U.S. 542), because state power, recognized by §14(b), begins *only with actual negotiation and execution of the type of agreement described by §14(b)*. Absent such an agreement, conduct arguably an unfair labor practice would be a matter for the [NLRB] under *Garmon*."]

NOTES

1. Does picketing for a union security provision invalid under state law violate §8(b)(2) of the NLRA? Would it violate the duty of fair representation, at least when a union with majority support is involved? Consider §8(a)(3), its proviso, and §14(b). If a state finds that picketing seeks a union security provision banned by state law, why should it be preempted from enjoining such picketing? Cf. *Garmon II*, supra p. 737. See generally Grodin & Beeson, State Right-to-Work Laws and Federal Labor Policy, 52 Calif. L. Rev. 95 (1964); Henderson, The Confrontation of Federal Preemption and State Right-to-Work Laws, 1967 Duke L.J. 1079.

2. Several years after a local voted a dues increase, all its members employed at one of a company's unionized plants stopped paying dues and later resigned. The local nevertheless spent almost $11,000 (in 1977) in order to represent those employees, prior to the local's decertification. During the 1977 negotiations for a renewal agreement, the local demanded a clause that would have required each nonunion employee, as a condition of

retaining his job, to pay a representation fee consisting of "a pro rata share of the costs directly related to enforcing and servicing the collective bargaining agreement," as determined by "an independent audit," but not to exceed the amount of union dues. The employer maintained that the union's demand contravened the state right-to-work law, which barred any employer from requiring an employee, as a condition of employment, to pay any dues, fees, or charges of any kind to any labor organization. The union insisted on its demand. The employer filed an 8(b)(3) charge, which led to the issuance of a complaint. What result? Cf. Journeymen & Apprentices, Plumbing & Pipe-fitting Indus. v. NLRB, 675 F.2d 1257 (D.C. Cir. 1982), *cert. denied*, 459 U.S. 1171 (1983).

3. Assume first that a state right-to-work law is not applicable and that a collective agreement provides that the union shall be the exclusive source for the referral of applicants for employment. May the union lawfully require nonunion applicants using the hiring hall to pay a fee reasonably related to the cost of providing such services? See NLRB v. Local 138, Operating Engrs., 385 F.2d 874 (2d Cir. 1967), *cert. denied*, 391 U.S. 904 (1968). Now assume that the state law set forth in Note 2 above is in effect. Would the legality of the user fees for nonunion members be affected? Does the imposition of such a fee violate the state law? If so, would §14(b) authorize a state to proscribe such fees?

4. In the absence of a union security provision, under what circumstances, if any, should a union be permitted to charge a nonmember all, or some of, the costs of processing his grievance, as a condition of taking it through the contractual grievance-arbitration process? Is this question essentially the same as the questions raised in Note 3 above? See Machinists, Local 697 (Canfield Rubber Co.), 223 N.L.R.B. 832 (1976). Cf. §19 of the NLRA, as amended.

3. Hiring Halls

The union-run hiring hall has been an important institution in industries such as construction, maritime, and longshoring, where employment is characteristically migratory and the composition of the employer's labor force shifts with the requirements of particular projects. In such industries, the hiring hall has served as a central clearinghouse for job seekers and job openings.

A union hiring hall could function to promote even-handed distribution of jobs, without discriminating in favor of union members. In practice, however, such halls have involved strong and obvious pressures to prefer union members. Indeed, hiring halls, in industries such as construction and maritime, have functioned on a closed shop basis. See generally Rains, Construction Trades Hiring Halls, 10 Lab. L.J. 363 (1959); Craig, Hiring-Hall Arrangements and Practices, 9 Lab. L.J. 939 (1958). Although the Taft-Hartley Act proscribed closed shops and discriminatory hiring halls, it has been an open secret that those proscriptions have been flouted. See The Closed Shop in Hiding, Fortune, Sept. 1951, p. 62; W. Haber & H. Levinson, Labor Relations and Productivity in the Building Trades 62, 71 (1956).

In the late 1950s the NLRB sought to close the gap between the mandates of the statute and prevailing practices. In order to promote equal job opportunities for union and nonunion applicants, the Board reformulated its substantive and remedial approach to hiring halls and other adjuncts to discrimination. Those efforts and their frustration by the courts are dealt with in the materials below.

Local 357, Teamsters v. NLRB
365 U.S. 667 (1961)

DOUGLAS, J. Petitioner union (along with the International Brotherhood of Teamsters and a number of other affiliated local unions) executed a three-year . . . agreement with California Trucking Associations, which represented a group of motor truck operators in California. The provisions of the contract relating to hiring of casual or temporary employees were as follows:

> . . . Casual employees shall, wherever the Union maintains a dispatching service, be employed only on a seniority basis in the Industry whenever such senior employees are available. An available list with seniority status will be kept by the Unions, and employees requested will be dispatched upon call to any employer who is a party to this Agreement. Seniority rating of such employees shall begin with a minimum of three months service in the Industry *irrespective of whether such employee is or is not a member of the Union.*
>
> Discharge of any employee by any employer shall be grounds for removal of any employee from seniority status. No casual employee shall be employed by an employer who is a party to this Agreement in violation of seniority status if such employees are available and if the dispatching service for such employees is available. The employer shall first call the Union or the dispatching hall designated by the Union for such help. In the event the employer is notified that such help is not available, or in the event the employees called for do not appear for work at the time designated by the employer, the employer may hire from any other available source. (Emphasis added.)

. . . One Slater was a member of the union and had customarily used the hiring hall. But in August 1955 he obtained casual employment with an employer who was party to the hiring-hall agreement without being dispatched by the union. He worked until sometime in November of that year, when he was discharged by the employer on complaint of the union that he had not been referred through the hiring hall arrangement.

Slater made charges against the union and the employer. . . . [T]he Board found that the hiring-hall provision was unlawful per se and that the discharge of Slater on the union's request constituted a violation by the employer of §8(a)(1) and §8(a)(3) and a violation by the union of §8(b)(2) and §8(b)(1)(A). . . . The Board ordered, inter alia, that the company and the union cease giving any effect to the hiring-hall agreement; that they jointly and severally reimburse Slater for any loss sustained by him as a result of his discharge; and that they jointly and severally reimburse all casual employees for fees and dues paid by them to the union beginning six months prior to the date of the filing of the charge. 121 N.L.R.B. 1629.

. . . [T]he Court of Appeals . . . set aside the portion of the order requiring a general reimbursement of dues and fees. By a divided vote it upheld the Board in ruling that the hiring-hall agreement was illegal per se. 275 F.2d 646. Those rulings are here on certiorari, one on the petition of the union, the other on petition of the Board.

Our decision in Carpenters Local 60 v. Labor Board[e] . . . is dispositive of the petition of the Board that asks us to direct enforcement of the order of reimbursement. The judgment of the Court of Appeals on that phase of the matter is affirmed.

The other aspect of the case goes back to the Board's ruling in Mountain Pacific Chapter, 119 N.L.R.B. 883. That decision, rendered in 1958, departed from earlier rulings and held, Abe Murdock dissenting, that the hiring-hall agreement, despite the inclusion of a nondiscrimination clause, was illegal per se:

> Here the very grant of work at all depends solely upon union sponsorship, and it is reasonable to infer that the arrangement displays and enhances the Union's power and control over the employment status. Here all that appears is unilateral union determination and subservient employer action with no aboveboard explanation as to the reason for it, and it is reasonable to infer that the Union will be guided in its concession by an eye towards winning compliance with a membership obligation or union fealty in some other respect. The Employers here have surrendered all hiring authority to the Union and have

---

[e][365 U.S. 651 (1961), ruling that §10(c) did not warrant the reimbursement order, which the Court described as "punitive," noting that no basis existed for concluding that all the casual employees, many of whom had been long-time union members, would have refused to pay dues to the union absent its violations of §8(b)(2). — Eds.]

given advance notice via the established hiring hall to the world at large that the Union is arbitrary master and is contractually guaranteed to remain so. From the final authority over hiring vested in the Respondent Union by the three AGC chapters, the inference of encouragement of union membership is inescapable.

Id., 896.

The Board went on to say that a hiring-hall arrangement to be lawful must contain protective provisions. Its views were stated as follows:

We believe, however, that the inherent and unlawful encouragement of union membership that stems from unfettered union control over the hiring process would be negated, and we would find an agreement to be nondiscriminatory on its face, only if the agreement explicitly provided that:

(1) Selection of applicants for referral to jobs shall be on a nondiscriminatory basis and shall not be based on, or in any way affected by, union membership, bylaws, rules, regulations, constitutional provisions, or any other aspect or obligation of union membership, policies, or requirements.

(2) The employer retains the right to reject any job applicant referred by the union.

(3) The parties to the agreement post in places where notices to employees and applicants for employment are customarily posted, all provisions relating to the functioning of the hiring arrangement, including the safeguards that we deem essential to the legality of an exclusive hiring agreement.

Id., 897.

The Board recognizes that the hiring hall came into being "to eliminate wasteful, time-consuming, and repetitive scouting for jobs by individual workmen and haphazard uneconomical searches by employers." Id., 896, n.8. The hiring hall at times has been a useful adjunct to the closed shop. But Congress may have thought that it need not serve that cause, that in fact it has served well both labor and management — particularly in the maritime field and in the building and construction industry. In the latter the contractor who frequently is a stranger to the area where the work is done requires a "central source" for his employment needs; and a man looking for a job finds in the hiring hall "at least a minimum guarantee of continued employment."

Congress has not outlawed the hiring hall, though it has outlawed the closed shop except within the limits prescribed in the provisos to §8(a)(3). Senator Taft made clear his views that hiring halls are useful, that they are not illegal per se, that unions should be able to operate them so long as they are not used to create a closed shop:

. . . The [NLRB] and the courts did not find hiring halls as such illegal, but merely certain practices under them. The Board and the court found that the manner in which the hiring halls operated created in effect a closed shop in violation of the law. Neither the law nor these decisions forbid hiring halls, even hiring halls operated by the unions as long as they are not so operated as to create a closed shop with all of the abuses possible under such an arrangement, including discrimination against employees, prospective employees, members of union minority groups, and operation of a closed union.

S. Rep. No. 1827, 81st Cong., 2d Sess., pp. 13, 14.

There being no express ban of hiring halls in any provisions of the Act, those who add one, whether it be the Board or the courts, engage in a legislative act. The Act deals with discrimination either by the employers or unions that encourages or discourages union membership. As respects §8(a)(3) we said in Radio Officers v. Labor Board, 347 U.S. 17, 42-43:

> . . . [T]his section does not outlaw all encouragement or discourage-ment of membership in labor organizations; only such as is accomplished by discrimination is prohibited. Nor does this section outlaw discrimination in employment as such; only such discrimination as encourages or discourages membership in a labor organization is proscribed.

It is the "true purpose" or "real motive" in hiring or firing that constitutes the test. Id., 43. Some conduct may by its very nature contain the implications of the required intent; the natural foreseeable consequences of certain action may warrant the inference. Id., 45. The existence of discrimination may at times be inferred by the Board, for "it is permissible to draw on experience in factual inquiries." Radio Officers v. Labor Board, supra, at 49.

But surely discrimination cannot be inferred from the face of the instrument when the instrument specifically provides that there will be no discrimination against "casual employees" because of the presence or absence of union membership. The only complaint in the case was by Slater, a union member, who sought to circumvent the hiring-hall agreement. When an employer and the union enforce the agreement against union members, we cannot say without more that either indulges in the kind of discrimination to which the Act is addressed.

It may be that the very existence of the hiring hall encourages union membership. We may assume that it does. The very existence of the union has the same influence. When a union engages in collective bargaining and obtains increased wages and improved working conditions, its prestige doubtless rises and, one may assume, more workers are drawn to it. . . . The truth is that the union is a service agency that probably encourages membership whenever it does its job well. But, as we said in Radio Officers v. Labor Board, supra, the only encouragement or discouragement of union membership banned by the Act is that which is "accomplished by discrimination." P.43.

Nothing is inferable from the present hiring-hall provision except that employer and union alike sought to route "casual employees" through the union hiring hall and required a union member who circumvented it to adhere to it.

It may be that hiring halls need more regulation than the Act presently affords. As we have seen, the Act aims at every practice, act, source or institution which in fact is used to encourage and discourage union membership by discrimination in regard to hire or tenure, term or condition of employment. . . . Yet, where Congress has adopted a selective system for dealing with evils, the Board is confined to that system. Where, as here, Congress has aimed its sanctions only at specific discriminatory practices, the Board cannot go farther and establish a broader, more pervasive regulatory scheme.

The present agreement for a union hiring hall has a protective clause in it, as we have said; and there is no evidence that it was in fact used unlawfully. We cannot assume that a union conducts its operations in violation of law or that the parties to this contract did not intend to adhere to its express language. Yet we would have to make those assumptions to agree with the Board that it is reasonable to infer the union will act discriminatorily. . . .

Affirmed in part and reversed in part.

Frankfurter, J., took no part in the consideration or decision of this case.

[The concurring opinion of Harlan, J., with whom Stewart, J., joined, is omitted.]

CLARK, J., dissenting in part.[1] . . . Lester Slater, the complainant, became a "casual employee" in the truck freight business in 1953 or early 1954. He approached an employer but was referred to the union hiring hall. There the dispatcher told him to see Barney Volkoff, an official of the union, whose office in the union headquarters building was some three miles away. Describing his visit to Volkoff, Slater stated that "[I] just give him [Volkoff] the money to send back East to pay up my dues back there for the withdrawal card, . . . and I went right to the [hiring] hall and went to work." . . . After some difficulty with one of his temporary employers (Pacific Intermountain Express), the hall refused to refer Slater to other employers. In order to keep employed despite the union hall's failure to dispatch him, Slater relied on a letter from John Annand, an International Representative of the union, stating that "you may seek work wherever you can find it in the freight industry without working through the hiring hall." It

---

[1] I agree with the Court's disposition of that part of the Board's petition seeking direct enforcement of the order of reimbursement.

was this letter that obtained Slater his employment with Los Angeles-Seattle Motor Express, where he was characterized by its dock foreman as being "a good worker." After a few months employment, the Business Agent of the union (Victor Karaty) called on the Los Angeles-Seattle Motor Express, advising that it could not hire Slater "any longer here without a referral card"; that the company would "have to get rid of Slater, and if [it] . . . didn't, that he was going to tie the place up in a knot, [that he] would pull the men off." Los Angeles-Seattle Motor Express fired Slater, telling him that "[We] . . . can't use you now until you get this straightened out with the union. Then come back; we will put you to work." He then went to the union, and was again referred to Volkoff who advised, "I can't do anything for you because you are out. You are not qualified for this job." Upon being shown the Annand letter, Volkoff declared "I am the union." On later occasions when Slater attempted to get clearance from Volkoff he was asked "How come you weren't out on that — didn't go on the picket line"? (Apparently the union had been on a strike.) Slater testified, "I told him that nobody asked me to. I was out a week. I thought the strike was on. The hall was closed. The guys told me there weren't no work." The landlady of Slater also approached Volkoff in an effort to get him cleared and she testified that "I asked Mr. Barney Volkoff what he had against Lester Slater and why he was doing this to him." And she quoted him as saying: "For a few reasons, one is about the P.I.E. [Pacific Intermountain Express] . . . [a]nother thing, he is an illiterate." She further testified that "he [Volkoff] didn't like the way he dressed. . . ." He therefore refused to "route" . . . Slater through the union hiring hall. . . .

The word "discrimination" in the section . . . includes not only distinctions contingent upon "the presence or absence of union membership," but all differences in treatment regardless of their basis. This is the "cause" portion of the section. But §8(a)(3) also includes an "effect" clause which provides that the intended or inherent effect of the discrimination must be "to encourage or discourage [union] membership." The section has, therefore, a divided structure. Not all discriminations violate the section, but only those the effect of which is encouragement or discouragement of union membership. Cf. Radio Officers v. Labor Board, 347 U.S. 17, at 43. . . . Each being a requirement of the section, both must be present before an unfair labor practice exists. On the other hand, the union here contends, and the Court agrees, that there can be no "discrimination" within the section *unless it is based* on union membership, i.e., members treated one way, nonmembers another, with further distinctions, among members, based on good standing. Through this too superficial interpretation, the Court abuses the language of the Congress and unduly restricts the scope of the proscription so that it forbids only the most obvious "hard-sell" techniques of influencing employee exercise of §7 rights. . . .

. . . I believe, as this Court has recognized, that "the desire of employees to unionize is directly proportional to the advantages *thought to be* obtained. . . ." *Radio Officers*, supra, at 46. (Emphasis added.) I therefore ask, "Does the ordinary applicant for casual employment, who walks into the union hall at the direction of his prospective employer, consider his chances of getting dispatched for work diminished because of his nonunion status or his default in dues payment?" Lester Slater testified—and it is uncontradicted—that "He [the applicant] had to be a union member; otherwise he wouldn't be working there . . . you got to have your dues paid up to date and so forth." When asked how he knew this, Slater replied, "I have always knew that." Such was the sum of his impressions gained from contact with the hall from 1953 or 1954 when he started to 1958 when he ended. The misunderstanding—if it is that—of this common worker, who had the courage to complain, is, I am sure, representative of many more who were afraid to protest or, worse, were unaware of their right to do so.

Of the gravity of such a situation the Board is the best arbiter and best equipped to find a solution. . . . It has resolved the issue clearly, not only here, but also in its 1958 Report which, as I have said, repeated its *Mountain Pacific* position "that a union to which an employer has so delegated hiring powers will exercise its power with a view to securing compliance with membership obligations and union rules." At p. 68. In view of Slater's experience, for one, the idea is certainly not farfetched. . . .

However, I need not go so far as to presume that the union has set itself upon an illegal course, conditioning referral on the unlawful criterion of union membership in good standing (which inference the majority today says cannot be drawn), to reach the same result. I need only assume that, by thousands of common workers like Slater, the contract and its conditioning of casual employment upon union referral will work a misunderstanding as to the significance of union affiliation unless the employer's abdication of his role be made less than total and some note of the true function of the hiring hall be posted where all may see and read. The tide of encouragement may not be turned, but it will in part at least be stemmed. As an added dividend, the inherent probability of the free-wheeling operation of the union hiring hall resulting in arbitrary dispatching of job seekers would to some significant extent be diminished.

I would hold that there is not only a reasonable likelihood, but that it must inescapably be concluded under this record, that, without the safeguards at issue, a contract conditioning employment *solely upon union referral* encourages membership in the union by that very distinction itself.

[Whittaker, J., joined in all except footnote 1 of this dissent; he would have added the reasons supporting the Board's direct reimbursement order set forth in his own dissent in a companion case, Carpenters Local 60 v. Labor Board, 365 U.S. 651, 660 (1961)].

NOTES

1. Assume that the Board's protective conditions had been based on §8(a)(1) and §8(b)(1)(A), rather than §8(a)(3) and §8(b)(2). Could the Board have properly balanced competing interests, as it generally does in applying §8(a)(1) to employer conduct not instigated by a union? Under this alternative approach, is it likely that the protective conditions would have been upheld? What of the back pay order against the union?

2. Suppose that the NLRB, during a rule-making proceeding, had shown that unions maintaining hiring halls have a disproportionately small percentage of minorities as members and users of the hall; hence, the NLRB had by rule required the safeguards invalidated in the principal case. Would there have been a stronger basis for holding that noncompliance with those requirements violated §8? Would *Local 357* now foreclose the adoption of those requirements by rule?

3. The NLRB has held that a union bylaw that bars union members from working with nonunion employees and that is known to unionized employers does not violate §8 in the absence of some direct inducement of the employer to discriminate in employment. American Federation of Musicians, 165 N.L.R.B. 798 (1967), *aff'd*, Glasser v. NLRB, 395 F.2d 401 (2d Cir. 1968). Is such a result realistic? Is it consistent with the Board's *Miranda* doctrine? See generally Note, 37 U. Chi. L. Rev. 778 (1970).

4. Prior to July 2, 1965, the effective date of Title VII of the Civil Rights Act of 1964, certain construction unions had barred blacks from both membership and job referrals through union-run hiring halls. Thereafter, the unions eliminated those restrictions but continued to base priority for referrals on a combination of the applicant's experience under collective agreements and in the construction trades generally. Experience under collective agreements was necessary for the highest referral priority. As a result of pre-1965 discrimination, blacks, regardless of their job qualifications, could not satisfy that requirement. Furthermore, they had also encountered difficulty in securing any construction experience because the unions had controlled most of the work and had discouraged union members from working with nonunion employees. The Board's General Counsel issues a complaint that the foregoing referral system violates §§8(a)(1), 8(a)(3), 8(b)(1)(A) and

8(b)(2); the charged parties rely on §8(f)(4) of the NLRA. What disposition? Cf. National Elec. Contractors Assn., 231 N.L.R.B. 1021 (1977). Suppose that the referral system is attacked as a violation of Title VII. What result? Cf. United States v. Sheet Metal Wkrs., 416 F.2d 123 (8th Cir. 1969); Kaplan v. IATSE, 525 F.2d 1354 (9th Cir. 1975). In applying §8(a)(1) and 8(a)(3) and 8(f)(4), what effect, if any, should the NLRB give to Title VII?

General Building Contractors Assn. v. Pennsylvania, 458 U.S. 375 (1982). The Operating Engineers Union, Local 542, by a ten-week strike in 1961, obtained an exclusive hiring hall from four area employer associations, who agreed to hire only operating engineers referred by the union from its current lists. Similar requirements were embodied in the local's agreements with employers who were not part of a multiemployer bargaining unit. The union also required its members to seek work only with the firms it designated. (The employers' subsequent unsuccessful efforts to eliminate those hiring hall provisions also triggered a strike.) Later agreements between the union and the employer associations contained a broad prohibition of discrimination against blacks, among others.

In a class action, the State of Pennsylvania and 12 black plaintiffs alleged, inter alia, that the union had engaged in a pattern of discrimination by denying blacks access to the union's referral lists and by referring them only to the worst paying jobs. The plaintiffs claimed that the union had violated both Title VII and 42 U.S.C. §1981.[f] The complaint also named the contractor-employers and their associations as defendants in the §1981 action. The employers were not, however, charged with a Title VII violation because of the failure to name them in the plaintiffs' complaint to the EEOC, a precondition to maintaining a federal court suit.

The trial court concluded that the union, because of its intentional discrimination and enforcement of practices with a disparate racial impact, had violated both Title VII and §1981. That court found, however, that the evidence failed to show that the employers, viewed as a class, had been aware of the union discrimination or had intended to discriminate. Nevertheless, the court held the employers liable under §1981 to an injunction but not for

---

[f] Section 1981, which has been construed to cover private action (as distinguished from only "state action"), such as a union's administration of a hiring hall, provides "All persons within the jurisdiction of the United States shall have the same right in every State and Territory to make and enforce contracts, to sue, be parties, give evidence, and to the full and equal benefit of all laws and proceedings for the security of persons and property as is enjoyed by white citizens, and shall be subject to like punishment, pains, penalties, taxes, licenses, and exactions of every kind, and to no other."

damages. The court of appeals, en banc, affirmed that judgment by an equally divided vote.

The Supreme Court reversed, with Justice Marshall, joined by Justice Brennan, dissenting, and Justice O'Connor, joined by Justice Blackmun, writing a separate concurrence, as did Justice Stevens. The Court reasoned this way: §1981 reaches only purposeful discrimination and not practices with merely a disparate impact. The employers were not vicariously liable for the union's intentional discrimination in the operation of the hiring hall. The hall had not served as the "joint agent" of the employers and the unions, for the employers' power (based on the collective bargaining agreement) to oppose the union's discrimination did not convert the union or the hiring hall into the employers' agent. There was, accordingly, no basis for the injunction, which, given the absence of employer liability and the substantial burdens it entailed, could not be justified as "minor or ancillary."

NOTES

1. Does the trial court's finding that the employers, albeit as a class, lacked knowledge of the discrimination involved seem plausible to you?

2. An employer, even though not guilty of intentional racial discrimination, may violate Title VII if he uses a method for selecting employees with a "disparate impact" on a protected group unless there is a "business necessity" for using the disputed method. See Griggs v. Duke Power Co., 401 U.S. 424 (1971). In *General Contractors*, what labor relations considerations bear on the business necessity defense? See Sears v. Atchison, Topeka & Santa Fe Ry. Co., 645 F.2d 1365 (10th Cir. 1981), *cert. denied sub nom.* United Transp. Union v. Sears, 456 U.S. 964 (1982), for a similar problem in the context of disputed seniority clauses, which one side unsuccessfully sought to change.

3. Consider whether the union or employers in *General Contractors* violated the NLRA. Cf. Houston Maritime Assn., 168 N.L.R.B. 615 (1967), *enforcement denied*, 426 F.2d 584 (5th Cir. 1970); Barton Brands Ltd. v. NLRB, supra p. 1138.

CHAPTER 12

REGULATION OF UNION GOVERNMENT AND ADMINISTRATION

The LMRDA (of 1959) broke new ground by subjecting important aspects of union government to direct federal regulation.[a] The McClellan Committee's disclosures[b] of corruption, misgovernment and oppression in some unions had provided the immediate impetus for that legislation, but its roots were considerably deeper. From the enactment of the Wagner Act to the end of the 1950s, the membership and power of unions had substantially increased. That growth sharpened old questions as to a special national responsibility for curbing abuses by institutions whose growth had been promoted by national policy.[c] Friends of unions and of collective bargaining had emphasized that responsibility and had long urged that neither state law nor internal union machinery provided adequate protection against infringements of "union democracy," members' civil liberties, and invidious barriers, such as those based on race, to membership and jobs.[d]

Such failures involved significant tensions within the traditional justification for the union movement. A commitment to democracy had been central to the rationale for unionization and collective bargaining. The democratic idea had been embodied in union constitutions;[e] it had also been

[a] The impact of Taft-Hartley on internal union affairs had been deliberately negligible and indirect. See §§8(a)(3), 8(b)(1), 8(b)(2), 8(b)(5), 9(c)(1)(A)(ii), 9(e)(1), and (now repealed) 9(f-h).

[b] This committee, which takes its popular name from its chairman, Senator John McClellan, was formally established as "The Senate Select Committee to Investigate Improper Activities in Labor-Management Relations," by S. Res. 74, 85th Cong., 1st Sess. (1957).

[c] As early as 1912, John R. Commons had urged that the corollary of state-compelled recognition of unions would be that "the State must strip [a union] of any abuses it may practice." See U.S. Commission on Industrial Relations, Final Report 374 (1915).

[d] See generally, Seidman, Emergence of Concern with Union Government and Administration, in Regulating Union Government 1, 5-7 (M. Estey, P. Taft, M. Wagner eds. 1964).

[e] See, e.g., AFL-CIO Constitution, Preamble and article II (1959).

For a 1959 study of union constitutions and their deficiencies with respect to nominations and elections, among other matters, see L. Bromwich, Union Constitutions (1959).

invoked in support of proposals for legal protection of the union movement. Unions were to bring democracy to the plant and to substitute the rule of law for the arbitrary power of the boss. Plainly, such high purposes are defeated if union autocracy is substituted for, or added to, managerial autocracy. Furthermore, it is difficult to justify the disruption and the costs associated with the legally protected bargaining system unless the union movement advances a generally accepted value. And of all the justifications for legal protection of unions in the 1930s, their contribution to industrial democracy seemed to have retained the greatest support.

It is one thing to agree that union democracy is good or, at least, that our symbolic code requires us to praise it. It is quite another matter to articulate its content and to devise and enforce implementing legislation. Unions are diverse and many-faceted institutions. They frequently seek "to combine within [themselves] two extremely divergent forms of social structure, that of an army and of a democratic town meeting." See Muste, Factional Fights in Trade Unions, in American Labor Dynamics 332-333 (J. Hardman ed. 1928); for a survey of attitudes regarding the content and the feasibility of union democracy, see A. Cook, Union Democracy: Practice and Ideal — An Analysis of Four Large Local Unions, ch. 1 (1963). Democratic structures might work not only against the solidarity and discipline necessary for an effective economic army but also against economic peace.[f] Finally, at the level of the international union, there were deep-seated structural obstacles to the formation of opposition parties and the promotion of responsiveness and accountability of the leaders to their constituents. The foregoing characteristics of unions had persuaded some students that legal intervention to promote union democracy was impracticable, particularly at the international level.[g] Plainly the LMRDA reflects a more optimistic view of the role

---

[f]National Planning Assns., Causes of Industrial Peace, Case Study No. 4, 57-58 (1953), quoted in Hays, The Union and Its Members: The Uses of Democracy, 11 N.Y.U. Conf. on Labor 35, 39 (1958). Similarly, where the members view the union as a democratic organ rather than as a marketer of labor services, there may be an increased unwillingness to ratify settlements agreed to by their bargaining representatives. There has been an increase in membership rejections of settlements following the enactment of the LMRDA. Some rejections may have been tactical maneuvers stimulated by the leadership or may have resulted from the leaders' evasion of their responsibilities. In any event, after the passage of the LMRDA, employers complained that unions had become "too democratic" and that union leaders were afraid to stand up to irresponsible rank-and-file demands because of the resultant danger of losing the next election. See D. McLaughlin & A. Schoomaker, The Landrum-Griffin Act and Union Democracy 181 (1979). But this fear appears to have been exaggerated. Id. at 185; Odewahn & Krislov, Contract Rejections: Testing the Explanatory Hypothesis, 12 Indus. Rel. 289, 294 (1973).

[g]See, e.g., Magrath, Democracy in Overalls: The Futile Quest for Union Democracy, 12 Ind. Lab. Rel. Rev. 503 (1959). But cf., Summers, The Usefulness of Law in Achieving Union Democracy, 48 Am. Econ. Rev. 44 (1958).

of law.[h] The law, having promoted freedom of association, was now to promote freedom within associations.

The LMRDA was, however, remarkably silent about one item crucial to the idea of industrial democracy, i.e., union practices with respect to admission of members. The first section of this chapter introduces the impact of state law, federal labor legislation, and Title VII of the Civil Rights Act of 1964 on that critical problem.

A. ADMISSION TO MEMBERSHIP

Under the orthodox common law view, unions, as "voluntary associations," were free to determine their own membership standards. See Blumrosen, Legal Protection Against Exclusion from Union Activities, 22 Ohio St. L.J. 21 (1961). As the materials below suggest, the orthodox view neglected two important considerations: First, unlike private associations generally, some unions, through the closed shop, excluded nonmembers from particular occupations.[i] Second, even when a union did not bar entry into jobs and the bargaining unit, the principle of majority rule barred nonmembers from negotiating for themselves while exclusion from membership deprived them of the opportunity to influence directly the shape of the bargain by which they were to be bound.

Under the prevailing view, a union constitution was treated as a "contract" between individual members and their union; hence, wrongful expulsions were actionable as breach of contract and also as a wrongful deprivation of an aggrieved member's property rights in the union's assets. These rationales were criticized as disregarding the social and economic interests affected by union regulation of membership, and especially so when a closed shop was combined with a closed union. See the classic article by Chafee, The Internal Affairs of Associations Not For Profit, 43 Harv. L. Rev. 993 (1930), suggesting use of the prima facie tort doctrine under which unions would be required to justify the harm intentionally inflicted by exclusion

---

[h] See Hartley, The Framework of Democracy in Union Government, 32 Cath. U.L. Rev. 13 (1982) (a survey of union structures and participation of individuals and minorities); J. Bellace, A. Berkowitz, & B. Van Dusen, The Landrum-Griffin Act: Twenty Years of Federal Protection of Union Members' Rights (1979) (hereinafter Bellace).

[i] As preceding materials indicated, the Taft-Hartley Act was designed generally to insulate job interests from union membership but failed to achieve that result in important employment sectors.

from membership. Nevertheless, courts generally adhered to the orthodox contract and property rationales and declined to monitor membership procedures. Judicial repudiation of, and limitations on, this restricting orthodoxy are illustrated below.

Directors Guild of America v. Superior Court
64 Cal. 2d 42, 409 P.2d 934 (1966)

[Plaintiff alleged that he had been offered, and then denied, a job as an assistant director for a TV series after his application for admission had been rejected by the defendant union solely because of its nepotistic policy. The union had maintained a closed shop through oral agreements with employers, bylaws banning members from working with nonmembers, and by threats of economic pressure against recalcitrant employers and employees, including plaintiff's prospective employer and his employees. In Count I, plaintiff alleged that because of the union's arbitrary denial of union membership to him and its coercive tactics, the employer did not hire him as an assistant director. Count II complained that the union had "tortiously interfered and prevented plaintiff from being able to enter into such advantageous employment contract." The court denied relief and declared: The plaintiff's claim essentially involved employment discrimination, a matter under the NLRB's exclusive jurisdiction. Had the plaintiff actually been employed he would have been entitled to relief against the union's arbitrary denial of admission under California precedents barring the coupling of a closed shop with a closed union, or with second class union membership. See James v. Marinship Corp., 25 Cal. 2d 721, 731, 155 P.2d 329, 335 (1945); Williams v. International Boilermakers, 27 Cal. 2d 586, 165 P.2d 903 (1946). The court added:]

TOBRINER, J. The decisions of this court thus recognize that membership in the union means more than mere personal or social accommodation. Such membership affords to the employee not only the opportunity to participate in the negotiation of the contract governing his employment but also the chance to engage in the institutional life of the union. Although in the case which involves interstate commerce the union must legally give fair representation to all the appropriate employees, whether or not they are members of the union, the union official, in the nature of political realities, will in all likelihood more diligently represent union members, who can vote him out of office, than employees whom he must serve only as a matter of abstract law.

Our decisions further recognize that the union functions as the medium for the exercise of industrial franchise. As Summers puts it, "The right to join a union involves the right to an economic ballot." (The Right to Join a Union (1947) 47 Colum. L. Rev. 33.) Participation in the union's affairs by the workman compares to the participation of the citizen in the affairs of his community. The union, as a kind of public service institution, affords to its members the opportunity to record themselves upon all matters affecting their relationships with the employer; it serves likewise as a vehicle for the expression of the membership's position on political and community issues. The shadowy right to "fair representation" by the union, accorded by the Act, is by no means the same as the hard concrete ability to vote and to participate in the affairs of the union.

The above grounds for condemnation of arbitrary rejection from membership apply as forcefully to the situation in which the union does not have a union shop contract as to that in which it does. . . . [T]he basis for membership lies in the right and desirability of representation, not in the union's economic control of the job.

Our analysis applies, however, only to union membership for those employed in the appropriate craft or industry. To hold that a union must admit *all* persons who seek membership but are not employed in the craft or industry whose employees are represented by the union would raise serious social and economic questions. Any such sweeping ruling would subject the union to an influx of unemployed persons who could distort its function from representation of those working in the relevant craft or industry to purposes alien to such objectives. It would set up for state courts a test as to the scope of the union's obligation of representation which would conflict with the [NLRB's] counterpart concept of the appropriate bargaining unit. It could gravely affect the basic structure of the union. Although we would hold that the union, even in the absence of the union shop must admit to membership all qualified employed applicants, the instant complaint, lacking such allegation of employment, must fail. . . .

NOTES

1. Would the applicability of §§8(a)(3) and 8(b)(2) of the NLRA turn on whether the plaintiff had actually been employed? If not, is there any justification for making that fact decisive for preemption?

2. Would the plaintiff's employment control whether the union had breached its duty of fair representation? Suppose that the plaintiff brings an action in a state or federal court, repeating the allegations made in the

principal case and alleging also the union's breach of that duty. What result? Cf. Vaca v. Sipes, supra p. 1145; Houston Maritime Assn., supra p. 1230.

3. Payne, an employee represented by the union in a plant covered by the NLRA, applied for union membership. His application was rejected because he refused to subscribe to the following oath: "I am not now affiliated with, and never will join or give aid, comfort, or support to any Revolutionary Organization." Payne's employment has not been affected by his nonmembership in the union, which has agreed to let him participate in ratification of collective bargaining agreements despite his nonmembership. Would the federal labor statutes or the federal Constitution give him a remedy against the union's refusal to admit him to membership? Cf. Hovan v. Carpenters, 704 F.2d 641 (1st Cir. 1983).

4. Suppose that Payne had been a member of the union but had been expelled under a regulation stating that "all Communists, Fascists, or members of other totalitarian organizations, or advocates of their ideas, are subject to expulsion." Payne, prior to expulsion, had been charged with spreading "Communist propaganda" and had been served with notice of the charges, given a hearing, and had not denied the charges. Does he have a basis under the LMRDA or state law for securing a restoration of his membership? Would it make a difference if the charges against him were based on statements he made while campaigning for union office? Cf. Turner v. Air Transport Lodge 1894, IAM, 590 F.2d 409 (2d Cir. 1978), cert. denied, 442 U.S. 919 (1979); see also Hurwitz v. Directors Guild, 364 F.2d 67 (2d Cir. 1966).

Local 53, Insulators & Asbestos Wkrs. v. Vogler, 407 F.2d 1047 (5th Cir. 1969). The union, which dominated employment and training in the area's asbestos and insulation trades, had restricted membership to sons or close relatives living in members' households and had required applicants to be approved by a majority of the members voting by secret ballot. Because of the union's deliberate limitation of membership, only approximately one-quarter of the workers it represented in collective bargaining were members. In a Title VII action, the court of appeals affirmed a temporary injunction against the union's nepotistic requirements and against discrimination in union membership and referrals. The court also upheld an order requiring the union to admit to membership three blacks and one Mexican, whose applications the union had denied; to develop objective criteria for determining the size of membership necessary to meet present and future needs of local industry; to suspend new membership in the interim; and to alternate referrals of blacks and whites for work, on a chronological basis.

NOTES

1. Insulators & Asbestos Workers, Local 53, 185 N.L.R.B. 642 (1970), involving the same basic situation addressed in the foregoing case, illustrates the overlap and the different significance of racial (and similar) factors under the NLRA and Title VII, respectively. The Board found a violation of §§8(b)(2) and (1)(A) in that the union in administering its hiring hall had discriminated in employment on the basis of union membership. Member Jenkins protested the Board's failure to find those violations for the additional reason that the discrimination had been based on race and national origin. The trial examiner had not passed on that ground out of comity to the district court, which had already issued its preliminary injunction. What of Jenkins' suggestion today?

2. In United Steelworkers v. Weber, 443 U.S. 193, 198 n.1 (1979), the Court stated: "Judicial findings of exclusion from crafts on racial grounds are so numerous as to make such exclusion a proper subject for judicial notice. [Citing numerous cases]." That notorious discrimination presumably has been a factor in judicial orders to unions to observe specified quotas for admission, acceptance into apprenticeship programs, or job referrals, despite the obstacles presented by §703(j), Title VII of the Civil Rights Act of 1964. (Students should examine that section.) See Rios v. Enterprise Assn. Steamfitters, Local 638, 501 F.2d 622, 630 (2d Cir. 1974); Edwards & Zaretsky, Preferential Remedies for Employment Discrimination, 74 Mich. L. Rev. 1 (1975). Compare Meltzer, The Weber Case: The Judicial Abrogation of the Antidiscrimination Standard in Employment, 47 U. Chi. L. Rev. 423, 430-434, 449-453 (1980). See also Firefighters Local 1784 v. Stotts, 104 S. Ct. 2576 (1984).

3. Suppose that practically all of the work force in a given industry is unionized but it is urged that restrictive union admission policies, coupled with a closed-shop tradition, have kept the work force too low. Are there any objective criteria for determining the appropriate size of the union, based on industry need? Can such determinations be made without assumptions about the appropriate wage rate, and is that assumption in turn affected by the number of workers available in the particular industry? Given the social problem involved, should courts be unduly concerned about this dilemma?

4. Senator McClellan's original bill (S. 1137, 86th Cong., 1st Sess. (1959)) had contained the following provision, which was dropped from the LMRDA: "Section 101 (2). . . . Every person who meets the reasonable qualifications uniformly prescribed by a labor organization shall be eligible for membership and admitted to membership in such organization." What would be the principal difference between such a provision and §703(c) of

Title VII of the Civil Rights Act of 1964? Would the enactment of Senator McClellan's proposal be desirable?

B. "DISCIPLINING" OF MEMBERS

Long before the LMRDA, state courts had developed several legal theories for setting aside union disciplinary action that was not warranted by the provisions of the union constitution and bylaws, that was contrary to "public policy," or that had involved a denial of a "fair hearing." State law, however, was criticized as chaotic and inadequate. See Summers, Legal Limitations on Union Discipline, 64 Harv. L. Rev. 1049, 1050 (1951); but cf. Cox, Internal Affairs of Labor Unions Under the Labor Reform Act of 1959, 58 Mich. L. Rev. 819, 835-837 (1960).

The LMRDA established a new federal source of protection for union members while preserving both state competence over union discipline and NLRB jurisdiction over union conduct that might be viewed as "discipline." See §§103, 603. The following materials will deal with the content, interaction, and coordination of those sources of regulation.

See generally T. Keeline, NLRB and Judicial Control of Union Discipline (1976); Wellington, Union Fines and Workers' Rights, 85 Yale L.J. 1022 (1976).

1. The Exhaustion Requirement

Detroy v. American Guild of Variety Artists
286 F.2d 75 (2d Cir.), *cert. denied*, 366 U.S. 929 (1961)

[Plaintiff, a performer who worked with a chimpanzee troupe, sued, under LMRDA §102, alleging that the American Guild of Variety Artists (AGVA) had violated his rights under §101(a)(5) by publishing his name on a "National Unfair List" without giving him notice or a hearing. This publication had been prompted by plaintiff's noncompliance with an arbitration award upholding a hotel's charge that plaintiff had breached his contract. The district court dismissed the complaint, relying on both the provision in §101(a)(4) concerning exhaustion of internal union remedies and the availability of reasonable AGVA procedures granting its members a hearing "within the four-month period permitted by law."]

LUMBARD, J. . . . Article XX of the Constitution of the AGVA

. . . establishes procedures whereby claims asserted against the union are heard and determined by its Board of Executive Committee. Thus, the first issue before us now is whether the proviso in §101(a)(4), which protects the right of a union member to sue his union, "Provided, That any such member may be required to exhaust reasonable hearing procedures (but not to exceed a four-month lapse of time) within such organization, before instituting legal or administrative proceedings against such organizations or any officer thereof," required of the appellant in this case that he first have recourse to the internal procedures established by the union's constitution. The exhaustion proviso of §101(a)(4) does not appear in §102, which grants members who claim that their rights under §101 have been infringed a federal forum in which to litigate their disputes with the union. It might also appear from the rejection by the House of Representatives of H.R. 8342, the bill originally reported out of the Committee on Education and Labor, which explicitly provided for exhaustion of internal remedies in §102, that Congress did not mean to have the exhaustion doctrine apply to the rights granted by §101, except where, as in the case of the right to sue, it was expressly provided. However, the broad language of the proviso in §101(a)(4) includes suits instituted against labor unions in any court on any claim. Absent a clear directive by Congress, the policy formulated over a course of time by courts reluctant to interfere in the internal affairs of private organizations should not be superseded. We hold, therefore, that the provision in §101(a)(4) applies, as well, to suits brought in the federal courts for violations of the rights secured by §101.

Judge Dimock in this case read §101(a)(4) as imposing upon the union member an absolute duty to exhaust union remedies before applying to the federal courts. The legislative history of the section indicates, however, that Congress had no intention of establishing such a rule.

. . . When read in light of the statements made on the floor of Congress by the authors of the statute, it appears clear that the proviso was incorporated in order to preserve the exhaustion doctrine as it had developed and would continue to develop in the courts, lest it otherwise appear to be Congress' intention to have the right to sue secured by §101 abrogate the requirement of prior resort to internal procedures. In addition, the proviso dictated an outside limit beyond which the judiciary cannot extend the requirement of exhaustion — no remedy which would require proceedings exceeding four months in duration may be demanded. We therefore construe the statute to mean that a member of a labor union who attempts to institute proceedings before a court or an administrative agency may be required *by that court or agency* to exhaust internal remedies of less than four months' duration before invoking outside assistance.

Section 102, under which the appellant instituted his proceeding, provides for enforcement by federal courts of rights secured by federal law. . . . In enforcing rights guaranteed by the new statute, . . . federal courts may develop their own principles regarding the time when a union's action taken in violation of §101 is ripe for judicial intervention. . . . The rules formulated by . . . state courts may suggest helpful avenues of approach, cf. Textile Workers v. Lincoln Mills, 1957, 353 U.S. 448, 457, but the authority granted to the federal courts by Congress to secure the rights enumerated in §101 of the 1959 Act is accompanied by the duty to formulate federal law regarding a union member's obligation to exhaust the internal union remedies before seeking judicial vindication of those rights.

If we look to the substantial body of state law on the subject, we find that the general rule requiring exhaustion before resort to a court has been almost entirely swallowed up by exceptions phrased in broad terms. . . . Summers, Legal Limitations on Union Discipline, 64 Harv. L. Rev. 1049, 1086-1092 (1951). Rather than decide whether exhaustion is proper by determining whether the union's action can be characterized as "void" (e.g., Tesoriero v. Miller, 1949, 274 App. Div. 670, 88 N.Y.S.2d 87) or as "affecting property rights" (e.g., Local Union No. 65 of Amalgamated Sheet Metal Workers, etc. v. Nalty, 6th Cir., 1925, 7 F.2d 100), we believe it preferable to consider each case on its own facts.

The Congressionally approved policy of first permitting unions to correct their own wrongs is rooted in the desire to stimulate labor organizations to take the initiative and independently to establish honest and democratic procedures. Other policies, as well, underlie the exhaustion rule. The possibility that corrective action within the union will render a member's complaint moot suggests that, in the interest of conserving judicial resources, no court step in before the union is given its opportunity. Moreover, courts may find valuable the assistance provided by prior consideration of the issues by appellate union tribunals. . . . Congress has provided a safeguard against abuse by a union of the freedom thus granted it by not requiring exhaustion of union remedies if the procedures will exceed four months in duration. But . . . if the state of facts is such that immediate judicial relief is warranted, Congress' acceptance of the exhaustion doctrine as applied to the generality of cases should not bar an appropriate remedy in proper circumstances.

. . . [T]he only hearing given the appellant before his name was placed on the National Unfair List was that of the arbitration proceeding. The union was not a party to arbitration, and the issue decided by the arbitrators was not whether the appellant should be disciplined by the union but whether he owed an obligation to an employer with whom he had contracted. It is undisputed that no hearing was held in which the appellant could respond to the union's intention of taking disciplinary action. Quite clearly, a hearing in which some liability between a union member and a third party is determined is not the type of hearing demanded by §101(a)(5). At no time was the appellant given the opportunity of arguing before the union's hearing board that placing him on the Unfair List exceeded the powers granted to the union by its constitution, nor could he raise other mitigating circumstances in response to an expressed intention to place his name on such a list. The facts on their face, therefore, reveal a violation of the rights guaranteed union members by §101(a)(5). If the question before us were whether the union's constitution authorized the listing of the appellant's name on an unfair list after a hearing with due procedural safeguards, a union tribunal might provide some insight to aid our decision. But no prior consideration by such a tribunal is necessary or helpful on the question whether the treatment of the appellant violated §101(a)(5).

[The court then emphasized that blacklisting virtually barred the plaintiff from employment; that his damages would be difficult to calculate; and that recovery of damages from either the union or its officers might well be impossible under New York law.]

Moreover, it is by no means clear that the union's own rules afforded the appellant a remedy within the organization. . . .

. . . [We] hold that where the internal union remedy is uncertain and has not been specifically brought to the attention of the disciplined party, the violation of federal law clear and undisputed, and the injury to the union member immediate and difficult to compensate by means of a subsequent money award, exhaustion of union remedies ought not to be required. The absence of any of these elements might, in light of Congressional approval of the exhaustion doctrine, call for a different result. The facts of this case, however, warrant immediate judicial intervention.

Nor can we agree with the union's claim that the listing of the appellant's name did not constitute discipline within the meaning of §101(a)(5). If a union such as the AGVA undertakes to enforce the contracts made by its members with employers, it does so because such enforcement is to the ultimate benefit of all the members, in that it promotes stability within the industry. A breach of contract or a refusal to abide by an arbitration award, therefore, is not damaging merely to the employer but to the union as well, and the union's listing of those of its members who do violate their contracts is an act of self-protection. In thus furthering its own ends the union must abide by the rules set down for it by Congress in §101(a)(5), and any member against whom steps are taken by the union in the interest of promoting the welfare of the group is entitled to these guarantees.

In passing on the motions for summary judgment and for a temporary injunction, the district court had before it only the complaint and the affidavits of the appellant and various officers of the union. The undisputed facts of the case require that a temporary injunction issue ordering the union to remove the appellant's name from its Unfair List where it is now retained in apparent violation of §101(a)(5). . . . . [Reversed.]

NOTES

1. The Supreme Court subsequently adopted the interpretation of §101(a)(4) reflected in the principal case. See NLRB v. Industrial Union of Marine & Shipbuilding Workers, 391 U.S. 418, 427-428 (1968).

2. A union, pursuant to a collective bargaining agreement requiring it to exclude from its hiring hall members fired by an employer for misconduct, excluded ten members for 90 days after they had been fired for engaging in an unauthorized strike. The ten sued under the LMRDA, alleging that the union had disciplined them without observing the procedures required by §101(a)(5). Seven plaintiffs admitted full and willing participation in the wildcat strike; three denied such participation. What ruling on defendant's motion to dismiss the claims of all plaintiffs on the ground that they had not suffered "discipline" within the meaning of the LMRDA? Is "discipline" under §101(a)(5) limited to action affecting the associational relationship (e.g., right to attend meetings and to vote) between a member and his union? Does "discipline" include any detriment imposed by a union on a member because of conduct as a union member or employee? In light of the purpose of §101(a)(5), should the question of whether a member has been "disciplined" depend on the existence of a genuine dispute over whether he has violated a valid union policy? Cf. Hackenburg v. Boilermakers, Local 101, 694 F.2d 1237 (10th Cir. 1982), with Detroy, supra. See Beaird & Player, Union Discipline of its Membership Under §101(a)(5) of Landrum-Griffin, 9 Ga. L. Rev. 383 (1975).

2.   Rationales For and Scope of Protection

Apart from internal union appeals, a variety of remedies may exist for improper union discipline of a member. The principal remedies arise from state law, the LMRDA, and the NLRA. Occasionally, there are also efforts, usually unsuccessful, to invoke the First Amendment. Similarly, when there is "conspiratorial activity," 42 U.S.C. §1985(3) has sometimes provided a remedy. See Brett v. Sohio Constr. Co., 518 F. Supp. 698 (D. Alaska 1981).

The materials below will explore the content, the rationale, and the interplay among these remedies. Although a particular case may focus on only one remedy, a pervasive question is the relative usefulness of each available remedy, as well as the availability of procedural mechanisms, such as pendent jurisdiction, for pursuing several remedies in the same lawsuit or concurrently before different tribunals, such as the NLRB and a state or federal court.

Finnegan v. Leu
456 U.S. 431 (1982)

BURGER, C. J. The question presented . . . is whether the discharge of a union's appointed business agents by the union president, following his election over the candidate supported by the business agents, violated the [LMRDA]. The Court of Appeals held that the Act did not protect the business agents from discharge. We granted certiorari to resolve Circuit conflicts, . . . and we affirm.

I

In December 1977, respondent Harold Leu defeated Omar Brown in an election for the presidency of Local 20 of the International Brotherhood of Teamsters, Chauffeurs, Warehousemen and Helpers of America, a labor organization representing workers in a 14-county area of northwestern Ohio. During the vigorously contested campaign, petitioners, then business agents of Local 20, openly supported the incumbent president, Brown. Upon assuming office in January 1978, Leu discharged petitioners and the Local's other business agents, all of whom had been appointed by Brown following his election in 1975. Leu explained that he felt the agents were loyal to Brown, not to him, and therefore would be unable to follow and implement his policies and programs.

Local 20's bylaws — which were adopted by, and may be amended by, a vote of the union membership — provide that the president shall have authority to appoint, direct, and discharge the Union's business agents. . . . The duties of the business agents include participation in the negotiating of collective-bargaining agreements, organizing of union members, and processing of grievances. In addition, the business agents, along with the president, other elected officers, and shop stewards, sit as members of the Stewards Council, the legislative assembly of the Union. Petitioners had come up through the union ranks, and as business agents they were also members of Local 20. Discharge from their positions as business agents did not render petitioners ineligible to continue their union membership.

Petitioners filed suit in the United States District Court, alleging that they had been terminated from their appointed positions in violation of the [LMRDA §§101(a)(1), 101(a)(2), 102, and 609]. The District Court granted summary judgment for respondents Leu and Local 20, holding that the Act does not protect a union employee from discharge by the president of the union if the employee's rights as a union member are not affected. 469 F. Supp. 832 (1979). . . . [T]he Sixth Circuit affirmed. . . .

II

The [LMRDA] was the product of congressional concern with widespread abuses of power by union leadership. The relevant provisions of the Act had a history tracing back more than two decades in the evolution of the statutes relating to labor unions. Tensions between union leaders and the rank-and-file members and allegations of union wrongdoing led to extended congressional inquiry. As originally introduced, the legislation focused on disclosure requirements and the regulation of union trusteeships and elections. However, various amendments were adopted, all aimed at enlarged protection for members of unions paralleling certain rights guaranteed by the Federal Constitution; not surprisingly, these amendments — ultimately enacted as Title I of the Act — were introduced under the title of "Bill of Rights of Members of Labor Organizations." The amendments placed emphasis on the rights of union members to freedom of expression without fear of sanctions by the union, which in many instances could mean loss of union membership and in turn loss of livelihood. Such protection was necessary to further the Act's primary objective of ensuring that unions would be democratically governed and responsive to the will of their memberships. . . .

Sections 101(a)(1) and (2) . . . , on which petitioners rely, guarantee equal voting rights, and rights of speech and assembly, to "[e]very *member* of a labor organization" (emphasis added). In addition, §609 of the Act renders it unlawful for a union or its representatives "to fine, suspend, expel, or otherwise discipline any of its *members* for exercising any right to which he is entitled under the provisions of this Act." (Emphasis added.) It is readily apparent, both from the language of these provisions and from the legislative history of Title I, that it was rank-and-file union members — not union officers or employees, as such — whom Congress sought to protect.

Petitioners held a dual status as both employees and members of the Union. As *members* of Local 20, petitioners undoubtedly had a protected right to campaign for Brown and support his candidacy. At issue here is whether they were thereby immunized from discharge at the pleasure of the president from their positions as appointed union *employees*.

III

Petitioners contend that discharge from a position as a union employee constitutes "discipline" [under] §609; and that termination of union employment is therefore unlawful when predicated upon an employee's exercise of rights guaranteed to members under the Act. However, we conclude that the term "discipline," as used in §609, refers only to retaliatory actions that affect a union member's rights or status *as a member* of the union. Section 609 speaks in terms of disciplining "members"; and the three disciplinary sanctions specifically enumerated — fine, suspension, and expulsion — are all punitive actions taken against union members as members. In contrast, discharge from union employment does not impinge upon the incidents of union membership, and affects union members only to the extent that they happen also to be union employees. See Sheridan v. Carpenters Local No. 626, 306 F.2d 152, 156 (CA3 1962). We discern nothing in §609, or its legislative history, to support petitioners' claim that Congress intended to establish a system of job security or tenure for appointed union employees.

Congress used essentially the same language elsewhere in the Act with the specific intent not to protect a member's status as a union employee or officer. Section 101(a)(5) states that "[n]o member of any labor organization may be fined, suspended, expelled, or otherwise disciplined" without enumerated procedural protections. The Conference Report accompanying S. 1555 as finally enacted, H.R. Conf. Rep. No. 1147, 86th Cong., 1st Sess., 31 (1959), 1 Leg. Hist. 935, explains that this "prohibition on suspension without observing certain safeguards applies only to suspension of membership in the union; *it does not refer to suspension of a member's status as an officer of the union*" (emphasis added). This too is a persuasive indication that the virtually identical language in §609 was likewise meant to refer only to punitive actions diminishing membership rights, and not to termination of a member's status as an appointed union employee.

We hold, therefore, that removal from appointive union employment is not within the scope of those union sanctions explicitly prohibited by §609.

IV

Our analysis is complicated, however, by the fact that §102 provides independent authority for a suit against a union based on an alleged violation of Title I of the Act. Section 102 states that

> [a]ny person whose rights secured by the provisions of this title have been infringed by any violation of this title may bring a civil action in a district court of the United States for such relief (including injunctions) as may be appropriate.

Although the intended relationship between §§102 and 609 is not entirely clear, it seems evident that a litigant may maintain an action under §102 — to redress an "infringement" of "rights secured" under Title I — without necessarily stating a violation of §609.

The question still remains, however, whether petitioners' "rights secured" under Title I were "infringed" by the termination of their union employment. Petitioners, as union members, had a right under §§101(a)(1) and (2) to campaign for Brown and to vote in the union election, but they were not prevented from exercising those rights. Rather, petitioners allege only an *indirect* interference with their membership rights, maintaining that they were forced to "choos[e] between their rights of free expression . . . and their jobs." See Retail Clerks Union Local 648 v. Retail Clerks International Assn., 299 F. Supp. 1012, 1021 (DC 1969).

We need not decide whether the retaliatory discharge of a union member from union office — even though not "discipline" prohibited under §609 — might ever give rise to a cause of action under §102. For whatever limits Title I places on a union's authority to utilize dismissal from union office as "part of a purposeful and deliberate attempt . . . to suppress dissent within the union," cf. Schonfeld v. Penza, 477 F.2d 899, 904 (CA2 1973), it does not restrict the freedom of an elected union leader to choose a staff whose views are compatible with his own.[11] Indeed, neither the language nor the legislative history of the Act suggests that it was intended even to address the issue of union patronage.[12] To the contrary, the Act's overriding objective was to ensure that unions would be democratically governed, and responsive to the will of the union membership as expressed in open, periodic elections. See Wirtz v. Hotel Employees, 391 U.S. 492, 497 (1968). Far from being inconsistent with this purpose, the ability of an elected union president to select his own administrators is an integral part of ensuring a union administration's responsiveness to the mandate of the union election. . . .

No doubt this poses a dilemma for some union employees; if they refuse to campaign for the incumbent they risk his displeasure, and by supporting him risk the displeasure of his successor. However, in enacting Title I of the Act, Congress simply was not concerned with perpetuating appointed union employees in office at the expense of an elected president's freedom to choose his own staff. Rather, its concerns were with promoting union democracy, and protecting the rights of union *members* from arbitrary action by the union or its officers. . . . [Affirmed.]

BLACKMUN, J., with whom BRENNAN, J., joins, concurring. . . .

I must assume that what the Court holds today is that the newly elected

---

[11] We leave open the question whether a different result might obtain in a case involving nonpolicymaking and nonconfidential employees.

[12] We think it virtually inconceivable that Congress would have prohibited the long-standing practice of union patronage without any discussion in the legislative history of the Act. . . . Had such a result been contemplated, it undoubtedly would have encountered substantial resistance. Moreover, Congress likely would have made some express accommodation to the needs of union employers to appoint and remove policymaking officials. . . .

president may discharge the union's appointed business agents and other appointed union member-employees who will be instrumental in evolving the president's administrative policies. See Elrod v. Burns, 427 U.S. 347 (1976); Branti v. Finkel, 445 U.S. 507 (1980).[j] Indeed, the Court uses the terms "staff," ante, . . . and "his own administrators," ibid. In addition, this particular union's bylaws expressly give the president plenary authority over the business agents. With that much, I have no difficulty.

On the understanding, but only on the understanding, that the Court by its opinion is not reaching out further to decide the same issue with respect to nonpolicymaking employees, that is, rank-and-file member-employees (a matter which, for me, presents another case for another day), I join the Court's opinion.

NOTE

Ms. Hodge, beginning in 1960, served as a secretary of a Teamsters local for 14 years and belonged to the union for the latter 12. She had wide-ranging responsibilities and access to confidential and sensitive information, including internal union charges against employees, collective bargaining proposals, and strike calls. In 1973, after a dispute over the local's handling of strike benefits, the local was placed under a trusteeship, pursuant to the union constitution. Thereafter, the local's officers, with whom Hodge had worked closely, were displaced. She, however, continued her previous role, with somewhat curtailed authority. An insurgent group, composed in part of former local officials, litigated the validity of the trusteeship and also fielded its own slate of candidates for office. The insurgents lost the election. The new administration fired Ms. Hodge because they believed she had voted for the insurgents. What is the likelihood that she would succeed in a suit for reinstatement or damages brought under the LMRDA? Compare Hodge v. Teamsters Local 695, 707 F.2d 961 (7th Cir. 1983), with NLRB v. Hendricks County Rural Elective Membership Corp., supra p. 713.

---

[j] [In *Branti*, the Court protected assistant public defenders against dismissal following the appointment of a Democratic public defender, to succeed his Republican predecessor, by the county legislature, control of which had switched to the Democrats. The Court declared that constitutional protection against patronage dismissals extended to "policy making" and "confidential" positions if party affiliation is not an appropriate requirement for the office involved. Three dissenters objected to the vagueness of the Court's standard, noting, e.g., the difficulty of determining whether it would protect a United States district attorney. See also Delong v. United States, 621 F.2d 618, 623-624 (4th Cir. 1980) (the *Elrod-Branti* principle extends to actions or threats that constitute a "constructive dismissal" because they force the public employee to choose between resignation and surrender of protected rights). — EDS.]

Newman v. Local 1101, Communications Wkrs., 570 F.2d 439 (2d Cir. 1978) (*Newman I*). Under Local 1101's bylaws, the power to govern the Local is shared by its Executive Committee (consisting of its six principal officers) and its Executive Board (consisting of those officers plus five business agents). The bylaws authorize the Committee and the Board to create steward positions and to fill them by appointment or by elections held within membership work units. The Committee is authorized to remove a steward, subject to veto by the Board or the membership. The Local's leadership created 1,000 stewardships, which were filled through work unit elections.

Newman, a vocal critic of the Local's leadership and a strong proponent of a more democratic union, was elected as one of four stewards for his work unit in September 1975. On December 2, 1976, the Executive Committee removed him as job steward, on the ground that his disruptive conduct at a union meeting the previous day had prevented the Local's president from discussing the CWA's preparations for upcoming negotiations with the Bell system. Despite a dispute over the factual basis for that charge, it was undisputed that Newman had vigorously opposed the Local's approach and advocated a more militant bargaining policy.

In an action brought under LMRDA §102 by Newman and 21 other members against the Local and various of its officers, the district court granted a preliminary injunction, ordering Newman's reinstatement and restraining the defendants from refusing to certify or from decertifying any member as a job steward because of his exercise of LMRDA rights. The district court, on the basis of the parties' affidavits, found that Newman had been removed because he had repeatedly expressed views in opposition to the union leadership and had sponsored resolutions, adopted by his work unit and presented by him at the December 1st meeting, advocating a more aggressive negotiating posture and formation of a strike committee. The district court concluded that Newman's removal had constituted both retaliation for his exercise of rights under §101(a)(2) and "unlawful discipline" under §609.

The court of appeals reversed and remanded. The court declared that a union member risks removal by conduct inconsistent with his duties resulting from his acceptance of a union position. The union may not, however, discipline a job steward "for the purpose of suppressing or chilling his exercize of free speech rights or that of others as members." The court added:

"The inquiry in each case, therefore, must be to determine whether a member's opposition to the union's programs or policies may be reasonably viewed as precluding him from acting effectively as its representative, and whether his removal from his official position would tend to prevent him or others from exercising their rights as members under Title I of LMRDA. The inquiry requires a close analysis of the nature of the union position in question, the extent of the allegedly unlawful discipline, and the motivation behind the removal. . . . Only where there is clear and convincing proof that the union action — in this case the decertification of Newman as a job steward — was 'part of a purposeful and deliberate attempt by union officials to suppress dissent within the union,' [Schonfeld v. Penza], 477 F.2d 904, should the federal court act under LMRDA."

The court also noted: ". . . [D]espite a prior decertification as a job steward and the union leadership's prior refusal to certify him after election to that office, Newman continued to exercise his free speech rights as a union member . . . in opposition to Local 1101's incumbent leadership. In view of this unique record, in which identical conduct by the defendants had not deterred Newman or any other union members from exercising their rights under LMRDA, we do not believe that judicial intervention is necessary or justified."

On remand, the district court ordered Newman's reinstatement. The court of appeals, affirming (*Newman II*), gave this summary of the findings below (597 F.2d 833 (1979)): Notwithstanding Newman's opposition, he had served faithfully as steward, explaining the leadership's position on policies with which he had disagreed, supporting various Local programs even though he had deemed them not in the Local's best interests, and generally carrying out the Local's directions. He had not disrupted the December 1 meeting, which, moreover, had been held when the Local was soliciting members' views about future policies. The purpose and effect of Newman's decertification "was not to discipline him for failure properly to perform his duties as job steward but to stifle not only Newman but members generally from exercising their rights openly to criticize the Local's management, to publish their views, and to run for office."

The court of appeals declared: "The district court applied the proper standards as outlined in our earlier decision and was 'not unmindful of the fine line which must be drawn between what might be termed insubordination on the one hand and freedom of speech on the other,' Wood v. Dennis, 489 F.2d 849, 855-56 (7th Cir. 1973), *cert. denied*, 415 U.S. 960 (1974). Moreover, although there was conflicting evidence . . . , Judge Knapp's key findings, being supported by evidence found by him to be credible, cannot be labelled clearly erroneous, F.R. Civ. P. 52(a). . . . We are not therefore dealing with the case of an appointed or elected official of a union who seeks 'to completely subvert the purpose of his employment by engaging in activities diametrically opposed to the performance of his specified duties,' Sewell v. Grand Lodge, 445 F.2d 545, 550-51 (5th Cir. 1971), *cert. denied*, 404 U.S. 1024 (1972). Nor does our affirmance preclude the Local from imposing upon its officers, stewards and other representatives, reasonable rules designed to assure that they will cooperate in implementing the management's policies or programs and in spreading its views or from removing a representative who fails to do so, provided the Local does nothing to inhibit the representative from exercising his rights under LMRDA as a member to criticize the Local's management or policies. . . ."

NOTES

1. Under *Newman II*, did the district court's findings appear to satisfy the chilling-purpose-or-effects test of *Newman I?* In light of the affirmance in *Newman II*, what appears sufficient to satisfy that test?

2. Is the approach in *Newman I and II* foreclosed by the Supreme Court's subsequent decision in Finnegan v. Leu? In that connection, would it be material if, under the bylaws, all stewards had been appointed? See Adams-Lundy v. Flight Attendants, 116 L.R.R.M. 2394 (5th Cir. 1984).

3. Are courts likely to be able to devise workable standards for distinguishing between "insubordination" by a union official and that official's exercise of "freedom of speech," qua member? Pertinent variables are explored in Pope, Free Speech Rights of Union Officials Under the LMRDA, 18 Harv. C.R.-C.L. L. Rev. 525 (1983).

4. A union removes a steward for filing (at the request of other employees) what higher union officials consider unjustifiable grievances against the company; the union removes another steward for filing, again at the request of another employee, charges against the union for breach of its duty of fair representation to other employees. Has the union violated the NLRA? Cf. NLRB v. Local 212, UAW, 690 F.2d 82 (6th Cir. 1982).

5. Suppose that the evidence shows both serious insubordination by an appointed union official and that discipline imposed on him by the union would tend to chill freedom of speech by the official and other members and was motivated in part by that purpose. What result if the official challenges his discipline? Cf. *Transportation Management*, supra p. 268; Connick v. Myers, 103 S. Ct. 1684 (1983).

Salzhandler v. Caputo
316 F.2d 445 (2d Cir.), *cert. denied*, 375 U.S. 946 (1963)

LUMBARD, J. . . . Salzhandler, a member of Local 442, Brotherhood of Painters, Decorators & Paperhangers of America, brought suit in the district court following the decision of a Trial Board of the union's New York

District Council No. 9 that he had untruthfully accused . . . Webman, the president of the local, of the crime of larceny. The Trial Board found that Salzhandler's "unsupported accusations" violated the union's constitution which prohibited "conduct unbecoming a member . . . ," "acts detrimental to . . . interests of the Brotherhood," "libeling, slandering . . . fellow members [or] officers of local unions" and "acts and conduct . . . inconsistent with the duties, obligations and fealty of a member."

Salzhandler's complaint alleged that his charges against Webman were an exercise of his rights as a member of the union and that the action of the Trial Board [violated] the LMRDA under which he was entitled to relief.

The undisputed facts developed during the trial in the district court amply support Salzhandler's claims for relief.

. . . [A]t the times in question [Salzhandler] was serving a three-year term [as financial secretary] which was to end June 30, 1962. His weekly compensation as an officer was $35, of which $25 was salary and $10 was for expenses. . . .

. . . In going over the union's checks in July 1960 Salzhandler noticed that two checks, one for $800 and one for $375, had been drawn to cover the expenses of Webman and one Max Schneider at two union conventions to which they were elected delegates. The $800 check, drawn on August 21, 1959 to Webman's order, was endorsed by Webman and his wife. The $375 check, drawn on March 4, 1960 to "Cash," was likewise endorsed by Webman and his wife. Schneider's endorsement did not appear on either check. Schneider had died on May 31, 1960.

On July 15, 1960 two checks, each for $6, were drawn as refunds of dues paid by Max Schneider and another deceased member. Such checks were ordinarily mailed to the widows. Webman, however, brought the two checks to Salzhandler and told him to deposit them in a special fund for the benefit of the son of Max Schneider. Salzhandler refused to do this because the checks were not endorsed. Thereafter Sol Feldman and W. Shirpin, . . . trustees of the local, each endorsed one of the checks and Salzhandler made the deposit as Webman had requested.

In November 1960 Salzhandler distributed to members of the local a leaflet which accused Webman of improper conduct with regard to union funds and of referring to members of the union by such names as "thieves, scabs, robbers, scabby bosses, bums, pimps, f-bums, [and] jail birds." Attached to the leaflet were photostats of the four checks. . . . Salzhandler wrote:

> The last convention lasted five days, Monday August 31, to Friday, September 4, 1959. The delegates of 442 presented their credentials Monday, August 31, and on Thursday, September 3, as soon as they got the mileage

fare, they disappeared. They were absent at Thursday afternoon session. The most the chairman should have gotten was a weeks pay and allowance — $250.00. The auditor's report shows he got $200 in pay and $300 in expenses — $500, or twice what was coming to him, and also $300 as expenses for the Business Agent. The check was made out to *Cash* for $800 (photostat enclosed). So was the voucher. It does not indicate that Max Schneider got any of it. The same goes for a check made out *only* to I. Webman on March 4, 1960 for another convention, where the chairman was to get $250, but got $375. It does not indicate Schneider got his share. Were the checks legal?

The leaflet also branded Webman as a "petty robber" of the two $6 checks. . . .

On December 13, 1960, Webman filed charges against Salzhandler with the New York District Council No. 9 . . . , alleging that Salzhandler had violated the union constitution, §267, by libeling and slandering him in implying that he, Webman, had not reimbursed Max Schneider for convention expenses, and that he had been a "petty robber" in causing the two $6 checks to be deposited in the Michael Schneider fund, rather than being paid over to the two widows. The charge went on to state that Salzhandler was guilty of "acts and conduct inconsistent with the duties, obligations and fealty of a member or officer of the Brotherhood" and that the net effect of the leaflet was untruthfully to accuse an officer of the union of the crime of larceny. For over six hours on the evening of February 23, 1961, Salzhandler was tried by a five-member Trial Board of the District Council. . . . Salzhandler was represented by a union member who was not a lawyer. At the trial, Webman introduced the leaflet. Salzhandler produced the photostats and was questioned by the Trial Board. Webman's witnesses testified that the convention expenditures were approved by the membership. Salzhandler produced three witnesses who testified that Webman had called members names as alleged in the leaflet.

Not until April 2, 1961 did Salzhandler receive notice of the Trial Board's decision and his removal from office and this was from a printed postal card mailed to all members: "By a decision of the Trial Committee . . . , Sol Saltzhandler [sic] is no longer Financial Secretary of Local Union 442."

Thereafter, on April 4, the District Council mailed to Salzhandler only the final paragraph of its five page "Decision" which read as follows:

It is our decision that Brother Solomon Salzhandler be prohibited from participating in the affairs of L.U. 442, or of any other Local Union of the Brotherhood, or of District Council 9, for . . . five (5) years. He shall not be permitted during that period to attend meetings of L.U. 442, to vote on any matter, to have the floor at any meeting of any other Local Union affiliated with the District Council, or to be a candidate for any position in any local Union or in the District Council. In all other respects, Brother Salzhandler's rights and obligations as a member of the Brotherhood shall be continued.

Salzhandler did not receive a copy of the full opinion of the Trial Board until after this action was commenced on June 14, 1961. . . . Salzhandler filed [timely] intraunion appeals with the Secretary-Treasurer of the Council and the General Secretary-Treasurer of the Brotherhood on April 12 and 28. At the time this action was brought, plaintiff had received no word regarding said appeals.

On May 15, 1961, Salzhandler attempted to attend a meeting of the local but was prevented from doing so by Webman. The complaint alleges that Webman assaulted Salzhandler and used violence in removing him. . . .

Judge Wham dismissed the complaint [based on LMRDA §102], holding that the Trial Board's conclusion that the leaflet was libelous was sufficiently supported by the evidence. He went further, however, and made an independent finding that the statements were, in fact, libelous. The court held, as a matter of law, that "The rights accorded members of labor unions under [LMRDA] Title I . . . do not include the right . . . to libel or slander officers of the union." We do not agree.

The LMRDA . . . was designed to protect the rights of union members to discuss freely and criticize the management of their unions and the conduct of their officers. The legislative history and the extensive [prior] hearings abundantly evidence the intention of the Congress to prevent union officials from using their disciplinary powers to silence criticism and punish those who dare to question and complain. The statute is clear and explicit. . . . [The court here quoted §§101(a)(1) and (2), 102, and 609.]

Appellees argue that just as constitutionally protected speech does not include libelous utterances, Beauharnais v. Illinois, 343 U.S. 250, 266 (1952), the speech protected by the statute likewise does not include libel and slander. The analogy to the First Amendment is not convincing. In Beauharnais, the Supreme Court recognized the possibility that state action might stifle criticism under the guise of punishing libel. However, because it felt that abuses could be prevented by the exercise of judicial authority, 343 U.S. at 263-264, the court sustained a state criminal libel statute. But the union is not a political unit to whose disinterested tribunals an alleged defamer can look for an impartial review of his "crime." It is an economic action group, the success of which depends in large measure on a unity of purpose and sense of solidarity among its members.

The Trial Board . . . consisted of union officials, not judges. It was a group to which the delicate problems of truth or falsehood, privilege, and "fair comment" were not familiar. Its procedure is peculiarly unsuited for drawing the fine line between criticism and defamation, yet, were we to adopt the view of the appellees, each charge of libel would be given a trial de novo in the federal court—an impractical result not likely contemplated by Congress, see 105 Cong. Rec. 6026 (daily ed. April 25, 1959) (colloquy between Senator Goldwater and Senator Clark)—and such a Trial Board would be the final arbiter of the extent of the union member's protection under §101(a)(2).[7]

In a proviso to §101(a)(2), there are two express exceptions to the broad rule of free expression. One relates to "the responsibility of every member toward the organization as an institution." The other deals with interference with the union's legal and contractual obligations.

While the inclusion of only two exceptions, without more, does not mean that others were intentionally excluded, . . . the legislative history supports the conclusion that Congress intended only those exceptions which were expressed.[8]

The expression of views by Salzhandler did not come within either exception in the proviso to §101(a)(2). The leaflet did not interfere in any way with the union's legal or contractual obligations and the union has never claimed that it did. Nor could Salzhandler's charges against Webman be construed as a violation of the "responsibility of every member toward the organization as an institution." Quite the contrary; it would seem clearly in the interest of proper and honest management of union affairs to permit

---

[7] See Summers, American Legislation for Union Democracy, 25 Mod. L. Rev. 273, 287:

"The most difficult problem arises when a member is expelled for 'slandering a union officer.' Union debates are characterized by vitriol and calumny, and campaigns for office are salted with overstated accusations. Defining the scope of fair comment in political contests is never easy, and in this context is nearly impossible. To allow the union to decide this issue in the first instance is to invite retaliation and repression and to frustrate one of the principal reasons for protecting this right—to enable members to oust corrupt leadership through the democratic process."

[8] As initially introduced before the Senate, the freedom of speech section was absolute in form. See 105 Cong. Rec. 5810 (daily ed. April 22, 1959). The section was in fact passed in that form. Id. at 5827. Later the question came to be reconsidered and the free speech section was amended to include the two express exceptions. Id. at 6030 (daily ed. April 25, 1959). In effect, the section as initially passed took away the power of unions to punish for expressions of views. The subsequent amendment restored that power in only two situations.

We are referred to certain statements made during the debate in the Senate which allegedly indicate that "reasonable restraints" on speech were intended. See, e.g., 105 Cong. Rec. 6022 (daily ed. April 25, 1959) (remarks of Senator Kuchel). We find these statements to be ambiguous and we are not persuaded that exceptions other than those specified were intended.

members to question the manner in which the union's officials handle the union's funds and how they treat the union's members. It is that interest which motivated the enactment of the statute and which would be immeasurably frustrated were we to interpret it so as to compel each dissatisfied and questioning member to draw, at the peril of union discipline, the thin and tenuous line between what is libelous and what is not. This is especially so when we consider that the Act was designed largely to curtail such vices as the mismanagement of union funds, criticism of which by union members is always likely to be viewed by union officials as defamatory.

The union argues that there is a public interest in promoting the monolithic character of unions in their dealings with employers. But the Congress weighed this factor and decided that the desirability of protecting the democratic process within the unions outweighs any possible weakening of unions in their dealings with employers which may result from the freer expression of opinions within the unions. . . .

. . . Here Salzhandler's charges against Webman related to the handling of union funds; they concerned the way the union was managed. The Congress has decided that it is in the public interest that unions be democratically governed and toward that end that discussion should be free and untrammeled and that reprisals within the union for the expression of views should be prohibited. It follows that although libelous statements may be made the basis of civil suit . . . , the union may not subject a member to any disciplinary action on a finding . . . that such statements are libelous. . . .

Accordingly, we reverse the judgment of the district court and direct entry of judgment for the plaintiff which, among other things, should assess damages and enjoin the defendants from carrying out any punishment imposed by the . . . Trial Board.

NOTES

1. Assume that in an identical case today a trial board would remove a Salzhandler from his office as financial secretary without, however, restricting his rights as member. Would an injunction against such removal be consistent with the Supreme Court's approach in Finnegan v. Leu, supra p. 1243?

2. Suppose that incumbent officers, acting on a union matter within their authority, libel a member. Would *Salzhandler* limit union discipline against the offending officers?

3. Consider whether the LMRDA provides a remedy to a member who, after proper notice and hearing, is fined or expelled for the following conduct:

(a) He circulates libelous statements about fiscal irregularities on the part of union officials among the general public and members of other unions while the union is on strike or while it is engaged in an organizational campaign. Cf. Brotherhood of Boilermakers v. Rafferty, 348 F.2d 307 (9th Cir. 1965).

(b) He campaigns for a rival union, which has filed an election petition with the NLRB. Cf. Lodge 702, IAM v. Loudermilk, 444 F.2d 719 (5th Cir. 1971). See also infra p. 1278, Note 2.

(c) He urges during a union meeting, and elsewhere, that an ongoing strike is in breach of contract and tries to start a back-to-work movement. Would it be material whether his construction of the agreement was right or wrong?

(d) He advocates "Communist ideas," thereby violating a provision of the union constitution barring members from "advocating . . . communism, fascism, nazism, or any other totalitarian philosophy . . . or giving support to these 'isms' or to movements . . . inimical to the union or its established policies and laws." Would it be material if the disputed advocacy occurred during a campaign for union office, during a union meeting, or at the work place? Cf. Turner v. Air Transport Lodge 1894, IAM, supra p. 1236.

4. In Semancik v. UMW, Dist. 5, 466 F.2d 144, 157 (3d Cir. 1972), the court upheld a permanent injunction against the union's enforcing its prohibition of "dishonest or questionable practices." The district had tried several times to enforce this provision against members who had opposed the incumbents in union elections. The court declared that the limitation imposed by *Hardeman*, infra p. 1292, on judicial review of substantive provisions did not extend to provisions so vague as to chill free speech and to be a potential means of harassing political opponents by selective enforcement. Should union constitutional provisions be invalidated unless they satisfy doctrines regarding vagueness and overbreadth developed for "state action" under the First Amendment? See Comment, Facial Adjudication of Disciplinary Provisions in Union Constitutions, 91 Yale L.J. 144 (1981).

Hall v. Cole, 412 U.S. 1 (1973). The respondent, at a regular membership meeting, introduced resolutions critical of the officers' undemocratic and short-sighted actions. These resolutions were defeated, and the union expelled the respondent from membership for violating a rule against "malicious vilification" of any officer. A federal district court ordered respondent's reinstatement; the court found no damages but ordered the union to pay him $5,500.00 in counsel fees. The Supreme Court, by Brennan, J., upheld that award, reasoning that §102 permits an award of fees and that the instant award was not an abuse of discretion. The Court observed that the respondent, by vindicating his own right to free speech guaranteed by §101(a)(2), had rendered a substantial service to the union as an institution and to its members. Accordingly, under the "common benefit theory," an award of counsel fees fell within the traditional equitable authority of federal courts. The Court rejected the contention that the express authorization of counsel fees in §§201(c) and 501(b) of the LMRDA, coupled with the absence of authorization in §102, indicates an intent to preclude fee-shifting under §102. The Court reasoned that §§201(c) and 501(b) are not part of Title I and deal with narrowly defined statutory problems, whereas §102 was premised on the need, under Title I, for remedies fashioned for a virtually infinite variety of circumstances; consequently, §102 embodied a broad judicial mandate to fashion "appropriate relief." White, J., with whom Rehnquist, J., joined, dissented. They urged that a clearer signal from Congress was needed to permit attorney-fee awards "in member-union litigation, which so often involves private feuding having no general significance. The award of fees in the occasionally successful and meritorious case will not be worth the litigation the Court's decision will . . . foster."

Mitchell v. International Assn. of Machinists
196 Cal. App. 2d 796, 16 Cal. Rptr. 813 (1961)

[The petitioners were represented by, and members of, the union. They had openly campaigned for an initiative measure seeking a state constitutional amendment banning union shops, which the union expressly opposed. The union expelled the petitioners for "conduct unbecoming a member." The trial court, finding no adverse effect on the petitioners' jobs, upheld the expulsions. The appellate court reversed.]

Fox, P. J. . . . It would seem proper to begin by dispelling two troublesome illusions. The first is that unions are purely voluntary organizations like Republicans, Democrats, Elks, and church groups. A modern labor union, both in structure and in function, bears little resemblance to other voluntary associations. . . . "It is this omnipotent analogy that leads the courts astray." (Williams, The Political Liberties of Labor Union Members, 32 Tex. L. Rev. 826, 829.) Unions can be distinguished from other voluntary organizations in many respects. Most importantly, a large part of their power and authority is derived from government which makes it exclusive bargaining agent. Further, they are not primarily social groups which require homogeneous views in order to retain smooth functioning. They are large, heterogeneous groups, whose members may agree on one thing only — they want improved working conditions and greater economic benefits. The union's power, when considered together with its source, imposes upon it reciprocal responsibilities toward its membership and the public generally that other voluntary organizations do not bear. . . .

Secondly, it cannot be assumed that the only value in membership is job retention. Even though a member may keep his job when expelled, his expulsion causes him to suffer a detriment the apprehension of which would no doubt have a coercive effect on the membership. First of all, it is not clear what his rights would be if he quit his job to seek another, at least in intrastate commerce. Also, he has a financial stake in the strike fund, perhaps a pension fund, and other funds to which he has contributed. Further, he is denied the right to participate in his union "government." Although the union is required by law to represent him impartially [*Steele*, supra p. 1127], he has no voice in how that representation is to be conducted. In addition, there are frequently social ramifications for a nonmember working among members that cannot be overlooked. All this is solely for the purpose of demonstrating that there *is* a real conflict which cannot be dismissed by the assertion that since a member is assured by federal legislation that loss of membership for a reason other than nonpayment of dues does not mean loss of job, he is free to do as he wishes. . . .

Other . . . cases involving . . . the extent of the limitation on personal rights imposed by union membership have been fairly well categorized by the writers. At one extreme there are the "treason" cases in which an individual's acts are patently antagonistic to the continued existence of the union as a collective bargaining agent. Company spies and dual unionists are two examples. . . . Similar cases are those in which members impair adherence to the collective bargaining agreement by violating work rules, working below scale, and engaging in wildcat strikes. (See Williams, supra, at p. 831.) The courts lose no time in such cases in upholding union discipline. At the other extreme are cases in which the courts frustrated union attempts to interfere with specific citizenship obligations. The Barbers were enjoined from expelling a member for enforcing Sunday laws against a fellow member (Manning v. Klein, 1 Pa. Super. 210). The Plumbers were prevented from expelling a member who, as a public official, refused to appoint another member as a plumbing inspector (Schneider v. Local Union No. 60, 116 La. 270 [40 So. 700]. Another union was compelled to reinstate a member who testified before the Interstate Commerce Commission against safety devices sought by the union. Other unions have been ordered to reinstate members who testified against the union in court.

Somewhere between these two extremes lies the small group of cases involving political activity by members, obligatory only in the moral sense, which the union as a whole opposes. Spayd v. Ringing Rock Lodge No. 665, 270 Pa. 67 [113 A. 70], involved an action by a member of the union to compel reinstatement following expulsion for violation of a rule prohibiting any member from using his influence to defeat any action taken by union officials concerned with legislation. Plaintiff was expelled because he signed a petition asking the Legislature to reconsider its adoption of the "full crew law." Using every legal theory available under the circumstances, the court held that the union's action violated plaintiff's property rights, the Constitution, and public policy. Concluding, the opinion states, at page 73 [113 A.], "The right here involved, and the voting franchise, are the only means by which peaceful changes in our laws and institutions may be sought or brought about, and they cannot, with safety to the state, or the whole body of the people, be gathered into the hands of the few for any purpose whatsoever." . . .

In deciding whether a union may, *under these facts*, be permitted to penalize a member for engaging in political activity which the union opposes, certain considerations must be brought to light: (1) the interest of the community and the individual in the latter's membership; (2) the importance to the community of the individual's untrammeled right to express himself on political questions; (3) the interest of the union in excluding obnoxious members; (4) the interest of the union in speaking with one voice; (5) the nature of the political activity and the manner of its conduct. As to the first consideration, the value of membership to the individual has already been demonstrated. And to the extent that industrial democracy is important to the community, its interest is also manifest. (Cox, Law and the National Labor Policy [1960] p. 110.)

With respect to the second, few subjects in the history of western civilization have drawn such a unanimity of support. In a dissenting opinion Mr. Justice Brandeis observed,

> The right of a citizen of the United States to take part, for his own or the country's benefit, in the making of federal laws and in the conduct of the Government, necessarily includes the right to speak or write about them; . . . Full and free exercise of this right . . . is ordinarily also his duty; for its exercise is more important to the Nation than it is to himself. (Gilbert v. Minnesota, 254 U.S. 325, 337-338). . . .

As to the union's interest in excluding obnoxious members, it would be completely unrealistic to assume that unions are composed of like-thinking individuals. It is only when dissident views are expressed in a forum where they have a chance of acceptance that the member becomes "undesirable." But expulsion cannot serve to quiet the individual. It can only serve to intimidate those who remain. While this, too, might be a legitimate objective under some circumstances, the very question to be decided is whether the community ought to tolerate that result in *these* circumstances.

As to the interest of the union in presenting a unified front, this cannot be gainsaid. And where activity of the union is directly designed to attain economic goals, such as the decision to strike or not to strike, or adherence to the collective bargaining agreement, judicial regard for this interest has already been demonstrated. And it is no doubt true that economic and political objectives of unions frequently cannot be treated as completely separate things. But still a distinction should be made in this context. Where purely economic activity is concerned, the community interest is not so deeply involved as it would be if the entire union membership in the nation were limited in its political expression (on matters of legitimate union interest) to the opinions of the majority or the union leadership. If this were the case we would be deprived of an immeasurably important source of political thought. Furthermore, so long as the individual member purports to represent only himself, and not his union, the union's public position is not diluted.

This brings us to the question of the nature of the political doctrine propounded and the manner in which it is advocated. We are not called upon to decide what the result would be if a member was expelled for advocating repeal of the Wagner Act or the abolition of unions. Only the right-to-work law is here involved. The union argues that it may reasonably consider such a law seriously inimical to its interests. This is certainly not an unreasonable position. . . . But there is substantial respectable opinion to the contrary. Cox, [Law and the National Labor Policy, 1960] at page 110 says, "The member who acts as a strikebreaker may be guilty of treason, but one can believe in right-to-work laws and remain a good trade-unionist." (See also Brandeis, Symposium on Peace with Liberty and Justice, 2 Nat. Civic Federation Rev. No. 2 [May 15, 1905] p. 16, cited in American Fed. of Labor v. American Sash & Door Co., 335 U.S. 538, at pp. 551 and 552. . . . There being such a disparity of opinion as to the long-run effect of voluntary unionism, the question becomes not whether the union is justified in its opinion, but whether the point is sufficiently debatable so that society's interest in the debate, together with the individual's right to speak freely on political matters, outweighs the union's interest in subduing public dissent among union members. . . .

It could not be more apparent where the balance lies. On this point, Cox, supra, page 111, has this to say:

It needs no argument to demonstrate the importance of freedom to pursue personal political activities. It begs the question to say that a man has a right to engage in whatever political activity he wishes but no right to be a union member. The question is whether there will be an excessive loss of freedom if unions are permitted to make political conformity the price of membership. Bearing in mind the size and importance of unions in industry as well as their growing interest in politics, it seems apparent that the total loss would be great indeed if a significant number of large labor organizations adopted the attitude of the International Association of Machinists. It would also work serious changes in our political system if individuals can be insulated from direct political action by the decisions of organized groups even though the decisions are reached by majority rule.

It is therefore clear that, at least where the political activity of the member is not patently in conflict with the union's best interests, the union should not be permitted to use its power over the individual to curb the advocacy of his political views.[7] . . . [Reversed.]

NOTES

1. Is the court's emphasis on whether a dissident's point is sufficiently debatable consistent with the quotation from Brandeis? With the values behind the First Amendment?

2. Any difference in result if plaintiffs had publicly supported a law banning strikes in defense industries, eliminating the principle of majority rule, or repealing the NLRA?

3. A union official, in his individual capacity, publicly supports the Republican candidate for President after the union's executive board has voted that the union should support the Democratic nominee. Would it be contrary to public policy to remove the dissenting official from his union office? To expel him from membership? Cf. Morgan v. Local 1150, IUE, 16

---

[7] . . . [W]ith respect to [an employer's] right to attempt to influence his employee's political activities, the California . . . Labor Code, §1101, reads: "No employer shall make, adopt, or enforce any rule, regulation or policy: . . .

"(b) Controlling, or directing, or tending to control or direct the political activities or affiliations of employees."

Section 1102 reads: "No employer shall coerce or influence or attempt to coerce or influence his employees through or by means of threat of discharge or loss of employment to adopt or follow or refrain from adopting or following any particular course or line of political action or political activity." [Footnote number relocated in text. — Eds.]

L.R.R.M. 720 (Super. Ct. Ill. 1945), *rev'd on other grounds*, 331 Ill. App. 21, 72 N.E.2d 59 (1946). Would the LMRDA invalidate that removal?

NLRB v. Allis-Chalmers Mfg. Co.
388 U.S. 175 (1967)

BRENNAN, J. . . . Employees at the [Wisconsin] plants of respondent Allis-Chalmers Manufacturing Company were represented by [UAW] locals. . . . Lawful economic strikes were conducted at both plants in support of new contract demands. In compliance with the UAW constitution, the strikes were called with the approval of the International Union after at least two-thirds of the members of each local voted by secret ballot to strike. Some members of each local crossed the picket lines and worked during the strikes. After the strikes were over, the locals [charged] these members . . . with violation of the International constitution and bylaws. The charges were heard by local trial committees in proceedings at which the charged members were represented by counsel. No claim of unfairness in the proceedings is made. The trials resulted in each charged member being found guilty of "conduct unbecoming a Union member" and being fined in a sum from $20 to $100. Some of the fined members did not pay the fines and one of the locals obtained a judgment in the amount of the fine against one of its members, Benjamin Natzke, in a test suit brought in the Milwaukee County Court. An appeal from the judgment is pending in the Wisconsin Supreme Court.

[Allis-Chalmers charged the locals with violating §8(b)(1)(A). The NLRB dismissed the complaint. A panel of the Seventh Circuit affirmed, but, after rehearing en banc, the court, three judges dissenting, withdrew the panel opinion, and held that the locals' conduct violated §8(b)(1)(A). The Supreme Court reversed.]

I

The panel and the majority en banc of the Court of Appeals thought that reversal of the NLRB order would be required under a literal reading of §§7 and 8(b)(1)(A); under that reading union members who cross their own picket lines would be regarded as exercising their rights under §7 to refrain from engaging in a particular concerted activity, and union discipline in the form of fines for such activity would therefore "restrain or coerce" in violation of §8(b)(1)(A) if the section's proviso is read to sanction no form of discipline other than expulsion from the union. The panel rejected that literal reading. The majority en banc adopted it, stating that the panel "mistakenly took the position that such a literal reading was unwarranted in the light of the history and purposes" of the sections, 358 F.2d, at 659, and holding that "[t]he statutes in question present no ambiguities whatsoever, and therefore do not require recourse to legislative history for clarification." Id., at 660.

It is highly unrealistic to regard §8(b)(1), and particularly its words "restrain or coerce," as precisely and unambiguously covering the union conduct involved in this case. On its face court enforcement of fines imposed on members for violation of membership obligations is no more conduct to "restrain or coerce" satisfaction of such obligations than court enforcement of penalties imposed on citizens for violation of their obligations as citizens to pay income taxes, or court awards of damages against a contracting party for nonperformance of a contractual obligation voluntarily undertaken. But even if the inherent imprecision of the words "restrain or coerce" may be overlooked, recourse to legislative history to determine the sense in which Congress used the words is not foreclosed. . . .

National labor policy has been built on the premise that by pooling their economic strength and acting through a labor organization freely chosen by the majority, the employees of an appropriate unit have the most effective means of bargaining for improvements in wages, hours, and working conditions. The policy therefore extinguishes the individual employee's power to order his own relations with his employer and creates a power vested in the chosen representative to act in the interests of all employees. . . .

Integral to this federal labor policy has been the power in the chosen union to protect against erosion [of] its status under that policy through reasonable discipline of members who violate rules and regulations governing membership. That power is particularly vital when the members engage in strikes. . . . Provisions in union constitutions and bylaws for fines and expulsion of recalcitrants, including strikebreakers, are therefore commonplace and were commonplace at the time of the Taft-Hartley amendments.[9]

To say that Congress meant in 1947 by the §7 amendments and §8(b)(1)(A) to strip unions of the power to fine members for strikebreaking, however lawful the strike vote, and however fair the disciplinary procedures and penalty, is to say that Congress preceded the Landrum-Griffin amendments with an even more pervasive regulation of the internal affairs of

[9]It is suggested that while such provisions for fines and expulsion were a common element of union constitutions at the time of the enactment of §8(b)(1), such background loses its cogency here because such provisions did not explicitly call for court enforcement. However, the potentiality of resort to courts for enforcement is implicit in any binding obligation. . . . It is also suggested that court enforcement of fines is "a rather recent innovation." Yet such enforcement was known as early as 1867. Master Stevedores' Assn. v. Walsh, 2 Daly 1 (N.Y.).

unions. It is also to attribute to Congress an intent at war with the understanding of the union-membership relation which has been at the heart of its effort "to fashion a coherent labor policy" and which has been a predicate underlying action by this Court and the state courts. More importantly, it is to say that Congress limited unions in the powers necessary to the discharge of their role as exclusive statutory bargaining agents by impairing the usefulness of labor's cherished strike weapon. It is no answer that the proviso to §8(b)(1)(A) preserves to the union the power to expel the offending member. Where the union is strong and membership therefore valuable, to require expulsion of the member visits a far more severe penalty upon the member than a reasonable fine. Where the union is weak, and membership therefore of little value, the union faced with further depletion of its ranks may have no real choice except to condone the member's disobedience. Yet it is just such weak unions for which the power to execute union decisions taken for the benefit of all employees is most critical to effective discharge of its statutory function.

. . . [W]hen the literal application of the imprecise words "restrain or coerce" . . . in §8(b)(1)(A) produces the extraordinary results we have mentioned we should determine whether this meaning is confirmed in the legislative history of the section.

II

The explicit wording of §8(b)(2), which is concerned with union powers to affect a member's employment, is in sharp contrast with the imprecise words of §8(b)(1)(A). . . . It is significant that Congress expressly disclaimed [in connection with §8(b)(2)] any intention to interfere with union self-government or to regulate a union's internal affairs. The Senate Report stated:

> The committee did not desire to limit the labor organization with respect to either its selection of membership or expulsion therefrom. But the committee did wish to protect the employee in his job if unreasonably expelled or denied membership. The tests provided by the amendment are based upon facts readily ascertainable and *do not require the employer to inquire into the internal affairs of the union.*

S. Rep. No. 105, 80th Cong., 1st Sess., 20, I Legislative History of the Labor Management Relations Act, 1947 (hereafter Leg. Hist.) 426. (Emphasis supplied.) . . .

What legislative materials there are dealing with §8(b)(1)(A) contain not a single word referring to the application of its prohibitions to traditional internal union discipline in general, or disciplinary fines in particular. On the contrary there are a number of assurances by its sponsors that the section was not meant to regulate the internal affairs of unions. . . .

It is true that there are references in the Senate debate on §8(b)(1)(A) to an intent to impose the same prohibitions on unions that applied to employers as regards restraint and coercion of employees in their exercise of §7 rights. However apposite this parallel . . . when applied to organizational tactics, it clearly is inapplicable to the relationship of a union member to his own union. Union membership allows the member a part in choosing the very course of action to which he refuses to adhere, but he has of course no role in employer conduct, and nonunion employees have no voice in the affairs of the union.

Cogent support for an interpretation of . . . §8(b)(1) as not reaching the imposition of fines and attempts at court enforcement is the proviso to §8(b)(1). It states that nothing in the section shall "impair the right of a labor organization to prescribe its own rules with respect to the acquisition or retention of membership therein. . . ." Senator Holland offered the proviso during debate and Senator Ball immediately accepted it, stating that it was not the intent of the sponsors in any way to regulate the internal affairs of unions. At the very least it can be said that the proviso preserves the rights of unions to impose fines, as a lesser penalty than expulsion, and to impose fines which carry the explicit or implicit threat of expulsion for nonpayment. Therefore, under the proviso the rule in the UAW constitution governing fines is valid and the fines themselves and expulsion for nonpayment would not be an unfair labor practice. Assuming that the proviso cannot also be read to authorize court enforcement of fines, a question we need not reach, . . . to interpret the body of §8(b)(1) to apply to the imposition and collection of fines would be to impute to Congress a concern with the permissible *means* of enforcement of union fines and to attribute to Congress a narrow and discrete interest in banning court enforcement of such fines. Yet there is not one word in the legislative history evidencing any such congressional concern. And . . . a distinction between court enforcement and expulsion would have been anomalous for several reasons. First, Congress was operating within the context of the "contract theory" of the union-member relationship which widely prevailed at that time. The efficacy of a contract is precisely its legal enforceability. . . . Second, as we have noted, such a distinction would visit upon the member of a strong union a potentially more severe punishment than court enforcement of fines, while impairing the bargaining facility of the weak union by requiring it either to condone misconduct or deplete its ranks. . . .

The 1959 Landrum-Griffin amendments . . . also negate the reach given §8(b)(1)(A) by the majority en banc below. "To be sure, what Congress did in 1959 does not establish what it meant in 1947. However, as another major step in an evolving pattern of regulation of union conduct, the 1959 Act is a relevant consideration. Courts may properly take into account the later Act when asked to extend the reach of the earlier Act's vague language to the limits which, read literally, the words might permit." [Labor Board v. Drivers Local Union, 362 U.S. 274, 291-292.] In 1959 Congress did seek to protect union members in their relationship to the union by adopting measures to insure the provision of democratic processes in the conduct of union affairs and procedural due process to members subjected to discipline. Even then, some Senators emphasized that "in establishing and enforcing statutory standards great care should be taken not to undermine union self-government or weaken unions in their role as collective bargaining agents." S. Rep. No. 187, 86th Cong., 1st Sess., 7. The Eighty-sixth Congress was thus plainly of the view that union self-government was not regulated in 1947. Indeed, that Congress expressly recognized that a union member may be "fined, suspended, expelled, or otherwise disciplined," and enacted only procedural requirements to be observed. [§101(a)(5).] Moreover, Congress added a proviso to the guarantee of freedom of speech and assembly disclaiming any intent "to impair the right of a labor organization to adopt and enforce reasonable rules as to the responsibility of every member toward the organization as an institution. . . ." [§101(a)(2).]. . . .

III

The collective bargaining agreements with the locals incorporate union security clauses. Full union membership is not compelled by the clause: an employee is required only to become and remain "a member of the Union . . . to the extent of paying his dues. . . ." The majority en banc below nevertheless regarded full membership to be "the result not of individual voluntary choice but of the insertion of [this] union security provision in the contract under which a substantial minority of the employees may have been forced into membership." 358 F.2d, at 660. But the relevant inquiry here is not what motivated a member's full membership but whether the Taft-Hartley amendments prohibited disciplinary measures against a full member who crossed his union's picket line. . . . Whether those prohibitions would apply if the locals had imposed fines on members whose membership was in fact limited to the obligation of paying monthly dues is a question not before us and upon which we intimate no view. . . . [Reversed.]

[The concurring opinion of White, J., is omitted.]

BLACK, J., whom DOUGLAS, HARLAN, and STEWART, JJ., join, dissenting. . . .

I

. . . [T]he Court in characterizing the union-member relationship as "contractual" and in emphasizing that its holding is limited to situations where the employee is a "full member" . . . , implies that by joining a union an employee gives up or waives some of his §7 rights. But the Court does not say that a union member is without the §7 right to refrain from participating in such concerted activity as an economic strike called by his union. Such a holding would be clearly unwarranted even by resort to the legislative history of the 1947 addition to §7 of "the right to refrain from any or all of such activities." According to Senator Taft, that phrase was added by the Conference Committee to "make the prohibition contained in §8(b)(1) apply to coercive acts of unions against employees who did not wish to join *or did not care to participate in a strike or a picket line*." 93 Cong. Rec. 6859, II Leg. Hist. 1623. (Emphasis added.)

. . . [T]he Court interprets the words "restrain or coerce" in a way directly opposed to their literal meaning, for the Court admits that fines are as coercive as penalties imposed on citizens for the nonpayment of taxes. Though Senator Taft, in answer to charges that these words were ambiguous, said their meaning "is perfectly clear," 93 Cong. Rec. 4021, II Leg. Hist. 1025, and though any union official with sufficient intelligence and learning to be chosen as such could hardly fail to comprehend the meaning of these plain, simple English words, the Court insists on finding an "inherent imprecision" in these words. And that characterization then allows the Court to resort to "[w]hat legislative materials there are." . . .

. . . The real reason for the Court's decision is its policy judgment that unions, especially weak ones, need the power to impose fines on strikebreakers and to enforce those fines in court. It is not enough, says the Court, that the unions have the power to expel those members who refuse to participate in a strike or who fail to pay fines imposed on them for such failure to participate; it is essential that weak unions have the choice between expulsion and court-enforced fines, simply because the latter are more effective in the sense of being more punitive. Though the entire mood of Congress in 1947 was to curtail the power of unions, as it had previously curtailed the power of employers, in order to equalize the power of the two, the Court is unwilling to believe that Congress intended to impair "the usefulness of labor's cherished strike weapons." I cannot agree with this conclusion or subscribe to the Court's unarticulated premise that the Court has power to add a new weapon to the union's economic arsenal whenever the Court believes that the union needs that weapon. That is a job for Congress, not this Court. . . .

II

Contrary to the Court, I am not at all certain that a union's right under the proviso to prescribe rules for the retention of membership includes the right to restrain a member from working by trying him on the vague charge of "conduct unbecoming a union member" and fining him for exercising his §7 right of refusing to participate in a strike, even though the fine is only enforceable by expulsion from membership. It is one thing to say that Congress did not wish to interfere with the union's power, similar to that of any other kind of voluntary association, to prescribe specific conditions of membership. It is quite another thing to say that Congress intended to leave unions free to exercise a court-like power to try and punish members with a direct economic sanction for exercising their right to work. Just because a union might be free, under the proviso, to expel a member for crossing a picket line does not mean that Congress left unions free to threaten their members with fines. Even though a member may later discover that the threatened fine is only enforceable by expulsion, and in that sense a "lesser penalty," the direct threat of a fine, to a member normally unaware of the method the union might resort to for compelling its payment, would often be more coercive than a threat of expulsion.

Even on the assumption that §8(b)(1)(A) permits a union to fine a member as long as the fine is only enforceable by expulsion, the fundamental error of the Court's opinion is its failure to recognize the practical and theoretical difference between a court-enforced fine, as here, and a fine enforced by expulsion or less drastic intraunion means. As the Court recognizes, expulsion for nonpayment of a fine may, especially in the case of a strong union, be more severe than judicial collection of the fine. But, if the union membership has little value and if the fine is great, then court-enforcement of the fine may be more effective punishment, and that is precisely why the Court desires to provide weak unions with this alternative to expulsion, an alternative which is similar to a criminal court's power to imprison defendants who fail to pay fines. . . .

The Court disposes of this tremendous practical difference between court-enforced and union-enforced fines by suggesting that Congress was not concerned with "the permissible *means* of enforcement of union fines" and that court-enforcement of fines is a necessary consequence of the "contract theory" of the union-member relationship. And then the Court cautions that its holding may only apply to court enforcement of "reasonable fines." Apparently the Court believes that these considerations somehow bring reasonable court-enforced fines within the ambit of "internal union affairs." There is no basis either historically or logically for this conclusion. . . . [T]here is not one word in the authorities cited by the Court that indicates that court enforcement of fines was commonplace or traditional in 1947, and, to the contrary, until recently unions rarely resorted to court enforcement of union fines. Second, Congress' unfamiliarity in 1947 with this recent innovation and consequent failure to make any distinction between union-enforced and court-enforced fines cannot support the conclusion that Congress was unconcerned with the "means" a union uses to enforce its fines. Congress was expressly concerned with enacting "rules of the game" for unions to abide by. 93 Cong. Rec. 4436, II Leg. Hist. 1206. As noted by the [NLRB] the year after §8(b)(1)(A) was passed, "[i]n that Section, Congress was aiming at means, not at ends." Perry Norvell Co., 80 N.L.R.B. 225, 239. . . . If the union here had attempted to enforce the payment of the fines by persuading the employer to discharge the nonpaying employees or to withhold the fines from their wages, it would have clearly been guilty of an unfair labor practice under §8(b)(2). If the union here, operating under a union shop contract, had applied the employees' dues to the satisfaction of the fines and then charged them extra dues, that, under Board decisions, would have been a violation of §8(b)(1)(A), since it would have jeopardized the employees' jobs. Yet here the union has resorted to equally effective outside assistance to enforce the payment of its fines, and the Court holds that within the ambit of "internal union discipline." . . .

 . . . I have already pointed to the impact that $100 per day court-enforced fines may have on an employee's job — they would totally discourage him from working at all — and I fail to see how court enforcement of union fines is any more "internal" than employer enforcement. The undeniable fact is that the union resorts to outside help when it is not strong enough to enforce obedience internally. And even if the union does not resort to outside help but uses threats of physical violence by its officers or other members to compel payment of its fines, I do not doubt that this too would be a violation of §8(b)(1)(A).

Finally, the Court attempts to justify court-enforcement of fines by comparing it to judicial enforcement of the provisions of an ordinary commercial contract — a comparison which, according to the Court's own authority, is simply "a legal fabrication." The contractual theory of union membership, at least until recently, was a fiction used by the courts to justify judicial intervention in union affairs to protect employees, not to help unions. I cannot believe that Congress intended the effectiveness of §8(b)(1)(A) to be impaired by such a fiction, or that it was content to rely on the state courts' use of this fiction to protect members from union coercion. Particularly is that so where the "contract" between the union and the employee is the involuntary product of a union shop. . . .

III

. . . [T]he Senate sponsors of §8(b)(1)(A) were primarily concerned with coercive organizational tactics of unions and . . . most of the examples of abuse referred to in the debates concerned threats of violence by unions against nonmember employees. But to say that §8(b)(1)(A) covers *only* coercive organizational tactics, which the Court comes very close to doing, is to ignore much of the legislative history. It is clear that §8(b)(1)(A) was intended to protect union as well as nonunion employees from coercive tactics of unions, and such protection would hardly be provided if the section applied only to organizational tactics. Also, it is clear that Congress was much more concerned with nonviolent economic coercion than with threats of physical violence. . . . Examples were given of cases where unions threatened to double the dues of employees who waited until later to join. It is difficult to see how fining a member is less coercive than doubling his dues, or how the one is "within the ambit of internal union affairs" and the other is not. After the bill was passed, in commenting on some of the abuses it was designed to correct, Senator Wiley said there are "instances in which unions . . . have imposed fines upon their members up to $20,000 because they crossed picket lines — dared to go to the place of employment." Twice during the debate, Senator Taft emphatically stated that the section guarantees employees who wished to work during a strike the right to do so. Though on neither occasion did he expressly limit his examples to organizational strikes, the Court reads them as having such a limited reference. . . .

V

[The union security clause] . . . made it necessary for all employees, including the ones involved here, to pay dues and fees to the union. But §8(a)(3) and §8(b)(2) make it clear that "Congress intended to prevent utilization of union security agreements for any purpose other than to compel payment of union dues and fees." [*Radio Officers' Union*], 347 U.S. 17, 41. If the union uses the union security clause to compel employees to pay dues, characterizes such employees as members, and then uses such membership as a basis for imposing court-enforced fines upon those employees unwilling to participate in a union strike, then the union security clause is being used for a purpose other than "to compel payment of union dues and fees." It is being used to coerce employees to join in union activity in violation of §8(b)(2).

The Court suggests that this problem is not present here, because the fined employees failed to prove they enjoyed other than full union membership, that their role in the union was not in fact limited to the obligation of paying dues. For several reasons, I am unable to agree with the Court's approach. Few employees forced to become "members" of the union by virtue of the union security clause will be aware . . . that they must somehow "limit" their membership to avoid the union's court-enforced fines. Even those who are brash enough to attempt to do so may be unfamiliar with how to do it. Must they refrain from doing anything but paying dues, or will signing the routine union pledge still leave them with less than full membership? And finally, it is clear that what restrains the employee from going to work during a union strike is the union's threat that it will fine him and collect the fine from him in court. How many employees in a union shop whose names appear on the union's membership rolls will be willing to ignore that threat in the hope that they will later be able to convince the [Board] or the state court that they were not full members of the union? By refusing to decide whether §8(b)(1)(A) prohibits the union from fining an employee who does nothing more than pay union dues as a condition to retaining his job in a union shop, the Court adds coercive impetus to the union's threat of fines. Today's decision makes it highly dangerous for an employee in a union shop to exercise his §7 right to refrain from participating in a strike called by a union in which he is a member in name only.

NOTES

1. In dealing with *Allis-Chalmers* and related problems, should the Board and courts have adopted the balancing approach followed (e.g., in *Republic Aviation*, supra p. 152; *Mackay*, supra p. 301; and *Great Dane*, supra p. 334), in passing on the legality under §8(a)(1) and (3) of employer measures designed to promote efficiency and maintain operations? If so, how should the balance be struck between the union's need for solidarity and the individual's interest in working without threat of fines or loss of union membership? See Archer, *Allis-Chalmers* Recycled: A Current View of a Union's Right to Fine Employees for Crossing a Picket Line, 7 Ind. L. Rev. 498 (1974).

2. A union fined its members $400 for working during an authorized and lawful strike and brought an action to recover the fines. During negotiations for a renewal agreement, the company insisted that a condition of any agreement was the cancellation of these fines and the acceptance of a clause barring the union and the company, by discipline, fine, or discharge, from interfering with the exercise of §7 rights, including the right to refrain from any of the activities protected by §7. Has the company violated §8(a)(5)? Cf. Universal Oil Products Corp. v. NLRB, 445 F.2d 155 (7th Cir. 1971).

NLRB v. Boeing Co.
412 U.S. 67 (1973)

[The parties' collective agreement, which included a maintenance of membership clause, expired on September 15, 1965. During an 18-day strike over a renewal agreement, 143 employees out of the 1,900 bargaining unit employees, crossed the picket lines and worked. Following the execution of a new agreement, the union duly charged the strike-breakers with violating the prohibition of the union constitution against "accepting employment . . . in an establishment in which a strike exists." Under appropriate union procedures, each strike-breaker was found guilty, fined $450.00 and barred from holding union office for five years. The employees' base pay for a 40-hour week ranged from $95 to $145. The union sued in a state court to collect these fines. The trial examiner, finding the fines excessive, upheld the company's §8(b)(1)(A) charge. The Board, however, dismissed the complaint, concluding that Congress had not authorized the NLRB to regulate the size of union fines.]

REHNQUIST, J. . . . In deciding [*Allis-Chalmers*] and [*Scofield*, infra] the Court several times referred to the unions' imposition of "reasonable" fines. . . . The Company contends, not illogically, that the Court's use of the adjective "reasonable" was intended to suggest to the Board that an unreasonable fine would amount to an unfair labor practice. . . .

. . . [W]e recede from the implications of the dicta in these earlier cases. While "unreasonable" fines may be more coercive than "reasonable" fines, all fines are coercive to a greater or lesser degree. The underlying basis for the holdings of *Allis-Chalmers* and *Scofield* was not that reasonable fines were noncoercive under . . . §8(b)(1)(A) . . . , but was instead that those provisions were not intended by Congress to apply to the imposition by the union of fines not affecting the employer-employee relationship and not otherwise prohibited by the Act. . . .

. . . While the line may not always be clear between [internal and external] matters . . . , to the extent that the Board was required to examine into such questions as a union's motivation for imposing a fine it would be delving into internal union affairs in a manner which we have previously held Congress did not intend. Given the rationale of *Allis-Chalmers* and *Scofield*, the Board's conclusion that §8(b)(1)(A) . . . has nothing to say about union fines of this nature, whatever their size, is correct. Issues as to the reasonableness or unreasonableness of such fines must be decided upon the basis of the law of contracts, voluntary associations, or such other principles of law as may be applied in a forum competent to adjudicate the issue. Under our holding, state courts will be wholly free to apply state law to such issues at the suit of either the union or the member fined.

. . . At least since 1954, it has been the Board's consistent position that it has "not been empowered by Congress . . . to pass judgment on the penalties a union may impose on a member so long as the penalty does not impair the member's status as an employee." Local 283, UAW, 145 N.L.R.B. 1097, 1104 (1964). . . . [S]uch a consistent and contemporaneous construction of a statute by the agency charged with its enforcement is entitled to great deference by the courts. . . .

The Court of Appeals and the Company have suggested several policy reasons why the Board should not leave the determinations of reasonableness entirely to the state courts. . . . [F]irst, more uniformity in the determination of what is reasonable will result if the Board suggests standards and, second, more expertise . . . will be brought to bear if the issue is decided by the Board rather than solely by the courts. Even if we were to concede the relevance of policy factors in determining congressional intent, we are not persuaded that the Board is necessarily the better forum for determining the reasonableness of a fine. . . .

. . . [I]n *Allis-Chalmers* . . . we stated that "state courts, in reviewing the imposition of union discipline, find ways to strike down 'discipline [which] involves a severe hardship.'" 388 U.S., at 193 n.32, quoting Summers, Legal Limitations on Union Discipline, 64 Harv. L. Rev. 1049, 1078 (1951). The Board assumed that in view of this statement, our reference to "reasonable" fines, when reasonableness was not in issue, in *Allis-Chalmers* and in *Scofield*, was merely adverting to the usual standard applied by state courts in deciding whether to enforce union-imposed fines. The Board reads these cases, therefore, as encouraging state courts to use a reasonableness standard, not as a directive to the Board.

Our review of state court cases decided both before and after our decisions in *Allis-Chalmers* and *Scofield* reveals that state courts applying state law are quite willing to determine whether disciplinary fines are reasonable in amount. Indeed, the expertise required for a determination of reasonableness may well be more evident in a judicial forum that is called upon to assess reasonableness in varying factual contexts than it is in a specialized agency. . . .

Nor is it clear . . . that the Board's setting of standards of reasonableness will necessarily result in greater uniformity in this area even if uniformity is thought to be a desirable goal. Since state courts will have jurisdiction to determine reasonableness in the enforcement context in any event, the Board's independent determination of reasonableness in an unfair labor practice context might well yield a conflict when the two forums are called upon to review the same fine.

. . . [T]he Board was warranted in determining that when the union discipline does not interfere with the employee-employer relationship or otherwise violate a policy of the [NLRA], the Congress did not authorize it "to evaluate the fairness of union discipline meted out to protect a legitimate union interest." . . . Reversed.

[Burger, C.J., dissenting, referred to the oddity of a union's supporting state court jurisdiction and stressed the need for uniformity and the Board's expertise. Douglas, J., joined by Blackmun, J., also dissented. He urged that the union — by fining employees more than they had earned during the strike — was, in effect, suspending them without pay after the strike — action that would plainly be unlawful if undertaken at the union's instigation. He noted that Board jurisdiction over the reasonableness of fines would mean publicly provided counsel for indigent and unsophisticated employees.]

Scofield v. NLRB
394 U.S. 423 (1969)

[A union rule barred union members on incentive pay from accepting payment during the regular pay period for production exceeding a union-imposed ceiling. The union required that such excess production be banked and drawn on only when employees had not reached the daily ceiling. The employer would, however, make over-the-ceiling payments during the regular pay period if an employee so requested. The union fined members making such requests; nonpayment of fines could lead to expulsion from membership for "conduct unbecoming a member." The employer had, without success, bargained for the union's abandonment of the ceiling. Under the parties' union security agreement, employees could pay a "service fee" rather than join the union. The union sued in a state court to collect fines of $50 to $100, which, along with a year's suspension from membership, the union membership had imposed on members who had requested and received prompt payment for over-the-ceiling production. The Court upheld the Board's dismissal of the complaint.]

WHITE, J. . . . Although the Board's construction of the section emphasizes the sanction imposed, rather than the rule itself, and does not involve the Board in judging the fairness or wisdom of particular union rules, it has become clear that if the rule invades or frustrates an overriding policy of the labor laws the rule may not be enforced, even by fine or expulsion, without violating §8(b)(1). In both *Skura*[7] and *Marine Workers*,[8] the Board was concerned with union rules requiring a member to exhaust union remedies before filing an unfair labor practice charge with the Board. That rule, in the Board's view, frustrated the enforcement scheme established by the statute and the union would commit an unfair labor practice by fining or expelling members who violated the rule.

[In *Marine Workers*[9]] the result reached by the Board was sustained, the Court agreeing that the rule in question was contrary to the plain policy of the Act to keep employees completely free from coercion against making complaints to the Board. Frustrating this policy was beyond the legitimate interest of the labor organization, at least where the member's complaint concerned conduct of the employer as well as the union.

Under this dual approach, §8(b)(1) leaves a union free to enforce a properly adopted rule which reflects a legitimate union interest, impairs no policy Congress has imbedded in the labor laws, and is reasonably enforced against union members who are free to leave the union and escape the rule. . . .

In the case at hand, there is no showing . . . that the fines were unreasonable or the mere fiat of a union leader, or that the membership of petitioners in the union was involuntary. Moreover, the enforcement of the rule was not carried out through means unacceptable in themselves, such as violence or employer discrimination. It was enforced solely through the internal technique of union fines, collected by threat of expulsion or judicial action. The inquiry must therefore focus on the legitimacy of the union interest vindicated by the rule and the extent to which any policy of the Act may be violated by the union-imposed production ceiling.

. . . [U]nion opposition to unlimited piecework pay systems is historic. Union apprehension, not without foundation, is that such systems will drive up employee productivity and in turn create pressures to lower the piecework rate so that at the new, higher level of output employees are earning little more than they did before. The fear is that the competitive pressure generated will endanger workers' health, foment jealousies, and reduce the work force. In addition, the findings of the trial examiner were that the ceiling served as a yardstick for the settlement of job allowance grievances, that it has played an important role in negotiating the minimum hourly rate and that it is the standard for "factoring" the hourly rate raises into the piecework rate.

[7] Local 138, Operating Engineers, 148 N.L.R.B. 679 (1964).
[8] Industrial Union of Marine & Shipbuilding Wkrs., 159 N.L.R.B. 1065 (1966).
[9] NLRB v. Industrial Union of Marine & Shipbuilding Workers, 391 U.S. 418 (1968).

The view of the trial examiner was that "in terms of a union's traditional function of trying to serve the economic interests of the group as a whole, the Union has a very real, immediate, and direct interest in it." 145 N.L.R.B., at 1135. . . .

The principal contention of the petitioners is that the rule impedes collective bargaining, a process nurtured in many ways by the Act. But surely this is not the case here. The union has never denied that the ceiling is a bargainable issue. It has never refused to bargain about it as far as this record shows. Indeed, the union has at various times agreed to raise its ceiling in return for an increase in the piece rate, and the ceiling has been regularly used to compute the new piece rate. . . . The company has repeatedly sought an agreement eliminating the piecework ceiling, an agreement which, had it been obtained, unquestionably would have been violated by the union rule. . . . [I]t has signed contracts recognizing the ceiling, has tolerated it, and has cooperated in its administration by honoring requests by employees to bank their pay for over-ceiling work. We discern no basis in the statutory policy encouraging collective bargaining for giving the employer a better bargain than he has been able to strike at the bargaining table. . . . The contract . . . leaves in the hands of the employee the option of taking full advantage of his allowances, performing only as an average employee and not reaching even the ceiling rate. At least there is nothing before us to indicate that the company disciplines individuals who work at only the machine rate or individuals who produce more but who choose not to exceed the union ceiling. The same decision can be made collectively by the union. Although it has agreed in the contract to a pay scale for production in excess of ceiling, that fact in the context of this case does not support an inference that the union has agreed not to impose the ceiling or that its action in announcing one is somehow contrary to the contract. And if neither union nor member is in breach of contract for establishing and adhering to the ceiling, it is equally clear that the rule neither causes nor invites a contract violation by the employer who stands ready to pay an employee for his over-ceiling production or to bank it at his request. . . .

This leaves the possible argument that because the union has not successfully bargained for a contractual ceiling, it may not impose one on its own members, for doing so will discriminate between members and those others who are free to earn as much as the contract permits. All members of the bargaining unit, however, have the same contractual rights. In dealing with the employer as bargaining agent, the union has accorded all employees uniform treatment. If members are prevented from taking advantage of their contractual rights bargained for all employees it is because they have chosen to become and remain union members. . . . [T]he price of obeying the [instant] rule is not as high as in *Allis-Chalmers*. There the member could be replaced for his refusal to report to work during a strike; here he need simply limit his production and suffer whatever consequences that conduct may entail. If a member chooses not to engage in this concerted activity and is unable to prevail on the other members to change the rule, then he may leave the union and obtain whatever benefits in job advancement and extra pay may result from extra work, at the same time enjoying the protection from competition, the high piece rate, and the job security which compliance with the union rule by union members tends to promote.

That the choice to remain a member results in differences between union members and other employees raises no serious issue under §8(b)(2) and §8(a)(3) . . . , because the union has not induced the employer to discriminate against the member but has merely forbidden the member to take advantage of benefits which the employer stands willing to confer. . . .

Marshall, J., took no part in the consideration or decision of this case.

[Black, J., dissented for the reasons set forth in his dissent in *Allis-Chalmers*.]

NOTES

1. A union unilaterally adopted a rule limiting its members, who had been painting an average of 11.5 rooms per week, to 10 rooms per week. The stated purpose of this rule was to reduce speed-up pressures and to protect the painters' health and the quality of their work. The governing collective bargaining agreement was silent about production quotas but specified a seven-hour day and five-day work week. While the union and employer argued over whether the union had violated the agreement, it expired. In subsequent bargaining that led to a strike, the parties, unable to agree on new provisions concerning production quotas, retained the old provisions. After the renewal agreement was executed, the union threatened members who violated its ten-room rule with expulsion. Some members stopped work after reaching that quota even though they had not worked a full 35-hour week. Production fell below the prior 11.5 average.

Has the union committed an unfair labor practice? What if the union's ceiling had been fixed at the prior average production rate, or if the employees had been on a piecework basis and the union had been trying to stretch out declining work? Cf. Painters District Council (Westgate Painting and Decorating Corp.), 186 N.L.R.B. 964 (1970), *enforced*, 453 F.2d 783 (2d Cir. 1971), *cert. denied*, 408 U.S. 930 (1972).

2. Are union fines (with or without court enforcement) unfair labor practices when imposed for a member's violation of a rule requiring activity unprotected by the NLRA, such as strikes or related activity in breach of a no-strike clause, or repeated and concerted refusals to engage in overtime? Cf. NLRB v. GAIZL Local 13-B, 682 F.2d 304 (2d Cir. 1982), *cert. denied*, 103 S. Ct. 1183 (1983). What if the union expelled rather than fined members for violating a union rule requiring participation in unprotected activity? Compare the Board's upholding expulsion of a member for filing a decertification petition while holding imposition of a fine collectible in court on account of such a filing to be an unfair labor practice. See Molders Local 125, 178 N.L.R.B. 208 (1969), *enforced*, 442 F.2d 92 (7th Cir. 1971); Marble Finishers Local 89 (Bybee Stone Co.), 265 N.L.R.B. 496 (1982).

3. A union fines a member ostensibly for his violation of the union's election rules but actually for opposing (unsuccessfully) the incumbent's reelection. Has the union violated the NLRA? Cf. Carpenters Local 22, 195 N.L.R.B. 1 (1972).

NLRB v. Granite State Joint Board, Textile Workers Local 1029, 409 U.S. 213 (1972). Shortly after the beginning of a strike, called pursuant to a membership strike vote, the union members voted unanimously (or virtually so) that any member aiding the employer during the strike would be subject to a $2,000 fine. After the strike ran for six weeks, two members resigned through a letter to the union; seven to twelve months later, 29 others resigned. The 31 resignees promptly returned to work, passing through the union's picket line. The union, after notice and hearing, fined them and sued to collect. The Supreme Court upheld the Board's finding of a §8(b)(1)(A) violation, stating, through Douglas, J.:

"[W]hen a member lawfully resigns from the union, its power over him ends. . . . Where a member lawfully resigns from a union and thereafter engages in conduct which the union rule proscribes, the union commits an unfair labor practice when it seeks enforcement of fines for that conduct. . . .

"The Court of Appeals gave weight to the fact that the resigning employees had participated in the vote to strike. We give that factor little weight. . . . Events occurring after the calling of a strike may have unsettling effects, leading a member who voted to strike to change his mind. The likely duration of the strike may increase the specter of hardship to his family; the ease with which the employer replaces the strikers may make the strike seem less provident. We do not now decide to what extent the contractual relationship between union and member may curtail the freedom to resign.

But where, as here, there are no restraints on the resignation of members, . . . §7 requires that the member be free to refrain in November from the actions he endorsed in May and that his §7 rights are not lost by a union's plea for solidarity or by its pressures for conformity and submission to its regime. . . ."

NOTE

In Booster Lodge 405, IAM v. NLRB, 412 U.S. 84 (1973), the union, although not restricting resignations during a strike, had expressly banned strike breaking by members. The union contended that this provision bound a member to continue in a strike called while he was a member, despite his later resignation. The Court, rejecting this contention, upheld the Board's decision that the union had violated §8(b)(1)(A) by fining resignees for their postresignation strike breaking and by suing to collect. The Court, invoking *Textile Wkrs.*, declared generally that a valid resignation freed a member from all associational obligations. The Court, however, stressed the absence of evidence that the union, before the ratification or beginning of the strike, had advised its members that resignation would not end their obligation to refrain from strike breaking. Blackmun, J., concurring, expressly relied on the union's apparent failure to give such notification.

Machinists Local 1327 *(Dalmo Victor),* 263 N.L.R.B. 984 (1982) (supplemental decision). Shortly before calling an economic strike against the employer, the local reminded its members of the following provision of its constitution:

> *Improper Conduct of a Member* . . . Accepting employment . . . in an establishment where a strike or lockout exists . . . without permission. Resignation shall not relieve a member of his obligation to refrain from accepting employment at the establishment for the duration of the strike or lockout within 14 days preceding its commencement. Where observance of a primary picket line is required, resignation shall not relieve a member of his obligation to observe the primary picket line for its duration if the resignation occurs during the period that the picket line is maintained or within 14 days preceding its establishment.

The Board first held that this provision did not restrict a member's right to resign but, instead, unlawfully attempted to restrict the postresignation conduct of ex-members. Accordingly, the Board concluded that the union had violated §8(b)(1)(A) by imposing court collectible fines on three members for resigning and returning to work eight months into a strike. The court of appeals, however, found the constitutional provision to be a permissible restriction on members' rights to resign. The court, accordingly, denied enforcement and remanded for a Board determination of the validity of the disputed provision, as construed by the court. See NLRB v. Machinists Local 1327, 608 F.2d 1219 (9th Cir. 1979).

The Board accepted as the law of the case the court's characterization of the disputed provision without, however, abandoning its own position that a restriction on postresignation conduct was involved. On the issue posed by the court, two Board members, Fanning and Zimmerman, reasoned this way: The Board must balance an employee's statutory right to refrain from concerted activity against a union's legitimate interest in collective self-help. Union rules differentiating between strike and strike-free periods unreasonably restrict a member's §7 right to resign. On the other hand, "in order to vindicate its interest in assessing its strength throughout . . . a strike and to protect [employees who are committed to a strike] . . . a union is entitled to reasonable notice of the effective date of resignations which occur immediately before or during a strike." Although declaring the disputed provisions unlawful, Members Fanning and Zimmerman announced a general approach, to operate absent "extraordinary circumstances," upholding "a rule which restricts a union member's right to resign for a period not to exceed 30 days after the tender of such a resignation. . . ."

Chairman Van de Water and Member Hunter agreed that the union's constitutional provision and the related fines were unlawful but rejected the 30-day rule, for these reasons: First, it is improper to balance away the employees' express §7 right in order to protect a union's interest in strike solidarity. Second, even if such balancing were proper, the 30-day rule slights the interests of individual employees, who might be strapped for money or worried about earlier replacement. Third, the rule ignores the Supreme Court's dichotomy between "internal" sanctions imposed on members and "external" sanctions imposed on nonmembers, including resignees. Finally, the 30-day waiting period constitutes an arbitrary compromise, beyond the Board's authority. Van de Water and Hunter delineated this approach for the future:

> Any union rule that restricts a member's right to resign is unreasonable and any discipline taken by a union against an employee predicated on such a rule violates §8(b)(1)(A). . . . [F]or a resignation to be valid, it must be in writing and is effective upon receipt by the union. Finally, . . . a union may not condition a resignation upon the payment of any dues or assessments.

Member Jenkins, dissenting, urged that the union's constitutional prohibition, viewed as a ban on resignations during a strike, was valid under the proviso to §8(b)(1)(A) and wholly consistent with *Allis-Chalmers* and subsequent Supreme Court opinions.

The Ninth Circuit upheld the union's rule, concluding that it met *Scofield*'s three-part test. The Court, while not disputing "the employee's §7 right to resign," rejected the view that it is unreasonable for the union to penalize, by court-collectible fines, a member's breach of certain crucial obligations, such as avoiding strike breaking. See Machinists Local 1327 v. NLRB, 725 F.2d 1212 (9th Cir. 1984). But see Patterns Makers' League v. NLRB, 724 F.2d 57 (7th Cir. 1983).

(In Machinists, Local 1414 (Neufeld Porsche-Audi, Inc.), 270 N.L.R.B. No. 209, 116 L.R.R.M. 1257 (1984), the Board considered the IAM's constitutional provision, supra p. 1279, as amended in 1981 so as to restrict a member's right to resign while a "primary picket" line was being maintained (or within 14 days preceding its establishment) if members were required to observe such a line. Finding that one Locki had violated the amended provision, the IAM had imposed a court-collectible fine of $2,250 for resuming work for the struck employer after participating in an economic strike for three months. Three Board members, endorsing the view expressed in *Dalmo Victor II* by Van de Water and Hunter, declared "that the Respondent's [1981] restriction on resignations . . . , as well as any other restriction a union may impose on resignation, is invalid, and [held] that the Respondent violated §8(b)(1)(A) by [fining] Locki. . . ."

Member Zimmerman, concurring in result, dissented from the overruling of *Dalmo Victor II*.)

NOTES

1. Does the §7 right to abstain from concerted activity control the issue of whether an employee, by accepting full membership or by voting for and participating in a strike, waives that right in accordance with the union constitution of which he has specific knowledge? If an open-ended obligation to avoid strike breaking arises from such voting or participation, would members be discouraged from taking an active role in union affairs, thereby undercutting a goal of the LMRDA?

2. If an employee may waive his §7 right, is there an acceptable basis in the Act for limiting his waiver to 30 days (rather than a shorter or longer period), even though a union constitution establishes a longer period? See

Comment, Union Power to Discipline Members Who Resign, 86 Harv. L. Rev. 1536 (1973).

American Broadcasting Cos. v. Writers Guild
437 U.S. 411 (1978)

[The respondent, Writers Guild of America, West, Inc. (the Guild), represents writers employed by producers of motion pictures for theaters and TV. The Guild has collective bargaining agreements with the petitioners, who are the Association of Motion Picture and Television Producers and the three principal TV networks (ABC, CBS, and NBC), which also produce TV films. In March 1973, the Guild, during a strike against petitioners over renewal agreements, picketed and, by highly publicized strike rules for its members, forbade crossing of picket lines and similar activity. Since Guild policy banned members' resignations until six months after completion of negotiations, a member disobeying strike rules risked union discipline.

Some Guild members — producers, editors, and others ("hyphenates") — perform primarily executive and supervisory functions, including grievance adjustment, but also do minor writing, which was expressly excluded from coverage by the Guild's agreement. Unions other than the Guild represent many hyphenates as to their primary work. Some of those unions, whose contracts with the petitioners contain no-strike clauses, urged the hyphenates to return to work despite the Guild's strike, as did the petitioners. Many hyphenates did return but did only their supervisory work, including grievance adjustment when necessary.

After its own hearings, the Guild, finding violations of its rules by the hyphenates, penalized them by suspensions, expulsion, and substantial fines, some as high as $50,000.

After customary NLRB proceedings, the ALJ concluded that the Guild had violated §8(b)(1)(B), reasoning this way: The hyphenates were "supervisors," and the Guild penalties had been triggered by the supervisors' performance, during the strike, of their usual work, including adjustment of (or openness to) grievances from employees working despite the strike. The Guild, by issuing strike rules designed to prevent hyphenates from working and by its disciplinary penalties, had "coerced . . . [the] employer in the selection of representatives for collective bargaining and the adjustment of grievances within the meaning of §8(b)(1)(B)."

A majority of a three-member NLRB panel adopted the ALJ's principal findings and conclusions, observing that Florida Power & Light Co. v. Electrical Wkrs., Local 641, 417 U.S. 790 (1974) (*FP&L*) had involved supervisors who had performed bargaining-unit work and hence did not apply where supervisors had been disciplined for doing only their ordinary supervisory work (including grievance-adjustments). The court of appeals (2-1), found *FP&L* controlling and denied enforcement.]

WHITE, J. As the Court has set out in greater detail in its comprehensive review of §8(b)(1)(B) in *FP&L*, the prohibition against restraining or coercing an employer in the selection of his bargaining representative was, until 1968, applied primarily to pressures exerted by the union directly upon the employer to force him into a multiemployer bargaining unit or otherwise to dictate or control the choice of his representative for the purpose of collective bargaining or adjusting grievances in the course of administering an existing contract. In San Francisco-Oakland Mailers' Union No. 18, International Typographical Union (Northwest Publications, Inc.), 172 N.L.R.B. 2173 (1968), however, the Board applied the section to prohibit union discipline of one of its member-supervisors for the manner in which he had performed his supervisory task of grievance adjustment. Although the union "sought the substitution of attitudes rather than persons, and may have exerted its pressures upon the [employer] by indirect rather than direct means," the ultimate fact was that the pressure interfered with the employer's control over his representative. "Realistically, the Employer would have to replace its foremen or face *de facto* nonrepresentation by them." *Oakland Mailers*, supra, at 2173.

The application of the section to indirect coercion of employers through pressure applied to supervisory personnel continued to evolve until the *FP&L* and *Illinois Bell*[18] cases [arose]. . . . In each of those cases, the union disciplined supervisor-members who had performed rank-and-file work behind a union picket line during a strike. In a companion case to *Illinois Bell*,[19] upon which *Illinois Bell* explicitly relied, the Board found an infraction of §8(b)(1)(B), broadly construing its purpose "to assure to the employer that its selected collective-bargaining representatives will be completely faithful to its desires" and holding that this could not be achieved "if the union has an effective method, union disciplinary action, by which it can pressure such representatives to deviate from the interests of the employer."[21] In like fashion, in *FP&L*, the Board held that fining supervisors for

[18] IBEW, Local 134 v. NLRB, 159 U.S. App. D.C. 242, 487 F.2d 1113, *rev'd on rehearing en banc*, 159 U.S. App. D.C. 272, 487 F.2d 1143 (1973), refusing to enforce IBEW, Local 134, 192 N.L.R.B. 85 (1971) (*Illinois Bell*), and IBEW Systems Council U-4, 193 N.L.R.B. 30 (1971) (*FP&L*).
[19] Local Union No. 2150, IBEW, and Wisconsin Electric Power Co., 192 N.L.R.B. 77 (1971).
[21] Id., at 78.

doing rank-and-file work during a work stoppage "struck at the loyalty an employer should be able to expect from its representatives for the adjustment of grievances and therefore restrained and coerced employers in their selection of such representatives." [22]

The Court of Appeals overturned both decisions of the Board, holding that although the section could be properly applied to union efforts to discipline supervisors for their performance as collective-bargaining or grievance-adjustment representatives, it could not reasonably be applied to prohibit union discipline of supervisors crossing picket lines to perform bargaining-unit work: "When a supervisor forsakes his supervisory role to do rank-and-file work ordinarily the domain of nonsupervisory employees, he is no longer acting as a management representative and no longer merits any immunity from discipline." 487 F.2d, at 1157.

This Court affirmed the judgment of the Court of Appeals:

> . . . [A] union's discipline of one of its members who is a supervisory employee can constitute a violation of §8(b)(1)(B) only when that discipline may adversely affect the supervisor's conduct in performing the duties of, and acting in his capacity as, grievance adjuster or collective bargainer on behalf of the employer.

417 U.S., at 804-805. The Court thus rejected the claim that "even if the effect of [union] discipline did not carry over to the performance of the supervisor's grievance adjustment or collective bargaining functions," it was enough to show that the result would be "to deprive the employer of the full allegiance of, and control over, a representative he has selected for grievance adjustment or collective bargaining purposes." Id., at 807. Assuming without deciding that the Board's decision in *Oakland Mailers* fell within the outer reaches of §8(b)(1)(B), the Court concluded that the *Illinois Bell* and *FP&L* decisions did not, because it was "certain that these supervisors were not engaged in collective bargaining or grievance adjustment, or in any activities related thereto, when they crossed union picket lines during an economic strike to engage in rank-and-file struck work." 417 U.S., at 805.

Subsequent to *FP&L*, . . . the Board directed its attention, as it understood *FP&L* to require, to the question whether the discipline may adversely affect the supervisor's conduct in performing his grievance-adjustment or collective-bargaining duties on behalf of the employer. In *Hammond Publishers*, supra, and *Triangle Publishers*, supra, the Board held that it [violated] §8(b)(1)(B) for a union to discipline a supervisor-member whose regular duties included the adjustment of grievances for crossing a

[22] 193 N.L.R.B., at 31.

picket line to perform his regular functions during a strike. See also Wisconsin River Valley Dist. Council (Skippy Enterprises, Inc.), 218 N.L.R.B. 1063 (1975). These cases rested on the Board's conclusion that such discipline imposed on the supervisor would have a "carryover" effect and would influence the supervisor in the performance of his adjustment functions after the strike and hence interfere with and coerce the employer in the choice of his grievance representative. . . . The *Triangle* decision was not challenged in the courts, but *Hammond* was enforced, 539 F.2d 242 (1976), as was *Skippy Enterprises*, 532 F.2d 47 (CA7 1976). . . .

We cannot agree with what appears to be the fundamental position of the Court of Appeals and the union that under §8(b)(1)(B), as the section was construed in *FP&L*, it is never an unfair practice for a union to discipline a supervisor-member for working during a strike, regardless of the work that he may perform behind the picket line. The opinion in *FP&L* expressly refrained from questioning *Oakland Mailers* or the proposition that an employer could be coerced or restrained within the meaning of §8(b)(1)(B) not only by picketing or other direct actions aimed at him but also by debilitating discipline imposed on his collective-bargaining or grievance-adjustment representative. Indeed, after focusing on the purposes of the section, the Court in *FP&L* delineated the boundaries of when that "carryover" effect would violate §8(b)(1)(B): whenever such discipline may adversely affect the supervisor's conduct in his capacity as a grievance adjustor or collective bargainer. In these situations — that is, when such impact might be felt — the employer would be deprived of the full services of his representatives and hence would be restrained and coerced in his selection of those representatives. . . .

Respondent objects that this construction of the Act impermissibly intrudes on the union's right to resort to economic sanctions during a strike. However, an employer also has economic rights during a strike, and the statute declares that, in the unrestrained freedom to select a grievance-adjustment and collective-bargaining representative, the employer's rights dominate. Ample leeway is already accorded to a union in permitting it to discipline any member, even a supervisor, for performing struck work — to carry that power over to the case of purely supervisory work is an inappropriate extension and interference with the employer's prerogative. The Board has so ruled, and . . . " '[t]he function of striking [the] balance to effectuate national labor policy is often a difficult and delicate responsibility, which the Congress committed primarily to the [NLRB], subject to limited judicial review.' " . . .

. . . [A]s to those hyphenates who reported for work, it is strenuously urged that there is no basis for concluding that the discipline imposed upon them would adversely affect the performance of their grievance-adjustment duties either during or after the strike. . . .

. . . [I]t does not strike us as groundless or lacking substantial evidence for the Board to conclude on this record that the discipline imposed would have the necessary adverse effect. Strike rules were distributed in February; the strikes against the Association began on March 4 and terminated June 24; the strikes against the networks began on March 29 and ended on July 12. Between April 6 and November 8 — both during and after the strikes — some 31 hyphenates who had worked during the strikes were charged with violating union rules, 15 hearings had been held prior to the closing of evidence in November 1973, and from June 25 to September 28, very substantial penalties were imposed in 10 cases although 9 have already been reduced on appeal. These penalties were widely publicized at the time of their imposition. Other charges were pending and remained to be tried when the record was closed in this case.

These penalties were meted out at least in part because the accused hyphenates had complied with the orders of their employers by reporting for work and performing only their normal supervisory functions, including the adjustment of grievances, during the strike. Hyphenates who worked were thus faced not only with threats but also with the *actuality* of charges, trial, and severe discipline simply because they were working at their normal jobs. And if this were not enough, they were threatened with a union blacklist that might drive them from the industry. How long such hyphenates would remain on the job under such pressure was a matter no one, particularly the employer, could predict.

Moreover, after the strike, with the writers back at work, the hyphenates who had worked during the strike still faced charges and trials or were appealing large fines and long suspensions. At the same time, they were expected to perform their regular supervisory duties and to adjust grievances whenever the occasion demanded, functions requiring them to deal with the same union which was considering the appeal of their personal sanctions. As to these supervisors, who had felt the union's wrath, not for doing rank-and-file work contrary to union rules, but for performing only their primary supervisory duties during the strike and who were in a continuing controversy with the union, it was not untenable for the Board to conclude that these disciplined hyphenates had a diminished capacity to carry out their grievance-adjustment duties effectively and that the employer was deprived of the full range of services from his supervisors. Such a hyphenate might be tempted to give the union side of a grievance a more favorable slant while the threat of discipline remained, or while his own appeal of a union sanction was pending. At the very least, the employer could not be certain that a fined hyphenate would willingly answer the employer's call to duty during a subsequent work stoppage, particularly if it occurred in the near future. For an employer in these circumstances to insure having satisfactory collective-bargaining and grievance-adjustment services would require a change in his representative.

As the Board has construed the Act from *Oakland Mailers* to *Triangle, Hammond*, and the cases now before us, such a likely impact on the employer constitutes sufficient restraint and coercion in connection with the selection of collective-bargaining and grievance-adjustment representatives to violate §8(b)(1)(B). In *FP&L* the Court declined the invitation to overrule *Oakland Mailers*, and we do so again. Union pressure on supervisors can affect either their willingness to serve as grievance adjustors or collective bargainers, or the manner in which they fulfill these functions; and either effect impermissibly coerces the employer in his choice of representative. . . .

Because we have concluded that the Board's construction of §8(b)(1)(B) is not an unreasonable reading of its language or inconsistent with its purposes, and because we cannot say that the Board's findings lacked substantial evidence, we must reverse the judgment of the Court of Appeals.

STEWART, J., with whom BRENNAN, MARSHALL, and STEVENS, JJ., join, dissenting.

The Court holds today that a labor union locked in a direct economic confrontation with an employer is powerless to impose sanctions on its own members who choose to pledge their loyalty to the adversary. Nothing in §8(b)(1)(B) or any other provision of the [NLRA] permits such a radical alteration of the natural balance of power between labor and management. . . .

In the present cases it is entirely clear that the union had no interest in restraining or coercing the employers in the *selection* of their bargaining or grievance-adjustment representatives, or in affecting the *manner* in which supervisory employees performed those functions. As the Court notes, . . . the union expressed no interest at the disciplinary trials in the kind of work that was done behind its picket lines. Its sole purpose was to enforce the traditional kinds of rules that every union relies on to maintain its organization and solidarity in the face of the potential hardship of a strike. Cf. NLRB v. Allis-Chalmers Mfg. Co., 388 U.S. 175, 181-184.

. . . [T]his Court today forbids a union from disciplining a supervisor-member who crosses its picket line — who clearly gives "aid and comfort to the enemy" during a strike . . . — solely because that action may have the incidental effect of depriving the employer of the hypothetical grievance-adjustment services of that particular supervisor for the duration of the strike. This ruling quite simply gives the employer the superior right to call on the loyalty of *any* supervisor with grievance-adjustment responsibilities, whenever the union to which the supervisor belongs calls him out on strike. In short, the Court's decision prevents a union with supervisory members from effectively calling and enforcing a strike.

Nothing in §8(b)(1)(B) permits such a sweeping limitation on the choice of economic weapons by unions that include supervisory employees among their members. On the contrary, as the Court clearly held in *FP&L*, supra, an employer's remedy if he does not want to share the loyalty of his supervisors with a union is to insist that his supervisory personnel not belong to a union; or if he does not welcome the consequences of his supervisors' union membership he may legally penalize them for engaging in union activities, . . . or "resolv[e] such conflicts as arise through the traditional procedures of collective bargaining." *FP&L*, supra, at 813.[4]

The sole function of §8(b)(1)(B) is to protect an employer from any union coercion of the free choice of his bargaining or grievance-adjustment representative. In prohibiting union interference in his choice of representatives for dealings with the union, this statutory provision does not in any way grant him a right to interfere in the union's relationship with its supervisor-members. The statute leaves the balance of power in equipoise. The Court's decision, by contrast, tips it measurably in favor of the employer at the most delicate point of direct confrontation, by completely preventing the union from enlisting the aid of its supervisor-members in a strike effort. It seems to me that the Court's reading of §8(b)(1)(B) is "fundamentally inconsistent with the structure of the Act and the function of the sections relied upon." American Ship Building Co. v. NLRB, 380 U.S. 300, 318.

Accordingly, I would affirm the judgment of the Court of Appeals.

NOTES

1. A union is engaged in a lawful strike for a renewal agreement covering statutory "employees." It inquires whether it would violate the NLRA by imposing fines on its supervisor-members for violating well-publicized union rules by performing the following kinds of work behind a lawful picket line: (1) only supervisory work, not including grievance-adjustment or collective bargaining §8(b)(1)(B) work; (2) only §8(b)(1)(B) work; (3) supervisory work plus a "minimal amount" of rank-and-file work; (4) approximately equal amounts of supervisory work and rank-and-file work. In the last two situations, would the amount of the strike-related increase in the rank-and-file work done by the supervisors be relevant? Would it also be relevant

---

[4] Alternatively, the employer may ease the dilemma of his supervisory employees by offering to provide their defense or to indemnify them against any fines that might be imposed by the union for a breach of strike discipline. Several of the employers in this case did in fact extend such offers to the hyphenates. . . .

whether they regularly performed §8(b)(1)(B) work? The divisions within the Board regarding the relevant factors for deciding such cases are reviewed in Glaziers & Glassworkers Local 1621 (Glass Management Assn.), 221 N.L.R.B. 509 (1975); see also Columbia Typographical Union No. 101 (Washington Post), 242 N.L.R.B. 1079 (1979); Teamsters Local 296 (Northwest Publications), 263 N.L.R.B. 778 (1982) (reaffirming the Board's "reservoir doctrine," under which a supervisor doing only supervisory work (without authority over collective bargaining or grievances) is a "representative" under §8(b)(1)(B); consequently, union discipline of a supervisor for performing such work violates that section). Consider also the significance of the factors discussed in connection with *Textile Workers*, supra p. 1278, and *Booster Lodge*, supra p. 1279.

2. A local union charged S, a front line supervisor, with violating both the local's working rules and the provisions of the collective agreement regarding working hours and wages, by working "off the clock" on certain pre-start activities. The company contended that those activities are necessary for efficient operation and are part of S's supervisory duties. Nevertheless, the union fined S $250, suspending $150 of the fine if he stopped working off the clock. Has the union violated §8(b)(1)(B)? Cf. Northwest Publications v. NLRB, 656 F.2d 461 (9th Cir. 1981) (noting that neither the ALJ nor the Board had reached the question of whether the supervisor was a "representative" within the scope of §8(b)(1)(B), the court refrained from deciding the question but suggested that "[w]hether a supervisor is currently a representative may not be material, if a union's disciplinary action be such as to chill a supervisor's willingness to undertake representative responsibilities").

3. *"Due Process" in Union Tribunals — and Judicial Review*

Cornelio v. Metropolitan Dist. Council of Philadelphia, United Bhd. of Carpenters & Joiners of America
243 F. Supp. 126 (E.D. Pa. 1965), *aff'd per curiam*, 358 F.2d 728 (3d Cir. 1966), *cert. denied*, 386 U.S. 975 (1967)

[Plaintiff's complaint alleged as follows: He had requested his local to petition the Council for arbitration of his discharge and that of 20 coemployees. The Council assigned two business agents, defendants B. T. Gray and G. Gushire, to investigate the charges set forth in the petition, which the local had prepared. Those agents failed to investigate those charges, but instead, at the instigation of Council official R. H. Gray, another defendant, solicited and secured statements from 11 of plaintiff's coworkers that they had heard the plaintiff defame union officials at the job site. Those statements formed the basis of the charges preferred by the business agents against the plaintiff. The plaintiff, restricted by the union constitution to representation only by a union member, was denied counsel of his own choice before the Council Trial Committee. That committee's recommendation — that plaintiff be fined $350 and suspended for five years from union activities, but not from membership — was ultimately adopted by the Council and affirmed by the general president approximately 18 months after the recommendation was made. The trial court dismissed the complaint for failure to state a claim.]

Longo, J. . . . The essence of plaintiff's complaint is that he did not make the defamatory statements[k] attributed to him; that the charges against him were false; that he was denied the opportunity to refute the charges because he was not accorded the full and fair hearing guaranteed him by §101(a)(5) of LMRDA . . . and that the resultant conviction and disciplinary action was unlawful. Plaintiff contends that he was denied [such a] full and fair hearing in that

(1) he was prejudiced by the fact that his accusers were persons of influence (business agents) within the union; and

(2) he was denied the right to be represented by "outside" counsel. . . .

Neither ground is sufficient, as a matter of law, to sustain a charge of deprivation of the full and fair hearing guaranteed by the LMRDA. . . .

The union Constitution provides . . . : "The accused and the accuser may appear before the Trial Committee either in person or by counsel (who shall be a member of the United Brotherhood), and shall be entitled to be present at all times when the Trial Committee is receiving evidence. . . ."[1]

This restriction, according to plaintiff, deprives him of the assistance of counsel and therefore denies him procedural due process.

The answer to the contention lies in the statement of the fundamental principle that the right to be represented by counsel, guaranteed by the Sixth Amendment to the Constitution of the United States, does not apply to hearings before labor unions. . . . All that a union member is entitled to in any controversy between him and the union is a fair hearing. This means only

---

[k] [On discipline for alleged defamation, contrast this case with *Salzhandler*, supra p. 1250. — Eds.]

[1] [Normally, union constitutions specifying a "right to counsel" also make professional attorneys and other outsiders ineligible to serve as counsel. See U.S. Bur. Lab. Stat., Dept. of Labor, Bull. No. 1350, Disciplinary Powers and Procedures in Union Constitutions 99 (1963). — Eds.]

that before any action is taken against him he must be informed of the charges and be given an opportunity to hear them and refute them.

Smith v. General Truck Drivers Union [181 F. Supp. 14, 17 (S.D. Cal. 1960)].

The legislative scheme for the protection of rights of individual members of labor unions clearly contemplates, at least in the first instance, a "within the family" procedure for resolving intraunion conflicts. So long as both the accuser and the accused are placed on a "roughly equal footing" . . . and are bound by the same restriction, the accused has no cause for complaint in the fact that he is limited to being represented at the trial by a member of the United Brotherhood family. Denial of assistance of counsel is of even less significance as it bears upon the requirement of "fair hearing" where, as here, the trial body is made up of union members who in all likelihood, will not be "learned in the law."

Plaintiff's other point, that a fair hearing was impossible because his accusers were persons of influence within the union is equally devoid of merit. There is nothing in either the LMRDA or in the union Constitution which evidences an intent to disqualify union officials from exercising the rights of membership, including the right to prefer charges against other members. Indeed, common sense and logic would dictate that union officials, who are vested by their fellow members with the responsibility for the proper administration of union affairs and enforcement of duly adopted rules and regulations, have such power. The only restriction which appears in the trial procedure set forth in the union Constitution is that one who is a party to or directly interested in any case, whether he be an officer or a member, is disqualified from serving as a member of the Trial Committee before which the case is to be heard. Such restriction . . . is essential to a fair hearing. . . . [T]hat plaintiff's accusers were business agents cannot, without more, constitute deprivation of the full and fair hearing to which he was entitled. . . .

NOTES

1. Judicial concern over the composition of union disciplinary tribunals has been reflected in cases invalidating discipline on the ground that members of such tribunals have prejudged the issues or have participated in prior proceedings. See, e.g., Cefalo v. Moffett, 333 F. Supp. 1283 (D.C. 1971), *relief modified*, 449 F.2d 1193 (D.C. Cir. 1971); Rosario v. Amalgamated Ladies' Garment Cutters' Union, Local 10, 605 F.2d 1228 (2d Cir.

1979), *cert. denied*, 446 U.S. 919 (1980) (improper under §101(a)(5)(C) for disciplinary charges to be retried, after remand, by previous hearing tribunal; the union appellate tribunal, although rejecting a claim that the principal accuser had participated in the trial body's deliberations, had vacated the convictions "to avoid any appearance of impropriety"). A governmental agency is not disqualified from rehearing charges after initial findings of misconduct are vacated. What characteristics of intraunion adjudication would you expect to enter into *Rosario's* barring such rehearings by a union tribunal? Section 101(a)(5) has also been invoked to support claims of the accused in union disciplinary proceedings that he is entitled to make a record of the proceedings when the union does not. Should such a claim be upheld even though bargaining over contract terms or grievance discussions is usually not recorded?

2. Members of the trial board, although not directly interested in the outcome of a disciplinary proceeding, may believe that officers with power over their economic lives may be vitally interested in the result. Is a "fair trial" likely in such circumstances? Cf. Curtis v. Stage Employees, Local 125, 687 F.2d 1024 (7th Cir. 1982).

3. Appeal to the membership assembled in convention has been criticized as resembling the "people's courts" of Soviet governments and as ignoring the lessons of history that independent courts are essential to protect individual rights against popular majorities as well as against the legislature and the executive. See Christensen, Union Discipline Under Federal Law: Institutional Dilemmas in an Industrial Democracy, 43 N.Y.U.L. Rev. 227, 249 (1968).

4. Some unions, notably the UAW, have established "public review boards," composed of outsiders, such as university personnel, arbitrators, and clergymen, to serve as a final appeal body with respect to union disciplinary decisions. See Oberer (the first Director of the UAW Board), Voluntary Impartial Review of Labor: Some Reflections, 58 Mich. L. Rev. 55 (1959); Brooks, Impartial Public Review of Internal Union Disputes: Experiment in Democratic Self-Discipline, 22 Ohio St. L.J. 64 (1961); Klein, Linn, Feller (separate articles), Public Review Boards, in Arbitration — 1974, Proc., 27th Ann. Meeting, Natl. Acad. of Arb. 189-235 (1975).

International Bhd. of Boilermakers v. Hardeman
401 U.S. 233 (1971)

BRENNAN, J. . . . Respondent . . . brought this action under §102 [LMRDA] in [federal] District Court . . . , [alleging] that in expelling him [from membership] the petitioner [union] violated §101(a)(5). . . . A jury awarded respondent damages of $152,150. The [Fifth Circuit] affirmed. 420 F.2d 485 (1969). We granted certiorari limited to the questions whether the subject matter of the suit was preempted because exclusively within the competence of the [NLRB] and, if not preempted, whether the courts below had applied the proper standard of review to the union proceedings. . . . We reverse.

. . . Respondent, George Hardeman, is a boilermaker. He was [in October 1960] a member of petitioner's Local Lodge 112. On October 3, he went to the union hiring hall to see Herman Wise, business manager of the Local Lodge and the official responsible for referring workmen for jobs. Hardeman had talked to a friend of his, an employer who had promised to ask for him by name for a job in the vicinity. He sought assurance from Wise that he would be referred for the job. When Wise refused to make a definite commitment, Hardeman threatened violence if no work was forthcoming in the next few days.

On October 4, Hardeman returned to the hiring hall and waited for a referral. None was forthcoming. The next day, in his words, he "went to the hall . . . and waited from the time the hall opened until we had the trouble. . . ." When Wise came out of his office to go to a local jobsite, . . . Hardeman handed him a copy of a telegram asking for Hardeman by name. As Wise was reading the telegram, Hardeman began punching him in the face.

Hardeman was tried for this conduct on charges of creating dissension and working against the interest and harmony of the Local Lodge, and threatening and using force to restrain an officer of the Local Lodge from properly discharging the duties of his office. The trial committee found him "guilty as charged," and the Local Lodge sustained the finding and voted his expulsion for an indefinite period. International union review of this action, instituted by Hardeman, modified neither the verdict nor the penalty. Five years later, Hardeman brought this suit alleging that petitioner violated §101(a)(5) by denying him a full and fair hearing in the union disciplinary proceedings.

I

We consider first the union's claim that the subject matter of this lawsuit is, in the first instance, within the exclusive competence of the [NLRB]. . . . [T]he critical question . . . is whether Hardeman was afforded the rights guaranteed him by §101(a)(5) of the LMRDA. If he was denied them, Congress has said that he is entitled to damages for the consequences of that denial. Since these questions are irrelevant to the legality of conduct under the [NLRA], there is no danger of conflicting interpretation of its provisions. And since the law applied is federal law explicitly made applicable to such circumstances by Congress, there is no danger that state law may come in through the back door to regulate conduct that has been removed by Congress from state control. Accordingly, this action was within the competence of the District Court.

II

. . . [Hardeman] was charged with violation of Art. XIII, §1, of the Subordinate Lodge Constitution, which forbids attempting to create dissension or working against the interest and harmony of the union, and carries a penalty of expulsion. He was also charged with violation of Art. XII, §1, of the Subordinate Lodge By-Laws, which forbids the threat or use of force against any officer of the union in order to prevent him from properly discharging the duties of his office; violation may be punished "as warranted by the offense." Hardeman's conviction on both charges was upheld in internal union procedures for review.

The trial judge instructed the jury that "whether or not he [respondent] was rightfully or wrongfully discharged or expelled is a pure question of law for me to determine." He assumed, but did not decide, that the transcript of the union disciplinary hearing contained evidence adequate to support conviction of violating Art. XII. He held, however, that there was no evidence at all in the transcript of the union disciplinary proceedings to support the charge of violating Art. XIII. This holding appears to have been based on the Fifth Circuit's decision in Boilermakers v. Braswell, 388 F.2d 193 (CA 5th Cir. 1968). There the Court of Appeals for the Fifth Circuit had reasoned that "penal provisions in union constitutions must be strictly construed," and that as so construed Art. XIII was directed only to "threats to the union as an organization and to the effective carrying out of the union's aims," not to merely personal altercations. 388 F.2d, at 199. Since the union tribunal had returned only a general verdict, and since one of the charges was thought to be supported by no evidence whatsoever, the trial judge held that Hardeman had been deprived of the full and fair hearing guaranteed by §101(a)(5). The Court of Appeals affirmed, simply citing Braswell. . . .

We find nothing in either the language or the legislative history of §101(a)(5) that could justify such a substitution of judicial for union authority to interpret the union's regulations in order to determine the scope of offenses warranting discipline of union members. Section 101(a)(5) began life as a floor amendment to S. 1555, the Kennedy-Ervin Bill, in the 86th Congress. As proposed by Senator McClellan, and as adopted by the Senate on April 22, 1959, the amendment would have forbidden discipline of union members "except for breach of a published written rule of [the union]." 105 Cong. Rec. 6492-6493. But this language did not long survive. Two days later, a substitute amendment was offered by Senator Kuchel, who explained that further study of the McClellan amendment had raised "some rather vexing questions." Id., at 6720. The Kuchel substitute, adopted the following day, deleted the requirement that charges be based upon a previously published, written union rule; it transformed Senator McClellan's amendment, in relevant part, into the present language of §101(a)(5). Id., at 6720, 6727. As so amended, S. 1555 passed the Senate on April 25. Id., at 6745. Identical language was adopted by the House, id., at 15884, 15891, and appears in the statute as finally enacted.

The Congress understood that Senator Kuchel's amendment was intended to make substantive changes in Senator McClellan's proposal. Senator Kennedy had specifically objected to the McClellan amendment because

> In the case of . . . the . . . official who bribed a judge, unless there were a specific prohibition against bribery of judicial officers written into the constitution of the union, then no union could take disciplinary action against [an] officer or member guilty of bribery. . . .
> . . . [W]e can trust union officers to run their affairs better than that.

Id., at 6491. Senator Kuchel described his substitute as merely providing "the usual reasonable constitutional basis" for union disciplinary proceedings: union members were to have "constitutionally reasonable notice and a reasonable hearing." Id., at 6720. After the Kuchel amendment passed the Senate, Senator Goldwater explained it to the House Committee on Labor and Education as follows:

> [T]he bill of rights in the Senate bill requires that the union member be served with written specific charges prior to any disciplinary proceedings but it does not require that these charges, to be valid, must be based on activity that the union had proscribed prior to the union member having engaged in such activity.

Labor-Management Reform Legislation, Hearings before a Joint Subcommittee of the House Committee on Education and Labor, 86th Cong., 1st Sess., pt. 4, p. 1595 (1959). And Senator McClellan's testimony was to the same effect. Id., pt. 5, pp. 2235-2236, 2251, 2285.

We think that this is sufficient to indicate that §101(a)(5) was not intended to authorize courts to determine the scope of offenses for which a union may discipline its members.[11] And if a union may discipline its

---

[11] State law, in many circumstances, may go further. See Summers, The Law of Union Discipline: What the Courts Do in Fact, 70 Yale L.J. 175 (1960). But Congress, which preserved state law remedies by §103 of the LMRDA was well aware that even the broad language of Senator McClellan's original proposal was more limited in scope than much state law. See 105 Cong. Rec. 6481-6489.

members for offenses not proscribed by written rules at all, it is surely a futile exercise for a court to construe the written rules in order to determine whether particular conduct falls within or without their scope.

Of course, §101(a)(5)(A) requires that a member subject to discipline be "served with written specific charges." These charges must be, in Senator McClellan's words, "specific enough to inform the accused member of the offense that he had allegedly committed." Where, as here, the union's charges make reference to specific written provisions, §101(a)(5)(A) obviously empowers the federal courts to examine those provisions and determine whether the union member had been misled or otherwise prejudiced in the presentation of his defense. But it gives courts no warrant to scrutinize the union regulations in order to determine whether particular conduct may be punished at all.

Respondent does not suggest, and cannot discern, any possibility of prejudice in the present case. Although the notice of charges with which he was served does not appear as such in the record, the transcript of the union hearing indicates that the notice did not confine itself to a mere statement of citation of the written regulations that Hardeman was said to have violated: the notice appears to have contained a detailed statement of the facts relating to the fight that formed the basis for the disciplinary action. Section 101(a)(5) requires no more.

III

There remains only the question whether the evidence in the union disciplinary proceedings was sufficient to support the finding of guilt. Section 101(a)(5)(C) of the LMRDA guarantees union members a "full and fair" disciplinary hearing, and the parties and the lower federal courts are in full agreement that this guarantee requires the charging party to provide some evidence at the disciplinary hearing to support the charges made. This is the proper standard of judicial review. We have repeatedly held that conviction on charges unsupported by any evidence is a denial of due process, Thompson v. Louisville, 362 U.S. 199, 206 (1960); . . . and . . . §101(a)(5)(C) may fairly be said to import a similar requirement into union disciplinary proceedings. Senator Kuchel, who first introduced the provision, characterized it on the Senate floor as requiring the "usual reasonable constitutional basis" for disciplinary action, 105 Cong. Rec. 6720, and any lesser standard would make useless §101(a)(5)(A)'s requirement of written specific charges. A stricter standard, on the other hand, would be inconsistent with the apparent congressional intent to allow unions to govern their own affairs, and would require courts to judge the credibility of witnesses on the basis of what would be at best a cold record.

Applying this standard to the present case, we think there is no question that the charges were adequately supported. Respondent was charged with having attacked Wise without warning, and with continuing to beat him for some time. Wise so testified at the disciplinary hearing, and his testimony was fully corroborated by one other witness to the altercation. Even Hardeman, although he claimed he was thereafter held and beaten, admitted having struck the first blow. . . . [T]here is no question but that the charges were supported by "some evidence."

Reversed.

[The concurring opinion of White, J., is omitted.]

DOUGLAS, J., dissenting. . . . Violation of Art. XIII of the constitution carries with it automatic expulsion. Violation of the bylaws would carry punishment "as warranted by the offense," which, I assume, would justify expulsion. For respondent to use force against Wise who was in charge of referral of men to jobs through the union hiring hall may well have been an attempt "to prevent him from properly discharging the duties of his office" within the meaning of Art. XII. But how an isolated fist fight could "create dissension" among union members or work against the union's interests in the other ways described in Art. XIII remains a mystery.

The finding of the union was the general one "guilty as charged." Under which provision — constitution or bylaw — it suspended him indefinitely is not made clear. Perhaps it was under only one or perhaps under both provisions.

In that posture the case is in the category of Stromberg v. California, 283 U.S. 359, where a conviction might have been valid under one charge but would have been invalid under the other; but the verdict being a general one, it was impossible to tell under which he was convicted. It is as much a denial of due process to sustain a conviction merely because a verdict of guilty *might* have been rendered on a valid ground as it is to send an accused to prison following conviction of a charge on which he was never tried. . . . Since the finding of "guilty as charged" had that infirmity, it could not stand; and the jury was justified in assessing damages for an unlawful expulsion.

NOTES

1. Does the limited judicial review prescribed by *Hardeman* give adequate weight to the limitations of union adjudicative machinery? Cf. NLRA §10(e).

2. Suppose that Hardeman had sued in state court, claiming a denial of "due process" in the lack of any evidence supporting the charge of violation of Art. XIII, §1 [re dissension] and invoking the argument voiced by the

dissent. Notwithstanding LMRDA §103, is there a plausible argument for preempting state jurisdiction over the claim?

C. LOCAL-INTERNATIONAL DISPUTES: TRUSTEESHIPS AND RELATED MATTERS[m]

United Bhd. of Carpenters v. Brown
343 F.2d 872 (10th Cir. 1965)

[Local 201 applied for the formation of a district council, to be composed of local unions located around Wichita, Kansas. Such a council was designed primarily to permit employees to work in the council area without paying a "service permit fee" that otherwise would be required, and to help provide personnel for area missile sites. Such a council would have substantially benefited the members of Local 201, because it was the biggest local in the area, but its territory included only three of the missile sites. After Local 201's members voted overwhelmingly for forming the council, it was established, with bylaws providing for a per capita tax of $4 as well as monthly dues of $8 per member, an increase of $2.20. The dues increase, following a vote in its favor, was defeated in two separate votes. Furthermore, Local 201's members also voted in favor of disaffiliating from the district council. The General President of the United Brotherhood, pursuant to his authority under the union constitution, ordered affiliation of Local 201 with the council and the increase in the local's dues. Upon the local's noncompliance, the international's executive board, after a hearing, recommended that (1) Local 201 "be placed under the complete supervision" of the General Office; (2) the supervisor should replace all the local's officers; and (3) the president's directive be obeyed. One Mack, appointed as trustee, took the foregoing actions and also negotiated a new collective agreement. Following related state court litigation, a federal district court held that the trusteeship was invalid and should be revoked and that the dues increase, not having been decided by secret ballot, was unlawful.]

HILL, J. . . . . Appellants contend that the judgment must be reversed and the action dismissed because plaintiffs have not exhausted the administrative remedy available to them under [§304(a)]. . . . The argument is that plaintiffs were required to first file a complaint with the Secretary of Labor in accordance with §304(a) and exhaust that remedy before proceeding in court with this lawsuit. There is authority to support that argument.

---

[m]See LMRDA, Title III, §§301-306.

E.g., Cox v. Hutcheson, 204 F. Supp. 442 (S.D. Ind. 1962). But, there is also authority supporting the view that a local union member need not exhaust the administrative remedy provided in §304(a) before bringing suit . . . under that section. Executive Board, Local Union No. 28, IBEW v. International Brotherhood of Electrical Workers, 184 F. Supp. 649 (D. Md. 1960). We believe the latter view is the better rule for the reasons set forth in Judge Watkins' excellent analysis . . . in [*Executive Board*, 184 F. Supp., at 655-659]. We . . . accordingly hold that appellants were not required to exhaust the administrative remedy provided in §304(a) before instituting this action. . . .

Appellants also contend that the judgment must be reversed and the action dismissed for the reason that the plaintiffs have failed to exhaust the internal remedies afforded by United Brotherhood's Constitution and Laws as required by §101(a)(4). . . . We do not agree. Section 101(a)(4) is applicable only where individual violations of the so-called Bill of Rights provisions are alleged and does not apply where, as here, the validity of a trusteeship is being challenged. . . . In any event, the requirement that internal remedies be exhausted is subject to certain exceptions that are applicable here. E.g., Calagaz v. Calhoon, 5 Cir., 309 F.2d 248; Harris v. International Longshoremen's Association, Local 1291, 3 Cir., 321 F.2d 801; Libutti v. Di Brizzi, 2 Cir., 337 F.2d 216.

The basic issue . . . is, of course, the validity of the trusteeship imposed upon Local 201 by United Brotherhood. . . . [Section 302] provides that a trusteeship may be established and administered by a labor organization over its subordinate body ". . . only in accordance with the constitution and bylaws of the organization which has assumed trusteeship. . . ." The statute is mandatory . . . and has . . . removed whatever inherent power an international union had prior to its enactment to impose such a trusteeship. Unless the constitution and bylaws of the parent organization make provision therefor, such organization has no power to establish a trusteeship over a subordinate body. . . . [No specific provision of the constitution and bylaws of United Brotherhood authorizes] it to impose a trusteeship on any of its subordinate local unions.

It is suggested, however, that United Brotherhood's power to impose the trusteeship in question may be derived from the general authority granted to it in sections 6B[10] and 6D[11] of its Constitution and Laws, as implemented

---

[10] "The right is reserved to the United Brotherhood through the International Body to regulate and determine all matters pertaining to the various branches and subdivisions of the trade."

[11] "The right is reserved to establish jurisdiction over any Local or Auxiliary Unions, District, State or Provincial Councils whose affairs are conducted in such a manner as to be detrimental to the welfare of the members and to the best interests of the International Body."

by the provision in section 10K, which empowers the General Executive Board ". . . to take such action as is necessary and proper for the welfare . . ." of the national union. Appellant's argument is that while its constitution and laws do not specifically grant it the authority to impose trusteeships, such authority may be implied from sections, 6B, 6D and 10K and that implied authority is sufficient. We do not agree. The legislative history of §302 . . . clearly discloses [Congress'] intent . . . ". . . that there should be a 'limitation on the right of internationals to place local unions in trusteeship'" and one of those limitations was that ". . . the trusteeship must conform to the constitution and bylaws of the labor organization." 2 U.S. Code Cong. & Adm. News, 86th Cong., 1st Sess., 1959, pp. 2333-2334. Obviously, a trusteeship cannot conform to the constitution and bylaws of a labor organization where, as here, the constitution and bylaws make no provision for trusteeships. We think the statute not only contemplates, but requires, more than some vague general reference to the effect that the parent organization shall have power to take such action as is necessary and proper for its welfare. It requires at the very least that the organization's constitution and bylaws set forth the circumstances under which a trusteeship may be established over its local unions and the matter or procedure in which it is to be imposed. . . .

A second limitation upon the imposition of trusteeships is that under §302 it must be for one of the following purposes: (1) To correct corruption or financial malpractice; (2) to assure the performance of collective bargaining agreements or other duties of a bargaining representative; or (3) to restore democratic procedures, or otherwise carry out the legitimate objects of the labor organization. Congress recognized that the use of trusteeships by an international union is a particularly effective device for the maintenance of order within the organization and that ". . . they have been widely used to prevent corruption, mismanagement of union funds, violation of collective bargaining agreements, infiltration of Communists; in short, to preserve the integrity and stability of the organization itself. . . ." But, Congress also recognized that ". . . in some instances trusteeships have been used as a means of consolidating the power of corrupt union officers, plundering and dissipating the resources of local unions, and preventing the growth of competing political elements within the organization." 2 U.S. Code Cong. & Adm. News, 86th Cong., 1st Sess., 1959, p. 2333. To preserve the legitimate use of trusteeships, Congress in enacting §302 enumerated the purposes for which a trusteeship could be imposed in a language of a broad and general nature. However, in order to prevent their misuse, Congress obviously intended those purposes to have limitations as well and therefore in determining whether a particular case meets the test, the statute must be construed in the light of the various other provisions of the Act.

The purpose of the Act as a whole is not only to stop and prevent outrageous conduct by thugs and gangsters but also to stop lesser forms of objectionable conduct by those in positions of trust and to protect democratic processes within union organizations. [LMRDA §1.] To accomplish that purpose, a "Bill of Rights of Members of Labor Organizations" was incorporated into the Act. . . . Thus, the rights of individual members of a labor union are protected by federal statute with a view to allowing those members to conduct local matters with a minimum of outside interference. . . .

. . . The trial court found, and the evidence confirms, that United Brotherhood established the trusteeship over Local 201 because it would not affiliate with the District Council and would not raise its dues. The court also found, and the evidence shows, that it was not imposed because of "dissension" within the local union. The result is that the trusteeship was established for the purposes of affiliating Local 201 with the District Council and raising the dues of its membership. In determining whether these are proper purposes under §302, we must remember that a majority of the local membership consistently voted against having anything to do with the District Council and on at least two occasions, by secret ballot, voted against the proposal to raise the monthly dues. We must also remember that [LMRDA §101 was] designed to afford them protection in that respect. Under these circumstances, we have no hesitancy in holding that the purposes for which this trusteeship was imposed do not fall within any of the categories set forth in §302. Beyond question, they do not come under the category of correcting corruption or financial malpractice and have nothing whatever to do with collective bargaining. It is also clear to us that the specified purposes are not within the category of restoring democratic processes or otherwise carrying out the legitimate objects of United Brotherhood. To the contrary, the imposition of the trusteeship in question could have no other effect than to stifle democratic processes by, in effect, voiding the results of the properly conducted elections on the issues involved. If we were to hold that the asserted purposes were proper, this court would be placed in the position of allowing a national union to establish a trusteeship over a local union because the members of the local union insisted upon exercising a right granted them by statute. This would in effect nullify and frustrate not only the plain purpose but the express terms of the Act.

It is true that there is a presumption as to the validity of a trusteeship for a period of eighteen months from the date of its establishment. [§304(c).] But, it is quite clear from the statute itself and from the legislative history that Congress intended for the presumption of validity to be available only where the trusteeship has been established ". . . in conformity with the procedural requirements of its [the labor organization's] constitution and bylaws and authorized or ratified after a fair hearing either before the executive board or before such other body as may be provided in accordance with its constitution or bylaws. . . ." [LMRDA §304(c)]. . . . Since the trusteeship in this case was not established in conformity with the constitution and bylaws, the presumption is not available to appellants.

We conclude that the trusteeship in question is invalid under the provisions of §302 . . . for two distinct and separate reasons.

[Here the court dealt with the effect of the prior state judgment, and distinguished between a "per capita tax" imposed on a local and "dues" covered by LMRDA §101(a)(3). It affirmed the judgment below invalidating the trusteeship but reversed, insofar as that judgment ordered the international to reimburse the local for payments made by the temporary officers; the state court had upheld those payments and its decision was res judicata in this proceeding.]

NOTES

1. Contrast the restrictiveness of the principal case with customary methods of interpretation that derive implied obligations and powers from collective bargaining agreements, legislative enactments, and federal and state constitutions. What justification, if any, is there for the greater restrictiveness of the principal case? Is that approach unduly inflexible? Cf. International Bhd. of Electrical Wkrs., Local 1186 v. Eli, 307 F. Supp. 495, 503-504 (D. Hawaii 1969).

2. An international union may take various steps that may restrict a local's autonomy or destroy it completely. The applicability of Title III to such steps turns on the content of "trusteeship," as defined in LMRDA §3(h). In light of that definition, consider under what circumstances the following acts would constitute the imposition of a "trusteeship":

(a) The international revokes the charter of a local for engaging in an economic strike forbidden by the international and charters a new local with jurisdiction embracing that of the "revoked" local. See the long and interesting saga reported in Parks v. IBEW, 314 F.2d 886 (4th Cir. 1963), cert. denied, 372 U.S. 976 (1963), and compare Local 2 v. International Bhd. of Telephone Workers, 261 F. Supp. 433 (D. Mass. 1966).

(b) An international directs the merger of one local with a considerably larger one. Cf. Brewery Bottlers Local 1345 v. International Bhd. of Teamsters, 202 F. Supp. 464 (E.D.N.Y. 1962); see also Musicians Local 10 v. American Federation of Musicians, 57 L.R.R.M. 2227 (N.D. Ill. 1964), upholding a trusteeship imposed in order to merge two racially segregated locals pursuant to a merger plan providing that during a transitional period specified officers should be elected by members formerly belonging to the smaller black local; cf. Daye v. Tobacco Workers Union, 234 F. Supp. 815 (D.D.C. 1964).

For a discussion of the applicability of Title III to the foregoing situations, see Beaird, Union Trusteeship Provisions of the [LMRDA] of 1959, 2 Ga. L. Rev. 469, 502-510 (1968). See generally, Anderson, Landrum-Griffin and the Trusteeship Imbroglio, 71 Yale L.J. 1460 (1962). Whether a merger or charter revocation also constitutes "discipline," triggering §101(a)(5), Title I, turns on whether members' rights to jobs, pensions, and other benefits are substantially protected. See Local 37 v. Sheet Metal Wkrs., 107 L.R.R.M. 3288 (8th Cir. 1981).

3. In Local 13410 v. Mine Workers, 475 F.2d 906 (D.C. Cir. 1973), the court referred to statements of legislative committees indicating that at common law a trusteeship was ordinarily invalid unless the subordinate body had been granted a fair hearing. The court emphasized that prior protections should not be diminished and that a hearing should be afforded before a trusteeship is imposed, except when the parent union reasonably believes that an emergency forecloses such a hearing. See Note, A Fair Hearing Requirement for Union Trusteeships Under the LMRDA, 40 U. Chi. L. Rev. 873 (1973).

4. Section 301 of the LMRA has served as a source of jurisdiction over (a) actions in which a local or a subordinate unit of an international claims that the international's action violates the union constitution (see Plumbers & Pipefitters v. Plumbers & Pipefitters, 452 U.S. 615 (1981)), and (b) over actions in which an international seeks injunctive relief to enforce a trusteeship compatible with Title III. See Brotherhood of Painters v. Brotherhood of Painters, Local 127, 264 F. Supp. 301 (N.D. Cal. 1966); Natl. Assn. of Letter Carriers v. Sombrolto, 449 F.2d 915 (2d Cir. 1971) (injunction will lie to enforce a trusteeship on a local about to violate both a no-strike pledge and the federal law against strikes by federal employees even if Norris-La-Guardia Act is assumed to be applicable to labor disputes involving postal employees).

Does it make any difference with respect to the force to be given to state law whether jurisdiction is based on §301, as distinguished from Title III of the LMRDA?

D.   FISCAL AND FIDUCIARY RESPONSIBILITY

In addition to disclosing corruption in some unions, the McClellan Committee reported the subversion of employee self-determination and independent collective bargaining through organization of, and secret payments to, "spontaneous" antiunion committees composed of employees; the replacement of militant unions by friendly ones; sweetheart contracts; and similar abuses by employers and labor relations consultants. See Select Comm. on Improper Activities in the Labor or Management Field, Interim Report, S. Rep. No. 1417, 85th Cong., 2d Sess. (1958).

The protection of dissent and of union elections provided by the LMRDA might indirectly curb such abuses on the part of union officials by encouraging exposure of misconduct and discipline or electoral defeat of offenders. The statute also mounted a more direct attack by means of the following interrelated measures: (1) provisions in Title V making certain financial malpractices federal criminal offenses (see §§501(c) and 503) and barring certain ex-convicts and Communists from holding office (see §504);[n] (2) reporting and disclosure requirements applicable to unions, their officers, and employers (see Title II); (3) the imposition of a general fiduciary obligation on union officials, enforceable under certain circumstances by a union member in the federal courts (see §501); (4) amendments to §302 of the LMRA; and (5) compulsory bonding of union personnel handling union finances and property. See §502.[o]

1. Reporting Requirements

Sections 203(b), 203(c), and 204(f) present a complex problem regarding the scope of the reporting requirement, a problem which is of particular interest to management lawyers and "labor relations counselors." With respect to lawyers, additional complications arise from §204, which, in general, exempts from disclosure information communicated to lawyers that is covered by the lawyer-client privilege.

Section 203(b) requires monthly and annual reports from "every person" who agrees with an employer "directly or indirectly (1) to persuade employees concerning their right to organize and to bargain collectively," or (2) to inform the employer of certain employee or union activities. Section

---

[n] In United States v. Brown, 381 U.S. 437 (1965), the Court (5 to 4) invalidated that section as a bill of attainder when applied to members of the Communist Party. As the dissenters observed, the Court did not attempt to distinguish laws barring felons from certain occupations "but would apparently save them." 381 U.S. at 469. Cf. De Veau v. Braisted, 363 U.S. 144 (1960), upholding a state statute (implementing an interstate compact) that in effect barred felons from holding union office.

[o] In 1965, §502 was amended to permit the use of a standard "honesty" bond rather than the more expensive "faithful performance bond," and to enlarge the number of eligible surety companies. Pub. L. No. 89-216, 79 Stat. 888, amending 29 U.S.C. §502.

203(c) provides, however, that "nothing in [§203] shall be construed to require any employer or other person to file a report covering the services of such person by reason of his giving or agreeing to give advice to such employer. . . ." Neither the language nor the legislative history of §203 discloses the impact of the exemption for advice on §203(b)'s reporting requirement.

The following situation illustrates the resultant interpretive problems. During an organizing campaign at A's plant, his lawyer (L) speaks to a captive audience of A's employees regarding their rights and vulnerability to replacement under the NLRA. Such speeches generally constitute "persuader" activity. L also gives A advice on his legal rights and obligations. In addition, L has been retained as a legal advisor by companies B, C, D, etc.; during the reporting period L has given them only advice of the kind generally exempted from disclosure by §203(c). The question is, however, whether L, because of his persuader activities for A, must report on his arrangements for giving advice to A and, more importantly, report on his arrangements regarding advice to B, C, D, regardless of their knowledge of L's persuader activities on behalf of A.

Courts have disagreed over the correctness of the Secretary of Labor's position, i.e., that L's persuader activities on behalf of Client A require L to report on his purely advisory arrangements for his other clients. See Donovan v. Master Printers Assn., 532 F. Supp. 1140 (N.D. Ill. 1981), aff'd, Master Printers Assn. v. Donovan, 699 F.2d 370 (7th Cir. 1983). How should that question be resolved? For arguments supporting the Secretary's position, see Beaird, Reporting Requirements for Employers and Labor Relations Consultants in the [LMRDA], 53 Geo. L.J. 267 (1965); but see Note, Two Views of a Labor Relations Consultant's Duty to Report under [§203, LMRDA], 65 Mich. L. Rev. 752 (1967).

Persuader activities by lawyers may also raise ethical problems. Thus the American Bar Association's Code of Professional Responsibility and Code of Judicial Conduct (1975), DR 7-104, provides:

Communicating With One of Adverse Interest

(A) During the course of his representation of a client a lawyer shall not:

    (1) Communicate or cause another to communicate on the subject of the representation with a party he knows to be represented by a lawyer in that matter unless he has the prior consent of the lawyer representing such other party or is authorized by law to do so.

    (2) Give advice to a person who is not represented by a lawyer, other than the advice to secure counsel, if the interests of such

person are or have a reasonable possibility of being in conflict
with the interests of his client.

Would DR 7-104 prohibit a lawyer, representing a company, from advising
its employees during an organizing campaign of the employer's rights under
§8(a)(5), his right to replace strikers, and to close down?

The disclosure requirements of Title II were apparently modeled on
the Securities Act of 1933. There are, however, reasons to question that
analogy. When the Securities and Exchange Commission has serious questions regarding the accuracy or adequacy of disclosure in a registration
statement, it can issue a stop order, which, for practical purposes, will prevent
the marketing of securities until the deficiencies are corrected. There is no
equally effective and prompt sanction under the LMRDA. Furthermore, the
larger volume of reports under the LMRDA will impose considerably larger
burdens on enforcement machinery. Despite the Secretary's authority under
§601, his investigative zeal may be diluted by his traditional role as the
representative of "labor," his occasional role as a super-mediator in collective bargaining, and his reluctance to intervene in factional disputes. In any
event, the disclosure requirements imposed by §§9(f) and (g) of the LMRA
(now repealed) produced a warehouse of unexamined reports and a dearth of
criminal prosecutions, which was striking in view of the abuses uncovered by
the McClellan Committee. Furthermore, commentators have generally
concluded that the disclosure requirements of Title II, although prompting
unions to keep more accurate and detailed records, have not significantly
affected unions' fiscal and auditing practices. See Bellace, at 95.

Supplementing the disclosure requirements is the investigative power
conferred on the Secretary of Labor by §601 of the LMRDA. See Marshall v.
Stevens People and Friends for Freedom, 669 F.2d 171 (4th Cir. 1981),
cert. denied sub nom. Ramsey v. Donovan, 455 U.S. 940 (1982), where the
court enforced a subpoena that called for production of (a) the names of
contributors to organizations opposed to unionization of J.P. Stevens Co.
and (b) the organizations' business and financial records. But the court,
relying on LMRDA §603(b), denied enforcement with respect to disclosure
of the names of nonsupervisory employees associated with, or contributing
to, such organizations.

A limited power to investigate is also granted to union members by
LMRDA §201(c), which entitles them "for just cause to examine any books,
records, and accounts necessary to verify" reports required of labor organizations by Title II of the Act. Similar rights existed at common law. See, e.g.,
Mooney v. Local 284, Bartenders Union, 48 Cal. 2d 841, 313 P.2d 857
(1957) (by analogy to shareholder's right to inspect corporate books for

"proper purpose," union member requesting accounting of expenses and income — after union had unexplained operating deficit for several months — entitled to inspect books without exhausting internal remedies). Regarding survival of common law rights, see LMRDA §§603(a), 205, and 201(c). For an exploration of problems arising under §201(c), see Fruit and Vegetable Packers and Warehousemen Local 760 v. Morley, 378 F.2d 738 (9th Cir. 1967); Landry v. Sabine Independent Seamen's Assn., 623 F.2d 347 (5th Cir. 1980). Insurgents, through §201(c), may secure information useful in criticizing and challenging incumbents. Furthermore, rival unions, reform groups, and employers may, through §205(a), secure similarly useful information through the reports that Title II requires unions to file annually with the Department of Labor. See D. McLaughlin & A. Schoomaker, The Landrum-Griffin Act and Union Democracy 162 (1979).

2. Fiduciary Obligations

Highway Truck Drivers & Helpers, Local 107 v. Cohen
182 F. Supp. 608 (E.D. Pa. 1960), *aff'd*, 284 F.2d 162
(3d Cir. 1960), *cert. denied*, 365 U.S. 833 (1961)

CLARY, J. . . . . [The LMRDA imposes a fiduciary responsibility on officers of a labor organization (§501(a)) and provides for enforcement by a suit in a federal district court (§501(b)).] The present [private] suit has been brought under §501(b) to enforce certain of these duties.

The moving parties are nine rank-and-file members of Highway Truck Drivers and Helpers, Local 107 [*Teamsters*], . . . who were given leave by this Court on November 12, 1959 to file a complaint against the defendants, the governing officers of Local 107. The complaint charged the defendants with a continuing mass conspiracy to cheat and defraud the union of large sums of money — the conspiracy alleged to have begun in 1954 and continued to the present time.

The defendants have yet to answer these very serious charges. Having been unsuccessful in first opposing the plaintiffs' petition for leave of this Court to sue, defendants now move to have the complaint dismissed. They are supported in this motion by counsel for Local 107, which has been allowed to intervene as a party defendant. This motion to dismiss is presently before the Court along with the plaintiffs' prayer for a preliminary injunction to prohibit the defendants from using union funds to defray the legal costs and other expenses being incurred by the defendants (and several other members of Local 107) in the defense of civil and criminal actions brought against them in the Courts of Pennsylvania and also the present suit in our own Court. The charges in these cases, in essence, grow out of the alleged activities of the defendants complained of here. The question of the preliminary injunction will be taken up after we resolve the motion to dismiss the complaint. . . .

The defendants' contention that those alleged wrongs which occurred *prior* to the enactment of §501 can not alone constitute a basis for recovery under that section, must be accepted. . . . [T]he principle that a statute which creates a new substantive right or duty will not, in the absence of clear legislative intent to the contrary, be construed to apply retrospectively, is too well established to admit of argument.

. . . [A]lthough the duties alleged to have been breached here have long been encompassed within the moral law, and presumably within the common law of the various states (although we would be hard pressed to substantiate this with case law in the labor field), these duties are new to *federal law*, on which the jurisdiction . . . of this Court to act is based. . . .

[The plaintiffs, urging that a federal remedy for misconduct antedating the LMRDA was warranted by the doctrine of the *Steele* case, supra p. 1127, and by the due process clause, had stressed that most of the local's agreements provided for a union shop and that, accordingly, the members had a federally protected right to have dues money used to advance proper union objectives and not for purely private gain. After rejecting those contentions, the court declared:]

Happily we need not base our opinion solely upon constitutional grounds. There is a more obvious reason why the plaintiffs' theory is of no avail here. The rights which §8(a)(3) of the Taft-Hartley Act confer, as well as the corresponding duties imposed by it . . . are rights and duties conferred upon the collective bargaining unit, i.e., *the union*. They are not conferred upon the individual officers of that union. Therefore, the plaintiffs really must argue that a federal law which confers numerous rights upon a *union*, must necessarily impose strict duty upon its *individual officers* not to spend the union's money for noncollective bargaining purposes. This does not follow. The language in the opinions relied upon by the plaintiffs speak in terms of the "duty of the union." Yet the whole tenor of the plaintiffs' complaint makes it evident that this suit is against the individual officers of Local 107 and not against the union. In their brief in opposition to Local 107's motion to intervene, the plaintiffs specifically state that "The Union itself . . . has no standing as a party litigant" since the plaintiffs appear as trustees ad litem for the union.

Nor do we view this as a mere technicality which has been corrected by the Court's Order allowing the union to intervene as a party defendant. It is evident that the plaintiffs' claim here is not against the union. The acts complained of were not acts of the union done on its behalf by an acting officer. If anything, they are acts done in flagrant breach of duty. If they were in fact done, they were done for the defendants own personal gain *at the expense of the union*. In such a suit against private individuals, the Taft-Hartley Act clearly does not confer federal jurisdiction. . . .

If the only matter before the Court were the motion to dismiss discussed above, the Court might be disposed to grant the motion. However, there is another facet to the case which prevents the dismissal of the action. That facet relates to the motion for a preliminary injunction to prohibit the defendants from using union funds to defray the expense of legal fees in civil and criminal actions which have been brought against them in the Courts of Pennsylvania as well as to defray legal costs of the present action. The charges in those cases, in essence, grow out of alleged misappropriation of funds by the officers, and the plaintiffs maintain that such expenditures are in violation of the fiduciary duties imposed upon officers of a labor union by §501(a) . . . , and that unless such expenditures are enjoined the union will suffer irreparable harm thereby. . . .

Shortly after the effective date of the Act and the institution of suits, criminal and civil, in the local Courts against the defendants, the union at a regular monthly meeting, with few dissenting votes, adopted a resolution authorizing the union to bear "Legal costs of such actions [against the officers] which are in reality not directed at our officers but are directed at us, the members of Local 107, our good contracts, our good wages and our good working conditions."

The question, therefore, which faces us is: Does the expenditure of union funds to pay for legal fees in the defense of both criminal and civil actions brought against the various defendant officers for an alleged conspiracy to cheat and defraud their union of large sums of money constitute a breach of that fiduciary duty imposed upon them by §501(a), notwithstanding the purported authorization of such expenditures by a resolution of the union membership passed at a regular union meeting?

At the hearing on the preliminary injunction, it was brought out that within the limit of some four or five weeks after the adoption of the resolution the union, pursuant to the resolution, paid upwards of $25,000 to the attorneys representing the defendants. It is also clear that counsel for the union has advised the officers that such expenditures are proper. We are, therefore, with the payment of those large sums of money already accomplished and threatened further payments about to occur, in a position factually to pass upon the merits of the plaintiffs' contention.[5] . . .

Section 501 . . . attempts to define in the broadest terms possible the duty which the new federal law imposes upon a union official. . . . It appears evident to us that [Congress] intended the federal courts to fashion a new federal labor law in this area, in much the same way that the federal courts have fashioned a new substantive law of collective bargaining contracts under §301(a) of the Taft-Hartley Act. . . . See Textile Workers Union of America v. Lincoln Mills, 1957, 353 U.S. 448. In undertaking this task the federal courts will necessarily rely heavily upon the common law of the various states. Where that law is lacking or where it in any way conflicts with the policy expressed in our national labor laws, the latter will of course be our guide. . . .

In determining whether or not the expenditures now sought to be enjoined violate the fiduciary responsibility of an officer of a labor organization we must necessarily determine the legal effect of the September 20th Resolution. . . .

The plaintiffs assert that the Resolution authorizing such expenditures is encompassed within the express prohibition of §501(a) against any "general exculpatory resolution." Although not expressly purporting to absolve the defendants of guilt, plaintiffs argue that the Resolution *in effect* does just this. Unfortunately the Act does not define the phrase "general exculpatory resolution."

The defendants take issue with the plaintiffs' interpretation. They maintain that the Resolution should be taken at face value, i.e., as a pledge of the union's faith in their officers and a pledge of financial aid to defend suits which are in reality directed at the union movement. . . .

A plain reading of the last sentence in §501(a) leads me to agree with the defendants, at least in their conclusion. On the other hand, it is not necessary for a resolution to read "The officers are hereby absolved of all responsibility created by the Act" before a court will strike it down as "exculpatory" under §501(a). Nor must a court accept at face value the stated purpose of a resolution when reason and common sense clearly dictate a different purpose. Nevertheless in my interpretation of §501(a), the Resolution under discussion is *not* one "purporting to relieve any [officer] of liability for breach of the duties declared by this section. . . ."

We must distinguish between a resolution which purports to *authorize*

---

[5] There has been no showing [by] the defendants that defendants . . . would be able to reimburse the union for funds expended in their behalf. . . . [I]n the circumstances the Court holds that a showing of irreparable harm (assuming the illegality of the payments) has been established.

action which is beyond the power of the union to do and for that reason in violation of §501(a) when done by an officer (such as the present Resolution) and a resolution which purports to *relieve* an officer of liability for breach of the duties declared in §501. At times this distinction may be a fine one. Very often the result will be the same. Nevertheless we feel that such a distinction should be made here unless the "exculpatory" provision is to be read as a mere "catch-all" phrase.

We turn then to the question of whether the September 20th Resolution is valid, i.e., conforms with the law of Pennsylvania and the Federal Labor laws. If it is inconsistent with either, we think it follows that the present expenditures by the defendants violate that provision in §501(a) which imposes upon them a strict duty to "expend [union funds] in accordance with its constitution and bylaws and any resolutions of the governing bodies adopted thereunder . . ."—since we read this sentence to authorize only those expenditures made pursuant to a *lawful* bylaw or resolution. . . .

[The court noted that the union's constitution did not specifically authorize the disputed expenditures.]

It is true that from the general objectives and purposes of a particular trade union, certain ancillary powers reasonably necessary for their attainment may be implied. In determining whether a particular act falls within this admittedly broad latitude of action, the Court must take into consideration all of the factors surrounding it, i.e., the stated purpose of the action, its immediate effect, its possible future benefit to the union, etc. This is necessary in order to determine whether the union, in light of the authority derived from its constitution, has a sufficient interest in the action to empower it to so act. If it has, a court of law will not interfere regardless of the wisdom or propriety of the act. If it has not, a court of law must intervene at the behest of a single union member. . . .

In [determining] whether a union has sufficient interest in criminal and civil suits brought against various officers for the theft of union funds, to spend large sums of its money on legal fees for those officers, the Court is admittedly without a Pennsylvania case directly on point. There are, however, two interesting English cases which . . . held that such expenditures were beyond the power of a union to make. Alfin v. Hewlett, 18 T.L.R. 664 [1902]; Orman v. Hutt, 1 Ch. 98 (1914) (c.a.). These cases are persuasive.

Furthermore we feel that those cases involving the use of corporate funds to pay for the defense of officers charged with misconduct in office are helpful. Although this question again has not been passed upon in Pennsylvania, several other jurisdictions when faced with the problem have concluded that such expenditures are improper. . . .

The only interest which Local 107 (as an organization dedicated to the objectives stated in its Constitution) would appear to have in the civil and criminal actions against these officers is an interest (1) in not losing the services of their officers (whom we must presume are competent) simply because someone wrongfully accuses them of misconduct, or (2) in not having men closely associated with their union (whose conduct somewhat reflects upon the union) convicted of serious wrongs when they are not in fact guilty of these wrongs, or (3) not having officers in their union accused of serious wrongs by antiunion people, simply because they are officers of a union.

Assume for a moment that one of these officers was accused of evasion of personal income taxes, would not Local 107 have exactly these same interests in the outcome of a suit? If in such a situation, a majority of the union were to pass a resolution affirming their confidence in that officer and asserting herein that the action by the United States was in reality an attempt "to break up and destroy our union [and therefore] be it resolved that Local 107 go on record to help our [officer] in every way possible in [this] court [matter] by having Local 107 bear the legal costs of such actions which [is] in reality not directed at our [officer], but [is] directed at us, the members of Local 107, our good contracts, our good wages, and our good working conditions," a proper court of law upon an objection by a union member would independently pass upon the power of Local 107 to spend its money, and even presuming the good faith of the membership in passing such a resolution, would properly enjoin the expenditure as outside the legitimate aims and purposes of Local 107 as expressed in its Constitution.

. . . [T]he Court feels that such expenditures to pay for the legal expenses incurred by the defendant officers in the criminal and civil suits brought against them individually are expenses to be borne by the officers themselves and are beyond the power of Local 107 to make. . . . [I]t follows that a mere majority vote at a regular union meeting can not authorize such expenditures. . . .

There is a further reason why the present Resolution is no defense here. Aside from its validity under Pennsylvania law, it is inconsistent with the aims and purposes of the [LMRDA] and violates the spirit of that Act. A stated purpose of the Act is "to *eliminate* . . . improper practices on the part of labor organizations . . . and their officers". (Emphasis added). To allow a union officer to use the power and wealth of the very union which he is accused of pilfering, to defend himself against such charges, is totally inconsistent with Congress's effort to eliminate the undesirable element which has been uncovered in the labor-management field. To allow even a majority of members in that union to authorize such action, when, if the charges made against these defendants are true, it is these very members whom the officers have deceived, would be equally inconsistent with the Act. If some of those members have not been deceived by the defendants, but because of the immediate gains in their income and working conditions which Local 107 has won for them, they are content to accept as officers anyone who produces immediate results, regardless of what other wrongs those officers may commit in so doing, this Court would still not feel constrained to bow to their will in the light of its duty both to those members of Local 107 who place honesty above material gain as well as to the millions of others in the labor movement whose cause would be seriously injured by such an attitude.

. . . [The defendants urge] that the plaintiffs are here asking us to do that which Congress specifically refused to do when it failed to adopt Subsection 107(b) of the original Senate version of the Labor Bill (The Kennedy-Ives Bill), which specifically prohibited "both unions and employers from directly or indirectly paying or advancing the costs of defense, of any of their officers . . . who [are] indicted for . . . any violation of any provision of the Bill." S. Rep. No. 187, 86th Cong., First Session, 1959, U.S. Code Cong. and Adm. News 1959, p. 2318.

. . . [T]here are reasons why we are not persuaded by their argument here.

First, the language contained in the Kennedy-Ives Bill is much broader than our holding in the present case. . . . That section quoted above would foreclose financial aid by the union to an officer in suits under the Act, under *any* circumstances. . . . That Congress refused to foreclose the right of a union under *any* circumstances to lend financial aid to an officer when sued under any section of the Kennedy-Ives Bill is not . . . a strong argument for the conclusion that under *no* circumstances could a union be prohibited from lending financial aid to an accused officer.

Second, in none of the cases cited by the defendants to support their argument as to the conclusion to be drawn from the omission of §107(b) were there two distinct bills involved. Here the Act finally passed by Congress (with modification) was the Landrum-Griffin House Bill and not the Kennedy-Ives Senate Bill. Strictly speaking, the Conference Committee did not amend the final Bill as to the provision in question, since it was never contained in it to begin with. Had the Kennedy-Ives Bill ultimately been adopted with §107(b) deleted, the defendants' argument would be more convincing.

Finally, even assuming that Congress intended to leave a union free to use its funds for the purpose of paying its officers legal expenses in actions brought against them under the new Act, if under the law of Pennsylvania, the state in which the union membership contractual relationship arose, such expenditures are illegal, a union officer could not consistent with his duty to the union (which duties ultimately flow from its Constitution) expend union funds for this purpose. This would follow unless we interpret the omission of this prohibition as creating an affirmative federal right in a union to so spend its funds, which right is intended to supersede any state law to the contrary. We flatly reject such an interpretation of the new Act. . . .

[After the principal case was returned to the district court for trial, the plaintiff sought recovery, on the union's behalf, of over $24,000 disbursed by the union for counsel fees incurred by the defendant-officers. Prior to a bench trial, conducted by Judge Body rather than Judge Clary, the international union had amended its constitution to authorize payment of all legal expenses incurred in defending officers of the international and local unions in criminal or civil proceedings if certain procedural requirements were met — as they were in this case. The court nevertheless required repayment of the $24,000 to the union, stating, 215 F. Supp. 938, at 940-941 (1963):]

Defendant urges that while the Local 107 resolution was ultra vires when these opinions were written, it has subsequently been validated by an amendment to the constitution of the international union. This view . . . completely disregards the statement in 284 F.2d at page 164 . . . that the resolution was "invalid because it authorized action beyond the powers of the union as derived from its constitution *and was inconsistent with the aims and purposes* of the [LMRDA]. . . ." (Emphasis supplied.) . . .

This clearly establishes the Act as the primary basis for prohibiting payment of defendants' attorney fees. Judge Clary was merely adding another string to his bow in holding the payments to be ultra vires. Assuming that string was broken by the constitutional amendment, without any doubt the Act itself is sufficient reason for requiring defendant to repay the money in question. . . .

. . . Defendants claim that any fees allocable to the criminal proceedings pending in Philadelphia are properly payable to defendants if they are exonerated, and that an order to repay now is premature. This position presupposes that a determination of exoneration is not only possible but that it is likely to occur, if at all, in the near future. We do not decide whether defendants may or can be exonerated, or whether exoneration authorizes the union to indemnify them. . . . The record shows nothing like exoneration to date. Defendants have been paid money, or received benefits, which they must return to the union. The money was improperly paid in the first instance. . . . Since the facts have not changed, there is no reason to delay repayment. Defendants should not be allowed to use union funds to assist them in their defense.

[This decision was affirmed, 334 F.2d 378 (3d Cir. 1964), *cert. denied,* 379 U.S. 921 (1964).]

NOTES

1. Plaintiff's counsel in the principal case, having secured an injunction against use of union funds for legal expenses and other purposes, filed a motion for counsel fees and expenses, pursuant to LMRDA §501(b). The court, in granting that motion, declared that Congress did not "intend this phrase to be narrowly construed to mean that a part of the money recovery effectuated and no other benefits conferred should be considered 'recovery.' . . . [O]therwise, what would be the inducement to the speedy prosecution of an action?" Although a little less than $25,000 had been recovered, the court allowed $38,000 in counsel fees. See Highway Truck Drivers & Helpers, Local 107 v. Cohen, 220 F. Supp. 735, 737 (E.D. Pa. 1963); Clark, The Fiduciary Duties of Union Officials under the LMRDA, 52 Minn. L. Rev. 437, 472-473 (1967) (questioning such liberality in awarding counsel fees).

2. Tucker v. Shaw, 378 F.2d 304 (2d Cir. 1967), raised the question of whether a union's regularly retained counsel could represent the union's officers in a suit brought against them under LMRDA, §501(a) and (b). The plaintiffs sought, among other relief, to recover, on behalf of the union, union funds allegedly diverted for the defendants' personal purposes. In barring the union's counsel from representing the officers, the court noted that the union's interest in the outcome of the litigation might well be adverse to that of the officers; that the attorney's familiarity with the facts involved in the litigation "might unfairly tip the scales against plaintiffs at the outset"; and that because of this familiarity with the facts, the attorney was a likely witness in the case. See also Yablonski v. UMW, 448 F.2d 1175 (D.C. Cir.), cert. denied, 406 U.S. 906 (1971); Weaver v. UMW, 492 F.2d 580 (D.C. Cir. 1973).

When independent counsel must be retained to represent the union's interest, who chooses such counsel?

Johnson v. Nelson, 325 F.2d 646 (8th Cir. 1963). The plaintiffs, after being disciplined by a local for activities protected by §101(a)(2) and (5) of the LMRDA, secured a revocation of that discipline pursuant to a binding settlement approved by a federal district court. Thereafter, the union filed new charges against the plaintiffs, which were dismissed by a Special Trial Board established pursuant to the judicially approved settlement. That board also recommended that the local pay the attorney fees and related expenses incurred by all parties in the union trials and the lawsuit; the local's membership approved that recommendation. The officers of the local refused, however, to pay the plaintiffs' legal fees incurred in the lawsuit, as distinguished from the union trials, and obtained the international's support of their refusal. After a fruitless request to the local's officers for the payment approved by the membership, the plaintiffs sued the local's president and treasurer under Title V, §501(a) and (b). In affirming the judgment that payment be made to the plaintiff, the court, relying on the legislative history, concluded that §501 should not be limited to responsibility for fiscal matters but should be liberally construed as encompassing all activities of union officials. The court, noting that the defendants had been motivated by personal animosity, concluded that under the circumstances, the international's directive had not been a justification, or even the reason, for the defendants' disregard of the resolution authorizing payment. A denial of recovery would, the court urged, discourage legal action to vindicate Title I rights.

NOTES

1. In *Johnson*, was the plaintiff suing "for the benefit of the labor organization," as those terms are used in §501(b)? Contrast with the expansive approach in that case Head v. Brotherhood of Ry. Clerks, 512 F.2d 398 (2d Cir. 1975); Agola v. Hagner, 556 F. Supp. 296 (E.D.N.Y. 1982).
2. Consider whether §501 should apply to alleged misconduct of the following kinds:
(a) Union officials generate liability for the union by a strike that flagrantly violates a no-strike pledge or the statutory proscription against secondary boycotts.
(b) Union officials enter into sweetheart contracts and are paid off by employers. (See Schonfeld v. Rarback, 61 L.R.R.M. 2043 (S.D.N.Y. 1965), with which cf. the view of the Second Circuit referred to in Note 1, supra; see also Echols v. Cook, 56 L.R.R.M. 3030 (N.D. Ga. 1962).
(c) Union officials, by massive mismanagement, bring about the actuarial insolvency of a union-established pension fund. Cf. Hood v. Journeymen Barbers, 454 F.2d 1347 (7th Cir. 1972).
3. See generally Determining Breach of Fiduciary Duty Under the LMRDA, 93 Harv. L. Rev. 608 (1980). See also Leslie, Federal Courts and Union Fiduciaries, 76 Colum. L. Rev. 1314 (1976).

3.   Labor Relations and Regulation of Employee Welfare and Pension Funds

Section 302 of the LMRA, an avowedly stop-gap measure, was designed to shield collective bargaining against bribery and extortion and to protect jointly-administered health and welfare funds against dissipation. Successive amendments to that section tightened proscriptions of bribery and extortion and expanded the purposes permissible for funds to which employers made payments and in whose administration unions shared.

Section 302 was also supplemented by the Welfare and Disclosure Act of 1958, which operated without regard to whether employee benefit plans resulted from collective bargaining. That Act—a weak disclosure measure—was expected to facilitate policing by private litigation; 1962 amendments added, inter alia, criminal penalties for gross abuses, such as embezzlement and kickbacks.

Several other federal statutes also have had a limited impact on health and welfare funds. LMRDA §501 has served as the basis for federal enforcement of fiduciary obligations of union trustees of health and welfare funds. See Hood v. Journeymen Barbers, 454 F.2d 1347 (7th Cir. 1972).

The Employee Retirement Income Security Act of 1974 (ERISA), responding to the loss of pensions by some employees, vastly expands federal regulation. It imposes far-reaching and complex standards regarding investments, funding, employee eligibility, disclosure, and reporting. It generally covers all private pension and welfare plans but permits the Labor Department to grant exemptions.

A significant interrelationship[p] between the regulation of such plans and the NLRA is reflected in NLRB v. Amax Coal Co., 453 U.S. 322 (1981), which dealt with the status of trustees selected by an employer under §302(c)(5) of the LMRA. Although that section refers to such trustees as "the representatives of the employer," the Court emphasized that the fiduciary duty of such trustees was directly antithetical to that of an agent of the appointing party. Hence, the Court, agreeing with the NLRB, ruled broadly that they were not employer "representatives for the purposes of collective bargaining" under NLRA §8(b)(1)(B); consequently, union insistence that management appoint or retain particular trustees for a §302(c)(5) trust does not violate §8(b)(1)(B).

Stevens, J., dissenting, urged that the Court could have rested on narrower grounds: first, that the UMW had been trying only to induce Amax to agree to the continued use of a multiemployer fund and was indifferent to the identity of that fund's management representatives; and, second, that Amax had participated in picking the management trustees of the multiemployer fund, from which Amax had withdrawn. Justice Stevens objected that the Court's opinion would be read as permitting a union "to exercize an economic veto over an employer's selection of the management trustees," under §302(c)(5). Although those appointees are fiduciaries, they frequently exercise broad discretion over questions such as level of employer contribu-

---

[p]See also Walsh v. Schlect, 429 U.S. 401 (1977), involving the interrelationship between §8(e) of the NLRA and §302(c)(5).

tions, eligibility requirements, and benefit standards, on which management and union representatives could legitimately differ. Consequently, the Court's approach undercuts the purposes behind the requirement in §302(c)(5)(B) for equal employer representation in fund administration.

The Court in *Amax* considered the applicability of §8(b)(1)(B) but not of §8(b)(3). Is §8(b)(3) violated by a union's strike to veto an employer's appointee or to press its own candidate?

Note: Regulation of Union "Political" Expenditures

Such regulation reflected the concern — that had led to earlier restrictions on corporations — about the corrupting impact of big money on politics. In the union context another purpose of regulation was emphasized — to protect dissenting members against "their money" being used to support candidates that they opposed. See generally Cohan, Of Politics, Pipefitters and Section 610: Union Political Contributions in Modern Context, 51 Tex. L. Rev. 936 (1973).

The pertinent regulation includes the following elements: Section 304, LMRA, which amended §313 of the Federal Corrupt Practices Act, proscribed contributions or expenditures by a corporation or labor organization in connection with federal elections. The Supreme Court has narrowly construed this Act, as applied to labor, partly to avoid constitutional issues. See United States v. CIO, 335 U.S. 106 (1948); Pipefitters Local 562 v. United States, 407 U.S. 385 (1972). *Pipefitters* involved expenditures in connection with federal elections; these expenditures were drawn from a union fund, administered by union officials, and collected through job site solicitations. Also used for nonpolitical purposes, the contributions were described as "assessments" by the union and calculated on the basis of hours worked. Although some contributors believed otherwise, employment or union membership did not depend on donations to the fund. In reversing the convictions below, the Supreme Court held that a legitimate political fund must be "separate from the sponsoring union only in . . . that there must be a strict segregation of its monies from union dues and assessments." It also held that union officials in soliciting must plainly indicate both the political purpose of the donations and that noncontributors would not suffer loss of membership, employment, or any institutional reprisal. Powell, J., joined by Burger, C.J., dissented, urging strongly that the conviction "accords with the plain language of the controlling statute."

Convictions for violating §304 have been rare. They include that of W. A. Boyle, the former president of the United Mine Workers. See United States v. Boyle, 482 F.2d 755 (D.C. Cir.), *cert. denied*, 414 U.S. 1076 (1973).

NOTES

1. The Federal Election Campaign Act of 1971 and 1974 imposed extensive regulations on federal campaign financing. Under the 1974 Act, "contributions by separate segregated funds" may not exceed $5,000 per candidate. See Pub. L. No. 93-443, §101(a), 88 Stat. 1263 (1974) (current version at 2 U.S.C. §441a (1982)). As the Court indicated in *Pipefitters*, that Act did not, however, limit unions and corporations with respect to expenditure categories permitted under §610, as amended in 1971, namely, communications by a union to its members or by a corporation to its stockholders, or the costs of establishing or administering a separate segregated fund. See Fleishman, The 1974 Federal Elections Campaign Act Amendments: The Shortcomings of Good Intentions, 1975 Duke L.J. 851.

2. In Buckley v. Valeo, 424 U.S. 1 (1976), the majority of a divided Court upheld the individual contribution limits, the disclosure and reporting provisions, and the public financing arrangements of the Federal Election Campaign Act of 1971, as amended in 1974. The Court, however, invalidated, as contrary to the First Amendment, the statutory limitations on campaign expenditures, on independent expenditures by individuals and groups, and on expenditures by a candidate from his personal funds. The Court also invalidated the statutory provisions for the appointment, without Presidential involvement, of a majority of the members of the Federal Election Commission. (Congress obviated the latter difficulty by enacting §101(a)(1) of Pub. L. No. 94-283 (S. 3065, May 11, 1976), codified as amended at 2 U.S.C. §437c(a)(1) (1982). Pub. L. No. 94-283, §321, codified as amended at 2 U.S.C. §441b (1982), also revised and incorporated 18 U.S.C. §610.) In Common Cause v. Schmitt, 512 F. Supp. 489 (D.D.C. 1980), *aff'd* 455 U.S. 129 (1982), the Court's reasoning in *Buckley* was extended to invalidate the statutory ceiling on expenditures by independent political committees. See Polsby, Buckley v. Valeo: The Special Nature of Political Speech, 1976 Sup. Ct. Rev. 1; Wright, Money and the Pollution of Politics: Is the First Amendment an Obstacle to Political Equality?, 82 Colum. L. Rev. 609 (1982) (a strong indictment of the Court's invalidation of the statutory limits on campaign expenditures, as distinguished from contributions, and of the "alarming influence of political action committees sponsored by special interests" on political contests); Forrester, The New Constitutional Right to Buy Elections, 69 A.B.A.J. 1078 (1983) (arguing that "*Buckley* and its offspring should be overruled"); and E. Drew, Politics & Money: The New Road to Corruption (1983) (concludes that money is playing a role in politics "different (i.e., vastly greater) in both scope and nature from anything that has gone before" and that post-Watergate federal campaign-finance laws are ineffectual, stimulating ingenious avoidance and

a myth of equal finances for candidates). But cf. M. Johnston, Political Corruption and Public Policy in America 140-171 (1982) (arguing that campaign finance reforms limit political expression without providing compensatory benefits, favor Democrats over Republicans, and enhance the advantages incumbents enjoy over challengers).

3. In Federal Election Commission (FEC) v. National Right to Work Commission (NRWC), 459 U.S. 197 (1982), the FEC charged that the NRWC, a Virginia nonprofit corporation without capital stock, had sought federal campaign contributions from non-"members," thereby violating §441b(a) of the Federal Election Campaign Act of 1971, as amended. That Act makes it unlawful for any corporation or any labor organization to make any "contribution or expenditure" in connection with a federal election or primary. Section 441b(b)(2) provides, however, that "contribution or expenditure" shall not include

> (A) communications by a corporation to its stockholders and executive or administrative personnel and their families or by a labor organization to its members and their families on any subject; (B) nonpartisan registration and get-out-the-vote campaigns by a corporation aimed at its stockholders and executive or administrative personnel and their families, or by a labor organization aimed at its members and their families; and (C) the establishment, administration, and solicitation of contributions to a separate segregated fund to be utilized for political purposes by a corporation, labor organization, membership organization, cooperative, or corporation without capital stock . . . ; [and that]
>
>   (C) This paragraph shall not prevent a membership organization, cooperative, or corporation without capital stock, or a separate segregated fund established by a membership organization, cooperative, or corporation without capital stock, from soliciting contributions to such a fund from members of such organization, cooperative, or corporation without capital stock.

The NRWC, which has publicized its opposition to compulsory unionism, established a separate segregated fund "to receive and make contributions on behalf of federal candidates." In 1976, NRWC sent solicitation letters to 267,000 former contributors to that fund, who responded with contributions of $77,000. The court of appeals held that "members," as used in §44lb(b)(4)(C), embraces "at least those individuals whom NRWC describes as its active and supporting members." The Supreme Court disagreed, holding that those individuals did not qualify as "members."

The Court reasoned this way: The pertinent legislative history, although limited, suggests that the term "members" should be understood to require a relatively enduring and independently significant financial or organizational attachment. So-called members of NRWC, however, although each receives a "membership" card, take no part in the operation of the corporation, elect no officials, and apparently have no meetings. Moreover, the NRWC's articles of incorporation disclaimed the existence of members. The determination by the court of appeals that NRWC's "members" include "anyone who has responded to one of the corporation's essentially random mass mailings" would render meaningless the statutory limitation to "members." The Court dismissed concerns that its narrow construction involved constitutional difficulties, noting that the regulation was warranted by the governmental interest in preventing both the actual corruption threatened by large financial contributions and the erosion of public confidence by the appearance of corruption. The Court also rejected the claim that §441b is too broad because its proscriptions extend to corporations and labor unions that lack great financial resources and that, like the NRWC, solicit only those who have proven to be "philosophically compatible" with the corporation's views. Cf. United Steelworkers v. Sadlowski, infra p. 1343.

4. In addition to the direct regulation embodied in §304, the Federal Regulation of Lobbying Act (1946), 2 U.S.C. §§261-270 (1964), requires unions to file reports of their spending with the Clerk of the House of Representatives if they solicit, collect, or receive money for the principal purpose of influencing federal legislation. Both the Supreme Court's narrow construction of that statute and the statutory exemptions have contributed to the failure of the filed information to give an adequate picture of lobbying in general or of lobbying by organized labor in particular. See H. Wellington, Labor and the Legal Process 223 (1968).

5. On the question of whether §501 of the LMRDA provides union members with private judicial remedies for union expenditures in violation of federal campaign laws, see McNamara v. Johnston, 522 F.2d 1157 (7th Cir. 1975), cert. denied, 425 U.S. 11 (1976).

E. ELECTIONS, REFERENDA, AND PARTICIPATORY INTERESTS

Prior to the enactment of the LMRDA, state regulation of union elections was hesitant, uneven, and ill-defined. A few courts avoided intervention by requiring a "property right" in the complainant and by holding that a member's interest in an election did not meet that requirement. Other courts, rejecting that requirement or finding it satisfied by a member's interest in union affairs, exercised their equity powers to police union elections. The basis for such intervention typically was vindication of the "contract" embodied in the constitution and bylaws — a rationale equally applicable to all forms of referenda. Although a handful of states had legislation dealing with union elections, it was generally limited in scope, sometimes invalidated on constitutional grounds, and was largely a dead letter. See Rezler, Union Elections: The Background of Title IV of LMRDA, in Symposium on LMRDA 475, 476-482 (R. Slovenko ed. 1961).

State courts had granted both preelection and postelection relief. Postelection remedies were generally deemed inadequate because the attendant delays permitted the incumbents to solidify their position. Courts were, moreover, reluctant to become involved in conducting a new election despite the availability, and the occasional use, of masters and receivers to handle details. See Summers, Judicial Regulation of Union Elections, 70 Yale L.J. 1221 (1961).

Titles I and IV of the LMRDA supplemented the protection of state law in order to promote free and democratic elections and equal opportunities of members to participate in internal union affairs. Under the best of circumstances, such legislation presents difficulties. It deals with institutions with diverse structures and traditions. It must strike a balance between individual and collective interests and between self-correction and governmental intervention. It must steer a course between essentially hortatory generalities and provisions so detailed as to foreclose reasonable adaptation to diverse institutional needs.

The legislative process from which the LMRDA emerged scarcely represented the best circumstances for grappling with the difficulties involved. The provisions of Title I were proposed from the floor and were, accordingly, denied the benefit of study by a legislative committee and its staff.[q] Those provisions were, moreover, not integrated with the provisions of Title IV, which overlapped and were also supported by different enforcement machinery. The debate in both houses was in general unenlightening and appeared sometimes to be deliberately obscurantist.[r] The resultant difficulties are reflected in the materials that follow. See generally Bellace, supra p. 1233; Note, Union Elections and the LMRDA: Thirteen Years of Use and Abuse, 81 Yale L.J. 407 (1972).

[q] See Cox, Internal Affairs of Labor Unions Under The Labor Reform Act of 1959, 58 Mich. L. Rev. 819, 833 (1960).
[r] See Smith, The Labor-Management Disclosure and Reporting Act of 1959, 46 Va. L. Rev. 195, 197-198 (1960). For an interesting analysis of the partisan pressures involved, see A. McAdams, Power and Politics in Labor Legislation (1964).

Local 3489, United Steelworkers of America v. Usery
429 U.S. 305 (1977)

BRENNAN, J. The Secretary of Labor brought this action in the District Court for the Southern District of Indiana under §402(b) of the LMRDA, to invalidate the 1970 election of officers of Local 3489, United Steelworkers of America. The Secretary alleged that a provision of the Steelworkers' International constitution, binding on the Local, that limits eligibility for local union office to members who have attended at least one-half of the regular meetings of the Local for three years previous to the election (unless prevented by union activities or working hours), violated §401(e). . . . The District Court dismissed the complaint, finding no violation of the Act. The [Seventh Circuit] reversed. 520 F.2d 516 (1975). We granted certiorari to resolve a conflict among Circuits over whether the Steelworkers' constitutional provision violates §401(e). . . . We affirm.

I

At the time of the challenged election, there were approximately 660 members in good standing of Local 3489. The Court of Appeals found that 96.5% of these members were ineligible to hold office, because of failure to satisfy the meeting-attendance rule. Of the 23 eligible members, nine were incumbent union officers. The Secretary argues, and the Court of Appeals held, that the failure of 96.5% of the local members to satisfy the meeting-at-tendance requirement, and the rule's effect of requiring potential insurgent candidates to plan their candidacies as early as 18 months in advance of the election when the reasons for their opposition might not have yet emerged,[5] established that the requirement has a substantial antidemocratic effect on local union elections. Petitioners argue that the rule is reasonable because it serves valid union purposes, imposes no very burdensome obligation on the members, and has not proved to be a device that entrenches a particular clique of incumbent officers in the local.

II

The opinions in three cases decided in 1968 have identified the considerations pertinent to the determination whether the attendance rule violates §401(e). Wirtz v. Hotel Employees, 391 U.S. 492; Wirtz v. Bottle Blowers Assn., 389 U.S. 463; Wirtz v. Laborers' Union, 389 U.S. 477.

---

[5] Regular meetings were held on a monthly basis. Thus, in order to attend half of the meetings in a three-year period, a previously inactive member desiring to run for office would have to begin attending 18 months before the election.

. . . The injunction in §401(e) that "every member in good standing shall be eligible to be a candidate and to hold office" is made expressly "subject to . . . reasonable qualifications uniformly imposed." But "Congress plainly did not intend that the authorization . . . of 'reasonable qualifications . . .' should be given a broad reach. The contrary is implicit in the legislative history of the section and in its wording. . . ." Wirtz v. Hotel Employees, supra, at 499. The basic objective of Title IV of the LMRDA is to guarantee "free and democratic" union elections modeled on "political elections in this country" where "the assumption is that voters will exercise common sense and judgment in casting their ballots." 391 U.S., at 504. Thus, Title IV is not designed merely to protect the right of a union member to run for a particular office in a particular election. "Congress emphatically asserted a vital public interest in assuring free and democratic union elections that transcends the narrower interest of the complaining union member." Wirtz v. Bottle Blowers Assn., supra, at 475; Wirtz v. Laborers' Union, supra, at 483. The goal was to "protect the rights of rank-and-file members to participate fully in the operation of their union through processes of democratic self-government, and, through the election process, to keep the union leadership responsive to the membership." Wirtz v. Hotel Employees, supra, at 497.

Whether a particular qualification is "reasonable" [under] §401(e) must therefore "be measured in terms of its consistency with the Act's command to unions to conduct 'free and democratic' union elections." 391 U.S., at 499. Congress was not concerned only with corrupt union leadership. Congress chose the goal of "free and democratic" union elections as a preventive measure "to curb the possibility of abuse by benevolent as well as malevolent entrenched leadership." Id., at 503. *Hotel Employees* expressly held that that check was seriously impaired by candidacy qualifications which substantially deplete the ranks of those who might run in opposition to incumbents, and therefore held invalid the candidacy limitation there involved that restricted candidacies for certain positions to members who had previously held union office. "Plainly, given the objective of Title IV, a candidacy limitation which renders 93% of union members ineligible for office can hardly be a 'reasonable qualification.' " Id., at 502.

III

. . . [W]e conclude that here, too, the antidemocratic effects of the meeting-attendance rule outweigh the interests urged in its support. Like the bylaw in *Hotel Employees*, an attendance requirement that results in the exclusion of 96.5% of the members from candidacy for union office hardly seems to be a "reasonable qualification" consistent with the goal of free and democratic elections. . . .

Petitioners argue, however, that the bylaw held violative of §401(e) in *Hotel Employees* differs significantly from the attendance rule here. Under the *Hotel Employees* bylaw no member could assure by his own efforts that he would be ineligible for union office, since others controlled the criterion for eligibility. Here, on the other hand, a member can assure himself of eligibility for candidacy by attending some 18 brief meetings over a three-year period. In other words, the union would have its rule treated not as excluding a category of member from eligibility, but simply as mandating a procedure to be followed by any member who wishes to be a candidate.

Even examined from this perspective, however, the rule has a restrictive effect on union democracy.[6] In the absence of a permanent "opposition party" within the union, opposition to the incumbent leadership is likely to emerge in response to particular issues at different times, and member interest in changing union leadership is therefore likely to be at its highest only shortly before elections. Thus it is probable that to require that a member decide upon a potential candidacy at least 18 months in advance of an election when no issues exist to prompt that decision may not foster but discourage candidacies and to that extent impair the general membership's freedom to oust incumbents in favor of new leadership.

Nor are we persuaded by petitioners' argument that the Secretary has failed to show an antidemocratic effect because he has not shown that the incumbent leaders of the union became "entrenched" in their offices as a consequence of the operation of the attendance rule. The reasons for leaderships becoming entrenched are difficult to isolate. The election of the same officers year after year may be a signal that antidemocratic election rules have prevented an effective challenge to the regime, or might well signal only that the members are satisfied with their stewardship; if elections are uncontested, opposition factions may have been denied access to the ballot, or competing interests may have compromised differences before the election to maintain a front of unity. Conversely, turnover in offices may result from an open political process, or from a competition limited to candidates who offer no real opposition to an entrenched establishment. But Congress did not saddle the courts with the duty to search out and remove improperly entrenched

---

[6] Petitioners argue that attendance at 18 relatively short meetings over three years is no very onerous burden on a union member. But this argument misconceives the evil at which the statute aims. We must judge the eligibility rule not by the burden it imposes on the individual candidate but by its effect on free and democratic processes of union government. Wirtz v. Hotel Employees, 391 U.S., at 499.

union leaderships. Rather, Congress chose to guarantee union democracy by regulating not the results of a union's electoral procedure but the procedure itself. Congress decided that if the elections are "free and democratic," the members themselves are able to correct abuse of power by entrenched leadership. Procedures that unduly restrict free choice among candidates are forbidden without regard to their success or failure in maintaining corrupt leadership.

Petitioners next argue that the rule is reasonable within §401(e) because it encourages attendance at union meetings, and assures more qualified officers by limiting election to those who have demonstrated an interest in union affairs, and are familiar with union problems. But the rule has plainly not served these goals. It has obviously done little to encourage attendance at meetings, which continue to attract only a handful of members.[8] . . .

As for assuring the election of knowledgeable and dedicated leaders, the election provisions of the LMRDA express a congressional determination that the best means to this end is to leave the choice of leaders to the membership in open democratic elections, unfettered by arbitrary exclusions. Pursuing this goal by excluding the bulk of the membership from eligibility for office, and thus limiting the possibility of dissident candidacies, runs directly counter to the basic premise of the statute. We therefore conclude that Congress, in guaranteeing every union member the opportunity to hold office, subject only to "reasonable qualifications," disabled unions from establishing eligibility qualifications as sharply restrictive of the openness of the union political process as is petitioners' attendance rule.

IV

Finally, petitioners argue that the absence of a precise statement of what the Secretary of Labor and the courts will regard as reasonable prevents the drafting of a meeting-attendance rule with any assurance that it will be valid under §401(e). The Secretary . . . has [declared]:

> Experience has demonstrated that it is not feasible to establish arbitrary guidelines for judging the reasonableness of [a meeting-attendance eligibility requirement]. Its reasonableness must be gauged in the light of all the circumstances of the particular case, including not only the frequency of meetings, the number of meetings which must be attended and the period of time over which the requirement extends, but also such factors as the nature, availability and extent of excuse provisions, whether all or most members have the opportunity to attend meetings, and the impact of the rule, i.e., the number

---

[8] Attendance at Local 3489's meetings averages 47 out of approximately 660 members. There is no indication in the record that this total represents a significant increase over attendance before the institution of the challenged rule.

or percentage of members who would be rendered ineligible by its application. 29 CFR §452.38(a)(1976).

Obviously, this standard leads to more uncertainty than would a less flexible rule. But in using the word "reasonable," Congress clearly contemplated exactly such a flexible result. Moreover, on the facts of this case and in light of *Hotel Employees*, petitioners' contention that they had no way of knowing that a rule disqualifying over 90% of a local's members from office would be regarded as unreasonable in the absence of substantial justification is unpersuasive.

Affirmed.

[Powell, J., joined by Stewart and Rehnquist, JJ., dissented on these grounds: The holding unwarrantably interfered with the union's right to manage its internal affairs. The record showed not entrenched leadership, but victories by nonincumbents who had won major as well as minor offices. Absent a stronger showing of abuse than had been made, the need for the disputed rule to serve the purposes urged by the union should be left to the union's judgment.]

NOTES

1. A predominantly white union with approximately 50,000 members, consisting primarily of public school teachers (but covered by the LMRDA), amended its constitution by majority vote so as to guarantee eight percent of the seats in its "Representative Assembly" (numbering approximately 600) to members of four minority groups — Blacks, Asians, Hispanics, and American Indians. If the regular election procedures did not place those minorities in eight percent of the assembly seats, the amendment directs the Board of Directors to appoint additional minority members to reach that goal. The amendment also increases the Board of Directors from 50 to 54, reserving the four new places for members of the same minority groups and providing that those places are to be in addition to those won by minorities through the regular procedures.

The Secretary of Labor sues for an injunction against the application of this amendment in an upcoming election, urging that it does not embody "reasonable qualifications uniformly imposed," under §401(e), and that it denies members the right to vote for candidates of their choice. How should the court rule? Would it be material if there were evidence that the union had in the past discriminated against members of the minority groups involved or that the proportion of those groups who were union members or public school teachers in the region involved was greater than eight percent? Cf.

Donovan v. Illinois Education Assn., 667 F.2d 638 (7th Cir. 1982)(reversing the court below and invalidating similar bylaws); with which cf. United Steelworkers v. Weber, 443 U.S. 193 (1979).

2. Procedural Issues Under §402(b):

(a) A union member protested that a local union had violated §401(e) by paying the per capita dues of selected delinquent members and permitting them to vote in a run-off election. The Secretary was permitted to challenge the general election, as well as the run-off, even though his complaint had alleged exhaustion of union remedies only with respect to the run-off. The controlling consideration for the Court was that the member's protest had given the union fair notice that the earlier election had had the same unlawful taint as the run-off. See Wirtz v. Local 125, Laborers Intl. Union, 389 U.S. 477 (1968). Cf. Hodgson v. Local Union 6799, 403 U.S. 333 (1971): An insurgent candidate for president of a local protested within the union against the use of its facilities to electioneer for the incumbent, who was reelected. Thereupon, the insurgent filed a complaint with the Secretary under LMRDA §402(a), renewing the objection filed with the union and, for the first time, objecting to a meeting attendance requirement imposed as a condition for eligibility for union office. The Secretary's action, under §402(b), attacked that eligibility requirement, inter alia. The Court, affirming the direction of a new election on another ground, held that the member's failure to protest the attendance requirement within the union precluded the Secretary's challenging it in a §402 action, at least where the protesting member had been aware of that requirement when he filed his protest with the union. Brennan, J., dissented. White, J., dissented, urging that the limitation recognized by the majority should apply only to the grounds for setting aside the prior election and not to the terms for a new election (assuming one were ordered on other grounds). The new election must conform to Title IV as well as the union's constitution and bylaws. This suggestion was embraced by the Court in Trbovich v. United Mine Workers, 404 U.S. 528, 537 n.8 (1972).

(b) In *Trbovich*, supra, the Court held that a union member, whose complaint to the Secretary of Labor had initiated the Secretary's Title IV challenge to an election, had a right to intervene in that action. The Court, however, noted that Title IV's legislative history indicates that, in making suit by the Secretary the exclusive postelection remedy, Congress intended (1) to screen out frivolous litigation and (2) to consolidate in one action all meritorious claims challenging a single election. Accordingly, the Court held that the scope of such intervention is limited to the allegations set forth in the Secretary's complaint. The Court added that "[t]here is no evidence whatever that Congress was opposed to participation by union members in the litigation so long as that participation did not interfere with the screening and centralizing functions of the Secretary."

(c) In Dunlop v. Bachowski, 421 U.S. 560 (1975), the Court ruled (1) that the Secretary of Labor must furnish the complainant and the court with a statement of the grounds for the Secretary's refusal to sue under §402(b) and the essential facts upon which his inferences are based, and (2) that such refusal is subject to limited judicial review under the "arbitrary and capricious" standard of §706(2)(A) of the Administrative Procedure Act. The Court emphasized, however, that judicial review should normally be confined to examining the statement of reasons and should not extend to challenges of the factual basis of the Secretary's findings as to the existence of violations or their impact on the election. The Court held that the Third Circuit had erred in authorizing a trial-type inquiry into the factual basis of the Secretary's conclusions. The Court, moreover, reserved the question as to the authority of the district court to order the Secretary to sue if his refusal were "arbitrary."

Rehnquist, J., agreed that a complaining member was entitled to a statement from the Secretary explaining his refusal to sue. He urged, however, that the requirement of "a brief statement" arose from the Administrative Procedure Act and was wholly independent of whether the Secretary's decision was reviewable. He dissented from the holding as to judicial review, finding it incompatible with "the exclusivity of the Secretary's role in the enforcement of Title IV." He also rejected efforts to distinguish cases recognizing the unreviewable discretion of the NLRB's general counsel to withhold an unfair labor practice complaint. In Bachowski, the Third Circuit had urged, as a ground for distinction, that the NLRA involved "vindication of societal or governmental interest, rather than the protection of individual rights."

Is the Third Circuit's basis for distinction convincing? See Bachowski v. Brennan, 405 F. Supp. 1227 (W.D. Penn. 1975) (on remand). See generally Note, Dunlop v. Bachowski and the Limits of Judicial Review under Title IV of the LMRDA: A Proposal for Administrative Reform, 86 Yale L.J. 885 (1977).

3. In Wirtz v. Hotel, Motel & Club Employees Union, Local 6, 391 U.S. 492 (1968) (referred to in both opinions in Local 3489), the Court considered the effect of §401(c)(2) on elections involving bylaws that restrict eligibility to a small percentage of members. The district court, in finding the outcome of the election "not affected" by the violation of §401, had relied on these factors: (a) the insurgents' poor electoral showing, (b) the absence of evidence that any ineligible nominees had been a proven vote-getter, (c) the lack of a substantial issue or grievance against the incumbents, and (d) the

overwhelming advantage enjoyed by the "Administration Party" because of
their full slate. Rejecting that reasoning, the Court suggested that in vote-
tampering situations, §401(2) should preclude invalidation of the election
when the margin of victory substantially exceeds the number of disputed
ballots. But the Court distinguished wholesale exclusion from the ballot,
stating (at 508):

> . . . None of the factors relied on is tangible evidence against the rea-
> sonable possibility that the wholesale exclusion of members did affect the
> outcome. Nothing in them necessarily contradicts the logical inference that
> some or all of the disqualified candidates might have been elected had they
> been permitted to run. The defeat suffered by the few candidates allowed to
> run proves nothing about the performance that might have been made by
> those who did not. The District Court properly perceived that the bylaw
> necessarily inhibited the membership generally from considering making the
> race, but held that any inference from this was disproved by "the heavy vote in
> favor of the administration candidates. . . . " Ibid. But since 93% of the
> membership was ineligible under the invalid bylaw it is impossible to know that
> the election would not have attracted many more candidates but for the bylaw.
> In short, the considerations relied on by the court are pure conjecture, not
> evidence. We therefore conclude that the prima facie case established by the
> violation was not met by evidence which supports the District Court's finding
> that the violation did not affect the result. . . .

4. The investigatory authority conferred on the Secretary by LMRDA
§601 extends to violations of Title IV, and his accompanying subpoena
authority has been held not to depend on the filing of a complaint by a union
member or a showing of probable cause. See Local 57, IUOE v. Wirtz, 346
F.2d 552 (1st Cir. 1965); Silberman and Dreiser, The Secretary and the
Law: Preballoting Investigations Under the Landrum-Griffin Act, 7 Ga. L.
Rev. 1 (1972); a reply to Rauh, LMRDA — Enforce It or Repeal It, 5 Ga. L.
Rev. 643 (1971).

Calhoon v. Harvey
379 U.S. 134 (1964)

BLACK, J. . . . The respondents, three members of District No. 1,
National Marine Engineers' Beneficial Association, filed a complaint in
Federal District Court against the union, its president and its secretary-treasurer, alleging that certain provisions of the union's bylaws and national
constitution violated the Act in that they infringed "the right of members of
defendant District No. 1, NMEBA, to nominate candidates in elections of

defendant, . . . guaranteed to each member of defendant, and to each plaintiff, by §101(a)(1). . . ." It was alleged that §102 . . . gave the District Court jurisdiction [over] the controversy. The union bylaws complained of deprived a member of the right to nominate anyone for office but himself. The national constitution in turn provided that no member could be eligible for nomination or election to a full-time elective office unless he had been a member of the national union for five years and had served 180 days or more of seatime in each of two of the preceding three years on vessels covered by collective bargaining agreements with the national or its subsidiary bodies. . . . [R]espondents asked that the union be enjoined from preparing for or conducting any election until it revised its system of elections so as to afford each of its members a fair opportunity to nominate any persons "meeting fair and reasonable eligibility requirements for any or all offices to be filled by such election."

The union moved to dismiss the complaint on the grounds that (1) the court lacked jurisdiction over the subject matter, and (2) the complaint failed to state a claim upon which relief could be granted. The District Court dismissed for want of "jurisdiction," holding that the alleged conduct of the union, even if true, failed to show a denial of the equal rights of all members of the union to vote for or nominate candidates guaranteed by §101(a)(1) . . . so as to give the District Court jurisdiction of the controversy under §102. The allegations, said the court, showed at most imposition of qualifications of eligibility for nomination and election so restrictive that they might violate §401(e) of Title IV by denying members a reasonable opportunity to nominate and vote for candidates. The District Court further held that it could not exercise jurisdiction to protect §401(e) rights because §402(a) . . . provides a remedy, declared by §403 to be "exclusive," authorizing members to vindicate such rights by challenging elections after they have been held, and then only by (1) first exhausting all remedies available with the union, (2) filing a complaint with the Secretary of Labor, who (3) may, after investigating the violation alleged in the complaint, bring suit in a United States district court to attack the validity of the election. The Court of Appeals reversed, holding that "the complaint alleged a violation of §101(a)(1) and that federal jurisdiction existed under §102." 324 F.2d 486, 487. Because of the importance of the questions presented and conflicting views in the courts of appeals and the district courts, we granted certiorari.

I

Jurisdiction of the District Court under §102 . . . depends entirely upon whether this complaint showed a violation of rights guaranteed by §101(a)(1), for we disagree with the Court of Appeals' holding that jurisdiction under §102 can be upheld by reliance in whole or in part on allegations which in substance charge a breach of Title IV rights. An analysis and understanding of the meaning of §101(a)(1) and of the charges of the complaint are therefore essential to a determination of this issue. Respondents charge that the bylaws and constitutional provisions referred to above infringed their right guaranteed by §101(a)(1) to nominate candidates. The result of their allegations here, however, is an attempt to sweep into the ambit of their right to sue in federal court if they are denied an equal opportunity to nominate candidates under §101(a)(1), a right to sue if they are not allowed to nominate anyone they choose regardless of his eligibility and qualifications under union restrictions. But Title IV, not Title I, sets standards for eligibility and qualifications of candidates and officials and provides its own separate and different administrative and judicial procedure for challenging those standards. And the equal-rights language of §101(a)(1) would have to be stretched far beyond its normal meaning to hold that it guarantees members not just a right to "nominate candidates," but a right to nominate anyone, without regard to valid union rules. . . .

[Section 101(a)(1)] is no more than a command that members and classes of members shall not be discriminated against in their right to nominate and vote. And Congress carefully prescribed that even this right against discrimination is "subject to reasonable rules and regulations" by the union. The complaining union members here have not been discriminated against in any way and have been denied no privilege or right to vote or nominate which the union has granted to others. They have indeed taken full advantage of the uniform rule limiting nominations by nominating themselves for office. It is true that they were denied their request to be candidates, but that denial was not a discrimination against their right to nominate, since the same qualifications were required equally of all members. Whether the eligibility requirements set by the union's constitution and bylaws were reasonable and valid is a question separate and distinct from whether the right to nominate on an equal basis given by §101(a)(1) was violated. The District Court therefore was without jurisdiction to grant the relief requested here unless, as the Court of Appeals held, the "*combined* effect of the eligibility requirements and the restriction to self-nomination" is to be considered in determining whether §101(a)(1) has been violated.

II

We hold that possible violations of Title IV of the Act regarding eligibility are not relevant in determining whether . . . a district court has jurisdiction under §102 of Title I. . . . Title IV sets up a statutory scheme governing the election of union officers, fixing the terms during which they hold office, requiring that elections be by secret ballot, regulating the handling of campaign literature, requiring a reasonable opportunity for the nomination of candidates, authorizing unions to fix "reasonable qualifications uniformly imposed" for candidates, and attempting to guarantee fair union elections in which all the members are allowed to participate. Section 402 . . . , as has been pointed out, sets up an exclusive method for protecting Title IV rights, by permitting an individual member to file a complaint with the Secretary of Labor challenging the validity of any election because of violations of Title IV. . . . It is apparent that Congress decided to utilize the special knowledge and discretion of the Secretary of Labor in order best to serve the public interest. Cf. San Diego Building Trades Council v. Garmon, 359 U.S. 236, 242. In so doing Congress, with one exception not here relevant, decided not to permit individuals to block or delay union elections by filing federal-court suits for violations of Title IV. Reliance on the discretion of the Secretary is in harmony with the general congressional policy to allow unions great latitude in resolving their own internal controversies, and, where that fails, to utilize the agencies of Government most familiar with union problems to aid in bringing about a settlement through discussion before resort to the courts. Without setting out the lengthy legislative history . . . , we are satisfied that the Act itself shows clearly by its structure and language that the disputes here, basically relating . . . to eligibility of candidates for office, fall squarely within Title IV . . . and are to be resolved by the administrative and judicial procedures set out in that Title.

Accordingly, the judgment of the Court of Appeals is reversed and that of the District Court is affirmed. . . .

Douglas, J. would affirm the judgment of the Court of Appeals for the reasons stated in its opinion as reported in 324 F.2d 486.

Stewart, J., whom Harlan, J. joins, concurring. This case marks the first interpretation by this Court of the significant changes wrought by the [LMRDA]. . . . At issue are subtle questions concerning the interplay between Title I and Title IV. . . . In part, both seem to deal with the same subject matter: Title I guarantees "equal rights and privileges . . . to nominate candidates"; Title IV provides that "a reasonable opportunity shall be given for the nomination of candidates." . . . [T]he two Titles of the legislation differ most substantially in the remedies they provide. If a Title I right is at issue, the allegedly aggrieved union member has direct, virtually immediate recourse to a federal court to obtain an adjudication of his claim and an injunction if his complaint has merit. Vindication of claims under Title IV may be much more onerous. Federal-court suits can be brought only by the Secretary of Labor, and then, only after the election has been held. . . .

The Court precludes the District Court from asserting jurisdiction over this complaint by focusing on the fact that one of the imposed restrictions speaks in terms of eligibility. And since these are "possible violations of Title IV of the Act regarding eligibility" they "are not relevant in determining whether or not a district court has jurisdiction under §102 of Title I. . . ." By this reasoning, the Court forecloses early adjudication of claims concerning participation in the election process. But there are occasions when eligibility provisions can infringe upon the right to nominate. Had the NMEBA issued a regulation that only Jesse Calhoon was eligible for office, no one could place great store on the right to self-nomination left to the rest of the membership. This Court long ago recognized the subtle ways by which election rights can be removed through discrimination at a less visible stage of the political process. The decisions in the Texas Primary Cases were founded on the belief that the equal right to vote was impaired where discrimination existed in the method of nomination. Smith v. Allwright, 321 U.S. 649; Nixon v. Herndon, 273 U.S. 536. . . . No less is the equal right to nominate infringed where onerous burdens drastically limit the candidates available for nomination. . . .

After today, simply by framing its discriminatory rules in terms of eligibility, a union can immunize itself from preelection attack in a federal court even though it makes deep incursions on the equal right of its members to nominate, to vote, and to participate in the union's internal affairs. . . .

Nonetheless, the Court finds a "general congressional policy" to avoid judicial resolution of internal union disputes. That policy, the Court says, was designed to limit the power of individuals to block and delay elections by seeking injunctive relief. Such an appraisal might have been accurate before the addition of Title I, but it does not explain the emphasis on prompt judicial remedies there provided. In addition to the injunctive relief authorized by §102 and the saving provisions of §103, §101(a)(4) modifies the traditional requirement of exhausting internal remedies before resort to litigation. Even §403 is not conclusive on the elimination of preelection remedies. At the least, state-court actions may be brought in advance of an election to "enforce the constitution and bylaws." And as to federal courts, it is certainly arguable that recourse through the Secretary of Labor is the exclusive remedy only after the election has been held.[6] By reading Title I rights so narrowly, and by construing Title IV to foreclose absolutely preelection litigation in the federal courts, the Court sharply reduces meaningful protection for many of the rights which Congress was so assiduous to create.[7] By so simplifying the

---

[6] See Summers, Pre-Emption and the Labor Reform Act — Dual Rights and Remedies, 22 Ohio St. L.J. 119, 138-139 (1961). It would be strange indeed if only state courts were available to enforce the federal law created by the Act during the pre-election period.

[7] The Court's reading of federal-court remedies available under Title I and Title IV is

tangled provisions of the Act, the Court renders it virtually impossible for the aggrieved union member to gain a hearing when it is most necessary — when there is still an opportunity to make the union's rules comport with the requirements of the Act.

My difference with the Court does not reach to the disposition of this particular case. Whether stated in terms of restrictions on the right to nominate, or in terms of limitations on eligibility for union office, I think the rules of a labor organization would operate illegally to curtail the members' equal right to nominate within the meaning of Title I only if those rules effectively distorted the basic democratic process. The line might be a shadowy one in some cases. But I think that in this case the respondents did not allege in their complaint nor demonstrate in their affidavits that this line was crossed. . . .

Local No. 82, Furniture & Piano Moving Drivers v. Crowley
104 S. Ct. 2557 (1984)

[While insurgents were seeking office, several members, including Crowley, were excluded from a meeting of the local (to nominate candidates for its executive board) because they could not produce a computerized receipt showing their dues payment. Another dispute concerned the office for which insurgent Lynch had been nominated. The insurgents claimed that he was a nominee for secretary-treasurer; but the incumbent secretary-treasurer, who was also presiding, declared himself the only nominee for that office and named Lynch as a nominee for president (as did the ballot). The local denied the protests of several members and distributed mail ballots (the traditional voting method), which were to be counted by December 13, 1980. On December 1, after the ballots had been distributed, the plaintiffs sued in a federal district court, alleging that the local and its officers, by the computerized receipts requirement, had violated (i) the plaintiffs' "equal rights . . . to nominate candidates [and] to attend membership meetings," under §101(a)(1); and (ii) their right to freedom of expression at union meetings, under §101(a)(2). They also alleged that the defendants had violated §101(a)(1) by excluding Lynch as a nominee for secretary-treasurer.

---

particularly restrictive because of the limited powers of the district judge once the balloting has occurred. Under §402(c), the court is confined to setting the election aside only if "the violation of §401 may have affected the outcome." For the aggrieved union member, this protection may be totally inadequate. The function of nominating a candidate is not always to gain the office. A faction may be vitally interested in appearing on the ballot merely to show that it is part of the political structure of the union. Under the Court's view, until such a faction approaches majority status, judicial relief in the federal courts will be absent. . . .

Under the district court's temporary restraining order of December 12, the ballots were to be sealed and delivered to the court. By that time, many if not most ballots had been returned and were to have been counted by the union the next day. Following hearings and negotiations, the court, invoking its jurisdiction under Title I, invalidated the ballots and selected outside arbitrators to conduct another election. The Secretary of Labor intervened on defendants' behalf in their appeal. Rejecting the argument that Title IV barred the relief granted below, the court of appeals affirmed. The Supreme Court reversed.]

BRENNAN, J. . . . To examine fully the relationship between the respective enforcement provisions of Title I and Title IV, . . . it is necessary first to summarize the relevant statutory provisions and Congress' principal purposes in their enactment. The LMRDA was "the product of congressional concern with widespread abuses of power by union leadership." Finnegan v. Leu, 456 U.S. 431, 435 (1982). Although the Act "had a history tracing back more than two decades," ibid., and was directly generated by several years of congressional hearings, see S. Rep. No. 187, 86th Cong., 1st Sess., 2 (1959), many specific provisions . . . did not find their way into the statute until the proposed legislation was fully considered on the floor of the Senate, 456 U.S., at 435, n.4. It should not be surprising, therefore, that the interaction between various provisions that were finally included in the Act has generated considerable uncertainty. . . .

Chief among the causes for this confusion is Title I . . . , which provides union members with an exhaustive "Bill of Rights" enforceable in federal court. . . . Title I is designed to guarantee every union member equal rights to vote and otherwise participate in union decisions, freedom from unreasonable restrictions on speech and assembly, and protection from improper discipline. . . .

As first introduced, . . . on the floor of the Senate, see 105 Cong. Rec. 6469-6476, 6492-6493 (1959), Title I empowered the Secretary of Labor to seek injunctions and other relief in federal district court to enforce the rights guaranteed to union members. A few days later, however, [this] McClellan amendment was replaced by a substitute amendment offered by Senator Kuchel. See id., at 6693-6694, 6717-6727. . . . [T]his substitute [provided] for enforcement of Title I through suits by individual union members in federal district court. Id., at 6717, 6720. As so amended, the legislation was endorsed in the Senate by a vote of 77-14, id., at 6727, and was quickly accepted without substantive change by the House, see H. R. 8400, 86th Cong., 1st Sess., §102 (1959). . . .

Standing by itself, this jurisdictional provision [§102] suggests that individual union members may properly maintain a Title I suit whenever . . . that title [has] been violated. At the same time, however, §102 explicitly limits the relief that may be ordered . . . to that which is "appropriate." . . .

Congress . . . included in Title IV an exclusivity provision that explains the relationship between the enforcement procedures established for violations of Title IV and the remedies available for violations of potentially overlapping state and federal laws. Relying on this provision [§403], and on the comprehensive nature of the enforcement scheme established by §402, we have held that Title IV "sets up an exclusive method for protecting Title IV rights," and that Congress "decided not to permit individuals to block or delay union elections by filing federal-court suits for violations of Title IV." [*Calhoon*,] [379 U.S.] at 140.

. . . This case requires . . . that we decide whether Title I remedies are available to aggrieved union members while a union election is being conducted.   ◆

It is useful to begin by noting what the plain language of the Act clearly establishes about the relationship between the remedies provided under Title I and Title IV. First, the exclusivity provision included in §403 of Title IV plainly bars Title I relief when an individual union member challenges the validity of an election that has already been completed.[16] Second, the full panoply of Title I rights are available to individual union members "prior to the conduct" of a union election. As with the plain language of most federal labor laws, however, this simplicity is more apparent than real. Indeed, by its own terms, the provision offers no obvious solution to what remedies are available during the course of a union election. . . .

Even if the plain meaning of the "already conducted" language of §403 could be read not to preclude other remedies until the actual tabulation and certification of ballots has been completed, we would hesitate to find such an interpretation determinative. First, such an approach would ignore the limitation on judicial remedies . . . included in Title I, which allows a district court to award only "appropriate" relief. Moreover, we have previously "cautioned against a literal reading" of the LMRDA. Wirtz v. Bottle Blowers Assn., 389 U.S., at 468. . . . [T]he statute was "the product of conflict and compromise between strongly held and opposed views, and its proper construction frequently requires consideration of its wording against its legislative history and in light of the general objectives Congress sought to achieve."

---

[16]. . . The exclusivity provision of Title IV may not bar post-election relief for Title I claims or other actions that do not directly challenge the validity of an election already conducted. See, e.g., Ross v. Electrical Workers, 513 F.2d 840 (CA9 1975) (common law tort claim); Amalgamated Clothing Workers Rank and File Committee v. Amalgamated Clothing Workers, 473 F.2d 1303 (CA3 1973) (Title I claim).

Ibid. . . . See *Sadlowski*, 457 U.S., at 111. Indeed, . . . this admonition applies with its greatest force to the interaction between Title I and Title IV . . . , if only because of the unusual way in which the legislation was enacted.

Nor does the legislative history . . . provide any definitive indication of how Congress intended §403 to apply to Title I suits while an election is being conducted. Throughout the legislative debate on this provision, the exclusivity of Title IV was predominantly, if not only, considered in the context of a union election, such as one held at a union meeting, that would take place for a discrete and limited period of time. Thus, Congress did not explicitly consider how the exclusivity provision might apply to an election that takes several weeks or months to complete. Moreover, the legislative history . . . on the meaning of §403 is largely derived from congressional action that occurred prior to the time that Title I was added to the LMRDA. . . .

Despite this absence of conclusive evidence in the legislative history, the primary objectives that controlled congressional enactment of the LMRDA provide important guidance for our consideration of the availability of Title I remedies during a union election. . . . [T]hroughout the congressional discussions preceding enactment of both Title I and Title IV, Congress clearly indicated its intent to consolidate challenges to union elections with the Secretary of Labor, and to have the Secretary supervise any new elections necessitated by violations of the Act. This strongly suggests that, even when Title I violations are properly alleged and proven, Congress would not have considered a court order requiring and judicially supervising a new election to be "appropriate" relief under Title I. At the same time, there is nothing in the legislative history suggesting that Congress intended to foreclose all access to federal courts under Title I during an election, especially when a statutory violation could be corrected without any major delay or disruption to an ongoing election. We therefore conclude that whether a Title I suit may properly be maintained by individual union members during the course of a union election depends upon the nature of the relief sought by the Title I claimants.

Throughout its consideration of the LMRDA, Congress clearly intended to lodge exclusive responsibility for postelection suits challenging the validity of a union election with the Secretary of Labor. . . .[20]

---

[20] This view is confirmed by the elaborate procedures eventually included in Title IV to ensure that the Secretary supervises any new elections and to minimize any other outside interference in union elections. See, e.g., [§402(a)] (requiring exhaustion of internal remedies before member may file complaint with the Secretary; also providing that challenged elections shall be presumed valid pending final decision on Title IV violation); [§402(c)] (requiring that

. . . Although the enactment of Title I offered additional protection to union members, including . . . various statutory safeguards . . . during . . . a union election, there is no direct evidence . . . that Congress believed that enforcement of Title I would either require or allow courts to pre-empt the expertise of the Secretary and supervise their own elections. In the absence of such legislative history, and given the clear congressional preference expressed in Title IV for supervision of new elections by the Secretary of Labor, we are compelled to conclude that Congress did not consider court supervision of union elections to be an "appropriate" remedy for a Title I suit filed during . . . a union election. §102.

That is not to say that a court has no jurisdiction over otherwise proper Title I claims that are filed during . . . a lengthy union election. The important congressional policies underlying enactment of Title I . . . likewise compel us to conclude that appropriate relief under Title I may be awarded by a court while an election is being conducted. Individual union members may properly allege violations of Title I that are easily remediable under that title without substantially delaying or invalidating an ongoing election. For example, union members might claim that they did not receive election ballots distributed by the union because of their opposition to the incumbent officers running for reelection. Assuming that such union members prove a statutory violation under Title I, a court might appropriately order the union to forward ballots to the claimants before completion of the election. To foreclose a court from ordering such Title I remedies during an election would not only be inefficient, but also would frustrate the purposes that Congress sought to serve by including Title I in the LMRDA. Indeed, eliminating all Title I relief in this context might preclude aggrieved union members from ever obtaining relief for statutory violations, since the more drastic remedies under Title IV are ultimately dependent upon a showing that a violation "may have affected the outcome" of the election, [§402(c)].

In sum, whether suits alleging violations of Title I . . . may properly be maintained during the course of a union election depends upon the appropriateness of the remedy required to eliminate the claimed statutory violation. If the remedy sought is invalidation of the election already being conducted with court supervision of a new election, then union members must utilize the remedies provided by Title IV. For less intrusive remedies sought during an election, however, a district court retains authority to order appropriate relief under Title I. . . .

. . . [T]hese proceedings demonstrate why they are inconsistent with

---

any new elections shall be conducted under the Secretary's supervision). [Footnote number relocated in text. — Eds.]

the policies underlying the LMRDA. For example, the temporary restraining order and preliminary injunction issued by the court delayed the union election that was originally scheduled for December 1980 for one full year. Among other consequences, this left the incumbent union officers in power beyond the scheduled expiration of their terms. Cf. §401(b) (officers shall be elected not less than once every three years). If the procedures under Title IV had been properly followed, the December 1980 election would have been presumed valid, see §402(a), and new officers would have replaced the incumbents. Moreover, the expertise of the Secretary in supervising elections was completely ignored. Not only did the court acting alone decide that a new election was required, but its order established procedures for that election and appointed an outside arbitrator to supervise their implementation. This action by the District Court directly interfered with the Secretary's exclusive responsibilities for supervising new elections, and was inconsistent with the basic objectives of the LMRDA enforcement scheme. . . . [Reversed.]

[Stevens, J., dissented on these grounds: The Court unjustifiably undermines the core purpose of Title I, which is to enlarge union members' protections, including their right to seek union office and to participate generally in union election campaigns. The Court's result is not justified by §403, which was designed to limit state power to invalidate union elections rather than to compel members to rely on the Secretary to vindicate Title I rights. Indeed, the addition of Title I and §102 reflected Congress' conviction that Title I rights should be enforced by private actions rather than through the Secretary. Under the Court's approach, which turns the statute and its legislative history on their head, the most serious violations of Title I cannot be adequately remedied, except through the Secretary's discretion. Calhoon v. Harvey does not require that approach. There, the Court held that §102 did not cover the complaint because it challenged the eligibility requirements for union office, and Title IV rather than Title I governed such requirements. Here by contrast, the insurgents established probable violations of §101.]

Driscoll v. International Union of Operating Engineers, Local 139, 484 F.2d 682 (7th Cir. 1973), *cert. denied*, 415 U.S. 960 (1974). Driscoll, a union member, after exhausting his internal union remedies, filed a complaint with the Secretary of Labor pursuant to §402, charging that §401 was violated by the union's requirement that all candidates for union office execute a non-Communist affidavit, and asking for invalidation of that requirement in future elections. The Secretary declined to sue, whereupon Driscoll filed an action alleging, inter alia, violations of §101(a)(1), (2), and

(5) of the LMRDA. The district court, relying on Calhoon v. Harvey, dismissed for want of jurisdiction under Title I over restrictions on eligibility for union office. Driscoll urged that *Calhoon* was not applicable because the affidavit requirement directly infringed his right to free speech protected by Title I. In rejecting that contention, the court of appeals held that plaintiff did not fall within the one exception to the "broad mandate of *Calhoon*" that the court was prepared to recognize: Title I jurisdiction would exist to protect what also appeared to be Title IV rights, when removal of union official and a declaration of his future ineligibility were part of a deliberate attempt to suppress dissent in the context of long-standing factionalism, as in Schonfeld v. Penza, 477 F.2d 899 (2d Cir. 1973), which sustained an injunction against disciplinary action and stayed the election of a successor for the removed officer.

NOTE

Under the Court's approach in *Crowley*, under what circumstances, if any, would a federal district court now be authorized to grant the plaintiff's prayer in a situation such as *Driscoll?* Suppose that the plaintiffs sued in a state court, alleging that the disputed requirement violated state law or the union constitution. Would the LMRDA foreclose state jurisdiction? Would a federal district court have pendent jurisdiction over such a claim?

Yablonski v. United Mine Workers, 305 F. Supp. 868 (D.D.C. 1969). In 1969, Jock Yablonski, a member of the UMW's Executive Board, announced his candidacy for the UMW's presidency, then filled by Tony Boyle. Before the election, the UMW's newspaper (the "Journal"), which the Union regularly sent to its members, gave Boyle an unusual amount of favorable coverage, while not even mentioning Yablonski's activities. Yablonski sued the UMW in a federal district court, alleging a violation of the LMRDA §§401(c) and 501, and requesting a temporary injunction directing the defendants to give Yablonski equal treatment in the future and to compensate for past inequality by devoting one-half of each of the next two issues to material that he supplied. The court found that the defendants had used the Journal as a campaign instrument for Boyle in violation of §401(c), and that the usual standards for injunctive relief had been satisfied. Nevertheless, the court denied the requested relief, reasoning this way: Section 401(c) did not authorize that relief, which was also barred by the First Amendment. Furthermore, §401(g) is enforceable only by the Secretary of Labor in a §402 action and, indeed, §401(g) might be violated by granting the specific relief requested by the plaintiffs. The court did, however, enjoin the defendants from discriminatory use of the membership lists and, specifically, from using the Journal so as to advance Boyle's candidacy.

The career of the *Yablonski* litigation suggests the limitations of pre-election relief against incumbents' abuse of their position for electioneering purposes. The original complaint was filed August 26, 1969. The district court's opinion was handed down September 15, 1969; an appeal resulted in a remand for clarification, which the district court issued November 4, just slightly more than one month before the December 9 election. See Yablonski v. United Mine Workers, 305 F. Supp. 876 (1969). That election, a much closer one than usual for the UMW, resulted in Yablonski's defeat by almost a two-to-one margin. The incumbents' exploitation of the Journal was, however, an important factor in the invalidation of the election. See Hodgson v. Mine Workers, 344 F. Supp. 17 (D.D.C. 1972), which describes the tactics used by the incumbents against Yablonski[s] — tactics reminiscent of the worst abuses of machine politics in American cities.

Yablonski, his wife, and his daughter were murdered after he had challenged the election through the union's internal procedures. In 1973, Boyle was linked to the conspiracy to kill the Yablonskis; he was subsequently convicted on three counts of first-degree murder. See Commonwealth v. Boyle, 498 Pa. 486, 447 A.2d 250 (1982). See also P. Clark, The Miners' Fight for Democracy: Arnold Miller and the Reform of the United Mine Workers 25-26 (1981).

NOTE

The relief granted in Hodgson v. Mine Workers, 344 F. Supp. at 36, included the following:

> Commencing with the July 1, 1972 issue of the UMWA Journal up to and including the last issue prior to the supervised election, equal space for the presentation of news concerning, and the political views of bona fide candidates will be made available in each issue under a format subject to the approval of the Secretary of Labor. Slates of candidates may combine their allotted space and present their views as a slate.

Is this relief compatible with the First Amendment? Cf. Miami Herald Publishing Co. v. Tornillo, 418 U.S. 241 (1974).

---

[s]See also Comment, Campaign Financing of Internal Union Elections, 128 U. Pa. L. Rev. 1094 (1980).

United Steelworkers v. Sadlowski, 457 U.S. 102 (1982). The Steelworkers have elected their officers by a vote of their members (numbering over one million in 1977). In the 1977 election, Sadlowski, an insurgent candidate for president of the Union, received substantial financial support from nonmembers, using the money in part for legal expenses incurred in attempting to protect his statutory rights. The insiders won and, alleging that outside support had violated LMRDA §401(g) (which bars "money of an employer [from being] contributed or applied to promote the candidacy of any person in an election" covered by Title IV), brought suit in a federal district court against a group of outside contributors. That suit was dismissed on these grounds: Section 402 makes investigations and civil actions by the Secretary of Labor the exclusive remedies for violations of §401(g); furthermore, the statutory remedies preclude state courts from adjudicating state tort claims, such as those relating to postelection disputes, that are inextricably intertwined with provisions of the federal Act. McBride v. Rockefeller Family Fund, 612 F.2d 34 (2d Cir. 1979), *cert. denied,* 445 U.S. 951 (1980).

In their 1978 convention of approximately 5,000 delegates, the Steelworkers, by a constitutional amendment, banned a candidate from soliciting or accepting "financial support, or any other direct or indirect support of any kind (except an individual's own volunteered personal time) from any nonmember." The district court, disposing of cross motions for summary judgment, invalidated this "outsider rule" in toto, as contrary to the right-to-sue provision of §101(a)(4). The Court of Appeals for the D.C. Circuit affirmed, without deciding whether that violation alone warranted an injunction against the rule in toto. The court upheld that broad relief after accepting appellee Sadlowski's argument, first raised on appeal, that the outsider rule also violated the "freedom of speech and assembly" provision of §101(a)(2). The court reasoned that §101(a)(2) puts essentially the same limits on labor unions with respect to outside campaign contributions as would the First Amendment if it applied to unions. The Supreme Court, speaking through Marshall, J., reversed (5-4).

The Court upheld the outsider rule under the proviso to §101(a)(2), noting that the rule is "rationally related to the union's legitimate interest in reducing outsider interference with union affairs." The Court observed that, although §101(a)(2) restates a principal First Amendment value — the right to speak one's mind, without fear of reprisal — "there is absolutely no indication that Congress intended the scope of §101(a)(2) to be identical to the scope of the First Amendment"; rather, the proviso, by incorporating a test of reasonableness, avoids the more stringent tests applied to governmental action under that Amendment.

Justice White, joined by the Chief Justice and Justices Brennan and Blackmun, vigorously dissented, on these grounds: The Court had failed to judge the rule with reference to the "paradigmatic situation" addressed by Congress in guaranteeing free elections — "a large union with entrenched, autocratic leadership bent on maintaining itself by fair means or foul" and having at its disposal the advantages of incumbency, including the union staff, which serves as a campaign organization, contributing and soliciting campaign funds; and access to membership lists as well as to the members themselves. In light of those considerations, the dissenters urged that the "absolute, unbending, no-contribution rule" was not a "reasonable restriction" on Sadlowski's right to speak, assemble, and run for union office.

NOTES

1. Does the Court in *Sadlowski* undercut the underlying purpose of its decision in Local 3489 v. United Steelworkers, supra p. 1323, i.e., to keep nomination channels open — presumably in order to encourage challenges to, and accountability of, incumbent officers?

2. The National Right to Work Legal Defense and Education Foundation is a tax-exempt, nonprofit organization that opposes "compulsory unionism." The Foundation has financed test cases brought by workers against labor unions, in order to challenge the obligation to pay dues or the use of compelled dues for "political activities." Many of the Foundation's contributors are either employers under contract with unions or competitors of such employers. A group of national labor unions sues in a federal district court for a declaratory judgment and an injunction, claiming that the Foundation is violating LMRDA §101(a)(4) by financing suits (other than as a party) brought by employees and union members against unions. The Foundation asks you whether the complaint states a claim. How would you advise them? What additional facts, if any, would you want? Cf. International Union, UAW v. National Right to Work Legal Defense & Education Foundation, Inc., 116 L.R.R.M. 2013 (D.D.C. 1984).

3. Plaintiff, invoking LMRDA §102, in a federal district court sued his union and certain of its officers in their individual capacities, alleging their violation of his rights under §§101(a)(2) and 101(a)(5), when, as retribution for his running (unsuccessfully) for union office, the union officers had denied him referrals through the union hiring hall. He seeks punitive as well as compensatory damages from both the union and the individual officers. Does §102 of the Act provide for personal liability of union officers whose actions violate §101, when those actions do not constitute a good faith effort to discharge their official union duties? Cf. LMRDA §§102 and 609, and Keene v. International Union of Operating Engrs., Local 624, 569 F.2d 1375 (5th Cir. 1978).

Gurton v. Arons, 339 F.2d 371 (2d Cir. 1964). In February 1964, Local 802 of the American Federation of Music (AFM) conducted a mail vote among its 28,000 members on whether future elections of the local's officers should be by a secret mail vote; 12,654 voted "yes"; 2,206 voted "no." Thereupon, plaintiffs Gurton and Rothstein proposed bylaw amendments to be considered at a membership meeting in May, which would have undercut the February referendum by conditioning voting eligibility on registration in person at the office of the secretary of the local in September, during regular business hours. Most of the local's members are not employed full time as musicians, and only a small proportion vote when members must vote in person. The plaintiffs' proposed amendment was designed to secure control of the local by full-time musicians, like themselves. The local's Executive Board initially refused to put the plaintiffs' resolutions on the agenda for the May meeting but finally did so — in compliance with an order by a federal district court. The 1,500 members present adopted those resolutions by majority vote. The local's officers appealed to the AFM's Executive Board, relying on a bylaw authorizing an appeal from a stand taken by a meeting "in violation of [AFM's] principles." The Executive Board nullified the resolutions as contrary to Article 12, §6 of the International's bylaws, which provided:

> A Local failing to enforce its own laws, or submitting to unjust, unfair or improper conditions forced upon it by the arbitrary ruling of packed meetings, or through the influence of members who control the situation, must, after a proper investigation, submit to such decision arrived at by the officers of the Federation as, in their opinion, may correct the situation.

The board reasoned that the plaintiffs' resolution had disenfranchised many members who, because they lived or worked out of town, would be unable to register in person. Consequently, the resolution, which frustrated the majority vote for a procedure that would maximize voting opportunities, was repugnant to the purpose underlying §6, i.e., avoidance of minority control. Relying on LMRDA §§101 and 501 for jurisdiction, the plaintiffs sued in the federal district court for a temporary injunction directing the local to give effect to their resolutions. The district court denied relief and was affirmed on appeal.

Hays, J. . . . "The only violation of §101 claimed . . . is a denial of the equal right to vote in elections or referendums. The plaintiffs argue that if they are not allowed to vote in accordance with the limitations on voting contained in the Rothstein and Gurton resolutions, they will be denied their *right* to vote. But the guaranty of the equal right to vote is surely not a general commission for the federal courts to review the constitution and by-laws of the union. As long as no claim is made that provisions of the constitution and by-laws are being applied in such a way as to deny equality in voting, there is nothing in §101 which authorizes consideration of those documents. Section 101 grants no power to the courts to examine into whether by-laws were lawfully adopted or repealed. See Calhoon v. Harvey, 85 S. Ct. 292 (1964); Robins v. Rarback, 325 F.2d 929 (2d Cir. 1963).

"It is equally clear that §501 of the LMRDA has no application to the present controversy. A simple reading of that section shows that it applies to fiduciary responsibility with respect to the money and property of the union and that it is not a catch-all provision under which union officials can be sued on any ground of misconduct with which the plaintiffs choose to charge them. . . .

"The provisions of the LMRDA were not intended by Congress to constitute an invitation to the courts to intervene at will in the internal affairs of unions. Courts have no special expertise in the operation of unions which would justify a broad power to interfere. The internal operations of unions are to be left to the officials chosen by the members to manage those operations except in the very limited instances expressly provided by the Act. The conviction of some judges that they are better able to administer a union's affairs than the elected officials is wholly without foundation. Most unions are honestly and efficiently administered and are much more likely to continue to be so if they are free from officious intermeddling by the courts. . . .

"In the present case, the controversy was handled within the union without any irregularity but with due regard for the procedures provided by the bylaws. The action taken by a meeting of members of the local was appealed in the regular course to the International Executive Board, which exercises the power of the international organization between conventions. . . . The provisions of the bylaws under which the International Board acted do not appear to us to be arbitrary or unreasonable and they are binding upon the plaintiffs as members of the union. . . . There seems to us to be nothing arbitrary or reprehensible in the union's supreme governing body, acting under the authority of the union's bylaws nullifying [the] action [by five percent of the membership disenfranchising a large majority of the members.] . . . Affirmed."

(The separate opinion of Lumbard, J., concurring, is omitted.)

NOTES

1. An arbitration board denied the grievances of plaintiffs, who had been discharged because, on the alleged advice of an IAM representative,

they had breached a no-strike clause. Plaintiffs attacked the award, asserting newly discovered evidence of an arbitrator's bias, but the union's president refused to support their challenge. Although plaintiffs met the union constitution's requirements for a special meeting, the local's president refused to call one. Moreover, at the next regular meeting he denied plaintiffs permission to ask the membership for support of their claim. Plaintiffs sue in a federal district court, claiming that the president's refusals violated their rights under §101(a)(2). The union moves to dismiss, urging that the allegations do not state a federal claim. What result? Cf. Yanity v. Benware, 376 F.2d 197 (2d Cir.), *cert. denied*, 389 U.S. 874 (1967) (dismissing a similar claim).

2. Suppose a special meeting had been called but had been adjourned as soon as the plaintiffs had sought to raise the arbitration question. Would §§101(a)(1) or (a)(2) have been violated? Must the right to call meetings be enforced to implement the provisions of those sections? If so, what result if the union constitution had not provided for special meetings? Are the provisions of the union constitution a source of rights federally protected under §101 rather than a potential limitation on such rights? Does §101(a) at least require that the union refrain from arbitrariness by calling meetings in accordance with the union's own rules? See generally Note, 81 Harv. L. Rev. 488 (1967), criticizing the decision in Yanity v. Benware, supra Note 1.

Young v. Hayes, 195 F. Supp. 911 (D.D.C. 1961). The IAM by majority vote at its quadrennial convention adopted 106 proposed amendments to its constitution. Part I of the ballot contained 47 amendments, all listed under Proposition 4, along with a statement that these amendments were mandatory under the LMRDA; and Part II, 59 amendments separately listed for voting. That ballot was sent to the local lodges and was adopted by a margin of almost 4 to 1 in a membership vote. Plaintiffs, local lodges and individual members, claimed a violation of LMRDA §101(a)(1) in that members, contrary to the union constitution, had been denied an opportunity to vote separately on each of the 47 amendments. The court found that the 47 amendments, although prompted by the LMRDA, had not been required by the Act and also found that their inclusion under Proposition 4 constituted an "abuse of discretion" and a violation of the union constitution. In invalidating those amendments, the court stressed that "mandatory" in the ballot was misleading and stated: "[T]he right to vote extended [by Title I] is not a mere naked right to cast a ballot. . . . [E]xtreme care should be taken to make sure every procedural safeguard is provided . . . , when amendments are . . . submitted . . . for vote and thus insure adherence to the union constitutional amending procedures. . . . [T]he membership should be fully informed as to amendments which . . . are affirmatively required by the Act . . . and . . . as fully informed and educated as is possible and consistent with orderly procedures. . . . "

NOTES

1. Is the court's result dependent on the provision in the union constitution limiting the "subject" of each amendment? If so, does the decision involve an unwarranted expansion of the protection provided by §101? If the court's decision does not rest on the provisions of the union constitution, does the decision mean that "equal rights to vote" include the right to be reasonably informed about the issues to be voted on and that federal courts, like the Securities and Exchange Commission with respect to proxy solicitation, are to scrutinize the adequacy of solicitation material submitted in connection with referenda?

2. Does LMRDA §501 impose a duty of full and fair disclosure on union officers with respect to matters submitted to the vote of the membership or their delegates at a convention? See Cefalo v. Moffett, 449 F.2d 1193 (D.C. Cir. 1971), but cf. Gurton v. Arons, supra; see also the *Johnson* case, supra p. 1315.

3. A union, by a simple majority vote of its members rather than the two-thirds plainly required by the union constitution, authorized a monthly assessment of $50 for failure to walk a picket line during a strike. Subsequently, the union imposed and collected such an assessment from Maverick, who had challenged the sufficiency of the vote. Has the union violated the LMRDA? Cf. Bunz v. Moving Picture Machine Operators, Local 224, 567 F.2d 1117 (D.C. Cir. 1977). Suppose that a union's leadership, in clear violation of a union constitution, imposed (rather than disregarded) a requirement of a super majority (e.g., for the creation of new offices). Would the union have violated the statutory requirement for equal voting rights as well as the union constitution?

American Postal Wkrs. Union, Headquarters Local 6885 v. American Postal Wkrs. Union
665 F.2d 1096 (D.C. Cir. 1981)

[The Postal Reorganization Act of 1970 (PRA) provided that the NLRA should be applicable to postal labor relations, to the extent that it is consistent with the PRA. The American Postal Workers Union (APWU) was created in July 1971, by the merger of four national unions, each representing one craft in the Postal Service. Negotiations between the APWU and the Postal Service produced the "National Agreement" in 1971; the Agreement was not submitted to union members for approval. In 1972 the APWU constitution was amended to include Article XIX, which required "[a]pproval [of future contracts] by a majority of the union members voting who are covered by the proposed agreement." At that time, the APWU represented only employees covered by the National Agreement. Beginning in 1973, the APWU was selected as the bargaining representative for some smaller, "non-mail processing units" in the Postal Service. The APWU interpreted Article XIX as applying only to national units; consequently, collective bargaining agreements negotiated for the "non-mail processing units" were not subject to ratification votes.

The APWU was certified in 1977 as the representative of the Postal Service's R&D employees in Rockville, Md. In 1978, as both sides prepared for fact finding after negotiations had been suspended, the APWU and the Postal Service reached a tentative agreement. A local union and its members sued in a federal district court. They alleged that by not submitting the proposed agreement to the local's members for ratification (and by related actions), the APWU (a) breached its promise to the local and violated Article XIX of its constitution, (b) violated LMRDA §101(a)(1), and (c) breached both its duty of fair representation and its fiduciary obligation. The trial court's summary judgment dismissed all claims against the union defendants. Plaintiffs appealed, and nonunion members of the bargaining unit, as intervenors, adopted those of appellants' arguments that applied to them.]

MIKVA, J. . . .

II.   THE RIGHT TO RATIFY

. . . We find no need to interpret article XIX of the APWU constitution or to rule on the reasonableness of appellees' construction. Even if appellants have no ratification right under the literal terms of the constitution, they do have such a right under section 101(a)(1) of the LMRDA. . . .

This provision itself accords no voting rights to a union membership, but it does mandate that rights given to some members be available to all. The Ninth Circuit has described section 101(a)(1) as protecting union members from "denial of a voting right given to any other member or class of members." *Stelling*, 587 F.2d at 1385. . . . The APWU has in effect created two classes of members, only one of which is entitled to ratify its collective bargaining agreements. Such classifications, unless within the scope of the statute's proviso regarding "reasonable rules and regulations," are impermissible under section 101(a)(1): "while a union may set up procedural and even substantive conditions or restrictions on the members' right to vote, it may not do so indefinitely or arbitrarily so as to establish a permanent special class of membership not entitled to an equal vote." Acevedo v. Bookbinders Local 25, 196 F. Supp. 308, 311 (S.D.N.Y. 1961). . . .

The APWU's refusal to permit Local 6885 to approve its contract, while requiring ratification votes on the national agreement, is therefore contrary to section 101(a)(1) if it cannot be justified as a "reasonable" distinction. In ruling for appellees on this issue, the court below held:

> Rather than discrimination, such a provision merely enables the unions to deal flexibly in their selection of bargaining methods. . . . (citing Byrom v. American Postal Workers Union, Civ. No. 78-4268, slip op. at 7 (S.D.N.Y. Oct. 2, 1979).) . . .

This rationale was more fully explained in *Byrom*, in which the court noted that contract ratification is a method of collective bargaining. The other general method of negotiating contracts — giving the bargaining representative final authority to bind the membership — may be more or less advantageous relative to the ratification method, depending on the circumstances of the particular situation. The court in *Byrom*, followed by the court below, inferred that Congress did not intend by section 101(a)(1) to limit a union's flexibility in selecting bargaining methods.

We are not persuaded that this notion of flexibility rises to the level of a "reasonable" justification for discriminating against non-mail processing units in the exercise of ratification rights. No evidence in the record explains why ratification was inappropriate for the Local 6885 bargaining agreement, or even for nonnational contracts generally. No differences between such contracts and the ratified national agreements were articulated by appellees, by the court below, or by the court in *Byrom*. In fact, there is no indication that the desire to preserve flexibility even motivated the discrimination challenged by appellants. Moreover, accepting this broad, general concept of flexibility as sufficient explanation for the disparate treatment here gives unions carte blanche to discriminate among members and substantially vitiates the force of section 101(a)(1). Cf. Alvey v. General Electric Co., 622 F.2d 1279, 1286 (7th Cir. 1980) (similar reasoning re union's asserted rationale of "uniformity").

What does emerge from the record is a mechanical adherence to prior practice with no rational policy justification. When the APWU constitution first provided for member ratification of collective bargaining agreements, the union represented only persons covered by the national contract. There was obviously no need for the framers of article XIX to consider whether a similar procedure should be followed in negotiating contracts for non-mail processing units, and article XIX referred exclusively to "national" agreements, negotiating teams, etc. As the union gradually undertook representation of nonnational units, this language was understandably interpreted to permit ratification only of national agreements. That construction was considered precedent and followed — with no apparent consideration of the reasonableness of the distinction. . . . The traditional interpretation was then "corrected" in 1978 when the union constitution was amended to permit ratification by non-mail processing units. . . .

If our historical analysis is accurate, the union's discrimination against appellants and their kind is not justified by any reasonable distinction between them and those union members given a right of ratification, and article XIX may not be deemed one of the "reasonable rules and regulations" permitted by section 101(a)(1). . . .

Our conclusion is corroborated by interpretations of the statute's reference to "reasonable rules and regulations" appearing in the case law and the legislative history. These sources indicate that a union may limit voting to active members, or to those in good standing, and may exclude those who have not belonged to the union for the requisite period of time. . . . Cf. 105 Cong. Rec. 15,536 (1959) (remarks of Rep. Thompson) (in favor of permitting unions to exclude inactive and supervisory members from vote).

In addition, section 101(a)(1) permits a union to limit participation in a specific vote to those whose interests are affected. See, e.g., *Alvey*, 622 F.2d at 1286-87; Fritsch v. District Council 9, Bhd. of Painters, 493 F.2d 1061, 1063 n.8 (2d Cir. 1974) (no right to vote for other locals' bargaining agents, who performed no duties for appellants); Williams v. International Typographical Union, 423 F.2d 1295, 1298 (10th Cir.), *cert. denied*, 400 U.S. 824 (1970); (those who only moonlight as printers have no "vital interest" in, and therefore no right to vote on, wage scales); *Acevedo*, 196 F. Supp. at 311 (separation of skilled and unskilled workers for . . . bargaining and representation).

. . . [C]ourts have, however, expressed disapproval of other classifications drawn by a union that operate to deny the right to vote to some members. In *Alvey*, for example, the union constitution permitted only members in good standing — those who had paid dues — to participate in union affairs. Laidoff members of the union were not permitted to pay dues and were therefore excluded from a vote to ratify revised seniority rules. The Seventh Circuit found this distinction unreasonable and noted that "discrimination is most invidious where, as here, it is applied to prevent a group of members from voting or even speaking on matters that vitally affect them." 622 F.2d at 1287. See Trail v. International Bhd. of Teamsters, 542 F.2d 961, 966 (6th Cir. 1976) (affirming refusal to dismiss section 101(a)(1) claim based on union's affording appellants ratification right only on national and central states agreements and denying vote on Michigan Rider, which also affected them). . . .

. . . [Appellants] have a very substantial interest . . . in the bargaining agreement governing their own employment. Once the union acted to permit some of its members to approve or reject their contracts, section 101(a)(1) directed that similar rights be given appellants — in the absence of a reasonable rationale for discriminating. Neither the vague, broad notion of flexibility nor the formalistic adherence to outmoded interpretations of article XIX's language provides sufficient justification for denying appellants an opportunity to ratify their contract. The court below therefore erred in granting summary judgment on this question. We remand for fuller consideration of the local's allegations and the union's defenses.[19]

[The court found that the facts here made inapplicable decisions that the duty of fair representation had been violated by a bargaining agent's failure to provide information important to a choice facing the membership. Since there was no evidence supporting the local's other fair representation claims, the district court's dismissal of those claims was affirmed.

Nichols, J., concurring in part and dissenting in part, objected to the last sentence of Part II of the majority opinion and n.19 on these grounds: The plaintiff's failure to move for a summary judgment below precluded the court of appeals from granting such a judgment. Nevertheless, on remand, except for the quantum of damages, there would be no triable issue regarding the violation of LMRDA §101(a)(1) or Article XIX of the union's constitution. He observed:]

It appears to me that the union officials who negotiated the contract placed themselves in a conflict of interests position by simultaneously negotiating with the same management some contracts that required ratification, and some that by their view did not. They would be under a strong temptation to make the inevitable concessions to management in the contracts not to be ratified, and obtain the plums in those that were to be. Any court sitting in equity, as the trial court was here, should not overlook these things. I would not exonerate any union official from breach of the duty of fair representation who voluntarily put himself in such a position unless he had shown by clear and convincing evidence that he had inflicted no harm. So the point is more relevant to what we say, perhaps, than to what we do. . . .

---

[19] . . . Courts . . . have not distinguished between §101(a)(1) and duty of fair representation claims. . . . As far as the members of Local 6885 are concerned, these claims appear to be interchangeable in this case, and their remedies duplicative. They may differ, however, in their remedial consequences for the intervening nonunion members of the unit. . . . If the district court concludes that appellants have stated a valid claim under §101(a)(1), the court should then determine the significance of that finding for intervenors' duty of fair representation allegations.

[On remand, in Local 6885 v. Postal Workers, 113 L.R.R.M. 2433 (D.D.C. 1982), the court granted the intervenors' (nonunion members') motion for summary judgment, reasoning as follows: Ratification was not an internal union affair but had important external ramifications on "perhaps the most important topic in any bargaining session — wages (merit pay increases and save grade provisions)." The court added:]

It certainly would not follow from this reasoning that the APWU would owe the interveners a duty of fair representation with respect to *any* union matter which had an effect, no matter how attenuated, on their wages or salaries. Here, however, the ratification phase had such direct consequences on the wages of the interveners that it must be considered to be inextricably connected with the bargaining phase. Thus, the duty of fair representation . . . would also extend, in this instance, to the ratification phase. If the Court were to rule otherwise, the duty of fair representation owed to the interveners in the bargaining phase would be seriously diluted, in the same way that the force of [§101(a)(1)] would be "substantially vitiate[d]" if the plaintiff local were not guaranteed the right of ratification that other locals were. Since the union admittedly breached its duty to the local with respect to the ratification phase, it was certainly foreseeable that the damages flowing from that breach would affect the non-member employees as well. If the union's failure to submit the contract for ratification showed a disregard of the interests of the local, it certainly also showed a similar disregard for the interests of the interveners.

NOTES

1. On remand, the district court appears to have rested its judgment for the intervenors, who were not union members, on the international's violation of rights conferred on union members by the Act and by the union constitution. (a) Is that approach justifiable? (b) Suppose that the union had submitted the tentative agreement for ratification at a meeting open only to union members. Would the union have violated its duty of fair representation? What if the proposed agreement had a different impact on union members and nonmembers? Or if the union had solicited the views of nonmembers and had advised the voting members accordingly? Cf. Pennsylvania Labor Relations Board v. Eastern Lancaster School District, 58 Pa. Commw. 78, 427 A.2d 305 (Pa. Commw. Ct. 1981).

2. (a) Even though a union constitution does not confer a ratification right, may such a right be derived from §101(a)(1) or from the duty of fair representation? See Aikens v. Abel, 373 F. Supp. 425 (W.D. Pa. 1974), with

which compare Branch 6000, Natl. Assn. of Letter Carriers v. NLRB, 595 F.2d 808 (D.C. Cir. 1979), supra p. 1144, Note 2.

(b) Would it be material if a union, although not required to do so by its constitution, had customarily requested ratification but, without any prior notice to its members, had failed to do so in connection with the negotiations and agreement in dispute? What impact, if any, might imposing a legal obligation on the basis of past practice have on a union's willingness to submit agreements voluntarily for ratification by the membership?

(c) Recognition of members' rights to ratification, whether derived from the LMRDA or the duty of fair representation, will raise questions regarding the content of such a right. Will it, for example, encompass a right to a secret ballot (which unions rarely recognize in this context)? Cf. LMRDA §101(3)(A) (secret ballot for dues increase).

3. An unpublished table compiled by the Office of Labor-Management Policy Development (May 1978) indicates that the national constitutions of 34 (or 47 percent) of the 72 national unions with 40,000 or more members require contract ratification by members. The bylaws of locals and intermediate union bodies give the same right to an unknown number of other employees. Many unions, without any formal requirement, have established traditions of member ratification. See Lahne, Union Contract Ratification Procedures, Monthly Lab. Rev., May 1968, at 7, 9.

TABLE OF CASES

INDEX